Inside AutoCAD® Release 12

By

Tom Boersma
Jim Boyce
Frank Conner
Rusty Gesner
Jeff Hester

Original Authors:

D. Raker
H. Rice

New Riders Publishing, Carmel, Indiana

Inside AutoCAD® Release 12

By Tom Boersma, Jim Boyce, Frank Conner, Rusty Gesner, and Jeff Hester

Original authors: D. Raker and H. Rice

Published by:
New Riders Publishing
11711 N. College Ave., Suite 140
Carmel, IN 46032 USA

All rights reserved. No part of this book may be reproduced or transmitted in any form or by any means, electronic or mechanical, including photocopying, recording, or by any information storage and retrieval system, without written permission from the publisher, except for the inclusion of brief quotations in a review.

Copyright © 1992 by New Riders Publishing

Printed in the United States of America 4 5 6 7 8 9 0

Library of Congress Cataloging-in-Publication Data

Inside AutoCAD Release 12 / by Tom Boersma ... [et al.].
p. cm.
"Original authors, D. Raker, H. Rice."
Includes index.
ISBN 1-56205-055-9 : $34.95
1. Computer graphics. 2. AutoCAD (Computer program).
I. Boersma, Tom. II. Raker, Daniel. III. Rice, Harbert.
IV. Title: Inside AutoCAD Release Twelve.
T835I4763 1992
620.0042'0285'5369—dc20 92-19826
CIP

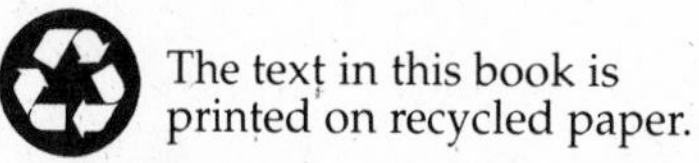

Publisher
David P. Ewing

Associate Publisher
Tim Huddleston

Acquisitions Editor
Brad Koch

Managing Editor
Cheri Robinson

Product Director
Rusty Gesner

Production Editor
Tim Huddleston

Editors
Margaret Berson
Peter Kuhns
Rob Lawson
Rich Limacher
Cheri Robinson
Nancy Sixsmith
Rob Tidrow
Lisa Wagner

Technical Editors
Robert Dunn
Scott Pesci

Editorial Secretary
Karen Opal

Acquisitions/Editorial Assistant
Geneil Breeze

Book Design and Production
William Hartman
Hartman Publishing

Proofreaders
JoAnna Arnott
Nancy Sixsmith

Indexed by
Sharon Hilgenberg

Composed in Palatino and Courier by
William Hartman
Hartman Publishing

About the Authors

Tom Boersma

Tom Boersma is a certified manufacturing engineer, an ATC trainer, and a CAD/CAM training specialist at Grand Rapids Community College in Michigan. He is a co-author of *Inside AutoCAD for Windows*, published by New Riders Publishing.

Jim Boyce

Jim Boyce has been involved with computers as a user, system administrator, programmer, and college educator. He was full-time faculty at Texas State Technical Institute for six years. Mr. Boyce currently is a free-lance author whose work appears regularly in a number of CAD- and computer-related magazines, including *CADalyst, CADENCE, MicroCAD News*, and *PC Magazine*. He is the author of *Maximizing Windows 3* and *Maximizing Windows 3.1*, co-author of *Inside AutoCAD for Windows*, and a contributor to *Inside AutoCAD, Sixth Edition*, published by New Riders Publishing. Mr. Boyce is a full press member of the Computer Press Association.

Frank Conner

Frank Conner is a CAD/CAM instructor in the Technology Division at Grand Rapids Community College. Mr. Conner was chairperson of the committee that developed the AutoCAD Certified Operator's Examination and also is a private consultant to the CAD/CAM industry. He attended Southwestern Michigan College and Grand Valley State University, and received his master's degree from Norwich University. Mr. Conner is listed in *Who's Who in the Computer Industry* and *Who's Who in Education*; he is a founding member of the AutoCAD Executive Training Center Council and a member of the Society of Manufacturing Engineers. Mr. Conner has authored four books on AutoSketch and has developed several training manuals relating to the CAD/CAM/CNC industry. He was a co-author of the *AutoCAD Student Workbook* and the *AutoCAD Student Workbook Instructor's Guide*, published by New Riders Publishing.

Rusty Gesner

B. Rustin Gesner is publishing director of New Riders Publishing in Gresham, Oregon. Prior to joining New Riders, he was founder and president of CAD Northwest, Inc., in Portland, Oregon. Mr. Gesner is a registered architect and formerly practiced the profession in Oregon and Washington after attending Antioch College and the College of Design, Art, and Architecture at the University of Cincinnati. Mr. Gesner is co-author of the New Riders books *Maximizing AutoCAD Volume I* (formerly titled *Customizing AutoCAD)* and *Volume II* (formerly titled *Inside AutoLISP*), *AutoCAD for Beginners*, *Inside AutoCAD*, and *Inside AutoCAD for Windows*.

Jeff Hester

Jeffrey Hester is an A/E CAD Coordinator for Fluor Daniel in Irvine, CA. He has ten years of architectural and structural design experience, and has used AutoCAD since 1985. Mr. Hester is a co-author of *AutoCAD 3D Design and Presentation* and *AutoCAD: The Professional Reference*, both published by New Riders Publishing. Mr. Hester juggles his time between developing PC-based 3D presentations and CAD management.

Daniel Raker

Daniel Raker is president of Design & Systems Research, Inc., a Cambridge, Massachusetts-based management consulting firm specializing in computer graphics applications and market research.

Harbert Rice

Harbert Rice, a graduate of Harvard University, was the founder of New Riders Publishing, the first and foremost publisher of books on AutoCAD.

New Riders Publishing extends special thanks to the following contributors to this book:

Kenneth W. Billing

Kenneth W. Billing has been consulting on AutoCAD networks, management, customization, AutoLISP programming, and presentation graphics since 1985. He is the author of *Managing and Networking AutoCAD*, published by New Riders Publishing.

Kevin Coleman

Kevin Coleman has been using AutoCAD and other computer graphics programs since 1985. He attended the University of Oregon.

Kurt Hampe

Kurt Hampe is a computer applications consultant and instructor in Louisville, KY. He has used AutoCAD professionally for six years.

Acknowledgments

The authors are grateful to all the editors at New Riders: Cheri Robinson, Nancy Sixsmith, Rob Tidrow, Rob Lawson, Lisa Wagner, Margaret Berson, Peter Kuhns, and Rich Limacher. Special thanks to Tim Huddleston for managing the editorial process.

Special thanks to Bill Hartman for designing this book, and for his speedy production and page layout work. Thanks, too, to Robert Dunn and Scott Pesci for their diligence in technical editing.

Rusty Gesner offers profuse thanks to numerous friends and colleagues at Autodesk for their encouragement and support over the past eight years. Rusty also thanks Patrick Haessly and Harbert Rice for their contributions to earlier editions of this book.

Trademark Acknowledgments

New Riders Publishing has made every attempt to supply trademark information about company names, products, and services mentioned in this book. Trademarks indicated below were derived from various sources. New Riders Publishing cannot attest to the accuracy of this information.

AutoCAD, AutoCAD Training Center, Autodesk, Autodesk Animator, AutoLISP, AutoShade, AutoSketch, ADI, and ATC are registered trademarks of Autodesk, Inc. The following are trademarks of Autodesk, Inc.: ACAD, Advanced Modeling Extension, Advanced User Interface, AME, ATLAST, AUI, AutoCAD Development Systems, AutoCAD SQL Extension, AutoCAD SQL Interface, Autodesk Training Center, AutoFlix, DXF, and 3D Studio. RenderMan is a registered trademark of Pixar used by Autodesk under license from Pixar.

Microsoft Windows, MS-DOS, OS/2, Windows Write, and Excel are trademarks of the Microsoft Corporation. IBM/PC/XT/AT, IBM PS/2 and PC DOS are registered trademarks of the International Business Machines Corporation. UNIX is a registered trademark of the AT&T Company.

Trademarks of other products mentioned in this book are held by the companies producing them.

Warning and Disclaimer

This book is designed to provide information about the AutoCAD Release 12 computer program. Every effort has been made to make this book as complete and as accurate as possible, but no warranty or fitness is implied.

The information is provided on an "as is" basis. The author and New Riders Publishing shall have neither liability nor responsibility to any person or entity with respect to any loss or damages arising from the information contained in this book or from the use of the disks or programs that may accompany it.

Contents at a Glance

Table of Contents

Part One: Getting Started

Part Two: Basic 2D AutoCAD Drafting

NRP

Part Three: Advanced 2D AutoCAD Drafting

Part Four: Advanced AutoCAD Features

Part Five: AutoCAD and 3D Drawing

NRP

Introduction

AutoCAD is a software phenomenon; its users far outnumber the users of any other CAD system. Since the introduction of AutoCAD, the program has grown from a small curiosity to a full-fledged CAD system by any set of standards. AutoCAD also has grown from a relatively simple program to a large and complex one. Even if you are new to AutoCAD, however, you do not need to be intimidated by its size and complexity. Over a million designers and drafters have learned to use AutoCAD; hundreds of thousands of them have mastered the program with the help of previous editions of *Inside AutoCAD*.

Inside AutoCAD Release 12 is your guide to a significant step in the evolution of AutoCAD. Release 12 has been dubbed "the user's release." Like most of the previous releases of AutoCAD, Release 12 adds many new features. The most noticeable new feature of Release 12 is the more productive design environment that results from enhancements to the user interface. Release 12 provides a more comprehensive set of pull-down menus and dialog boxes, an integrated screen menu, and several improvements in input and editing that make AutoCAD easier and more intuitive to use.

Inside AutoCAD Release 12 helps you take advantage of the many features that AutoCAD Release 12 offers over previous versions of AutoCAD. In this

book, you learn how to use the following features, which are new to, or improved in, AutoCAD Release 12:

- **More dialog boxes.** Release 12 includes easy-to-use dialog boxes for many kinds of operations and for virtually all settings. The enhanced dialog boxes make AutoCAD easier to learn and use than ever before.
- **Better menus.** The main menu is gone, replaced by a File pull-down menu. The pull-down menu is better organized and more complete than the old main menu, and features nested child sub menus for related sets of commands and options. The screen menu automatically displays pages of options for every command, whether you enter the command by menu or from the keyboard.
- **Enhanced object selection.** You can use several new methods to more quickly, easily, and precisely select objects to edit. These methods include automatic windowing and selecting objects crossing irregular lines, or selecting windows with irregular boundaries.
- **Noun/verb editing.** You can now select entities, then specify the command to edit them with.
- **Grips editing.** You can select entities and then pick geometric points (like object snap points) on them to drag them around and modify them by, using several of the most common editing operations.
- **Locked layers.** You can lock layers to leave them visible, while preventing object selection or editing on them.
- **Plotting.** Plotting is greatly improved in Release 12, with dialog-box control, your choice of any number of alternative plotters or plot configurations, and optional plot preview.
- **PostScript.** You can use, plot, and export PostScript fonts and fills for publishing-quality graphics.
- **Graphics file formats.** AutoCAD Release 12 can import PostScript, TIFF, GIF, and PCX graphics files; and can export these and other common graphics-file formats.
- **Dimensioning.** AutoCAD Release 12 makes dimensioning fast and easy through a new set of sub menus (which give you fast access to dimensioning commands) and a dialog box (for setting variables and managing styles). You no longer need to remember all those cryptic variable names.
- **Linetypes.** Broken linetypes now display with polylines of all types.

- **Automated boundary and hatch generations.** You can automatically generate complex boundary polylines defined by multiple entities, and you can then hatch those boundaries.
- **Regions.** You can create editable single-entity flat objects from polylines and circles, and then extract properties such as area, perimeter, centroid, bounding box, moment of inertia, products of inertia, principal moments, and radius of gyration.
- **Rendering and shading.** Release 12's built-in rendering and shading features enable you to create presentations within AutoCAD, without using another program, such as AutoShade.

Who Should Read this Book—and How

Whether you are a new or experienced AutoCAD user, *Inside AutoCAD Release 12* is your most complete combined introduction, tutorial, and reference manual to AutoCAD Release 12.

The Benefits of this Book to New AutoCAD Users

This book requires no previous AutoCAD experience; it takes you from the beginning level and makes you an expert. If you are new to AutoCAD, you can skim through the book for an overview. After that, you should read all the chapters and work through the exercises. The drawing exercises teach you how to use the program's interface, commands, menus, and dialog boxes. Remember that this book requires no previous DOS experience; if you need more information on the basics of DOS before you start working with AutoCAD, start by reading Appendix B.

You will find that this book covers AutoCAD Release 12 more completely that any other single available document. Study the book well and you will become expert in the program's use. After you have completed Parts One and Two, you will be ready to take advantage of the book's benefits to experienced users.

The Benefits of this Book to Experienced AutoCAD Users

Even if you are experienced with previous releases of AutoCAD, Release 12 has enough new features to make this book valuable to you. Although you can skim through parts of the book, you should explore the new dialog boxes and menus in Chapter 2 and the new editing techniques in Chapter 6, then delve into Parts Three and Four to add advanced 2D drawing and editing techniques to your repertoire.

If you have been using only AutoCAD's 2D features, you also may want to use Part Five of this book to expand into 3D surface and solid modeling. You will find discussion and tips in Appendixes A and B that will help you optimize the performance of both AutoCAD and DOS. Appendix C introduces you to AutoCAD customization.

If You are Upgrading from AutoCAD Release 11

This book is written specifically for the Release 12 version of AutoCAD. If you are upgrading from AutoCAD Release 11, AutoCAD Release 12 offer you many new features, including those described earlier. This book provides comprehensive coverage of these new features.

If You are Upgrading from AutoCAD Release 10

You also will find a great deal of useful information in this book if you are upgrading from AutoCAD Release 10. If you are making this upgrade, you will find an enormous number of added features and enhancements in Release 12, and these features are comprehensively covered in this book. They include paper space, dimension styles, new text alignments, external references, new 3D-input methods, and a new 3D polyface surface entity.

You can use paper space to easily compose multiple-view 2D or 3D drawing sheets, so that when you plot, what you see on the screen is what you get on paper. You can use external references (xrefs) to insert one drawing into another, protecting the inserted drawing from being edited while ensuring that the other drawing updates automatically when the inserted drawing is edited. You can use dimension styles to create and control dimensioning standards and to protect associative dimensions from accidental changes during editing.

The Benefits of this Book to All Readers

No matter how proficient you are with AutoCAD or your computer, and no matter how you read this book, you will revisit it again and again as a reference manual. You will find *Inside AutoCAD Release 12* indispensable as you use it to find explanations and examples of specific commands and techniques. You may also refer to the table of AutoCAD system variables in Appendix C.

How this Book is Organized

Inside AutoCAD Release 12 is organized for both the beginner and the experienced AutoCAD user. The book is designed both as a tutorial to help new users learn to master AutoCAD Release 12, and as a reference guide that you can use over and over, long after you have mastered the basics of the program. To accomplish these goals, the book is organized into parts, each of which covers a specific group of concepts and operations.

Inside AutoCAD Release 12 starts with the basics of two-dimensional CAD drafting and ends with the construction and presentation of three-dimensional models. The exercises and discussions do not assume that you have any prior knowledge of CAD in general or of AutoCAD in particular. Further, you do not need any knowledge of programming. If you study the entire volume, however, you will be able to use AutoCAD Release 12 for 2D drafting, 3D modeling, and presentation. Further, you will be able to customize AutoCAD Release 12 so that it works in a way that best suits your unique needs.

Part One: Getting Started

The three chapters in Part One teach you some basics and prepare you to begin drawing in AutoCAD Release 12. You learn how to start the AutoCAD Release 12 program, set up AutoCAD to follow the exercises, and set up specific drawing parameters in the drawing editor. The chapters familiarize you with the AutoCAD drawing editor and interface. At the end of Part One, you are ready to begin creating and editing drawings in AutoCAD.

Chapter 1 teaches you how to set up your system for running AutoCAD. (You can get more detailed information about DOS from Appendix B or a DOS reference guide.) The chapter also shows you how to set up AutoCAD Release 12 for the exercises in this book, and how to install the optional *Inside AutoCAD Release 12* disk (referred to as the *IA DISK*). The drawings on the disk can save you time while you work through the exercises. Even if you are an experienced AutoCAD or DOS user, you need to create a special command line and to specify directories, so that AutoCAD can work in sync with this book's exercises.

Although Chapter 2 teaches a few basic AutoCAD drawing and editing commands, the chapter's real purpose is to teach you about the AutoCAD Release 12 interface. Chapter 2 identifies and discusses the parts of the drawing screen, and covers the various menus and methods of command entry, including the use of pull-down menus, pop-up menus, and dialog boxes. Chapter 2 also shows you how to use AutoCAD's on-line help system.

Chapter 3 covers drawing setup. CAD, like manual drafting, requires some planning and setup before you actually start drawing. Although several basic drawing commands are used in the exercises, Chapter 3 emphasizes the setting up of layers, linetypes, colors, and drawing units.

When you complete Part One, you will be familiar with your AutoCAD drafting system so that you can begin learning how to draw productively in Part Two.

Part Two: Basic 2D AutoCAD Drafting

Part Two covers basic 2D drafting. To produce good 2D drawings, you need to know how to control the accuracy of AutoCAD's drawing tools. Part Two teaches you how to control the drawing display and how to create and edit 2D drawings.

Chapter 4 shows you how to use AutoCAD's snap, grid, object snaps, and other accuracy aids. These tools assist you in creating extremely precise drawings. You also learn how to control the standard AutoCAD coordinate system and to create your own coordinate system.

In Chapter 5, you learn how to control the drawing window so that you can draw and arrange images of any size on the screen. You develop a mastery of single and multiple views in the drawing area, and learn to control the

amount of the drawing that is being displayed. The chapter also demystifies the concept of paper space, which is the bridge between your computer and the paper.

Chapter 6 covers several basic drawing commands and introduces several of the editing features that are new to Release 12. New users will find these editing methods intuitive and easy to use; experienced AutoCAD users may need to study this chapter more carefully and practice to break old habits and take advantage of new and more efficient ways to create and edit drawings.

Chapter 7 shows you how to use every remaining 2D drawing command, so that you can draw virtually anything you want.

Chapter 8 comprehensively covers all the features of the basic editing commands introduced in Chapter 6 for moving, copying, rotating, arraying, and mirroring existing entities in your drawings. Editing goes beyond fixing mistakes and making changes; in fact, you often can draw more efficiently by editing existing entities than you can by creating new ones.

Part Three: Advanced 2D AutoCAD Drafting

Part Three of *Inside AutoCAD Release 12* introduces many new and advanced features of AutoCAD. The previous chapters cover several basic commands and features; this section teaches you how to use those commands more efficiently and to improve your drawing versatility. Additional advanced commands are covered, and Part Three offers in-depth coverage of dimensioning and plotting. You learn drawing-construction techniques, how to create and insert drawing symbols, dimensioning techniques, and how to prepare drawings for plotting and presentation. By the time you complete Part Three, you will know all of AutoCAD's 2D commands and many drawing and editing techniques, tips, and tricks for producing accurate, professional-looking 2D drawings.

Chapter 9 covers advanced editing commands that enable you to use many methods to extend, stretch, trim, scale, and offset existing objects. In this chapter, you also learn several additional methods for creating new objects.

Chapter 10 describes a wide range of drawing tips and techniques. This chapter combines commands from the previous chapters and shows you how to use construction lines and point filters to build accurate drawings

quickly. You also learn how to use all the AutoCAD UNDO features so that you can easily try different edits without wasting time.

Chapters 11 and 12 show you how to use AutoCAD blocks (symbols) and xrefs (externally referenced files). In Chapter 11, you learn how to save drawing time and file space by using blocks to insert repetitive objects in your drawings. You also learn how to update your drawings quickly and easily by redefining blocks. Chapter 11 also teaches the use of external references. Xrefs are insertions into a drawing that reference the contents of other drawing files. Xrefs coordinate the cooperative editing of a master drawing by enabling several people to work on parts of it simultaneously. Xrefs also make drawings smaller by storing parts in their own separate drawing files; the master file updates automatically if the referenced file is edited.

Chapter 12 is another techniques chapter, teaching the application of blocks, xrefs, and other drafting techniques to the creation of a drawing. In this chapter, you draw a complete site plan.

Chapter 13 shows how to compose and plot your drawings the way you want them. You learn how to use paper space to compose drawings, making multiple-view plotting a cinch. Chapter 13 also includes dozens of plotting tips.

Chapter 14 contains techniques for dressing up your drawings with hatching, linetypes, and free-hand sketching. This chapter closes by examining AutoCAD's inquiry commands, which tell you what, where, and when you are drawing.

Chapter 15 covers the basic use of AutoCAD's dimensioning settings and commands to dimension your drawings. (Advanced dimensioning is discussed in Chapter 17.)

When you complete Part Three, you will have learned how to create complex 2D drawings, from initial setup to final plot.

Part Four: Advanced AutoCAD Features

Part 4 introduces you to new and more advanced features of AutoCAD Release 12. Part 4 shows you how to customize and tailor AutoCAD to your specific needs—from storing nongraphic information in your drawings, to

customizing and using advanced dimensioning, to using AutoCAD data and images in conjunction with other applications.

Chapter 16 teaches you how to use AutoCAD's attribute entities as tags that you attach to blocks in your drawing to maintain information about various items. If you are creating a drawing that details the equipment in a factory, for example, you can use attributes to keep track of cost, function, manufacturer, purchase date, maintenance data, and other types of information about the equipment. Chapter 16 also shows you how to extract data from the attributes in a drawing. You can use the extracted data to create reports, bills of materials, or to otherwise collect and analyze data.

Chapter 17 shows you how to set variables and how to create and use dimension styles to customize and control dimensions so that they meet your standards. Chapter 17 also covers several of AutoCAD's advanced dimensioning capabilities, such as ordinate, chain, and datum dimensioning.

Chapter 18 describes techniques and commands for importing and exporting AutoCAD data and images to and from other programs. AutoCAD Release 12 can import and export PostScript, PCX, TIFF, and GIF files, as well as export several other industry-standard graphics-file formats. This opens up some new ways to use AutoCAD, such as for desktop publishing and presentation work. Chapter 18 also covers two file standards for CAD data exchanges: Autodesk's DXF and the international IGES file formats. The capability to copy a drawing or part of a drawing to another document can save considerable time in developing training materials, manuals, reports, and other documents.

When you finish Part Four, you will be able to extract data from your drawings, customize your dimensioning methods, and exchange graphic and nongraphic data with other users and programs.

Part Five: AutoCAD and 3D Drawing

Part Five covers 3D modeling, from planar 2D entities to extruded 2D entities, to true 3D surface entities. You learn how to create, edit, and display models. You can use 3D models to create complex shapes or find intersections and other design relationships that are difficult or impossible to draw manually.

Chapter 19 teaches you how to use the user coordinate system (UCS) to position construction planes anywhere in 3D space. You can draw on these construction planes by using standard 2D AutoCAD drawing commands, creating a 3D model from extruded 2D entities. Chapter 19 also teaches you to control your viewpoint and viewports to visualize your model in 3D, and to view your model more realistically with hidden lines removed.

Chapter 20 introduces 3D entities, such as 3D polylines, 3D faces, and 3D surface meshes. You learn to use the basic 3D surface commands as well as AutoLISP-defined commands that create 3D objects, such as boxes, wedges, cones, and spheres. You also use surface shading to view your 3D model quickly and clearly.

Chapter 21 shows you how to move around in and present your 3D drawings. You learn to dynamically adjust your 3D viewpoint and create perspective views to help you plan and preview 3D presentations. You learn to put dynamic views, slides, and scripts together to create a walk-through presentation.

Chapter 22 covers shading and rendering for study and presentation. AutoCAD Release 12 includes powerful rendering capabilities that formerly required another program such as AutoShade. With these features, you can create realistic images of surfaced 3D models. The AutoCAD Render commands, covered in Chapter 22, show how to create shaded images, beginning with an explanation of the fundamentals of rendering.

Chapter 23 covers 3D solid modeling with the Advanced Modeling Extension (AME) (available at an additional cost). Solid modeling represents 3D objects more accurately than surface modeling does, enables you to add and subtract 3D objects to build your object, and includes mass properties information that you can extract. Although solid modeling does not entirely replace the traditional 3D drawing techniques, it certainly introduces some exciting new capabilities to AutoCAD.

By the time you finish Part Five, you will be an expert in AutoCAD Release 12, from 2D to 3D.

The Appendixes

Inside AutoCAD Release 12 also has three useful appendixes.

Appendix A covers AutoCAD installation, configuration, and troubleshooting.

Appendix B covers the basics of using DOS and improving the performance of your computer system.

Appendix C describes techniques and commands for customizing AutoCAD to add commands and macros, define external commands and command abbreviations, and use prototype drawings to save time and avoid entering repetitive steps manually. Appendix C also includes a useful table of AutoCAD's system variables.

How To Use the Tutorials

Each chapter is divided into a series of exercises, each of which teaches one or more AutoCAD commands. Explanatory text accompanies each exercise, putting commands and techniques into context, explaining how commands behave, and showing you how to use different options. If you just read the text and exercises, and look at the illustrations, you will learn a great deal about the program. But if you want to gain a greater mastery of AutoCAD Release 12, you need to sit down at a computer that is equipped with AutoCAD Release 12 and work through the exercises.

Where To Find Specific Topics

You should work through each part of the book in order, but you can choose specific topics, if you want. The optional IA DISK enables you to enter the exercise sequence at several different points in most chapters. If you want to begin immediately, examine the following Quick Start Guide to locate key topics and techniques.

Wherever you start, you should first do the setup (and optional IA DISK installation) exercises in Chapter 1 so that your system setup corresponds with the directions and illustrations in the exercises.

Table 1.1
Quick Start Guide to Inside AutoCAD Release 12

If you want to:	*Turn to:*
Set up to use the book and IA DISK	Chapter 1
Set up AutoCAD Release 12	Chapter 1
Install or configure AutoCAD Release 12	Appendix A
Learn to use DOS	Appendix B
Use menus and dialog boxes	Chapter 2
Use various forms of input	Chapter 2
Set up drawings	Chapter 3
Use the user coordinate system (UCS) in 2D	Chapter 4
Use the user coordinate system (UCS) in 3D	Chapter 19
Use multiple views (viewports) in 2D	Chapter 5
Use multiple views (viewports) in 3D	Chapter 19
Use MVIEW (paper space) viewports in 2D	Chapters 5 and 13
Use MVIEW (paper space) viewports in 3D	Chapter 19
Learn 2D drawing commands	Chapters 2, 6, and 7
Use 2D drawing commands to draw 3D objects	Chapters 10 and 19
Learn 3D drawing commands	Chapters 19, 20, and 21
Edit 2D drawings	Chapters 8, 9, and 10
Edit 3D drawings	Chapters 19, 20, and 21
Render and shade 3D drawings	Chapter 22
Create 2D regions and 3D solids models	Chapter 23
Extract material and mass properties	Chapter 23
Create 2D drawings from 3D entities	Chapter 19 and 23
Plot 2D and 3D drawings	Chapter 13
Compose paper space drawing sheets to plot	Chapters 13 and 19
Use blocks (symbols and parts) in drawings	Chapters 11 and 12
Use external references (xrefs)	Chapters 11 and 12
Add attribute information to drawings	Chapter 16
Dimension drawings	Chapters 15 and 17
Customize dimensioning	Chapter 17
Use associative dimensions and styles	Chapter 17
Control 3D views and perspectives	Chapters 19 and 21
Customize menus and buttons	Appendix C

Using the Optional IA DISK

The best way to use *Inside AutoCAD Release 12* is to work through every exercise in sequence. You can work through selected exercises to cover topics of particular interest, but many exercises require drawings that were created in earlier exercises or chapters. In most cases, you can create the drawing you need without investing too much time and effort. But you can more easily choose exercises to perform without backtracking if you use the optional IA DISK. This disk contains exercise drawings that have been saved at various stages of completion. Whenever you see the disk symbol at the beginning of an exercise, you know that you can find the appropriate drawing on the IA DISK.

When this icon appears, you see instructions that tell you how to use the IA DISK to complete an exercise.

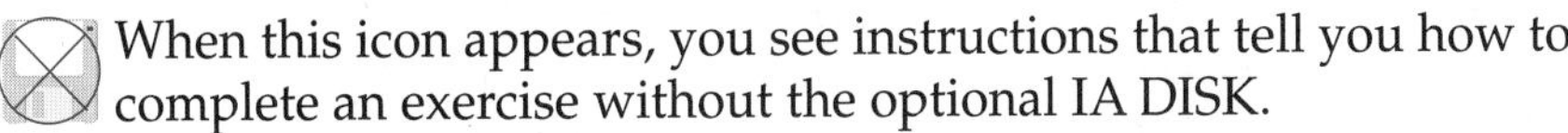

When this icon appears, you see instructions that tell you how to complete an exercise without the optional IA DISK.

Chapter 1 shows you how to set up directories on your hard disk for use with *Inside AutoCAD Release 12*. The setup is designed so that the IA directory structure and exercises will not interfere with your normal AutoCAD settings or any other work you are doing. Chapter 1 also explains how to install the drawing and support files included in the IA DISK.

A Special Note to AutoCAD Instructors

Several editions of *Inside AutoCAD* have been used for classroom instruction, and *Inside AutoCAD Release 12* is equally suitable for classroom use. Each chapter begins with a brief description of its contents and tells the student what he should be able to learn from it. Each chapter ends with a summary.

Following the Book's Conventions and Exercises

The conventions used for showing various types of text throughout this book are, insofar as possible, the same as those used in the *AutoCAD*

Reference Manual. These conventions are shown in this section. Some conventions, such as the use of italics to introduce a new term, are pretty simple. Others, such as those used in the exercises, are worth a closer look.

Exercises

A sample exercise follows. You do not need to work through it, but you should study the format so that you will know what to expect from the exercises throughout the book. Most exercises are preceded or followed by one or more illustrations, which were captured from the screen during an actual exercise. Exercises are arranged in two columns, with direct instructions on the left and explanatory notes on the right. Lengthy explanations sometimes extend across both columns. The numbers shown in circles refer to points in the illustrations (see fig. I.1).

A Sample Exercise

Continue in the SAMPLE drawing from the previous exercise.

`Command:` *Press F9 to turn on snap*	Activates snap mode
`Command:` *Choose* Draw, *then* Circle, *then* Center, Radius	Issues the CIRCLE command from the Circle child menu
`_circle 3P/2P/TTR/<Center point>:` *Pick point at ① (see fig. I.1)*	Specifies the circle's center point
`Diameter/<Radius>: 3↵`	Draws a 6" circle
`Command:` *From the screen menu, choose* DRAW, *then* LINE:	Issues the LINE command
`From point:` *From the pop-up menu, choose* Center	Specifies the CENter object snap
`center of` *Pick the circle at ②*	Starts the line at the circle's center
`To point:` *Pick at ③*	Draws the line
`To point: 3,5↵`	Specifies the coordinates that you typed
`To point:` *Press Enter*	Ends the Line command

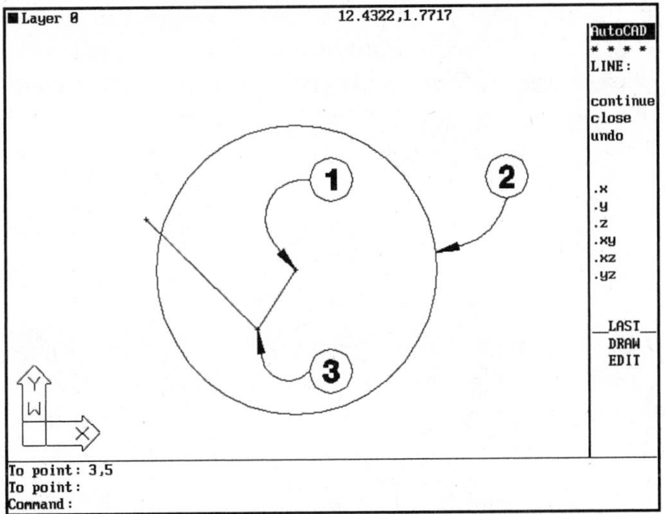

Figure I.1:

A sample exercise illustration.

The AutoCAD Release 12 interface uses many of the elements used by other modern programs with a GUI (Graphical User Interface). When you see an instruction such as "`Command:` *Choose* Item" in an exercise, it means to move the pointer to the top of the screen, which displays a menu bar, then move the pointer to the item on the menu bar, and click the left mouse button. This displays a pull-down menu—a list of menu items from which you can choose commands and options. When you move your pointer to an item and choose it, a command is issued, or a child sub menu or a dialog box appears.

When the exercise tells you to "*Choose* Draw, *then* Circle," you should choose the Draw pull-down menu, then the Circle item from it. If a pull-down menu or dialog box is currently displayed, *Choose* refers to an item on it.

The *screen menu* is the menu that appears at the right side of the drawing area. All instructions to choose from the screen menu are prefaced with "*From the screen menu, choose....*" Instructions to use the pop-up menu (which appears at the pointer's location when you press a certain pointer button) are prefaced with "*From the pop-up menu, choose....*" Otherwise, the exercises assume that you will use the pull-down menu. See Chapter 2 for more information on using menus and dialog boxes. You can choose any menu or dialog box item, whether it is text or an icon, by moving the pointer to the item and clicking the left mouse button. If you are not already familiar with the AutoCAD interface, Part One introduces you to it.

In some cases, you will see the symbol ↵ in the exercises. Your computer may have a key labeled Enter, or one labeled Return, or one with an arrow symbol. In any case, ↵ means that you need to press the key that enters a return (generally by using the little finger of your right hand).

You often enter commands from the keyboard. Similarly, point coordinates, distances, and option keywords often must be typed. The exercise text generally indicates when typed input is required by showing it in blue text following a prompt, such as `Command:` **`UNITS`** ↵ or `To point:` **`3,5`** ↵. You should type the input as it appears, and then press Enter.

Early in the book, you will notice that exercises contain copious prompts and explanations of what is (or should be) happening as you enter commands. Later exercises often omit prompts that are issued by commands that have become routine and explanations of familiar effects.

Many exercises end with an instruction to end or save the drawing. You may not want to end a drawing, because some chapters can be completed in one or two sittings. You should save your drawings when instructed, however, because doing so helps you build a habit of saving drawings at regular intervals. If you want to proceed at a leisurely pace, you can end your drawing whenever you see the Save instruction, and reload it later. If you want to take a break where a save or end instruction is not shown, just close and save or end your drawing and reload it later.

Notes, Tips, and Warnings

Inside AutoCAD Release 12 features many special "sidebars," which are set apart from the normal text by icons. The book includes three distinct types of sidebars: "Notes," "Tips," and "Warnings." These passages have been given special treatment so that you can instantly recognize their significance and so that you can easily find them for future reference.

A *note* includes "extra" information that you should find useful, but which complements the discussion at hand instead of being a direct part of it. A note may describe special situations that can arise when you use AutoCAD Release 12 under certain circumstances, and may tell you what steps to take when such situations arise. Notes also may tell you how to avoid problems with your software and hardware.

A *tip* provides you with quick instructions for getting the most from your AutoCAD system as you follow the steps outlined in the general discussion. A tip might show you how to conserve memory in some setups, how to speed up a procedure, or how to perform one of many time-saving and system-enhancing techniques.

A *warning* tells you when a procedure may be dangerous—that is, when you run the risk of losing data, locking your system, or even damaging your hardware. Warnings generally tell you how to avoid such losses, or describe the steps you can take to remedy them.

Exercises and Your Graphics Display

The authors created this book's illustrations by capturing screen displays during the process of performing the exercises. All screen displays were captured from systems using standard VGA display controllers set for the 640×480-pixel resolution. Text-font settings were customized to produce pleasing printed illustrations. If your system has a super-VGA or EGA card, or another high-resolution display controller, your screen displays may not exactly match the illustrations. Menus and screen elements may appear larger or smaller than they do in the illustrations, and you may want to zoom in or out further than the instructions indicate. You should learn from the outset, in fact, that you must adjust to the task at hand and the resources available. You may find that entities are easier to see if you use different colors than instructed in the exercises, especially if you are working with a white background rather than a black background.

You probably will find the drawing image clearer if you use the AutoCAD Release 12 CONFIG command to set your video display to use a black drawing background. See your *Interface, Installation, and Performance Guide* or Appendix A for more information on configuration.

What You Need To Use this Book

To use *Inside AutoCAD Release 12*, you need the following software and hardware, at the very least. This book assumes the following:

- You have a computer with both AutoCAD Release 12 and PC DOS/ MS-DOS 3.0 or later installed and configured. DOS 5.0 or later is highly recommended. Appendix A provides more specific information and recommendations on system requirements, and on installing and configuring AutoCAD Release 12.
- You have at least 3M of free hard disk space left after you have installed and configured AutoCAD Release 12.
- You have a graphics display and pointing device configured to work with AutoCAD.
- You are familiar with PC DOS/MS-DOS and can use the basic DOS commands and utilities (if not, see Appendix B).

Handling Problems

As you work through the exercises in *Inside AutoCAD Release 12*, you may experience some problems. These problems can occur for any number of reasons, from input errors to hardware failures. If you have trouble performing any step described in this book, take the following actions:

- Check the update text file on the IA DISK.
- Try again. Double-check the steps you performed in the previous exercise(s), as well as earlier steps in the current exercise.
- Check the settings of any AutoCAD system variables that were modified in any previous exercise sequences. (See the system variables table in Appendix C for a listing of all system variables.)
- See the troubleshooting section of Appendix A.
- Check the *AutoCAD Reference Manual* or the AutoCAD Release 12 online help.

If none of the above suggestions help, call New Riders Publishing (503-661-5745), *only* if the problem relates to a specific exercise, instruction, or error in the book. Otherwise, try the following for further help:

- Call your AutoCAD dealer.
- Log in to the Autodesk forum on Compuserve, and ask or search for help.

Other AutoCAD Titles from New Riders Publishing

New Riders Publishing offers the widest selection of books on AutoCAD available anywhere. Although the following titles are oriented to the command-line interface rather than the Windows interface, their contents still apply to AutoCAD Release 12.

Inside AutoCAD Release 12 is written for the beginning to intermediate AutoCAD user. If you prefer a beginning tutorial, see *AutoCAD Release 12 for Beginners*. It covers the 80 percent of AutoCAD that most users use in everyday work, packaged in an easy-to-use text.

For comprehensive coverage of the several Autodesk products that can be used to create 3D designs and presentations, see *AutoCAD 3D Design and Presentation*. The book includes coverage of AutoCAD 3D, AME solid modeling, AutoShade, RenderMan, Autodesk Animator Pro, 3D Studio, and AutoFlix.

If you want to turn your AutoCAD drawings into animated presentations—or if you just want to draw cartoons—see *Inside Autodesk Animator*.

If you want to customize AutoCAD to work your way, see *Maximizing AutoCAD, Volume I* and *Maximizing AutoCAD, Volume II*. *Volume I—Customizing AutoCAD with Macros and Menus*—covers all aspects of customization short of writing programs in AutoLISP or the C language. *Volume II—Inside AutoLISP*—covers applications development using AutoLISP programs, menus, dBASE, and includes and introduction to ADS programming in the C language.

If you want a quick yet comprehensive reference, see the *New Riders' Reference Guide to AutoCAD Release 12*.

If you want a tutorial workbook or need to pass the Certified AutoCAD Operator's Exam, see the *AutoCAD Student Workbook*. The workbook is designed specifically to help new AutoCAD users prepare for this exam.

If you manage other AutoCAD users, with or without a network, see *Managing and Networking AutoCAD*. This book provides a comprehensive discussion of the issues facing an AutoCAD manager or network administrator.

If you do technical drafting in 2D or 3D, see *AutoCAD Drafting and 3D Design*. It is written around ANSI Y14.5M standards.

If you want a comprehensive reference volume on AutoCAD, see *AutoCAD: The Professional Reference*. This generous volume covers everything from basic commands to customization.

Contacting New Riders Publishing

The staff of New Riders Publishing is committed to bringing you the very best in computer reference material. Each New Riders book is the result of months of work by authors and staff, who research and refine the information contained within its covers.

As part of this commitment to you, the NRP reader, New Riders invites your input. Please let us know if you enjoy this book, if you have trouble with the information and examples presented, or if you have a suggestion for future editions.

Please note, however, that the New Riders staff cannot serve as a technical resource for AutoCAD Release 12 or any other applications or hardware. Refer to the documentation that accompanies your programs and hardware for help with specific problems. Your AutoCAD dealer can provide general AutoCAD support.

If you have a question or comment about any New Riders book, please write to NRP at the following address:

New Riders Publishing
Prentice Hall Computer Publishing
Attn: Associate Publisher
11711 N. College Avenue
Carmel, IN 46032

We will respond to as many readers as we can. Your name, address, or phone number will never become part of a mailing list or be used for any other purpose than to help us continue to bring you the best books possible.

If you prefer, you can FAX New Riders Publishing at the following number:

(317) 571-3484

Thank you for selecting *Inside AutoCAD Release 12*!

Part One

Getting Started

The process of getting started is often one of the most challenging aspects of learning to use new software. Perhaps you are new to the computer-aided drafting (CAD) environment or to AutoCAD, or perhaps you do not have much experience with computers. Part One of *Inside AutoCAD Release 12* shows you how to set up your system for use with this book's exercises and how to begin working in the AutoCAD drawing editor.

How Part One is Organized

Part One includes three chapters, which take you through the basics of setting up, starting, and drawing in AutoCAD. In these chapters you learn how to set up AutoCAD so that you can follow the book's exercises, begin and save drawing files, and set up specific drawing parameters in the drawing editor. These chapters cover the following five basic topics:

- Starting up AutoCAD
- Setting up AutoCAD for the exercises in this book

- Learning the parts of the AutoCAD drawing editor
- Using the AutoCAD menus
- Beginning to draw in AutoCAD

After you get grounded in these topics in Part One, you will have the necessary background for learning the core of AutoCAD's drawing and editing commands, which are discussed in Part Two.

Understanding the Need for Proper Setup

Chapter 1 shows you how to set up AutoCAD so that you can easily duplicate this book's exercises. You can draw these exercises from scratch every time, or you can use the drawing files that are included on this book's optional disk. This disk (called the *IA DISK* throughout this book) contains AutoCAD drawing files that have been specially prepared for use with the book's exercises. By using these disk files, you can better concentrate on the material in the chapter because the drawing being discussed generally continues at the point of creation shown in the file. The disk is also helpful if you do not follow the chapters in order, or if you want to go at any time to some particular topic of interest. Chapter 1 gives you instructions on installing the disk.

Setting Up for the Drawing Exercises

This book instructs you to run AutoCAD from a special directory, which you will create in Chapter 1. That directory will contain a special AutoCAD configuration file, as well as your exercise drawings. You should set up and use the special directory for the following reasons:

- The tutorials are easier to follow if you are working with the same path names that are shown in the exercises.
- If you run the exercises from their own directory, they do not interfere with any existing drawings or settings that you already are using on your system.
- By learning how to set up a special directory, you can set up AutoCAD for other special situations in the future, such as varying hardware or multiple projects.

Chapter 1 teaches you how to create a batch file to start AutoCAD from the special directory that you set up. By the end of Chapter 1, you should have your system all ready to begin drawing with AutoCAD.

Moving around in the Drawing Editor

Chapter 2 explains the basics of interacting with the AutoCAD program. The chapter's exercises show you how to begin a drawing, how to enter points and coordinates, and how to save your drawing.

Chapter 2 describes the important parts of the drawing screen and explains their functions. AutoCAD sometimes seems more complex than it is because it offers several ways to access the same command. AutoCAD Release 12 provides a more user-friendly interface than earlier releases of the program because of the increased use of pull-down menus and dialog boxes, which enable you to select items graphically. Chapter 2 is designed to help you navigate through the various menu systems and dialog boxes, and to introduce you to the different methods of command entry.

Throughout this book, the exercises show you various methods of command entry. Remember, however, that you do not need to master all the methods at once. Determine the method that makes the most sense to you, and concentrate on that until you feel ready to try some of the others.

Learning AutoCAD's Editing and Help Facilities

Among the first AutoCAD commands this book introduces are the editing tools, such as ERASE and UNDO. If you are new to AutoCAD, you probably will make mistakes often and want to correct them quickly. Even users who have mastered the AutoCAD software still use the editing tools often. The on-line help function enables you to access information that explains the use of commands and the function of available command options. The help system is another good feature to learn early. AutoCAD Release 12's on-line help system offers even more help than was previously practical.

Creating Your First Drawings

Chapter 3 introduces several basic drawing commands, in tutorial fashion, to help you with the beginning drawings. Because AutoCAD can work in so many different applications and disciplines, drawing parameters are very important. Chapter 3 explains standard CAD terms as it introduces you to the basic commands. Drawing layers, linetypes, colors, and drawing units are covered, and the chapter helps you practice setting up related drawings. Chapter 3 also makes several comparisons between "manual drafting" and CAD drafting to help you visualize the similarities and differences between the two types of drafting.

The goal of Part One is to familiarize you with the AutoCAD drafting system. When you are done with Part One, you should be comfortable enough with AutoCAD to start learning to draw productively.

Setting Up

*I*nside AutoCAD Release 12 is a tutorial about AutoCAD. This chapter helps you set up the AutoCAD program on your computer, and then guides you as you explore the program's working relationship with the operating system. Appendix A gives you detailed instructions on loading and configuring the AutoCAD software; this chapter helps you start AutoCAD with the right parameters and control its operating characteristics.

Even if you are an experienced DOS user and have some experience with AutoCAD, you need to make some preparations before moving on to any of the following chapters. You should start by performing several exercises in this chapter, beginning with the "Making the IA Directory" exercise, which appears in a later section.

Setting Up AutoCAD for this Book's Exercises

The setup for *Inside AutoCAD Release 12* requires you to create a directory—named IA—on your hard disk. *Inside AutoCAD Release 12* makes use of an optional disk, called the IA DISK. If you do not have the IA DISK, see the Introduction for a description of the disk and for instructions on obtaining it. The book and disk are designed to ensure that the AutoCAD settings you

use for the book's exercises do not interfere with any other AutoCAD settings or projects that you may have under way.

Creating Directories

This book assumes that you are using the DOS operating system version 3.3 or later, that you are running AutoCAD on a hard disk drive named drive C, and that you have a directory structure similar to the one shown in the following exercise and figure 1.1.

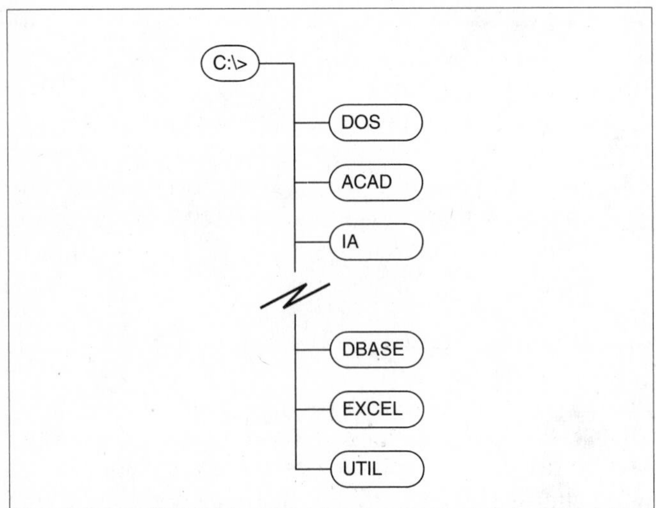

Figure 1.1: The directory structure for *Inside AutoCAD Release 12.*

When this book shows a DOS prompt, the prompt includes the current path. When drive C's root directory is the current directory, for example, the DOS prompt looks like this:

```
C:\>
```

When the IA subdirectory is the current directory, the prompt looks like this:

```
C:\IA>
```

If you want your DOS prompt to show the current path, you can enter the line **PROMPT=PG** at the DOS command line. You also can modify the prompt permanently by putting this line in your system's AUTOEXEC.BAT file.

Your drive letter or subdirectory names may differ from those shown in this book. If they do, substitute your drive letter and directory names wherever you encounter drive letters (such as C) or the directory names (such as \ACAD) in the book. If you are using an operating system other than DOS, your directory creation and setup will differ from those shown in the following pages. Even so, you should set up a directory structure that is similar to the one shown in this chapter.

Making the IA Directory

The book's setup also assumes that you work in the IA directory. You need to make an IA directory on your hard disk and then place a copy of your AutoCAD configuration file into this directory. By copying the configuration file into the working directory, you create a self-contained AutoCAD environment. To begin this task, make the hard disk's root directory the current directory. In the following exercise, you make the IA directory.

Before you begin the following exercise, note that the input you type at the `C:\>` command prompt is shown in `blue text`. After you type the blue input, press Enter to execute the command.

Making the IA Directory

Change to the root directory of drive C and perform the following steps:

`C:\> MD \IA↵`	Creates the directory
`C:\> DIR *.↵`	Displays a list of directory names, as shown in the following listing

```
Volume in drive C is DRIVE-C

Directory of  C:\

ACAD     <DIR>  12-01-88   11:27a
DOS      <DIR>  12-01-88   11:27a
IA       <DIR>  12-01-88   11:27a
```

Your disk may show other directories, as follows:

```
123      <DIR>  12-01-88   11:27a
DBASE    <DIR>  12-01-88   11:27a

5 File(s) 48753472 bytes free
```

The ACAD subdirectory contains the AutoCAD program files, configuration files, and standard support files. The DOS subdirectory contains the DOS operating-system files. The IA subdirectory contains the configuration files, prototype drawings, and other support files that are required for the *Inside AutoCAD Release 12* exercises. Your directory listing almost certainly will be different from the one shown here.

Setting Up the AutoCAD Configuration Files

AutoCAD requires a *configuration file*—a file named ACAD.CFG—which specifies the hardware devices (such as video display cards and plotters) that you use with AutoCAD. This file is created the first time you run AutoCAD. The following exercise assumes that AutoCAD's configuration file resides in the ACAD directory. If your configuration file is not in the ACAD directory, substitute the correct directory name for \ACAD in the following exercise. By copying the ACAD.CFG file to the IA directory, you establish a separate AutoCAD configuration for this book. If AutoCAD has not yet been configured, see Appendix A of this book or your AutoCAD *Interface, Installation and Performance Guide* for more information on configuring the program.

Configuring AutoCAD is a simple process of answering a series of prompts to tell AutoCAD what devices you are using, how they are connected, and your preferences for several optional settings that control AutoCAD's behavior.

Copying the AutoCAD Configuration File to the IA Directory

C:\> **CD \acad** ↵	Make the ACAD directory current
C:\ACAD> **COPY ACAD.CFG \IA**↵ 1 File(s) copied	Copies the AutoCAD configuration file from the ACAD directory to the IA directory

Installing the IA DISK

Now you are ready to install the IA DISK files. To save you typing and drawing setup time, the disk provides starting drawings for many of the

exercises. These drawings enable you to skip material you already know. If, for example, you want to learn about dimensioning but do not want to first create a drawing to dimension, you can simply begin adding dimensions to an existing drawing from the disk.

Installing the IA DISK

First, put the IA DISK in drive A.

`C:\ACAD>` **`CD \IA`**↵	Makes the IA directory current
`C:\IA>` **`A:IA-LOAD`**↵	Executes the IA DISK's installation program

Follow the prompts that appear next. If you have any problems, see the README.TXT file on the IA DISK. You can display the README.TXT file by changing to the IA DISK's drive and entering MORE<README.TXT at the DOS prompt.

Using a Batch File To Start AutoCAD

Now you can create a simple batch file that starts AutoCAD so that it does not conflict with your current AutoCAD setup, and which keeps your drawing exercise files in one place. The batch file loads AutoCAD directly from your ACAD directory to avoid conflict with any ACAD.BAT batch file that you might already have. The batch file avoids conflicts by ensuring that the settings of two of AutoCAD's environment variables—named ACAD and ACADCFG—are correctly set when you run AutoCAD and then are cleared when you exit from AutoCAD. This section shows you how to make a batch file named IA.BAT to use with the directory you have created for the IA DISK. For more explanation of start-up batch files and of the settings shown in this section, see Appendix A.

If you are using an operating system other than DOS, you can create a similar shell file rather than the batch file. See the AutoCAD *Interface, Installation and Performance Guide* for details.

After you create the IA.BAT batch file, you can start AutoCAD from any directory by entering \IA at the DOS prompt. The backslash enables you to

enter the IA batch command from any directory; if the IA.BAT file is placed in a directory on your path, you can omit the backslash.

The IA batch file sets the ACAD, ACADDRV, and ACADCFG settings, makes the IA directory current, and starts AutoCAD. When you exit from AutoCAD, the batch file clears ACAD, ACADDRV, and ACADCFG and returns you to the root directory. Your configuration may require additional settings. The IA.BAT file requires at least the following nine lines:

```
SET ACADDRV=\acad\DRV
SET ACADCFG=\IA
SET ACAD=\acad\SUPPORT;\acad\SAMPLE;\acad\FONTS;\acad\ADS
CD \IA
\acad\ACAD %1 %2
SET ACAD=
SET ACADCFG=
SET ACADDRV=
CD \
```

In the fifth line of the file, the `%1` and `%2` are *replaceable parameters*. These parameters are used in batch files as place holders for any command-line options that a program might take. Because AutoCAD can take two optional parameters (which can set a default drawing or script or enter AutoCAD's configuration when you start AutoCAD), this batch file includes two place holders. See the AutoCAD *Interface, Installation and Performance Guide* for more information.

The sample IA.BAT file supports the default directories suggested by the AutoCAD installation program. If your AutoCAD support files are not installed in the AutoCAD program directory, or your font, support, sample, and ADS files (if installed) are not in the acad\FONTS, acad\SAMPLE, acad\SAMPLE, and acad\ADS directories, then change the `SET ACAD=` line. If your device drivers are not in the acad\DRV directory, change the `SET ACADDRV=` line. If your font, sample, and support files are combined in the acad\SUPPORT directory, for example, delete `;\acad\SAMPLE` and `;\acad\FONTS`, and use `SET ACAD=\acad\SUPPORT;\acad\ADS`.

Your System's Requirements

Your system may require you to add other lines to the IA.BAT file. If you use multiple drives, add a line to change to the drive that contains the IA

directory (drive C, for example) before the line `CD \IA`. If you are using any AutoCAD ADI device drivers (for your video board, for example, or for your digitizer), you need to add commands to execute the device drivers just before the `\acad\ACAD` line.

If your system is already configured and running AutoCAD and it needs such settings, you should find them in your AUTOEXEC.BAT file or in an AutoCAD startup batch file, such as the ACAD386.BAT file that the 386 DOS version of the AutoCAD installation program creates. If so, copy them to the IA.BAT file. Similarly, if you already have AutoCAD set up with a startup batch file that makes any memory or swap-disk configuration settings, you need to add them to your IA.BAT file. Do not, however, add any additional lines beginning with SET ACAD= or SET ACADCFG=. For more information, see Appendix A

The following are some examples of typical additional configuration lines:

```
SET SVADICFG=C:\acad\DRV\SVADI.CFG
DS800R11 -I -X
SET DGPADI=DIGIDRV
SET ACADDRV=C:\acad\DRV
```

If your AutoCAD program files are not in a directory named \ACAD, then substitute your directory name for `acad` where shown in lowercase letters in the preceding listings and the following exercise.

Creating the IA.BAT File

The best way to create your batch file is to use a word processor or text editor in ASCII-text mode. If you prefer, however, you can use the following technique, which utilizes the DOS COPY command. This technique copies the characters you type at the keyboard to create the specified IA.BAT file. The keyboard is referenced as CON in the exercise because it (along with the video device) is the CONsole—the default DOS input/output device.

As you create your version of the IA.BAT file, be sure to make any changes and add any extra lines you need. To enter the ^Z character shown in the exercise, hold down the Ctrl (Control) key while you press Z, and then press Enter.

Creating the IA.BAT Batch File

`C:\ACAD>` **`CD\`**↵	Returns to the root directory
`C:\>` **`COPY CON IA.BAT`**↵	Creates a file named IA.BAT containing the following lines of keyboard input
`SET ACADDRV=\acad\DRV`↵	Sets the ACADDRV environment variable
`SET ACADCFG=\IA`↵	Sets the ACADCFG environment variable

The following line sets the ACAD environment variable:

`SET ACAD=\acad\SUPPORT;\acad\SAMPLE;\acad\FONTS;\acad\ADS`↵	
`CD \IA`↵	Makes IA the current directory
`\acad\ACAD %1 %2`↵	Starts the AutoCAD program
`SET ACAD=`↵	Clears the ACAD setting
`SET ACADCFG=`↵	Clears the ACADCFG setting
`SET ACADDRV=`↵	Clears the ACADDRV setting
`CD \`↵	Returns to the root directory after you exit from AutoCAD
`^Z`↵	Ends the COPY command and creates the IA.BAT file
`1 File(s) copied`	Confirms that the IA.BAT file was written to disk

Now you can start an *Inside AutoCAD Release 12* session from any directory on your hard drive simply by entering **\IA**. For more information on the startup batch file's settings, see Appendix A.

If the root directory is on the path specified by your AUTOEXEC.BAT file, you can omit the backslash and just enter **IA**. If you want to keep your root directory uncluttered, you can move the IA.BAT file to any other directory on your path.

Using the IA Batch File

With these file-handling chores out of the way, you can now use the IA.BAT file to start up AutoCAD.

Starting AutoCAD

C:\> \IA↵ Begins AutoCAD

If you have the IA DISK, a dialog box displays a message about the disk, including any last-minute information. Click on the up and down arrows at the right of the text listing to scroll up and down through the text. Click on the OK button when through to close the dialog box and display a new drawing.

Your screen displays a new drawing (see fig. 1.2)

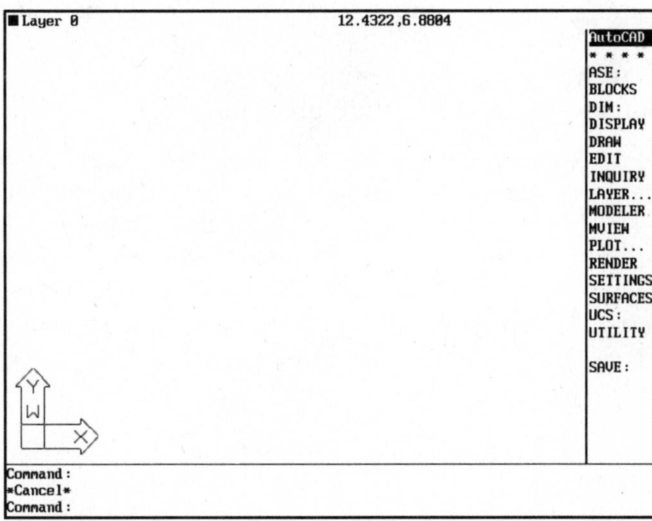

Figure 1.2: A new, empty AutoCAD drawing.

NOTE

If your system displays a `Bad command or filename` error message when you try to start AutoCAD with the IA batch file, make sure that you have specified the correct path to the AutoCAD executable file. If AutoCAD is installed on a different drive than the IA subdirectory, you must also put the correct drive letter before the first backslash on the `\acad\ACAD %1 %2` line of the IA batch file. If the ACAD.EXE file is located in the ACAD12 directory on drive E, for example, use the following command:

```
E:\ACAD12\ACAD %1 %2
```

As soon as you enter \IA from the operating system, the batch file takes control of your computer. The batch file makes IA the current directory, and the AutoCAD program displays the opening screen.

Setting the Defaults for the Exercises

To make absolutely sure that you are using the same default settings in AutoCAD as this book uses, take the steps shown in the following exercise to set up AutoCAD so that it does not use a prototype drawing. A *prototype drawing* is a drawing that AutoCAD uses as a template for creating a new drawing. All the AutoCAD settings that are stored in a drawing file, other drawing information, and any entities are transferred to the new drawing from the prototype. Without a prototype drawing, AutoCAD begins all new drawings with the same settings as the initial default ACAD.DWG. See Appendix C for more information on prototype drawings.

If you move the crosshair cursor to the top of the screen, the pull-down menu bar appears. The File pull-down menu gives you the choice of creating or editing drawings, plotting drawings, configuring AutoCAD, and using special utilities. To choose the File menu and New menu items specified in the exercise, move your cursor to highlight the specified item and click the pick button (generally the left-most or lowest-numbered button on your pointing device).

Starting a New Drawing

Move the cursor to the top of the screen	Displays the pull-down menu bar
Choose File	Displays the File pull-down menu
Choose New	Displays the Create New Drawing dialog box (see fig. 1.3)
Click on the box to the left of **N**o Prototype, *then on* **R**etain as Default	Places Xs in the boxes, turning on their settings
Choose **O**K	Closes the dialog box and saves your settings
Move the cursor to the top of the screen	Displays the pull-down menu bar
Choose Settings	Displays the Settings menu

Choose Selection Settings	Displays the Entity Selection Settings dialog box
If any of the boxes below Selection Modes *contains Xs, click on the boxes to clear them*	Clears selection modes
Choose **O**K	Closes the dialog box and saves the settings
Choose Settings, *then* Grips	
Click on **E**nable Grips *to clear x from box*	Turns off grips
Choose **O**K	
Choose File, *and then* exit AutoCAD	Ends this AutoCAD session

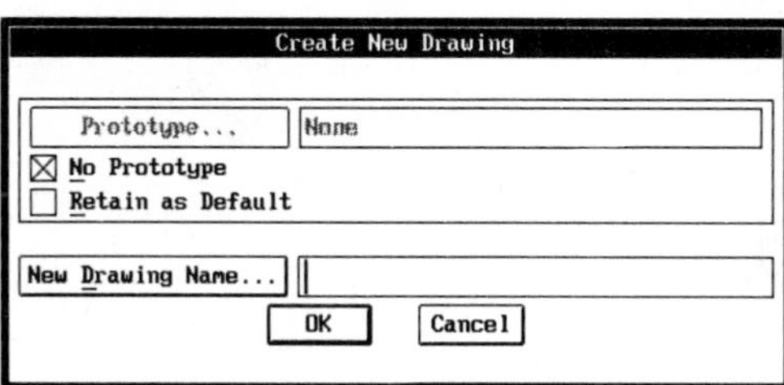

Figure 1.3: The Create New Drawing dialog box.

If you jump from chapter to chapter, set PICKADD to zero and PICKDRAG to one for all chapters after Chapter 6.

You can enter the NEW command at the AutoCAD `Command:` prompt. You can access many of AutoCAD's commands from the pull-down and screen menus, as well as from the command line. The commands sometimes act differently, however, depending on the way you access them. The differences between command-access methods are discussed as you learn about AutoCAD's commands and menus in the next chapter.

You can use the REINIT command to bring up the Re-initialization dialog box. Here, you can reinitialize your digitizer or mouse if it becomes inactive for some reason. You also can reinitialize your plotter if you forget to turn it on before starting AutoCAD. If your screen becomes "scrambled," reinitialize it by pressing Ctrl-C three times, then typing REINIT and pressing Enter, then pressing S, then the spacebar, and then Enter again. For more information on reinitializing various devices, see Appendix A.

Summary

Now that you have set up AutoCAD for the *Inside AutoCAD Release 12* exercises, your work with this book will not interfere with your usual AutoCAD configuration, and you will be ready to perform the exercises in this book.

Chapter 2 begins by placing you back into the AutoCAD drawing editor and showing you how to begin drawing. The various parts of the graphics screen are explained, and you are introduced to the menus and dialog boxes that contain many AutoCAD commands.

2

Getting To Know How AutoCAD Works

You probably are already familiar with manual drafting and design techniques or with CAD techniques used in programs other than AutoCAD. The drawing techniques and design methods you use in AutoCAD, however, are much the same as those used in manual drafting (and with other CAD programs); only the tools are different. Learning to use those tools is as simple as learning to use AutoCAD's user interface. In this chapter, you learn about the components that make up AutoCAD's drawing editor, and put them to use to create a few simple drawings.

Using the Drawing Editor

One of the best ways to learn AutoCAD is to begin a drawing and start using some of the commands. In this chapter, you open a new CAD drawing file, draw some lines and text, and save the file. By taking these steps, you learn how to access commands from AutoCAD's menus, and to become familiar with AutoCAD's use of the keyboard and pointing device.

When introducing new commands, this book emphasizes the use of pull-down menus, which seem to be the easiest interface for a new user. AutoCAD's pull-down menus are similar to those in other software packages. Figure 2.1 shows an example of an AutoCAD pull-down menu. Unless otherwise specified in the exercises, the instructions refer to the pull-down menus. The complete AutoCAD Release 12 pull-down menu system is shown in the menu map at the back of this book. Most of the commands used in the following exercises are covered more completely in later chapters. This chapter focuses more on methods of choosing commands and learning the drawing editor layout than on the specific commands themselves.

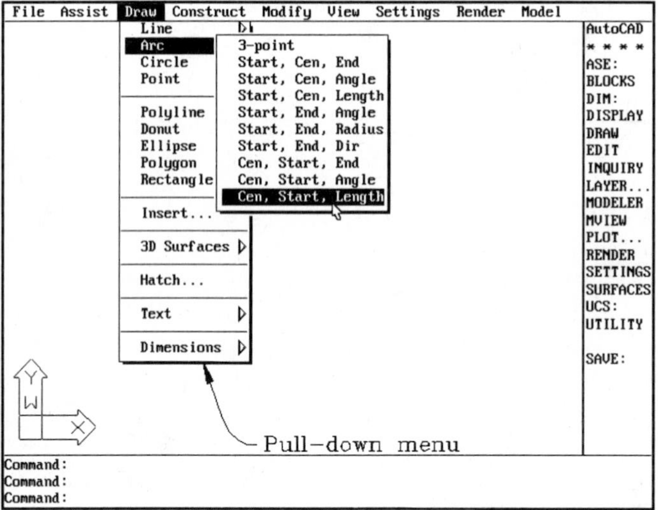

Figure 2.1:

An AutoCAD pull-down menu.

This chapter also examines AutoCAD's other forms of command input, including command-line entry, the use of shortcut-key definitions, and the screen menu. You learn about these types of command entry to gain a balanced overview of the many ways in which you can issue commands and choose options.

The exercises in this book often instruct you to use your pointing device to perform certain functions on the graphics screen. This pointing device could be a mouse, digitizer tablet, or the keyboard's cursor keys. The button most often used is the *pick* button. This usually is the mouse's left button or the lowest-numbered button (1 or 0) on the digitizer puck or stylus. You use this button to pick a menu selection, click on a dialog box selection, or select

an entity on the graphics screen. Sometimes you must *double-click* the input device if you want to choose a selection in a dialog box. This requires pressing the pick button twice in rapid succession. When the term *drag* is used, you must hold down the pick button while you move the cursor to another location.

Beginning a New Drawing

If you followed the exercises in Chapter 1, you can start AutoCAD by entering IA at the operating system prompt. This runs the IA.BAT batch file that you created in Chapter 1. After the AutoCAD logo and software identification information appear, the drawing editor is displayed, as shown in figure 2.2.

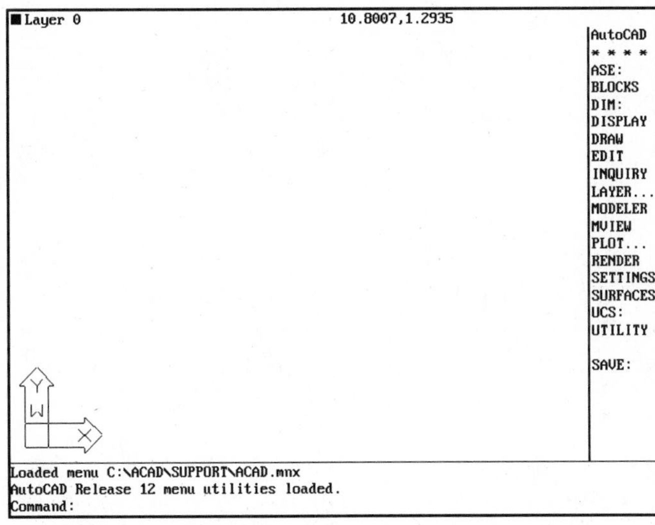

Figure 2.2:

The AutoCAD drawing editor.

If you choose File from the pull-down menu, and then New, AutoCAD displays the Create New Drawing dialog box shown in figure 2.3. You can type your new drawing's name in the blank input box, which contains the blinking cursor. If you click on the New Drawing Name button, another dialog box appears, enabling you to choose an existing file name. This dialog box enables you to replace an existing drawing with the new one, or to edit the selected name and create a similarly named drawing. You also can create a drawing with no name, and then name it later by using the SAVE command or the Save As pull-down menu option.

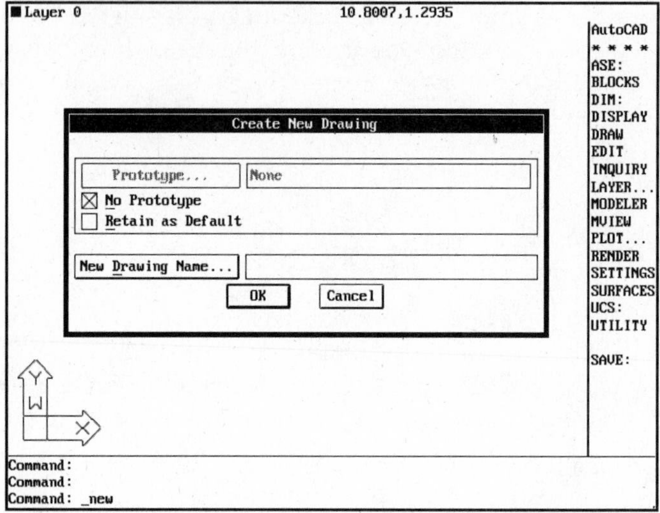

Figure 2.3:

The Create New Drawing dialog box.

When a dialog box appears on-screen, you can remove it only in two ways. That is, you can accept it or cancel it. Click on OK to accept the current entries in the box, or click on the Cancel button to ignore any changes to the current settings. You can press Enter to accept the dialog box if the OK button is highlighted or shadowed. You can press either Esc or Ctrl-C to cancel the dialog box.

When a dialog box is on the screen, you can click on an appropriate text box to enable keyboard entry or corrections to the current settings. You can click on an on/off setting to modify the existing setting. You will find more detailed information on the use of dialog boxes near the end of this chapter.

NOTE

For your drawing names, you can use alphabetical characters, numbers, and most symbols, but no spaces. AutoCAD adds a file-name extension of DWG when it stores the drawing on disk, creating drawing file names such as CHAPTER2.DWG. Remember: because AutoCAD takes care of the extension (DWG), you should not enter it.

In the following exercises, you begin a new drawing file named CHAPTER2. AutoCAD sets up a new drawing file called CHAPTER2.DWG in the IA directory of your current drive (all exercises in this book assume that you are using drive C).

Starting a New Drawing

`Command:` *Choose* File, *then* New, *type* `CHAPTER2` *in the* New Drawing Name *edit box, and then choose* OK	Begins a new drawing named CHAPTER2 in the \IA directory

The new drawing is created in \IA because the IA.BAT batch program makes \IA the default directory when you start AutoCAD.

You also can execute the NEW command by typing NEW and pressing Enter at the `Command:` prompt. When you use the NEW command, you can press Enter in response to the drawing name prompt to clear the existing drawing database from memory and start a new, unnamed drawing. The following exercise lets you practice starting a new drawing without assigning a name.

Clearing the Drawing Database

`Command:` **`NEW`**↵	Displays the Create New Drawing dialog box
Press Enter	Clears the drawing database without assigning a name to the drawing

As you just saw, AutoCAD lets you start a new drawing without naming it right away. When you issue the SAVE command, AutoCAD prompts for a drawing name if there is no current name. The SAVEAS command enables you to save the existing file under a different name.

Now that you have used the pull-down menu and have seen a dialog box, along with typing a command at the keyboard, you are ready to begin drawing with AutoCAD.

Starting To Draw

Try moving the pointer around in the graphics screen. The AutoCAD drawing editor, as shown in figure 2.4, has several different parts. The largest part of the screen is the center area, called the *drawing area*. The *screen menu* is on the right side of the drawing area, and the *pull-down menu bar* appears along the top of the screen. The *status line*, which also appears across the top of the drawing screen, shows the current active layer and the coordinate readouts. When you move the pointer onto the status line, it changes to display the pull-down menu bar. Several lines of text appear at the bottom of the screen. This text is referred to as the `Command:` *prompt*.

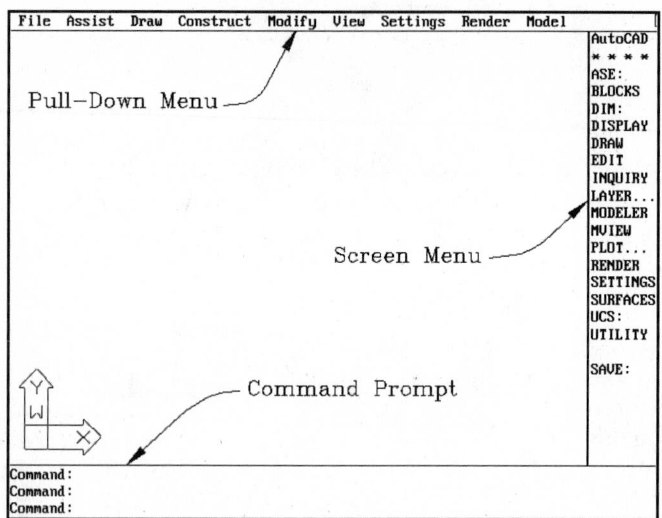

Figure 2.4:

The AutoCAD drawing editor.

You can access the pull-down menu by moving the pointer to the appropriate menu heading and then clicking on it. When the pull-down menu appears, you click on one of the menu's items to execute the command. When you click on some items in a pull-down menu, a *cascading menu* (also called a *child menu*) or dialog box appears to help you execute the command.

In the following exercise, you use a pull-down menu to issue AutoCAD's LINE command, and then experiment with drawing lines.

Drawing Your First Line

`Command:` *Choose* Draw, *then* Line, *then* 1 Segment	Starts the LINE command for a single segment
`Command: line From point:` *Move the cursor and click near* ① *in figure 2.5*	Picks the line's starting point

Move the crosshairs and see a line trailing behind them.

`To point:` *Pick a point near* ②	Specifies the line's end point, then ends the LINE command

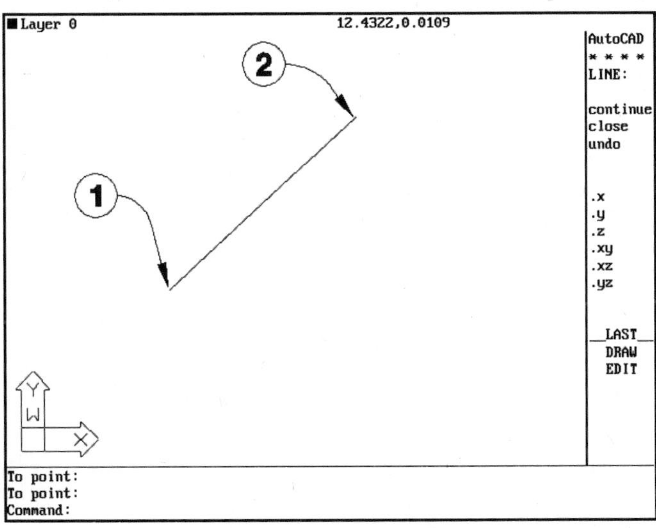

Figure 2.5:

Drawing a line.

The 1 Segment menu item terminates the LINE command after a single segment is drawn. Normally, the LINE command continues until you end it, as the following exercise shows. In the next exercise, you continue drawing lines by repeating the LINE command. If you press Enter at the `Command:` prompt, the last command is repeated; in this case, you can press Enter to reissue the normal LINE command.

Continuing the LINE Command

`Command:` *Press Enter*	Repeats the previous command
`LINE From point:` *Press Enter*	Starts a new line at the first line's end point
`To point:` *Pick a point near* ① *in figure 2.6*	Specifies the end point of the new line segment
`To point:` *Pick a point near* ②	Specifies the next line segment's end point
`To point:` *Press Enter*	Ends the LINE command

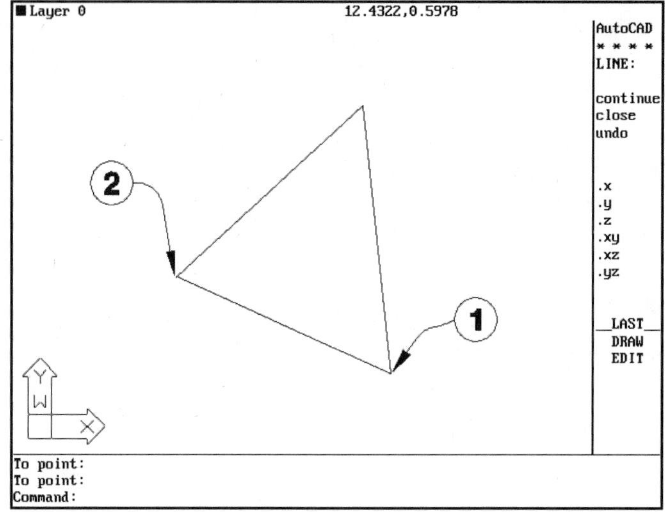

Figure 2.6:

Continuing the line.

TIP

On most systems, you also can press a mouse or digitizer cursor button to simulate the pressing of the Enter key. This is called AutoCAD's button number 1 and is generally the right button on a mouse or the lowest-numbered button (after the pick button) on a digitizer. On many digitizers, the pick button is marked with a 1 and AutoCAD button 1 is marked with a 2. On must digitizer stylii, the puck button is built into the stylus' point and is clicked by pressing the point against the tablet surface. AutoCAD button 1 is often a small button on the barrel of the stylus. AutoCAD button 1 is referred to as the Enter button throughout this book.

You can see that AutoCAD's LINE command is simple and straightforward. When you issue the LINE command, AutoCAD begins the process of recording the two end points of a line segment. If you press Enter at the `From point:` prompt, AutoCAD continues drawing lines, starting the next line at the last end point of the previous line.

You can issue the normal LINE command by repeating the command, entering **LINE** at the `Command:` prompt, by using the Segments pull-down menu option, or by choosing the LINE: screen-menu option. You can draw another line segment every time you see a `To point:` prompt. AutoCAD helps you visualize the next segment's location by *rubber-banding*, or trailing a segment between your last point and the cursor.

TIP

If you press Ctrl-C, Enter, or the spacebar, AutoCAD ends the LINE command and returns to the `Command:` prompt.

Entering Points and Coordinates in AutoCAD

Why is it so easy to draw in AutoCAD? You start the program, which takes you immediately into the drawing editor, then you begin entering points. It does not matter whether you enter points by picking them with your pointer or by entering them at the keyboard. The reason for this ease of use is that AutoCAD uses a standard Cartesian coordinate system and recognizes various types of drawing geometry.

The World Coordinate System (WCS)

When you enter the drawing editor, you enter a coordinate system called the *World Coordinate System* (referred to throughout this book as the *WCS*). When AutoCAD asks you to enter a point, you either locate the point with your pointing device or enter the point's coordinates from the keyboard. The system's coordinates consist of a horizontal X displacement and a vertical Y displacement (and a Z displacement for 3D). These coordinates are called *absolute coordinates*. Although absolute coordinate points are specified with parentheses (3,4) in textbook geometry by convention, coordinates typed at the keyboard in AutoCAD are separated only by a comma, such as 3,4. Both the X and Y are measured from a zero base point that is initially set at the lower left corner of your screen. This base point's coordinates are 0,0.

The User Coordinate System (UCS)

If you look at the lower left corner of your screen, you see an icon near point 0,0. This icon, shown in figure 2.7, is the *UCS icon*. "UCS" stands for *User Coordinate System*. The UCS enables you to establish your own coordinate system and shift your base point in your drawing by changing the position of the coordinate system. You make extensive use of the UCS when you work in 3D, but for now, leave it at the default position.

The default UCS is called the World Coordinate System (the WCS).

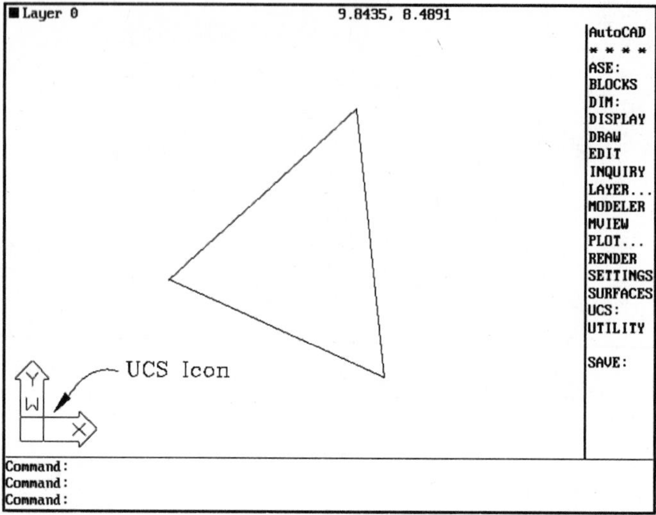

Figure 2.7:

The drawing editor with the UCS icon.

The WCS X axis is horizontal, left to right, and the Y axis is vertical, down to up. If you look closely at the UCS icon, you see that the X arrow points to the right on the X axis, and the Y arrow points up the Y axis. The "W" on the Y arrow means that you are currently in the default World Coordinate System. The UCS icon displays other information about your location in 3D. The UCS icon, for example, displays a "+" when the icon is shown at the UCS origin (0,0). The box in the icon's corner indicates the Z-axis direction, which is covered later, in the chapters on 3D.

If you find the UCS distracting when you are working in 2D, you always can turn it off. The following exercise shows you how to turn it off and on. The UCSICON On, Off, and OR selections on the Settings menu turn the UCS icon on and off, and cause it to display at the origin.

Turning the UCS Icon Off and On

`Command:` *Choose* Settings, *then* UCS, *then* Icon, *then* Off	Turns off the icon
`'setvar Variable name or ?: ucsicon`	AutoCAD displays the command sequence as the commands are executed
`New value for UCSICON <1>: 0`	

`Command:` *Choose* Settings, *then* UCS, *then* Icon, *then* On	Turns the icon back on
`'setvar Variable name or ? <UCSICON>: ucsicon`	
`New value for UCSICON <0>: 1`	

You can enter the UCSICON command at the `Command:` prompt, if you like. In addition to the On/Off/Origin options, the All option enables the setting to affect the UCSICON in all the views in a multiple-view drawing screen setup.

Finishing the Practice Exercise

In the next exercise, you continue using the pull-down menus to add some text to the drawing, and then zoom in closer to see it. Enter the text and coordinate values shown in the exercise, and complete the entry by pressing Enter.

Adding Text and Using ZOOM

`Command:` *Choose* Draw, *then* Text, *then* Dynamic	Begins the DTEXT command
`_dtext Justify/Style/<Start point>: C↵`	Specifies the Center justification option
`Center Point: 6,3.25↵`	Specifies absolute coordinates
`Height <0.2000>: .05↵`	Sets the text height
`Rotation angle <0>:` *Press Enter*	Accepts the 0 rotation angle
`Text: Welcome To INSIDE AutoCAD↵`	Enters the text string
`Text:` *Press Enter*	Ends the DTEXT command

Where is the welcome? You must zoom in closer to see it.

`Command:` *Choose* View, *then* Zoom, *then* Window	Issues the ZOOM command with the Window option
`Command: _'zoom All/Center/Dynamic/Extents/Left/ Previous/Vmax/Window/<Scale(X/XP)>: w`	
`First corner:` *Pick at* ① *(see fig. 2.8)*	Specifies the zoom window's first corner
`Other corner:` *Pick a point at* ②	Zooms the display (see 2.9)

`Command:` *Press Enter*	Repeats the ZOOM command
`'ZOOM All/Center/Dynamic/Extents/Left/ Previous/Vmax/Window/<Scale(X/XP)>:` **ALL**↵	Specifies the All option
`Regenerating drawing.`	Returns to the full magnification

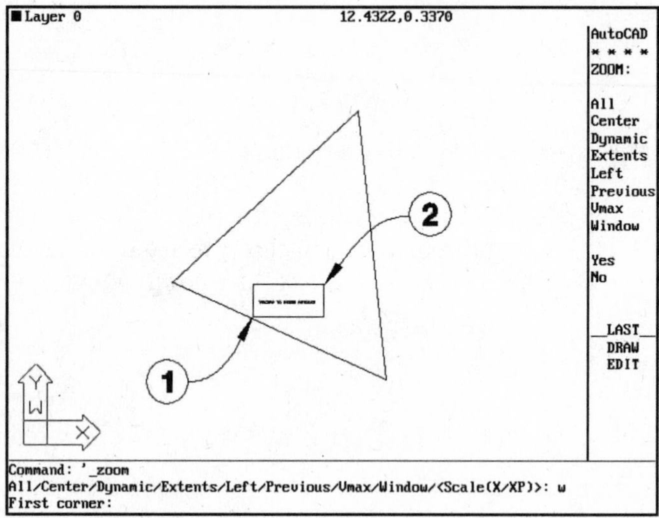

Figure 2.8:
Small text prior to ZOOM Window.

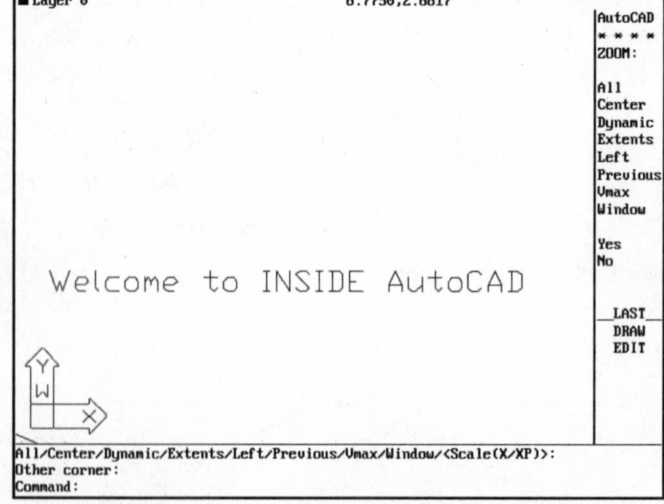

Figure 2.9:
The magnified text after ZOOM Window.

You may have noticed a leading underscore (_) in front of commands issued from the menu. This underscore character is part of AutoCAD's method of making foreign-language translations of menus easier, but you can simply ignore it.

You have started a new drawing file and created some lines and text by using AutoCAD's pull-down menus. Now you can complete your first pass through the drawing editor by saving your first effort.

Saving a Drawing File

AutoCAD provides several commands and selections on the File pull-down menu that write the drawing as a file on a permanent storage device, such as a hard drive. Your work is saved with a DWG file-name extension. AutoCAD further secures your work by renaming the previous version of the drawing file (if one exists) with a BAK extension.

The File menu's Save and Save As selections and the SAVE command write a DWG file and then return to the drawing editor so that you can continue working on the current file. The Save selection executes the QSAVE command, which automatically saves the drawing under the existing name, as shown at the `Command:` prompt in figure 2.10.

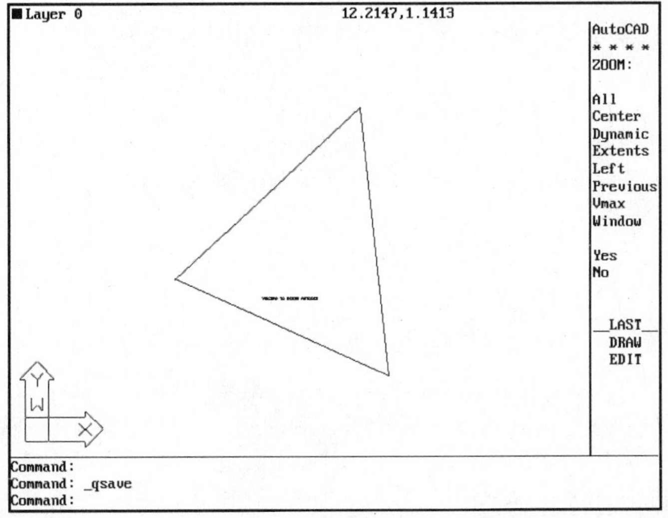

Figure 2.10: The QSAVE command, issued by the Save menu item.

The Save As item gives you the option of saving your current drawing session under the current name or under a file name of your choice. Press Enter to accept the default name shown at the `Command:` prompt or type in a new name to save the drawing to a different file name. The Save As menu selection displays the File dialog box to enable graphic selection of file names, drives, and directories.

Saving Your File

`Command:` *Choose* File, *then* Save As	Issues the SAVEAS command and opens the Save Drawing As dialog box
Click in the File *edit box, type* `CHAPTER2`, *then choose* OK	Saves the drawing as CHAPTER2.DWG

The File menu features several other options, two of which you can use when opening and closing a drawing file. The Exit AutoCAD item enables you to exit from AutoCAD. If there are unsaved changes, the Drawing Modification dialog box appears. This dialog box enables you to save the current changes, discard the changes, or cancel out of the dialog box and return to the drawing editor.

The File menu's Recover option attempts to restore a damaged drawing file. This also is attempted if you choose the drawing file under the Open menu selection.

You have just navigated the most basic route through AutoCAD. You have started a new drawing file, used a few drawing commands, and saved your work. Now it is time to take a more detailed look at AutoCAD's user interface.

Communicating with AutoCAD

When you choose menu items, you can glance at the `Command:` prompt at the bottom of your screen to see what information AutoCAD needs (such as a start point), or what action to take (such as selecting objects). Then watch the center of the graphics screen for the action. You also can use the status line to keep track of AutoCAD.

The Status Line

If you look at the top of the drawing editor, in the area used by the pull-down menu, you see the status line. This line contains a combination of text and numbers. Here you find information about how AutoCAD is set up and how it reacts when you issue certain commands. Think of the status line as a medical monitor that gives you AutoCAD's vital signs. Figure 2.11 shows the current color box, the layer name, Snap and Ortho (when they are active), and the coordinate readout. The letter P also appears to the right of Snap if paper space is active.

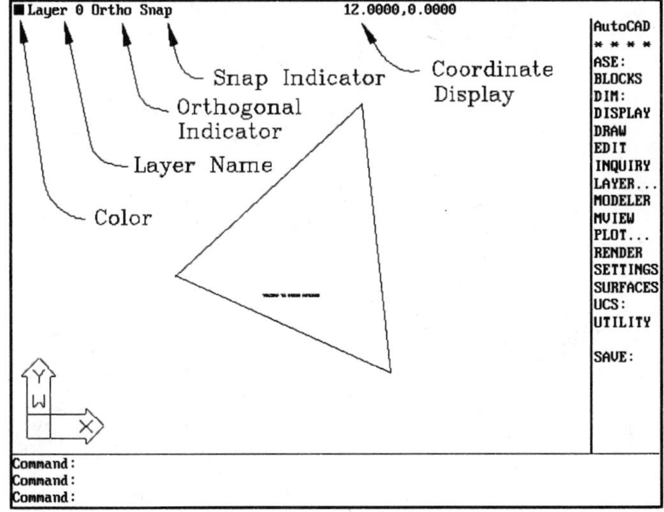

Figure 2.11: The AutoCAD status line and some of its components.

The Coordinate Display

The status line's *coordinate display* is helpful when you need to determine drawing positions. These numbers represent the current or last coordinate position defined. When you move the pointer around with the coordinate setting turned off, these numbers do not change; rather, they continue to identify the last point you entered as part of a command or picked with the cursor. The F6 key acts as a switch to activate the coordinate display, so that the coordinates continually update as the crosshairs move around the screen.

Move the cursor to the lower left corner, and the coordinates approach 0,0. When a command that accepts coordinates is active and at least one point

has been entered, the F6 key really enables three different choices. The display mode switches from off to polar coordinates to absolute coordinates. The polar coordinates are displayed only when you are using a drawing command.

The Command Line

As you work with the AutoCAD program, you come to know what it expects from you and how it reacts when you do something. Many AutoCAD commands set up new drawing environments to receive additional commands. AutoCAD uses the bottom part of the screen to tell you what it is doing. This communication channel is called the `Command:` prompt. The `Command:` prompt is usually three lines, depending on your configuration. The `Command:` prompt shows AutoCAD's prompts and your responses or input. It keeps track of your latest communication with AutoCAD.

AutoCAD has a flexible command and menu structure. You can issue any AutoCAD command by typing the command name at the keyboard in response to the `Command:` prompt.

As you type, the letters appear after the `Command:` prompt. In order to execute any typed command, you must press Enter to let AutoCAD know that you are finished typing. (This key might be called the Return key on some systems.) If AutoCAD cannot interpret what you have typed, it lets you know after you press Enter.

Entering Commands at the `Command:` Prompt

`Command:` **`LI`** ↵	Issues an incorrect command name
`Unknown command. Type ? for list of commands.`	AutoCAD indicates that it does not recognize the command as you have typed it
`Command:` **`LINE`** ↵	Issues the LINE command with the correct spelling
`From point:` *Pick any point*	
`To point:` *Pick any point*	
`To point:` *Press Enter*	Ends the LINE command

Remember that you must press Enter to enter input you have typed, such as **LINE** for the LINE command. You also can use the spacebar or the Tab key rather than Enter, unless AutoCAD is expecting a text string (such as when you are using the TEXT command).

The Text Screen

In addition to the `Command:` prompt, AutoCAD can display a full screen of `Command:` prompt text, as shown in figure 2.12. You can press the F1 key to switch AutoCAD between the text screen (this is called running in text mode) and graphics screen (graphics mode). Sometimes, a command (such as SHELL) causes the text screen to appear. Press F1 to switch back to the graphics screen.

```
To point:

Command:

Command:

Command:

Command:

Command:

Command:

Command:

Command: Li
Unknown command.  Type ? for list of commands.

Command: LINE
From point:
To point:
To point:

Command:
```

Figure 2.12:
The AutoCAD text screen.

Switching between Text and Graphics Modes

`Command:` *Press F1*	Displays the text screen
`Command:` *Press F1*	Displays the graphics screen

If you look closely at the text screen, you see the last sequence of commands that you have typed (or picked from the menu). You can use this text window to look back through a set of `Command:` prompts to see what you

have done. If you are interrupted by a phone call, for example, you can view the text window to easily find your place and get started again.

Correcting Errors

AutoCAD is forgiving. The worst thing that can happen when you mistype a command name is that AutoCAD warns you that it does not recognize the command as you typed it. Then AutoCAD gives you another chance or prompts you to get help.

If you notice a typing error before you press Enter, press the Backspace key on the keyboard to erase the characters. Then you can retype the entry. If you just want to start over, you can press Ctrl-X to display `*Delete*`, ignore all previous characters on the line, and get a blank new line to enter what you intended.

If you start the wrong command, and it is already showing on the `Command:` prompt, you can press Ctrl-C one or more times to cancel any command and return to the `Command:` prompt.

Using the ERASE Command

AutoCAD also forgives you if you draw something that you do not want or if you put an object in the wrong place.

You can remove an entity by using the ERASE command, and then you can redraw the entity. When you use ERASE, the crosshairs change to a *pick box*. You move the pick box until it touches the entity that you want to remove. Select the entity by clicking on it with your pointing device's pick button.

AutoCAD offers you other ways to select entities and other ways to salvage errors without erasing. For now, however, ERASE is enough to get you out of a jam if you get stuck with a screen filled with lines that you do not want.

In the following exercise you erase the `Welcome...` text on your screen. You find the ERASE command in the Modify menu.

Using ERASE To Remove an Entity

`Command:` *Choose* View, *then* Zoom, *then* Window	Begins the ZOOM command with the Window option
`_'zoom All/Center/Dynamic/Extents/Left/ Previous/Vmax/Window/<Scale(X/XP)>: w`	
`First corner:` *Pick a point at the lower left corner of the text*	Locates the zoom window's first corner
`Other corner:` *Pick a point at the upper right corner of the text*	Locates the window's second corner
`Command:` *Choose* Modify, *then* Erase, *then* Single	Issues the ERASE command with the Single option
`_erase`	
`Select objects: si`	
`Select objects:` *Place the pick box on the "W" of Welcome, as shown in figure 2.13, and click the pick button*	Selects the object to be erased and erases the text
`Select objects: 1 found`	

Figure 2.13:

Selecting text for erasing.

The Single menu choice issues ERASE with the Single option, prompts you to select an object, and immediately erases it. You then can select the Single menu choice again to erase another entity. If you enter **ERASE** at the `Com-`

`mand:` prompt or use the Select menu choice, ERASE lets you select many entities and then erases them at the same time. You can choose Oops to bring back the last entity group erased. You also can enter E at the `Command:` prompt to issue the ERASE command. If you want to try the screen menu, you can find the ERASE command under the EDIT group.

Using the UNDO Command

Sometimes, you may discover you that have executed many commands, and yet your drawing is not turning out quite right. You may have made a crucial mistake, and you may need to back up in your drawing session to the point where the error was made. You can use AutoCAD's UNDO command to step back, one command at a time. This can be more helpful than just erasing, because the UNDO command undoes not only entities, but also the zooms and screen settings that you may have changed along the way.

The following exercise introduces you to the UNDO command.

Using UNDO To Reverse an Erasure

`Command:` *Choose* Assist, *then* Undo	
`Command: _U GROUP`	Makes the text reappear
`Command:` *Choose* Assist, *then* Redo	Makes the text disappear again
`Command: _redo`	

The Assist pull-down menu has two selections that control undoing: Undo and Redo. The Undo selection issues the U command, which cancels the last command or *group*. Any menu choice, even if it issues several commands, is considered one group and is undone in one step. In most cases, this means only the last command. If you repeat a command (such as CIRCLE) several times in succession, however, you can use U to undo several items at the same time. AutoCAD also features the UNDO command, which offers additional controls (these are covered in later chapters).

The Redo selection issues the REDO command, which undoes U and UNDO. Although you can select Undo repeatedly to back up step-by-step, you can use Redo only once, immediately after U or UNDO.

It is often just as convenient to enter a U from the keyboard as it is to select the UNDO command from a menu.

Getting Help from AutoCAD

Help is almost always available in AutoCAD. The only drawback to the AutoCAD help feature, however, is that often when you need help, you may not understand enough about the HELP command's features to really use them. The following sections show you the various ways to access on-line help.

You can find the Help command in the Assist pull-down menu. When you issue the HELP command, AutoCAD first displays instructions for using the HELP dialog box (see fig. 2.14). Enter the command's name and AutoCAD provides an explanation of that command. If you click on Index, AutoCAD displays the Help Index dialog box, and lists all commands matching the text in the Pattern edit box. This pattern is initially set to *, which matches all command names. This may be a good starting point if you are not familiar with the commands. Another way to use the HELP command is to issue it while using the command about which you want to learn more. A description of how to use the command is given, and the command continues. This is called *context-sensitive* help.

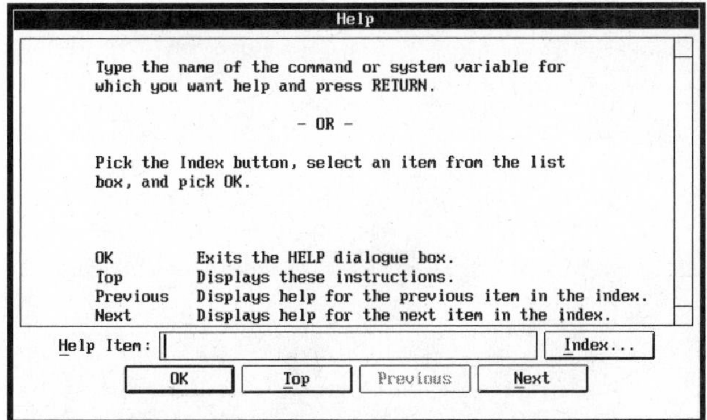

Figure 2.14:

The Help dialog box.

In the following exercise, you request help while using the COPY command. Note that you can use a question mark (?) as an abbreviation for the HELP command. In this case, you are using the HELP command as a *transparent* command; that is, you are issuing the HELP command while another command is active. When a command runs transparently, it runs while another command is active. You can issue a command transparently by preceding the command's name with an apostrophe ('). You can enter the apostrophe from the keyboard to issue a transparent command.

Using HELP To Get Help

`Command:` *Choose* Assist, *then* Help!	
`Command:'?`	Displays the Help dialog box

The Help dialog box appears with an alphabetical list of commands, as shown in figure 2.14.

In the Help Item *edit box, enter* `LINE`↵	Displays the Help page for the LINE command
Choose OK	Closes the Help dialog box
`Command:` *Choose* Construct, *then* Copy	Starts the COPY command
`_copy`	
`Select objects:` *Choose* Assist, *then* Help!	

AutoCAD displays a Help screen for object selection, as shown in figure 2.15.

Choose the down-arrow scroll button	Scrolls through the `COPY,Select_objects:` help item

The down-arrow scroll button is the small button with an arrow on it pointing down, at the far right of the list box.

Choose OK	Closes the Help dialog box
`Resuming _COPY command.`	
`Select objects:` *Press Ctrl-C*	Cancels the COPY command

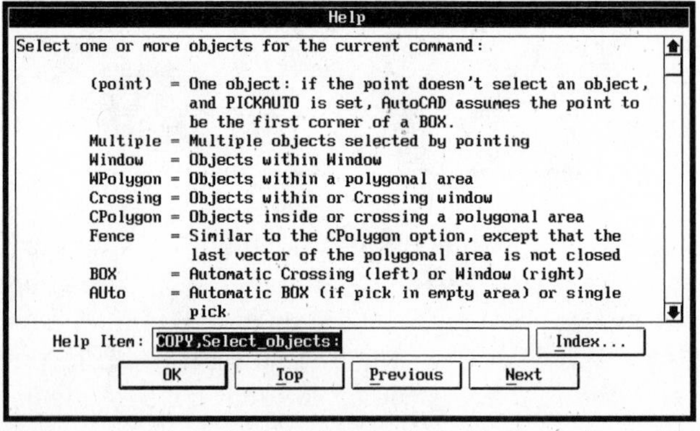

Figure 2.15:

The COPY, *Select_objects:* help screen.

Most dialog boxes contain a Help button, which you can choose to display the Help dialog box.

Using Other Help Features

The large window in the Help dialog box displays Help text. To view the rest of the text, click on the up- or down-arrow buttons on the scroll bar at the right side of the dialog box to scroll up or down. You also can drag the slider box between the arrows up or down to quickly move through the text. As shown earlier, you can type the command's name in the Help Item box to display that command in the window.

Help Dialog Box Buttons

Several other buttons in the Help dialog box are useful for moving through the help text. The Next button skips to the next topic, and the Previous button skips to the previous topic. The Top button takes you back to the beginning of Help.

The Index button opens another dialog box, which contains a list of all the commands for which help is available. You can quickly scan through this list by using the up- and down-arrow buttons or the slider box. It is much easier to find a command in this list than it is to look in the actual help text. To further narrow the search, you can enter a pattern in the Pattern box.

The following exercise shows you how to use the help index to view information about specific commands and procedures.

Getting Help for a Command

`Command:` *Choose* Assist, *then* Help!	Displays the Help dialog box
Click on Index	Displays the Help Index dialog box
Double-click in the Pattern *edit box*	Highlights the * in the edit box
Enter `C*` ↵	Displays only Help entries that begin with the letter C
Double-click on CIRCLE	Displays the Help screen for the CIRCLE command (see fig. 2.16)

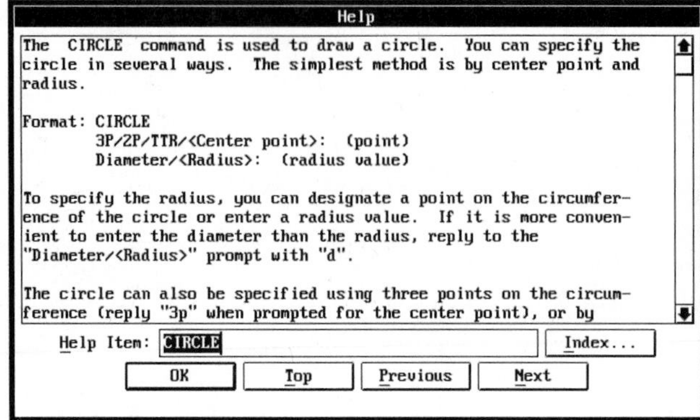

Help
The CIRCLE command is used to draw a circle. You can specify the circle in several ways. The simplest method is by center point and radius.
Format: CIRCLE
3P/2P/TTR/<Center point>: (point)
Diameter/<Radius>: (radius value)
To specify the radius, you can designate a point on the circumference of the circle or enter a radius value. If it is more convenient to enter the diameter than the radius, reply to the "Diameter/<Radius>" prompt with "d".
The circle can also be specified using three points on the circumference (reply "3p" when prompted for the center point), or by
Help Item: CIRCLE
Index...
OK
Top
Previous
Next

Figure 2.16:

The CIRCLE command's Help screen.

You also can request help with a specific procedure. This feature is explained in the next exercise.

Getting Help for Point Entry

Choose Index	Displays the index screen
Double-click in the Pattern *edit box*	Highlights the * in the edit box
Enter `PO*` ↵	Displays only Help entries that begin with the letters *PO*
Double-click on the POINTS *entry*	Displays the Help screen for point entry
Choose OK	Closes the Help dialog box

Figure 2.17 shows a portion of the help for point entry.

Using the File Menu

You learned in earlier exercises how to use several of the command options under the File pull-down menu. The New selection enables you to name a

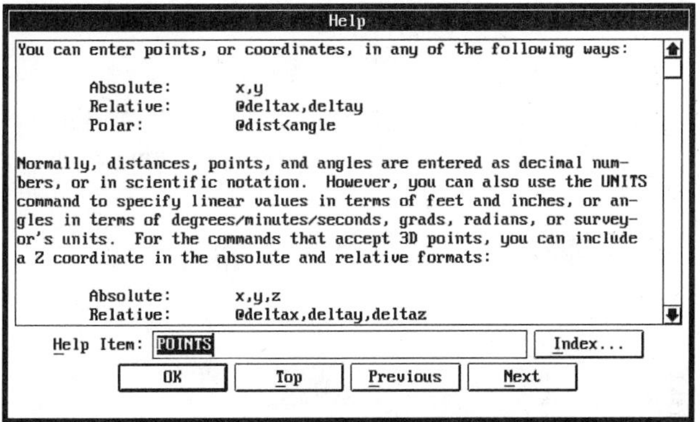

Figure 2.17:

Help for point entry.

new file when you create it. The Save option enables you to save the file again under that name. By choosing Save As, you can rename the file as it is being saved. Unless you are interested in the prototype drawing file options in the Create New Drawing dialog box, it is really not necessary to name a drawing initially because AutoCAD prompts for a file name as soon as you try to save the drawing.

Opening an Existing File

If you want to load an existing drawing into the drawing editor, choose Open from the File pull-down menu; the Open Drawing dialog box appears. Use the up and down arrows or drag the slider box to find the appropriate drawing file's name, and then double-click on that name. The Read Only Mode button enables you to view a file but not to modify it. Of course, you can always enter the name in the File edit box, or click on the Type It button to type the file name on AutoCAD's command line if you already know it.

You learned in earlier exercises how to begin a new drawing and assign it a name, and how to save a drawing after you have made changes to it. The next exercise shows you how to open an existing drawing file and save it with a new name—two functions you may frequently perform.

Opening an Existing Drawing

`Command:` *Choose* File, *then* Open	Displays the Drawing Modification dialog box (see fig. 2.18)
Choose **D**iscard Changes	Discards changes you made to the drawing and opens the Open Drawing dialog box
Double-click on CHAPTER2 *in the* **F**iles: *list box (see fig. 2.19)*	Loads the drawing CHAPTER2 into the graphics editor

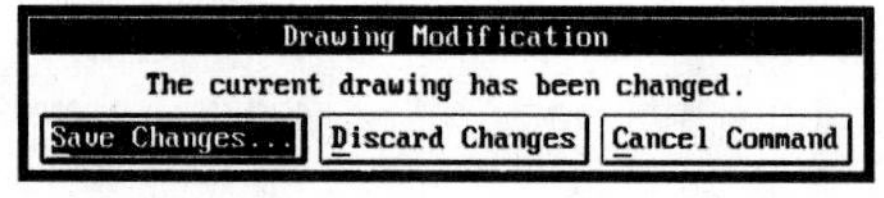

Figure 2.18:

The Drawing Modification dialog box.

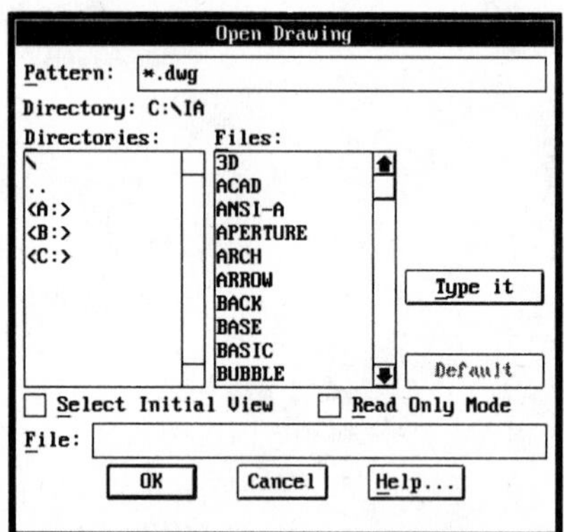

Figure 2.19:

The Open Drawing dialog box.

In the next exercise, you save the drawing with a new name.

Saving a File to a New Name

`Command:` *Choose* File, *then* Save As	Displays the Save drawing as dialog box
`_saveas` *Type* `CHAP2-B`, *then choose* OK	Saves the drawing to a new file and closes the dialog box
`Current drawing name set to C:\IA\CHAP2-B.`	
`Command:` *Choose* File, *then* New, *then* OK	Clears the drawing database without assigning a drawing name
`Command:` *Choose* File, *then* Open	Displays the Open Drawing dialog box

The drawing you saved earlier with the SAVEAS command, CHAP2-B, appears in the Open Drawing dialog box.

Choose Cancel	Closes the dialog box

Specifying File Patterns

After you have used AutoCAD for some time, you will probably have many drawings in your drawing directories. It can be time-consuming to hunt through all of the file names in the Open Drawing dialog box, so AutoCAD provides a means of displaying only the file names you want to view. The default pattern displayed in the box is `*.dwg`. If you only want four-character file names to appear, you can enter a pattern of ????.DWG. Or a pattern of PROJ5*.DWG shows only those files that begin with the characters PROJ5. The following exercise illustrates the use of patterns.

Using File-Name Pattern Filters

`Command:` *Choose* File, *then* Open	Displays the Open Drawing dialog box
Double-click in the Pattern *edit box*	Highlights the *.DWG entry
Enter `C*.DWG`↵	Lists only drawing names that begin with the letter C
Choose Cancel	Aborts the command

Changing Directories

You can see from the previous exercise that the Pattern edit box is very useful for viewing only specific drawings in the selected directory. But what do you do when the drawing you want to load is not in the current directory? Use the Directories list box. The directory window enables you to choose the appropriate directory. Click on the up or down arrows on the scroll bar, or drag the slider box to view the entire list. The arrow buttons in the scroll bar at the right edge of the list box act much like the up- and down-arrow keys on your keyboard. Each click of a scroll arrow button moves the entries in the list box by one item at a time. The slider box, which is located on the scroll bar between the two arrow buttons, enables you to dynamically drag the contents of the list past the viewing window. Double-click on the two dots (..) at the top of the list to move one level closer to the root directory.

Try loading a drawing from the AutoCAD SAMPLE directory in the next exercise.

Loading Drawings from Other Directories

`Command:` *Choose* File, *then* Open	Displays the Open Drawing dialog box
Double-click on .. in the Directories *list box*	Changes to the parent directory
Double-click on ACAD *in the* Directories *list box*	Selects the AutoCAD directory

If AutoCAD is installed in a directory other than \ACAD on your system, substitute the appropriate directory in the previous step.

Double-click on SAMPLE	Selects the \ACAD\SAMPLE directory
Use the down button in the Files *list box to locate the entry* SHUTTLE	
Double-click on SHUTTLE *in the* Files *list box*	Loads the drawing SHUTTLE.DWG from the \ACAD\SAMPLE directory (see fig. 2.20)

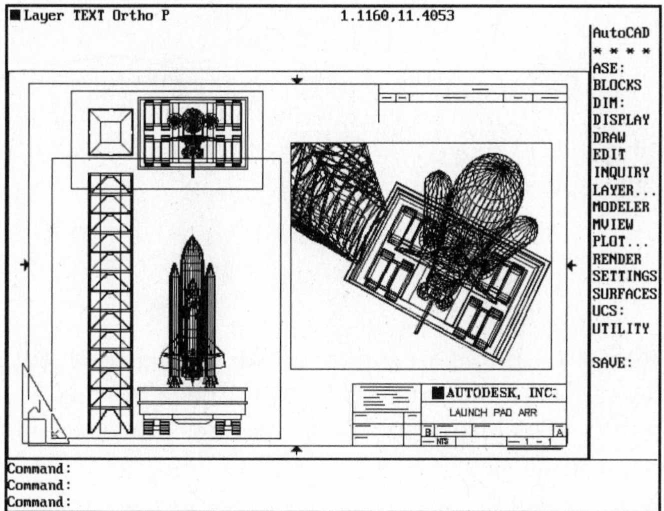

Figure 2.20:
The SHUTTLE drawing.

In the next exercise, you close out the SHUTTLE drawing and load another file from the \IA directory.

Re-loading CHAPTER2 from the \IA Directory

`Command:` *Choose* File, *then* Open	Displays the Open Drawing dialog box
Double-click on .. *in the* Directories *list box*	Selects the \ACAD directory
Double-click on .. *in the* Directories *list box*	Selects the root directory
Double-click on IA *in the* Directories *list box*	Selects the \IA directory
Double-click on CHAPTER2	Loads the drawing CHAPTER2.DWG

Using Other File Menu Options

In addition to commands that enable you to open and save drawing files, the File menu includes commands that perform many other actions. Several of these commands are examined in more detail in other chapters; however, you may be curious as to what these commands do and when you might need them.

Plot

The Plot option, (see Chapter 13), enables you to plot the current drawing. When you choose Plot, AutoCAD displays the Plot dialog box, in which you can select the plotting device and examine or change the many parameters and settings associated with plotting.

About AutoCAD

The About AutoCAD option displays a dialog box of information about your copy of AutoCAD, and displays the contents of the file ACAD.MSG, if the file exists. You can customize the ACAD.MSG file to provide additional information about your company, special operating instructions, or any other information you choose.

Exit AutoCAD

The Exit AutoCAD option does just what its name implies; it exits from AutoCAD and returns to the operating system. If you prefer a quicker way to exit AutoCAD, enter the QUIT command at the AutoCAD `Command:` prompt. The QUIT command performs the same function as the Exit AutoCAD option in the File menu. If unsaved data exists, the Drawing Modification dialog box enables you to save or discard the changes.

Configure

The Configure option steps you through AutoCAD's interactive configuration, which defines to AutoCAD the hardware you are using. The menu header, shown in figure 2.21, gives information ranging from your AutoCAD version and serial number to your current hardware selections. If someone else installed your software, you may want to copy this hardware information, in case you have to reconfigure the software in the future. This configuration also tells who owns your program's license and from which dealer it was obtained; this is the dealer who is required to provide you with support. See Appendix A for more details about the Configure option.

```
          A U T O C A D (R)
Copyright (c) 1982-92  Autodesk, Inc.  All Rights Reserved.
Release Q.0.33 (5/4/92) 386 DOS Extender
Serial Number:  118-10007017
ALPHA VERSION -- NOT FOR RESALE
Licensed to:    Jim Boyce, New Riders Publishing
Obtained from:  Autodesk - 415-331-2354

Configuration menu

  0.  Exit to drawing editor
  1.  Show current configuration
  2.  Allow detailed configuration

  3.  Configure video display
  4.  Configure digitizer
  5.  Configure plotter
  6.  Configure system console
  7.  Configure operating parameters

Enter selection <0>:
```

Figure 2.21:
Configuration settings.

Utilities

The Utilities option enables you to perform disk-file maintenance operations. The File Utilities dialog box enables you to perform many common file maintenance chores from within the drawing editor. This is especially helpful if you have not learned how to maneuver about in your computer's operating system. Four of the dialog box's options—List files, Delete file, Copy file, and Rename file—are commands every CAD operator needs to use. The Unlock file option unlocks a file that was accidentally left locked by the file-locking function, which enables only one session to edit the drawing at a time. Choosing any of these options opens the appropriate dialog box, enabling the selections of directories, files, and pattern names.

You also can perform general maintenance on your files and directories—such as copying, renaming, and deleting files—by using the corresponding commands directly from the operating system. There is no harm in doing so; they perform the same tasks. Table 2.1 lists AutoCAD's file-maintenance commands and their DOS-command equivalents.

NOTE

If you get a `Waiting for file: ... Locked by ... Press Ctrl-C to cancel.` message, make absolutely sure that no one else is using the file. If you are positively sure that no one else is using it, the file may have been left locked accidentally. If so, you can use the Unlock option to unlock it. File locking enhances security on networks.

Table 2.1
AutoCAD File Utility Commands

Command	*Equivalent DOS Command*
List files	DIR
Copy file	COPY
Rename file	REN
Delete file	DEL
Unlock file	none
Exit	none (returns to the `Command:` prompt)

You also can access the AutoCAD file utilities from the drawing editor by entering FILES at the `Command:` prompt.

The Compile *shape/font file* option is not covered in this book. This option is used for creating custom text fonts. See *Maximizing AutoCAD, Volume I,* (New Riders Publishing) or the *AutoCAD Reference Manual* for details.

The Recover option is for salvaging a drawing file that AutoCAD does not load because it has detected an error in the file.

Import/Export, Xref, and Applications Menu Options

The Import/Export functions, which are covered extensively in Chapter 18, enable AutoCAD to exchange data with other software. This import/export feature supports common translation file formats, such as DXF, IGES, and PostScript.

Xref is a function that enables the external reference of other drawings and links to be created between drawing databases. This is an extension of blocking techniques and is explained in Chapter 12.

You can choose the Applications option to bring up a dialog box that enables you to load AutoLISP and AutoCAD Development System (ADS) files.

Now that you have used some of AutoCAD's pull-down menus and entered commands at the `Command:` prompt, you are ready to examine the other ways in which you can issue commands and control AutoCAD.

Comparing AutoCAD's Menus

Menus are the interface by which you communicate with AutoCAD. You do not need to remember all the commands and their options and modifiers. Instead, you use the menu system to choose commands with a pointing device. The AutoCAD menus are organized to make navigation through the software as simple as possible, although the commands themselves require a certain amount of study and practice before you feel comfortable using them.

AutoCAD has more than 150 commands, most of which feature numerous options. Most of these commands relate to specific functions such as drawing, editing, or dimensioning. Because many users are somewhat handicapped when it comes to typing, AutoCAD provides an ACAD.MNU file that offers five alternative ways to enter commands from menus:

- Pull-Down Menu
- Screen Menu
- Tablet Menu
- Button Menu
- Pop-Up Menu

In addition to these menus, AutoCAD provides many dialog boxes through which you can make and control input. Menus provide a convenient way to organize and group commands so that they can easily be chosen and executed. You have already used the pull-down menu; the rest of this chapter examines all the menus, as well as dialog boxes.

Most menu items are programmed first to cancel any existing commands before executing the new one. This means that you can execute a command while another one is still active, and the first one is canceled.

AutoCAD's standard menus give you many different ways to execute some of the same commands. You should try all the types of menus available to see which menu method you prefer. Feel free to experiment with the menus as you proceed with this chapter. Note that, in addition to the five methods of command entry listed earlier, you also can enter complete commands directly at the `Command:` prompt, and you can use the command shortcut keys that are defined in the file ACAD.PGP.

Pull-Down Menus

The pull-down menu was introduced in AutoCAD Release 9. This feature was added to make AutoCAD work more like many of the other software packages that had adopted pull-down menus. The menu bar presents a list of titles that indicate the types of selections available in each pull-down menu. The names of the nine pull-down menus appear at the top of the screen in the drawing editor.

Many pull-down menu selections open a child menu to help with sub-command selection, as shown in figure 2.22. Some AutoCAD pull-down menus present dialog boxes for commands with multiple settings and groups of related commands. Many people find pull-down menus easier to use than screen menus because each submenu occupies a different spot on the screen.

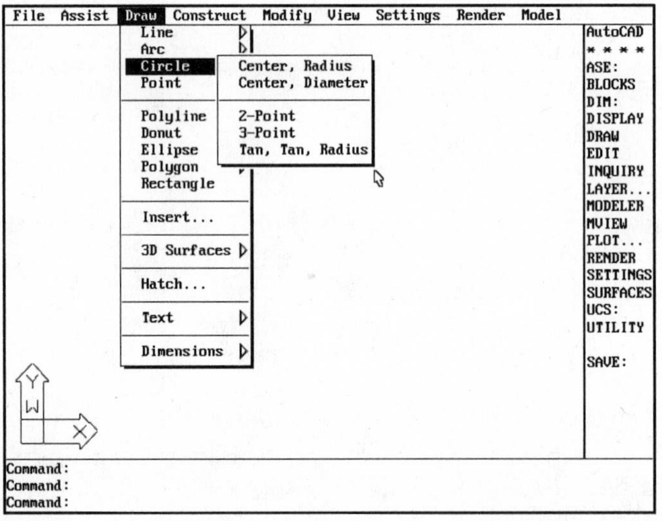

Figure 2.22:

The Draw pull-down menu and the Circle child menu.

Unless otherwise specified, the instructions in this book's exercises refer to the pull-down menus.

Here are some minor points you should remember about the pull-down menus.

- If a pull-down selection is followed by three dots (such as Hatch...), that selection calls up a dialog box or an AutoLISP program.

- Selections followed by an arrow, such as Dimensions, call up *child*, or cascading, menus. You can either click on the menu option to open the child menu, or highlight the right edge (the menu arrow) with the cursor arrow. When you choose a pull-down menu item a second time, the previous cascading menu command is automatically highlighted, so you can just double-click the pull-down menu name if you want to use the same command again. If you want a different selection from a child menu that is already displayed, click on the pull-down to open the menu, move the cursor to the right of the menu area (leaves the child menu open), then come back into the main pull-down menu from either side or into the child menu from the right side to select the option you want. This enables you to select a new option without closing, and then reopening, the child menu.

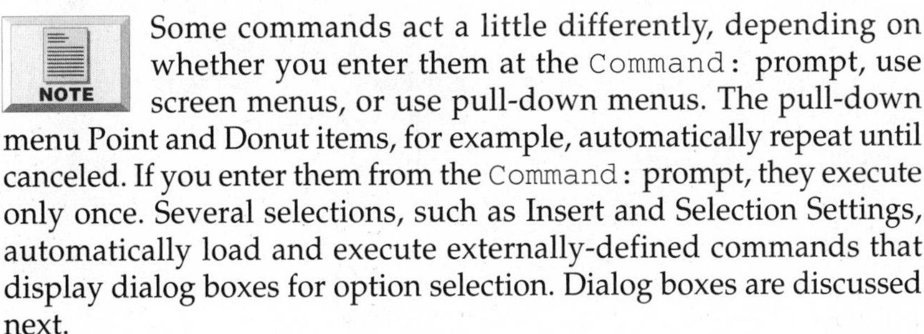

NOTE

Some commands act a little differently, depending on whether you enter them at the `Command:` prompt, use screen menus, or use pull-down menus. The pull-down menu Point and Donut items, for example, automatically repeat until canceled. If you enter them from the `Command:` prompt, they execute only once. Several selections, such as Insert and Selection Settings, automatically load and execute externally-defined commands that display dialog boxes for option selection. Dialog boxes are discussed next.

Dialog Boxes

AutoCAD's dialog boxes offer a unique and convenient way to view and adjust certain AutoCAD settings, to enter and edit text strings, and to enter file names. Although dialog boxes are usually brought up through menu selections that contain their commands, you also can access them by entering their command names at the `Command:` prompt. Most names begin with DD, such as DDEMODES. Table 2.2 lists the commands that use dialog boxes.

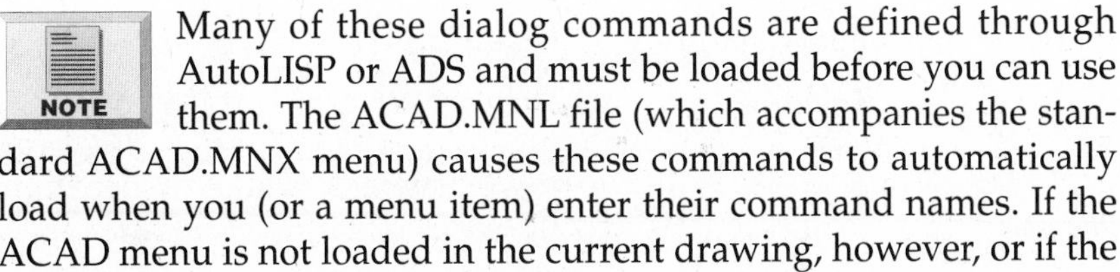

NOTE

Many of these dialog commands are defined through AutoLISP or ADS and must be loaded before you can use them. The ACAD.MNL file (which accompanies the standard ACAD.MNX menu) causes these commands to automatically load when you (or a menu item) enter their command names. If the ACAD menu is not loaded in the current drawing, however, or if the

ACAD.MNL file is not on the AutoCAD search path, these commands are not auto-loaded when you try to use them. If you use a different menu file, it needs an MNL file that contains the contents of ACAD.MNL. For example, if your menu is MYOWN.MNU (or MNX), you need a corresponding MYOWN.MNL file that includes the contents of ACAD.MNL.

Table 2.2
Commands that Issue Dialog Boxes

Command	*Pull-Down Menu Selection*	*Purpose*
DDEMODES	Entity Modes	Sets layer, color, linetype, and other default properties for new entities
DDLMODES	Layer Control	Creates layers, sets their default properties, and controls visibility
DDRMODES	Drawing Aids	Controls snap, grid, modes, and isometric settings
DDATTE		Edits attributes in blocks
DDUCS	Named UCS	Controls the User Coordinate Systems
DDEDIT		Edits text entities or attribute definitions
DDIM	Dimension Style	Sets dimensioning styles and variables
DDGRIPS	Grips	Controls Autoedit grips
DDSELECT	Selection Settings	Enables entity-selection settings to be changed
DDOSNAP	Object Snap	Controls running object snaps
DDINSERT	Insert	Assists in block insertion
DDRENAME		Enables names of blocks, layers, views, and so on, to be renamed
DDATTEXT		Controls attribute extraction
DDATTDEF		Helps in defining attributes
DDUNITS	Units Control	Controls all the units options
DDCHPROP	Properties	Helps to change entity properties
ALL FILE	Various	Display and scroll through lists of file names

When a dialog box appears on the screen, it shows a list of settings and their current values. Some settings are on/off boxes with a check to indicate when they are on. You click on the box with the pointer's pick button to turn a setting on or off. Other boxes display values such as names, colors, or distances. You change these edit boxes by highlighting and editing them or by entering a new value. Some values, such as file or layer names, are presented in list boxes, which may only show a portion of a long list. These list boxes have scroll bars at the right side to scroll up and down the lists. A typical dialog box, such as the one that defines drawing tools, is shown in figure 2.23.

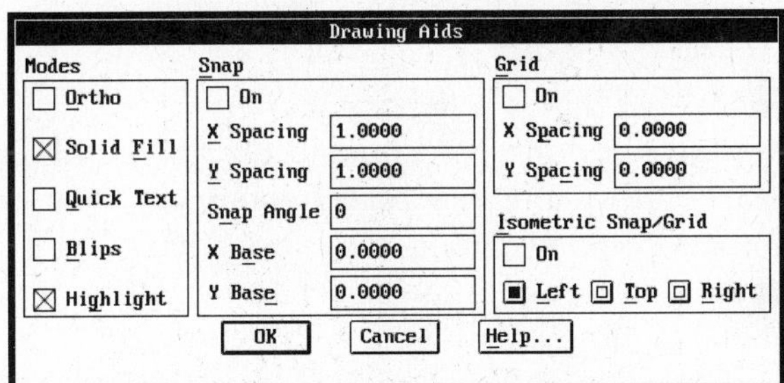

Figure 2.23:

The Drawing Aids dialog box.

Although dialog boxes duplicate the functions of other commands, they provide clearer and more convenient control over complex commands or groups of commands. You will find additional explanations and practice exercises for dialog boxes later in this chapter.

Icon Menus and Image Buttons

AutoCAD also can display menu selections as graphic images in a special type of dialog box, called an *icon menu*. AutoCAD uses slide files to construct these special menus. When AutoCAD displays an icon menu, you choose a menu item by clicking on a graphical representation of the selection (an *icon*). AutoCAD executes the corresponding selection like any other menu selection. The Previous and Next buttons flip through other pages of icons. AutoCAD has a number of preset icon menus, such as those used for hatch patterns, as shown in figure 2.24.

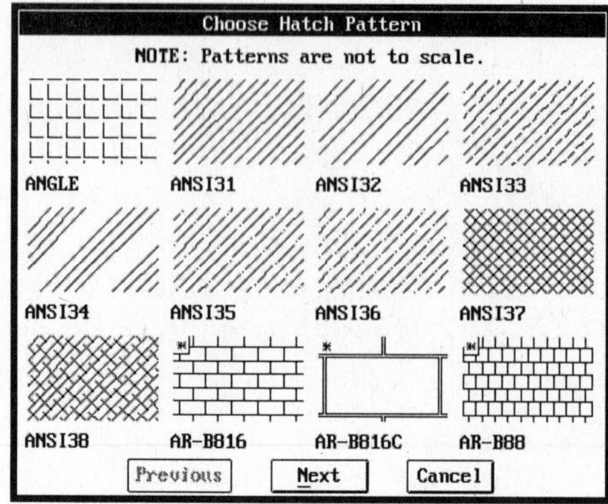

Figure 2.24:

The Choose Hatch Pattern dialog box.

Icon menus sometimes show only a selection of icons in addition to the Previous, Next, and Cancel buttons, with no additional controls on the dialog box associated with the icons. Other icon menus include a text list box at the left of the dialog box, which describes each icon's function. In addition to selecting an icon, you also can select a description from the list, and the associated icon is automatically selected, as well.

AutoCAD also uses other dialog boxes that can display images. These dialog boxes use image buttons to graphically illustrate command options. *Image buttons* are very much like standard control buttons, except that they display pictures rather than words. Dialog boxes containing image buttons function very much like icon menus; that is you click on an image button to issue a command function associated with the button, just as clicking on an icon issues a command or selects an option.

The Screen Menu

The *screen menu* appears on the right side of the screen in the drawing editor. Recall that you make your screen menu selections by highlighting the item with your pointing device and pressing the pick button. A *branch* is an item that activates another AutoCAD submenu. The groupings of menu pages are for convenience only and have no effect on AutoCAD's command structure. If you get lost, just choose AutoCAD at the top of any screen menu. This choice returns you to the initial screen menu, called the *root menu*, and restores the initial pull-down menu bar.

Exercise instructions referring to screen menus assume that their menu selections are currently visible on the screen menu. If not visible, choose the AutoCAD selection at the top of the screen menu.

When you choose a menu item, it changes menu pages or sends a command, option, or a series of commands to AutoCAD for execution. This command execution is the same as if you had typed the input. You may remember from using the pull-down menu that screen menus are often activated from the pull-down selections to help you with command options. In this way, AutoCAD's screen menus are context-sensitive, changing appropriately as you select pull-down menu items.

Keyboard Access to the Screen Menu

You also can access the screen menu from the keyboard. The keyboard offers two methods of screen menu selection. The first method is to press the menu cursor key (usually Ins) to highlight a menu selection. Use the up- and down-arrow keys to move the highlighted bar to the menu item you want and press Ins again (or press Enter) to choose the item.

The second method of accessing the screen menu from the keyboard is to start typing characters of the menu selection at the `Command:` prompt. As you type, the menu label beginning with the characters you type becomes highlighted. Most selections are highlighted by typing one or two characters, and then you press Enter or Ins to execute the selection.

Screen Menu Conventions

As you move through the screen menus, notice that the DIM:, LAYER:, UCS:, and SAVE: selections are followed by colons. These selections often branch to a new menu page and always start the command. Any selection that automatically starts a command has a colon after the menu label. Many commands require subcommands in order to complete their chores. These subcommands usually are listed in lowercase letters. As you flip through menu pages, remember that you always can return to the root menu by choosing AutoCAD at the top of the menu page.

At the bottom of most menu pages are shortcut branches that enable you to return to your LAST menu page or to the DRAW and EDIT menu pages. Some menu pages offer more selections than can fit on one page. In such cases, the next and previous selections flip forward and back through pages to access all the selections available.

Finally, every menu page has * * * * below the AutoCAD selection. This selection presents you with a menu page containing choices for HELP, U (Undo), REDO, REDRAW, SETVAR, and object snaps. *Object snaps* are aids for drawing objects. Chapter 4 covers the object snap options.

Menus are a powerful tool in AutoCAD, giving you flexibility in command entry. With a little practice, you should soon find your preferences. Many users, however, prefer to use a tablet menu, as described in the next section.

The Tablet Menu

AutoCAD comes with a standard tablet menu that performs many of the same functions as the screen and pull-down menus. Figure 2.25 shows the complete tablet menu. The tablet menu offers a few advantages over the other menu options. You can easily remember where to find tablet menu selections, and you always can find them without flipping through menu pages. The tablet menu also includes graphic images to help you identify your selection. Many selections from the tablet menu call the appropriate screen menu pages to help you in your subcommand option selections.

To bring up AutoCAD's standard tablet menu, you need to run through a small set of configuration steps. See Appendix A for help in configuring the AutoCAD standard tablet menu.

Button Functions

Nearly everyone uses some type of pointing device with AutoCAD—usually a mouse or tablet puck (see fig. 2.26). AutoCAD reserves one button on the puck or mouse for picking points and choosing screen and tablet menu items. This is the button that tells AutoCAD to pick a point or select an object where the cursor or crosshairs are positioned on the screen.

A mouse usually has two or three buttons, and a puck can have up to sixteen buttons. The position of the pick button varies with the device. The second button acts as an Enter key. Most of the other buttons are assigned to do the same duties as the function keys and control settings explored in the next chapter.

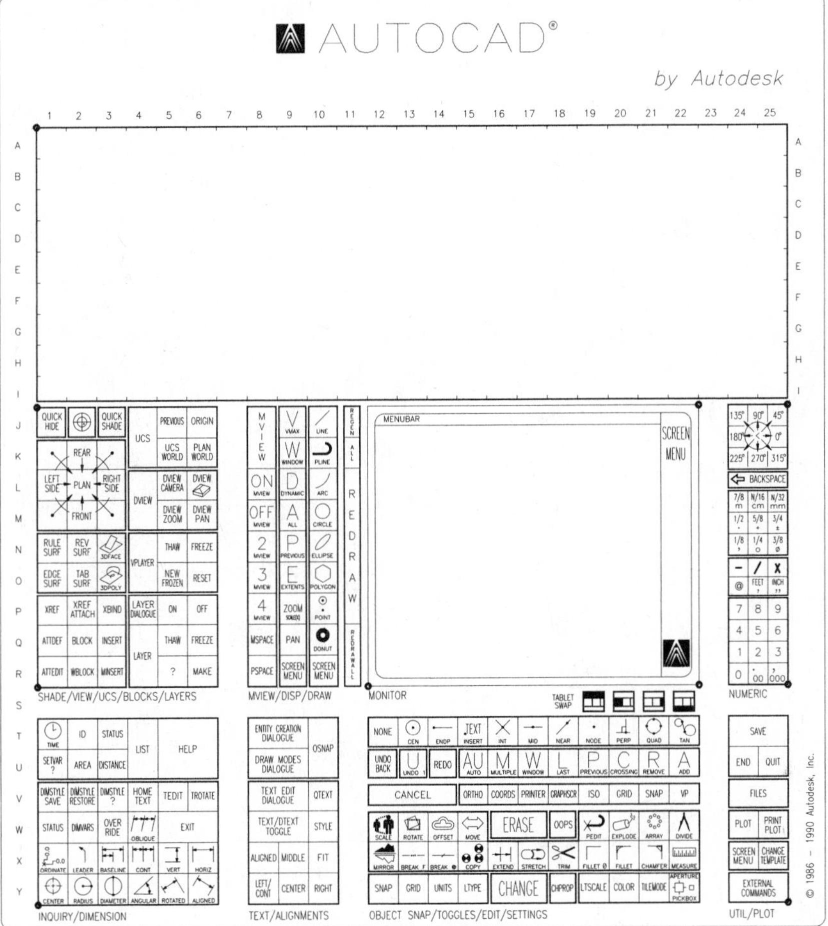

Figure 2.25:

The AutoCAD tablet menu.

Pop-Up Menu

AutoCAD button 2 displays the pop-up (cursor) menu on the screen at the pointer position. This enables easy access to the object snap modes and point filters. AutoCAD button 2 is usually the middle button on a three-button mouse. If you use a two-button mouse, you can hold down Shift while you press the right button to display the pop-up menu. On a digitizer puck, AutoCAD button 2 is the next-lowest numbered button after the pick button and the Enter button. AutoCAD button 2 is referred throughout this book as the *pop-up button*.

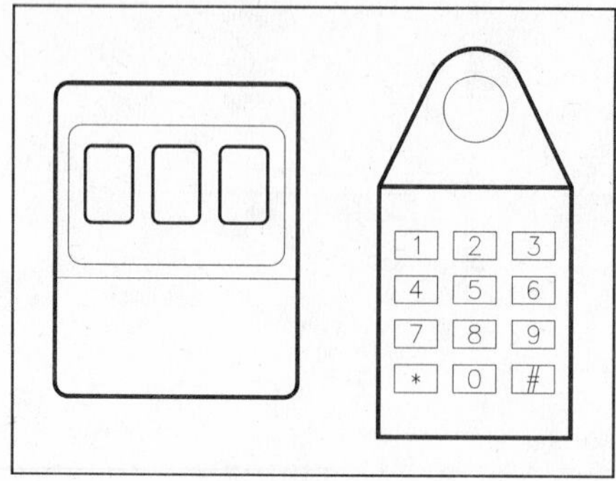

Figure 2.26:

A typical mouse and puck.

Buttons Menu

Some digitizing pucks and other input devices have sixteen or more buttons. AutoCAD's standard menu file, ACAD.MNU, also includes a buttons menu that assigns additional functions to the buttons on pointing devices that have more than four buttons. AutoCAD assigns these auxiliary button as follows:

Button Function	*Effect*
^B	Snap
^O	Ortho
^G	Grid
^D	Coordinate Display
^E	Isoplane
^T	Tablet On/Off

You can assign the buttons to execute other menu selections by creating a custom button menu. For details on creating button menus, see *Maximizing AutoCAD, Volume I,* (New Riders Publishing) or Appendix C of this book.

Using Keyboard Commands versus Menus

Many experienced users think that keyboard command entry can be just as fast if not faster than menus. This is particularly true if you use AutoCAD's *command alias* feature. A command alias is an abbreviation that you can use

instead of typing the entire command name. When you use an alias, AutoCAD replaces it with the full command name and executes the command normally. To execute the Circle command from a menu, for example, you pull down the Draw menu or choose the DRAW screen menu, then choose the Circle icon or CIRCLE items. Or, you can merely type a C, press Enter, and be done with it. Some of AutoCAD's standard abbreviations are shown in table 2.3.

Table 2.3
Keyboard Command Abbreviations

Alias	*Command*	*Alias*	*Command*
A	ARC	LA	LAYER
C	CIRCLE	M	MOVE
CP	COPY	P	PAN
DV	DVIEW	PL	POLYLINE
E	ERASE	R	REDRAW
L	LINE	Z	ZOOM

These abbreviations cover only a few of AutoCAD's many commands, but you can easily create your own abbreviations by modifying the ACAD.PGP file. This procedure is explained in Appendix C, and a more comprehensive IA-ACAD.PGP file is included on the optional IA DISK. You can use that file or create your own custom ACAD.PGP file for your most frequently used commands.

AutoCAD offers a similar keyboard shortcut for command options. Instead of flipping through menus for command options, you can abbreviate virtually any command option to the one or two letters that are unique for that option at the current prompt. For example, recall the ZOOM prompt:

```
All/Center/Dynamic/Extents/Left/Previous/Vmax/Window/<Scale(X/XP)>:
```

Earlier, the ZOOM Window menu item you used responded to this prompt with merely a W, not with the entire word WINDOW. You need only type the characters that are shown as uppercase in AutoCAD prompts to execute an option.

The purpose of this book is to teach you AutoCAD thoroughly, so you want to become intimately familiar with the AutoCAD commands. Pull-down menu selection is emphasized because that is probably the easiest interface for a new user. After you learn the commands, you can decide if keyboard entry, abbreviations, or other menus are better for you.

AutoCAD's standard menus are general purpose, but you may do specific types of drawings for which custom menus are much more efficient. You can purchase custom menus for many different applications (see your AutoCAD dealer). Or you can create your own custom menus, as comprehensively covered in *Maximizing AutoCAD, Volume I,* (New Riders Publishing).

Most users find that a combination of keyboard commands or abbreviations and menu selections works out well.

The following section thoroughly covers the use of dialog boxes. As more software packages are starting to use a Windows type of dialog box, it becomes easier for a user to learn several software packages. If you are new to the type of dialog boxes that AutoCAD uses, this next section should be of special interest.

Using Dialog Boxes

Dialog boxes are more convenient than AutoCAD's other data-entry methods because they enable you to view or change several items at a time. In addition, dialog boxes are the only way to view a list of files when you need to specify a file name.

Entering Text in Dialog Boxes

The Open Drawing dialog box and other file dialog boxes in AutoCAD are almost identical to the Save Drawing As dialog box, which is shown in figure 2.27. This dialog box, which contains most of the dialog box features, appears when you enter the SAVE command if you have not yet named the current drawing. Dialog box features that are not part of the Save Drawing As dialog box are explained after the following exercise.

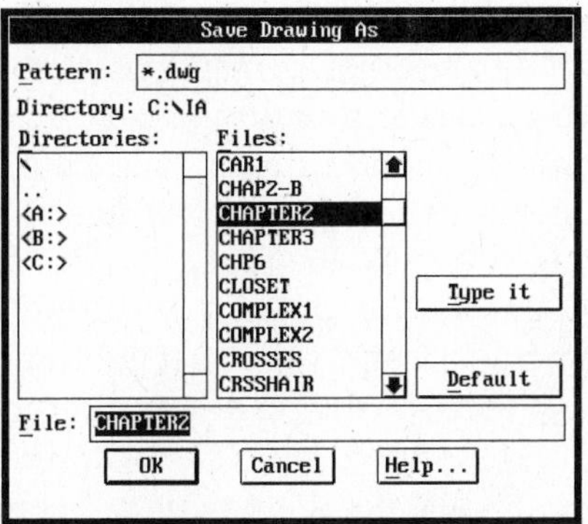

Figure 2.27:

The Save Drawing As dialog box.

You use *edit boxes* in dialog boxes to enter text and values such as file, color, layer names, distances, or scale factors. In the Save Drawing As dialog box, the long rectangular box immediately above the OK button is an edit box. This edit box is highlighted when the Save Drawing As dialog box appears. To highlight an edit box that is not currently highlighted, click on it. Your keyboard's Tab key also moves between the edit boxes and buttons, highlighting each one as you move to it. If the edit box or button name has a single underlined letter, that letter can be typed from the keyboard to highlight that location. The underlined T in the Type it button is a shortcut key. If an edit box is in the text-entry mode, you must hold down Alt while typing the shortcut key.

When an edit box is highlighted, the characters you type replace the current value. If you want to edit the current value instead of replacing it, click on the edit box or press one of the cursor-control keys. A vertical-bar text cursor appears to mark the current character-entry position. The cursor-control keys are the four arrow keys and the Home and End keys. The left- and up-arrow keys move the text cursor one character to the left; the right- and down-arrow keys move it to the right. The Home and End keys move the text cursor to the beginning and end of the line. The Backspace and Del keys delete the character before and after the current text cursor position. Any characters you type are inserted at the current text-cursor position. If the value is too long to fit into the edit box, it scrolls to the left or right. You can use the cursor keys to scroll the text in the box.

When you have the desired text in the edit box, you can accept it by pressing Enter or by clicking on the OK button. OK, Cancel, Type it and Default are examples of dialog box buttons. A *button* is an object that immediately

executes an action when you click on it. Some buttons, such as the **S**et Color button in the Layer Control dialog box, open child dialog boxes, which you use to enter new values. You can select a button by clicking on it or by using its shortcut key (if it has one). In the file dialog boxes, the OK button accepts the current settings, exits, and performs the file action, and the Cancel button exits without making changes. The Enter and Esc keys also are shortcut alternatives to OK and Cancel buttons. If AutoCAD does not accept your new value, it is invalid and you must edit it or cancel the change. The **T**ype it button closes the dialog box and returns you to the `Command:` prompt, and the **D**efault button restores all settings in the file dialog box to what they were when the dialog box appeared.

Using Dialog Box Lists

You also can enter a file name and make selections in dialog boxes by selecting from lists. To select an item in the list, click on it or use the cursor keys to move up and down the list. If you double-click on an item, the same action occurs as when you select the item and press Enter. When you double-click on a file name in the file list box, the file name is selected and a file action occurs on the chosen item. In the file dialog boxes, the file name you choose from the list appears in the file name edit box. Edit and list boxes that are linked this way are called *combo boxes.*

If an item is gray in a dialog box, it usually means the item currently is not relevant or cannot be selected.

The list of directory names below the **D**irectories label also is a list box. When you select a directory from it, its name appears on the line above the list box. You can, however, use the **F**ile edit box to change directories. If you preface the text you enter in the **F**ile edit box with a backslash, AutoCAD interprets it as a directory name rather than a file name, changing the current directory and the contents of the file name and directory lists.

The other type of list box found in some dialog boxes is the *pop-up list.* When you click on the pop-up (arrow) icon at the right of a pop-up list, the list box appears below the pop-up box. After the list is highlighted, you can use the cursor keys to scroll up and down the hidden list, or select an item by pressing the key of that item's first character.

Filtering File Names in a File Dialog Box

The line above the Directories list and the File edit box shows the current defaults for the directory and file name. The Pattern edit box, at the top of the dialog box, enables you to specify file patterns to show in the list. You can filter the file names that are to be listed in the file name list box by entering DOS wild cards and text strings in the pattern edit box.

Using File Dialog Boxes

When you save your drawing, use the Save Drawing As dialog box to try out various dialog box features. The following exercise tests the features found in this dialog box. If your AutoCAD program directory is not named ACAD, substitute your directory's name for \ACAD in the next exercise.

Saving a Drawing with the Save Drawing As Dialog Box

Continue from the previous drawing, with CHAPTER2.DWG loaded.

`Command:` **`SAVE`** ↵	Displays the Save Drawing As dialog box

The File edit box is highlighted and displays CHAPTER2, the Files name list shows CHAP2-B.DWG, and the current directory is C:\IA. Other files from the IA Disk also appear in the list.

Double-click on .. in the Directories *list box, then double-click on* ACAD	Changes to the \ACAD directory and redisplays the file and directory lists
Double-click in the Pattern *edit box, then enter* ***.***	Filters the file-name list to display all the files in the \ACAD directory
Click twice on the scroll bar under the slider box to page down the list	
Click on the scroll bar above the slider box button to page up the list	
Click on the down arrow to scroll down one line	
Click on any file name	Displays the name in the File edit box

Click on the right end of the File *edit box and press Backspace four times*	Positions the text cursor and deletes the file extension
Click on the Default *button or press* Alt-D ↵	Restores CHAPTER2 and \IA defaults

You could click on the OK button or press Enter at this point to save to the default, but instead, try the Type it button.

Click on the Type it *button or press* Alt-T ↵	The dialog box disappears and a file-name prompt appears
`Save current changes as <C:\IA\CHAPTER2>:` *Press Enter*	Saves the drawing

As you invest time in your drawings, they become more valuable and you need to save them frequently. Your work is not secure until it is saved to a file on the hard disk, with periodic backups copied to another disk or tape.

MS-DOS file names are limited to eight characters. As you work in AutoCAD, it helps to think ahead about naming and organizing your drawing files. Create file and directory names that help identify the contents of the files. Try to anticipate how you are going to sort your files in the DOS environment. For example, in file lists, PROJ01 and PROJ02 sort in order with PROJ??, but PROJ1 sorts after PROJ02. When you use SAVE to record your work-in-progress, you can adopt a temporary naming convention for saving several levels of backup files: PTEMP01, PTEMP02, and so on.

Choose File, then Save As to display the Save File As dialog box. Some commands, such as BLOCK and INSERT, do not display a file dialog box unless you request it by entering a tilde (~) at the prompt for a file name.

You can turn the file dialog box feature off by setting the FILEDIA AutoCAD system variable to 0. With the file dialog box turned off, all file menu selections and commands prompt for the file name on the `Command:` prompt. If you have the file dialog box feature turned off, you can still pop up file dialog boxes when you want to use them by entering a tilde (~) when prompted for a file name.

Using Other Dialog Box Features

The file dialog boxes contain all dialog features except check boxes, radio buttons, and horizontal slider bars. Figure 2.28 illustrates check boxes and radio buttons in the Drawing Aids dialog box (choose Settings, then Drawing Aids).

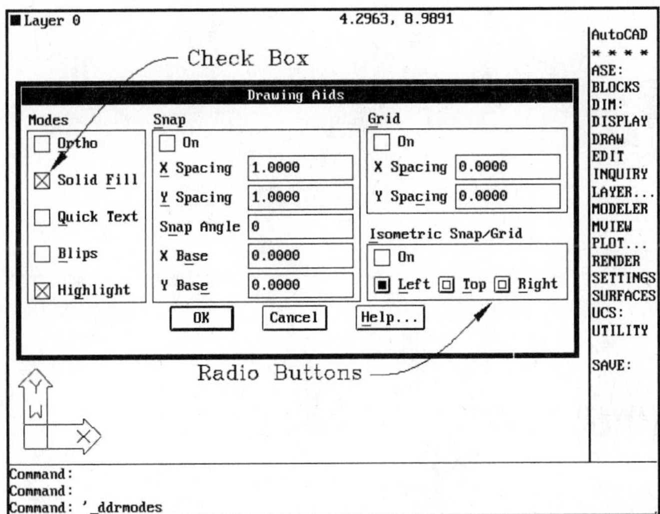

Figure 2.28:

Check boxes and radio buttons in the Drawing Aids dialog box.

Check boxes are on/off switches that appear near key words labeling items that can only be on or off, such as the Grid On or Snap On items in the Drawing Aids dialog box. If an X mark appears in the box, it is on; if the box is blank, it is off. You click on the box to turn it on or off. *Radio buttons* are groups of settings—only one radio button can be on at any one time. Radio buttons appear as a group of circles or squares enclosed in a box, with a black dot indicating which button is on, such as the ISOMETRIC SNAP/GRID group in the Drawing AIDS dialog box.

Slider bars are horizontal sliders that control values. They function the same as list box scroll bars. Figure 2.29 shows a slider in the Grips dialog box (choose Settings, then Grips). The slider controls the size of AutoCAD grip boxes. The slider bar can be dragged by your input device, or you can click on the arrows to adjust the grip size. A sample of the size is shown beside the slider.

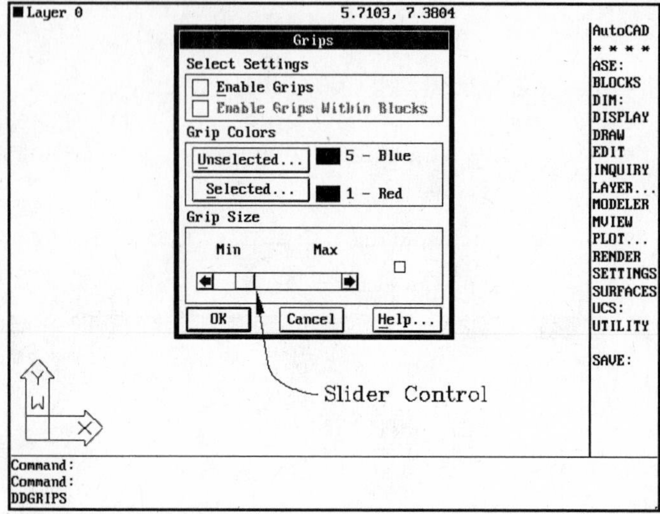

Figure 2.29:

Sliders in the Grips dialog box.

Ending Your Work

Save your work now by using the END command. The END command makes a backup file from your previously saved file, stores the up-to-date copy, and exits the drawing editor. The END command saves the drawing to the current drawing file name. You can type in the END command at the `Command:` prompt or access it from the File menu by choosing the Exit AutoCAD option. In previous releases of AutoCAD, the QUIT command left the drawing editor and discarded any unsaved changes. In Release 12, the QUIT command still warns you that you have unsaved changes and enables you to save them before exiting.

At times, you may need your drawing files to be as small as possible for archiving or exchanging with others. You can sometimes reduce the size of an AutoCAD drawing file by ending twice. That is, end your drawing once, reload it, and end it a second time. When you erase objects in a drawing, they are not actually removed from the drawing database until the drawing is loaded the next time. The process of double-ending a drawing completely purges the drawing of deleted entities. This can save disk space, especially after an extensive editing session.

Summary

You have had a chance to set up AutoCAD and experiment with the drawing editor by entering a few commands. AutoCAD is cooperative. It only takes action when you tell it to do something. AutoCAD lets you know that it is waiting for your input with the `Command:` prompt or other prompts on the prompt line.

Help is always available to you from the pull-down menu, if you type **Help** or **?** at the `Command:` prompt, or if you type **'Help** or **'?** when you are in commands. If you get stuck drawing, you can always undo a command, erase your drawing, or leave the drawing unsaved and start over.

Now that you know your way in and out of AutoCAD, you can move on to organizing AutoCAD's drawing environment and experimenting with using menus. Chapter 3 introduces you to more of the drawing and editing commands in AutoCAD.

NRP
Chapter 2

3

Setting Up an Electronic Drawing

The preparation required for drawing in AutoCAD is much like preparation for drawing on a drafting board. In manual drafting, you select drawing tools to fit your particular drawing; for instance, you might select a 1/16" scale. Similarly, you set up parameters in AutoCAD to fit your particular drawing. That is, you create custom tools to use with AutoCAD. After you set up the proper units, scale, linetype, sheet size, and text, you can begin drawing.

If you take time to set up AutoCAD before you start your drawing, you can save your settings and use them in future drawings, which saves preparation time.

This chapter continues to discuss the AutoCAD menus that were introduced in Chapter 2 and shows you how to set up AutoCAD for drawing. You also learn how to save settings in a prototype drawing.

Organizing Your Drawing Setups

A few differences exist between the process of organizing an electronic drawing and the preparation of a manual drawing. Before you prepare an

electronic drawing sheet, you need to understand how an electronic drawing's scale, layers, and drawing entities are different from their manual-drawing counterparts. For this reason, take a moment to become familiar with scale, layers, and entities.

Understanding Full-Scale Electronic Drawings

In AutoCAD, drawing elements are stored in real-world units. AutoCAD can track your drawing data in fractions or decimals, in meters, millimeters, feet, inches, or just about any unit of measurement that you want to use.

When you draw on a drafting board, you usually create the drawing to fit a specific sheet size or scale. The text, symbols, and line widths are generally about the same size from one drawing to another.

In AutoCAD, however, this process is reversed. You always draw the image at actual size (full scale) in real-world units. The only time you need to worry about scale is during plotting. At plot time, AutoCAD enables you to scale your full-size electronic drawings up or down to fit the plot sheet. You must, therefore, plan ahead for scaling a full-size AutoCAD drawing and make settings that adjust the scale of the text, symbols, and line widths so that they plot at an appropriate size.

A bolt that is two inches long may look ten inches long when it is blown up on the screen, but AutoCAD regards the drawing as being two inches long, no matter how you show it or plot it. To help you get comfortable with electronic scaling, this chapter illustrates setups with different units and sheet sizes.

Working with Electronic Layers

Even in manual drafting, almost everything you design and draw can be thought of as being separated into layers. Printed circuit boards have layers. Buildings are layered by floors. Even schematic diagrams have information layers for annotations. A virtually unlimited number of electronic layers are available in AutoCAD to give you more flexibility and control in organizing your drawing than you would have in manual drafting.

If you have ever done manual drafting, you may have used transparent overlays to separate your drawings into physical layers. Think of AutoCAD's electronic layers in 2D as transparent sheets that are laid

one over the other. When you are working in 2D, you are looking down through a stack of sheets (see fig. 3.1). You can see your entire drawing as it is being built from the superimposed sheets. A single sheet may be pulled out to examine or modify, or you can work with all the layers at once.

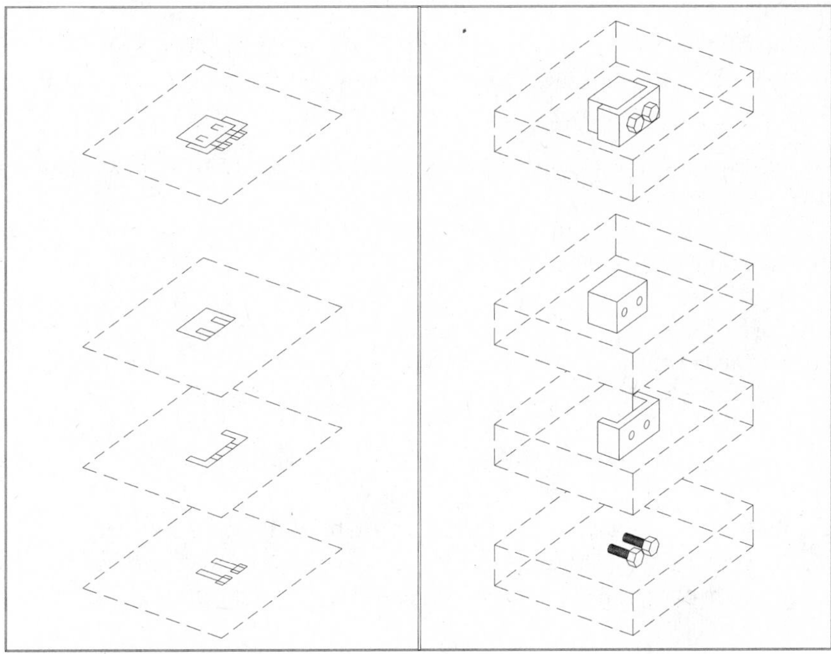

Figure 3.1:

2D and 3D layers.

In 3D, layers become more of an organizational concept and have less physical resemblance to overlays. Any layer can contain any group of objects, which may be superimposed in space to co-exist with other objects on other layers. In 3D, you should think of each layer as containing a unique class of objects. You can look at all layer groups together, or you can look at any combination by specifying the layers you want to see.

Each layer can have any color and linetype associated with it. When you set up your AutoCAD layers, you need to determine which parts of the drawing you are going to place on each layer and what color and linetype you are going to use with each layer. You can make as many or as few layers as you need.

Understanding Entities and Properties

When you use AutoCAD's drawing tools to draw on one of these electronic layers, you create a *drawing entity*. Lines, circles, and text are examples of entities. In addition to its geometric location, each entity has an associated color, layer, and linetype. 3D entities also have thickness and elevation. AutoCAD calls these associations *properties*. Color is commonly used in AutoCAD to control the line weight of entities when they are plotted. You can preset each layer's color and linetype.

One part of preparing for an AutoCAD drawing is determining how you will group entities on layers and what colors and linetypes to use when you construct drawing entities. The simplest (and in many cases, the best) way to organize a drawing is to use layers to control the properties of entities. If you are going to draw a gizmo by using red dashed lines, you can draw it on the red dashed-line layer. Many of these decisions are determined by drawing standards that you previously may have established. If you need to make exceptions, AutoCAD enables you to change the properties of any entity, regardless of its layer.

If you are not using color in your plotted and printed output, you may want to use color to control line weight in your plots. Plotter pens are assigned by entity color. Plotting and color-control for plotting are discussed in Chapter 13.

Setting Up a Drawing

You can find most of the setup tools you need on the Settings pull-down menu (see fig. 3.2) and on the two pages of the SETTINGS screen menu.

When you begin a new drawing, AutoCAD makes several assumptions about drawing setup, including display and input units, scale, and linetype. These pre-established settings are called *defaults*.

AutoCAD sets up many default settings by reading a prototype drawing, which is stored on your hard disk. The AutoCAD prototype drawing, which comes with your AutoCAD software, is called ACAD.DWG. By telling AutoCAD to use no prototype drawing (as you did in Chapter 1), you begin new drawings with all the defaults found in the original ACAD.DWG.

The standard ACAD.DWG prototype assumes that you want to draw entities on layer 0. By default, layer 0 has white, continuous lines. (These

Figure 3.2:

The Settings pull-down menu and first page of the SETTINGS screen menu.

may appear inverted as black lines on a white background on some systems, but AutoCAD still treats them as white lines.) The ACAD.DWG also assumes a default system of measurement display (called *units*) that uses decimal units and initial drawing limits of 12 units in the X direction and 9 units in the Y direction. The drawing *limits* define your intended drawing area.

When you set up your drawing, you actually are modifying settings that were passed by AutoCAD from the prototype drawing into your new drawing. As you set up your drawing, AutoCAD shows you the default values in brackets at the `Command:` prompt. You can accept the default values by pressing Enter. You also can create one or more custom prototype drawings and tell AutoCAD the prototype drawing you want to use for these defaults. This technique is demonstrated later in this book.

Determining a Scale Factor and Drawing Limits

How do you calculate the scale you need? First, establish your system of units. Second, determine a scale factor. A *scale factor* is a setting that enables you to produce a plot at the size you want from a drawing that you have created at actual size (*full scale*). You set your electronic sheet so that you can draw at full scale.

The following sections show you how to tailor AutoCAD settings by examining an architectural drawing and an engineering drawing. After you become familiar with these sample drawings, you learn how to set up layers by creating a simple one-to-one scale drawing.

First, you must determine a drawing scale factor, and then you use it to calculate the following AutoCAD settings:

- Sheet size (limits)
- Line width
- Text height
- Symbol size
- Linetype scale

The limits setting is the most important setting affected by a scale factor because it is the AutoCAD equivalent of sheet size. You set the drawing's limits during the initial drawing setup; other drawing effects are set later.

Determining Scale Factor and Sheet Size

Sheet size is calculated in much the same way as in manual drafting, except that you use the resulting scale ratio to scale up the sheet size to fit around the full-scale size of your drawing. Then, when you plot the drawing, you scale everything back down by the same factor. In traditional drafting, the drawing is scaled down to fit within the sheet.

If you are working with an architectural calculation for a floor plan that is 75 feet by 40 feet, you may want the drawing to be scaled at 1/4" = 1' (12"). What is your scale factor, and what size electronic sheet are you going to use? The size of your electronic sheet is set by the limits that you choose. The limits are determined by the X,Y values of the lower left and upper right corners of your electronic sheet.

If you convert your drawing scale to a ratio of 1:*n*, then *n* is your scale factor. If you already have selected a drawing scale, you can easily determine the scale factor. Thus, in this example, because you are working at 1/4" = 1'-0", your scale factor is 48. The mathematics look something like this:

1/4:12/1 converts to 1:48/1 or 1:48 for a scale factor of 48.

If, on the other hand, you select a drawing scale of 3/8" = 1'-0", your drawing scale factor is 32. The math looks like this:

3/8:12/1 converts to 1:96/3 or 1:32 for a scale factor of 32.

Calculating a Sheet Size for a Known Scale and Object Size

Use your scale factor to determine your electronic drawing limits by running some test calculations on possible plotting sheet sizes. You set the limits by multiplying the sheet size by your scale factor. Follow this sample set of calculations:

Size of floor plan	*75" × 40'*
Scale	*1/4" = 12"*
Determine scale factor	*48*

Now, test a 17-by-11-inch sheet:

17" × 48 = 816" or 68'

11" × 48 = 528" or 44'

A 17" × 11" sheet equals 68' × 44' at 1/4" to 12" scale.

This sheet size is too small because the 75' × 40' drawing does not fit on the sheet. Now test a 36-by-24-inch sheet:

36" × 48 = 1728" or 144'

24" × 48 = 1152" or 96'

A 36" × 24" sheet equals 144' × 96' at 1/4" to 12" scale.

This should work with plenty of room for dimensions, notes, and a border.

In this example, you determined your limits by the number of units that fit across a standard sheet (D size, 36" × 24", because 144' across 36" at 1/4" = 12"). If you have to fit the drawing to a predetermined sheet size, start with that size and the size of what you are drawing, and then calculate the scale factor from them:

36" × 24" sheet and 75' × 40' object:

75' equals 900" (75' × 12" per foot)

36":900" (ratio of sheet size to object size)

36":900" equals a ratio of 1:25

Next lowest scale is 1:24, or 1/2:12, which is 1/2" = 1' scale

Your limits do not actually limit the size of your drawing. Think of AutoCAD's limits as an electronic fence, which AutoCAD uses to warn you if you draw outside your boundary. This boundary is an ideal way to represent a sheet size. It gives you a frame of reference for zooming or

plotting. If you need to draw outside the electronic sheet, you can expand the sheet by resetting the limits.

Setting the Drawing's Limits

How do you get these settings into AutoCAD? You can set limits manually or you can use an AutoCAD setup routine that sets limits automatically. The setup routine uses the limits you choose as it steps you through the calculations for sheet size and scale. In the exercises that follow, you use an automatic limits setup on an architectural sheet, and then you try the UNITS and LIMITS commands to set up an engineering drawing. Later in this chapter you learn how to set limits manually.

Setting Limits Automatically

When you choose Layout from the View pull-down menu, the MV Setup item loads and executes an AutoLISP program that sets up your limits. This program also draws a border around the drawing or inserts a complex title block. The border is drawn around the perimeter of the sheet as a reference line that matches your limits. This border is not intended to be plotted but shows your sheet edges. MVSETUP also includes another option that sets up the drawing in paper space with optional viewports and inserts a complex title block. Paper space and optional viewports are covered in Chapter 5. Figure 3.3 shows the menu selection sequence used for MVSETUP.

To get started, follow the steps in this exercise to begin AutoCAD, create a new drawing, and step through setting up AutoCAD:

Using MVSETUP To Prepare an Architectural 1/4"-Scale Drawing

Start AutoCAD by using the IA.BAT batch program.

`Command:` *Choose* File, *then* New	Opens the Create New Drawing dialog box
Type `ARCH` *and press Enter or click on* OK	Creates a new drawing named ARCH in the current directory
`Command:` *Choose* View, *then* Layout, *then* MV Setup	Loads and initiates the MVSETUP command

`mvsetup Auto: (load mvsetup)`

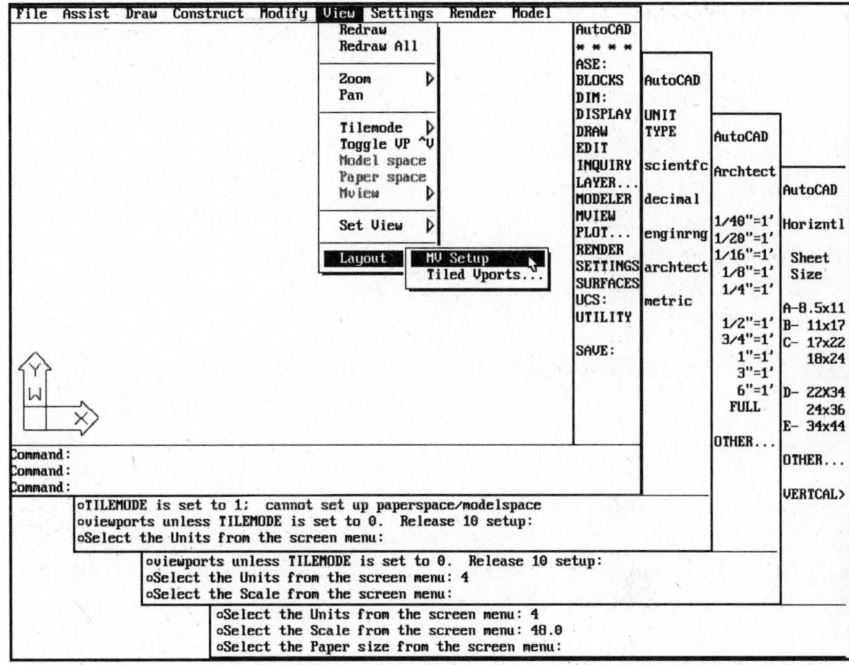

Figure 3.3:

The MVSETUP menus.

`C:MVSetup loaded. Type` **MVS** `or` **MVSETUP** `to set up your drawing. Paperspace/Modelspace is disabled. The pre-R11 setup will be invoked unless it is enabled. Enable Paper/Modelspace? <Y>:` **N**↵

`TILEMODE is set to 1; cannot set up paperspace/modelspace viewports unless TILEMODE is set to 0. Release 10 setup:`

`Select the Units from the screen menu:` *Choose* architect

`Select the Scale from the screen menu:` *Choose* 1/4"=1'

`Select the Paper size from the screen menu:` *Choose* 24×36 — Completes the setup

`Command:` *From the top of the screen menu, choose* AutoCAD — Displays the root screen menu

---

A border is drawn around the drawing.

Setting Units

AutoCAD offers units that are suitable for nearly any normal drawing practice. If you normally use architectural units, use AutoCAD's architectural units. Choose your system of units by using the Units Control option from the Settings pull-down menu. The process of setting units does two things for your drawing. First, it sets up the input format for entering distances and angles from the keyboard. Second, it sets up the output format that AutoCAD uses when displaying and dimensioning distances and angles.

The AutoCAD Units Control dialog box gives you control over the unit options. The next exercise shows you how to complete a detailed description of the units you want to use.

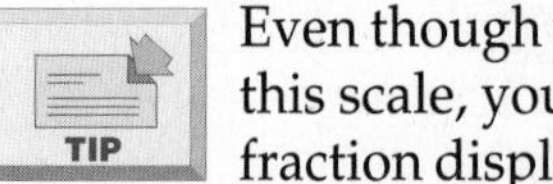

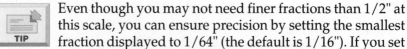

Even though you may not need finer fractions than 1/2" at this scale, you can ensure precision by setting the smallest fraction displayed to 1/64" (the default is 1/16"). If you set this Precision option in the Units area to 1/2", everything you draw is rounded to 1/2" when displayed, even if the dimension is not accurate. Individual errors in drawing are less likely but may cause cumulative errors. Set the option to 1/64" to make drawing errors more likely to show up. Then, if a coordinate displays as 49/64" when it should be 1", you know that it is not drawn correctly.

Figure 3.4 shows the Units Control dialog box with the default settings. The default setting for zero angle is usually to the right or east. The default setting for angle measurement is counterclockwise. Use these default settings in your setup.

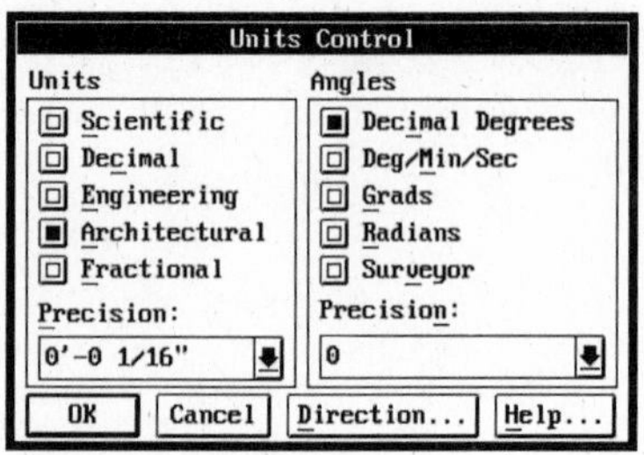

Figure 3.4:

The AutoCAD Units Control dialog box specifies various unit settings.

Using Units To Set Up an Architectural Drawing

`Command:` *Choose* Settings, *then* Units Control	Displays the Units Control dialog box
Choose the Architectural *radio button in the* Units *area*	Selects Architectural units
Click on the Precision *pop-up list box in the* Units *area, then select* 0'-0 1/64"	Changes precision from 1/16" to 1/64"
Choose the Decimal Degrees *radio button in the* Angles *area*	Selects Decimal Degrees angles
Click on the Precision *pop-up list box in the* Angles *area, then select* 0.00	Changes the angular measurement precision from 0 to 2
Choose Direction	Opens the Direction Control dialog box
Choose the East *radio button in the* Angle 0 Direction *area*	Specifies East (right of screen) as the direction of angle 0
Choose the Counter-Clockwise *radio button*	Measures angles counterclockwise from 0
Choose OK, *then* OK *again*	Closes both dialog boxes
`Command:` *Move the cursor and pick a few points, noting the coordinate display in the status bar*	
`Command:` *Choose* File, *then* Save	Saves your changes to ARCH.DWG

After you set the units, the coordinates display shows feet, inches, and fractions. If the format of the current coordinate is too long to fit in the coordinates display area, it displays in scientific units, such as `1.704450E+03,95'-9 51/64"`.

If the active coordinate display is off, you can press F6 to turn it on.

Usually, you set units only once for a drawing, but you can change units in the middle of a drawing.

Fractional units represent inches by default, but the inch marks (") are not shown. You can use fractional units for units other than inches by adjusting dimensioning and plot setups.

Entering and Displaying Values in Various Units

No matter what units you use, you can enter values in integer, decimal, scientific, or fractional formats. When using architectural or engineering units, you can input values as feet, inches, or both. AutoCAD assumes that the value is in inches unless you use a foot mark (') to indicate feet. You can omit the inches mark ("), and if the inches value is zero, you do not need to type anything. The values 2'0" or 2'0 or 2' or 24" are all equivalent in engineering units. Notice that no space is allowed between the foot and inch value. Because the inch mark is optional, you need to specify only the foot mark. Thus, to signify one foot, three inches, you can enter 1'3" or 1'3.

Use a hyphen to separate fractions, as in 1'3-1/2. You must enter fractions without spaces (1-3/4 rather than 1 3/4) because AutoCAD reads a press of the spacebar as a press of the Enter key. The input format and display format differ. You input 1'3-1/2" but AutoCAD displays this value as `1'-3 1/2"`. You can force feet and inches, angles, and fractions to display in the same form as their entries by setting the UNITMODE system variable to 1. To do so, just enter **UNITMODE** at the `Command:` prompt and then change the value to **1**.

Using the Limits Command

In the previous exercises, you used AutoCAD's automatic limits setup to configure an AutoCAD drawing. Next, you are going to follow the steps in a setup sequence for the engineering sheet by using AutoCAD's individual settings commands for units and limits.

Determining a Scale for a Known Object and Sheet Size

Consider an engineering example as a second case for setting limits. If a 24-inch manhole cover needs to be drawn on an 8 1/2-by-11-inch sheet, how do you compute your scale factor and determine your electronic limits? Try the following "trial-and-error" method:

Size of manhole cover	*24" diameter*
Sheet size	*11" × 8 1/2"*

Test a scale of 1/2" = 1" scale, which is a scale factor of 2 (1 unit = 2 units):

$$11'' \times 2 = 22''$$
$$8\text{-}1/2'' \times 2 = 17''$$

A scale factor of 2 gives 22" × 17" limits; this scale factor is too small. The 24-inch manhole cover drawing will be too large for the sheet of paper.

Test a scale of 1/4" = 1" scale, which is a scale factor of 4 (1 unit = 4 units):

$$11'' \times 4 = 44''$$
$$8\text{-}1/2'' \times 4 = 34''$$

These limits of 44" by 34" should work.

For this example, select engineering units: feet and inches with the inch as the smallest whole unit. Engineering fractions are decimals of an inch. This time, use the SETTINGS item from the screen menu to issue the UNITS command.

Using UNITS To Set Engineering Units for a Drawing

Choose File, *then* New, *and enter* `ENGR` ↵	Begins a new drawing named ENGR
`Command:` *From the screen menu, choose* SETTINGS, *then* next, *then* UNITS:	Starts the UNITS command

```
_UNITS
Report formats:        (Examples)

  1. Scientific        1.55E+01
  2. Decimal           15.50
  3. Engineering       1'-3.50"
  4. Architectural     1'-3 1/2"
  5. Fractional        15 1/2

With the exception of Engineering and Architectural formats,
these formats can be used with any basic unit of measurement.
For example, Decimal mode is perfect for metric units as well
as decimal English units.

Enter choice, 1 to 5 <2>: 3↵
Number of digits to right of decimal point (0 to 8) <4>: 2↵
```

```
Systems of angle measure:         (Examples)
  1.  Decimal degrees              45.0000
  2.  Degrees/minutes/seconds      45d0'0"
  3.  Grads                        50.0000g
  4.  Radians                      0.7854r
  5.  Surveyor's units             N 45d0'0" E
Enter choice, 1 to 5 <1>: Press Enter

Number of fractional places for display of angles (0 to 8) <0>: 2 ↵
Direction for angle 0.00:
  East    3 o'clock  =   0.00
  North  12 o'clock  =  90.00
  West    9 o'clock  =  180.00
  South   6 o'clock  =  270.00
Enter direction for angle 0.00 <0.00>: Press Enter

Do you want angles measured clockwise? <N> Press Enter
Command: Press F1                          Switches AutoCAD from text
                                           mode to graphics mode
```

By entering **UNITS** at the `Command:` prompt, you issue the same command you would by selecting UNITS: from the screen menu. If you enter **DDUNITS** at the `Command:` prompt or choose Units Control from the Settings pull-down menu, AutoCAD displays the AutoCAD Units Control dialog box. The Units Control dialog box appears in an exercise later in this chapter.

Setting Limits

After you establish your drawing's units, use the Drawing Limits option from the Settings pull-down menu to set sheet boundaries for your drawing. AutoCAD displays the following prompt to indicate the default location for the lower left corner of the screen:

```
<0'-0.00",0'-0.00">
```

By default, AutoCAD specifies that the lower left boundary of your intended drawing area is X = 0 and Y = 0. You can enter a new lower left corner by assigning new X,Y coordinates. In the following exercise, you accept the default lower left corner by pressing Enter and then enter your estimated limits of 44",34" for the upper right corner.

Setting Limits for an Engineering Drawing Sheet

`Command:` *Choose* Settings, *then* Drawing Limits	Starts the LIMITS command

`'_limits`
`Reset Model space limits:`
`ON/OFF/<Lower left corner ><0'-0.00", 0'-0.00">:` *Press Enter*
	Accepts the default location for the lower left corner

`Upper right corner <1'-0.00", 0'-9.00">:`**`44",34"`**↵	Sets the limits for the upper right corner

You also can issue the LIMITS command by entering **LIMITS** at the `Command:` prompt or by choosing SETTINGS and then LIMITS: from the screen menu.

Unfortunately, AutoCAD does not insert a border around the drawing area when you set limits manually. You need the border to see the drawing's limits. The following steps solve this problem by setting a drawing grid. A grid also is useful for estimating coordinate values and distances.

Setting a Grid To Display the Drawing's Limits

`Command:` *Choose* Settings, *then* Drawing Aids	Displays the Drawing Aids dialog box
Click the On *check box in the* Grid *area*	Turns on the grid
Double-click in the X Spacing *edit box, then enter* `1"` ↵	Sets the grid spacing to 1"
Choose OK	Closes the dialog box and displays the grid
`Command:` *Choose* View, *then* Zoom, *then* All	Zooms so that limits and the grid cover the drawing area
`Command:` *Press Enter*	Repeats the ZOOM command
`ZOOM` `All/Center/Dynamic/Extents/Left/ Previous/Vmax/Window/ <Scale(X/VP)>:` **`.75`**↵	Zooms so that the limits and the grid cover 75 percent of the drawing window
`Command:` *Choose* File, *then* Save	Saves the drawing as ENGR.DWG

The grid that appears provides a boundary for your scaled drawing, as shown in figure 3.5.

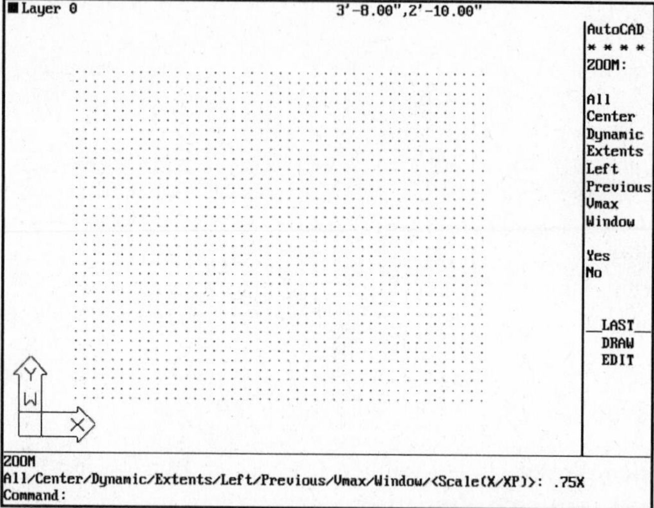

Figure 3.5:

The limits shown by a grid.

The area covered by the grid is the defined limits, representing an 8 1/2-by-11-inch plotting sheet at 1/4" = 1" scale. If you draw outside the grid, you are drawing outside the area that represents the intended plot area. Later in this chapter you learn how to use the Drawing Aids dialog box to set the grid and other drawing settings.

In the preceding exercise, you issued the ZOOM command by selecting the Zoom item from the View pull-down menu. You also can issue the ZOOM command by entering **ZOOM** at the `Command:` prompt or by choosing ZOOM: from the DISPLAY screen menu.

When you set drawing limits to match your plotting sheet's size, remember that plotters grip a portion of the sheet's edge during plotting. Make sure that your drawing allows enough room at the borders for your plotter. A safe margin is from 1/4" to 1 1/4", depending on the plotter brand and the amount of the paper's edge it grips.

Turning On the Limits Warning

You may have noticed the ON/OFF prompt for the LIMITS command. When you turn on limits checking, AutoCAD does not allow you to draw outside the limits. When limits checking is on, AutoCAD checks each point you specify to determine whether the point is within the drawing's established limits. If the point is outside the limits, AutoCAD prevents you from drawing to the point (as in creating a line that passes beyond the limits). The following exercise shows you how to test this capability.

Although your limits represent a plot area of 8 1/2" by 11", they cover 44" by 34" in real-world units. Try drawing a 24-inch diameter circle to represent the manhole cover and see if it fits within your limits.

Testing Your Drawing Scale Factor and Limits

`Command:` *Choose* Settings, *then* Drawing Limits

`_limits`
`Reset Model space limits:`

`ON/OFF/<Lower left corner <0'-0.00",0'-0.00">:` *From the screen menu, choose* ON	Turns on limits checking

The following steps draw a circle for the outside of the manhole cover:

`Command:` *Choose* Draw, *then* Circle, *then* Center, Radius

`_circle 3P/2P/TTR/<Center point>:` *Try to pick a point outside the grid*

`**Outside limits`	AutoCAD rejects the point because it is outside the limits
`3P/2P/TTR/<Center point>:` **`22,17`** ↵	Specifies a center point inside the limits
`Diameter/<Radius>:` **`12`** ↵	Specifies the circle's radius so that the circle remains within the limits

The manhole should fit neatly on the drawing, as shown in figure 3.6.

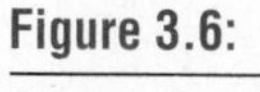

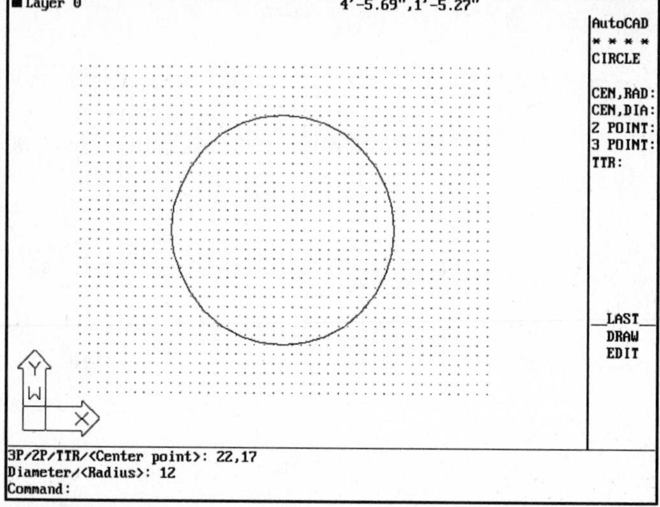

Figure 3.6:

A manhole, drawn with a circle.

The Circle selection on the Draw pull-down menu displays a cascading menu with several choices, each of which issues the CIRCLE command and the appropriate option for its method of specifying a circle. For example, the Center, Diameter menu item issues a CIRCLE command and the Diameter option. You also can issue the CIRCLE command and options from the screen menu by choosing DRAW, then CIRCLE, and then one of the circle options. Enter **CIRCLE** at the `Command:` prompt to issue the CIRCLE command alone, without options.

Setting Other Drawing Effects

Other settings, such as text height and symbol scale, are based on your drawing standards. If you have a drawing standard, you should adjust AutoCAD's settings to match your specifications. Just as you set your electronic sheet size to accommodate the manhole cover, you can adjust text, symbols, and line width so that they are in proportion to sheet size. You can easily configure these settings if you have a drawing scale factor. Simply determine the size you want your text, symbols, and other elements to be when the drawing is plotted, then multiply that size by the scale factor.

The following examples are for the manhole cover:

Plotted Size	×	*Scale Factor*	=	*Electronic Size*
0.2" Text height	×	4	=	0.8"
1/2" Bubble	×	4	=	2" diameter (or 1" radius)
1/16" Line width	×	4	=	1/4"

AutoCAD also provides a variety of linetypes, such as hidden and dashed. You adjust linetypes by using the LTSCALE command to set the correct scale factor for the desired linetype. Like text and symbols, LTSCALE should be set for the plotted appearance, not how it looks on the screen. Linetype scale is largely a matter of personal preference, but setting it to your scale factor is a good starting point. Linetype selection is discussed in detail later in this chapter.

The following exercise shows you how to add scaled text, a bubble callout (the number 1 in a circle), and a circle (the inner lip of the manhole) to your manhole cover. In the exercise, you use a hidden linetype to add the circle to your drawing.

Setting Text Height, Symbol Size, and Linetype Scale

`Command:` *Choose* View, *then* Zoom, *then* All	Zooms to the grid and limits
`Command:` *Press F6*	Turns on coordinate display
`Command:` *Press F9*	Turns on snap
`Command:` *Choose* Draw, *then* Text, *then* Dynamic	
`_dtext Justify/Style/<Start point>:` **`M`**↵	Specifies Middle text justification
`Middle point:` **`23,3`**↵	
`Height <0'-0.20">:` **`.8`**↵	
`Rotation angle <0.00>:` *Press Enter*	
`Text:` **`MANHOLE COVER`**↵	

Move the text cursor by using the coordinate display to pick the point 1'-3.00",0'-3.00".

`Text:` **`1`**↵	
`Text:` *Press Enter*	Ends the DTEXT command
`Command:` *Choose* Draw, *then* Circle, *then* Center, Radius	
`_circle 3P/2P/TTR/<Center point>:` **`15,3`**↵	

`Diameter/<Radius>:` **1**↵

Before drawing the inner lip, set the current linetype to HIDDEN.

`Command:` *From the screen menu, choose* AutoCAD, *then* SETTINGS, *then* LINETYP:	Starts the LINETYPE command
`'_LINETYPE`	
`?/Create/Load/Set:` **L**↵	Specifies the Load option
`Linetype(s) to load:` **HIDDEN**↵	Displays the Select Linetype File dialog box
Double-click on ACAD *in the* Files *list box*	Loads the HIDDEN linetype from ACAD.LIN
`Loading linetypes: HIDDEN`	
`?/Create/Load/Set:` *Press Enter*	
`New entity linetype (or ?) <BYLAYER>:` **HIDDEN**↵	
`?/Create/Load/Set:`↵	
`Command:` *Choose* Draw, *then* Circle, *then* Center, Radius *and draw a circle at 22,17 with an 11" radius*	

The circle has a hidden linetype, but you need to adjust the linetype scale to see it.

`Command:` **LTSCALE**↵	Issues the LTSCALE command
`New scale factor <1.0000>:` **4**↵	Sets the linetype scale to the drawing's scale factor
`Regenerating drawing.`	

The partially completed manhole with text, a bubble, and an inner lip should look like the drawing in figure 3.7.

Like the LINETYPE command, the LTSCALE command also appears on the screen menu (choose SETTINGS, then next, then LTSCALE:), or you can enter **LINETYPE** or **LTSCALE** at the `Command:` prompt to access these commands. You can make a linetype active by using the Set option under the LINETYPE command or as part of the LAYER command.

As you can see from the exercise, after you calculate a drawing scale factor for your drawing's plot scale and sheet size and you calculate the drawing's limits, it is relatively simple to adjust text height and linetype scale proportionally to that drawing scale factor. The important thing to remember is that this drawing scale factor does not scale the drawing in AutoCAD; you still draw things full-size. The scale is only a factor that you apply to individual commands to size symbols, linetypes and text appropriately for their eventual plotted output.

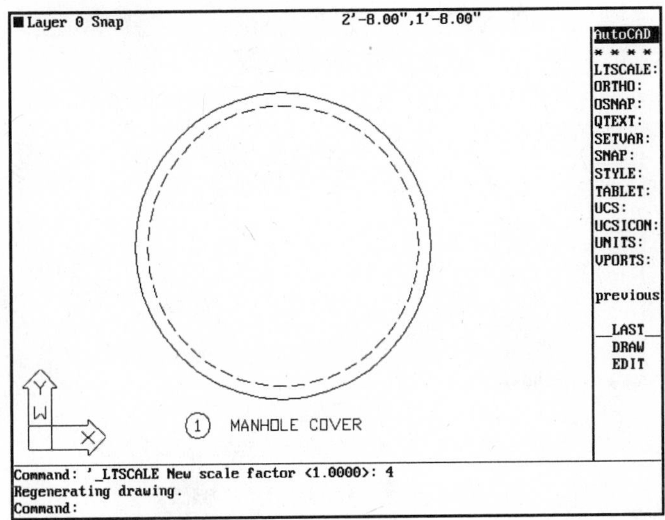

Figure 3.7:

The manhole with text, symbol, and a linetype.

A linetype scale of 0.3 to 0.5 times your drawing scale factor usually yields the best plotted output but may not be visually distinguishable on screen. You may need to set a linetype scale for drawing and later reset it for plotting.

If you have a printer (or plotter) installed on your system and you have AutoCAD configured for that printer (see your *Interface, Installation, and Performance Guide* or Appendix A), take a moment to make a quick plot before continuing. If you do not have a printer available, skip to the section on layers.

Making a Quick Plot

If you have a printer configured in AutoCAD, the following exercise enables you to print a hard copy of the manhole drawing. Do not be too concerned about the plotting sequence; it is explained in detail in the plotting chapter. The plot shows how all the calculations that you made provide a plotted drawing at 1/4-inch scale. The following exercise reflects settings for an HP LaserJet printer, but will work for any 8 1/2-by-11-inch or larger printer or plotter. Figure 3.8 shows the Plot Configuration dialog box, which you use in the following exercise to specify plot options.

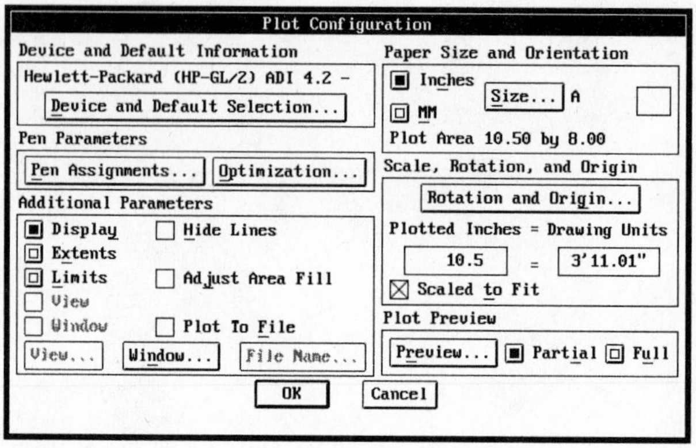

Figure 3.8

The Plot Configuration dialog box.

Making a Quick Plot on a Printer

`Command:` *Choose* File, *then* Plot	Displays the Plot Configuration dialog box (see fig. 3.8)
`Command: _plot`	
Click on the Limits *radio button in the* Additional Parameters *area*	
Double-click in the Plotted Inches *edit box in the* Scale, Rotation, and Origin *area, and then enter* `1`	
Double-click on the number in the Drawing Units edit box, then enter `4`	Specifies a plot scale of 1:4
Choose OK	

```
Effective plotting area:  10.50 wide by 8.00 high
Position paper in plotter.
Press RETURN to continue or S to Stop for hardware setup
```

Press Enter	Starts the plot
`Regeneration done 100%`	Displays progress
`Plot complete`	

After you issue the preceding commands, your plotted output should resemble the manhole in figure 3.9.

The right side of the plot may be cropped and your plotting area may differ from that shown in the exercise, depending on the size of your printer or plotter. Nevertheless, you should be able to apply a drafting scale to your printout and measure a 24" circle at 1/4 scale and 0.2"-high text with a 0.25" bubble.

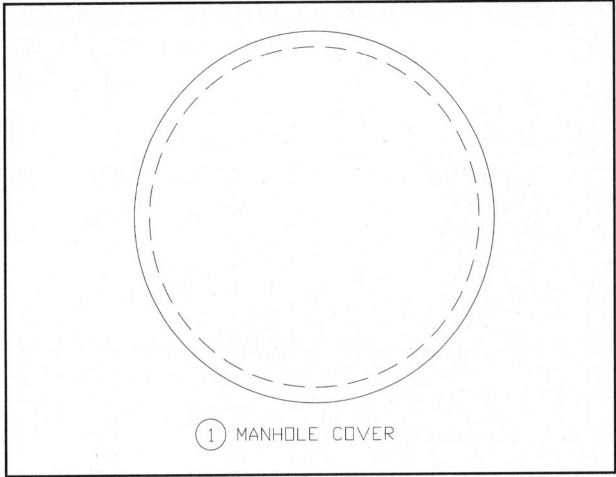

Figure 3.9:

A 1/4-scale plot of the manhole.

When beginning a new drawing, AutoCAD has defaults that enable you to start drawing immediately. It is wise, however, to start by first setting up drawing parameters, such as units and limits. Layering of entities also is important when creating a drawing with a well-organized data base. The next section shows you how to set up layers, as well as other important drawing elements.

Setting Up Layers, Colors, and Linetypes

In the following exercise, you begin a new drawing by using engineering units and limits for an 8 1/2-by-11-inch sheet with a drawing scale factor of 1 (full scale). In this exercise you use the Units Control dialog box (DDUNITS command) rather than the UNITS command. In this drawing, you create a new list of layers, and you set colors and linetypes by using the Layer Control dialog box.

Setting Up Units and Limits

`Command:` **`NEW`** ↵	Opens the Create New Drawing dialog box
Enter `CHAPTER3` ↵	Begins a new drawing

`Command:` *Choose* Settings, *then* Units Control	Displays the Units Control dialog box
Choose the Engineering *radio button, then click on the* Precision *pop-up list box in the* Units *area, and choose* 0.00	Specifies Engineering units
Choose the Decimal Degrees *radio button, then click on the* Precision *pop-up list box in the* Angles *area, and choose* 0.00	Specifies Decimal angular measurement
Choose OK	Closes the dialog box
`Command:` *Choose* Settings, *then* Drawing Limits	
`'_limits`	
`Reset Model Space limits`	
`ON/OFF/<Lower left corner <0'-0.00",0'-0.00">:` *Press Enter*	Defaults to 0,0
`Upper right corner <1'-0.00", 0'-9.00">:` **`11,8.5`** ↵	
`Command:` **`Z`** ↵	Issues a shortcut key for the ZOOM command
`ZOOM All/Center/Dynamic/Extents/Left/ Previous/Vmax/Window/<Scale(X/XP)>:` **`A`** ↵	Performs a ZOOM All
`Regenerating drawing.`	
`Command:` *Choose* File, *then* Save	Saves the drawing as CHAPTER3.DWG

The drawing is ready for the next exercise, in which you learn how to set up layers.

Understanding Layers

Layers help you control and organize your drawing. If your drawing becomes too dense or complicated, you can turn off selected layers so that they do not interfere with your work. If you later need to draw certain parts that you did not anticipate, you can create new layers for those parts.

As described earlier in this chapter, layers are comparable to overlay drafting on transparent sheets. You create your drawing by building it on a family of sheets (layers). Each layer has a name, a default color, and a linetype. You can work on any layer. Although editing commands such as ERASE work on any number of layers at once, you can draw on only one layer at a time. The layer you currently are using is called the *current* layer.

When you draw an entity, it is attached to the current layer. The current layer name is displayed at the left of the status line, as shown in figure 3.10. The new drawing you started in the preceding exercise uses layer 0—the default layer from the ACAD.DWG prototype drawing—as the current layer.

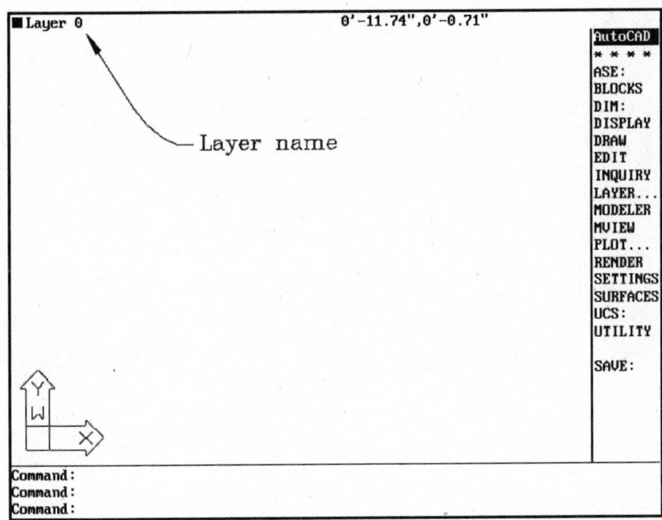

Figure 3.10:

The current layer's name, displayed in the status line.

The Layer Control dialog box, which appears in figure 3.11, contains every available tool for defining and setting up new layers. You can modify the properties of existing layers separately or in groups. This dialog box is important if you need to create drawings to specific layering standards or if you want to control the drawing display and plotted output. You can access the Layer Control dialog box in one of three ways:

1. Choose the Settings pull-down menu, then choose the Layer Control option.
2. Enter the DDLMODES command at the `Command:` prompt.
3. Choose LAYER from the screen menu.

To use the dialog box transparently, use the menus or enter 'DDLMODES in the middle of another command. If you change settings transparently, however, the changes may not affect all current commands. You also can change layer settings by using the LAYER command, which is discussed later in this chapter.

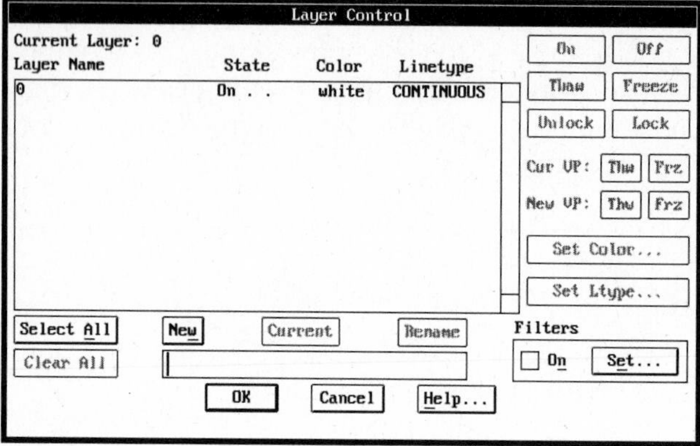

Figure 3.11:

The Layer Control dialog box.

In the Layer Control dialog box, layer 0 is shown with AutoCAD's default drawing properties: white, continuous lines. Layer 0 is fine for experimenting, and it has some special properties that will be explained later, but for most drawing work you should set up your own layers.

Understanding Layering Conventions

Like other drawing parameters, layer setup is a matter of standard practice and style. Layers are most often used to separate different types of objects in your drawing. You may place drawing components on one layer, for example, and their dimensions on another layer. Try to anticipate the types of layers that you want to separate. The following list shows a sample set of layers:

Objects on Layer	*Layer Name*
Components	OBJ01
Dimensions	DIM01
Symbols/Annotations	ANN01
Text	TXT01
Title Sheets	REF01

You can create an unlimited number of layers, but for most applications, 10 to 20 layers is more than enough. When you name your layers, it helps to apply DOS-style naming conventions and use wild cards to organize them. Layer names can be up to 31 characters long, but the status line shows only

the first eight characters. You can use letters, digits, dollar signs ($), hyphens (-), and underscore (_) characters in your layer names. AutoCAD converts all layer names to uppercase.

Many different layer-naming schemes are currently in use. Some code the color, linetype, and line weight. Others specify the trade and work location, such as ARCH-FLR01 or ELEC-CLG03. One popular convention codes layers with the Construction Specifications Institute (CSI) material code. Whatever scheme you use, remember three things:

1. Coordinate with anyone with whom you may be trading drawings, such as consultants and subcontractors.
2. Whatever types of information you code in your names, always put the same type of information in the same column (character position) so that you can select groups of layers by using wild cards. If you use a layer-naming scheme of ARCH-FLR01 and ARCH-FLR03, for example, you can select all floor plan layers by using the wild cards ????-FLR?? or all architectural layers by using ARCH*. If you name the second floor A-2NDFLR, however, you cannot select it with the same wild cards.
3. Make the scheme expandable, so that it accommodates growth. When you draw a three-story building, for example, use two characters for floor numbers so that the naming scheme is compatible with the 33-story building you design a year later.

Autodesk has even attempted to coordinate all the registered third-party software developers with layer-naming guidelines that prohibit different packages from interfering with each other when used on the same project.

For more information and recommendations on layer-naming schemes, see *Managing and Networking AutoCAD*, by New Riders Publishing.

Using the Layer Control Dialog Box

You must instruct AutoCAD to draw on the proper layer. You can use the Layer Control dialog box to create layers, to control which layers of the drawing are displayed, and to determine which layer becomes the current drawing layer. The LAYER command and the Layer Control (DDLMODES) dialog box set the following properties for the specified layer or layers:

- **Current.** This property makes the specified layer the current layer; new entities are then are placed on this layer.

- **On.** This property makes the layer visible.
- **Off.** This property makes the layer invisible.
- **Color.** This property defines a single default color so that anything drawn on the specified layer is the specified color, unless an entity color overrides it.
- **Ltype.** This property defines a single default linetype for the specified layer. Lines (and other drawing elements) drawn on the specified layer take on the default linetype unless you override it.
- **Freeze.** This property makes the layer invisible so that AutoCAD ignores all the layer's entities during regeneration. This setting increases the performance of AutoCAD searches and displays.
- **Thaw.** This property unfreezes layers.
- **Lock.** This property changes the layer property so that it is visible, but the entities cannot be altered or deleted.
- **Unlock.** This property restores a locked layer back to its original state.

The ability to freeze and thaw layers by viewports also is available and is covered in Chapter 5's discussion of paper space.

Creating New Layers

The drawing file you created earlier has only one layer. In the following exercise, you define several more layers, change the default parameters, and then save them for future use. The target layers are shown in table 3.1.

Table 3.1
Layer Configuration Table

Layer Name	*State*	*Color*	*Linetype*
0	On	7 (White)	CONTINUOUS
CIRCLE	On	3 (Green)	CONTINUOUS
PARAGRAM	On	6 (Magenta)	CONTINUOUS
SQUARE	On	2 (Yellow)	CONTINUOUS
TEXT	On	4 (Cyan)	CONTINUOUS
TRIANGLE	On	1 (Red)	CONTINUOUS

When you create new layers in the Layer Control dialog box, you can enter several names if they are separated by commas without spaces.

Creating New Layers

`Command:` *Choose* Settings, *then* Layer Control	Displays the Layer Control dialog box
Type `CIRCLE,PARAGRAM,SQUARE,TEXT,TRIANGLE`	
Click on the Ne**w** *button*	Creates the new layers, named CIRCLE, PARAGRAM, SQUARE, TEXT, and TRIANGLE

The layer information should now appear in the dialog box, as shown in figure 3.12. Because you did not set any properties for the new layers, AutoCAD automatically set them with the same defaults as layer 0. Each layer is color 7 (white) with a continuous linetype.

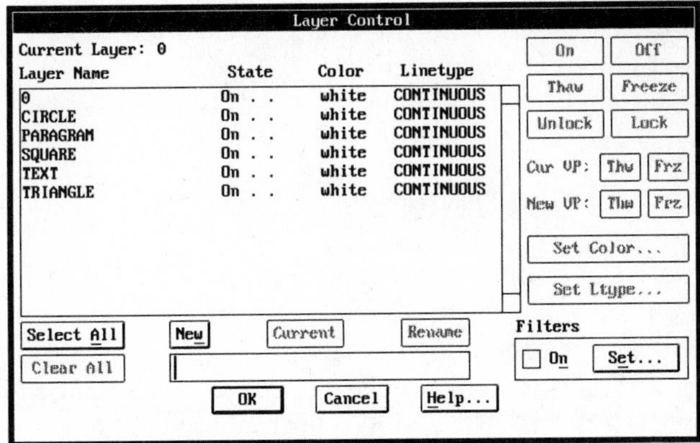

Figure 3.12:

The newly defined layers, as shown in the Layer Control dialog box.

Understanding Layer Color

A layer has only one color, but several layers can have the same color. Color is assigned to layers by names or numbers (up to 255 different colors). Colors commonly are used to assign plotting line weights to objects in the drawing. AutoCAD uses the following naming and numbering conventions for seven standard colors:

Color Number	*Color*
1	Red
2	Yellow
3	Green
4	Cyan
5	Blue
6	Magenta
7	White

NOTE

Colors with numbers higher than 7 do not have names, and their availability depends on your video card and display. You can see colors with numbers higher than 7 by loading the CHROMA or COLORWH drawings from the AutoCAD SAMPLE disk (and probably from the SAMPLE directory). You also can see CHROMA by viewing the slide named ACAD(CHROMA), and you can see COLORWH by viewing the COLORWH slide. The VSLIDE command is explained later in the book.

Modifying Layer Properties

You can easily change layer properties by using the Layer Control dialog box. The **O**n and O**f**f buttons and the **T**haw and Free**z**e buttons control the visibility of the currently selected layer(s). The **S**et Color and Set **L**type buttons display child dialog boxes (see fig. 3.13), which assign color and linetype to the selected layers. The **C**urrent button makes a single selected layer current. (Chapter 5 discusses the use of the Cur VP Thw and Frz and New VP Thw and Frz buttons.) You must select a layer before you can modify its properties. To select or deselect a layer, click on the layer's name in the list box. You can select or deselect all the drawing's layers at the same time by clicking on the Select **A**ll and Clea**r** All buttons.

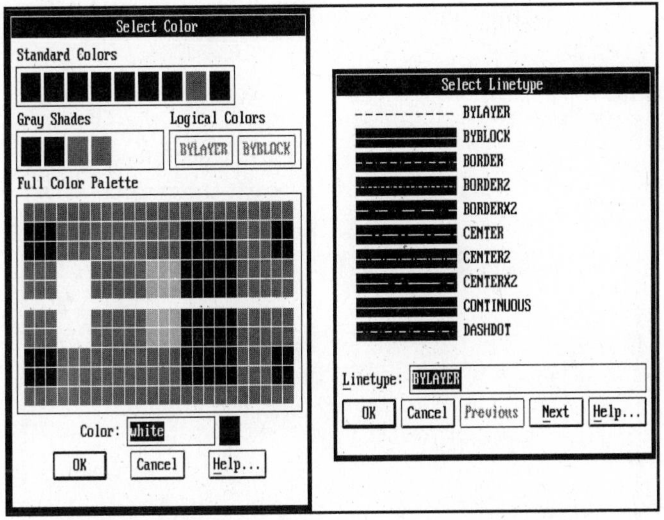

Figure 3.13:

The Select Color and Select Linetype dialog boxes.

The Select Color dialog box enables you to graphically select colors for layers. You can click on a color box to select a color, or enter its name in the Color edit box. The Select Linetype dialog box enables you to graphically select a linetype to assign to a layer. As with the Select Color dialog box, you also can enter the linetype by name in the Linetype edit box.

Setting Layer Color

In the following exercise, you set the layer colors in your drawing.

Setting Layer Colors

Continue from the preceding exercise with the Layer Control dialog box open.

Click on CIRCLE *in the list box, then click on* Set Color	Selects the CIRCLE layer and displays the Select Color dialog box
Click on the green box in the Standard Colors *area, then choose* OK	Changes CIRCLE's color to green in the Layer Control dialog box list
Click on CIRCLE	Deselects the layer

Repeat this process by selecting each layer and then setting its color to match the colors listed in figure 3.14.

Click on the OK *button*	Saves the new layer and color settings and exits from the Layer Control dialog box

Layer Control

Current Layer: 0

Layer Name	State	Color	Linetype
0	On . .	white	CONTINUOUS
CIRCLE	On . .	green	CONTINUOUS
PARAGRAM	On . .	magenta	CONTINUOUS
SQUARE	On . .	yellow	CONTINUOUS
TEXT	On . .	cyan	CONTINUOUS
TRIANGLE	On . .	red	CONTINUOUS

On Off Thaw Freeze Unlock Lock
Cur VP: Thw Frz
New VP: Thw Frz
Set Color...
Set Ltype...
Select All New Current Rename
Clear All
Filters
On Set...
OK Cancel Help...

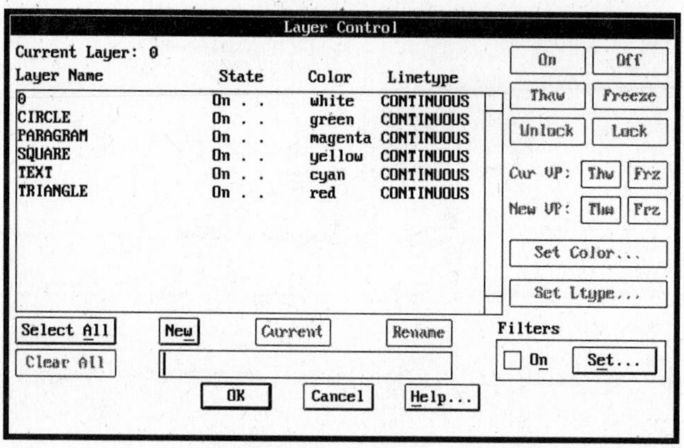

Figure 3.14:

The Layer Control dialog box with new color settings.

You also can specify a color in the Select Color dialog box by entering its name or number in the Color edit box.

Setting Layer Linetype

If you use the LAYER command to set linetypes, they are automatically loaded from the ACAD.LIN file, which contains AutoCAD's linetype definitions. Before the linetypes can be displayed and selected in the Layer Control dialog box, however, they must be loaded. You can use the Load option from the LINETYP: command on the SETTINGS screen menu to load ACAD.LIN, which usually resides in the ACAD subdirectory. Until you learn the individual names, it is easiest to specify files by using the asterisk wild-card character (*), which loads all linetypes. Figure 3.15 shows the standard linetypes.

Each of the linetypes has corresponding double-scale and half-scale linetypes, such as DASHED2 for a half-scale dashed line and DASHEDX2 for a double-scale dashed line. The half-scale linetypes all end in 2 and the double-scale linetypes end in X2.

DASHED
HIDDEN
CENTER
PHANTOM
DOT
DASHDOT
BORDER
DIVIDE
CONTINUOUS

Figure 3.15:
AutoCAD's standard linetypes.

In the following exercise, you load and set new layer linetypes.

Setting Layer Linetypes

`Command:` *From the screen menu, choose* SETTINGS, *then* LINETYP:, *then* Load	
`_LINETYPE ?/Create/Load/Set: _LOAD`	
`Linetype(s) to load: *↵`	Specifies all linetypes and displays the Select Linetype File dialog box
Double-click on ACAD	Specifies the file \ACAD\ACAD.LIN

`Linetype BORDER loaded.`
`Linetype BORDER2 loaded.`
`Linetype BORDERX2 loaded.`
`Linetype CENTER loaded.`
`Linetype CENTER2 loaded.`
`Linetype CENTERX2 loaded.`
`Linetype DASHDOT loaded.`
`Linetype DASHDOT2 loaded.`
`Linetype DASHDOTX2 loaded.`
`Linetype DASHED loaded.`
`Linetype DASHED2 loaded.`
`Linetype DASHEDX2 loaded.`
`Linetype DIVIDE loaded.`
	AutoCAD reports its progress as it loads the new linetypes

```
Linetype DIVIDE2 loaded.
Linetype DIVIDEX2 loaded.
Linetype DOT loaded.
Linetype DOT2 loaded.
Linetype DOTX2 loaded.
Linetype HIDDEN loaded.
Linetype HIDDEN2 loaded.
Linetype HIDDENX2 loaded.
Linetype PHANTOM loaded.
Linetype PHANTOM2 loaded.
Linetype PHANTOMX2 loaded.
```

`?/Create/Load/Set:` *Press Enter*	Ends the LINETYPE command
`Command:` *Choose* Settings, *then* Layer Control	Displays the Modify Layer dialog box
Click on CIRCLE, *then click on* Set **L**type	Displays the Select Linetype box
Choose **N**ext, *click on the* DASHED *linetype example, then choose* OK	Assigns the dashed linetype to the CIRCLE layer

Repeat this process to assign a HIDDEN linetype to the PARAGRAM layer. The layer settings should duplicate those in figure 3.16.

Choose OK	Saves new layer and linetype settings
`Command:` *Choose* File, *then* Save	Saves the drawing

Figure 3.16:

The Layer Control dialog box with new linetype settings.

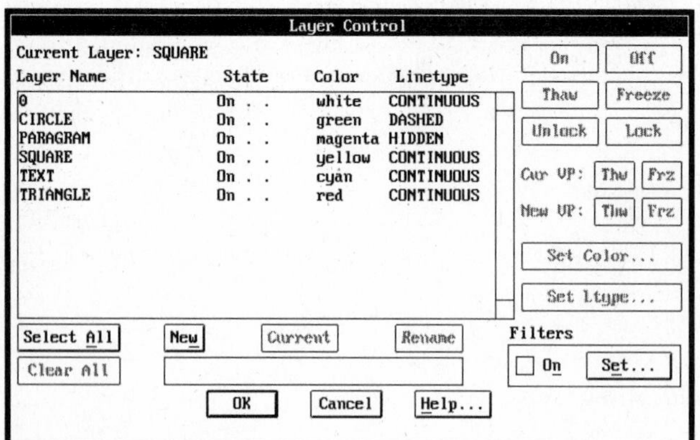

You can create your own custom linetypes by using the LINETYPE command. See Appendix C for details.

You now have a complete set of layers. You can modify their other properties by choosing the layers and selecting the appropriate buttons in the Layer Control dialog box.

Choosing the Current Layer

As you learned earlier, the current drawing layer name always appears at the left end of the status line. To make a different drawing layer active, select only that layer in the Layer Control dialog box, then click on the Current button to make that layer current. After you click on the OK button to exit from the dialog box, that new current layer's name appears in the status line.

You can change layer settings at any time while you work in the drawing. If you alter the properties of layers (such as linetype or color), AutoCAD regenerates the drawing window to reflect these changes when you exit from the LAYER command.

Making Layers Invisible

In the exercise that follows, you learn how to turn a layer off and then on again. If you turn off the current layer, AutoCAD prompts you to reconfirm the action. Remember that you have to see what you are drawing!

Follow the steps to draw a square with lines, and then turn the SQUARE layer off and on.

Setting a Current Layer and Layer Visibility

`Command:` *Choose* Settings, *then* Layer Control	Displays the Layer Control dialog box
Select SQUARE *and click on* Current	Displays `Current layer: SQUARE` at the upper left of the dialog box
Click on OK	Exits and displays a yellow box (to show the current layer's assigned color) and the layer name SQUARE on the status line

`Command:` *Choose* Draw, *then* Line, *then* Segments, *and draw a square in the upper left corner of the drawing area* (see fig. 3.17)	
`Command:` *Choose* Settings, *then* Layer Control, *select* SQUARE, *click on* Off, *then* OK	An alert box warns that the current layer is turned off
Click on OK	Accepts the warning and the square disappears
`Command:` *Press Enter*	Redisplays the dialog box
Select SQUARE, *choose* **O**n, *then* OK	Turns the SQUARE layer back on

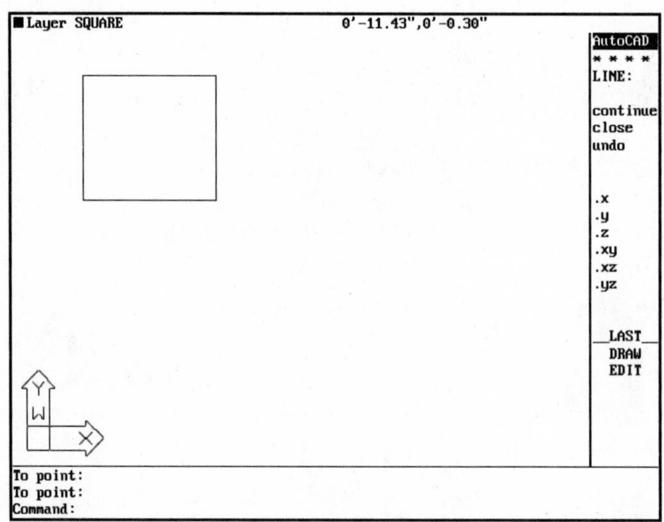

Figure 3.17:

A drawn square and the current layer's name on the status line.

If you are drawing but you cannot see anything happening, make sure that you have not turned off the current layer.

You also can make a layer invisible by freezing it. When a layer is frozen, the entities on it do not display, regenerate, or print. This arrangement means that your drawing refreshes more quickly after you invoke a command (such as ZOOM) that requires a regeneration. The disadvantage of freezing layers is that layers have to regenerate when you thaw them. The thawing process takes a little longer to perform. For this reason, freeze layers only when you know you will not need to display, regenerate, or print the frozen layer for a while.

Locking Layers

Another nice feature to use with layered entities is the Lock option. The Lock option enables you to view the locked layer's entities but not select them for editing. In a complex drawing, you can lock the layers that are not being used, making entity selection much easier. Also, when you give a drawing file to another person for reference or review, you can lock some layers to avoid unwanted changes. The Unlock option unlocks selected layers that have been locked.

Using the LAYER Command

Although the dialog box usually is easier to use, you can use the LAYER command to create layer names, set color and linetype, control layer visibility, and display layer status. The LAYER command displays the following prompt:

```
?/Make/Set/New/ON/OFF/Color/Ltype/Freeze/Thaw/LOck/Unlock:
```

The ON, OFF, Color, Ltype, Freeze, Thaw, LOck, and Unlock options offer the same settings as their Layer Control dialog box counterparts. The Make option creates a new layer and makes it the current layer. The New option creates new layers. With the New, ON, OFF, Color, Ltype, Freeze, Thaw, LOck, and Unlock options, you can enter multiple layer names separated by commas. The Set option sets the layer you specify as the new current layer. Try using the LAYER command to experiment with setting layers. You can access the LAYER command by entering LAYER at the `Command:` prompt.

Testing Drawing Layer Properties

In the last few exercises, you created a working drawing file that uses real units, limits, and a foundation of layers. How do you know that all these layers work? You just saw the yellow square on the SQUARE layer. In the following exercise, you make the CIRCLE layer current and draw a circle to see how entities adopt other layer settings. After drawing the circle, you save the drawing by naming it to a new file called WORK. This drawing is used as the prototype drawing in the next chapter on drawing accuracy. After saving the drawing near the end of the exercise, you use the LAYER command to change the color of the CIRCLE layer to blue, then enter U to undo the change.

Testing Layers and Saving the WORK Drawing

Continue from the preceding exercise, in the CHAPTER3 drawing.

`Command:` **`LAYER`**↵	Starts the LAYER command

`Command: LAYER ?/Make/Set/New/ON/OFF/`
`Color/Ltype/Freeze/Thaw/LOck/Unlock:`
From the screen menu, choose Set
	Tells AutoCAD that you want to set a new current layer

`SET New current layer <SQUARE>:` **`CIRCLE`**↵	
`?/Make/Set/New/ON/OFF/Color/Ltype/` `Freeze/Thaw/LOck/Unlock:` *Press Enter*	Makes CIRCLE the current layer
`Command:` *Choose* Draw, *then* Circle, *then* Center, Radius *and pick two points, placing the circle in upper right corner of the drawing*	
`Command:` *Choose* File, *then* Save As, *and enter* **`WORK`**↵	Saves the file with the name WORK.DWG
`Command:` **`LAYER`**↵	

`Command: ?/Make/Set/New/ON/OFF/`
`Color/Ltype/Freeze/Thaw/LOck/Unlock:`
From the screen menu, choose Color
	Specifies the Color option

`Color:` **`BLUE`**↵	Specifies blue
`Layer name(s) for color 1 (blue)` `<CIRCLE>:` *Press Enter*	
`?/Make/Set/New/ON/OFF/Color/Ltype/` `Freeze/Thaw/LOck/Unlock:` *Press Enter*	Makes the circle blue
`Command:` **`U`**↵	Undoes the color change
`LAYER`	

After you draw the circle, your drawing should look like figure 3.18. You should have a yellow square and a green dashed circle.

You also can make all layer settings and create new layers by using the LAYER command.

As the next section explains, you do not have to use layers to control all the properties of all your entities. You can just as easily modify the color and linetype properties associated with individual drawing entities.

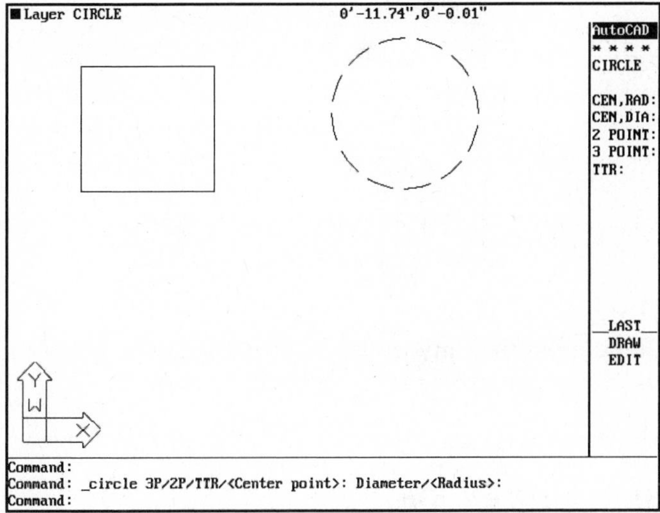

Figure 3.18: The square and circle on their respective layers.

Setting Color and Linetype by Entity

You have seen how to control an entity's color or linetype by drawing it on an appropriate layer. You also can set color and linetype explicitly by overriding the layer's defaults and setting an individual entity's color and linetype. You must use separate commands to make these individual changes.

You can use the Entity Creation Modes dialog box (the DDEMODES command) to control the current entity color, linetype, and layer settings. The dialog box appears in 3.19. The Color and Linetype buttons display the same Select Color and Select Linetype child dialog boxes as the Layer Control dialog box. The Layer button displays a Select Layer dialog box, in which you can review layer settings or double-click on a layer to make it current.

To display the Entity Creation Modes dialog box, you can enter **DDEMODES** at the `Command:` prompt or you can choose Entity Modes from the Settings pull-down menu. You also can choose SETTINGS and then DDEMODES from the screen menu. To use the dialog box transparently, you can use the menus or enter **'DDEMODES** while another command is active. You also can use the COLOR and LINETYPE commands to ensure that an entity receives the color and linetype you want.

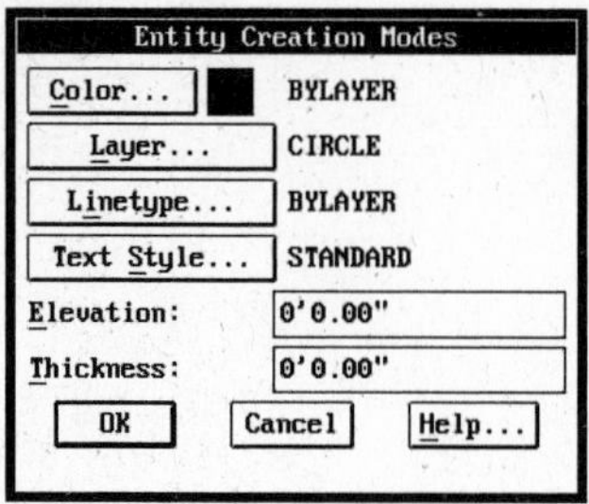

Figure 3.19:

The Entity Creation Modes dialog box.

Remember that any transparent changes you make to settings may not affect all current commands.

Understanding Entity Colors

You can use the Entity Creation Modes dialog box to control the current entity color, linetype, and layer settings. You also can use the COLOR command to ensure that an entity receives the color you want. If you use the COLOR command to set the default entity color to a specific color (rather than by layer), the subsequently created entities take on *explicit* colors. Explicit colors are not affected by the entity's layer or by changes to the layer. When you create a new entity, AutoCAD assigns the current entity color setting to the new entity. When you change the current entity color, it does not affect entities that already exist—only entities that are created after you set the color.

You can set an individual entity's color to any valid color name or number. (Remember you can have 1 to 255 colors, but only the first seven have names.) By default, AutoCAD sets colors by layer. When color is set to BYLAYER, AutoCAD does not store new entities with a specific color. Instead, it gives new entities the color property according to layer, which causes any new entity to adopt the color that is assigned to its layer.

Another color setting is the BYBLOCK color. Chapter 10 covers BYBLOCK assignments.

Take a look at the color settings in your new drawing. Then, take the following steps to change the color to red by using the Entity Creation Modes dialog box, as shown in figure 3.19. You will see in the exercise that the

default color is set to BYLAYER. After you change the color, you draw another circle to see how the explicit color settings override the layer setting.

Using the Entity Creation Modes Dialog Box

Continue with the WORK drawing from the preceding exercise.

`Command:` *Choose* Settings, *then* Entity Modes	Displays the Entity Creation Modes dialog box
Click on the Color *button*	Brings up the Select Color dialog box
Click on box 1, RED, *then* OK	Sets the current color to red and exits from the Select Color dialog box
Click on OK	Exits from the Entity Creation Modes dialog box
`Command:` *Choose* Draw, *then* Circle, *then* Center, Radius *and pick two points below the first circle*	Draws a circle

Your drawing should show a red dashed circle, in addition to the green dashed circle and yellow square, as shown in figure 3.20.

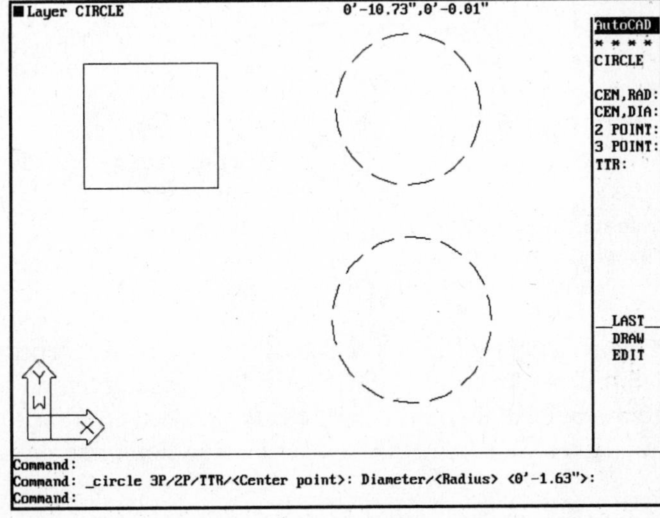

Figure 3.20: A second circle added to the drawing.

In the preceding exercise, you used the pull-down menus to set the current color. If you prefer, you can enter **COLOR** at the `Command:` prompt or choose SETTINGS, then COLOR: from the screen menu. You simply enter a new entity color at the COLOR command's `New entity color <BYLAYER>:` prompt.

Understanding Entity Linetypes

After reading about entity colors, you might guess that linetype settings have a similar control. Take a look at the Linetype option in the Entity Creation Modes dialog box. This option enables you to set an explicit linetype that overrides the layer's default for all entities that you create after you change the setting. You also can set the linetype to BYLAYER, so that new entities use the layer's default linetype.

The linetype choices are displayed in the Select Linetype dialog box, as shown in figure 3.21. A sample of the highlighted linetype appears in the box. The next exercise shows you how to change the linetype setting independently of the layer setting.

Setting Entity Linetypes

Continue with the WORK drawing from the preceding exercise.

`Command:` *Choose* Settings, *then* Entity Modes, *then click on* Linetype	Displays the Entity Creation Modes and Select Linetype dialog boxes
Click on CONTINUOUS, *then* OK, *then click on* OK *again*	Sets the current linetype to continuous and exits from both dialog boxes
`Command:` *Choose* Draw, *then* Circle, *then* Center, Radius *and pick two points beneath the square*	Draws another circle

You should have three circles. The last one is drawn with a red continuous line, even though it is on the CIRCLE layer, which is set to green with dashed lines. (Remember that you changed the individual entity color to red in the previous exercise.) The drawing should now look like the sample in figure 3.22.

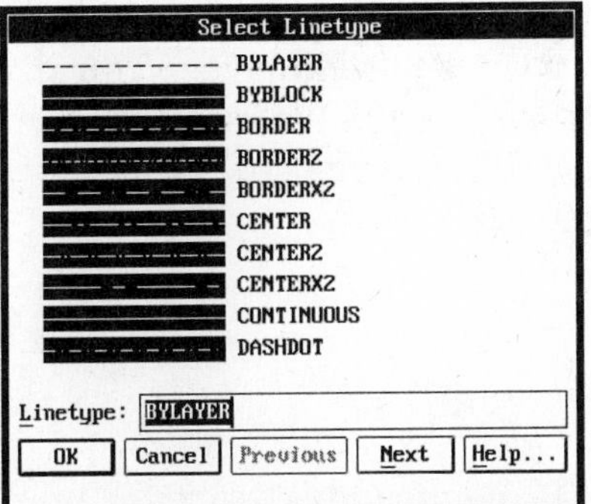

Figure 3.21:

The Select Linetype dialog box.

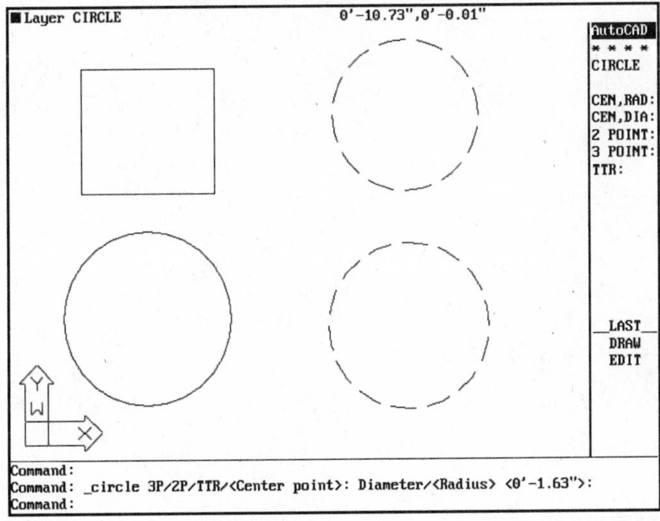

Figure 3.22:

The third circle with the continuous linetype.

You also can use the LINETYPE command to set the current linetype; enter **LINETYPE** at the `Command:` prompt or choose SETTINGS, then LINETYP: from the screen menu. The LINETYPE command displays the following prompt:

```
?/Create/Load/Set:
```

You can load linetypes, as you did earlier. To load the linetypes, you can enter a **?** to list linetypes, create new linetypes (as discussed in Appendix C), or enter an **S** to set a new current linetype. To set a new current linetype, enter its name at the `New entity linetype <current linetype>:` prompt, which appears when you select the Set option.

Explicit color and linetype settings stay in effect, even when you change current layers. You should not mix explicit color and linetype settings with layer settings, or the drawing may become too confusing. Try to stick with one system of control, with few exceptions.

Changing Entity Properties

The COLOR and LINETYPE commands change the properties only for new entities that are drawn after you change the color and linetype settings. But you also can change the properties of existing entities. To do so, you can use the CHPROP (CHange PROPerties) command. After you select the objects whose properties you want to change, AutoCAD asks which properties you want to modify. You can use CHPROP to change the following properties:

- Color
- Layer
- Linetype
- Thickness

Thickness is a property associated with 3D entities. You will read more about thickness in Chapter 19.

In the following exercise, you use CHPROP to change a circle's layer and color.

Using CHPROP To Change Layer and Color

`Command:` *From the screen menu, choose* AutoCAD, *then* EDIT, *then* CHPROP:

`CHPROP Select objects:` *Select the green circle (the first circle)*

`1 found.`

`Select objects:` *Press Enter* — Ends object selection

`Change what property (Color/LAyer/LType/Thickness) ?` *From the screen menu, choose* LAyer

`New layer <CIRCLE>:` **`SQUARE`**↵ — Gives the circle the properties of the SQUARE layer

`Change what property (Color/LAyer/LType/Thickness) ?` *From the screen menu, choose* Color	
`COLOR New color <BYLAYER>:` *From the screen menu, choose* red	Specifies the color number for red
`Change what property (Color/LAyer/LType/Thickness) ?` *Press Enter*	Turns the circle red

Like many other commands in AutoCAD, you can issue the CHPROP command can by typing it or by choosing it from the screen or pull-down menu. You also can use a dialog box to change properties.

Using a Dialog Box To Change Properties

When you choose the Modify pull-down menu, then Change, then Properties, the Change Properties dialog box appears if entities have previously been selected. (You also can enter **DDCHPROP** at the `Command:` prompt to display the dialog box.) If you have not yet created a selection set, DDCHPROP prompts you to select objects, then displays the dialog box after the objects are selected. The next exercise demonstrates the use of the DDCHPROP command. Figure 3.23 shows the Change Properties dialog box.

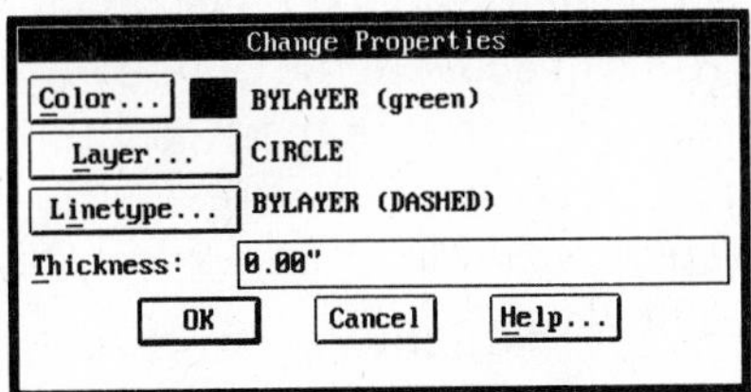

Figure 3.23:

The Change Properties dialog box.

Using DDCHPROP To Change Entity Properties

`Command:` *Choose* Modify, *then* Change, *then* Properties	Starts the DDCHPROP command
`Select objects:` *Pick the red, hidden circle*	
`1 found`	
`Select objects:` *Press Enter*	Opens the Change Properties dialog box

Click on Color, *then click on the magenta color box, then on* OK	Selects magenta
Click on OK	Makes the circle magenta
`Command:` **U**↵	Undoes the change

The DDCHPROP command may be a little easier to use than CHPROP because of the way options are graphically displayed in the dialog box. The color and linetype dialog boxes are helpful and the layer list is extremely useful because it is often difficult to remember the layer names (and to spell them correctly) when typing them in. You also can click on the dialog box's Help button if you forget how to use the command.

You also can use the Modify <entity> dialog box, which is opened by the Entity item on the Modify pull-down menu, to change properties and other aspects of existing entities. See Chapter 6 for details.

Using the RENAME Command

The RENAME command changes the names of existing drawing objects, such as blocks or layers. The Rename dialog box provides a convenient tool for renaming such items. You can activate the dialog box by entering **DDRENAME** at the `Command:` prompt or by choosing RENAME:, then Dialogue from the UTILITY screen menu. The dialog box enables you to select the item's category, such as Block. A list box displays the existing name. You then can enter a new name in the edit box.

In the following exercise, you practice using the RENAME command.

Using DDRENAME To Rename Drawing Objects

Continue with the WORK drawing from the preceding exercises.

`Command:` *From the screen menu, choose* UTILITY, *then* RENAME:	Starts the RENAME command
`RENAME Block/Dimstyle/LAyer/LType/Style/UCS/VIew/VPort:` *From the screen menu, choose* Dialogue	Starts the DDRENAME command and opens the Rename dialog box

Select the Layer option from the Named Objects list box.

Click on TRIANGLE *in the* Items *list box*	Selects the TRIANGLE layer for renaming
Click in the Rename To: *edit box and type* `TRI`, *then click on* Rename To:	Renames the TRIANGLE layer to TRI
Choose OK	Closes the dialog box

`1 Layer(s) renamed.`

When the RENAME command is issued, the prompt offers a selection of items that you can rename. These items include blocks, dimension styles, layers, linetypes, styles, user coordinate systems, views, and viewports. Many of these items have not yet been discussed in this book, but are covered in later chapters. After you specify a category, such as Block, you first specify the item's old name. Then you specify the new name to replace it.

Using the STATUS Command

In the following exercise, you use the STATUS command to check your current entity property defaults. You cannot use STATUS to change those default settings. The STATUS command displays its information in a text screen.

Using Status To Get a Drawing Status Report

`Command:` *Choose* Assist, *then* Inquiry, *then* Status	Displays a text screen with status information

Notice the following three lines in the status display (see fig. 3.24):

```
Current layer:       CIRCLE
Current color:       1 (red)
Current linetype:    CONTINUOUS
- Press RETURN for more ->
Total conventional memory:432K   Total Extended memory:5420K
Swap file size: 0K bytes
```

`Command:` *Press F1 to switch back to graphics mode*

```
7 entities in C:\IA\WORK
Model space limits are X:  0'-0.00"   Y:  0'-0.00"  (Off)
                       X: 0'-11.00"   Y:  0'-8.50"
Model space uses       X:  0'-1.10"   Y:  0'-0.97"
                       X:  0'-9.74"   Y:  0'-8.21"
Display shows          X:  0'-0.00"   Y:  0'-0.00"
                       X: 0'-11.75"   Y:  0'-8.50"
Insertion base is      X:  0'-0.00"   Y:  0'-0.00"   Z:  0'-0.00"
Snap resolution is     X:  0'-1.00"   Y:  0'-1.00"
Grid spacing is        X:  0'-0.00"   Y:  0'-0.00"

Current space:        Model space
Current layer:        CIRCLE
Current color:        1 (red)
Current linetype:     CONTINUOUS
Current elevation:  0'-0.00"  thickness:  0'-0.00"
Fill on  Grid off  Ortho off  Qtext off  Snap off  Tablet off
Object snap modes:    None
Free disk: 10795008 bytes
Virtual memory allocated to program: 5276K
Amount of program in physical memory/Total (virtual) program size: 100%
-- Press RETURN for more --
Total conventional memory: 360K      Total extended memory: 5420K
Swap file size: 0K bytes
Command:
```

Figure 3.24:

The status display.

The top of the status report shows your drawing limits. The status report lists the current layer, current color, and current linetype, followed by additional information about your settings. These settings become more important as you read through the book. For now, remember that you can access this information and that AutoCAD keeps track of all the data.

Modifying and Viewing System Variables

AutoCAD has about 175 variables that are saved with a drawing. These variables cover everything from the units settings to dimensioning options. Fortunately, the default settings in the ACAD.DWG drawing file are established to enable you to start drawing without many adjustments. You will probably never need to use many of the variables in the drawings you create.

You can type all the system variables at the `Command:` prompt, just as you can enter any AutoCAD command. You already have changed several of the variables, however, by making changes to dialog boxes or screen-menu selections.

You can use the SETVAR command to set and view the values of AutoCAD's system variables. You also can enter the names of system

variables directly at the `Command:` prompt to set their values. The following exercising demonstrates the use of the SETVAR command.

Using SETVAR To Change System Variables

Continue with the WORK drawing from the preceding exercises.

`Command:` **`SETVAR`**↵	Issues the SETVAR command
`Variable name or ?:` **`BLIPMODE`**↵	
`New value for BLIPMODE <1>:` **`0`**↵	Turns off BLIPMODE, so that blip marks do not appear when you pick points
`Command:` *Choose* Draw, *then* Line, *then* Segments	
Draw a few lines, noting that blips do not appear when you pick points	
`To point:` *Press Ctrl-C*	Cancels the LINE command
`Command:` **`U`**↵	Undoes the LINE command
`Command:` **`U`**↵	Undoes the BLIPMODE change

This chapter does not explain all the AutoCAD system variables. Instead, they are covered throughout the book as they apply to different commands. You cannot directly change the value of some system variables because they are *read-only variables*; you can see their value, but AutoCAD does not allow you to change it. You can update such variables by making changes in other areas of your drawing or configuration.

Keeping Your Work Safe

You have been working on the CHAPTER3 drawing for some time, but you may not have saved it yet. If your system's power failed suddenly or some other event occurred to cause you to lose the changes you have made, you would not lose much; CHAPTER3 is not a very important or complex drawing. If you were working on a real drawing with a real deadline, however, you could not take lost work so lightly. This section shows you how to ensure that you do not lose changes to your drawing during an editing session.

In the following exercise, you specify an interval (in minutes) for AutoCAD's automatic file-saving feature. You specify the interval through the SAVETIME system variable. The variable's initial default setting is 120 minutes.

Using SAVETIME To Set Autosave Frequency

Continue with the WORK drawing from the preceding exercises.

`Command:` **`SAVETIME`**↵	Accesses the SAVETIME system variable
`New value for SAVETIME <120>:` **`15`**↵	Sets autosave to 15-minute intervals
`Automatic save to C:\IA-ACAD\AUTO.SV$`	An automatic save occurs
`Command:` *Choose* File, *then* Exit AutoCAD, *and discard your changes*	Exits from AutoCAD

Automatic saves are made to the file name AUTO.SV$ in the current directory. If you need to recover a drawing from the saved file, rename AUTO.SV$ with a DWG extension, such as WHEW.DWG, and open it as a drawing.

You have finished setting up drawing parameters in AutoCAD. This will seem much easier after you have had a little more practice and a better understanding of how AutoCAD works.

Summary

The exercises in this chapter illustrate the manner in which AutoCAD uses setup commands. AutoCAD begins new drawings by reading many default settings from a prototype drawing named ACAD.DWG. The proper setup of a drawing file requires you to set up units, limits, and a working set of layers. AutoCAD saves you time by offering dialog boxes, defaults, and wild-card options in place of elaborate keyboard entry during your setup.

Several key concepts can help you establish a good drawing setup. Use an appropriate drawing scale factor to set your drawing limits for your electronic sheet size. You also can use AutoCAD's automatic setup routines to select your final sheet size and to set your drawing's limits. You can scale text, linetype, and symbols using your drawing scale factor.

You should organize your layers to hold different types of objects. Adopt a layer-naming convention that enables you to organize your drawing's names with wild cards. The current layer is the active drawing layer. The status line always shows the current layer. Default drawing properties for color and linetype are set using the BYLAYER variable. You can explicitly override BYLAYER color and linetype using the COLOR and LINETYPE commands. You also can change properties associated with existing entities by using the CHPROP command. If you are uncertain as to which properties are current in your drawing, use the Entity Creation Modes dialog box or the STATUS command to help you keep track.

The drawing tasks you performed in this chapter were not very accurate—you simply picked points on the screen rather than entering exact measurements and coordinates. In the next chapter, you learn to use many of AutoCAD's commands and tools to prepare very accurate drawings. Because accuracy is extremely important in CAD drawings to ensure proper dimensioning, Chapter 4 will be of special interest to you.

Part Two

Basic 2D AutoCAD Drafting

Two-dimensional (2D) drawings are the workhorses of drafting and design. To obtain good 2D drawings by using AutoCAD, you need to know the basics of object creation and editing. You also need to know how to control AutoCAD's graphics display screen. Part Two of *Inside AutoCAD Release 12* teaches you the basic techniques for producing accurate, professional-looking 2D drawings. In the following five chapters, you learn basic drawing and editing techniques, as well as tips and tricks that help you produce the kind of high-quality drawings you want and expect from AutoCAD.

How Part Two is Organized

Part Two includes five chapters that take you from the coordinate system and object snap techniques, through controlling your

AutoCAD graphics environment, to basic two-dimensional drawing and editing commands. These chapters cover the following five subjects:

- Understanding AutoCAD's coordinate systems
- Using object snap features and electronic drawing aids
- Controlling the graphics display
- Using the basic drawing and editing commands
- Creating graphic entities

These topics prepare you for the more advanced drawing and editing commands and techniques in Part Three.

Understanding the Coordinate System

One important feature of an electronic CAD program is its capability to maintain an accurate database of graphic entities. Chapter 4 explains the importance of accuracy in CAD drawings and the importance of avoiding bad drawing habits. As your first step in learning to create accurate entities, you must develop an understanding of how to use the coordinate system.

Chapter 4 shows you how to create precise drawings by using AutoCAD's object snaps and other electronic drawing aids. You learn how to control your location in the drawing file and how to create your own coordinate system.

Using the Display Commands

If you know how to control the AutoCAD display, you can save time and frustration when you work with complex drawings. Chapter 5 shows you how to work with a single-viewport and a multiple-viewport drawing area. You also learn how to use zooms and pans to control the displays in the drawing area. The chapter demystifies the concept of paper space, which is the bridge between your computer and the paper. When you are done with Chapter 5, you should be able to set up views and display your work in multiple viewports. You also learn how to zoom in to the view to see fine details, to zoom out to see the big picture, and to save your drawing views and viewports for future use.

Understanding Basic Drawing and Editing

The 80/20 rule can easily be applied to using AutoCAD; that is, you probably can achieve 80 percent of your initial drawing requirements by using only 20 percent of the available commands. Chapter 6 introduces the drawing and editing commands that enable you to quickly start creating a drawing. The drawing and editing exercises in Chapter 6 are easy to follow because they use Release 12's new grip editing features to grab onto and modify geometric objects by points such as center, end and midpoints. This should give you the confidence you need to produce useful drawings and continue learning more AutoCAD commands.

Creating AutoCAD Graphic Entities

Graphic entities are the building blocks of CAD drawings. Chapter 7 includes complete coverage of all the graphic entities you can create in AutoCAD. Although you may not immediately see a need for all these types of entities, the chapter's drawing exercises show you how entities can be used to reduce the number of steps necessary to complete a drawing. The more time you spend with AutoCAD, the more similarity you can see in the way all entity-creation commands operate. Before long, the commands' prompts should be all you need to remind you of the information that is necessary to create an entity.

Editing Graphic Entities

Many entities need to be edited after they are created. AutoCAD's real power and flexibility lie in the program's editing capabilities. In fact, many experienced AutoCAD drafters spend more time using editing commands than drawing commands. Chapter 8 explains many common editing commands and provides some examples that show you when and how to use them. Chapter 8 also explains more about the object-selection process and shows you how to control selection sets so that you can edit exactly the objects you want. The chapter's exercises also teach you how to create multiple copies of objects arranged in a particular way, to rotate and trim objects in a variety of ways, and to change an entity's properties.

4

Drawing Accurately

Given a straight edge and a ruler, a drafter can locate a point on a drawing sheet with some degree of accuracy; the drafter then can use that point as a location for drawing more objects. In this chapter, you learn how AutoCAD's electronic tools replace manual-drafting tools for locating points and maintaining drawing accuracy.

Some of the benefits of AutoCAD's tools stand out immediately. You never need to clean up eraser shavings, you work at the proper scale, and you never need to lend your 30/60 triangle. Other benefits are not as apparent, such as the 100-percent accuracy of straight edges and triangles, the precise mathematically-defined curves, and electronically-flexible graph paper to trace over as a guide.

Examining Electronic Drawing Aids

The first step in creating accurate drawings is to locate your drawing points. One way to locate them accurately is to enter coordinates from the keyboard. Although you may know some of the coordinate values to start a drawing, you rarely have complete information for entering all your drawing points. Besides, this method of coordinate entry is grueling, tedious work and leaves you open to making typing errors.

Most of the time, you can pick drawing points without any help from AutoCAD. As you saw in the last chapter, however, it is hard to pick points accurately. AutoCAD provides two methods for controlling the movement of your cursor so that you can accurately select pick points. The first method is to use the grid and snap functions; the second is to use the object snap functions (see fig. 4.1).

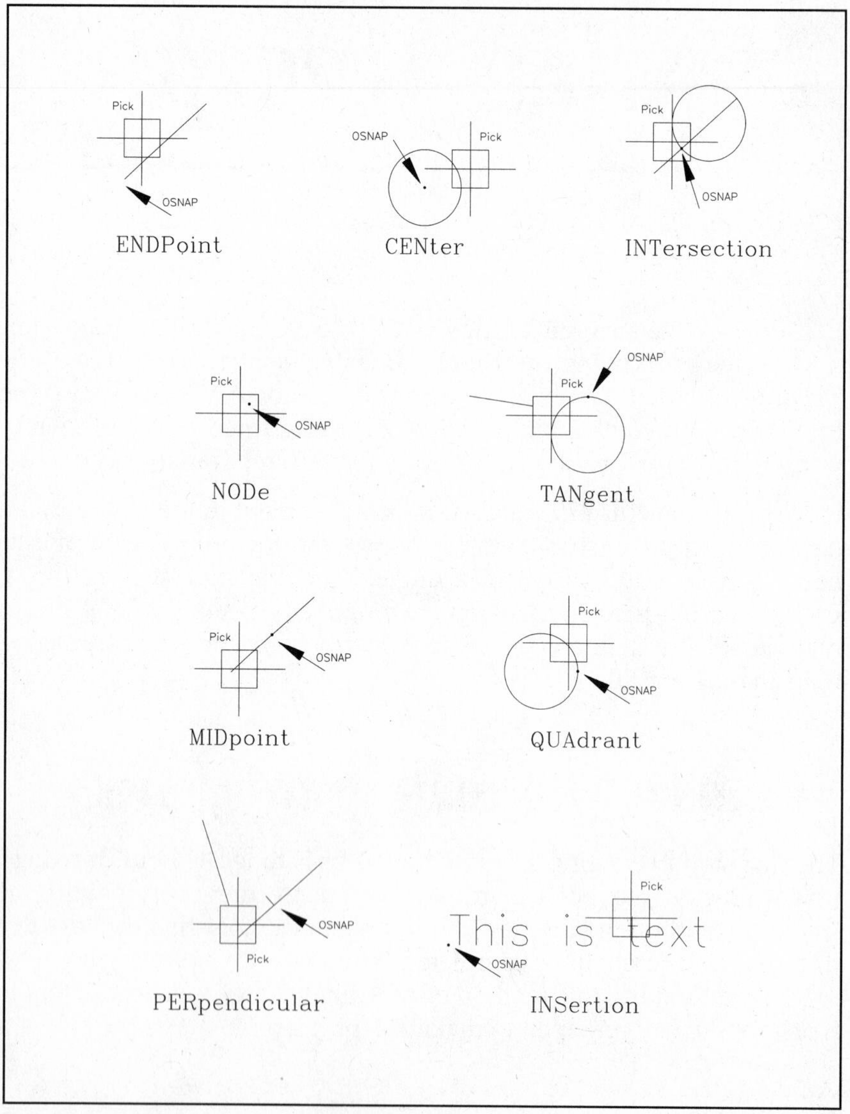

ENDPoint CENTer INTersection

NODe TANgent

MIDpoint QUAdrant

PERpendicular INSertion

Figure 4.1:
Object snap targets and the points they pick.

AutoCAD has two other drawing-accuracy aids: ortho mode and XYZ point filters. When AutoCAD is in ortho mode, you can draw or input points only orthogonally—in other words, at right angles to previous points or lines. Ortho mode is discussed in detail in this chapter. For information on XYZ point filters, see Chapter 10.

Understanding Grid and Snap

AutoCAD is accurate to at least 14 significant digits. If you pick your drawing points without some form of control, however, AutoCAD must translate the cursor's pixel position into the current drawing units. That is, AutoCAD must approximate the coordinates you actually want. If you try to pick the point 2.375,4.625, for example, you may get such numbers as 2.3754132183649,4.6248359103856. If you set the coordinate display to show only three decimal places, these numbers falsely appear to be rounded accurately, but AutoCAD stores them internally with their true precision—with several more decimal places of "inaccuracy." Even if you visually align the crosshairs with the grid or other objects, you seldom locate the desired point with complete accuracy.

You can control your pick points by using grid and snap. AutoCAD's grid serves as a visible template that shows the location of a set of points, but it does not round the input points to accurate locations. *Snap* is an invisible grid template that controls the points that you select with your cursor. If you set snap to 0.5, then you can select only points that fall on 0.5-unit increments.

You can most easily control pick points by coordinating AutoCAD's grid and snap capabilities. If you set them equally, you can select only grid points. If you set the snap increments to half the grid increments, you can select only the grid points themselves or points that lie halfway between the grid points. You control the accuracy of your point selection by using snap; grid enables you to keep track visually of the points you are snapping to.

Understanding Object Snaps

As your drawing becomes more complex, points on circles, arcs, and intersections of angled lines no longer fall directly on grid and snap points. AutoCAD offers a set of tools called *object snaps* (also called *geometric snaps*) to help you accurately pick such points. To understand object snaps, remember that objects such as lines have middle and end points, and circles have center, quadrant, and tangent points. When you draw, you often attach lines to these points.

AutoCAD's *object snaps* are geometric filters that enable you to select your drawing-attachment points. If, for example, you want to draw to an intersection of two lines, you can set the object snap to filter for intersections, and then pick a point close to the intersection. The point snaps to the precise intersection of the lines. Although it takes a little time to get used to setting object snaps, they are the best way to maintain geometrically accurate drawings.

Examining the Drawing Accuracy Tools

Drawing accuracy is controlled by the GRID, SNAP, ORTHO, and OSNAP commands and by the Drawing Aids dialog box. This dialog box is accessed from the Drawing Aids item in the Settings pull-down menu (see fig. 4.2); when you select Drawing Aids, the Drawing Aids dialog box appears, as shown in figure 4.3. The commands also are found on the SETTINGS screen menu. You also can turn Grid, Snap, and Ortho on and off by using function keys and Ctrl-key combinations. If Ortho or Snap is active, the word `Ortho` or `Snap` (or both) appears near the left side of the status line.

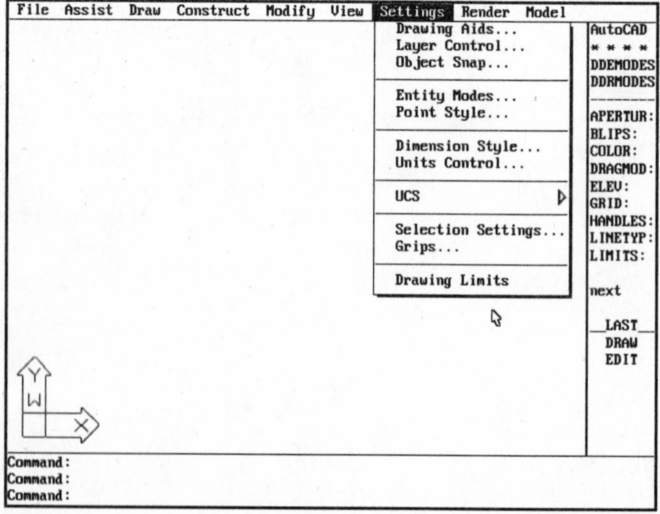

Figure 4.2:

The Settings pull-down menu and first page of the SETTINGS screen menu.

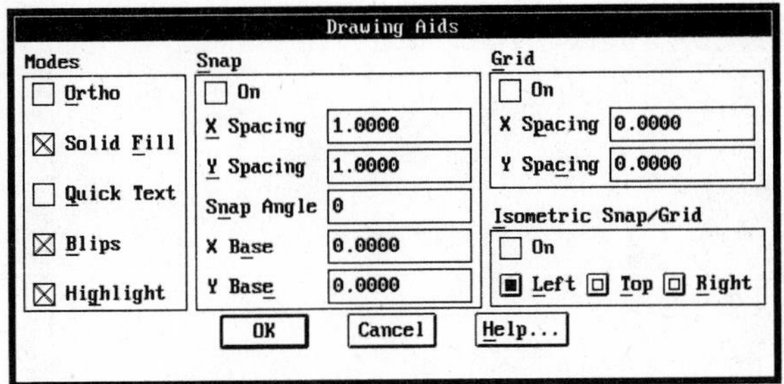

Figure 4.3:

The Drawing Aids dialog box.

Using Drawing Aids

In the following exercise, you use a technique of starting a new drawing so that its settings are equal to one of the drawings from the IA DISK. This new drawing uses the defaults of the IA7WORK drawing from the IA DISK as a prototype instead of using the ACAD.DWG settings as shown in Chapter 3. AutoCAD begins with a copy of the specified prototype drawing, giving it the new name you specify. If you do not have the IA DISK, follow the exercise's instructions to load the WORK drawing from Chapter 3.

Reloading the WORK Drawing File

In AutoCAD, choose File, then New, then enter WORK=IA7WORK.

Choose YES *to replace the existing* WORK *drawing.*

In AutoCAD, choose File, then Open, then enter `WORK`, then erase the square.

`Command:` *Choose* Settings, *then* Layer Control, *verify that your settings match those shown in table 4.1, and then choose* OK

Your drawing should look like figure 4.4, which shows a single circle located in the upper right corner of your graphics drawing area.

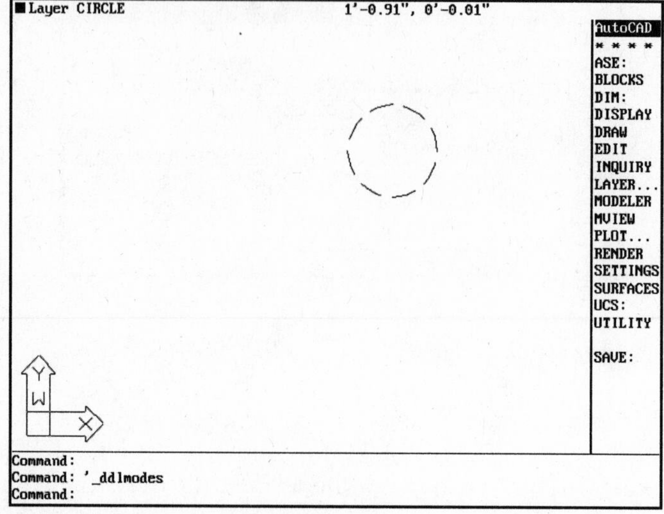

Figure 4.4:

The WORK drawing.

Table 4.1
WORK Drawing Settings

UNITS	Engineering, 2 decimal places, 2 fractional places for angles, defaults all other settings.		
LIMITS	0,0 to 11,8.5		
Layer Name	***State***	***Color***	***Linetype***
0	On	7 (White)	CONTINUOUS
CIRCLE	On/Current	3 (Green)	DASHED
PARAGRAM	On	5 (Magenta)	HIDDEN
SQUARE	On	2 (Yellow)	CONTINUOUS
TEXT	On	4 (Cyan)	CONTINUOUS
TRIANGLE	On	1 (Red)	CONTINUOUS

The drawing's current layer is CIRCLE. In the following exercise, you draw a few points on the CIRCLE layer.

Controlling Drawing Points

The POINT command is the simplest of AutoCAD's drawing commands. This command inputs a single drawing point. Try it with the coordinate values shown in the following exercise. To see the actual point entity, you must perform a display redraw after you create the point.

Using the POINT Command

`Command:` *Choose* Draw, *then* Point	Starts the POINT command
`Command: _point Point: 3,6.25↵`	Displays a small blip mark at the specified coordinate
`Command: _point Point:` *Press Ctrl-C*	Cancels the POINT command
`Command:` *Choose* View, *then* Redraw	Leaves only a dot

First, a mark appears at the specified coordinates. This mark is actually larger than the point itself, which you drew with the POINT command. This mark is a construction marker (or *blip*) for the point. The REDRAW command clears the construction marker and leaves a small green dot, or *point entity.* (You may not easily see the point, but it is there.) You can be certain of its location because you typed the absolute X,Y coordinate values. (REDRAW is discussed further at the end of this chapter.)

Determining the Accuracy of Pick Points

Picking a point accurately with your cursor is difficult. To help track your cursor, you can turn on your coordinate display by pressing Ctrl-D or F6. Then, as you move the cursor, the digital readout of your coordinates should display the crosshair cursor's current X,Y location. Figure 4.5 shows the coordinate display to the right on the status line.

Try the following exercise to see how accurately you can pick your drawing points. To test your pick point, use the coordinate display and the ID Point selection from Inquiry on the Assist pull-down menu. Try to pick at coordinates 3.25,5. ID Point simply displays the picked point's coordinates.

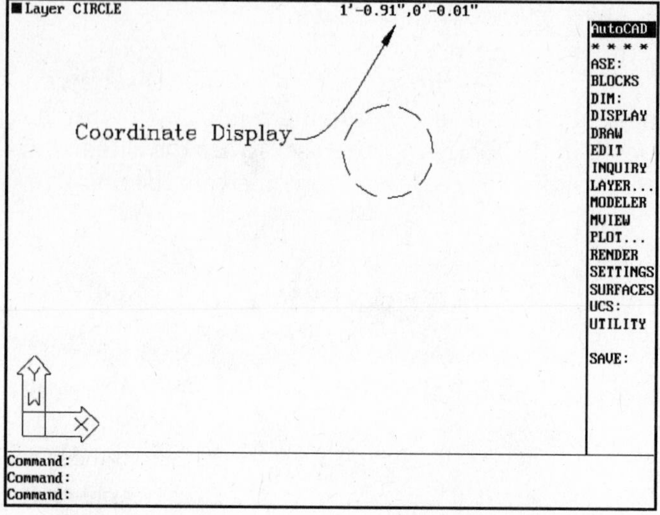

Figure 4.5:

The coordinate display.

Using ID To Test Pick Points

Press F6 to make sure that your coordinate display is turned on.

`Command:` *Choose* Assist, *then* Inquiry, *then* ID Point	Issues the ID command transparently
`'_id Select point:` *Try picking a point at exactly 0'-3.25",0'-5.00" on the coordinate display*	
`X = 3.24"  Y = 5.03"  Z = 0.00"`	Your point may differ

ID Point shows the X, Y, and Z position of your pick point. Try a few more points. As you can see, it is nearly impossible to accurately pick the point you want. Without some form of control over the points you pick, a drawing can contain many inaccurate points.

The ID command and the coordinates display may claim that the point is exactly at 3.25,5.00. When you change your units to six or eight decimal places, however, you see that AutoCAD really is rounding off an inaccurate point.

Although the coordinate display shows coordinates with the full precision set by the UNITS command, instructions to pick points at specific coordinates are generally abbreviated in this book's exercises.

Leading and trailing zeros, and feet and inch marks that are not required for point entry may be omitted. For example, rather than "pick at 0'-3.25",0'-5.00"," you may be instructed to "pick at 3.25",5.00"" or to "pick or enter 3.25,5."

Using the Grid Display

To get accurate points, first set up a grid template that helps you see points on the screen. A *grid* consists of a series of construction points that appear on the screen, but which are not part of the drawing file. Grids serve as a frame of reference while you draw.

You set up a grid by using the GRID command or the Drawing Aids dialog box. In the next exercise, you set up a one-inch grid. If you move the crosshairs and try to pick a grid point with the ID command, you can see that grid points do not actually control input points.

Using GRID To Set Up a Grid

`Command:` *Choose* Settings, *then* Drawing Aids	Displays the Drawing Aids dialog box
In the Grid *area, click on the* On *check box*	Turns on the grid
Double-click in the X Spacing *box and enter* `1`, *then choose* OK	Sets X to 1" and defaults Y to X, then displays the grid

The one-inch grid appears, as shown in figure 4.6.

Now use the ID command to try to pick a point that lies exactly on one of the grid marks.

`Command:` **`ID`**↵

`Point:` *Try picking on the grid at exactly 7.00",5.00"*

AutoCAD displays the following message, which shows the exact location of the point you just picked:

```
X = 0'--6.99" Y = 0'--4.99"  Z = 0'--0.00"
```

While the message confirms that you did pick a point, it also shows that the point is not precisely located on the grid. The message you see on your screen may be different from this one.

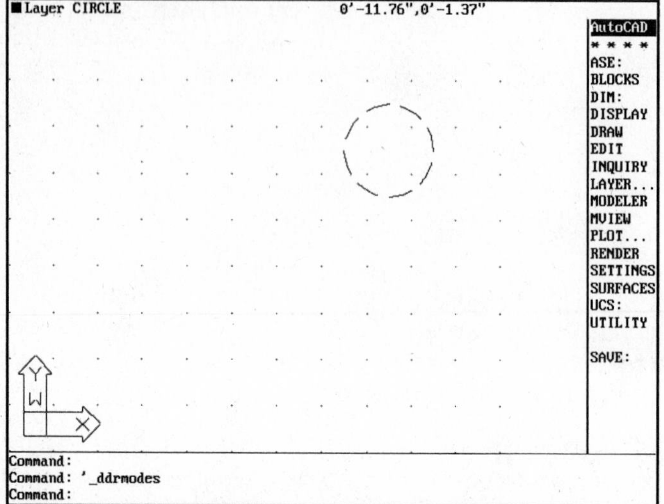

Figure 4.6:

A grid, added to the WORK drawing.

TIP The grid helps you visualize distances and see drawing limits. The grid, however, is only a visual aid, and does not affect point entry or cursor movement. When you set the grid spacing, avoid setting a grid that is too dense (that is, one whose markers are too close together). A too-dense grid obscures the drawing and causes screen redrawing to operate slowly.

Because you have several options in setting up a grid, you are not limited to creating square grids. You can, for example, change the grid spacing to give different X,Y aspect ratios. Figure 4.7 shows a grid with a 2X:1Y aspect ratio.

You can set the grid by using the Drawing Aids dialog box or the GRID command. The GRID command prompt appears with the following options:

```
Grid spacing(X) or ON/OFF/Snap/Aspect <0'--0.00">:
```

These options perform the following functions:

- **Grid spacing (X).** This option sets the X,Y grid increment and activates it. If you enter 0, AutoCAD makes the grid equal to the snap spacing, changing automatically when snap changes. If you enter a number followed by an X, AutoCAD sets the grid to the current snap increment times the specified number.
- **ON.** This option makes the grid visible.
- **OFF.** This option makes the grid invisible.

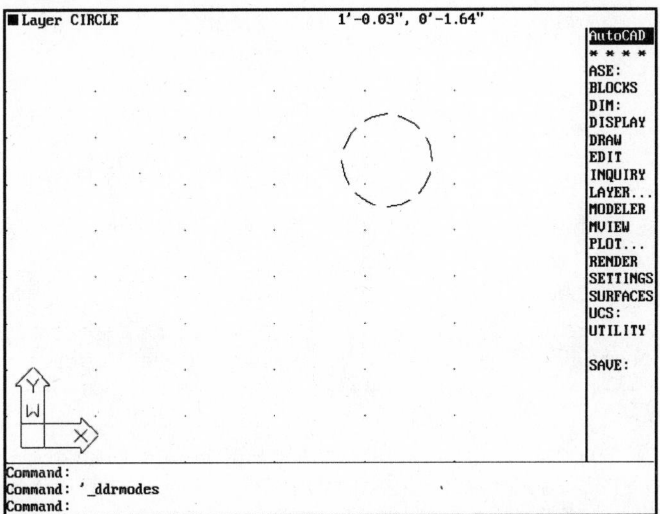

Figure 4.7:

A grid with a 2X:1Y aspect ratio.

- **Snap.** This option sets the grid increment so that it is equal to the current snap increment (when you enter `0` or `1X` for the grid spacing, for example), except that the Snap option does not automatically change the grid as snap changes.
- **Aspect.** This option enables you to set different increments for grid's horizontal and vertical markers.

You can press Ctrl-G or F7 to turn the grid on and off.

Setting Snap Points

The SNAP command sets the smallest increment that AutoCAD will recognize when you move the cursor. If you turn snap on and set a spacing value, you notice that your cursor moves with a jerking motion; it jumps from snap point to snap point instead of tracking smoothly. Think of setting snap as setting your smallest drawing increment. When you set snap-spacing values, all drawing pick points are forced to multiples of your snap values.

A good practice is to set your snap to some fraction of your grid spacing. AutoCAD normally aligns snap points with the grid. As you draw, you can easily "eyeball" points that are 1/4 to 1/5 the distance between grid points.

In the following exercise, you set the snap increment to 0.25", or 1/4 of your grid spacing.

Using SNAP To Set Snap Points

`Command:` *Choose* Settings, *then* Drawing Aids	Displays the Drawing Aids dialog box
In the Snap *area, click on the* On *check box*	Turns on snap
Double-click in the X Spacing *box, enter* `.25`*, and click on* OK	Defaults the Y spacing so that it equals the X spacing

The word `Snap` appears on the left side of the status line, indicating that snap is on, and the coordinates display accurately in 1/4-inch increments (see fig. 4.8). Try moving the cursor around. The crosshairs now jump to the snap increments.

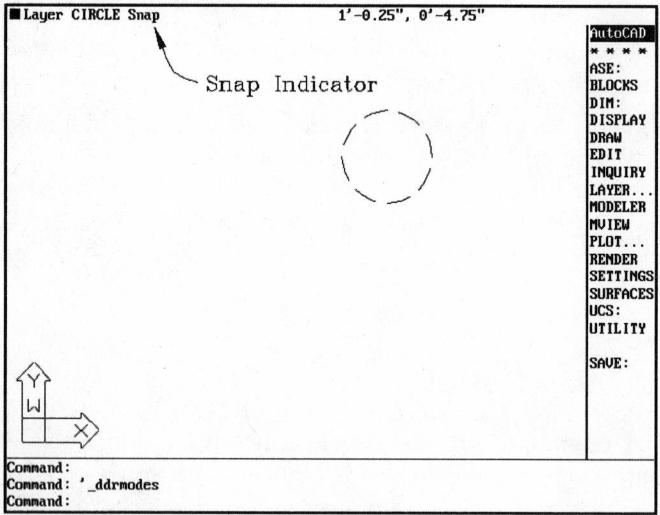

Figure 4.8:
The status line shows that snap is on.

NOTE

You can turn snap on and off by pressing Ctrl-B or F9. Turning snap off is helpful if you want to select an object at a point to which you cannot snap.

Using Snap Points To Draw Objects

After you set a snap value, you can draw accurately, as long as the object you want to draw is on a snap point. The status line shows the correct crosshair position as it rounds the X,Y values to 0.25".

In the following exercise, draw a 2"×2" square with the lower left corner at 0'-7.50",0'-1.00". Use the coordinate display to help you pick the points used in the following exercise. As you pick points, notice that the cursor snaps to the snap increments.

Using SNAP To Draw a Square

`Command:` *Choose* Settings, *then* Layer Control, *make* SQUARE *the current layer, and click on* OK

`Command:` *Choose* Draw, *then* Line, *then* Segments — Issues the LINE command

At the `Command: _line From point:` prompt, use the coordinates display to pick the point 0'-7.50", 0'-1.00". This starts the line and updates the coordinates display to show a distance and an angle, as in `0'--1.500"<0.00`.

`To point:` *Press F6, then pick point 0'-9.50",0'-1.00"*	Changes coordinates back to X,Y display, then draws the line
`To point:` *Pick point 0'-9.50", 0'-3.00"*	Draws a line
`To point:` *Pick point 0'-7.50", 0'-3.00"*	Draws a line
`To point:` *Pick point 0'-7.50", 0'-1.00"*	Finishes the square
`To point:` *Press Enter*	Ends the LINE command

After you finish, your drawing should look like the one shown in figure 4.9.

The *X,Y to distance<angle* coordinate display options seen in this exercise are discussed later in this chapter.

As you work with the GRID and SNAP commands, you probably will need to adjust the grid and snap settings as you zoom, so that you can work in greater detail. If you start with a snap at 1 unit and a grid at 5 units on a whole drawing, you may need to reset your snap to 1/4 units and your grid to 1 unit when you zoom to work on a portion of the drawing.

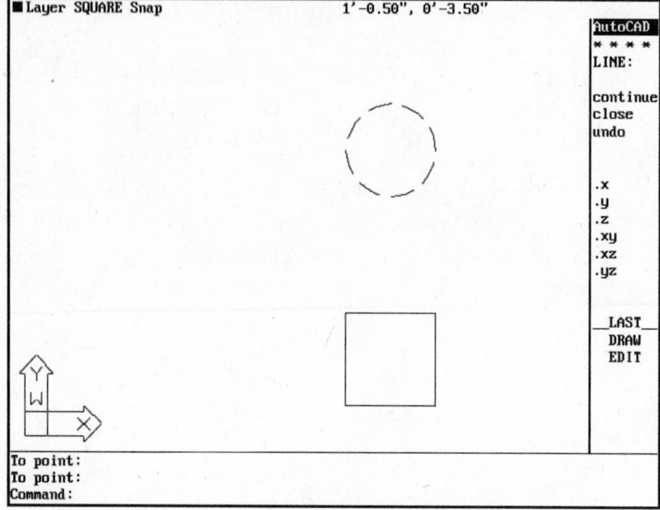

Figure 4.9:

A square drawn with the SNAP command.

You can coordinate your snap and grid spacing to suit your needs. Make it a practice to set your grid and snap, and then leave them on most of the time. If you do not pick your drawing points with snap (or object snap) on, your drawings will not be accurate.

You can use the dialog box or the SNAP command to set snap. The SNAP command provides the following options:

```
Snap spacing or ON/OFF/Aspect/Rotate/Style <0'--0.00">:
```

You can use the following options to set snap spacing:

- **Snap spacing.** This option prompts you for a value to set the snap increment and to turn on snap.
- **ON.** This option turns on snap.
- **OFF.** This option turns off snap. This is the initial default setting
- **Aspect.** This option prompts for different horizontal (X) and vertical (Y) snap increments (except in isometric mode; see the description of the Style option).
- **Rotate.** This option prompts you to specify an angle and a basepoint, around which you can rotate the snap grid (and crosshairs). See the discussion of Ortho (later in this chapter) for an example.
- **Style.** This option prompts for Standard or Isometric style. Standard sets the normal (default) snap style; Isometric sets an isometric snap grid style by aligning the snap points to a 30-, 90-, or 150-degree grid.

You use isometric snaps to draw in the standard isometric planes. Press Ctrl-E one or more times to rotate the current isometric drawing plane from top to right, then to left, and then back to top.

Using Ortho Mode as a Special Snap

If you are drawing horizontal and vertical lines, you can place an additional constraint on your cursor movements by turning on ortho mode. "Ortho" stands for *orthogonal* and limits cursor movement to right angles from the last point. When ortho is on, any lines you enter with the cursor are aligned with the snap axes. In effect, you can draw only at right angles. To turn on ortho, you can use the Drawing Aids dialog box, the ORTHO command, F8, or Ctrl-O.

Ortho is easy to use and helpful any time you draw sets of horizontal and vertical lines. In the following exercise, you access the ORTHO command, and then draw another square around the square you just drew. When you turn on ortho, `<Ortho on>` appears at the `Command:` prompt. As you draw the square, the cursor is limited to vertical and horizontal movement, which makes it easy to get true 90-degree corners. The rubber-band cursor that normally trails from the last point to the intersection of the crosshairs now goes from the last point to the nearest perpendicular point on the X or Y crosshairs.

As you pick points, notice that you do not actually need to place the cursor on the correct X and Y coordinates. The cursor need only be aligned along one axis, either X or Y, depending on the desired location of the next point.

After you draw the square, undo it and turn off ortho; you will use this drawing again later to practice using AutoCAD's object snaps.

Using ORTHO To Draw a Square

`Command:` *Choose* Draw, *then* Line, *then* Segments	
`Command: _line From point:` *Pick* ① *at 7.00",0.50" (see fig. 4.10), then move the cursor around*	Starts the line and rubber bands freely
`To point:` *Press F8 to turn on Ortho*	
`To point: <Ortho on>` *Move cursor around, then pick* ② *at 10.00",0.50"*	Rubber bands orthogonally and draws the line

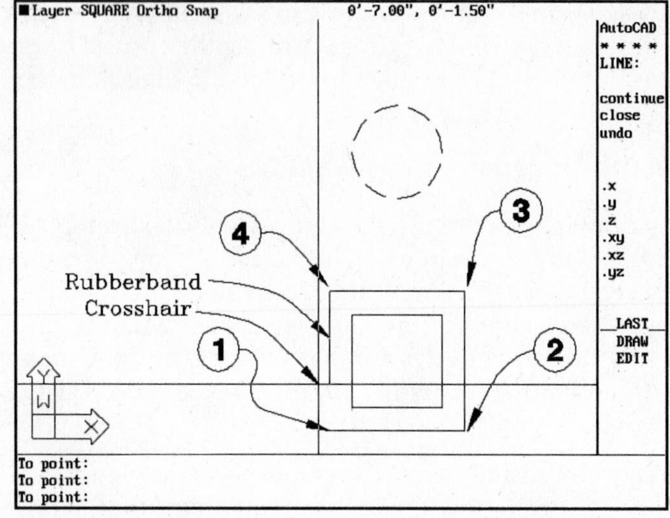

Figure 4.10:
Using Ortho to draw a square.

`To point:` *Pick ③ at 10.00",3.50"*	
`To point:` *Pick ④ at 7.00",3.50"*	
`To point:` *From the screen menu, choose* close	Closes the series of lines and ends the LINE command
`Command:` *Choose* Assist, *then* Undo	Removes the four lines and turns off ortho mode; `Ortho` disappears from the status line

If you turn on or off a mode such as Ortho, Snap, or Grid in the middle of a command, and later undo the command, the active setting also is undone.

Examining Coordinate Entry

If you enter coordinates from the keyboard, they override the Snap and Ortho drawing controls (but not object snap). You may often enter coordinates from the keyboard as you set up drawings or as you draw at specific points or known distances that are relative to known points.

The Z distance or Z angle is assumed to be zero, unless otherwise specified.

Using Absolute Coordinates

If you know the exact coordinates of your point or its distance and angle from the 0,0 drawing origin, you can use the keyboard to enter coordinates in several formats. All of these formats are known as *absolute coordinates* or *explicit coordinates*.

Absolute Cartesian coordinates treat coordinate entry as X and Y displacements from 0,0 (or X,Y,Z from 0,0,0 in 3D). For example, the absolute Cartesian coordinates 6,5,4 place a point that is 6 units along the positive X axis, 5 units along the positive Y axis, and 4 units along the positive Z axis from the 0,0,0 base point. The default position for 0,0 is at the lower left of your limits and drawing area, but you can locate it anywhere by using the UCS command. If your displacement is positive, you do not need to use a plus (+) sign. Negative displacement is left and down on the screen. You must use a minus (-) sign for negative displacements. In figure 4.11, the points are located by the Cartesian distances X, Y, and Z.

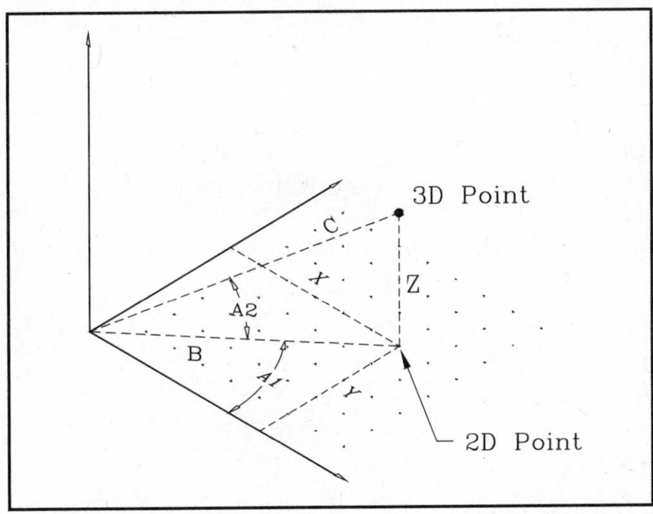

Figure 4.11:
Various forms of coordinate entry.

Absolute Polar coordinates also treat 2D coordinate entry as a displacement from 0,0, but you specify the displacement as a distance and angle. The distance and angle values are separated by a left-angle bracket (<). Positive angles are counterclockwise, relative to 0 degrees as an imaginary horizontal line extending to the right of 0,0. In figure 4.11, the 2D point is located using B and A1, as in B<A1. In this system of coordinate entry, 90 degrees is

vertically above, and 180 degrees is horizontally left (see fig. 4.12). The value 2<60, for example, is two units from 0,0 along a line at 60 degrees from the X axis in the X,Y plane.

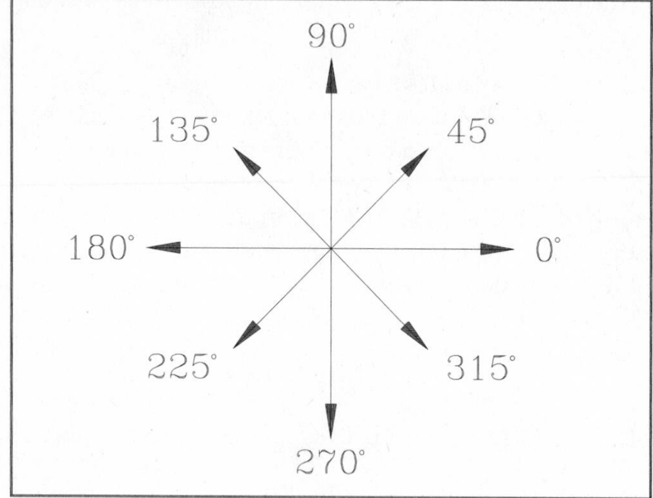

Figure 4.12:
Default units angle directions.

Absolute Spherical coordinates are 3D polar coordinates, and are specified as a distance and two angles. The first angle is from 0,0 in the X,Y plane, and the second angle is the angle toward the Z axis up or down from the X,Y plane. In figure 4.11, the 3D point is located using spherical coordinates by distance C and angles A1 and A2, as in C<A1<A2. For example, 2<60<45 specifies a point 2 units from the 0,0,0 origin along a line at 60 degrees from the X axis in the X,Y plane and at 45 degrees up toward the Z axis from the X,Y plane.

Absolute Cylindrical coordinates also are for 3D use. They are like polar coordinates, but also use a height in the Z axis above or below the X,Y plane. In figure 4.11, the 3D point is located using cylindrical coordinates by distance B, angle A1, and distance Z, as in B<A1,Z. For example, 2<60,3 specifies a point 3 units vertically above the 2D (polar) point that is 2 units from the 0,0,0 origin, along a line at 60 degrees from the X axis in the X,Y plane.

In the following exercise you review the use absolute Cartesian coordinates, which you already have used several times, and try absolute polar coordinates as you draw a triangle at the upper left corner of the drawing.

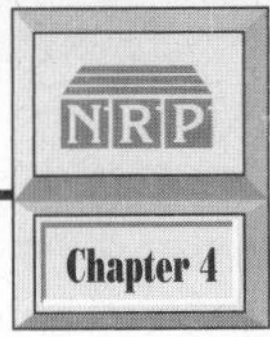

Specifying Points with Absolute Coordinates

Continue working in the WORK drawing.

`Command:` *Choose* Settings, *then* Layer Control, *and TRIANGLE the current layer*	
`Command:` *Choose* Draw, *then* Line, *then* Segments	
`Command: _line From point: 1.25,5.25↵`	Specifies an absolute Cartesian point
`To point: 3,7.5↵`	Specifies an absolute Cartesian point
`To point: 7.08<47.86↵`	Specifies an absolute polar point
`To point:` *From the screen menu, choose* close	Closes the triangle

The triangle appears in the upper left part of the drawing area, as shown in figure 4.13.

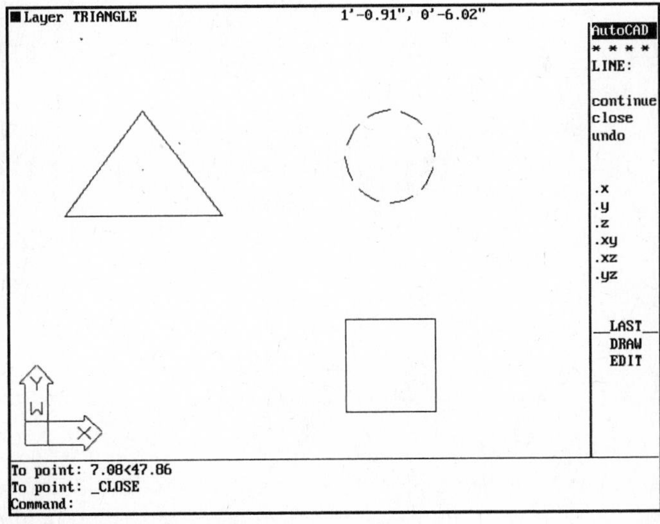

Figure 4.13:

A triangle, drawn with absolute coordinates.

The preceding exercise uses simple points, but in a real drawing they are harder to calculate. If you examine the drawing database closely, you find that the third point (5 times the square root of 2 at 45 degrees) does not align exactly with the first point because it is entered with two decimal places of precision.

Absolute coordinates can locate the first point of an object in the drawing, but relative coordinates are usually better for locating subsequent points. Relative polar coordinates can be picked easily by using the cursor with the coordinate display.

Using the Coordinates Display To Track Polar Coordinates

The precision capability of the SNAP, GRID, and ORTHO commands often is sufficient for accuracy, but drawing is easier if you know how far the cursor is from the last point. You can use the cursor to pick polar coordinates; you can track your cursor movements for polar input by switching the coordinate display to polar mode. To activate the coordinate display, press F6 or Ctrl-D. Figure 4.14 shows the polar coordinates display.

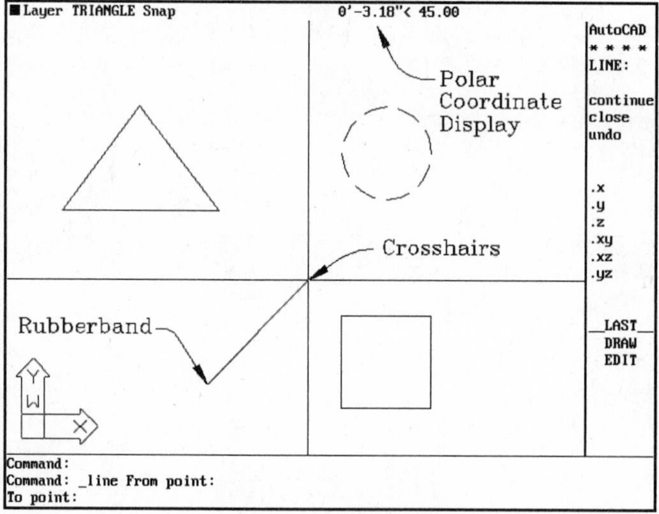

Figure 4.14: Displaying polar coordinates.

The coordinate display has three modes. The default mode is static coordinates, or off. *Static coordinates* display an X,Y coordinate, which is updated only when a new point is picked.

When you press F6 once, you get the second mode, in which the X,Y display is constantly updated as you move the cursor. This second, constantly updated mode has a "split personality" in most commands. When the crosshairs pull a rubber-band line, such as in a LINE command, the second mode automatically switches into a *polar distance<angle* display relative to

the last point. This mode is the most frequently used mode because it enables you to pick the initial point for a command with absolute X,Y coordinates and to pick subsequent points with relative polar points.

The third mode locks the coordinates into X,Y display. (This works only in a command that shows a polar display.) If you press F6 a third time, the coordinates display is locked into X,Y mode. If this sounds confusing, it is! Press F6 once or twice until you get the coordinate display you want.

Using Relative Coordinates

Often you may know the X,Y or X,Y,Z distance, or the distance and angle from a previous point to a point you want to enter, but you may not know the point's displacement from 0,0. Any method of entering coordinates also can be used relative to the last point entered in your drawing, instead of relative to 0,0. To enter a relative point, enter an at symbol (@) to precede the first number.

Relative coordinates treat the last point of coordinate entry as a temporary 0,0,0 (stored in the LASTPOINT system variable). If you want to add a horizontal line segment to be two units in the X direction and one in the Y direction from the previous point, enter **@2,0**. Relative polar, spherical, and cylindrical coordinates specify displacement with distance(s) and angle(s). For example, the relative polar @2<60 is 2 units at 60 degrees.

If you want to enter a new point at the last point, you can use a zero distance, such as @0,0 or @0<*nn* (*nn* can be any angle). This is the same as the last point. A simpler way to enter a new point at the last point is to enter an @ without any number or angle. AutoCAD interprets this symbol as specifying the last point.

> **TIP** Issue the ID command at the `Command:` prompt to draw relative to a point that is not the last point used in the drawing. The ID command enables you to pick the point you want to work relative to, and it becomes the new last point. You also can check and change the last point with the LASTPOINT system variable.

In the following exercise, try relative, Cartesian, and polar coordinate entry by drawing a parallelogram. You use the keyboard and the cursor to specify relative polar coordinates. Use the following exercise sequence for your input values.

Drawing with Relative Coordinates

Continue from the previous triangle exercise (work relative to its last point).

`Command:` *Choose* Settings, *then* Layer Control, *and make PARAGRAM the current layer*	
`Command:` *Choose* Draw, *then* Line, *then* Segments	
`Command: _line From point:` *Use the coordinate display to pick absolute Cartesian coordinates 0'-4.25", 0',1.00"*	Starts LINE and changes the coordinate display to polar display
`To point:` **`@2.25<60↵`**	Specifies relative polar coordinates
`To point:` **`@--3,0↵`**	Specifies relative Cartesian coordinates
`To point:` *Using the coordinate display, pick relative polar coordinates @ 0'-2.25"<240.00*	
`To point:` *Press F6, then use the display to pick absolute Cartesian coordinates 0'-4.25",0',1.00"*	Changes the coordinate display to absolute X,Y coordinates
`To point:` *Press Enter*	Ends the LINE command
`Command:` *Choose* File, *then* Save	Saves the drawing

After you finish, your drawing should look like figure 4.15.

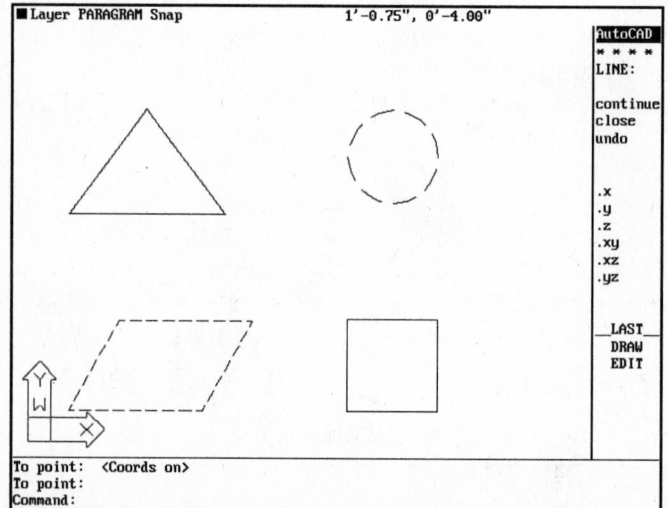

Figure 4.15:

A parallelogram, drawn with relative coordinates.

Do not let the coordinate display fool you; it displays with as much or as little precision as you set when you issue the UNITS or DDUNITS commands. A polar display is rarely precise at angles other than 90-degree increments. For example, 2.10<60 is more likely 2.0976325 at 60.351724 degrees, or some such.

Creating Your Own Coordinate System

So far you have been using AutoCAD's default coordinate system, the *World Coordinate System*, (WCS). You can create your own coordinate system by using the UCS command. The UCS command enables you to position the 0,0 origin anywhere, so that you can work relative to any point you want. You also can rotate the X,Y (and even Z) axes to any angle in 2D or 3D space (see fig. 4.16). Although the *User Coordinate System* (*UCS*) was developed for use in 3D drawing, it also can be useful for 2D-drawing applications.

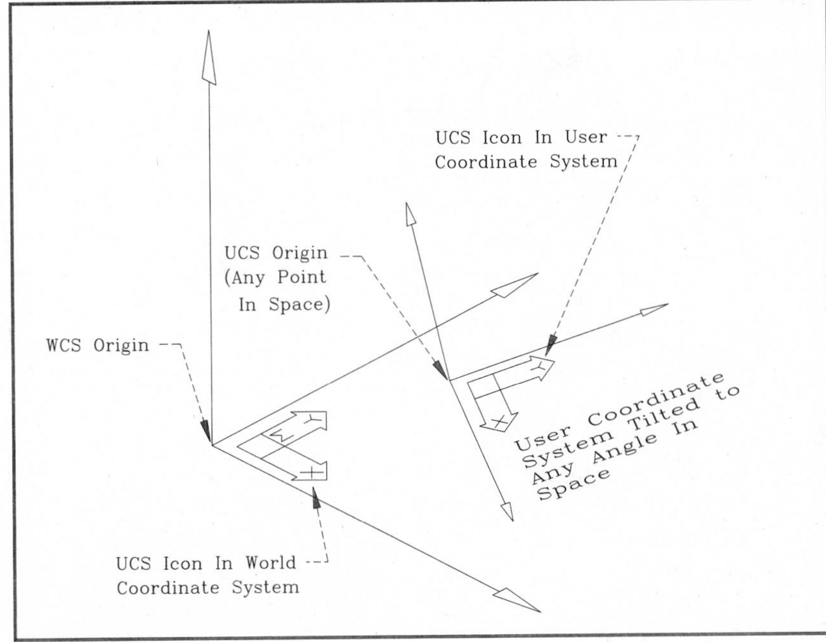

Figure 4.16:

A User Coordinate System and the World Coordinate System.

The following two examples and their exercises show you a few of the UCS command's capabilities. The first uses the UCS command to change the location of the 0,0 origin point and the direction of the X and Y axes in your drawing. The second changes the location of 0,0 and keeps the X and Y directions in the default directions. When you draft in 2D, you frequently encounter cases in which you have drawing data relative to known positions. Large sets of offset data or datum-dimensioned work are common examples. To handle this type of drawing, you can set your UCS origin to the known position, input the drawing data relative to the UCS's 0,0 origin, and then return your UCS to its original (default) world setting.

You can modify or change the current UCS by using either the UCS command or the UCS Control dialog box (the DDUCS command—see fig. 4.17). The Settings pull-down menu contains a single UCS menu item, which offers a number of child menus from which you can set or select UCS options. The Named UCS and Presets menu items on the first UCS child menu offer two UCS dialog box options: UCS Control (the UCS Control dialog box) and UCS Presets (an icon menu of preset UCS orientations for 3D work). These options are available through typed commands and on the UCS: screen menu.

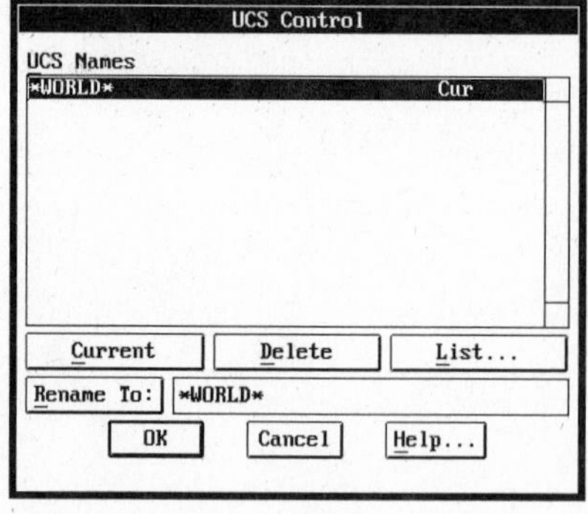

Figure 4.17:

The UCS Control dialog box.

The UCS icon (the X,Y arrows at the lower left corner of the drawing editor) helps you keep track of the UCS by showing the orientation of the X and Y axes. You can set the icon so that it appears aligned on the 0,0,0 origin of the UCS, if there is room in the drawing window. When the UCS icon is set to the origin, and it can fit there, a plus mark appears. If the icon cannot fit at the origin, it appears at the lower left without a plus mark. The UCS icon's appearance is controlled by the UCSICON command or the Icon selection on the UCS child pull-down menu. AutoCAD also offers a UCSICON: selection and a UCS: selection on the SETTINGS screen menu, as well as a UCS: selection on the root screen menu.

Now, make sure that your UCS icon is on. In the following exercise, you use the UCS command to rotate your drawing's coordinate system 90 degrees and set the 0,0 origin near the lower right corner. When you specify the new UCS's coordinates, you specify them in terms of the current coordinate system. Use the coordinates display to pick the new origin.

Using UCS To Create a User Coordinate System

`Command:` *Choose* Settings, *then* UCS, *then* Icon, *then* Origin	Sets the UCS icon to origin
`'setvar Variable name or ? <>: ucsicon` `New value for UCSICON <1>: 3`	
`Command:` **`Z`**↵	Issues the shortcut key for the ZOOM command
`ZOOM All/Center/Dynamic/Extents/Left/ Previous/Vmax/Window/<Scale(X/XP)>:` **`.8`**↵	Zooms out so that you can watch the UCS icon jump to the origin
`Command:` **`U`**↵	Undo to zoom back
`Command:` *Choose* Settings, *then* UCS, *then* Origin	Issues the UCS command with the origin prompt
`Origin point <0,0,0>:` *Pick the absolute point 10.25,.5*	Relocates the UCS and the icon to the lower right
`Command:` *Choose* Settings, *then* UCS, *then* Axis, *then* Z	Issues the UCS command with the Z rotation angle prompt
`Rotation angle about Z axis <0.00>:` **`90`**↵	Reorients the UCS so that the X axis points up

As shown in figure 4.18, the new coordinate system and icon appear in the lower right corner of the drawing editor.

To see the effect of the changed origin, move the crosshairs and watch the coordinates display. They should show 0,0 at the lower right corner, a vertical X direction, and a horizontal Y direction.

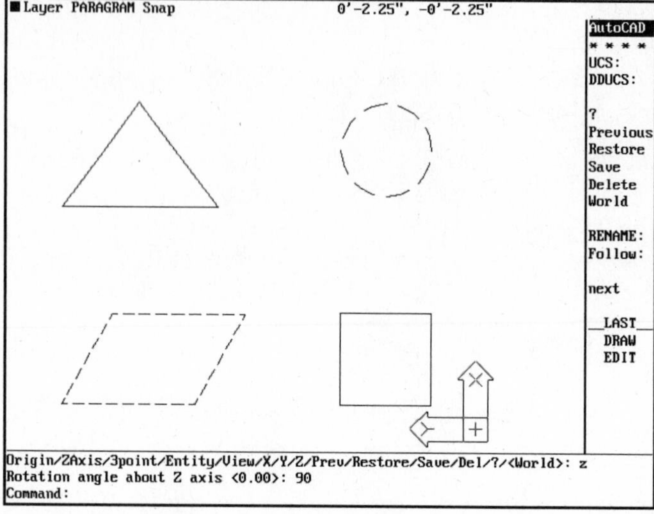

Figure 4.18:

The new User Coordinate System.

The process of offsetting the origin is straightforward, but you may ask what effect rotating the UCS around the Z axis has on your 2D drawing. Imagine that you are standing on the X axis, looking down at your drawing with your left arm extended to the left to grip a pole rising up from 0,0. Walk forward through 90 degrees and kick the X axis as you walk. You just rotated around the Z axis by 90 degrees. To AutoCAD, the Y axis is North. If you draw a building that fits on the drawing best with North pointing to the left, you find it easier to work if you rotate the UCS. Similarly, if you are datum-dimensioning a part from its lower right corner, you can relocate and rotate its UCS.

Try out the new UCS by making a border around your drawing. Use the following exercise as a guide.

Drawing a Border in a UCS

`Command:` *Choose* Settings, *then* Layer Control, *and make TEXT the current layer*

`Command:` *Choose* Draw, *then* Line, *then* Segments

`_line From point: 0,0`↵	Starts the line at the lower right corner
`To point:` *Turn on Ortho, then pick relative polar coordinates @7.50<0.00*	Draws the right border

`To point:` *Pick the relative polar coordinates @ 9.75<90.00*

Notice that "up" is now to the left (see fig. 4.19).

`To point:` *Pick the relative polar coordinates @ 7.50<180.00*

`To point:` *Pick the relative polar coordinates @ 9.75<270.00*

`To point:` *Turn off Ortho and press Enter* — Ends the LINE command

`Command:` **`UCS`** ↵

`Origin/ZAxis/3point/Entity/View/X/Y/Z/Prev/Restore/Save/Del/?/<World>:` *Press Enter* — Restores the World Coordinate System

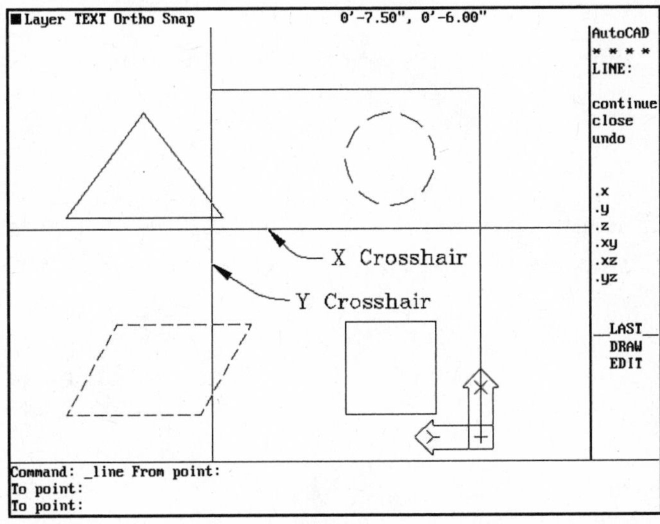

Figure 4.19:

The border in progress.

If you use the UCS command, rather than the UCS Control dialog box, you see the following prompt:

`Origin/ZAxis/3point/Entity/View/X/Y/Z/Prev/Restore/Save/Del/?/<World>:`

The UCS Control dialog box, the menu items in the Axis child menu, and the UCS Orientation dialog box in effect issue the UCS command with the appropriate options preset. You learn how to use all these options in Part Two, which covers 3D. You can use the following subset of options with most two-dimensional applications:

- **Origin.** This option specifies a new X,Y,Z origin point relative to the current origin.
- **Z.** This option rotates the X,Y axes around the Z axis.
- **Prev.** This option steps back to the previous UCS. You can back up through as many as ten previously used UCSs.
- **Restore.** This option sets the UCS to a previously saved UCS.
- **Save.** This option enables you to store the current UCS under a name, which you specify.
- **Del.** This option removes a saved UCS.
- **?.** This option lists previously saved UCSs by name to display point of origin and orientation.
- **<World>.** This option indicates that, by default, the UCS is set to the WCS. Press Enter to accept this option.

The following UCSICON command options control the display of the UCS icon:

- **ON.** This option turns on the UCS icon.
- **OFF.** This option turns off the UCS icon.
- **All.** This option displays the UCS icon in all multiple viewports.
- **Noorigin.** This option displays the UCS icon at the lower left corner of the viewports.
- **ORigin.** This option displays the UCS icon at the 0,0 origin of the current UCS, unless the origin is out of the drawing area or is too close to the edge for the icon to fit. The icon then appears at the lower left corner.

In the following exercise, you change the location of your UCS origin to midway up the drawing. Then you add some text to the drawing.

Using UCS To Change the Origin Point

`Command:` *Choose* Settings, *then* UCS, *then* Origin	
`Origin point <0,0,0>:` **`5.5,4.25`**↵	Sets a new origin
`Command:` *Choose* Draw, *then* Text, *then* Dynamic	Issues the DTEXT command (see Chapter 7 for more details)
`_dtext Justify/Style/<Start point>:` **`C`**↵	Specifies the Center justification option
`Center point:` **`0,0`** ↵	

`Height <0'--0.20">: .25` ↵	
`Rotation angle <0.00>:` *Press Enter*	
`Text:` **`Welcome To INSIDE AutoCAD`** ↵	Displays the text
`Text:` *Press Enter*	Accepts the text

Your drawing should look like figure 4.20.

`Command:` **`UCS`** ↵	Begins the UCS command
`Origin/ZAxis/3point/Entity/View/X/Y/Z/ Prev/Restore/Save/Del/?/<World>:` *Press Enter*	Restores the World Coordinate System
`Command:` *Choose* Settings, *then* Layer Control, *and make layer 0 the current layer*	
`Command:` *Choose* File, *then* Save As, *then type* **`BASIC`** *and choose* OK	Saves the drawing under the name BASIC, for use in the next chapter

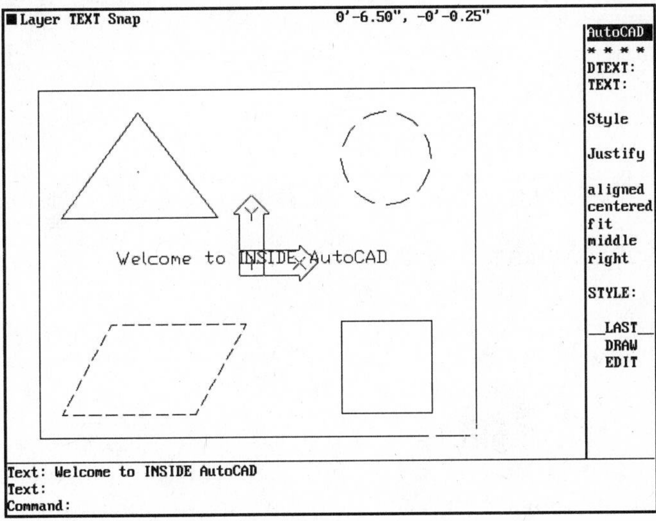

Figure 4.20:

Text centered at the current UCS origin.

The UCS icon now should be located at the lower left of the display. Each shape should have the color and linetype of its appropriately named layer. Your grid should be 1 unit and snap should be .25 units. If needed, make corrections and save your drawing again as BASIC. You use this drawing again in the following exercises and in the next chapter on display controls.

If you want to take a break, this is a good stopping point. In fact, whenever you save or quit a drawing, you can safely take a break. For the rest of the

chapter, you use the BASIC drawing as a scratch drawing to see how object snaps work.

Snapping to Entities: Object Snaps

Snap is useful if you want to draw an element that fits the snap increments. You can draw almost anything because of the many absolute or relative coordinate-entry options. If you need to align new points, lines, and other objects with geometric points on entities that you already have drawn, however, you need an easier method.

Suppose, for example, that you want to start a new line at the exact end point of an existing line, and it does not fall at a snap point. Or suppose that you want to pick a tangent point to a curve or pick the intersection of two lines that do not fall on a snap point. For both of these examples, you need to use object snaps. The OSNAP command enables you to edit existing entities and to add new entities with precision. OSNAP provides a choice of geometric points that you can snap to by using object snap.

Using the OSNAP Command To Pinpoint a Location

AutoCAD's OSNAP command and filter modes calculate the attachment points you need to make accurate drawings. You tell AutoCAD which object snap attachment mode(s) to use—such as INT for INTersection. After you pick a point or enter coordinates near the geometric point you want, AutoCAD snaps to the precise attachment point.

At the beginning of the chapter, figure 4.1 shows all the filter modes you can use for picking different attachment points on objects. The geometric shapes that make up your BASIC drawing give you the opportunity to exercise all these object snap options.

Using Overrides versus Running Modes

You can use object snaps as single-pick *override* filters, or you can set a *running* object snap mode that is active until you are prompted for object selection or until you turn it off. You select object snaps as *overrides* (which interrupt the current running mode) by using the pop-up menu or the screen menu that appears when you select the * * * * item at the top of the screen menu (see figure 4.21). You can make the pop-up menu appear at the cursor's location by pressing the third button on your input device. This is the middle button on a three-button mouse (the lowest-numbered button after the pick and Enter buttons on a digitizer cursor). On many pointing devices, this button is marked with a 3; this book refers to it as the *pop-up button*. You also can access the pop-up menu by pressing button 2 (the Enter button) while holding down the Shift key. You can find the OSNAP command on the SETTINGS screen menu or on the Running Object Snap dialog box under the Settings pull-down menu. The object snap options are the same for both overrides and running modes. You also can specify object snaps from the keyboard.

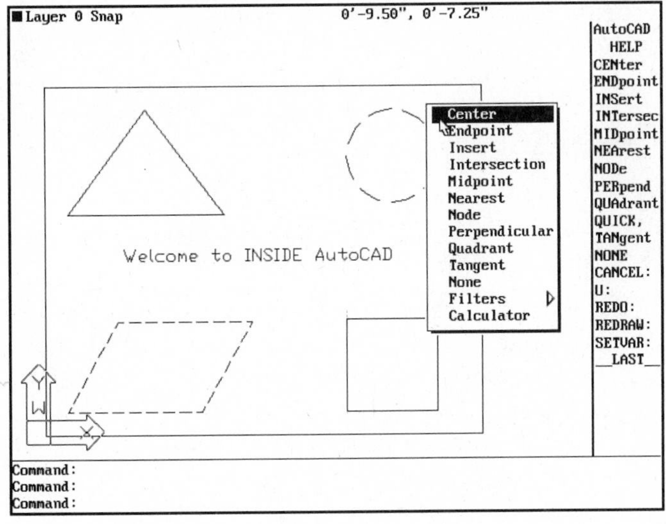

Figure 4.21:

The pop-up and * * * * object snap menus.

If you type the object snap modifiers, just enter the first word or the first three or four characters, such as MID or PER. If you are using ENDPoint, get in the habit of entering ENDP rather than END, to avoid accidentally ending your drawing.

Using Object Snaps as Single-Pick Filters

To learn how overrides work, you use the NODe and ENDPoint object snaps in the following exercise to draw a line from the point entity (the first point you drew in the drawing) in the triangle to the corner of the triangle. NODe snaps to a point entity, not to the triangle's geometric node.

Using the NODe and ENDPoint Object Snaps

`Command:` *Press F9 to turn off Snap*	
`Command:` *Choose* Draw, *then* Line, *then* Segments	
`_line From point:` *Press the pop-up button, then choose* Node	Displays the pop-up menu and specifies the NODe object snap
`nod of` *Pick point ① near the point entity in the triangle (see fig. 4.22)*	Snaps to the point entity
`To point:` *From the pop-up menu, choose* Endpoint	Issues the ENDPpoint object snap override
`endp of` *Pick point ② near the triangle's corner (see fig. 4.22)*	Snaps to the end point (see fig. 4.23)
`To point:` *Press Enter*	Ends the LINE command

Figure 4.23 shows the result.

You have used object snap successfully. If a pick fails to find an object to snap to when an override mode is set, AutoCAD warns you and reprompts for the point, discarding the object snap setting.

A dense drawing can have several attachment points close to your pick point. If you want to snap to an intersection, AutoCAD may find one, but it may not be the intersection you want. Object snap uses a tolerance or *target* box to identify the points it considers as candidates for the snap attachment (see fig. 4.24). This tolerance is controlled by an *aperture* box, which is an

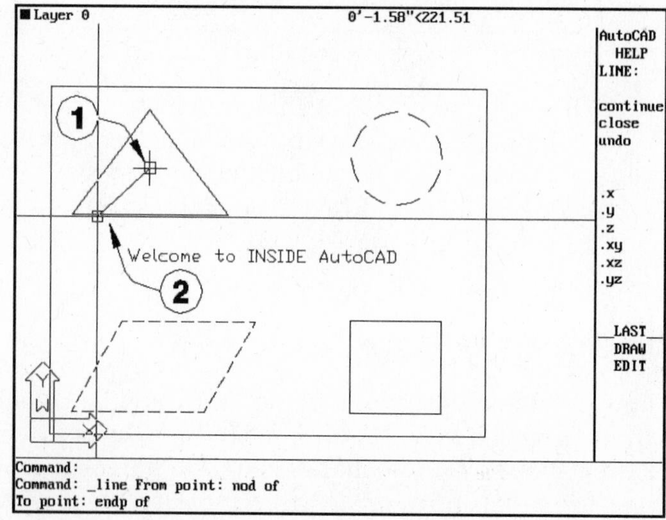

Figure 4.22:

Using the NODe and ENDPoint object snaps.

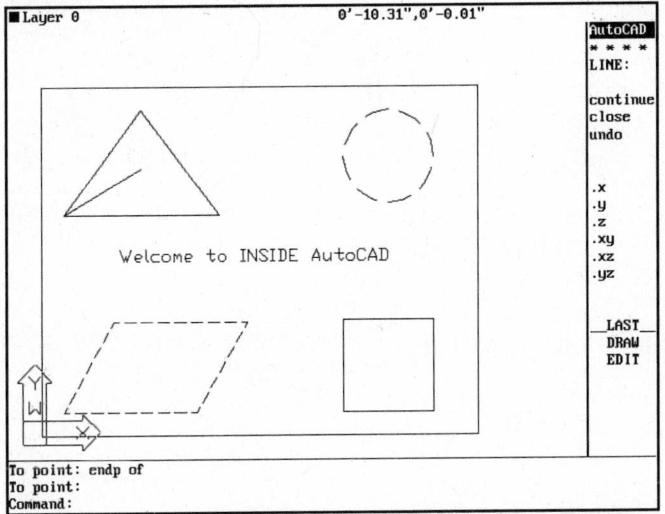

Figure 4.23:

The line drawn with object snaps.

electronic bull's-eye that homes in on object snap points. AutoCAD uses the object snap only for objects that fall within the aperture. You should size your aperture according to the entities you are selecting, the drawing's zoom settings, the display resolution, and the drawing density.

Setting the Aperture and Picking a Point

In the following exercise you set the aperture to control the size of the crosshairs' bull's-eye. You can use the APERTURE command or the APERTUR: selection from the SETTINGS screen menu. You also can adjust the aperture by using a slider bar in the Running Object Snap dialog box. To access this dialog box, choose Object Snap from the Settings pull-down menu.

Using Aperture To Set the Osnap Target

Continue in the BASIC drawing from the previous exercise.

`Command:` *From the screen menu, choose* SETTINGS, *then* APERTUR:	Issues the APERTURE command
`Command: _APERTURE`	
`Object snap target height (1--50 pixels) <10>:` *From the screen menu, choose* 5	Sets the aperture's size to five pixels from the center point

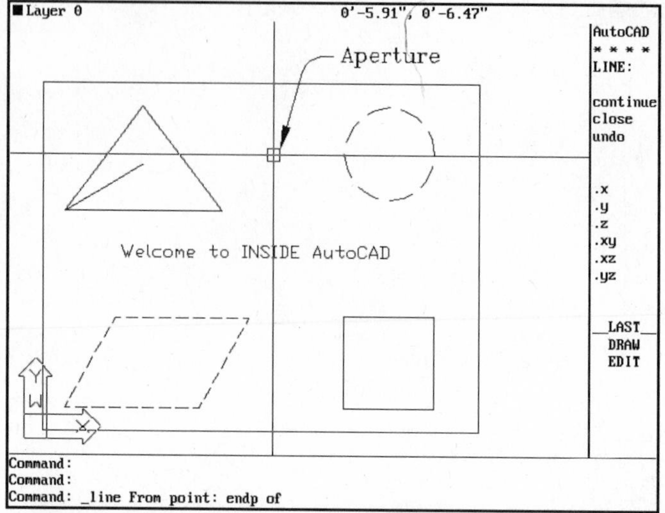

Figure 4.24:

The object snap aperture.

A *pixel* is the smallest dot that your screen can display. Four to six pixels (the default value is ten) give a good target size, depending on the resolution of your display. The size is measured from the aperture's center, so five pixels make a ten-pixel-high aperture box. Try a few different values to see how comfortable you feel with larger and smaller apertures.

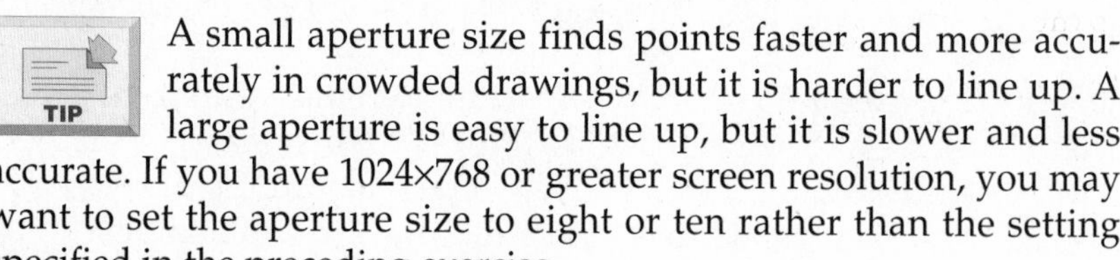

A small aperture size finds points faster and more accurately in crowded drawings, but it is harder to line up. A large aperture is easy to line up, but it is slower and less accurate. If you have 1024×768 or greater screen resolution, you may want to set the aperture size to eight or ten rather than the setting specified in the preceding exercise.

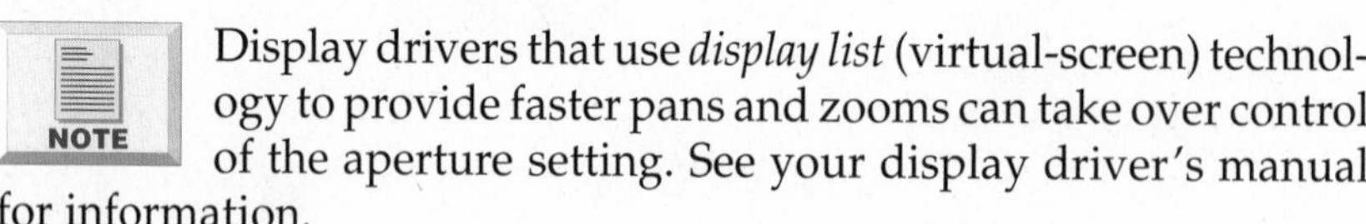

Display drivers that use *display list* (virtual-screen) technology to provide faster pans and zooms can take over control of the aperture setting. See your display driver's manual for information.

The following exercises demonstrate the operation of the remaining object snaps. These object snaps include INTersection, MIDpoint, PERpendicular, INSert, TANgent, CENter, QUAdrant, and NEAr. The point that INSert finds on a text entity depends on the type of justification that was used to create the text.

Completing the Object Snap Options

`Command:` `L`↵	Issues the LINE command
`Command: LINE From point:` `@`↵	Starts the line from the last point that was specified
`To point:` *From the pop-up menu, choose* Intersection	Issues the INTersect object snap
`int of` *Pick* ① *near the intersection of the parallelogram (see fig 4.25)*	Finds the intersection of the two selected lines
`To point:` *From the pop-up menu, choose* Midpoint	Issues the MIDpoint object snap
`mid of` *Pick* ② *or anywhere on the triangle's base line*	Finds the midpoint
`To point:` *From the pop-up menu, choose* Perpendicular	Issues the PERpendicular object snap
`per to` *Pick* ③ *or anywhere on the triangle's right side*	Finds perpendicular from base to side
`To point:` *From the screen menu, choose* * * * * *, then* INSert	Displays the screen menu of object snaps and issues the INS override
`INSERT of` *Pick* ④ *or anywhere on the text*	Finds the center text insertion point
`To point:` *From the pop-up menu, choose* Tangent	Issues the TANgent object snap
`tan to` *Pick* ⑤ *on the circle's upper left side (see fig. 4.26)*	Finds the tangent point
`To point:` *From the pop-up menu, choose* Center	Issues the CENter object snap
`cen of` *Pick* ⑥ *or anywhere on the circle*	Finds the circle's center point
`To point:` `QUA` ↵	Issues the QUAdrant object snap
`of` *Pick* ⑦ *near the circle's bottom*	Finds the 270-degree quadrant point
`To point:` *From the pop-up menu, choose* Nearest	Issues the NEArest object snap
`nea to` *Pick* ⑧ *or anywhere on the line from the text to the circle*	Finds the closest point to the point you picked
`To point:` *Press Enter*	Ends the LINE command

Your drawing should now look like figure 4.27.

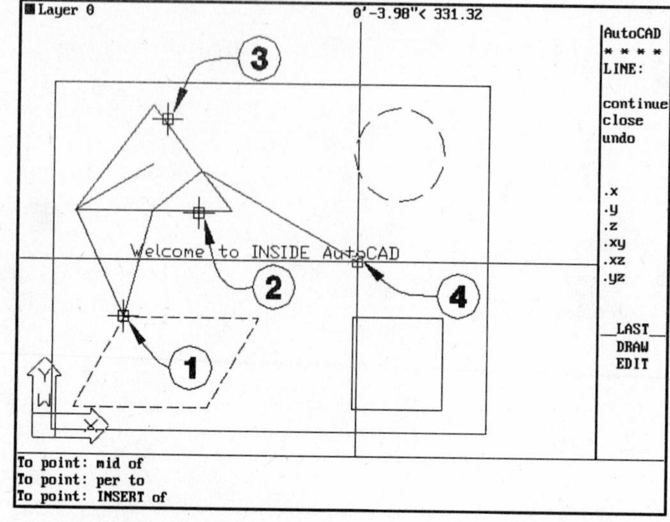

Figure 4.25: Using the INTersection, MIDpoint, PERpendicular, and INSert object snaps.

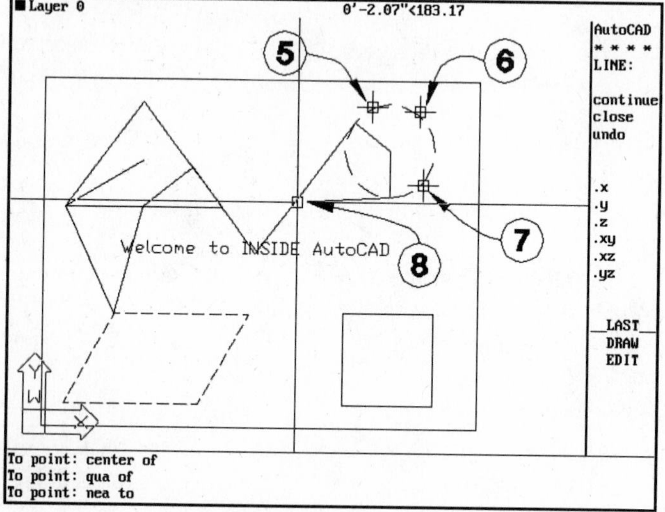

Figure 4.26: Using the TANgent, CENter, QUAdrant, and NEAr object snaps.

Using QUIck To Optimize Osnap

When you use an object snap, AutoCAD must search every object in the drawing window to find all the objects that cross the aperture box. The program then calculates potential points for all qualified objects to find the best (closest) fit for the object snap you issue. This process can take some time if the drawing contains many objects.

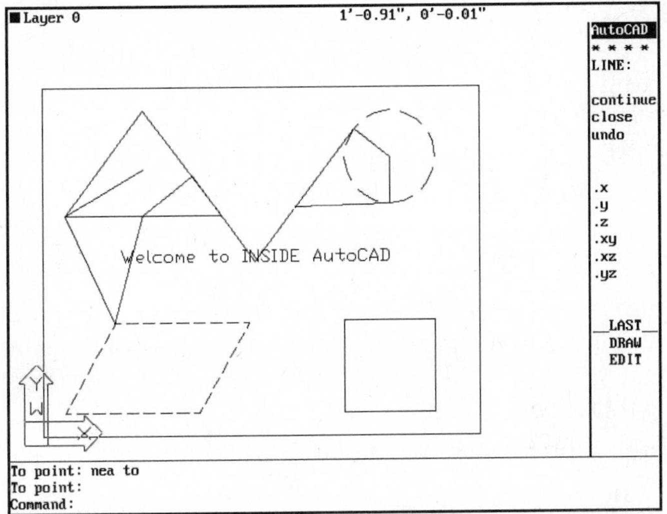

Figure 4.27:

The completed line, drawn with object snaps.

You can shorten the object snap search process by reducing the size of the aperture to keep extraneous objects out of the target. You also can use the QUIck object snap option, which enables AutoCAD to take the most recently created object that meets your object snap criteria, instead of doing an exhaustive search and comparison to find the closest object. You invoke QUIck by using it as a prefix for other object snap option(s), such as QUI,INT for a quick intersection.

When you invoke QUIck, AutoCAD occasionally finds a different fit from the one you want. If this happens, simply cancel the current command and start the object snap process again without the QUIck modifier. The following list explains all the OSNAP options, including the QUIck modifier:

- **CENter.** This option snaps to the center of an arc or circle.
- **ENDPoint.** This option snaps to the nearest end point of a line or arc.
- **INSert.** This option snaps to the origin of text, attributes, and symbols (block or shape) that have been inserted into the drawing file. (You learn more about blocks, shapes, and attributes in Chapter 11.)
- **INTersection.** This option snaps to the nearest intersection of any combination of two lines, arcs, or circles.
- **MIDpoint.** When you choose the MIDpoint option, AutoCAD snaps to the midpoint of a line or arc.
- **NEArest.** This option snaps to the nearest point on an entity. This is generally an endpoint, a tangent, or a perpendicular point.
- **NODe.** This option snaps to a point entity.

- **PERpendicular.** This option snaps to a point on a line, arc, or circle that, for the picked entity, would form a perpendicular (normal) line from the last point to the picked entity. The resulting point need not even be on the entity.
- **TANgent.** This option snaps to a point on an arc or circle that forms a tangent to the picked arc or circle from the last point.
- **QUAdrant.** This option snaps to the closest 0-, 90-, 180-, or 270-degree point on an arc or circle.
- **QUIck.** This option forces all other object snap options to find the first potential target quickly. The point QUIck chooses is not necessarily the closest target. QUIck finds the potential point that is on the most recently qualified object in the target box.
- **NONe.** This option removes or overrides any running object snap.

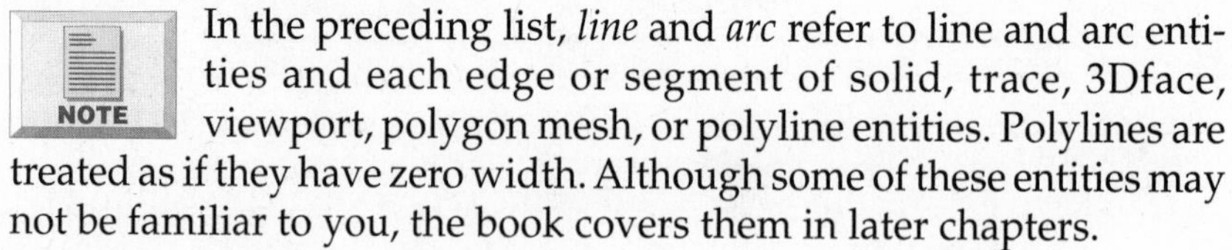

In the preceding list, *line* and *arc* refer to line and arc entities and each edge or segment of solid, trace, 3Dface, viewport, polygon mesh, or polyline entities. Polylines are treated as if they have zero width. Although some of these entities may not be familiar to you, the book covers them in later chapters.

Generally, references to object snap modes are abbreviated to their first three letters throughout the rest of the book.

In previous exercises, you used object snaps as overrides in the middle of the LINE command to fine-tune line end points. This override mode temporarily sets up an object snap aperture condition to complete the task at hand. Frequently, however, you may need to use the same mode or combination of modes repeatedly. For this reason, AutoCAD enables you to set running modes.

Using a Running Mode Object Snap

An object snap condition that is set to be in effect until you change it is called a *running mode*. You use the OSNAP command to set running object snap modes. Running mode object snaps remain in effect until you replace them with another running mode setting or until you temporarily override them. If a pick fails to find an object to snap to when a running mode is set, AutoCAD finds the point it would have found if no object snap mode were set. Unlike SNAP, GRID, and ORTHO, the OSNAP command is not transparent; fortunately, overrides are transparent. Use the NONe override to temporarily suppress a running mode.

If a running object snap is on, the crosshairs have a bull's-eye aperture during point entry and object selection.

In the following exercise, you draw a diamond in the square by using a running MID object snap mode.

Using a Running Object Snap To Put a Diamond in a Square

`Command:` *Choose* Settings, *then* Object Snap	Issues the DDOSNAP command and displays the Running Object Snap dialog box
`Command:` *Check the* Midpoint *check box, then choose* OK	Sets MID as the running object snap mode
`Command:` *Choose* Draw, *then* Line, *then* Segments	Displays the aperture box
`From point:` *Pick point* ① *on the top line (see fig. 4.28)*	Snaps to the midpoint of the line
`To point:` *Pick point* ② *on the right line*	Snaps to the midpoint
`To point:` *Pick point* ③ *on the bottom line*	Snaps to the midpoint
`To point:` *Pick point* ④ *on the left line*	Snaps to the midpoint
`To point:` *Pick point* ⑤ *on the top line*	Snaps to the midpoint
`To point:` *Press Enter*	Ends the LINE command
`Command:` **OSNAP** ↵	Issues the OSNAP command
`Object snap modes:` **NONe** ↵	Resets the running object snap mode to NONe

You can specify two or more running or override modes at once; AutoCAD finds the calculated point of whichever mode is closest to the crosshairs. Specify multiple modes by checking multiple check boxes in the Running Object Snap dialog box. If you use the OSNAP command at the `Command:` prompt, include multiple object snap modes on the `Command:` prompt and separate them with commas, as in END,MID,CEN.

The INT,ENDP,MID running object snap mode should cover most of your object selection requirements.

Use the override modes whenever the need arises; they override running modes. Set up a running object snap whenever you repeatedly use the same object snap mode(s).

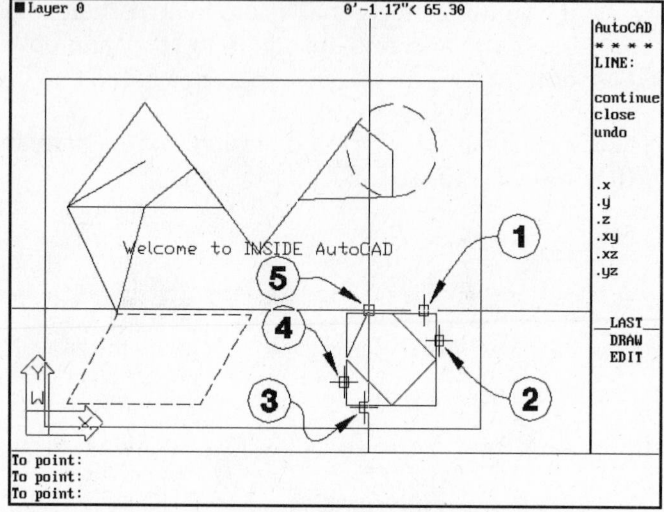

Figure 4.28:

Drawing with a running MIDpoint object snap.

Using REDRAW and BLIPMODE for a Clean Drawing Window

As you worked through the object snap exercises, you probably noticed that when you entered a point (either with a cursor or from the keyboard), AutoCAD places a small cross (blip) on the screen. As you draw, you fill up the drawing area with real drawing entities (such as lines and circles) and construction markers. A few blips are useful for keeping an eye on where you have been (or might want to go again), but they become distracting if they accumulate on the screen.

As you draw, erase, and move entities, pieces of lines and entities seem to disappear. Although they usually are still there, a gap is left in the underlying entity's representation in the drawing window after you erase or move an entity that overlaps another.

You can use the REDRAW command to clean up the drawing, redraw underlying entities, and get rid of blips. Erase a line and try it.

Using REDRAW To Clear Up the Drawing Window

`Command:` *Choose* Modify, *then* Erase, *then* Single	
`_erase Select objects: si`	
`Select objects:` *Pick a point on the line from the triangle to the center of the text*	Erases the line

The line is gone (see fig. 4.29). Part of the triangle also seems to be gone.

`Command:` *Choose* View, *then* Redraw	Redraws the drawing window: the blips are gone and the triangle is okay (see fig. 4.30)
`Command:` *Choose* File, *then* Exit AutoCAD, *then* Discard Changes	Discards changes to the drawing

The display appears as before in figure 4.30, but without the blip marks.

If you do not need blips, you can use the BLIPMODE command to suppress construction markers. You can prevent AutoCAD from drawing these temporary markers by turning off BLIPMODE. To suppress blips, set BLIPMODE's value to 0.

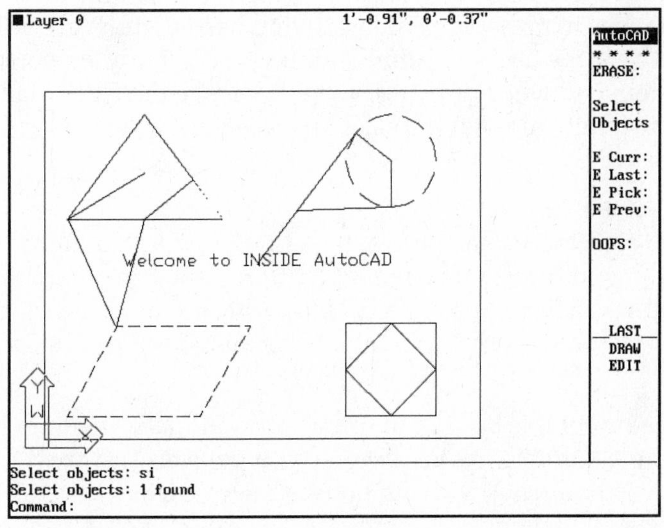

Figure 4.29:
The display after ERASE and before REDRAW.

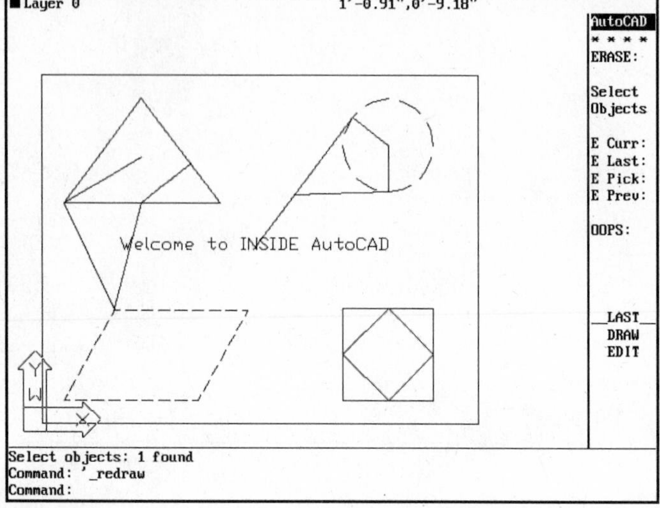

Figure 4.30:

The display after REDRAW.

Summary

A trick for ensuring accurate drawing is to use relative and polar points, with the coordinate display used for reference. Use the GRID command to give you a frame of reference; use the SNAP command to limit your crosshairs and picks to preset increments. If you need to draw at 90-degree increments, activate the ORTHO command. If you need to align your coordinate system with your drawing, you can change the UCS. Many users find it helpful to jot down notes or make up a checklist to keep track of these display settings.

To construct geometrically accurate objects, use coordinate entry and Osnap for snapping to objects. You can invoke the Osnap options temporarily as an override to any point-picking command. A running object snap mode sets up a full-time mode and aperture that you can still override. Try to find a good aperture setting to control the reliability and speed of your object snap searches.

Throughout the rest of this book, you often see coordinates given in response to prompts with the exercises. You can type them and press Enter, or you can pick the coordinates with the pointing device if you are sure the pick is accurate. Remember that the crosshairs position is only accurate with snap on or with object snap. Use object snap at every opportunity you can. Your drawing productivity will improve, and you can be confident that your work is accurate. Now that you have had a chance to experiment with object snaps, move on to learning how to get around in AutoCAD.

5

Controlling the Graphics Display

Whether you set your drawing limits to represent a drawing that is 2' × 3' or 2000' × 3000', your computer's screen is not large enough to give you a one-to-one view of the drawing file. In this chapter, you learn how to use AutoCAD's tools to control your location in the display, your future location, and your movement from one location to another.

In AutoCAD, your display becomes a *viewport* into your drawing, enabling you to zoom in and out, and to move around the drawing. You actually have been working in a viewport all along—a single viewport that uses the entire drawing area. In this chapter, you learn to use multiple viewports, as shown in figure 5.1, to see several parts of your drawing simultaneously, and to scale the viewports to different sizes for eventual plotting.

AutoCAD's display controls make drawing easier. Basic display-control commands, such as ZOOM and PAN, function in AutoCAD just like their photographic counterparts. The ZOOM command enables you to magnify your drawing to do detailed work. PAN enables you to slide your drawing from side-to-side so that you can work on large objects without having to return to a full-drawing view to determine your location in the drawing. Simple controls, such as REDRAW and REGEN, enable you to clean up your drawing or display its most current view.

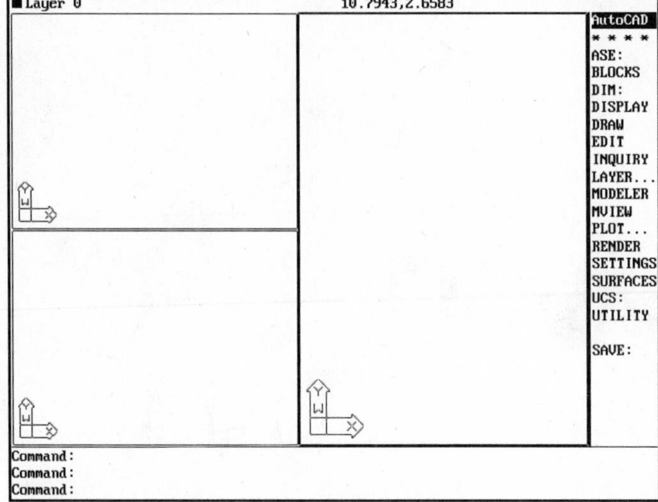

Figure 5.1:

The drawing area, divided into three viewports.

To make drawing easier, you can open multiple viewports in the drawing area to display your model at different scales and from different viewpoints. You also can use these viewports to display areas of your model that normally are not visible at the same time, such as both ends of a long part. You can see your entire object in a single viewport, for example, while you zoom in to work on a drawing detail in a second viewport. A parts schedule can be viewed in one viewport while you check your drawing annotations in another. You can even set many of AutoCAD's controls—such as snap, grid, and the UCS icon—differently in each viewport. When you save your drawing, the viewport setup is saved with it so that you do not need to re-create the viewports every time you load the drawing.

The display-control tools are located on the View pull-down menu and the DISPLAY screen menu, as shown in figure 5.2.

Setting Up the Display Controls

You do not need an elaborate drawing to get a feel for display controls; the simple geometric shapes in the BASIC drawing (which you saved in Chapter 4) work well enough for you to practice getting around the drawing area. If you are using the optional IA DISK, the drawing named IA7BASIC.DWG is identical to the BASIC drawing. If you have the IA DISK

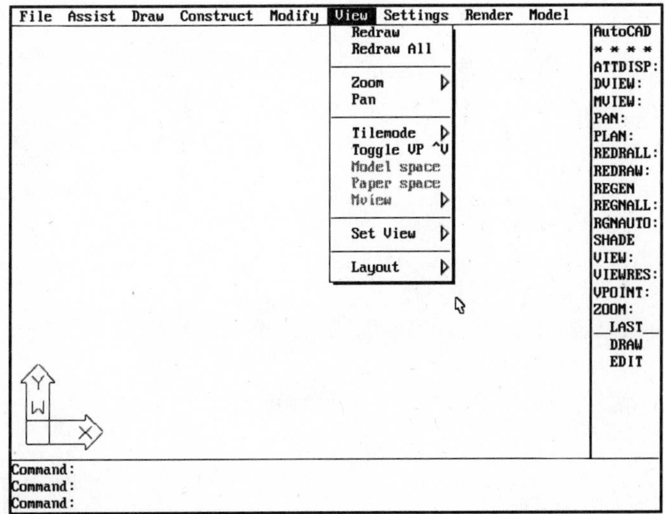

Figure 5.2:

The View pull-down and DISPLAY screen menus.

and you did not save the BASIC drawing from Chapter 4, you can use the Create New Drawing dialog box to load IA7BASIC as BASIC. Table 5.1 shows the settings that you should use for the BASIC drawing.

Table 5.1
BASIC Drawing Settings

GRID	SNAP	ORTHO	UCS	UCSICON
On	On	Off	World	On

UNITS	Engineering, 2 decimal places, 2 fractional places for angles, defaults all other settings.
LIMITS	0,0 to 11,8.5

Layer Name	*State*	*Color*	*Linetype*
0	On/Current	White	CONTINUOUS
CIRCLE	On	Green	DASHED
PARAGRAM	On	Magenta	HIDDEN
SQUARE	On	Yellow	CONTINUOUS
TEXT	On	Cyan	CONTINUOUS
TRIANGLE	On	Red	CONTINUOUS

Loading the BASIC Drawing

Choose File, then New, and enter BASIC=IA7BASIC as the new drawing's name.

Open the BASIC drawing, which you created in Chapter 4, and verify the settings shown in Table 5.1.

Your drawing should look like figure 5.3 and match the settings in table 5.1.

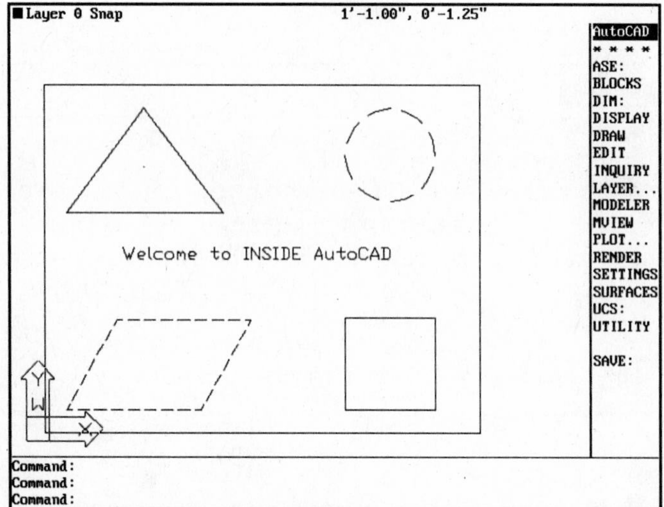

Figure 5.3:
The BASIC drawing.

Using ZOOM To Control the Drawing Display

Now that the drawing is loaded and visible in the drawing editor, suppose that you want to look more closely at the triangle. To do this, you need to zoom in on the drawing. The most common way to tell AutoCAD what part of the current drawing you want to enlarge is to pick diagonal corners of a box or *window* around the area of interest. Use the ZOOM command with the Window option to zoom in on your drawing.

Zooming In with Zoom Window

Do the following exercise to become more familiar with the ZOOM command's Window option. You do not need to pick exact coordinates; just indicate roughly the area you want to see in more detail.

Using ZOOM Window

`Command:` *Choose* View, *then* Zoom, *then* Window	Issues the ZOOM command with the Window option
`Command:_'zoom`	
`All/Center/Dynamic/Extents/Left/ Previous/Vmax/Window/<Scale(X/XP)>: w`	
`First corner:` *Pick* ① *(see fig. 5.4)*	Sets the window's lower left window
`Other corner:` *Pick* ②	Sets the window's upper right corner

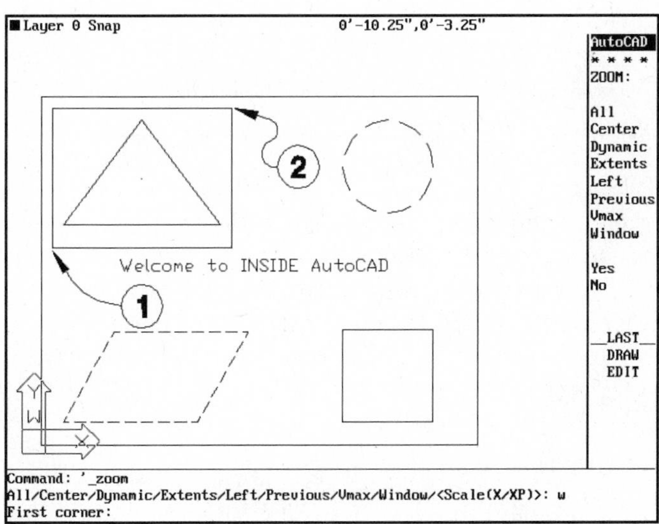

Figure 5.4:

Creating a Zoom Window.

Notice that after you pick the first corner, instead of the normal crosshairs, your cursor changes to a *rubber-band* box. As soon as you pick the second corner, AutoCAD repaints the drawing area with the area you enclosed in the window, as shown in figure 5.5. The corners that you pick guide AutoCAD in determining the new area to display. This area usually is not exactly the same shape as originally displayed because AutoCAD maintains its 1:1 X and Y display aspect ratio, regardless of the aspect ratio (proportions) of the window you specify.

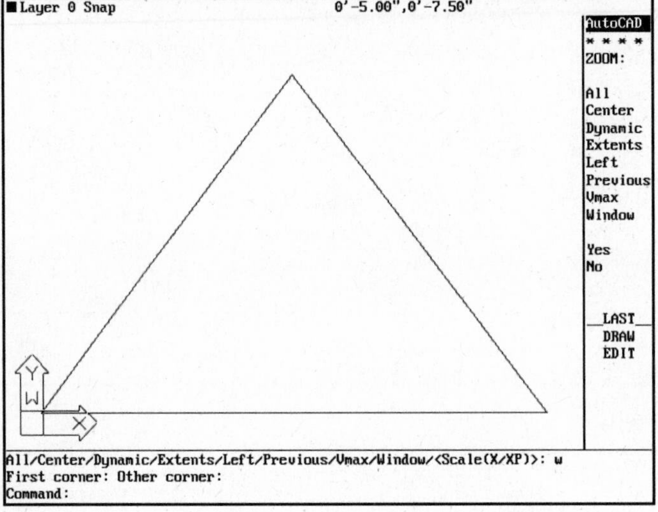

Figure 5.5:

The view of the drawing after ZOOM Window.

The following exercise shows you how to zoom closer to the upper point of the triangle by creating another zoom window. After you pick the new corners, AutoCAD redraws the drawing area. It is not necessary to specify the Window option. When the ZOOM command is issued, you can automatically start a window simply by picking a point on the screen.

Using ZOOM Window To Zoom Closer

`Command:` **`ZOOM`**↵

`All/Center/Dynamic/Extents/Left/Previous/Vmax/Window/<Scale(X/XP)>:` *Pick the window's lower left corner (see fig. 5.6)*

`Other corner:` *Pick the upper right corner (see fig. 5.6)*

After you pick the upper right corner, AutoCAD redraws the screen and magnifies the top of the triangle, as shown in figure 5.7.

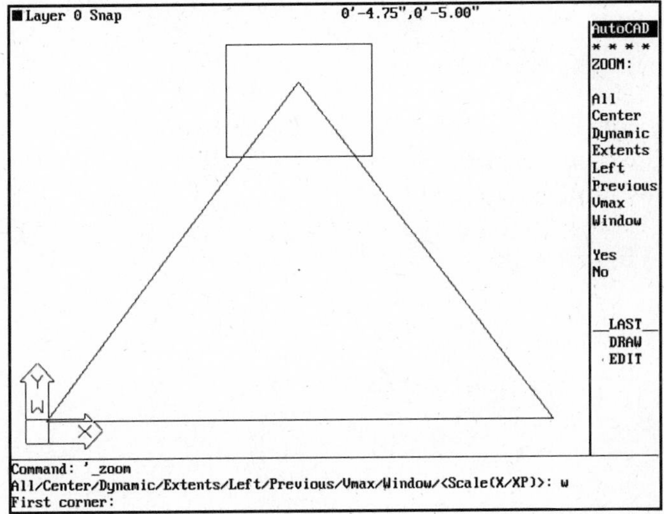

Figure 5.6:
The ZOOM Window.

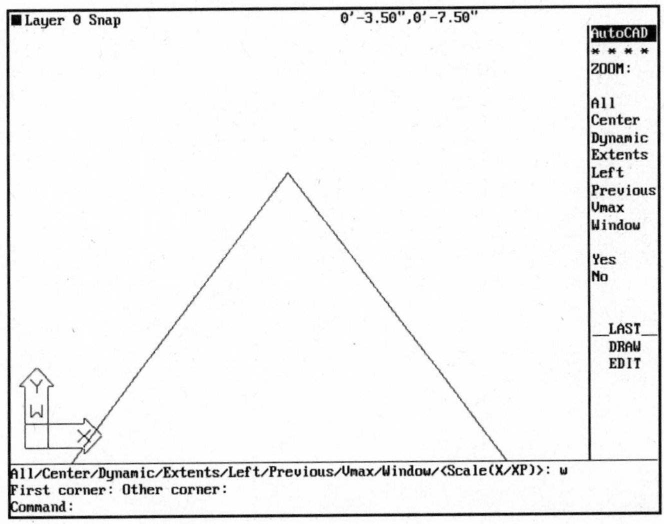

Figure 5.7:
The triangle's magnified top, after the second zoom.

How far can you zoom in? Suppose, for example, that you draw the entire solar system at full scale, which is about 7,000,000,000 miles across. If you draw the solar system with enough detail, you can position your view at the outskirts of the galaxy and zoom in close enough to read a book on a desk. AutoCAD is capable of such drawings because it is precise within at least 14 significant digits. Try zooming in on your drawing once more, before you zoom back to a full view.

Zooming Out with Zoom All

If you want to zoom back out to view the entire drawing after you have zoomed in on it, you can use ZOOM command's All option. The All option is the easiest way to return to the full display of your drawing file. The following exercise shows you how to zoom back out to the drawing's extents after having zoomed in on a detail.

Using Zoom All

`Command:` *Choose* View, *then* Zoom, *then* All — Issues the ZOOM command with the All option

```
Command: _zoom
All/Center/Dynamic/Extents/Left/Previous/
Vmax/Window/<Scale(X/XP)>: a
Regenerating drawing.
**Redisplay required by change in
drawing extents.
```

Your on-screen view of the drawing should appear as it did when you started. When AutoCAD executes the ZOOM command with the All option, it regenerates and repaints the current viewport with everything in the drawing file. If you draw within the drawing limits, ZOOM All returns the display screen to its limits. If your drawing exceeds the limits you set for it, ZOOM All zooms beyond the limits to display everything in the drawing file.

Examining other Zoom Options

As you have seen, the Window and All options enable you simply to move in closer to and move back from your drawing. The ZOOM command, however, is one of AutoCAD's most powerful and versatile display-control commands, and features several useful options, including the following:

- **All.** In 2D (plan view), this option displays the drawing's limits or extents, whichever is larger. In a 3D view, All displays the drawing's extents.
- **Center.** This option zooms to the center point and displays the height (in drawing units) or the magnification that you specify. Pick a new center and press Enter to *pan* (move the display at the current zoom magnification). The center point you pick becomes the viewport's center. To keep the center point unchanged and to change the display height or magnification, press Enter at the new center point prompt instead of specifying a new point.
- **Dynamic.** This option graphically combines the PAN command with the ZOOM command's All and Window options. Dynamic displays an image of the entire generated portion of your drawing, and you use the cursor to tell AutoCAD where to zoom. Dynamic can zoom in or out, or it can pan the current viewport. Dynamic is explained in more detail later in this chapter.
- **Extents.** This option displays all the drawing entities as large as possible in the current viewport.
- **Left.** This option zooms to the lower left corner and displays the height (in drawing units) or the magnification that you specify. The point you specify becomes the new lower left corner of the current viewport. In all other ways, Left works in the same way as Center.
- **Previous.** This option restores a previous display for the current viewport, whether it was generated by the ZOOM, PAN, VIEW, or DVIEW commands. AutoCAD stores up to ten previous views for each viewport; you can step back through them by repeatedly using the Previous option.
- **Vmax.** This option zooms to the currently generated virtual screen, to display the maximum possible drawing area without a regeneration.
- **Window.** This option zooms to the rectangular area you specify by picking two diagonally opposite corner points. When you issue the ZOOM command, you can automatically begin a zoom window by picking a point on the screen. Unless the X,Y proportions of the window you specify exactly match the proportions of the viewport, a little extra width or height of the image shows.
- **Scale(X/XP).** This option requires you to enter a magnification factor for AutoCAD to use in zooming. The Scale option is the default. In other words, you can type a scale factor without specifying the Scale option. If you enter a number, such as 2, you create a zoom scale that is twice what is shown by the limits. If you specify a scale factor

followed by an X—such as .8X—you create a view with a scale of .8 of the existing view. The XP option is for a scale relative to paper space.

NOTE: Zooms occasionally require a drawing regeneration. The ZOOM command's All and Extents options always cause a drawing regeneration and sometimes causes two regenerations. Such regenerations are not a problem in small or simple drawings, but large or complex drawings can take a long time to regenerate. If you use the ZOOM command's Previous or Vmax options, you can often avoid forcing AutoCAD to regenerate your drawing.

Keeping Track of Zoom Displays

Every time you zoom in or out, AutoCAD keeps track of the previous display, up to ten zooms. In the following exercise, you learn how to use the Left, Center, and Previous options.

Using ZOOM Left, Center, and Previous

`Command:` *From the screen menu, choose* DISPLAY, *then* ZOOM:	Starts the ZOOM command
`Command: _'ZOOM`	
`All/Center/Dynamic/Extents/Left/ Previous/Vmax/Window/<Scale(X/XP)>:` **L↵**	Specifies the Left option
`Lower left corner point:` *Pick near the point 2.50,2.00 or enter the coordinates*	Sets the lower left corner
`Magnification or Height <0'-8.50">:` **4.5↵**	Specifies the window height and zooms (see fig. 5.8)
`Command:` *Press F9 to turn off Snap*	
`Command:` *Press Enter*	Repeats the ZOOM command
`_'ZOOM`	
`All/Center/Dynamic/Extents/Left/ Previous/Vmax/Window/<Scale(X/XP)>:` **C↵**	Specifies the Center option
`Center point:` *Pick a point on the letter W*	Sets the window's center point
`Magnification or Height <0'-4.50">:` **.5↵**	Specifies the window height and zooms in on the drawing (see fig. 5.9)
`Command:` *Press Enter*	Repeats the ZOOM command

_'ZOOM	
All/Center/Dynamic/Extents/Left/ Previous/Vmax/Window/<Scale(X/XP)>: P↵	Zooms back to the previous view
Command: *Press Enter*	Repeats the ZOOM command
_'ZOOM	
All/Center/Dynamic/Extents/Left/ Previous/Vmax/Window/<Scale(X/XP)>: P↵	Zooms to the previous view

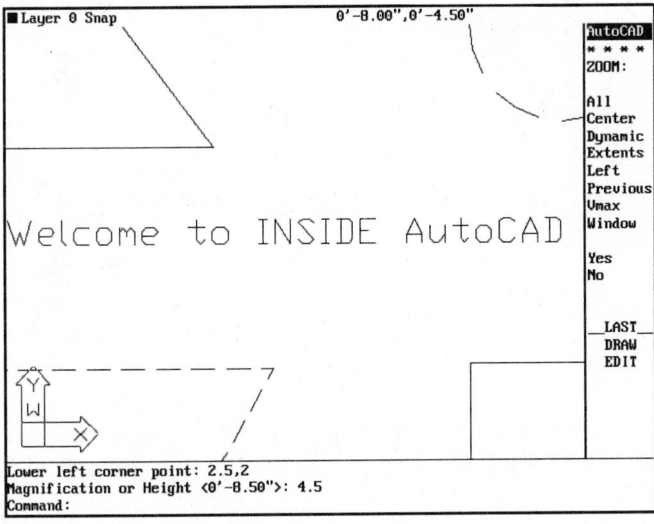

Figure 5.8:

The result of the ZOOM command's Left option.

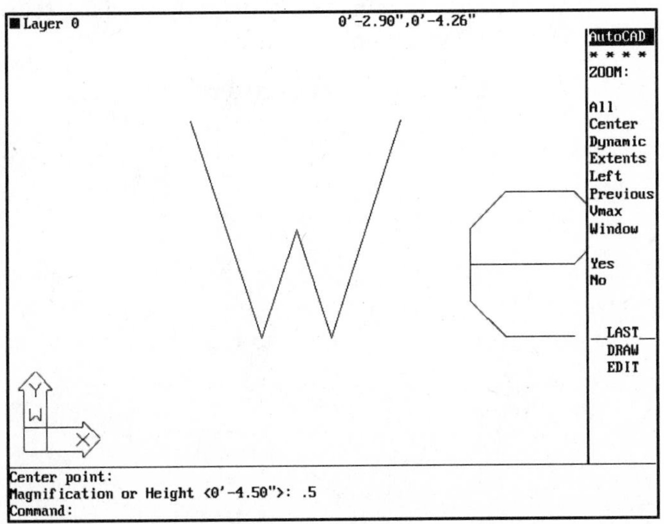

Figure 5.9:

The result of the ZOOM command's Center option.

If all went well, you should end up where you started, with a full view of your drawing.

The Previous option does not necessarily zoom out. It simply returns to a previous view, whether larger or smaller than the current view, including views created by the PAN and VPOINT commands.

You may have noticed a speed difference in zooms that regenerate the drawing and those that do not. In a complex drawing, this time difference can be considerable. To control drawing regenerations, you need to understand how ZOOM works. The following section explains AutoCAD's virtual screen.

Understanding AutoCAD's Virtual Screen

To understand the ZOOM command, you need to understand the relationship of REDRAW, REGEN, and the virtual screen. When you load a new drawing or use the REGEN command, AutoCAD recalculates the current view to its full 14 places of precision. The program calculates this as if the display were a 32,000×32,000-pixel display screen, or the *virtual screen*. The virtual screen contains the last regeneration, or recalculation, of the graphic database. AutoCAD translates this calculated image to your actual display area and redraws the current viewport. AutoCAD can perform a redraw quickly, several times as quickly as a regeneration. This translation is what occurs when you use the REDRAW command, turn on the grid, turn on layers, or change other settings that cause a redraw.

Many kinds of zooms require only a redraw, not a regeneration. The drawing does not regenerate as long as you do not zoom outside of the current virtual screen or zoom so far into tiny detail that AutoCAD cannot accurately translate from the virtual screen. When a zoom occurs without a regeneration, it occurs at redraw speed.

If you want your zooms to be fast, then you need to avoid regenerations. Zooming in to a larger magnification usually is no problem. The easiest way to control regenerations when zooming out is to use the ZOOM Dynamic option.

Using the ZOOM Dynamic Option

You have used the basic two-step process of zooming in on your drawing with a window and zooming back out by using the ZOOM command's All option. What if you want to magnify a small portion of the drawing while you already are zoomed in to a different section? The ZOOM command's Dynamic option enables you to control and display your zoom window in a single step without having to use the ZOOM command's All option.

AutoCAD actually has three display subsets. When you work with a dynamic zoom, these subsets are shown in the current viewport. AutoCAD uses the following display sets:

- **Drawing extents.** Displays everything in the drawing file.
- **Generated area.** Displays a portion (up to all) of the drawing file that AutoCAD has regenerated. This is the virtual screen.
- **Current view.** Displays a portion (up to all) of the generated data that currently appears in the current viewport.

When you select a dynamic zoom, you can see all three of these areas graphically in the current viewport before you make a decision on the next view.

Figure 5.10 shows four rectangular areas outlined on the diagram. The first three show the entire drawing extents (white or black), the currently generated virtual screen (four red corners), and the current view (green or magenta). The extents are the limits, unless you draw beyond the limits.

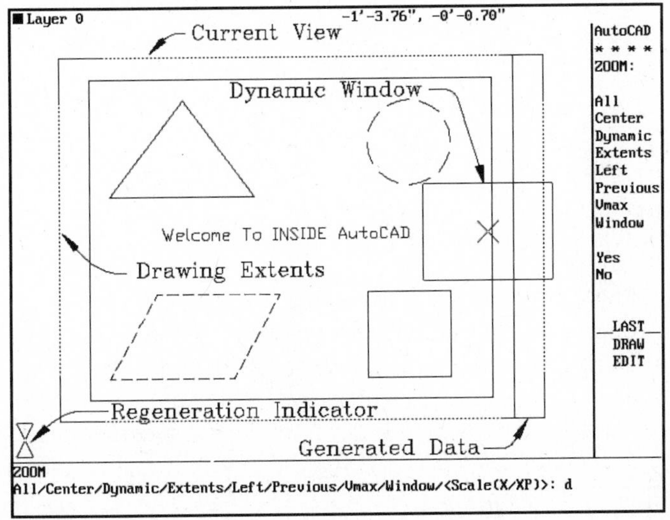

Figure 5.10: The ZOOM command's Dynamic option controls.

The fourth rectangular area is a dynamic window (white or black) that you can move with your pointer. Use this dynamic window to select the next view you want to see.

If you select your next view from the area bounded by the *generated* data, the next view appears in redraw speed. If you select your next view to include data from outside the currently generated data, your zoom requires a regeneration of the entire drawing file as AutoCAD calculates the part of the drawing file you want to see in your next view. When you move the pointer outside the generated drawing file area, a little hourglass appears on the lower left part in the current viewport indicating that regeneration is occurring. If you zoom in greater than 50 times the current view, AutoCAD must regenerate the drawing.

In the following exercise, you learn how to use the ZOOM command's Dynamic option. You first must use the ZOOM command's All option and then zoom in to magnify your drawing by a factor of three. Then call up the ZOOM command's Dynamic display.

Using ZOOM Dynamic

`Command:` *Choose* View, *then* Zoom, *then* All	Zooms to the drawing limits
`Command:` *Press Enter*	Repeats the ZOOM command

`_ZOOM`
`All/Center/Dynamic/Extents/Left/`
`Previous/Vmax/Window/<Scale(X/XP)>: 3↵`
	Magnifies the display by a factor of three (see fig. 5.11)

`Command:` *Press Enter*	Repeats the ZOOM command

`_ZOOM`
`All/Center/Dynamic/Extents/Left/`
`Previous/Vmax/Window/<Scale(X/XP)>: D↵`
	Displays the ZOOM command's Dynamic controls (see fig. 5.12)

Your display should look like figure 5.12. By moving your pointer around, you can drag the dynamic viewing window around as if it were held by the X handle in the middle of the window. Your pointer also controls the window's size. When you click your pointing device's button, an arrow appears within the dynamic viewing window and enables you to control the window's size. When you move the arrow to the right, you make the window larger; move the arrow to the left to make the window smaller.

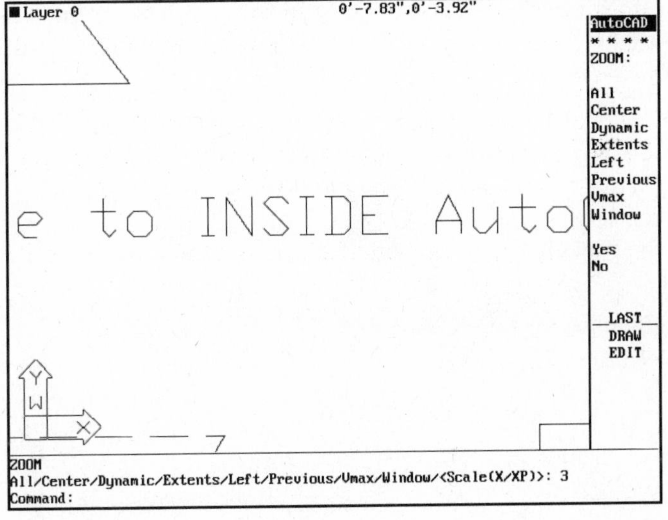

Figure 5.11:

The BASIC drawing magnified three times.

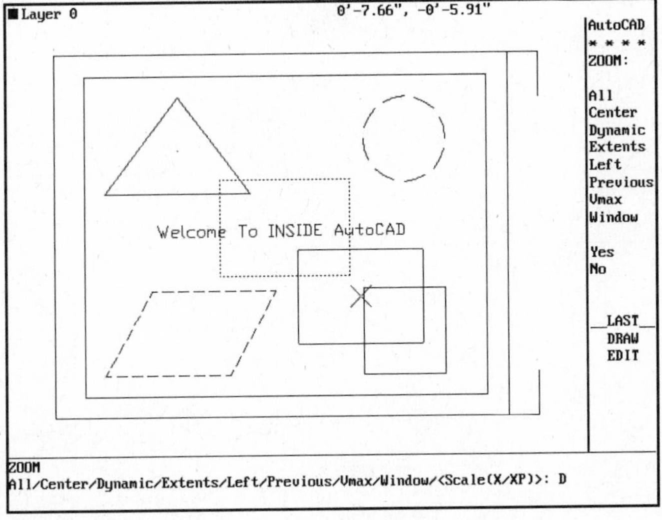

Figure 5.12:

The beginning of the ZOOM command's Dynamic option.

When the window is the size you want, click again to lock in the size. You click the pointer button to move between the dynamic window size and its location.

After you capture the desired viewing area in the window, press Enter while holding the dynamic viewing window in place to select it. AutoCAD zooms to that new window.

Continuing with the ZOOM Dynamic Command

Continue from the previous exercise, with the ZOOM command active.

`All/Center/Dynamic/Extents/Left/`
`Previous/Vmax/Window/<Scale(X/XP)>:` D

Drag the dynamic window around with the X handle shown at ① in figure 5.13	
Click the pointer button	Switches to dynamic window sizing
Move the window horizontally by dragging it to ② in figure 5.14	Stretches and shrinks the dynamic window
Click the pointer button	Switches to dynamic location control
Line up the dynamic viewing window (see ③ in fig. 5.15)	Encloses the circle
Hold the pointer in place, and press Enter or right-click	Displays the view shown in figure 5.16

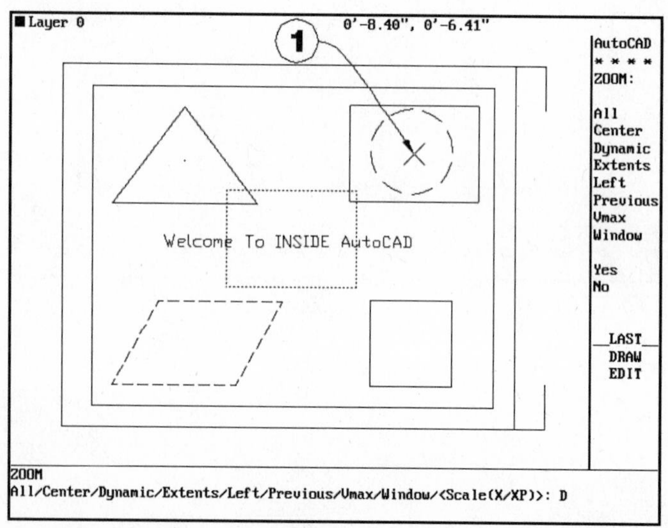

Figure 5.13:

Moving the current view.

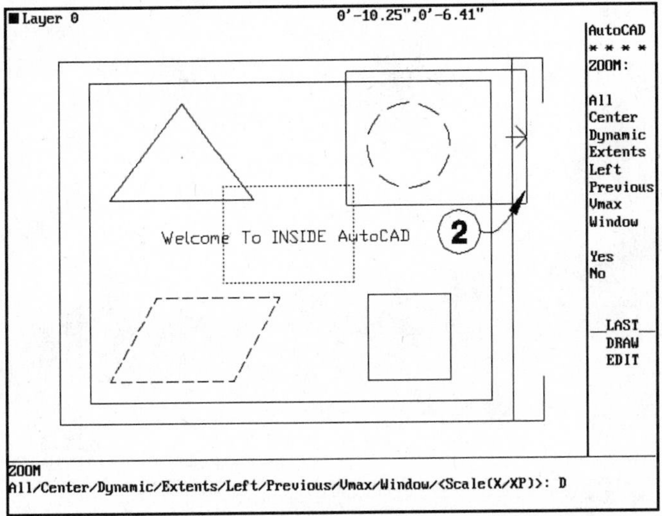

Figure 5.14:

Resizing the current view.

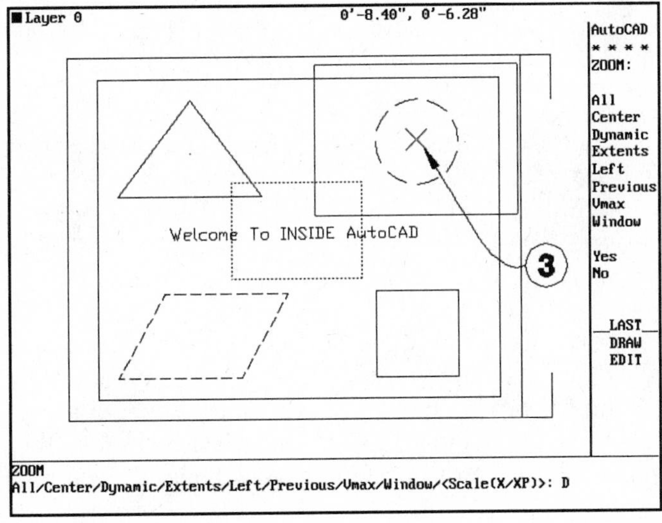

Figure 5.15:

The viewing window that encloses the circle.

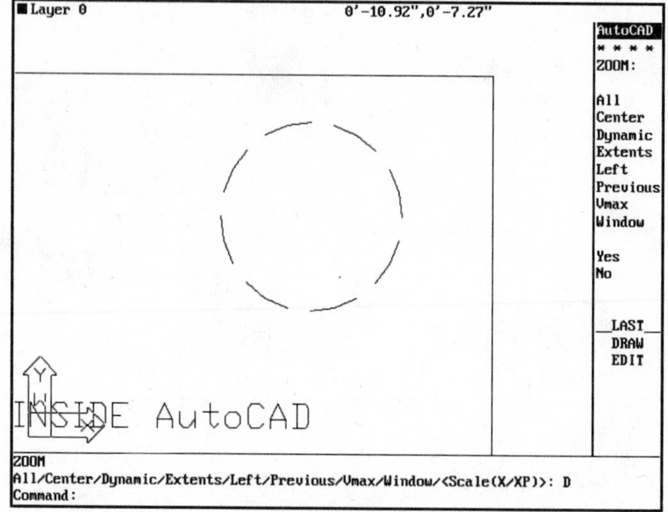

Figure 5.16:

The display after using the ZOOM command's Dynamic option.

You might shrink the dynamic window so far that you see only the arrow or X. If this happens, you need to enlarge the window with the pointer to regain a visible window.

You can do your own style of the Dynamic option of ZOOM by using the other ZOOM options and cutting them short. You can, for example, start the Previous option and cut it short by pressing Ctrl-C as soon as you see enough to decide where to go next. Then follow with your intended zoom.

Now try zooming back out by using the ZOOM command's Extents option in the following exercise. The Extents and All options zoom out as far as needed, even beyond the limits, to display everything in the drawing file. Unlike All (which never zooms to a smaller area than the limits), the Extents option zooms to the smallest area possible that displays all the entities in the drawing.

Using ZOOM Extents

`Command: Z ↵`	Issues the ZOOM command
`All/Center/Dynamic/Extents/Left/ Previous/Vmax/Window/<Scale(X/XP)>: E ↵`	Magnifies the drawing to the edge of the drawing border

Your screen should look like the one shown in figure 5.17.

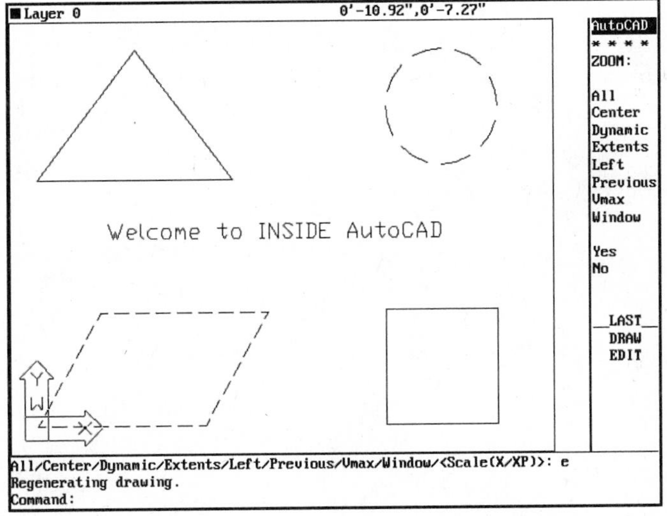

Figure 5.17:

The drawing after using ZOOM Extents.

Always use the ZOOM command's Extents option just before you end your drawing session. Extents acts as a check to let you know if you have drawn anything outside your limits. You can cut the zoom short by pressing Ctrl-C.

You might notice that you can use the ZOOM command's Dynamic option to move your current view from side to side without changing the magnification. This movement is called *panning*. AutoCAD also has a PAN command, which you can use just for panning.

Using PAN To Move around in the Drawing

The PAN command enables you to view other areas of the drawing by moving the drawing across the current viewport. If you are zoomed in to a given area of the drawing and you need to draw outside the current viewport, the PAN command enables you to shift the drawing to display the area you need to see. The PAN command behaves just like a camera pan. It enables you to move around the drawing at your current magnification.

To use the PAN command, you must supply AutoCAD with a *displacement*. A displacement is defined by two points, which determine the distance and direction of the pan. When you specify two points to identify a displacement, you specify a point at which AutoCAD picks up the drawing (the *first* displacement point) and then specify another point at which the drawing will be placed (the *second* displacement point). Your display crosshairs trail a line from the first to the second displacement point, showing you the pan's path.

In the following exercise, use the PAN command to isolate the square in the upper left corner of your drawing area.

Using PAN for Display

`Command:` *Choose* View, *then* Pan	Issues the PAN command
`Command: _'pan displacement:` *Pick a point at* ① *(see fig 5.18)*	Specifies the first displacement point
`Second point:` *Pick a point at* ②	Specifies the second point and pans the view

Your screen should look like the one shown in figure 5.19.

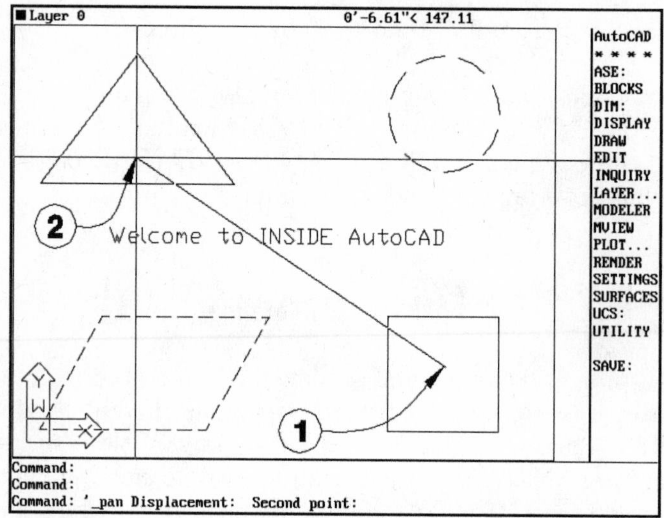

Figure 5.18:
Using the PAN command to show displacement.

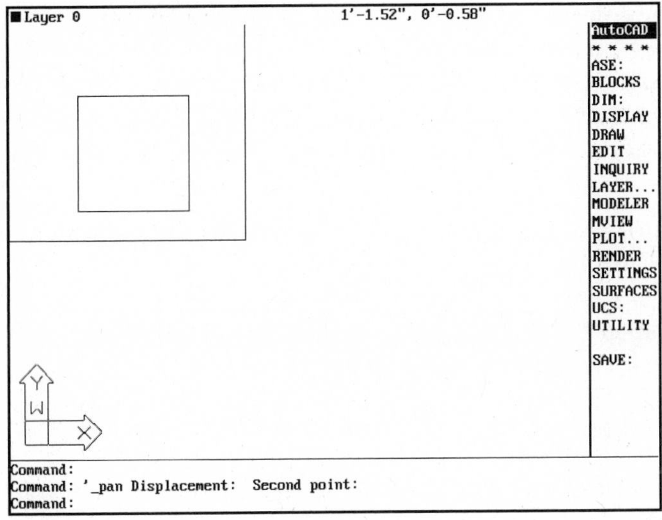

Figure 5.19:

The view after the PAN command.

When you use the ZOOM command's Dynamic option with a constant window size, it functions in much the same manner as the PAN command. You also can do limited panning by using the Center and Left ZOOM options and by keeping the same height.

Using VIEW To Name and Save Working Views

As you work on a drawing, you may find that your zooms and pans frequently return to the same drawing views. You can save time by saving and recalling your zooms and pans.

Suppose, for example, that you are going to concentrate your work on the sample drawing's square for the next few hours. Periodically, you want to zoom out to work in other areas, but most of the time you are zoomed in to the square. Instead of picking a window around the square every time you want to zoom to this area, you can store this view with a name, and then use the name to restore that view whenever you need it.

A stored window is called a *named view.* To save a view, use the VIEW command to name and store it. You can select VIEW from the DISPLAY screen menu, or you can enter **VIEW** at the `Command:` prompt. You can display the View Control dialog box by entering **DDVIEW** or choosing Named view from the Set View child menu on the View pull-down menu. The following exercise shows you how to use AutoCAD's VIEW command and save a view named SQUARE. After saving the view, you zoom out and then restore the view.

Before you begin the following exercise, zoom to the area of the drawing shown in figure 5.20.

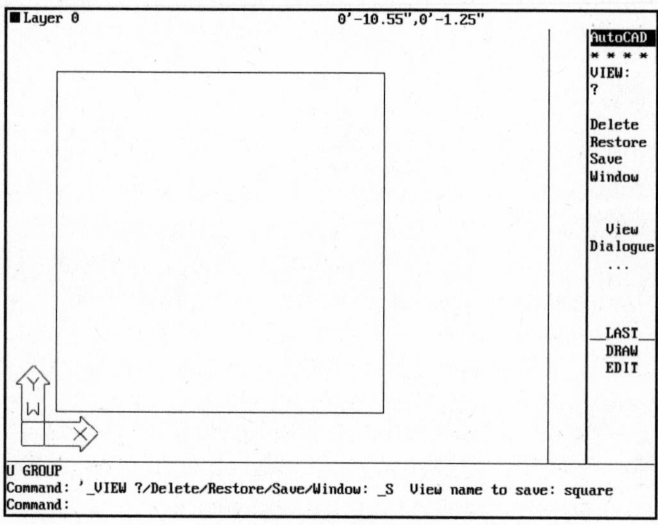

Figure 5.20:

The saved and restored view named SQUARE.

Using VIEW To Save and Restore a View

`Command:` *From the screen menu, choose* DISPLAY:, *then* VIEW:, *then* Save	Starts the VIEW command with Save option
`Command:_'VIEW ?/Delete/Restore/Save/ Window:_S View name to save:` **SQUARE**↵	Saves the current view under the name SQUARE
`Command:` *Choose* View, *then* Zoom, *then* All	Returns to full view (see fig. 5.21)
`Command:` *From the screen menu, choose* DISPLAY:, *then* VIEW:, *then* Restore	Starts the VIEW command with the Restore option
`Command:_'VIEW ?/Delete/Restore/Save/ Window: _RESTORE View name to restore:` **SQUARE** ↵	Restores the saved view named SQUARE as shown in figure 5.20

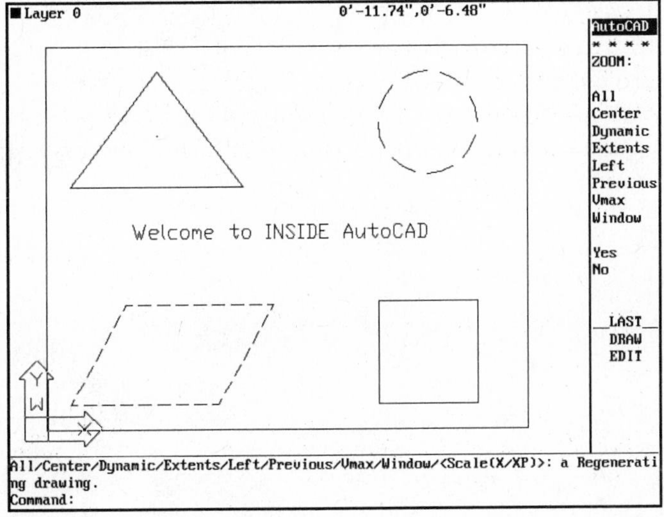

Figure 5.21:

The view after using the ZOOM command's All option.

Useful named views are L for Limits or A for All. Both are easy to type and can be used instead of issuing the ZOOM command's All option to avoid regenerations. Use a standard named view called PLOT for consistency in plotting.

The VIEW command has the following five options:

- **?.** This option displays a list of all saved viewport configurations when you enter an asterisk (*). The ? option lists a specific set of views when you enter names with wild cards. The list includes an M or P with the view's name to indicate whether the view is defined in model space (M) or paper space (P).
- **Delete.** This option prompts you to enter the name of a view to delete. You can use wild cards to delete a group of views.
- **Restore.** This option enables you to enter the name of a saved view to display it in the current viewport.
- **Save.** This option saves the current viewport's view.
- **Window.** This option enables you to define a window to save as a view by specifying its corners. You also can enter a name for the view.

You can rename an existing view by using the RENAME command or the Rename dialog box (DDRENAME command). The RENAME command is described in Chapter 3.

If you use the ZOOM command's Center option, press Enter to default the center point, enter **.8X**, and then save the view as **A** or **ALL**. This configuration provides a margin of safety in avoiding zoom and pan regenerations. Then use the VIEW command's Restore option to restore the All view, rather than the ZOOM command's All or Dynamic options.

When many view names are being saved and restored, the View Control dialog box is a very useful tool (see fig. 5.22). Enter **DDVIEW** or choose Named View from the Set View child menu on the View pull-down menu to display this dialog box. The list box shows all the existing named views. You use the radio buttons to restore a named view, create a new view, delete an existing view, or see a description of a view's general parameters. The edit box enables you to type in or change view names. As is the case with most dialog boxes, you can choose OK to accept the most recent changes in the dialog box; select Cancel to disregard the changes.

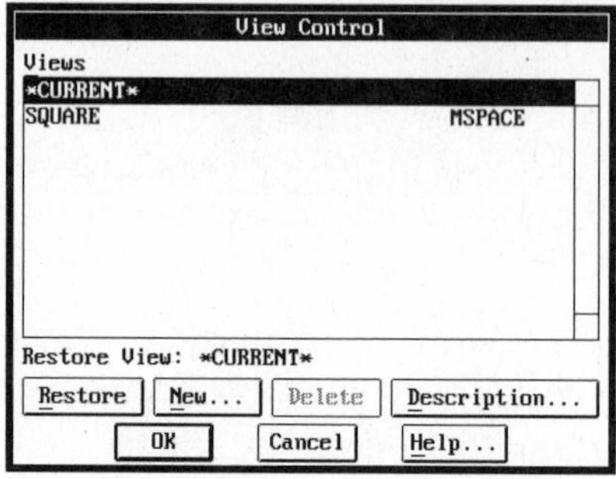

Figure 5.22:
The View Control dialog box.

In the following exercise, you use the View Control dialog box to restore and save named views of the drawing.

Using DDVIEW to Work with Views

`Command:` *Choose* View, *then* Zoom, *then* All	Returns to full view
`Command:` *Choose* View, *then* Set View, *then* Named View	Starts the DDVIEW command and displays the View Control dialog box
Click on SQUARE *in the view list box, then choose* Restore, *then* OK	Restores the view named SQUARE and closes the dialog box

`Command: U↵`	Undoes the VIEW command and returns to previous view
`Command:` *Zoom in on the parallelogram*	
`Command:` *Choose* View, *then* Set View, *then* Named View	Starts the DDVIEW command and displays the View Control dialog box
`DDVIEW`	
Click on the New *button, then type* `PARA`, *and choose* Save View	Saves the view with the name PARA
Choose OK	Closes the dialog box
`Command:` *Press Enter*	Repeats the DDVIEW command

The two views, PARA and SQUARE, appear in the View Control dialog box.

Choose Cancel	Closes the View Control dialog box

The View Control dialog box also can list information such as clipping data, twist angle, and view size. This information may be especially helpful for shading or rendering; you can access it by choosing the Description button. View names also can be deleted if they are no longer needed. (Remember to click on the Help button if you forget how some of these options work.)

Controlling Display Size and Resolution

As your drawing files become larger, you need to control the display size and resolution of your drawing. This means that you have to be conscious of the amount of your drawing you want AutoCAD to keep active at any one time. In using dynamic zooms, you have seen that AutoCAD keeps three different sets of drawing data active: the drawing extents, generated data, and the current view.

When your drawing file is small and uncomplicated, all these subsets usually are one and the same. As your drawing file gets larger, only portions of the file are generated, and it becomes more efficient to display only portions of your drawing. You usually use redraw (fast) speed to move from one view to another in the generated portion of the drawing file by using a PAN or ZOOM command. To call up a view that contains non-generated data, however, requires a regeneration of a different set of data and takes more time.

Using VIEWRES To Control Smooth Curves and Regeneration

The AutoCAD VIEWRES (VIEW RESolution) command controls the speed of your zooms and regenerations in two ways. First, it turns fast zoom on and off. *Fast zoom* means that AutoCAD maintains a large virtual screen so that it can do most pans and zooms at redraw speed. If fast zoom is off, all pans and zooms cause a regeneration. Second, VIEWRES determines how fine the curves should be. When circles or arcs are tiny, AutoCAD needs to display only a few straight lines to fool your eye into seeing smooth curves. When arcs are larger, AutoCAD needs more segments (or vectors) to make a smooth arc. The VIEWRES circle zoom percent tells AutoCAD how smooth you want your curves, and AutoCAD determines how many segments are needed to represent what is to be displayed.

In the following exercise, you learn how to alter the displayed smoothness of the circle by generating fewer segments. To see the effect, you need to change the circle's layer to a continuous linetype.

Using VIEWRES To Control Resolutions

`Command:` *Choose* View, *then* Zoom, *then* All	Displays the entire drawing
`Command:` *Choose* Modify, *then* Change, *then* Properties	Issues the DDCHPROP command
`Select objects:` *Select the circle and change its linetype to CONTINUOUS*	
`Command:` **`VIEWRES`**↵	
`Do you want fast zooms? <Y>:` *Press Enter*	Accepts the fast zoom default
`Enter circle zoom percent (1-20000) <100>:` **`5`**↵	
`Regenerating drawing.`	Displays the circle as an octagon
`Command:` *Press Enter*	Repeats the VIEWRES command
`VIEWRES Do you want fast zooms? <Y>:` *Press Enter*	
`Enter circle zoom percent (1-20000) <100>:` **`100`** ↵	
`Regenerating drawing.`	Redisplays the round circle

Figures 5.23 and 5.24 demonstrate the effect of VIEWRES on circles.

The trade-off for fast zoom is that when a regeneration is required, AutoCAD takes longer to regenerate the drawing than if fast zoom is off. AutoCAD takes longer because it must regenerate a larger area.

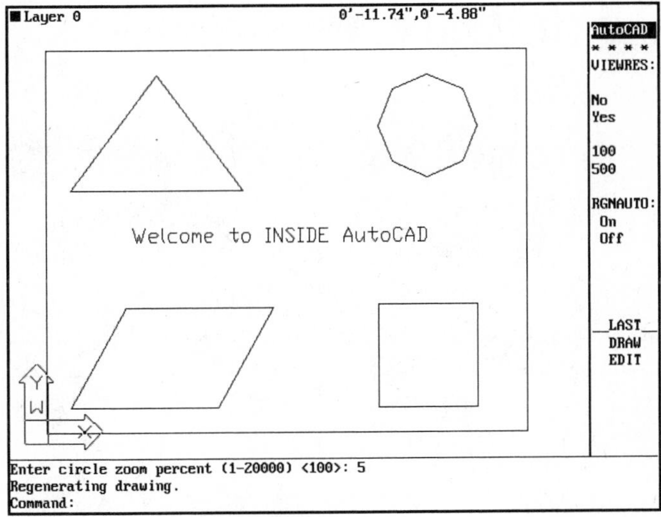

Figure 5.23:

The circle before the VIEWRES command.

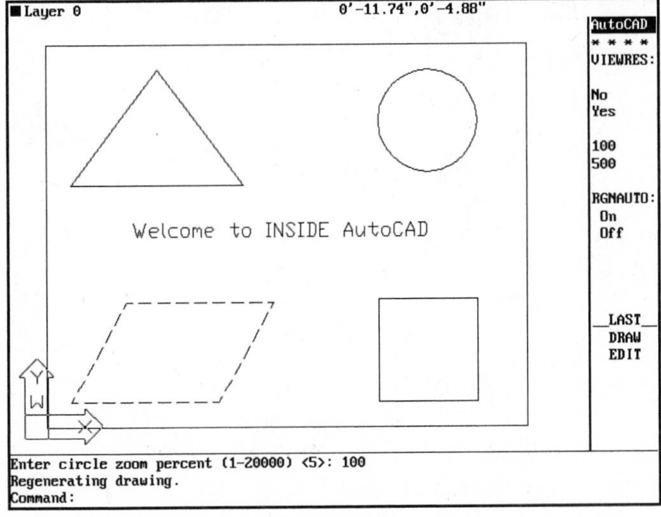

Figure 5.24:

The circle after the VIEWRES command.

If you turn fast zoom off, the ZOOM command's Dynamic option and all other pans and zooms always cause a drawing regeneration. Although you probably never should turn off fast zoom, you might find that AutoCAD is more efficient when zooming large text-filled drawings or doing work that often causes regenerations even if fast zoom is on. In addition, if VIEWRES is set to too high a number, it may cause slow regenerations.

Using REGEN To Control Data Generation

You have seen that the VIEWRES command and some zooms cause AutoCAD to regenerate the drawing. When the drawing file is full of many entities, particularly text, arcs, and circles, regeneration takes a long time.

You can force a regeneration of the display and drawing file by using the REGEN command. You can use REGEN to make AutoCAD recalculate the virtual screen at a particular current view so that your dynamic zoom display shows only the desired part of the drawing. To use REGEN, enter **REGEN** at the `Command:` prompt. AutoCAD displays the message `Regenerating drawing.` while the drawing regenerates.

To keep AutoCAD from regenerating extraneous data, freeze layers that you are not using. Thaw the layers when you need them.

Using REGENAUTO To Control AutoCAD's Regeneration

When you zoom, pan, or view, you usually want AutoCAD to make sure that everything in the drawing file is displayed accurately. Because large drawings can take a long time to regenerate, however, you may not want AutoCAD to regenerate when you are busy drawing or editing.

You can use the REGENAUTO command to determine when AutoCAD regenerates the drawing. When REGENAUTO is off, AutoCAD avoids regeneration unless absolutely necessary. When necessary, AutoCAD first stops and asks if you want to regenerate. The REGEN command, however, always overrides REGENAUTO and forces AutoCAD to regenerate the drawing.

The disadvantage of turning off REGENAUTO is that reset linetype scales, redefined symbols, and changed text styles do not automatically display with their new settings until you regenerate the drawing. After you are comfortable with these items in AutoCAD, not seeing every change as it occurs is a small penalty to pay for the time savings of keeping REGENAUTO turned off in complex drawings.

The QTEXT command displays text as only a box outline so that drawings regenerate quickly. Chapter 7 discusses the use of QTEXT.

Using Transparent Commands

You can use the PAN, ZOOM, and VIEW commands (as well as REDRAW) while most other AutoCAD commands are active. When you issue a command while a previously issued command is active, the second command is said to be operating *transparently.* You can issue a *transparent* command by placing a leading apostrophe (') before the command's name. Recall that you can get transparent 'HELP the same way. Often the pull-down menu selections issue commands with the apostrophe included.

In the following exercise, draw a line and issue a transparent 'VIEW and 'ZOOM. Then look for the double angle bracket (>>) at the `Command:` prompt. The double bracket shows that the current command is suspended.

Using Transparent VIEW and ZOOM

`Command:` *Issue the ZOOM command with the All option*

`Command:` *Choose* Draw, *then* Line, *then* Segments

`_line From point:` *Pick any point in the triangle*

`To point:` **'VIEW↵** — Specifies a transparent command

`>>?/Delete/Restore/Save/Window:` **S↵** — Indicates that another command is suspended with the >> prompt

`>>View name to save:` **A↵** — Saves the current view and completes the VIEW command

`Resuming _LINE command.`

`To point:` *Choose* View, *then* Zoom, *then* Window

`_'zoom`	Begins a transparent ZOOM with the Window option
`>>Center/Dynamic/Left/Previous/Vmax/ Window/<Scale(X/XP)>: w`	
`>>First corner:` *Pick ① (see fig. 5.25)*	
`>>Other corner:` *Pick ②*	Completes the ZOOM command
`Resuming _LINE command.`	
`To point:` *Pick any point inside the circle*	
`To point:` **'VIEW↵**	Starts the VIEW command transparently
`>>?/Delete/Restore/Save/Window:` **R↵**	
`>>View name to restore:` **A↵**	Restores view A without regenerating
`Resuming _LINE command.`	
`To point:` *Press Enter*	Ends LINE command

You may have noticed that the transparent ZOOM prompt omits the All and Extents options. The options are left out because they cause regenerations.

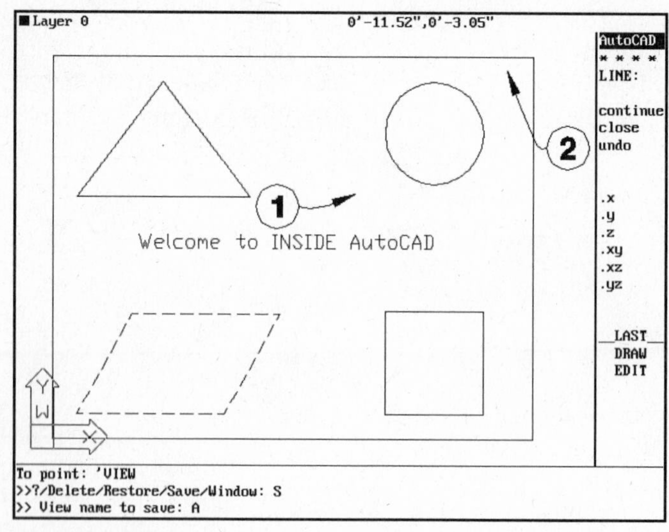

Figure 5.25:
A LINE command suspended by issuing a transparent VIEW command.

Displaying Multiple Viewports

So far, all the display controls used in these exercises have looked in on your drawing with a single drawing view in a single viewport. AutoCAD, however, also can display multiple views of your drawing simultaneously in the graphics window. In effect, you divide your drawing area into windows called *viewports* and display different views of your drawing in each of them.

You have been working in a viewport all along—a single viewport that covers the entire drawing area. Multiple viewports work just as if you divide your drawing area into rectangles, making several different drawing areas instead of one. You can have up to 16 viewports visible at one time while still retaining your screen and pull-down menus and `Command:` prompt area.

You can work in only one viewport at a time. The viewport you are using is called the *current viewport*. You make a viewport current simply by clicking in it. When a viewport is current, its border is thicker than the others and the cursor appears as it normally does in a single viewport display. When you work in any viewport, use your normal display controls just as if you are working with a single viewport. You can retain zoom, pan, grid, and snap settings for that viewport. The key point, however, is that the images shown in multiple viewports are multiple images of the same data. You are not duplicating your drawing; rather, you are just putting its image in different viewports.

Because the viewports look onto the same *model* or drawing, you can draw from viewport to viewport. You can start a line in one viewport, click on another viewport to make it current, and then complete the line. AutoCAD rubber bands your line segment across the viewports.

Multiple viewports are essential in 3D modeling to give you concurrent views of your model from different viewpoints. You can, for example, display plan, elevation, and isometric views of your model. Viewports also offer advantages over a single view display in some common 2D drafting situations, such as multiview drawings or drawings with multiple plotted scales. When you are faced with the problem of detailing different areas of a large drawing or you need to keep one area of your drawing (such as a title block or bill of materials) in constant view, use viewports to divide your drawing area.

Two types of viewports are available in AutoCAD—*tiled* viewports (see fig. 5.26) and *untiled* viewports (see fig. 5.27). Untiled viewports (referred to as *mview viewports* because they are defined by the MVIEW command) are much more flexible and must be created in an environment called *paper space.* Tiled viewports were the first type of viewports available in AutoCAD; mview viewports were added in Release 11. Because mview viewports are more natural and similar to manual drafting, this book emphasizes their use.

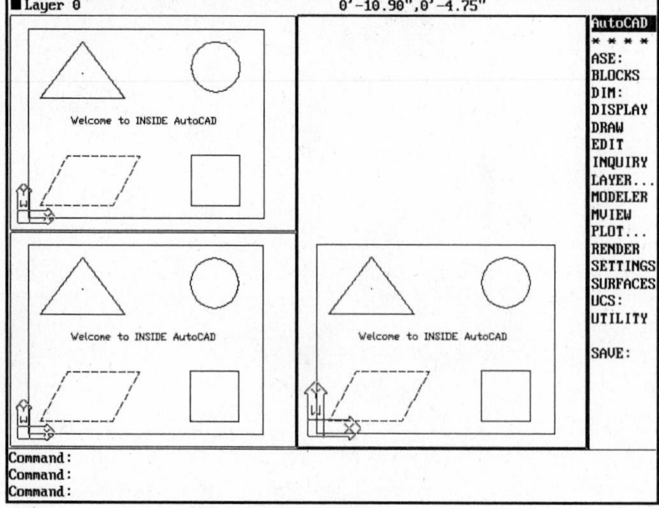

Figure 5.26:

Tiled viewports.

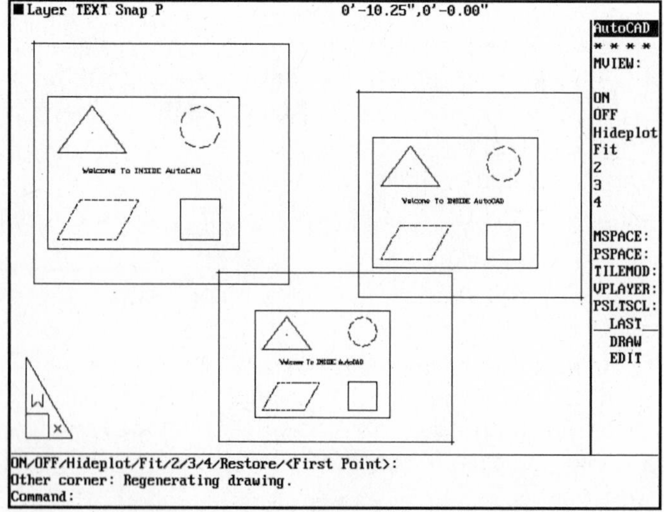

Figure 5.27:

Untiled (MVIEW) viewports.

Understanding Paper Space and Model Space

Model space is the drawing environment that exists in any viewport, whether it is a single full-size viewport, one of several tiled viewports, or an mview viewport entity in paper space. Think of *paper space* as an infinitely large sheet of paper on which you can arrange viewports that show your model. Although model space is a three-dimensional environment, paper space is a two-dimensional environment for arranging views of your model for display or plotting.

Whether you are creating two-dimensional or three-dimensional models, you do most of your drawing in model space. You draw in paper space when you add standard items, such as title blocks and sheet borders, and some types of dimensioning or annotation. Paper-space dimensioning and annotation are essential in 3D work.

You view paper space only in plan view, which reinforces the two-dimensional nature of paper space. You can draw 3D objects in paper space, but with no way to view them because it makes little sense to do so.

Working in Paper Space

Along with paper space comes a new type of viewport—mview viewports. *Mview viewports* can be any size; they do not have to touch (as tiled viewports do), and they even can overlap one another. You can think of viewports as glass windows into your drawing that can be either open or closed. If you are in paper space, the window is closed and, although you can still see through it, you cannot reach through it to make changes to the entities behind it. But you can move and edit the window frame itself. When you are in model space, the current viewport window is open and you can work with the entities shown inside to edit them or draw more entities. You cannot modify the window frame in model space, however, only the entities inside the frame. You also cannot have more than one of those windows open (current) at a time.

You can draw anything in paper space that you can draw in model space, except that 3D objects look flat. Paper space is similar to another semi-independent drawing that overlays your entire group of viewports. What you draw in paper space appears over, but not in, your viewports. You can snap by using object snap commands from paper space to the model-space contents of the underlying viewports. You cannot, however, snap by using

object snap commands from model space to paper space. Zooms cause more regenerations in paper space because paper space uses no virtual screen.

When you are working in paper space, viewports are like any other entity. You can, for example, edit the boundary of the viewport itself. Indirectly, that can affect the view of the model shown in the viewport. If you make the paper space viewport larger by stretching it, you might see more of the model. If you make the paper space viewport smaller, some of the model might disappear behind the boundary of the viewport. You can use the MOVE command to move a viewport around without affecting other viewports. You can change the color of a viewport's boundary box by using the CHPROP command, and you can erase a viewport just like any other AutoCAD entity. All these changes can be made in paper space.

When you return to model space, you can select individual viewports and edit individual entities that show up in those viewports. You cannot, however, edit the viewport frame's size, color, or other attributes.

Examining the Command Set for Mview Viewports

Three primary commands and one system variable enable you to enter and use viewports in paper space. The TILEMODE system variable must be set to 0 (off) before you can enter paper space. Then you use the MVIEW command to create viewports. To enter model space so that you can work in these viewports, use the MSPACE command. Use the PSPACE command to return to paper space to edit viewports, to add title blocks or annotation, or to set up for plotting. All these commands and several preset options are on a child menu displayed by choosing View and then Mview from the pull-down menu.

Entering Paper Space and Creating Viewports

When you begin a drawing in AutoCAD, the display shows a single viewport by default, unless you are using a prototype drawing that has been set up for multiple viewports. The system variable TILEMODE is set to 1 (on) by default, which gives you only tiled viewports. As you just saw, to enter paper space, you must set TILEMODE to 0. When you are in paper space and you set TILEMODE back to 1, AutoCAD returns to model space with one or more tiled viewports.

To activate paper space, choose View, then TILEMODE, and then Off from the pull-down menu. This sets TILEMODE to 0. You also can access the MVIEW command from the DISPLAY screen menu or enter it at the `Command:` prompt. The letter `P` appears at the left side of the status line when paper space is active.

The following example uses the BASIC drawing from Chapter 4 or the drawing named IA7BASIC.DWG from the optional IA DISK. If you do not have the IA DISK, load the BASIC drawing that you created in Chapter 4. This exercise shows you how to enter paper space, create a few mview viewports, then draw some lines and experiment with object selection in paper space.

Creating Viewports in Paper Space

Choose File, *then* New , *then* Discard Changes, *and enter* `BASIC=IA7BASIC` ↵	Restarts the drawing BASIC.DWG
`Command:` *Choose* File, *then* Open, *then* Discard Changes, *and enter* `BASIC`, *and verify that the drawing has the settings shown in Table 5.1*	
`Command:` *Choose* View, *then* Tilemode, *then* Off	Sets TILEMODE to 0 and enters paper space

The drawing image disappears until you create viewports.

`Command:` *Choose* View, *then* Mview, *then* Create Viewport	Starts the MVIEW command

`Command: _mview`
`ON/OFF/Hideplot/Fit/2/3/4/Restore/`
`<First Point>:` *From the screen menu, choose* Fit
	Fits a viewport to fill the display area and redisplays the drawing image

`Command:` *Perform a ZOOM with the Center option, center point 12,0 and height 19*	Displays the viewport shown in figure 5.28
`Command:` *Choose* View, *then* Mview, *then* 2 Viewports	Issues the MVIEW command with the 2 option

`Command: _mview`
`ON/OFF/Hideplot/Fit/2/3/4/Restore/`
`<First Point>: _2`	

`Horizontal/<Vertical>: H`↵	Specifies a Horizontal divider between viewports
`Fit/<First Point>:` *From the pop-up menu, choose* Intersection	Specifies the INTersect object snap mode

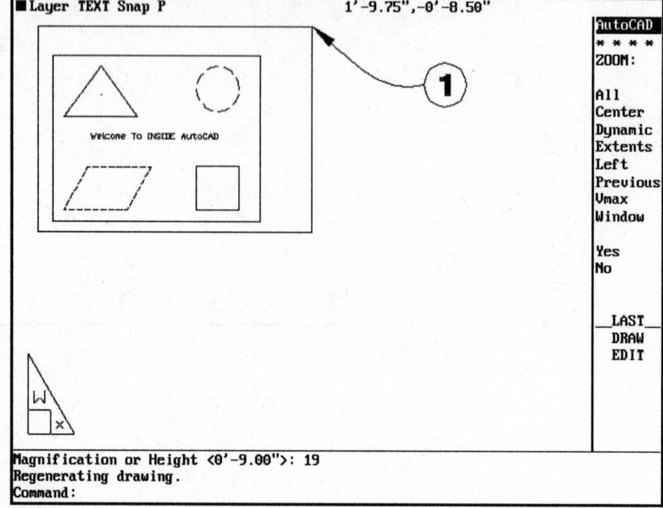

Figure 5.28:

The first paper space viewport.

`int of` *Pick the viewport's upper right corner at ① in figure 5.28*	Sets the first corner of the new viewport pair
`Second point:` **`24,-9`**↵	Sets the viewport's other corner
`Regenerating drawing.`	Displays the drawing image in two new viewports (see fig. 5.29)
`Command:` *Choose* File, *then* Save	Saves the current drawing
`Command:` *Choose* Draw, *then* Line, *then* Segments, *and draw a few lines across two or three viewports*	
`Command:` **`E`**↵	Issues shortcut key for the ERASE command
`Select objects:` *Select the lines you just drew*	Selects the lines
`Select objects:` *Select the circle or text*	Ignores entities in the viewports
`Select objects:` *Press Enter*	Erases only the selected lines

You cannot select the entities in the viewports unless you are in model space. The viewports themselves, however, are erased if you select their borders while in paper space.

If you set TILEMODE to 1 to exit from paper space after you already have created viewports, the viewports remain defined. You can redisplay them later by setting

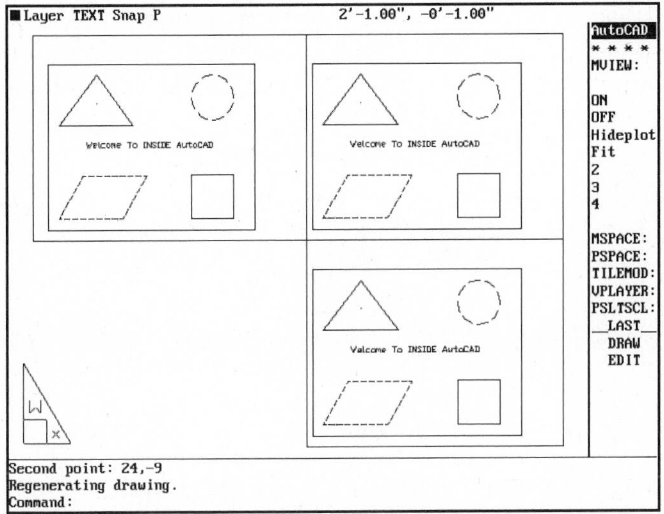

Figure 5.29:

Three mview viewports.

TILEMODE to 0, or by choosing View, then TILEMODE, and then Off from the pull-down menu.

The MVIEW command gives you the following options for creating and controlling viewports in paper space:

- **First point.** This option enables you to specify two diagonally opposite corner points to define a new viewport, which becomes the current viewport.
- **ON.** This option makes all model space entities in the selected viewports visible.
- **OFF.** This option makes all model space entities in the selected viewports invisible.
- **Hideplot.** This option enables you to select the viewports from which 3D hidden lines are to be removed during plotting.
- **Fit.** This option creates a single viewport the size of the current paper space view.
- **2/3/4.** This option creates two, three, or four viewports.
- **Restore.** This option creates an arrangement of mview viewports that matches the appearance of a tiled viewport configuration that has been saved by using the VPORTS command. (MVIEW cannot save and restore mview viewport configurations.)

When you create viewports by using the Fit, 2, 3, or 4 options, the viewports appear tiled, but you can move them apart and resize them by using commands such as STRETCH and MOVE.

NOTE

The MVSETUP program, which is included with AutoCAD, can set up multiple viewports, adjust limits, and insert a title block. You can load this LISP program by entering **MVS** at the `Command:` prompt, or from the pull-down menu by selecting View, then Layout, then MV Setup.

Drawing in Multiple Viewports

The following exercise begins by entering model space and setting the upper left viewport as current. By zooming in on the triangle and drawing lines to points that are no longer visible in that viewport, you can see some of the benefits of drawing with multiple viewports.

Drawing with Multiple Viewports

Continue in the BASIC drawing from the previous exercise.

`Command:` *Choose* View, *then* Model space	Switches from paper space to model space and displays the UCS icon in each viewport
`Command:` *Click in the upper left viewport*	Makes the upper left viewport the current viewport
`Command:` *Zoom in on the triangle (see fig 5.30)*	
`Command:` *Choose* Settings, *then* Drawing Aids, *and set the grid to .25*	
`Command:` **L** ↵	Issues the LINE command
`LINE From point:` *Pick a point that is approximately in the center of the triangle (notice the rubber-band cursor)*	Starts the line
Click in the upper right viewport (notice rubber-band cursor)	Changes the current viewport
`To point:` *Choose* View, *then* Zoom, *then* Window, *and transparently zoom in on the circle (see fig 5.31)*	
`Resuming _LINE command.`	
`To point:` *Pick a point that is approximately in the center of the circle, as shown in figure 5.31*	Continues the line

`To point:` *Click in the bottom right viewport, then pick the approximate center of the square, as shown in figure 5.32*	Makes the viewport current and continues the line
`To point:` *Pick the approximate center of the parallelogram shown in figure 5.33*	Continues the line
`To point: C↵`	Closes the line in the triangle

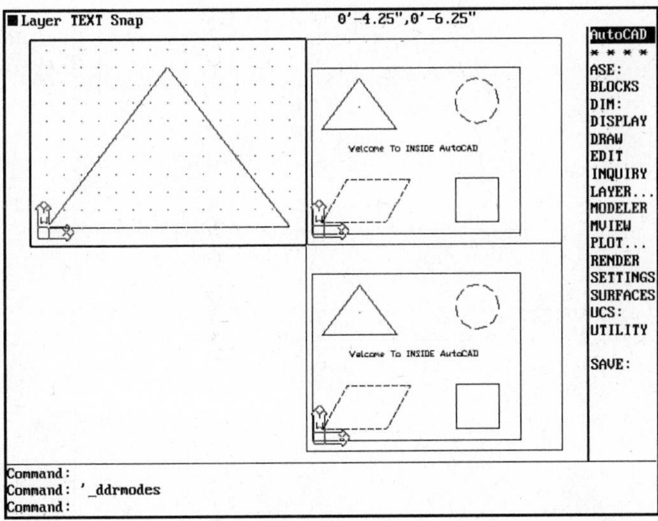

Figure 5.30:

The left viewport zoomed, displaying a small grid.

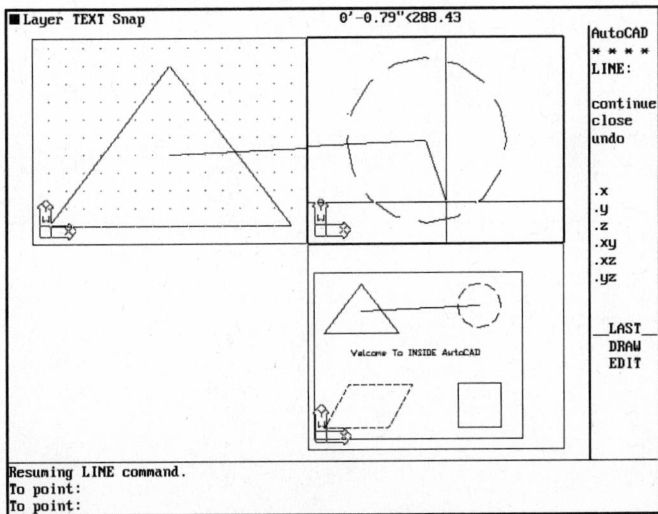

Figure 5.31:

The upper right viewport with the first line.

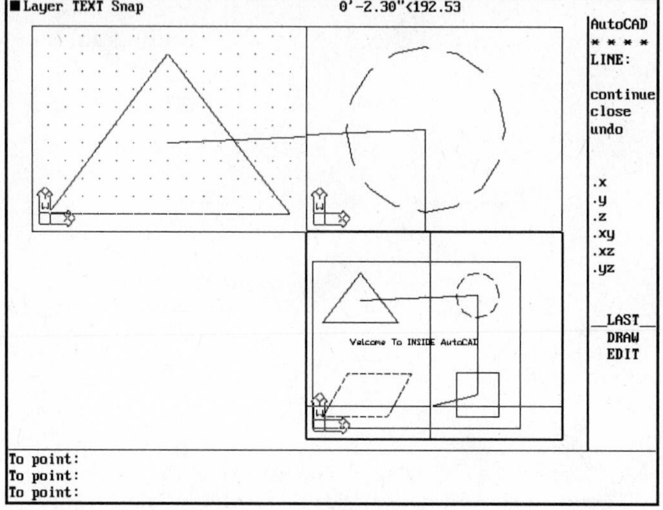

Figure 5.32:

The bottom right viewport with the continuing line.

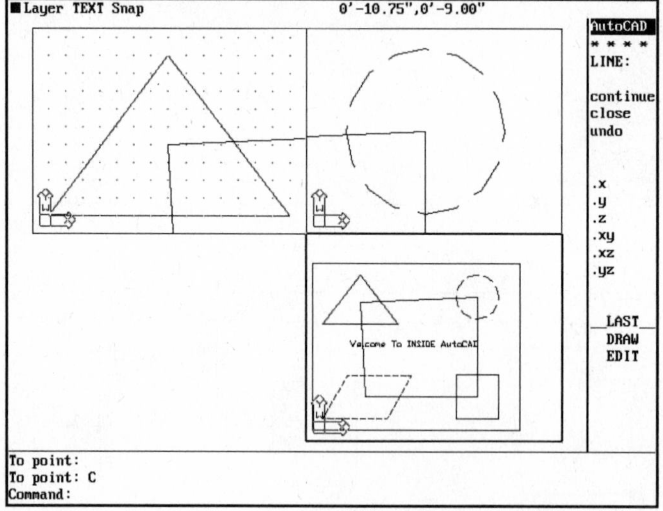

Figure 5.33:

The complete line shown in all the viewports.

When you are done, the upper viewports should show portions of the completed lines and the bottom viewport should show the whole drawing.

Editing Mview Viewports

In model space, any actions you make, such as erasing or copying, affect the model in the current viewport rather than the viewport itself. When you are working in paper space, the only entities you can access are the boundary boxes around each viewport and any entities you created or inserted in paper space. The key to understanding viewports in paper space is that when you are working in paper space you cannot make any changes to the model—just to the viewport. To make changes to the model, you have to enter model space. Occasionally, you may want your edit commands to change the viewport itself, rather than the model that is displayed inside it. You might, for example, create a viewport that is not quite large enough to display all of the view that is supposed to appear in it at a certain scale for plotting. Use AutoCAD's STRETCH command to resize the viewport while in paper space.

AutoCAD recognizes the boundary box around the viewport as a single entity. If you select one line of the boundary box, the entire viewport is selected. Because the viewports are recognized as single entities, you can move, copy, erase, and scale them. (These editing commands are covered in detail in the chapter on editing. For now, just follow the exercise steps.)

You also can place the viewports on different layers. If the color for a viewport is set to BYLAYER, the boundary box displays at whatever color has been assigned to the layer. You also can change the color of the boundary box lines by using the CHPROP command and by providing an explicit color for the viewport. A change to the layer or color of the boundary does not affect the image inside the viewport, just the boundary box. If you want to plot a drawing without plotting the viewport boundary boxes, place the boundaries on a layer that can be turned off for plotting.

The next exercise continues with the BASIC drawing that was modified in the last exercise and uses AutoCAD's editing commands to change the viewports (see Chapters 6-9 for details on the editing commands).

Editing Mview Viewports

Continue in the BASIC drawing.

`Command:` *Choose* View, *then* Paper space	Redisplays the triangle paper space UCS icon
`Command:` *Choose* Modify, *then* Stretch	Issues the STRETCH command with the Crossing option
`Select objects to stretch by window...`	
`Select objects: crossing`	
`First point:` *Pick at ① near the left viewport (see fig. 5.34)*	
`Second point:` *Pick at ②, across the viewport's bottom left corner*	Selects a corner of the viewport
`Select objects:` *Press Enter*	Ends object selection
`Base point:` *Pick point ③ on bottom edge of viewport (see fig. 5.34)*	Sets the base point of the stretch
`New point:` *Pick point near ④*	Specifies the displacement and stretches the viewport to about twice its original height
`Command:` *Choose* Modify, *then* Move	Issues the MOVE command
`Select objects:` *Pick each viewport on its boundary, and then press Enter*	Selects all three viewports
`Base point or displacement:` *Pick at ⑤ outside bottom left of left viewport*	Sets the move's "from point"
`Second point of displacement:` **`0,0`** ↵	Moves the viewports into positive X,Y coordinate space
`Command:` *Choose* View, *then* Zoom, *then* All	Shows the entire drawing
`Command:` **`CHPROP`** ↵	
`Select objects:` *Pick the upper right viewport's boundary and press Enter*	Selects the viewport to change
`Change what property (Color/LAyer/LType/Thickness) ?` **`C`** ↵	Specifies the Color option
`New color <BYLAYER>:` **`RED`** ↵	Specifies the new color
`Change what property (Color/LAyer/LType/Thickness) ?` *Press Enter*	Ends the command and changes the viewport's color
`Command:` *Choose* Modify, *then* Erase, *then* Single	
`Select objects: si`	
`Select objects:` *Pick the lower right viewport*	Erases the viewport
`Command:` *From the screen menu, choose* OOPS:	Restores the erased viewport
`Command:` *Save the drawing*	

The results are shown in figure 5.35.

You can see how easy it is to change mview viewports. Just remember that if you want to change the viewport, you have to be in paper space. If you want to change the model, you have to be in model space.

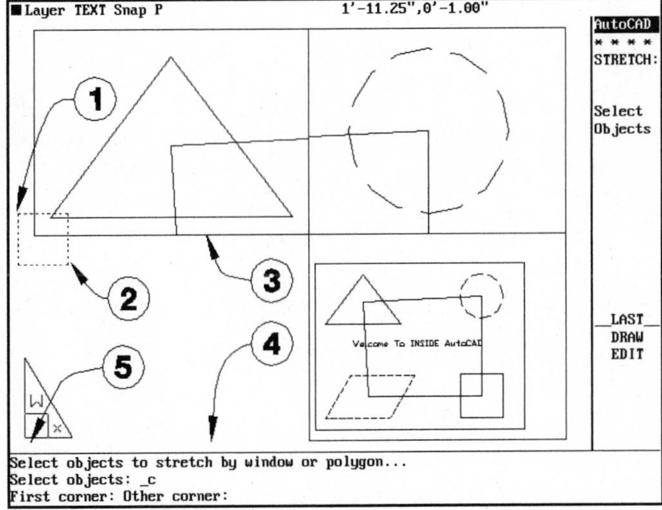

Figure 5.34:

The unedited mview viewports.

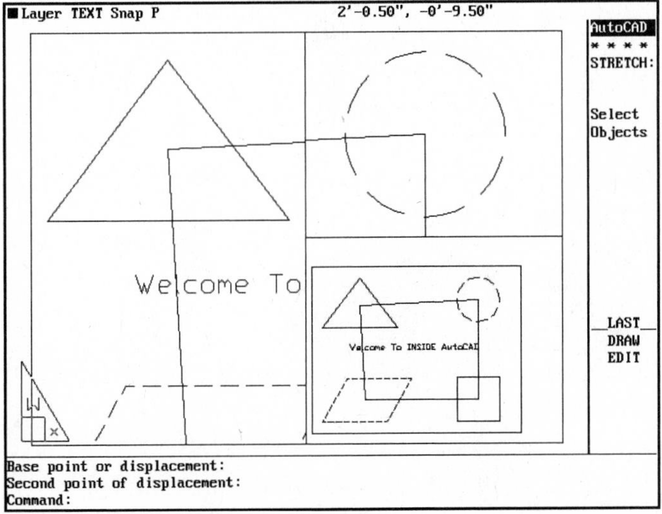

Figure 5.35:

The edited mview viewports.

Using VPLAYER To Control Layer Visibility

Normally, when you freeze a layer, that layer disappears from every viewport because the LAYER command affects layers globally. With mview viewports (not tiled viewports), you can control the layer visibility in individual viewports by using the VPLAYER (ViewPort Layer) command.

Unlike the LAYER command, VPLAYER only affects the way layers appear in a single viewport. This enables you to select a viewport and freeze a layer in it while still enabling the contents of that layer to appear in another viewport. VPLAYER settings affect only the visibility of layers in viewports when TILEMODE is set to 0 (paper space). If you switch back to a single or tiled model view by setting TILEMODE to 1 (tiled viewports), the global layer settings take precedence over any VPLAYER settings.

The VPLAYER command can be executed from either paper space or model space. If you are in model space and use the Select option, the graphics window temporarily switches to paper space so that you can select a viewport. The following exercise uses the VPLAYER command from model space.

The BASIC drawing is a good starting point for this exercise because it is relatively simple and contains entities drawn on different layers.

Controlling Layer Visibility Using VPLAYER

Continue in the BASIC drawing, or open it again.

`Command:` **`MS`** ↵	Enters model space
`Command:` *Choose* View, *then* Mview, *then* Vplayer	Begins the VPLAYER command
`Command: _vplayer ?/Freeze/Thaw/Reset/ Newfrz/Vpvisdflt:` *From the screen menu, choose* Freeze	Specifies the Freeze option
`Layer(s) to Freeze:` **`CIRCLE`** ↵	
`All/Select/<Current>:` **`S`** ↵	AutoCAD prompts for viewports to select
`Switching to Paper space.`	
`Select objects:` *Pick the upper right viewport and press Enter*	Selects the viewport
`Switching to Model space.`	

`?/Freeze/Thaw/Reset/Newfrz/Vpvisdflt:` *From the screen menu, choose* Freeze	
`Layer(s) to Freeze:` **PARAGRAM**↵	
`All/Select/<Current>:` **S**↵	
`Switching to Paper space.`	
`Select objects:` *Pick the lower right viewport and press Enter*	
`Switching to Model space.`	
`?/Freeze/Thaw/Reset/Newfrz/Vpvisdflt:`**F**↵	Specifies the Freeze option
`Layer(s) to Freeze:` **TEXT**↵	
`All/Select/<Current>:` **S**↵	
`Switching to Paper space.`	
`Select objects:` *Select the left viewport and press Enter*	
`Switching to Model space.`	
`?/Freeze/Thaw/Reset/Newfrz/Vpvisdflt:` ↵	Ends the VPLAYER command
`Regenerating drawing.`	Redisplays the viewports with selected layers frozen in each (see fig. 5.36)

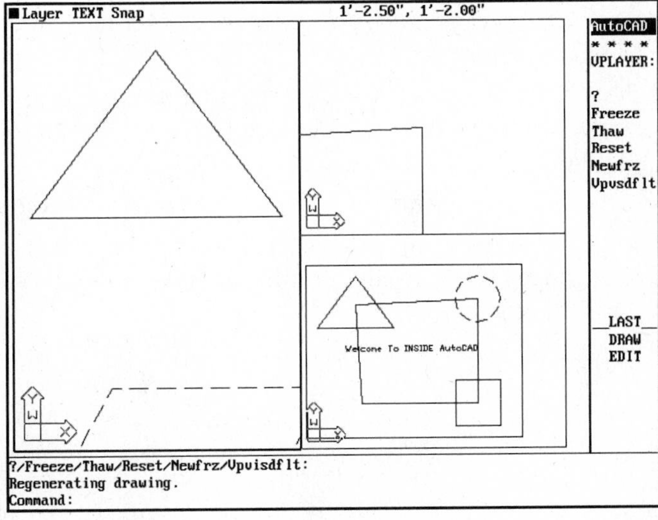

Figure 5.36:
Using VPLAYER to freeze layers.

After you use VPLAYER, although a layer is frozen in each of the viewports, the data on it still appears in the other viewports.

Understanding VPLAYER Options

The VPLAYER command gives you a number of options for selectively controlling layer visibility, as well as creating new layers. The options are available in VPLAYER:

- **?.** This option lists the current viewport's frozen layers. In model space, this option prompts for a viewport selection, temporarily switching to paper space.
- **Freeze.** This option enables you to specify layer name(s) to freeze and to specify the viewport(s) in which to freeze them.
- **Thaw.** This option enables you to specify layer name(s) to thaw and to specify the viewport(s) in which to thaw them.
- **Reset.** This option enables you to specify layer name(s) to restore the current default visibility setting for the specified layer(s) and specify the viewports in which to reset them. The default is set by the Vpvisdflt option.
- **Newfrz.** This option enables you to specify name(s) to create new layer(s) that are frozen in all viewports. You can enter more than one name, separated by commas.
- **Vpvisdflt.** This option enables you to specify layer name(s) and Frozen or Thawed (the default) to set the current visibility defaults for the specified layer(s) in subsequently created viewports.
- **All.** This option specifies all mview viewports, whether visible or not.
- **Select.** This option enables you to select one or more mview viewports. If model space is current, the graphics window switches to paper space for the selection.
- **Current.** This option specifies the current viewport.

Controlling Dialog Box Viewport Layers

You also can use the Layer Control dialog box (choose Settings and then Layer Control, or enter the DDLMODES command) to control layers in mview viewports.

Controlling Layer Visibility Using VPLAYER

Continue in the BASIC drawing from the preceding exercise.

`Command:` *Choose the left viewport to make it active*	
`Command:` *Choose* Settings, *then* Layer Control; *choose the* TRIANGLE *layer,* Cur VP Frz, *then* OK	Displays the layer Control dialog box (see fig. 5.37) and freezes TRIANGLE

Notice that the TRIANGLE layer is frozen in the left viewport.

`Command:` *From the Layer Control dialog box, choose the* TRIANGLE *layer, then* Cur VP Thw, *then* OK	Thaws the layer in the current viewport

```
Layer Control
Current Layer: TEXT
Layer Name        State        Color     Linetype
0                 On . . . .   white     CONTINUOUS
CIRCLE            On . . . .   green     DASHED
PARAGRAM          On . . . .   magenta   HIDDEN
SQUARE            On . . . .   yellow    CONTINUOUS
TEXT              On . . C .   cyan      CONTINUOUS
TRIANGLE          On . . . .   red       CONTINUOUS

On  Off  Thaw  Freeze  Unlock  Lock
Cur VP: Thw Frz
New VP: Thw Frz
Set Color...  Set Ltype...
Select All  New  Current  Rename  Filters
Clear All   On  Set...
OK  Cancel  Help...
```

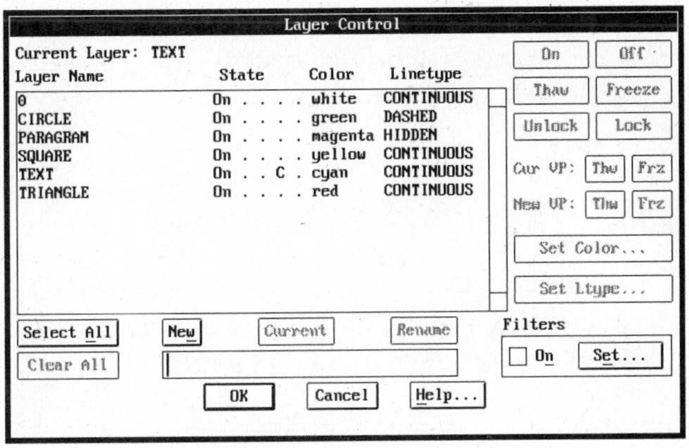

Figure 5.37:
The Layer Control dialog box.

Whereas using the VPLAYER command is a more powerful and versatile method of turning layers off and on in different mview viewports, the Layer Control dialog box is a little easier because it enables graphic selection of the layers. The dialog box method can be cumbersome to perform many changes at once because the viewport must first be selected before opening the dialog box.

In paper space, the Layer Control dialog box displays the settings of the current viewport, which, in this case, is the current left viewport.

The Cur VP: Thw and Frz (CURrent ViewPort THaW and FReeZe) buttons control the freeze and thaw status of selected layers in the current viewport. The New VP: Thw and Frz buttons control the freeze and thaw status of selected layers for new viewports. These buttons set the layer(s) so that it is

automatically frozen in subsequently created viewports. You might choose to do this when setting up several new viewports in a complex drawing. By clicking on the buttons after selecting layers, you can change the states of the current or new viewports. If you are in paper space, the change applies to the paper space view itself, not to any of the viewports.

Notice the four columns in the State column (the On column and several columns of dots). The first column shows the global on and off settings for each layer; the second column shows the global freeze and thaw settings; the third column shows the current viewport settings; and the fourth column shows the new viewport settings. A dot in a column for a layer indicates that the layer is thawed for that setting. A letter indicates that the layer is off or frozen for that setting. Use O for a global on or off setting; F to make a global Freeze; C for Cur VP: Frz; and N for New VP: Frz.

The following exercise shows you tiled viewports and how to convert them to mview viewports. By setting TILEMODE back to 1 (on), the drawing area changes back to a single tiled viewport.

Using TILEMODE To Exit from Paper Space

`Command:` *Choose* View, *then* Tilemode, *then* On	Turns on TILEMODE
`New value for TILEMODE <0>: 1`	Displays all the layers in a single tiled viewport
`Command:` *Save the drawing*	

When you exit from paper space, all the layers display in the default single-tiled viewport, regardless of their VPLAYER settings.

Choosing between Mview Viewports and Tiled Viewports

What is so special about mview viewports? You can work on simultaneous multiple views of your drawing in tiled viewports, but AutoCAD restricts the way you can size tiled viewports. You can resize and place mview viewports, however, any way that you want. Mview viewports also enable you to control layers selectively by viewport, rather than globally in all tiled

viewports. If you use mview viewports, you can freeze a layer in one viewport and leave it thawed in another viewport. You can plot several mview viewports simultaneously in paper space to create a multiview drawing, but only one tiled viewport can be plotted at a time.

To fill the screen with a view when working in a mview viewport for an extended period of time, turn TILEMODE on with a single tiled viewport.

Using Tiled Viewports

Most, if not all, of your modeling and drawing can be done by using mview viewports. Sometimes, however, you might want to use AutoCAD's tiled viewports for model space work. As you work through the following exercises, keep in mind that all of the drawing features found in tiled viewports, such as the capability to draw from one viewport to another, also are inherent in mview viewports.

The VPORTS command controls tiled viewports. It divides the AutoCAD graphics area into windows. Like mview viewports, each tiled viewport contains a unique view of the drawing. Unlike mview viewports, however, tiled viewports must touch at the edges and they cannot overlap one another. You cannot edit, rearrange, or turn individual tiled viewports on or off. The other limitation of tiled viewports is in layer visibility—VPLAYER and the VP Frz settings of the Layer Control dialog box do not work in tiled viewports. You must use the LAYER command or global settings in the Layer Control dialog box to freeze layers in tiled viewports, and then the corresponding layers in all viewports are affected.

Tiled viewports are created by using the VPORTS command. Make sure the TILEMODE system variable is set to 1 (on), then enter **VPORTS** or select VPORTS: from the SETTINGS screen menu. VPORTS offers several command options that you can use to build your display by adding, deleting, and joining viewports. After you have the viewports you want, you can save and name the group. A group of viewports is called a *configuration*. Use the same naming conventions to name your configuration that you use for layer names. You can have up to 31 characters, and you can use three special characters ($, -, and _) in your names. Most of the options in VPORTS are similar to the MVIEW command. The capability to save and restore named tiled viewports are the only advantages tiled viewports have

over mview viewports. You later learn how to apply tiled viewport capabilities to paper space.

The VPORTS command offers the following options:

- **Save.** This option saves and names the current viewport configuration (up to 31 characters).
- **Restore.** This option restores any saved viewport configuration. Enter a specific name to restore, enter an asterisk to display a list of all saved viewport configurations, or use any wild cards to list a specific set of names.
- **Delete.** This option deletes a saved viewport configuration.
- **Join.** This option combines the current viewport with a selected viewport. The two viewports must be adjacent and form a rectangle.
- **SIngle.** This option changes the screen to a single viewport and displays the view of the current viewport.
- **?.** This option enables you to enter an asterisk to list all named viewport configurations, or use wild cards to list a specific set of viewports.
- **2.** This option divides the current viewport into a horizontal or vertical pair of viewports.
- **3.** This option divides the current viewport into three viewports. This is the default option.
- **4.** This option divides the current viewport into four viewports.

Creative use of the 2, 3, 4, and Join options often is needed to get the arrangement you want. In the following exercise, use VPORTS to divide your drawing area into three viewports by using the BASIC drawing from Chapter 4 or IA7BASIC.DWG from the optional IA DISK.

Begin the exercise by opening the existing BASIC drawing or set TILEMODE to 1 in your current drawing (see fig. 5.38). Then divide your drawing area in half. Next, divide the top half into three viewports. Finally, join the top three viewports into two viewports so that you end up with a configuration of two up and one below.

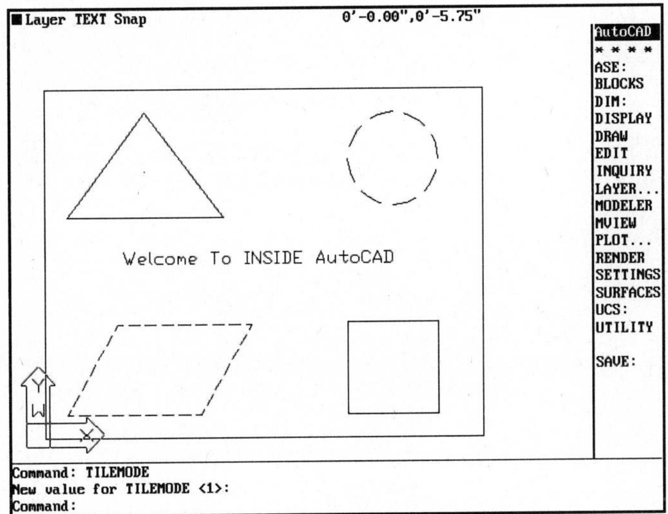

Figure 5.38:

The TILEVP drawing before viewports.

Using VPORTS To Get Multiple Views

Choose File, New, Discard Changes, *and enter* `TILEVP=IA7BASIC`↵ — Starts a new drawing called TILEVP

Open the existing drawing named BASIC (from Chapter 4), and make sure the drawing has the settings shown in table 5.1, or continue from the preceding exercise.

`Command:` **`TILEMODE`**↵	
`New value for TILEMODE <1>:` *Press Enter*	Confirms that TILEMODE is set to 1
`Command:` *From the screen menu, choose* SETTINGS, *then* next, *then* VPORTS:	Starts the VPORTS command
`Command: _VPORTS`	
`Save/Restore/Delete/Join/SIngle/?/ 2/<3>/4:` **`2`**↵	Specifies the 2 viewport option
`Horizontal/<Vertical>:` **`H`**↵	Specifies Horizontal
`Regenerating drawing.`	Divides the drawing area, as shown in figure 5.39
`Command:` *Press Enter*	Repeats the VPORTS command

`_VPORTS`	
`Save/Restore/Delete/Join/SIngle/?/` `2/<3>/4:` **3** ↵	
`Horizontal/Vertical/Above/Below/Left/` `<Right>:` **V**↵	Divides the current (upper) viewport into 3 vertical viewports (see fig. 5.40)
`Command:` *Press Enter*	
`_VPORTS`	
`Save/Restore/Delete/Join/SIngle/` `?/2/<3>/4:` **J**↵	Specifies the Join option
`Select dominant viewport <current>:` *Press Enter*	Accepts the top right viewport as dominant
`Select viewport to join:` *Pick the top center viewport*	Merges the two viewports (see fig. 5.41)

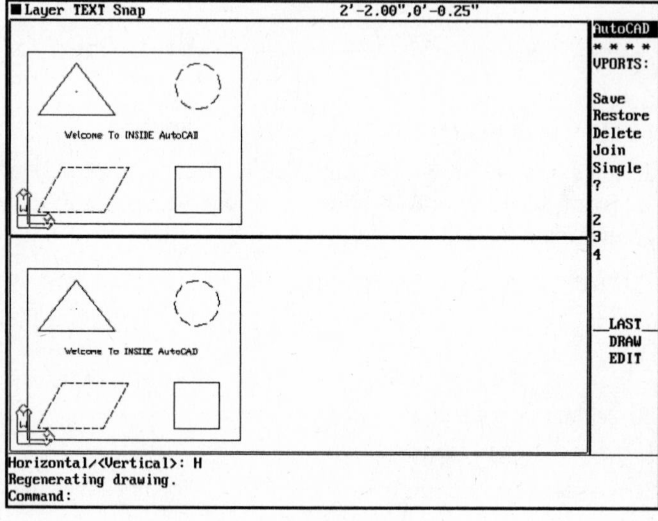

Figure 5.39:

The drawing with two viewports.

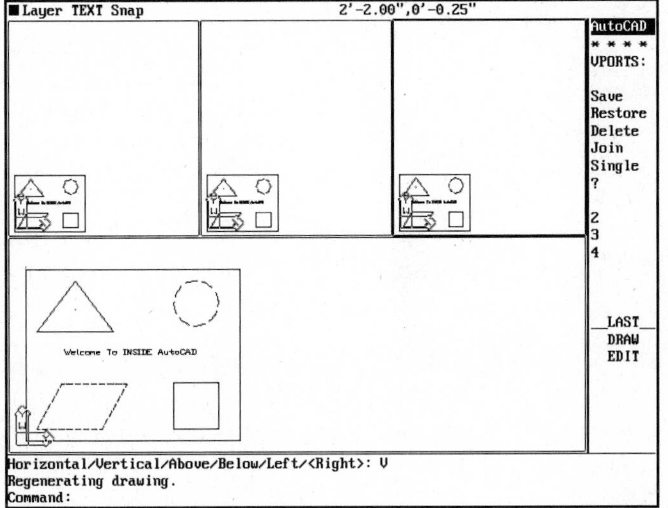

Figure 5.40:

The top viewport divided three times.

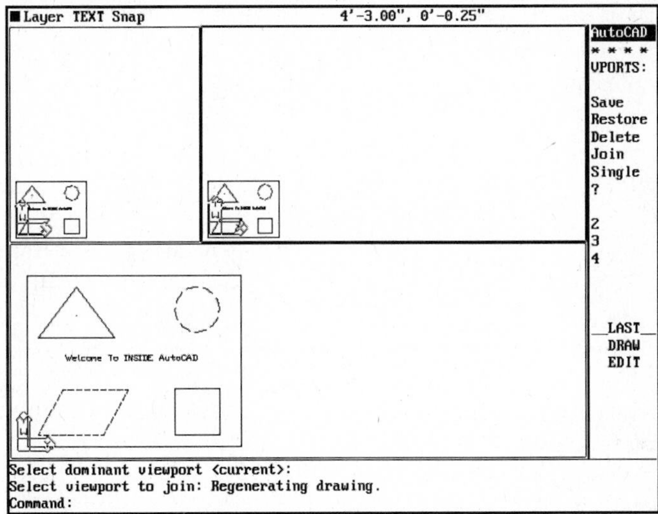

Figure 5.41:

Joining the top left and top center viewports.

All viewports that are being joined inherit the current settings of the dominant viewport.

In the following exercise, you save your viewport configuration, return your drawing to a standard single-viewport display, and restore the named viewport configuration.

Saving a VPORT Configuration

`Command:` **`VPORTS`** ↵	
`Save/Restore/Delete/Join/SIngle/ ?/2/<3>/4:` **`S`**↵	Specifies the Save option
`?/Name for new viewport configuration:` **`BASIC`**↵	Saves the viewport configuration as BASIC
`Command:` *Press Enter*	
`VPORTS`	
`Save/Restore/Delete/Join/SIngle/ ?/2/<3>/4:` **`SI`**↵	Regenerates the drawing with a single viewport
`Command:` *Press Enter*	
`Save/Restore/Delete/Join/SIngle/?/2/ <3>/4:` **`R`**↵	
`?/Name of viewport configuration to restore:` **`BASIC`**↵	
`Regenerating drawing.`	Regenerates the drawing with the BASIC viewport configuration
`Command:` *Quit AutoCAD*	

When you use the SIngle option, the resulting viewport inherits the settings of the current viewport.

You can translate previously saved tiled viewports into mview viewports. To do so, use the Restore option of the MVIEW command while you are in paper space.

Saving and Restoring Mview Viewports

The VPORTS and VIEW commands cannot save and restore mview viewports. When you save and restore named views in paper space, any viewports currently in the views are visible, just like any other entity. If the arrangement of viewports is changed since the view was saved, the former arrangement is not restored. You can, however, save and restore mview viewports by using the BLOCK, INSERT, and MVIEW commands. (The BLOCK and INSERT commands are covered in detail in Chapter 11.)

To save an arrangement of viewports while in paper space, make a block of the viewport entities you want to save by using an insert base point of 0,0 and any name you want.

To restore a previously saved (blocked) arrangement of viewports while in paper space, insert the saved block of the viewport entities by using an insert point of 0,0 and prefacing the name with an asterisk. Then use the MVIEW command to turn them on (they insert turned off) and select all the viewports. Before you insert the saved viewports, you probably want to erase any current viewports. The next chapter includes an exercise with an example of this technique.

To save an arrangement of viewports to use in other drawings, use the WBLOCK command, rather than the BLOCK command. To import viewports into other drawings, use the INSERT and MVIEW commands as previously described. You also can create several groups of viewports in paper space and pan around to the set in which you want to work.

Using REDRAWALL and REGENALL

When you use multiple viewports and you want to redraw or regenerate all the ports, use the REDRAWALL or REGENALL commands. The standard REDRAW and REGEN commands only affect the current viewport. REDRAWALL also can be performed transparently.

You can delete the BASIC and TILEVP drawings because they are not used again in this book.

Summary

AutoCAD offers many ways to get around the AutoCAD display. Display commands frame different aspects of your drawing and viewports give you multiple views. The following tips may help you get around on your display.

ZOOM gives you more (or less) detail. The most common zoom-in method is Window. Window is the most intuitive and convenient way to specify what the next view contains. The most common zoom-out methods are All and Previous, or named views. When zooming out, use ZOOM Dynamic or a view named ALL to get you there in a single step. ZOOM Dynamic enables you to choose your next zoom display view. ZOOM Extents gives you the biggest view possible of your drawing file. Use ZOOM Extents at the end of a drawing session to make sure that you have not drawn outside your limits.

A PAN displacement gives a nearby view while you are still at the same magnification. When moving from one side of the drawing file to another, use ZOOM Dynamic to see the whole view and to help you locate your next view. ZOOM Dynamic is more intuitive than PAN and gives you feedback on how long it takes to generate your requested image. The VIEW command saves and restores zoomed-in windows. Take the time to use names and store views for drawing efficiency.

Watch how often you regenerate your drawing file. A REDRAW cleans up construction and refreshes the image without regenerating the drawing. Remember, VIEWRES optimizes display generation by trading looks for speed. The REGEN command gets you the latest look at what is in the drawing file. Automatic drawing regeneration is controlled by using REGENAUTO.

The time it takes to name and save standard working views and viewport configurations is worthwhile if you are using multiple views. As your drawings become more complex, named views save you time in editing and plotting.

Use mview viewports to see multiple views of your drawing. Use multiple viewports when you need to do detailed (zoomed-in) work while still looking at your whole drawing or when you need to see a schedule or reference part of your drawing.

The next chapter introduces you to editing, which is a new topic. In Chapter 6 you learn how to select entities for editing, learn to use basic editing techniques to modify the drawing, and learn to use a feature that is new in Release 12—grips.

6

Basic Drawing and Editing

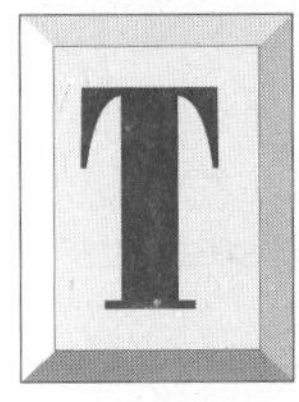

This chapter is designed to teach you how to create a drawing in AutoCAD. If you have worked through the previous chapters, you should be comfortable with the following procedures:

- Opening existing drawing files, as well as naming and saving new files
- Entering commands from the keyboard or choosing them from the pull-down or screen menus
- Using object snaps and coordinate input
- Manipulating the graphics display
- Setting up a drawing file with the proper units, limits, and other common settings

Learning all of these steps may have been more involved than you expected in preparation for CAD drafting. But establishing a solid foundation of good AutoCAD habits prevents you from having to "unlearn" bad habits that come from trying to draw without understanding how AutoCAD was meant to be used. Now comes the part you have been waiting for: creating a real drawing. This chapter focuses on the basic drawing and editing commands that you first use in creating and modifying graphic entities.

A fundamental difference between manual drafting and CAD drafting is that, in manual drafting, the end product is the sheet of paper with the design shown on it. With CAD, the end product is the graphic database, with hard copy plots used as one means of sharing that data with others. Creating a CAD drawing involves the use of graphic entities, such as lines, arcs, and circles. These entities can be edited and changed as needed to contain the exact geometric shape and properties required of them.

A few of the drawing commands and editing-command options are used in this chapter to introduce you to drawing and editing and to illustrate how powerful, yet easy to use, this software is. A single view in Model Space is all that is needed to view a part, but you can use the ZOOM and PAN commands to show the part at a scale that is easiest for you to work with.

Figure 6.1 shows a drawing of the tool plate you work on in this chapter.

Table 6.1 shows the settings for the TOOLPLAT drawing.

The following exercise begins a new drawing called TOOLPLAT. If you are using the IA DISK for a prototype, the settings should be the same as table 6.1. If you are not using the IA DISK, then change your layers and settings to match the table.

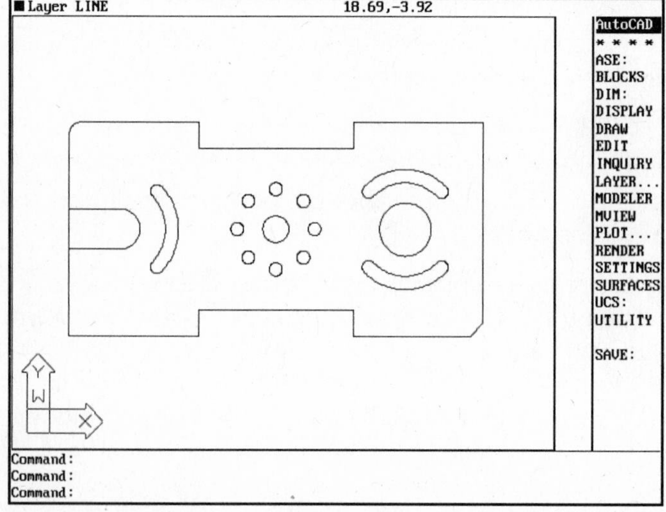

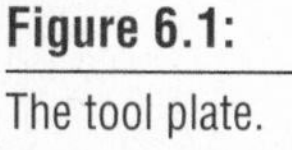
Figure 6.1:
The tool plate.

Table 6.1
TOOLPLAT Drawing Settings

COORDS	*GRID*	*SNAP*	*UCSICON*
On	.5	.25	ORigin

UNITS	All illustrations show decimal units, 2 decimal places, 0 fractional places for angles, default all other settings.
LIMITS	–1,–1 to 20,12 in model space
Viewports	One mview viewport 8.5"×11.0"

Layer Name	*State*	*Color*	*Linetype*
0	On/	7 (White)	CONTINUOUS
ARC	On	4 (Cyan)	CONTINUOUS
LINE	On/Current	2 (Yellow)	CONTINUOUS
CIRCLE	On	1 (Red)	CONTINUOUS

Setting Up the TOOLPLAT Drawing

Start AutoCAD, using the IA.BAT batch program.

Use the NEW command to begin a new drawing named `TOOLPLAT=IA7CHAP6`.

Begin a new drawing called TOOLPLAT *and refer to table 6.1 for the settings.*
Issue a ZOOM with the Extents option.

`Command: MS ↵` Switches to model space

Issue a ZOOM with the All option, then verify the settings shown in table 6.1.

The LINE command is one of the most often-used entity-creation commands in AutoCAD. It can be issued by entering LINE (or L), by choosing Line and an option from the Draw pull-down menu, or by choosing LINE: from the DRAW screen menu.

Using the LINE Command

You already used the LINE command several times in previous chapters, but you have not used all of its options and techniques for drawing lines. If you use the LINE command, AutoCAD records the two endpoints of each line segment. Remember that you can enter points by using the following methods:

- Use the pointer and crosshairs to pick points
- Use snap, ortho, and object snaps to control your point picking
- Enter coordinates at the keyboard: absolute or relative, Cartesian, polar, spherical, or cylindrical

In the following exercises, you practice using object snap and the various forms of typed and picked coordinate entry presented in Chapter 4.

After a line is created from two endpoints (regardless of how they were entered), AutoCAD assumes that you want to continue drawing lines until you end the LINE command and return to the `Command:` prompt.

The LINE command has three useful options: continue, Undo, and Close. The continue option enables you to pick up the last point of the most recent line to start a new line segment. Press Enter in response to the `From point:` prompt to continue. Undo and Close are specified by entering a **U** or a **C** at the `To point:` prompt. Undo eliminates the last line segment of the current command and backs up one point so you can try the line segment again. Close makes a polygon by drawing a segment from your last endpoint, closing it to the first point of the line series drawn by the current LINE command.

Choosing Line from the Draw pull-down menu offers several choices. The Segments item (which issues the default LINE command) continues to prompt for additional endpoints, while the 1 Segment option exits after a single line is drawn. The Double Lines option uses a LISP routine to create double lines at a specified width. (See Chapter 12 for its use.)

In the next exercise, use the Line options in the Draw pull-down menu to draw part of the perimeter of the tool plate. Use a mixture of absolute coordinate entry, relative point selection, and polar selection. Your drawing should look like figure 6.2 when you finish the exercise.

Using the LINE Command

`Command:` *Choose* Settings, *then* Layer Control	Opens the Layer Control dialog box
Select the LINE *layer, then click on* Current, *then choose* OK	Makes LINE the current layer
`Command:` *Choose* Draw, *then* Line, *then* Segments	Issues the default LINE command (multiple segments)
`_line From point:` **`0,0`**↵	Starts the line with an absolute coordinate
`To point:` **`5,0`**↵	Specifies an absolute coordinate and draws a line
`To point:` **`@0,1`**↵	Draws relative to the last point
`To point:` **`@6<0`**↵	Specifies a relative polar point
`To point:` *Pick the relative polar point 2.00<270*	Draws a 2" line at 270 degrees
`To point:` **`U`**↵	Removes the last line
`To point:` *Pick the relative polar point 1.00<270*	Draws a 1" line at 270 degrees
`To point:` *Pick the relative polar point 4.50<0*	Draws a 4.5" line at 0 degrees
`To point:` **`@.5,.5`**↵	Draws a .5" chamfer
`To point:` *Press Enter*	Ends the LINE command

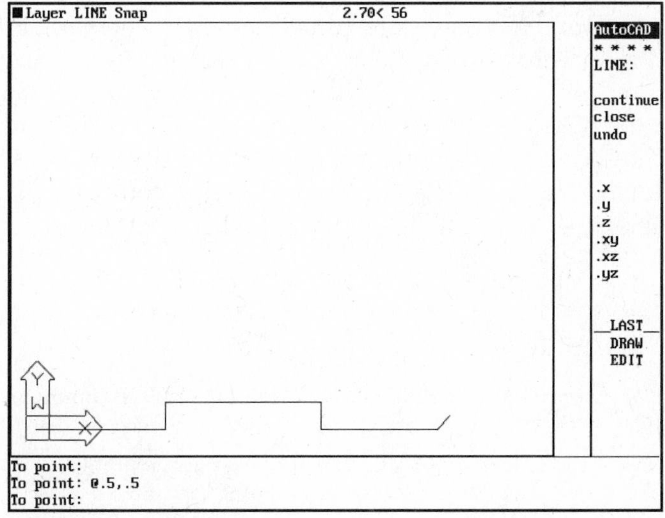

Figure 6.2:

The tool plate perimeter started with LINE.

The Undo option is a very convenient method of stepping back, one line segment at a time, during the LINE command. Each time U is entered or Undo is chosen, AutoCAD backs up one segment. This can be done several times in a row. After the LINE command is ended, a U or UNDO command undoes all the segments created during the previous command.

Before continuing with the tool plate perimeter, take a moment to examine the options for the LINE command.

LINE Options

The following list summarizes the LINE command options:

- **Continue.** Choose the continue option from the screen menu or press Enter at the `From point:` prompt to continue a line from the endpoint of the most recent previously drawn line or arc.
- **Close.** Enter C (Close) or choose Close from the screen menu at the `To point:` prompt to close a series of line segments. This option creates a line from the last segment's endpoint to the first point of the series.
- **Undo.** Press U at the `To point:` prompt to undo the last line segment, back to the previous point.

You can keep undoing as long as you are in the LINE command and have not exited the command by pressing Enter, the spacebar, or Ctrl-C.

Next, complete the perimeter of the tool plate using the LINE command. Instead of the pull-down menu, however, use a combination of the screen menu and command line to issue and control the LINE command. Your completed perimeter should look like figure 6.3 when completed.

Using a Variety of Line Methods

`Command:` *From the screen menu, choose* DRAW, *then* LINE:	Starts the LINE command
`_LINE From point:` *Press Enter*	Uses the last point as a starting point
`To point:` **16,8↵**	
`To point:` **11,8↵**	

`To point:` *Pick the relative polar point 1.00<270*

`To point:` *Pick the relative polar point 6.00<180*

`To point:` **`@1<90`**↵

`To point:` *Pick the relative polar point 5.00<180*

`To point:` *Enter* `C` *or, from the screen menu, choose* close	Closes to the first point in the series

The line closes to the first point in the previous command series, not to the beginning of your perimeter as you may have expected.

`Command:` **`U`**↵	Undoes all lines from the previous LINE command
`Command:` **`REDO`**↵	Brings back the lines
`Command:` *Choose* Modify, *then* Erase, *then* Single	Starts the ERASE command with the Single option
`_erase Select objects: si`	
`Select objects:` *Pick the last diagonal line*	Erases the line and ends the ERASE command
`Command:` **`LINE`**↵	Starts the LINE command
`From point:` *From the pop-up menu, choose* Endpoint	Selects the ENDP object snap
`endp of` *Pick at ① (see fig. 6.3)*	
`To point:` *From the pop-up menu, choose* Endpoint, *then pick at ②*	Draws the last line
`To point:` *Press Enter*	Ends the LINE command

Use the PAN command to position the tool plate at the center of the viewport.

`Command:` **`QSAVE`**↵	Saves the drawing

NOTE

Any time you draw a few line segments and want to close them into an irregular polygon, use Close. (Close creates a closed series of line entities; to make a regular polygon as a single polyline entity, use the POLYGON command. See Chapter 7 for more details.) Just press Enter or Ctrl-C at the `To point:` prompt if you want to terminate the command without closing to the first point.

In later exercises, you draw the slot at the left of the tool plate, add fillets to the upper corners, and chamfer the lower left corner. For now, you need to learn the ARC and CIRCLE commands.

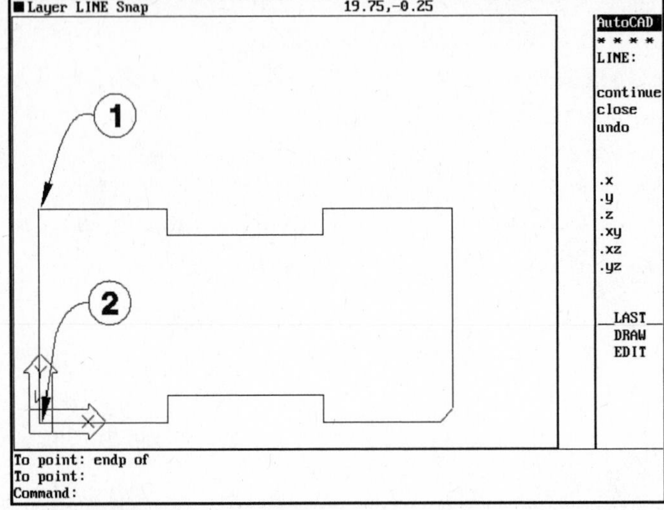

Figure 6.3:

The completed tool plate perimeter.

Creating Circles and Arcs

Unlike lines, circle and arc entities require more than two simple endpoints. You can create arcs and circles in at least a dozen different ways. Regardless of the parameters (like endpoints, angles, directions, or chords) that you enter to create the entity, arcs and circles are stored as the simplest possible geometry. A circle is stored as a center point and a radius. An arc is a center point, a radius, a start angle, and an end angle. Using this geometric information, AutoCAD can regenerate accurate curves at the best possible resolution and smoothness that your system can display or plot.

Getting To Know Circles

If you choose the Circle option from the Draw pull-down menu, AutoCAD displays a child menu that lists five circle creation methods. Why so many? Different drafting tasks provide different information about where circles should go. Most often, you know the center point and the radius or diameter. In these cases, you use this information to create the circle. The following list contains the circle options:

- **Center point.** Type or pick the center point, and CIRCLE prompts for a diameter or radius. This option is the default.

- **Diameter.** Use this option to enter a distance or pick two points to show a distance for the diameter.
- **Radius.** Use this option to enter a distance or pick two points to show a distance for the radius.
- **3P.** Use this option to specify the circumference with three points.
- **2P.** Use this option to specify two diameter points on the circumference.
- **TTR.** Use this option to select two lines, circles, or arcs that form tangents to the circle, and then specify the circle's radius.

As demonstrated in figure 6.4, you can create a circle in at least five ways. Which method do you choose? If you know whether you have a radius, diameter, or points, you can pick the correct option from the menu. If you do not have this information, entering the CIRCLE command from the keyboard enables you to pick your options in midstream.

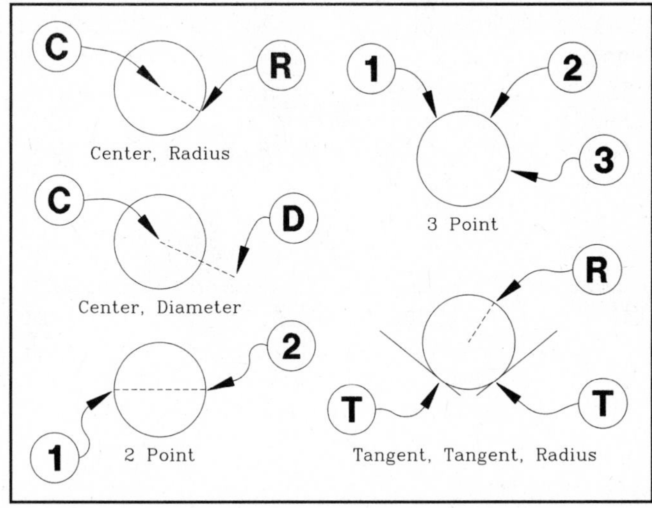

Figure 6.4:
Five different ways to draw circles.

Notice the difference between Center point/Diameter and 2P. Both options enable you to specify a diameter, but if you pick the second point with Center point/Diameter, it merely shows the diameter's distance, and the circle does not draw through the point. If you pick two points with 2P, you see a circle appear between those two points with the distance as the diameter. 2P enables you to draw a diameter circle the way most people intuitively think about diameter.

In the next exercise, you draw a few circles using the Center, Radius option for the first circle and Center, Diameter for the second circle. Figure 6.5 shows what your drawing should look like after the next exercise.

Using the CIRCLE Command

Continue with the TOOLPLAT drawing from the previous exercise.

`Command:` *Choose* Settings, *then* Layers, *and make the* CIRCLE *layer current*	
`Command:` *Choose* Draw, *then* Circle, *then* Center, Radius	Starts the CIRCLE command
`_circle 3P/2P/TTR/<Center point>:` *Pick or enter point 8.00,4.00*	Specifies the circle's center
`Diameter/<Radius>: .5`↵	Draws a circle with a .5" radius
`Command:` *Choose* Draw, *then* Circle, *then* Center, Diameter	Issues the CIRCLE command with the Diameter option
`_circle 3P/2P/TTR/<Center point>:` *Pick or enter point 13.00,4.00*	Specifies the circle's center
`Diameter/<Radius>: <.50> _dia Diameter <1.00>: 2`↵	Draws a circle with a 2" diameter

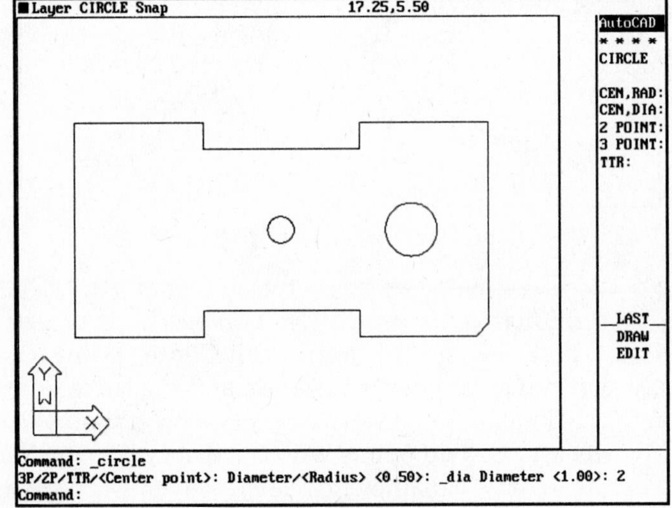

Figure 6.5:

Circles added to the tool plate.

If you pick a center point with the Center, Radius option, AutoCAD gives you the option of selecting a radius or diameter. If you pick a coordinate as the radius, as you did for the first circle, you get a circle through the radius point. Enter **D** instead to show the diameter prompt. Picking a coordinate then gives you a circle by the center point/diameter method. If you select the Circle, Diameter option, AutoCAD automatically enters the diameter option for you.

If you enter **2P**, **3P**, or **TTR** at the center point prompt, you get one of those options, and AutoCAD prompts you for the necessary points to complete the circle.

You also can access the CIRCLE command from AutoCAD's DRAW screen menu or from the command line. Use CIRCLE in the screen menu along with the 2P and 3P options to draw a few more circles. Figure 6.7 shows the result of the next exercise.

Drawing 2-Point and 3-Point Circles

`Command:` *From the screen menu, choose* AutoCAD, *then* DRAW, *then* CIRCLE, *then* 2 POINT:	Starts the CIRCLE command with the 2P option
`_CIRCLE 3P/2P/TTR/<Center point>: _2P` `First point on diameter:` *Pick or enter absolute point 9.25,4.00*	Specifies the first point on the diameter
`Second point on diameter: DRAG`	Automatically uses the DRAG option to request the second point
Pick or enter point 9.75,4.00	Draws a .5" circle
`Command:` *Use ZOOM and pick window points ① and ② (see fig. 6.6)*	Zooms in on the hole pattern
`Command:` *From the* DRAW *screen menu, choose* CIRCLE 3 POINT:	Starts the CIRCLE command with the 3P option
`_CIRCLE 3P/2P/TTR/<Center point>: _3P` `First point:` *Pick or enter point 7.75,2.50*	Specifies the first point on the diameter
`Second point:` *Pick or enter point 8.00,2.25*	Specifies the second point on the diameter
`Third point: DRAG`	Issues the DRAG option to request a third point

Drag the cursor to dynamically resize the circle, then pick or enter point 8.25,2.5 to complete the circle (see fig. 6.7).

`Command: U↵`	Undoes the last circle

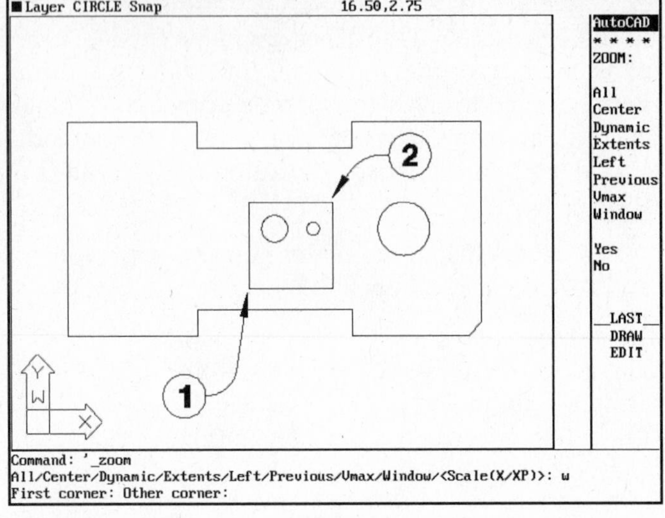

Figure 6.6:

Zoom points for the circles.

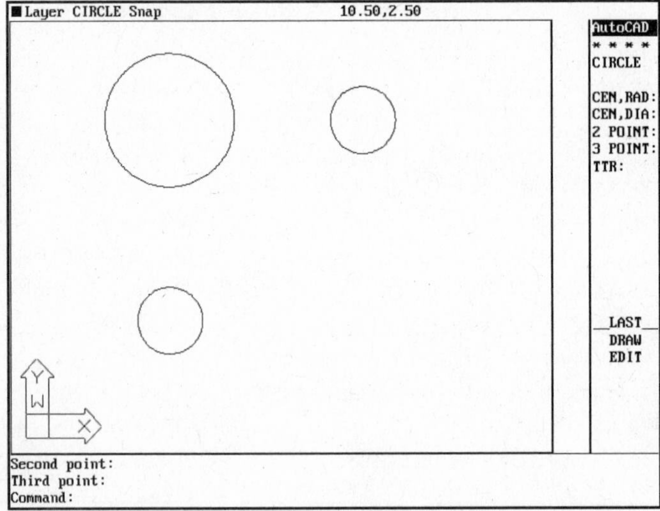

Figure 6.7:

Circles drawn with the 2P and 3P options.

Although the menu automatically issued the DRAG option, it is not necessary because drag is on by default. You also can issue the CIRCLE command and options from the AutoCAD command prompt or use the **C** shortcut command. Use this method, along with the TTR option, to draw a few more circles.

Using the TTR Circle Option

`Command:` *Perform a ZOOM with the Previous option*	Displays the entire tool plate
`Command:` **`CIRCLE`**↵	Starts the CIRCLE command
`3P/2P/TTR/<Center point>:` **`T`**↵	Specifies the TTR option
`Enter Tangent spec:` *Pick the line at point ① in figure 6.8*	Selects the first tangent line
`Enter second Tangent spec:` *Pick the line at point ②*	Selects the second tangent line
`Radius <0.25>:` **`.5`**↵	Draws a 1" circle tangent to the two lines
`Command:` **`C`**↵	Issues the CIRCLE command
`3P/2P/TTR/<Center point>:` **`T`**↵	Specifies the TTR option
`Enter Tangent spec:` *Pick the line at point ② (see fig. 6.8)*	Selects the first tangent line
`Enter second Tangent spec:` *Pick the line at point ③*	Selects the second tangent line
`Radius <0.50>:` *Press Enter*	Uses the default to draw a tangent circle

Save the drawing

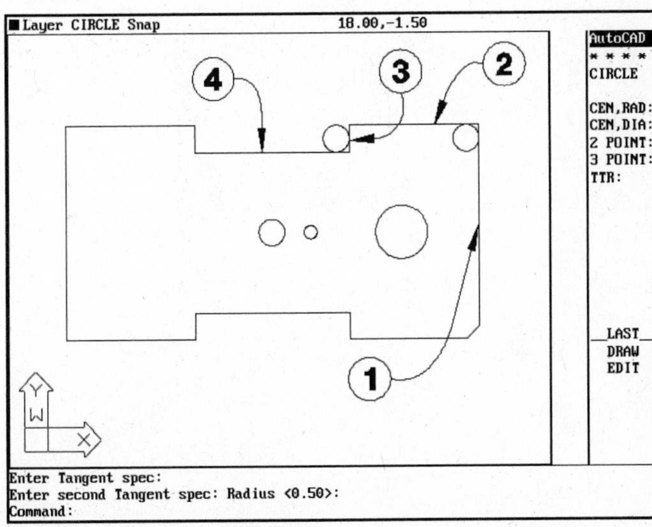

Figure 6.8:

Circles drawn using the TTR option.

It would really be much easier to use the FILLET command instead of the CIRCLE command with the TTR option, but it was good practice using the CIRCLE command. You often find that there are several ways to accomplish a task in AutoCAD, and you must decide which one seems the easiest for you.

The CIRCLE command has many options, depending on what information you have about the circle. When using AutoCAD properly, you never need to calculate (or worse yet, guess) the information for correctly drawing a circle. Using the proper option and the right object snaps should give you a very accurate circle. You later learn how to trim and break apart circles; however, it is sometimes easier just to draw an arc. Arcs are explained in the following section.

Using Three-Point Arcs

If you thought there are many ways to create circles, there are even more ways to create arcs; and AutoCAD offers nearly every possible geometric method for creating them.

The most straightforward way to create arcs is with the three-point default of the ARC command. It works about the same way as a three-point circle. The first point is the arc's beginning; the second and third points define the arc's curve. The last point and first point define the chord of the arc. AutoCAD automatically drags the arc, unless you have turned drag off. You can turn drag off using the DRAGMODE system variable.

The ARC command can be issued from the DRAW screen menu, accessed from the Draw pull-down menu, or entered at the `Command:` prompt. The pull-down menu has a child menu, much like the CIRCLE command, with all of the options listed.

Draw the arc for the guide slot at the left of the tool plate using a three-point arc (see fig. 6.9).

Drawing 3-Point Arcs

Make ARC the current layer

`Command:` *Choose* Draw, *then* Arc, *then* 3-point	Issues the ARC command
`_arc Center/<Start point>:` *Pick or enter point 2.00,3.25*	Starts the arc

`Center/End/<Second point>:` *Pick or enter point 2.75,4.00*	Picks a second point

Move the cursor on the screen, noting how the arc drags from the first point through the second point.

`End point:` *Pick or enter point 2.00,4.75*	Draws the arc

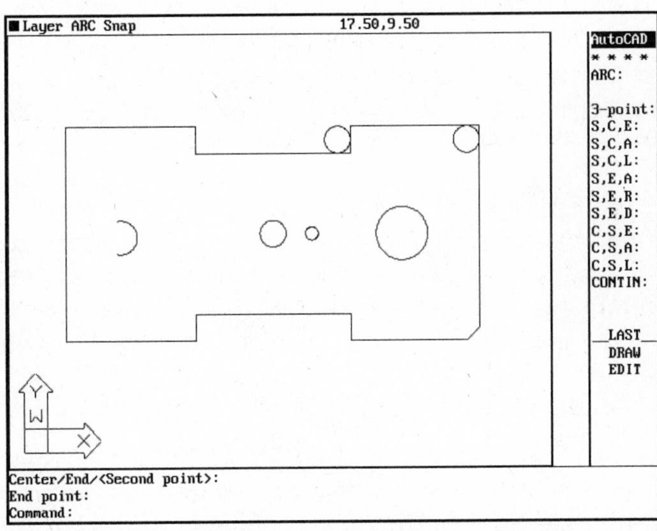

Figure 6.9:

A three-point arc for the guide slot.

Make sure that you feel comfortable with the way AutoCAD uses drag to help you decide where the three-point arc is going to fall. After you enter the first two points, drag is automatically turned on by the menu item. When the DRAGMODE command is set to Auto, which is the default, drag helps you see the results of the command before it is finished. Experiment by dragging the crosshairs during drawing and editing commands.

Next, draw the fillet for the upper left corner of the tool plate using the Start, Center, End option. Instead of using the pull-down menu option, however, use the AutoCAD command line to experiment with the ARC prompts.

Drawing Arcs with Start, Center, End

`Command: ARC ↵`	
`_ARC Center/<Start point>:` *Pick or enter point 0.50,8.00*	Begins the arc
`Center/End/<Second point>: C↵`	Specifies the Center option
`Center:` *Pick point 0.50,7.50*	Specifies the center point

Move the cursor, noting how the arc dynamically follows the third point.

`Angle/Length of chord/<End point>:` *Pick relative polar point 0.50<180*	Draws the arc

As shown in the previous exercise, you can enter points by typing coordinates or by picking from the screen with the help of the coordinate display. Remember the first rule of using AutoCAD: read the command prompt. When you use commands with as many options as ARC offers, reading the default prompt and the available options is the only way to know what type of data AutoCAD is looking for. In many cases, a coordinate can be entered for the default response or another option can be chosen. These options are explained more fully in the following section.

The ARC command has eight options: the default start point, continue, Center, End point, Angle, Radius, Direction, and Length of chord. These options can be grouped by common functions (see fig. 6.10) to provide ten ways to draw arcs. Try some of these arc options on your SCRATCH layer.

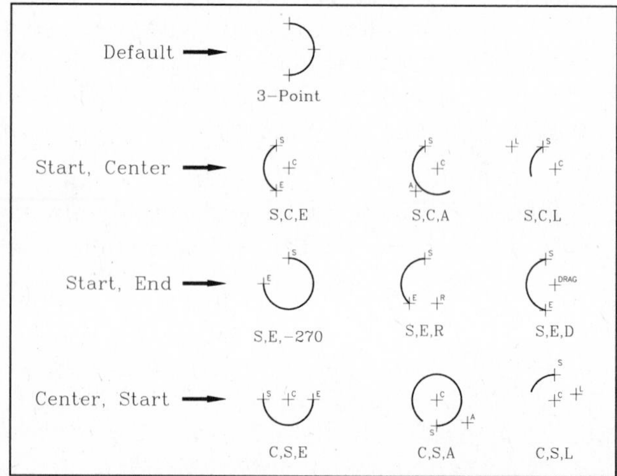

Figure 6.10:
Ten different ways to draw arcs.

Using the Arc Options

There are several different options for drawing arcs, and some of those options have variations that enable you to choose the easiest order of input. An example of that input order is center—start—end versus start—center—end. The following list explains some of the arc options.

- **3-Point.** This option creates an arc that passes through three specified points. The first point is the start point, the third point is the endpoint, and the second point is any other point lying on the arc.
- **Start,Center.** This option requires an arc starting point and the center point of the arc. This option group has a third parameter, which completes the arc by specifying an endpoint, an angle, or a length of chord.
- **Start,End.** This option enables you to define the starting and ending points of the arc first, and then to define how the arc is to be drawn. You define the arc with an angle, radius, direction, or center point.
- **Center,Start**. This option enables you to first identify the center of the arc, and then the start point. The arc is completed by supplying an angle, length of chord, or endpoint.
- **Continue.** This option is a further default—invoked by pressing Enter at the first arc prompt or by choosing CONTIN from the arc screen menu—that starts a new arc tangent to the last line or arc drawn. Similarly, pressing Enter at the first prompt of the LINE command starts a new line at the end of the last arc.

You can select any of the ten arc methods from the pull-down, screen, or tablet menus. The options are abbreviated by mnemonic letters. If you are entering arc commands from the keyboard, you find the commands have common beginnings according to their class (Start,Center; Start,End; Center,Start; and so on).

You can choose your options midstream and select one arc-creation method over another by entering ARC and the options from the keyboard. If you begin an arc with a picked point, your construction methods narrow to those that begin with Start; if you begin with C, AutoCAD restricts you to options that accept the center point first, and so on.

To finish your examination of the ARC command, use the Angle option, polar point specification, and the CONTINUE: screen menu item to draw one of the radial slots on the tool plate. When you have completed the slot, add a line to the guide slot at the left of the tool plate.

Drawing Arcs with Angles, Polar, and Continue

`Command:` *From the screen menu, choose* C,S,A:	Issues ARC with the Center, Start, and Angle options
`_ARC Center/<Start point>: _C Center:` *Pick or enter point 13.00,4.00*	Locates the arc's center
`Start point:` **`@2.25<225`**↵	Locates the arc's start point
`Angle/Length of chord/<End point>: _A` `Included angle: DRAG`	Menu issues Angle and DRAG options

Move the cursor, noting that graphical included angle input is measured from zero degrees, not from the start of the arc.

`Included angle:` **`90`**↵	Draws the arc
`Command:` *From the screen menu, choose* CONTIN:	Issues ARC with the Continue option
`_ARC Center/<Start point>:` `End point: DRAG`	Continues the arc from the end of the last arc drawn

Move the cursor, noting that the dynamic arc is always tangent to the previous arc.

`End point:` **`@.5<135`**↵	Draws the arc
`Command:` *Press Enter*	Repeats the ARC command
`_ARC Center/<Start point>:` **`C`**↵	Specifies the Center option
`Center:` *Pick or enter point 13.00,4.00*	Locates the center
`Start point:` *From the pop-up menu, choose* Endpoint, *and pick at ① (see fig. 6.11)*	Locates the start point
`Angle/Length of chord/<End point>:` **`A`**↵	Specifies the Angle option
`Included angle:` **`-90`**↵	Draws the arc clockwise

Next, continue with another tangent arc.

`Command:` *From the screen menu, choose* CONTIN:	
`Endpoint: DRAG` *From the pop-up menu, choose* End point, *then pick ②*	Closes the slot with another arc
`Command:` **`L`**↵	Issues LINE command
`From point:` *Pick or enter point 2.00,4.75*	Starts the line
`To point:` *From the pop-up menu, choose* Perpendicular, *then pick ③*	Draws a line
`To point:` *Press Enter*	Ends the LINE command

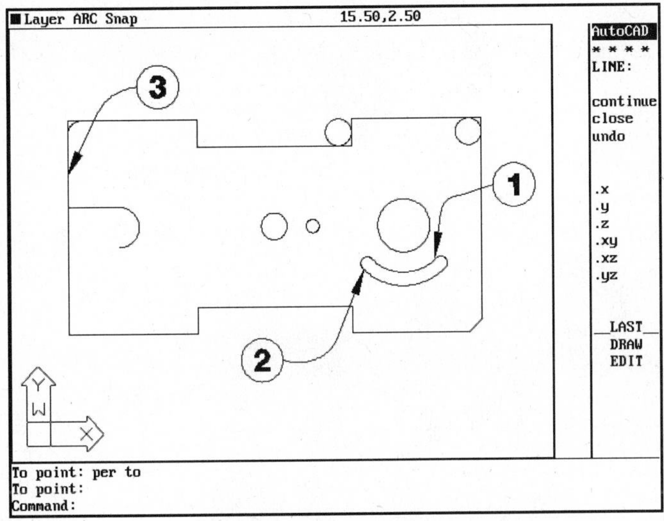

Figure 6.11:

The slots added to the tool plate.

Instead of trying to memorize every option of the ARC command, try to understand what combinations of data—start point, center point, radius, and so on—are needed to define an arc. Usually three pieces of data must be given for AutoCAD to accurately draw an arc. The reason so many options are given is to make sure that you can describe the arc based on the information you have, without having to calculate or guess at unknown information.

Your TOOLPLAT drawing is far from complete, but you are now familiar with all of the options for the LINE, ARC, and CIRCLE commands and have used many of these options in the TOOLPLAT drawing. You may feel, however, that the order and manner in which you created the drawing was a bit haphazard. Actually, it was by design. Now you can experiment with some of the very powerful features that are new to AutoCAD in Release 12—autoediting and grips—to complete the TOOLPLAT drawing.

Using Grips and Autoediting Modes

The remainder of this chapter explains and demonstrates some of the editing techniques you need to finish the drawing. In CAD drafting, editing means much more than erasing entities or correcting mistakes. Editing commands are often used in conjunction with entity-creation commands to make your drawings easy to create, yet very accurate. AutoCAD's editing commands have many options suitable for different situations. The following exercises introduce the basic options of each editing command, using the autoediting method with grip controls.

Think of *grips* in AutoCAD as being convenient locations on each entity to help control and manipulate that entity. Each entity has several grip points which can be chosen very accurately (without specifying object snap modes) by picking in the grip box. For instance, the grip points on a line are the endpoints and the midpoint (see fig. 6.12). When the GRIPS system variable is set to 1 (on—the default), the grips appear on an entity when that entity is selected at the `Command:` prompt.

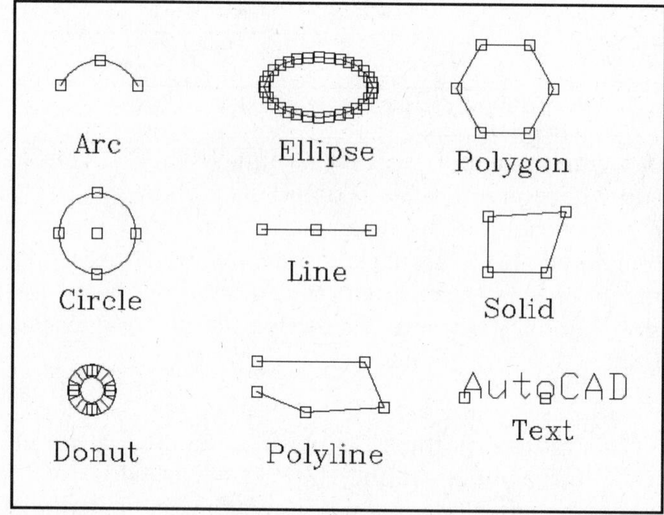

Figure 6.12:
Common entity grip locations.

When you click on a visible grip, it becomes "hot" (selected) and displays highlighted. A hot grip becomes a base point for one of the autoediting modes to manipulate the entity. *Autoediting modes* are a special group of common editing commands that are available when a base grip is chosen. These modes are briefly explained in the following list.

- **Stretch.** The stretch mode enables entities to be modified by moving one or more grips to another location while leaving the other part of the entity in its original location. This can easily change the size or shape of an entity or a group of entities. In some cases, the stretch mode moves an entity.

- **Move.** The move mode relocates entities from a base point to another specified location. The size and orientation does not change.
- **Rotate.** This mode enables objects to be rotated around a specified base point. The angle can be entered or specified by dragging.
- **Scale.** The scale mode enables entities to be scaled up or down by a given scale factor about a specified base point. Scale factors can be directly entered, dragged to size, or given, using the reference option.
- **Mirror.** Selected entities can be mirrored about a line formed by the base point grip and another selected point.

All of these autoediting modes have several things in common. First of all, when entities are selected and a base grip is chosen to issue the command, you can choose the proper mode by entering the first two letters of the mode (SC for scale, for example) or by pressing Enter or the spacebar to switch between the modes. If you want to make a copy while executing an autoediting mode, use the copy option or hold down the shift key while making multiple second point picks. The Undo option undoes the last edit, and the eXit option exits the autoediting modes. These modes are similar to the commands, such as STRETCH and MOVE, which are discussed in the next chapter.

The following exercises introduce you to selecting and editing entities using grips. Zoom in on the upper left corner of the tool plate and stretch the top and side lines to the ends of the arc to form a proper fillet for the corner.

Stretching Lines with Grips

Continue with the TOOLPLAT drawing from the previous exercises and use ZOOM with the Window option to show the drawing area.

`Command:` **`GRIPS`**↵	Accesses GRIPS system variable
`New value for GRIPS <0>:` **`1`**↵	Turns on grips
`Command:` *Turn on Snap by pressing F9*	
`Command:` *Pick a point on the upper left arc*	Selects and highlights the arc and displays its grips points
`Command:` *Pick line at ① (see fig. 6.13)*	Selects and highlights the top line, and displays grips
`Command:` *Pick grip at ②*	Enters stretching autoediting mode
`** STRETCH **` `<Stretch to point>/Base point/Copy/ Undo/eXit:` *Pick arc's grip at ③*	Stretches the line to the arc endpoint

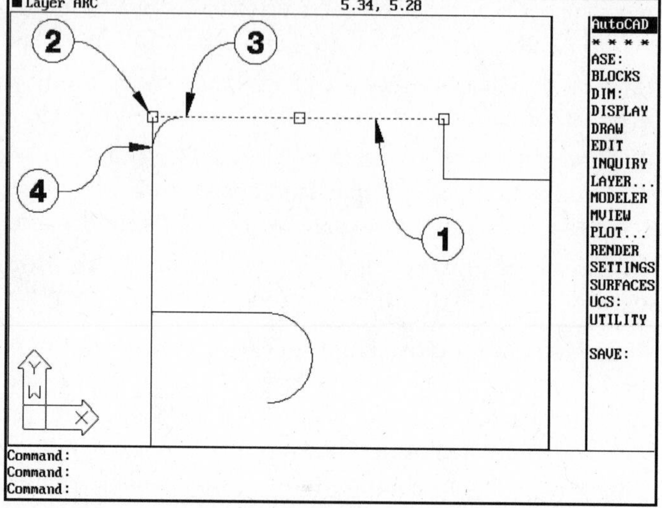

Figure 6.13:

Grip points and pick points.

NOTE: If you miss the entity when picking, a rubber-band box (a window) appears from the pick point. Pick again at the same point, and then try again. Window selection is covered later in this chapter.

The previous exercise could have used the End point object snap to lock the line onto the endpoint of the arc. Because the cursor automatically snaps to grips, however, there is generally no need to use object snaps when editing with grips. (Some entities do not provide grips for certain object snaps, so you need to use object snaps occasionally.) The trick to eliminating object snaps for editing, and even for drawing, is to first select the entities to snap to as well as the entities to edit, which displays all their grips. Then, click on the grips of the entities to edit, which makes their autoedit grips hot. You then can snap to any of the displayed grips without using object snap modes. The hot grips remain hot until the autoedit operation is completed or canceled by pressing Ctrl-C. All the grips remain displayed until you enter a command or press Ctrl-C at the `Command:` prompt.

Depending on the autoediting mode being used, either only hot entities or all highlighted entities are affected. To better control editing with grips, you must understand AutoCAD's selection settings and methods. The next section explains them.

Controlling GRIPS and Selection Parameters

Remember that the GRIPS system variable must be on for autoediting modes to function. The Grips dialog box can be displayed by the DDGRIP command or by choosing Grips from the Settings pull-down menu. Putting a check mark in the Enable Grips check box turns on the GRIPS system variable; clearing the box turns it off. The grip size, which works similarly to object snap aperture size, can easily be adjusted with the slider bar. The color of both displayed and selected grips also can be specified in this dialog box.

Controlling Selection with DDSELECT

Two other settings, Use Shift to Add and Press and Drag, improve the versatility and interaction of editing with grips. They are found in another dialog box called Entity Selection Settings (see fig. 6.14). The DDSELECT command brings up this dialog box, or you can choose Selection Settings from the Settings menu. The other settings in this dialog box are covered in Chapter 8.

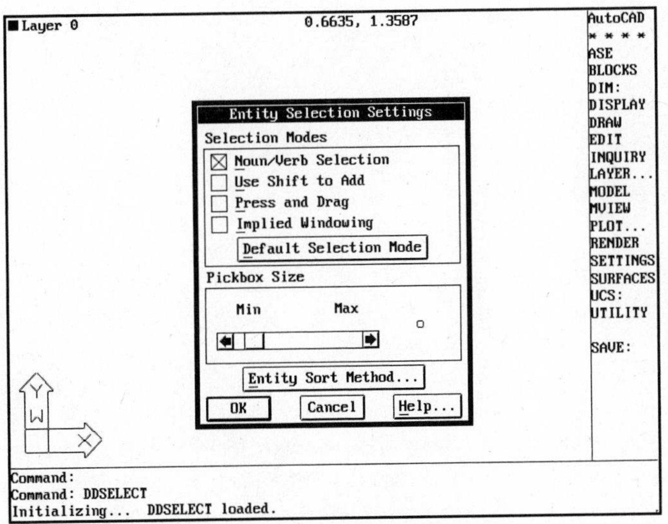

Figure 6.14:

The Entity Selection Settings dialog box.

AutoCAD editing modes and commands operate on a *selection set* of entities that you select. The current selection is generally indicated by highlighting the entities. The Use Shift to Add setting controls how entities are added to the selection set (the same as the PICKADD system variable). When this is on, (1—the default), entities are added to the selection set as they are selected. When this is off (0), newly selected entities replace the existing selection set, unless you hold down the shift key as you select them. Whether PICKADD is on or off, holding down Shift and selecting currently highlighted entities removes those entities from the selection set. To add entities when PICKADD is off, hold down the shift key while selecting entities. Experiment with using PICKADD off in the following exercise.

Controlling Selection

Continue with the TOOLPLAT drawing from the previous exercise.

`Command:` *Pick any entity*	Highlights the entity and starts a selection set
`Command:` *Pick two other entities*	Highlights the entities and adds them to the set
`Command:` *Shift-pick one of the highlighted entities*	Removes the entity from the set
`Command:` *Choose* Settings, *then* Selection Settings	Displays the Entity Selection Settings dialog box
Put a check mark in the Use Shift to Add *check box, then choose* OK	Turns PICKADD off (0) and exits
`Command:` *Pick any entity*	Clears the selection set (leaving grips on) and starts a new set
`Command:` *Pick any other entity*	Clears the selection set again and starts another new set
`Command:` *Shift-pick two other entities*	Adds the entities to the existing set
`Command:` *Shift-pick a highlighted entity*	Removes the entity from the set

When you are selecting entities, it is obvious whether PICKADD is off or on. How you have it set really depends on your personal preference, but once you are used to it, you will probably find it more versatile to have it off. Remember to use the shift key to unselect entities or, when PICKADD is off, to select additional entities.

The exercises throughout the rest of this book assume that PICKADD is off.

As an alternative to pressing Ctrl-C to clear a selection set or to clear grips (press twice to clear both), you can pick in a clear area of the screen to clear the selection set or remove grips from the screen. When you do so, you are actually selecting a window or crossing-window of empty space in the drawing to clear the selection set. You must pick twice. If your first pick finds an entity, it selects the entity. If, however, the first pick misses, it sets the base corner of a rubber-banded window or crossing box. A second pick completes the window or crossing selection. A window selects all entities totally enclosed within its box; a crossing selects all entities within the box or that cross its box. You pick window points left-to-right, and the rubber-band box is shown solid; you pick crossing points right-to-left, and the rubber-band box is dashed. If the selection set is already empty, or if you just emptied it with a window or crossing selection of empty space, making another window or crossing selection removes all grips from the display. The following exercise demonstrates this technique.

Clearing the Selection Set and Grips

Continue with the TOOLPLAT drawing from the previous exercise. You should have a few entities selected.

`Command:` *Pick points ① and ② (see fig. 6.15)*	Clears the selection set
`Command:` *Pick points ① and ② again*	Clears the grip markers from the screen

The previous exercise should have cleared the grip boxes from the screen. This often needs to be done to keep the drawing area from becoming to cluttered.

Window and crossing selections, including clearing a selection set and grips using the preceding method, are easier if you change the way AutoCAD makes window and crossing selections. The next section explains why.

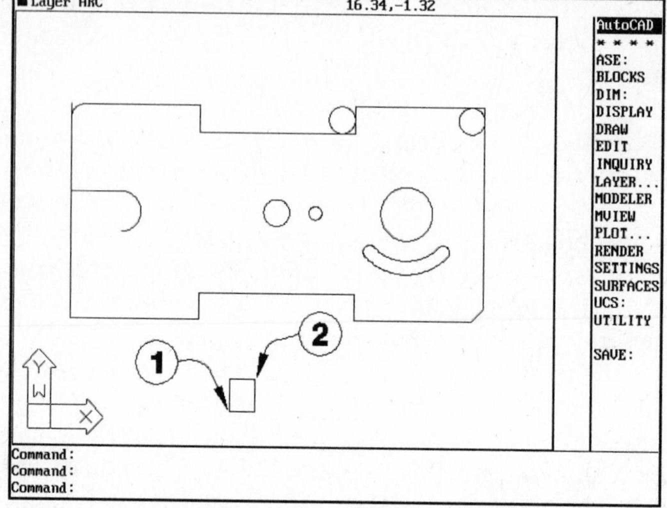

Figure 6.15:

Selecting empty space.

Controlling Press and Drag

Prior to Release 12, AutoCAD always required two picks to show a window. Most software using a graphical interface enables window selection by pressing and holding the button at the first point, dragging to the second point, and then releasing the button. The Entity Selection Settings dialog box now offers a choice in the way a window or crossing is specified. When the Press and Drag box is checked (the PICKDRAG system variable is on, set to 1), a window is created by pressing the pick button, moving to the other corner of the window, and releasing. Even if you are used to the old two-pick method, once you get used to Press and Drag you will find it faster and more efficient. It also behaves the same as other software you may use and enables you to clear selection sets or grips with a single pick. Try this technique in the next exercise.

Controlling Click and Release

`Command: DDSELECT↵`	Displays the Entity Selection Settings dialog box
Put a check mark in the Press and Drag *checkbox, then choose* <u>O</u>K	Turns on PICKDRAG and exits
`Command:` *Click and hold button 1 at ① (see fig. 6.16), drag to ②, and release button 1*	Creates a crossing window selection

`Command:` *Click and hold button 1 at ③, drag to ④, and release*	Creates an enclosed window selection, clears the previous selection set, and starts a new set
`Command:` *Click once in empty space*	Clears the selection set
`Command:` *Click again in empty space*	Removes grip markers

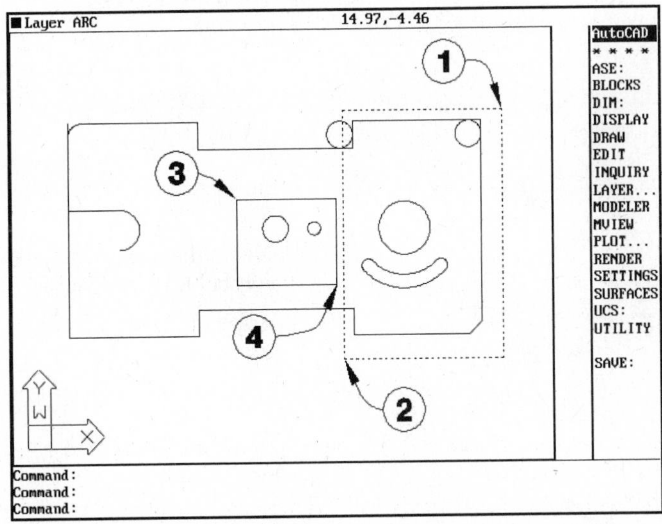

Figure 6.16: Selection points for click and release.

NOTE

Throughout the rest of the book, Press and Drag (PICKDRAG 1) is the default window/crossing selection mode. The exercises direct you to use a crossing or window selection—remember to use the click/hold/drag technique to select as directed.

Controlling Aperture Size

The pickbox size that appears on the crosshairs can easily be adjusted by clicking on and dragging the box on the horizontal slider in the Entity Selection Settings dialog box. It also can be set using the PICKBOX system variable or chosen from the APERTUR: option of the SETTINGS screen menu. The size is called out in pixels and usually ranges between 5 and 15, depending on your graphics resolution. Use whatever is comfortable for your display and pointing device.

Editing with the Autoediting Modes

Now that you have an understanding of GUI Selection Syntax and Click and Release options, you are ready to put them to work to simplify your editing tasks. The following exercises continue the use of stretch autoediting mode and show you how to snap to specific points by using just grips. This can be a great time saver over using the regular object snaps and usually involves fewer steps.

Continue with the TOOLPLAT drawing from the previous exercise.

`Command:` *Pick the arc at ① (see fig. 6.17)*	Selects the arc and displays its grips
`Command:` *Pick line at ②*	Clears the previous set, selects the vertical line, and shows grips
`Command:` *Pick grip at ③*	Grips the line and enters stretch mode
`** STRETCH **`	
`<Stretch to point>/Base point/Copy/ Undo/eXit:` *Pick the lower left grip on the arc at ① in fig. 6.18*	Snaps the line to the arc endpoint

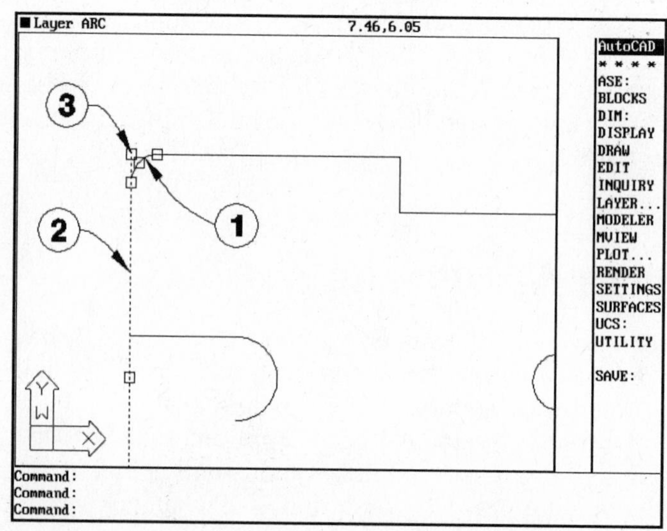

Figure 6.17:
Grip and entity selection points.

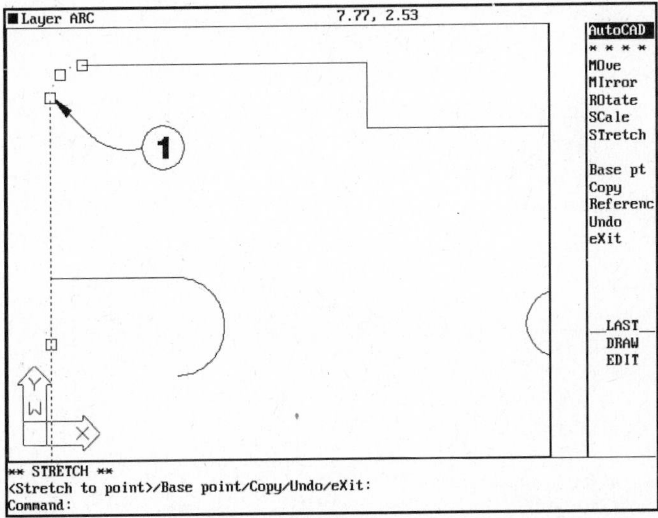

Figure 6.18:

TOOLPLAT after stretching lines.

The stretch autoediting mode affects other entities as well. With a few exceptions, which depend on which grip you pick, the Stretch autoediting mode changes the shape of entities. In the next exercise, you change one of the arcs in the radial slot.

Stretching Arcs with Autoedit

Zoom to the previous view with ZOOM P.

`Command:` *Pick the lower arc of the radial slot at ① (see fig. 6.19)*	Selects the arc and displays grips
`Command:` *Pick the midpoint grip*	Grips the midpoint and stretch mode
`** STRETCH **`	Changes the arc shape
`<Stretch to point>/Base point/Copy/Undo/eXit:` *Pick any point below the original grip location*	
`Command:` *Pick the left endpoint grip on the arc*	Grips the endpoint and enters stretch mode
`** STRETCH **`	Changes the arc's shape
`<Stretch to point>/Base point /Copy/Undo/eXit:` *Pick any point below the original grip location*	
`Command: U↵`	Undoes the first change
`Command: U↵`	Returns the arc to its original shape

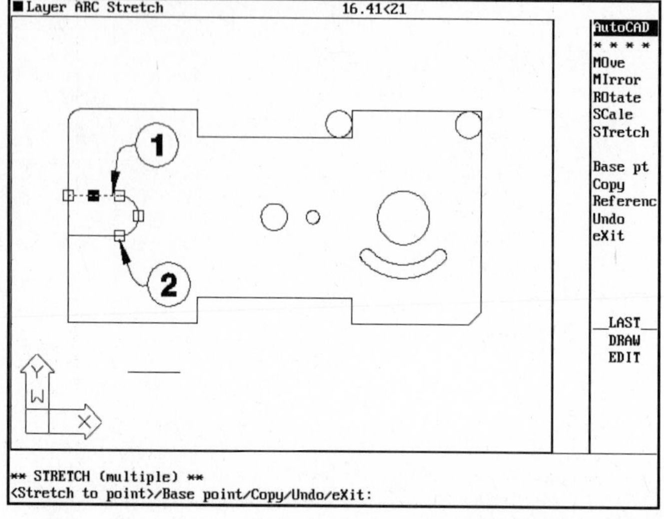

Figure 6.19:
Copying with stretch autoediting mode.

Copying and Moving with Stretch Autoediting Mode

The stretch autoediting mode can be used to move an entity, change an endpoint, or resize an entity, depending on what type the entity is and which grip is selected. Picking one grip point on an entity may not have the same effect as picking one of the other grip points. Selecting the end of a line stretches the line, for example, whereas picking the middle grip moves it. You also can use the Copy option or hold the shift key down while choosing the second point to create copies while stretching.

Experiment with these methods and options, and use the copy option of the stretch autoediting mode to complete the guide slot at the left of the tool plate.

Copying with Autoediting modes

`Command:` *Pick line at ① (see fig. 6.19)*	Selects the line and displays grips
`Command:` *Pick the mid grip on the line*	Grips line and enters stretch mode, moving line
`** STRETCH **` `<Stretch to point>/Base point/Copy/Undo/eXit:` *Pick a point above the tool plate*	Moves the line
`Command:` **R**↵	Issues the REDRAW command

`Command:` *Enter* `U` *twice*	Undoes the REDRAW and autoedit move
`Command:` *Select the guide slot arc*	Selects and displays grips
`Command:` *Pick at* ①	Clears the arc from the set, selects the line, and displays its grips
`Command:` *Pick the line's midpoint grip*	Grips the line and enters stretch autoediting mode, moving the line
`** STRETCH **` `<Stretch to point>/Base point/Copy/` `Undo/eXit:` `B` ↵	Specifies the Base Point option
`Base point:` *Pick the right grip*	Changes the base (move from) point, still moving the line
`** STRETCH **` `<Stretch to point>/Base point/Copy/` `Undo/eXit:` `C`↵	Specifies the Copy (multiple stretch) option
`**STRETCH (multiple) **` `<Stretch to point>/Base point/Copy/` `Undo/eXit:` *Pick the bottom grip on the arc at* ②	Copies the line
`<Stretch to point>/Base point/Copy/` `Undo/eXit:` *Pick another point below the base plate*	Copies the line again
`<Stretch to point>/Base point/Copy/` `Undo/eXit:` `U`↵	Undoes the last copy
`<Stretch to point>/Base point/Copy/` `Undo/eXit:` *Press Enter*	Exits from autoediting mode
`Command:` `QSAVE`↵	Clears the selection sets and grips, and saves the drawing

You can exit from the multiple autoediting modes by pressing Enter, the spacebar, Ctrl-C, or by entering an X. When not in multiple mode, you can exit from autoediting by pressing Ctrl-C or by entering an X.

Because it is so versatile—capable of stretching, moving, and copying objects—the stretch mode is the first of the autoediting modes to appear when you choose a grip to enter autoediting mode. The move autoediting mode works similarly to stretch and is explained in the next section.

Using the Move Autoediting Mode

Instead of using the stretch autoediting mode to move something, try using the move mode. To do so, enter MO (for MOve) at the autoedit prompt or press the spacebar once, and the move mode prompt appears. Specifying a point moves the selected entity or entities the distance between the base point (the grip you selected) and the specified point. If you want a base point other than the selected grip, the base point option enables a new base point to be specified, as was done in the preceding exercise. You can specify points by any combination of grips, object snaps, or by entering the coordinates.

TIP

If you are trying to move or stretch a grip point a small distance, the desired point may fall within the grip box of the gripped point, preventing you from picking the desired point. In such cases, just move or stretch the grip to an out-of-the-way point, pick the grip again, and then pick the desired point, which is now clear of the grip.

Try using the move autoediting mode in the next exercise.

Using Move Autoediting mode

`Command:` *Pick, drag, and release to select from ① to ② (see fig. 6.20)*	Selects the radial slot and displays grips
`Command:` *Pick either large arc's mid grip*	Enters stretch mode
`** STRETCH **` `<Stretch to point>/Base point/Copy/ Undo/eXit:` *Press Enter*	Switches to move mode
`** MOVE **` `<Move to point>/Base point/Copy/ Undo/eXit:`	

Move the cursor and note that the entire radial slot (the entire selection set) now moves with the cursor.

Pick any point below the tool plate	Relocates the slot
`Command: U↵`	Undoes the move

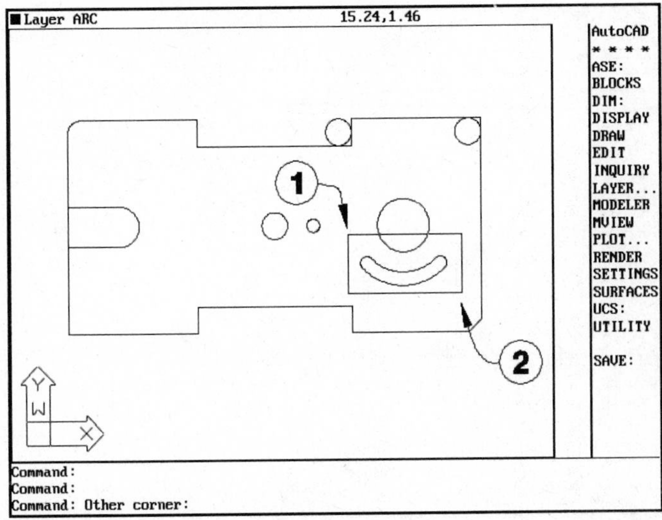

Figure 6.20:

The selection points for the slot.

Like stretch mode, one or more copies can be made from the original by using move mode. Use the copy option or hold down the shift key while picking the point to copy to. The next exercise uses the copy option with move mode.

Copying with Move Autoediting Mode

`Command:` *Select a window from* ① *to* ② *(see fig. 6.20)*	Selects the radial slot and displays grips
`Command:` *Pick either of the large arc's grips*	Enters stretch mode
`** STRETCH **` `<Stretch to point>/Base point/Copy/Undo/eXit:` *Press spacebar*	Switches to move mode
`** MOVE **` `<Move to point>/Base point/Copy/Undo/eXit: C↵`	Specifies the copy (multiple) option
`** MOVE (multiple) **` `<Move to point>/Base point/Copy/Undo/eXit:` *Pick two points below the tool plate (see fig. 6.21)*	Copies two new slots to below the tool plate
`<Move to point>/Base point/Copy/Undo/eXit:` *Press Enter*	Exits from autoediting mode
Save the drawing	

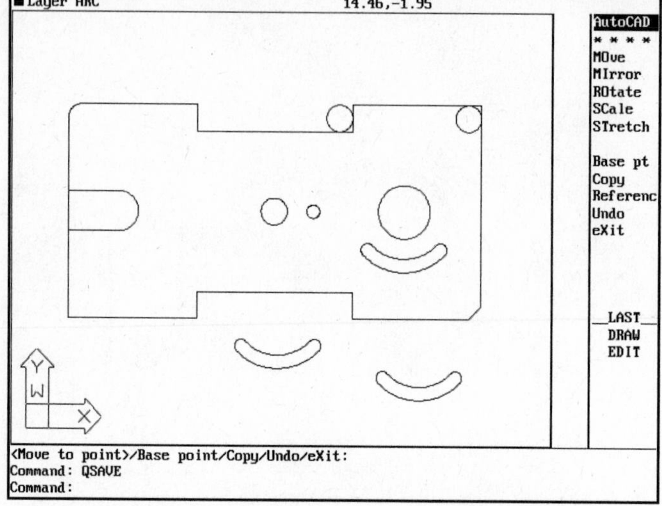

Figure 6.21:

Two copies of the radial slot.

The previous exercise showed how the move option of autoedit is used and how multiple copies can be made if necessary. It is important to have all of the entities to be included in the command selected, as well as to have any additional grips displayed that may be needed for point selection. Rotate mode is shown next.

Rotating with Autoediting Mode

It is often more convenient to draw a shape in a normal orientation and then rotate it or rotate and copy it into a different orientation than it is to draw it at an odd angle. The rotate mode enables selected entities to be rotated about a base point. The default base point is the selected grip. You can use the base point option to specify a different one. You enter rotate mode by pressing Enter or the spacebar twice or by entering **RO** (ROtate). You are then prompted for a rotation angle. Entering a positive angle produces a counterclockwise rotation by that amount; entering a negative angle produces a clockwise rotation.

The autoediting modes, in order , are stretch, move, rotate, scale, and mirror. Autoedit rotates through the modes, in order, when you press Enter, the spacebar, or the Enter button on your pointing device. If you press Enter when in mirror

mode, it puts you back in stretch mode again. You also can pick the modes and options from the screen menu.

Try using the rotate option in the following exercise.

Rotating and Moving Entities with Autoedit

Continue with the TOOLPLAT drawing from the previous exercise.

`Command:` *Select a window from* ① *to* ② *(see fig. 6.22)*	Selects the radial slot and displays its grips
`Command:` *Pick either large arc's midpoint grip*	Highlights grip and enters stretch mode

`** STRETCH **`
`<Stretch to point>/Base point/Copy/`
`Undo/eXit:` *Press the spacebar twice*
	Switches to rotate mode

`** ROTATE **`
`<Rotation Angle>/Base point/Copy/`
`Undo/Reference/eXit:`	

Move the cursor, and note that the slot rotates dynamically as you do so.

`<Rotation angle>/Base point/Copy/` `Undo/Reference/eXit:` **90**↵	Rotates the entities 90 degrees counterclockwise

Now, using figure 6.23 as a guide, move the slot into position at the left of the tool plate.

`Command:` *Pick either of the mid grips*	Enters stretch mode

`** STRETCH **`
`<Stretch to point>/Base point/Copy/`
`Undo/eXit:` *Press the spacebar once*
	Switches to move mode

`** MOVE **`
`<Move to point>/Base point/Copy/`
`Undo/eXit:` *From the screen menu, choose* Base pt
	Prompts for a base point

`Base point:` *From the pop-up menu, choose* Center, *then pick either of the large arcs*	Sets the base point at the arc's center
`<Move to point>/Base point/Copy/` `Undo/eXit:` *From the pop-up menu, choose* Center, *and pick center of guide slot arc*	Moves the slot to a new location

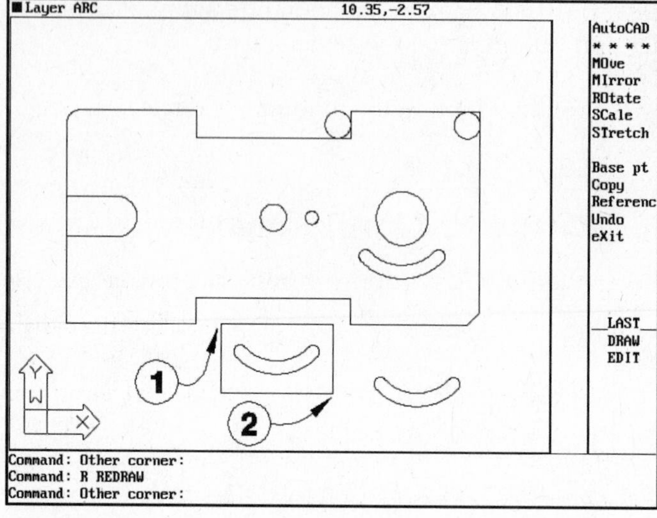

Figure 6.22:
Slot selection and grips.

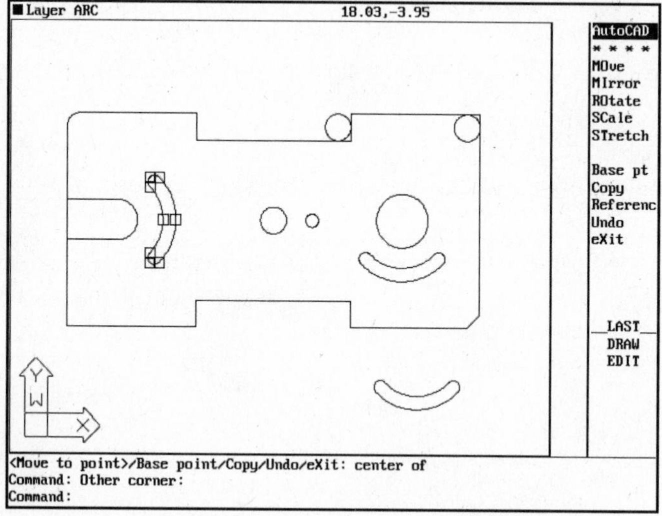

Figure 6.23:
The rotated and relocated slot.

The rotate and move options of the autoedit command were used to orient the slot and move it to the proper location. Object snaps were used, instead of grips, because arc centers do not have grips. Remember that picking an empty window once clears the selection set and doing it a second time

removes the visible grips. You use that technique again in the following exercise.

Next, use the copy option of the rotate autoediting mode to complete the hole pattern at the center of the tool plate.

Rotating and Copying with Autoedit

`Command:` *Double-click at ① (see fig. 6.24)*	Clears the selection set and grips
`Command:` *Pick the circle at ②*	Creates the set and displays grips
`Command:` *Pick the circle at ③*	Clears the previous set, selects the circle, and displays grips
`Command:` *Pick the circle's center grip ③*	Enters stretch mode
`** STRETCH **` `<Stretch to point>/Base point/Copy/Undo/eXit:` *Press Enter twice*	Switches to rotate mode
`** ROTATE **` `<Rotation angle>/Base point/Copy/Undo/Reference/eXit:` **B↵**	Prompts for a base point
`Base point:` *Pick center grip of circle ②*	Sets the rotation base point
`<Rotation angle>/Base point/Copy/Undo/Reference/eXit:` **C↵**	Specifies the copy option
`** ROTATE (multiple) **` `<Rotation angle>/Base point/Copy/Undo/Reference/eXit:` **45↵**	Makes the first copy at 45 degrees
`<Rotation angle>/Base point/Copy/Undo/Reference/eXit:` **90↵**	Makes the next copy at 90 degrees
`<Rotation angle>/Base point/Copy/Undo/Reference/eXit:` **135↵**	Makes the next copy at 135 degrees
`<Rotation angle>/Base point/Copy/Undo/Reference/eXit:` **180↵**	Makes the next copy at 180 degrees
`<Rotation angle>/Base point/Copy/Undo/Reference/eXit:` *Press Enter*	Exits from autoediting mode
`Command:` **QSAVE↵**	Clears grips and the selection set, and saves the drawing

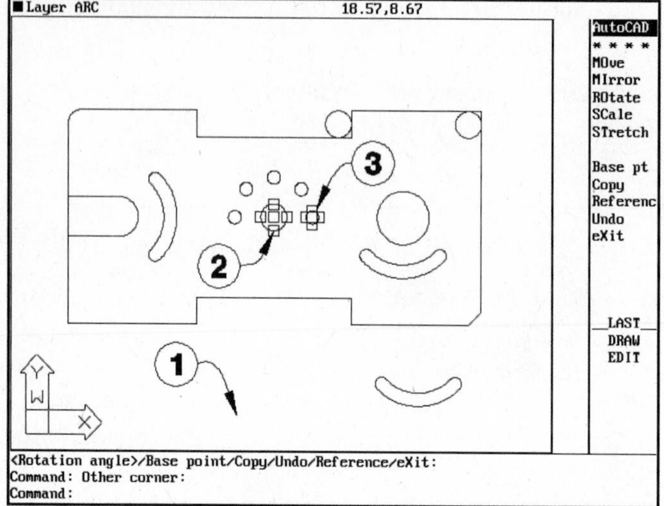

Figure 6.24:

Circles copied with Rotate Autoediting mode.

The rotate option of the autoedit command is convenient for changing the orientation of entities or creating circular patterns. Most of its options—base point, copy, undo, and exit—work the same as with the other autoediting modes. The reference option enables you to specify the current rotation and then the new rotation desired. This works well when you do not know the incremental distance between the old and new rotation. See Chapter 8 for details. In this drawing, some of the work which can be accomplished by rotating also can be done with mirroring.

Mirroring Entities with Autoediting Mode

The mirror mode creates a mirror image of the selected entities over a chosen mirror line. The mirror line is defined with endpoints of the base point and a selected second point. The base point is assumed to be the selected grip, unless a different grip is specified with the base point option. If Ortho is on, you can easily pick a second point for a horizontal or vertical mirror line. The copy option creates a mirrored copy of the original entities; otherwise the original entities are transformed. Enter MI (MIrror) at the autoedit prompt or cycle through the options by pressing Enter, the Enter button of the pointing device, or the spacebar to access the mirror mode.

Try the mirror autoediting mode on the tool plate. Mirror the right-hand radial slot to make a copy above the hole.

Mirroring Entities with Autoediting mode

`Command:` *Select the circle at ③*	Creates the set and shows grips
`Command:` *Select a window from ① to ② (see fig. 6.25)*	Selects the radial slot and displays grips
`Command:` *Pick one of the grips on the slot*	Enters stretch mode
`** STRETCH **` `<Stretch to point>/Base point/Copy/Undo/eXit:` *Press Enter 4 times*	Switches to mirror mode
`** MIRROR **` `<Second point>/Base point/Copy/Undo/eXit:` **B**↵	Prompts for a base point
`Base point:` *Pick center grip of the circle at ③*	Specifies the new base point
`<Second point>/Base point/Copy/Undo/eXit:` *Pick the circle's right grip at ③*	Locates the second point directly to the right of the base point and mirrors the slot

Because you did not use the copy option, the original slot was deleted.

`Command:` **U**↵	Undoes the edit
`Command:` *Select the circle at ③*	Creates the set and shows grips
`Command:` *Select a window from ① to ② (see fig. 6.25)*	Selects the radial slot and displays grips
`Command:` *Pick one of the grips on the slot*	Enters stretch mode
`** STRETCH **` `<Stretch to point>/Base point/Copy/Undo/eXit:` *Press the spacebar 4 times*	Switches to mirror mode
`** MIRROR **` `<Second point>/Base point/Copy/Undo/eXit:` **B**↵	
`Base point:` *Pick the center grip of ③*	
`<Second point>/Base point/Copy/Undo/eXit:` **C**↵	Specifies the copy option
`** MIRROR (multiple) **` `<Second point>/Base point/Copy/Undo/eXit:` *Pick the circle's right grip at ③*	Copies and mirrors in one operation
`** MIRROR **` `<Second point>/Base point/Copy/Undo/eXit:` *Press Enter*	Exits from autoedit
Save the drawing	

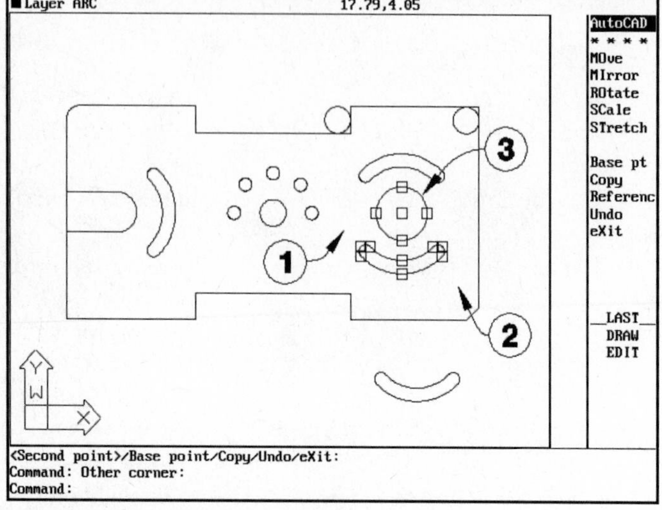

Figure 6.25:

Slot created using Mirror Autoediting mode.

Using the Shift Key To Copy

Next, use the mirror mode to complete the hole pattern at the center of the tool plate. This time, instead of using the Copy option, press Shift as you pick the second point. Using Shift is an alternate way to copy with autoedit.

Finishing the Hole Pattern

`Command:` *Pick the circle in the center of the hole pattern*	Creates the set and displays grips
`Command:` *Select a crossing window from points ① to ② (see fig. 6.26)*	Selects 3 circles and displays grips
`Command:` *Pick any one of the grip points on the small holes*	Enters stretch mode
`** STRETCH **`	
`<Stretch to point>/Base point/Copy/Undo/eXit:` **MI**↵	Enters mirror mode
`** MIRROR **`	
`<Second point>/Base point/Copy/Undo/eXit:` **B**↵	
`Base point:` *Pick the center hole's center grip*	Sets a new base point

`** MIRROR **` `<Second point>/Base point/Copy/Undo/eXit:` *Shift-pick (hold down the shift key and pick) the right grip of the center hole*	Copies while picking second point
`** MIRROR (multiple) **` `<Second point>/Base point/Copy/Undo/eXit:` *Press Enter*	Exits autoedit mode

Your drawing should look like figure 6.27.

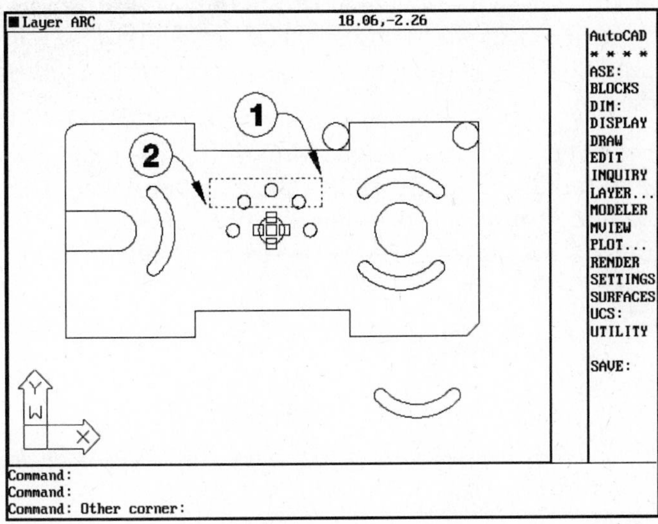

Figure 6.26:

Crossing selection of circles.

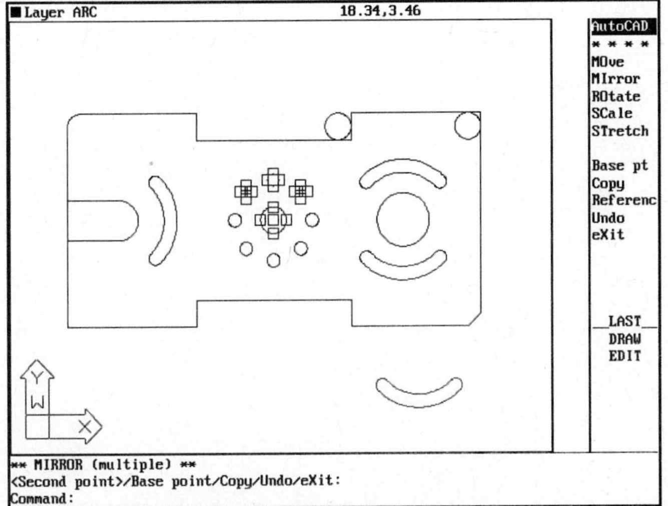

Figure 6.27:

Completed hole pattern with grips.

Look for opportunities to use the mirror option in your drawings to save time when creating entities. Remember to properly specify the two points that form the mirror line. Also, determine whether the Copy option is needed.

Scaling with Autoedit

Scaling is another editing feature that is a great time saver. You may need to use the scale mode of autoedit to create blown-up views, scale standard shapes up or down, or change from an inch base to a metric base entity. Like the rotate mode, scaling is done from a base point, which, unless otherwise specified, is the selected grip point.

Next, assume that an engineering change requires that you scale down the size of the hole and radial slots at the right side of the tool plate. The pattern is proportional to its original size—just smaller. Use the scale autoediting mode in the following exercise to scale the slots to 3/4 of their original size.

Using Scale Autoediting mode

`Command:` *Double-click in empty space*	Clears the selection set and grips
`Command:` *Pick a crossing window from ① to ② (see fig. 6.28)*	Selects slots and circle using crossing box
`Command:` *Pick center grip of center circle*	Enters stretch mode
`** STRETCH **` `<Stretch to point>/Base point/Copy/Undo/eXit:` *Press spacebar 3 times*	Switches to scale mode
`** SCALE **` `<Scale factor>/Base point/Copy/Undo/Reference/eXit:` *Move the cursor*	Dynamically scales entities in proportion
`<Scale factor>/Base point/Copy/Undo/Reference/eXit: .75↵`	Scales entities to 3/4 original size

Save the drawing. It should now look like figure 6.29.

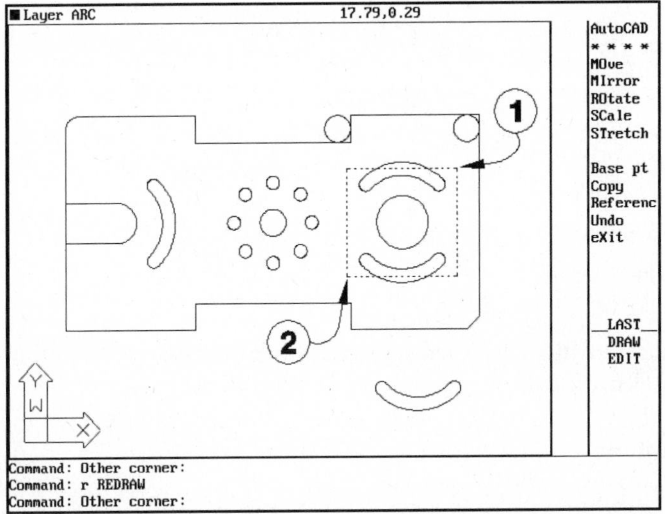

Figure 6.28:

Crossing selection of slots.

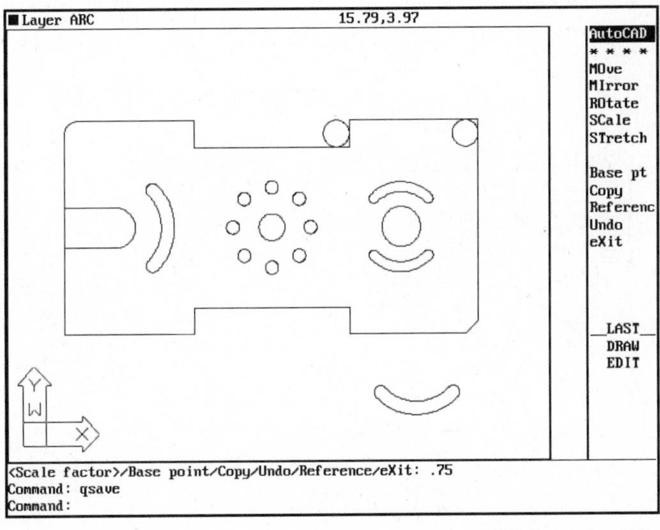

Figure 6.29:

Scaled slot pattern.

Because the proper scale—usually full—is so important in a CAD data base, be sure to scale entities to their proper size. The scale mode is handy for scaling text, title blocks, borders, and so on to finish off a drawing. The autoediting modes have the same effect on text as on other graphic entities. You can scale, copy, move, and rotate text just like any other entity.

The next section further explains the entity selection options you may want to explore.

Changing Entities with DDMODIFY

Earlier in this chapter, you used the autoediting modes to modify entities. Chapter 8 shows you how to use many of AutoCAD's other editing commands, as well as other aspects of the autoediting modes. To give you a taste of single-entity editing, the chapter finishes with a look at the DDMODIFY command, which enables you to change many of the characteristics of individual drawing entities by using dialog box controls.

The DDMODIFY command is an editing command that lists information about the selected entity. It also enables you to change the selected entity. It is issued by the Entity option of the Modify pull-down menu. The change options are slightly different, depending on the entity selected. In the case of the circle shown in figure 6.30, the radius can be changed by changing the value in the edit box. The center coordinates can be changed this way as well, or the **P**ick Point option can be used to select a new center point. If you click on Cancel instead of on OK, any changes made are disregarded.

Try the DDMODIFY command in the following exercise.

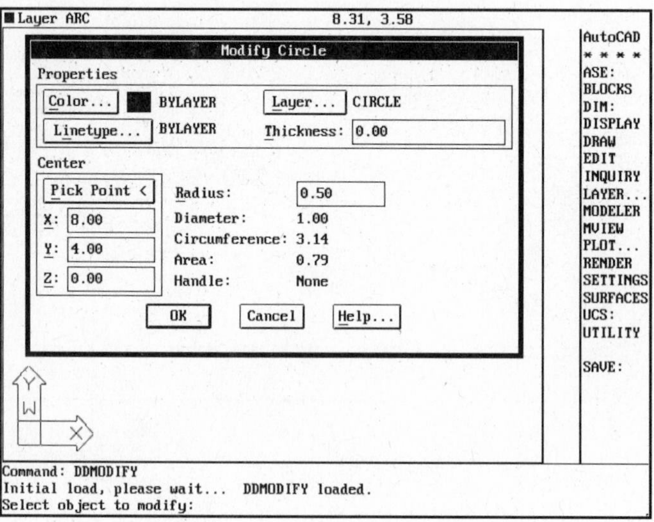

Figure 6.30:

A sample dialog box opened by DDMODIFY.

Using DDMODIFY To Change Entities

Continue with the TOOLPLAT drawing from the previous exercise.

`Command:` *Choose* Modify, *then* Entity	Autoloads and starts the Modify command
`Select object to list:` *Pick the 1" circ in the middle of the tool plate*	Opens the Modify Circle dialog box
Double-click in the <u>R</u>adius *edit box, then enter* `1.5`	Highlights and replaces the radius data in the dialog box
Choose OK	Closes the dialog box and changes the circle's radius
`Command:` *Press Enter*	Repeats the DDMODIFY command
`Select object to list:` *Pick the same circle*	Opens the Circle dialog box
Double-click in the <u>R</u>adius *edit box, then enter* `0.5`	Replaces the radius data in the dialog box
Click on Pick Point	Prompts for a new center point
`Center point:` *Pick a point near the top of the screen*	Relocates the circle and returns to the Circle dialog box
Choose Cancel	Closes the dialog box and undoes the changes to the circle

Quit AutoCAD and discard the last changes to the drawing.

The DDMODIFY dialog box also controls properties such as linetype, layer, and color of the selected entity. Choosing one of these options displays a child dialog box for the appropriate selections.

Summary

This chapter showed you how to create a drawing by using just a few of the basic drawing and editing commands. The LINE and CIRCLE commands are often used in CAD drafting. You learned some similarities between the way the drawing commands operate. They can be issued from a pull-down or screen menu. Entering commands from the keyboard is sometimes the most efficient method, if you can remember how to type the command. Commands that have shortcut keys are easiest to type.

Remember to read the command line to see what type of input AutoCAD is looking for. Points can be specified by coordinates, or by choosing them from the screen with object snaps or grips. AutoCAD offers several options for the arc and circle commands, so that you can draw them with whatever information you have. The option of absolute, relative, or polar coordinates also gives you powerful drawing capabilities without having to use a calculator to obtain unknown information. Try not to pick points from the screen unassisted, or your drawing accuracy can suffer.

Many more drawing and editing techniques are explained in the following chapters. The first challenge is to master the drawing and editing commands themselves, then start to develop a style of CAD drafting that best fits your needs. Each time you complete a drawing, you will think of ways to draw it more efficiently the next time. Eventually, you find the techniques that perform best for your line of work.

Chapter 7 explains more of the entity-creation commands that you commonly use for your drawings. A drawing containing more detail and a greater variety of graphic entities is used to illustrate the use of these commands. Turn to Chapter 7 to learn more about graphic entities.

Graphic Entities

Just as you find collections of tools around a manual drafting board for making lines, text, and curves, AutoCAD gives you a collection of electronic tools to perform similar functions. This chapter continues to discuss AutoCAD's drawing commands. You use these tools to build the drawing shown in figure 7.1. Each command creates an *entity,* which is the most fundamental piece of a drawing. The LINE command, for example, creates a line entity; the ARC command creates an arc entity. These drawing entities are sometimes called *graphic primitives* (see fig. 7.2). Primitives are the primary entities from which more complex components, symbols, and whole drawings are built. You may, for example, make an annotation bubble symbol from primitive line, circle, and text entities.

On paper, your drawing is static. As seen in Chapter 6, AutoCAD graphic entities are *dynamic*. An AutoCAD arc, for example, has handles so that you can move it. Text has changeable height, width, and slant. Lines have two endpoints, but when two lines cross, AutoCAD can find the exact intersection.

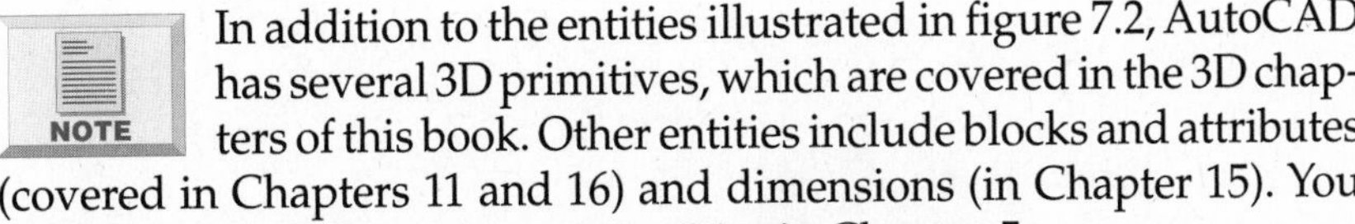

In addition to the entities illustrated in figure 7.2, AutoCAD has several 3D primitives, which are covered in the 3D chapters of this book. Other entities include blocks and attributes (covered in Chapters 11 and 16) and dimensions (in Chapter 15). You already learned about viewport entities in Chapter 5.

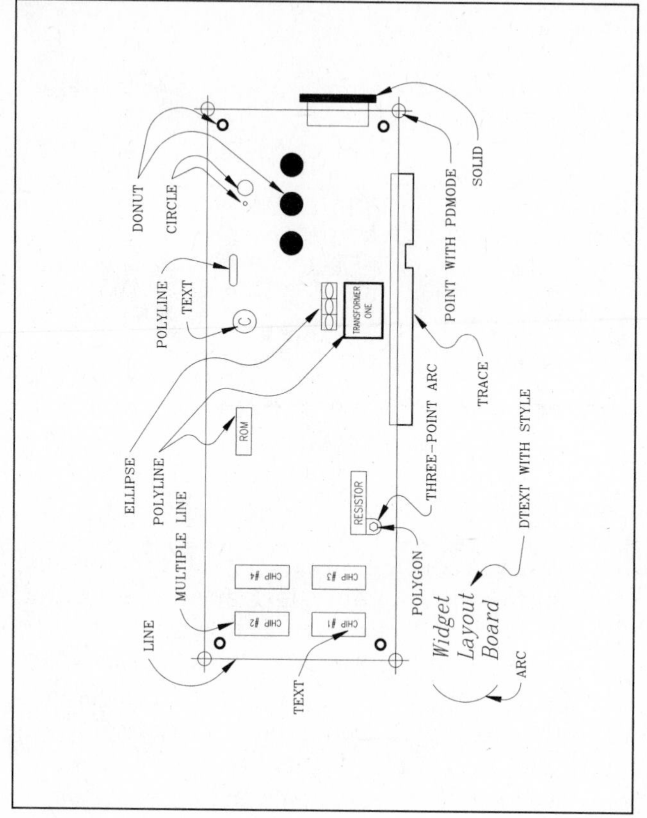

Figure 7.1:

Entities used in the WIDGET drawing.

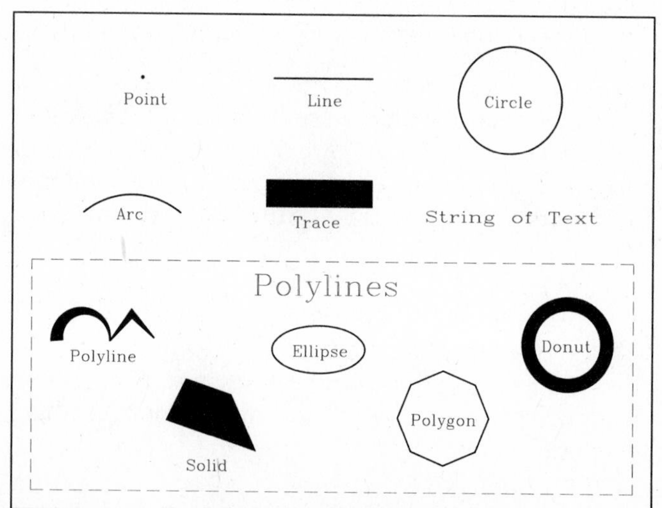

Figure 7.2:

Graphic primitives in AutoCAD.

Establishing Drawing Tools and Drawing Goals

Chapter 6 introduced you to the LINE, ARC, and CIRCLE commands. The POINT and DTEXT commands were used briefly in earlier chapters. These commands and their associated commands — PLINE, DONUT, POLYGON, ELLIPSE, TRACE, TEXT, and SOLID — are used in this chapter.

The principal drawing commands are on the Draw pull-down menu (see fig. 7.3); all the drawing commands are on the screen menu. To access these screen menu commands, select DRAW from the root screen menu. You also can use a tablet menu if you have one configured in AutoCAD (see Appendix A).

Several of the command items on the Draw pull-down menu are modified commands. You can preset parameters for these commands using system variables and the Entity Modes options in the Settings pull-down menu.

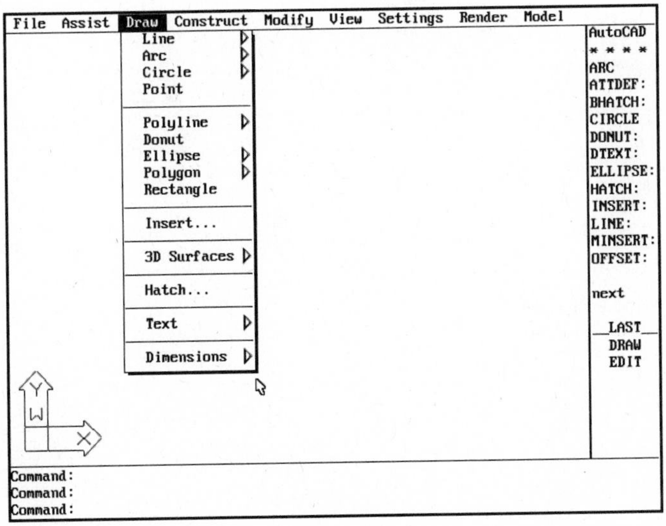

Figure 7.3:

The DRAW screen menu and Draw pull-down menu.

The goals for this chapter are two-fold. The first goal is to learn about different graphic entities and how they are used. The second goal is to work through a drawing that contains more features than the one in Chapter 6. In the exercises, you use graphic entities to build a design by drawing a widget controller circuit board layout. In the next chapter, you manipulate your drawing using AutoCAD's powerful editing commands, which enable you to move, copy, and change entities.

By the end of the next chapter, you should have a complete widget layout on your drawing area and an understanding of AutoCAD's drawing and primary editing commands. The widget may only faintly resemble a real board layout, but it does contain all of the primitive 2D entities of AutoCAD. Figure 7.1 shows the entities that you use to create the widget drawing.

Setting Up for Drawing Entities

To start, you must create a new drawing. You can create the WIDGET drawing with the settings shown in table 7.1.

Table 7.1
WIDGET Drawing Settings

COORDS	*GRID*	*SNAP*	*UCSICON*
On	.5	.1	ORigin

UNITS	Engineering, 2 decimal places, 2 fractional places for angles, default all other settings.
LIMITS	0,0 to 11,8.5

Layer Name	*State*	*Color*	*Linetype*
0	On/Current	7 (White)	CONTINUOUS
BOARD	On	2 (Yellow)	CONTINUOUS
HIDDEN	On	1 (Red)	HIDDEN
PARTS	On	4 (Cyan)	CONTINUOUS
Text	On	3 (Green)	CONTINUOUS

The following exercise uses the technique described in Chapter 5 for saving and restoring paper space viewports. The BLOCK and INSERT commands are covered in detail in Chapter 11.

Setting Up for the WIDGET Drawing

Start AutoCAD using the IA.BAT batch program.

`Command:` *Choose* File, *then* New, *and enter* **`WIDGET=IA7WIDGE`** ↵	Starts a new drawing called WIDGET

Begin a new drawing called WIDGET and use the settings shown in table 7.1.

`Command:` *Choose* View, *then* Zoom, *then* All	
`Command:` *Choose* View, *then* Tilemode, *then* Off	Switches to paper space
`Command:` *Choose* View, *then* Mview, *then* 3 Viewports	Issues MVIEW with 3 viewports
`_mview ON/OFF/Hideplot/Fit/2/3/4/Restore/<First Point>: _3`	
`Horizontal/Vertical/Above/Below/Left/<Right>:` **`A`**↵	Specifies a large viewport above the others
`Fit/<First Point>:` *From the screen menu, choose* Fit	Fits the viewports to the drawing area
`_FIT Regenerating drawing.`	

Next, use the BLOCK and INSERT commands to save and restore the viewports.

`Command:` *From the screen menu, choose* BLOCKS, *then* BLOCK:	Issues the BLOCK command
`_BLOCK Block name (or ?):` **`3VIEW`** ↵	
`Insertion base point:` **`0,0`**↵	
`Select objects:` *Pick point* ① *(see fig. 7.4)*	Specifies the window's first point

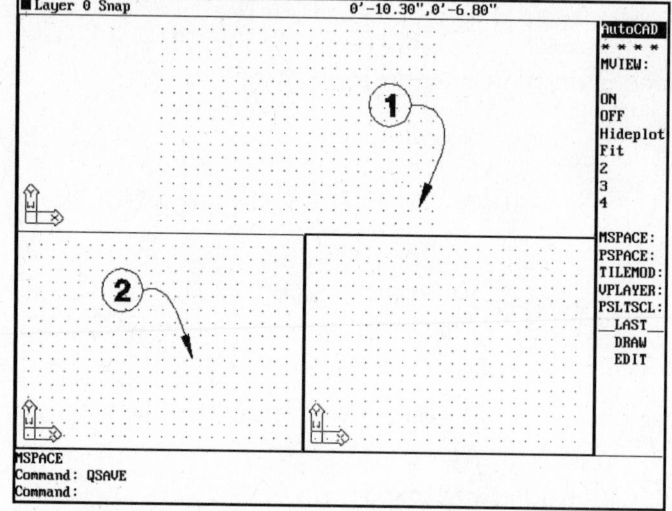

Figure 7.4:

The drawing with restored paper space viewports.

`Other corner :` *Pick* ②	Selects with a crossing window
`3 found`	
`Select objects:` *Press Enter*	
`Command:` *Choose* Draw, *then* Insert	Opens the Insert dialog box
Click on **B**lock	Opens the Blocks Defined in this Drawing dialog box (see fig. 7.5)
Double-click on 3VIEW	Specifies the name of the block to insert
Click on the **E**xplode *check box*	Explodes the block on insertion
Click on **O**K	Closes the dialog box and continues the INSERT command
`Insertion point: 0,0↵`	Specifies the block's origin
`X scale factor <1> / Corner / XYZ:` *Press Enter*	
`Y scale factor (default=X):` *Press Enter*	
`Rotation angle <0.00>:` *Press Enter*	

You cannot see the viewports' contents until you turn them on again.

`Command:` *Choose* View, *then* Mview, *then* Viewport ON	Turns on the viewports
`ON/OFF/Hideplot/Fit/2/3/4/Restore/ <First Point>: ON`	

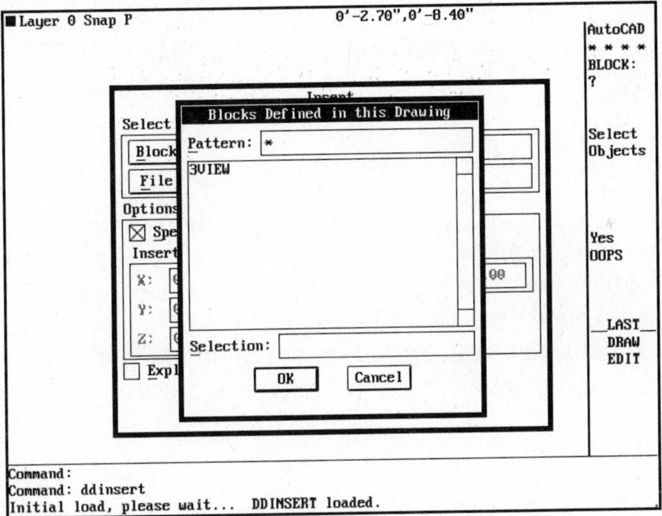

Figure 7.5:

The Blocks Defined in this Drawing dialog box.

`Select objects:` *Pick the same corner points as earlier*	Selects the viewports with a crossing window
`3 found`	
`Select objects:` *Press Enter*	
`Regenerating drawing.`	
`Command:` **`MS`** ↵	Issues the MSPACE command and switches to model space
`Command:` **`QSAVE`** ↵	Saves the drawing

After you finish, your current layer should be layer 0. The crosshair cursor should be active in the upper viewport because it is current.

Using a Scratch Layer To Experiment

Each exercise in this chapter shows you how to use one or more drawing command options for each graphic entity. As you work through this chapter's exercises, you use each drawing command. Some commands, such as PLINE and DTEXT, have several options that you can explore on your own. If you want, you can make a layer named SCRATCH on which to experiment (it is not used in the basic widget drawing). If your practice entities get in the way, simply turn off the SCRATCH layer.

Using Snap and Object Snaps

The drawing-entity exercises show absolute or relative coordinate values for drawing or picking points. You can snap to any of these points, or you can pick the points in the drawing window by using snap and grid and by following the coordinate display. If you are unsure about a coordinate value, you can always pick or enter the value shown in the exercise. If you enter the values from the keyboard, you can omit any trailing zeros or inch marks.

Establishing the Reference Points

The point is the most fundamental drawing entity. Points are helpful in building a drawing file. Although points are hard to see, you can control their size and use them as drawing reference points. In the following exercise, you lay out the four reference points for the widget board by using the POINT command, and then use the Point Style dialog box to set a point type that is easier to see.

Setting a Point Type

Make the top viewport active by clicking in it.

`Command:` *Choose* Draw, *then* Point	Issues the POINT command
`_point Point:` **`2.50",3.30"`** ↵	Puts a small blip at the point
`_point Point:` *Press Ctrl-C*	Cancels the POINT command
`Command:` **`R`** ↵	Redraws, leaving only a dot
`Command:` *From the screen menu, choose* POINT:, *then* TYPE	Accesses the Point Style dialog box

Double-click on the icon in the second row, third column, from the upper left corner.

`Command:` *Choose* Draw, *then* Point

`Point:` **2.5,5.8** ↵	
`Point:` **9.5,5.8** ↵	
`Point:` **9.5,3.3** ↵	
`Point:` *Press* Ctrl-C	Cancels the POINT command
`Command:` **REGENALL** ↵	Regenerates to redisplay the first point

`Regenerating drawing.`

`Command:` *Choose* View, *then* Zoom, *then* Window *and pick corner points that enclose the points you drew in the top viewport*

After you zoom out, your drawing area should look like figure 7.6.

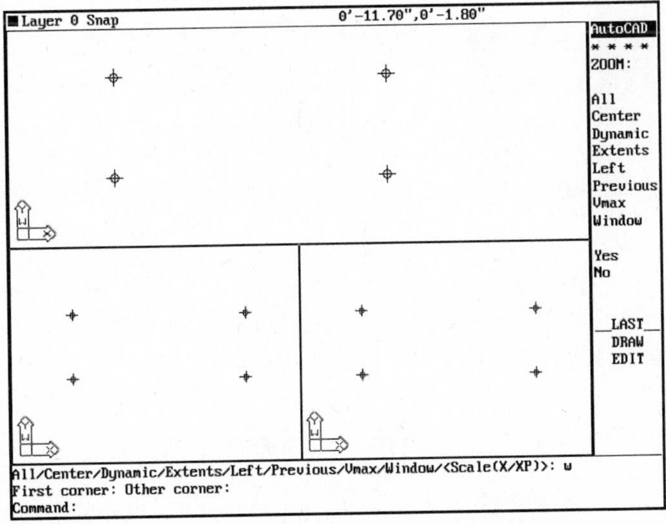

Figure 7.6:

Use PDMODE to change point styles.

When you drew the first point, a mark appeared in the drawing window. This mark is actually larger than the point that you placed — it was simply the construction marker (blip) for the point. The REDRAW command cleared the construction marker and left a small, white dot — the default point type — in the drawing.

Resetting your point display mode gave you the circle-with-cross points. You can set about 20 combinations of point types by using the Point Style dialog box, as shown in figure 7.7. You can also enter PDMODE as a system variable and change it directly by entering a new value.

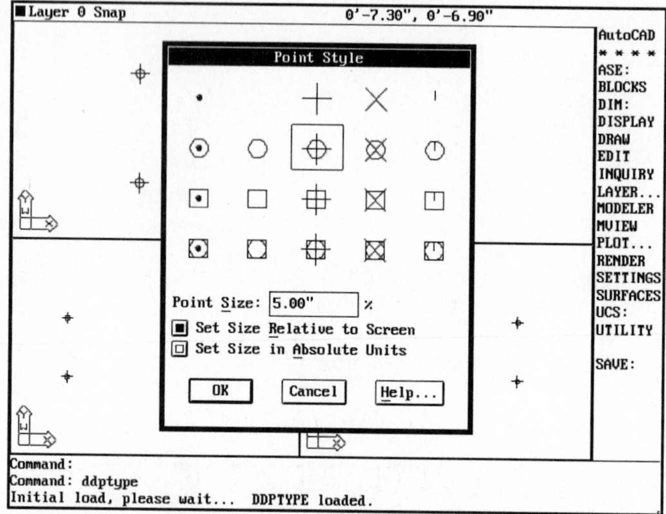

Figure 7.7:

Some of the point styles available in AutoCAD.

You control the size of the points by using the PDSIZE system variable. Set PDSIZE to a positive number to place its height in current drawing units. Set PDSIZE to a negative number to make its point size a consistent percentage of drawing window area or current viewport height, regardless of the zoom factor. For example, a setting of 8 makes points eight units high; a setting of -8 makes points eight percent of the drawing window area or current viewport height. You can change the point size from the POINT screen menu, the Point Style dialog box, or you can enter PDSIZE to change it.

A reference layer that is set up with points or a few lines helps organize your drawing file when you place other elements. After you finish making your placements, turn off the reference layer. You also can snap to a point using the NODe object snap. Points are useful to include as snap nodes in blocks (blocks are discussed in Chapter 10).

Continue the drawing exercise by using the LINE command. This important drawing command was used in several earlier chapters, and is it fully explained in Chapter 6.

Drawing the Board Outline

`Command:` *Choose* Settings, *then* Layers, *choose the BOARD layer, click on* Current, *and then* OK	Opens the Layer dialog box and makes BOARD the current layer
`Command:` **`DDOSNAP`** ↵	Opens the Running Object Snap dialog box
Click on the Node *checkbox, then choose* OK	Sets the running object snap mode to NODe
`Command:` **`L`** ↵	Issues the LINE command
`LINE From point:` *Pick the point entities in the order drawn in the previous exercise*	
`To point:` *From the screen menu, choose* Close	Completes the rectangle
`Command:` **`OSNAP`** ↵	Issues the direct command to set the object snap
`Object snap modes:` **`NONE`** ↵	Turns off the current running object snap

You also can use the DDOSNAP command to deselect NODe and turn off running object snap.

When you have completed the previous exercise, your drawing should resemble figure 7.8.

Drawing Rectangles

In the steps that follow, you add a port to the widget's right side to see how the RECTANG (rectangle) command functions. If you know the coordinates for two of the rectangle's corners, you can use the RECTANG command more quickly than drawing four separate lines. RECTANG is an AutoLISP defined command, defined by the ACAD.MNL file. RECTANG is on the Draw menu and actually creates one Polyline instead of four separate line segments.

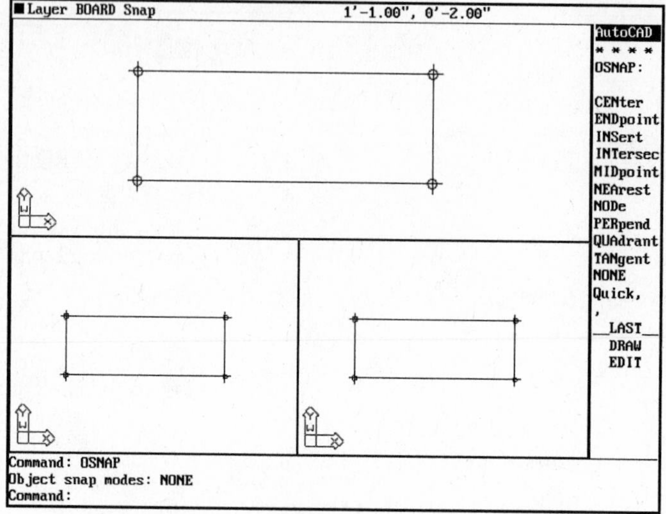

Figure 7.8:

The completed widget board layout.

Drawing a Port Connector

`Command:` *Choose* Draw, *then* Rectangle	Issues the RECTANG command
`First corner:` *Pick the absolute point 9.30,3.70*	
`Other corner:` *Pick the absolute point 9.60,4.50*	

The rectangle is really a single polyline, which is a special type of entity covered later in this chapter. Your drawing should look like figure 7.9 after you finish drawing the port connector.

As you know, you can press Enter to repeat the previous command. You also can make AutoCAD automatically repeat commands.

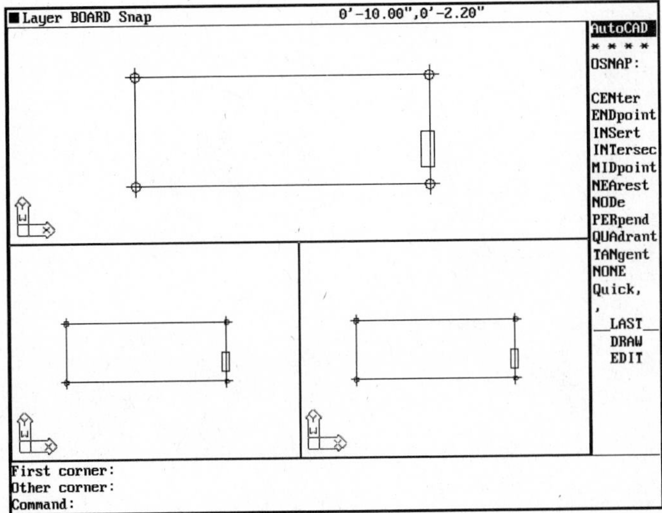

Figure 7.9:

The widget board with the port added.

Using MULTIPLE To Repeat Commands

You can repeat commands automatically by preceding them with the MULTIPLE command. Use the MULTIPLE command in the following exercise to fill up the left side of the widget board. In the steps, the MULTIPLE command draws four rectangles by repeating the LINE command. These rectangles are RAM chips, and, as you draw them, you practice various forms of coordinate entry.

Using the MULTIPLE Command To Repeat Commands

Click in the bottom left viewport to make it current.

`Command:` *Choose* Settings, *then* Layers, *and make PARTS the current layer*

`Command:` *Using ZOOM, pick window points surrounding the left side of the board (see fig. 7.10)*

`Command:` **`MULTIPLE LINE`** ↵

Notice that no `Command:` prompt appears when you press the spacebar after typing MULTIPLE.

`From point:` *Pick the absolute point 2.80,3.70*	
`To point:` *Pick the relative polar point @0.70<90.00 (press F6 if necessary to display coordinates in polar mode)*	
`To point:` *Pick the relative polar point @.3<0*	
`To point:` *Pick the relative polar point @0.70<270.00*	
`To point: C ↵`	Closes the line and MULTIPLE starts a new LINE command
`LINE From point:` *Pick the absolute point 2.80,4.70*	
`To point: @0,.7 ↵`	Specifies a relative Cartesian point
`To point:` *Pick the relative polar point @0.30<0.00*	
`To point: @.7<-90 ↵`	Specifies a relative polar point
`To point: C ↵`	Closes and starts LINE again
`LINE From point: 3.4,4.7 ↵`	
`To point:` *Pick or enter the relative polar points @.7<90 to @.3<0 to @.7<270 and enter* `C` *to close*	
`Line From point:` *Pick the absolute points 3.4,3.7 to @.7<90 to @.3<0 to @.7<-90 and enter* `C` *to close*	
`Line From point:` *Press Ctrl-C*	Cancels the MULTIPLE LINE command
`Command:` *Save the file*	

Your drawing should resemble the one shown in figure 7.10.

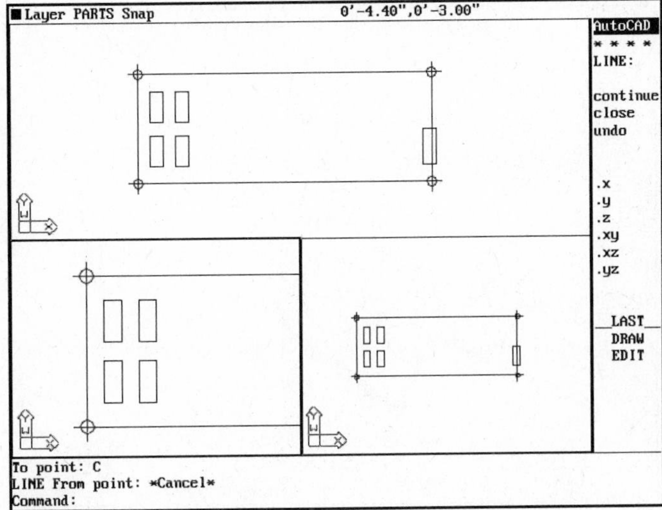

Figure 7.10:

The widget board with RAM chips added.

Drawing with TRACE

TRACE is a bommand which operates similar to LINE except for the Width option. You draw traces just like you draw lines, with a From point and a To point. AutoCAD first asks you how wide you want the trace. As figure 7.11 illustrates, you can create any desired width of traces. When you draw traces, AutoCAD lags one segment behind in displaying the trace because it must calculate the miter angle between the previous trace segment and the next segment.

Try using TRACE to draw a connector on the lower right side of the widget by typing or picking the points.

Using TRACE To Draw a Wide Line

Click in the top viewport to make it current.

`Command:` *Choose* Settings, *then* Layers, *and make* BOARD *the current layer*

`Command:` **`TRACE`** ↵ — Starts the TRACE command

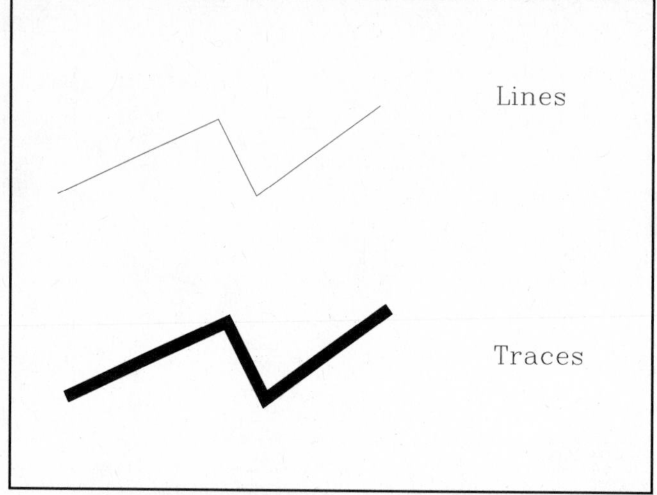

Figure 7.11:

Lines and traces.

`Trace width <0'-0.05">:` **`.01`** ↵	
`From point:` **`5.5,3.3`** ↵	
`To point:` *Pick the relative polar point @.2<270*	
`To point:` *Pick the relative polar point @2<0*	
`To point:` *Pick the relative polar point @.1<90*	
`To point:` *Continue with @.3<0 to @.1<270 to @.9<0 to @.2<90*	
`To point:` *Press Enter*	Ends the TRACE command
`Command:` *Use LINE to add an interior line from 5.50,3.30 to @.1<90 to @3.2<0 to @.1<270*	Draws the wide part of the connector (see fig. 7.12)
`Command:` *Use ZOOM, then specify window points surrounding the left end of trace and line*	Zooms in for a closer look at the trace and line
`Command:` **`U`** ↵	Undoes the zoom

Your drawing should look like figure 7.12

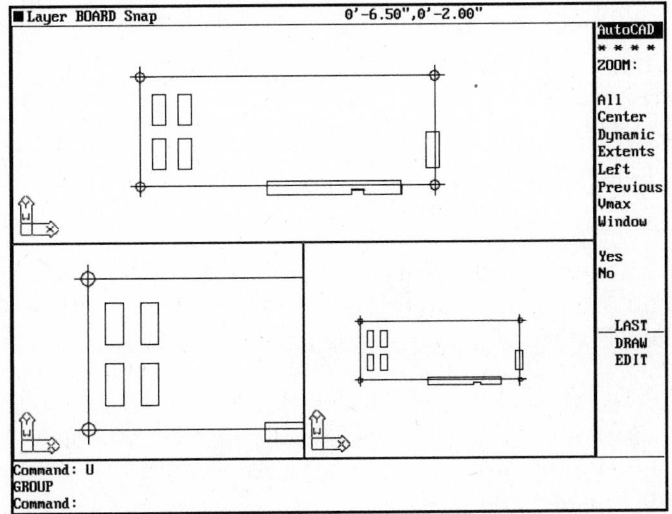

Figure 7.12: The connector, drawn with TRACE.

You should see a noticeable thickness to the trace (see fig. 7.13). Numerous wide traces slow down regenerations, redraws, and plots. Read about the FILL command later in this chapter to see how to turn off temporarily the interior filling of traces and how to increase regeneration speed.

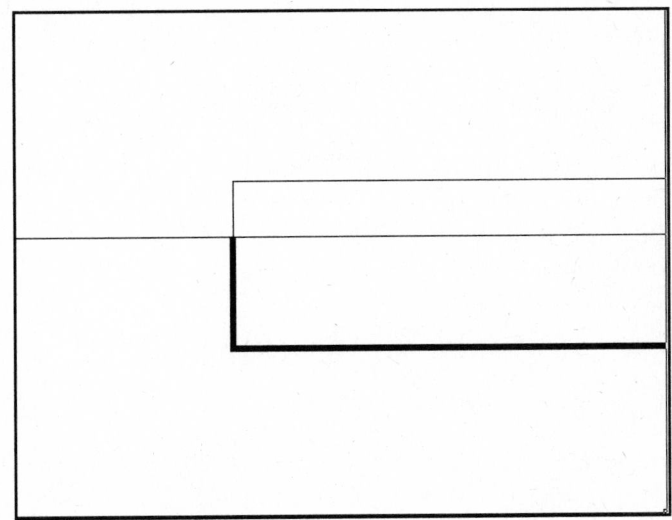

Figure 7.13: A close-up view of the line and trace.

Traces do have limitations. You cannot, for example, perform the following actions:

- Curve a trace
- Close a trace
- Continue a trace
- Undo a trace segment

To create thick lines, use either colors assigned to thick plotter pens or the PLINE command (covered later in this chapter). If you need mitered ends and corners, use TRACE.

To create a finished end using a miter, draw an extra segment and erase it. The remaining segment will have a mitered end, depending on the direction of the trace that is added to the finished end.

Because traces are stored the same way as four-sided solids, snapping to them is limited. Object snap INT and ENDP both find the corners. MID finds the middle of any side. You can use MID, but not ENDP, on the end of a trace to find the original From and To points.

Exploring More ARC and CIRCLE Options

To continue this drawing, experiment with the ARC and CIRCLE commands. These commands, already covered in Chapter 6, have many options, depending on what information you have available on these entities.

Drawing the Capacitors

`Command:` *Choose* Settings, *then* Layers, *and make* PARTS *the current layer*	
`Command: MULTIPLE CIRCLE ↵`	Issues a repeating CIRCLE command
`3P/2P/TTR/<Center point>: 6.80,5.30 ↵`	Sets the center point
`Diameter/<Radius>: 0.15 ↵`	Sets the radius

`CIRCLE 3P/2P/TTR/<Center point>:` **`2P`** ↵	Specifies the 2P method for the center of the switch
`First point on diameter:` **`8.40,5.30`** ↵	
`Second point on diameter:` **`8.60,5.30`** ↵	
`CIRCLE 3P/2P/TTR/<Center point>:` **`8.30,5.30`** ↵	Specifies the center point for the switch contact
`Diameter/<Radius><0'-0.10">:` **`D`** ↵	
`Diameter<0'-0.2">:` **`.05`** ↵	
`CIRCLE 3P/2P/TTR/<Center point>:` *Press Ctrl-C*	Stops the MULTIPLE command

Three circles, as shown in figure 7.14, have now been added to the drawing.

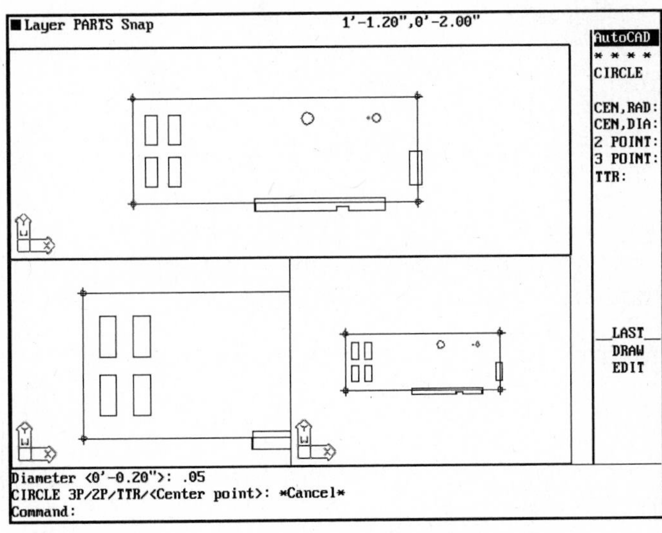

Figure 7.14:

Capacitors drawn with circles.

In the following exercise, you use the ARC command to draw part of the logo.

Using ARC with Start Point, End, and Direction

Make the bottom right viewport current.

`Command:` *Choose* Settings, *then* Layers, *and make TEXT the current layer*

`Command:` *Use ZOOM and window the lower left quarter of the viewport (see fig. 7.15)*

`Command:` *Choose* Settings, *then* Drawing Aids, *and set the X and Y grid spacing and snap to .05 units*

`Command:` *Choose* Draw, *then* Arc, *and then* 3-Point

`arc Center/<Start point>:` *Pick the absolute point 2.2,2.8. at ① (see fig. 7.15)*

`Center/End/<Second point>:` *Pick the second point 2.0,2.35 at ②* — Drag comes on automatically

`Endpoint:` *Pick the endpoint 2.2,1.9 at ③*

In the next exercise, you zoom in closer in the lower left viewport, and then use the LINE and ARC commands to draw the resistor.

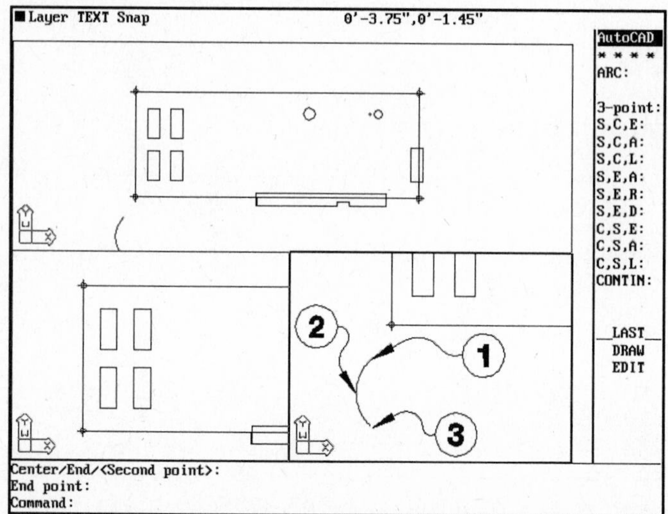

Figure 7.15:

A three-point arc for a future logo.

Drawing a Resistor

Make the bottom left viewport current.

`Command:` *Choose* Settings, *then* Layers, *and make* PARTS *the current layer*

`Command:` *Use ZOOM and pick window points at 3.90,3.40 and 5.10,4.20*

`Command:` **`DDVIEW`** ↵ — Opens the View Control dialog box

Click on New and save the view with the name RESISTOR.

`Command:` *Start the LINE command, draw from 4.1,3.9 to @.8<0 to @.2<270 to @.8<180, and enter* `C` *to close*

`Command:` *Press Enter, then draw a line from 4.10,3.60 to @.1<90*

`Command:` *Press Enter, then draw a line from 4.30,3.60 to @.1<90*

`Command:` *Choose* Draw, *then* Arc, *and then* Start,End,Dir

`Center/<Start point>:` *From the pop-up menu, choose* Endpoint — Specifies the ENDPoint object snap

`endp of` *Pick the endpoint of first line at ① (see fig. 7.16)*

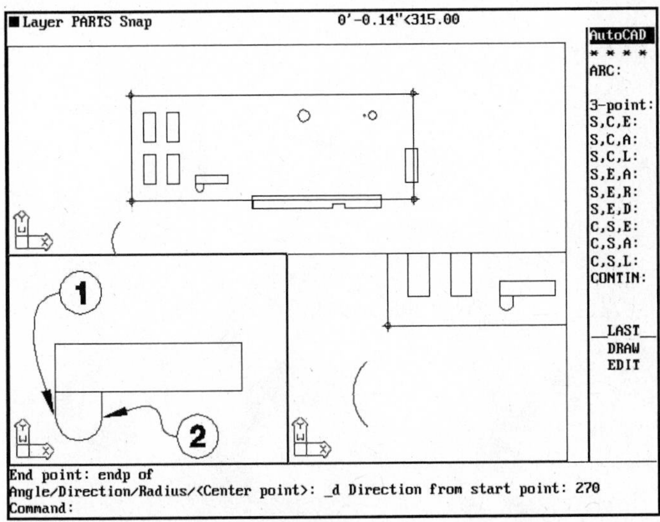

Figure 7.16:

A resistor with a Start,End,Direction arc.

`Center/End/<Second point>:` `_e`

`Endpoint:` *From the pop-up menu, choose* Endpoint

`endp of` *Pick the endpoint of the last line at* ②

`Angle/Direction/Radius/<Center point>:` **D**

`Direction from start point:` **270**, *or drag and pick point at 270 degrees*

`Command:` *Choose* View, *then* Zoom, *then* Previous

You explored the most common entities — the line, arc, and circle — in Chapter 6 and in this chapter. Given what you already know about entities, how would you create thick lines or thick, tapered lines, other than by using the TRACE command? Can you draw a continuous series of lines and arcs? Can you make a closed polygon with three straight sides (lines) and one curved side?

Creating Polylines

To draw these symbols, consider using the PLINE command to draw polylines. Instead of creating multiple lines to get a thick line, or creating independent arcs and then connecting them to lines, you can create a polyline. Some samples of polylines are shown in figure 7.17.

Figure 7.17:

You can create many kinds of polylines.

Polylines versus Lines

Polylines are different from independent line entities created using the LINE command, which visually appear to be joined. AutoCAD treats a multisegment polyline as a single drawing entity. Polylines can include both line and arc segments connected at vertices (endpoints). Information such as tangent direction and line width is stored at each vertex.

Polylines offer two advantages over lines. First, polylines are versatile. They can be straight or curved, thin or wide, one width or tapered. You can, for example, draw a curved leader with an arrowhead as a single polyline.

Second, the fact that a polyline is a single entity makes editing operations easier and reduces errors if you use crosshatching or work in 3D. You can edit a polyline by selecting any segment because all of a polyline's segments are selected. In contrast, if you want to copy one of the RAM chip rectangles made up of four individual line entities in the widget drawing, you must select each individual line segment. If you crosshatch or create 3D objects from 2D lines, you must have edges that connect. Objects drawn with lines and arcs can have tiny gaps that cause hatch or 3D errors. Use polylines to draw any closed or connected object or polygon, particularly if you anticipate hatching it or working with your drawing in 3D.

You already created a polyline by choosing Rectangle from the Draw menu. Use the PLINE command to create another widget rectangle, the ROM chip, in the center of the board.

Using PLINE To Draw a ROM Chip

Make the bottom right viewport current.

`Command:` *Choose* Settings, *then* Drawing Aids, *and set snap to .1"*	
`Command:` *Choose* View, *then* Pan, *and center the board in the viewport (see fig. 7.18)*	
`Command:` *Choose* Draw, *then* Polyline, *then 2D*	Starts the PLINE command
`_pline From point:`**`5.10,5.2`**`↵`	Starts the polyline
`Current line-width is 0'-0.00"`	
`Arc/Close/Halfwidth/Length/Undo/Width/<Endpoint of line>:` **`@0,0.2`** `↵`	

```
Arc/Close/Halfwidth/Length/Undo/
Width/<Endpoint of line>:
@.6<0 ↵
Arc/Close/Halfwidth/Length/Undo/
Width/<Endpoint of line>:
```
Pick the point @.2<270
```
Arc/Close/Halfwidth/Length/Undo/
Width/<Endpoint of line>:
```
From the screen menu, choose Close — Ends the polyline

After you choose Close, your drawing should look like figure 7.18.

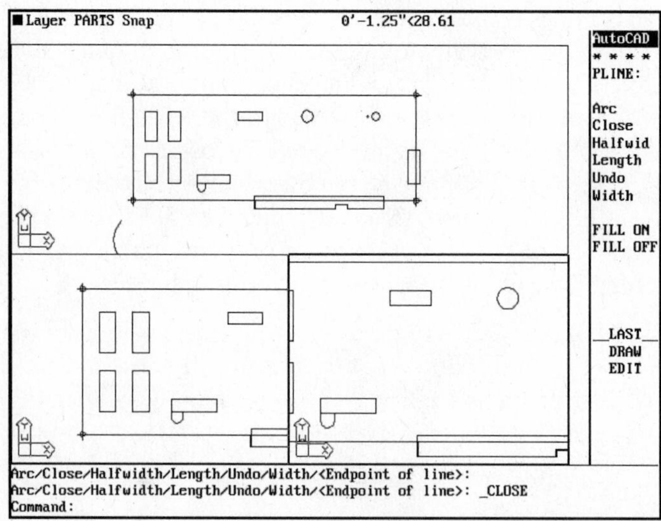

Figure 7.18:
A ROM chip drawn with PLINE.

This new rectangle looks similar to the RAM chips on the left. In the next chapter, you are shown that this single ROM chip entity includes all four segments, whereas the other rectangles actually are four separate entities.

Because PLINE can draw two basic kinds of segments, straight lines and curves, some PLINE prompts are similar to the line and arc prompts. If you draw straight polyline segments, prompts such as Endpoint, Close, and

Undo appear. Check out the possibilities on the PLINE prompt line. The following list describes the PLINE options:

- **Arc.** This option switches from drawing polylines to drawing polyarcs and issues the polyarc options prompt.
- **Close.** This option closes the polyline by drawing a segment from the last endpoint to the initial start point, and then exits from the PLINE command.
- **Halfwidth.** This option prompts you for the distance from the center to the polyline's edges (half the actual width).
- **Length.** This option prompts you to enter the length of a new polyline segment. AutoCAD then draws the new segment at the same angle as the last polyline segment or tangent to the last polyarc segment.
- **Undo.** This option reverses the changes made in the last drawn segment.
- **Width.** This option prompts you to enter a width (default 0) for the next segment to create polylines. To taper a segment, define different starting and ending widths. After drawing the tapered segment, AutoCAD draws the next segment with the ending width of the tapered segment.
- **Endpoint of line.** This option prompts you, as the default, to specify the endpoint of the current line segment.

The Arc option presents another set of options, including some familiar arc prompts, such as Angle/CEnter/Radius, Second pt, and Endpoint of arc.

The PLINE Arc options include the following:

- **Angle.** This option prompts you to enter the included angle (a negative angle draws the arc clockwise).
- **CEnter.** This option prompts you to specify the arc's center.
- **Close.** This option closes the polyline by connecting the initial start point to the last endpoint with an arc segment, and then it exits the PLINE command.
- **Direction.** This option prompts you to specify a tangent direction for the segment.
- **Halfwidth.** This option prompts you to specify a halfwidth, the same as for Line options.
- **Line.** This option switches back to Line mode.
- **Radius.** This option prompts you to specify the arc's radius.

- **Second pt.** This option selects the second point of a three-point arc.
- **Undo.** This option undoes the last drawn segment.
- **Width.** This option prompts you to enter a width, the same way as for Line mode.
- **Endpoint of arc.** This option prompts you to specify the endpoint of the current arc segment. This option is the default.

Although drawing lines and arcs with PLINE is similar to drawing the equivalent elements using LINE and ARC, note several important differences. First, you get all the prompts every time you enter a new polyline vertex. Second, additional prompts, such as for Halfwidth and Width, control the width of the segment. When a polyline has width, you can control the line fill by turning FILL on or off. Third, you can switch back and forth from straight segments to curved segments, and add additional segments to your growing polyline.

Using PLINE To Draw Arcs and Wide Lines

You can try using these extra polyline features by putting two more objects on your widget. Create a diode (the little narrow object with arcs on both ends) by combining line and arc segments. Then draw a rectangular transformer using a wide polyline. The diode is located between the circles at the top and the transformer near the bottom center of the board. Continue working in your right viewport. When you start PLINE, the first prompt is for drawing straight segments. Using the Arc option displays the Arc prompts in the polyline command.

Using PLINE To Draw a Diode and a Transformer

`Command:` *Choose* View, *then* Pan, *and pick points to show the right end of the board in the viewport (see fig. 7.19)*

`Command:` *Choose* Draw, *then* Polyline, *then* 2D

`_pline From point:` *Pick the absolute point 7.30,5.40*	
`Current line-width is 0'-0.00" Arc/Close/Halfwidth/Length/ Undo/Width/<Endpoint of line>:` **`@0.30,0`** ↵	Draws a line segment
`Arc/Close/Halfwidth/Length/Undo/ Width/<Endpoint of line>:` **`A`** ↵	Specifies the Arc option
`Angle/CEnter/CLose/Direction/Halfwidth/ Line/Radius/Second pt/Undo/Width/ <Endpoint of arc>:` **`A`** ↵	Specifies the Angle option
`Included angle:` **`180`** ↵	
`Center/Radius/<Endpoint>:` **`@0.10<90`** ↵	Draws an arc segment
`Angle/CEnter/CLose/Direction/Halfwidth/ Line/Radius/Second pt/Undo/Width/ <Endpoint of arc>:` **`L`** ↵	Specifies the Line option
`Arc/Close/Halfwidth/Length/Undo/Width/ <Endpoint of line>:` **`@0.30<180`** ↵	Draws a line segment
`Arc/Close/Halfwidth/Length/Undo/Width/ <Endpoint of line>:` **`A`** ↵	Specifies the Arc option
`Angle/CEnter/CLose/Direction/Halfwidth/ Line/Radius/Second pt/Undo/Width/ <Endpoint of arc>:` **`CL`** ↵	Closes the polyline with an arc segment

You can zoom in for a better look. Afterward, select UNDO or issue ZOOM with the Previous option.

After you complete the preceding exercise, your drawing should look like figure 7.19.

Next, draw the transformer with a wide polyline by using a preset width. The PLINEWID system variable enables a polyline width to be specified for any subsequent polylines.

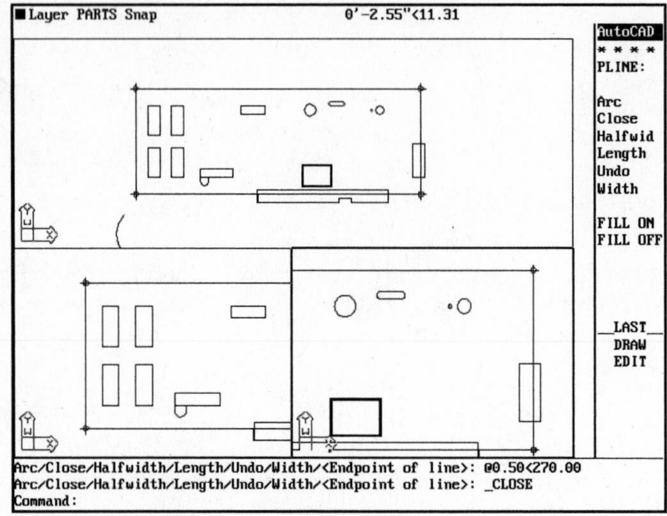

Figure 7.19:

A diode and a transformer drawn with polylines.

Drawing a Polyline with a Preset Width

`Command:` **`PLINEWID`** ↵	Presets the width
`New value for PLINEWID <0'-0.00">:` **`.02`** ↵	
`Command:` **`PL`** ↵	Starts the PLINE command
`From point:` *Pick the absolute point 6.60,3.50*	
`Current line-width is 0'-.02"`	
`Arc/Close/Halfwidth/Length/Undo/Width/ <Endpoint of line>:` **`@0.50<90.00`** ↵	
`Arc/Close/Halfwidth/Length/Undo/Width/ <Endpoint of line>:` **`@0.70<0.00`** ↵	
`Arc/Close/Halfwidth/Length/Undo/Width/ <Endpoint of line>:` **`@0.50<270.00`** ↵	
`Arc/Close/Halfwidth/Length/Undo/Width/ <Endpoint of line>:` *From the screen menu, choose* Close	
`Command:` *Save the drawing*	

You also can preset PLINEWID for the RECTANG command you used earlier in this chapter.

With polylines you can create complex objects; PEDIT enables you to modify a polyline without redrawing it from scratch. See Chapter 9 for more information on PEDIT.

The Rectangle item on the Draw menu is one of several commands in AutoCAD that enable you to create a polyline instead of individual entities.

Creating Donuts, Polygons, and Ellipses

You can use polylines to create many different objects. AutoCAD has several commands that use the basic polyline entity to draw different symmetrical closed shapes. The DONUT, POLYGON, and ELLIPSE commands take advantage of the power of the simpler PLINE command.

Creating Donuts

As you can imagine, the DONUT command creates an entity that looks like a donut. Donuts can have any inside and outside diameter. In fact, as figure 7.20 demonstrates, a donut with a 0 inside diameter is a filled-in circle; this shape is a good dot.

In the following exercise, put three filled dots on the right of the board as capacitors. Then put regular donuts at each corner of the widget as ground holes.

Using DONUT To Create Donuts

`Command:` **DONUT** ↵

`Inside diameter <0'-0.50">:`**0**↵ — Sets the donut's inside diameter to 0, creating a solid dot

`Outside diamter <0'-1.00">:`***.3*** ↵

`Center of doughnut:` *Pick the absolute point 8.80,4.70*

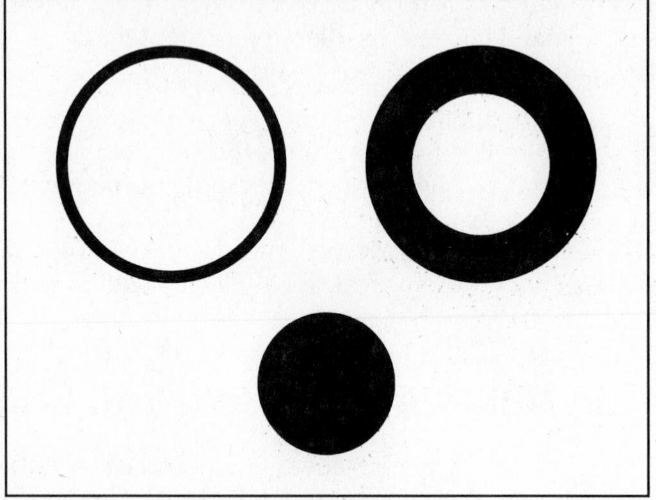

Figure 7.20:
Some examples of donuts.

`Center of doughnut:` *Pick the absolute point 8.30,4.70*	
`Center of doughnut:` *Pick the absolute point 7.80,4.70*	
`Center of doughnut:` *Press Enter*	Ends the command
`Command:` *Press Enter*	Repeats the command
`DONUT Inside diameter <0'-0.00">:` **`0.1`** ↵	Specifies a new interior diameter
`Outside diameter <0'-0.30">:` **`0.15`** ↵	
`Center of doughnut:` *Pick the absolute point 9.30,5.60*	
`Center of doughnut:` *Pick the absolute point 9.30,3.50*	
Click in the top viewport	Makes the top viewport current
`Center of doughnut:` *Pick the absolute point 2.70,3.50*	
`Center of doughnut:` *Pick the absolute point 2.70,5.60*	
`Center of doughnut:` *Press Enter*	Ends the DONUT command

Your drawing should look like figure 7.21.

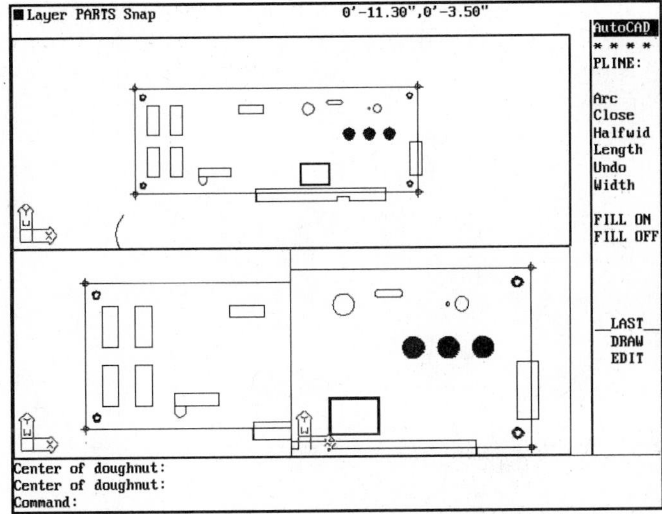

Figure 7.21:
Using DONUT to add parts.

As you can see, DONUT keeps on prompting for the center of the donut until you press Enter to exit the command.

You can type **Donut** or **Doughnut**; AutoCAD accepts either spelling.

The donut that AutoCAD constructs is not a new primitive. The donut is actually a polyline that has the following three polyline properties: it is made of arc segments, it has width (you set the widths by entering the inside and outside diameter), and it is closed.

Drawing Regular Polygons

If you want multisegmented polygons with irregular segment lengths, use polylines or closed lines. If you want nice, regular polygons, use the POLYGON command. A polygon is actually another polyline in disguise. POLYGON gives you two ways to define the size of your figure (see fig. 7.22). You can show the length of one of the edges or define it relative to a circle. The polygon can then be inscribed in or circumscribed about the circle.

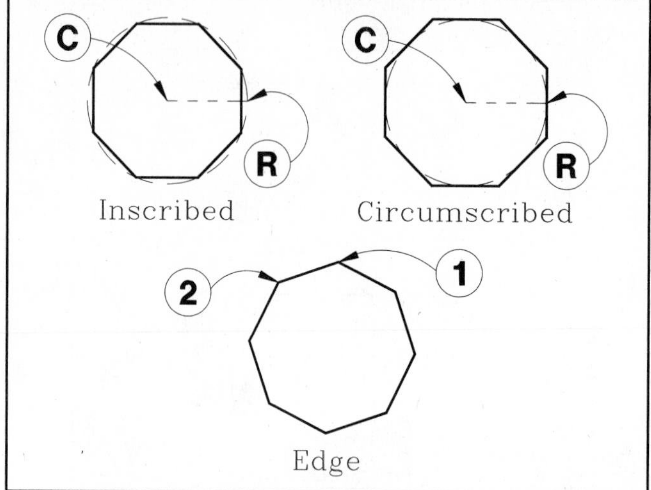

Figure 7.22:
Two basic ways to draw polygons.

Six-sided polygons make good hex nuts. In the next exercise, put a six-sided polygon in the mounting tab on the bottom of the resistor.

Using POLYGON To Draw Regular Polygons

Make the bottom left viewport current and restore the RESISTOR view.

`Command:` *Choose* Draw, *then* Polygon, *then* Circumscribed

`_polygon`
`Number of sides <4>:` **`6`** ↵

`Edge/<Center of polygon>:` *From the pop-up menu, choose Center*

`center of` *Pick anywhere on the arc*
`Radius of circle:` **`.05`** ↵ — Draws a hexagon

After you enter the polygon's radius, the hexagon should resemble the one shown in figure 7.23.

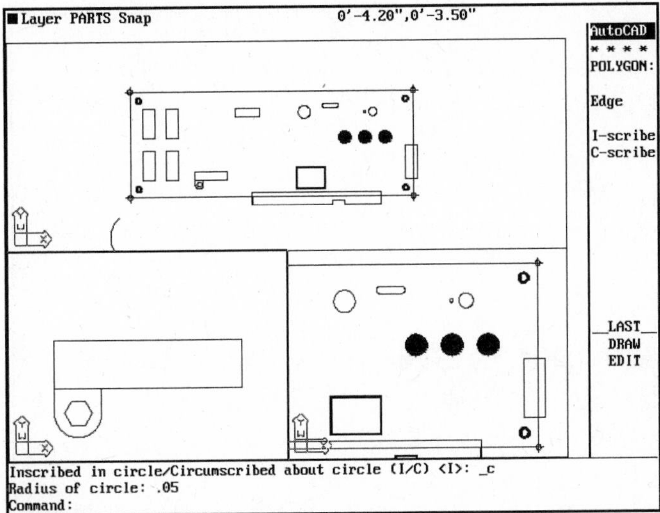

Figure 7.23:

Drawing a polygon on the resistor.

If you know the center point, the inscribed or circumscribed method is probably what you need. The edge method is handy for aligning an edge of the polygon with existing objects. The *edge* method generates a polygon that continues counterclockwise from two edge endpoints that you select. If you want to see a slow circle, draw a polygon with 1000 edges.

Drawing an Ellipse

The ELLIPSE command creates a polyline in disguise. AutoCAD first prompts you for the major axis, defined by two endpoints or the center and one endpoint. You then can define the minor axis by distance or rotation, or by dragging the ellipse if you pick the point or angle. Figure 7.24 shows the various ellipse-creation methods.

In the next exercise, you create a rectangle just above the transformer and put three ellipses in it. This part is called a *jumper*.

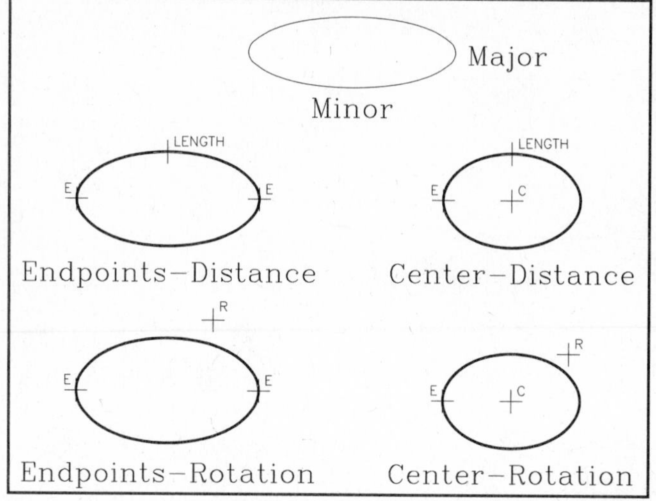

Figure 7.24:
Some examples of ellipses.

Using ELLIPSE To Draw a Jumper

Make the bottom right viewport current.

`Command:` *Use ZOOM and window to show the area just above the transformer (see fig. 7.25)*	
`Command:` **`PL`** ↵	Issues the PLINE command
`Command:` *Choose* Settings, *then* Drawing Aids, *and set snap to .05"*	
`From point:` **`6.70,4.10`** ↵	
`Current line-width is 0'-0.02"`	
`Arc/Close/Halfwidth/Length/Undo/ Width/<Endpoint of line>:` *From the screen menu, choose* Width	
Set width to zero and draw to @0.2<90 to @0.6<0 to @0.2<270 and close	
`Command:` *Start the LINE command and use snap to create two lines that divide the rectangle in thirds*	
`Command:` *Choose* Draw, *then* Ellipse, *then* Center, Axis, Axis	Issues the ELLIPSE command with Center and Axis options

`_ellipse <Axis endpoint 1>/Center: _c`	
`Center of ellipse:` *Pick the absolute point 6.80,4.20*	Places the center point
`Axis endpoint:` *Pick the polar point @0.10<0.00*	Specifies the axis' endpoint
`<Other axis distance>/Rotation:` *Pick polar point @0.05<270.00*	Specifies the other axis' endpoint
`Command:` *Press Enter*	Repeats the ELLIPSE command
`<Axis endpoint 1>/Center:` *Pick the absolute point 6.90,4.20*	Specifies the axis' start point
`Axis endpoint 2:` *Pick the polar point @0.20<0.00*	Places the axis' endpoint
`<Other axis distance>/Rotation:` *Pick the polar point @0.05<270.00*	Sets the other axis' endpoint and length

Next, draw an end/rotation ellipse in the right box.

`Command:` *Press Enter*	Repeats the ELLIPSE command
`<Axis endpoint 1>/Center:` *Pick the absolute point 7.10,4.20*	Specifies the axis' start point
`Axis endpoint 2:` *Pick the polar point @0.20<0.00*	Specifies the axis' endpoint
`<Other axis distance>/Rotation:` *From the screen menu, choose* Rotation	Specifies the Rotation option
`_ROTATION Rotation around major axis:` **60** ↵	
`Command:` *Save the drawing*	

After you finish, your drawing should look like figure 7.25.

ELLIPSE is the last type of polyline. If you want to try more polylines, create a layer named SCRATCH and experiment on this layer.

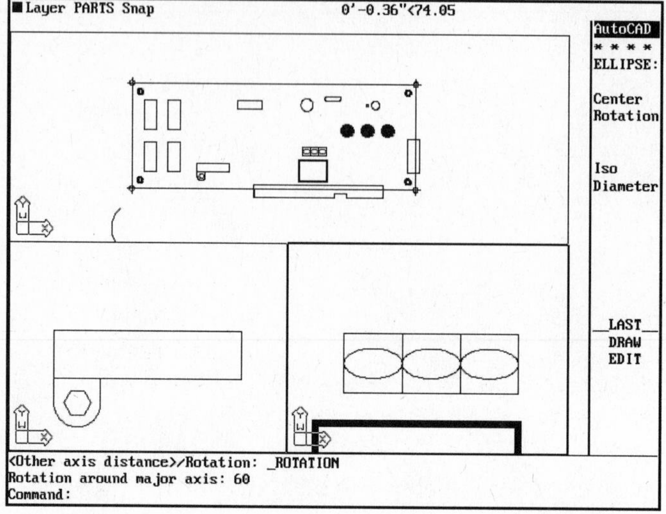

Figure 7.25:

A jumper created with the ELLIPSE command.

Creating Solids

The SOLID command creates a filled-in polygon — a two-dimensional boundary (polygon) filled with color. This area is defined by three or four points that form a triangular or quadrilateral shape. You can construct more complex shapes by continuing to add vertices. The order in which you enter vertices and the spatial relationship between these points determines the solid's appearance (see fig. 7.26). If you try to create a quadrilateral shape from four points, you might mistakenly create a bow tie. Nine times out of ten, users first create bow ties and butterflies instead of quadrilaterals.

Do not confuse the SOLID command, which has been around for many years, to the relatively new concept of AME solid modeling. The advanced modeling extension of AutoCAD is a three-dimensional, solid modeling addition to AutoCAD.

In the following exercise, use SOLID to create a vertical solid at the outer edge of the port on the right side of the widget.

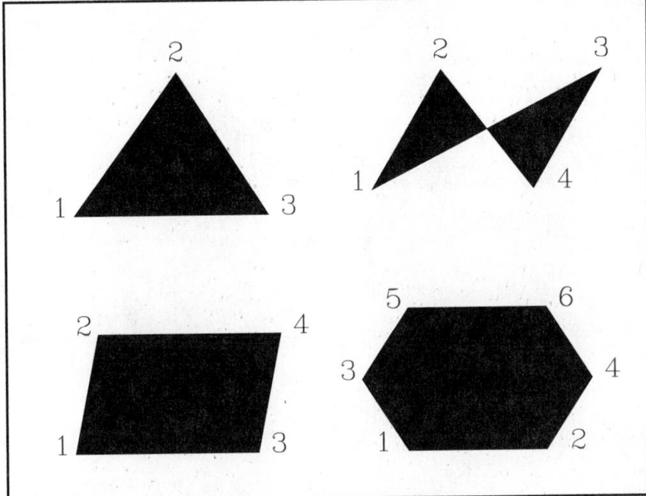

Figure 7.26:

Examples of solids.

Using SOLID To Make a Solid Shape

`Command:` *Choose* View, *then* Zoom, *then* Dynamic, *and magnify the area around the port (see fig. 7.27)*	
`Command:` *Enter* **`SNAP`**, *and set snap spacing to .1*	
`Command:` **`SOLID`** ↵	
`First point:` *Pick the absolute point 9.60,4.60*	
`Second point:` *Pick the absolute point 9.70,4.60*	
`Third point:` *Pick the absolute point 9.60,3.60*	
`Fourth point:` *Pick the absolute point 9.70,3.60*	Draws the solid and prompts for more
`Third point:` *Press Enter*	Ends the SOLID command

Your drawing should resemble figure 7.27, showing the solid filled area around the port.

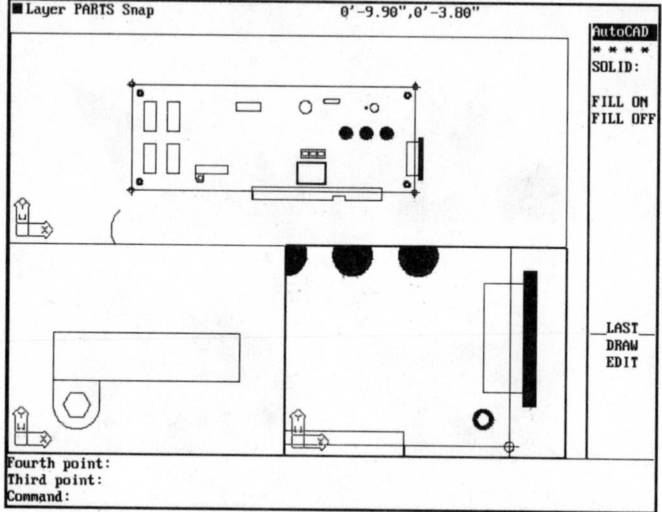

Figure 7.27:

Enhancing the port with a solid.

If you keep entering points, SOLID keeps prompting for new third and fourth points, drawing new solids from the previous third and fourth points to the new points.

After solids and traces are created, they are identical except in name. Both types of entities fill and snap with object snaps in the same way.

Using Fill Control with Solids, Traces, and Polylines

When the FILL command is turned off, it reduces solids, polylines, and traces to single-line outlines of their boundaries. If FILL is on, solids, polylines, and traces are filled-in on the screen and at plotting time.

Turn off FILL to decrease redraw, regeneration, and plotting times.

The FILL command is either on or off. The steps that follow show you how to turn on and off the widget's filled entities.

Using the FILL Command

```
Command: FILL ↵
ON/OFF <ON>: OFF ↵                     Turns off FILL
```

The FILL command does not affect existing entities until after the next regeneration. To see the effect of FILL, regenerate the drawing now.

```
Command: REGENALL ↵                    Regenerates all viewports
Command: FILL ↵
ON/OFF <OFF>: ON ↵                     Turns FILL back on
```

Figure 7.28 shows the WIDGET drawing with FILL off.

Notice the pie-shaped sections in the donuts in figure 7.28. When fill is off, each polyline segment shows as an outline.

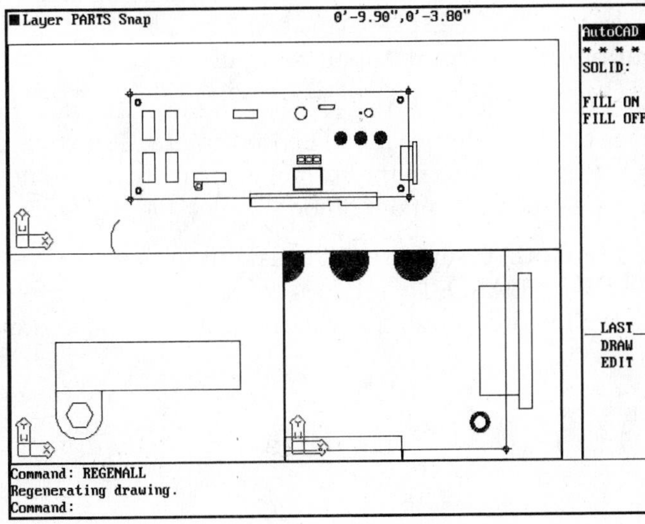

Figure 7.28:

Fill off.

Using AutoCAD's Text Commands

The rest of this chapter explains the commands associated with placing text in a drawing. AutoCAD text has a set of default parameters that define how text is placed and stored. You must select a beginning point for your text, a height for the characters, and the way the text is to be placed and formatted. Then you enter the characters. You already used text in its default AutoCAD form.

Style Settings

If you draw the letter A, you need 7, 19, or more line strokes, depending on the font. Rather than store each stroke of a character in a string of text, AutoCAD stores characters in special files called shape files. *Shape files* efficiently store each character definition as a series of *vectors* (directions and distances). These shape files are compiled into even more efficient binary SHX files, from which AutoCAD can rapidly extract character information for display. In translating text from the compiled shape files to your screen or plotter, AutoCAD passes the text through several filters that incorporate your preferences for the appearance of the text.

Text style is the set of parameters AutoCAD uses in translating text from a shape into strokes on the plotter or pixels on the monitor. A text style is a named collection of instructions in the current drawing that does not change the original shape file font definition.

As you have seen, AutoCAD supplies many default settings. The default text style is called STANDARD. This style is defined with the simple TXT font and with default width, rotation angle, and justification (alignment).

Using STYLE To Create and Maintain Text Styles

Use the STYLE command to create new styles or change the parameters for existing styles. The job of setting your style is really part of the setting-up process. Set your styles early in the drawing before you get into any intensive text input.

Because the default TXT font used in the STANDARD style is a bit awkward, use the following exercise to respecify the font used with your STANDARD style.

Using STYLE To Modify a Text Style

`Command:` *Enter* `NEW`*, then enter,* `WIDGET=IA7WIDG2` *and press Enter to overwrite the existing WIDGET drawing*

Continue with the WIDGET drawing

`Command:` **`STYLE`** ↵

`Text Style name (or ?) <STANDARD>:` *Press Enter*	Accepts the default name (STANDARD) as the style to modify

When the Select Font File dialog box appears, change to the subdirectory in which the AutoCAD font files are located (usually \ACAD or \ACAD\FONTS), select the ROMANS.SHX font file, and click on OK.

`Existing style.`	
`Height <0'-0.00">:` *Press Enter*	Accepts the 0 default for variable height
`Width factor <1.00>: .8` ↵	Makes the style narrower
`Obliquing angle <0.00>:` *Press Enter*	
`Backwards? <N>:` *Press Enter*	
`Upside-down? <N>:` *Press Enter*	
`Vertical ? <N>:` *Press Enter*	
`STANDARD is now the current text style.`	

Now your STANDARD style uses the ROMANS font and is slightly narrower than normal.

To help you select fonts graphically, AutoCAD has a Select Text Font dialog box with pages of icons from which you can select your text styles. Two pages are shown in figures 7.29 and 7.30. All of the standard AutoCAD fonts are included in the icon pages. Select a font from the icons to create a new style, with the same style name as the font.

To get to these icons, choose Text from the Draw pull-down menu, then choose Set Style.

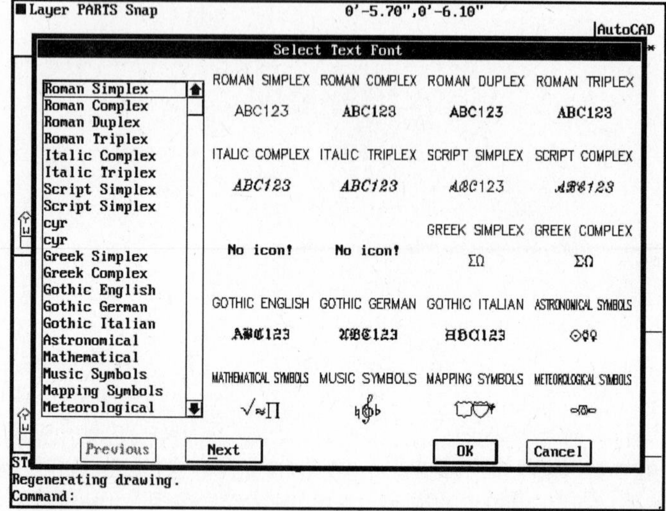

Figure 7.29:

The first icon page for creating text styles.

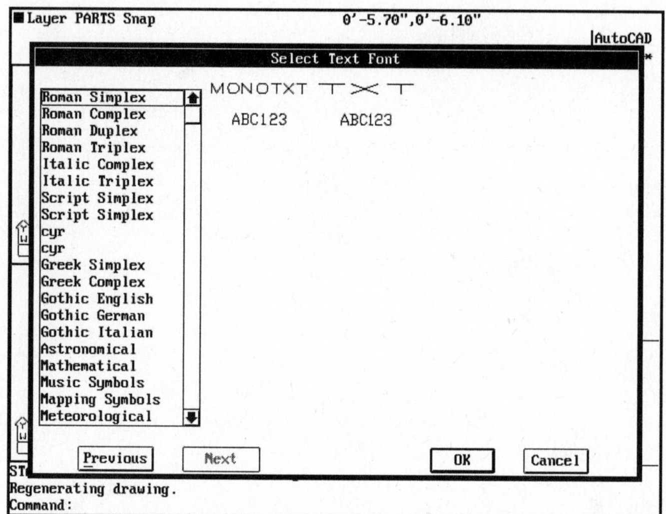

Figure 7.30:

The second icon page for creating text styles.

Style Options

As figure 7.31 shows, AutoCAD offers several text style parameters. The following are the text style options:

- **Style name.** This option prompts you to name a new style to create or an existing style to edit. This style becomes the current default.
- **?.** This option lists named styles defined in the current drawing. You can enter an asterisk (the default) to list all named styles or use wild cards to list a specific set of styles.
- **Font.** This option prompts you to choose a font file name for the style to reference using the Select Font File dialog box for the style to reference. The default <TXT> references the TXT.SHX file.
- **Height.** This option prompts you to specify text height for a fixed height style, or enter 0 (the default) for a variable height style. Text commands do not prompt for height unless you use a variable height style.
- **Width factor.** This option prompts you for a width factor to expand or condense text (default 1 = normal).
- **Obliquing angle.** This option prompts you to specify a number to slant the text characters, italicizing them (default 0 = vertical). To slant toward the right, use a positive number; to slant toward the left, use a negative number. Use small angles; a little slant looks like a lot.
- **Backwards.** This option mirrors text horizontally.
- **Upside-down.** This option mirrors text vertically.
- **Vertical.** This option orients text vertically, one character below.

Notes on Style

Here are some notes on using the AutoCAD STYLE command:

- Style definitions for AutoCAD are maintained in a tables section of the drawing database file. You can store many styles in a single drawing file. These styles affect only the current drawing.
- If you are using the STYLE command, press ?, then press Enter in response to the text style name prompt to see a list of the styles currently defined and stored in the drawing file.

Text style parameters			
Width factor 0.75	→	ABC 123	ROMANS
Width factor 1.00	→	ABC 123	
Width factor 1.25	→	ABC 123	
Oblique angle 0	→	ABC 123	
Oblique angle 10	→	*ABC 123*	VERTICAL
Oblique angle 20	→	*ABC 123*	
Oblique angle 45	→	*ABC 123*	
Upside down	→	ABC 123	
Backwards	→	ABC 123	

Figure 7.31:

Examples of text styles.

- If you give a new name in response to the text style name prompt, AutoCAD creates a new style in the style table.
- If you give an existing style name in response to the text style name prompt, AutoCAD assumes that you want to change or edit the existing style. It prompts you for all the style parameters and offers the old settings as defaults.
- If you change the Font or Vertical option of a style that is currently defined in the drawing file, AutoCAD regenerates the drawing. Any existing text of that style is updated with the new style definition. Changes to all other options are ignored for existing text.

Do not bother to define a standard set of styles each time you start a new drawing. You can add your standard styles to your standard prototype drawing (see Chapter 17 and Appendix C). Or, you can save them as part of another drawing file and insert them as a block (this will not override any existing definitions in an existing drawing). See Chapter 12 for more information.

Dynamic Text versus Regular Text

After you create the styles you want for your drawing, AutoCAD offers two commands that you can use to input the text: DTEXT and TEXT. Either command places text. The only difference is that DTEXT does it *dynamically,* enabling you to see each character in the drawing as it is typed.

If you use TEXT, AutoCAD waits for all your text input and then places the text in the drawing when you exit the TEXT command.

To get started with TEXT (and to see the new style definition), label the resistor in the lower left part of the widget in the next exercise.

Using TEXT To Add Labels

Make the bottom left viewport current

`Command:` *Choose* Settings, *then* Layer Control *and make the* TEXT *layer current*	
`Command:` **`TEXT`** ↵	
`Justify/Style/<Start point>:` **`J`** ↵	Issues the full justification prompt
`Align/Fit/Center/Middle/Right/TL/TC/TR /ML/MC/MR/BL/MC/BR:` **`M`** ↵	Specifies the Middle option
`Middle point:` *Pick the absolute point 4.50,3.80*	
`Height <0'-0.20">:` **`.1`** ↵	
`Rotation angle <0.00>:` *Press Enter*	
`Text:` **`RESISTOR`** ↵	Displays the text after you press Enter

Save the drawing

Your drawing should now look like figure 7.32.

Notice that the prompt options are the same as for the DTEXT command you used earlier.

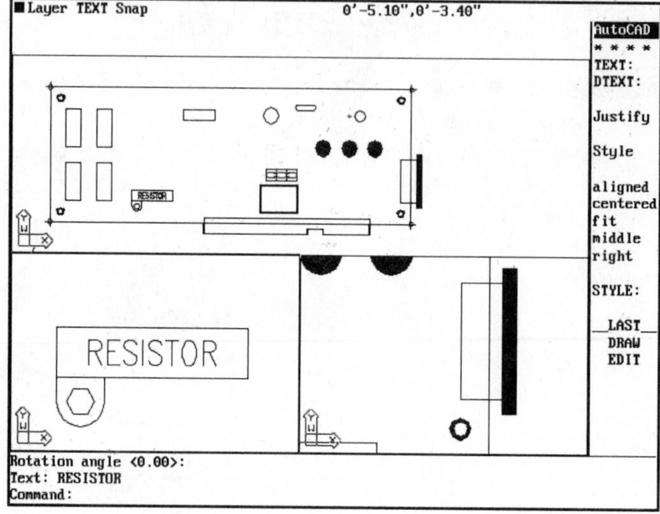

Figure 7.32:

The resistor, labeled with TEXT.

Formatting Text

The first thing AutoCAD wants to know about the text is how you want to format it. You have several options for formatting your text:

- **Justify.** This option issues the prompt for text justification.
- **Style.** This option enables you to specify a new text style default. The style must already be created with the STYLE command.
- **Start point.** This default option prompts you to specify a point for the default bottom left justification.
- **Press Enter.** This option highlights the last text entered and prompts for a new text string when you press Enter at the prompt. AutoCAD places the new text directly below the highlighted text, using the same style, height, and rotation. You also can pick a new point with DTEXT before you enter the text.
- **Height.** This option prompts you to specify the text height (the default is 0.2). You are not prompted for height when using Align justification or any text style with a predefined height.
- **Rotation angle.** This option prompts you to specify the text placement angle (the default is 0).
- **Text.** This option prompts you to enter the text string.

Text Justification

Justification (or alignment) specifies the way in which the text is aligned, relative to the start and optional endpoint(s) you give it. You have used Middle, Center, and the default Left justifications. The justification prompt shows the complete list:

```
Align/Fit/Center/Middle/Right/TL/TC/TR/ML/MC/MR/BL/BC/BR:
```

The following list describes each of these options:

- **Align.** Specify the beginning and ending points of the text baseline. The text height is scaled so that the text between these points is not distorted.
- **Fit.** Specify the beginning and ending points of the text baseline. The text width is distorted to fit the text between these points without changing the height.
- **Center.** Specify a point for the horizontal center and the vertical baseline of the text string.
- **Middle.** Specify a point for the horizontal and vertical midpoint of the text string.
- **Right.** Specify a point for the bottom right baseline of the text string.
- **TL.** Specify a point for the left of the text string, aligned with the top of the tallest character.
- **TC.** Specify a point for the center of the text string, aligned with the top of an uppercase character.
- **TR.** Specify a point for the right side of the text string, aligned with the top of an uppercase character.
- **ML.** Specify a point for the left side of the text string, aligned halfway between the top of an uppercase character and the text baseline.
- **MC.** Specify a point for the center of the text string, aligned halfway between an uppercase character and the bottom of the text baseline.
- **MR.** Specify a point for the right side, between the top of the an uppercase character and the text baseline.
- **BL.** Specify a point for the left side of the text string, aligned at the bottom of a descender.
- **BC.** Specify a point for the center of the text string, aligned at the bottom of a descender.

- **BR.** Specify a point for the right side of the text string, aligned at the bottom of a descender.

Figure 7.33 presents a graphical depiction of each option.

Start Point (Left Justified)
Align
Fit
Center
Middle
Right (Right Justified)
TL (Top Left)
TC (Top Center)
TR (Top Right)
ML (Middle Left)
MC (Middle Center)
MR (Middle Right)
BL (Bottom Left)
BC (Bottom Center)
BR (Bottom Right)

Figure 7.33:
Text justification options.

The TL, TC, TR, ML, MC, MR, BL, BC, and BR justifications are the nine possible combinations of the Top, Middle, and Bottom vertical justifications and the Left, Center, and Right horizontal justifications. The default Left and the simple Center and Right justifications are all baseline justifications, which could have fit into this same matrix if B was not already taken by Bottom. Fit, TL, TC, TR, ML, MC, MR, BL, BC, and BR-justified text cannot be used with vertical text styles; the others work vertically or horizontally.

Middle-justified text (unlike ML, MC, and MR) floats vertically, depending on whether the particular text string includes uppercase characters or characters with descenders. The other options have three vertical positions relative to a standard text cell height. The Standard cell height is the height of a capital letter. The options TL, TC, TR, ML, MC, MR, BL, BC, and BR each maintain vertical text positioning, regardless of the string entered. Middle is designed to always be centered in both axes, for use in bubbles and similar applications. The other justifications are designed to be consistent results for most other applications.

If you respond to the DTEXT (or TEXT) start point prompt by pressing Enter, the new text starts one line below the last text you entered in the drawing. The new text assumes the height, style, and justification of the previous text, even if you have used intervening AutoCAD commands.

Using DTEXT To Place Text

DTEXT can be more flexible to use than TEXT. Input for DTEXT is always shown left-justified on the screen, regardless of the chosen format. The justification is corrected after the command is finished. You also can reposition the box cursor on the drawing area at any point during text entry by picking a new point with your crosshairs. This feature enables you to place text throughout your drawing with a single DTEXT command. The trade-off for this flexibility in picking new points is that the menus are disabled.

What happens if you make a mistake entering text? If you are using DTEXT, you can backspace and correct your errors as you type. If you do not realize that you have a mistaken text entry until you see it in the drawing window, do not panic — all is repairable. You learn to edit text in the next chapter. For now, just undo the text and try again.

Input more text with DTEXT by labeling other parts of the widget. Add text by entering the justifications and starting points shown, and either type or drag answers to the height and angle prompts. Start on the left and label the RAM chips with Middle/Left text. Figure 7.34 shows the labeled chips.

Using DTEXT To Label the Widget Drawing

`Command:` *Choose* View, *then* Zoom, *then* Dynamic, *and zoom to enclose the RAM chips*

`Command:` *Enter* `SNAP`, *and set Snap to 0.05*

`Command:` *Choose* Draw, *then* Text, *then* Dynamic — Issues the DTEXT command

`_dtext Justify/Style/<Start point>: J ↵`

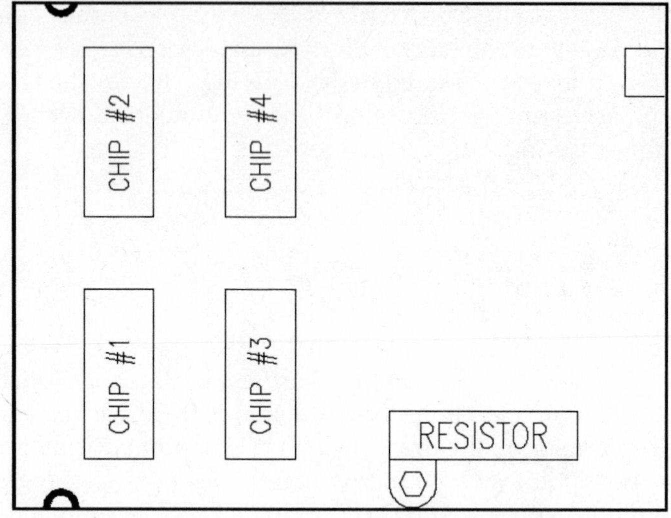

Figure 7.34:
Detail of the chip labels.

`Align/Fit/Center/Middle/Right/TL/TC/ TR/ML/MC/MR/BL/BC/BR:` **`ML`** ↵	Specifies the Middle-Left option
`Middle/left point:` *Pick at 2.95,3.8*	
`Height <0'-0.10">:` **`.08`** ↵	
`Rotation angle <0.00>:` **`90`** ↵	
`Text:` **`CHIP #1`** ↵	Displays the text, but does not yet justify it
Move the cursor by picking at point 2.95,4.8	
`Text:` **`CHIP #2`** ↵	
Move the cursor by picking at point 3.55,3.8	
`Text:` **`CHIP #3`** ↵	
Move the cursor by picking at point 3.55,4.8	
`Text:` **`CHIP #4`** ↵	
`Text:` *Press Enter*	Ends the DTEXT command and redisplays the justified text

Pan or zoom to the center of the board.

`Command:` **`DTEXT`** ↵	Starts the DTEXT command

`Justify/Style/<Start point>:` **M** ↵	Specifies the Middle option
`Middle point:` *From the pop-up menu, choose* Center	Specifies the CEN object snap mode
`center of` *Pick any point on the circle shown in fig. 7.35*	
`Height <0'-0.08">:` **.15** ↵	
`Rotation angle <90.00>:` **0** ↵	
`Text:` **C** ↵	
`Text:` *Press Enter*	
`Command:` *Press Enter*	Reissues the DTEXT command
`Justify/Style/<Start point>:` **F** ↵	Specifies Fit justification
`First text line point:` *Pick the absolute point 6.65,3.80*	Specifies the left end of the text string
`Second text line point:` *Pick the polar point @0.60<0.00*	Specifies the right end
`Height <0'-0.15">:` **.08** ↵	
`Text:` **TRANSFORMER** ↵	Displays the text, but not yet justified
`Text:` *Press Enter*	Draws the text so that it is squeezed between points; ends the DTEXT command
`Command:` *Press Enter*	Repeats the DTEXT command
`Justify/Style/<Start point>:` **C** ↵	Specifies Center justification
`Center point:` *Pick the absolute point 6.95,3.65*	
`Height <0'-0.08">:` *Press Enter*	
`Rotation angle <0.00>:` *Press Enter*	
`Text:` **ONE** ↵	
`Text:` *Press Enter*	
`Command:` *Press Enter*	Repeats the DTEXT command
`Justify/Style/<Start point>:` **MC** ↵	Selects the Middle-Center justification option
`Middle point:` *Pick the absolute point 5.40,5.30*	
`Height <0'-0.08">:` *Pick the polar point @0.10<90.00*	

`Rotation angle <0.00>:` *Press Enter*	
`Text:` **`ROM`** ↵	
`Text:` *Press Enter*	
`Command:` **`REDRAWALL`** ↵	Gets rid of blips and cleans up the screen

Figure 7.35 shows the results of this exercise.

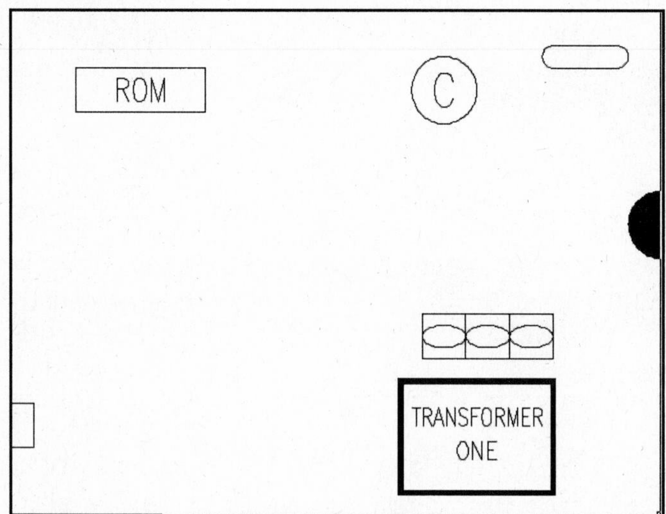

Figure 7.35:

Detail of the new labels.

AutoCAD never forgets. Its default prompts you during the text commands show your previous parameter settings. You can speed parameter entry by pressing Enter to accept the defaults.

Next, try the Middle, Fit, Center, and Middle/Center justifications.

DTEXT automatically lines up successive lines of text, one under the other, if you press Enter after each line. If you press Enter at the first text prompt, lines of text align with the previous text entered. Before trying this technique in the next exercise, change your text style to one with an oblique slant to give the widget drawing a title with a unique look.

Defining an Oblique Text Style

Make the bottom right viewport current and zoom to the logo in the lower left corner of the board (see fig. 7.36). Then take the following steps to create a new style for the title.

Command: **STYLE** ↵

Text Style name (or ?) <STANDARD>: **TITLE** ↵

New style.

After the Select font file dialog box appears, change to the subdirectory that contains ROMANC.SHX and select ROMANC.SHX.

Height <0'-0.00">: **.2** ↵	Specifies a fixed height
Width factor <1.00>: **.8** ↵	Makes the font thin
Obliquing angle <0.00>: **15** ↵	Slants the font 15 degrees

Backwards? <N>: *Press Enter*

Upside-down? <N>: *Press Enter*

Vertical ? <N>: *Press Enter*

TITLE is now the current text style.

Next use the TITLE style and have DTEXT automatically line up the words "Widget," "Circuit," and "Board" under one another. After you finish, change your drawing window to a single view and zoom for a good look.

Creating Successive Lines of Text

Command: *Choose* Draw, *then* Text, *then* Dynamic, *or enter* **DTEXT**

Justify/Style/<Start point>: *Pick or enter absolute point 2.50,2.60*	Left-justifies the text at the picked point

Rotation angle <0.00>: *Press Enter*

Text: **Widget** ↵

Text: **Layout** ↵

Text: **Board** ↵

Text: *Press Enter*

Make the top viewport current	
Command: **TILEMODE** ↵	Accesses the TILEMODE system variable
New Value for TILEMODE <0>: **1** ↵	Returns to a single viewport
Command: *Issue ZOOM with the Extents option*	Fills the display with the drawing
Regenerating drawing.	
Save the drawing	

Your drawing now should resemble figure 7.36.

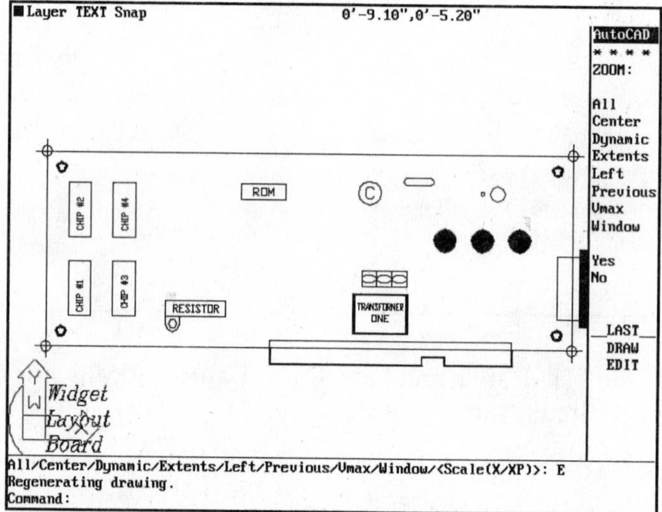

Figure 7.36:

A zoomed widget board with text.

Two more special, quick text topics await you. But first, here are some points to remember about text entry.

- Whenever you want to jog your memory, enter J at the first text prompt to see the full justification prompt. You do not, however, need the full prompt to use any of its justifications. You can enter any of them at the first prompt. Often, you can set height and angle once (as you set up your drawing file for example) and press Enter to use these defaults for all future text use.
- You also can use object snap modes to help you place your text. To add a line to existing text, use DTEXT with object snap mode INSert, pick the existing text, and enter only a space on the first line. Then press Enter to space down for the next line.

- You can enter text upside down by using an angle definition to the left of the starting point (180 degrees).

The default height shown in the TEXT command is rounded off to your units setting and may not accurately display its true value.

Using Special Text Characters

Occasionally, you may need to use special symbols or angle text on a drawing. This section describes how to create some special effects. If you want to practice some of the special text examples, use your SCRATCH layer.

Text Underscore and Overscore

You use underscores, superscripts, and special symbols regularly in text strings on drawings. You do not find these symbols on standard keyboards. Figure 7.37 shows some special text. The underscored and overscored text in the illustration was entered into the DTEXT command, as follows:

```
Text: %%u88%%u %%o88%%o
```

You can enter the special character switches, %%u (underline) and %%o (overscore), any time you are typing a text string in response to the text prompt.

Angled versus Vertical Text

Most text reads horizontally from left to right. Sometimes, however, you may want text that reads top to bottom.

You can use the normal DTEXT or TEXT command parameters to rotate or align your text at any angle. If you want your text to read vertically, you can create a style and give it a vertical orientation. A vertical orientation aligns characters one below the other. You can give all standard AutoCAD fonts a vertical orientation.

SPECIAL TEXT CHARACTERS		
%%%	Forces single PERCENT sign	%
%%p	Draws PLUS/MINUS symbol	88±
%%u	UNDERSCORE mode on/off	88
%%o	OVERSCORE mode on/off	88
%%c	Draws DIAMETER symbol	88ø
%%d	Draws DEGREE symbol	88°
%%nnn	Draws ASCII character	

Figure 7.37: Examples of special text.

Quick versus Fancy Text

As your drawing file fills up with drawing entities, it takes longer and longer to zoom, redraw, or regenerate the drawing window. Sooner or later, you want to cut down the regeneration time. AutoCAD offers two options for speeding up text display. First, you can do all your text work in a simple font, such as TXT, while you are creating the drawing or while you are making test plots. When creating the final plot, you can enhance the drawing by replacing the simple font with a more elegant font, such as ROMANC. You save time during initial drawing editor work, but your drawings still look good with the last-minute font change.

Because font-character definitions differ in width, and font respecification does not attempt to compensate, you may find the new fancy text does not fit where you placed the old simple text.

A second option (to speed regeneration time) is to use the AutoCAD QTEXT command. QTEXT (for Quick TEXT) enables you to temporarily replace the display of text with a rectangle outlining its position.

The QTEXT Command

QTEXT is available from the keyboard or from the SETTINGS screen menu. It does not replace text until the next regeneration. Try using the QTEXT command on the widget drawing.

Looking at QTEXT

Command: **QTEXT** ↵

ON/OFF <Off>: **ON** ↵

Command: **REGEN** ↵ — Replaces the text with boxes (see fig. 7.38)

Regenerating drawing.

Command: **QTEXT** ↵

Turn off Qtext

Exit from AutoCAD

Figure 7.38 shows the widget drawing with QTEXT turned on.

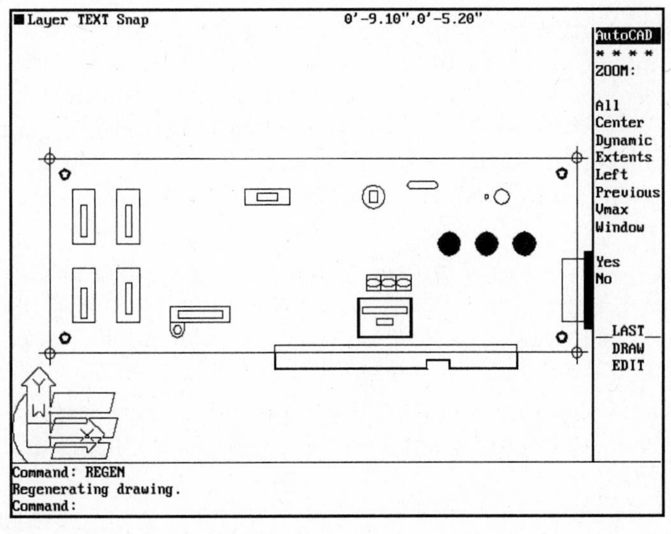

Figure 7.38:

The widget after Qtext is turned on.

The text regenerates when you reload the drawing in the next chapter. Notice that QTEXT did not accurately represent the justification and text line lengths. To do so, AutoCAD must do the full text display calculations, and that would save little time over normal text display.

Summary

In this chapter, you covered much material. Pull-down, screen, and tablet menus (if you use one) are becoming familiar, like road signs in a new town. Although the number of side streets for different drawing commands may seem endless, you are beginning to understand how the primary drawing commands get you almost all the way to your destination.

You may put aside learning additional commands and options until you need them or have some extra time to explore AutoCAD. If you like Sunday drives into the country, AutoCAD enables you to "wander" through some of the less frequently used commands without letting you stray too far off the beaten path.

Here are some reminders about the entities you used in this chapter:

- Points are useful reference locators for a later object snap. They can be displayed in various sizes and styles.
- Lines are the pillars of the drawing community. Connected lines are the norm; press Enter to stop a connected line run. Continue starts a line at the last endpoint. Close makes a polygon by returning a connected line series to the first point. Take advantage of TRACE's mitered edge to get angled ends for fat lines. Otherwise, you will find PLINE superior to TRACE for every other purpose.
- CIRCLE requires minimal information to generate full circles. Center point/radius is the most common circle-creation method. A three-point arc is the most convenient to create. The start,center series also is useful.
- Polylines enable you to create single graphic elements composed of linear and curved segments. Donuts, polygons, and ellipses are made from polylines.
- Text gets to the drawing window through a filtering process that controls style, justification, height, and rotation. DTEXT dynamically places text as you key characters at the keyboard. Style gives you flexibility in creating type styles that are tailored to your needs. The

justification options give control over placement. Keep text on its own layer or use QTEXT to keep redraw and regeneration times to a minimum as drawing files expand.

Think ahead about the sequence for entering Solid vertices. It can be difficult to avoid drawing a bow tie.

In this chapter, you began earnest work on a real drawing. Every entity that you used works the same in a 3D drawing, although AutoCAD has a few more graphic entities especially designed for 3D, which you will see in a later chapter.

You have already mastered setting layers, drawing lines and circles, and inserting text. By the end of the next chapter, this drawing will be a complete, four-layer, full-color widget layout drawing.

8

Introduction to Editing

The one certainty in the drawing business is change. Change this! Change that! Drawing revision numbers keep mounting! If you are to use AutoCAD successfully, you must become familiar with the program's editing functions. In fact, you may find yourself spending more time editing existing drawings than creating new ones.

So far in this book, you have spent most of your tutorial time creating new drawing entities. Chapter 6 used the basic options of several editing commands in the form of grip editing. AutoCAD, however, includes several more powerful and versatile editing commands and options. In this chapter, you expand your drawing knowledge by using more of AutoCAD's editing commands and options.

The benefits of electronic drawing editing are simple. When you master AutoCAD's editing capabilities, you can stay on top of changes to your project without falling behind in your drawings. You can erase, move, copy, and resize individual objects quickly without disturbing other entities in the drawing. You also can create multiple copies of objects—and even arrange those copies in an arrayed pattern—with minimal original entry. Figure 8.1, for example, shows how simple editing techniques can enhance a drawing. You learn how to make these changes to the widget drawing in this chapter.

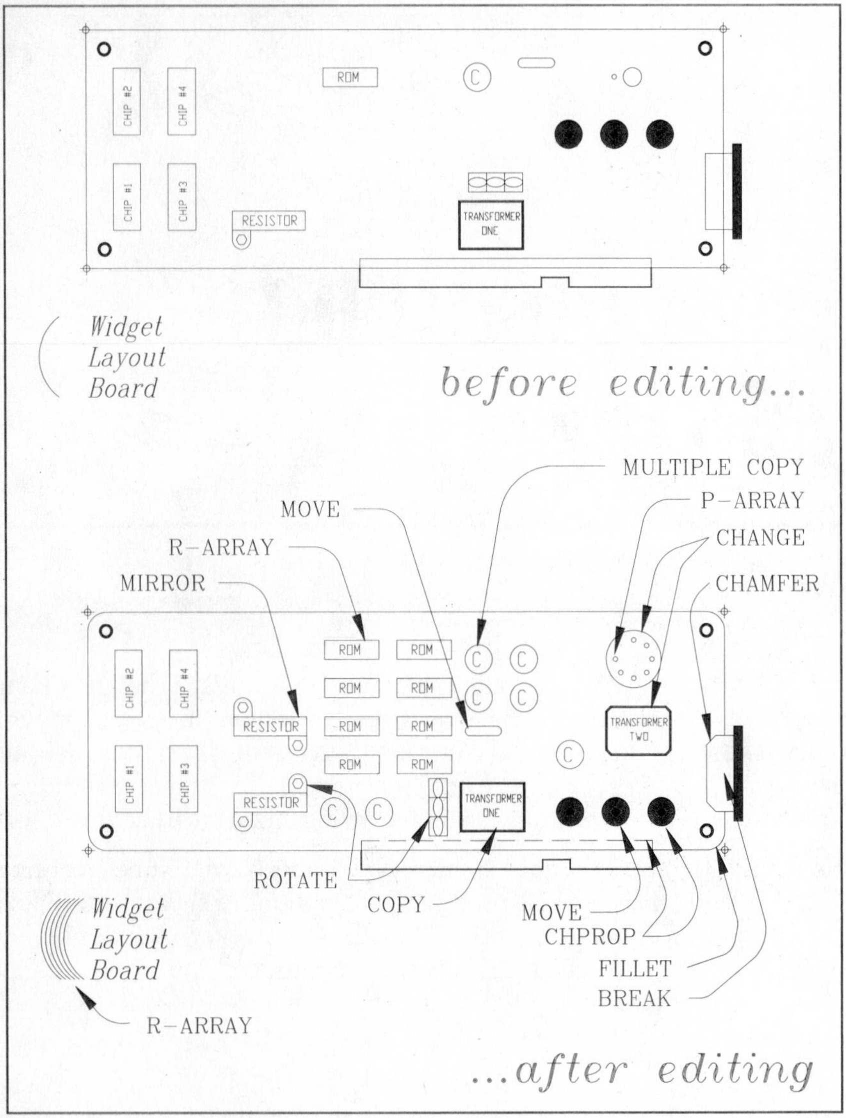

Figure 8.1:
The widget drawing, before and after editing.

You can perform three basic kinds of activities when you edit a drawing: changing, copying, and erasing entities within your drawing. You can change an existing entity's location, layer, and visual properties, such as color and linetype. You also can *break* entities by deleting portions of line

and arc segments. Breaking an entity reduces its length or divides it into multiple entities. You can copy entities, either one at a time or in an arrayed pattern. You also can erase entities to get rid of previous mistakes.

AutoCAD offers more advanced editing functions—such as trimming, extending, stretching, and scaling—as well as some editing construction techniques. The following chapters cover these advanced functions. This book's 3D chapters cover 3D variations of these editing commands.

Exploring the Editor's Toolkit

Most of AutoCAD's editing commands are gathered on the Modify pull-down menu and the EDIT screen menus (see fig. 8.2). The Settings pull-down menu includes settings for some of the editing commands. The Construct pull-down menu also contains commands that are sometimes thought of as editing commands.

This chapter discusses the basics of editing. In the following exercises, you are shown ways to change both the spatial (location) and appearance (color and linetype) properties of existing entities. To perform these simple editing functions, you need to use only a few basic editing commands.

File Assist Draw Construct Modify View Settings Render Model
Entity...
Erase
Break
Extend
Trim
Align
Move
Rotate
Rotate 3D
Scale
Stretch
Change
Explode
PolyEdit
Edit Dims
AutoCAD
* * * *
ARRAY:
ATTEDIT:
BREAK:
CHAMFER:
CHANGE:
CHPROP:
COPY:
DDATTE:
DDEDIT:
DDMODIFY
DIVIDE:
ERASE:
EXPLODE:
next
LAST
DRAW
EDIT
Command:
Cancel
Command:

Figure 8.2:

The Modify pull-down and the EDIT screen menus.

The basic editing commands form two groups. The first group, which changes the location, quantity, and orientation of objects, includes the following commands:

Command	*Function*
MOVE	Moves selected objects
ROTATE	Rotates selected objects about a base point
COPY	Creates one or more copies of selected objects
MIRROR	Creates a reverse copy of selected objects
ARRAY	Creates a rectangular or polar array of selected objects

You have already used the grip-editing mode of these basic commands, but have not used all of their options. In this chapter, you explore these commands and all their options, as well as these additional commands used for editing objects:

Command	*Function*
BREAK	Removes a portion of the selected object
CHAMFER	Inserts a chamfer segment between two continuous lines or polylines
FILLET	Inserts a fillet arc between two continuous lines, two polyline segments, or all segments of an entire polyline

In addition to these two groups of commands, this chapter shows you how to use the ERASE command to delete entities and offers further practice with the various grip editing modes that you examined in Chapter 6.

How Editing Commands Work

Most editing commands involve a four-step process. Before you actually edit an object, you must think about the kind of edit you want to do, which objects you want to edit, and how you want to edit them. The process includes these steps:

1. Issue the editing command
2. Select the entities
3. Enter the appropriate parameters and pick points
4. Watch the edit as it takes place on-screen

Noun/verb selection of entities means that the entities (the nouns) are selected before the verb (the command) is issued. This method of entity selection is different than the verb/noun process, in which entities are not selected until after the command is issued.

When you invoke an editing command, AutoCAD switches to object-selection mode. In object-selection mode, you tell AutoCAD which entity or entities you want to edit. Most commands require you to select one or more objects. You can, however, reverse the order of steps 1 and 2 in Release 12, if the PICKFIRST system variable is on (set to 1). This enables the entities to be selected before issuing the command. PICKFIRST is turned on by a check in the Noun/Verb Selection box in the Entity Selection Settings dialog box. This dialog box is displayed with the DDSELECT command or by choosing Selection Settings from the Settings menu. Setting PICKFIRST on adds versatility to editing; you can pick first, or you can still perform editing by first issuing the EDIT command, and then selecting entities. A pick box is displayed on the cursor at all times when either GRIPS or PICKFIRST is turned on.

Although many editing commands work well with noun/verb selection, this method of selection is not compatible with editing commands, such as FILLET or TRIM. Such commands ignore the PICKFIRST selection set.

The following section describes how to build a selection set, whether you pick first or issue the editing command first.

Selecting Before Editing

In AutoCAD, you have the option of selecting entities before an editing command is issued (noun/verb), or first issuing the command and then selecting entities. With the PICKFIRST system variable turned off (0—the default), the method is "verb, then noun." You issue the ERASE command, for example, then pick the entities you want to erase.

With PICKFIRST turned on, the method is "noun, then verb." You select the entities you want to erase, then issue the ERASE command, which erases the entities without any other input from you. The next exercise demonstrates both of these methods and shows how to select between the two.

Selecting Before Editing

Open the TOOLPLAT drawing from the end of Chapter 6.

`Command:` **`PICKFIRST`** ↵	Accesses PICKFIRST system variable
`New value for PICKFIRST <1>:` **`0`** ↵	Turns off PICKFIRST mode
`Command:` **`ERASE`** ↵	Starts the ERASE command

Select two circles ① and ②, and extra radial slot (see fig. 8.3). Remember to use Shift to add the second circle and the slot to the selection set.

`Select objects:` *Press Enter*	Erases the entities
`Command:` **`U`** ↵	Brings the entities back
`Command:` **`PICKFIRST`** ↵	Accesses the PICKFIRST system variable
`New value for PICKFIRST <0>:` **`1`** ↵	Turns on PICKFIRST mode
`Command:` *Select the circles and the slot again*	Displays grips
`Command:` **`ERASE`** ↵ 6 found	Erases the selection set without additional input

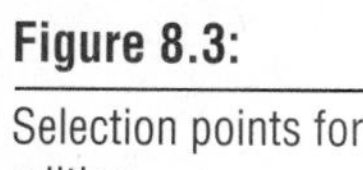

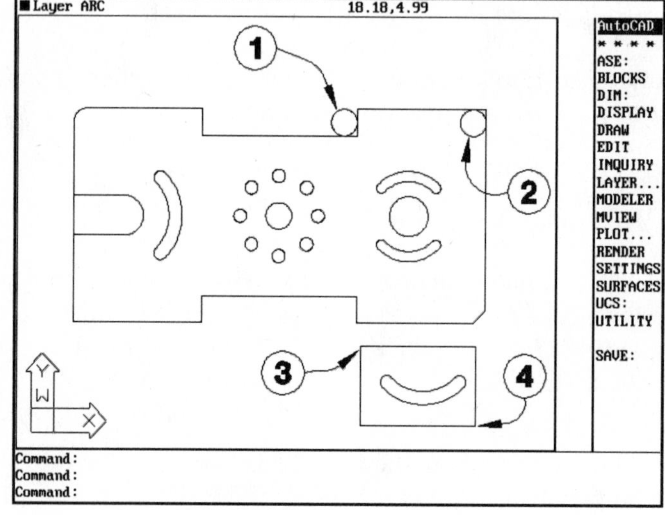

Figure 8.3:

Selection points for editing.

Building the Selection Set

AutoCAD offers over a dozen ways to collect objects for editing. You can, for example, pick individual objects or enclose a group of objects within a window. As you select objects, AutoCAD sets up a temporary selection set and highlights the objects by temporarily changing their colors, making them blink, or giving them dotted lines. This highlighting enables you to confirm that you have selected the correct entities. If you make an error at the `Select objects:` prompt, AutoCAD prompts you with all the available modes. When you have selected all the desired objects, press Enter to end object selection and continue the editing command.

The selection process also is controlled by a system variable called PICKADD. When this is set to 0 (off), selecting additional entities replaces the ones already selected. Selecting with PICKADD off clears the selection set and starts a new one, unless you hold down Shift. Holding down Shift while choosing additional entities adds them to the existing group. To remove previously selected entities from the selection set, hold down Shift as you select them. If you select a group that contains both unselected and previously selected entities, with Shift down, the unselected ones are added, but the previously selected ones are not removed. If PICKADD is set to 1 (on), entities are automatically added to the selection set as they are chosen, but you can still use Shift to remove entities from the set. A check mark in the Use Shift to Add box of the Entity Selection Settings dialog box indicates that PICKADD is off.

AutoCAD provides the following methods for adding objects to a selection set:

- **Object pick.** This method enables you to pick individual objects. This is the default option. When picking, AutoCAD finds the most recently created object that falls within or crosses the pick box. If snap and object snap are used together, AutoCAD snaps first, then performs the object snaps from that snapped point.
- **Window.** This method adds objects within the corners of a window you specify. AutoCAD selects only those objects that are enclosed entirely within the window. Lines that are overlapped by the window edge are considered within this window.
- **Last.** This method adds the last object created to the selection set.
- **Crossing.** This method works the same as Window, except that Crossing also includes any object that is partially within (or crossing) the window.

- **Remove.** This method switches to Remove mode, so that you can remove selected objects from the selection set (not from the drawing). You also can use Shift when you select to remove objects from the set.
- **Add.** This method switches from Remove mode back to normal, so that you again can add to the selection set. If PICKADD is off, you also can use Shift to add selected objects to the set.
- **Multiple.** This method enables you to pick multiple objects in close proximity and speeds up selection by enabling multiple selections without highlighting or prompting. An extra Enter is required to complete the multiple selection and return to normal object selection.
- **Previous.** This method selects the entire preceding selection set (from a previous command) as the current selection set.
- **Undo.** This method undoes or reverses the last selection operation. Each U undoes one selection operation.
- **Wpolygon.** This method is similar to Window selection but enables you to draw an irregular polygon to select objects. All entities completely within the polygon are selected.
- **Cpolygon.** This method is similar to the Crossing selection but enables you to draw an irregular polygon to select objects. All entities inside or crossed by the polygon are selected.
- **Fence.** This method enables you to draw an unclosed polyline fence with which to select objects. All objects touched by the fence line are selected.
- **ALL.** This method selects all entities in the drawing that are not on a layer which is locked or frozen.

When do you use which mode? The default option, Object Pick, is fast and simple, even for picking three or four objects, and it requires no mode setting. Last and Undo are obvious. Previous is great for repeated operations on the same set of objects, like a copy and rotate operation.

Sometimes objects are so close to each other that you cannot pick the one you want; AutoCAD just keeps finding the same object over and over again. If this happens, use Multiple and pick repeatedly, and AutoCAD finds multiple objects within the pickbox. Then remove from the set the object(s) you do not want.

A number of editing commands, such as FILLET, TRIM, and EXTEND, require individual entity selection, part or all of the time. In these cases, you must select your objects by picking them instead of Crossing, Window, and so on.

Windows and Crossing Modes Settings

You can choose between Window and Crossing, depending on which option best extracts the group you want from the crowd, simply by the order in which you pick the two corner points. In grips editing, as you saw in Chapter 6, picking left to right makes a window and right to left makes a crossing window. If the PICKAUTO system variable is on (1), object selection during editing commands behaves in the same way as grips editing selection. If it is off (0), you must use the W and C options. PICKAUTO on is indicated by a check in the Implied Windowing box of the Entity Selection Setting dialog box. PICKAUTO on causes object selection to automatically enter window/crossing mode if the first pick does not find an object to select.

The Window selection process ignores the portions of objects that fall partly outside of the current drawing window. If all visible portions of an object are in the Window box, it is selected.

The Wpolygon, Cpolygon, and Fence options are powerful tools for building complex selection sets, particularly when selections must be made in a crowded area of the drawing. These selection methods take longer to implement than the Window and Crossing options, but they are more flexible and can actually save steps.

The PICKDRAG system variable, explained in Chapter 6, controls whether one or two picks are needed to show a window. If PICKDRAG is set to 1 (on), press down on the pick button at the first corner and hold it down while you drag the window. When this variable is set to 0 (off), a window requires a pick at both corners. This setting is shown in the Entity Selection Settings dialog box as Click and Drag.

Setting Object Selection Behavior

You already set PICKADD off (the Use Shift to Add box is checked in the Entity Selection Settings dialog box) and PICKDRAG on (Click and Drag is checked) in Chapter 6. To take advantage of the flexibility of Noun/Verb Selection, you need to turn PICKFIRST on by putting a check in the Noun/Verb Selection box. You also should turn PICKAUTO on by putting a check in the Implied Windowing box, or you may find the difference between the behavior of grips mode editing selection and selection during editing commands to be confusing.

In the next exercise, set these two selection controls on and leave them on for the rest of the exercise in this book.

Additional Selection Set Options

AutoCAD has three other selection set options: BOX, AUto, and SIngle. These options are designed primarily for use in menus and offer no real advantages over the options discussed in the preceding list when specifying modes from the keyboard. Note that BOX, AUto, and SIngle are used by some of the pull-down menu items in the following exercises.

- **BOX.** This option combines Window and Crossing into a single selection. To pick the points of your box (window) from left-to-right is the same as a Window selection; right-to-left is the same as a Crossing selection.
- **AUto.** This option combines individual selection with the BOX selection. This selection performs the same as BOX, except that if the first pick point finds an entity, that single entity is selected and the BOX mode is aborted. AUto mode is always on if the PICKAUTO system variable is on (1).
- **SIngle.** This option works in conjunction with the other selection options. If you precede a selection with SIngle, object selection automatically ends after the first successful selection without having to use the Enter that is normally required to exit object selection.

When specifying modes from the keyboard, you know how you intend to select the object(s), so you can use Window, Crossing, or just pick the object(s) with PICKAUTO on, rather than use BOX or AUto.

Setting Up for Editing

This chapter uses the WIDGET drawing created in Chapter 7. You also can use the IA7WIDG3.DWG drawing file from the IA DISK. In the following exercise, you create a new file, WIDGEDIT, in which you try out the editing options.

Setup for Editing the WIDGEDIT Drawing

Start AutoCAD with the IA.BAT batch program.

Open the WIDGET drawing from Chapter 7.

`Command:` *Choose* File, *then* New, *and enter* `WIDGEDIT=IA7WIDG3`

Table 8.1
Setup for Editing the Widget Drawing

COORDS	*GRID*	*SNAP*	*UCSICON*
On	.5	.1	OR

UNITS	Engineering, 2 decimal places, 2 fractional places for angles, default all other settings
LIMITS	0,0 to 11,8.5
VIEW	Saved as RESISTOR

Layer Name	*State*	*Color*	*Linetype*
0	On	7 (White)	CONTINUOUS
BOARD	On	2 (Yellow)	CONTINUOUS
HIDDEN	On	1 (Red)	HIDDEN
PARTS	On	4 (Cyan)	CONTINUOUS
TEXT	On/Current	3 (Green)	CONTINUOUS

You should have a full-screen view of the widget. The following exercises do not make use of the viewports stored with the widget drawing, but you can use viewports in the exercises. You can restore the viewports by using TILEMODE=0. Your current layer is not important to the exercises—editing commands work on any layer. If you want additional practice using indi-

vidual editing commands, use a layer named SCRATCH, make it the current layer, create some new entities, and practice the editing command on the entities. After you finish, undo, erase, or freeze the SCRATCH layer and continue with the widget drawing.

Making Some Quick Moves

The process of making a move is quite simple. You grab what you want and move it where you want it. Try moving the solid donuts by using a Window selection. When you are prompted for a base point or displacement, pick a base point. After you pick this point, you can drag the selection set by using your pointer and pick a second displacement point to place the objects. As the ? in the exercise demonstrates, any time you want to see the full object selection options prompt, you can display it by entering a question mark (or any other irrelevant input).

Selecting and Windowing Donuts To Move

Choose Selection Settings from the Settings menu. Make sure the check boxes in the Noun/Verb Selection box and the Implied Windowing box are turned on.

`Command:` *Choose* Modify, *then* Move	Begins the Move command
`Command: _MOVE`	
`Select objects:` **?**↵	

`*Invalid selection*`
`Expects a point or Window/Last/`
`Crossing/BOX/ALL/Fence/Wpolygon/`
`Cpolygon/Add/Remove/Multiple/`
`Previous/Undo/AUto/SIngle/Implied`
	Displays a full selection prompt because ? was invalid input

`Select objects:` *Pick the left donut (see fig. 8.4)*	
`1 found.`	
`Select objects:` **W**↵	Specifies window selection mode
`First corner:` *Click and hold button 1 at ① (see fig. 8.4)*	
`Other corner:` *Drag to second corner at ② and release button 1*	Selects the right two donuts with a window
`2 found.`	
`Select objects:` *Press Enter*	Tells AutoCAD that you are through selecting objects

`Base point or displacement:` *Pick any point near the donuts*	Specifies the "from" point of the move
`Second point of displacement:` *Use coordinate display to pick at polar point 1.00<270*	Specifies the "to" point and completes the move (see fig. 8.5)

After you move the donuts, they should appear near the bottom of the widget, as seen in figure 8.5.

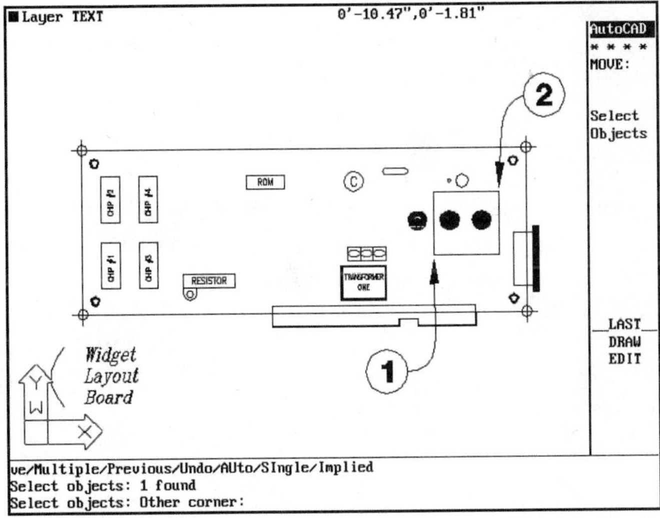

Figure 8.4:
Selecting donuts with a window for Move.

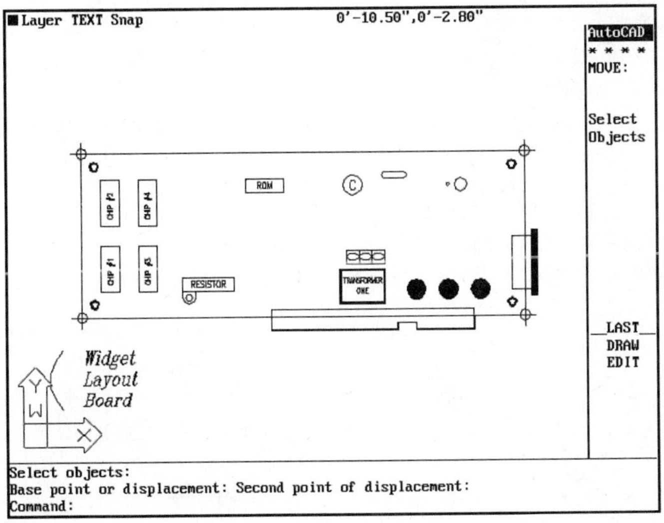

Figure 8.5:
The donuts after being moved.

Although, with Implied Windowing (PICKAUTO) on, you did not need to use the Window option to select a window, sometimes using the Window or Crossing option explicitly is essential. Implied Windowing and AUtomode will find an object within the pickbox (if any), instead of entering Window/Crossing selection. If there is such an object at the corner of the desired window selection area, you must use the W or C options to make your selection.

As you see, object selection and moving is easy. After you select the donuts with a window, they are highlighted. You tell AutoCAD you are through collecting by pressing Enter in response to the `Select objects:` prompt. After you finish selecting, pick your displacement points, and your donuts are moved.

Another way to control which entities are selected by a pick is to change the pick-box size by changing the PICKBOX system variable. Enter PICKBOX, and then enter a new value. You also can change the pick box size transparently in the middle of a command by using 'SETVAR or 'PICKBOX, but the change does not take effect until the second following pick. The DDSELECT dialog box controls the pick-box size as well.

Moving With Noun/Verb Selection

The previous exercise using the MOVE command can also be done using the Noun/Verb selection process. Try selecting the three donuts with a window and then issuing the MOVE command. You will not be prompted to select entities because AutoCAD recognizes that it has already been done. The next exercise demonstrates that method of moving the donuts.

Using Move With the Noun/Verb Selection

`Command:` **`U`**↵	Undoes the previous MOVE command
`Command:` *Select the three donuts using a window*	Selects the entities
`Command:` **`MOVE`**↵	Issues the MOVE command
`MOVE 3 found`	
`Base point or displacement:` **`0,-1`**↵	Specifies a displacement
`Second point of displacement:` ↵	Moves the donuts

You also can use Move grip mode to move objects, just as you did in Chapter 6. Undo the previous MOVE command, and then perform the same edit by using Move grip mode.

Using Move Grip Mode

`Command: U↵`	Undoes the previous MOVE command
`Command:` *Select the three donuts using a window*	Displays grips
`Command:` *Pick one of the grips*	Enters stretch mode

`** STRETCH **`
`<Stretch to point>/Base point/Copy/`
`Undo/eXit: MO↵`
	Switches to move mode

`** MOVE **`
`<Move to point>/Base point/Copy/`
`Undo/eXit: @1<270`
	Moves the donuts

The Grip editing feature combines several of the most common editing commands into one command with different mode options. Grip editing always begins in the stretch mode. Pressing Enter or the spacebar switches between the various modes. Typing in the shortcut keys may be a quicker method of accessing the proper mode. The modes and the shortcut keys are as follows:

- **MO.** Move
- **MI.** Mirror
- **ST.** Stretch
- **SC.** Scale
- **RO.** Rotate

One of the most difficult parts of learning AutoCAD is that the software offers so many ways of doing things. Editing is no exception. Although moving an entity seems simple, there are many ways of defining the distance, or *displacement*, to move it.

Displacement and Drag

When you change the location of objects in a selection set, you use a displacement. If you know the absolute X,Y, or polar displacement, you can enter it at the `Base point or displacement:` prompt. Entering **0,-1** or **1<270** (do not preface the displacement with an @), for example, duplicates the move you just did. Then press Enter, instead of a value, at the `Second point:` prompt to tell AutoCAD to use the first value as an absolute offset.

Often, you want to show a displacement by entering two points. Think of the first point (base point) as a handle on the selection set. The second point is where you want to put the handle of the set down. The *displacement* is an imaginary line from the base point to the second point. AutoCAD calculates the X and Y differences between the base and second points. The new location of the object(s) is determined by adding this X,Y displacement to its current location.

AutoCAD does not actually draw a displacement line; it gets the information it needs from the displacement points. When you pick displacement points on the screen, AutoCAD shows a temporary rubber-band line trailing behind the crosshairs from the first point to the second.

As you move the donuts, an image of the selection set also follows the crosshairs. AutoCAD provides a visual aid to help you pick your second displacement point. This action is called *dragging*. Without dragging, it sometimes can be difficult to see if the selection set fits where you want it.

When you set a base point, try to pick a base point that is easy to visualize (and remember). If the base point is not in, on, or near the contents of the selection set, you appear to be carrying the selection set around magically without touching it. Sometimes you use object snap mode to move the points to a different but related object. Otherwise, it is a good idea to make this drag anchor (base-displacement point) a reference point, such as an object snap point on one of the objects.

Using DRAGMODE

When you edit large selection sets, you may want to control dragging. You can turn dragging on or off by using the DRAGMODE system variable. The default for DRAGMODE is Auto, which causes AutoCAD to drag everything that makes sense. Turn DRAGMODE on to be more selective about

what you drag. If DRAGMODE is on, and you want to drag while using a command, type Drag and press Enter before picking the point that you want to drag. The option Off turns DRAGMODE off entirely and ignores a previously typed Drag.

Add and Remove Modes for the Selection Set

You often need to remove objects from a selection set when too many objects are in the set. Although, with Use Shift to Add on (PICKADD off), you rarely need to use them, AutoCAD has two modes for handling selection set contents: an Add mode and a Remove mode. In Add mode, the default `Select objects:` prompt appears. If you pick individual objects or use any other object-selection mode, such as Window or Last, the objects are placed in the selection set. If Shift Add is on, Remove mode overrides it, but Add mode has no effect other than ending Remove mode.

You also can press R (for Remove) in response to the normal Add mode prompt. When the `Remove objects:` prompt appears, remove objects from the selection set by using any type of object selection in the Remove mode. Press A to return to Add mode.

Using a Crossing Window

A second type of window-object selection is a *crossing window,* which selects everything that falls within your selection window or crosses the boundary of the window. Crossing is handy when you want to select objects in a crowded drawing. The number of picks (one or two) that are required to show a window depends on whether the PICKDRAG system variable is 1 or 0. This setting is also known as Click and Drag in the Entity Selection Setting dialog box. AutoCAD also differentiates between objects in the window and objects crossing the window. Some advanced editing commands, such as the stretch command, treat selected objects in the window differently from those crossing the window boundary.

The next exercise uses a polar displacement to combine a crossing window and the Remove mode to move the ROM chip. Select the capacitor and the ROM chip together by using Crossing, and then remove the capacitor from the selection set. (The *capacitor* is the circle containing a C.)

Using Crossing, Add, and Remove Selection Set Modes

`Command:` *Click in an empty area of the drawing*	Clears the selection set
`Command:` **`M`**↵	Issues the MOVE command
`Command:` **`MOVE`**	
`Select objects:` *Click and hold at ① (see fig. 8.6)*	
`Other corner:` *Drag to ② and release*	Selects the objects with a crossing window
`4 found.`	Highlights four objects
`Select objects:` **`R`**↵	Begins Remove mode
`Remove objects:` *Pick the circle*	
`1 found, 1 removed`	Removes the circle from the selection set
`Remove objects:` *Pick the text character C*	
`1 found, 1 removed`	Removes the C from set
`Remove objects:` *Press Enter*	Ends selection
`Base point or displacement:` **`1.1<270`**↵	Specifies a polar displacement
`Second point of displacement:` *Press Enter*	Uses the previous input as the displacement

As figure 8.7 shows, this operation moves the chip and leaves the capacitor in its original location.

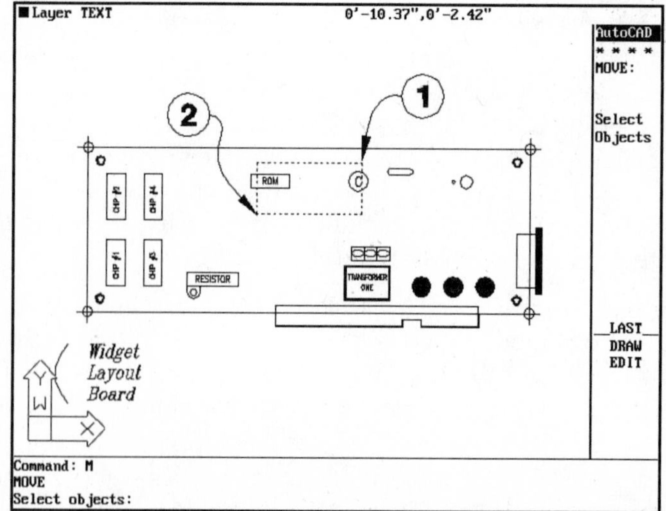

Figure 8.6:

Using a crossing window to move objects.

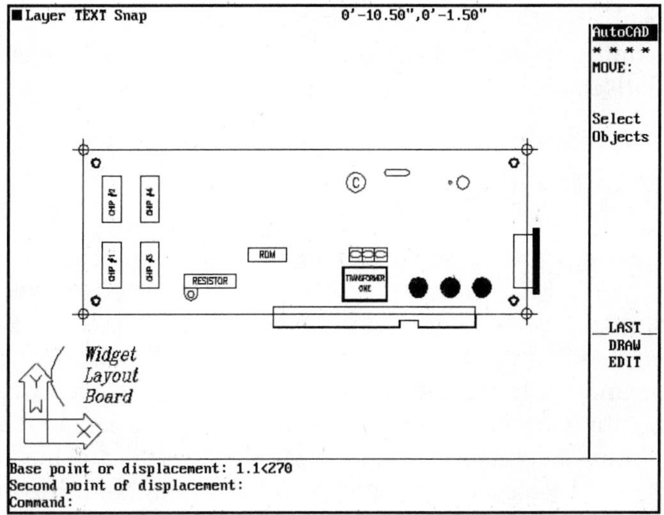

Figure 8.7:

The ROM chip in its new location.

Next, use automatic selection and the Move Grip mode to perform the same edit again.

Removing Entities with Shift to Add

`Command:` U↵	Undoes the previous MOVE command
`Command:` *Click and hold at ① (see fig. 8.6), drag to ② and release*	Selects the capacitor and ROM with a crossing window and displays grips
`Command:` *Hold shift, then select a window around the capacitor*	Removes the capacitor from the selection set
`Command:` *Pick any of the ROM's grips*	Enters stretch mode
`** STRETCH **` `<Stretch to point>/Base point/Copy/Undo/eXit:` *Press Enter*	Enters Move mode
`** MOVE **` `<Move to point>/Base point/Copy/Undo/eXit:` @1.1<270	Moves the ROM chip

This exercise used a relative point to define the move distance because the Grip modes do not support the displacement option. You also can enter a displacement with the Base point option and a second point.

Understanding the Selection Set

In a complex drawing, you may notice the time it takes AutoCAD to search through the drawing file for entities that qualify for the selection set. Every time you select more objects for the selection set, AutoCAD shows the number you selected and the number it actually found. These numbers are not always the same, for two reasons. First, you can select objects that do not qualify for editing. Second, you may have already selected an entity. In the latter case, AutoCAD informs you that it found a duplicate. In all cases (except Multiple mode selections), AutoCAD uses the highlighting feature to show you what is currently in the selection set.

To speed up the selection of very large selection sets, turn the HIGHLIGHT system variable off. To do so, enter HIGHLIGHT and set it to 0 (off). If you do so, select carefully because you cannot tell what objects are selected. Highlight off is useful for selecting large, easily defined portions of the drawing. Also, consider using the DDSELECT dialog box to set Entity Sort Method to fit your selection situation. (Entity Sort is discussed later in this chapter.)

Using the SIngle Option for Object Selection

Menu items—such as Erase, then Single on the Modify pull-down menu—expect you to select exactly one object, so they use the SIngle mode of object selection. As soon as an object (or group of objects) is selected, object selection ends without having to press Enter. Try SIngle and an absolute displacement to move the diode from the top of the widget down to the left. Remember that the diode was made with a polyline. The diode selects and moves as a single entity.

Using the SIngle Option for Object Selection

`Command:` *Choose* Modify, *then* Move	
`Command: _move`	
`Select objects: SI↵`	Specifies single object selection mode
`Select objects:` *Pick any point on the diode*	
`1 found.`	Highlights the diode and completes the selection set
`Base point or displacement: -.6,-.9 ↵`	Specifies a negative absolute displacement
`Second point of displacement:` *Press Enter*	Uses the preceding input as the displacement

Save the drawing

Figure 8.8 shows the diode in its new location.

You can precede any of the object selection modes with SI (for SIngle), but SIngle was designed primarily for use in menu macros.

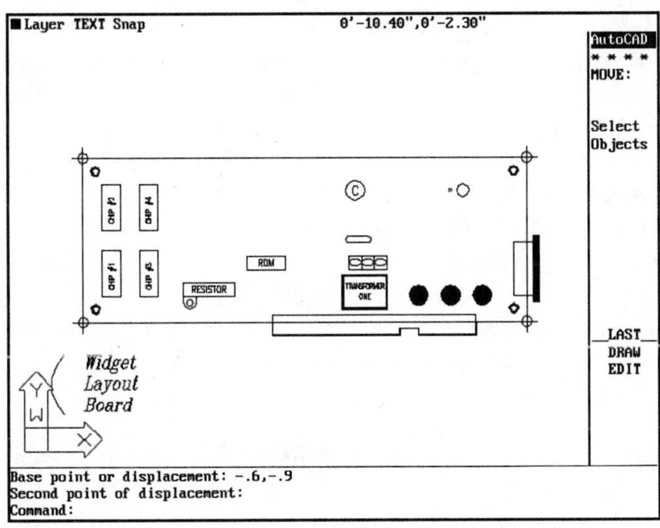

Figure 8.8:

The diode's new location.

Using the Previous Selection Set Option

The Previous selection option is helpful when you cancel an editing command or use several commands on the same selection set. Previous object selection reselects the object(s) that you selected in your previous editing command.

Previous enables you to edit the preceding set without having to individually select its objects again. Previous is different from the Last option, which selects the last created object visible in the drawing area. Previous does not work with some editing commands, such as STRETCH, in which a window, crossing, or point selection is required.

Controlling Entity Sorting

Unlike earlier versions of AutoCAD, which always sorted entities in their order of creation, Release 12 normally uses an oct-tree (octal tree) method of sorting the entity data base. Entity sorting affects the order in which entities are found by object selection and object snapping; and affects the order in which they are displayed or output by redraws, regenerations, MSLIDE, plotting, and PostScript output. The old method of sorting favored the most recently created entities during selection and object snapping, and displayed or output entities in their order of creation. The oct-tree method sorts, selects, displays, and outputs entities in grid arrangement. The oct-tree method divides the drawing up into rectangular areas, making object selection and object snapping much faster because they need only consider the local area instead of the whole drawing. These areas are visually evident during a redraw or regen of a complex drawing because AutoCAD redraws or generates each area in turn.

If you want to see the effect of an oct-tree sort, create a 50-row-by-60 column array of circles and perform a ZOOM All.

In most cases, the order of the entities is of little consequence. For cases in which the order matters, you can use the Entity Sort Method dialog box—illustrated in figure 8.9—to override oct-tree sorting and consider the order of creation for specific operations.

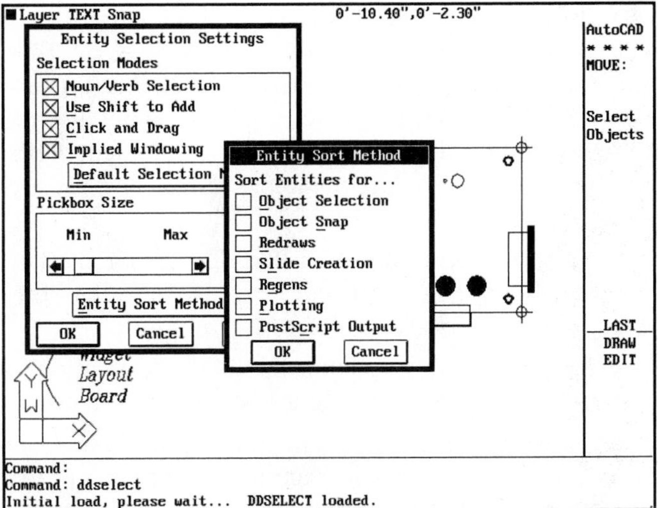

Figure 8.9:

The Entity Sort Method dialog box.

To display the Entity Sort Method dialog box, first enter DDSELECT or choose Settings, then Selection Settings, and then choose Entity Sort Method. The Entity Sort Method options and the operations they affect are as follows:

- Object Selection. When picking an entity with oct-tree sorting on, if several entities fall within the pickbox, it is hard to predict which entity will be found. With oct-tree sorting off, the most recent entity will be found. When you are editing recent entities, as is often the case, setting oct-tree off will help select them. When making a window or crossing selection with oct-tree on, entities will be selected in an unpredictable order. With oct-tree off, they will be selected in the reverse of the creation order. This sometimes makes a difference when creating a block; for example, if the block contains attributes which need to prompt in a specific order, you need to control their order of selection.
- Object Snap. As with Object Selection, oct-tree affects the finding of entities when object snapping. Turn it off when using the QUIck object snap option if you want the most recent entities to be predictably found.
- Redraws. If the order in which entities appear on the screen during a redraw really matters to you, turn oct-tree off to make them appear in their order of creation. Because many zooms merely redraw instead of regenerating, this might be important to you. If, for example, you first

draw a basic part outline, framework, or building grid in your drawings, you can use it to locate your zooms. With oct-tree off, that first-drawn outline, framework, or grid appears first. You can do a rough zoom, cut the zoom short with a Ctrl-C, and then zoom, use the outline, framework, or grid to zoom more precisely. With oct-tree on, the order of appearance is less predictable.

- Slide Creation. As with redraws, oct-tree controls the order of appearance of objects in slides created by MSLIDE. This order is often important in a complex slide; a presentation might look odd if all the windows of a building appeared before the wall outlines.
- Regens. As with redraws, oct-tree controls the order of appearance of objects during regens. See the preceding Redraw discussion.
- Plotting. Because AutoCAD's plot routine, and many plotters, perform their own vector sorting, oct-tree is generally not important to plotting. If, however, you are plotting to an image file format, you may want to control the order of appearance, as discussed in the preceding Slide Creation option.
- PostScript Output. As with slides and plotting to image files, if you need to control the order of appearance in the PostScript file, set oct-tree off.

Setting oct-tree off for any option causes only that option's operations to use the old-style sorting; other operations still use an oct-tree sort. When an option box in the Entity Sort Method dialog box is checked, it sets oct-tree off for that option. The SORTENTS system variable stores the current oct-tree sort setting; see Appendix C for more information.

Using the COPY Command

The basic COPY command is similar to the MOVE command. The only difference between a copy and a move is that COPY leaves the original objects in place.

In the steps that follow, use a Wpoly (Window Polygon) selection to copy the widget's transformer and capacitor. Wpoly provides a multisided window for selection. Try canceling the command and using Previous to reselect the selection set that is to be copied.

Using the COPY Command, Wpoly, and Previous

`Command:` *Choose* Construct, *then* Copy	Begins the COPY command
`Command: _copy`	
`Select objects:` **WPOLY**↵	Specifies Wpolygon mode
`First polygon point:` *Pick at* ① *(see fig. 8.10)*	Starts polygon selection
`Undo/<Endpoint of line>:` *Pick at* ②	Continues selection
`Undo/<Endpoint of line>:` *Pick points* ③ *through* ⑦	Creates the polygon
`Undo/<Endpoint of line>:` *Place the cursor at*⑧*, and press Enter*	Closes the polygon
`5 found`	Highlights and selects the transformer and ROM
`Select objects:`	Ends selection
`<Base point or displacement>/Multiple:` *Press Ctrl-C*	Cancels the COPY command
`Command:` *Press Enter*	Repeats the COPY command
`Command:` **COPY**	
`Select objects:` **P**↵	Uses the previous selection set
`5 found`	Highlights the transformer and ROM
`Select objects:` *Hold shift, and a window around the capacitor*	Removes ROM from the selection set
`2 found, 2 removed`	
`Select objects:` *Press Enter*	
`<Base point or displacement>/Multiple:` *From the pop-up menu, choose* Intersection	
`int of` *Pick the transformer's lower left corner*	Specifies the "from" point
`Second point of displacement:` **8.20,4.30**↵	Copies the transformer

Figure 8.11 shows the board with the newly copied transformer.

Remember, you can always use object snap and snap modes to help you get an exact displacement location or to help select objects for the selection set.

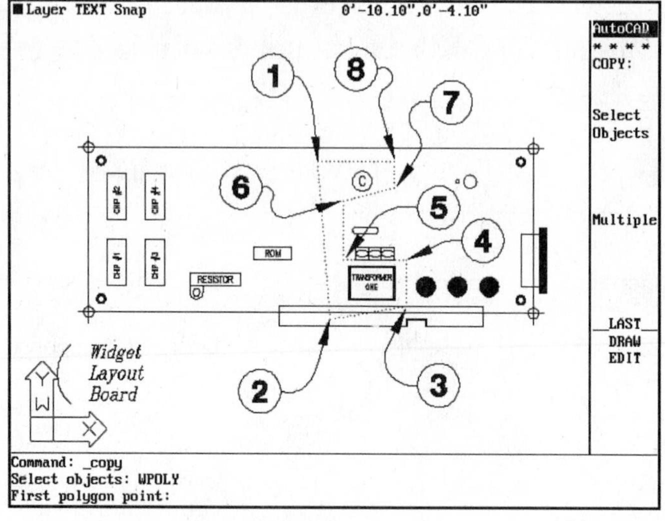

Figure 8.10:

Selecting the transformer and capacitor.

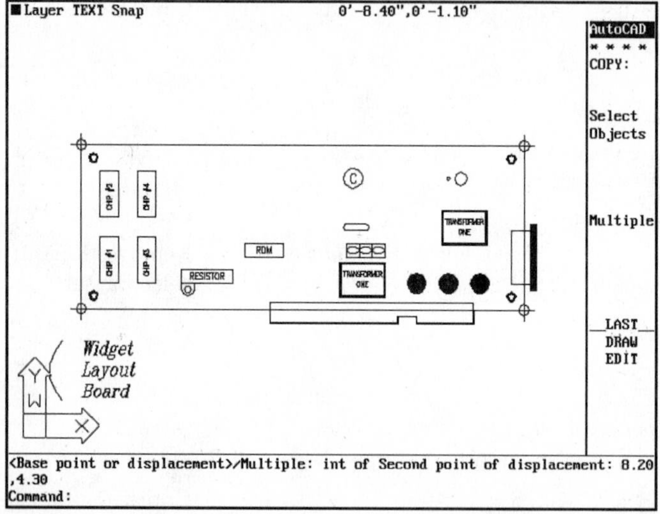

Figure 8.11:

The copied transformer.

NOTE Now that you have practiced using object selection, most exercises in the rest of the book omit the `nnn found` and `Select objects:` *Press Enter* prompts and their responses. Most exercises simply tell you what to select, leaving you to complete the selection set on your own.

Using the COPY Command Options

The COPY command options are similar to the MOVE options. COPY options include displacement points identification, object-selection options, and a new option: Multiple, which stands for multiple copies. (Do not confuse the new Multiple option with Multiple object selection.)

Working with the COPY Multiple Option

The Multiple option of the COPY command enables you to copy the contents of your selection set several times, without having to respecify the selection set and base point. If you respond to the `Base point or displacement:` prompt by typing **M**, AutoCAD reprompts for base point, then repeatedly prompts you for multiple `Second point of displacement:` points. Press Enter to get out of the Multiple loop.

Follow the steps in the next exercise to make multiple copies of the capacitor. Put three copies next to the original capacitor and put one copy between the transformers. Finally, put two more copies next to the resistor on the bottom of the board. The polar coordinates shown are for your reference. To maintain accuracy, the coordinates are all snap points. As you begin the next exercise, your drawing should look like figure 8.12.

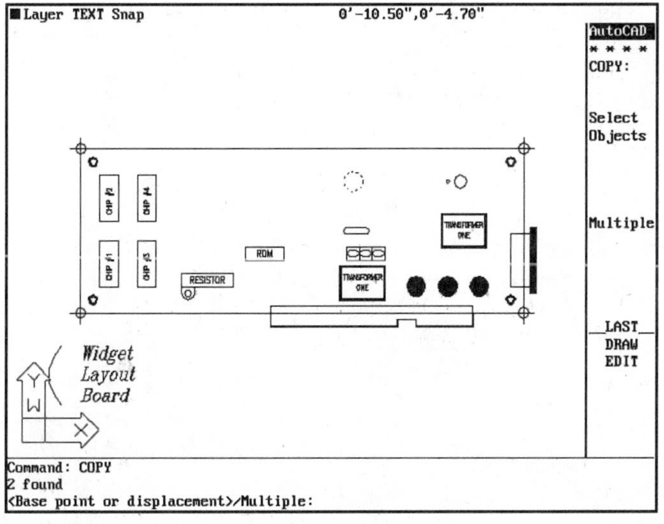

Figure 8.12:

Before the multiple copy.

Using COPY Multiple To Make Copies of the Capacitor

`Command:` *Select the capacitor with a window*	
`Command:` **`COPY`**↵	
`2 found`	Selects the preselected set
`<Base point or displacement>/Multiple:` *Enter* **`M`** *or choose* Multiple *from the screen menu*	Invokes the Multiple Copy option
`Base point:` *From the pop-up menu, choose* Center, *then select the circle*	
`Second point of displacement:` *Pick at polar point 0.40<270.00*	Makes the first copy
`Second point of displacement:` *Pick at polar point 0.50<0.00*	Makes another copy
`Second point of displacement:` *Pick at polar point 0.64<321.34*	
`Second point of displacement:` *Pick at polar point 2.26<225.00*	
`Second point of displacement:` *Pick at polar point 1.94<235.49*	
`Second point of displacement:` *Pick at polar point at 1.41<315.00*	
`Second point of displacement:` *Press Enter*	Exits from the Copy option

Figure 8.13 shows the copies.

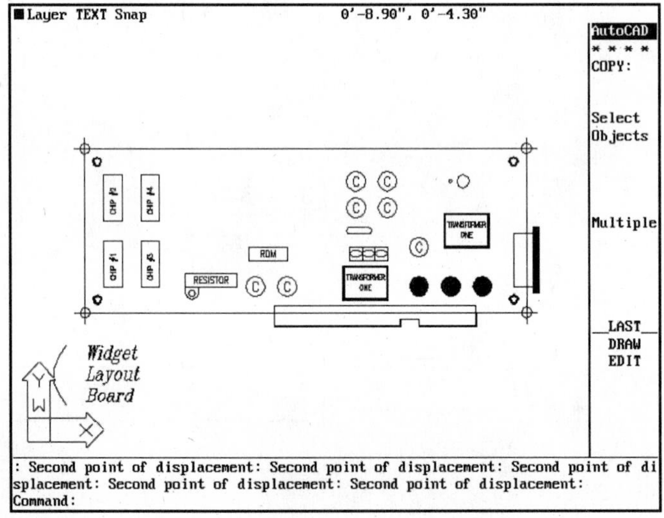

Figure 8.13:

Detail of the completed multiple copy.

Using ARRAY To Make Multiple Copies in a Pattern

Making arrays is another type of multiple copying. Often, you want to make multiple copies of an object or group of objects in a regular pattern. Suppose, for example, you have a rectangle that represents a table in a cafeteria. If AutoCAD were capable of placing the table every nine feet in the X direction and every 14 feet in the Y direction, you could make five rows and eight columns of tables. Another example of the usefulness of arrays is when you draw evenly spaced bolt holes around the circumference of a tank top.

The ARRAY command functions similarly to the COPY command. Unlike COPY, however, ARRAY makes a regular pattern of entities instead of making individually placed copies of the selection set. You determine the number of copies and the repetition pattern. The two basic array patterns are rectangular and polar.

Using Rectangular Arrays

You make a *rectangular array* by specifying the number of rows and columns you want and an X,Y offset distance. You can have a single row with multiple columns, a single column with multiple rows, or multiple rows and columns.

You can show the displacement between rows or columns by picking two points at the `Distance between rows (--):` and `Distance between columns (|||):` prompts. You also can specify the offsets by entering positive or negative offset values (see figs. 8.14 and 8.15). The *offset distance* is the X and Y direction from the original selection set. Entering negative values produces an array in the negative X or Y (or both) directions. A positive X value generates columns to the right; a negative X value generates columns to the left. A positive Y value generates rows up; a negative Y value generates rows down.

Try making a rectangular array by using the ROM chip.

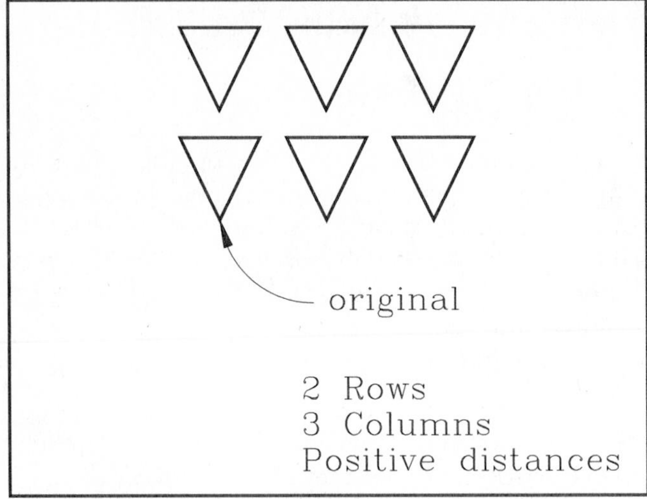

Figure 8.14:
Positive array offsets.

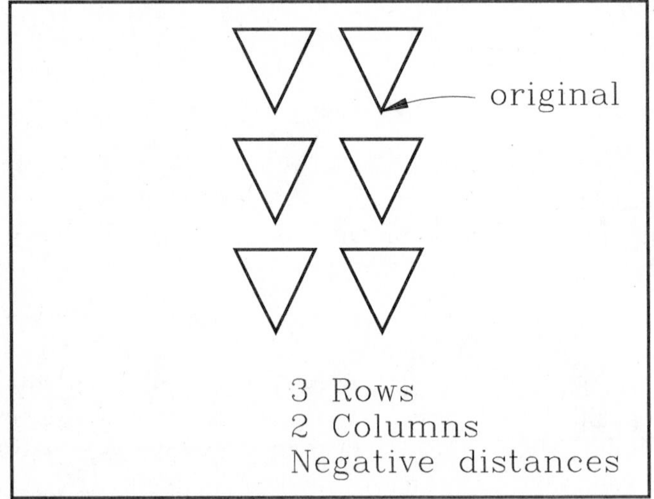

Figure 8.15:
Negative array offsets.

Using ARRAY To Make a Rectangular Array

`Command:` *Select the ROM chip and its text*	
`Command:` *Choose* Construct, *then* Array	Begins the ARRAY command
`Command: _array 2 found`	Selects the preselected set
`Rectangular or Polar array (R/P) <R>:` *Press Enter or choose* Rectang *from the screen menu*	Specifies a rectangular array
`Number of rows (--) <1>: 4↵`	
`Number of columns (|||) <1>: 2↵`	
`Distance between rows (--): 0.40↵`	
`Distance between columns (|||): 0.80↵`	Draws the array (see fig. 8.16)

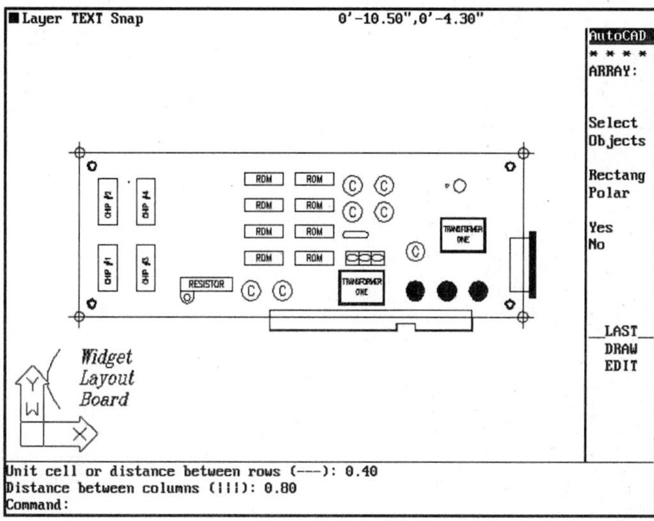

Figure 8.16:

The completed rectangular array.

If you set up a big array (with many rows and columns), AutoCAD asks if you really want to repeat the selection set that many times. If an array gets too big, you can stop it by pressing Ctrl-C, and then reverse the array by using UNDO.

ARRAY is useful, even if you want to make only one row or column of entities. This command is quicker than COPY Multiple.

In the following exercise, make a set of logo arcs next to the widget layout text at the bottom left area of your drawing. This is the single-row array of arcs shown in the next example.

Making a Single-Column Array

`Command:` **`ARRAY`**↵	
`Select objects:` *Pick the logo arc*	
`Rectangular or Polar array (R/P) <R>:` *Press Enter*	
`Number of rows (--) <1>:` *Press Enter*	Accepts the default value of one row
`Number of columns (|||) <1>:` `6`↵	Specifies six columns
`Distance between columns (|||):` `0.05`↵	Draws the array (see fig. 8.17)

Figure 8.17:
Detail of the logo after the array.

Using Polar Arrays

In *polar arrays*, you place copies of the entities in the selection set around the circumference of an imaginary circle or arc. Polar arrays are useful for creating mechanical parts, such as gear teeth or bolt patterns. Figures 8.18 and 8.19 show examples of regular and rotated circular arrays.

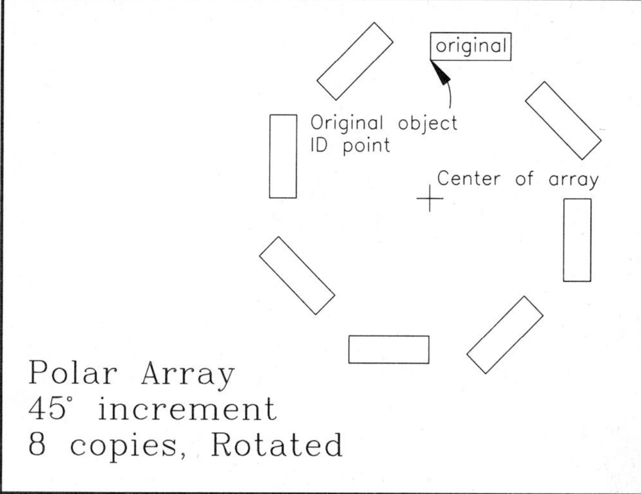

Figure 8.18:
A rotated polar array.

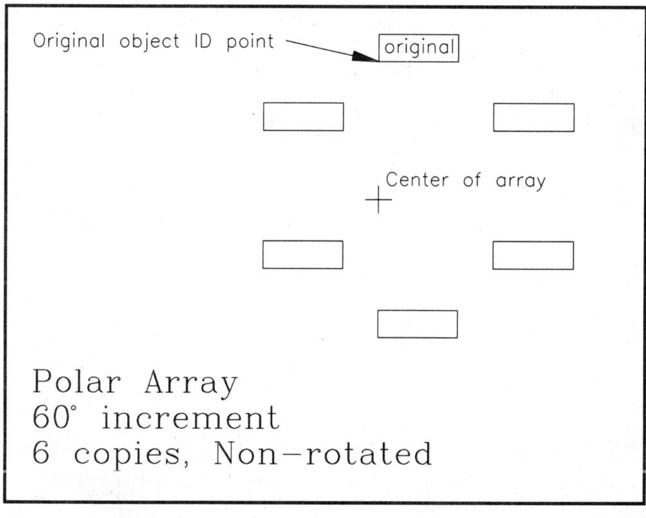

Figure 8.19:
A nonrotated polar array.

When you form a polar array, you specify the number of items you want in the array, the angle you want to fill, and whether or not you want the items rotated. One *item* is one copy of the selection set to be arrayed. When you count your items, remember to include the original. You can array around a full circle or part of a circle. If you array around part of a circle, you need one more item than the total arc angle, divided by the incremental angle. If, for example, you are arraying 90 degrees, and you want the items at 30-degree increments, you need 90/30 + 1 = 4 items.

The following exercise shows how to array the contact around 270 degrees of a circle. You need seven items (270/45 + 1 = 7). The contact is the small circle to the left of the switch (large circle) on the right side of the widget. It does not matter whether you rotate the contact as it is copied because you are arraying circles.

Using Polar Array on Switch Contacts

`Command:` *Select the small circle to the left of the switch as shown by* ①

`Command:` **`ARRAY`**↵

`1 found`

`Rectangular or Polar array (R/P):` *Enter* `P` *or choose* Polar *from the screen menu*	Specifies a polar array
`Center point of array:` *From the pop-up menu, choose* Center	
`center of` *Pick any point on the large circle*	Specifies the center of the array

`Number of items:` **`7`**↵

`Angle to fill (+=ccw, -=cw) <360>:` **`270`**↵

`Rotate objects as they are copied? <Y>` *Press Enter*

Figure 8.20 shows a zoomed view of this array.

If you array a line (using a polar array) twice around its midpoint or four times around its endpoint, you create a cross. A large number of lines creates a sunburst.

If an array can rotate entities, AutoCAD also must be able to rotate individual entities.

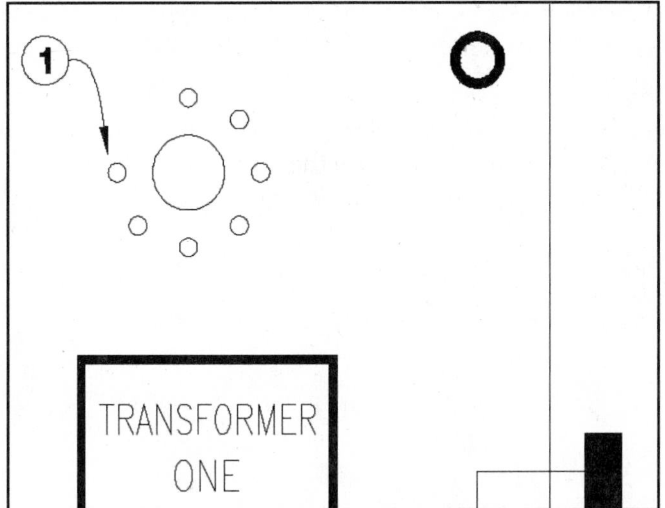

Figure 8.20:
Detail view of the switch after the array.

Turning Entities by Using the ROTATE Command

The ROTATE command enables you to turn existing entities at precise angles. ROTATE, like MOVE, requires you to specify a first point as a base point. This rotation base point does not need to be on the object that you are rotating—you can put it anywhere and AutoCAD turns your selected entities relative to the base point. Nevertheless, be careful when you use ROTATE; it is easy to become confused with rotation base points (such as bad drag handles) that are not on the entities you intend to rotate. After you specify the base point, give a rotation angle. Negative angles produce clockwise rotation; positive angles produce counterclockwise rotation (assuming the default direction setting in units).

An alternate way to specify an angle is to use a reference angle. You can change the angle of an entity by giving AutoCAD a reference angle that should be set equal to the new angle. You can say, for example, "Put a handle on 237 degrees and turn it to 165." This is often easier than calculating the difference (72 degrees clockwise) and entering that number at the prompt. You need not even know the actual angles; you can pick points to indicate angles. To align with existing objects, use object snaps when picking the points of the angle(s).

Try two rotations in the next two exercises. First, use ROTATE to reposition the jumper. The *jumper* is the rectangular object with three ellipses in it, located just above the transformer. Rotate the jumper into position vertically at the left of the transformer.

Using the ROTATE Command

`Command:` *Choose* Modify, *then* Rotate	Begins the ROTATE command
`Command: _rotate`	
`Select objects:` *Select the jumper with a window from ① (see fig. 8.21) to ②*	
`Base point:` **6.45,4.3** ↵	
`<Rotation angle>/Reference:` **-90** ↵	Specifies the rotation angle

Figure 8.22 shows the rotated jumper.

Throughout much of the rest of the book, as in the preceding exercise, exercises simply tell you what to select and omit the full set of prompts and responses.

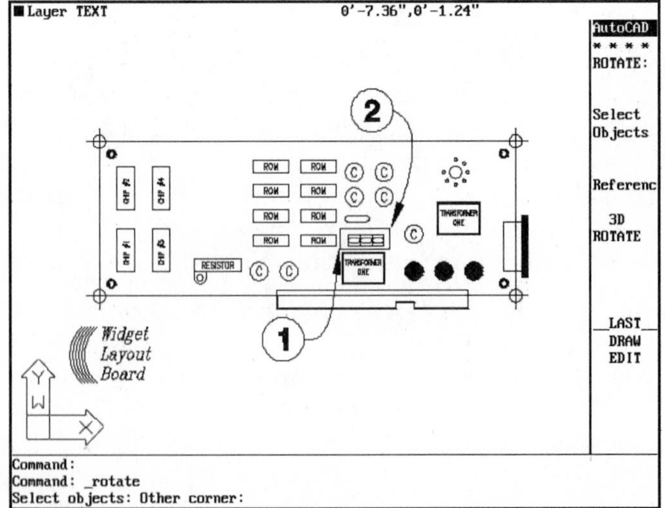

Figure 8.21: Selecting the jumper with a window.

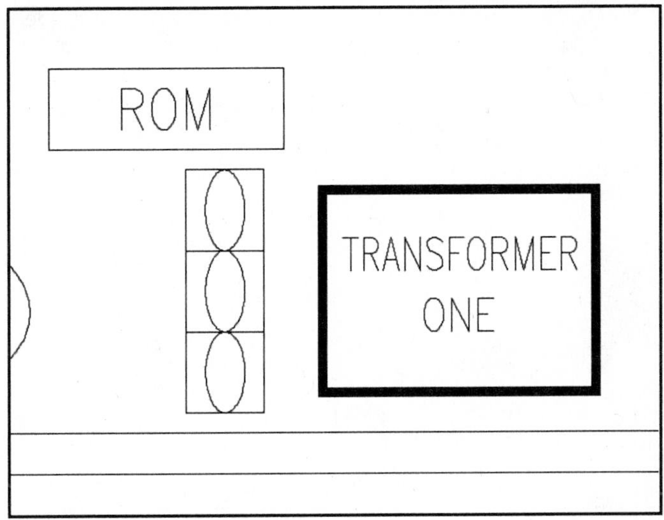

Figure 8.22:

Detail of the jumper after being rotated.

Next, you combine a Copy operation and a Rotate operation to place another mounting tab and nut above the resistor. This Copy and Rotate technique is an efficient trick. You can accomplish the task by first using the COPY command, then the ROTATE command, but it is easier to use the Copy option of Rotate Grip mode—you then only have to perform one operation, instead of two.

Using the Copy and Rotate Technique

`Command:` *From the screen menu, choose* DISPLAY, *then* VIEW:, *and then* Restore

`Command:` **`'VIEW`**

`?/Delete/Restore/Save/Window: _RESTORE`
`View name to restore:` **`RESISTOR`**↵

First, select the entities.

`Command:` *Select the tab and nut with a window from ① (see fig. 8.23) to ②*

`Command:` *Pick any one of the grips* — Enters stretch mode

`** STRETCH **`
`<Stretch to point>/Base point/Copy/`
`Undo/eXit:` **RO**↵
	Switches to rotate mode

`** ROTATE **`
`<Rotation angle>/Base point/Copy/Undo/`
`Reference/eXit:` **C**↵
	Specifies the Copy option

`** ROTATE (multiple) **`
`<Rotation angle>/Base point/Copy/Undo/`
`Reference/eXit:` **B**↵
	Specifies the Base point option

`Base point:` *Pick point 4.50,3.80*	
`<Rotation angle>/Base point/Copy/Undo/` `Reference/eXit:` *Pick point 0.50<180*	Copies the entities
`<Rotation angle>/Base point/Copy/Undo/` `Reference/eXit:` *Press Ctrl-C*	Cancels rotate Grip mode

After you complete this exercise, your drawing should look ike figure 8.24.

The preceding exercise shows how handy Copy and Rotate can be for avoiding redrawing entities in new positions.

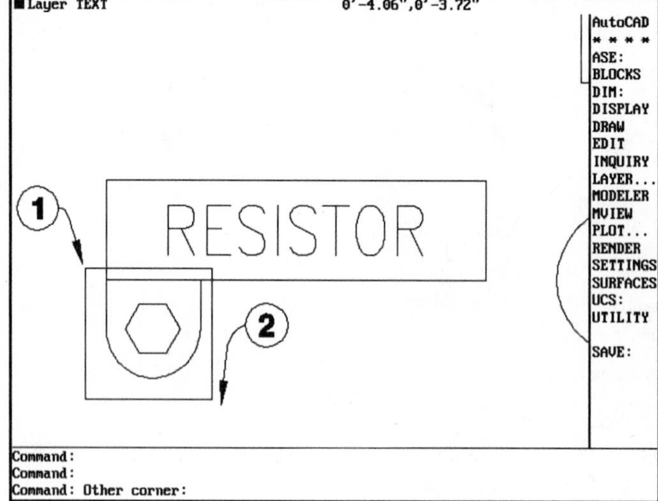

Figure 8.23:

Selecting a resistor tab and nut with window.

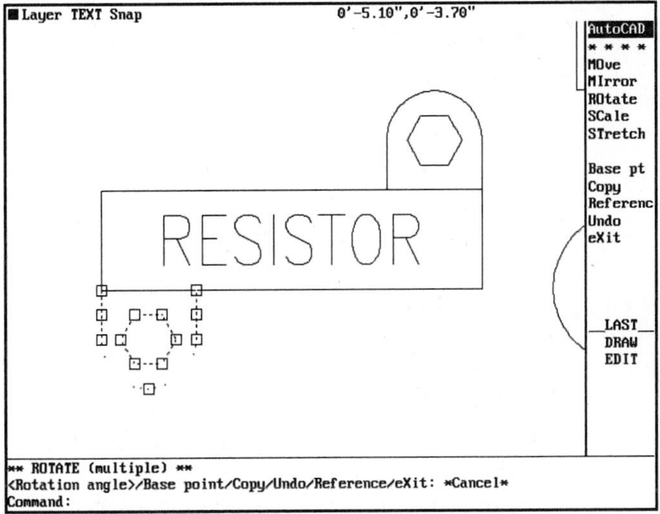

Figure 8.24:

A nut after you use the Copy and Rotate options.

Copying through the Looking Glass

The MIRROR command creates a mirrored copy of objects. You can mirror the contents of a selection set at any angle. MIRROR prompts you to identify a selection set; it then initiates a mirror operation. AutoCAD prompts you for the beginning and endpoint of a mirror line. The line can be in any direction. If you want a perfect 180-degree flip, use Ortho to help you create an orthogonal mirror line. If you want mirroring at a precise angle, use relative polar coordinates (@8<60, for example) or use a rotated snap or UCS.

Finally, AutoCAD asks if you want to keep the original entities in place or to delete them. Think of this as copying or moving the contents of the selection set through the mirror.

If you have text in your selection set (as the example does), you need to consider whether you want to pass the text through the mirror unchanged or mirrored. If you do not want text mirrored, set the MIRRTEXT system variable to 0, enabling graphics, but not text, to be inverted.

Mirror the resistor you have been working on, keeping the original. Set the MIRRTEXT system variable to 0 so that text is not mirrored.

Using MIRROR To Mirror the Resistor

`Command:` **`MIRRTEXT`**↵	
`New value for MIRRTEXT <1>:` **0** ↵	Turns off MIRRTEXT
ZOOM Previous.	
`Command:` *Choose* Construct, *then* Mirror	Starts the MIRROR command
`Command: _mirror`	
`Select objects:` *Select the resistor with a window from 4.00,3.40 to 5.00,4.20*	
`First point of mirror line:` *Pick at 5.00,4.20*	
`Second point:` *Turn on Ortho, then pick any point to the left*	Specifies the mirror line
`Delete old objects? <N>` *Press Enter*	Mirrors the resistor and retains the original

Save and continue or end and take a break.

Figure 8.25 shows a zoomed view of the mirrored resistor and the location of the mirror line.

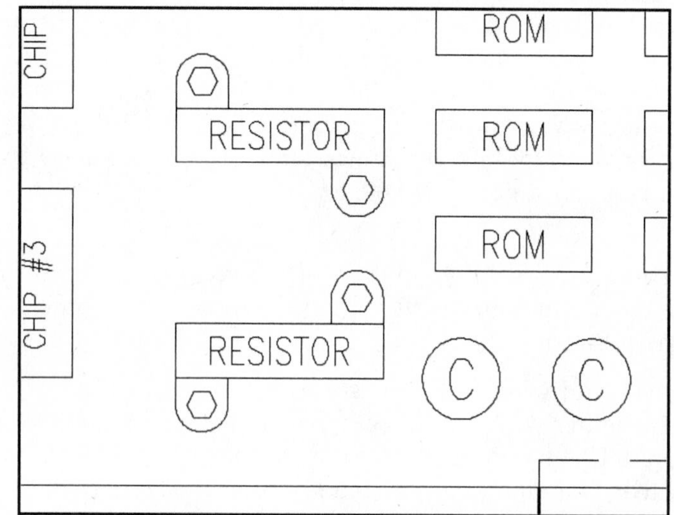

Figure 8.25: Detail of the resistor after being mirrored.

So far, the editing commands that you have worked with are variations on a theme—moving or copying single entities, or making multiple copies of entities. The next group of editing commands involves deleting portions of entities, or—in the case of ERASE—deleting entire entities.

Deleting and Restoring by Using ERASE and OOPS

Like a hammer, the ERASE command can be a constructive tool. But, like a hammer, you must watch how you use it. The ERASE command has been the scourge of many drawing files.

The following exercise uses ERASE and its complement, the OOPS command. OOPS is prominently displayed on the ERASE screen menu. OOPS uses no prompts; it just restores whatever was last obliterated with ERASE.

In the steps that follow, get rid of the original resistor by using ERASE. You can reload your WIDGEDIT drawing or continue from the preceding exercise. In either case, your drawing now should resemble figure 8.26.

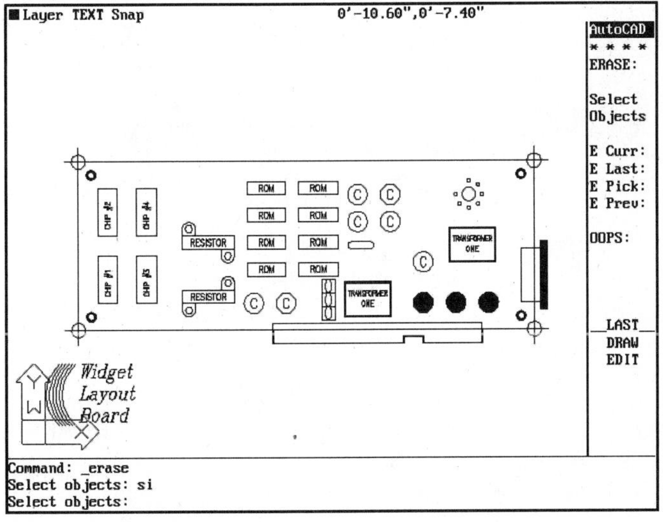

Figure 8.26:

The layout board before erasing.

Using ERASE

Command: *Choose* Modify, *then* Erase, *then* Single

Command: _erase

Select objects: si

Select objects: *Use a window to select the top resistor*

13 found — Deletes the resistor immediately (see fig. 8.27), without repeating the Select objects: prompt

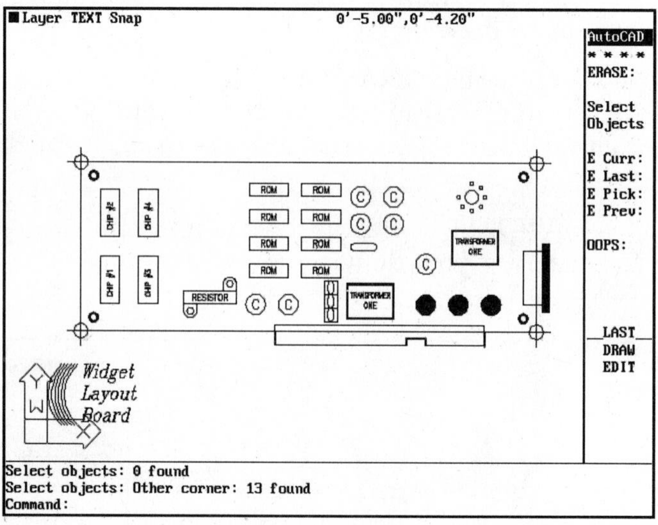

Figure 8.27:

The completed erase.

When you use the Erase option on the Modify pull-down menu, the ERASE command uses the Auto and SIngle object selection modes to act immediately on each selection, and then it automatically repeats. If you enter **ERASE** at the Command: prompt or use the screen menu, ERASE uses normal object selection and does not automatically repeat.

Every time you execute an erase, AutoCAD keeps a copy of what you erased, in case you want to bring it back into the file by using OOPS. Only the most recent erasure is kept ready. Try OOPS now to restore your resistor by choosing OOPS: from the screen menu.

OOPS enables you to recover from the unthinkable. After you have mistakenly deleted an entity from your drawing, you can recover the last deletion (under most circumstances) by using OOPS, even if you have used other commands since then. However, the OOPS command does not recover an entity after you plot or end and then resume a drawing.

Using BREAK To Cut Objects

BREAK cuts existing objects in two or erases portions of objects. Use any of the standard selection-set techniques to let AutoCAD know which entity you want to break. The safest way to select the object you want is by picking it. AutoCAD uses the pick point as the start of the break and prompts you for the second point. Crossing, Window, or Previous breaks the most recently selected entity. Unless you select by picking, you are then prompted for the first point (the start of the break) and second point (the end of the break). If you pick the same point again, AutoCAD cuts your object in two at the selected point, but does not delete any of it.

The process of picking does not work as well when breaking between intersections because AutoCAD may select the wrong entity. You can pick the object to be broken at another point, and then respecify the first break point. To do this, enter an **F** at the initial `Second point:` prompt, and AutoCAD reprompts you for the first point.

The following exercise breaks out the line at the port on the right side of the widget.

Using BREAK To Break a Line

`Command:` *Choose* Modify, *then* Break, *then* Select Object, 2 Points	Begins the BREAK command
`Command: _break Select object:` *Pick at* ① *(see fig. 8.28)*	Specifies what to break and the default first break point
`Enter second point (or F for first point):` F	Issues the First option
`Enter first point:` *From the pop-up menu, choose* Intersection, *then pick at* ②	Specifies the first break point
`Enter second point:` *From the pop-up menu, choose* Intersection, *then pick at* ③	Locates the break's endpoint and completes the break (see fig. 8.29)

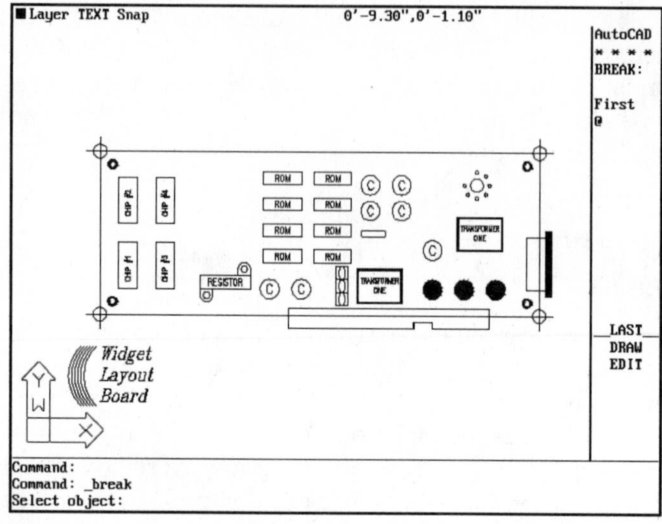

Figure 8.28:
The board before breaking.

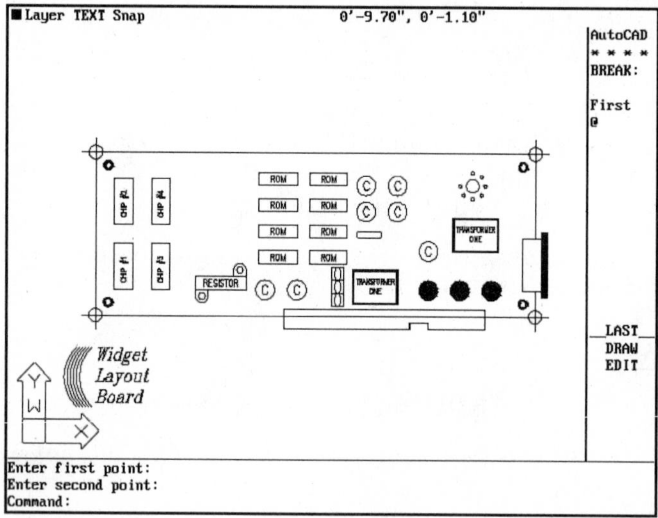

Figure 8.29:
The board after breaking.

BREAK works on lines, arcs, circles, traces, and polylines (including polygons and donuts). Take care to select the first and second points in counterclockwise order when breaking circles and arcs. Closed polylines need a little experimentation. BREAK's effects depend on the location of the polyline's first vertex. The break cannot extend across this vertex. If a point is off the entity, it acts as if you used object snap NEArest. If one point is off

the end of an arc, line, trace, or open polyline, that end is cut off instead of breaking the entity in two.

Rounding Edges Using the FILLET Command

A *fillet* is a tangent arc swung between two lines to create a round corner. The FILLET command is simple; AutoCAD asks you to identify the two lines that you want joined. You identify the lines by picking them. AutoCAD then shortens or extends the lines and creates a new arc for the fillet corner.

You can specify the radius of the arc to create the fillet corner. The default radius is 0. The fillet radius you set becomes the new default. The most common use for FILLET is to round corners, but a fillet with a zero radius (the original default) is good for cleaning up underlapping or overlapping lines at corners. FILLET with a zero radius creates a corner but does not create a new entity (see fig. 8.30). You pick the portions of the line that you want retained, and AutoCAD trims the other ends.

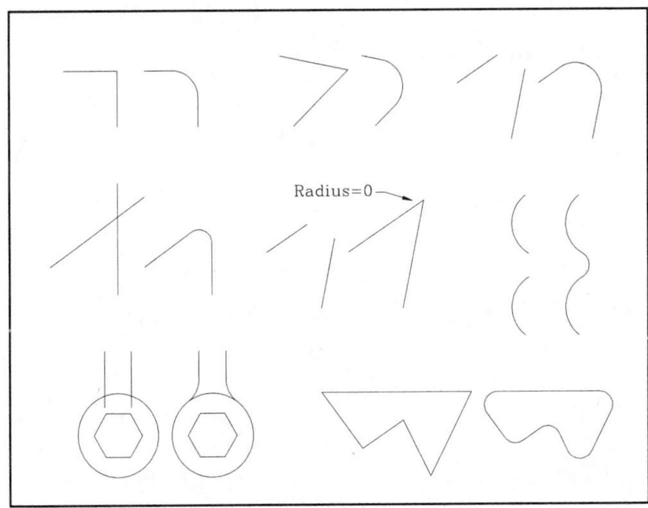

Figure 8.30:
Examples of fillets.

FILLET works on any combination of two arcs, circles, and non-parallel lines; or on a single polyline. You can select lines or a polyline by using Window, Last, or Crossing, but the results may be unpredictable. Selection by picking is safer and is required for arcs or circles. Arcs and circles have more than one possible fillet and are filleted closest to the pick points.

Try filleting the four corners of the layout board. First, set a default fillet radius with the Radius option, and then fillet the board.

Using FILLET To Round Corners

`Command:` *Choose* Construct, *then* Fillet	Begins the FILLET command
`_fillet Polyline/Radius/<Select first object>:` **R↵**	Sets radius
`Enter Fillet radius<0'-0.00>:` **.25↵**	
`Command:` *Press Enter*	Repeats FILLET command
`FILLET Polyline/Radius/<Select first object>:` *Pick a line at one corner of the widget board*	
`Select second object:` *Pick the other line*	Builds a fillet arc between the selected lines
`Command:` *Press Enter*	Repeats the FILLET command

Fillet each of the three remaining corners.

`Command:` **R↵**	Redraws the screen

Your board's corner should resemble the one shown in figure 8.31.

When fillets have the same radius arc (as in the preceding exercise), you can speed up the edit by preceding FILLET with the Multiple command to make multiple fillets.

AutoCAD offers two ways to fillet polylines: one vertex or all vertices. If you select the polyline by Window, Crossing, or Last, the most recent vertex is filleted. If you pick two points on adjacent segments, the vertex between those segments is filleted. If you enter a `P` at the first fillet prompt, you are prompted to select a polyline and all of its vertices are filleted. Try this technique in the following exercise by using the CHAMFER command, which works much like the FILLET command.

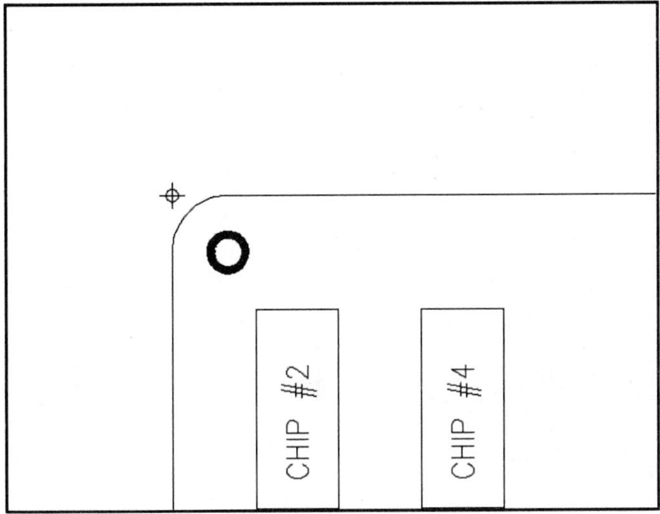

Figure 8.31:

Detail of a filleted corner.

Applying the CHAMFER Command

A *chamfer* is a beveled edge that is easy to add. CHAMFER works only on two lines or a single polyline. To get the chamfer, you supply a chamfer distance along each line that you want to join, rather than an arc radius. The distance that you supply is the cut-back distance from the intersection of the lines (see fig. 8.32).

Try two sets of chamfers. First, chamfer all four corners of the second transformer polyline with 45-degree chamfers (equal distances). Then, chamfer two corners on the right side port.

Using CHAMFER on the Layout Board

`Command:` *Choose* Construct, *then* CHAMFER	Begins the CHAMFER command
`Command: _chamfer`	
`Chamfer Polyline/Distances/ <Select first line>: D↵`	Specifies the Distances option
`Enter first chamfer distance <0'-0.0">: .05↵`	Resets the first distance

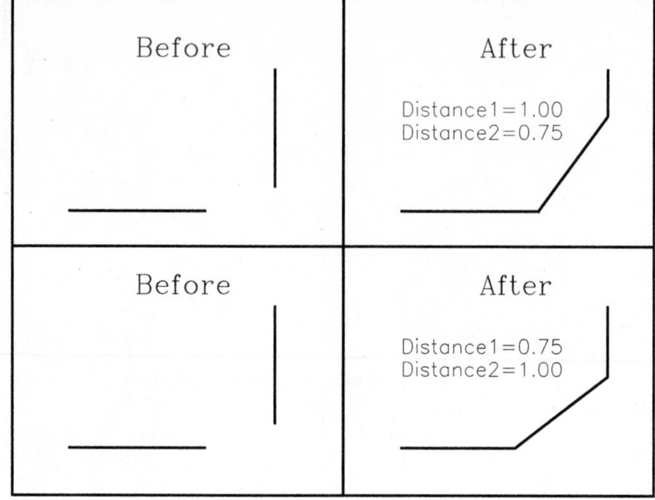

Figure 8.32: Examples of chamfered line intersections.

`Enter second chamfer distance <0'-0.05">:` *Press Enter*	Accepts the new first distance as the default second distance
`Command:` *Press Enter*	Repeats CHAMFER
`Polyline/Distances/<Select first line>:` *Enter* **`P`** *or choose* polyline *from the screen menu*	
`Select 2D polyline:` *Select the transformer polyline on the right*	Chamfers all four vertices in one pick
`4 lines were chamfered`	
`Command:` *Press Enter*	Repeats CHAMFER
`Chamfer Polyline/Distances/ <Select first line>:` **`D↵`**	Enters the Distances option
`Enter first chamfer distance <0'-0.05">:` **`.1↵`**	Resets the first distance
`Enter second chamfer distance <0'-0.10">:` *Press Enter*	Accepts the new first distance as the default second distance
`Command:` *Press Enter*	Repeats CHAMFER
`Chamfer Polyline/Distances/ <Select first line>:` *Select the top horizontal port line*	
`Select second line:` *Select the vertical port line*	
`Command:` *Press Enter*	Repeats CHAMFER
`Chamfer Polyline/Distances/ <Select first line>:` *Select the bottom horizontal port line*	
`Select second line:` *Select the vertical port line*	

As you can see from the exercise, it is easy to chamfer polylines. All four corners of the transformer were modified at the same time (see fig. 8.33).

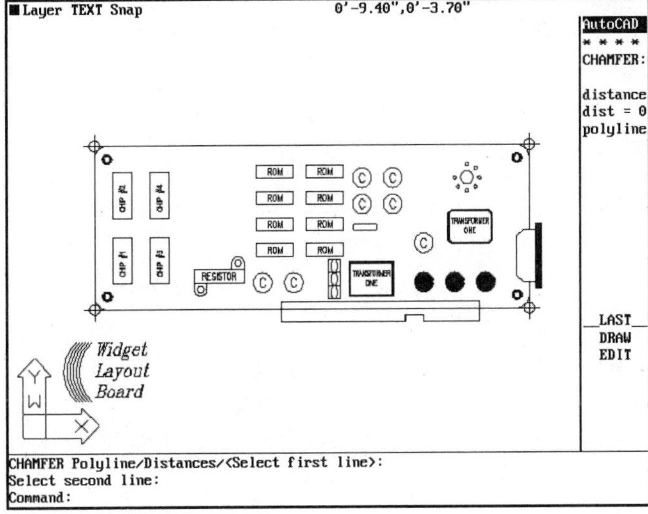

Figure 8.33: The transformer and port after chamfering.

The following sections discuss the CHANGE and CHPROP commands, which modify existing entities.

Modifying Entities by Using the CHANGE Command

The CHANGE command can selectively edit one or more parameters that give a drawing entity its identity, location, and appearance in the drawing file. Use CHANGE in 2D drawings to modify entity points, text, or attribute definitions (see Chapter 16); and use a second command, CHPROP (discussed in the next section), to modify appearances. CHPROP works in both 2D and 3D.

When you select objects to change, AutoCAD prompts you for the points and parameters that are changeable for the entities that you select. These points and parameters vary with the type of entity.

The CHANGE command affects different entities in the following ways:

- **Lines.** Change point, which is the default for the change command, changes the endpoint of a line. If several lines are selected, their nearest endpoints converge at the picked change point. If Ortho is on, lines are forced orthogonal, instead of converging.
- **Circles.** Change point alters the circumference of an existing circle, forcing it to pass through the change point, while keeping the same center point.
- **Text (and attribute definitions).** Change point alters the location, rotation angle, height, style, and text string. CHANGE acts as a second chance to reset your text parameters.
- **Blocks.** CHANGE enables you to alter the insertion point or rotation angle. (See Chapter 11.)

If you select several different entities, even different types, CHANGE ignores any change point you pick; it instead cycles through the entities in the order selected, prompting for the appropriate changes.

Entities on a locked layer are not altered by the editing commands. This is a good way to protect certain entities and helps to make a well-organized drawing.

First, use CHANGE to change the text of the second transformer from "ONE" to "TWO." Then, change the diameter of the switch circle on the right side of the board. Figure 8.34 shows the board before these changes are made.

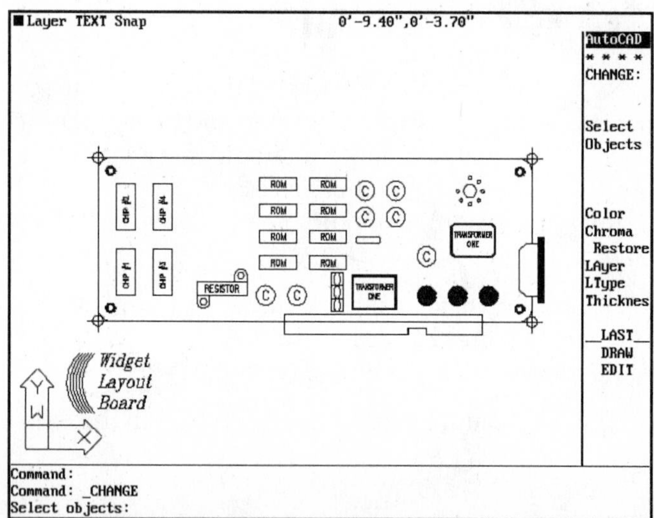

Figure 8.34:

The text and circle before changes.

Using CHANGE To Modify the Layout Board

`Command:` *From the screen menu, choose* EDIT, *then* CHANGE:	
`Command: _CHANGE`	
`Select objects:` *Select the text string* ONE *in the transformer on the right*	
`Properties/<Change point>:` *Press Enter*	
`Enter text insertion point:` *Press Enter*	Keeps the same point
`Text style: STANDARD` `New style or RETURN for no change:` *Press Enter*	Displays current and prompts for new style
`New height <0'-0.08">:` *Press Enter*	Keeps the same height
`New rotation angle <0.00>:` *Press Enter*	Keeps the same angle
`New text <ONE>:` **TWO**↵	Changes ONE to TWO
Now, change the diameter of the switch.	
`Command:` *Press Enter*	Repeats the command
`Select objects:` *Select the center switch circle inside the array*	
`Properties/<Change point>:` *Pick point 8.20,5.30*	Specifies a new circumference point and changes the circle

Figure 8.35 shows a zoomed view of the changed switch and transformer.

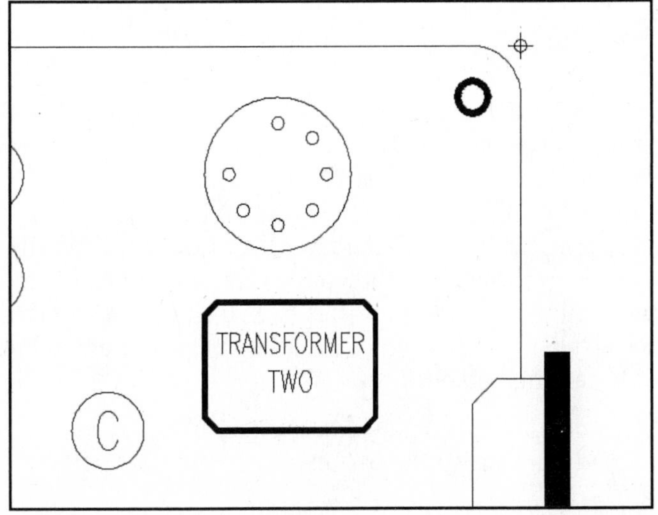

Figure 8.35: Detail of the switch and transformer after changes.

You also can use CHANGE to modify the properties of entities. Using CHANGE to modify properties in 2D drawings works fine, but it may not always work in 3D drawings. That is why AutoCAD offers the CHPROP command, which always works.

When you redefine an existing text style by using STYLE, only changes to the font and vertical orientation affect existing text. You can use the CHANGE command to force existing text to reflect modifications to width, height, obliquing angle, and so on. If you enter a style name at the new style prompt, AutoCAD updates all text parameters, even if the style name entered is the same as the currently defined style. Press Enter to leave all parameters unchanged.

Using CHPROP To Change Properties

CHPROP changes properties in a 2D or 3D drawing. So far, you have changed the location, size, or shape of entities already in place. In the next section, you learn how to change their properties.

As discussed in Chapter 3, all entities have properties that you can edit. These properties are the following:

- Color
- Layer
- Linetype
- Thickness

When you created the lines in your widget drawing, you gave them a color and linetype. You created the individual widget parts on the layer PARTS with both entity color and linetype BYLAYER. (PARTS has a cyan [4] default color and a continuous default linetype.) When you created the parts, these entities picked up their characteristics from the layer defaults. While you were editing these lines, they retained their BYLAYER color and linetype. At this point, the widget's entities have 0 elevation and thickness. These properties apply to 3D drawings. (You learn about them in Part Five, which covers 3D drawing and editing.)

The CHPROP command is the best way to change the properties of entities that you have already drawn. In the first exercise, you use CHPROP to

change the interior connector line's layer property to the HIDDEN layer. The object-selection prompts are abbreviated in this exercise and in most of the remaining exercises. After you select the objects, you see a prompt for the property that you want to change.

Using CHPROP To Change Layers

`Command:` *Select the connector lines using a window*	
`Command:` *From the screen menu, choose* EDIT, *then* CHPROP:	
`Command: _CHPROP 10 found`	
`Change what property (Color/LAyer/ LType/Thickness) ?` **LA**↵	Specifies the Layer property
`New layer <BOARD>:` **HIDDEN**↵	Specifies HIDDEN, and then reprompts for other properties
`Change what property (Color/LAyer/ LType/Thickness) ?` *Press Enter*	Completes the changes (see fig. 8.35)

Your drawing should show red, hidden connector lines (see fig. 8.36). The linetype and color properties are still BYLAYER.

Entity color and linetype properties can be independent of layer. In fact, an entity can have any color or linetype.

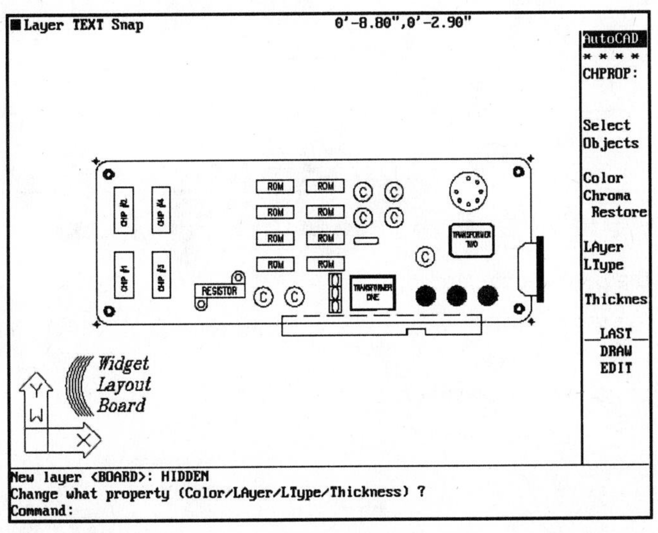

Figure 8.36:

The connector after the layer change.

Using the Change Properties Dialog Box

The Change Properties dialog box is a very convenient alternative to the CHPROP command (see fig. 8.37). It is displayed by entering DDCHPROP or by choosing Change, and then Properties from the Modify pull-down menu. The four existing properties are displayed with child dialog boxes for selecting new properties instead of typing them. This is very useful, in a drawing with too many layers, to easily type the new layer name at the CHPROP prompt.

Change the entity color of the three donuts (the solid dots) by using the DDCHPROP dialog box. Then, take one last look at your widget layout drawing with all its edits.

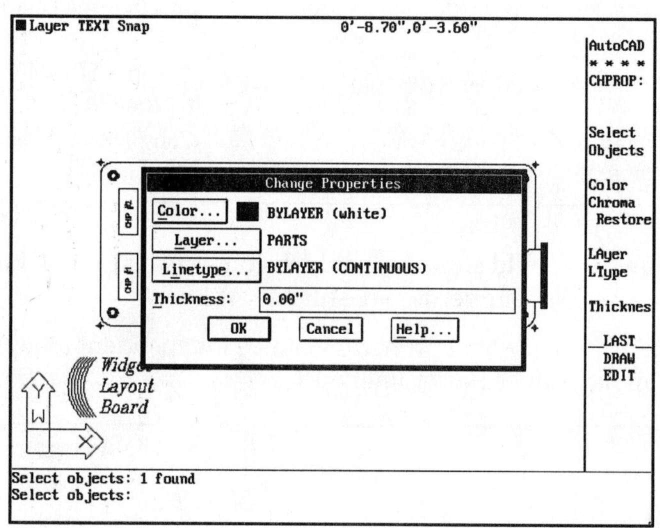

Figure 8.37

The Change Properties dialog box.

Using DDCHPROP To Change the Color of Donuts

Continue from the preceding exercise.

`Command:` *Choose* Modify, *then* Change, *then* Properties	Starts the DDCHPROP command
`Select objects:` *Select the three solid dots*	Displays the Change Properties dialog box
Click on Color	Displays the Select Color dialog box

`New color <BYLAYER>:` *Click on the magenta box, then click on* OK	Selects magenta and returns to the Change Properties dialog box
Click on OK	Closes dialog box and executes change

ZOOM All, then save the drawing.

Now, the donuts are magenta, overriding the cyan PARTS layer default.

CHPROP provides an easy method for changing entity properties. For organized controlled drawings, it is usually best to work with color and linetype by layer settings. Instead of changing color and linetype properties, try expanding and redefining the layers you set up in your drawings.

Another dialog box is available, which enables changing of properties and entity geometry, such as points and radii. The DDMODIFY command first prompts for an entity to be selected, shows all of its properties and coordinate data, and enables the entity to be changed. This dialog box, almost a combination of the CHANGE and CHPROP commands, also can be displayed by choosing Entity from the Modify pull-down menu. Unlike CHANGE, CHPROP, and DDCHPROP, which can modify several entities at one time, DDMODIFY only modifies a single entity.

As promised, you now have a full four-color widget layout board (see fig. 8.38). Save this drawing; you can use it later when you experiment with plotting in Part Three.

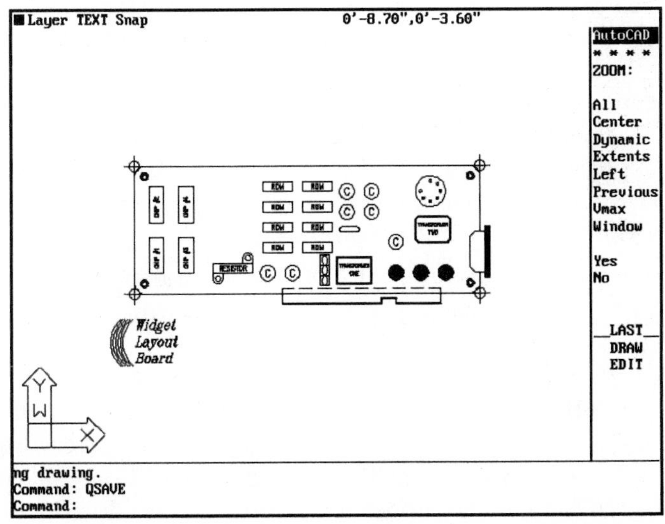

Figure 8.38:

The completed WIDGEDIT drawing.

You can now delete the WIDGET, PSPLOT, MVPLOT, and VPLAYER drawings; you no longer need them.

Summary

You can see how important editing is in constructing a drawing. In the beginning of the chapter on graphic entities, you learned that drawings are dynamic. With a first course in editing under your belt, you can see just how dynamic a drawing can be.

Are you ready for the next engineering change order? The following Editor's Guide to Editing will help keep you prepared:

- Plan ahead for editing. When you first set up a drawing, think about how you are going to use your multiple layers. If you have everything on one layer, editing can be complicated. Think about repetitive features and building blocks. Draw it once, copy it forever. Start by defining your basic components and building your drawing up from there.
- Use all of the editing commands. Try to use grips when possible to simplify editing. Use snap, Ortho, and object snaps to set up your MOVE and COPY displacements. MIRROR and ARRAY can help you complete a repetitive drawing in a hurry. Be careful with ERASE. To avoid disasters, you can always use OOPS and UNDO.
- Learn to use all of the object-selection options, including using the Remove option and using the shift key with object selection. All selection-set options have their roles. Last and Previous can be used when you realize that AutoCAD did what you said, not what you meant. The object-picking method is best for detail work, especially with object snap. If you want to edit most of the entities at once, use the All option, then Remove the entities you did not want to include.
- Window is powerful, but it does not do it all. Remember, what you see in the window is what goes into the selection set. You can use Crossing as a knife to slice out a selection set. BOX and SIngle are best for menu macros, as you will see when you get to customization. The use of AUto is a good habit. You can use it as a window, a crossing, or just to select an object. The WPOLY window is nice when a rectangular window will not enclose the entities. Previous saves time in repetitive editing. Do not forget, a U undoes the last object selection operation.

- Think ahead about individual edits. Use display control to keep your field of view small and your concentration level high. Do not get caught setting up the base point of a displacement, only to find that the second point is off the screen (if that happens, cancel, zoom, and try again). Do not underestimate the power of the CHANGE command. It really is an effective tool. Changing an endpoint is often easier than erasing and then adding a new line segment. You can almost always change text style, height, or rotation more easily than you can erase and replace it. Use CHPROP when you need to change the layer, color, and linetype properties of existing entities. When you are unsure of the change options, try DDCHPROP or DDMODIFY for a more graphic interface.
- Watch the current layer name on the status line. Note the edit prompts on the prompt line; it is easy to start creating a selection-set window while the prompt line is waiting for you to enter **W** to initiate the window selection. Use the F1 key, which changes from the text screen to the graphics screen and back again, to see AutoCAD's status.

So far, you have looked at some of AutoCAD's basic editing commands. The next chapter moves on to more advanced editing commands that you use with electronic drafting techniques to get more productivity from editing your drawings.

Part Three

Advanced 2D AutoCAD Drafting

In previous chapters, you learned how to use AutoCAD's many basic drawing features to create and edit various types of drawings. You also learned how to control the graphics display and how to use the coordinate system and electronic drawing aids to draw entities accurately.

Part Three of *Inside AutoCAD Release 12* introduces you to the program's new and more advanced features. The following seven chapters show you how to use these features in the most productive ways. The chapters cover Release 12's new advanced commands and show you how to use the AutoCAD dimensioning and plotting tools, which enable you to produce finished drawings.

How Part Three is Organized

Part Three contains seven chapters, which cover the following three topics:

- Advanced drawing and editing commands
- Grouping entities together to create symbols and insertable drawing files (such as overlays, backgrounds, and title blocks)
- Preparing and printing your drawing

When you finish Part Three, you will be able to produce and plot nearly any type of 2D drawing.

Advanced Drawing and Editing

Chapter 9 covers AutoCAD's more advanced editing commands, which enable you to extend, stretch, trim, scale, and offset objects. The chapter also shows you how to edit polylines to create continuous drawing lines. These advanced editing techniques are extremely productive in 2D drafting, and they are essential in the 3D environment.

All this book's drawing and editing chapters offer tips and tricks, but Chapter 10 is a "pure techniques" chapter. It shows you how to combine construction lines, electronic point filters, and editing commands to build accurate drawings quickly. Chapter 10 also teaches you how to place editing marks and controls in your editing sequences, so that you can try different edits without wasting time. Chapter 10 also teaches you how to take advantage of AutoCAD's undo functions.

As you apply AutoCAD's drawing and editing commands to your drawings, you may begin to recognize patterns in your own command usage. The trick for improving productivity is to learn the drawing and editing commands that enable you to build fast, accurate drawings, and then to incorporate these editing sequences and techniques into your daily AutoCAD work. If you are looking for advanced editing techniques, you can learn them by working through Chapters 9 and 10.

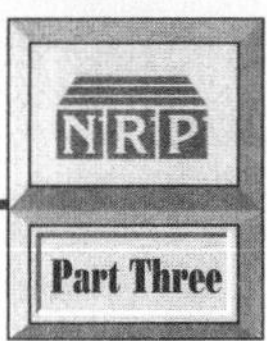

Blocks (Symbols) and Reference Files

AutoCAD enables you to save groups of entities as symbols, which AutoCAD calls *blocks*. You can save drawing time and file space by learning how to use blocks to insert repetitive objects in your drawings. Chapter 11 shows you how to use blocks and how to update your drawings quickly and easily by redefining the blocks. This chapter also introduces you to the basics of external reference files (xrefs). An *xref* is a drawing that refers to other drawing files for some of their information. Reference files coordinate the cooperative editing of a master drawing by enabling several people to work on component parts of it simultaneously.

Chapter 12 continues with block usage by teaching you construction techniques with blocks and xrefs. The exercises in this chapter involve developing a site plan—called "Autotown"—with houses, trees, and cars. The chapter shows how quickly you can develop a drawing by using much existing geometry.

Presentation and Plotting

Chapter 13 teaches you a variety of methods for successfully plotting output. You learn how and when to use paper space to compose drawings and to make multiple-view plotting a cinch. You also discover dozens of plotting tips. Chapter 14 explains techniques for using hatching and linetypes, and for doing free-hand sketching in AutoCAD. This chapter concludes with a discussion of AutoCAD's inquiry commands, which tell you what you are drawing, as well as where and when you are drawing it. Chapter 15 guides you through the basics of AutoCAD's dimensioning commands and settings. (Advanced dimensioning is discussed in Chapter 17.)

9

Advanced Editing

To take advantage of AutoCAD's power, you need to combine AutoCAD's editing commands with CAD drafting techniques. Although the editing commands you learned in the last chapter help speed up your drafting, the editing commands and techniques discussed in this chapter enable you to change the way you create your drawings. You can use advanced editing commands, such as EXTEND, STRETCH, TRIM, and OFFSET for more than copying and moving entities. These commands build on AutoCAD's geometrical recognition of the entities in your drawing. By combining these commands with construction techniques, such as setting up construction lines, parallel rules, and construction layers, you can make a rough draft of a drawing quickly, and then finish it perfectly.

Besides construction techniques, this chapter shows you the way to use polylines and PEDIT to create continuous two-dimensional lines. Continuous polylines are important for AutoCAD's hatch patterns and 3D, and they provide continuity when you form three-dimensional faces and meshes. If your two-dimensional drawing has breaks in its line profile, you cannot form a complete three-dimensional surface. Figure 9.1 shows a 3D mesh formed from a continuous polyline.

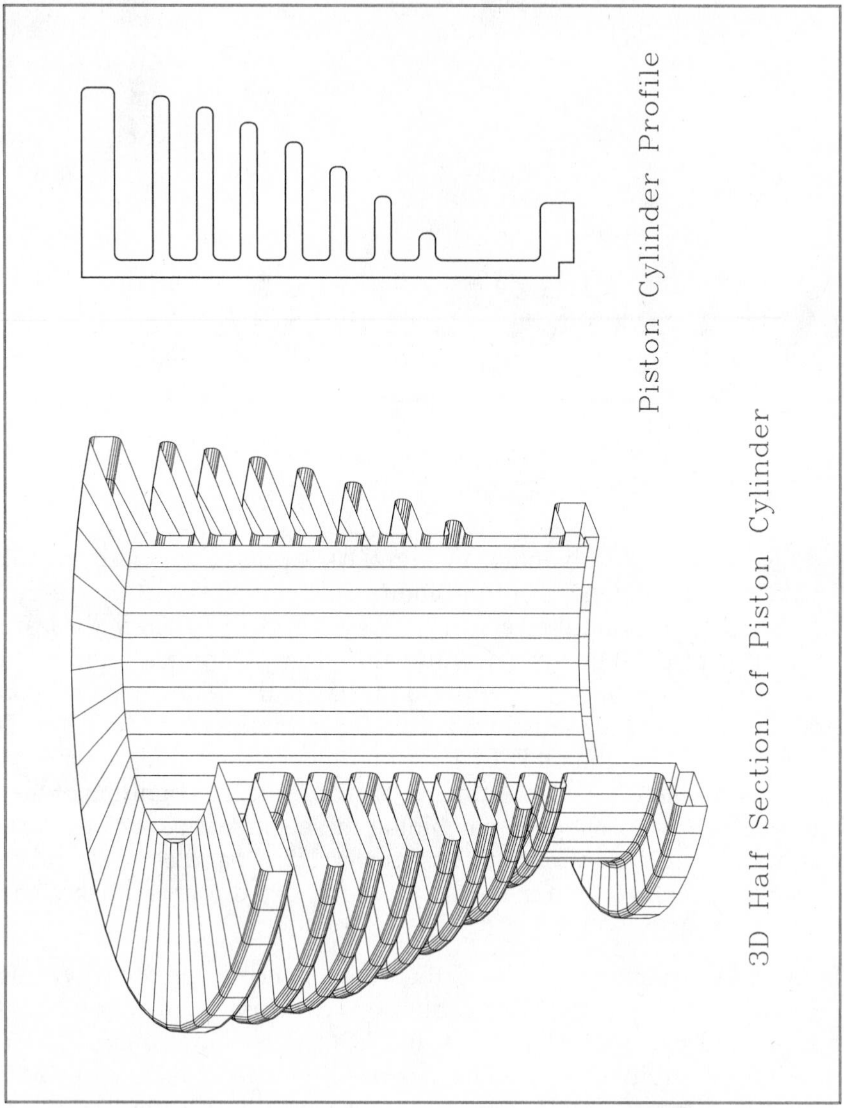

Figure 9.1:
3D-piston cylinder and profile.

Before you work with 3D drawings, you must master basic 2D skills, such as drawing polylines and using PEDIT to modify new polylines and convert or join existing entities. The exercises in this chapter show you how to use PEDIT and other advanced editing commands to combine entity creation and CAD construction techniques into a single drawing process.

The editing commands covered in this chapter's exercises include EXTEND, OFFSET, SCALE, STRETCH, TRIM, and PEDIT. The trick to using these advanced editing commands is to plan ahead. The operations of commands such as EXTEND, STRETCH, and TRIM can involve a number of entities. These commands require more setup and more planning for the way you are going to use them. PEDIT, for example, requires continuity to join lines and arcs.

Setting Up the Cylinder Drawing

The drawing that you create in this chapter's exercises is the piston cylinder profile (see fig. 9.2). The full cylinder is approximately 10 by 14.60 inches.

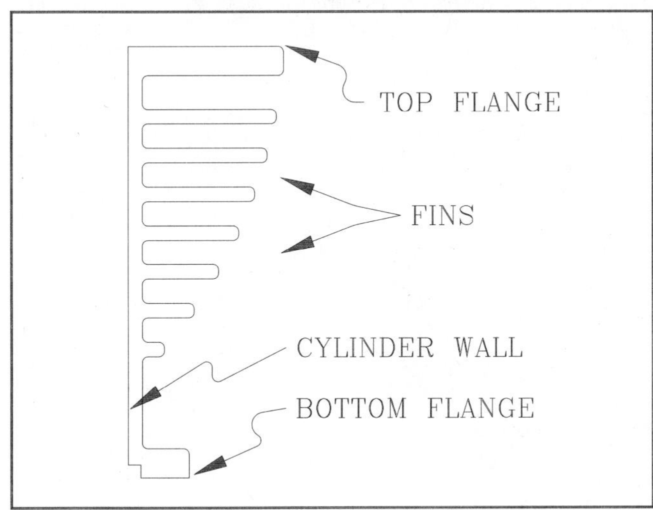

Figure 9.2:
A cylinder profile target drawing.

The following sample calculations estimate a drawing scale factor and set a sheet size:

```
Finned Piston Cylinder Wall    14.60" × 10.00"
Plot sheet size  11" × 8 1/2"
Test 1/2" = 1" scale is a scale factor of 2.
11" × 2 = 22" and 8 1/2" × 2 = 17"    22" × 17" limits
```

In the steps that follow, create a new drawing called CYLINDER. Use the default decimal units (each unit represents one inch). If you dimension this drawing, you can use the AutoCAD dimensioning feature to add inch marks automatically. Set your limits at 22×17. Use the settings shown in table 9.1 to help you complete your setup. If you are using the IA DISK, begin your CYLINDER drawing by setting it equal to \IA\IA7CYLIN.

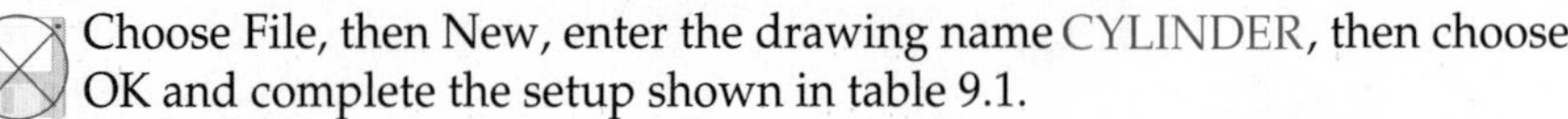

Setup for CYLINDER Drawing

Choose File, then New, enter the drawing name CYLINDER=IA7CYLIN and choose OK.

Choose File, then New, enter the drawing name CYLINDER, then choose OK and complete the setup shown in table 9.1.

Set the 2D layer current.

Table 9.1
Cylinder Drawing Settings

COORDS	*GRID*	*SNAP*	*ORTHO*
On	1	0.1	ON

UNITS	Default decimal units, 2 digits to right of decimal point, default all other settings.
LIMITS	0,0 to 22,17
ZOOM	Zoom All

Layer Name	*State*	*Color*	*Linetype*
0	On	7 (White)	CONTINUOUS
2D	On/Current	1 (Red)	CONTINUOUS
3D	On	3 (Green)	CONTINUOUS

If you want to practice individual editing commands, create a layer named SCRATCH. Create some entities on this layer, try out some editing variations, then freeze your SCRATCH layer and pick up again where you left off with the exercise sequences.

Using Lines and Polylines To Rough-In a Drawing

Start to create the cylinder by roughing-in the section profile of the cylinder in the following exercise. First, use a polyline to draw the top, side, and bottom of the cylinder. Then draw one line and array it to form the construction lines for what later becomes the cylinder fins. Finally, draw an arc on the right side as a construction line to help form the ends of the fins. Your current layer is 2D.

Using PLINE, LINE, and ARC To Rough-In the Cylinder Wall

`Command:` *Choose* Draw, *then* Polyline, *and choose* 2D	Issues the PLINE command
`Command: _PLINE`	
`From point:` *Pick point 17,12*	
`Current line-width is 0.00`	
`Arc/Close/Halfwidth/Length/Undo/Width/<Endpoint of line>:` **`@3<180`** ↵	
`Arc/Close/Halfwidth/Length/Undo/Width/<Endpoint of line>:` **`@8<270`** ↵	
`Arc/Close/Halfwidth/Length/Undo/Width/<Endpoint of line>:` **`@1<0`** ↵	
`Arc/Close/Halfwidth/Length/Undo/Width/<Endpoint of line>:` *Press Enter*	
`Command:` *Enter* `L`*, and draw a line from 14.00,11.00 to @1<0*	Issues the LINE command and draws the line
`Command:` *Select the line you just drew, then choose* Construct, *and* Array	Selects the line and starts the ARRAY command
`Command: _array 1 found`	Finds the preselected line

`Rectangular or Polar array (R/P) <R>:` *From the screen menu, choose* Rectang	
`Number of rows (--) <1>:` **7** ↵	
`Number of columns (|||) <1>:` *Press Enter*	
`Unit cell or distance between rows (--):` **-.8**↵	Makes six copies of the line at .8 spacing
`Command:` *Enter* **A**, *then draw an arc from 17,12 to 16.1,8.7 to 14,5.7*	Issues the ARC command and draws the arc

Your drawing should resemble the one shown in figure 9.3.

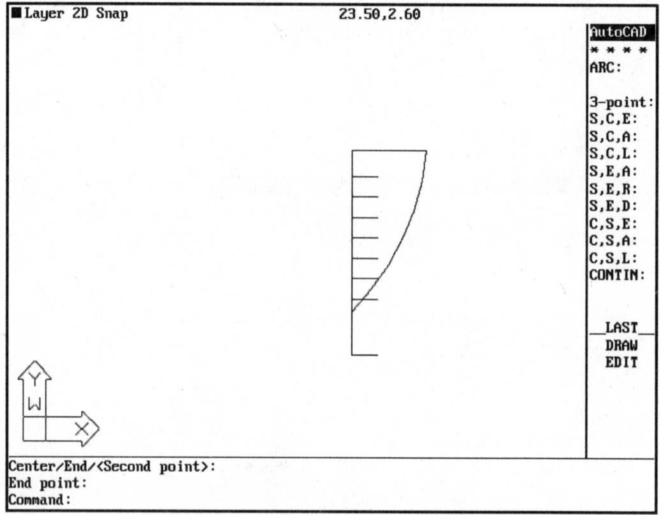

Figure 9.3:
The rough construction lines of a cylinder wall.

Your arc should extend down from the polyline endpoint on the top right, intersect the first line that you drew, and intersect the polyline on the left a little more than halfway between the bottom and the intersected line. This arc is a construction line boundary that you use to form the cylinder fins. The fin lines are formed by extending the lines to the arc.

Extending Entities

To extend the lines to the arc, use the EXTEND command, which extends lines, polylines, and arcs. The boundary edge(s) can be lines, polylines, arcs, circles, and viewport entities (when in paper space). Use normal object selection to select the boundary edge(s) to which you want to extend, then pick the objects that you want to extend. You must pick individually each object to extend. You cannot use other modes to fill a selection set full of objects that you want to extend, and then extend them all at once. Objects to extend are ignored unless EXTEND can project them to intersect a boundary object.

Use EXTEND if you do not know the drawing intersection points or if you do not want to calculate them. In these cases (and in the current exercise), it is easier to use a construction line and then extend the entities. EXTEND has a few constraints: you cannot extend closed polylines or shorten objects (use the TRIM command to shorten lines).

In the following exercise, use EXTEND to lengthen the fin lines until they meet the construction arc.

Using EXTEND To Extend Lines to an Arc

Use ZOOM Window and zoom to view shown in figure 9.4.

`Command:` *Choose* Modify, *then* Extend	Issues the EXTEND command
`Command: _extend` `Select boundary edges(s)...`	
`Select objects:` *Pick the arc and press Enter*	
`<Select object to extend>/Undo:` *Pick each of the seven short lines at the endpoint closest to the arc*	Extends all the lines except the bottom one
`Entity does not intersect an edge.`	Fails to extend
`<Select object to extend>/Undo:` *Press Enter*	Exits from the EXTEND command

The zoomed view and extended lines should look like figure 9.4.

The EXTEND command cannot adjust the bottom line because it crosses the arc. You can use TRIM on this line, but you use STRETCH instead in a later exercise to attach the line and the arc. In another later exercise, you use TRIM for something more complicated.

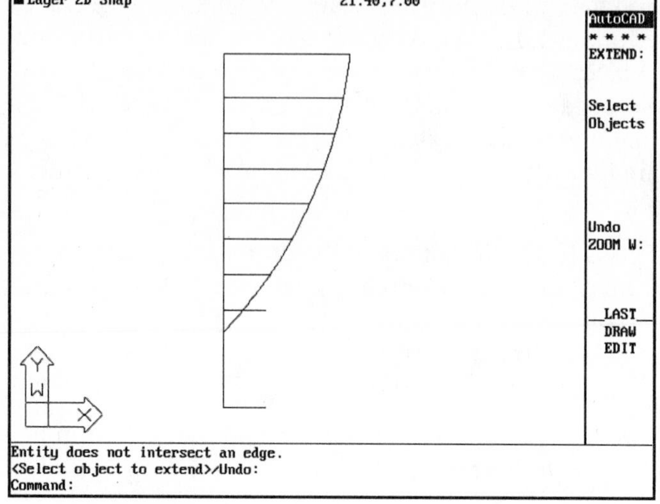

Figure 9.4:
Extending lines to the arc.

Using the OFFSET Command

The cylinder wall and each cylinder fin is made up of parallel lines. The OFFSET command enables you to create parallel drawing lines you pick each entity individually that you want to offset and AutoCAD creates a parallel copy.

You cannot offset some types of entities. Entities that you can offset include lines, arcs, circles, and 2D polylines. Polylines include donuts, ellipses, and polygons. Each offset creates a new entity with the same linetype, color, and layer settings as the original entity. Polylines also have the same width and curves.

You can use two techniques to offset entities. You can provide an offset distance and then indicate the side of the offset. You can input values or pick a point to show the offset distances, but you must use a pick to show the side for placement. Offset distances cannot be negative values.

The second way to offset entities (the default) is to pick the entity you want to offset and then pick a point through which the entity is to be offset. If the through point falls beyond the end of the new entity, the offset is calculated as if the new entity extended to the through point, but it is drawn without that imaginary extension.

In the following exercise, use OFFSET with a through point to create a double cylinder wall and to double the lines that form the fins. After you offset these lines, close the ends of the wall and fins.

Using OFFSET To Create Wall and Fin Lines

Use ZOOM to zoom to view shown in figure 9.5.

`Command:` *Choose* Construct, *then* Offset	Issues OFFSET with the default distance

`Command: _offset`
`Offset distance or Through <Through>: .3`
Press Enter
	Sets a default for the distance

`Select object to offset:` *Pick polyline on the left*	
`Side to offset?` *Pick any point to the left of the polyline*	Draws a new parallel polyline
`Select object to offset:` *Pick one of the fin lines*	Draws a new parallel line
`Side to offset?` *Pick any point above the line*	
`Select object to offset:` *Continue to offset the fin lines, picking each offset above the selected line*	
`Command:` *Choose* Settings, *then* Object Snap, *check the* Endpoint *box, and choose OK*	Sets the running object snap to ENDPoint
`Command:` *Enter* `L`, *and draw vertical lines closing ends of each pair of fin lines, including top and bottom*	Issues the LINE command and draws lines
`Command:` *Choose* Settings, *then* Object Snap, *clear the* Endpoint *checkbox, and choose* OK	Sets the running object snap to NONe
`Command: QSAVE ↵`	Saves the drawing

Figure 9.5 shows the cylinder with its offset lines, but before the lines are closed. Figure 9.6 shows the cylinder with its closed polylines.

You can use OFFSET to offset lines and polylines (as you saw in the preceding exercise), and you also can use OFFSET to form concentric circles.

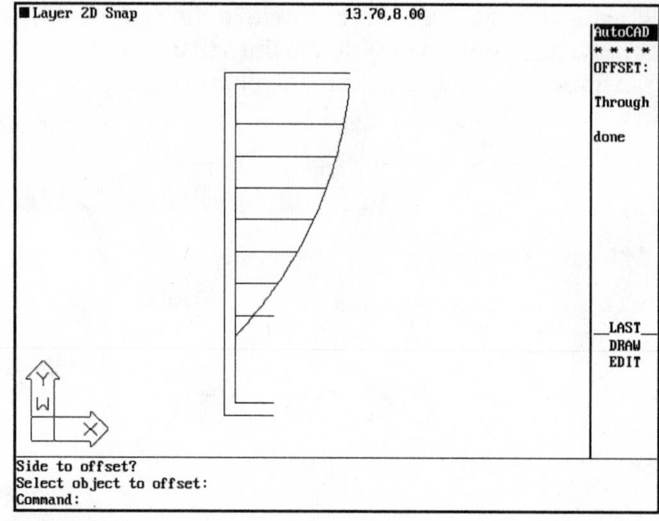

Figure 9.5:

The cylinder after offset.

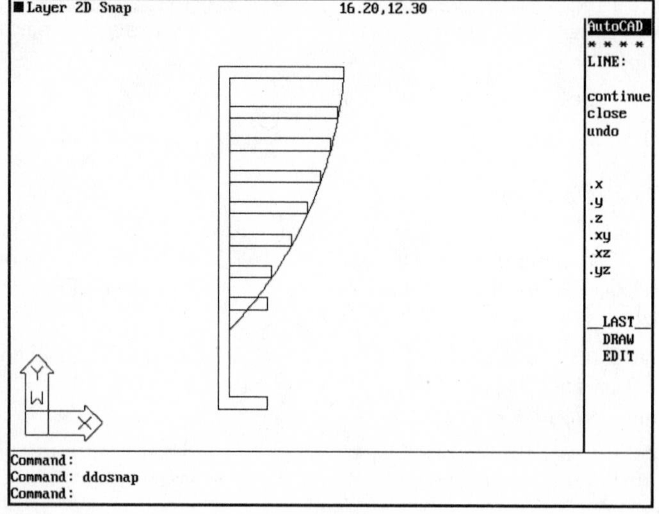

Figure 9.6:

The cylinder with connecting lines.

NOTE

OFFSET forms a new entity by drawing the entity parallel to the original entity. OFFSET cannot form a new entity inside an arc or circle if the offset distance exceeds the original radius. (You cannot create a negative radius.) Donuts, polygons, and arc or short segments in other polylines are treated similarly. OFFSET attempts to duplicate small zig-zag segments and loops with

polylines, but you may get confused results. Use PEDIT to clean up offset polylines if you do not like the results.

In the exercise that follows, you learn how to thicken the flanges and shorten the bottom fin by using the STRETCH command.

Using STRETCH for Power Drawing

The STRETCH command enables you to move and stretch entities. You can lengthen entities, shorten them, and alter their shapes.

When you use STRETCH, most often you use a crossing window. After you select your objects with a crossing window (see fig. 9.7), you show AutoCAD where to stretch your objects with a displacement, a base point, and a new point. Everything that you selected inside the crossing window moves, and entities crossing the window are stretched. The expression *inside the window* means that all of an object's endpoints or vertex points are within the window. The expression *crossing the window* means that one or more points are inside and one or more points are outside the window.

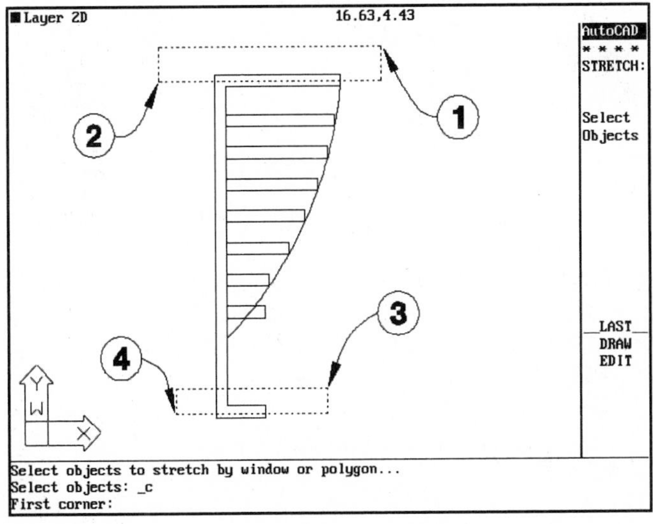

Figure 9.7:

Crossing windows to stretch flanges.

The STRETCH command uses the crossing window selection set. (A window moves entities, but it does not stretch them.) If you want to leave untouched any objects that fall within the crossing window, you can use the Remove mode to remove them from the selection set. With a window, you can add only objects you want moved to the new destination. If you use Crossing or Window to add or remove entities, the results may not be what you want because STRETCH only recognizes the most recent Crossing or Window selection.

STRETCH interacts differently with different entities. In the following exercise, use STRETCH on lines and polylines by widening the top and bottom of the cylinder.

Using STRETCH To Widen the Flanges

`Command:` *Choose* Modify, *then* Stretch	Issues STRETCH with a Crossing selection
`Command: _stretch` `Select objects to stretch by window or polygon...`	
`Select objects:` **`_c`**	
`First corner:` *Pick at point* ① (see fig. 9.7), *drag to* ②, *release, and press Enter*	Sets the crossing window
`other corner: 2 found`	
`Base point:` *Pick any point*	
`New point:` *Pick or enter point at* `@.3<90`↵	Stretches the flange
`Command:` *Press Enter*	Repeats the command
`STRETCH` `Select objects to stretch by window or polygon ...`	
`Select objects:` *Pick the upper right corner at* ③, *drag to* ④, *release, and press Enter*	Selects the bottom flange
`Base point:` *Pick any point*	
`New point:` *Pick or enter point at* `@.3<90`↵	

After you finish, your drawing should resemble the one shown in figure 9.8.

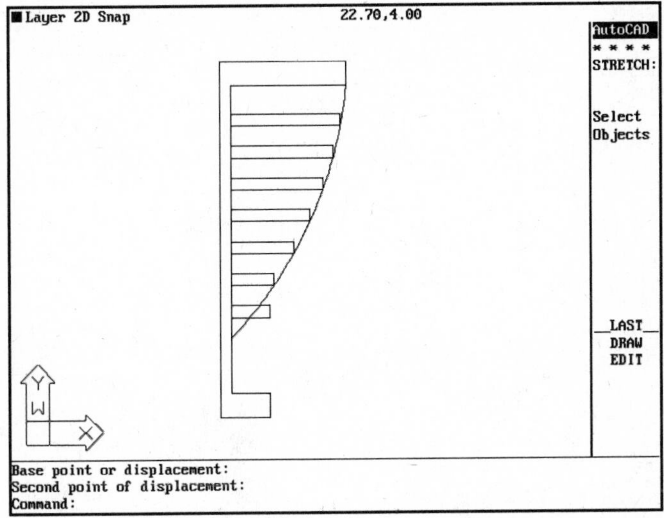

Figure 9.8:

The top and bottom flanges after being stretched.

Unlike the MOVE and COPY commands, STRETCH does not accept absolute X,Y or polar displacements. When you use MOVE or COPY, and enter an X,Y or dist<angle value at the first prompt, it becomes an absolute displacement if you press Enter at the second point prompt. The STRETCH equivalent to an absolute displacement is picking any point for the base point and then typing relative coordinates, such as @0,-7.5.

Use STRETCH again in the following exercise to shorten the bottom fin so that it is in line with the arc.

Using STRETCH To Shorten the Fin

`Command:` *Choose* Modify, *then* Stretch

`Command: _stretch`
`Select objects to stretch by window...`
`Select objects: _c`

`First corner:` *Pick corners at* ① *and* ② *(see fig. 9.9) and press Enter*

`Base point:` *Pick at* ③

`New point:` *From the popup menu, choose* Intersection, *then pick the intersection of the arc and line at* ④ — Shortens the fin

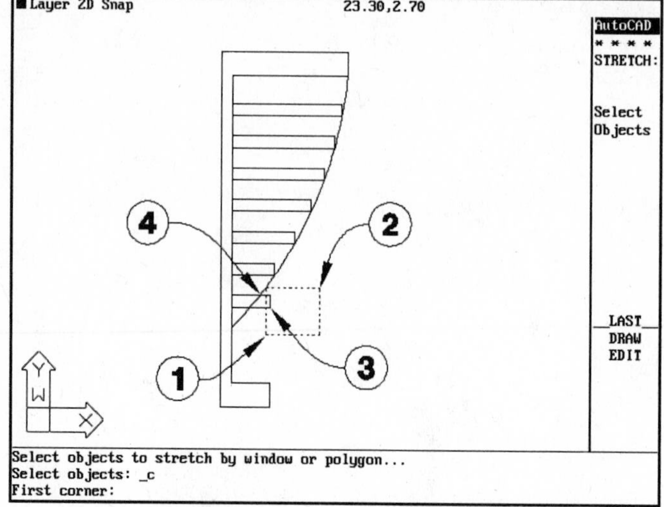

Figure 9.9:

A crossing window for stretching the fin.

When you are finished, the bottom fin should look like the one in figure 9.10.

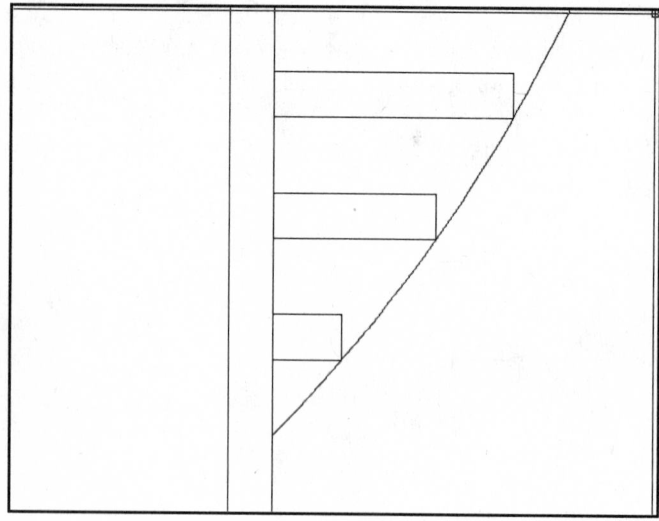

Figure 9.10:

A detail of the stretched fin.

As you work through the steps in the preceding exercise, you notice that the construction arc is highlighted by the crossing window, but it does not change with the stretch. The arc is not moved or stretched because its endpoints are not enclosed in the window. STRETCH operates differently with different entities.

Some significant points to remember when you use STRETCH with entities follow:

- The endpoints or vertex points of lines, arcs, polyline segments, viewports, traces, and solids determine what is stretched or moved.
- The center points of arcs or polyline arcs are adjusted to keep the sagitta constant. The *sagitta* is the altitude or distance from the chord midpoint to the nearest point on the arc.
- Viewport contents remain constant in scale.
- The location of a point, the center of a circle, or the insertion point of a block, shape, or text entity determine whether these entities are moved. These points are never stretched.

Using TRIM in Quick Construction

Frequently, you need to trim existing lines in a drawing. If you are working with a large number of entities, breaking individual entities is tiresome and cumbersome. You can get the same results faster by using TRIM. As with EXTEND, TRIM makes use of boundary entities that include lines, arcs, circles, polylines, and, in paper space, viewports. The entities that you select as your boundary edge become your cutting edge. After you select your cutting edge, you pick the individual entities that you want to trim. You can trim lines, arcs, circles, and polylines. Other entity types are ignored by the TRIM command; therefore, you can select extra objects that are in the area.

Figure 9.11 shows the trimmed interior lines of the top three cylinder fins. Compare those fins with the untrimmed ones, and then use TRIM in the following steps to cut the interior lines of all cylinder fins. You may have to turn off snap (F9) to pick the lines you want to trim.

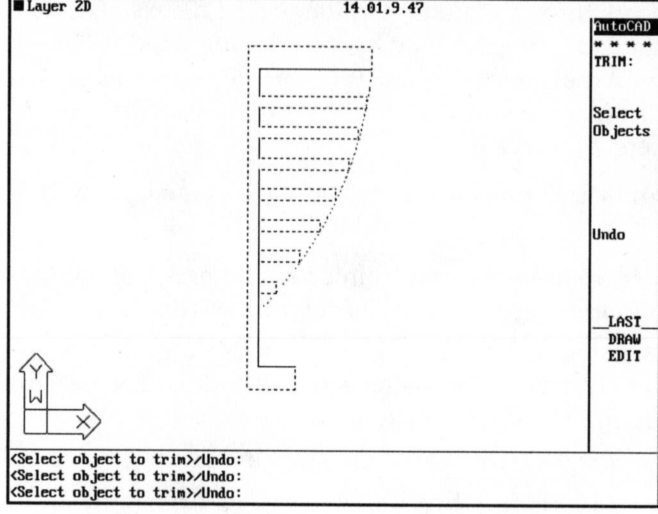

Figure 9.11:

A cylinder with three fins trimmed.

Using TRIM To Cut Fin Lines

Command: **TRIM** ↵	Issues the TRIM command
Select cutting edge(s)...	
Select objects: **ALL** ↵	Selects all the entities in the drawing
26 found Select objects: *Press Enter*	
<Select object to trim>/Undo: *Turn snap off, then pick a point on the cylinder wall between fin lines*	Trims the cylinder wall line
<Select object to trim>/Undo: *Continue picking until all the cylinder wall fin lines are trimmed*	
If you make an error, enter U *to undo it*	
<Select object to trim>/Undo: *Turn snap on, then press Enter*	Ends the command

The results of trimming the interior walls of the cylinder are shown in figure 9.12.

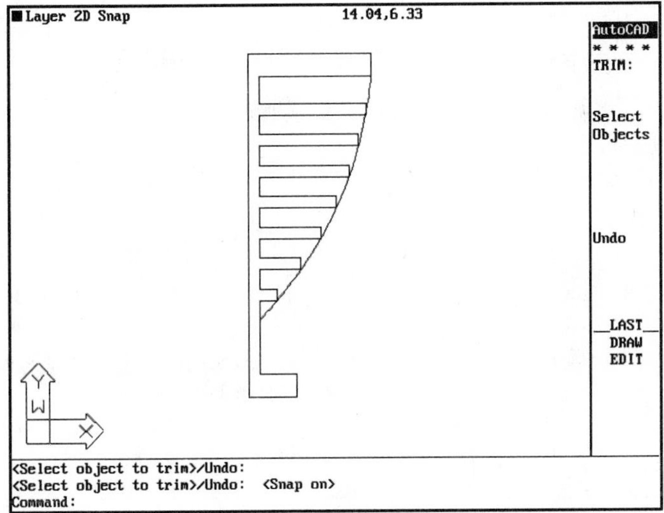

Figure 9.12: A cylinder after trim.

The same entity can be a cutting edge and be cut as an object to trim. After it has been trimmed, it is no longer highlighted, but it still functions as a cutting edge.

Using the SCALE Command

Occasionally, you may use the wrong drawing symbol and text scale or you may have to change an object's size in mid-drawing. The SCALE command enables you to shrink or enlarge objects that you already placed in your drawing. When you rescale drawing objects, you use a scale factor to change the size of entities around a given base point. The base point you choose remains constant in space; everything around it grows or shrinks by your scale factor. You can enter an explicit scale factor, pick two points to show a distance as a factor, or specify a reference length. To use a reference length, define a length (generally on an entity), and then specify the length you want it to become.

The piston cylinder is supposed to be 10 inches high. In the following exercise, use SCALE with the Reference option to change the cylinder profile to make it exactly 10 inches. After you finish, save your drawing.

Using SCALE To Enlarge the Cylinder

`Command:` *Choose* Modify, *then* Scale	Issues SCALE
`Command: _scale`	
`Select objects:` **`ALL`** ↵	
`Base point:` *Pick at* ① *(see fig. 9.13)*	
`<Scale factor>/Reference:` **`R`**↵	Specifies the Reference option
`Reference length <1>:` *Pick at* ① *(see fig. 9.13)*	Indicates the first point of the original reference length
`Second point:` *Pick at* ②	Defines the original reference length
`New length:` **`10`**↵	Resizes to exactly 10" (see fig. 9.14)

ZOOM All, then save the drawing and continue, or end and take a break.

TIP The scale base point also is the base point of the new length in the Reference option. If you want to show the length by picking points on another object, place the base point there, scale the selection, then use the MOVE command to adjust its location. Use Previous to select the object scale and object snaps to specify the move.

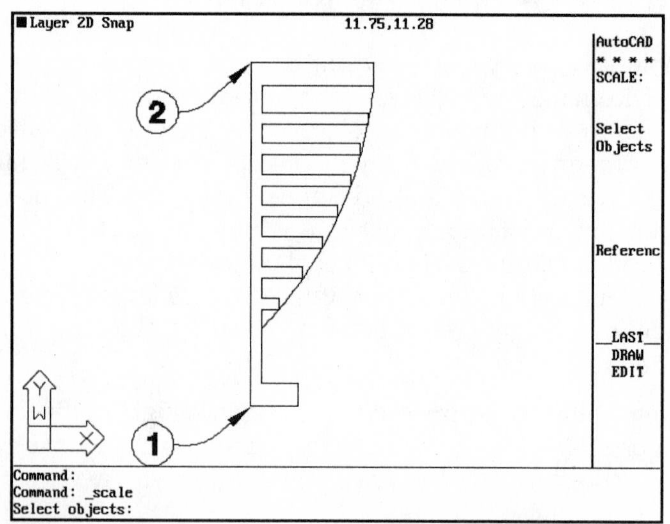

Figure 9.13:

A cylinder profile with pick points before scaling.

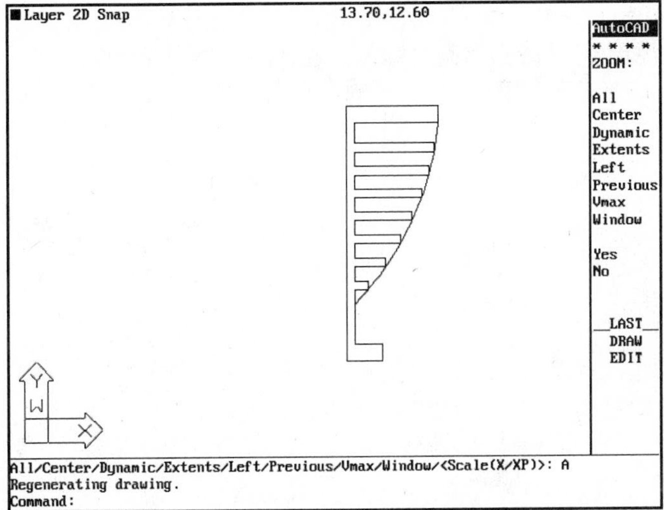

Figure 9.14:

A cylinder profile after scale and before zooming.

Now is a good time to introduce a new method of entity selection—filters. *Filters* enable you to include and exclude specific types of entities from your object selection sets. The next section explains the method you use.

Controlling the Selection Set

With all of the selection set options available for entity selection, it is still sometimes difficult and time-consuming to select the right entities in a very complex drawing. Entity-selection filters enable you to select only those entities that have been specified in the filter description. Common filters can include entity type, color, layer, or coordinate data. Although the concept of specifying filters is simple, the process may seem confusing because AutoCAD provides so many filter specifications and options for using them. The Entity Selection Filter dialog box, which contains all of these options, can be displayed by choosing Object Filters from the Assist pull-down menu (see fig. 9.15). Entering the FILTER command also displays the dialog box, and you can enter 'FILTER to use it transparently in another command when prompted for entity selection.

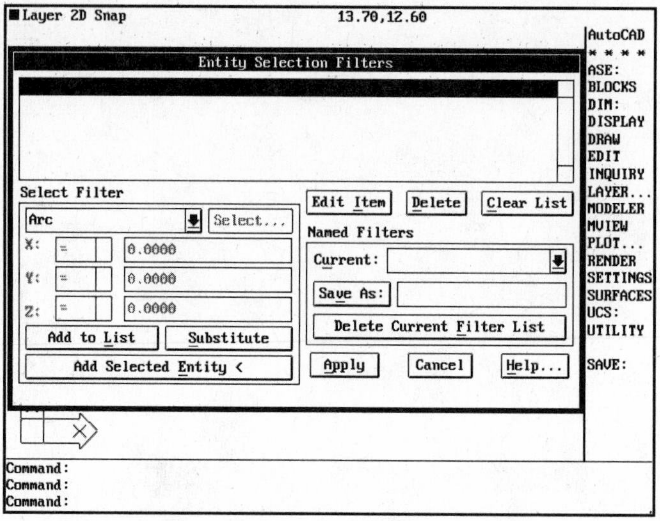

Figure 9.15
Entity Selection Filters dialog box.

Using Entity Selection Filters

You can specify entity-selection filters by choosing an item from the drop-down list under Select Filter, then clicking on the Add to List button. That filter then appears in the large display area at the top of the dialog box. You can repeat this process to add more filters. If you want to save the filter list to use at a later time, enter a name (up to 18 characters) in the edit box next to Save As and then click on the Save As button. You can find and retrieve all of the defined filter names in the list box next to the Current button. Choosing Apply closes the dialog box and prompts for object selection using the current filter. Choosing Cancel leaves the dialog box without applying the filter.

Try using entity filters in the following exercise.

Selecting Objects by Using FILTERS

Continue with the CYLINDER drawing from the previous exercise.

`Command:` **`SAVEAS`** ↵

Save the drawing with the name `FILTERS`.

`Current drawing name set to C:\IA\FILTERS.`

You now can make changes to the FILTERS drawing to experiment with object filters, then reopen the drawing CYLINDER to continue with it in later exercises.

`Command:` *Choose* Assist, *then* Object Filters	Opens the Entity Selection Filters dialog box
With Arc *displayed in the Select Filter drop-down list box, choose* Add to List	Adds the arcs to the entity filter list
Choose Apply	Closes dialog box and prompts to select objects
`Command:`	
`Select objects:` *Select a window enclosing all of the entities in* the drawing	Creates a selection set, but filters out everything except the arc
`33 found`	
`32 were filtered out.`	
`Select objects:` *Press Enter*	Ends object selection
`Command:` **E** ↵	Starts the ERASE command
`Select objects:` **P** ↵	Selects the previous set
`1 found`	
`Select objects:` *Press Ctrl-C*	Cancels the ERASE command

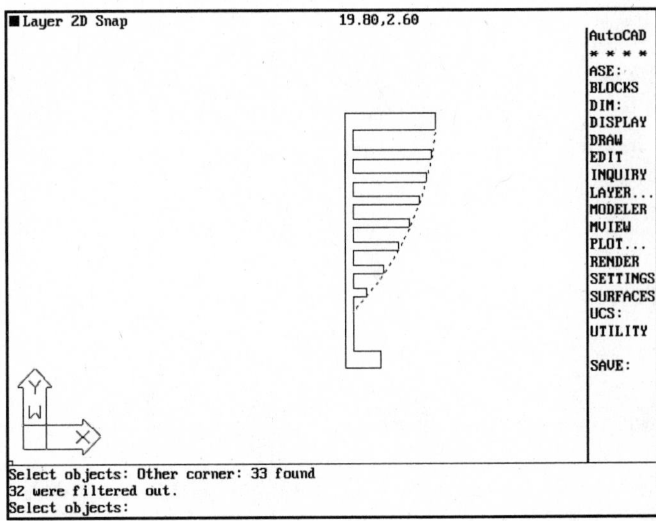

Figure 9.16

Arc selected using filters.

Remember that when a filter is active, only the selected entities that conform to that filter are selected; all other entities are disregarded. In the previous exercise, the prompt displayed the number selected and the number filtered out by the active filter. Only the arc entity was selected. The Previous select set option can be used to recall those entities during a subsequent editing command, or you can use 'FILTER transparently.

In the filters dialog box, you can create a list of filters to apply. After a filter has been added to the list, it can be highlighted by clicking on it. You may need to follow this procedure before you use the Delete, Edit Item, or Substitute button. The following exercise continues to define and use entity filters.

Filtering Specific Entity Characteristics

In addition to the entity filters, coordinate information can be specified to further filter the entities. Click on the X, Y, and Z coordinate boxes to specify entity data, such as start and endpoints of lines or arc radius and center points. These coordinate descriptions are found in the select filter list box, as are properties such as layer, color, and linetype. To give additional clarification to these filters, relational operators can be specified with the coordinate data. The more commonly used ones include equal (=), not equal (!=), less than (<), and greater than (>). Placing these operators in the small edit box next to the coordinates specifies how the coordinates are to be used. Try these in the following exercise, which selects lines whose X,Y endpoints are greater than 16.5,16.1.

Filtering Specific Entity Characteristics

`Command:` *Choose* Assist, *then* Object Filters	
Choose ClearList	
Scroll through the Select Filter *drop-down list box to find and select* Line End	Displays the Line End in Select Filter edit box
Click on = *in the box beside* X: *in the* Select Filter *area*	Opens a drop-down list box of logical operators
Select greater than (>)	Closes the drop-down list
Double-click on 0.0000 *in the* X: *row, then type* **`16.5`**	Highlights and replaces 0.0000

Click on = *beside* Y: *in the* Select Filter *area, then choose* < — Selects a logical operator

Double-click on 0.0000 *in the* Y: *row, then type* `16.1`

Choose Add to List — Adds Line End selection to filter list

Choose **A**pply — Closes the dialog box and prompts for object selection

`Select objects:` **`ALL`** ↵ — Selects lines that fit the search criteria (see fig. 9.17)
`33 found`
`23 were filtered out.`

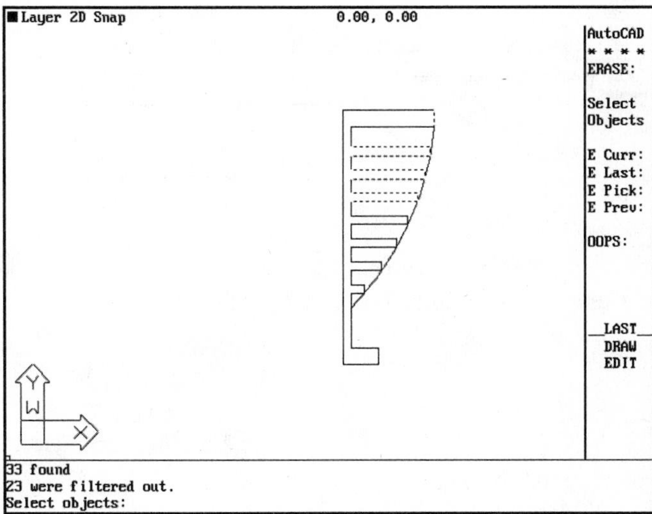

Figure 9.17: Lines selected using logical operators.

Using Conditional Testing

The entity filters can become extremely flexible when conditional testing is applied between the filters. This logic is the same logic that LISP or other similar programming languages use. The four grouping operators—AND, OR, XOR, NOT—each have a Begin and End option. It is important that they are balanced and are used in pairs. These operators are also selected from the Select Filter drop-down list and can be applied to the other properties or coordinates. Try it in the next exercise.

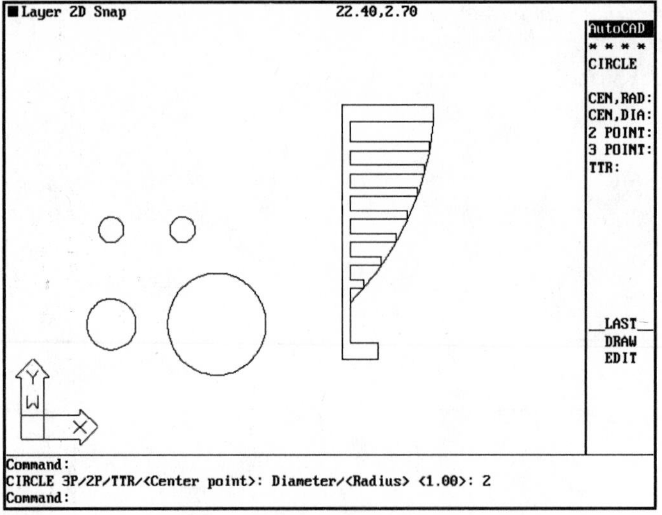

Figure 9.18:

Four circles for conditional testing.

Using Conditional Tests

Use the CIRCLE command to draw two circles with a 0.50" radius, a third circle with a 1.00" radius, and a fourth circle with a 2.00" radius (see fig. 9.18).

`Command:` *Select the 2" radius circle*	Creates the selection set and displays grips
`Command:` **`CHPROP`** ↵	Starts the CHPROP command with the 2" radius circle selected
`Change what property (Color/LAyer/LType/Thickness) ?` **`C`** ↵	
`New color <BYLAYER>:` **`Y`** ↵	
`Change what property (Color/LAyer/LType/Thickness) ?` *Press Enter*	Ends the command and changes the circle to yellow
`Command:` *Choose* Assist, *then* Object Filters	
Choose ClearList	
From the filter selection list, select Circle, *then* choose Add to List	Adds Circle to the filter list
From the filter selection list, select ** Begin NOT, *then choose* Add to List	Adds ** Begin NOT to the filter list

From the filter selection list, select Circle Radius, *then double-click on* 0.0000 *in the X: row, type* **1**, *and choose* Add to **L**ist	Sets the filter to exclude any circle with a radius of 1"
From the filter selection list, select ** End NOT, *then choose* Add to **L**ist	Ends the NOT operation
From the filter selection list, select ** Begin NOT, *then choose* Add to **L**ist	Adds ** Begin NOT to the filter list
From the filter selection list, select Color, *then choose* S**e**lect, *click on the standard yellow box, choose* OK, *then* Add to **L**ist	Sets the filter to exclude any circle with color 2 (yellow)
From the filter selection list, select ** End NOT, *then choose* Add to **L**ist	Ends the NOT operation

Use the scroll button beside the filter list to view the entire filter list, then enter 1 AND YELLOW in the Save As edit box and choose the S**a**ve As button to save the filter list.

Choose **A**pply	Prompts for object selection
`Select objects:` *Window select all of the circles, then press Enter*	
`4 found` `2 were filtered out.`	Selects only the .5" circles

To create a filter set by selecting multiple entity types, use OR. Do not use AND. To select lines and arcs, for example, use * Begin OR, Entity = Line, Entity = Arc, and ** End OR. AND would attempt to find entities that were simultaneously lines and arcs—a geometric impossibility. OR finds all entities that are lines or arcs.

You can apply filters from within another command. In fact, the true power of using filters comes from using them within another command. This process is similar to accessing the pop-up menu for point filters or object snaps when a command is prompting to select objects. Enter 'FILTER as a transparent command when you are asked to select objects. The last exercise in entity filters demonstrates this procedure.

Using Filters Within a Command

`Command: E ↵`	Begins the ERASE command
`Select objects: (FILTER) ↵`	Opens the Entity Selection Filters dialog box, with 1 and Yellow shown as current in the Named Filters area
Click on Apply	Resumes the ERASE command with entity filter selection
`Select objects: ALL ↵`	
`46 found` `44 were filtered out.`	
`Select objects:` *Press Enter*	Erases the two small circles

Entity filters are like Styles, Views, Layers, Coordinate Systems, and many other features in AutoCAD. You can define and then save filters with a name that you specify, so that you can later recall and use them again. Although setting up filters may seem to take much effort, filters will increase your productivity as you become more familiar with them. If your drawings are really not that complicated, or if you do not see the need to use entity filters, using locked layers might be a little easier to master.

Selecting with Locked Layers

Another new feature of AutoCAD Release 12 is its capability to lock a layer. In Chapter 3 you learned that turning a layer off removes it from your display, and freezing it also removes it from the active entity group, which must be recalculated during screen regenerations. What if you want to see the entities on a certain layer but do not want to select and modify them? Lock the layer. You can still object snap to them and list them. Changing the color and linetype is all that you can do to modify entities on locked layers, however. Layers can be locked and unlocked the same way you turn them on and off. An L appears under the State column of a locked layer. The following exercise illustrates this concept.

Controlling Selection with Locked Layers

`Command:` *Select the 2" radius circle*	Creates the selection set and displays grips
`Command:` **`CHPROP`** ↵	Starts the CHPROP command with the 2" radius circle selected
`Change what property (Color/LAyer/ LType/Thickness) ?` **`LA`**↵	
`New layer <2D>:` **`3D`**↵	
`Change what property (Color/LAyer/ LType/Thickness) ?` *Press Enter*	Ends the command and changes circle to layer 3D
`Command: DDLMODES` ↵	Opens the Modify Layer dialog box
Select layer 3D, click on Lock, *then choose* OK	Locks layer 3D
`Command:` **`E`** ↵	Begins the ERASE command
`Select objects:` *Window-select all of the circles*	
`2 found` `1 was on a locked layer.`	
`Select objects:` *Press Enter*	Erases the 2" circles, but ignores the 2" circle on the locked layer

If your drawings have the entities well organized by layer, the concept of locking layers should be easy to apply. If you have trouble isolating groups of entities by layer, using better drawing organization will help you. Now that you have explored some of the additional entity-selection options, continue with the cylinder drawing.

The cylinder drawing you are constructing in this chapter is a mixture of polylines and lines. In the next section, you practice editing by changing polyline width. The next section also shows you how to form a new polyline by joining the individual entities that make up the cylinder profile.

Controlling Polylines by Using PEDIT

Polylines can contain a complex continuous series of line and arc segments. Because of this complexity, AutoCAD provides the PEDIT command, which you use only to edit polylines. PEDIT also contains a large list of

subcommands for polyline properties. To manage this list, AutoCAD divides PEDIT into two groups of editing functions. The primary group of functions works on the whole polyline you are editing and the second group works on vertices connecting segments within the polyline.

The PEDIT command has more restrictions when you edit three-dimensional polylines, as you will see in the chapter on 3D. Although you are now concentrating on editing two-dimensional polylines, you learn how to form a three-dimensional polyline mesh from two-dimensional polylines at the end of this chapter.

The primary PEDIT options are as follows:

- **Close/Open.** This option adds a segment (if needed) and joins the first and last vertices to create a continuous polyline. When the polyline is open, the prompt shows Close; when closed, the prompt shows Open. A polyline can be open, even if the first and last points coincide and it appears closed. A polyline is open unless you use the Close option when you draw it, or later use the PEDIT Close option.
- **Join.** This option enables you to add selected arcs, lines, and other polylines to an existing polyline. Their endpoints must coincide exactly to be joined.
- **Width.** This option prompts you to specify a single width for all segments of a polyline. The new width overrides any individual segment widths that are already stored.
- **Edit vertex.** This option presents a set of options for editing vertices and their adjoining segments.
- **Fit.** This option creates a smooth curve through the polyline vertices.
- **Spline.** This option creates a curve controlled by, but not usually passing through, a framework of polyline vertices. The type of spline and its resolution are controlled by system variables.
- **Decurve.** This option undoes a Fit or Spline curve back to its original definition.
- **Ltype gen.** This option rengenerates the polyline by using current system variable settings.
- **Undo.** This option undoes the most recent editing function.
- **eXit.** This option is the default <X> and exits PEDIT to return you to the command prompt.

Using PEDIT Join To Create a Polyline

In the following exercise, use PEDIT to join the cylinder lines into a single closed polyline. Use a window to select all entities that you want to join. After you create the polyline, increase its width to .02 inch. In the final steps of the exercise, exit the PEDIT command and use FILLET to fillet all the corners in the polyline profile.

Using PEDIT To Join and Change a Polyline

Reload your CYLINDER drawing by using the OPEN command, then use ZOOM Window to zoom in on the cylinder profile.

`Command:` *Select the construction arc, then enter* `E`	Erases the arc
`Command:` *Choose* Modify, *then* PolyEdit	Issues AI_PEDITM, an AutoLISlP-defined prompt for object selection
`Command: ai_peditm`	
`Select objects:` *Select the bottom line of one of the middle fins and press Enter*	Issues the PEDIT command with that selection
`PEDIT Select polyline`	Uses the selection set
`Entity selected is not a polyline`	
`Do you want to turn it into one? <Y>` *Press Enter*	Converts the line to a polyline
`Open/Join/Width/Edit vertex/Fit/Spline/Decurve/Ltype gen/Undo/eXit <X>:` *From the screen menu, choose* Join	
`_JOIN Select objects:` **`ALL`** ↵	Creates a closed polyline
`35 segments added to polyline Open/Join/Width/Edit vertex/Fit/Spline/Decurve/Ltype gen/Undo/eXit <X>:` *From the screen menu, choose* Width	
`Enter new width for all segments:` **`.02`** ↵	Increases the lineweight (see figs. 9.19 and 9.20)
`Open/Join/Width/Edit vertex/Fit/Spline/Decurve/Ltype gen/Undo/eXit <X>:` *Press Enter*	
`Command:` *Choose* Construct, *then* Fillet	
`Command: _fillet Polyline/Radius/<Select first object>:` *From the screen menu, choose* radius	

`Enter fillet radius <0.00>:` **0.125** ↵	
`_FILLET Polyline/Radius/<Select first object>:` *From the screen menu, choose* polyline	
`_POLYLINE Select 2D polyline:` *Pick the polyline*	Fillets all corners (see figs. 9.21 and 9.22)

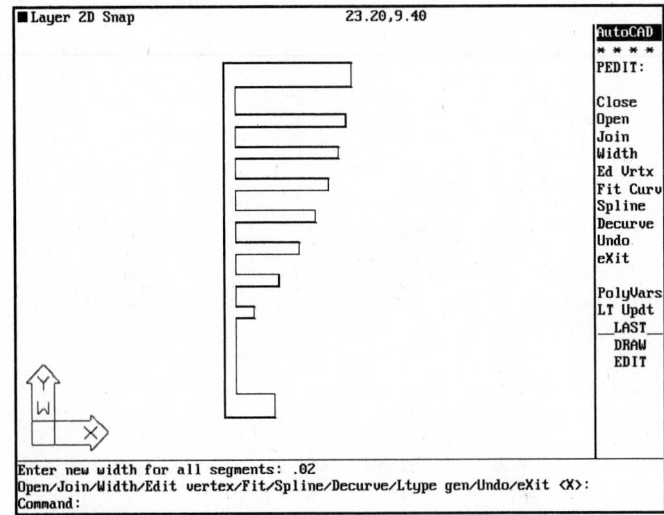

Figure 9.19:

The joined polyline with changed width.

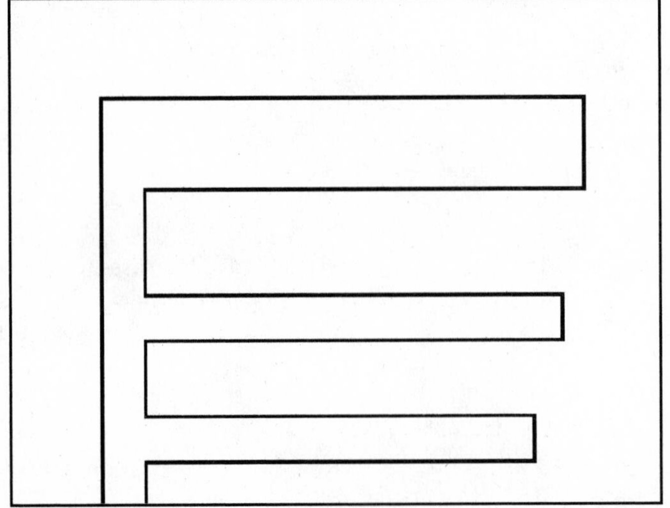

Figure 9.20:

Detail of the widened polyline.

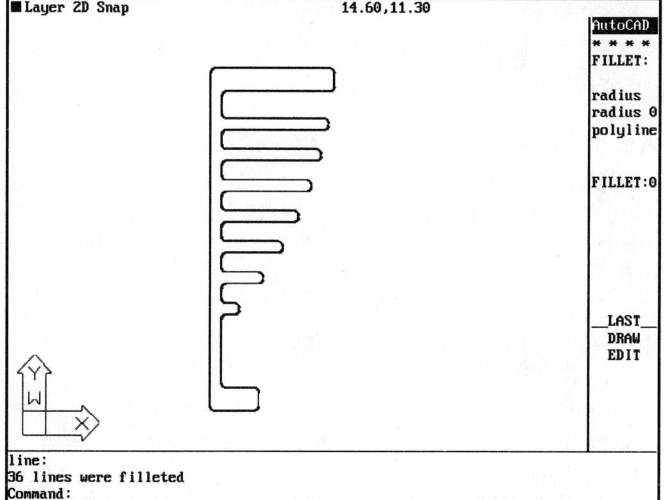

Figure 9.21: The polyline after being filleted.

Figure 9.22: Detail of the filleted polyline.

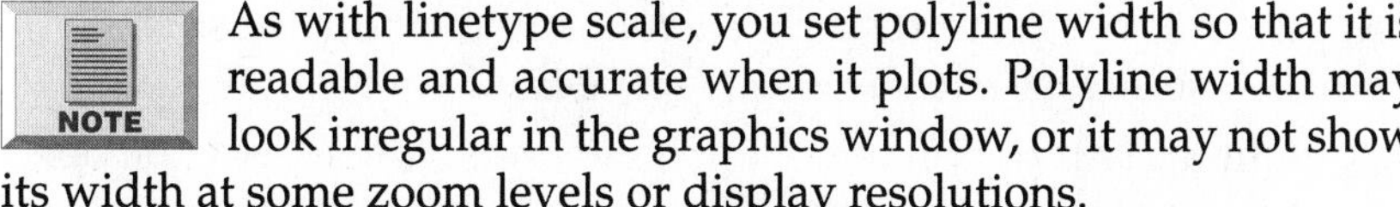

As with linetype scale, you set polyline width so that it is readable and accurate when it plots. Polyline width may look irregular in the graphics window, or it may not show its width at some zoom levels or display resolutions.

Two common edits involve joining polylines and changing their width properties. Later in this chapter, you learn how to use other PEDIT options, including the curve fit options.

The process of joining polylines is tricky—it can fail if the endpoints of the entities do not coincide exactly. Problems can be caused by not using snap and object snaps when drawing, and by occasional round-off discrepancies. Edit or replace stubborn entities by using object snap mode to select the adjacent endpoints, and then use PEDIT again. A good way to make endpoints coincide is to use the FILLET command with a zero radius.

Each polyline segment belongs to, and is controlled by, the preceding vertex. The Edit vertex option makes available a separate set of Edit vertex subcommands. When you use these commands, the current vertex of the polyline is marked with an X. This X shows you the vertex you are editing. Move the X until you mark the vertex you want to edit.

Options for the Pedit Edit vertex command are as follows:

- **Next/Previous.** This option moves the X marker to a new current vertex. Next is the initial default.
- **Break.** This option splits the polyline into two, or removes segments of a polyline at existing vertices. The first break point is the vertex on which you invoke the Break option. Use Next/Previous to access another vertex for the second break point. The Go option performs the break.

The BREAK command usually is more efficient than invoking PEDIT Break, unless curve or spline fitting is involved.

- **Insert.** This option adds a vertex at a point you specify following the vertex currently marked with an X. This option can be combined with Break to break between existing vertices.
- **Move.** This option changes the location of the current (X-marked) vertex to a point you specify.
- **Regen.** This option forces a regeneration of the polyline so that you can see the effects, such as width changes, of your vertex editing.
- **Straighten.** This option removes all intervening vertices from between the two you select, replacing them with one straight segment. It also uses the Next/Previous and Go options.

- **Tangent.** This option sets a tangent to the direction you specify at the currently marked vertex to control curve fitting. The tangent is shown at the vertex with an arrow, and can be dragged or entered from the keyboard.
- **Width.** This option sets the starting and ending width of an individual polyline segment to the values you specify.
- **eXit.** This option exits vertex editing and returns to the main PEDIT command.

Using PEDIT Edit Vertex Options

After you form a polyline, you often need to move a vertex or straighten a line segment. Try these two edits in the steps that follow by removing two of the fillets. Remove one fillet at the top left of the cylinder profile and another on the bottom flange. After you access the PEDIT Edit Vertex option, move the X to mark the desired segment. Use the Move option to move the top left vertex to the corner. This move creates a small bump at the corner from the existing fillet arc segment. You can use a transparent 'ZOOM to better view the bump. Use the Straighten option to make a 90-degree corner and eliminate the bump.

Using PEDIT Vertex Editing To Remove Fillets

`Command:` *Choose* Modify, *then* PolyEdit	
`Select objects:` *Select the polyline and press Enter*	
`Close/Join/Width/Edit vertex/ Fit/Spline/Decurve/Ltype gen/ Undo/eXit <X>:` *From the screen menu, choose* Ed Vrtx	Displays an X on the current vertex
`Next/Previous/Break/Insert/Move/ Regen/Straighten/Tangent/Width/ eXit <N>:` *From the screen menu, choose* Next *or press Enter, and repeat until the X is located as in figures 9.23 and 9.24*	Moves the current vertex along the polyline
`Next/Previous/Break/Insert/Move/ Regen/Straighten/Tangent/Width/ eXit <N>:` *Choose* Move *from the screen menu*	Specifies the Move option and the vertex location
`Enter new location:` *Enter or pick polar point @0.12<180*	Creates a bump, as shown in figure 9.25

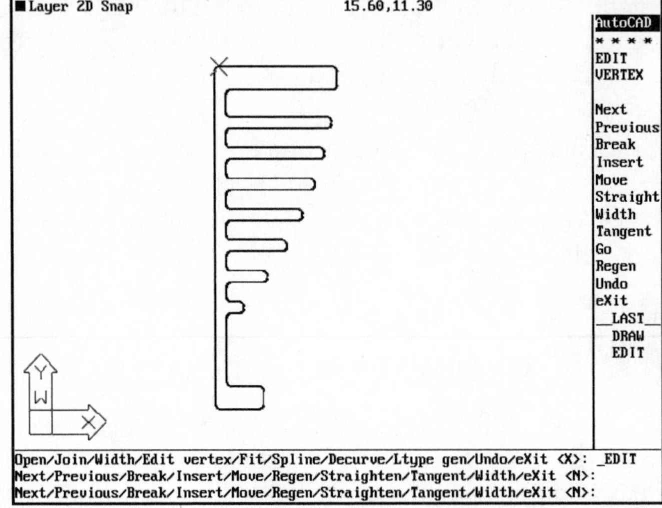

Figure 9.23:

The location of the edit X before the move.

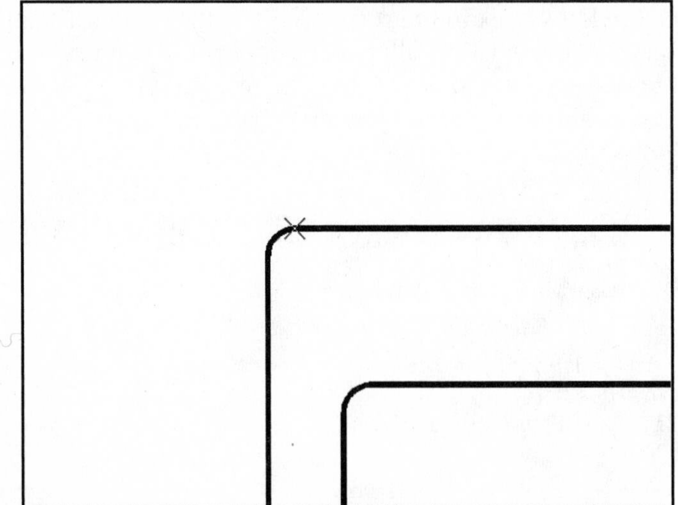

Figure 9.24:

Detail before the move.

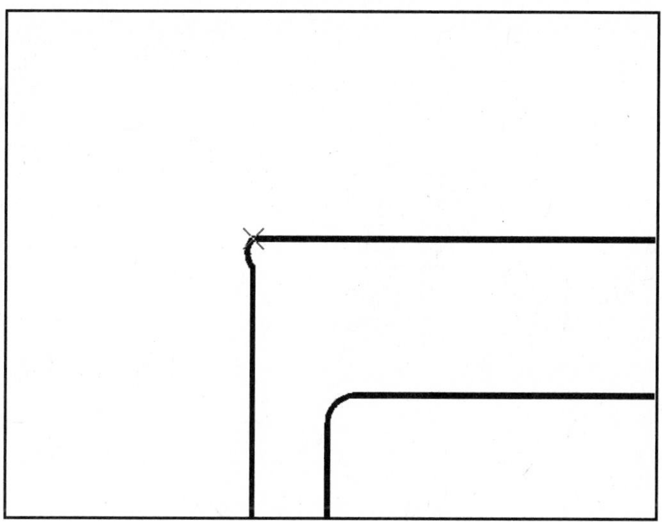

Figure 9.25

Detail after the move, before straightening.

In the next steps, you straighten the bump. Use 'ZOOM if you want to see the bump better, then zoom back out.

`Next/Previous/Break/Insert/Move/ Regen/Straighten/Tangent/Width/eXit <N>:` *From the screen menu, choose* Straight	
`Next/Previous/Go/eXit <N>:` *Press Enter*	Moves the X below the bump
`Next/Previous/Go/eXit <N>:` *Press Enter*	Moves X to match figure 9.26
`Next/Previous/Go/eXit <P>:` *From the screen menu, choose* Go	Straightens the line (see figure 9.27)
`Next/Previous/Break/Insert/Move/ Regen/Straighten/Tangent/Width/ eXit <N>:` *Stay in the command for the next exercise*	

If you make a mistake, exit the Edit vertex mode to the primary PEDIT mode and use the Undo option. Then re-enter Edit vertex mode and continue your work. The UNDO command undoes all operations of the Edit vertex session. When you finish editing a long polyline with a number of steps, exit and re-enter Edit Vertex mode occasionally to protect your work.

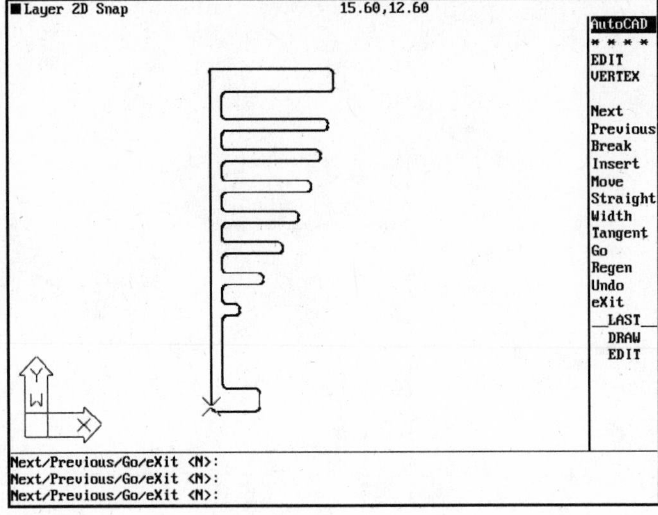

Figure 9.26:

The location of the X before straightening.

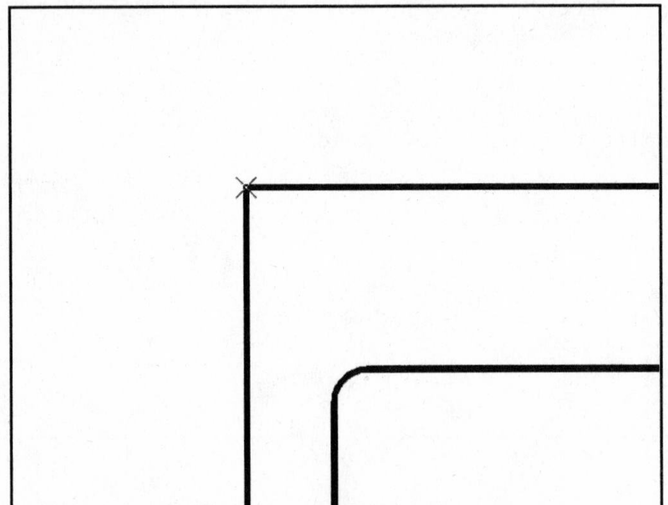

Figure 9.27:

After straightening.

You can repeat the preceding Move and Straighten options to clean up the lower right corner.

Straightening the Lower Right Corner

Continue in the PEDIT command from the previous exercise.

`Next/Previous/Break/Insert/Move/ Regen/Straighten/Tangent/Width/ eXit <N>:` *From the screen menu, choose* Next *three times*	Moves the X to match figures 9.28 and 9.29
`Next/Previous/Break/Insert/Move/ Regen/Straighten/Tangent/Width/ eXit <N>:` **`M`**↵	
`Enter new location:` **`@0.125<0`**↵	Creates a bump (see fig. 9.30)
`Next/Previous/Break/Insert/Move/ Regen/Straighten/Tangent/Width/ eXit <N>:` **`S`**↵	
`Next/Previous/Go/eXit <N>:` *From the screen menu, choose* Next *twice*	Moves the X to match figure 9.31
`Next/Previous/Go/eXit <N>:` **`G`** ↵	Straightens the line (see fig. 9.32)
`Next/Previous/Break/Insert/Move/ Regen/Straighten/Tangent/Width/ eXit <N>:` *Stay in the command for the next exercise*	

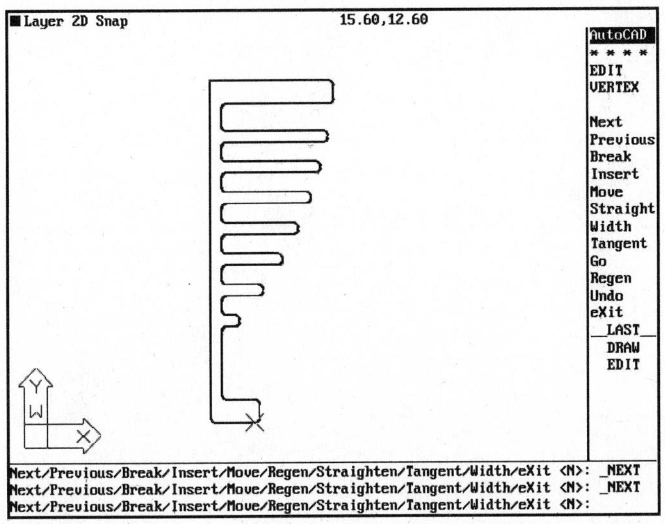

Figure 9.28:

The location of edit X before the second move.

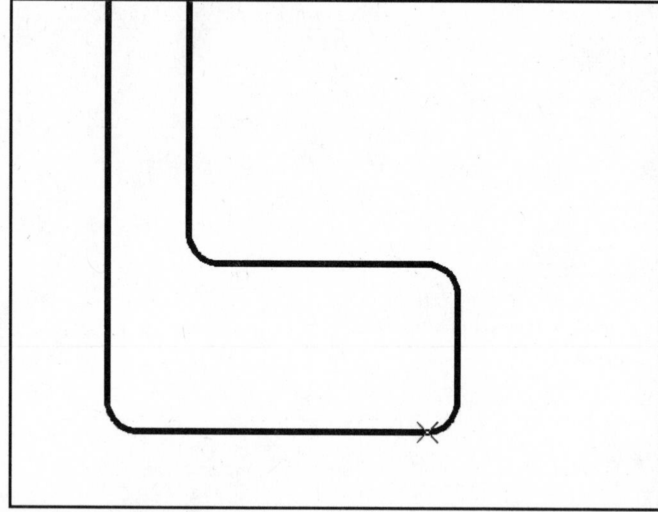

Figure 9.29:

Before the move.

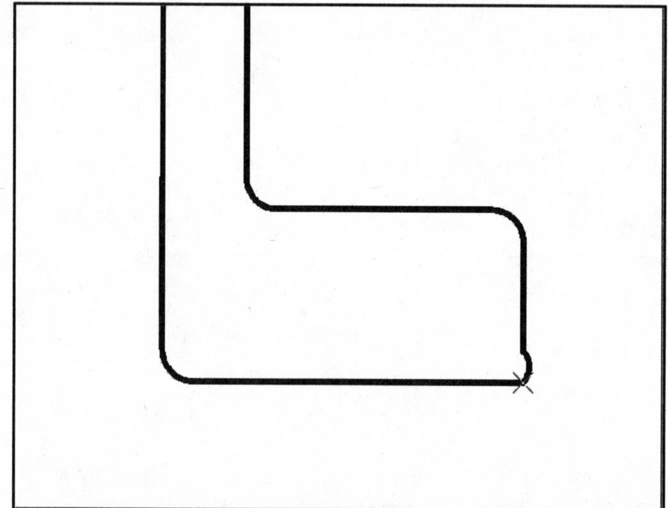

Figure 9.30:

After the move, before straightening.

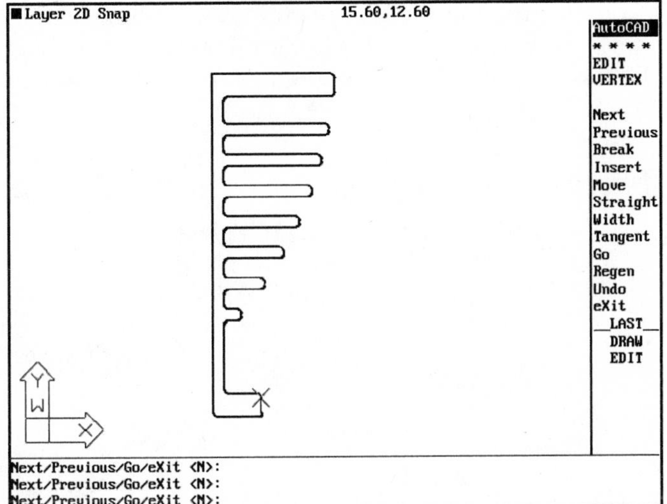

Figure 9.31:

The location of the X before the second straightening.

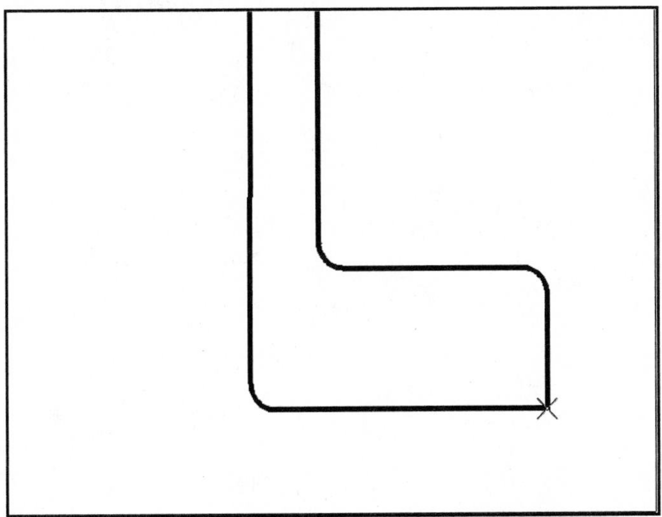

Figure 9.32:

After straightening.

You can add a vertex to an existing polyline. In the following exercise, add a notch to the lower left corner of the cylinder profile. The following editing sequence uses the Insert and Move vertex options to perform two moves and one insertion.

Using PEDIT To Add a Notch

Continue in the PEDIT command from the previous exercise.

`Next/Previous/Break/Insert/Move/ Regen/Straighten/Tangent/Width/ eXit <N>:` *From the screen menu, choose* Previous, *then press Enter*	Moves the X to match figures 9.33 and 9.34; notice the default change from N to P
`Next/Previous/Break/Insert/Move/ Regen/Straighten/Tangent/Width/ eXit <P>:` *From the screen menu, choose* Move	
`Enter new location:` **`@0.175<90`** ↵	Makes a bump, as shown in figures 9.35, 9.36
`Next/Previous/Break/Insert/Move/ Regen/Straighten/Tangent/Width/ eXit <P>:` *Choose* Insert *from the screen menu*	Prompts for a new vertex point
`Enter location of new vertex:` *Pick polar point at 0.30<0*	Makes a V-notch (see fig. 9.37 and 9.38, 0.175 + 0.125 = 0.3" notch)
`Next/Previous/Break/Insert/Move/ Regen/Straighten/Tangent/Width/ eXit <P>:` *From the screen menu, choose* Next *twice*	Moves the X to the vertex shown in figure 9.38
`Next/Previous/Break/Insert/Move/ Regen/Straighten/Tangent/Width/ eXit <N>:` *From the screen menu, choose* Move	
`Enter new location:` **`@0.175<0`** ↵	Squares off the notch (see fig. 9.39)
`Next/Previous/Break/Insert/Move/ Regen/Straighten/Tangent/Width/ eXit <N>:` *From the screen menu, choose* eXit	Exits from Edit vertex mode
`Open/Join/Width/Edit vertex/Fit/ Spline/Decurve/Ltype gen/Undo/ eXit <X>:` *Press Enter*	Exits from PEDIT
`Command:` **`QSAVE`** ↵	

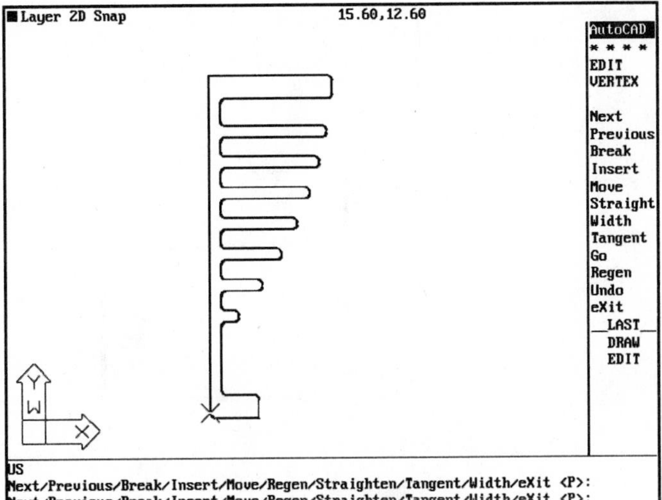

Figure 9.33:

The location of the X before the move.

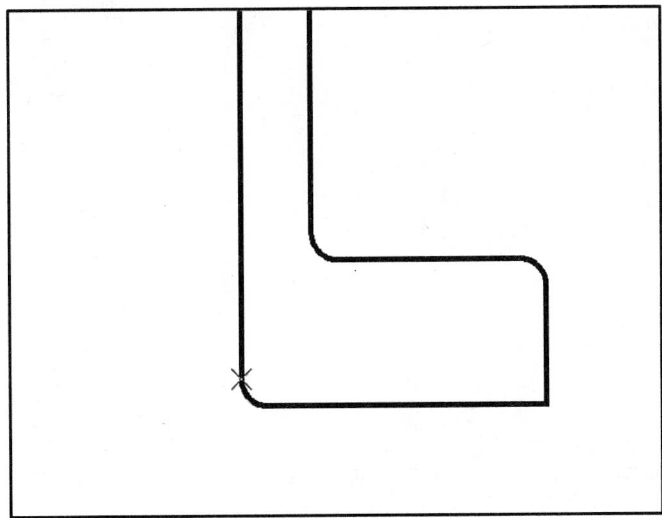

Figure 9.34:

Before the move.

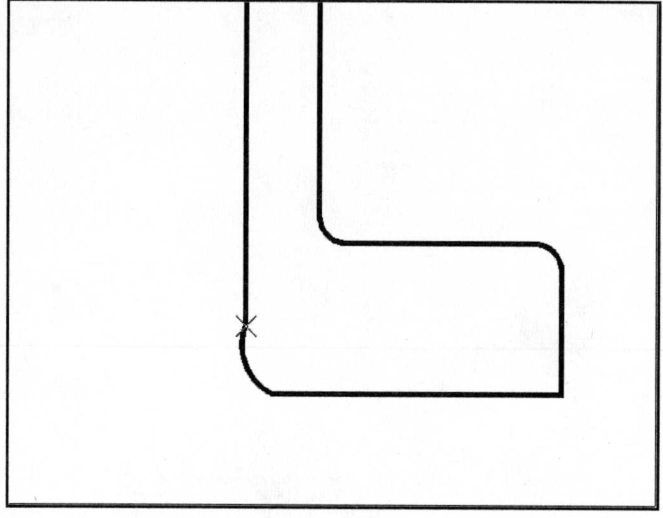

Figure 9.35:

After the move, before the insert.

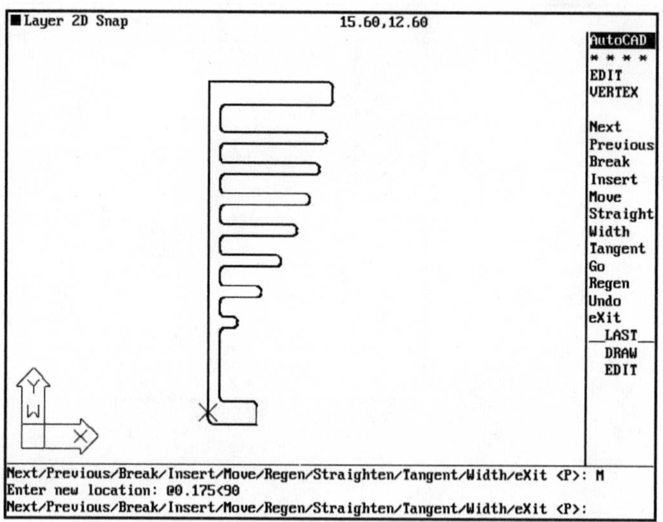

Figure 9.36:

The location of the edit X before insert.

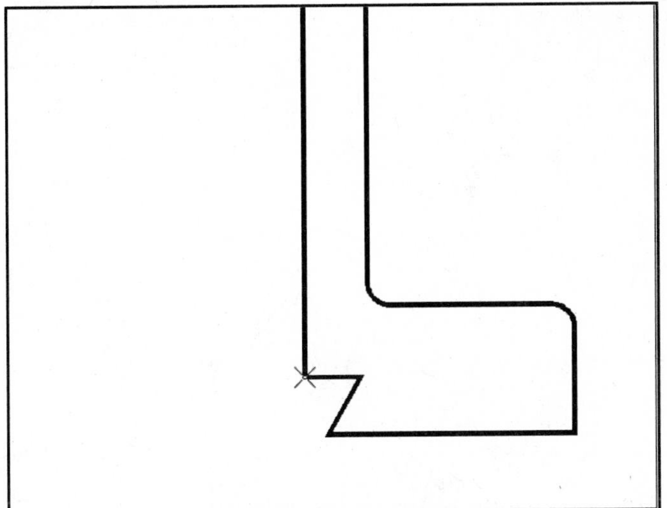

Figure 9.37:

After the insert, before the second move.

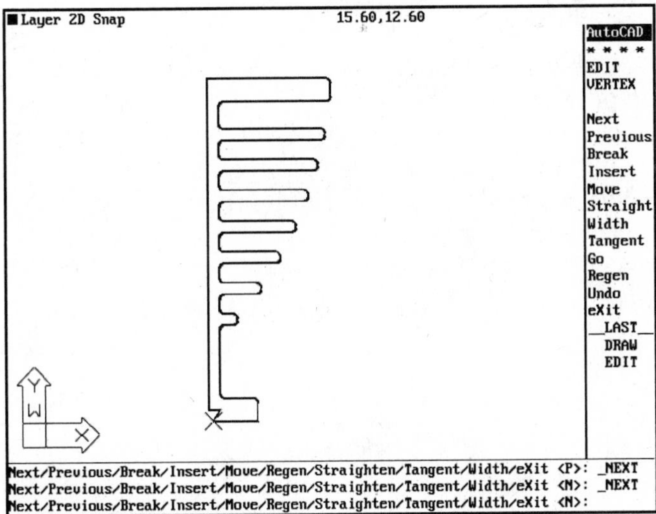

Figure 9.38:

The location of the edit X before the second move.

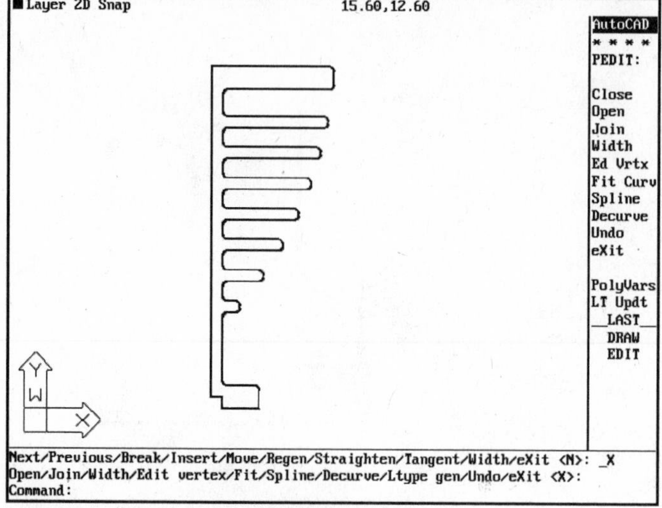

Figure 9.39:

The completed cylinder, with the notch.

Using EXPLODE on Polylines

If you must extensively edit a polyline, it may be easier to edit the vertices or to explode the polyline into individual segments, and then to rejoin the segments after you perform your edits. The EXPLODE command breaks a polyline into its individual segments. One disadvantage of using EXPLODE is that polylines lose their width and tangent information after they are exploded. EXPLODE locks in curves and splines by converting the polyline to many arcs or small straight lines. If wide polylines are exploded, only their center lines show (see fig. 9.40). If you explode the cylinder's polyline, 72 entities emerge.

Using PEDIT Fit and Spline Curves

The PEDIT command provides two options for making polyline curves that pass through control points: a fit curve and a spline curve. As you see in the next exercise, the cylinder profile dramatically shows the different results between fit curves and spline curves. A *fit curve* passes through vertex control points and consists of two arc segments between each pair of vertices (see fig. 9.41). A *spline curve* interpolates between control points but does not usually pass through the vertices (see fig. 9.42). The framework of vertices is called the *spline frame*.

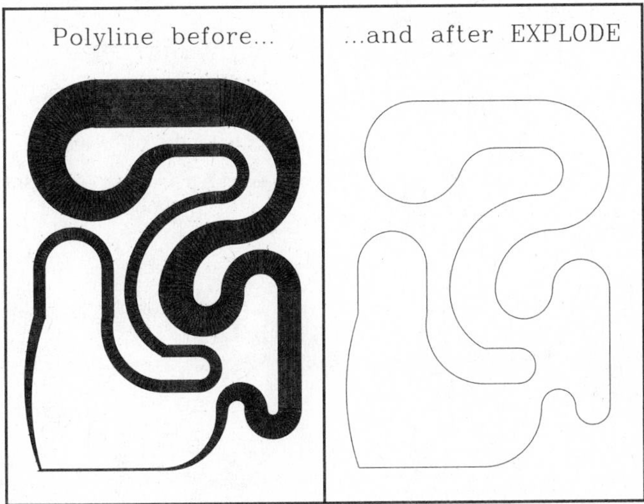

Figure 9.40:

A polyline before and after explosion.

PEDIT spline curves create arcs or short-line segments approximating the curve of the arc. To help you visualize a spline curve, AutoCAD provides a system variable called SPLFRAME. You can set SPLFRAME to 1 to show you the reference frame and vertex points for a spline curve. The fineness of the approximation and type of segment is controlled by the SPLINESEGS system variable. The numeric value controls the number of segments. A positive value generates line segments; a negative value creates arc segments. Arcs are more precise, but slower. The default is 8.

You can generate two kinds of spline curves: a quadratic b-spline (type 5) or a cubic b-spline (the default, type 6). Both spline curves are controlled by the SPLINETYPE system variable.

In the next exercise, try both fit and spline curves by using the cylinder fins as your control points. After you generate the spline curve, turn SPLFRAME on to see the reference frame for the curve. The exercise shows you how to regenerate the drawing within the PEDIT command, to make the frame visible. After you finish, use the Undo option to restore the original cylinder profile. Be careful using the Decurve option; it removes the fillets in the drawing. If you try it, undo to recover the fillets.

Using PEDIT To Make a Fit and a Spline Curve

`Command:` *Choose* Modify, *then* PolyEdit	
`Select objects:` **L**↵	Selects the polyline
`Open/Join/Width/Edit vertex/Fit/ Spline/Decurve/Ltype gen/Undo/ eXit <X>:` *From the screen menu, choose* Fit Curv	Creates a fit curve, as shown in figure 9.41
`Open/Join/Width/Edit vertex/Fit/ Spline/Decurve/Ltype gen/Undo/ eXit <X>:` *From the screen menu, choose* Spline	Creates a spline curve, as shown in figure 9.42
`Open/Join/Width/Edit vertex/Fit/ Spline/Decurve/Ltype gen/Undo/ eXit <X>:` **'SPLFRAME** ↵	
`>>New value for SPLFRAME <0>:` **1**↵	Turns on frame
`Resuming PEDIT command.`	

The frame does not appear until you use Edit vertex to regenerate the polyline.

`Open/Join/Width/Edit vertex/Fit/ Spline/Decurve/Ltype gen/Undo/eXit <X>:` *From the screen menu, choose* Ed Vrtx	
`Next/Previous/Break/Insert/Move/Regen/ Straighten/Tangent/Width/eXit <N>:` *From the screen menu, choose* Regen	Regenerates the image to display the frame (see fig. 9.43)
`Next/Previous/Break/Insert/Move/Regen/ Straighten/Tangent/Width/eXit <N>:` *From the screen menu, choose* eXit	Exits from Edit vertex mode
`Open/Join/Width/Edit vertex/Fit/ Spline/Decurve/Ltype gen/Undo/ eXit <X>:` *From the screen menu, choose* Undo	Undoes frame display
`Open/Join/Width/Edit vertex/Fit/ Spline/Decurve/Ltype gen/Undo/eXit <X>:` *From the screen menu, choose* eXit	Exits from PEDIT
`Command:` **U**↵	Undoes the PEDIT, restoring the original cylinder profile

Figure 9.43 shows a spline curve with its associated frame.

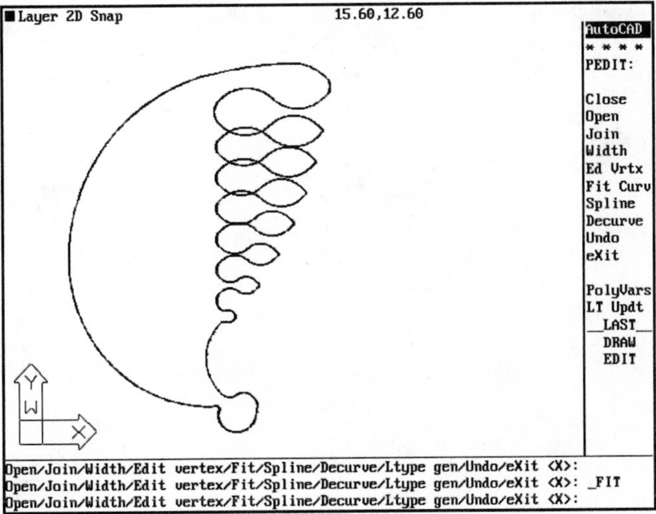

Figure 9.41:

The piston cylinder after fit curve.

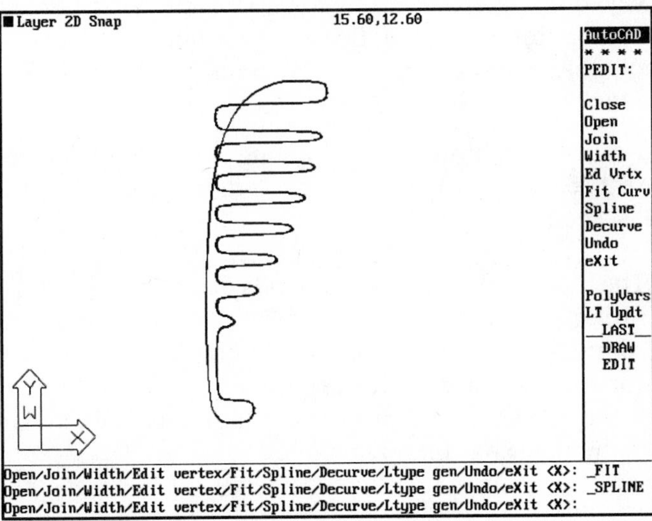

Figure 9.42:

The piston cylinder after spline curve.

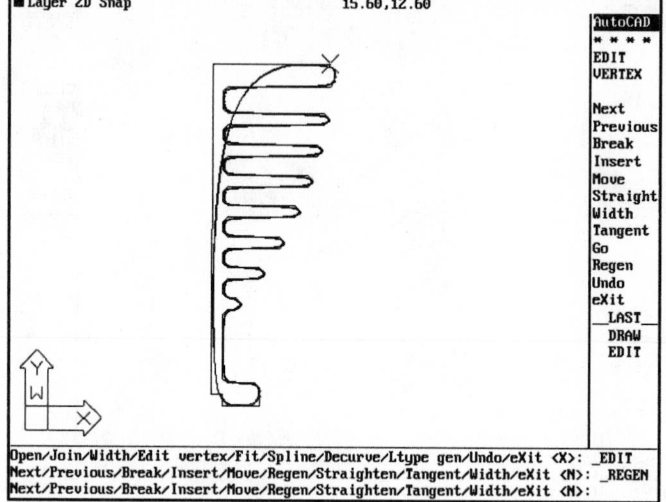

Figure 9.43:

A spline curve with frame.

When you displayed the reference frame for spline curves, the original cylinder profile and points appeared. If you are editing a spline curve and you need to know the location of the control points, use the SPLFRAME system variable to view your frame of reference.

After you undo your curve fitting, your drawing should look like the original in figure 9.38. Although you have moved, stretched, and curved the polyline, it still is a continuous polyline.

NOTE

The BREAK and TRIM commands make curve- and spline-fitting permanent. The PEDIT Break option and EXTEND command enable subsequent polyline edits to decurve and refit curves or splines. Curve-fit and spline-fit polylines can become complex. See the *AutoCAD Reference Manual* for their quirks and interactions with other editing commands.

Controlling Polyline Linetype Generation

When broken linetypes are used with polylines, short and spline or curve fit segments may appear continuous because there is not enough space between vertices to display the broken line pattern. In such cases, you can use the PLINEGEN system variable to control how the linetype is generated.

When the variable is set to 0 (off—the default) each vertex of the polyline starts the linetype pattern over again. When PLINEGEN is set to 1 (on) the linetype pattern is generated uniformly over the whole polyline. This will display a uniform linetype pattern across vertices, but sometimes corners fall in a gap in the pattern. The PLINEGEN variable controls linetype generation of new polylines. To change existing polylines, use the Ltype gen option of PEDIT to change the linetype generation. Both of these methods are used in the following exercise and illustrated in figures 9.44 and 9.45.

Controlling Polyline Linetype with PLINEGEN

Continue with the CYLINDER drawing from the previous exercise.

`Command:` *Select the polyline*	Displays grips
`Command:` **`CHPROP`** ↵	

`1 found`
`Change what property (Color/LAyer/`
`LType/Thickness) ?`**`LT`** ↵	

`New linetype <BYLAYER>:` **`HIDDEN`** ↵	
`Change what property (Color/LAyer/` `LType/Thickness) ?` *Press Enter*	Changes the polyline to a hidden linetype (see fig. 9.44)
`Command:` **`PLINEGEN`** ↵	
`New value for PLINEGEN <0>:` **`1`** ↵	
`Command:` **`PEDIT`** ↵	
`Select polyline:` **`L`** ↵	Selects Last

`Open/Join/Width/Edit vertex/Fit/`
`Spline/Decurve/Ltype gen/Undo/`
`<X>:`**`L`** ↵
	Specifies the Ltype generation option

`Full PLINE linetype ON/OFF <OFF>:` **`ON`** ↵	Renerates the polyline with a uniform linetype (see fig. 9.45)

`Open/Join/Width/Edit vertex/Fit/`
`Spline/Decurve/Ltype gen/Undo/`
`eXit <X>:` *Press Enter*
	Exits from PEDIT

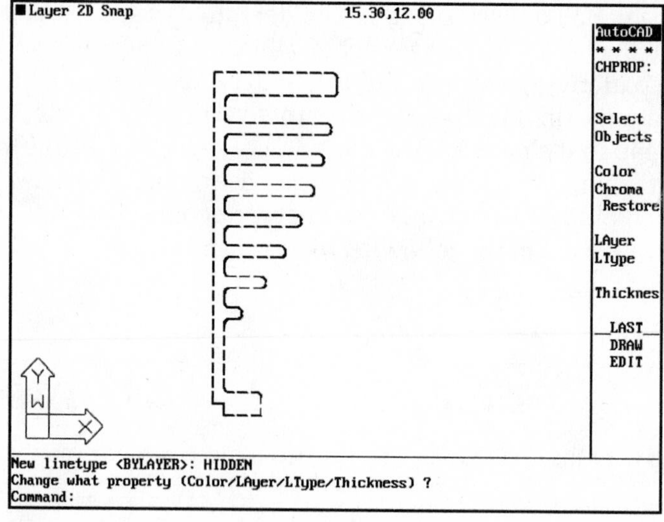

Figure 9.44:

The polyline with a per-segment linetype.

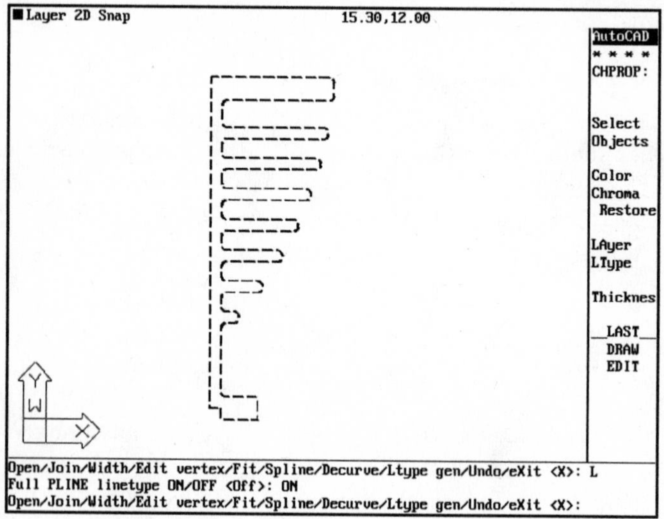

Figure 9.45:

The polyline with a smooth linetype.

Using PLUD

An AutoLISP-defined command called PLUD (short for PolyLine UpDate) can be used to control linetype generation. PLUD asks you whether you want to use the Full or Segment approach to generate linetypes in a polyline. You then are prompted to select a polyline. This routine is a combination of PLINEGEN and the Ltype gen option of PEDIT. This feature is used in the following exercise.

Controlling Polyline Linetypes with PLUD

`Command:` **`PLUD`** ↵	Loads and issues the PLUD command
`Full/Segment <Full>:` **`S`** ↵	
`Select objects:` *Pick the polyline, then press Enter*	Changes the linetype, as shown in figure 9.44
`Select objects:` *Press Enter*	
`1 Polyline(s) updated.`	
`Command:` *Press Enter*	Repeats PLUD command
`PLUD Full/Segment <Full>:` *Press Enter*	Accepts default
`Select objects:` *Pick the polyline, then press Enter*	Changes the linetype, as in figure 9.45
`Select objects:` *Press Enter* `1 PoLyline(s) updated`	

The system variable PLINEGEN should be set in your prototype drawing for the setting that works out best in your drawings. If you need to change a polyline you already created, use the PLUD command.

Another command that should be discussed with creating and editing polylines is XPLODE, which breaks apart polylines. You can, of course, use BREAK or TRIM, or you can use the XPLODE command, which is explained next.

Using the XPLODE Command

The XPLODE command is an AutoLISP-defined command that you can use to break up complex entities, such as polylines, blocks, and dimensions into simpler entities like lines, arcs, and text. Although complex entities are usually preferred, they must sometimes be broken apart to change or regroup them. The XPLODE command, which must be loaded before it can be used, is similar to the EXPLODE command except that it gives you more control over what happens to the color, layer, and linetype of the entities created after they are broken up. The following options are available with this command:

- **All.** This option enables all of the properties to be changed for the entities created from the XPLODE command.
- **Color.** This option enables you to set the color of the component entities or use the BYlayer choice.
- **LAyer.** This option enables a layer to be specified. The default is the current layer.
- **LType.** Similar to the LAyer option, any loaded linetype can be named or the default will be the current linetype.
- **Explode.** The default option Explode works like the regular XPLODE command.

Try the XPLODE command in the following exercise. You must load it before use.

Using the XPLODE Command

`Command: (LOAD "XPLODE")` *Press Enter* `C:XPlode loaded. Start command with XP or XPLODE.`	Loads XPLODE
`Command:` **`XP`** ↵	Begins XPLODE
`Select entities to XPlode.` `Select objects:` *Select the polyline*	
`All/Color/LAyer/LType/Inherit from parent block/<Explode>:` **`ALL`** ↵	
`New color for exploded entities.` `Red/Yellow/Green/Cyan/Blue/Magenta/White/BYLayer/BYBlock/<BYLAYER>:` **`W`** ↵	Chooses White for the exploded entity color

`Enter new linetype name. BYBlock/BYLayer/CONTinuous/ HIDDEN/<BYLAYER>:` **CONT** ↵	Chooses the continuous linetype for exploded entities
`XPlode onto what layer? <2D>:` *Press Enter*	Leaves entities on their current layer
`Entity exploded with color of 7, linetype of CONTINUOUS, and layer 2D`	

The polyline exploded into individual lines and arcs on layer 2D, and the entity's color and linetype changed to white, continuous. Next verify that the profile is no longer a polyline.

Checking the Results of EXPLODE

`Command:` **E** ↵	Begins ERASE
`Select objects:` *Select one of the fin line segments, then press Enter*	Erases the line
`Command:` **U** ↵	Undoes ERASE
`Command:` **U** ↵	Undoes XPLODE
`Command:` **CHPROP** ↵	
`Select objects:` *Select the polyline and press Enter*	
`Change what property (Color/LAyer/ LType/Thickness) ?` **LT** ↵	
`New linetype <HIDDEN>:` **BYLAYER** ↵	
`Change what property (Color/LAyer/ LType/Thickness) ?` *Press Enter*	Changes the polyline linetype

Use caution with the XPLODE command. Unless you are changing visible properties, it is hard to see if the command really worked. You may need to use XPLODE repeatedly to explode through nested levels of complex entities. Careless use of XPLODE may disable the database updating in some drawings. Exploded dimensions cannot be updated, exploded polylines will lose special properties, and exploded blocks will have no attributes.

Using REVSURF To Create a 3D Surface Mesh

You can use your cylinder profile to create a 3D surface mesh. The following exercise guides you through a quick 3D setup. The steps use a 3D viewpoint that looks down at the cylinder, so that you can see the surface mesh as it is formed. You use a 3D entity command called REVSURF to form the surface mesh, which forms a polyline surface mesh from the two-dimensional polyline that makes up the cylinder profile.

Do not worry about fully understanding the commands or the sequence used to create the 3D cylinder. Try the exercise to see how easily a complex 3D part is created. After you finish, save your drawing as 3DCYLIND.

Using REVSURF To Make a Quick 3D Mesh

Reopen drawing CYLINDER (discarding changes), or continue from the "Using PEDIT To Add a Notch" exercise.

`Command:` *Turn off grid with F7, then ZOOM All*	
`Command:` *Use the* LINE *command to draw from absolute point 10,15 to polar point @13<270*	Defines axis of rotation line

Use the LAYER command or Modify Layer dialog box to set layer 3D current.

`Command:` **`SURFTAB1`** ↵	
`New value for SURFTAB1 <6>:` **`24`** ↵	Sets the vertical mesh density
`Command:` **`SURFTAB2`** ↵	
`New value for SURFTAB2 <6>:` **`4`** ↵	Set the horizontal mesh density
`Command:` **`WORLDVIEW`** ↵	
`New value for WORLDVIEW <1>:` **`0`** ↵	Sets for viewpoints relative to UCS
`Command:` *Choose* Draw, *then* 3D Surfaces, *and choose* Surface of Revolution	Issues REVSURF
`Command: _revsurf`	
`Select path curve:` *Pick the polyline cylinder profile*	
`Select axis of revolution:` *Pick near the bottom of the rotation axis line*	
`Start angle <0>:` *Press Enter*	

`Included angle (+=ccw, -=cw) <Full circle>:` **`180`** ↵	Draws a half-cylinder surface

Use the LAYER command or Modify Layer dialog box to freeze layer 2D.

`Command:` *Choose* Settings, *then* UCS, then Axis, then X	Issues the UCS command with prompt for rotation
`Rotation angle about X axis <0>:` **`-90`** ↵	
`Command:` *Choose* View, *then* Set View, *then* Viewpoint, *then* Presets	Displays the Viewpoint Presets dialog box
Double-click in the X **A**xis *edit box and enter 255, then double-click in* XY **P**lane *edit box and enter* `17`*, then choose OK*	Sets angle above XY plane to 17 degrees and displays view like the one in figure 9.46
`Command:` *Choose* File, *then* Save As, *then enter* `3DCYLIND` *and choose* **O**K	Saves under new name

If you like the results shown in figure 9.46, see the 3D exercise in Part Five.

To cut down on computing time, the exercise only created a half-section of the cylinder. You can revolve the polyline 360 degrees to draw the full cylinder. If you have 5 minutes to an hour to kill (depending on your machine's speed), invoke the HIDE command to get rid of the hidden lines (see fig. 9.47).

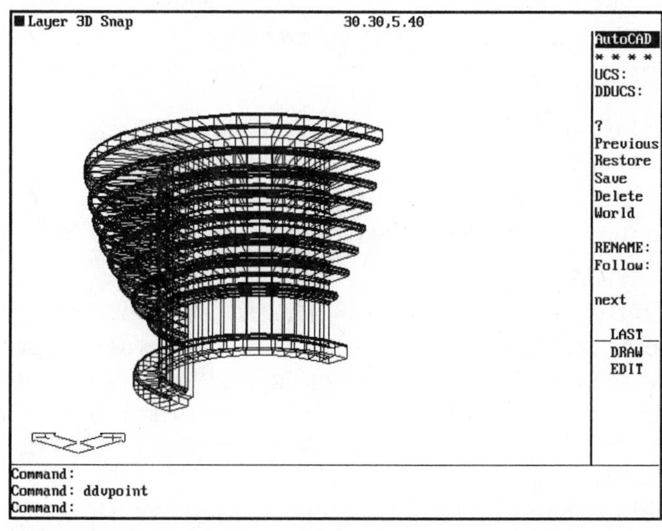

Figure 9.46:

A 3D half-section of a cylinder.

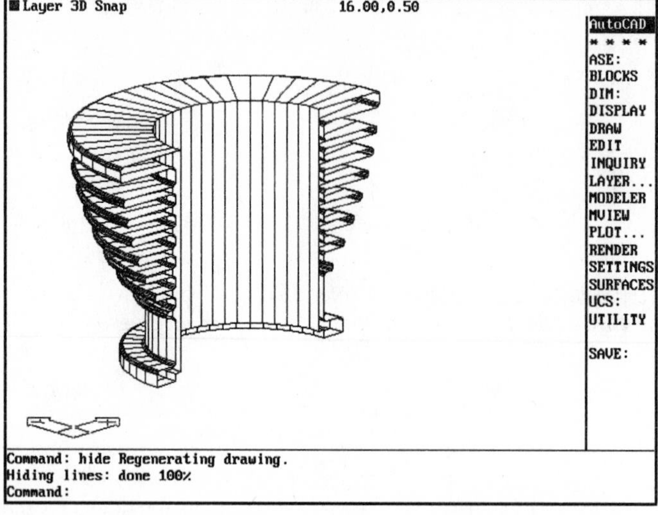

Figure 9.47:

A piston half-cylinder after Hide.

Using Hide To View Cylinder

`Command:` *Choose* Render, *then* Hide, *and from the screen menu, choose* YES	Issues HIDE
`Command: Hide Regenerating drawing.` `Hiding lines: done nn%`	Redisplays the drawing with hidden lines removed

Quit AutoCAD and discard the changes to the drawing.

You see how powerful 3D editing commands are—it is easy to create the complex cylinder surface mesh from your cylinder's two-dimensional polyline. Continuity becomes important in 3D. To show the effect of discontinuity, the cylinder polyline was nicked in two places. The cylinder then was revolved with REVSURF to form a 3D surface mesh.

The nicked profile is shown in figure 9.48. The two Xs mark the places at which the polyline was broken. The resulting 3D image is shown in figure 9.49. As you can see, the 3D mesh formation halts at the break points. The nicked 2D profile looks almost the same as your original profile, but it gives vastly different results when you form a 3D surface image.

NOTE

You can erase the CYLINDER drawing; you will not need it again.

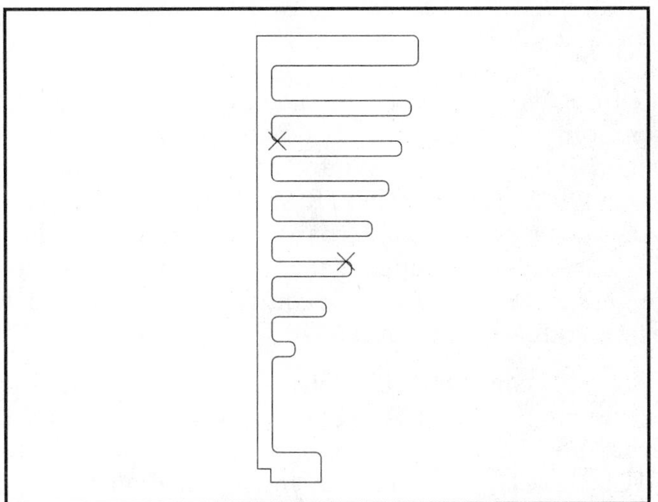

Figure 9.48:

A broken 2D polyline.

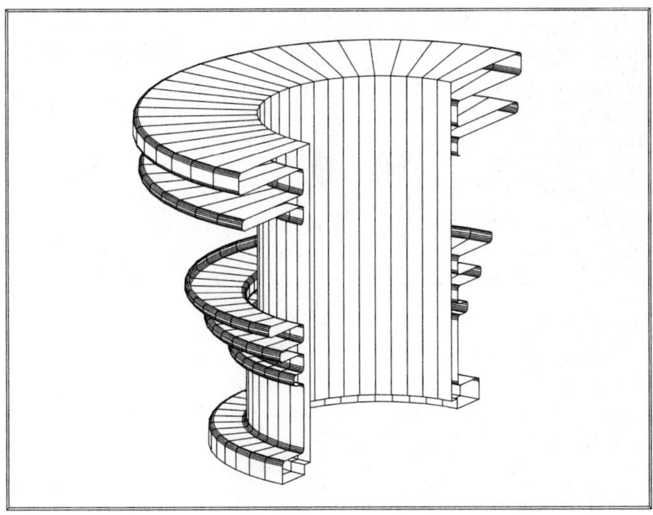

Figure 9.49:

A 3D half cylinder with a nicked polyline.

Summary

After you start editing, your drawings become dynamic. You now have an advanced editing course under your belt and you see that the editing process itself can give you added power and control. The editing commands—EXTEND, OFFSET, STRETCH, TRIM, SCALE, and PEDIT—are new tools that do not have exact counterparts in the manual world. These editing commands operate on multiple entities. When you combine these advanced editing tools with the electronic equivalent of construction lines, you can create fast, accurate drawings.

One trick to using these commands is to plan ahead. Do not get trapped into traditional thinking. It would have been a laborious process to draw the cylinder profile line-by-line and point-by-point. Plan on using EXTEND, OFFSET, STRETCH, and TRIM to rough-in your drawing. Then use PEDIT to get the details you want for more detail.

A second trick to using these new editing commands is to think about how the drawing is constructed. As you work with the more complex commands, the behind-the-scenes construction is almost as important as the appearance of the final drawing. You saw how two little nicks in a 2D polyline drastically effect a 3D object.

10

Drawing Construction Techniques

The process of learning individual AutoCAD commands is an important step for becoming proficient in CAD drafting. The real challenge, however, is to use the drawing and editing tools in a productive manner to create CAD drawings. Often, many ways to approach a drawing project are possible. Past experiences with manual drafting or using other CAD software can determine the AutoCAD methods that work well for you.

Using Advanced Construction Methods

This chapter is about methodology—it shows you ways to combine many of the drawing and editing commands that you learned in previous chapters with construction lines, point filters, and undo marks. You learn how to use these powerful tools rapidly and efficiently in constructing your drawings.

Point Filters and Construction Lines

Point filters are construction tools. The best way to visualize point filters is to consider them as invisible construction lines. Figure 10.1 compares construction lines and point filters. Construction lines are as important in CAD as they are in manual drafting. When you use a construction line to help draw an entity, you are really looking for the X- or Y-coordinate value of existing geometry.

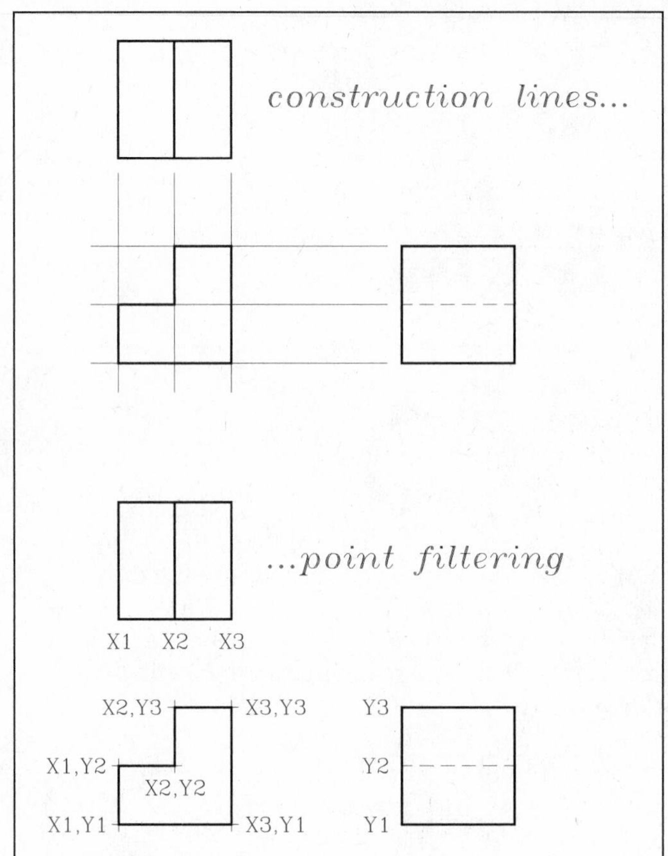

Figure 10.1:

Construction lines and point filter techniques.

Point filters give you the advantages of construction lines without requiring extra work ahead of time. Point filters enable you to indicate the coordinate values of the existing geometry and eliminate the need for drawing a construction line. After you become accustomed to using point filters, they can increase your drawing productivity.

The following drawing exercise, called MOCKUP, demonstrates the use of these construction techniques. If you are using the IA DISK, you have the MOCKUP drawing setup stored as the IA7MOCK drawing. A second drawing on the disk, IA7MOCK2, has the completed left view of the flange. Point filters are used to help construct the section view on the right. If you want to jump directly to the section on point filters, turn to "Using XYZ Point Filters for Section Construction," in this chapter and use the IA7MOCK2 drawing as your starting drawing.

UNDO Marks

You have seen the U or UNDO commands reverse the effects of a previous command. The U command is issued by the Undo option of the Assist menu, and the UNDO command is found on the EDIT screen menu. As you design and draft, you often try alternatives that may or may not work well. These alternatives often involve a long series of commands. Although you can undo repeatedly to back up and try again, it is often easier to place a mark in your drawing session at the beginning of the alternative branch, so that you can backtrack to that editing point in a single step. *Undo marks* are like editing bookmarks in your drawing. After placing a mark, you can try a command sequence, go back to your mark if it does not work, and then try an alternate sequence.

You place a mark by choosing Mark from the UNDO command on the EDIT menu. When Back is chosen from the UNDO command options, AutoCAD backs up through the previous commands until the mark is found. Each time you start a drawing session, AutoCAD keeps track of every command you execute by writing it to a temporary file on disk. This temporary file records all of your moves whenever you are in the drawing editor. You do not find this file on disk when you finish an editing session because it is a hidden file. At the end of a session, AutoCAD wipes it out and cleans up the disk. While you are in an editing session; however, you can play this sequence in reverse, undoing each command, or you can redo parts of your past command sequence if you undo too much.

If you have a printer hooked up to your system, you can get a hard copy of all command prompts and your responses by echoing your screen output to a printer. With your printer on and ready to print, press Ctrl-Q to turn on and off printer echo.

The Mark and Back options, as well as several other options, are seen when the UNDO command is typed or chosen from the EDIT screen menu.

Editing Tools

In addition to point filters and UNDO, this chapter's exercises also use the OFFSET, ARRAY, TRIM, FILLET, CHAMFER, CHANGE, CHPROP, and PEDIT editing commands, as well as the various grip modes. If you need to review these commands, refer to the two previous editing chapters and to Chapter 6.

Setting Up for the Mockup Drawing

The mockup drawing is actually a plan and section view of a flange. As in the widget drawing, you do not have to know anything about flanges to learn the basic concepts of undo marks, construction lines, and point filters. The dimensions needed to create the drawing are shown in figure 10.2.

Although this drawing probably would be drawn in decimal units, fractional units are used here, as shown in table 10.1. Set your drawing limits to 34 inches by 22 inches. The plotting scale factor is 1:2 for a 17"×11" final drawing.

Setting Up the Mockup Drawing

Choose File, then New, and enter `MOCKUP=IA7MOCK`.

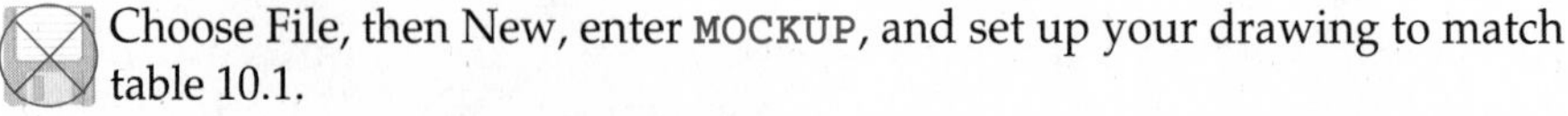

Choose File, then New, enter `MOCKUP`, and set up your drawing to match table 10.1.

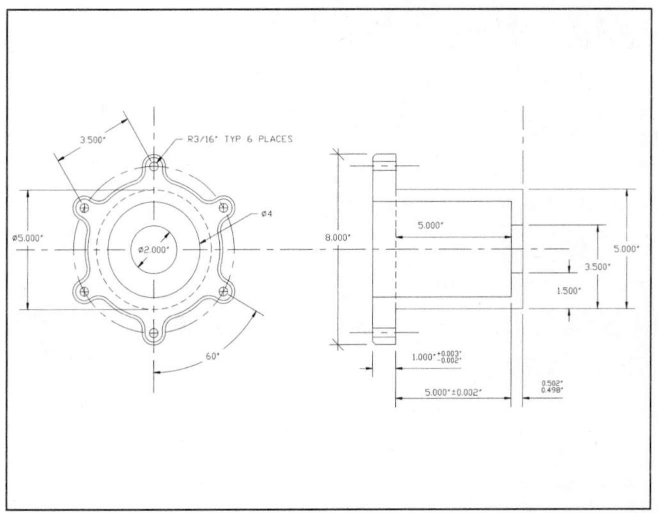

Figure 10.2:
A dimensioned mockup drawing.

Table 10.1
Mockup Drawing Settings

COORDS	*GRID*	*LTSCALE*	*ORTHO*	*SNAP*
On	1	1	ON	.5

UNITS	Set UNITS to 5. Fractional, 64ths denominator. Default the other Units settings.
LIMITS	Set LIMITS from 0,0 to 34,22.
ZOOM	Zoom All.
VIEW	Save view as A.

Layer Name	*State*	*Color*	*Linetype*
0	On	7 (White)	CONTINUOUS
CENTER	On/Current	1 (Red)	CENTER
DIMS	On	2 (Yellow)	CONTINUOUS
HIDDEN	On	4 (Cyan)	HIDDEN
PARTS	On	3 (Green)	CONTINUOUS

Using Construction Lines

The first step in making the mockup is to rough-in the construction lines. Create these lines by using your CENTER layer as a background layer. This defines the two major sections of the drawing. You then can use the PARTS layer to draw the flange and its section view.

Using OFFSET To Create Construction Lines

Use the LINE command to draw a line from 4,13 to @24<0, then another line from 10,7 to @12<90.

`Command:` *Choose* Draw, *then* Circle, *then* Center, Radius, *and draw a 3" radius circle at 10,13 (see fig. 10.3)*	
`Command:` *Choose* Construct, *then* Offset	
`Offset distance or Through <Through>:` **16**↵	Specifies the offset distance
`Select object to offset:` *Pick the vertical line*	
`Side to offset?` *Pick any point to the right of line*	Shows which direction to offset
`Select object to offset:` *Press Enter*	Ends the command
`Command:` *Press Enter*	Repeats the OFFSET command
`_OFFSET Offset distance or Through <16>:` *Offset circle to outside with distance 1 to create a 4" radius circle (see fig. 10.4)*	

The two circles on your screen are temporary construction lines that help you form the complex entity that makes up the perimeter of the flange.

Look at figure 10.2 again. The perimeter of the top flange is a polyline with six lugs sticking out, so it is difficult to draw this entire perimeter as a single polyline. The next three exercises show you how to create one-sixth of the perimeter, array this to get the basic perimeter, and then form a polyline by joining all of the adjoining entities.

Because you are creating several entities to represent the top flange and because you are also using several different editing commands, this is a

good place in the drawing sequence to put an undo mark in your drawing file. If the next three sequences produce undesirable results, you can easily come back to this point.

Use UNDO to place a mark in your drawing, and then resume construction of the lug that sticks out from the top of the flange perimeter. Construct the lug on your PARTS layer.

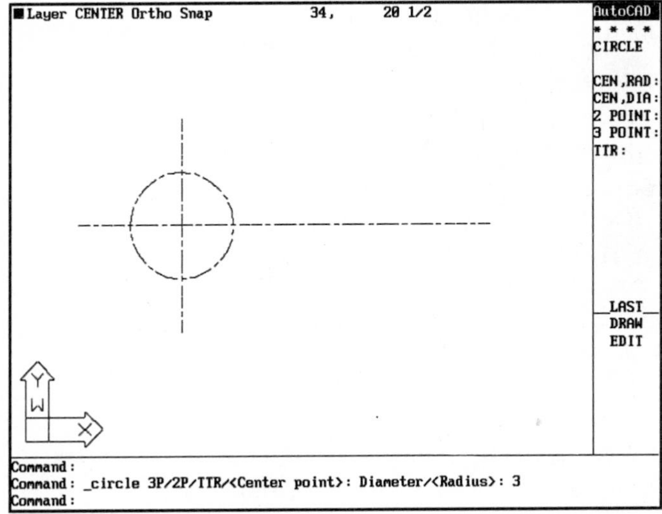

Figure 10.3:

The construction lines and circle.

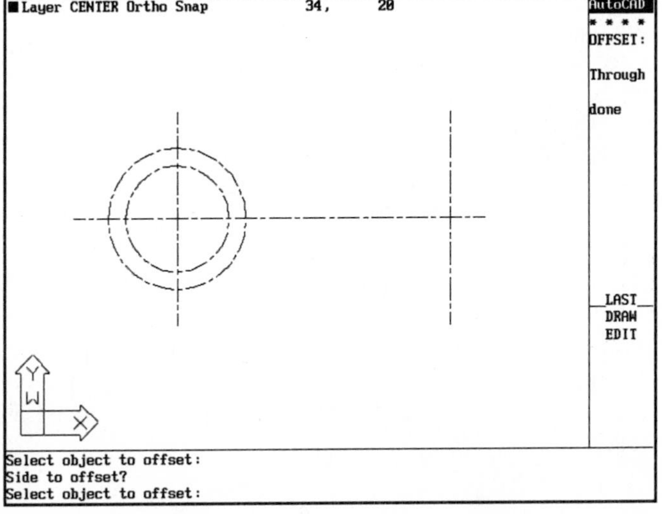

Figure 10.4:

An offset of the circle and line.

Using Construction Entities To Draw a Lug

`Command:` *From the screen menu, choose* EDIT, *then* next, *then* UNDO:, *then* Mark	Places a mark
`Command:` **`Zoom`**↵	
Zoom to the view shown in figure 10.5.	
`Command:` **`DDLMODES`**↵	
Make PARTS the current layer.	
`Command:` *Choose* Draw, *then* Circle, *and then* 2-Point	
`circle 3P/2P/TTR/<Center point>: _2p`	
`First point on diameter:` *Pick at* ① *in figure 10.5*	
`Second point on diameter:` *Pick at* ②	
`Command:` *Choose* Draw, *then* Circle, *then* Center, Diameter, *pick at* ③ *for the center, and enter* **`3/8`** *for the diameter*	
`Command:` **`L`** ↵	Starts the LINE command
Make sure SNAP is on, so the start and end points of the next two lines can be easily picked from the screen. Draw the two lines shown in figure 10.6, starting at ④ and ⑤.	
`Command:` **`QSAVE`** ↵	Saves the drawing

This is a good place in the drawing to experiment with undoing and redoing commands.

Controlling AutoCAD's UNDO

AutoCAD provides several commands to make changes or to correct mistakes made during the drawing process. Many of these commands have already been mentioned, and they are now demonstrated in this exercise. The most-used editing command, ERASE, is easy to use; and the OOPS command quickly brings back entities that are accidentally erased.

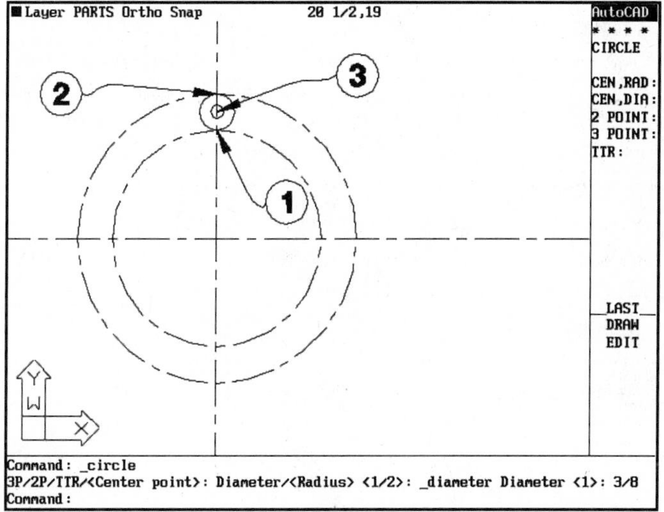

Figure 10.5:

Lug construction after circles.

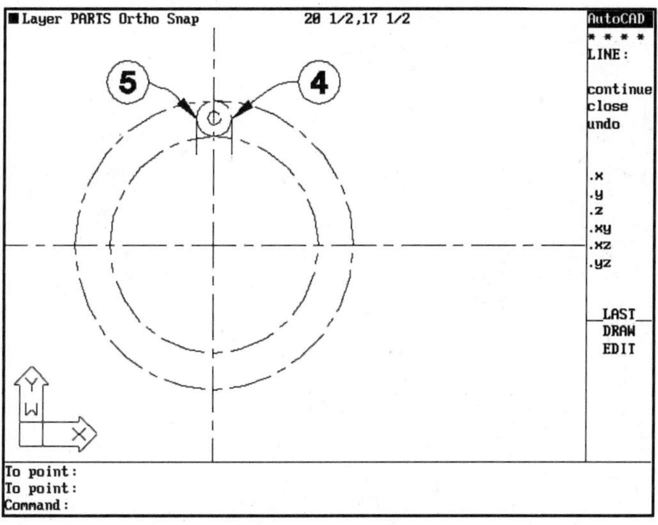

Figure 10.6:

Lug construction after lines.

Erasing the last item you drew, however, is only part of the process of going back through your drawing file. When you decide to go back, it is often to undo a whole sequence of draw and edit commands.

The U Command

The U command is a "mini-undo," which backs up by one step or command. Whatever you did immediately before issuing the U command is undone when you type U. Unlike the OOPS command, however, U works many times, stepping back through each previous last command, one by one. In this sense, U is similar to the Undo option in LINE or PLINE, which deletes line or polyline segments by going back one segment at a time. You can even undo an OOPS or an ERASE by using the U command.

The UNDO Command

The UNDO command, when entered or selected from the EDIT screen menu, offers more control than does the U command. By using UNDO, you can specify the number of steps you want to return. You also can set marks or group a series of commands together, so that if the process does not work, you can undo the whole series at once.

The REDO Command

If you issue REDO immediately after the UNDO command, REDO reverses, or cancels, the UNDO. Thus, you can experiment if you are not sure how far back you want to go. You can do something drastic, UNDO 20 commands for example, and then recover with a REDO. You can even play back your drawing sequences with UNDO (see fig. 10.7), and then use REDO to show or teach someone else what you have done.

Use the following illustrations and exercise sequence to test the U, UNDO, and REDO commands. When the test is complete, your drawing should look the same as it does now.

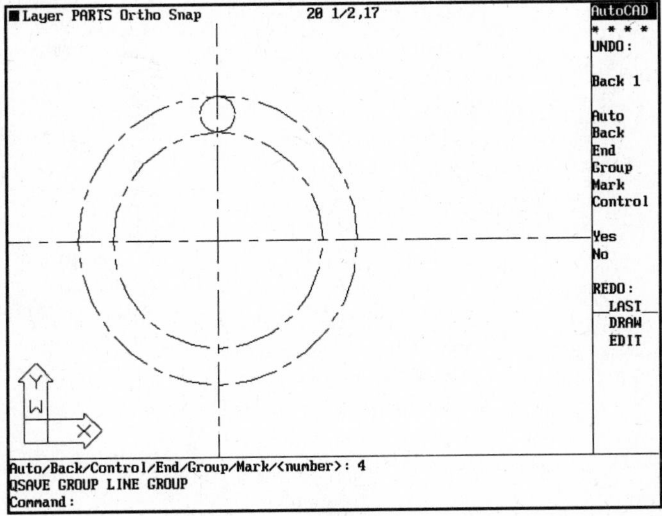

Figure 10.7:

Mockup after an Undo 4.

Using U, UNDO, and REDO on an Editing Sequence

`Command:` *Choose* Assist, *then* Undo	Undoes the last command
`_U QSAVE`	Shows the last command it undid
`Command:` *Choose* Assist, *then* Redo	Reverses the U command
`-redo`	
`Command:` **UNDO** ↵	
`Auto/Back/Control/End/Group/Mark /<number>:` **4** ↵	Undoes the last four commands
`QSAVE LINE GROUP GROUP`	
`Command:` *Choose* Assist, *then* Redo	Reverses the UNDO command
`-redo`	
`Command:` **UNDO** ↵	
`Auto/Back/Control/End/Group/Mark/ <number>:` **B** ↵	Backs up to the previously set mark (see fig. 10.8)
`QSAVE LINE GROUP GROUP DDLMODES ZOOM`	
`Mark encountered`	
`Command:` *Choose* Assist, *then* Redo	Reverses the UNDO command

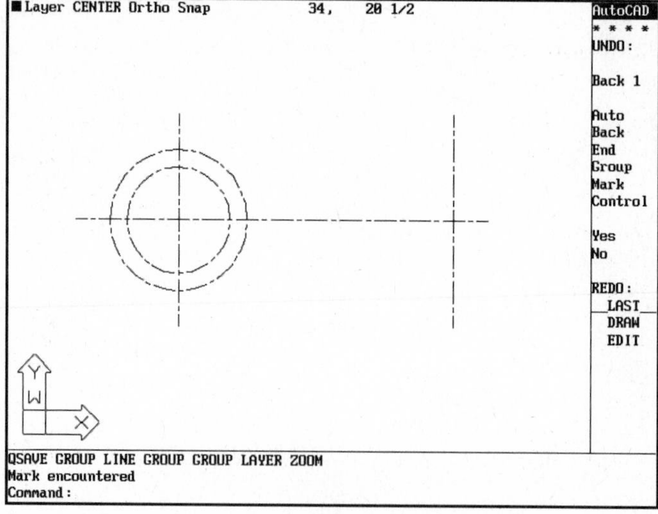

Figure 10.8:
MOCKUP after an UNDO Back.

If you accidentally undo too much and you cannot recover the data, reload your saved drawing. Although UNDO showed QSAVE as an undone command, commands that write to the disk are never actually undone. The UNDO Back option used in the exercise, is only one of six options that control UNDO. The following section lists the UNDO options.

UNDO Options

- **<number>.** This option enables you to enter a number, and AutoCAD steps back by that many steps.
- **Auto.** An ON/OFF setting, the Auto option affects menu items only. Sometimes, a single menu item creates or edits many entities. Normally, everything done by one command is one step back in Undo. If Auto is set to ON (the default), it causes an entire menu item to be treated as a single step by making it an undo *group*.
- **Back** and **Mark.** The UNDO Back option undoes until it returns to the beginning of the editing session, an undo mark, or a PLOT command (because they re-initialize the undo file as if beginning the editing session at that point). If no mark has been placed, you get a warning, `This will undo everything. OK <Y>`. Respond with a Yes or

No. You set an undo mark by executing the UNDO command with the Mark option. This option is available from the UNDO screen menu by choosing Mark. You can mark as many times as you like, each time setting a stop for the next UNDO Back.

- **Control.** The creation of the temporary undo file can take a large amount of disk space. The Control option enables you to specify how active the temporary file is with the following three options: All/None/One. All is the default. None turns UNDO off. One limits UNDO to just one step back. When set to One, none of the other UNDO options are available. All restores UNDO to its full function.
- **Group** and **End.** Like Back and Mark, the Group and End options put boundaries on the series of commands in the temporary file, so that you can undo the series in one step. You begin a group with the Group option, end the group with the End option, and then continue working. Later you step back using U or UNDO <number>. When the backstep gets to an End, the next UNDO step wipes out everything between the End and Group markers as a single step.

Be careful not to undo too much. Any settings during a command, including toggles or transparent commands, are undone with the main command. Although UNDO can wipe out your entire drawing in one step, you can save it if you catch it immediately with REDO.

In the exercises in the rest of the book (and in your own work), place undo marks to give yourself additional checkpoints in the editing session. If you then need to retry a sequence, you can easily step back and do it.

Using Array Techniques To Construct the Flange Perimeter

Continue drawing the flange. First, finish the lug by using the TRIM command, which is easier than trying to calculate the exact arc and line lengths that make up the lug. It also ensures that all the end points match.

Using TRIM To Draw First Lug of Flange

`Command:` *Press F9*	Turns off snap (Ctrl-B has the same effect)
`Command:` *Choose* Modify, *then* Trim	
`_trim Select cutting edge(s)...`	
`Select objects:` *Select the 3" circle at ①, shown in figure 10.9, and the lines at ② and ③*	
`Select objects:` *Press Enter*	Completes the cutting edge selection
`<Select object to trim>/Undo:` *Pick the line at ②*	Trims the line
`<Select object to trim>/Undo:` *Pick the line at ③*	
`<Select object to trim>/Undo:` *Pick the circle at ④*	
`<Select object to trim>/Undo:` *Pick the circle at ⑤*	
`<Select object to trim>/Undo:` *Press Enter*	Finishes the TRIM command
`Command:` *Press F9*	Turns snap back on

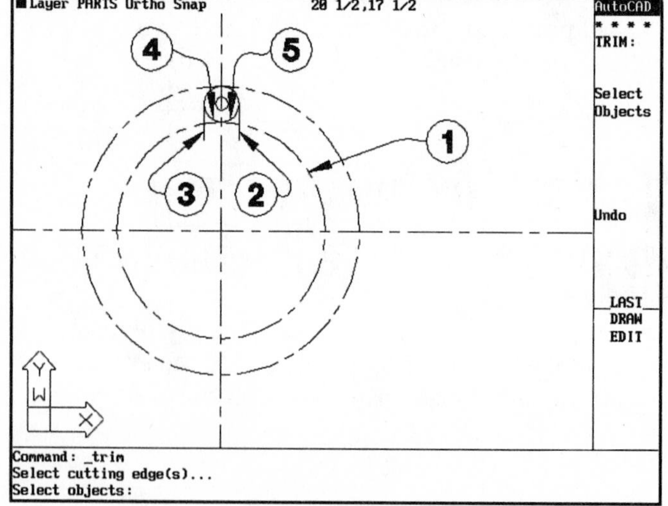

Figure 10.9:

Picks for the circle and line trim.

The first lug is now complete, as shown in figure 10.10. The perimeter in the target drawing showed the lug in six places. You can array the lug now and draw the remaining entities between the arrayed lugs, but it is more efficient to create one-sixth of the perimeter and then perform the array.

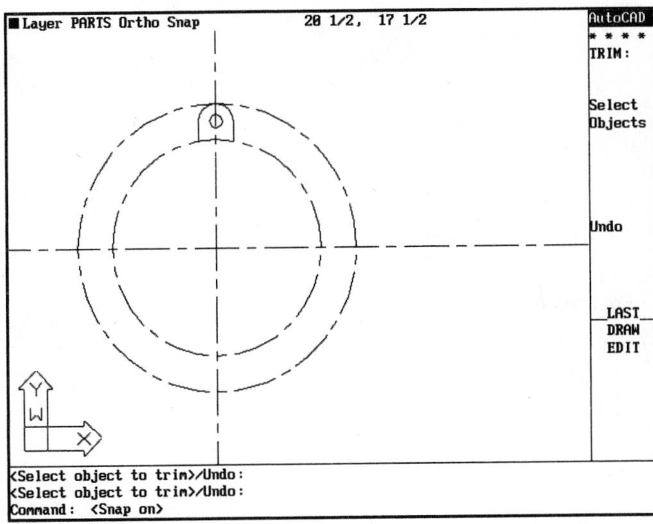

Figure 10.10:

A completed lug after trimming.

Completing a One-Sixth Portion To Array

AutoCAD's editing commands are used here to do the calculation and construction. Use the rotate autoedit mode to set up a one-sixth segment of the circle. Then use the ARC and FILLET commands and object snaps to complete the segment.

Using Autoedit Rotate and ARC To Construct a Perimeter Segment

`Command:` *Select the short lug line on the right side (see fig. 10.11)*	Displays grips
`Command:` *Pick any grip*	

`** STRETCH **`
`<Stretch to point>/Base point/Copy/`
`Undo/eXit: RO↵`
	Enters rotate mode

`** ROTATE **` `<Rotation angle>/Base point/Copy/Undo/ Reference/eXit:` **`B`** ↵	Issues the base point
`Base point:` **`10,13`** ↵	
`** ROTATE **` `<Rotation angle>/Base point/Copy/Undo/ Reference/eXit:` **`60`**↵	Rotates the lug line 60 degrees counterclockwise
`Command:` *Choose* Draw, *then* Arc, *then* Start, Cen, End	
`ARC Center/<Start point>:` *From the pop-up menu, choose* Endpoint	
`endp of` *Pick at* ① *(see fig. 10.12)*	
`Center/End/<Second point>:_c Center:` *From the pop-up menu, choose* Intersection	
`int of` *Pick at* ②	Picks the arc's center
`Angle/Length of chord/<End point>:` *From the pop-up menu, choose* End point	Picks the arc's endpoint
`ENDP of` *Pick at* ③	

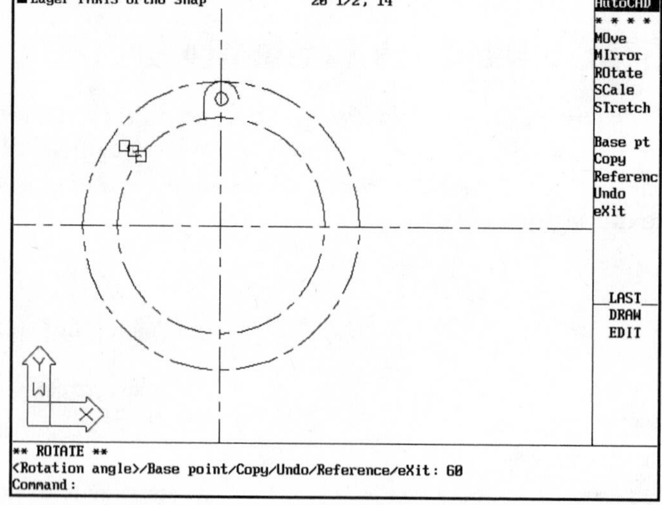

Figure 10.11:

The rotated lug line.

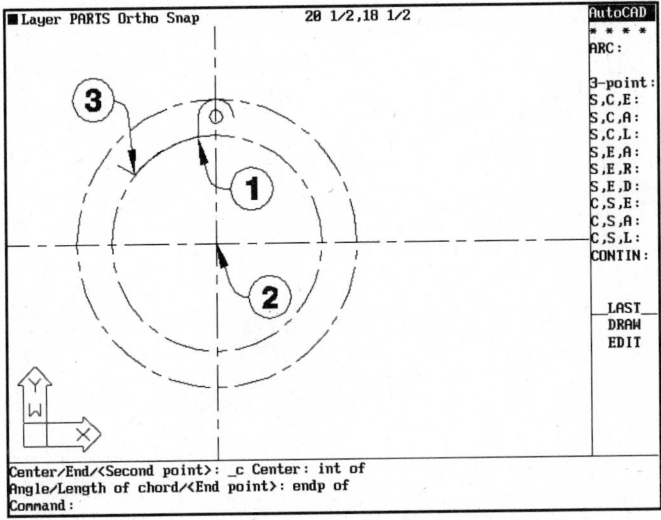

Figure 10.12:

The arc completes a one-sixth segment.

Using FILLET To Complete the Perimeter Segment

`Command:` *Turn off snap with F9*

`Command:` *Choose* Construct, *then* Fillet, *and set fillet radius to 1/2 inch*

`Command:` *Press Enter* — Reissues FILLET

`FILLET Polyline/Radius/<Select first object>` *Pick the arc at ① and the line at ② (see fig. 10.13)* — Fillets the arc and line

If you have difficulty selecting the small arc instead of the large arc, use DDLMODES to temporarily lock the CENTER layer.

`Command:` *Press Enter and pick the line at ③ and the arc at ④ (see fig. 10.14)*

You now are ready to create the perimeter by arraying the one-sixth segment. If you followed the construction sequence, all the entity points should line up. Notice that you have made only one trivial calculation: dividing the circle into sixths (60 degrees). By using object snaps and editing commands, you let AutoCAD do all the hard calculations and locations.

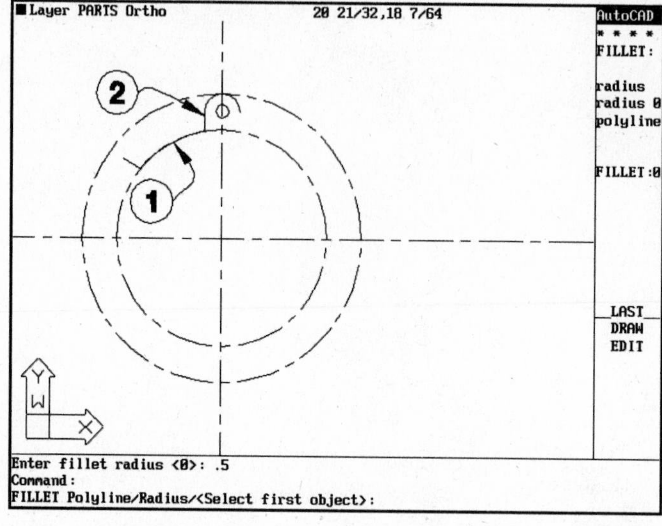

Figure 10.13:

Picks for the first fillet.

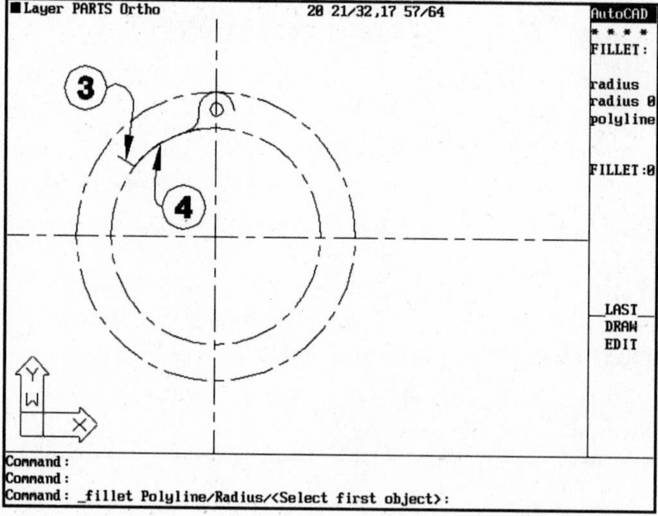

Figure 10.14:

Picks for the second fillet.

Using ARRAY and PEDIT To Create the Perimeter

Use a polar array to replicate the one-sixth segment to complete the perimeter of the flange (see fig. 10.15). Then, use PEDIT with the Join option to group the entity segments into a single polyline. After you have joined the segments, create two circles in the interior of the flange.

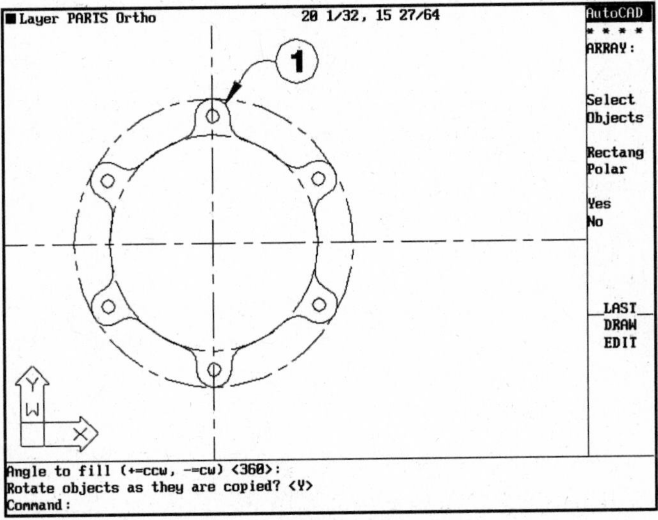

Figure 10.15:

The top flange after the array.

Using ARRAY and PEDIT To Complete the Flange

`Command:` *Use FILTER or a window to select all the green entities*	Displays grips
`Command:` *Choose* Construct, *then* Array	
`_array 7 found`	
`Rectangular or Polar array (R/P) <R>:` **P** ↵	
`Center point of array:` *From the pop-up menu, choose* Intersection, *then pick at 10,13*	Specifies the center intersection
`Number of items:` **6** ↵	
`Angle to fill (+=ccw, -=cw) <360>:` *Press Enter*	Specifies a full circle
`Rotate objects as they are copied? <Y>` *Press Enter*	Creates the array (see fig. 10.15)

Next, you join the flanges.

`Command:` *Choose* Modify, *then* PolyEdit

`Select objects:` *Pick first arc created on top flange at ① in figure 10.15*

`Select objects:` *Press Enter*

`Entity selected is not a polyline`

```
Do you want to turn it into one? <Y>
```
Press Enter

```
Close/Join/Width/Edit vertex/Fit/
Spline/Decurve/Ltype gen/Undo/
eXit <X>: J ↵
```

`Select objects:` **`ALL`** ↵	
`47 found`	Join ignored the extra entities
`Select objects:` *Press Enter*	
`35 segments added to polyline`	Creates a single polyline

```
Open/Join/Width/Edit vertex/Fit/
Spline/Decurve/Ltype gen/Undo/
```
`eXit <X>:` *Press Enter*

Next, draw the inside wall of the flange and the center hole in the bottom of the part.

Draw a 4" diameter circle at 10,13 and a 2-1/2"-diameter circle at 10,13.

Your drawing now should resemble figure 10.16.

The PEDIT Join option requires that each entity endpoint match the adjacent endpoint exactly. If you do not get a complete join, undo it and try again.

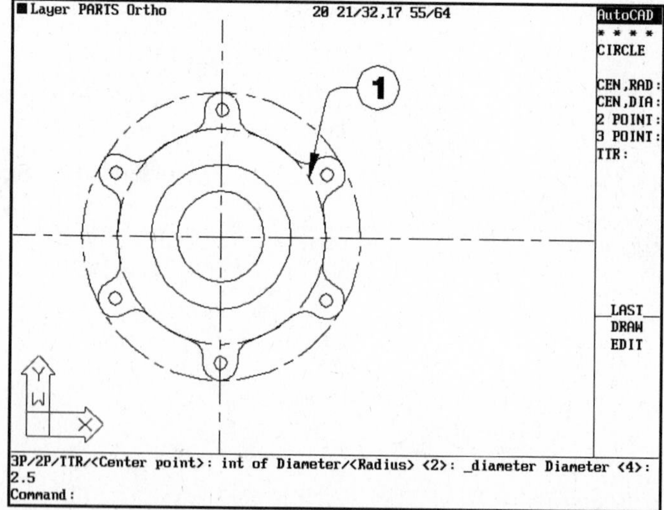

Figure 10.16:

Circles complete the top flange.

You can use a far-off drawing corner, viewport, or a scratch UCS for background construction, putting together pieces of a drawing that you can later move, copy, or array into place.

Editing by Recycling Entities

You can save drawing time by recycling surplus construction circles, rather than by creating new ones. Change the inner construction circle's layer (linetype) and radius to make a hidden line for the outer wall, and then change the outer circle's radius to make a bolt ring center line (see fig. 10.17). You could use both the CHPROP (or DDCHPROP) and CHANGE commands, but a single DDMODIFY command can do it all.

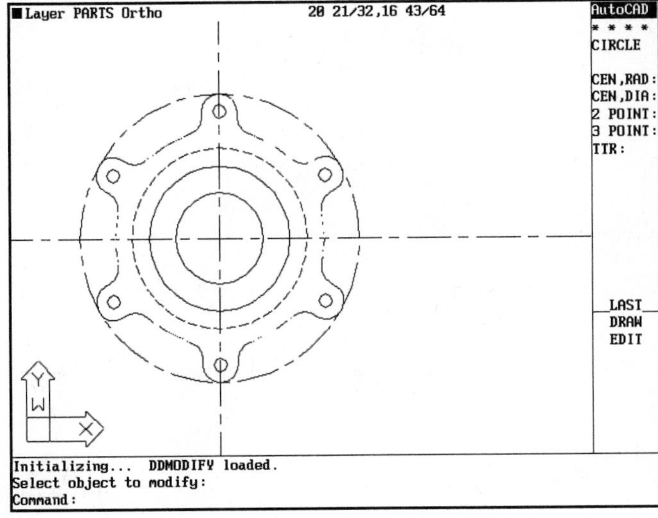

Figure 10.17:

The changed construction circle layer and radius.

Using DDMODIFY and CHANGE To Complete Top View

`Command:` *Choose* Modify, *then* Entity

`Select objects:` *Select center line construction circle at ① (see fig. 10.16) and press Enter*	Selects circle and opens Modify Circle dialog box
Click on Layer, *select* HIDDEN, *then click on* OK	Changes the circle layer to HIDDEN

Double-click in the **R**adius *edit box, type 2.5, and choose OK*	Resets radius, closes dialog box, and modifies circle
`Command:` *Press Enter to repeat DDMODIFY and change the radius of the outside circle to 3-1/2" (see fig. 10.18)*	
`Command: R ↵`	Redraws
`Command: QSAVE ↵`	

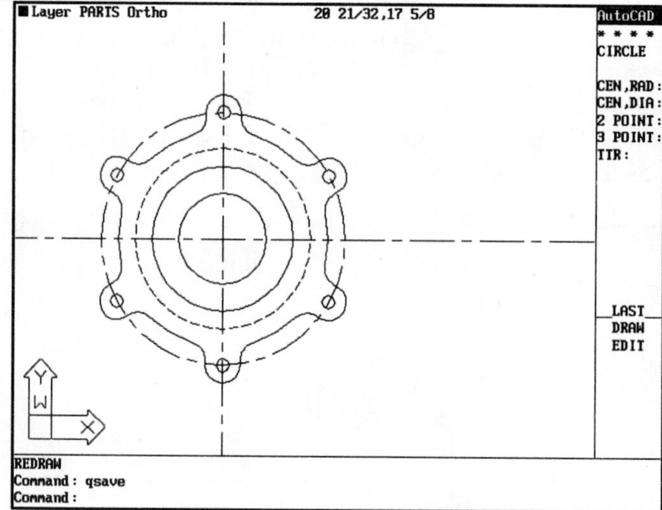

Figure 10.18:
The changed construction circle radius.

As the exercise shows, you still can type decimal entry when using fractional units (see fig. 10.17).

The plan view of the flange is finished. This is a good point to take a break before using XYZ point filters to construct the section view of the flange.

Using XYZ Point Filters for Section Construction

In figure 10.19, most of the geometry you need to draw the section view on the right already exists in the plan view. You can draw an accurate section quickly by aligning the new section lines with intersections of the lines and

entities making up the plan view. You cannot draw the lines by simply aligning your crosshair cursor, however, because most of the intersection points are not on snap increments.

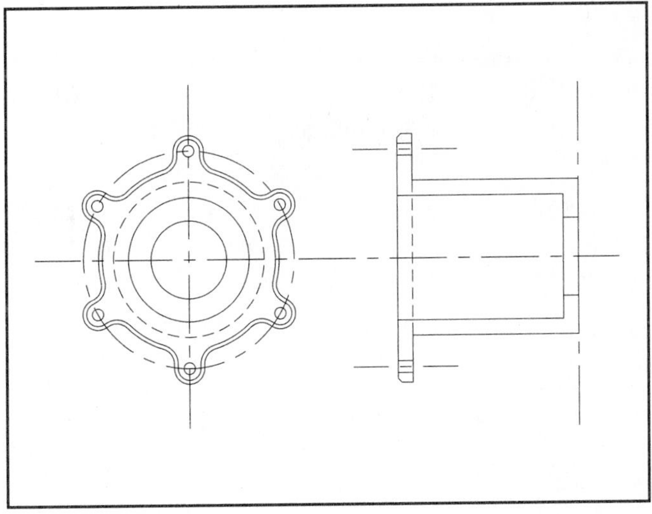

Figure 10.19:

A mockup target drawing.

Using XYZ point filters makes this alignment an easy procedure. Point filters enable you to pick X, Y, and Z coordinates independently. Although Z filtering is extremely useful in 3D drawings, it can be ignored for now.

Resume your MOCKUP drawing by comparing your setup to the table at the front of the chapter. If you are using the IA DISK, use the IA7MOCK2 drawing, which contains the completed plan view of the flange. Your current layer should be PARTS. Restore View A to start the drawing.

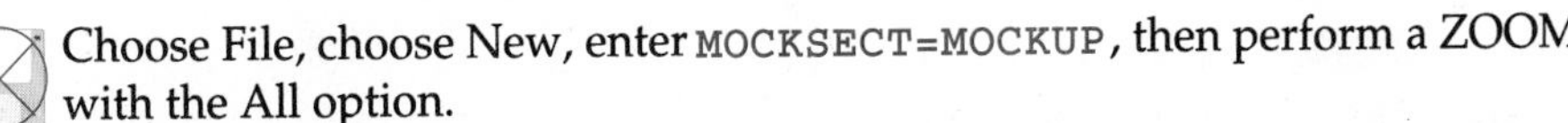

Setting Up for XYZ Point Filters

Choose File, choose New, and enter `MOCKSECT=IA7MOCK2`.

Choose File, choose New, enter `MOCKSECT=MOCKUP`, then perform a ZOOM with the All option.

To use point filters, precede a point that you pick (or enter) with a .X or .Y (pronounced dot-X or dot-Y). The dot (period) distinguishes the point filter from command options that begin with an X or Y. AutoCAD then takes only the specified coordinate from the following point, and prompts you for the other coordinate values.

When you specify a .X value, for example, you pick a point, or snap with object snap to an entity, that has the X value you want. AutoCAD then tells you that you need a Y value. You can pick, type, or use an object snap to get the Y value, which gives you the X,Y intersection point.

Since the flange is symmetrical, you only need to draw half of the section view, and then mirror the other half. Use the next exercise sequence with X and Y filters to create the lower half of the section, as shown in figures 10.20 through 10.23.

Using XYZ Point Filters To Draw a Section View

`Command:` *Zoom into area shown*	
`Command:` *Choose* Settings, *then* Object Snap, *check the* Intersection, *and* End point *check boxes, then choose* OK	Sets running INT, ENDP object snap
`Command:` *Turn off snap*	
`Command:` **APERTURE** ↵	
`Object snap target height (1-50 pixels) <5>:` **6** ↵	Adjusts the size of the aperture box
`Command:` **L** ↵	
`From point:` *From the pop-up menu, choose* Filters, *then* .X	
`.X of` *Pick anywhere on vertical base line at ① (see fig. 10.20)*	
`(need YZ):` *Pick intersection of hole and vertical center line at ②*	
`To point:` **@-.5,0** ↵	Draws the first line
`To point:` **.X** ↵	
`of` *Pick left side of last line drawn at ③*	
`(need YZ):` *Pick inside of flange circle and vertical center line at ④*	Draws the second line
`To point:` **@-5.5,0** ↵	Draws the third line (see fig. 10.21)

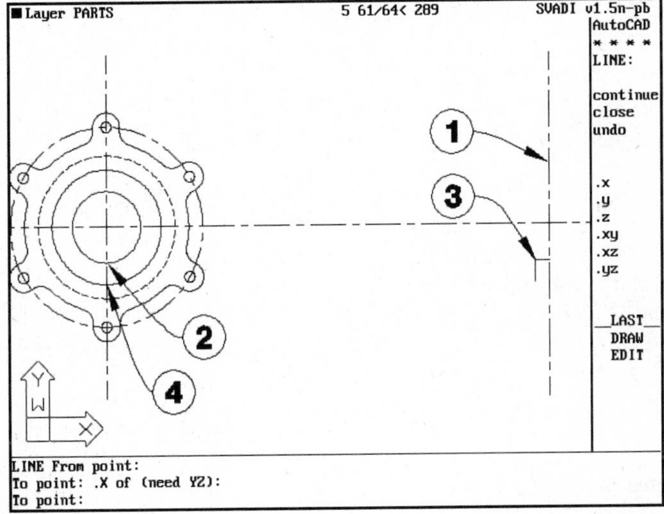

Figure 10.20:

The first and second lines of the section.

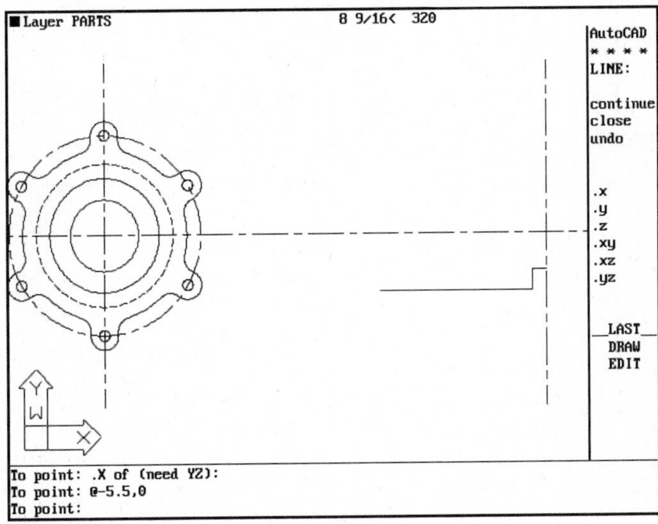

Figure 10.21:

The third line of the section.

`To point:` *From the pop-up menu, choose* Filters, *then* .X	
`.X of` *Pick left side of last line drawn at ⑤ in figure 10.22*	
`(need YZ):` *Pick intersection of arc and vertical center line at ⑥*	Draws the fourth line (see fig. 10.22)
`To point:` **`@1/2,0↵`**	Draws the fifth line
`To point:` **`.X↵`**	
`of` *Pick right side of last line drawn at ⑦ (see fig. 10.23)*	
`(need YZ):` *Pick intersection of hidden circle and vertical line at ⑧*	Draws the sixth line
`To point:` *From the pop-up menu, choose* Perpendicular	Uses PER to override running object snap
`per to` *Pick anywhere on vertical base line at ⑨*	
`To point:` **`C↵`**	Closes to the beginning point

You used both command line entry and the pop-up menu to select the .X filter. The point filters also can be found on the LINE screen menu. Try each method to see which is most efficient for you.

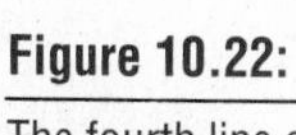

Figure 10.22:

The fourth line of the section.

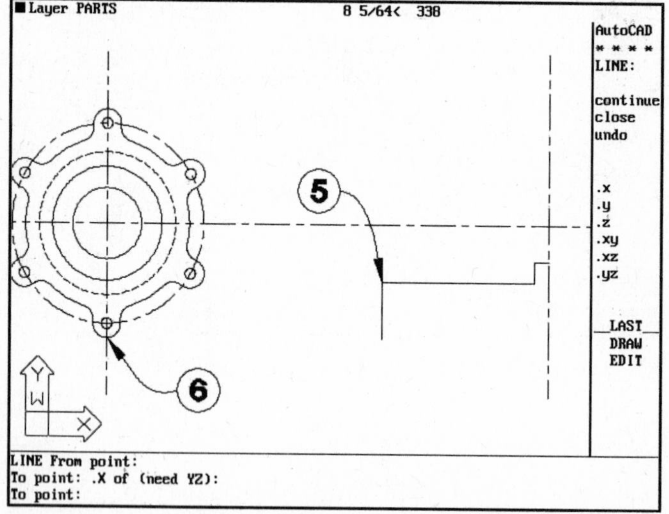

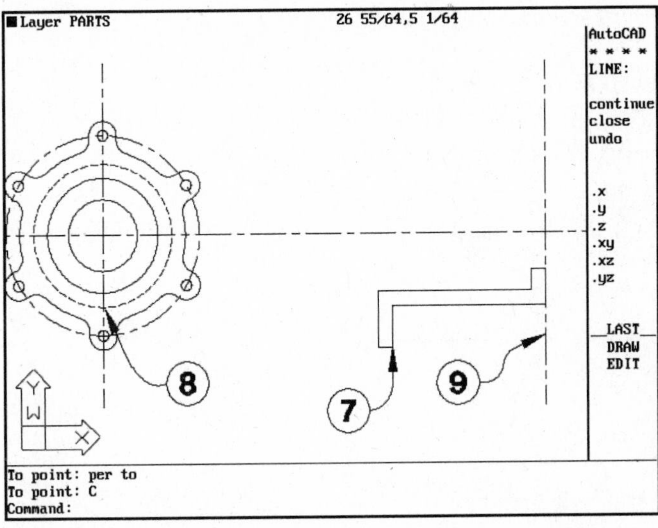

Figure 10.23:

A completed section.

Your screen should now show half a section view of the mockup part. Next, you complete the section half by using XYZ filters to add the lines for the hole in the top flange.

Using XYZ Filter To Draw a Hole in the Section View

`Command:` **`L↵`**	Issues the LINE command and displays filters on the screen menu
`From point:` *From the screen menu, choose* .x	
`.x of` *Pick line of top flange in the section view at ① (see fig. 10.24)*	
`(need YZ):` *Pick where the drilled hole and center line intersect at ②*	
`To point:` *From the pop-up menu, choose* Perpendicular	
`per to` *Pick line in the section view at ③*	
`To point:` *Press Enter*	
`Command:` *Enter* `L`*, and repeat the process for the line at the bottom of the hole*	
`Command:` *Press Enter*	Repeats the LINE command
`From point:` **`.X↵`**	Begins center line for hole

`of` *Pick a point about 1" to the right of the bottom flange at ④ (see fig. 10.25)*

`(need YZ):` *Pick center of lug hole at ⑤*

`To point:` *Turn on ortho, pick a point 1" to the left of the top flange at ⑥, then turn off ortho*

`To point:` *Press Enter*

Select the last line drawn, then use the CHPROP or DDCHPROP command to change it to the CENTER layer.

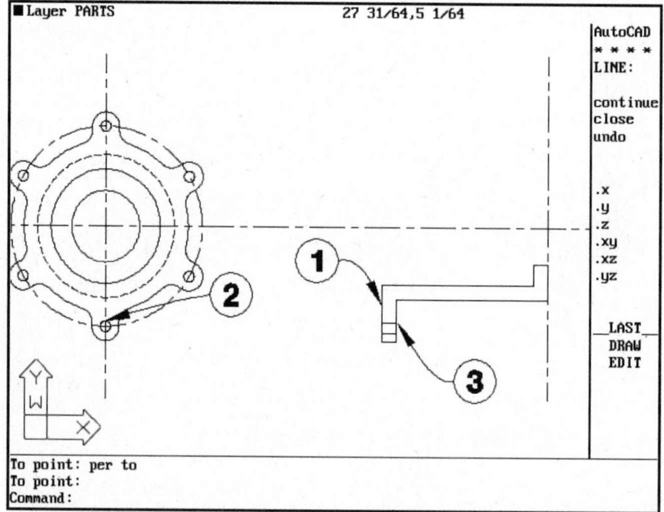

Figure 10.24:

A section view with hole lines.

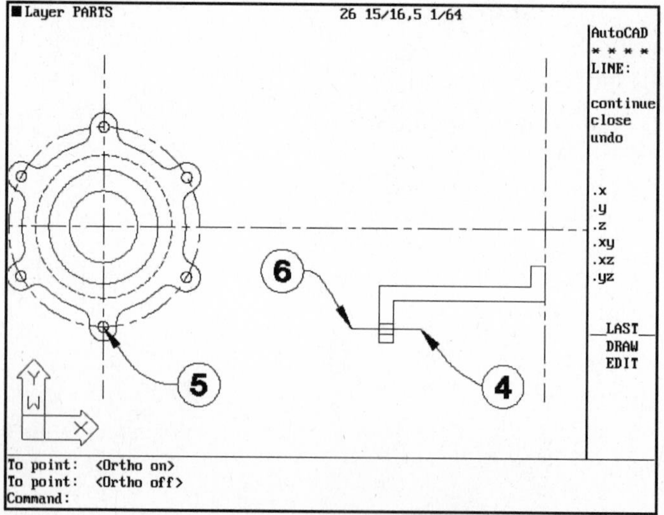

Figure 10.25:

A center line through hole.

In the following exercise, to get the rest of the section view, mirror the lower half and add four more lines.

Completing the Section View

`Command:` *Window-select the section and center line, then pick a grip*	Enters stretch grip mode

`** STRETCH **`
`<Stretch to point>/Base point/Copy/`
`Undo/eXit:` **MI** ↵
	Switches to mirror grip mode

`** MIRROR **`
`<Second point>/Base point/Copy/`
`Undo/eXit:` **B** ↵	

`Base point:` *Pick a point on the horizontal center line (see fig. 10.26)*	

`** STRETCH **`
`<Stretch to point>/Base point/Copy/`
`Undo/eXit:` **C** ↵
	Enters Copy mode

`** STRETCH (multiple) **`
`<Stretch to point>/Base point/Copy/`
`Undo/eXit:` **@1<0** ↵	

`** STRETCH (multiple) **`
`<Stretch to point>/Base point/Copy/`
`Undo/eXit:` *Press Enter*	

Use DDLMODES or LAYER to set the HIDDEN layer current.

`Command:` *Choose* Draw, *then* Line, *then* 1 Segment, *and draw a hidden line from* ② *to* ③ *(see fig. 10.27)*

Use DDLMODES or LAYER to make PARTS the current layer.

`Command:` *Draw the three lines at* ④	Completes the section
`Command:` *Choose* Settings, *then* Object Snap, *clear the* End point *and* Intersection *check boxes, then choose* **OK**	Resets object snap to NONE
`Command:` **QSAVE** ↵	Saves to the default drawing

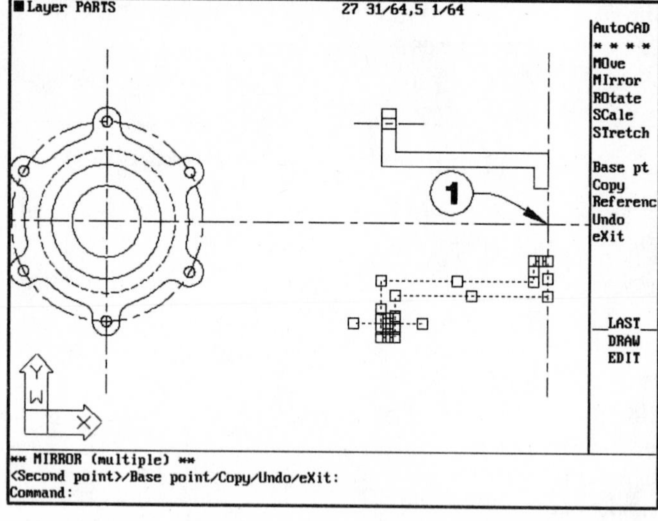

Figure 10.26:

The section after mirroring.

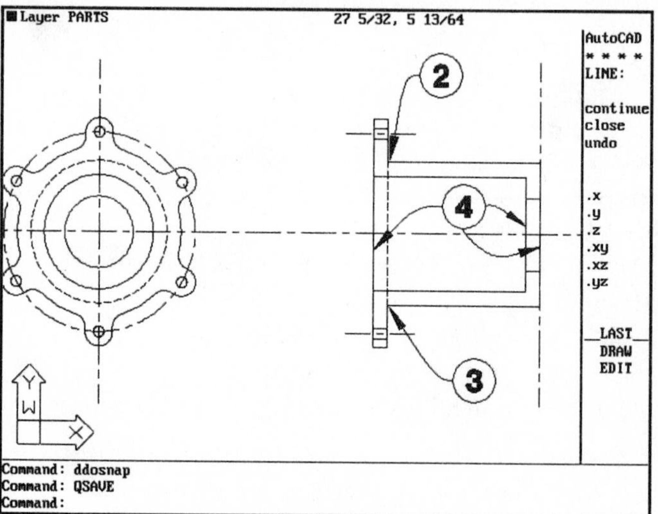

Figure 10.27:

The completed section.

The target flange has a chamfer. Take a moment to chamfer the section view, and then add the chamfer to the plan view by offsetting the perimeter. The following illustrations and exercise can help you do this procedure.

Chamfer Edge of Flange

Zoom to the view shown in figure 10.28.

`Command:` *Choose* Construct, *then* Chamfer	
`_chamfer Polyline/Distances /<Select first line>:` *From the screen menu, choose* distance	
`_D Enter first chamfer distance <0>: 1/8` ↵	
`Enter second chamfer distance <1/8>:` *Press Enter*	
`_CHAMFER Polyline/Distances/ <Select first line>:` *Pick top flange line at* ① *(see figs. 10.28 and 10.29)*	
`Select second line:` *Pick end flange line at* ②	Chamfers the lines
`Command:` *Press Enter*	Repeats the command
`_CHAMFER Polyline/Distances/<Select first line>:` *Pick top flange line at* ③	
`Select second line:` *Pick end flange line at* ④	
`Command:` *Choose* Construct, *then* Offset	
`Offset distance or Through <16>: 1/8` ↵	Changes the offset distance
`Select object to offset:` *Pick any perimeter point on the top flange in the plan view*	Selects the entity to offset
`Side to offset?` *Pick a point inside the perimeter*	
`Select object to offset:` *Press Enter*	

Save the drawing.

Figures 10.30 and 10.31 show the plan view of the flange with the new offset.

You use this MOCKSECT drawing later when you practice dimensioning.

You can delete the MOCKUP drawing, which is no longer needed.

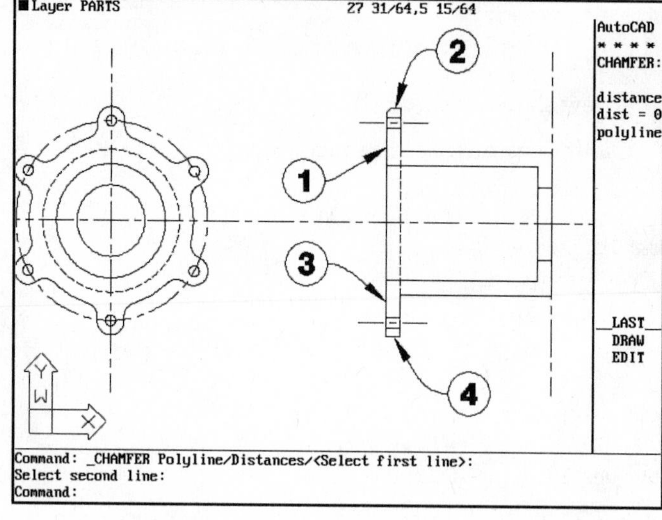

Figure 10.28:

The section after chamfering.

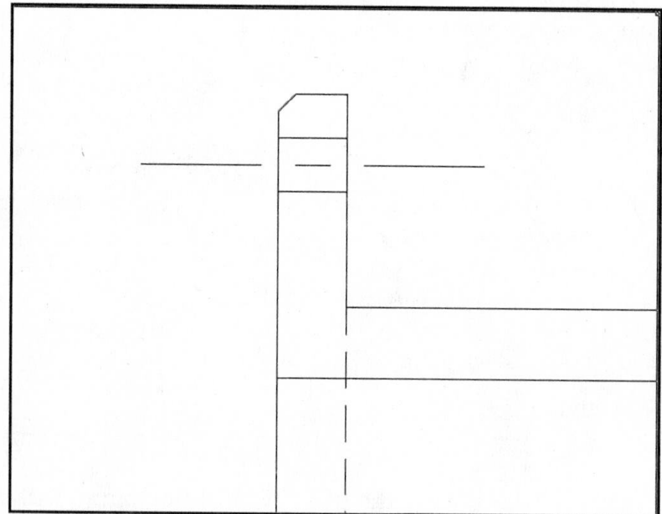

Figure 10.29:

Detail of the chamfer.

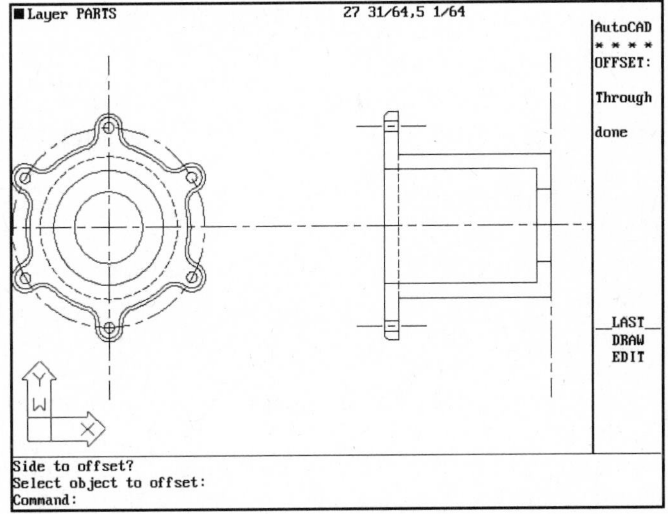

Figure 10.30:

The top view after offsetting.

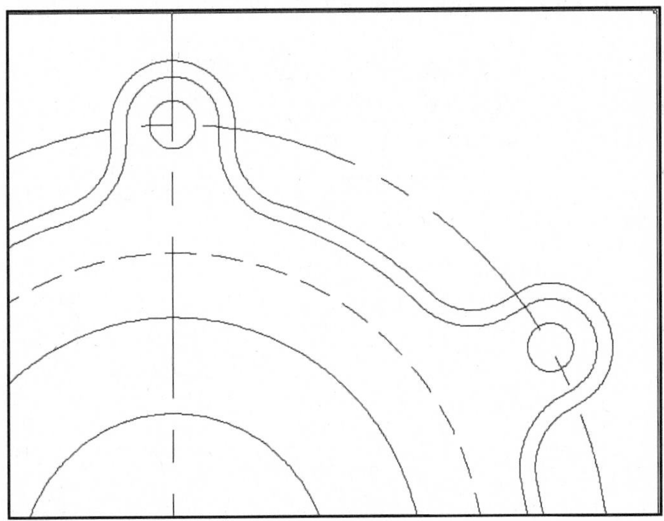

Figure 10.31:

Detail of the offset.

Defining Boundaries with BPOLY

A very fast and easy way of defining a boundary around the inside of a group of entities is with the BPOLY (Boundary POLYline) command. This command brings up the Polyline Creation border dialog box (see fig. 10.32). The easiest way to use the command is to choose the Pick Points button which accepts the default values in the dialog box and prompts you to choose an internal point. AutoCAD then draws a polyline around the area you selected, assuming that it is closed off with entities. To speed up the process and to give you more control over it, you may choose the Make New Boundary Set button which enables you to select the entities that AutoCAD uses in determining a boundary. Ray casting allows additional control by enabling you to specify which direction to search from the selected point for entities to form the boundary. BPOLY also is used as part of the BHATCH command; see Chapter 14 details on BHATCH.

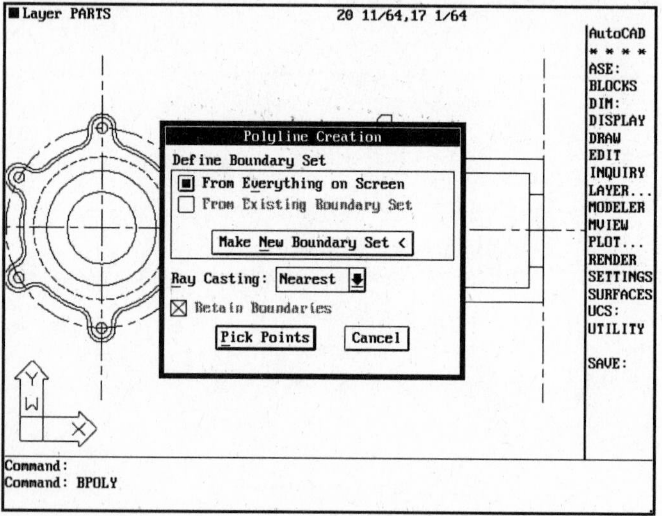

Figure 10.32:

The BPOLY Polyline Creation dialog box.

Next, use the BPOLY command to create an outline of a partial shim for the flange. After you create the shim outline, move it above the two existing views of the flange. To stop MOVE from finding the original entities, lock layers PARTS and CENTER.

Defining Boundaries with BPOLY

Continue with the MOCKSECT drawing from the previous exercise.

`Command:` *Select the circle at ①, (see fig. 10.33), then enter* `E`	Erases hidden circle

Enter DDLMODES, then create a new layer named SHIM with color yellow, and set it current. Lock layers PARTS and CENTER.

`Command:` **`BPOLY`** ↵	Opens the Polyline Creation dialog box
Choose Pick Points	Prompts for point
`Select internal point` *Pick at ② (see fig. 10.34)*	

`Selecting everything...`
`Selecting everything visible...`
`Analyzing the selected data...`
	Searches for and highlights boundary

`Select internal point` *Pick at ③, ④, and ⑤ (see fig. 10.34)*	
`Select internal point` *Press Enter*	Creates four boundary polylines
`Command:` **`M`**↵	Begins MOVE command
`Select objects:` *Select a window enclosing the entire flange front view*	Selects entities on unlocked SHIM layer
`15 found` `11 were on a locked layer.`	
`Select objects:` *Press Enter*	
`Base point or displacement:` *From the pop-up menu, choose* Intersection, *then pick intersection of center lines at center of flange*	
`Second point of displacement:` *Pick a point near 17,20*	

Pan to the view shown in figure 10.34.

Quit the drawing, discarding the changes

The BPOLY command saved considerable time and effort, and created a polyline that could be moved away and further modified into another part of the drawing. Generating Computer Numerical Control (CNC) tool paths from a mechanical part drawing is something for which this command is well suited. Boundary polylines are used later to automatically define hatch boundaries.

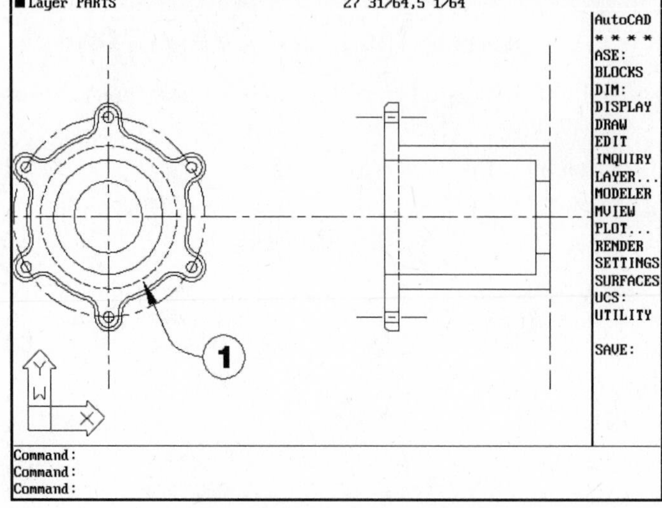

Figure 10.33:

The rlange Before BPOLY.

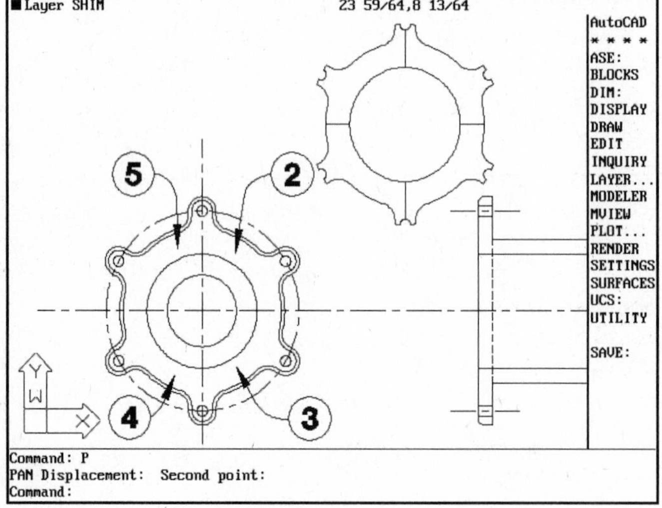

Figure 10.34:

The shims added to the flange drawing.

Summary

AutoCAD's drawing construction tools are as much a frame of mind as they are a framework of commands and options. In the course of constructing the mockup, you learned ways to drop construction lines, use a construction underlayer, and trace over construction lines. You also learned ways to use point filters—combining them with object snaps to create a section view.

There is never only one way to build an AutoCAD drawing. In fact, the opposite is true—you always can find other ways to build the same drawing. The trick is to find the methods that work most intuitively and efficiently for you.

You can plan ahead and save many unnecessary steps, and you can recycle entities to save erasing and drawing again. Try to envision well in advance the commands you are going to use. If you can visualize the construction technique ahead of time, your drawing productivity increases dramatically.

You can use point filters and construction lines to line up entities, and you can use construction lines for center lines, base lines and lines to align large numbers of points. You can use point filters for entity alignments, and you can use object snaps to help pick filtered points. Set up one or more layers for your construction lines. Construction lines do not have to be linear—use arcs and circles for angular or curved tracing. A few extra construction lines can make your drawing life easier.

You can use the UNDO command to protect your work sequences and REDO can rescue—but only immediately after an UNDO. Marks and Groups help control undos and make going back easier. Watch out for PLOT when you plan to undo. Going back to a mark is no substitute for saving regularly. Frequent saves are still the best way to protect your drawing file.

Would it be useful if you could save the contents of the selection set and use it as a rubber stamp whenever you need it? You can—with blocks, which is the topic of the next chapter.

11

Grouping Entities into Blocks

In this chapter, you learn how to create, store, and use blocks. The process of grouping entities into blocks enables you to repeat them easily and efficiently in one or more drawing files and to make them into permanent symbols in a symbol library.

You also learn to work with *external reference files (xrefs)*, which are similar to blocks. Xrefs make work-group drafting (in which several people work on different parts of the same drawing) simple and less error-prone—xrefs are the key to effective distributed design. Externally-referenced drawing files, when attached to a master drawing as an xref entity, become visible in that drawing without adding their data to the master drawing file. Xrefs are more efficient than blocks, and they automatically update drawings when changes are made. (Xrefs are examined as a separate topic following the section on blocks.)

Using Block Parts, Symbols, and Features

Figure 11.1 illustrates an entire town that was created from different types of drawing blocks. *Blocks* group individual entities together and treat them as one object. Symbols and drawing parts are typical candidates for such groups (see fig. 11.2). *Parts*, such as a car or desk, represent real objects, drawn full-size or at one-unit scale. *Symbols*, such as section bubbles, electrical receptacles, or welding symbols, are symbolic objects, which you can scale appropriately for plot size.

Figure 11.1:

The Autotown drawing with simple and complex blocks.

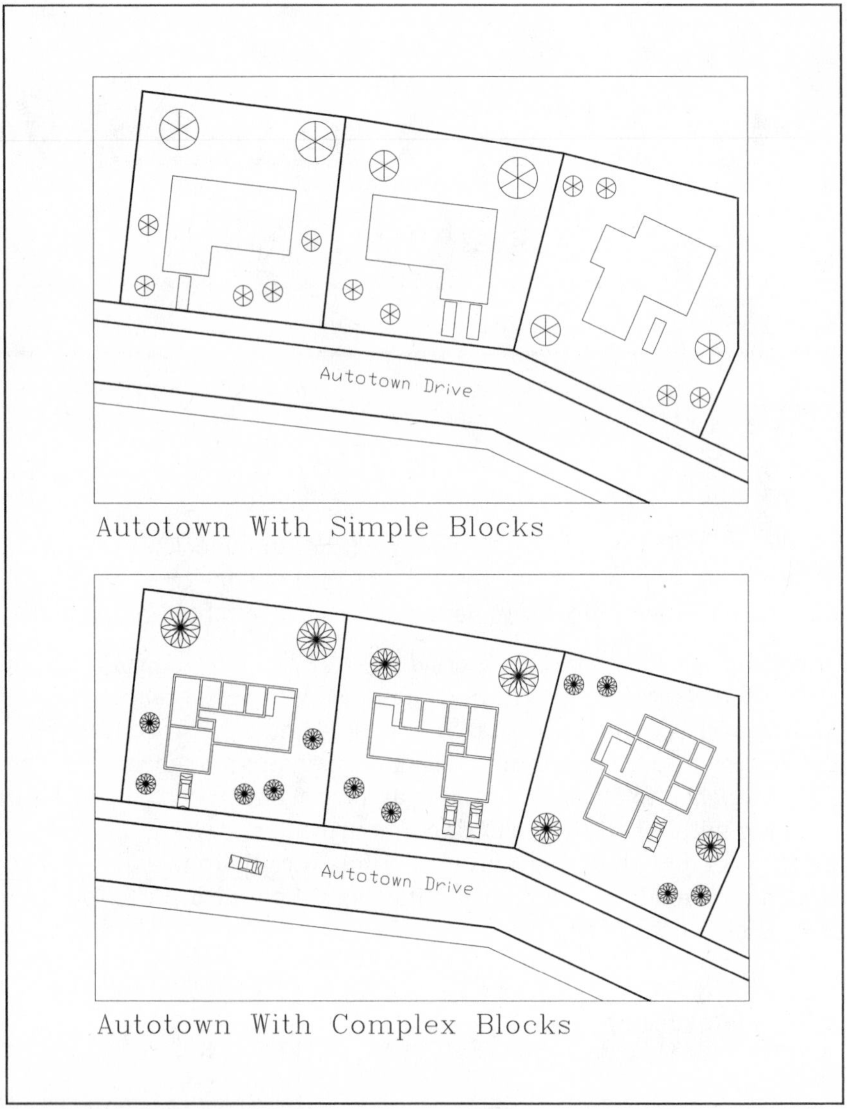

Autotown Drive

Autotown With Simple Blocks

Autotown Drive

Autotown With Complex Blocks

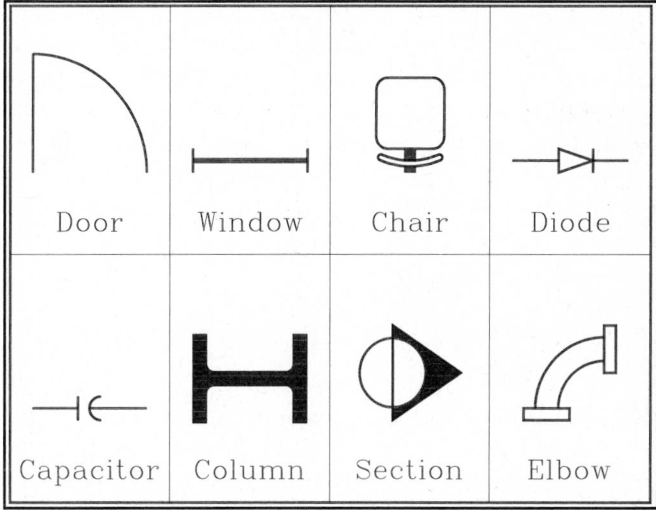

Figure 11.2:

Some common symbols and parts.

To move or copy symbol objects as individual drawing entities, you collect the individual entities into a selection set. As drawings become crowded, however, it becomes more difficult to select the entities you want. Selection is much easier if the entities are grouped together as a block. A block is saved with a name and can be reused in the same drawing later or reused in other drawings.

AutoCAD blocks enable you to operate on the group as a whole. Entities in blocks stick together; move one part of the block and the whole block moves. You can, of course, break up a block by exploding it if you need to edit it.

Block Speed and Versatility

Libraries of frequently used blocks speed the process of creating AutoCAD drawings. A *library* can consist of many individual drawing files, each used as a single block; a few files, each containing many blocks; or a combination of both. To build such a library takes time, but it dramatically reduces design time for future projects.

Besides their convenience, blocks provide additional drawing and editing benefits. A block insertion is faster than redrawing the same objects 20 times in 20 different drawings or copying those objects 20 times in the same drawing. When you insert blocks into your drawing file, you can change their scale and rotation. You can use one block, such as a window or bolt head, to represent many different sizes of the same object instead of using multiple instances of the block. This method enables you to build your drawing quickly by modifying simple blocks. You also can globally replace one block with another, revising an entire drawing with a single command.

Block Efficiency and Storage

One of the biggest advantages in using blocks is that they help minimize a drawing's file size. A smaller file takes less disk space and uses less memory when it loads. When you draw 100 lines, for example, you add 100 entities to your drawing. When you make a block containing 100 lines, AutoCAD creates a block definition containing 100 entities. This block of 100 lines is then stored as one entity in the drawing file. When you insert a block in your drawing, you add only one new entity—a reference to the block definition.

If you insert a block containing 100 lines into your drawing in 12 places, AutoCAD must store only 112 entities. These 112 entities include 100 lines in the block definition and 12 block references for the visible references. Without blocks, if you draw and copy 12 groups of 100 lines, you add 1200 entities to your drawing file. Blocks can save huge amounts of disk space.

Following the Block Exercises

You can use this chapter's exercises in two ways. First, the exercises in the early part of the chapter guide you through the basic block commands, including writing blocks to disk files and redefining blocks in a drawing. If you do not have the IA DISK, you need to create these blocks for the final Autotown exercise in Chapter 12.

Second, the section on xrefs guides you through creating, attaching, detaching, controlling, and converting xrefs. The exercises in this section are independent from the rest of the chapter.

In the following chapter, you apply the usage of these, as well as additional blocks in a techniques exercise.

Examining Block Editing Tools

The process of grouping entities into blocks is quite simple. You use the BLOCK command to create a block definition, INSERT to place a block reference in a drawing, and WBLOCK to store a block's entities as a separate drawing file on disk. You find INSERT, BLOCK, and WBLOCK with two other block commands, BASE and MINSERT, on the BLOCKS screen menu. In addition, INSERT can be found under the pull-down Draw menu.

This chapter uses commands from the screen menu; the next chapter explains using INSERT from the pull-down menu.

In addition to these block commands, you learn in this chapter about three additional commands that you use with blocks: EXPLODE, DIVIDE, and MEASURE. These three commands are located on the EDIT screen menus.

AutoCAD has another type of symbol entity, called a *shape*. Text is a special form of the shape feature. To learn more about shapes, see *Maximizing AutoCAD, Volume I* (New Riders Publishing).

Setting Up for Blocks

The next exercise helps you set up a drawing to create some simple blocks that you need for developing Autotown in the next chapter. "Autotown" is a simple site plan that encompasses three building lots along an elegant street known as "Autotown Drive." The drawing uses feet and decimal inches. Set your drawing limits at 360'×240'—a 36"×24" D-size sheet plotted at 1" = 10'.

Setting Up for the Blocks Exercise

Choose File, *then* New, *then* No Prototype, *and enter* `\IA\IABLOCKS`. *Set up your drawing as shown in table 11.1.*

Table 11.1
Blocks Drawing Settings

AXIS	*COORDS*	*GRID*	*SNAP*	*UCSICON*
OFF	ON	10'	6"	OR
UNITS	Engineering, 2 decimal places, decimal degrees, default all other settings.			
LIMITS	0,0 to 360', 240'			

Your current layer should be layer 0. Before you can do anything, you need to draw some objects (on layer 0) that will be made into blocks.

Making Objects for Blocks

The first objects you make for Autotown are symbols of a car and a tree. To draw these symbols, issue the ZOOM command, and then use the Center option to zoom to the center of the screen with a height of 15'. Draw the car by using the dimensions shown in figure 11.3.

Zoom by using the Center option below the car with a height of 8", set snap to .25, and then draw a 1"-diameter tree, as shown in figure 11.4

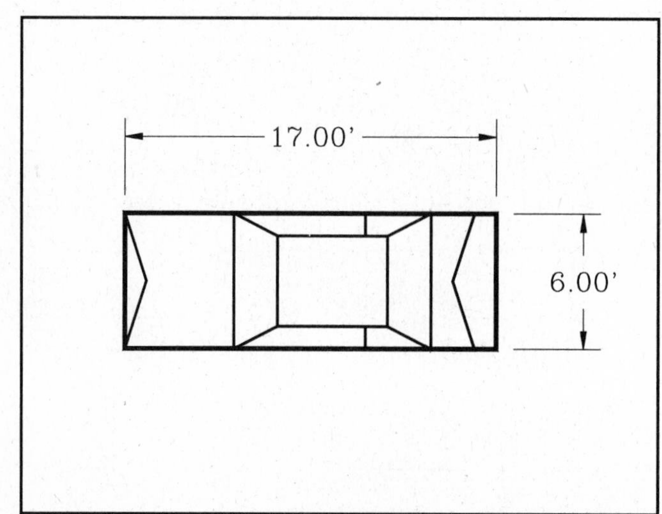

Figure 11.3:
A car for the block exercise.

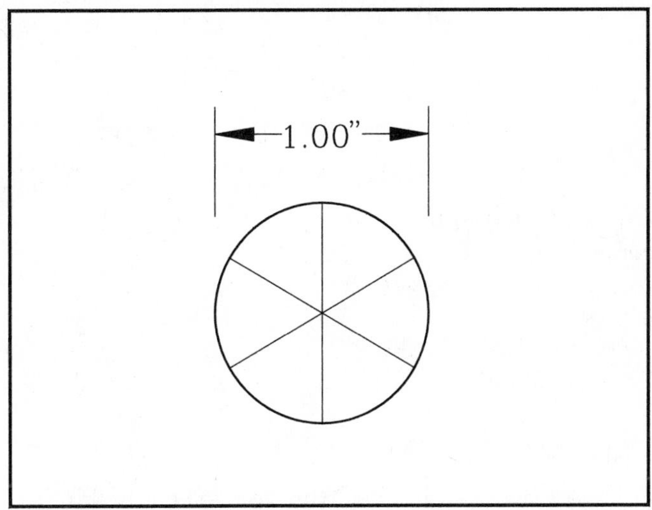

Figure 11.4:
A tree for the block exercise.

The car is drawn and inserted full-size, but the tree is drawn small (one unit in diameter), so that it can be scaled easily to make different sizes of trees when you insert it.

The BLOCK Command

Turn the car and tree into blocks by following the steps in the next exercise. When you execute BLOCK, AutoCAD first prompts you for a block name. Name the blocks TREE1 and CAR2. AutoCAD then prompts you for an insertion *base point*, which is the reference point that you later use to put the block in a new location. After you identify a base point, select the entities that form the blocks.

Using Block To Create Your First Blocks

`Command:` *From the screen menu, choose* BLOCKS, *then* BLOCK:	Issues the BLOCK command
`Block name (or ?):` **`TREE1`** ↵	Specifies the block name TREE1
`Insertion base point:` *Pick the center of the tree*	
`Select objects:` *Select all the trees (see fig. 11.5)*	
`Select objects:` *Press Enter*	Stores the block

`Command:` *Choose* View, *then* Zoom, *and then* Previous	
`Command:` *Choose* Settings, *then* Drawing Aids, *and set* Snap *back to 6"*	
`Command:` **`BLOCK`**↵	
`Block name (or ?):` **`CAR2`**↵	Specifies the block name CAR2
`Insertion base point:` *Use the MID object snap and pick the front of the car at ① (see fig. 11.6)*	
`Select objects:` *Use a crossing window to select all the car's entities*	
`Select objects:` *Press Enter*	Ends object selection

The blocks are displayed in figures 11.5 and 11.6.

You now should have a blank drawing. After you selected each drawing's entities, they disappeared. The entities are not lost; they are stored safely in memory as two blocks named CAR2 and TREE1.

AutoCAD keeps track of all blocks in an invisible part of the drawing file called the *block table*. When you used the BLOCK command, it created a definition of the car and the tree and stored the definitions in the block table (see fig. 11.7). Each block definition defines the entities associated with the block name. When you save the drawing, the block definitions are stored as part of the drawing file.

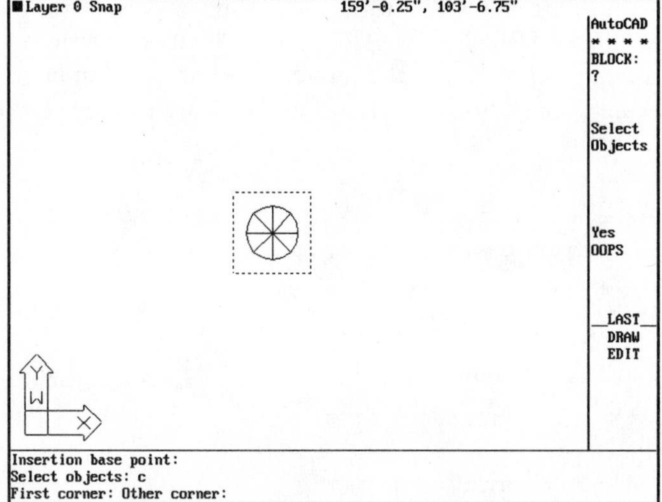

Figure 11.5:
The tree block.

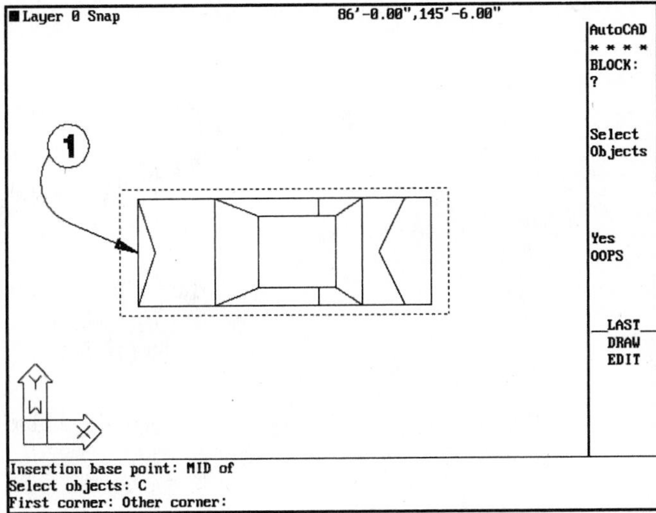

Figure 11.6:

The car block.

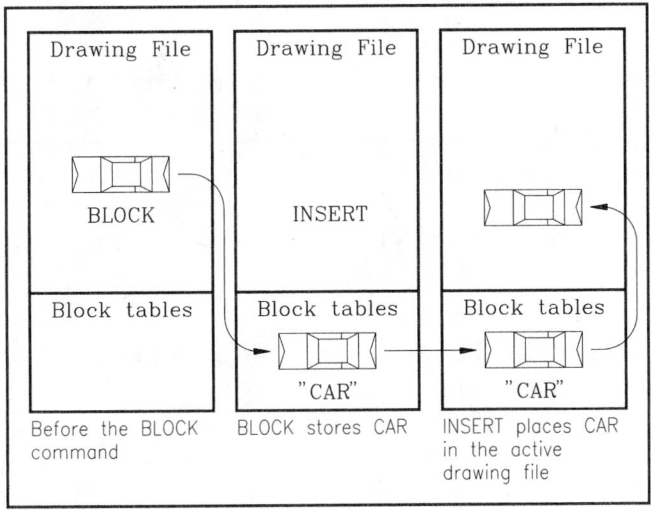

Figure 11.7:

BLOCK and INSERT with a block table area.

Using the INSERT Command

Leave the tree in storage for now (in memory). To get the car back, use the INSERT command to insert the car from the block table into the active part of the drawing file. First, AutoCAD wants to know which block you want to insert. If you respond with a question mark, AutoCAD lists the names of all the blocks currently defined in the table area of your drawing. The following steps look at these names.

Using INSERT ? To List Block Names

`Command:` *From the screen menu, choose* AutoCAD	
`Command:` *From the screen menu, Choose* BLOCKS, *then* INSERT:	Issues the INSERT command
`Block name (or ?):` *From the screen menu, choose* ?	Specifies the List option
`Block(s) to list <*>:` *Press Enter*	Displays the defined blocks in the text window

```
Defined blocks.
CAR2
TREE1
User     Unnamed
Blocks   References
   2         0
```

`Command:` *Press F1*	Switches AutoCAD from text mode back to graphics mode

In addition to selecting the INSERT: item from the screen menu, you can issue INSERT by entering INSERT at the `Command:` prompt.

Using INSERT To Insert the Car Block

Use Zoom with the left option, picking the left corner at 168',110' with a height of 40'	
`Command:` **`INSERT`** ↵	
`Block name:` **`CAR2`** ↵	
`Insertion point:` *Drag the car and pick at 174',118'*	
`X scale factor <1>/Corner/XYZ:` *Press Enter*	Defaults the X scale factor to 1:1
`Y scale factor <default=X>:` *Press Enter*	Defaults the Y scale factor to 1:1
`Rotation angle <0.00>:` *Press Enter*	Inserts the car with 0 rotation (see fig. 11.8)

Next, you copy the car.

`Command:` *Choose* Construct, *then* Copy	Copies the car
`Select objects:` *Select the car and press Enter*	
`<Base point or displacement>/ Multiple:` **`@`**↵	Specifies the last point
`Second point of displacement:` **`@30'<0`**↵	Copies the car with a polar displacement (see fig. 11.9)

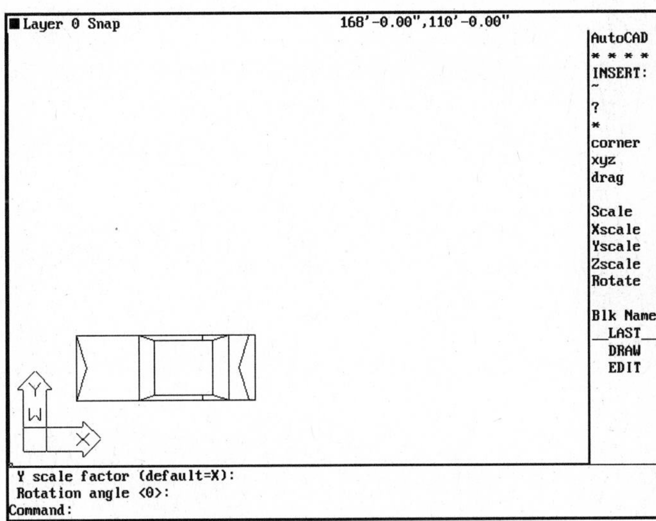

Figure 11.8:

The inserted car.

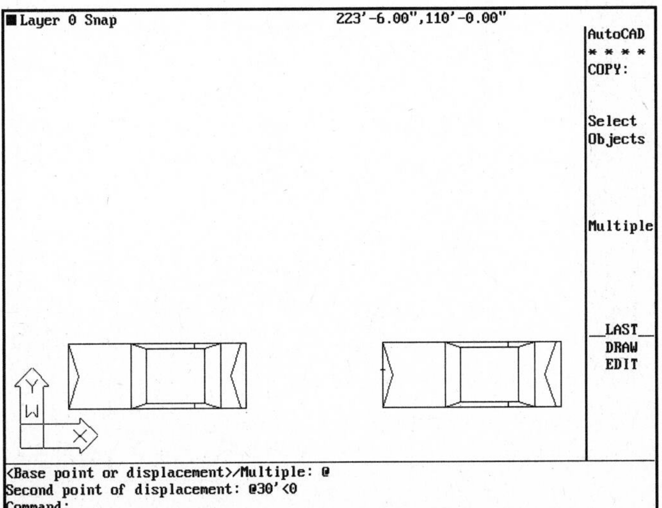

Figure 11.9:

The copied car.

Your car returns to the screen after you insert CAR2, but the car you see is not the same individual entity as your original car. When you copied the car, you selected it with a single object pick. After you insert a block in your drawing, you can move and copy it as a single entity.

What events occurred when the block was inserted? INSERT did three things: it created a block reference to the block definition, it left the original block definition in the block table area, and it drew an image representing the entities that make up the block definition.

You can insert not only blocks that you created in the current drawing but also any drawing file saved on disk. A previously saved drawing inserts as a block in the current drawing. The saved drawing's origin becomes the insertion base point, unless you set another base point by using the Base command (discussed later in this chapter).

The process of inserting a drawing creates a new block definition containing all the entities of that drawing. If AutoCAD cannot find a block that you know you have on disk, check its location against the list of directories (see Appendix A) that AutoCAD searches for files.

Scaling and Rotating Block Insertions

When you insert a block reference, you can enter different values for the block's scale and rotation. You can scale by entering X and Y scale factors. The default scale prompt for the Y factor uses the X factor you enter to simplify the process of scaling your drawing symbol to a 1:1 ratio. You can use different X and Y scales by entering different responses (the XYZ option is for 3D control). You also can give an angle of rotation by entering an angle or by dragging the rotation and picking a point.

Try two modified car block insertions. First, insert your car by using different X and Y scales. Use the values given in the following exercise to elongate the car to make it look like a stretch limousine. Second, insert another car at an angle. If you make a mistake, use UNDO or ERASE LAST to remove the block insertion.

Using INSERT with Scale and Rotation Changes

Command: **INSERT**↵

Block name: **CAR2**↵

Insertion point: *Pick at 174',128'*

X Scale factor <1>/Corner/XYZ: **1.5**↵ — Applies an X scale of 1.5 to the block

Y Scale factor <default=X>: **1**↵ — Keeps the Y scale at 1

Rotation angle <0.00>: *Press Enter* — Accepts the default rotation of 0.00 (see fig. 11.10)

Next, you use INSERT and leave the scale factor at 1, but rotate the car 45 degrees.

Command: **INSERT**↵

Block name (or ?)<CAR2>: **CAR2**↵

Insertion point: *Pick at 205',128'*

X Scale factor <1>/Corner: *Press Enter*

Y Scale factor <default=X>: *Press Enter*

Rotation angle <0.00>: **45**↵ — Applies a rotation angle of 45 degrees (see fig. 11.11)

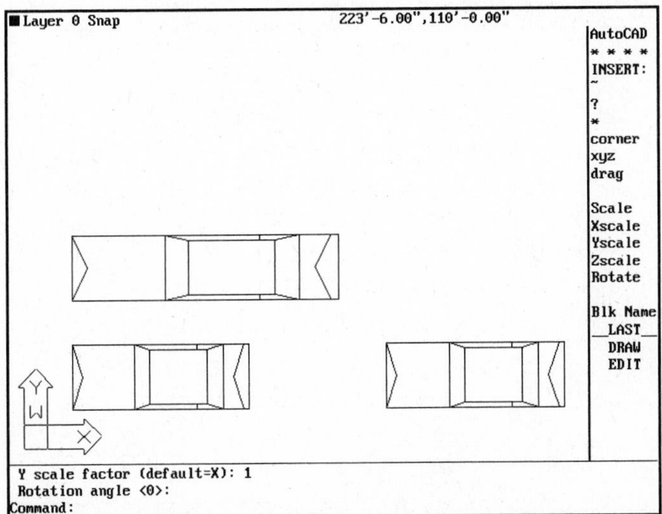

Figure 11.10:

A stretched limousine.

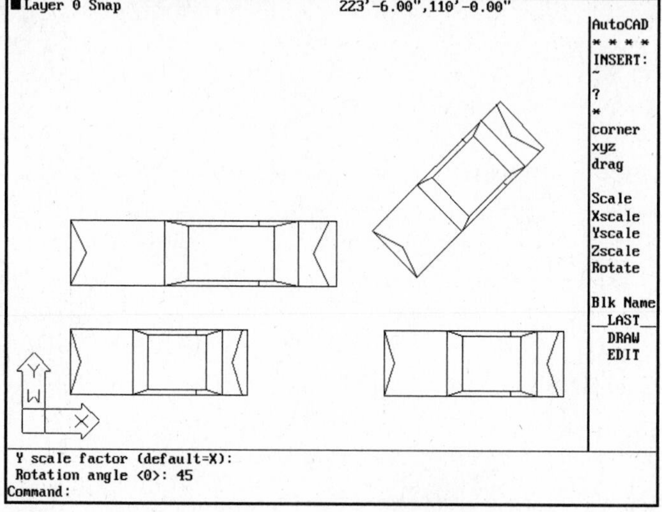

Figure 11.11:

An angled car.

What happened when you inserted blocks this time? The INSERT command again made references to the block table, which was modified by the scale and rotation values. These modifications are visible in the image of the car in the active drawing (see fig. 11.12).

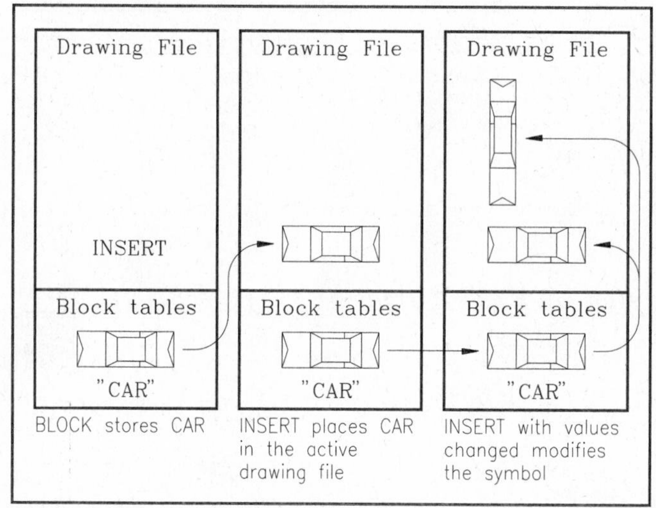

Figure 11.12:

A car drawing inserted with changes.

A handy trick for inserting objects that normally are horizontal or vertical is to use your pointer to pick a rotation angle with ortho (Ctrl-O) turned on. This method limits the rotation angle to 0, 90, 180, or 270 degrees.

While entering the scale values in the preceding exercise, you may have noticed a second option, called Corner. When you use the Corner option to enter your scale values, you can scale the block by indicating the X and Y size of a rectangle. The insertion point is the first corner of the rectangle. Drag and pick the other corner to determine scale. AutoCAD uses the width as the X scale and the height as the Y scale. The width and height are measured in current drawing units.

You do not need to type a C to use corner point scaling—if you move the mouse at the X scale prompt, you see the block being dynamically scaled. The Corner option is used in menus because it limits scale input to corner point-picking and issues an `Other corner:` prompt.

Whether you use keyboard scale entry or the Corner option, you can specify negative scale factors to mirror the block's insertion, turn it upside-down, or both.

Be careful with corner point scaling. The dragged scale is relative to one unit (1") square, and it works well if your block definition is about one unit in size. If your block definition is many drawing units in size (like CAR2), however, even a small rectangle gives a large scale factor.

When you use a corner scale input, use snap or object snap to control accuracy. Corner scale input is most useful when inserting unit scale blocks, such as parts (see figs. 11.13 and 11.14).

Using Unit Scale To Make Flexible Blocks

At first, you may think the capability to scale and rotate blocks during insertion is an option used only occasionally. However, these features are valuable parts of the INSERT command that are used over and over.

The trick of effective block scaling is to create your parts in a 1×1-unit cell. When you insert a block, you can then stretch or shrink it. The block is good at any scale with any insertion-scale factor. You can, for example, store a door or window part so that the endpoints are on the left and right edges of

the unit cell. You can then insert the symbol with appropriate scale factors to fill the area you need. If you draw a unit block at 1" and you want to insert it scaled to 3', remember that you use a scale factor of 36, not 3.

To illustrate the versatility of one-unit blocks, insert the tree in the following steps and scale it down to a bush.

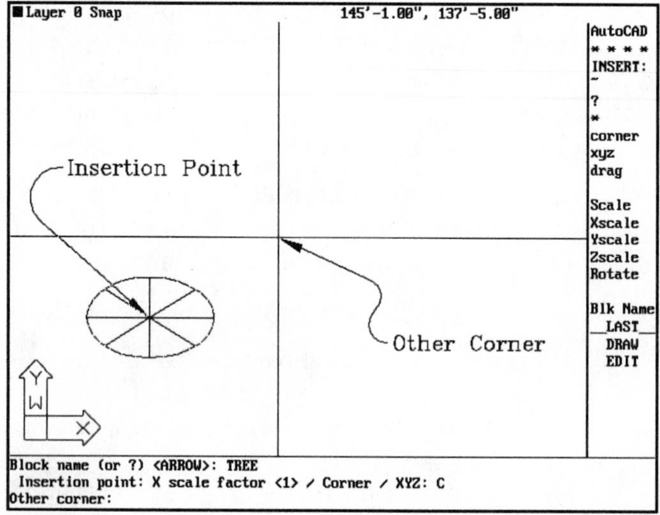

Figure 11.13:

A one-unit tree block inserted with corner scaling.

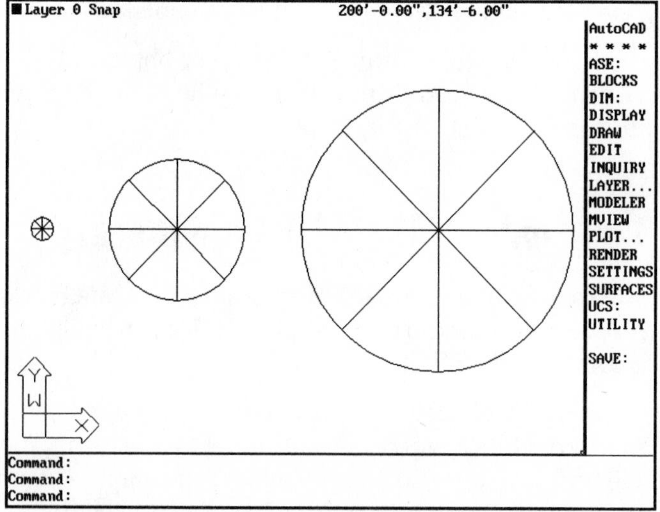

Figure 11.14:

A one-unit tree inserted at 12", 6', and 12'.

Using Corner Point Scaling to Insert a One-Unit Block

`Command:` *From the screen menu, choose* BLOCKS, *then* INSERT:

`INSERT Block name (or ?)<CAR2>:` **`TREE1↵`**

`Insertion point:` *Pick any clear point*

`X scale factor <1> / Corner/XYZ:` **`C↵`** Specifies the Corner option

`Other corner:` *Drag it to a good bush shape and size, then pick other corner*

`Rotation angle <0>:` *Press Enter*

Next you create a block called BUSH, which you can use again later.

`Command:` **`BLOCK↵`**

`BLOCK Block name (or ?):` **`BUSH↵`**

`Insertion base point:` *Pick the center of the bush*

`Select objects:` *Pick the bush*

`Select objects:` *Press Enter*

One-unit blocks are extremely useful. You can create libraries full of one-unit parts and then insert them at different sizes, depending on the situation. Do not create whole libraries full of different sizes of windows or bolts—create a single one-unit part, and then insert it at whatever scale you need.

Using Preset Scales

You have inserted blocks by specifying an insertion point, a scale, and an angle. It is possible to preset the scale factor and rotation angle before selecting the insertion point. When you preset the block's scale and angle, insertion point dragging is suspended until you finish setting those options. You then see the block's scale and angle as you drag it to pick the insertion point.

Try making one more stretch limousine by using preset values.

Using INSERT with Preset Scales

Command: **INSERT**↵	
Command: Block name: **CAR2**↵	
Insertion point: **X**↵	Specifies the X scale preset option
X scale factor: **1.3**↵	Presets the X scale value
Insertion point: **Y**↵	Specifies the Y scale preset option
Y scale factor: **1**↵	Presets the Y scale value
Insertion point: **R**↵	Specifies the rotation preset option
Rotation angle: **180**↵	Presets the rotation angle value
Insertion point: *Drag the car around, then pick at 196',138'*	

The newly inserted car appears in figure 11.15.

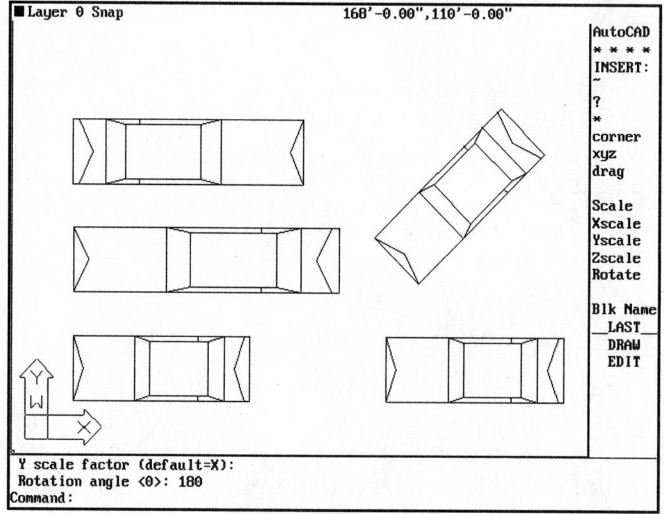

Figure 11.15:
A stretch limousine inserted with a preset scale.

Preset Scale and Rotation Options

Several options for presetting values are available, but they are not shown as prompts during the INSERT command. The following list displays every option.

- **Scale** and **PScale.** These options prompt for scale factor—preset to X, Y, and Z axes.
- **Xscale** and **PXscale.** These options preset only an X-scale factor.
- **Yscale** and **PYscale.** These options preset only a Y-scale factor.
- **Zscale** and **PZscale.** These options preset only a Z-scale factor.
- **Rotate** and **PRotate.** These options preset the rotation angle. Enter this value from the keyboard or by picking two points.

Type the first one or two characters of the preset option to tell AutoCAD what you want to preset.

The letter P stands for preliminary, not preset. Options prefixed with a P establish a preliminary scale and rotation value to aid in insertion. After the insertion point is selected, the normal prompts are displayed so that you can change the preset values.

Preset scale factors have limitations. You cannot mix fixed presets (such as Xscale) with preliminary presets (such as PYscale). If you try to mix them, the preliminary presets become fixed, and AutoCAD does not prompt you again for their values.

Preset options work best when you use them in custom menu macros. Macros can apply preset options transparently, which simplifies the task of placing the Block by using dragging in the INSERT command.

Inserting Blocks as Individual Entries

You use the BLOCK command to collect entities into a single group. When you insert the block in a drawing file, the insertion is a single entity. When you erase a block, the whole block (but not its stored definition) is erased. The same holds true for moving and copying blocks.

When is a block not a block? A block is not a block when it is **Inserted* or exploded.

After you insert a block, you may want to individually edit the different entities that make up the block. As you learned earlier, however, individual entities lose their identities when they are stored as a block.

What if you want to edit a block after you insert it? To edit individual pieces of a block after insertion, AutoCAD provides an option for the INSERT command. Place an asterisk (*) in front of a block name when you insert it to tell AutoCAD to break the block back into its individual entities. This is commonly called an *insert-star* or *star-insertion*. A star-insertion (denoted as **insertion*) does not insert a block reference; it duplicates the original entities of the block definition. Unlike using COPY to duplicate entities, a *insertion enables you to modify the scale and rotation of the copy.

The insertion of a separate drawing file into the current drawing creates a block in the current drawing unless the *insertion option is used. The *insertion option inserts only individual entities without creating a block.

Zoom in to your drawing in the next exercise and insert the car in the clear area of the drawing. To prove that the new car is really a collection of separate entities, change it into a sports car. Use some editing commands on the *inserted car and create a car as complex as you like, making sure it differs from the original. The car is used in a later exercise.

Using *INSERT* To Break Blocks into Components

Zoom in to a height of 15' in a clear area.

`Command:` **`INSERT`** ↵	
`Block name:` **`*CAR2`** ↵	Inserts the block as individual entities
`Insertion point:` *Pick a point near the left of the screen, then choose the default scale and rotation*	
`Command:` *Choose* Modify, *then* Erase, *then* Select, *and erase the windshield line and two lines on the trunk and hood*	
`Command:` *Choose* Modify, *then* Stretch, *and stretch the rear glass toward the back to make the roof smaller*	
`Command:` *Choose* Draw, *then* Arc, *then* 3 Point *and draw a new windshield*	
`Command:` *Choose* Construct, *then* Fillet, *and use the FILLET command to round the corners of the car with a 6" radius*	
`Command:` *Choose* View, *then* Zoom, *then* Previous	
`Command:` *Choose* File, *then* Save	Saves the file

The *inserted car block is shown in figure 11.16. The newly created sports car appears in figure 11.17.

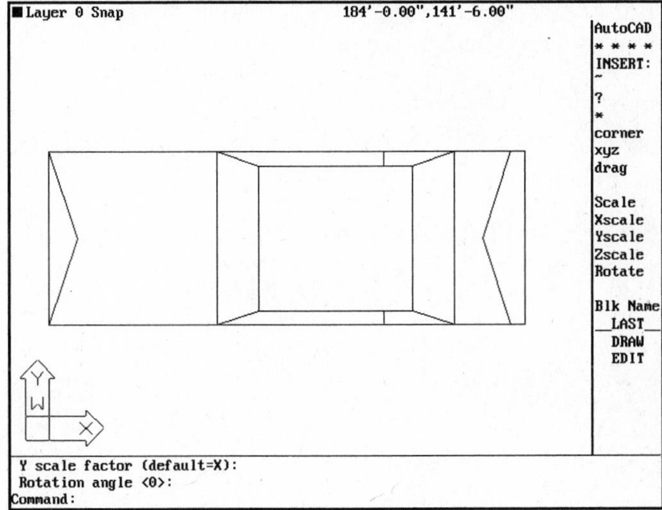

Figure 11.16:

The *inserted car.

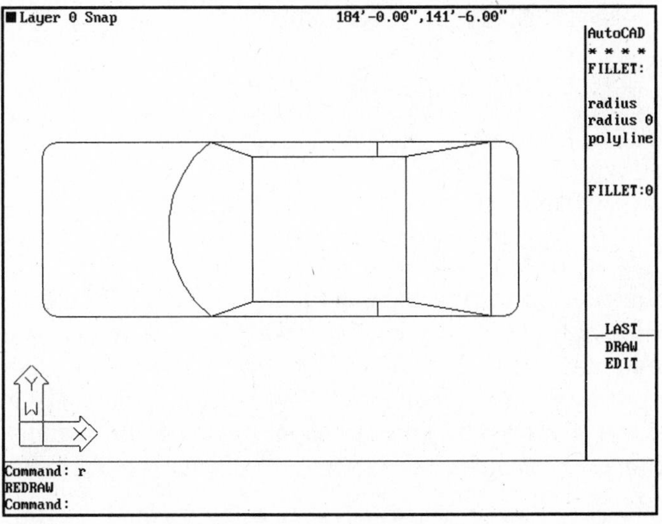

Figure 11.17:

A sports car.

When you use the star option to insert a block, AutoCAD restricts your flexibility in rescaling the objects as they are placed. You only can specify a single, positive scale factor in the * mode. Negative and unequal X and Y scales are not allowed. You can, however, rescale your *inserted blocks with STRETCH, SCALE, EXTEND, and other editing commands after insertion.

If you place a complex *inserted block in the wrong place, use UNDO to get rid of all the pieces.

What if you want to modify a block after it has already been inserted? You explode it.

Using the EXPLODE Command

You can use another command similar to INSERT to modify blocks that have already been inserted. The EXPLODE command separates a block back into its original entities. To test this command, try exploding the first car you inserted on the bottom left of your drawing.

Using EXPLODE To Explode a Block

`Command:` *From the screen menu, choose* EDIT, *then* EXPLODE	
`Select object:` *Pick the first car in the lower left corner*	Redraws the block as it explodes
`Select object:` *Press Enter*	

The exploded car pieces look identical to the image before the explosion. Some components of the drawing, such as byblock, color, linetype, and layer assignments, may change because they can come undone when you explode a block. If an exploded block includes nested blocks, only the outer level of the nest is broken up by the explosion. (Nesting and byblock properties are examined a little later in this section's discussion of block properties.)

Some entities cannot be exploded. You cannot explode an *inserted block, for example, because it already is exploded. You cannot explode a block that has been inserted by the MINSERT command, mirrored blocks, or a block with different X-, Y-, and Z-scale factors.

Using the MINSERT Command

A block is more than a block when the MINSERT command is used to insert it. Suppose you want to put many cars (or desks, printed circuit board drill locations, or other symbols you may have stored as blocks) in your drawing. You can insert one copy of the block and then use ARRAY to make several columns and rows.

The MINSERT command provides another option. Think of MINSERT (Multiple INSertion) as a single command that combines inserts and rectangular arrays. (You cannot use polar arrays with MINSERT.) MINSERT differs from ARRAY—each entity generated by ARRAY is an individual entity in the drawing file—it can be edited, deleted, copied, or even arrayed individually. Each component of the block that MINSERT generates is part of a single inserted block. You cannot edit the individual component blocks.

Use MINSERT in the following steps to fill your drawing with cars. Continue the steps by panning to the right side of your drawing to access a clear space. After you insert the cars by using MINSERT, use ERASE with the Last option to get rid of them.

Using MINSERT To Insert a Block

`Command:` *Choose* View, *then* Pan, *pick a point and specify a displacement of @60'<180*	
`Command:` *From the screen menu, choose* BLOCKS, *then* MINSERT:	Issues the MINSERT command
`Block name (or ?) <*CAR2>:` **CAR2** ↵	
`Insertion point:` *Pick a point in the lower left corner*	
`X Scale factor <1>/Corner/XYZ:` *Press Enter*	
`Y Scale factor <default=X>:` *Press Enter*	
`Rotation angle <0>:` *Press Enter*	
`Number of rows (---) <1>:` **4** ↵	
`Number of columns (|||) <1>:` **2** ↵	
`Unit cell or distance between rows (---):` **8'** ↵	
`Distance between columns (|||):` **19'** ↵	Displays eight cars, arranged in two columns (see fig. 11.18)
`Command:` *Choose* Modify, *then* Erase, *then* Last *to see that all the cars are tied to one another*	

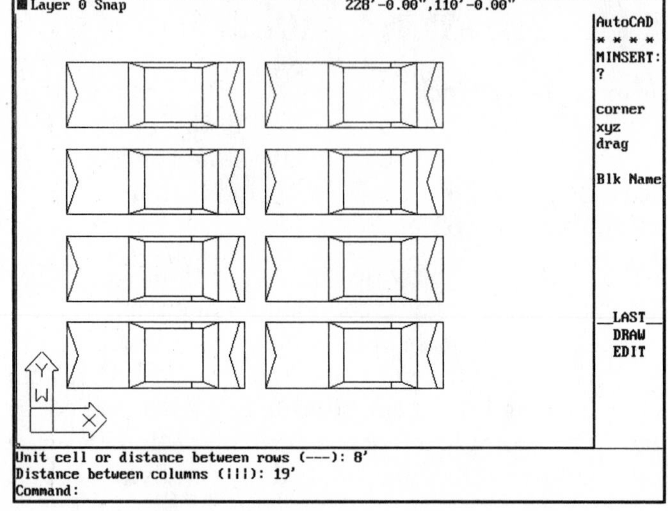

Figure 11.18:

Some cars drawn with MINSERT.

When you specify a rotation in MINSERT, the array is rotated and the individual blocks maintain their position in the array.

MINSERT is an efficient way to place multiple copies of a block in a drawing file. In an array, every entity occurrence takes up disk space. If you insert by using MINSERT, the block reference occurs only once and includes information about the number of rows, columns, and spacing of elements.

Two additional commands, DIVIDE and MEASURE, can be used to insert multiple copies of a block.

Using the DIVIDE Command

Blocks often need to be placed in a drawing at set intervals. You can use the DIVIDE command to divide an entity, such as a polyline, into parts of equal length, and to then insert a block at the division points. DIVIDE does not actually break the polyline (or other entity); it marks only the divisions. You can divide lines, arcs, circles, and polylines.

In the steps that follow, learn the use of the DIVIDE command by creating a new car block from CAR2 in the same space in which you erased the cars that were inserted with the MINSERT command. Call this new car block

CAR3 and change its insertion point so that the cars are set back from the polyline when they are inserted. Next, create a polyline. The direction in which you draw the polyline determines the side in which the cars are inserted. Finally, use DIVIDE to divide the polyline into five segments and then insert the new car blocks.

Using DIVIDE To Insert a Car Block

`Command:` **`INSERT`**↵	
`Block name:` **`CAR2`**↵	
`Insertion point:` *Pick a point in the center of the drawing and accept the default scales*	
`Rotation angle <0>:` **`-90`**↵	Rotates the car 90 degrees
`Command:` **`BLOCK`**↵	
`Block name (or ?):` **`CAR3`**↵	
`Insertion base point:` **`@0,3'`**↵	Places the insert point 3' in front of the car
`Select objects:` **`L`**↵	
`1 found.`	
`Select objects:` *Press Enter*	Creates CAR3 as a nested block containing CAR2
`Command:` *Choose* Draw, *then* Polyline, *then* 2D *and draw a polyline from 275',133' to @22'<180 to @ 17'<–90*	Draws the polyline (see fig. 11.19)
`Command:` *Choose* Construct, *then* Fillet, *and fillet the corner with a radius of 12'*	

Next, you divide the block along the polyline.

`Command:` *Choose* Construct, *then* Divide	
`Select object to divide:` *Pick the polyline*	Specifies the object to be divided
`<Number of segments>/Block:` **`B`**↵	Allows a block to be named to insert during the divide
`Block name to insert:` **`CAR3`**↵	Specifies the block to be inserted
`Align block with object? <Y>` *Press Enter*	Aligns the block to the orientation of the polyline
`Number of segments:` **`5`**↵	Specifies the number of blocks to be inserted

After you finish, your drawing should have four cars, one between each of the five segments (see fig. 11.20). Each inserted block is a separate entity.

You can divide a line or polyline even if you do not use blocks. The DIVIDE command inserts point entities that you can snap to by using NODe. You can make them display more visibly by using Pdmode and Pdsize.

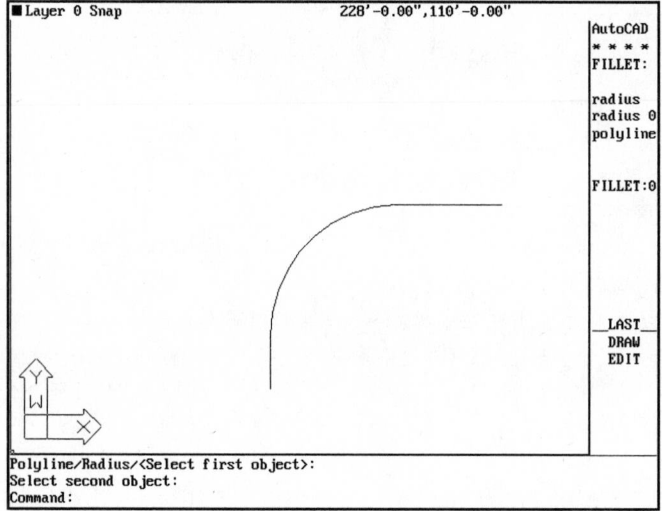

Figure 11.19:

A polyline for DIVIDE.

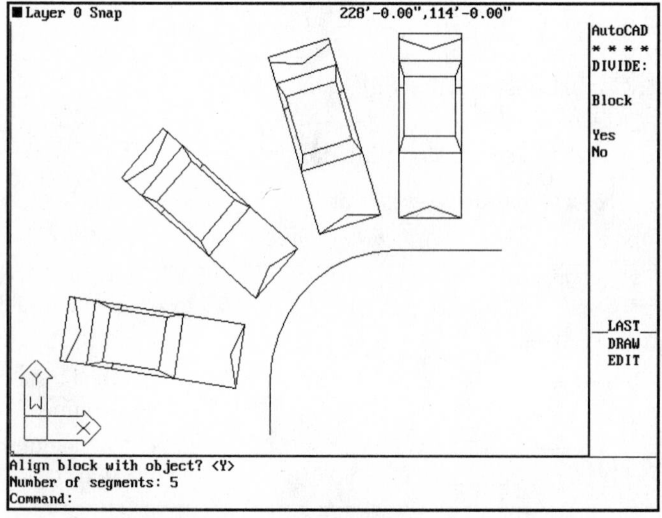

Figure 11.20:

Some cars inserted with DIVIDE.

When you use DIVIDE to insert blocks (or points), AutoCAD saves the inserted entities as a Previous selection set. You can select the group again for editing by using the Previous selection set option. If, for example, you want to change the layer of the cars, you can select all of them by using the Previous option when prompted to select objects in CHPROP.

You can use a construction entity for your block inserts, and then erase it after you perform your DIVIDE (or MEASURE) insert.

DIVIDE (and MEASURE) do not enable you to scale a block. If you want to insert the original one-unit size trees, for example, you create a larger block and insert it or rescale each block after it is inserted.

Using the MEASURE Command

The MEASURE command works like DIVIDE, but, instead of dividing an entity into equal parts, MEASURE enables you to specify the segment length. After you specify a block name to insert and a segment length (either by entering a value or by picking two points), AutoCAD inserts the block at the segment-length intervals.

Are you getting tired of placing cars in your drawing? Try adding some bushes to the parking area by following the next exercise.

Using MEASURE To Insert BUSH Blocks

`Command:` *Choose* Construct, *then* Measure	To measure the bush along the polyline
`Select object to measure:` *Pick the polyline*	
<Segment length>/Block: **B**↵	Prompts for the block's name
`Block name to insert:` **BUSH**↵	Specifies the block to be inserted
Align block with object? <Y>: *Press Enter*	
`Segment length:` **60**↵	Places a bush every five feet

As figure 11.21 shows, your enhanced parking area is beginning to look more realistic.

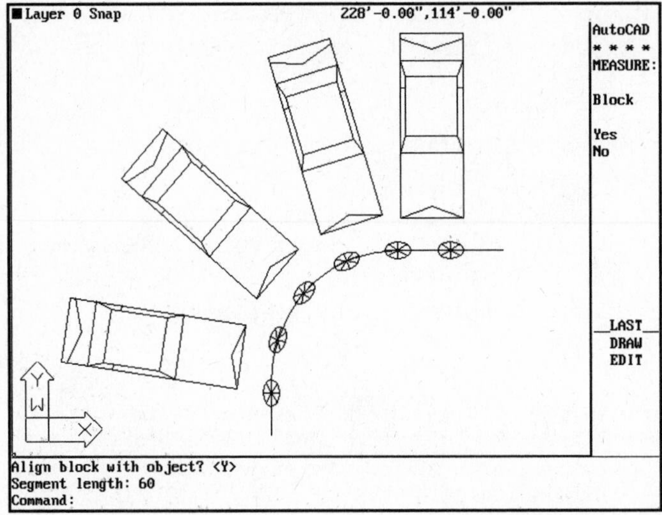

Figure 11.21: Some bushes inserted by using the MEASURE command.

Like DIVIDE, MEASURE works with blocks or points; it forms a Previous selection set that you can use for subsequent editing.

Using the WBLOCK Command

So far, the blocks you have created and stored in the block table have been self-contained in the current drawing file. The blocks are stored in this drawing when you save it or end it. Whenever you work in this drawing file, these block definitions are available. Sooner or later, however, you need to copy blocks from one drawing file to another drawing.

Sending Blocks to Disk as Drawing Files

WBLOCK enables you to save any block in your current drawing as a separate drawing file on disk. You also can use WBLOCK to select a set of entities and write them to a separate drawing file without making them into a block in the current drawing. Any block or selection set can be stored as a separate drawing file, and any drawing file can be inserted as a block.

The drawing file created by WBLOCK is a normal drawing that contains the current drawing settings and the entities that make up the block definition. The entities are normal drawing entities and are not defined as a block in the new file.

Store CAR2 as a separate file called CAR2.DWG and store TREE1 as the file TREE1.DWG.

Using WBLOCK To Write a Block to Disk

`Command:` *From the screen menu, choose* BLOCKS, *then* WBLOCK:

Enter `CAR2`↵ *in the* **F**ile *edit box*	Names the new file
`Block name: =`↵	Specifies a block name equal to the file name

`Command: WBLOCK`↵

Enter `TREE1`↵ *in the* **F**ile *edit box*

`Block name: =`↵

If you have a block that you use often, use WBLOCK to save it to a disk file. Group these new symbols into library subdirectories to organize them.

To insert (or *INSERT) CAR2.DWG into another drawing file, use the INSERT command and specify the block by using its disk file name, CAR2. Figure 11.22 shows how this process works.

Using WBLOCK with Entity Selection To Create a File

You can make a block file without first creating a block. When the block name prompt appears, press Enter instead of giving an existing block name. You are prompted for an insertion-base point and object selection. You can use any of the standard object-selection techniques with WBLOCK to select items for storing to disk. When you finish and press Enter, the entities are copied to the disk file you specified.

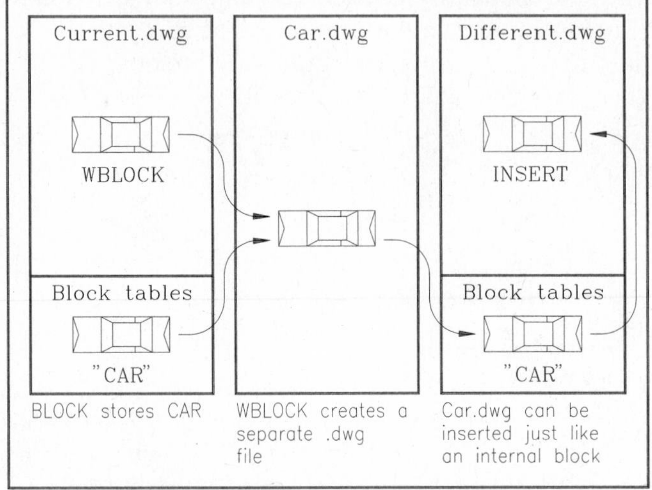

Figure 11.22:
WBLOCK and INSERT.

The entities are not defined as a block in the current drawing unless you also insert them. The drawing file created by WBLOCK is a normal drawing, containing the selected entities and current drawing settings. The entities are not defined as a block in the new file.

In the following exercise, use WBLOCK to store the sports car to the file called MY-CAR. When you use BLOCK or WBLOCK, the selected entities are erased. You can use OOPS to restore them, just as you can use it to restore entities deleted by the ERASE command. After you create the drawing file, use UNDO or OOPS to bring the entities back.

Using Entity Selection to Create a Block Drawing File

Use Zoom Previous or Dynamic, or pan to see the sports car.

`Command:` **`WBLOCK`** ↵

Enter **`MT-CAR`** *in the* File *edit box*

`Block name:` *Press Enter* — Prompts you to select the objects for the new file

`Insertion base point:` *Pick the car's front midpoint*

`Select objects:` *Select all the sports car's entities*

`Select objects:` *Press Enter*

`Command:` **`OOPS`** ↵ — Returns the car to the drawing

Just as you can insert an entire drawing file as a block, you can use WBLOCK to store an entire current drawing to disk as a new file.

Remember that the drawing file created by WBLOCK is like any other drawing file. WBLOCK does not create any blocks—it creates a drawing file that contains the entities that you select or that make up an existing block.

Using WBLOCK* To Write Most of a Drawing

If you respond to the WBLOCK block name prompt with an asterisk, it writes most of the entire current drawing to a disk file. AutoCAD does not write any unused named things that are referenced by entities, such as blocks, text styles, layers, or linetypes. Drawing-environment settings for UCSs, views, and viewport configurations, however, are written.

Using WBLOCK* To Write All of a Drawing

`Command:` **`WBLOCK`**↵	
Enter **`AUTOCITY`** *in the* File *edit box*	
`Block name:` **`*`**↵	Writes the drawing to a new file on disk

Like the PURGE command, WBLOCK* often is used to purge unused blocks. If you use WBLOCK* with the same file name as the current drawing, AutoCAD prompts if you want to replace it. If you answer Yes and then quit the current drawing, the current drawing is saved without any unused blocks. This trick is commonly called a *wblock star*. Be careful when you use WBLOCK* for this purpose; it also deletes unused layers, linetypes, and text styles.

Using the PURGE Command

As you work with blocks, you can build up extraneous blocks in the block table by inserting them and then later deleting them. Use the PURGE command to remove unused block definitions from the block table of the current drawing file.

PURGE only works in an editing session before you modify your drawing database, either by creating a new entity or by editing an existing entity. PURGE is selective and prompts you extensively. When you invoke this command, it provides information on the blocks stored in the block table area and asks you explicitly if you want to delete any of the listed blocks. You also can use PURGE to clean out unused layers, views, or styles—anything that you named during a drawing editor session. A good drawing habit is to use PURGE before you back up a drawing. To use PURGE, load your drawing and issue PURGE as the first command.

Using the BASE Command

When you create drawing files that you later might use as blocks, you need an easy way to control their insertion-base points. The BASE command creates an insertion-base point in a drawing file, enabling you to control its insertion point in another file. The *base point* is an insertion handle like the insertion-base point on a regular block. (It is not an entity or visible point.) If you make a drawing, store it on disk, and later insert it in another drawing, the insertion-base point defaults to 0,0 unless you specify a base point. Figure 11.23 shows how the BASE command works.

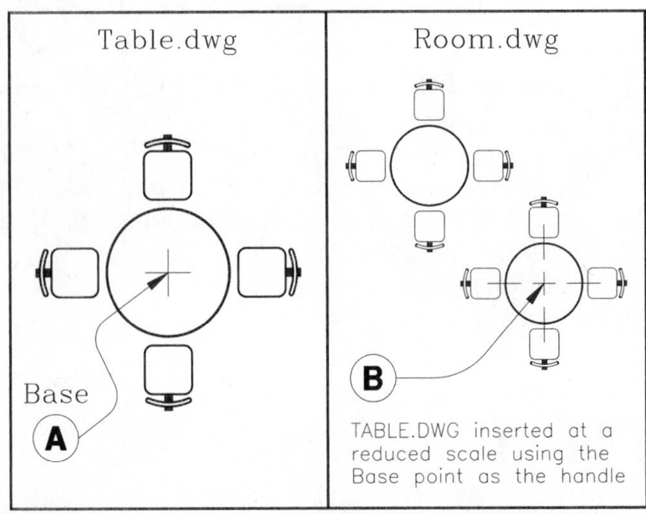
Table.dwg
Room.dwg
Base
A
B
TABLE.DWG inserted at a reduced scale using the Base point as the handle

Figure 11.23:

Inserting a drawing into another drawing.

Naming Conventions for Blocks

As your list of blocks and drawing files grows, you find that you need some organization and structure for naming your blocks. Give your blocks useful names. For example, CAR1 and CAR2 are better than C1 and C, but not as descriptive as VWBUG and PORSCHE.

Although AutoCAD enables you to choose block names up to 31 characters long, make your block names the same number of characters (or fewer) than what your operating system allows for file names. You later may want to store them by using WBLOCK. A block name that is an allowable file name enables you to specify = for the file name instead of typing it. You also can use common prefixes for similar classes of blocks (and drawings), so that you can use wild cards.

Keep an alphabetical log of block names in a disk text file and print it out as it changes so that you do not accidentally insert the wrong block or duplicate block names.

Defining Block Structure

Blocks are powerful tools and using them can make drawing easier. You should be aware of two additional block properties when you use blocks: blocks can include other blocks and blocks can include entities on different layers.

Nesting Blocks

A block can be made up of other blocks; this is called *nesting*. You can place a block inside a block inside a block. AutoCAD does not place a limit on the number of block-nesting levels, although editing nested blocks can get confusing if you go more than a few levels deep. (When you created the BUSH block, it contained a TREE1 block as a nested block.)

To include one block in another block, select the first block when you create the second. You can use standard editing commands with nested blocks, such as ARRAY, COPY, and MOVE, just as you use them with normal blocks.

Nested blocks further increase the efficiency and control of blocks. The BUSH block contains only one entity (the TREE1 block), instead of one circle and three lines. In figure 11.24, the chair is a nested block; the outer TABLE block only needs to contain four block references, instead of all the entities that make up each chair. Another advantage to nesting the TABLE block is that the CHAIR block can be redefined (changed) easily and independently of the TABLE block definition.

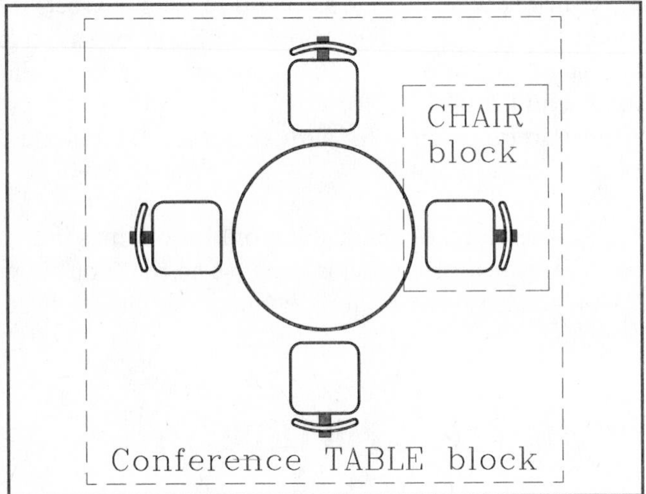

Figure 11.24:
An example of a nested block.

Blocks and Layers

When you work with blocks and layers, you need to know on which layers the entities are located in the block definition. In the blocks you have used so far, all the entities have been drawn on layer 0. You can, however, create a block with entities on different drawing layers (see fig. 11.25). You can, for example, create a block with graphic entities on layer ABC and text on layer XYZ. When you create the block, AutoCAD stores the entities inside the block on their appropriate layers.

When you insert multiple-layer blocks, each entity in the block displays, according to the color and linetype of the layer on which the entities were created. Entities included in a block can have color or linetype specification set to Bylayer (the default), Byblock, or by explicit color or linetype settings. If the current drawing file does not contain all layers in the block, the layers

are created in the new drawing when the block is inserted. Figure 11.26 shows a block insertion with an entity that retains its original explicit color when inserted on a different active layer.

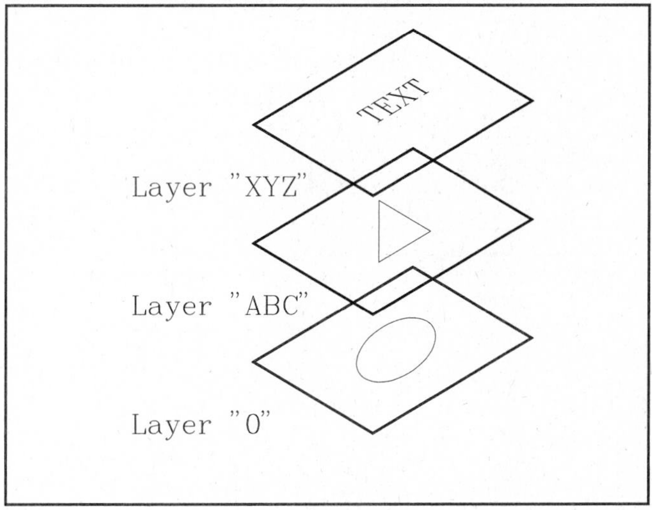

Figure 11.25:
A block can have entities on many layers.

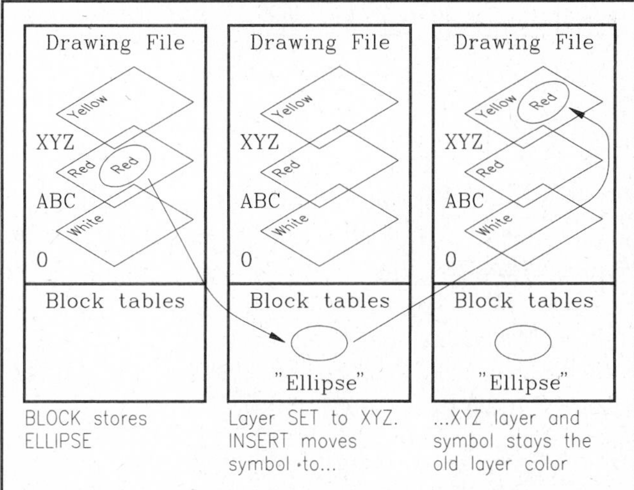

Figure 11.26:
An example of a block retaining its original layer's color.

Using Layer 0's Special Block-Insertion Properties

If you create entities on layer 0, store them in a block, and then insert the block on a different active layer (the entities move to the active layer). If any entities in the block have explicit color or linetype, they retain the customization. If the BYLAYER command is used, however, to set color, linetype or both, the entities adopt the default layer settings of the layer on which they are inserted (see fig. 11.27). In other words, blocks made from layer 0 Bylayer entities act as chameleons—they adopt the colors of their drawing environment, unless they have explicit settings.

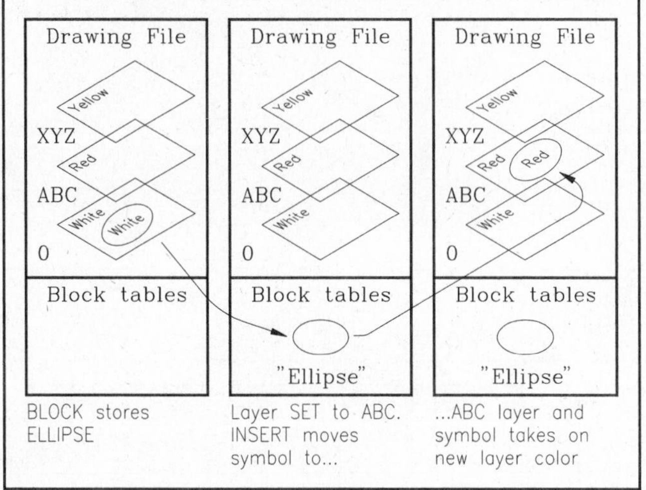

Figure 11.27:

An example of a block adopting a new layer's color.

NOTE: When you use a *insertion, or when you explode a block containing any entities that were on layer 0 at the time the block was created, the entities return to layer 0 and resume their original color and linetype.

Using Byblock Colors and Linetypes

Entities created by using the Byblock property (or existing entities changed to Byblock by using CHPROP) can take advantage of the special features of layer 0. Byblock entities take on any current entity color and linetype settings when the block is inserted, whether explicit (like red), Bylayer, or

even Byblock (for nesting). Byblock entities are completely flexible, unlike blocked layer 0 Bylayer entities, which are predestined to assume only the default color, linetype, or both, of the layer on which the block is inserted.

Working with Blocks and Frozen Layers

You may insert a block with multiple-layer entities on a layer, freeze the layer, and suddenly the block disappears from view. How does this happen?

When you give a block an insertion-base point, that invisible reference point is defined in the block at the time it is created. The reference point anchors the block into the drawing file by its insertion point coordinates. When you insert a block, AutoCAD does not insert all the information that makes up the block—only a block reference back to the invisibly-stored block definitions. Thus, whatever layer you use to insert the block contains the block reference at the insertion point. When you freeze the layer, you suppress the block reference, even though the block has entities on other layers that you have not frozen.

Substituting and Redefining Blocks

The properties discussed in previous sections sound good in theory, but what about some practical techniques? This first section on blocks ends with two useful block techniques: using substitute blocks and redefining blocks. The Autotown block exercises show you how to substitute working blocks and perform block redefinitions.

Substituting Block Names

As you insert a block, you can assign a different block name by using an equal sign. You can use an assignment, such as IA-TREE=TREE1, to tell AutoCAD to use the block name IA-TREE with the graphic information stored in the TREE1.DWG file on disk. The TREE1 symbol is then inserted in your drawing with the name IA-TREE. The substitution of the IA-TREE name in your current drawing ensures that you do not accidentally overwrite blocks in your drawing.

Redefining Blocks

If a block name already exists in your drawing, reinserting it with an equal sign redefines all existing insertions of the block.

To see how block redefinition works, replace all CAR2 blocks with MY-CAR blocks (the sports car you saved to disk). You can use the INSERT command to replace blocks and to insert them. You do not have to complete the INSERT command to redefine existing blocks. Cut the command short by pressing Ctrl-C, and the redefinition occurs.

Using INSERT To Redefine Blocks

Zoom or pan as needed to view all the cars.

`Command:` **`INSERT`** ↵	
`Block name:` **`CAR2=MY-CAR`** ↵	Replaces CAR2 with MY-CAR from the disk
`Insertion point:` *Press Ctrl-C*	Cancels the command
`*Cancel*`	
`Command:` Choose File, then Save	

Figure 11.28 shows the redefined blocks.

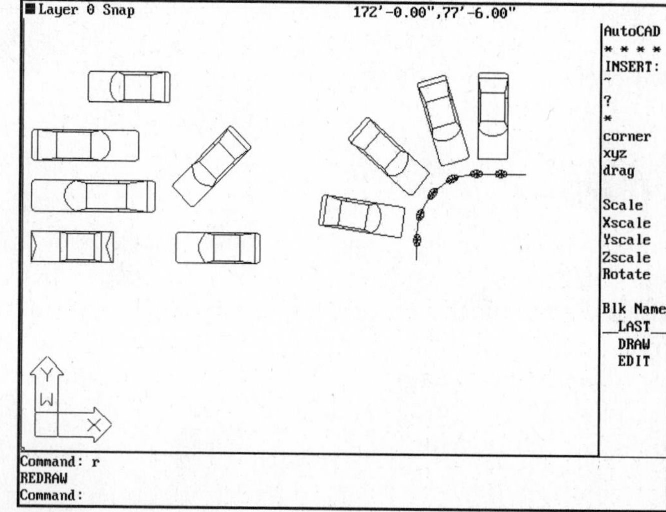

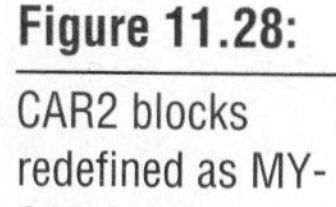

Figure 11.28:

CAR2 blocks redefined as MY-CAR blocks.

You should see sports cars all over the place. To replace cars with a few different cars may seem trivial. On the other hand, if you have a minor revision to make on a block that occurs several hundred times in a drawing, replacing blocks becomes no trivial matter. You can replace all your blocks globally by using a revised block in a single insertion redefinition.

If you are satisfied with a certain part of a drawing (or part on a layer), and you may not be working on that part for a while, make a WBLOCK of it and replace it with a simple block to improve redraw speed and reduce drawing clutter. When you are ready, put the drawing back together by inserting the block with an equal sign.

Using External References (Xrefs) for Design Distribution

Assume that your building design team consists of four people—one is working on the building's structure and floor plan, one on the electrical system, one on the plumbing and other facilities, and the other on the interior design.

These people need to know the basic outline of the building and the location of walls, doors, windows, and other features. They cannot wait for the floor plan to be finalized and completely drawn—they must get to work right away to stay on top of the project. If any change is made to the floor plan, the rest of the team must know it as soon as possible.

The best way to solve this problem is for each person on the team to insert the floor plan into their drawings as an xref. Every time a drafter loads his drawing to work on it, the latest revision of the floor plan automatically loads. If a wall has moved, the drafter knows it right away and can respond to the change.

Even if you do not design buildings, this example should give you ideas for ways to incorporate xrefs into your own applications.

Xrefs (external references) are collective entities similar to blocks. They can contain multiple entities, such as lines and arcs. You can insert xrefs in your drawing as you do blocks, and you can select them as a single entity, whether the xref contains one entity or a hundred.

Unlike blocks, which condense multiple drawing entities to a single entity in a drawing file, xrefs remove drawing entities altogether from the drawing file.

When you create a block that contains 100 lines, your drawing database contains an entry for each of those lines, including each line's layer setting, color setting, and linetype. You cannot list this data, even if you list the drawing database's contents. Although the data is buried in the block-definition table, data for all 100 lines is still in memory. When you insert more copies of your block onto your drawing, you duplicate only the block reference, not the original data. But the original lines always have to be in the block definition table for the block to exist.

Using Xrefs for Efficiency

Xrefs remove the need to store block data in a drawing. Xrefs do exactly what their name implies—they reference external drawings. When you insert an xref, you are inserting only its name. A few other bits of information also are inserted that AutoCAD needs in order to display an image of the xref in the drawing. The entities that make up the image are still located on disk in the drawing file referenced by the xref. Your drawing file saves only a reference to the external reference file.

Xrefs are like ghost images of other files. You can use them to insert images of parts and symbols into your drawing without actually inserting the data that make up the part or symbol. Like blocks, you can snap to objects in the xref. If your blocks contain hundreds of drawing entities and you insert an xref instead of a block, entities can be removed from each drawing file, which makes file sizes much smaller.

Using Xrefs To Control Drawings

Another reason to use xrefs is the control they offer. When several people work on parts of the same drawing, these parts can be incorporated into one master drawing as xrefs. By inserting the separate files as xrefs, the drafters ensure that every time the master drawing is loaded or plotted, the latest revisions to the referenced drawings automatically are used. The TABLET.DWG file on the Release 12 sample disk is one example that uses three referenced drawings (TABLET-A, B, and S).

Xrefs ensure that parts automatically are updated throughout an entire library of drawings. If you have parts that change from time to time and they need to be updated to the latest revision in a number of existing drawings, you can use block redefinition, one block and one drawing at a time. If you insert them as xrefs instead, they automatically update whenever a drawing is loaded or plotted.

Using Xrefs with Options

Xrefs are best when used to save common parts that may be revised during your project. The use of xrefs can significantly reduce the errors normally associated with copying data from one drawing to another. As you now know, xrefs always reflect the most current revision of the data they reference—if you make a change to the xref's source file, that xref is updated in every drawing in which it is referenced.

The following command options can be used with XREF:

- **?.** The ? option lists the xrefs in the current drawing. Press Enter to accept the default asterisk for a complete list, or use wild-card characters to specify a specific set of names.
- **Bind.** This option enables you to enter a single xref name or several xref names, separated by commas. You also can use wild cards in the current drawing to make one or more xrefs permanent by converting them to blocks. You also can use wild cards in the current drawing.
- **Detach.** This option enables you to enter a single xref name, enter several xref names separated by commas, or use wild cards to remove xrefs from the drawing.
- **Path.** This option enables you to enter a single xref name, enter several xref names separated by commas, or use wild cards to change the directory path of attached xrefs.
- **Reload.** This option enables you to enter a single xref name, enter several xref names separated by commas, or use wild cards to update xrefs to the latest versions of their referenced files without exiting the current drawing.
- **Attach.** This option enables you to enter a drawing file name to attach it to the current drawing as an xref.

The commands for using xrefs are issued by the XREF: and XBIND: items on the BLOCKS screen menu and found as Xref under the File pull-down menu.

In the following exercise, attach an xref to a drawing. Begin a new drawing named XSYMBOL. Then draw a new symbol on a layer called SYMLAYER (see fig. 11.29). After you save the drawing, attach the drawing as an xref in a new drawing.

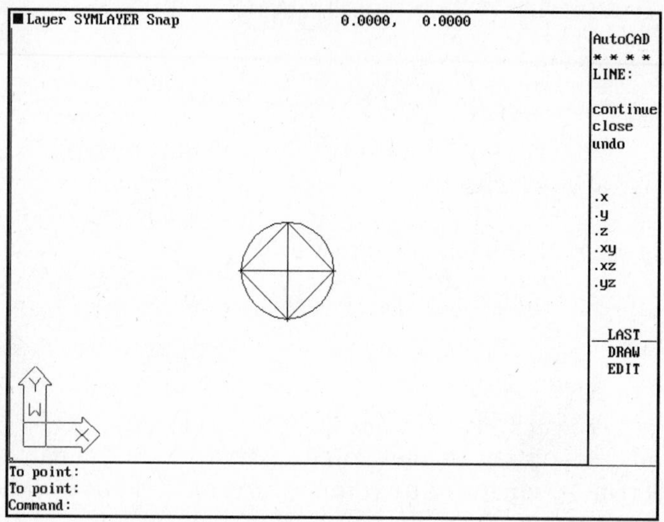

Figure 11.29:

A symbol on layer SYMLAYER in XSYMBOL drawing.

Attaching an Xref to a Drawing

`Command:` *Choose* File, *then* New, *and enter* `\IA\XSYMBOL`

Make a red layer named SYMLAYER and make it the current layer. Turn on snap and draw the symbol shown with 1" radius.

`Command:` *From the screen menu, choose* BLOCKS, *then* BASE, *and pick the center of the object*	Sets the insertion point
`Command:` *Choose* File, *then* Save	
`Command:` *Choose* File, *then* New, *and enter* `\IA\XTEST`	
`Command:` *Turn on snap and the coordinate display*	
`Command:` *Choose* File, *then* Xref, *then* Attach	Issues XREF with the Attach option

`Xref to Attach:` *Choose* XSYMBOL *and* OK — Specifies the xref's name

`Attach Xref XSYMBOL: XSYMBOL`

`XSYMBOL loaded.`

The rest of the prompts are identical to the prompts for the INSERT command.

`Insertion point:` **`5,5↵`**

`X scale factor <1> / Corner / XYZ:` *Press Enter*

`Y scale factor (default=X):` *Press Enter*

`Rotation angle <0>:`*Press Enter* — Attaches and displays the xref

`Command:` *Choose* File, *then* Save

You can see that attaching an xref is similar to inserting a block—xrefs function like blocks. If you select any part of the xref by using the ERASE command, the entire xref is deleted, as if it were a block. You cannot explode an xref to edit its entities, but, unlike blocks, you can edit the external file. When you update an xref file, you affect every drawing in which that file is referenced.

Using Xrefs for Workgroup Design Distribution

One reason xrefs were designed was to facilitate work-group design. You can allocate different parts of a large project to members of your design team and combine all the pieces at the end to make the final project. Use the XSYMBOL drawing in the next exercise as an example of xref's capability to provide automatic updates. Load it, then add two more circles to it and save the drawing. Finally, load XTEST again to see XSYMBOL as it automatically updates.

Updating an Xref

`Command:` *Choose* File, *then* Open, *and enter* **`\IA\XSYMBOL`**

`Command:` *Choose* Draw, *then* Circle, *then* Center, Radius, *and add two concentric circles around the symbol*

`Command:` *Choose* File, *then* Save

`Command:` *Choose* File, *then* Open, *and enter* **`\IA\XTEST`**	
`Resolve Xref XSYMBOL: XSYMBOL`	Loads and displays the current revision when you load the drawing
`XSYMBOL loaded.`	

When you load a drawing that contains xrefs, AutoCAD automatically reloads any external references. You loaded XSYMBOL, changed it, then ended it. When you loaded the drawing that contained XSYMBOL as an xref, the updated version of XSYMBOL appeared in the file automatically.

If you are part of a design team, you probably are on a network with other designers. What happens to your xrefs if someone edits a file you have referenced in your drawing while you are still working on the drawing? Nothing happens, unless you reload the xref.

Reloading Xrefs

You can reload xrefs in two ways. The first way, which you just used, is to load the drawing again. The other way is to use the XREF Reload option. When AutoCAD asks you which xrefs you want to reload, you can specify one or more xrefs by name or type * to reload them all.

In the following steps, change the original XSYMBOL external file by drawing a new square symbol (see fig. 11.30), and use WBLOCK to overwrite its file. Then reload XSYMBOL in your XTEST drawing to update it (see fig. 11.31). XTEST still should be loaded.

Reloading an Xref after its File Changes

Issue the LAYER command and make a layer named SYMLAYER. Set the new layer's color to yellow and the linetype to dashed. Then make the new layer current. Draw a 2"-square symbol with an X through it.

`Command:` *From the screen menu, choose* BLOCKS, *then* WBLOCK:	Displays the Create Drawing File dialog box
Enter the file name **`XSYMBOL`**, *pick the center of the square as the insertion point, and select the six lines in the square as the entities to define the block*	Saves the square and overwrites the existing file

`Command:` *Choose* File, *then* Xref, *then* Reload	Issues XREF with the Reload option
`Xref(s) to reload: *`	Updates all xrefs

```
Xref(s) to reload: *
  Scanning...
Reload Xref XSYMBOL: XSYMBOL
XSYMBOL loaded.  Regenerating drawing.
```

The updated xref appears in figure 11.31.

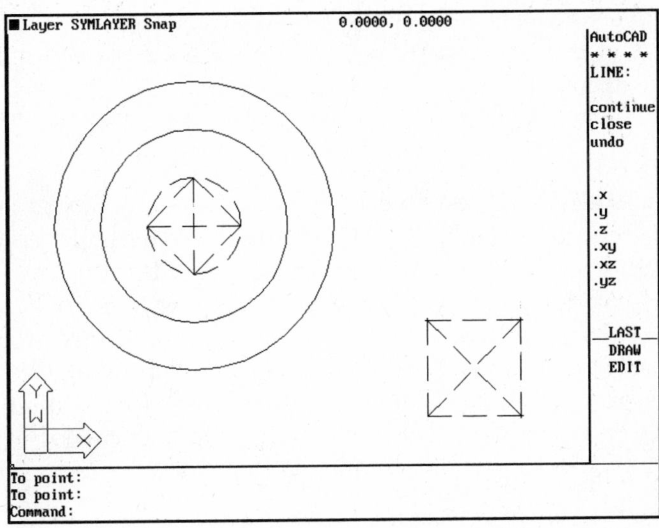

Figure 11.30: The new square symbol before using the WBLOCK command.

Figure 11.31: The xref symbol after updating.

When you reload xrefs, AutoCAD scans your drawing for xrefs and rereads the XSYMBOL drawing file from disk. AutoCAD then updates the symbol in the current drawing.

In an earlier exercise, you used WBLOCK to create a new SYMLAYER layer. This layer was created before storing the symbol to make its layer name match the original xrefs.

Understanding Xref Layers

When you insert a block into a drawing, any layers in the block's definition are added to the drawing. If a layer in a block already exists in the drawing, and the entities are set by using the BYLAYER command, the block's entities take on the characteristics of the existing drawing layer.

Xrefs work a little differently than blocks. When you attach an xref that contains layers other than layer 0, AutoCAD modifies the xref layer names to avoid duplication. A vertical bar (|) prefixes the xref layer names to separate the prefix from the layer name. You created the XSYMBOL data on layer SYMLAYER. When you attach XSYMBOL as an xref, AutoCAD renames SYMLAYER as XSYMBOL | SYMLAYER in the drawing in which the xref is attached. The renaming of the layers prevents the xref's entities from taking on the characteristics of existing layers in the drawing.

In the steps that follow, check the layers in XTEST to see that the layer has been renamed.

Listing Xref Layers

`Command:` *From the screen menu, choose* LAYER: — Displays the Layer Control dialog box

Layer name	*State*	*Color*	*Linetype*
0	On...	White	CONTINUOUS
SYMLAYER	On...	Yellow	CONTINUOUS
XSYMBOL | SYMLAYER	On...	Yellow	XSYMBOL | DASH

Choose OK *to exit from the* Layer Control *dialog box*

`Command:` *Choose* File, *then* Save

Layer 0 is the exception to xref layer renaming. As with block insertions, any data in xref files that reside on layer 0 loads on layer 0 in the current drawing; it assumes any settings you have assigned to layer 0.

Removing Xrefs from Drawings

A block's definition remains in memory, even after all visible insertions are erased. If you erase an xref, the reference to the external file still is in your drawing. When the drawing is reloaded, AutoCAD looks for the external file, even though visibly it does not appear.

Use XREF's Detach option to remove the xref from your drawing. The following steps use Detach to remove XSYMBOL from your XTEST drawing.

Detaching an Xref from a Drawing

Command: **XREF**↵

?/Bind/Detach/Path/Reload/<Attach>: **D**↵

Xref(s) to Detach: **XSYMBOL**

Scanning... — Detaches the xref; it is no longer part of your drawing

Using Bind with Xrefs

Sometimes you want to make your xref data a permanent part of your drawing, instead of a reference to an external file. When you finish a project and want to archive it, for example, separate xref files force you to archive all the drawings referenced in the main drawings. If the xref drawings are not available when you try to load your drawing, AutoCAD displays an error message that says it cannot find the xrefs. Without xrefs, AutoCAD cannot load and display them as part of the drawing. If you bind the xrefs, they are converted into permanent blocks in the drawing file.

Whenever you remove a drawing from its original environment (when you copy it onto a floppy disk for distribution to a client or contractor, for example), you either must bind the xrefs or include the xref drawings.

Binding xrefs is usually the safest method unless you send drawings to a consultant as a work in progress.

Return to the XTEST drawing and use the Bind option to make the xref XSYMBOL a permanent part of the drawing.

Using Bind To Make an Xref Permanent

`Command:` *Choose* File, *then* Xref, *then* Attach

`Xref to Attach:` *Choose* XSYMBOL

`Attach Xref XSYMBOL: XSYMBOL`

`XSYMBOL loaded.`

`Insertion point:` **`5,5`**↵

`X scale factor <1> / Corner / XYZ:` *Press Enter*

`Y scale factor (default=X):` *Press Enter*

`Rotation angle <0>:` *Press Enter*

`Command:` **`XREF`**↵

`/?/Bind/Detach/Path/Reload/<Attach>:` **`B`**↵

`Xref(s) to bind:` **`XSYMBOL`**

`Scanning...`

The Bind option merges xrefs into the drawing file in which they are contained. The xref becomes a standard block in the drawing. After it is bound, you can explode it and manipulate it just as you can any other block created or inserted directly in the drawing. To prove the XSYMBOL is now an ordinary block, you can explode and edit it, or list it with the BLOCK or INSERT command ? option.

Bind also changes the layers that belong to xrefs. It replaces the vertical bar (|) in the layer name with $*n*$ (*n* is a number). If you list the drawing layers again, layer XSYMBOL|SYMLAYER has been renamed XSYMBOL0SYMLAYER. When AutoCAD renames binded layers, it first uses 0 for the number. If a layer by that name already exists, AutoCAD substitutes a 1. AutoCAD continues trying higher numbers until it reaches a unique layer name. You can use the RENAME command to change these strange layer names to whatever layer name you like.

If you want to insert a drawing as a block into your current drawing (and there are conflicting layer names), attach the drawing as an xref first, then bind it as a block. This step preserves the incoming block's unique layers.

In addition to ensuring unique layer names, AutoCAD prevents xrefs and blocks from having the same names.

Controlling Xref Name/Block Conflicts

If you try to attach XSYMBOL again, the following error message appears:

```
** Error: XSYMBOL is already a standard block in the current
drawing. *Invalid*
```

If you need to attach the XSYMBOL xref again, you can substitute a different name in the current drawing as you do for blocks. Another option is to use RENAME to rename the XSYMBOL block to remove the conflict. To see which file name is referenced by an xref already loaded with a substitute name, use the ? option. You also can use the BLOCK command's ? option to view information on blocks and xrefs.

In the next exercise, attach XSYMBOL by using the name XSYM2=XSYMBOL. Then use the XREF ? option, the BLOCK ? option, and the LAYER ? option to list the new name.

Attaching an Xref with a Substitute Name

`Command:` **`XREF`**↵	
`?/Bind/Detach/Path/Reload/<Attach>:` *Press Enter*	
`Xref to Attach <XSYMBOL>:` **`XSYM2=XSYMBOL`**↵	Makes XSYM2 the xref name and XSYMBOL the external file name
`Attach Xref XSYM2: XSYMBOL` `XSYM2 loaded.`	
`Insertion point:` *Pick 9,5 and accept the default scale and rotation*	
`Command:` **`XREF`**↵	Prompts for names to list
`?/Bind/Detach/Path/Reload/<Attach>:` **`?`**↵	Lists all xrefs
`Xref(s) to list<*>:` *Press Enter*	

```
     Xref Name                    Path
-----------------------      ---------------
  XSYM2                          XSYMBOL
Total Xref(s): 1
```

Press F1 to return to the graphics screen

`Command:` *From the screen menu, choose* AutoCAD

`Command:` *From the screen menu, choose* BLOCKS, *then* BLOCK:, *and then* ?

`Blocks(s) to list<*>:` *Press Enter* — Lists all blocks

```
Defined blocks.
  XSYM2                                          Xref: resolved
  XSYMBOL
User      External       Dependent     Unnamed
Blocks    References     Blocks        Blocks
    1          1             0             0
```

Press F1 to return to the graphics screen

`Command:` *From the screen menu, choose* Layer — Displays the Layer Control dialog box, with the following listing:

Layer name	*State*	*Color*	*Linetype*
0	On...	White	CONTINUOUS
SYMLAYER	On...	Yellow	DASHED
XSYM2 I SYMLAYER	On...	Yellow	XSYM2 I DASHE
XSYMBOL0SYMLAYER	On...	Yellow	XSYMBOL0D

Choose OK *to exit from the* Layer Control *dialog box*

When you listed the xrefs by using XREF and BLOCK, XSYM2 appeared as the xref name in the current drawing. XSYMBOL appeared as its path which is the externally-referenced file name.

Although you can attach an xref with an equal sign, you cannot redefine an existing xref as you can for blocks. You can rename an xref, however, by using the Block option of the RENAME command. If you do so, the following RENAME warning appears:

```
Caution! XSYM2 is an externally referenced block.
Renaming it will also rename its dependent symbols.
```

What are dependent symbols, and what do XSYM2 I DASHED linetype and Xdep: XSYM2 mean in the list from the preceding exercise?

Understanding Xref's Dependent Symbols

Layers, linetypes, text styles, blocks, and dimension styles are symbols; that is, they are arbitrary names that represent things such as layers or styles (not to be confused with graphic symbols such as TREE1). The symbols that are carried into a drawing by an xref are called *dependent symbols* because they depend on the external file, rather than on the current drawing for their characteristics.

To avoid conflicts, dependent symbols are prefixed in the same manner as XSYM2 | SYMLAYER and XSYM2 | DASHED. The only exceptions are unambiguous defaults like layer 0 and linetype CONTINUOUS. You can vary text style STANDARD, however, which means it is prefixed.

Prefixed dependent symbols also apply to nested xrefs. If the external file XSYMBOL includes an xref named TITLEBLK, for example, the external file has the symbol name XSYMBOL | TITLEBLK if XSYMBOL is attached to another drawing. If TITLEBLK includes the layer LEGEND, it gets the symbol XSYMBOL | TITLEBLK | LEGEND. Xrefs may be nested deeply (xrefs within xrefs), or a drawing may contain many xrefs.

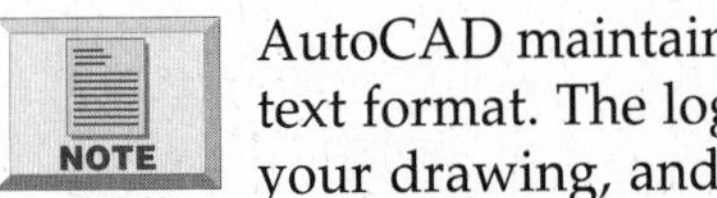

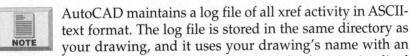

AutoCAD maintains a log file of all xref activity in ASCII-text format. The log file is stored in the same directory as your drawing, and it uses your drawing's name with an XLG extension. The log file continues to grow as the drawing is edited over many sessions. Occasionally, you may want to delete all or part of the log file to save disk space.

To protect the integrity of an xref, AutoCAD limits the capability to change dependent symbols in your current drawing. You cannot make an xref the current layer and draw on it, for example, as you can with a standard drawing layer. You can modify an xref's appearance, however, by changing the color, linetype, and visibility of an xref's layer. Any changes you make are only temporary. The xref reverts to its original state when it is reloaded, even if you save the drawing after making changes to an xref's layer settings.

You can selectively import these dependent symbols into your current drawing.

Using XBIND To Bind Dependent Xref Symbols

In an earlier exercise, you used the Bind option of XREF to convert XSYMBOL from an xref to a block. AutoCAD converted all the layers and data in the xref's file to become part of the new block.

You also can use the XBIND command to bind only portions of an xref to the current drawing. Use XBIND if you only want to bring in a text style, block, or layer defined in the xref without binding the entire xref.

To see how XBIND works, bind only the SYMLAYER layer in XSYMBOL, not the entire xref. Only the layer is bound, not the data drawn on that layer.

Binding Only Parts of an Xref by Using XBIND

`Command:` *From the screen menu, choose* BLOCKS, *then* XBIND:

`Block/Dimstyle/LAyer/LType/Style:`
From the screen menu, choose Layer

`Dependent Layer name(s):`
XSYM2|SYMLAYER ↵

```
   Scanning...
Also bound linetype XSYM2$0$DASHED:
it is referenced by layer
XSYM2$0$SYMLAYER.
```

`1 Layer(s) bound.`

Use DDLMODES or LAYER to see that the layer and linetype have been bound and renamed with (0) rather than (|).

`Command:` *Choose* File, *then* Save

In addition to any symbols you explicitly bind by using XBIND, linetypes and other symbols that can be bound to one another are automatically bound to the current drawing. A linetype bound to a layer is one example of binding linetypes and symbols. The entities (lines and so on) contained in the xref are not bound to the drawing. If you bind a block, however, you can then use INSERT to insert it in the current drawing.

You can transfer blocks and other symbols from one drawing to your current drawing. To do this, attach the drawing on disk as an xref, bind what you need, detach the xref, and rename the block.

Use BIND if you want to bind the entire xref to make it a block. Use XBIND if you only want to bind layer, linetype, dimension styles, nested blocks, or text styles without binding any actual entities in the xref.

Summary

Without blocks, you cannot keep track of all the individual components that make up even a simple drawing. Blocks help you organize your drawing by grouping useful collections of entities.

Xrefs give the same benefits as blocks, but they work with multiple drawings. Xrefs are most useful for keeping file size to a minimum and for ensuring that a drawing has the most up-to-date revision of the parts it contains. Xrefs act like blocks, and you can consider them special types of blocks. If controlling the proliferation of common data, keeping drawing size down, and decreasing disk usage are critical problems, use xrefs.

A well-planned system usually includes a well-organized library of blocks. Do not be afraid to create blocks when you need them. If you find that you are copying the same group of unblocked objects all the time, make them blocks. If you need a new block similar to an existing block, explode the old block, edit it, and make it a new block with a new name.

Use drag to see how a block is going to fit as you insert it. Use preset scale and rotation to see the block accurately as you drag it. Plan ahead to make groups of insertions so that you can use AutoCAD's insertion default prompts instead of typing block names and options over and over.

Use MINSERT, MEASURE, and DIVIDE to place many blocks with one command. Use an INSERT* or EXPLODE command to reconvert your blocks into their individual entities.

Block redefinitions can be a big time saver. If you are doing a project that requires a schematic or simple layout to precede a more accurate and detailed drawing, a global replacement can automate an entire

drawing-revision cycle. You also can update a drawing by redefining obsolete blocks or by using xrefs instead of blocks.

Be careful when you insert from a disk file. Existing named symbols and objects and their parameters take precedence over incoming ones. When you insert from a disk file, all named objects and symbols in the outside file get copied into the receiving file. If a layer (or style) already exists in the receiving drawing, it takes precedence. This may change text styles in the newly inserted parts or add to the current drawing file. To avoid that possibility, insert your parts as xrefs. Any duplicate layer names or other dependent symbols in the incoming drawing are thus renamed, avoiding duplication. Then, if you need the data to become a permanent part of your drawing, use XREF BIND or XBIND to make it permanent.

Use PURGE or a `Wblock *, Quit` sequence to keep your drawing file clean. PURGE is selective, but `Wblock *, Quit` wipes out all unused blocks. To remove unused xref definitions, use XREF DETACH.

You now have a basic understanding of blocks and xrefs. In the next chapter you apply these commands in the development of a housing site plan.

As you will see in the next chapter, there is no single tool in AutoCAD that enables you to develop a large, complex drawing more easily than blocks and external references. Once you have drawn an object, you never need to develop it again. Blocks' capability to be redefined is the single most powerful tool for most users of AutoCAD.

12

Construction Techniques with Blocks and Xrefs

In this chapter, you use blocks and xrefs to develop a site plan that contains houses, trees, and cars. This site plan is called Autotown. The Autotown exercises will show you how quickly you can develop a drawing through the application of existing geometry.

In addition to leading you through a further exploration of blocks and xrefs, the Autotown exercises teach you several techniques. One of these techniques involves the use of an extra AutoLISP command—DLINE—which draws double lines. If you have the IA DISK, you have several options before you continue with the Autotown exercises. These options are described later in this chapter. If you do not have the disk, you need to perform the Autotown set up exercises in this chapter.

The "Laying Out Autotown Drive and Lots" exercise lays out the site plan and demonstrates drawing-input techniques in surveyor's units. This site plan is available on the IA DISK. If you do not want to try surveyor's units, you can skip the exercise.

Follow the steps in the "Attaching the Site Layout as an Xref" exercise even if you have the IA DISK. This exercise shows you how to edit the Autotown drawing you saved and attach the site plan layout drawing file as an xref.

The "Creating Blocks for Autotown" sequence creates a set of simple and complex blocks, which you can use for subsequent exercises. You need the CAR2 and TREE1 blocks from Chapter 11 to perform this exercise. If you have the IA DISK, you can create the additional blocks, or you can use blocks from the disk.

In the "Aligning Working Blocks with a UCS" exercise, you practice inserting and redefining blocks, substituting block names, and setting temporary UCSs to align the blocks when they insert.

In the exercises called "Using DDINSERT to Insert Car Blocks" and "Grouping Blocks with BMAKE," you use dialog boxes to create and insert blocks. In these exercises, you complete the first stage of Autotown's development.

In the "Using Grips with Blocks" exercise, you change the xref that defines the site plan. After you make this change, some of the trees do not fit on the property. By using grips, you reposition the trees so that they again are within the property lines.

Before you begin to work with the Autotown exercises, however, you must set up and save the Autotown drawing file.

Setting Up Autotown

To prepare for the Autotown exercises, you must first start a site plan layout drawing named ATLAYOUT. The drawing uses feet, decimal inches, and surveyor's angles. Set your drawing limits at 360'×240'. The drawing is sized to fit a 36"×24" (D-size) sheet plotted at one inch equal to ten feet.

Set up the Autotown drawing according to the settings shown in table 12.1.

Table 12.1
ATLAYOUT Drawing Settings

Coords	*Grid*	*Snap*	*Ucsicon*
ON	10'	6"	OR

UNITS	Engineering, 2 decimal places, angles in surveyor's units, default all other settings.
LIMITS	Set LIMITS from 0,0 to 360',240'
ZOOM	Zoom ALL
VIEW	Save the view as All

Layer Name	*State*	*Color*	*Linetype*
0	On	7 (White)	CONTINUOUS
PLAN	On	4 (Cyan)	CONTINUOUS
SITE	On/Current	3 (Green)	CONTINUOUS

Use table 12.1 as a guide for the following exercise.

Setting Up ATLAYOUT and Saving Autotown.DWG

Choose File, *then* New, *choose* No Prototype, *and enter* `\IA\ATLAYOUT` *in the* Name *input box*

Set up the drawing by using the settings listed earlier. Make sure that SITE is the current layer. In the next step, you save the drawing with the name Autotown for use in later exercises.

`Command:` *Choose* File, *then* Save As, *and enter* **`AUTOTOWN`** ↵

Next, save the drawing with the name ATLAYOUT; continue working in this drawing.

`Command:` *Choose* File, *then* Save As, *select* ATLAYOUT, *then choose* Yes *to replace it*

Next, you can give the drawing a border and add the street by using the PLINE and DLINE commands.

Using DLINE To Draw Double Lines

The DLINE command draws a continuous double line by using straight or arc line segments. You can assign the width of the lines at any time. You can leave the end of the lines *capped* (closed) or open. The key element of this command is that it automatically cleans up intersecting lines as they are drawn. Like the LINE and PLINE commands, DLINE uses a rubber-band line (called the *dragline*) to show where the current segment is being drawn.

You can use the following command options with DLINE:

- **Break.** This option enables you to specify (by entering either the On or Off suboption) whether you want DLINE to create a gap between intersecting lines.
- **Caps.** This option controls caps at the end of double lines. You can specify Both to place a cap on both ends; End places one on the last end; None draws no caps; Start places a cap on the beginning end; and Auto places caps on any open ends.
- **Dragline.** This option lets you specify where the original line is placed, in relation to the offset line. You can choose from Left, Center, or Right.
- **Offset.** This option starts a new double line a relative distance from a base point, which usually is at an existing double line.
- **Snap.** This option gives you the choice of three suboptions: On, Off, and Size. On and Off specify whether the DLINE command enables you to snap to existing objects. The Size suboption determines the area (in pixels) to search for an object to snap to when you select a point.
- **Undo.** This option reverses the last operation.
- **Width.** This option enables you to specify the perpendicular distance between the two double lines.
- **start point.** This option lets you specify the double line's first point.

To issue the DLINE command, choose the Draw pull-down menu, then choose Line, then Double Lines. Otherwise, you can enter **DLINE** at the `Command:` prompt.

Laying Out Autotown Drive and Lots

Begin by adding the border polylines, then use DLINE for the streets.

Command: *Choose* Draw, *then* Polyline, *then* 2D, *and draw the border from 12'6,15' (with a width of 1') to 347'6,15' to 347'6,225' to 12'6,225' and close it*	
Command: *Choose* Draw, *then* Line, *then* Double Lines	Issues the DLINE command
Dline, Version 1.11, (c) 1990-1992 by Autodesk, Inc. Break/Caps/Dragline/Offset/Snap/ Undo/Width/<start point>: **C**↵	Specifies the Caps option
Draw which endcaps? Both/End/None/Start/<Auto>: **N**↵	Specifies no Caps
Break/Caps/Dragline/Offset/Snap/ Undo/Width/<start point>: **D**↵	Specifies the Dragline option
Set dragline position to Left/Center/Right/ <Offset from center = 0.00'>: **C**↵	Specifies the dragline in the center of the double lines
Break/Caps/Dragline/Offset/Snap/ Undo/Width/<start point>: **W**↵	Specifies the Width option
New DLINE width <0.05">: **600**↵	Sets the width to 600 inches
Break/Caps/Dragline/Offset/Snap/ Undo/Width/<start point>: **6',91'**↵	Specifies the drag line's starting point
Arc/Break/CAps/CLose/Dragline/Snap/ Undo/Width/<next point>: **221',65'9**↵	Specifies the next point
Arc/Break/CAps/CLose/Dragline/Snap/ Undo/Width/<next point>: **335'8,4'6** ↵	Specifies the next point
Arc/Break/CAps/CLose/Dragline/Snap/ Undo/Width/<next point>: *Press Enter*	Ends the DLINE command

To finish the road in the following steps, use DLINE again with an offset of 360 to create the road with a curb line. Then use TRIM to remove all the excess line segments.

Command: **DLINE**↵	Issues the DLINE command
Break/Caps/Dragline/Offset/Snap/ Undo/Width/<start point>: **W**↵	
New DLINE width <50'>: **360**↵	Sets the offset width to 360 inches

`Break/Caps/Dragline/Offset/Snap/ Undo/Width/<start point>:` **6',91'**↵	Specifies the start point for the center drag line
`Arc/Break/CAps/CLose/Dragline/Snap/ Undo/Width/<next point>:` **221',65'9**↵	
`Arc/Break/CAps/CLose/Dragline/Snap/ Undo/Width/<next point>:` **340'3,1'7**↵	
`Arc/Break/CAps/CLose/Dragline/Snap/ Undo/Width/<next point>:` *Press Enter*	Ends the DLINE command
`Command:` *Choose* Modify, *then* Trim, *and trim all the lines that extend beyond the border*	
`Command:` *Choose* File, *then* Save	

Your drawing should resemble the one shown in figure 12.1.

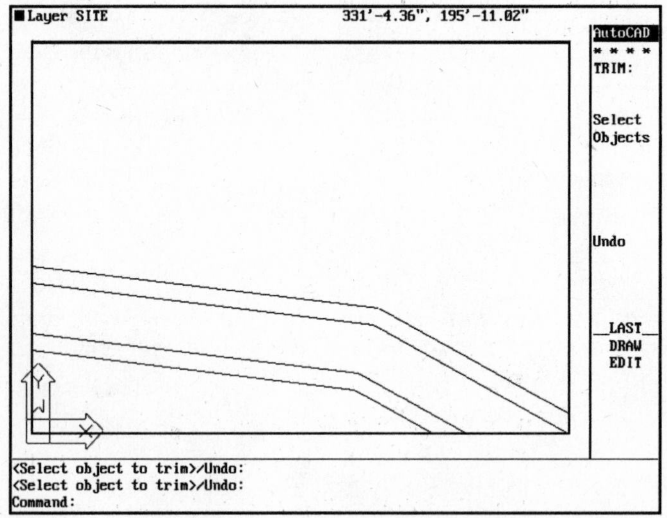

Figure 12.1:

The Autotown border and drive.

In manual drafting, converting and using surveyor's units is always a nuisance. As you will see in the following section, AutoCAD can convert these figures for you.

Using Surveyor's Angles

Autotown's setup contains surveyor's angles. AutoCAD still accepts normal decimal angle input for surveyor's angles and enables you to enter

a simple N, S, E, or W for 90-, 270-, 0-, and 180-degree angles. You can specify angles in survey nomenclature, such as N14d52'00"E for north 14 degrees, 52 minutes and 00 seconds east. In the next exercise, you use surveyor's angles to draw the lot lines for the three lots. You also use object snap modes as you pick drawing points.

Using Surveyor's Angles To Draw Autotown's Lot Lines

`Command:` **`LINE`**↵	Starts the LINE command
`From point:` *Use the INTersect object snap to pick the bend in the road* at ① *(see fig. 12.2)*	Specifies the starting point
`To point:` **`@100'2.5<N14d52'E`**↵	Draws a line 100' long at a direction of 14 degrees north and 52 minutes east
`To point:` **`@112'5.5<N80d47'W`**↵	Draws a line 112' long at a direction of 80 degrees north and 47 minutes west
`To point:` *Use the PER object snap to pick the north side of the road at* ②	
`To point:` *Press Enter*	Ends the LINE command
`Command:` **`LINE`**↵	
`From point:` *Use the INT object snap to pick the northwest corner of the center lot at* ③	
`To point:` **`@105'<N82d57'W`**↵	Draws a line 150' long at a direction of 82 degrees north and 57 minutes west
`To point:` *Use the PER object snap to pick the north side of the road at* ②	
`To point:` *Press Enter*	
`Command:` **`LINE`**↵	
`From point:` *Use the INT object snap to pick the northeast corner of the center lot at* ④	
`To point:` **`@91'8<S76d7'E`**↵	Draws a line 91' long at a direction of 76 degrees south and 7 minues east
`To point:` **`@74'<S`**↵	Draws a line 74' long to the south
`To point:` *Use the PER object snap to pick the north side of the road at* ⑤	
`To point:` *Press Enter*	

Your lot should now look like the lot in figure 12.2.

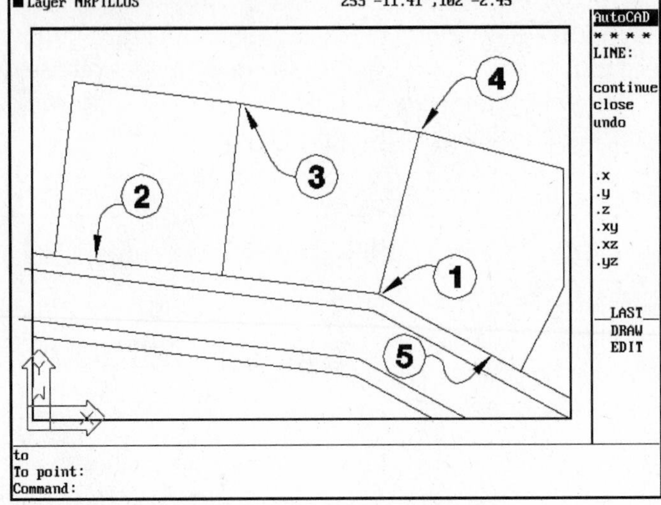

Figure 12.2:

Autotown with surveyed lot lines.

In the following steps, you finish the site layout by using DTEXT to finish the road.

To align text with an existing object, use an object snap to set the text angle, then pick the real location to place the text.

Using DTEXT To Label the Road

`Command:` *Choose* Settings, *then* Drawing Aids, *and set snap to 1'*	
`Command:` **`DTEXT`** ↵	
`Justify/Style/<Start point>:` *Use the INT object snap to pick the southwest corner of the center lot*	Sets one point to specify the angle
`Height <0.2000>:` **`6'`** ↵	
`Rotation angle <E>:` *Use INT to pick the southeast corner of the center lot*	Completes the angle specification
`Text:` *Pick at absolute point 133',75' with the crosshairs*	Specifies the real location
`Text:` **`Autotown Drive`** ↵	

`Text:` *Press Enter* — Ends the DTEXT command

`Command:` *Choose* Settings, *then* Drawing Aids, *and set snap back to 6"*

`Command:` *Choose* File, *then* Save

Figure 12.3 shows Autotown's new road and lots.

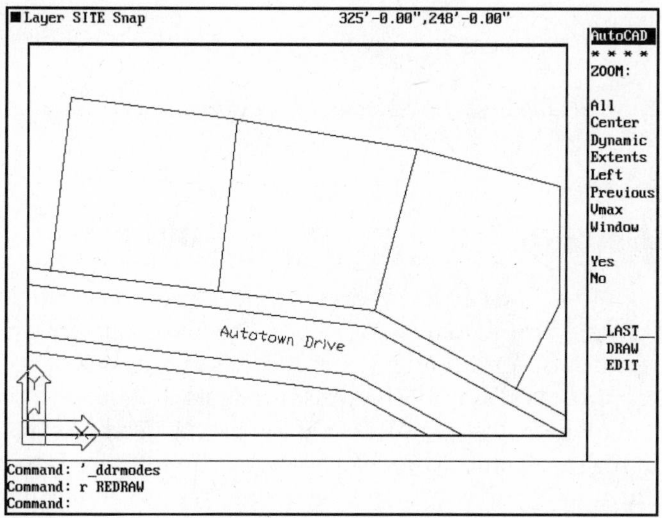

Figure 12.3:

The completed Autotown Drive, with text.

Using the Site Layout as an Xref

In the following exercise, you open the Autotown setup drawing and attach the site layout drawing to it as an xref. If you modify the site layout drawing, the changes automatically update in the finished Autotown drawing.

Attaching the Site Layout as an Xref

Choose File, *then* Open, *and enter* `\IA\Autotown` ↵

Make layer 0 current by using LAYER: *or* Layer Control

`Command:` *Choose* File, *then* Xref, *then* Attach

Choose ATLAYOUT, *then* OK	
`Attach Xref ATLAYOUT: ATLAYOUT`	
`ATLAYOUT loaded.`	
`Insertion point:` **0,0**↵	Specifies the origin as the xref's insertion point
`X scale factor <1> / Corner / XYZ:` *Press Enter*	Accepts the default scale and rotation angles
`Y scale factor (default=X):` *Press Enter*	
`Rotation angle <E>:` *Press Enter*	
`Command:` *Choose* File, *then* Save	

Using DLINE and WBLOCK To Prepare Autotown's Blocks

To study siting options, you can insert and arrange houses and site improvements as blocks. Throw in a car or two to dress up your presentations. You will not see much difference in regenerations and redraws of the Autotown drawing because it only contains three lots. If Autotown had three dozen lots, however, the complexity of the blocks used would make a big difference in regeneration and redraw speeds. The solution is to use matching pairs of simple and complex blocks and then use redefinition to swap them. Use the simple blocks during site design, then substitute the complex blocks for presentation plots.

You already have two blocks—CAR2 and TREE1—that you created in Chapter 11. Six other blocks are required in order to continue with the Autotown exercises. If you have the IA DISK, you also have the six other blocks and can skip to the following section, which shows you how to use a UCS to insert blocks. If you do not have the IA DISK, you must create the other six blocks. Even if you have the IA DISK, you may want to perform these exercises to get some practice with the DLINE and WBLOCK commands. If you have the disk and still want to follow these exercises, overwrite the disk blocks when you use WBLOCK to store your creations. Start with a floor plan and use figure 12.4 as a guide. The DLINE command breaks (or cleans up) all intersecting lines. If you make a mistake, issue the UNDO command.

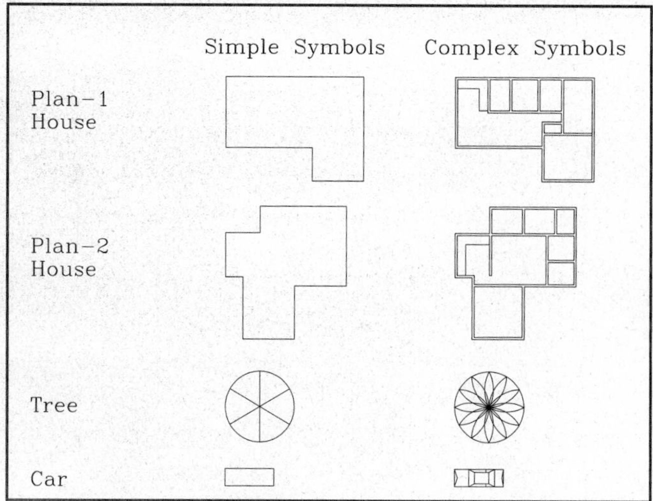

Figure 12.4:

Examples of simple and complex blocks.

Creating Blocks for Autotown

Zoom in on one of the lots as a construction area. Draw the SIMPLE1 floor plan with the dimensions shown in figure 12.5.

Next, you save the SIMPLE1 floor plan as a block, by using the WBLOCK command.

`Command:` *From the screen menu, choose* WBLOCK, *then* BLOCKS	Creates a block

Use WBLOCK *to store the floor plan as* SIMPLE1

In the following steps, you draw the COMPLEX1 floor plan, as shown in figure 12.6. Use the DLINE command to create the object, using the same dimensions you used in the SIMPLE1 floor plan.

`Command:` *Choose* Draw, *then* Line, *then* Double lines	
`Break/Caps/Dragline/Offset/Snap/ Undo/Width/<start point>:` **D↵**	
`Set dragline position to Left/Center/Right/ <Offset from center = 0.00">:` **L↵**	Places dragline to the left of the original line
`Break/Caps/Dragline/Offset/Snap/ Undo/Width/<start point>:` **W↵**	
`New DLINE width <5'>:` **6↵**	Specifies the width

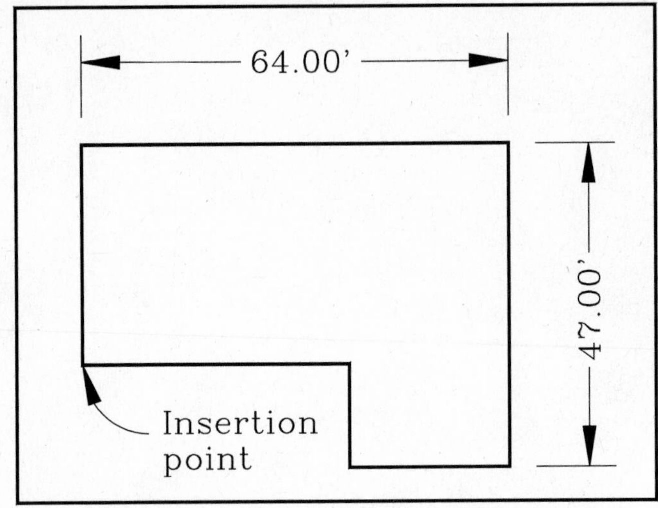

Figure 12.5:

The SIMPLE1 floor plan.

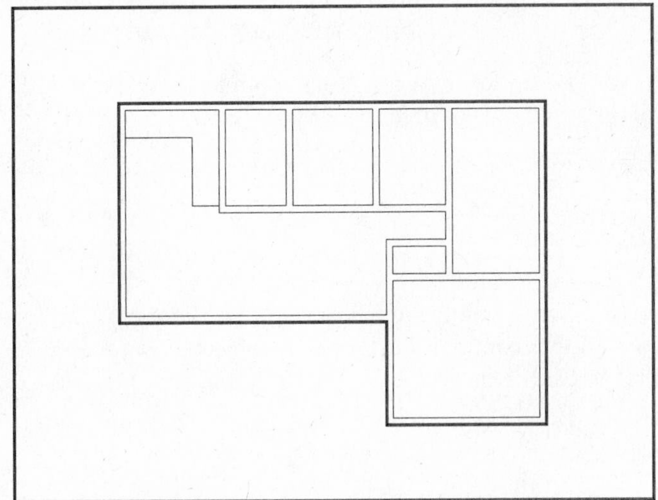

Figure 12.6:

The COMPLEX1 floor plan.

Break/Caps/Dragline/Offset/Snap/ Undo/Width/<start point>: *Pick a point for the upper left corner of the floor plan*	
Arc/Break/CAps/CLose/Dragline/Snap/ Undo/Width/<next point>: **@64'<0** ↵	
Arc/Break/CAps/CLose/Dragline/Snap/ Undo/Width/<next point>: **@47'<-90** ↵	
Arc/Break/CAps/CLose/Dragline/Snap/ Undo/Width/<next point>: **@20'<180** ↵	
Arc/Break/CAps/CLose/Dragline/Snap/ Undo/Width/<next point>: **@10'<90** ↵	
Arc/Break/CAps/CLose/Dragline/Snap/ Undo/Width/<next point>: **@44'<180** ↵	
Arc/Break/CAps/CLose/Dragline/Snap/ Undo/Width/<next point>: **CL** ↵	Closes the double-line polygon

In the following steps, you use DLINE with the Offset option to draw the interior wall section shown in figure 12.7

Command: **DLINE** ↵	
Break/Caps/Dragline/Offset/Snap/ Undo/Width/<start point>: **O** ↵	Specifies the Offset option
Offset from: *Use the INT object snap to pick the corner of the plan at ①*	Specifies the base from which to offset the second line
Offset toward: *Use the INT object snap to pick the corner to the right of the intersection at ②*	Sets the offset direction
Enter the offset distance <13'-7.00">: **15'** ↵	Sets starting point for the double line, defining the room's size
Arc/Break/CAps/CLose/Dragline/Snap/ Undo/Width/<next point>: **@15'<-90** ↵	
Arc/Break/CAps/CLose/Dragline/Snap/ Undo/Width/<next point>: **@35'<0** ↵	
Arc/Break/CAps/CLose/Dragline/Snap/ Undo/Width/<next point>: *Use the PER object snap to pick the top inside wall line*	

Finish COMPLEX1 by using DLINE to draw additional double-line walls. Because SNAP is set to 6, you can pick points for the starting and ending points of the double lines. Next, use WBLOCK to store the floor plan as COMPLEX1.

Use LINE and WBLOCK to create and save the SIMPLE2 floor plan with the dimensions shown in figure 12.8.

Use DLINE and WBLOCK to create and save the COMPLEX2 floor plan shown in figure 12.9. Make the floor plan as complex as you like.

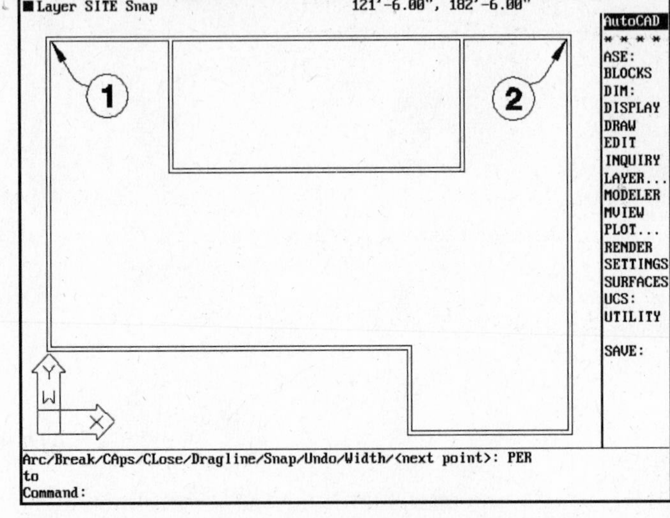

Figure 12.7:

Interior walls in the COMPLEX1 floor plan.

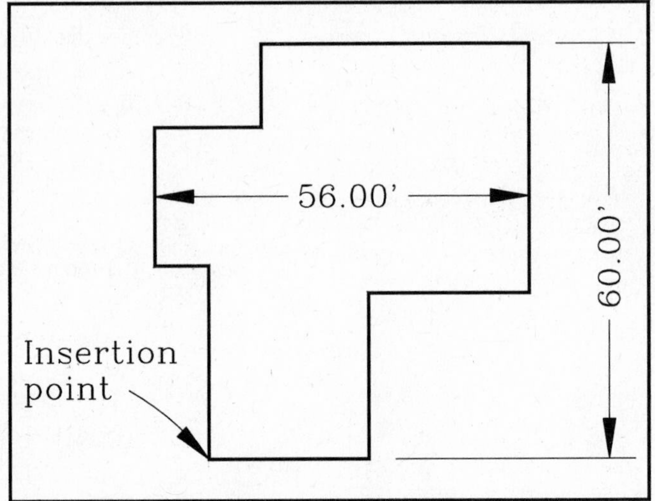

Figure 12.8:

The SIMPLE2 floor plan.

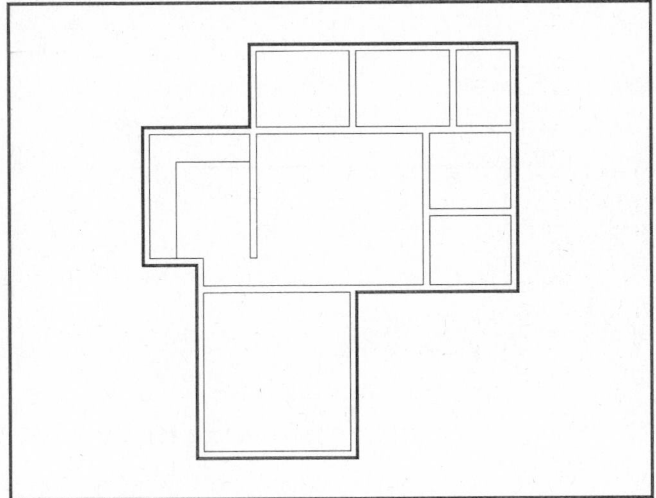

Figure 12.9:

The COMPLEX2 floor plan.

In the following steps, you continue by making a simple car and a complex tree. You already have CAR2 and TREE1 from Chapter 11.

Draw the CAR1 symbol with the dimensions shown in figure 12.10.

Use WBLOCK to store the car symbol as CAR1.

Zoom in and set snap to .125 to draw the TREE2 tree symbol one unit (1") in diameter (see fig. 12.11).

Use WBLOCK to store the tree symbol as TREE2.

`Command:` *From the screen menu, choose* Display, *then* VIEW:, *then* Restore, *and then enter* **ALL** ↵	Restores the view named ALL

Now that you have finished the blocks, you can build the rest of the subdivision.

Using a UCS To Insert Blocks

To insert the houses, set a UCS at the corner of each lot. This setting helps align the house plan in relationship to the lot. As you insert each block, substitute a working name (such as PLAN-1=SIMPLE1). This substitution tells AutoCAD to use the SIMPLE1.DWG drawing file on disk, but to name the block PLAN-1 in the drawing. The preliminary subdivision is shown in figure 12.12.

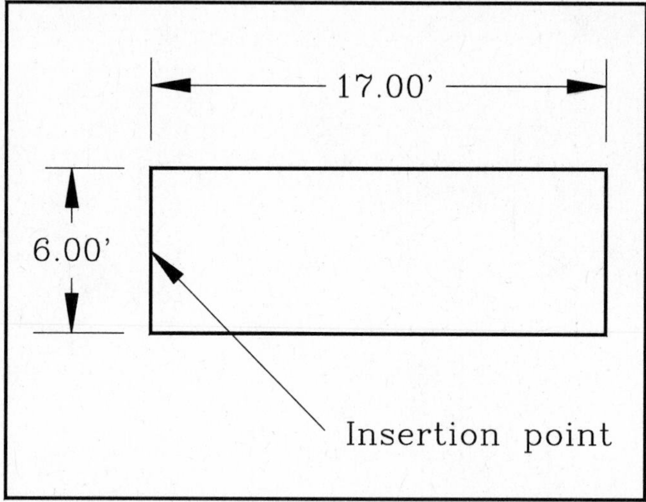

Figure 12.10

The CAR1 simple car symbol.

Figure 12.11:

The TREE2 complex tree symbol.

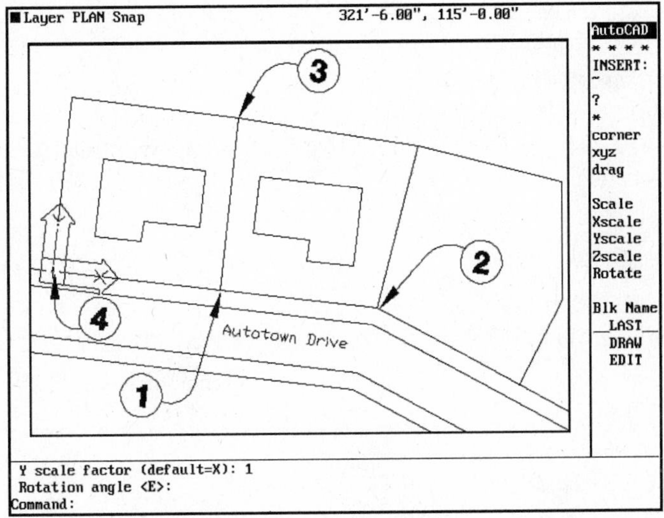

Figure 12.12:

Autotown with the first two floor plans.

Aligning Working Blocks with a UCS

`Command:` *Choose* Settings, *then* Layer Control, *and make PLAN the current layer*

`Command:` *From the screen menu, choose* UCS:, *then* next, *then* 3point

`Origin point <0,0,0>:` *Use INT to pick the lower left corner of the lot at ① (see fig. 12.12)*

`Point on positive portion of the X-axis <131'-3.02", 101'-5.66", 0'-0.00">:`
Use INT to pick the lower right corner of the lot at ②

`Point on positive-Y portion of the UCS X-Y plane <131'-2.13", 101'-6.66", 0'-0.00">:`
Use INT to pick the upper left corner of the lot at ③

Next you insert the SIMPLE1 plan on the center lot as PLAN-1.

`Command:` **`INSERT`** ↵

`Block name (or ?):` **`PLAN-1=SIMPLE1`** ↵ — Inserts the SIMPLE1 block and renames it PLAN-1 upon insertion

`Insertion point:` **`17',36'`** ↵

Accept the scale and rotation defaults

`Command:` *From the screen menu, choose* UCS:, *then* next, *then* Origin

Use the INT object snap to pick the left lot at lower left corner at ④

Next, you use a –1 X scale to insert a flipped PLAN-1 on the west lot. You do not need an = sign because the previous insertion defined PLAN-1 in your drawing's block table.

`Command:` **`INSERT`** ↵

`Block name (or ?)<PLAN-1>:` *Press Enter*

`Insertion point:` **`88',36'`** ↵

`X scale factor <1> / Corner / XYZ:` **`-1`** ↵ — Flips the block with the negative scale

`Y scale factor (default=X):` **`1`** ↵

`Rotation angle <E>:` *Press Enter*

`Command:` *From the screen menu, choose* UCS:, *then* next, *then* Origin *and set the origin for the east lot at the lower left corner (⑤ in fig. 12.13)*

Next, you use the Z option with the INT object snap to rotate about the Z axis, making the X axis parallel to the front lot line.

`Command:` *From the screen menu, choose* UCS, *then* next, *then* Z

`Rotation angle about Z axis <E>:` *Use* the *INT object snap to pick the lower left corner of the lot at ⑤*

`Second point:` *Use INTersect to pick the lower right corner of the lot at ⑥ (see fig. 12.13)*

Use INSERT to insert PLAN-2=SIMPLE2 on the east lot at 25'6,28', with an east rotation

---

No subdivision is complete without a few cars scattered around. In the next section, you insert several cars by using the DDINSERT command.

Using the Insert Dialog Box

The DDINSERT command displays the Insert dialog box for the insertion of BLOCKS. To issue the command, choose Insert from the Draw pull-down menu.

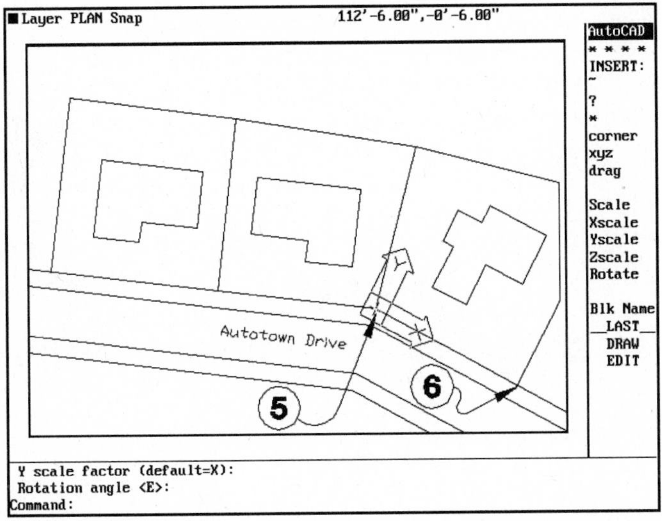

Figure 12.13:
Autotown with the last floor plan.

This dialog box has the same options as the INSERT command. You can choose the buttons for **B**lock and **F**ile to display a second dialog box with the available blocks or drawing files. You also can type the name in the input box. The **S**pecify Parameters on Screen box enables you to see all the block options. The **E**xplode block option performs the same function as *INSERT.

During the following insertion, you make the file CAR1 equal to the BLOCK CAR.

Using DDINSERT To Insert Car Blocks

`Command:` *From the screen menu, choose* UCS:, *then* World	Restores the World UCS
`Command:` *Choose* Draw, *then* Insert	Displays the Insert dialog box
Click on the **F**ile *button and select* CAR1, *then* OK	Specifies the file to insert
Enter `CAR` *in the* **B**lock *input box*	Specifies the block name to insert the file as
Choose OK	Displays the normal INSERT options for input

Pick your own insertion points, stretch the scales or use the defaults, and drag the angles. Figure 12.14 shows one possible arrangement for the cars. Use INSERT or DDINSERT to insert CAR for the remaining cars.

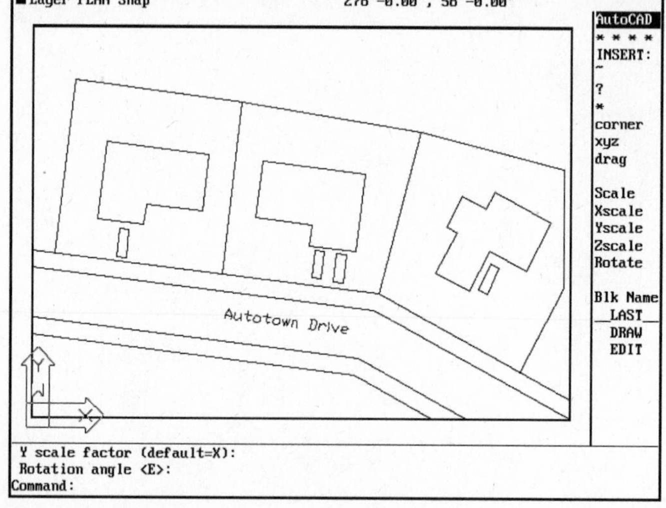

Figure 12.14:

Autotown with some inserted cars.

Using Preset Scale Insertions

After you finish inserting the cars, spruce up the subdivision with various trees. Remember that you drew the tree block with a one-unit (1") diameter. In the following exercise, you use different scale values to create trees with different diameters. Enter the desired diameter in inches because scale does not accept feet—only a factor by which it scales. Preset the scale factors because it is hard to place 1" trees accurately with drag before they are scaled. The trees then display at the desired scale as you drag them.

Using Preset Scale To Insert Trees

Command: **INSERT**↵

Block name (or ?) <CAR>: **TREE=TREE1**↵ — Renames TREE1 as TREE upon insertion

Insertion point: **S**↵ — Specifies the preset scale options

Scale factor: **240**↵ — Creates a tree 20' in diameter

Insertion point: *Pick a point (see fig. 12.15)*

Rotation angle <E>: *Press Enter*

Continue inserting more large trees with a 20' diameter. Use TREE as the inserted block name.

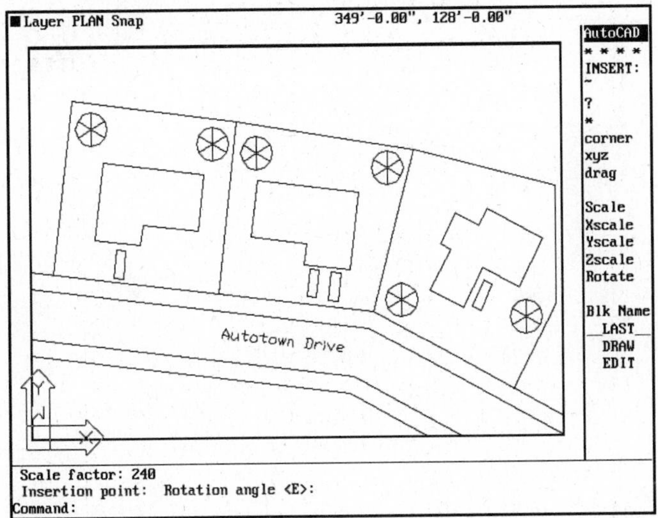

Figure 12.15: Autotown with some trees.

Using BMAKE To Group Blocks

In developing a drawing, it can be productive to group several existing blocks as nested blocks in a single block. You then can insert this new block throughout the drawing.

Figure 12.16 shows three similarly arranged trees in the corner of each lot. In the following exercise, you insert one group of trees, make them into a block named 3-TREES, and then insert the new block into each of the lots. You use the AutoLISP-defined command BMAKE to define the 3-TREES block. The BMAKE command enables you to define blocks through a dialog box. This command is not built into the menus; you must load it before use. You load BMAKE by issuing the APPLOAD command or by choosing the Application item from the File pull-down menu.

Making and Inserting Nested Blocks with BMAKE

`Command:` **`INSERT`**↵	
`Block name (or ?) <CAR>:` **`TREE`**↵	
`Insertion point:` **`SCALE`**↵	
`Scale factor:` **`60`**↵	
`Insertion point:` *Pick a point in the left lot*	Inserts one of the three trees
`Rotation angle <E>:` *Press Enter*	
`Command:` *Choose* INSERT *and add two more trees to develop the pattern as seen in figure 12.16.*	

Now that you have created one set of trees, group them into a block and insert them in the drawing.

`Command:` *Choose* File, *then* Applications, *then* <u>F</u>ile	Displays the Select LISP/ADS dialog box
Double-click on the \, *then* ACAD, *then* SAMPLE *in the* Directories *list*	Displays files in the \ACAD\SAMPLE subdirectory
Double-click on BMAKE, *then choose* <u>L</u>oad	Specifies BMAKE and loads it

The AutoLISP command BMAKE is now available in the drawing; you can issue the command by entering **BMAKE** at the `Command:` prompt. The BMAKE command defines a block in the same way as the BLOCK command, but BMAKE utilizes a dialog box to let you specify the block's parameters.

`Command:` **`BMAKE`**↵	
Pick the Select <u>P</u>oint *button*	Prompts for on-screen selection of insertion point
`Insertion base point:` *Pick a point in the middle of the three trees*	Defines an insertion point
Pick the <u>S</u>elect Objects *button*	Prompts for on-screen selection of the object to be included in the block
`Select objects:` *Select the three trees*	Specifies the objects for the block
`Select objects:` *Press Enter*	
Enter `3-TREES` *in the* Block Name *input box as the name of the block*	Defines the block's name
Pick the OK button to close the dialog box	

Use INSERT to place the block 3-TREES in the two lots. Use the Rotate option to place the block in the lot on the right, as shown in figure 12.16.

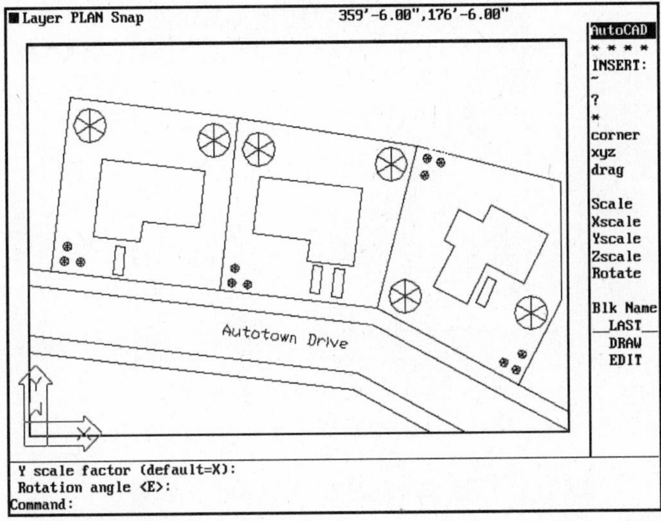

Figure 12.16:

Autotown with all the trees.

You are finished with Autotown's simple symbols. If you try different arrangements, drawing regeneration is quick because you inserted simple blocks. Before you redefine them with the complex blocks for presentation, review the blocks in your drawing and on your hard drive.

Displaying Blocks and Drawing Files

As you use AutoCAD, there are times when you need a list of the blocks and files that are available. Although it is very important that you give your blocks meaningful names, you may forget a block's name from time to time. Or you may make a typing error during the BLOCK command. When this happens, you may need to find out what you actually named the block. For these and many other reasons, you may need to display a list of block names or drawing files.

Use Block, a ?, and Utility from the Draw pull-down menu to look at your drawing directory files. Use the ? option of the BLOCK command to list blocks in a drawing; use the FILES command to list drawing files. The File List dialog box appears, as shown in figure 12.17. Your files may differ from those shown in figure 12.17.

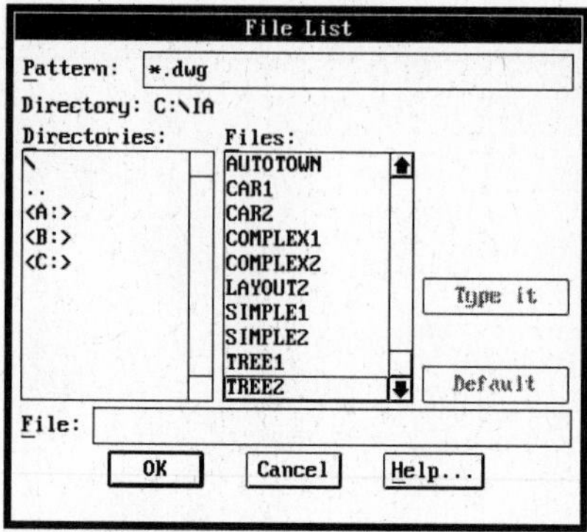

Figure 12.17:

The File List dialog box.

Displaying Blocks and Drawing Files

`Command:` *Choose* File, *then* Utilities, *and then* List Files	Displays the File List dialog box (see fig. 12.17)
Choose Cancel, *then* Exit *to return to the drawing editor*	

```
Command: BLOCK↵
Block name (or ?): ?↵
Block(s) to list <*>: Press Enter
Defined blocks.
 ATLAYOUT           Xref: resolved
 CAR
 PLAN-1
 PLAN-2
 TREE
 3-TREES
 User   External   Dependent  Unnamed
Blocks  References  Blocks   Blocks
  5     1       0       0
```

Press F1 to return to the graphics screen

Each working block has two corresponding drawing files that you created by using WBLOCK. The working blocks in the current drawing have simple PLAN-1, PLAN-2, TREE, and CAR names because you used an equal sign when you inserted them (as in PLAN-1=SIMPLE1). Maintain the files

(created with WBLOCK) separately to keep track of the simple and complex symbols. The BLOCK command also lists the xref site layout.

Redefining Blocks

You can use block redefinition to swap complete blocks for the currently inserted simple blocks. To redefine blocks, use the equal-sign option of the INSERT command. You do not have to complete the INSERT command; cut it short by pressing Ctrl-C, and the redefinition occurs.

Using Insert = To Redefine Blocks

Command: **INSERT**↵

Block name : **PLAN-1=COMPLEX1**↵

Block PLAN-1 redefined

Regenerating drawing.

Insertion point: *Press Ctrl-C to cancel*

Your drawing should now look like figure 12.18.

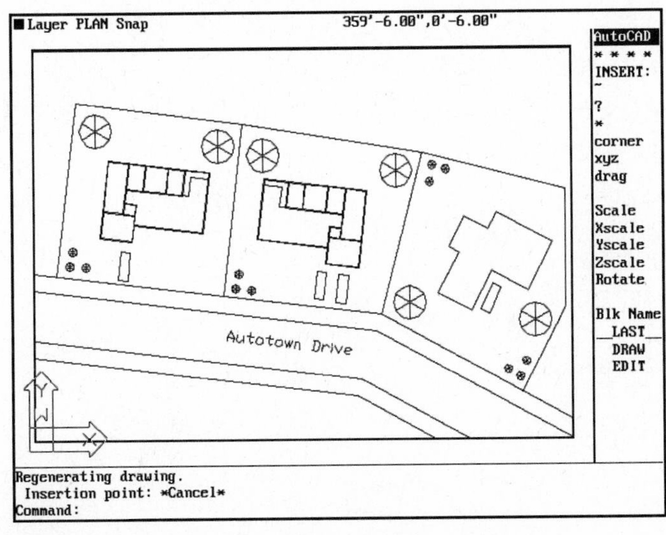

Figure 12.18: Updating PLAN-1 in Autotown.

If you must redefine several blocks, waiting for the regeneration each time is a nuisance. Turn REGENAUTO off until you finish. When you turn REGENAUTO back on, it will perform a single regeneration.

In the following steps, you redefine the rest of the drawing's working blocks. Refer to figure 12.19 as you work.

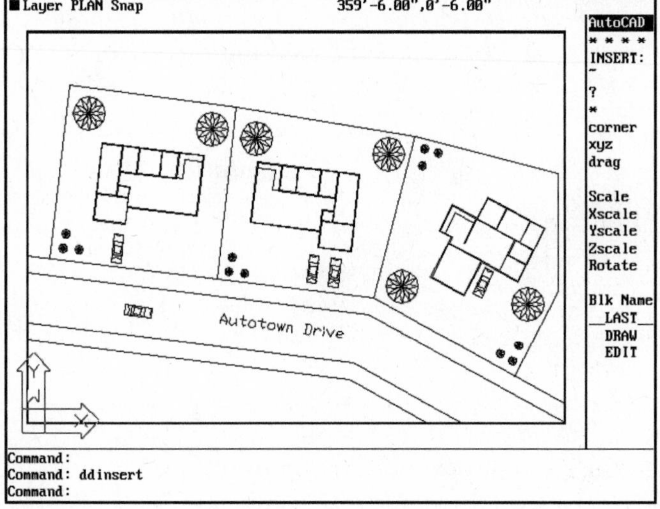

Figure 12.19:

Autotown with complex blocks.

Completing the Block Redefinitions with REGENAUTO Off

`Command:` **`REGENAUTO`**↵	
`ON/OFF <On>:` **`OFF`**↵	Turns off automatic regenerations
Use INSERT to insert PLAN-2=COMPLEX2 *and cancel the INSERT command*	
Use INSERT to insert TREE=TREE2 *and cancel the INSERT command*	
Use INSERT to insert CAR=CAR2 *and cancel the INSERT command*	
`Command:` **`REGENAUTO`**↵	
`ON/OFF <Off>:` **`ON`**↵	Turns automatic regeneration back on and regenerates

In the following steps, you insert one final car along the road (see fig. 12.19).

Command: **INSERT**↵

Block Name (or ?) <CAR>:↵

Insertion point:**90'6,81'**↵

X scale factor <1> / Corner / XYZ:↵

Y scale factor (default = x):↵

Rotation angle <E>:**172**↵

Command: *Choose* File, *then* Save

All the blocks are now redefined in the drawing. The last insertion used the new CAR=CAR2 block definition.

Updating the Externally Referenced Site Plan

In the following drawing, the site plan is from the drawing ATLAYOUT, which is attached with XREF. As explained in Chapter 11, the primary advantage of using an xref over a block is that you can modify the xref drawing independently from the drawing in which it is attached. When this happens, you can reload the xref or, the next time the drawing is opened, the xref is scanned and updated. Try updating the site plan file, then reload Autotown to see the changes.

Updating an Xref

Command: *Choose* File, *then* Open, *then double-click on* ATLAYOUT	Loads the externally referenced file

Next, you use the STRETCH command to change the plan.

Command: **STRETCH**↵

Select objects: **C**↵

Pick points to develop a crossing window across the top of the lots (see fig. 12.20)

Select objects: *Press Enter*

`Base point or displacement:` *Press Enter*	
`Second point of displacement:` **`@15'<S12dW↵`**	Stretches the lot lines
`Command:` *Choose* File, *then* Save	Saves changes
`Command:` *Choose* File, *then* Open, *then double-click on* Autotown	Reloads AUTOTOWN

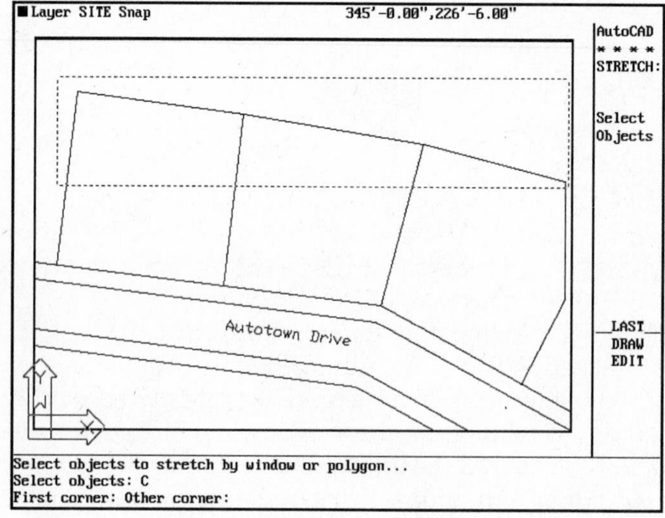

Figure 12.20:
Creating a crossing window for STRETCH.

When you reopened Autotown, the changes to ATLAYOUT placed your trees over the property line. You can use grip-editing techniques to move the trees.

Grips are available in blocks just as in any entity. To access grips within a block, use the Grip dialog box and turn on both Enable Grips or Enable Grips Within Blocks. Enable Grips places one grip at the insertion point of the block. Enable Grips Within Blocks displays grips attached to all the entities in the BLOCK.

Grip-Editing Blocks

`Command:` *Choose* Settings, *then* Grips	
Click on both the Enable Grips, *and* Enable Grips within **B**locks *boxes so that an X is displayed within both boxes, then choose* OK	Displays all grips within the entities of a block
`Command:` *Pick one of the trees*	Displays the tree's grips
Pick one of the tree's grips	Makes the grip hot
Drag inside the property line and click	Moves the tree
Use grips to move the remaining trees	
`Command:` *Choose* File, *then* Save	

Take one last look at Autotown (see fig. 12.21). Your finished Autotown drawing has about 200 entities. If you had created the drawing without blocks and xrefs, it would have about 1000 entities. As you can see, blocks and xrefs are efficient tools for drawing in AutoCAD.

You now can delete all the files created in this chapter except Autotown and ATLAYOUT.

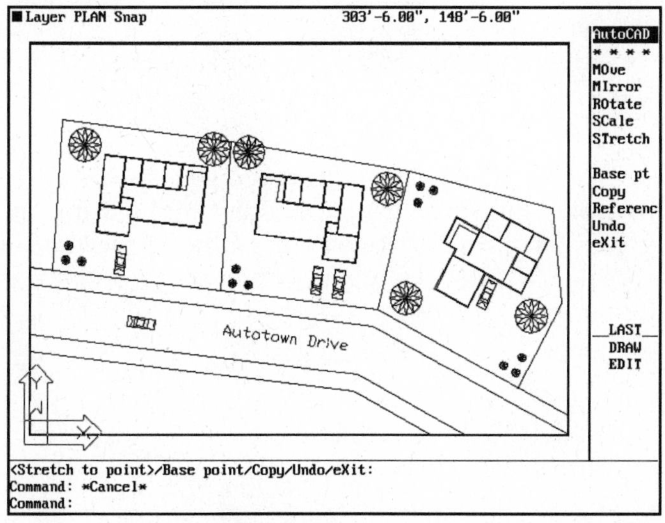

Figure 12.21: The finished Autotown drawing.

Summary

AutoCAD's blocks feature enables you to develop a large detailed drawing quickly and reduces the number of entities in the drawing.

Use the technique of first adding simple block representations to the drawing. After the drawing is complete, using = to update to a more detailed symbol keeps the computer from slowing down during the design process. You end up with a sophisticated-looking drawing quickly.

Grouping blocks within BLOCKS and creating nested BLOCKS aids in reducing drawing time. After a grouping pattern is recognized and stored, you can use INSERT to develop the geometry.

Dialog boxes for BLOCK and INSERT help you develop a drawing. These features can be particularly helpful for specifying BLOCK names. As with all dialog boxes, however, typing the command and options is often much faster.

Use the XREF command any time a drawing (or symbol) is to be shared by many drawings, and you plan to change the drawing during the development of any new drawing. An xref drawing enables all drawings to have immediate access to the most current version of the referenced drawing or symbol. If you do not plan to make changes (such as with an electrical symbol), use the BLOCKS command.

Grips are available with blocks, just as they are within singular entities. Use grips to quickly manipulate blocks with a drawing. Remember that, because blocks are single objects, some modifications are not possible.

You have created a lot of drawing data—it is now time to plot it. Although CAD replaces manual drafting in many ways, you generally need to have a paper copy of your drawing. As in manual drafting, the drawing must be scaled to fit on a piece of paper and may require different view and linetype characteristics. The next chapter explores plotting and composition of finished drawings.

13

Sheet Composition, Scaling, and Plotting

A CAD drawing is fundamentally different from a drawing created with paper and pencil. The final product of a manual drawing is the sheet of paper on which it is drawn. The final product of a CAD drawing actually is a database that represents all of the graphic entities and text associated with the drawing. AutoCAD's drawing editor builds a collection of data in memory. When you save your drawing, that data — lists and tables full of coordinates, numbers, and other information — is stored in a file on disk. Visually, this database has no resemblance at all to a drawing. When you edit the drawing, AutoCAD represents the data in the drawing editor by reading the database and issuing instructions that convert the data into the image you see. Figure 13.1 shows a sample printed drawing.

The process of generating a plot is similar to that of representing a drawing on-screen. Instead of converting the data into pixels on your monitor, however, AutoCAD translates the information into a raster or vector image that a plotter can understand. After you initially set up the plotter, these commands for a vector plotter usually amount to little more than moving a pen up and down and from one coordinate to another on the paper. If the pen is down when the command is issued, a line is drawn. Many little line segments combine to plot arcs and text.

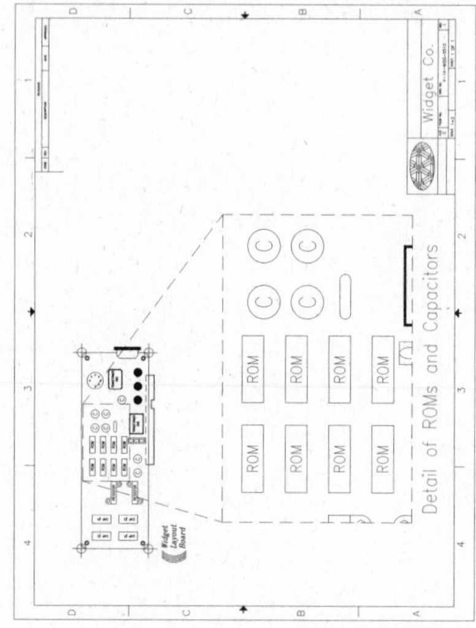

Figure 13.1:
A detail viewport and layout plotted from paper space sheet.

Fortunately, AutoCAD takes care of translating the data in your file into plotter commands. All you have to do is set up the plotter, select the drawing, tell AutoCAD what to plot, and watch it plot. So many plotters and printers are available that it would be impractical to cover here the configuration and setup of each one, especially because most output devices control many of the plotting parameters and functions from the plotter, rather than through AutoCAD. This chapter focuses on composing your drawing for plotting and on actually creating plots.

Getting Ready To Plot

The task of plotting involves more than just issuing the PLOT command. When you install AutoCAD, you have to tell AutoCAD the type of plotter you have, how the plotter is connected, and what default settings to use. When you draw, you have to compose your finished drawing for plotting. When you plot, you have to load paper into the plotter, put in the right type of pens for the plotting media you are using, and make sure the plotter is ready to start receiving information. When you finally issue the PLOT command, you have to check each of its parameters to make sure it is correct for that particular plot. With the drawing file ready to plot, you issue the PLOT command, which passes the data through with parameters that control the size and appearance of the finished plot, convert the data into plotter commands, and send them to the plotter.

Configuring AutoCAD for Your Output Device

AutoCAD must be properly configured for your output device. This can be accomplished by choosing Configure from the File pull-down menu, or by entering the CONFIG command, and then using Option 5, Configure plotter. Device configuration is covered in more detail in Appendix A. Before you try to configure an output device, you may have to know certain information about the device such as model number, emulation capabilities, and communications parameters. Consult your output device manufacturer's instructions and your *AutoCAD Interface, Installation and Performance Guide.*

The plotter configuration option of AutoCAD offers the following options:

- **Add** a plotter to the configuration.
- **Delete** a plotter from the active configuration list.
- **Change** a plotter configuration.
- **Rename** a plotter configuration.

Multiple Plotter and Printer Configurations

The CONFIG command can configure AutoCAD for one or more output devices and file formats. During configuration, you can assign your own special device names to any plotter, output device, or file format CONFIGURATION. The PLOT command conveniently enables you to select, from a list, what CONFIGURATION you want to use for a given plot.

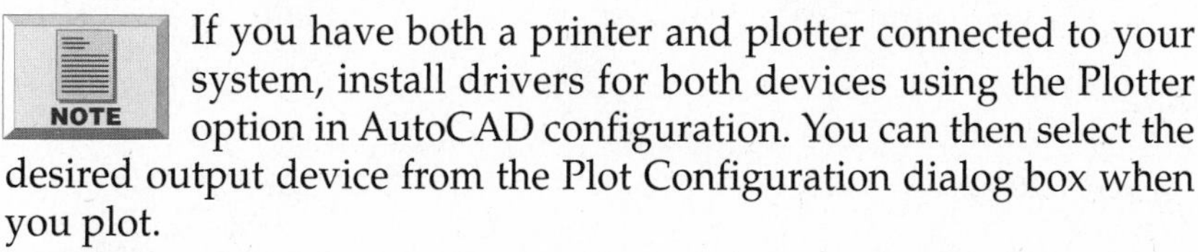

If you have both a printer and plotter connected to your system, install drivers for both devices using the Plotter option in AutoCAD configuration. You can then select the desired output device from the Plot Configuration dialog box when you plot.

NOTE

If you reconfigure AutoCAD, write or print out the current configuration in case the settings are accidentally lost or overwritten. You can use Ctrl-Q to copy screen output to the printer. Pressing Ctrl-Q a second time turns off printer output.

The plotting examples in this chapter are based on a generic D-size (34X22) plotter and a generic printer. Your default pen speed, sheet size, and linetypes may vary from the examples in this book, but these settings do not affect the exercises. If you want to change some of the configuration settings for your output device, you can set different values during the PLOT command.

First-Time Checklist

The following checklist outlines items you should check when you configure your plotter initially:

- Is the plotter plugged in?
- Is the plotter connected to the correct port on the computer?
- Does the interface cable between the plotter and computer match the connections shown in the AutoCAD installation manual?
- Has the plotter been configured in AutoCAD?
- Are the software configuration settings correct?
- Does the plotter self-test run properly and does the drawing output look OK?
- Is the paper alignment correct and do the pens operate properly?

If you are using a printer instead of a plotter, or a smaller plotter, most of the discussion in this chapter still applies. Some printers (such as PostScript printers) are configured as plotters. If you do not have a printer or plotter but can carry a floppy disk to a system with one, you can plot to a disk file and then copy it to the plotter. This process is covered later in this chapter.

If your plotter or printer requires an ADI driver for AutoCAD that was not supplied by Autodesk, see the manufacturer's instructions and be sure to add any required commands to your CONFIG.SYS or AUTOEXEC.BAT files.

Every-Time Checklist

The plotting process involves two steps: setting up the plotter to run, and readying your drawing file with the proper scale and other plotter assignments in AutoCAD. After you have configured the plotter in AutoCAD, you

only need to check and adjust parameters such as paper size and pen selection when you plot. Use the following checklist.

- Is the paper or other media loaded and properly aligned in the plotter? Does it move freely without striking the wall, cables, or other obstructions?
- Is the plotter adjusted for that size of paper?
- Are the pens in the holder? Are they primed and flowing freely? If the plotter uses removable carousels, is the correct carousel in the plotter? Does the carousel type match the pen type? Are the correct pens for the media being used, and is the speed set so the pens work without skipping?
- If the plotter shares a single COM port with another device such as a digitizer, has the selection switch been switched to the plotter or has the cable been connected to the plotter?
- Does the plotter need to be in Remote mode to sense incoming commands?

Try performing a plot based on the following procedures.

Accessing the PLOT Command

AutoCAD offers a number of ways to access the PLOT command. You can plot by choosing Plot from the File pull-down menu and specifying the plotting options. Choosing that sequence, as shown in figure 13.2, outputs the current drawing. You also can select the PLOT command from the screen menu or enter it at the `Command:` prompt. All these methods bring up the Plot Configuration dialog box, shown in figure 13.4, if the system variable CMDDIA is on (set to 1 — the default). If CMDDIA is set to 0, you are prompted for the plot options at the command line. Later in the chapter you learn how to plot without first bringing up the drawing. This is done if you start AutoCAD by entering the command **ACAD -P** at the operating system prompt.

The PRPLOT command, found in previous releases of AutoCAD, is no longer valid. Printers are supported along with plotters through the standard Plot Configuration dialog box.

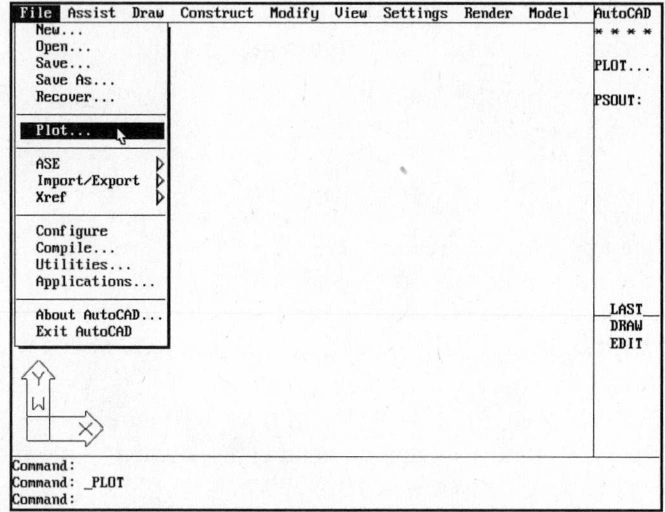

Figure 13.2:

The PLOT command on the pull-down and screen menus.

The Plot Configuration dialog box sets parameters and plots a drawing. Many of these parameters are the same as in the CONFIG command's plotter option, and you can use the Plot Configuration dialog box to select from any configured devices. However, if you need to add a new device, or delete or rename an existing one, use the CONFIG command, not PLOT.

You also can use scripts to run plots automatically. The SCRIPT command is on the UTILITY screen menu. The task of plotting from a script file is covered later in this chapter.

Creating a Checkplot To Fit the Paper

When you plot a drawing to fit, AutoCAD calculates a ratio between the width of the drawing area you specify and the width of the plotting area. AutoCAD performs the same calculation for the height of the drawing area and the height of the plotting area. The larger of the two dimensions determines the actual size of the plot. Because the drawing is plotted in proportion to its true size, some blank space may be left on the plot either for the width or height, depending on which proportion is smaller. The following exercise shows the prompts for a printer that is configured as a LaserJet in AutoCAD. If you are configured for a plotter or PostScript printer, this exercise should work fine. You can plot to the default device or choose another device from the dialog box, if one is available.

Begin by plotting the drawing extents in the following exercise. You are fitting them to the sheet, rather than scaling the drawing to a specific size. If you plot by using the Extents and Fit options, everything in the drawing is plotted as large as possible on the paper. Use the WIDGEDIT drawing from Chapter 9. If you did not create that file, you can use any drawing because it is plotted to fit the paper. Your plotting area dimensions probably differ from the numbers shown in the exercise, but your plot should appear similar to that shown in figure 13.3.

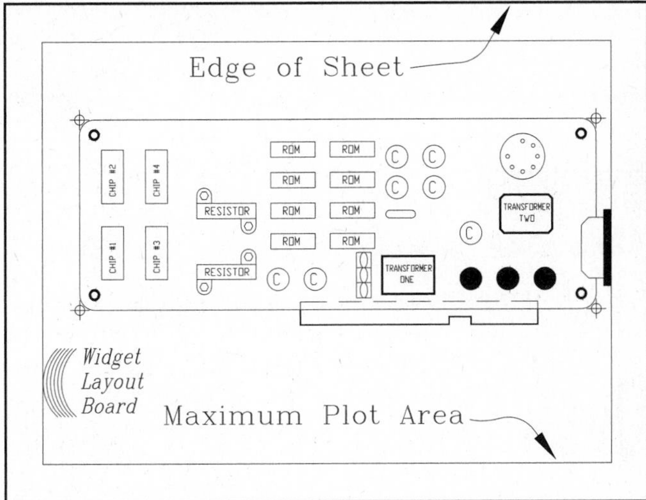

Figure 13.3: The WIDGEDIT drawing, plotted with extents, and scaled to fit.

Plotting the Extents To Fit the Paper

Start AutoCAD using the IA.BAT batch program.

Open drawing file WIDGEDIT, then ZOOM with the Extents option.

`Command:` *Choose* File, *then* Plot	Displays the Plot Configuration dialog box (see fig. 13.4)
`Command: _plot`	
Click on the Extents *radio button in the* Additional Parameters *area*	Specifies the area of the drawing to plot
Put a check mark in the Scaled to Fit *check box in the* Scale, Rotation, and Origin *area*	Scales the plot to fit the paper

Make sure your printer or plotter and paper are ready.

Click on OK	Starts PLOT command
`Effective plot area: 10.50 wide by 5.51 high`	
`Position paper in plotter. Press RETURN to continue or S to Stop for Hardware setup:` *Press Enter*	Starts the plot
`Regeneration done: nn`	AutoCAD cycles through the drawing, displaying the percent finished in place of nn at left, and displays "Plot Complete" on the command line

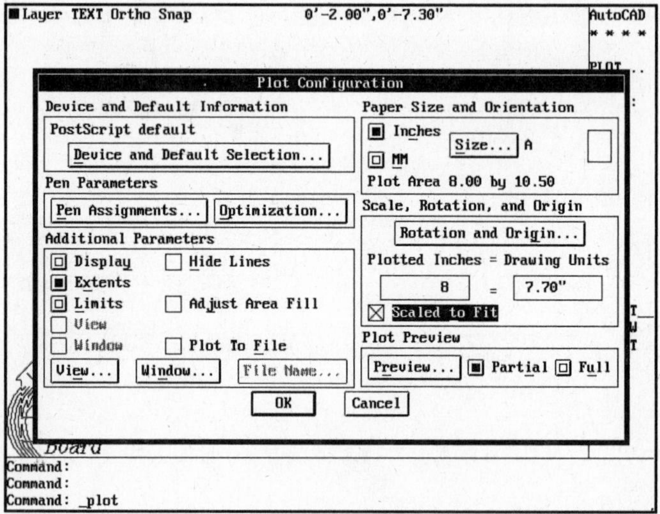

Figure 13.4:

The Plot Configuration dialog box.

If you used the WIDGEDIT drawing, your plot should resemble the one shown in figure 13.3. If the drawing plotted extremely small, perform a ZOOM Extents on the drawing, then replot. The drawing may need to be rotated to best fill the sheet on your printer or plotter; you learn how to rotate plots later in this chapter.

Take advantage of plotting to a printer to make quick, easy, and inexpensive checkplots. If your printer has high enough resolution, it also is useful for 11"×8 1/2" detail prints.

The steps described in the preceding exercise are basically what it takes to get a plot. But you should compose your plot before you even turn on the plotter.

Composing and Finishing a Drawing for Plotting

The WIDGEDIT drawing makes a nice plot, but it is not a finished drawing. A finished drawing is composed with a title block and usually includes more than one view of the object it represents. Often, detailed views are included — views that may be at different scales than the original drawing. A finished drawing often includes annotations and dimensions. Some layers, like construction layers, for example, may be turned off. Finished drawings usually include more than one line weight — usually controlled by plotting with different pens.

In the plot you just did, AutoCAD's defaults were used for all of the plotting-control parameters. Most finished drawings require changing one or more of those parameters for each plot. These parameters include:

- **Select the Part of the Drawing to Plot.** This parameter selects how much of the drawing to plot by choosing the Display, Extents, Limits, View, or Window radio buttons.
- **Select the Plotting Area.** This parameter specifies a sheet size, such as C, D, and so on, for plotting area, or specifies a custom plot size by plot length and width if you are using an odd-sized sheet or need the plot to be a certain finished size. Either option is selected by clicking on the Size button.
- **Select the Plot Scale.** This parameter checks the Scaled to Fit check box to scale the drawing to fill the plotting area, proportional to the model, but not to any certain scale. To plot to a specific scale, enter values in the Plotted Inches and Drawing Units edit boxes.

Paper space makes it easy to finish and compose a drawing for plotting. You simply treat paper space as an electronic sheet of paper, sized to match your plotter media, and compose your drawing. When you plot, what you see in the graphics window is what you get in the plot — at the full precision and resolution of your plotter.

Finishing and composing a drawing without paper space is more complicated. Model space is the environment in which you model your design, whether 2D or 3D. In model space, you can plot only the current viewport. You need to do some manual cut-and-paste operations by using commands such as COPY, SCALE, and TRIM to plot several views of a drawing on one sheet of paper from model space.

Think ahead about leaving room for a border and a title block. Set the drawing limits equal to the paper size and plot Limits, sizing and positioning your title block and border margins to compensate for the area the plotter needs to grasp the paper.

Controlling What To Plot

When you compose a drawing, your first consideration should be to decide what to plot. Many times, whether from model space or paper space, you want to plot only a portion of your drawing. You may, for example, need a checkplot of only one viewport or of part of a viewport. If you use layers and colors to segregate your data, you may want to plot only certain layers, areas, or colors. The LAYER command controls which layers are plotted. The PLOT command enables you to specify how much of the drawing to include in the plot and to control how colors plot. The PLOT command also enables you to move the location of the plot on the paper, scale the plot, and fit it to the paper, giving you fine control over the finished plot, even without paper space.

The PLOT command has five options that control how much of the drawing will plot. The Plot Configuration dialog box gives you the choice of Display, Extents, Limits, View, or Window. Anything that falls outside the selected area is clipped and not plotted. The following list describes what each choice does:

- **Display.** This option uses the image currently displayed in your graphics window to determine what to plot. Everything inside the area of the current viewport is plotted. (Remember, paper space itself or a single full-drawing area view in paper space is considered a viewport.)

- **Extents.** This option specifies to plot the extents of your drawing. This option, used in coordination with Fit, plots everything visible in the drawing to fit the paper.
- **Limits.** This option specifies to plot everything in the drawing limits.
- **View.** This option specifies to plot a named view that you have previously saved. You can save a number of different views with different names, then use View to plot each one by name. You can save an appropriate view named PLOT in every drawing, which makes plotting easy to standardize.
- **Window.** This option enables you to define a rectangular window around the area of the drawing you want to plot. Normally, you use the Window option only when you are plotting or printing with the drawing loaded into the drawing editor. If, however, you select Window when plotting or printing from a *freeplot* session (a session started with ACAD -P), you can use the Window button to specify the coordinates of the opposing corners of the window to determine what to plot.

Setting the Plotting Scale

In the first exercise, you plotted the WIDGEDIT drawing to fit the paper in the plotter. Although this gave you a plotted image proportional to the original model, it was not set to any specific scale. Most of the time your drawings do need to be plotted to scale.

In paper space, you compose your drawing in paper space limits that equal your sheet size and plot the drawing at full scale.

In model space, sizing your plot to a particular scale is more involved but fairly straightforward. You size your plot by finding a ratio between the actual size of the model and the scale at which you want it to plot. Suppose, for example, that you have a house plan drawn to actual size, and you want to plot it at a scale of 1/4"=1'-0". When you specify a plot scale in the PLOT command, you enter the corresponding scale in units that AutoCAD can interpret, instead of typing Fit. In this case, you could can either **1/4"=1'0** or **1=48**, and the drawing plots to that scale. Optionally, you can enter the same value in decimal form, such as **.25=12**, or **.020833=1**. This scales the model correctly, but what about scaling the annotations?

Scaling Annotations, Symbols, and Dimensions

How can you determine what size your text, bubbles, and dimensions will plot? The key is to understand that everything in your model is related to model space or real-world dimensions. You almost always draw objects actual size, and scale them when it is time to plot. In the preceding example, the house plan would have been drawn actual size. Suppose, for example, that you want your text to plot 1/8" high. If you create your text and other annotations at 1/8", the dimensions and notes would be so small relative to the house plan itself that you could not read them. It would be like standing 200 feet above the house while trying to read a newspaper resting on the ground.

When you create your dimensions and text, you need to know at what size you will eventually plot the drawing. In this example, you want to determine the relationship between 1/8" on the paper and the size of the text in the model. If 1/4" on paper equals 12" in the model, then 1/8" equals 6", so text and dimensions should be drawn 6" high in this drawing to plot 1/8" on paper at this scale. Dimension text and symbols are scaled similarly.

Consider one more example. If you find that your house plan is too big to fit on the paper at 1/4" = 1'-0", you might decide to scale the drawing to 3/16" = 1'-0" instead. But, you still want all of the text to plot 1/8" high. 1/8" is two-thirds of 3/16" (2/16 compared to 3/16), and 8" is two-thirds of 12", so you need 8" text to get 1/8" high characters on paper.

These same scales apply to text and annotations that you put on your model in model-space viewports-even if you compose the final drawing in paper space. Later, some paper space alternatives are explored.

Table 13.1 shows the model text size needed to achieve a specific plotted text size at some common scales.

Composing a Title Block in Model Space

Drawing in full scale brings up the problem of how to place a D-size sheet border and title block around a model that may be a hundred feet wide. The answer is simple: create the title block full size (34X22 or 36X24 for a D-size sheet). Then insert it as a block in your drawing by using the inverse of the scale that you would use to plot the drawing.

Table 13.1
Common Text Sizes at Various Scales

Scale	*Plotted Text Size*	*Text Size (Model)*
1/8"=1'-0"	1/8"	12"
	3/16"	18"
	1/4"	24"
3/16"=1'-0"	1/8"	8"
	3/16"	12"
	1/4"	16"
1/4"=1'-0"	1/8"	6"
	3/16"	8"
	1/4"	12"
1/2"=1'-0"	1/8"	3"
	3/16"	4.5"
	1/4"	6"
1"=1'-0"	1/8"	1.5"
	3/16"	2.25"
	1/4"	3"
1 1/2"=1'-0"	1/8"	1"
	3/16"	1.5"
	1/4"	2"
1:2	.125"	.25"
	.1875"	.3875"
	.25"	.5"
1:10	.125"	12.5"
	.1875"	18.75"
	.25"	25"
2:1	.125"	.0625"
	.1875"	.09375"
	.25"	.125"

Consider the same example shown earlier — a house plan drawn actual size that needs to go on a D-size sheet at a scale of 1/4" = 1'-0". You enter a scale of 1/4"=1'0 (equal to 1:48) when prompted for a scale in Plot. Your title block also is drawn actual size, only 34" or 36" wide. When you insert the title block by using the INSERT command, it has to be scaled up proportionally to the model. So if you insert the title block drawing into the model and scale it 48 times larger to fit around the plan of the house, it scales back to its original size when the drawing is plotted.

Model Space Alternative: Faking Paper Space

Another approach would be to scale the model drawing down and insert it into the title block before you plot. This approach has the advantage of always plotting at a standard 1=1 scale, and it enables you to preview the "what you see is what you will plot" image in the graphics window. It also makes it much easier to combine multiple scales of details in a single drawing. You can do this in two ways.

One solution is to do it in a single drawing file. First, create a block of your entire drawing; do not use the OOPS command to bring back the erased entities. Next, insert your title block at 1=1 scale on its own layer and zoom to the title block. Then, insert your entire drawing into the title block on the title block layer at the scale that you would have used to plot it in the previously discussed method. In this example, you would insert it at 1/48. If you later need to make changes to the drawing model, freeze the title block layer, *Insert the drawing block at 1=1 scale, zoom out and make changes, and reblock it to the same name. When you thaw and zoom back to the title block layer, you find the changes because of the block redefinition.

A second solution is to create a separate 1=1 scale title block drawing and insert the model drawing file into it at the appropriate scale. If you make changes to the model drawing file, re-insert it with an equal sign to redefine it in the title block drawing.

In either case, you plot the results at full scale. If you need to add annotations or title text, you do it at the real-world scale you want it to be in the plot. This method makes multiple model views or detail with varying scales in one drawing easier, but it is not as easy as using paper space.

Plotting Multiple Model Views or Details

Multiple model views or details with varying scales in one drawing are easy to compose in paper space. Set up each desired view or detail in its own viewport, scale it, and plot everything at once from paper space. That full process is covered later in this chapter.

You can fake the paper space technique by inserting a block for each desired view or detail into your 1=1 title block. Scale each insertion as if you were plotting it to scale by itself. As you see in the 3D chapters, you can use UCSs when you write your blocks to disk to create varying viewpoints of the same model. Then you can insert these into a single title block.

A third alternative is to scale and plot each view or detail separately, but all on the same sheet of paper. This alternative requires the capability to position each plot where you want it on the plotter sheet.

Positioning the Plot on Paper

Whichever way you compose and scale your plot, whether you plan to plot it all at once or plot separate views or details on the same sheet of paper, your next decision is how to place the plot on the paper.

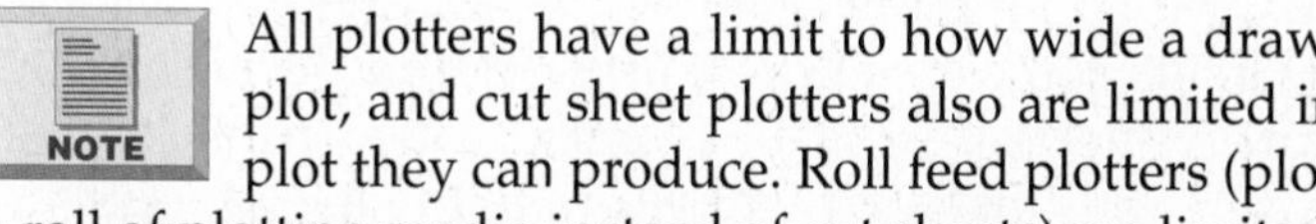

All plotters have a limit to how wide a drawing they can plot, and cut sheet plotters also are limited in how long a plot they can produce. Roll feed plotters (plotters that use a roll of plotting media instead of cut sheets) are limited as to width, but often can plot a drawing as long as the length of the media on the roll. Because cut sheet plotters are much more common than roll feed plotters, cut sheet plotters are used in the following discussion.

Plot Origin versus Area-to-Plot Origin

A plotter's starting pen position is the *plotter origin*. The plot places the lower left corner of the area to plot (display, extents, limits, view, or window) at the plotter origin. On a pen plotter, the plotter origin usually is at or near the lower left corner of the paper. For a printer plotter, it is the upper left corner. If you tell AutoCAD to rotate the plot, the origin changes. The rectangular boundary that defines the maximum plotting area for a plotter is called its *hard clip limits*. If you place a point in each of the opposite corners of the hard clip limits, one of the points becomes the plotter origin.

You can determine your plotter's origin and hard clip limits by separately plotting a vertical line and a horizontal line (length is not important). Plot them on the same sheet by using Extents and Fit. Both options start at the plotter origin and extend to the X or Y limits.

As already mentioned, AutoCAD normally places the lower left corner of the part of the drawing you specify to plot at the plotter origin. To plot the drawing at a particular point on the sheet, as you would to plot multiple views separately, tell AutoCAD to move the plotter origin. Do this by specifying an X,Y displacement in plotter units at the plot origin prompt or in the Plot Rotation and Origin dialog box. By specifying a different displacement for each view or detail, you can plot multiple images on a sheet, one at a time.

Plot Standardization

Even normal plots (one per sheet) are easier if you standardize the relationship of the plotter origin to the lower left corner of the area you specify to plot. You standardized the book's drawings by setting limits to the sheet size (in drawing units). If your plotter can plot the full sheet from edge to edge, you can plot limits at the default plot origin (home position at the lower left corner of the sheet). But most plotters grip a portion of the paper during the plot. This means that the lower left corner of the paper is not at the plotter origin, so you cannot plot limits to scale. You still can get an accurately scaled plot by doing a window plot or by plotting a named view. Set the lower left corner of the window or view in the drawing at an offset from the lower left corner of the limits. This offset should be equal to the distance from the lower left corner of the sheet to the plotter origin for your plotter. Unless you are plotting at full scale, you need to convert this offset to drawing units (offset times scale factor). Set the upper right corner to encompass the area you want to plot; anything outside the window or view (or outside your plotter's hard clip limits) will be clipped. Make sure any title block you use fits in the window or view and is within your plotter's hard clip limits.

By using a view named PLOT, you can standardize plotting at the appropriate scale at the default plotter origin. You can further standardize your plotting by combining this technique with using paper space or the fake paper space method. That way, you always plot a view named PLOT at full scale at the default plotter origin.

Plotting a Standard View Named PLOT to Scale

To see how this works and to practice plotting a drawing to scale, plot the WIDGEDIT drawing from Chapter 7 again. WIDGEDIT was created with 11"×8.5" limits, matching an A-size sheet at 1=1 scale or a C-size (22×17) sheet at 2=1 scale (twice real size). You will plot it at 2=1 scale. If you did not create the drawing, substitute the WIDGET drawing from Chapter 6, the IA7WIDG3 drawing from the IA DISK, or any other drawing with 11"×8.5" limits.

Assume that the generic plotter's origin is offset 1/2" in the X axis and 3/4" in the Y axis from the lower left corner of the sheet. This makes your offset .25,.375 (.5,.75 divided by a 2:1 plot-to-drawing scale). You can place the lower left corner of your PLOT view at .25,.375 to place the 0,0 point of your limits precisely at the corner of the plot sheet. If your plotter origin offset is different, substitute your X,Y offset divided by 2. If you are using a printer or if your maximum sheet size is smaller than C-size, plot to an A-size sheet at 1:1 scale and adjust your offset to match.

As in the earlier plot, your plot area may differ from that shown in the preceding PLOT command.

Plotting WIDGEDIT to Scale and Moving the Origin

Open the drawing file WIDGEDIT, then ZOOM All.

`Command: VIEW ↵`	
`?/Delete/Restore/Save/Window: W↵`	
`View name to save: PLOT↵`	Names the view
`First corner: .25,.375↵`	Sets the first window corner (substitute your calculated offset)
`Other corner: 11,8.5 ↵`	Sets the other corner and saves the view

Draw a border, using a 2D polyline, no larger than half your hard clip limits, centered on the image.

Set the PDMODE system variable to 0 and by using POINT, draw a point at your calculated offset point.

`Command:` *Choose* File, *then* Plot	Opens the Plot Configuration dialog box
Choose the View *button*	Opens the View Name dialog box
Double-click on PLOT in the View Name list	Selects the view, closes the dialog box, and turns on the **V**iew radio button
Choose the **S**ize *button, then select* A *if you are plotting to a printer, or* C *if you are plotting to a plotter, then choose* OK	Sets the paper size
Click on the Rotation and Origin *box and click on the* 90 *radio button if you are using a printer*	Sets the plot orientation on the paper
Turn off the Scaled to Fit *check box*	Allows the scale to be set
Double-click in the Plotted Inches *edit box and enter* `1` *and press Enter for A-size, or enter* `2` *and press Enter for C-size*	Sets the appropriate scale
Choose **O**K	Closes the dialog box

`Effective plotting area: 21.00 wide by 16.00 high`

`Position paper in plotter.`

Make sure your printer or plotter and paper are ready.

`Press RETURN to continue or S to Stop for Hardware setup:` *Press Enter*	Starts the plot

`Regeneration done: nn`

When the plot finishes, close the drawing and discard your changes.

The widget should have plotted at twice its real-world size for C-size, or at its exact size for A-size, with the lower left corner of the border exactly at your plotter origin and the lower left limits at the sheet corner as shown in figure 13.5.

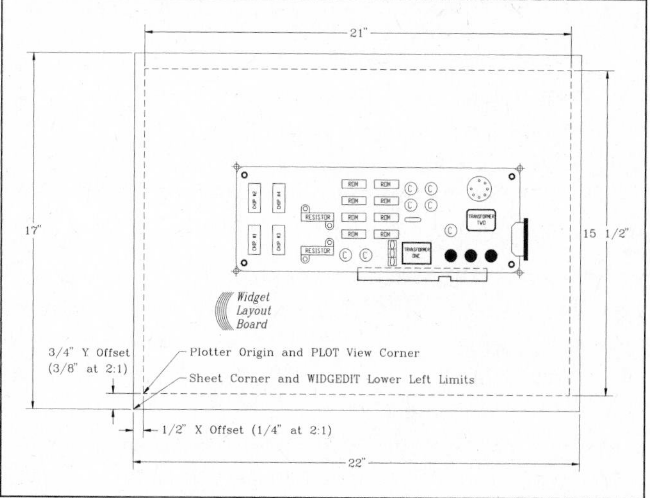

Figure 13.5:

Plot offset for WIDGEDIT at 2=1 scale.

If your plotter offset is too large and your hard clip limits are too small to accommodate your standard title sheet, perhaps you can expand them.

Expanding the Plotting Area

Sometimes your drawing does not fit in the hard clip limits, perhaps by a fraction of an inch. In some cases, the hard clip limits of the plotter can be expanded by increasing the plot area half an inch or more. Check your plotter documentation to see if your plotter offers an expanded mode. Usually, expanded mode is controlled by a small switch on the plotter. Expanded mode moves the location of the 0,0 plotter origin to the corner of the expanded area.

Sometimes, the expanded plotter origin comes too close to the pinch wheels that hold the paper against the plotter drum, at times even moving past the wheels. If this happens with an ink plot, the wheels smear anything drawn inside their area. To eliminate this problem, you can adjust the plotter origin away from the pinch wheel by entering a small origin offset.

You may find that composing a plot in paper space is even easier than using the technique just described.

Composing a Plot in Paper Space

One of paper space's primary functions is to make plotting easier, particularly in 3D work. The process you go through each time you take your drawing from the design stage to a finished plot is pretty much the same. The following checklist gives you an idea of what steps to take after your design is drawn.

- Enter Pspace and use MVIEW to create as many viewports as you need for the various views and details you want to plot. If your viewports exceed 15, turn them on, 15 at a time, and plot twice on a single sheet, or put details in separate drawing files and insert them or attach them as externally-referenced files in paper space before plotting. You also can create and draw in viewports that you do not intend to plot, to work on the main or master model from which the other views are derived. You can do the bulk of your design work now or after planning the arrangement of views in the title sheet.
- Insert your title sheet into paper space at full scale or attach it as an externally referenced file. Put it on its own layer so you can freeze it as you work on your drawing. Plan how the viewports to be plotted are to be arranged and scaled in the title sheet. You can draw construction lines on a layer that will not be plotted to keep track of your arrangement. Freeze the title sheet layer.
- Enter model space and create or finish drawing your views and details. Compose each view to be plotted as if it were a separate drawing in its own viewport. You do not need to have the viewports in their final arrangement as you work — arrange and size them for drawing convenience. But keep the planned scale and size of each in mind, particularly as you add annotations. You can control layers independently in each viewport, so annotations for one do not show up in others. Finish the model, complete with most dimensions, notes, and other details.
- Enter paper space and thaw your blank title sheet. Erase or freeze the layers of viewports that will not be plotted.
- Resize, stretch, and move the viewports to be plotted to match your planned arrangement in the sheet.
- Enter model space and use the ZOOM command's *n*XP option (*n* is your scale value) to scale each view or detail to the correct plotted scale. This technique is covered in the next section.

- Re-enter paper space. Add any annotations or dimensions that you want to do in paper space (dimensions can be automatically scaled to the viewport's contents). Insert any details or attach any externally-referenced files that are stored as separate drawing files. (These could be ordinary blocks or blocked viewports. If they are viewports, you have to turn them on.) Fill in your title block information.
- Create a view named PLOT with its lower left corner offset to match your plotter's offset. Restore the view. What you see is what you will get. Make any final layer on/off or freeze/thaw adjustments.
- Use the PLOT command to plot the PLOT view at full scale.

If you plot by using the Display option and have multiple viewports set, you get a plot of whatever is displayed in the current viewport.

The procedure outlined earlier introduced something new: zooming relative to paper scale.

Scaling Viewports Relative to Paper Scale

In the ZOOM command, entering a scale factor, followed by XP causes the image to display relative to your paper scale. (The XP stands for *times paper scale.*) If you enter a factor of 1XP, the viewport displays the image at full scale (1=1) relative to your paper. When you plot the drawing at full scale from paper space, the viewport plots at the scale factor specified by ZOOM with the XP option. A zoom factor of .5XP causes the image in the viewport to display at half size.

You determine the ZOOM XP scale as a decimal scale factor in the same manner that you figure scale if you were plotting that viewport by itself. If, for example, you want a view of your model at 1/4" = 1'-0", which is 1:48, divide 1 by 48 to get 0.020833 and enter 0.020833XP at the ZOOM command as your scale factor.

After you use the ZOOM XP option, be careful not to do other zooms in or out in model space. PAN is safe and good for fine-tuning the view. If you use ZOOM with the Dynamic option for panning, be sure that you do not change the size of the zoom box.

Scaling a viewport like this only makes sense if you are working in model space (Mspace). ZOOM with the XP option still works in paper space or tiled viewports, but its effect is identical to the ZOOM X option in those cases.

Setting Up Paper Space Views for Plotting

Whether you used tiled or untiled viewports, you model your design in one or more model space viewports, and then compose your title block sheet in paper space for plotting as outlined earlier.

If all of your views and details require more than one title sheet, you can insert more than one copy of your title block and then open viewports accordingly on each sheet. You can define plot views by using names like PLOT1, PLOT2, and so on. If you have more than 15 total viewports, you have to use MVIEW to turn them on and off as you plot the different plot views. This keeps you from having to duplicate the model in separate files for each sheet.

The composition of a sheet involves more than haphazardly opening viewports on the page and scaling the views inside them. You can overlap viewports if you want. You can turn viewport frames off by layer control if you do not want them to plot. Their contents still plot unless their appropriate layers are frozen.

Try to compose a new plot and arrange the viewports. Use the WIDGEDIT drawing from Chapter 9 again, or you can substitute the WIDGET drawing from Chapter 7, the IA7WIDG3 drawing (if you have the IA DISK), or any other drawing with 11"×8.5" limits. Compose two viewports on a 22"×17" sheet and plot it at full scale. One viewport contains a full view of the widget board, and the other shows a 4X detail view. If you do not have a C-size plotter or larger plotter, compose it on an 11"×8.5" sheet. A simple polyline border can be drawn to represent the title block sheet that normally would be inserted or attached. Before you pan and zoom the viewports, your drawing should look like the one shown in figure 13.6.

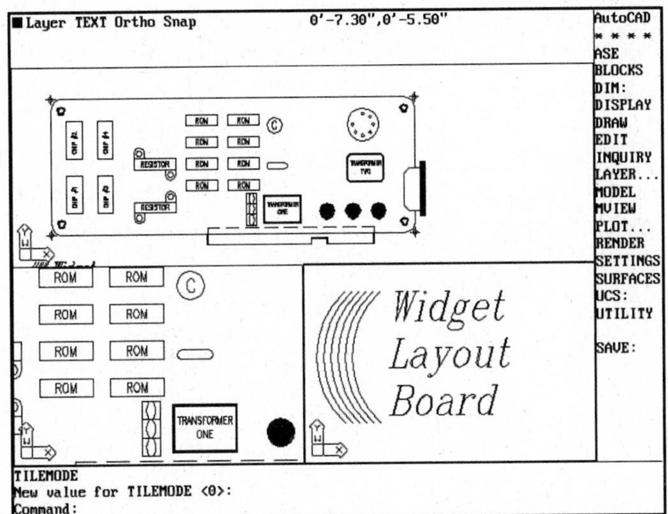

Figure 13.6:

The widget in paper space; before rearranging the viewports.

Composing a Plot in Mview Viewports

Begin a new drawing named `PSPLOT=IA7WIDG4`.

Choose File, then New, and enter `PSPLOT=WIDGEDIT`.

`Command:` **`TILEMODE`** ↵	
`New value for TILEMODE <1>:` **`0`**↵	Turns off TILEMODE
`Regenerating drawing.`	Displays Viewports from Chapter 7
`Command:` *Select all three viewports, then issue the* ERASE *command*	Leaves blank paper space sheet
`Command:` *Choose* Settings, *then* Drawing Limits, *and set limits from 0,0 to 11,8.5 for A-size or from 0,0 to 22,17 for C-size*	Sets paper space limits, independent from model space

ZOOM with the All option.

If you are using an A-size sheet, set snap to .125 and use PLINE to draw a border from .5,.375 to 10.5,.375 to 10.5,8.125 to .5,8.125 and close it.

If you are using a C-size sheet, set snap to .25 and use PLINE to draw a border from 1,.75 to 21,.75 to 21,16.25 to 1,16.25 and close it

`Command:` *Choose* View, *then* Mview, *then* Create Viewport	Issues MVIEW command
`ON/OFF/Hideplot/Fit/2/3/4/Restore/` `<First Point>:` *From the pop-up menu, choose* Intersection	
`int of` *Pick the upper left hand corner of the border at ① (see fig. 13.7)*	
`Other corner:` *Enter* **9,4.5** *for A-size or* **18,9** *for C-size*	Displays widget in a viewport
`Command:` *Press Enter*	Repeats MVIEW
`ON/OFF/Hideplot/Fit/2/3/4/Restore/` `<First Point>:` *Enter* **3.5,1** *for A-size or* **7,2** *for C-size*	
`Other corner:` *From the pop-up menu, choose* Intersection	
`int of` *Pick lower right corner of upper viewport at ②*	Displays widget in a another viewport
`Command:` **MS** ↵	Enters model space and allows the contents of the viewports to be zoomed and panned
`Command:` *Click on upper viewport*	Makes it active
`Command:` **Z** ↵	
`All/Center/Dynamic/Extents/Left/Previous/` `Vmax/Window/<Scale(X/XP)>:` *Enter* **.5XP** *for A-size or* **1XP** *for C-size*	Scales the image to .5=1 or 1=1 relative to paper space
`Command:` *Use ZOOM Center and pick the center point on the image, then press Enter at the height prompt*	Centers the image without changing the default height (see fig. 13.7)
`Command:` *Click on lower right viewport and use ZOOM 2XP for A-size or 4XP for C-size*	Makes it active and scales its image to 2=1 or 4=1

Command: *Use ZOOM Center and pick the middle of the eight ROMs, and then press Enter at the height prompt*	Pans the image without changing the default height (see fig. 13.7)

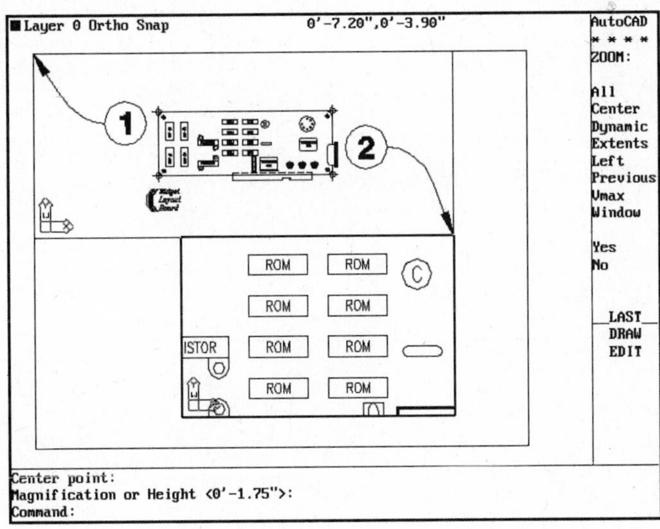

Figure 13.7:

Widget viewports arranged and scaled.

Normally, you add annotations and other finishing touches to each viewport by using unique layers to prevent visibility in other viewports. If you have done that, you also may want to add annotations in paper space. You can use object snaps when in paper space to snap to objects in viewports. This helps align and position your paper space objects and annotations.

Use the MVIEW Hideplot option in 3D work to specify which viewport(s) should have hidden lines removed when plotted.

In the following exercise, turn the viewport frames off and tie the 4X scale viewport to the full image with two dashed rectangles and dashed zoom lines, as shown in figure 13.8. This shows where the 4X image comes from.

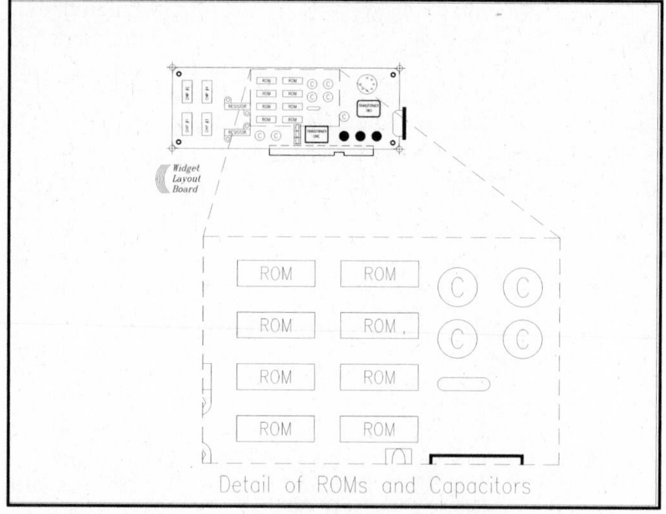

Figure 13.8:

The plotted widget with two viewports.

Annotating in Paper Space

`Command:` **`PS`** ↵	Re-enters paper space
`Command:` **`LINETYPE`** ↵	
`?/Create/Load/Set:` **`L`** ↵	
`Linetype(s) to load:` **`DASHED`** ↵	Pick ACAD from the SUPPORT directory
`Linetype DASHED loaded`	
`?/Create/Load/Set:` *Press Enter*	
Load DASHED from the ACAD.LIN file in your AutoCAD support directory	
`Command:` *Enter* **`DDLMODES`**, *then create layer DONTPLOT and turn it off, then create layer DASHED and set it current, with linetype DASHED*	Uses Layer Control dialog box to create and set layers
`Command:` *Using PLINE with INT object snap, trace over frame of bottom viewport*	Draws dashed box
`Command:` *Type* **`DDCHPROP`** *and press Enter, select both viewports (remove the polyline from theset), then use the LAyer option to place them on the DONTPLOT layer*	Makes viewport borders invisible

Command: *Enter* **LTSCALE**, *and set linetype scale to .5*	Regenerates with new linetype scale

Next, create a 1/4 scale duplicate of the polyline box and move it over the widget board in the upper viewport.

Command: *Select the dashed viewport outline*	Starts a selection set
Command: *Pick the lower left grip*	Enters stretch mode
** STRETCH ** <Stretch to point>/Base point/Copy/Undo/eXit: **SC** ↵	Switches to scale mode
** SCALE ** <Scale factor>/Base point/Copy/Undo/Reference/eXit: **C**↵	Specifies Copy option
** SCALE (multiple) ** <Scale factor>/Base point/Copy/Undo/Reference/eXit: **.25** ↵	Creates 1/4 scaled copy
** SCALE (multiple) ** <Scale factor>/Base point/Copy/Undo/Reference/eXit: *Press Enter*	Exits grip mode
Command: *Select the 1/4 scale dashed box, then pick its lower left grip*	Selects box and enters stretch mode
** STRETCH ** <Stretch to point>/Base point/Copy/Undo/eXit: **MO** ↵	Switches to move mode
** MOVE ** <Move to point>/Base point/Copy/Undo/eXit: *Move 1/4 scale box over the part of upper image that matches the 4X view (see fig. 13.8)*	
Command: *Enter* **L**, *then draw two lines connecting the two boxes*	Shows 4X detail zooming from full widget image

You can add any annotations and title text you want while in paper space by using the DTEXT command with text height set to the actual desired text height in the plot.

Finally, you create a plot view and plot the drawing.

Use the VIEW command's Window option to create a view named PLOT, setting lower left corner of window at your calculated plotter offset and setting upper right corner to encompass the border.

Save the drawing.

`Command: PLOT↵`	Opens Plot Configuration dialog box
Click on View, select PLOT, *then choose* OK	Selects view PLOT
Click on OK	Plots the drawing

The advantage of annotating in paper space is that you do not have to scale at plot time. You draw your model at real size, compose your plot sheet at full size, and plot it at 1=1. The only scaling is setting the viewport zoom scale relative to paper space for the plot. The disadvantage of annotating in paper space is that the annotation is not tied to the viewport contents.

Now that you know how to set up your title block and viewports manually, you may appreciate the fact that AutoCAD can automate this creation and insertion of title blocks and viewport configurations.

Automating Your Plot Setup Using MVSETUP.LSP

The MVSETUP.LSP routine is an AutoLISP-defined command accessed from the Layout option of the View pull-down menu. If you chose not to install all files when you installed AutoCAD, you may not have MVSETUP.LSP on your system. If not, copy the file MVSETUP.LSP from your original AutoCAD BONUS disk into your AutoCAD directory, your IA directory, or any directory on AutoCAD's support path.

To use MVSETUP.LSP, choose View, then Layout, then MV Setup from the pull-down menu. The first time you use MVSETUP, it takes longer than subsequent uses because MVSETUP sets itself up on your system. The first time each title block size is used also takes longer because MVSETUP builds the title block from scratch. The routine offers you the option of saving the title blocks to disk, so it can speed up sheet layout in subsequent uses. After you initially load MVSETUP, you can execute it in the current drawing as a command with the name MVS.

MVSETUP has options for aligning, creating, and scaling viewports, and for inserting a title block. Not all of these apply to your initial setup, so you may use MVSETUP more than once on each drawing.

Use MVSETUP in the following exercise to insert a title block and viewports in the WIDGEDIT drawing. If you are using a C-size or larger plotter, insert a C-size title block (see fig. 13.9); otherwise insert an A-size title block. Save the title block it creates for use later in the book.

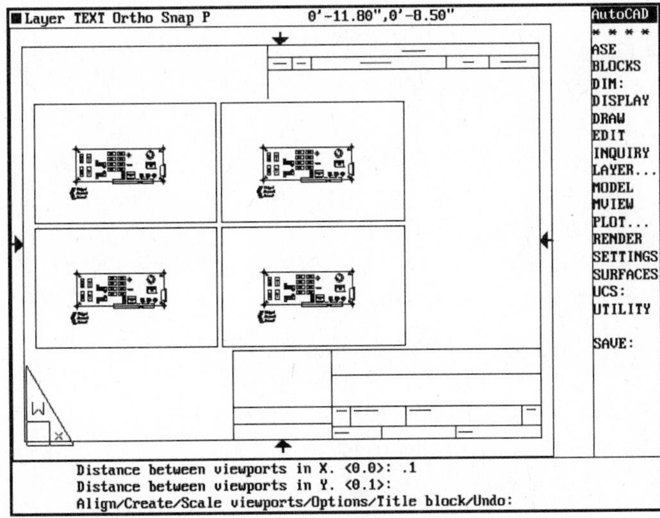

Figure 13.9:

A title block and viewports inserted by MVSETUP.

Setting Up a Widget Plot with MVSETUP

Enter `NEW`, then enter the file name `MVPLOT=IA7WIDG4`.

Enter `OPEN`, then enter the file name `WIDGEDIT`.

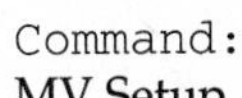

`Command:` *Choose* View, *then* Layout, *then* MV Setup	Loads and issues MVSETUP command
`Initializing... MVSETUP loaded.`	Executes MVSETUP automatically

`Paperspace/Modelspace is disabled. The pre-R11 setup will be invoked unless it is enabled. Enable Paper/Modelspace? <Y>: ↵`

`Regenerating drawing.`	Displays three existing viewports

First, you need to delete the existing viewports, then you need to insert a title block.

`Align /Create /Scale viewports/Options/Title block/Undo:` **T**↵	Specifies title block option
`Delete objects/Origin/Undo/<Insert title block>:` **D**↵	Specifies the Delete option
Select the objects to delete: Select all existing viewports	Deletes viewports
`Delete objects/Origin/Undo/<Insert title block>:` *Press Enter*	Displays title block insertion choices

```
Available title block options:
0:      None
1:      ISO A4 Size(mm)
2:      ISO A3 Size(mm)
3:      ISO A2 Size(mm)
4:      ISO A1 Size(mm)
5:      ISO A0 Size(mm)
6:      ANSI-V Size(in)
7:      ANSI-A Size(in)
8:      ANSI-B Size(in)
9:      ANSI-C Size(in)
10:     ANSI-D Size(in)
11:     ANSI-E Size(in)
12:     Arch/Engineering (24 x 36in)
13:     Generic D size Sheet (24 x 36in)
```

`Add/Delete/Redisplay/<Number of entry to load>:` *Enter* `7` *for A-size or* `9` *for C-size*	Inserts A-size or C-size title block
`Create a drawing named ansi-c.dwg? <Y>:` *Press Enter*	Saves title block for later

Next, you need to delete the existing viewports, and then insert new VIEWPORTS ones.

`Align/Create/Scale viewports/Options/Title block/Undo:` **C**↵	Specifies the Create option
`Delete objects/Undo/<Create viewports>: D`	Specifies the Delete option
`Select the objects to delete:` *Select all*	Deletes viewports

existing viewports

`Delete objects/Undo/` `<Create viewports>:` *Press Enter*	Displays viewport layout choices

`Available Mview viewport layout options:`
`0:     None`
`1:     Single`
`2:     Std. Engineering`
`3:     Array of Viewports`	

`Redisplay/<Number of entry to load>:` **3** ↵	Specifies Array option
`Bounding area for viewports. Default/` `<First point >:` *Enter* **.5,7** *for A-size or* **1,16** *for C-size*	Specifies upper left corner
`Other point:` *Enter* **8,2.2** *for A-size or* **16,2.5** *for C-size*	Specifies lower right corner
`Number of viewports in X. <1>:` **2** ↵	
`Number of viewports in Y. <1>:` **2** ↵	
`Distance between viewports in X. <0.0>:` *Enter* **.1** *for A-size or* **.5** *for C-size*	Specifies viewport spacing
`Distance between viewports in Y. <0.5>:` *Press Enter (defaults to X spacing)*	Creates 2x2 array of viewports with .1 or .5" spacing

Finally, scale the upper right viewport relative to paper space.

`Align/Create/Scale viewports/Options/` `Title block/Undo:` **S**↵	Specifies Scale option
`Select objects:` *Select the upper right viewport, then press Enter*	Enters model space to zoom view
`Enter the ratio of paper space units to model space units...`	
`Number of paper space units. <1.0>:` *Press Enter for A-size or enter* **2** *for C-size*	
`Number of model space units. <1.0>:` *Press Enter*	Scales A-size view 1:1 or C-size 2:1 (see fig. 13.10)
`Align/Create/Scale viewports/Options/` `Title block/Undo:` *Press Enter*	Exits MVSETUP

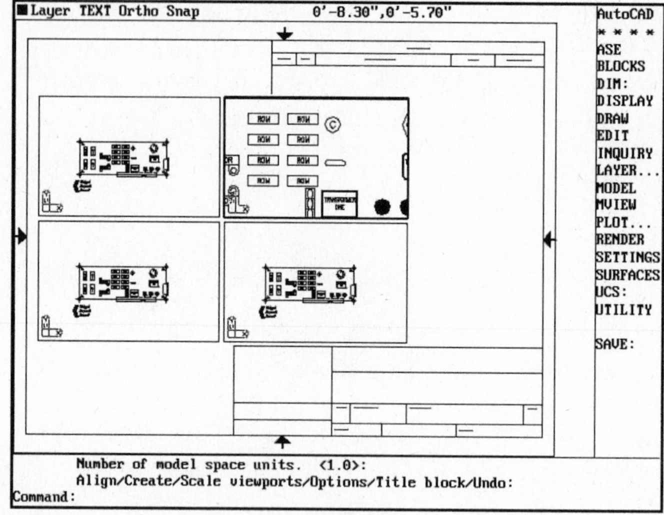

Figure 13.10:

Viewports scaled by MVSETUP.

You now have a title block that shows four viewports of WIDGEDIT. If it is C-size, the upper right viewport has a plot scale of 2:1, as shown in figure 13.10. But that is not all MVSETUP can do. You can use MVSETUP automatically to align images in two different viewports.

The Std. Engineering MVIEW viewport layout option sets up standard top, front, right, and 3D isometric viewports and viewpoints of a 3D model.

Aligning Viewport Images

Often, you want common elements in adjacent views of your drawing to line up with each other. This alignment particularly is important in multiview 3D plots. Although you can do this manually, MVSETUP makes it much easier. To use MVSETUP to align your images, start in paper space and zoom in on the two bottom viewports. Enter model space and misalign the bottom left viewport with PAN so that the viewports approximate figure 13.11. Then use MVSETUP to realign the image between the two viewports. When you finish the following command sequence, your drawing window should look like the one shown in figure 13.12.

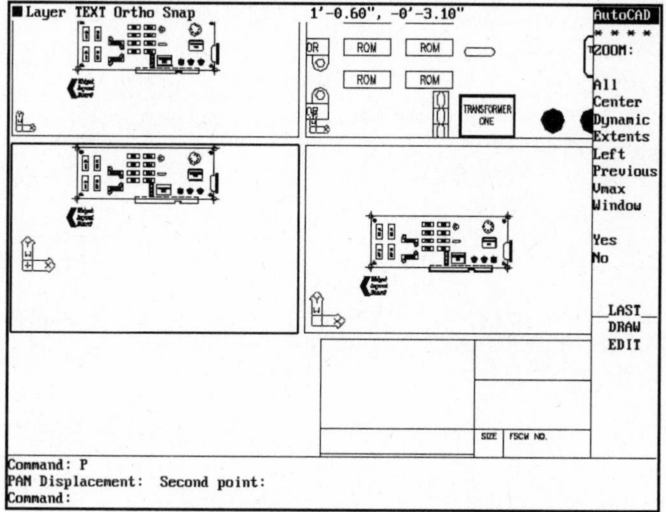

Figure 13.11:

Misaligned images.

Realigning Views With MVSETUP

Continue from the preceding exercise.

`Command:` *Use* ZOOM Window *to zoom in on two bottom viewports (see fig 13.11)*	
`Command:` *Enter* **`MS`**, *then click on the bottom left viewport*	Enters model space and makes viewport current
Command: *Enter* P, *then pan the viewport contents up a little*	Issues PAN command and misaligns images (see fig. 13.11)

Next, use MVSETUP to realign the two views.

`Command:` **`MVS`** ↵	Executes MVSETUP
`Align/Create/Scale viewports/Options /Title block/Undo:` **`A`**↵	Specifies the Align option
`Angled/Horizontal/Vertical alignment /Rotate view/Undo?` **`H`** ↵	Specifies Horizontal
`Basepoint:` *Pick the end point of a line in the left viewport*	

`Other point:` *Click in right viewport, and then pick the end point of a corresponding line*	Pans right viewport up to match left (see fig. 13.12)
`Angled/Horizontal/Vertical alignment /Rotate view/Undo?` *Press Enter*	
`Align/Create/Scale viewports/Options /Title block/Undo:` *Press Enter*	Exits MVSETUP

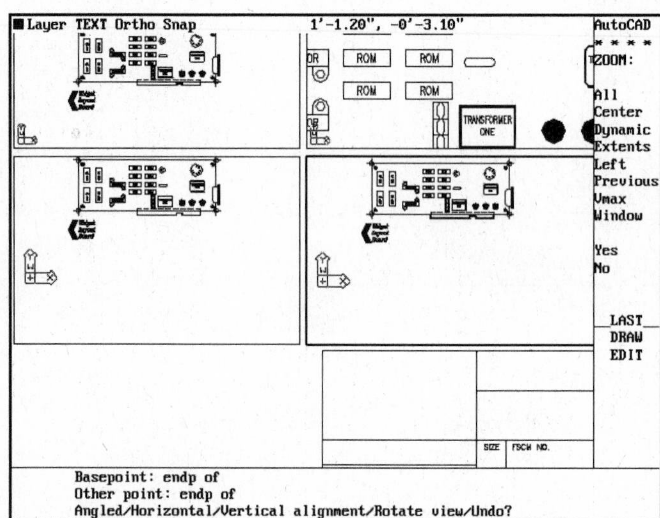

Figure 13.12:
Images realigned by MVSETUP.

Now, your viewport images should be lined up again. When PAN, ZOOM, and other operations misalign views and change the scale of a drawing that you have already composed for plotting, you should realign and rescale all your views just before plotting.

Customizing MVSETUP

You can customize the MVSETUP setup routine to use your own title blocks, custom viewport layouts, and more. Its defaults are contained in an ASCII file named MVSETUP.DFV, which contains instruction on how to customize it. The easiest form of customization is to simply edit the standard title block drawings it creates, making them conform to your standards and adding your standard title text.

Controlling Layer Visibility in Plots

Several references have been made to controlling layer visibility when plotting. You have seen how you can place mview viewports on layers that you turn off to prevent their plotting. AutoCAD works like overlay drafting, turning on and off combinations of layers to view the drawing data you need to see. This layer control gives you great flexibility in getting a number of finished plots out of a single drawing file. The layers that are on and thawed get plotted, and the layers that are off or frozen do not get plotted. Because layer control is more sophisticated in mview viewports in paper space than it is in tiled viewports or model space, that concept is examined first.

Layer Control in Paper Space

The capability to control your plot by layer is one of the most important aspects of plotting. Used properly, this technique can save you from duplicating work and filling up your disk with duplicate drawings. The following discussion uses a facilities plan as an example, but the same concept applies to nearly any type of drawing you create in AutoCAD.

Suppose, for example, that a site plan and a floor plan exist, as well as electrical, piping, and equipment layouts. This master facilities plan is used to create five separate plots — one for each of the areas listed. Five copies of the drawing could be made, erasing everything except what is needed in each, but that presents some major problems. If a change is made to the facility, all five drawings must be revised. Plus, if you make a change to one of the drawings, it is difficult to see how it affects the other areas if they are detailed on separate drawings. That does not have to be a problem.

The five different systems on the master drawing are all separated onto different layers. When you work on the drawing, you can leave all of the layers turned on so that all of the pertinent information is displayed. Any change to the electrical system, for example, shows conflicts with the other systems.

To plot the finished drawings, you can create five different title sheets in paper space and named plot views, one for each finished plot. Then, opening model space viewports on each sheet, position and scale the model images for each, adding any additional notation or details needed. Use the

LAYER command to freeze the unnecessary layers for each sheet when you plot it. If you freeze a layer in one viewport, AutoCAD freezes it in all. Of course, the work of all that freezing and thawing as you go from view to view to work or plot becomes a nuisance. To get around that problem, you can use the VPLAYER (View Port LAYER) command or the Layer Control dialog box to freeze layers selectively in one viewport without affecting other viewports.

The same principles apply to any multiview drawing in which you have annotations and dimensions that are specific to the views in each viewport. You just freeze those annotation layers in all other viewports.

In Chapter 5, both methods were discussed and you used the VPLAYER command. Try the Layer Control dialog box in the following exercise (see fig. 13.13). The Cur VP buttons control the freeze/thaw status of layers in the current viewport, and the New VP buttons control whether layers are frozen or thawed in the subsequently created viewports.

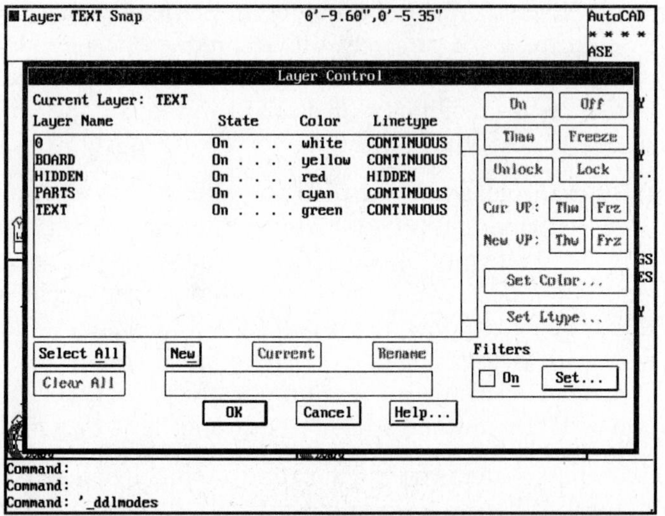

Figure 13.13:

Modify Layer dialog box.

The WIDGEDIT drawing shown in figure 13.14 is used again in the next exercise to see how the Layer Control dialog box selectively freezes layers, as shown in figure 13.15.

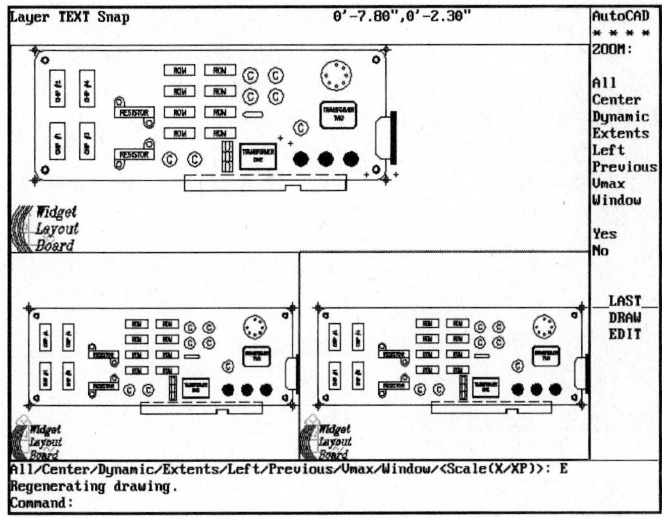

Figure 13.14: WIDGEDIT before freezing layers.

Freezing Layers Selectively with VPLAYER

Enter `NEW`, discard changes, then enter `VPLAYER=IA7WIDG4`.

Enter `OPEN`, discard changes, then enter `WIDGEDIT`.

`Command:` *Set TILEMODE to 0, then enter* `MS`	Enters paper space, and then model space
`Command:` *Use* ZOOM Extents *in each viewport, then click in lower right viewport*	Leaves right viewport current
`Command:` `DDLMODES` ↵	Opens Layer Control dialog box
Set layer 0 current, and review layer list (see fig. 13.13)	
Choose Clear All, *select the PARTS layer in the list box, and click on* Cur VP Frz	Freezes PARTS in current viewport

The dialog box now displays a C on the PARTS line in the fourth column under the State title in the layer list box.

Choose OK	Redisplays without cyan parts in lower right viewport

`Command:` *Click in lower left viewport*	Sets it current
`Command:` *Press Enter, then select the BOARD layer in the list box, and click on* Cur VP Frz	Repeats DDLMODES command and freezes BOARD in current viewport

The dialog box now displays a C on the BOARD line (but not on the PARTS line) in the State column in the layer list box.

Choose OK	Redisplays without yellow board in lower left viewport
`Command:` *Click in upper viewport*	Sets it current
`Command:` *Press Enter, then select the TEXT layer in the list box, and click on* Cur VP Frz, *then* OK	Repeats DDLMODES, freezes TEXT in current viewport and redisplays without green text in upper viewport

Quit AutoCAD and discard changes to the drawing.

Although you have frozen each of the main layers in one of the viewports, those layers still are visible in the other two viewports.

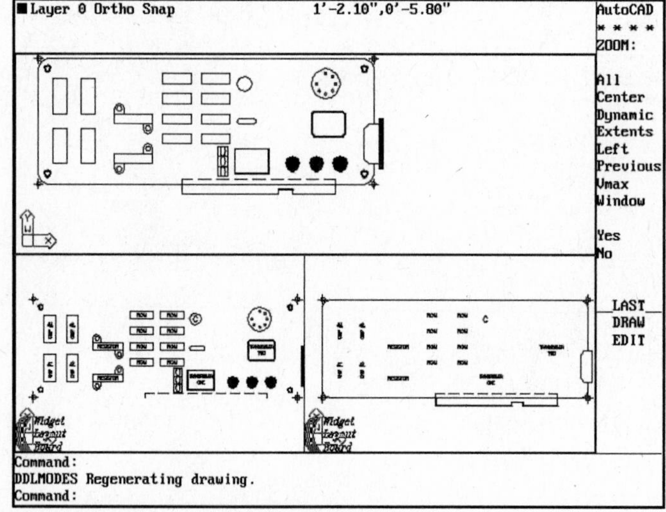

Figure 13.15:
WIDGEDIT after freezing layers.

Even without mview viewports, you can achieve control over layers almost as well, but it requires more effort.

Controlling Layers in Model Space or Tiled Viewports

In model space, you can control only your layers globally — a change to a layer's visibility affects all views. To compose your drawing for plotting, make sure the data you want to plot is on a different layer from the data that you do not want. By using the facilities plan example, you would start with the same model (each of the different systems for the facility would be on separate layers). You can use the LAYER command to turn on and off or freeze and thaw the correct layers for each desired combination of layers when you plot it. The key to doing this successfully is in knowing what to separate from what. Too many layers usually are better than too few layers.

To create a title block for each sheet, for example, put the blank title block and common text on a layer by itself. Create unique layers for title block text that differs from sheet to sheet. Place common data, such as the building outline, on a layer by itself and turn it on for all plots. Make sure that any data that is unique to a certain sheet is either on the layer for its system or on a layer by itself. That enables you to turn it on or off when you need it to plot. You can ease the nuisance of turning layers on and off, or freezing and thawing, by naming layers to enable you to use wild-card character filters to specify groups of names.

Using Other Methods to Plot

While the Plot Configuration dialog box is a nice addition to AutoCAD Release 12, it is sometimes advantageous to plot from the command line. Scripts use command line plotting, so, if you want to write a script for unattended plotting, you need to be familiar with the prompts. The defaults are listed on-screen and you have several options to go into some of the detailed areas, if you want them. The system variable called CMDDIA controls whether the PLOT command brings up the dialog box or shows the prompts at the `Command:` line. The default value is 1 (on) to display the dialog box, although plotting from a script file by-passes the dialog box no matter what CMDDIA is set to. This variable is demonstrated in the next exercise.

Another method of plotting which is new to AutoCAD is the *freeplotting* feature. This is a MODE *module* that is started from the operating system prompt, similar to starting AutoCAD, but is dedicated to plotting. Freeplotting is started by using a -p modifier when starting AutoCAD. On some systems you would enter **\ACAD\ACAD -p** at the DOS prompt. The screen looks like AutoCAD, but most commands do not function. In a networking situation, starting this MODE is not counted by the server authorization as an active copy of AutoCAD. Slides can be viewed in this MODE as well as previewing plots and running script files for plotting.

Freeplot commands include the following:

ABOUT	HELP	SCRIPT
COMPILE	PLOT	STATUS
CONFIG	QUIT	TEXTSCR
DELAY	REINIT	TIME
FILE	RESUME	VSLIDE
GRAPHSCR	RSCRIPT	

If you use the Plot Configuration dialog box in freeplot mode, you can use the Full Preview option to see and pan or zoom a drawing.

Try the next exercise by using the CMDDIA system variable and the Freeplotting module.

Using Freeplot Mode

`Command:` **`CMDDIA`**↵	
`New value for CMDDIA <1>:` **`0`**↵	Turns off command dialog boxes
`COMMAND:` **`QUIT`**↵	Exits AutoCAD
From the DOS prompt, type **`CD \IA`** ↵	Changes to IA directory
Type **`\ACAD\ACAD -P`** ↵	Starts AutoCAD in freeplot mode

If AutoCAD is installed in a directory other than \ACAD, or is installed on a drive other than the one containing the \IA directory, substitute the appropriate path in the previous step.

`Command:` **`LINE`**↵	Issues LINE command
`** Command not allowed. AutoCAD was invoked only to plot. **`	

You can issue only a limited set of commands in freeplot mode.

If you later want to turn on AutoCAD's dialog box input, just set CMDDIA=1. First, however, read through the next section to learn about pen assignment, and then plot a drawing in freeplot mode without the Plot Configuration dialog box.

Controlling Pens, Line Weights, and Linetypes

Another dimension of plotting, which often is carried over from manual drafting, is to use a variety of line weights and colors. Many drawings require different line weights or colors to communicate the content of the drawing. New CAD users often settle for a single line weight, not realizing they can use different pens on one plot even with a single-pen plotter. If you use a single-pen plotter, AutoCAD prompts you to change pens.

You can control three factors with drawing colors. You can plot with different pens (for different colors or sizes of pens), with different plotter linetypes, and with different pen speeds. (A *plotter linetype* is defined internally in the plotter, independently of AutoCAD's *software linetypes*.) You can control any of these three factors easily because AutoCAD separates the plot data by color. Everything that is the same color on your drawing plots by using the same pen number, plotter linetype, and pen speed. If you have not organized specific parts of the drawing by entity or layer color, use the CHPROP command to regroup them.

Pen Color

If you use the PLOT command to assign pen number 1 to the drawing color red, everything that is red in your drawing plots with pen number 1. Then you place a red pen in pen slot number 1 (or place a red pen in the pen holder when prompted to do so for single-pen plotters). If you want pen number 1 to plot with thick black lines, put a thick black pen in slot number 1. Drawing colors do not necessarily have to match plot colors. The task of plotting with different sizes of pens is exactly the same as that of plotting

with different colors of pens. Just use drawing color as a logical alias for line weight and assign the same pen number to each color that needs to be plotted at the same line weight. You can assign more than one drawing color to a particular pen number. You could, for example, assign blue and red to pen number 1. Then, anything in the drawing that is either blue or red would plot with pen number 1. To avoid frequent swapping of pens, AutoCAD's plot optimization sorts by pen number as it generates the plot data.

Plotter Linetype

The second plot factor you can control with drawing color is plotter linetype. Many plotters can generate internal plotter linetypes. They do not have anything in common with AutoCAD's linetypes so do not confuse the two. You can assign a linetype for each drawing color in the PLOT command. The linetype is specified by a number. Plotter linetype 0 is continuous, which is the default. If you enter a linetype number for a certain drawing color, AutoCAD plots all entities with that drawing color by using that plotter linetype. Be careful to avoid plotting entities that have a software linetype other than continuous with a plotter linetype other than continuous; the result is an inconsistent combination of the two. The pros and cons of software versus plotter linetypes are covered after the exercise. Plotter linetypes are assigned to drawing color independently of pen numbers, so more than one pen can use the same linetype, and one pen can use more than one plotter linetype. Some plotters have internally programmable linetypes/pen assignments that override AutoCAD's plot settings.

Pen Speed

The final plot factor you can control with drawing color is pen speed. The best speed varies with the pen type, size, type of ink, and plotting media. Use trial and error to set the fastest speeds that plot consistently. Pen speed is assigned to drawing color independently of pen numbers and plotter linetypes. The pen speed numbers are in cm/second. Some plotters have internally programmable speed/pen assignments that override AutoCAD's settings.

Try plotting from the command line in the next exercise and note the many settings that can be viewed and adjusted if necessary.

Plotting with Different Colors, Line Weights, and Linetypes

Continue from the previous exercise in freeplot mode. For a multipen plotter, place different colored pens or different size pens in slots 1, 2, and 3. For a single-pen plotter, place a pen in the plotter, and you are prompted to change pens at the appropriate time. After you prepare the plotter for plotting, just plot the Limits to Fit.

Command: **PLOT** ↵	Issues PLOT command and opens the Open Drawing File dialog box
Scroll through the file list to select WIDGEDIT, *or type* **WIDGEDIT** *in the* File *edit box, then choose* OK	Selects file to plot but does not load the drawing file

AutoCAD switches to text screen, and logo information appears.

```
What to plot — Display, Extents, Limits,
View or Window <D>: L ↵
Number of copies = 1
Plot device is Hewlett-Packard (HP-GL/2) ADI 4.2 - by Autodesk
Description: HP DraftMaster
Plot optimization level = 4
Plot will NOT be written to a selected file
Sizes are in Inches and the style is landscape
Plot origin is at (0.00,0.00)
Plotting area is 44.72 wide by 35.31 high (MAX size)
Plot is NOT rotated
Area fill will NOT be adjusted for pen width
Hidden lines will NOT be removed
Scale is 1=1.00"
Do you want to change anything? (No/Yes/File/Save) <N>: Y ↵
Do you want to change plotters? <N> Press Enter
How many copies of this plot would you like? , 1 to 99 <1>: Press
Enter
Pen widths are in Inches.
Entity      Pen  Line  Pen      Pen   Entity      Pen  Line  Pen
Pen
Color       No.  Type  Speed   Width  Color       No.  Type
Speed  Width
```

```
1 (red)        1    0    36   0.010       9        1    0
36   0.010
2 (yellow)     2    0    36   0.010      10        2    0
36   0.010
3 (green)      3    0    36   0.010      11        3    0
36   0.010
4 (cyan)       4    0    36   0.010      12        4    0
36   0.010
5 (blue)       5    0    36   0.010      13        5    0
36   0.010
6 (magenta)    6    0    36   0.010      14        6    0
36   0.010
7 (white)      7    0    36   0.010      15        7    0
36   0.010
8              8    0    36   0.010      16        8    0
36   0.010
Linetypes:  0 = continuous line
           1 = .................................
            2 = —   —   —   —
            3 = —    —    —    —
           4 = ——. ——. ——. ——.
            5 = — -  — -  — -  — -
            6 = - - - - - - - - - - - - - -
            7 = — .. — .. — .. — ..
            8 = - .-. - .-. - .-. - .-.
Do you want to change any of the above parameters? <N> Y ↵
Enter values, blank=Next, Cn=Color n, Sn=Show n, X=Exit
 Layer        Pen  Line  Pen    Line
 Color        No.  Type  Speed  Width
1 (red)        1     0    36   0.010      Pen number <1>: Press
Enter
1 (red)        1     0    36   0.010      Line type <0>: Press
Enter
1 (red)        1     0    36   0.010      Pen speed <36>: Press
Enter
1 (red)        1     0    36   0.010      Pen width < 0.01>: Press
Enter
2 (yellow)     2     0    36   0.010      Pen number <2>: Press
Enter
```

2 (yellow) 2 0 36 0.010 Line type <0>: **2** ↵

2 (yellow) 2 2 36 0.010 Pen speed <36>: *Press Enter*

2 (yellow) 2 2 36 0.010 Pen width < 0.01>: *Press Enter*

3 (green) 3 0 36 0.010 Pen number <3>: *Press Enter*

3 (green) 3 0 36 0.010 Line type <0>: **4** ↵

3 (green) 3 4 36 0.010 Pen speed <36>: *Press Enter*

3 (green) 3 4 36 0.010 Pen width < 0.01>: *Press Enter*

4 (cyan) 4 0 36 0.010 Pen number <4>: **X** ↵

Write the plot to a file? <N> *Press Enter*

Size units (Inches or Millimeters) <I>: *Press Enter*

Plot origin in Inches <0.00,0.00>: *Press Enter*

Standard values for plotting size

Size	Width	Height
ANSI paper sizes		
A	10.50	8.00
B	16.00	10.00
C	21.00	16.00
D	33.00	21.00
E	43.00	33.00
F	40.00	28.00
DIN/ISO paper sizes		
A4	11.20	7.80
A3	15.60	10.70
A2	22.40	15.60
A1	32.20	22.40
Max and User paper sizes		
MAX	44.72	35.31

Enter the Size or Width,Height (in Inches) <MAX>: *Press Enter*

Rotate plot clockwise 0/90/180/270 degrees <0>: *Press Enter*

Adjust area fill boundaries for pen width? <N> *Press Enter*

Remove hidden lines? <N> *Press Enter*

```
Specify scale by entering:
Plotted Inches=Drawing Units or Fit or ? <1=1.00">: F ↵
Effective plotting area:  44.72 wide by 34.56 high
Position paper in plotter.
Press RETURN to continue or S to Stop for hardware setup   Press Enter
Regeneration done nn
Plot complete.
Command: QUIT ↵                              Exits freeplot and AutoCAD
```

Your plotted drawing should look like the one shown in figure 13.16.

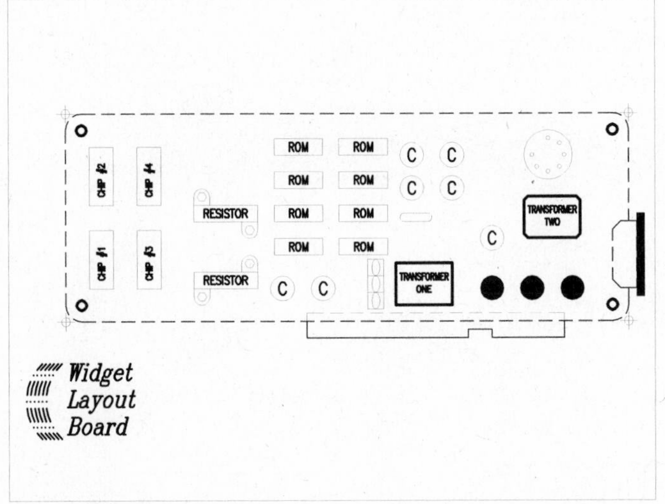

Figure 13.16: The widget plotted with plotter linetypes and line weights.

The color, pen, linetype, and speed parameters have three more options, which were not used in the preceding exercise. If you enter an S, it redisplays the settings made up to that point. If you enter C in which *n* is a color number, the dialog jumps to that color number. Enter C with no number to jump to the next color. If you enter an asterisk in front of a pen number, linetype number, or pen speed, such as *3 for pen 3, PLOT *it* assigns that setting is assigned to the current color and all higher numbered colors.

Plotter Linetypes, Software Linetypes, and Pen Widths

Plotter linetypes have advantages and disadvantages over software linetypes. Plotter linetypes are independent of scale, although you have to calculate and set an appropriate linetype scale for software linetypes. Wherever possible, you should use AutoCAD's software linetypes, but only lines, circles, arcs, and two-dimensional polylines accept software linetypes. Short polyline segments or spline and curve fit polylines generally plot continuous because the distance between vertex end points usually is too short to break the line. AutoCAD linetypes intelligently adjust to balance between end points, so corners always are closed. Plotter linetypes often fail to close at corners but do work well for polylines with short segments or curves. Consider using plotter linetypes when you need curved polyline linetypes or a special effect like applying a linetype to 3D meshes or even text. If you use a plotter linetype, make sure your entities are drawn in a unique color for that linetype only.

The pen width setting (default 0.010) in the PLOT command does not directly affect the pen selections. This setting controls the spacing of the closely spaced lines that AutoCAD plots to fill wide polylines, solid entities, and traces. Set it to match the smallest pen used to plot these entities to avoid gaps. The pen width setting also affects text. If plotted text shows partial skips in characters, or if characters run together, check your pen width plot setting. Too large a value causes these symptoms.

The *line weight* of PostScript printers (which are configured as plotters) is controlled by the pen width setting; 0.005 works well for 300 dpi printers.

Pen Motion Optimization

To minimize pen changes and time spent in pen-up moves (between the end of one line and the start of the next), AutoCAD includes configurable plot optimization. The settings are as follows:

0. No optimization
1. Adds end point swap
2. Adds pen sorting
3. Adds limited motion optimization

4. Adds full motion optimization
5. Adds elimination of overlapping horizontal or vertical vectors
6. Adds elimination of overlapping diagonal vectors

Each successive level of optimization includes the features of the preceding levels. The default is 4: end point swap, pen sorting, and full motion optimization. Some plotters do their own internal optimization, which may be more efficient. Items 5 and 6 are primarily for 3D work because then you may have many overlapping lines in a plot. You can adjust the level of optimization by reconfiguring your plotter, after first selecting item 2. Allow detailed configuration from the configuration menu. See your AutoCAD *Installation and Performance Guide* for details.

Plot settings can really take time and effort to set up correctly. To change them each time you plot can be time-consuming; it would be nice if you could save settings and reuse them.

Controlling Pen Assignments from a Dialog Box

The Pen Assignments dialog box, which you access by clicking on the Pen Assignments button in the Plot Configuration dialog box, enables you to control pen number, linetype, speed, and width. You turn the CMDDIA system variable back on (1) to access the Plot Configuration dialog box in the next exercise. Figure 13.17 shows the Pen Assignments dialog box.

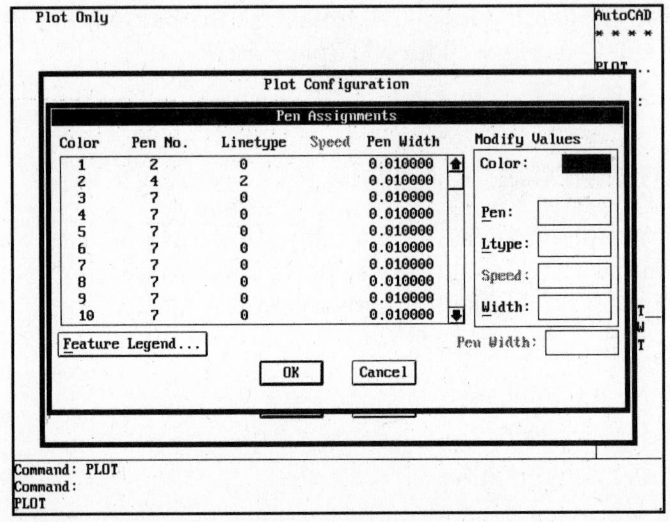

Figure 13.17:

The Pen Assignments dialog box.

Try using the Pen Assignments dialog box in the next exercise to change some pen number and linetype assignments for your next plot.

Using the Pen Assignments Dialog Box

Use the IA batch file to restart AutoCAD WITHOUT FREEPLOT MODE.

Enter `NEW`, discard changes, then enter `PENBOX=IA7WIDG4`.

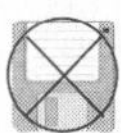

Enter `OPEN`, discard changes, then enter `WIDGEDIT`.

Command: **CMDDIA** ↵	
New value for CMDDIA <0>: **1** ↵	Turns on command dialog boxes
Command: **PLOT** ↵	Displays the PLOT CONFIGURATION DIALOG BOX *Open Drawing File dialog box*
Click on the File Name *button and enter* `WIDGEDIT`, *then choose* OK	*Displays Plot Configuration dialog box and specifies drawing to plot*
Click on Pen Assignments	Opens the Pen Assignments dialog box
Click on color 1 in the list box	Displays values for pen assignment in Modify Values area
Double-click in the Pen *edit box, then enter* 2	Assigns pen 2 to color 1
Click on color 1, then click on color 2	Deselects color 1 and selects color 2
Double-click in the Pen *edit box, then enter* 4	Assigns pen 4 to color 2
Double-click in the Ltype *edit box, then enter* 2	Assigns linetype 2 to color 2
Choose OK	Closes dialog box and returns to Plot Configuration dialog box

At this point, you could change other settings or choose OK to plot. Instead, choose Cancel to cancel the plot.

Quit AutoCAD, discarding changes.

The previous exercise demonstrated using the Plot Configuration dialog box to change pen color and linetype settings when CMDDIA is set to 1.

The previous exercise demonstrated using the Plot Configuration dialog box to change pen color and linetype settings when CMDDIA is set to 1.

Saving Default Plot Settings

AutoCAD maintains your most recent plot parameters from plot to plot and from one AutoCAD session to the next in the ACAD.CFG file. This is convenient; you do not have to reset all of the settings if it takes several attempts to get a plot correct, or if you use the same settings day in and day out. You may need several different sets of standard settings, or you may need to use more than one type of plotter. AutoCAD provides three ways to save and restore settings and plotter configurations.

You can configure several different output devices in AutoCAD or you can simply configure one device several times with different settings. Each configuration can be saved under a different name, and each time that configuration is used to plot, the same settings used the last time are remembered.

You can use configuration subdirectories to save and use several sets of defaults. At the beginning of the book, the IA directory was set as the configuration directory. You can create as many configuration directories as you like, in exactly the same manner as you created IA. You can change the configuration for each plotter or set of standards with the SET ACADCFG= line in the different batch files, and AutoCAD remembers the settings from plot to plot.

You also can use scripts to store and execute standard plot setups. *Scripts* give you a way to make AutoCAD push its own buttons. Scripts are like the macros you find in many other programs; they are really nothing more than automated input that simulates strings of keystrokes. AutoCAD users often overlook the fact that scripts can start and run plots. Scripts have the unique ability of being started outside the drawing editor. You can use a script, for example, to load a drawing, create some entities, and then end the drawing. You can use any input for scripts that you can use in your drawings or in AutoCAD's configuration menus. You can reconfigure plotters with scripts. You can end one drawing and start another, edit it, plot it, end it, and so on. If you have a specific set of operations to run on a group of drawings, you can use a script file to batch process the drawings.

You also can run a script from inside the drawing editor. If you have four standard plotting sequences, each requiring resetting parameters in the PLOT command, you can create four standard scripts, one for each setup. If you set up a standard view to plot named PLOT, your script might look like the example shown in table 13.2. This script is provided on the IA DISK as DPLOT.SCR. It plots to a D-size sheet at a 1=1 scale. (The right-hand comments are not part of the script file.) The script file to run your plotter may be slightly different. You can try entering the responses (listed in table 13.2) to a plot at the command line with CMDDIA turned off to see if they run your plotter.

Table 13.2
A Standard Plot Script

PLOT	The Plot command
V	View
PLOT	Plot view name
Y	Yes, change some parameters
N	No, do not change pen/color/linetypes
N	No, do not plot to file
I	Inches
0,0	Origin
D	Size
N	No, do not rotate
0.01	Pen width
N	No, do not adjust for pen width
N	No, do not hide
1=1	Scale
Add a blank line	Starts the plotter
Add a blank line	Returns to the drawing

If you named the preceding script DPLOT.SCR, you could run the script from the `Command:` prompt by using the following commands:

```
Command: Script ↵
Script file <SCRTEST>: DPLOT ↵
```

AutoCAD runs through the PLOT command, plots the drawing, and returns to the drawing editor after the plot is complete. If you have the IA DISK, examine (and modify) the script to adapt it to your own use. If you do not have the disk, you can create the script by using a text editor. Do not input the comments shown on the right in table 13.2.

Plotting to a File and Spooling

What if you do not have a plotter? Or you are at home and the plotter is at work? Or you need to create a plot file to import into a desktop publishing program?

Sometimes you may want to plot your drawing to a file, rather than to a plotter or printer. When you plot to a file, AutoCAD issues the same plot commands that it would if you were plotting to a plotter. The only difference is that AutoCAD redirects those commands to a file on disk, instead of to the plotter.

You may, for example, have a plot spooling program that enables you to plot multiple drawings one after the other without user intervention. (Plot spooling programs are discussed later in this chapter.) In that case, you plot your drawing to a file, instead of sending it to the plotter. Then, the plot spooler can pick up the file and send it to the plotter.

You also may want to plot to a file when you are transferring your drawings to other programs, such as desktop publishing programs or presentation graphics programs. Many programs import HP-GL or PostScript plot files. HP-GL files contain plot commands for Hewlett-Packard plotters. Even if your plotter is not a Hewlett-Packard plotter, you can configure AutoCAD for an HP plotter and plot an HP-GL file to disk. Then, you can import your plots into PageMaker, Ventura Publisher, and other graphics programs.

The task of plotting to a file is simple. When you issue the PLOT command, one of the questions AutoCAD asks you is whether you want to plot to a file or not. If you answer yes, AutoCAD redirects the plot commands to the file name you specify. If you need a special type of file, such as an HP-GL file, remember to first select the correct plotter by using the Configure option from the pull-down menu.

A plot spooler is a program that can control access to a plotter by one or more workstations and queue multiple plot requests through a single plotter. Because there are as many different possibilities for spooling as there are spoolers, this book cannot go into much depth about each one. Most spoolers, however, share some common features.

SPOOL is an acronym for Simultaneous Peripheral Output On-Line. On a single-user system, the spooler receives your plot as fast as AutoCAD can send it and trickles it out to the plotter, so you can go on working instead of waiting for the plotter to finish. Plot and print spoolers also enable several people to access a single device. The spooler logs their requests and schedules their plot or print into a queue to be printed when the device is available. Spooling is an integral part of UNIX and most other multi-user/multiprocessing operating systems and networks. Third-party programs are available for DOS systems that can handle spooling.

Depending on the spooler you are using, you may need to plot your drawing to a file first, then direct the file to the spooler as a job request. See the documentation that comes with your spooler for specifics on installing and using it.

Plotting Tips

The following sections offer some general advice on plotting. The visible quality of finished plots is as dependent upon the media and pens you use as it is upon properly controlling AutoCAD. Also, by knowing your plotting device well, you are capable of producing the fastest and highest quality plots possible.

Plotting Media

The type of media you use depends on the plotter, the project, and whether you need a checkplot or finished drawing. For checkplots, you usually can use the least expensive type of paper you can put through the plotter. Large cut sheets are relatively inexpensive if you purchase them in 1000-sheet quantities. But to really save money, buy a roll of butcher paper from your local paper supplier. Roller-ball pens or fiber-tip pens usually are best for checkplots. Because butcher paper is not smooth, roller-ball pens work better than fiber-tips, which tend to bleed through this type of paper.

The choice of vellum and mylar depend mainly on personal preference and the nature of the project. Some types of vellum and mylar do not work well with the inks used in plotter pens. Major drawing media suppliers have special vellum and mylar for use in plotters.

Pen Type, Speed, and Force

Three types of pens are common for plotting: roller-ball, fiber-tip, and ink pens. Roller-ball and fiber-tip pens are disposable, and ink pens are available in both disposable and refillable types. Four factors affect the efficiency of your pens — speed, acceleration, force, and point quality. You can change the speed of most plotters, as well as the force that is applied to the pen against the media. Many plotters use a default speed and force settings for the type of pen it thinks is installed. But you can override those settings to fine-tune your plot.

Pen speed typically is expressed in inches per second (ips) or centimeters per second (cps or cm/sec). Acceleration is stated in G-force. Acceleration is important because with short segments, text, and curves, the pen has little room to get up to full speed. Roller-ball pens offer the fastest acceleration, which is why they are ideal for checkplots. Roller-ball pens can go as high as 60 cps with good results. Fiber-tip pens often work best around 40 to 50 cps, and slowing their speed does not affect the quality much, either. With ink pens though, fine-tuning the speed and acceleration often makes a difference. Normally, ink pens plot well anywhere from 10 cps to 30 cps. Jewel tips outwear tungsten or ceramic, which outwear stainless, but all pens wear out eventually. Mylar wears tips much faster than vellum. Cross-grooved tips (not single grooved) can plot at higher speeds than plain tips.

Keeping Your Plotter and Pens Working

Most plotters are fairly maintenance-free (see your manufacturer's instructions for specifics). You can, however, do a few things every month or so for preventive maintenance. The first is to keep the roller and pinch wheels clean. The pinch wheels press the paper against the roller, and the roller moves the paper in and out of the plotter. Keep the pinch wheels clean of paper particles with a stiff toothbrush. The other item to check is the paper sensors (if your plotter uses photo-diodes to measure the ends of the paper when you load it). If so, two holes are in the plate over which the paper

moves, one in back and one in front. These holes have glass covers to keep dust and paper fibers out. When the covers get dirty, you may have problems loading the paper. Use a cotton-tipped swab with a little alcohol on it to clean the covers.

The secret to pen maintenance is to keep them capped, even if your pens normally sit in a pen carousel. Ink pens sometimes need a little extra care. The disposable pens usually come with caps that have a small rubber cushion inside, which keeps the tip from drying out and clogging. Even so, you may want to place capped pens in a carousel or sealed container with a damp sponge. Then a quick tap of the top end of the pen (not the tip) should get it running again. Finally, do not try to refill disposable pens; the nibs wear out too soon to make reusing them worthwhile.

Solving Plotter Problems

Even after you set everything up correctly, plots fail. The reasons are often simple, but it is the nature of plotting for things to go wrong. The following sections describe a few frequent plotter problems and some possible solutions.

No Communication between Computer and Plotter

Sometimes after you issue the PLOT command, and AutoCAD gives you an error message saying the plotter is not responding. This usually means that the computer cannot make contact with the plotter. If this happens, check for the obvious first and use the checklist from the beginning of this chapter. If AutoCAD still fails to plot, you may have a bad cable. Although it does not happen often, cables sometimes just go bad. Or someone might have accidentally pulled the cable and disconnected one of the contacts in the connector at one end of the cable. With a spare pretested cable available, you can confirm or rule out cabling problems with a simple swap.

Paper Jams

Paper jams usually are caused by misaligning the paper or by having one of the pinch wheels half-on, half-off the sheet. If one pinch wheel is completely

off the paper, the paper jams. Make sure the edges of the sheet are square with each other, or the plotter can not measure it properly and may try to run it out past the pinch wheels, causing a jam. Check and adjust or replace worn rollers.

No More Ink or a Pen Skips

The most irritating occurence when you plot is to run out of ink or have the pen skip in the middle of the plot. If this happens, do not remove the sheet from the plotter. You can replot over the original. The next step is to get the pens working again. You might as well check them all while you are at it. If the plot is a relatively short one, just issue the PLOT command again, and AutoCAD plots over the entities. If you are plotting a drawing that takes a long time to plot, resave the drawing, then erase the entities that plotted the first time. Then, reissue the PLOT command to finish the plot.

Wrong Linetypes

If lines plot with a different linetype than you expected or if the scale of dashed linetypes seems wrong, check to see if plotter linetypes are specified in the PLOT command's default settings. If the linetype for a color is anything other than 0, those entities plot by using the plotter's internal linetypes instead of AutoCAD's linetypes. If the scale of your lines is off, check the drawing's LTSCALE setting and adjust it for correct plotting.

Summary

Now you have followed the CAD drafting process from start to finish: setting up a new drawing, creating and editing entities, and finally, plotting. Continue to explore AutoCAD Release 12 by mastering the commands in Chapter 14 which add many enhancements to your drawings. Hatching with AutoCAD is very powerful and can be used in many creative ways to dress up your drawings.Many examples of this are shown in the next chapter. Creative use of linetypes is also explained, including how to define your own new linetypes. Freehand sketching is also available in AutoCAD, if you like to give drawings a personal touch.

Finally, a good portion of Chapter 14 explains all of the inquiry commands. Once you have a CAD drawing which is properly drawing to scale, you will be pleasantly suprised at how easy it is to obtain information such as area, perimeters, distances, and entity properties. Turn to Chapter 14 now and see for yourself.

14

Drawing Enhancements and Inquiry

Up to this point, your drawings have been simple. If you want to make your drawings look more professional, you can enhance them with patterns, shading, annotation, dimensioning, and linetypes. Figure 14.1 shows some of AutoCAD's hatch patterns and styles that you might use. You also may need to sketch in freehand or trace lines, such as contours in the Autotown site plan. You have already learned text annotation, and dimensioning is the topic of the next chapter. The rest you learn in this chapter.

You also learn how to use AutoCAD's inquiry commands to get information about your drawings and their entities. You have already used the ID, HELP, and STATUS commands. This chapter discusses the AREA, DBLIST, DIST, ID, LIST, and TIME commands. You are also introduced to the Region Modeler and how it applies to retrieving drawing database information.

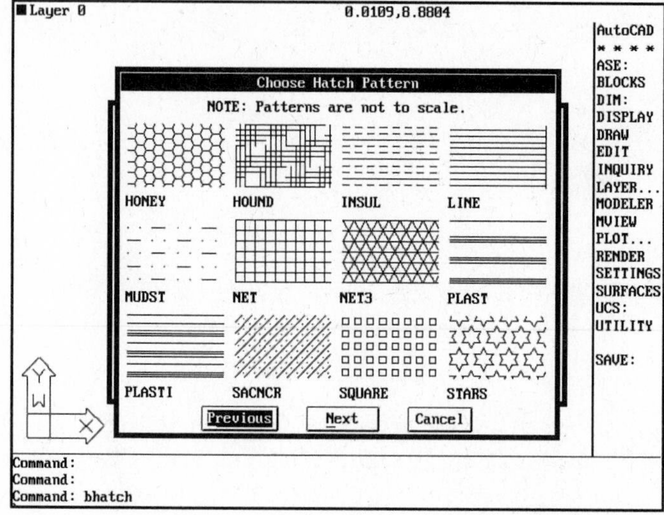

Figure 14.1:

Some AutoCAD hatch patterns and styles.

The discussion of hatching was deferred until after the blocks chapter, because AutoCAD's hatch patterns are really a type of blocks. When you use the HATCH command to place a pattern, such as a brick pattern in a walkway area, you are really inserting a block with the brick pattern.

Hatches are specialized blocks. They do not share the efficiency or easy insertion-point control of normal AutoCAD blocks, and they require some care in setting up boundaries. Good results may require a little practice.

Otherwise, the basic scaling and rotating techniques that you have learned about inserting blocks also apply to placing hatch patterns. AutoCAD's standard hatch patterns are sized as unit blocks. When you insert these patterns in your drawing, you scale and rotate the pattern. If you are composing your drawing in paper space, you can have AutoCAD automate hatch scaling.

Because you normally want to fit these patterns in predefined areas in your drawing, the focus of this chapter is to give you a set of techniques to help you define the boundaries that control the insertion of the hatch block. These boundaries can be defined by using POLYLINE to develop a boundary, BREAK to segment the area into a contiguous boundary, or by using BHATCH. The BHATCH command stands for *boundary hatch* and uses the same dialog box and methods as BPOLY to create a boundary by "tracing" the entities surround a selected point within the drawing.

Setting Up for Drawing Enhancements

The hatching and sketching exercises in this chapter represent a suburban renewal project for Autotown. You are going to pave the road, brick the sidewalk, add detail to some yards with hatching, and improve the drainage by sketching some contour lines.

To select a hatch pattern, you may type the name within the HATCH command, or use the dialog box with the BHATCH command. To know what hatch patterns are available within the HATCH command, you can enter a ? within the command. Doing this displays a listing of all the hatch pattern names and a description. The BHATCH command displays the hatch patterns with an icon menu. You can select the hatch pattern by pointing and picking the icon of the desired pattern.

You can use the IA7HATCH drawing from the IA DISK or recycle the AUTOTOWN drawing that you saved at the end of Chapter 10. To use this drawing, open ATLAYOUT first and STRETCH the property lines back to their approximate original location using @15'<N20dE. Add two more layers called SCRATCH and HATCH and check the other settings in table 14.1. You also bind the ATLAYOUT drawing to the current drawing and explode it so you can select its component entities when you hatch. If you have the IA DISK, ATLAYOUT is already stretched, bound, and exploded.

Your drawing should appear similar to figure 14.2 as you begin.

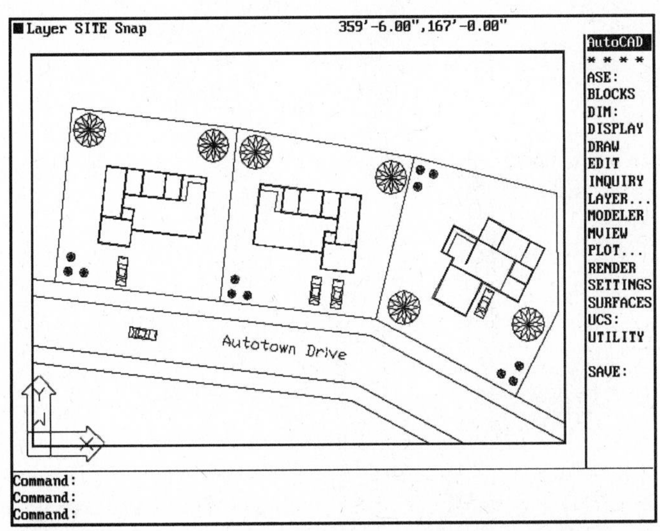

Figure 14.2:

The Autotown drawing.

Table 14.1
Autotown Drawing Settings

APERTURE	COORDS	GRID	SNAP	ORTHO	UCSICON
5	On	10'	1	OFF	OR

UNITS	Engineering units, 2 decimal places, surveyor's angles, default angle 0.
LIMITS	0,0 to 360',240'
ZOOM	Zoom All.
VIEW	View saved as ALL.

Layer Name	*State*	*Color*	*Linetype*
0	On	White	CONTINUOUS
ATLAYOUT0PLAN	On	Blue	CONTINUOUS
ATLAYOUT0SITE	On	Green	CONTINUOUS
HATCH	On	Magenta	CONTINUOUS
PLAN	On	Blue	CONTINUOUS
SCRATCH	On/Current	White	CONTINUOUS
SITE	On	Green	CONTINUOUS

Setting Up for Enhancing Autotown

`Command:` *From the screen menu, choose* BLOCKS, *then* XREF:
`?/Bind/Detach/Path/Reload/<Attach>:` **B**↵

`Xref(s) to bind:` **ATLAYOUT**↵ — Binds ATLAYOUT as a BLOCK
`Scanning...`

`Xref(s) to bind:` **IA7ATLAY**↵ — Binds IA7ATLAY as a BLOCK
`Scanning...`

Choose File, then New, and enter AUTOTOWN=\IA\IA7HATCH, replacing your previous AUTOTOWN drawing.

Choose File, then Open, and enter \IA\AUTOTOWN. Stretch the lots, create the HATCH and SCRATCH layers and check the other settings shown in table 14.1. Set layer SCRATCH current.

`Command:` **`STRETCH`** ↵	Starts the STRETCH command
Select objects: *Pick points to select a crossing window across the top of the lots as you did in Chapter 12*	Issues crossing Selects the objects to STRETCH
`Base point or displacement:` *Press Enter*	Specifies the basepoint at the last point picked
`Second point of displacement:` **`@15'<N20dE`** ↵	Stretches the lots 15 feet North, 20 degrees East

Use MOVE or grips move mode to reposition the trees.

`Command:` *From the screen menu, choose* BLOCKS, *then* XREF:
`?/Bind/Detach/Path/Reload/<Attach>:` **`B`** ↵

`Command:` *From the screen menu choose* EDIT, *then* EXPLODE, *and then select the border*	Explodes ATLAYOUT block into individual entities

Although the road and sidewalk appear to touch the border because the border is a PLINE with width, it does not at all locations. To select intersections and to use HATCH, you need to have closed areas. Use EXTEND to create the required closed borders.

`Command: EXTEND` ↵	
`Select boundary edge(s) ...`	Specifies line to extend to
`Select Objects:` *Choose the border*	
`<Select object to extend>/Undo:` *Pick each of the eight lines that define the road and sidewalk to the border*	Extends lines to the border

The drawing appears the same; however, the lines now intersect.

The process of hatching often requires building boundaries to control your hatch inserts. You are starting with the SCRATCH layer current, and you build your hatch boundaries there. You also can use it as a pure scratch layer to experiment with any of the predefined hatch patterns that seem interesting to you.

Autotown would look better if the road had some character. The next exercise shows you how to view the hatch patterns by name that are available to locate a brick pattern for the road.

Examining the Patterns Stored in ACAD.PAT

To view the patterns in ACAD.PAT by name with the HATCH command, use a ?, as shown in the following exercise.

Viewing Hatch Patterns

Command: *From the screen menu, choose* DRAW, *then* HATCH	Starts the HATCH command
`Pattern (? or name/U, style) <U>:` ?↵	Displays the name and description of available HATCH patterns
`Pattern(s) to List <*>` *Press Enter*	Displays all HATCH patterns

Press Ctrl-C, then press Enter to cancel the command

You should see a listing of HATCH pattern names and their descriptions similar to figure 14.3. When you are in the HATCH command, entering the name of a HATCH pattern places this pattern in the drawing. A sample image of each of these patterns can be found in the Appendix of the *AutoCAD Release 12 Reference Manual*. Later in the chapter, you are introduced to the BHATCH command that enables you to view and select pattern images.

```
ANGLE          - Angle steel
ANSI31         - ANSI Iron, Brick, Stone masonry
ANSI32         - ANSI Steel
ANSI33         - ANSI Bronze, Brass, Copper
ANSI34         - ANSI Plastic, Rubber
ANSI35         - ANSI Fire brick, Refractory material
ANSI36         - ANSI Marble, Slate, Glass
ANSI37         - ANSI Lead, Zinc, Magnesium, Sound/Heat/Elec Insulation
ANSI38         - ANSI Aluminum
AR-B816        - 8x16 Block elevation stretcher bond
AR-B816C       - 8x16 Block elevation stretcher bond with mortar joints
AR-B88         - 8x8 Block elevation stretcher bond
AR-BRELM       - Standard brick elevation english bond with mortar joints
AR-BRSTD       - Standard brick elevation stretcher bond
AR-CONC        - Random dot and stone pattern
AR-HBONE       - Standard brick herringbone pattern @ 45 degrees
AR-PARQ1       - 2x12 Parquet flooring: pattern of 12x12
AR-RROOF       - Roof shingle texture
AR-RSHKE       - Roof wood shake texture
-- Press RETURN for more --
```

Figure 14.3:

Some HATCH pattern names and descriptions.

Using the HATCH Command

You use the brick pattern to add detail to the Autotown street. The most important part of creating a hatch is defining the boundary for the pattern. The HATCH command requires a boundary consisting of a closed polygon or contiguous entities. To use the HATCH command to fill an area, you must completely define a closed boundary. When you define a boundary, avoid overlapping and open-ended intersections, or your pattern can spill out of bounds.

One method is to use a polyline to trace over the perimeter of the area you want to hatch. This method eliminates the uncertainty of whether your drawing has any questionable endpoints (like the endpoints where Autotown Drive meets the border line) or your fill area is open or closed. Create such boundaries on a scratch layer so they do not affect the rest of the drawing.

Create a boundary for Autotown Drive by tracing over the perimeter of the road with a polyline. Use object snaps to help pick the endpoints.

Using HATCH To Insert a Brick Pattern

Set a running INT object snap, and then use the PLINE command to trace the perimeter of the area of the road. Use the PLINE Close option to create an accurate closed boundary. Set the running object snap back to NONE after you are done.

`Command:` *Use the LAYER command and set* HATCH *current*	
`Command:` *From the screen menu, choose* DRAW, *then* HATCH:	Starts the HATCH command
`Pattern (? or name/U, style) <U>:` **`BRICK`** ↵	Specifies a BRICK pattern
`Scale for pattern <1.0000>:` **`120`** ↵	Scales the pattern by a factor of 120
`Angle for pattern <0.0000>:` **`45`** ↵	Specifies an angle of 45 degrees for the pattern
`Select objects:` *Select polyline boundary, text, and car in road*	Specifies the boundary for the HATCH
`Select objects:` *Press Enter*	Draws the hatch
`Command:` *Press F7*	Turns off grid (see fig. 14.4)
`Command:` *Choose* View, *then* Zoom, *then* Window, *and zoom in on the car in the road*	

Look closely at your bricked drive. What is wrong with the car? (Look at figure 14.5.)

The Hatch Donut-and-Hole Problem

The brick hatch pattern drew directly over the car in the road. This classic hatching problem is called the *donut-and-hole* problem. If you select something as simple as a circle or rectangle, the HATCH command fills it in, stopping the pattern at the edges. If you want to fill in a more complex boundary that also contains other objects, you need to tell the HATCH command not to draw the hatch pattern across those objects. A boundary

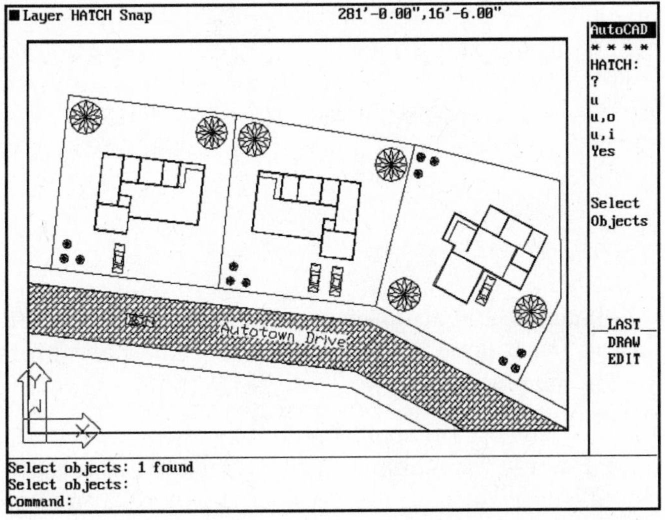

Figure 14.4:
Autotown with a bricked drive.

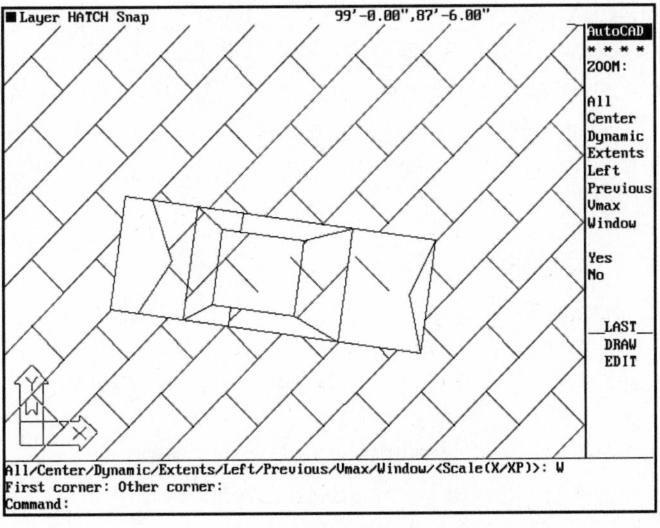

Figure 14.5:
Detail of the car.

inside another boundary, such as a circle (hole-and-donut), is called a *nested boundary.*

The HATCH command tries to decide what is the donut and what is the hole when it is figuring out where to hatch. In the Autotown Drive case, the text is a hole, but the car is a number of holes. (Text is treated as if surrounded by an invisible boundary.) AutoCAD normally hatches by starting

the pattern at the perimeter boundary and stopping at the next boundary, and then starting again at the next boundary. The car is made up of many lines, creating many interior boundaries, so the pattern fills over parts of the car. The HATCH command offers three hatch style options to help solve this problem.

HATCH Prompts and Options

As you work with hatches, you also need to set the scale and angle to get the effects you want. The following lists the HATCH command prompts and options that you have to work with:

- **Pattern...name...** This option enables you to enter a predefined hatch pattern name. Precede the name with an asterisk to insert the hatch as individual line entities instead of as a block reference. You also can append a comma and style code to the name.
- **?.** This option displays a list of all defined hatch pattern names and their descriptions. You can use wild cards for a specific list.
- **U.** This option creates a user-defined array or double-hatched grid of straight lines. You answer the following prompts to define the pattern:

```
Angle for crosshatch lines <0>:

Spacing between lines <1.0000>:

Double hatch area? <N>
```

- **,style.** This option enables you to append a comma and style code to the hatch pattern name, unless you want the default Normal style. The style code determines the way nested boundaries are hatched. The three style choices are the following:
  - **N.** Normal (the default) hatches every other boundary
  - **O.** Outermost hatches only the area between the outermost boundary and the next inner boundary
  - **I.** Ignore hatches everything inside the outermost boundary, ignoring inner boundaries
- **Scale for pattern <1.0000>.** This option establishes scale. Most predefined patterns are designed to look correct at a scale of 1 when plotted at 1:1 scale. In paper space, use a scale of 1. In model space, scale the pattern to the inverse of the plot scale. Enter a factor as *scale*XP to scale the hatch to match what you get by using *scale* in paper

space. In an mview viewport that is scaled to paper space with ZOOM XP, you can enter the hatch scale as 1XP.

- **Angle for pattern <0>.** This option enables you to enter the rotation angle — pick two points to show the angle.
- **Select objects.** This option specifies objects to define the hatch boundaries. Each boundary should consist of a contiguous series of entities. If you select a block, all entities in it are considered hatch boundaries. Mview viewport borders can be selected as hatch boundaries. If you select text, attributes, shape, trace, or solid entities, the hatch stops at their perimeters unless you use the Ignore style. The perimeters for text, attributes, and shapes include a small margin space to ensure readability. For hatching complex areas or areas without clearly defined boundaries, trace the perimeter with a polyline on a reference layer and select the polyline as the boundary. If you select entities that are not parallel to the current UCS, the boundaries are projected to and hatched in the current construction plane of the current UCS.

Using HATCH Outermost

Try the Outermost option to repave the road, as in figure 14.6. The HATCH command considers only the entities you select when it calculates the interior boundaries, so be sure to select all interior objects you do not want hatched.

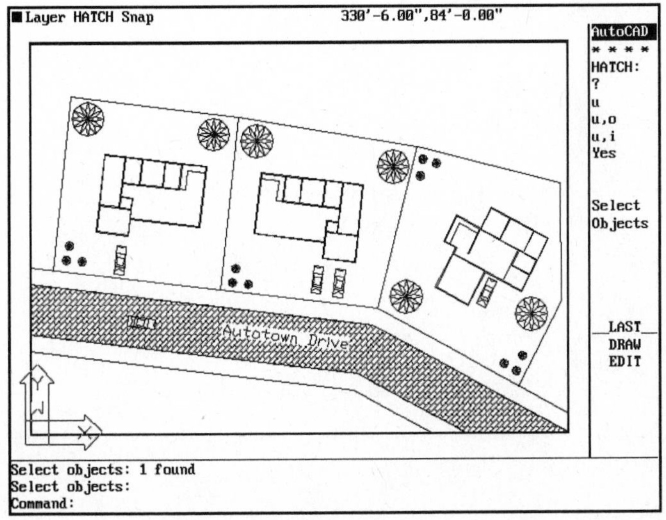

Figure 14.6:

Autotown Drive, properly bricked.

Using HATCH Outermost To Hatch Around Objects

`Command:` *Choose* View, *and then* Zoom, *then* Previous	Zooms to the previous display
`Command:` *Choose* Modify, *then* Erase, *then* Last	Erases the last hatching
`Command:` *From the screen menu, choose* DRAW, *then* HATCH:	Starts the HATCH command
`Pattern (? or name/U, style) <U>:` **`BRICK,O`**↵	Specifies a BRICK pattern with the Outermost style
`Scale for pattern <120.00>:`↵	Scales the pattern by a factor of 120
`Angle for pattern <N45d0'0"E>:`↵	Specifies an angle of 45 degrees for the pattern
`Select objects:` *Select polyline boundary, text, and car in road*	Specifies the boundary for the HATCH
`Select objects:` *Press Enter*	Draws the hatch

Figure 14.7 shows the results of this exercise.

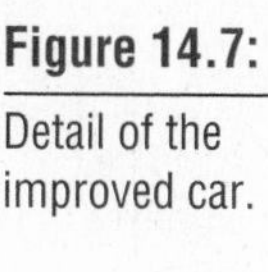

Figure 14.7:

Detail of the improved car.

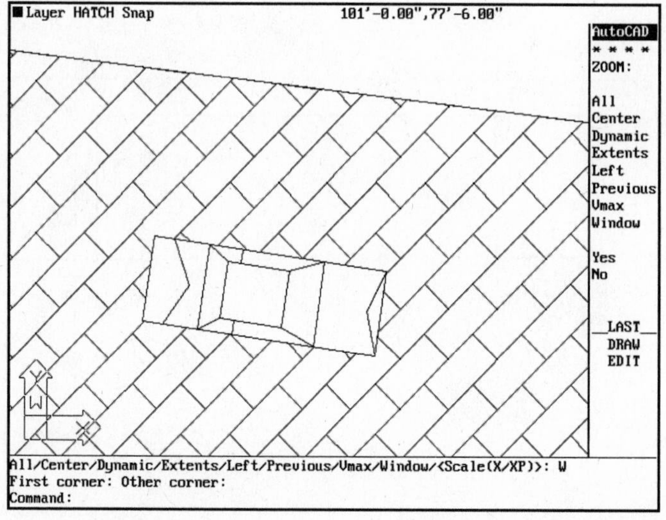

Breaking Existing Entities for a Hatch Boundary

In the Autotown drawing, you place a grass pattern between the three lot lines and the drawing border. In this case, it is easier to break the four intersections where the border and the outer lot lines meet Autotown Drive than it is to trace the entire lot and border perimeters.

In this exercise, use BHATCH and pick the segments as the hatch boundary and fill the area with a grass pattern. Figure 14.8 and the following exercise show the break points on Autotown Drive's polyline.

The BHATCH command works in the same way as the HATCH command, except it uses a dialog box and has additional options for defining hatch boundaries in the same way as BPOLY. You issue the BHATCH command by selecting Hatch under the Draw pull-down menu.

Using BREAK and BHATCH To Insert a Hatch Pattern

`Command:` *Choose* Modify, *then* Break, *then* Select Object, Two Points	
`Select object:` *Pick the border near (not at) point ① (see fig. 14.8)*	Selects the object to BREAK
`Enter second point (or F for first point):`**`_first`**	
`Enter first point:` *Use the* ENDP *object snap to pick point ①*	Specifies the first point to break the object
`Enter second point:` *Choose* @ *from the screen menu*	Picks at the first point and breaks line
Repeat the Break command for sidewalk at point ②, border at point ③, and sidewalk at point ④, using First for first point and the ENDPoint *object snap and* @	

`Command:` *Choose* Draw, *then* Hatch	Starts the BHATCH command
Choose the Hatch Options *button, then* Normal	Resets the style option to Normal
Choose the Pattern *button*	Displays first page of available patterns
Choose Next *twice, then click on the* Grass *image*	Displays and selects the pattern
Enter `120` *in the Scale input box*	Specifies the pattern scale
Enter `0` *in the Angle input box*	Specifies the pattern angle
Choose the OK *button*	Returns to the Boundary Hatch dialog box
Choose the Select Objects *button*	Redisplays the drawing area
`Select Objects:` *Select the border polyline, two broken ends of sidewalk, and all six lot lines adjoining hatched area shown in figure 14.8*	Specifies the HATCH boundary
`Select Object:` *Press Enter*	
Choose the Apply *button*	Draws the pattern in the drawing

You may notice that the grass slightly overlaps the wide border polyline. Hatch draws its pattern to the center line of wide polylines.

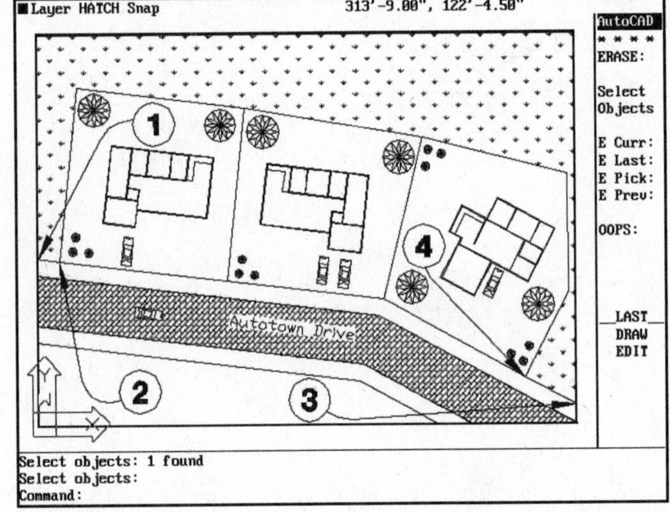

Figure 14.8:

Inserted grass pattern in Autotown.

Exploring the BHATCH Options

When using the BHATCH command, notice that there are several options in addition to the normal HATCH command options. You used the Pick Points option to pick a point inside the grass boundary area. The BHATCH command developed a polyline around the selected area. This polyline is temporary for use during the BHATCH command unless you choose Advanced Options and set Retain Boundaries to keep the border polyline after the HATCH pattern is added to the drawing.

After using Hatch Options in BHATCH, to set the type of pattern, angle, scale, and hatching style, you can use Pick Points to create a border. To use the Pick Points option with the BHATCH command, the area to HATCH must be a closed area. The entities need not connect at endpoints, but they must intersect. If they do not, you see an error message telling you that the boundary is not closed. To be sure of finding the correct boundary, pick the point near one line of the boundary. View Selections shows the selected entities (or boundaries) before hatching. The Preview Hatch option displays the hatch pattern in the drawing, enabling you to change any of the hatch options (or cancel the command) before the hatch pattern is applied. The Apply button draws the final pattern and exits.

Use BHATCH and the Pick Points option to place a Brick Stone sidewalk along the road. To use the Pick Points option with the BHATCH command, the area to hatch must be a closed area. The entities need not connect at endpoints, but they must intersect. If they do not, you get an error message telling you the boundary is not closed.

The BHATCH command works the same way as the HATCH command except that it uses a dialog box and can define hatch boundaries in the same way as BPOLY. You issue the BHATCH command by selecting Hatch under the Draw pull-down menu.

Hatching the Sidewalk

`Command:` *Choose* Draw, *then* Hatch

Choose the Hatch Options *button*

Choose the **Pattern** *button* — Displays the available patterns

You can use the Select Objects option in BHATCH to add boundary-defining entities to the selection set created by Pick Points. Select Objects also can be used to select a set of contiguous objects to hatch in exactly the same way as at the HATCH commands's `Select objects:` prompt.

Choose Next, *then* Brstone	Displays and selects the pattern
Enter `60` *in the Scale input box*	Specifies the pattern scale
Enter `45` *in the Angle input box*	Specifies the pattern angle
Choose the OK *button*	Returns to the Boundary Hatch dialog box
Choose the Pick Points *button*	Displays drawing to pick a point inside the area to hatch
`Select internal point` *Pick a point inside the sidewalk area (see fig. 14.9)*	Calculates and highlights hatch boundary
`Select internal points` *Pick a point inside the sidewalk area on the opposite side of the road*	Specifies another boundary
`Select internal points` *Press Enter*	Returns to the dialog box
Choose the Preview Hatch *button*	Displays the potential HATCH pattern on-screen
`Press RETURN to continue` *Press Enter*	Returns to the BHATCH dialog box
Choose the Apply *button*	Draws the hatch pattern

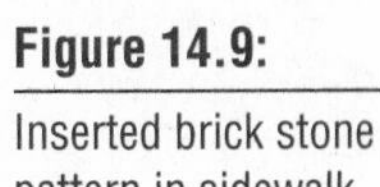

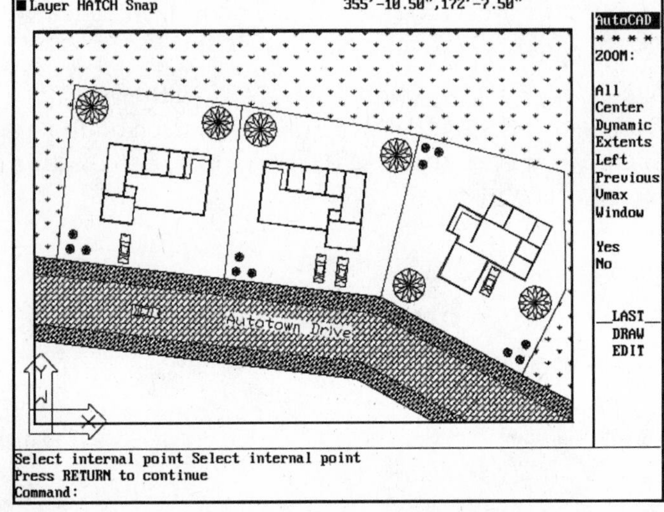

Figure 14.9:

Inserted brick stone pattern in sidewalk.

When using the BHATCH command, you must be able to see all the entities on-screen that are used to define the boundary by using the pick points option to define a boundary. If you need to hatch a very narrow area, or are working on a large drawing, the Advanced Options dialog box enables you to create a selection set from which the hatch boundary is made. Creating a selection set for Pick Points to consider speeds up the process in a complex drawing; otherwise, Pick Points considers all entities on the screen.

When picking internal points to create a BHATCH border, select the point inside the area near an entity that defines the area. By default, BHATCH selects the nearest object. The Advanced Options dialog box enables you to control how the Pick Point option locates the first entity for the boundary (by default, the nearest entity. Use the Ray Casting dialog box to change this so that a ray is projected in an +X, -X, +Y, -Y direction from the selected point.

In this exercise, you use BHATCH to pick a point inside the area to fill with a grass pattern, and BHATCH generates the boundary. Figure 14.8 and the following exercise show the break points on Autotown Drive's polyline.

Hatching Complex Areas

Next, show some mud on the east lot. This presents a more difficult hatch problem because you want to fill around the house, tree, and car blocks. This lot can only be hatched by tracing boundaries around the objects in the lot. The Outermost hatch style does not work; the result of using Outermost (note the missing hatch in some areas) is illustrated in figure 14.10.

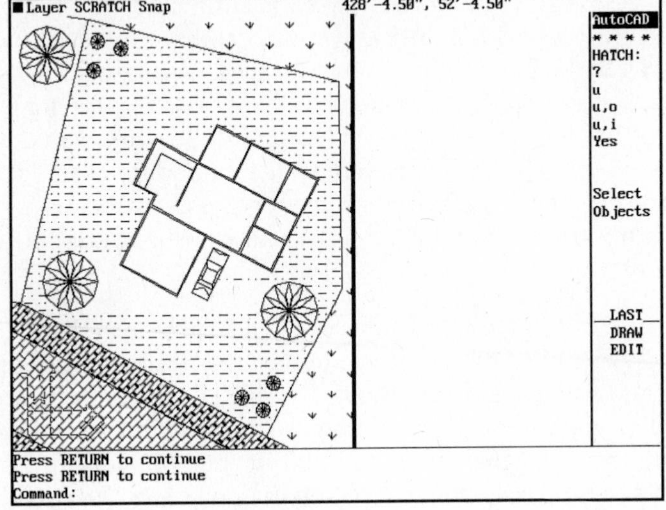

Figure 14.10:

Imperfect HATCH Outermost.

To insert the mud hatching properly, first trace the interior features with a polyline, and then hatch it using the BHATCH command with the MUDST hatch pattern.

Hatching Complex Boundaries

`Command:` *Issue the LAYER command and make* SCRATCH *the current layer*

`Command:` *Choose* View, *then* Zoom, *then* Window, *and then zoom in on the east (right) lot*

Set running object snap to INT, use PLINE to trace the perimeters of the house and car, and set object snap to QUA

`Command:` *Choose* Draw, *then* Circle, *then* 2-point *to draw circles around each tree*

Issue the LAYER command, turn off layer PLAN, and set HATCH current

Set running object snap back to NONE.	
`Command:` *Choose* Settings, *then* Entity Modes. *Set color to YELLOW, then Choose the* OK *button, and then the* OK *button again.*	
`Command:` *Choose* Draw, *then* HATCH	
Choose Hatch **O**ptions, *then* **N**ormal	Defines the hatch style
Choose the **P**attern *button*	Displays the available patterns
Choose Next *three times, then choose* Mudst	Displays and selects the pattern
Enter `120` *in the Scale input box*	Specifies the pattern scale
Enter `0` *in the Angle input box*	Specifies the angle
Choose the OK *button*	Returns to the Boundary Hatch dialog box
Choose the Pick Points *button*	
`Select internal points:` *Pick a point inside the lot, not inside a tree, house, or car*	
`Select internal points:` *Press Enter*	Returns to the dialog box
Choose the Select Objects *button*	Specifies the option to select the boundary objects on-screen
`Select Objects:` *Select the outline of the trees, car and house*	Specifies additional hatch boundaries
`Select Object:` *Press Enter*	
Choose the Appl**y** button	Draws the hatch pattern
`Command:` *Issue the LAYER command and turn PLAN on*	
`Command:` *Choose* Settings, *then* Entity Modes, *then the* Color *button, and set color back to BYLAYER*	
`Command:` *Choose* File, *then* Save	

The result appears in figure 14.11.

You can see that hatching complex areas can be a lot of work.

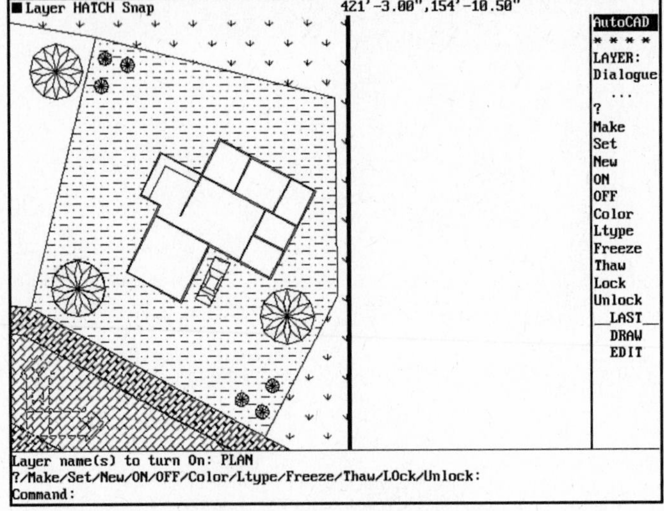

Figure 14.11:

A better hatch with traced boundaries.

TIP

When creating blocks you are likely to hatch around, draw a boundary on a scratch layer around the entities to be blocked before you create the block. When you insert the blocks, they already have boundaries included with them. Turn layers on and off as needed to get just the boundary visible, and then hatch.

TIP

When creating simple and complex block pairs for redefinition, make sure you have good clean hatch boundaries in the simple blocks. Then you can hatch before you redefine simple blocks with complex blocks.

So far, you have used both the Normal and Outermost hatch styles. The third style option ignores any interior boundary. If you want to test the Ignore hatch style, make the SCRATCH layer current and experiment with it.

If you place a pattern with the wrong scale or angle, you can always use Erase Last or U to get rid of the pattern and try again. Press Ctrl-C to stop a pattern fill in progress. Any other editing of hatches, however, is more complicated.

Editing Hatch Patterns

You probably noticed that a single Erase Last command erases an entire hatch pattern. Hatch patterns are *unnamed blocks* with insertion points at 0,0. Normal editing commands like MOVE, COPY, and ARRAY operate on the entire patter,n just like on a named block. If you hatch multiple areas in a single HATCH command and then try to move them individually, the hatches move as a group.

If you want to edit individual lines in a pattern, explode the pattern or use the asterisk option before the pattern name when you hatch it. *BRICK, for example, works just like an *insertion of a block. Because *hatch creates lots of little lines, an Undo is the best way to get rid of an erroneous *hatch.

The 0,0 insertion point of hatches causes a problem with Stretch. Stretch ignores hatch patterns, blocks, and text unless the insertion point is included in the selection window. For hatches, this means that you must include 0,0 in your window to get Stretch to move it.

Several items are worth noting when deciding whether to explode hatches or insert them with an asterisk (*HATCH). If you explode hatches, the bits and pieces migrate to layer 0, making it easy to select and modify the entities if you keep layer 0 clean. The use of *Hatch places hatch entities on the current layer. A normal hatch creates an unnamed block definition, containing all the hatch's lines and a block reference. When you explode the hatch, the drawing temporarily contains twice as much data. You get a new set of individual lines, but the block definition remains until the drawing is ended and reloaded. The use of HATCH creates a set of individual lines, but no block definition, so it uses less data.

Because HATCH uses blocks to group the lines as one entity, every use of the HATCH command creates a unique block definition. Normally, blocks save data storage space through multiple insertions of the same object. But the simultaneous hatching of identical multiple areas with the same pattern does not save data space. If you copy a hatch, however, the copy uses the same block definition and saves space.

When you are hatching several identical areas, hatch one and copy it several times to save data storage space.

Customizing Hatch Patterns

One more technique is useful when using the HATCH command. Assume that you want to use some simple parallel lines as a shading pattern to fill a boundary. Immediately after you invoke the HATCH command, pick the U option from the screen menu or tablet, or press U. U stands for *User-specified* hatch pattern. This hatch option enables you to create parallel or perpendicular crossed-line patterns.

The U option with zero or 90-degree rotation is good for ruling or gridding areas such as pavement, ceiling plans, or section cuts. Use the U option in the next exercise, in which you also explore controlling hatch alignment.

Controlling Hatch Alignment

So far, you have used hatches to fill an area and to indicate a type of material. The precise alignment of the pattern relative to objects in the drawing is not important in these uses. When hatches are used to lay out patterns such as for pavement, floor tile, or ceiling grids, however, the alignment is critical.

The base point of a hatch pattern's alignment is at 0,0 of the current UCS. You can relocate your UCS or use the Snap command's Rotate option to relocate your hatchiinsertion point, rather than letting it default to 0,0. The best option is to relocate the UCS.

Assume you live in the house on the muddy east lot, and you want to turn your garage into a family room. You want to tile it with a user-defined hatch of 36×36 carpet tiles. If you set a hatch angle to match the family room angle, its alignment with the walls is made purely by chance. A better method is to set the UCS to the lower left corner of the family room, and then hatch it. You may have to adjust the UCS and perform the hatch again to center the tile pattern and balance the cut-edge pieces.

Aligning a Hatch U Pattern with a UCS

`Command:` *Choose* View, *then* Zoom, *then* Window, *and zoom in to the garage/family room (see fig. 14.12)*	
`Command:` *From the screen menu choose* AutoCAD, *then* UCS, *then* next, *then* 3point, *and pick points* ①, ②, *and* ③ *with INT object snap (see fig. 14.12)*	Sets UCS to corner of room
`Command:` *Choose* Draw, *then* Hatch	
Choose Hatch **O**ptions	
Choose **U**ser Defined Pattern (U)	Specifies a user defined hatch pattern
Enter `0` *in the* `A`ngle *input box*	Aligns the HATCH with the UCS and the walls
Enter `36` *in the* `S`pacing *input box*	Sets spacing for 36×36 carpet tiles
Choose **D**ouble Hatch	Places a cross hatch in the drawing
Choose the OK *button*	Returns to the Boundary Hatch dialog box
Choose **P**ick points	
`Select internal points` *Pick a point inside the room*	
`Select internal points` *Press Enter*	Returns to the dialog box
Choose the Apply *button*	

Now that you have added the hatch pattern, save the drawing.

`Command:` *Choose* File, *then* Save *to save the file to disk*

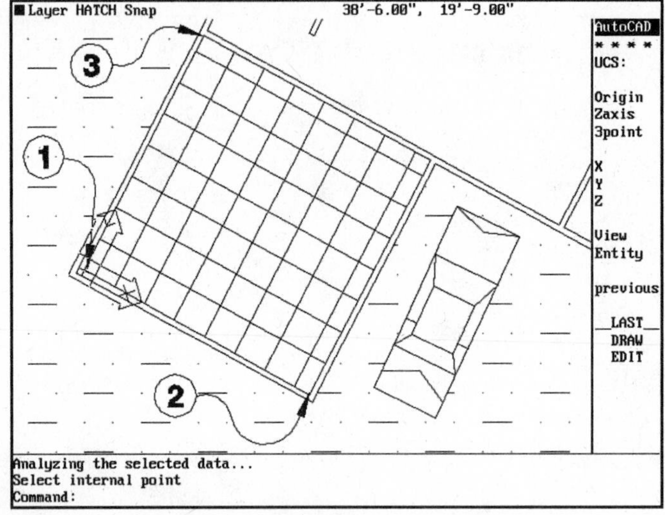

Figure 14.12:

Hatching tiles in the family room.

User-defined hatches are not restricted to simple patterns. Try hatching in different linetypes and at different linetype scales to generate some interesting patterns.

You can create your own hatch patterns like the linetype you create in the next section. The process of creating hatch patterns is much more complex than creating linetypes. You can learn how to create hatch patterns in *Maximizing AutoCAD, Volume I* (New Riders Publishing).

Using Linetypes and Linetype Scales

Do not overlook the opportunity of enhancing drawings by using AutoCAD's standard linetypes or by creating and using your own custom linetype patterns. Every linetype is a pattern of spaces, short-line segments, or dots. You create your own patterns using the LINETYPE command. LINETYPE affects only lines, arcs, circles, and polylines, and those entities in blocks.

The LINETYPE or LAYER commands set different linetypes. You control the overall scale of these patterns with LTSCALE. The easiest way to select linetypes is to use the Settings pull-down menu and then Entity Modes. Then, click on the Linetype button. The Select Linetype dialog box appears (see fig. 14.13), which graphically displays all currently loaded linetypes. You must use the LINETYPE command or the Ltype option of the LAYER command, however, to load linetypes before they show up in the dialog box. The LINETYPE command has a ? option to list any or all linetypes in any linetype file.

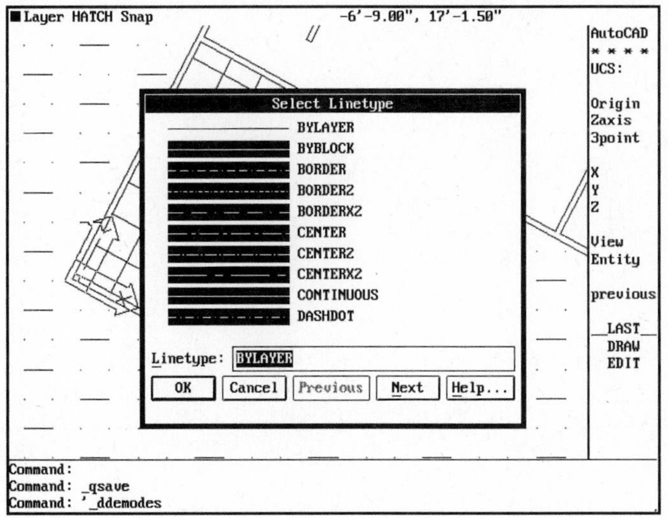

Figure 14.13:

The Select Linetype dialog box with standard linetypes.

LTSCALE Controls Line Pattern Spacing

You have used the LTSCALE command to adjust linetype scales. If you do not remember how LTSCALE works, review the following examples.

Each standard line pattern is defined to look good when plotted at full scale when LTSCALE is set to 1, the default. By setting LTSCALE to the desired scale factor, you can condense or stretch the pattern. Use your drawing scale factor as a starting scale, although you may need to adjust it slightly to personal preference or standards. Set LTSCALE for the plot appearance, not the screen appearance. Whatever setting meets your standards, remember to adjust it for your drawing scale for other than 1=1 plots. For example, a 1/4" = 1'-0" plot with a 0.375 standard linetype scale yields 48X.375 = 18 as the actual setting.

You can have only one linetype scale, which is applied to all linetypes. However, each of the standard linetypes comes in three variants — a standard scale pattern with a name such as PHANTOM, a half-scale pattern with a name such as PHANTOM2, and a twice-scale pattern with a name such as PHANTOMX2. Many users find the half-scale variants best for most purposes. Figure 14.14 shows how several of the standard, half-scale, and twice-scale linetypes look at different linetype scales.

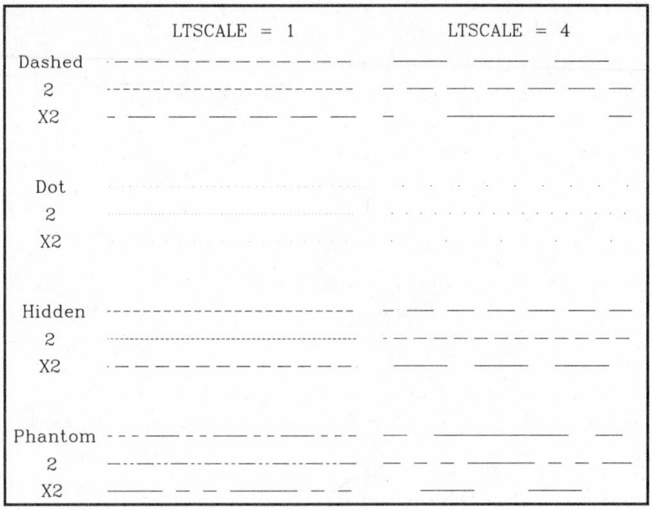

LTSCALE = 1
LTSCALE = 4
Dashed
2
X2
Dot
2
X2
Hidden
2
X2
Phantom
2
X2

Figure 14.14:

Ltscale and linetype examples.

If your lines generate slowly or appear continuous, instead of broken, try resetting LTSCALE higher.

In complex drawings with a lot of patterned linetypes, your regenerations may get rather slow. To speed things up, you can temporarily use continuous linetypes while drawing, and then change them to the correct linetypes before plotting.

Creating Your Own Linetypes

Autotown is getting a new gas line. Rather than use a standard linetype to draw it, the next set of exercises show you how to make your own linetype (named GASLINE), scale it, and then use it to draw the proposed gas line.

The LINETYPE command enables you to define your own dot-and-dash pattern and store that pattern in a linetype file. AutoCAD's standard linetypes are stored in a disk file named ACAD.LIN. You can add linetypes to ACAD.LIN or create your own file, like the MYLINES.LIN file in this exercise.

First, you create a new linetype, GASLINE, and store it. GASLINE consists of a dash, then five dots, and so on. The process is explained after the exercise.

Using LINETYPE To Create a Linetype

Continue from the preceding exercise, or from the Setting Up... exercise at the beginning of the chapter.

`Command:` *From the screen menu, choose* AutoCAD, *then* SETTINGS, *then* LINETYPE	Starts the LINETYPE command
`?/Create/Load/Set:` *From the screen menu choose* Create	Creates a newlinetype
`Name of linetype to create:` **`GASLINE`**↵	Specifies the name of the new linetype
Enter **`MYLINES`** *in the* File Name *text box, and then choose the* OK *button*	Specifies the DOS file where the linetype is stored
`Creating new file`	
`Descriptive text:` **`GASLINE _____ ..... _____ .....`**	Simulates the linetype with five underscores and periods
`Enter pattern (on next line):`	
`A,.4,-.1,0,-.1,0,-.1,0,-.1,0,-.1,0,-.1`↵	Specifies a .4 unit dash, then five zeroes for five dots, with .1 unit gaps between ends
`New definition written to file.`	
`?/Create/Load/Set:` ↵	Exits the LINETYPE command

The linetype has been created and stored but is not yet loaded.

What went on in the linetype definition sequence? Here is an explanation of the prompts and responses.

Name of linetype to create — Name of the linetype you want tocreate. Use a good descriptive name for the linetype to make it easy to identify later.

File for storage of linetype — Name of the disk file where the linetype definition is to be stored. It is safer to store linetype definitions in your own file, rather than to use the ACAD.LIN file where AutoCAD stores the standard linetypes. If you want them all in one file, copy the ACAD.LIN file to your name, and then add your linetypes to it.

Descriptive text — What you see when you issue a ? query to list the named linetypes. The pattern is a dot-and-dash representation of the linetype that shows on a text screen. Just type underscores (___) and periods (. . .) as descriptive text.

Enter pattern (on next line) — AutoCAD is asking for the actual definition of the linetype pattern to repeat when it draws the line. You separate values with commas. The pattern codes include:

- **The A,** — is entered for you. A is the alignment code to balance the pattern between end points. No other alignments are currently supported.
- **A positive number** — like .4. The positive number gives the unit length of a pen downstroke. The first stroke must be pen down; it is the maximum line length that appears as the first segment.

- **A negative number** — like -.1. The negative number gives the unit length of a pen upstroke. In other words, it is the length of the blank space.
- **A zero** — represents a dot.

After you have stored one or more linetypes in a linetype file, you can load the linetypes for use. Load these linetypes with the Load option of the LINETYPE command. You can list several names with commas between names. Use wild cards, such as * and ?, to load several or all linetypes at once. The process of loading a linetype does not set it current. You use the LAYER command to set it for layers or the LINETYPE Set option to set the linetype as an explicit entity linetype.

Try loading and setting GASLINE.

Using LINETYPE To Load a Linetype

`Command:` *From the screen menu choose AutoCAD, then* SETTINGS, *then* LINETYPE:	
`?/Create/Load/Set:` **`L`** ↵	Loads linetypes from a file
`Linetype(s) to load:` **`*`**↵	Loads GASLINE more quickly than entering the name
Press Enter at the Select Linetype File dialog box, accepting the default file name	
`Linetype GASLINE loaded.`	
`?/Create/Load/Set:` **`S`** ↵	Sets the default linetype
`New entity linetype (or ?) <BYLAYER>:` **`GASLINE`** ↵	Specifies the new default linetype
`?/Create/Load/Set:` *Press Enter*	Sets GASLINE current

After it is loaded, a linetype is stored in the drawing, and, unlike text font and xref files, the drawing file does not need to reference the linetype file in order to use it. You also can use the Entity Creation Modes Select Linetype dialog box to set the current entity linetype.

Any entities that you create now show the new GASLINE linetype. Try drawing the gas line between the curb and setback property line on the north side of Autotown Drive.

Testing and Scaling a Linetype

`Command:` *From the screen menu, choose* AutoCAD, *then* UCS, *then* World	Sets UCS to World
`Command:` *From the screen menu, choose* AutoCAD, *then* DISPLAY, *then* VIEW:, *then* Restore, *and enter* `ALL`	Restores view ALL

Issue the LAYER command and set layer SCRATCH *current and freeze* HATCH

`Command:` *Choose* Draw, *then the* Polyline, *then* 2D, *and draw a line between the curb and property lines, border to border*

The line looks as if it is continuous.

`Command:` *From the screen menu, choose* AutoCAD, SETTINGS, *then* next, *then* LTSCALE:

`New scale factor <1.0000>:` **`120`**

`Regenerating drawing.`

The linetype is still too small to be sure it is right (see fig. 14.15).

Zoom in close enough to see the dots

Now it looks correct (see fig. 14.16). It should plot fine at 1"=10'.

`Command:` *Choose* View, *then* Zoom, *then* Previous

Erase the gas line

`Command:` *Choose* File, *then* Save

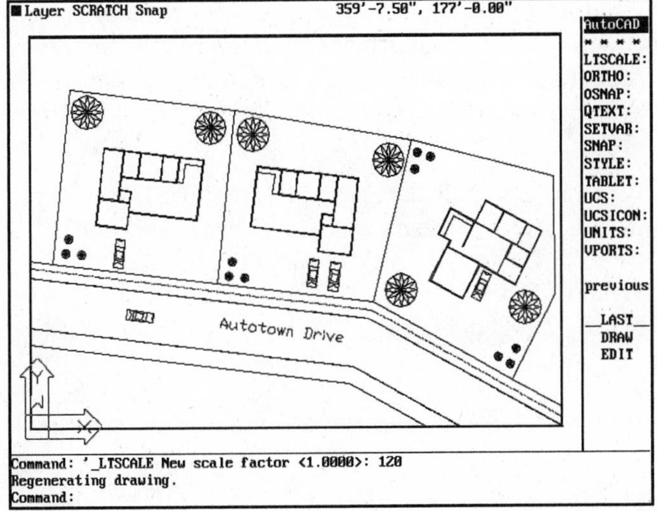

Figure 14.15:

GASLINE at Ltscale 120.

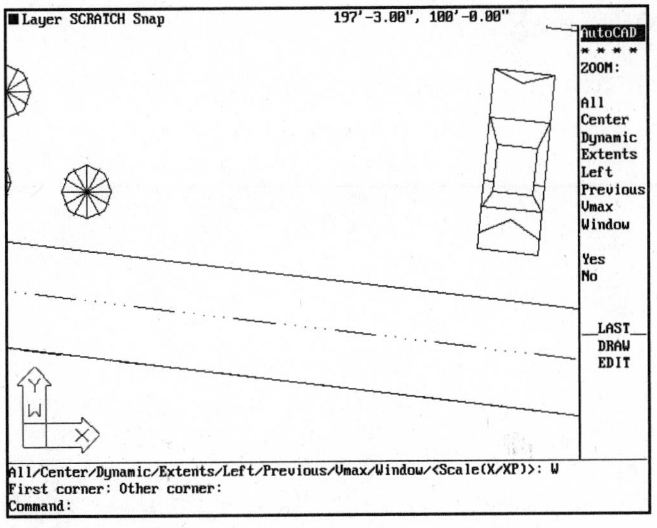

Figure 14.16:

GASLINE zoomed.

Just like text, properly scaled linetypes are not always legible when you are working on your drawing. When you are zoomed way out or in, they may appear continuous or invisible.

If you cannot discern linetypes on-screen in large-scale drawings, you may want to set a temporary linetype scale for screen appearance. Just remember to set it back to the correct scale before plotting.

Like replacing blocks and styles, loading a new definition of a linetype causes a regeneration and replaces old linetypes with new unless you suppress regeneration using REGENAUTO. Adjustments to LTSCALE do not affect existing entities until after a regeneration.

Complete the Autotown drawing by sketching some contour lines between the road and the lower border, to redirect the drainage away from the east lot and its new family room.

Drawing Freehand Using SKETCH

The SKETCH command enables you to draw lines freehand, without being bothered by point specification and other alignment or input parameters. You sketch just as you would doodle or draw on a piece of paper. SKETCH also is useful for tracing curves such as contour lines.

How SKETCH Works

AutoCAD stores sketch entities in the drawing file as successive short-line segments. It draws wherever you move your cursor, as you move it. Because AutoCAD does not know where your sketching may lead, both you and the program have to take precautions to keep the amount of sketch information from getting out of hand. Just a few quick motions of the cursor in sketch mode can create a huge number of short segments in the drawing file.

To help AutoCAD keep sketch information under control, you tell it how short a line segment to use for storing your sketch data. This is known as the *record increment*. AutoCAD stores a new segment every time your pointer moves more than the record increment away from the last stored segment end point. Try to keep the record increment as large as possible to minimize the number of lines.

The record increment is in current drawing units, but the effect on your input coordination also depends on the area your mouse or digitizer cursor has to move in your currently zoomed view. For example, if the width of your screen represents 300 feet (3600 inches), and the screen pointing area on your digitizer is six inches wide, a 60-inch increment means your sketch segments are five feet and that AutoCAD records a new segment every time you move your pointing device about one-tenth of an inch (six inches times 60 inches, divided by 3600 inches).

Mice that have variable speed vary in their mouse-to-screen scaling — move them at a steady speed for best results.

You also have to let AutoCAD know when to consider the sketching pointer up (off the paper) or down (sketching). AutoCAD keeps all sketch input in a temporary buffer until you press **R** to record it into the drawing file database. You can press **E** to erase sketched lines before you record them. If you record sketched lines, AutoCAD turns them into regular line (or polyline) entities.

Using SKETCH To Make Contour Polylines

Try making some contour lines using the SKETCH command. This example was chosen because it is a common and extremely useful application of SKETCH. To get smooth contour curves, you need to sketch with polylines rather than with lines (the default). Use the SKPOLY system variable to switch SKETCH from lines to polylines. If SKPOLY is 0, SKETCH draws lines. If it is 1, SKETCH draws polylines.

Polylines can be easily stretched and edited, but their biggest advantage is that you can curve fit polylines and get a smooth curve. When you set SKPOLY to sketch polylines, set your record increment larger than you would when you sketch with lines. Use an increment one-half the smallest radius or turn that you sketch. This may seem too large until you apply a curve fit to it.

Try sketching the contour lines. It takes a little time to get the hang of sketching, so do not be shy about undoing or erasing and trying again. Do not worry if your sketch ends extend over the drive and border lines. You

can trim the loose ends later. Set the linetype back to continuous because broken linetypes do not work well for short-line segments, like those that SKETCH creates. Set up SKETCH in the following exercise, and then sketch and edit the contour polylines.

Using SKETCH and Skpoly To Draw Contour Lines

Continue from the preceding exercise, or from the Setting Up... exercise at the beginning of the chapter.

Command: *Choose* View, *then* Zoom, *then* Window, *and then zoom to the area shown in figure 14.17*	
Command: *Choose* Settings, *then* Entity Modes, *and then the* Linetype *button*	
Choose CONTINUOUS, *then choose* OK, *and then choose* OK *again*	Selects continuous linetype
Command: ***SKPOLY*↵**	Access the SKPOLY system variable
New value for SKPOLY <0>: ***1*↵**	Sets SKETCH to draw polylines
Command: *From the screen menu choose* DRAW, *then* next, *and then* SKETCH	
Record increment <0'-0.10">: ***60*↵**	Specifies the length of a sketch line segment
Sketch. Pen eXit Quit Record Erase Connect.	
Click to put pen down and move cursor to sketch a line	Begins sketching
<pen down>	
Click to pick pen up	Stops sketching
<pen up> *Press* R	Records the line
1 polyline with 14 edges recorded.	
Press X	Exits SKETCH

Next, smooth the sketch polyline.

Command: *Choose* Modify, *then* Polyedit	
Select objects: **L ↵**	Selects the last entity

`Select objects:` *Press Enter*

`Close/Join/Width/Edit vertex/Fit curve/`
`Spline curve/Decurve/Undo/eXit <X>:`
Choose Fit Curve *from the screen menu*

Performs a fit curve on the sketch line

`Close/Join/Width/Edit vertex/Fit curve/`
`Spline curve/Decurve/Undo/eXit <X>:`
Press Enter

Draw the remaining contours shown and fit curves to them.

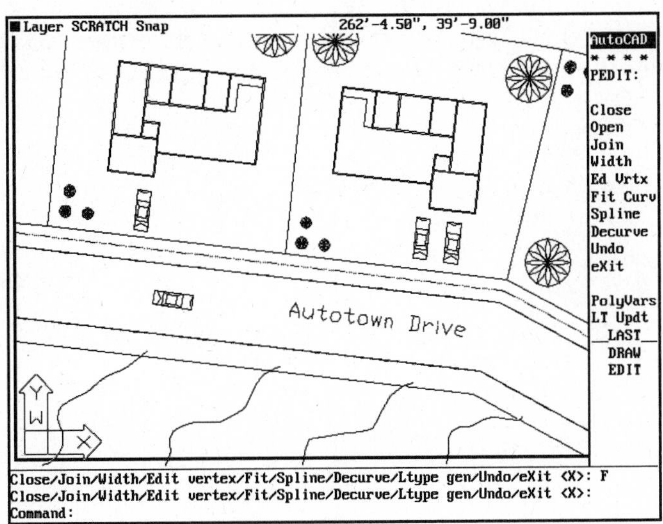

Figure 14.17:
Autotown with sketched contours.

SKETCH Options

When you are in the SKETCH command, all other input is ignored, except for the sketch mode controls (and toggles like F8 for ortho and F9 for snap). To control SKETCH using the following options, press the first character of the option without pressing Enter.

- **Pen.** This option tells AutoCAD the pointer is up or down. Just type **P**, without pressing Enter, to change the toggle. You also can click to cause the pen to be up or down.
- **eXit.** This option records the sketch segments you have been creating in the drawing file and gets you back to the command prompt. You also can exit by pressing the spacebar or Enter, which does the same thing as eXit.

- **Quit.** This option leaves SKETCH without storing the segments you have been creating. Pressing Ctrl-C does the same thing.
- **Record.** This option keeps you in SKETCH, but stores the segments you have been creating so far in the drawing file. This function is just like a save, but after you record, segments that get stored are not available for Erase from SKETCH.
- **Erase.** This option erases any unrecorded segment from a point you pick to the last segment drawn.
- **Connect.** This option connects the pen to the end of the last endpoint of an active sketch chain. You also can use normal AutoCAD editing techniques to connect finished sketch lines to other elements after you finish the sketch.

Now, trim any loose sketch ends, and the finished lines should resemble those shown in figure 14.18.

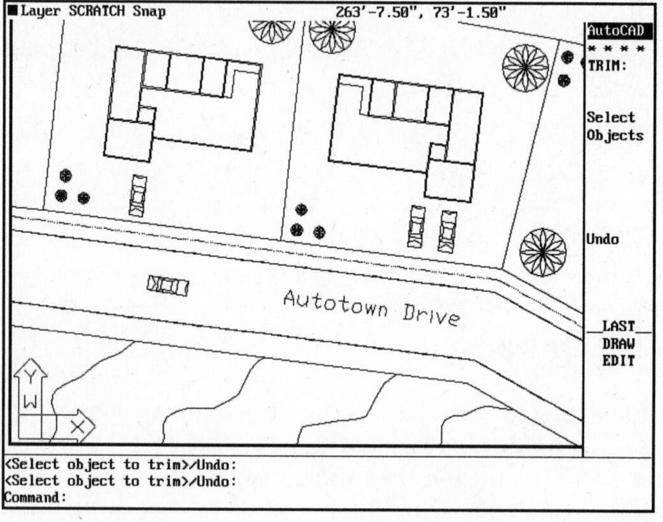

Figure 14.18:
The sketched lines after trimming.

Using TRIM To Trim Sketch Polylines

`Command:` *Choose* Modify, *then* Trim

`Select cutting edge(s)...`
`Select objects:` *Select the road and border lines*

`Select objects:` *Press Enter*

`<Select object to trim>/Undo:` *Select the overlapping ends of the sketch lines*

`Command:` *Choose* View, then Set View, *choose* AutoCAD, *then* DISPLAY, *then* Named view, *select* ALL, *then choose* Restore, *then* OK — Restores view ALL

Issue the LAYER command and thaw layer HATCH *if you want to view the complete drawing*

`Command:` Choose *File*, then *Save*

The added contour lines were the last step in Autotown's suburban renewal. Your drawing should now resemble figure 14.19.

Not everyone feels confident about freehand drawing skills. If you would rather trace, AutoCAD provides a way to trace contours (or any kind of data) from an existing paper drawing.

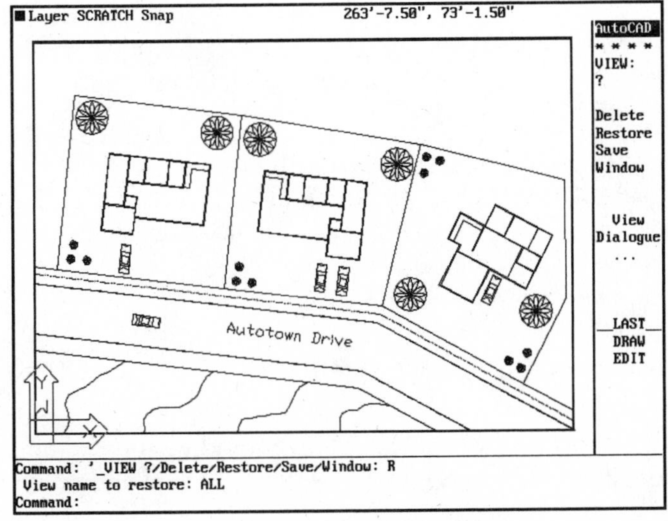

Figure 14.19: The enhanced Autotown.

Tracing and Digitizing Using the Tablet

If you have a digitizer, you can use it to trace and digitize drawings into AutoCAD. AutoCAD has two modes for using digitizers: the screen pointing mode you usually use and a calibrated digitizing mode. You use the calibrated digitizing mode to establish a relationship between points on a drawing taped to the tablet and points in your AutoCAD drawing. After that relationship has been calibrated, you can pick points in the AutoCAD drawing fairly accurately by digitizing the corresponding points on the paper drawing. Although this is not as accurate as creating a new drawing entirely from accurate coordinate and measurement data, it is often the only efficient way to import existing drawing data.

Digitizing is well-suited to tracing contours, which do not demand absolute precision, with sketched lines. Digitizing is not limited to sketching, however. You can use the full range of drawing commands and controls, even inserting blocks at datum points picked on the tablet.

To digitize, first use the CAL (calibrate) option of the Tablet command. It prompts you for two known points on the paper drawing and for the drawing coordinates to assign to them. After calibration, the relationship between the drawing and tablet is maintained even if you pan and zoom. The X and Y axes are calibrated with equal scales. If the tablet drawing is distorted (as are many paper drawings), you can compensate after tracing by blocking the results and inserting them with differing X and Y scales. If your paper drawing does not fit on the tablet menu's screen pointing area, you can reconfigure the tablet to use its full area for digitizing. To exit the calibrated tablet mode, use the Tablet command's OFF option; to re-enter tablet mode, use ON. You also can switch between tablet mode and screen pointing mode with F10 or Ctrl-T.

You are not going to change the Autotown drawing any more, but you are now going to use AutoCAD's inquiry commands to take another look at it. Autotown has defined distances and areas that make it a good practice drawing for retrieving information.

Using Inquiry Commands

AutoCAD's inquiry commands are useful for providing information about drawings. When lines are placed into a drawing file, they often represent

distances and locations with real world relationships. To help the person reading the drawing understand these spatial implications is part of creating a good drawing.

You have used the ID, HELP, and STATUS commands in earlier chapters. With these and other inquiry commands, you can measure, identify, and generally find out what is in a drawing file. AutoCAD already has much of the spatial information that you may need built into the drawing. The DISTANCE and AREA commands, for example, return line distances and polygon area values from the Start an inquiry session with a look at AutoCAD's timing features, and set the clock to see how long this last section of the chapter takes to examine.

Using TIME To Track Your Drawing Time

Unlike the other inquiry commands, TIME is really a management tool. TIME gives you a list of times and dates about your drawing and editing sessions. This information includes the current system time; the date and time a drawing was created; the date and time of the last update; time in the editor; and elapsed time.

Choose the TIME command, and set time ON. This acts as an elapsed timer that you can check at the end of these inquiry exercises to measure your time spent in the drawing editor.

These inquiry exercises can use any version of the Autotown drawing, as long as it has the lot lines in it. If you are starting after a break, reload your AUTOTOWN drawing. If you are jumping into the chapter at this point, do the quick "Setting Up for Enhancing Autotown" exercise at the beginning of the chapter, and then the following exercise. Start by turning on an elapsed timer built into the TIME command.

Using TIME To Track Your Drawing Time

Choose File, then Open, then enter `\IA\AUTOTOWN`.

`Command:` *From the screen menu, choose* INQUIRY, *and then* TIME

Your dates and times can vary from those shown.

```
Current time:             05 Jan 1992 at 10:29:27.000
Drawing created:          02 Jan 1992 at 12:17:08.000
Drawing last updated:     04 Jan 1992 at 14:10:23.000
Time in drawing editor: 0 days 1:49:15.000
Elapsed timer:            0 days 1:49:15.000
Timer on.
```

`Display/ON/OFF/Reset:` **R**	Resets the elapsed timer
`Timer reset.`	
`Display/ON/OFF/Reset:` *Press Enter*	
`Command:` *Press F1*	Returns the graphics screen

You also can access the time data with AutoLISP, which enables you to create drawing time management and billing programs.

Check the elapsed time after you look at the other inquiry commands. The simplest inquiry, ID, deserves a second look.

Using the ID Command

You have used ID before to locate points. ID returns the X,Y,Z location of a point.

The ID command is useful for resetting the last point without drawing anything, so you can use relative coordinates from the reset point. The last point is stored as the system variable LASTPOINT.

Use ID to reset the last point.

Using ID To Reset LASTPOINT

`Command:` *Issue the LAYER command, and set layer* 0 *current and freeze the* SCRATCH *and* HATCH *layers*	
`Command:` **LASTPOINT** ↵	Directly accesses the SETVAR LASTPOINT

`New value for LASTPOINT <168'-6.00", 46'-6.00",0'-0.00">:` *Press Enter*	Displays LASTPOINT value, yours may be different
`Command: ID↵`	
`Point:` *Use the ENDP object snap and pick point at ① (see fig. 14.20)*	IDs the point
`ENDP of X: 142'-5.95" Y: 205'-0.89" Z: 0'-0.00"`	Returns the exact location
`Command: LASTPOINT↵`	
`New value for LASTPOINT <142'-5.95", 205'-0.89",0'-0.00">:` *Press Enter*	Displays new values set by ID

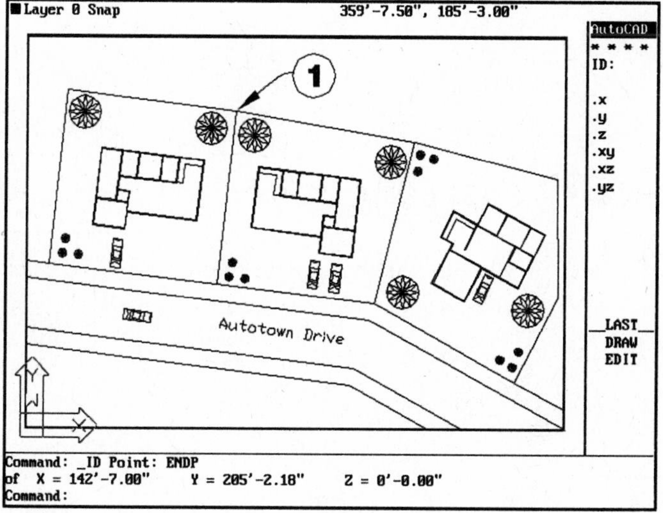

Figure 14.20:
ID corner point between lots.

Using DIST To Get Line Lengths—and More

DIST gives the 3D distance between two points, its angles in and from the X,Y plane, and the X, Y, and Z offset distances. The measured distance is stored as the system variable DISTANCE.

Assume you need to check the length of the lot line between the east lot and the middle lot. Use object snaps for accuracy, and DIST gets you this information.

Using DIST To Get a Lot Line Length and Angle

`Command:` *Choose* Assist, *then* Inquiry, *then* Distance	Issues DIST command transparently
`'_dist First point:` *Use the ENDP object snap to pick corner of lot at ① (see fig. 14.21)*	
`Second point:` *Use the ENDP object snap to pick corner of lot at ②*	Displays distances and angles

```
Distance = 100'-2.50", Angle in X-Y Plane =
S 14d52'0" W, Angle from X-Y Plane = E
Delta X = -25'-8.53", Delta Y = -96'-10.25",
Delta Z = 0'-0.00"
```

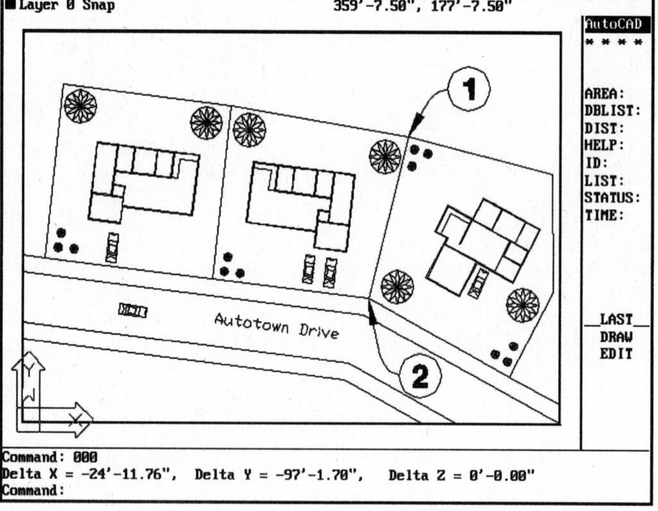

Figure 14.21:

Distance of lot lines.

You also can issue DIST from the screen menu by choosing AutoCAD, then INQUIRY, and then DIST.

If units are set to decimal degrees, DIST displays the angle in decimals, such as 255.1333.

Next, survey the perimeter and areas.

Using AREA To Get Area and Perimeter Values

AREA gives you the area surrounded by a straight-sided polygon, defined by temporary points that you pick. Or, you can select an entity such as a polyline or circle, and AREA automatically calculates its area, including curves. AREA keeps a running total that you can add to or subtract from to calculate complex areas or groups of areas. In the Add or Subtract mode, the AREA command stays active until you exit it by pressing Enter. Add and Subtract only accumulate in the current command; each use of the AREA command restarts from 0. The area is stored as the system variable AREA, and the calculated perimeter is stored as the system variable PERIMETER.

Try surveying the area and perimeter of the east lot, using object snaps for your pick points.

Using AREA To Calculate a Lot and Perimeter Area

`Command:` *Set a running object snap of INT,END*

`Command:` *Choose* Assist, *then* Inquiry, *then* AREA

`<First point>/Entity/Add/Subtract:`
Pick corner of the lot at ① (see fig. 14.22)

`Next point:` *Pick corner of the lot at ②*

`Next point:` *Pick corner of the lot at ③*

`Next point:` *Pick corner of the lot at ④*

`Next point:` *Pick corner of the lot at ⑤*

`Next point:` *Press Enter* Closes the boundary

`Area = 1634309.43 square in. (11349.3710 square ft.), Perimeter = 418'-2.67"`

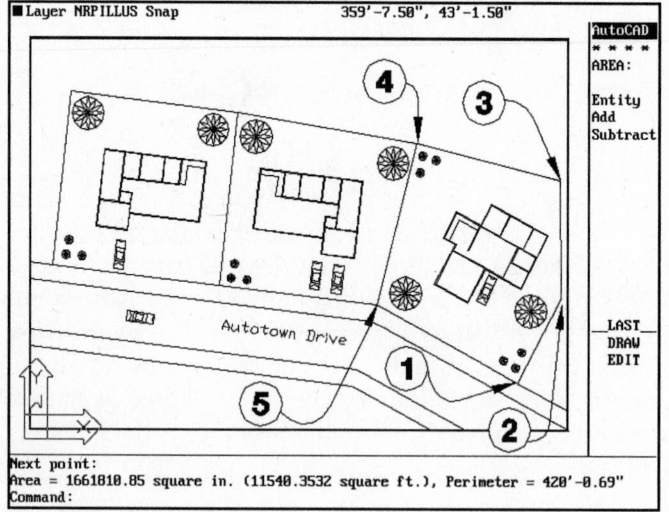

Figure 14.22:

Getting the area of the east lot.

You also can issue AREA from the screen menu (choose INQUIRY, then AREA:). You also can get an area just by picking an entity. AREA recognizes polylines and circles. Use the Entity option when you need the area of an existing or curved boundary. Use BPOLY or PLINE to trace a temporary polyline over your drawing if you need to define the boundary.

If you hatched the muddy east lot, try getting the area of the east house by picking the hatch boundary you drew around it earlier.

Using AREA To Find the Area of the East House

`Command:` *Sets running object snap to NONE*

Issue the LAYER command and thaw layer SCRATCH

`Command:` *From the screen menu,* choose INQUIRY, *then* AREA

`<First point>/Entity/Add/Subtract:` *Choose* Entity *from the screen menu*

`Select circle or polyline:` *Select polyline boundary around house*

`Area = 340992.00 square in. (2368.0000 square ft.), Perimeter = 232'-0.00"`

An area is always a closed calculation. AutoCAD assumes a closure line between the first and last pick points of your area boundaries. Likewise, when you select an open polyline, AREA treats it as if it were closed.

You can access the last-calculated area, distance, and perimeter values using the SETVAR command.

Using the AREA and PERIMETER System Variables

`Command:` **`SETVAR`** ↵

`'setvar Variable name or ?<LASTPOINT>:` **`AREA`**

`AREA = 340992.00 (read only)` Shows the area in square inches

`Command:` **`SETVAR`** ↵

`'setvar Variable name or ?<AREA>:` **`DISTANCE`** ↵

```
DISTANCE = 100'-2.50" (read only)
Command: SETVAR↵
'setvar Variable name or ?<DISTANCE>:
PERIMETER↵
PERIMETER = 232'-0.00" (read only)
```

Using LIST and DBLIST Inquiry Commands

AutoCAD has two other inquiry commands that you should know about: LIST and DBLIST. LIST gives a complete list of entities that you select, including where the entities are located. The LIST command gives the closed area of a closed polyline, including curves. LIST also lists the length of selected polylines. The length equals the perimeter reported by AREA if it is closed.

LIST is often used to check the block name, dimension style, color, layer, or pertinent coordinate points of existing entities, so you can use this information for drawing new entities. The following exercise lists information about a block and a polyline.

List Entity Data

`Command:` *Choose* Assist, *then* Inquiry, *then* List

`Select objects:` *Select car and the polyline border around it in east lot*

```
        POLYLINE  Layer: SCRATCH          The polyline data
                  Space: Model space      begins
        Closed
  starting width  0'-0.00"
    ending width  0'-0.00"
        VERTEX    Layer: SCRATCH          Polyline continues
                                          with four vertexes
                  Space: Model space
     at point, X=297'-3.17"  Y=108'-8.77"   Z= 0'-0.00"
  starting width  0'-0.00"
    ending width  0'-0.00"
```

Three more vertices are listed, then:

`END SEQUENCE  Layer: SCRATCH` `Space: Model space`	The polyline ends
`area  15120.00 sq in (105.0000 sq ft)`	Saved in AREA system variable
`perimeter 46'-0.00"`	Saved in PERIMETER system variable
`BLOCK REFERENCE Layer: PLAN`	Displays the block data
`Space: Model space`	
`CAR`	Displays the block name

```
   at point, X=300'-0.00"  Y=107'-6.00"  Z= 0'-0.00"
      X scale factor    1.0000
      Y scale factor    1.0000
  rotation angle 245d19'23"
      Z scale factor    1.0000
```

Command: *Press F1* — Returns to the graphics screen

You also can access LIST from the screen menu (choose INQUIRY, then LIST:). The color and linetypes also are listed when they are anything other than the default BYLAYER.

DBLIST gives a complete data list of every entity in the drawing file. After you issue a DBLIST command, you might never do it again. Issuing this command causes the entire database to scroll by the screen. Cancel with Ctrl-C to stop this display.

Using TIME To Get Elapsed Editing Time

Finish up this chapter by looking at TIME again to see how long you spent in this editor session.

Using TIME To Get Elapsed Drawing Time

`Command:` *From the screen menu, choose* INQUIRY, *then* TIME:

```
Current time:              05 Jan 1992 at 10:29:27.000
Drawing created:           02 Jan 1992 at 12:17:08.000
Drawing last updated:      04 Jan 1992 at 14:10:23.000
Time in drawing editor: 0 days 1:49:15.000
Elapsed timer (on):              0 days 0:13:00.000
```

The elapsed time is about 13 minutes.

`Display/ON/OFF/Reset:` *Press Enter*

`Command:` *Choose* File, *then* Exit AutoCAD

A test of these inquiry features took about 13 minutes in the drawing editor.

Using The Region Modeler as an Inquiry Tool

The Region Modeler can be a very powerful tool for finding out database information about a drawing. This information can include basic information such as area and perimeter. In addition, you can obtain advanced information. The advanced information includes the bounding box, centroid, moments of inertia, product of inertia, radii of gyration, and principal moments. This information can be useful for making engineering decisions. Chapter 23 introduces additional uses for these commands.

The object in figure 14.23 has been drawn with PLINES and CIRCLES.

Using the Region Modeler, the keyway, shaft, and internal perimeters circles were subtracted. The external perimeter circles have been unioned. The resulting geometry is shown in figure 14.24.

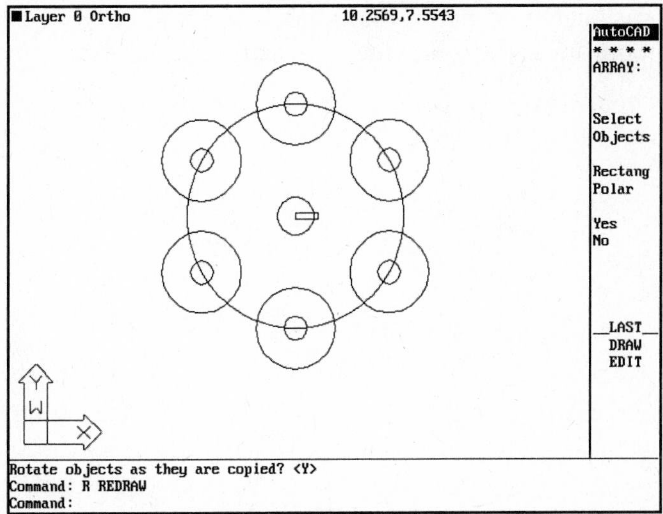

Figure 14.23:

The object drawn with PLINES and CIRCLES.

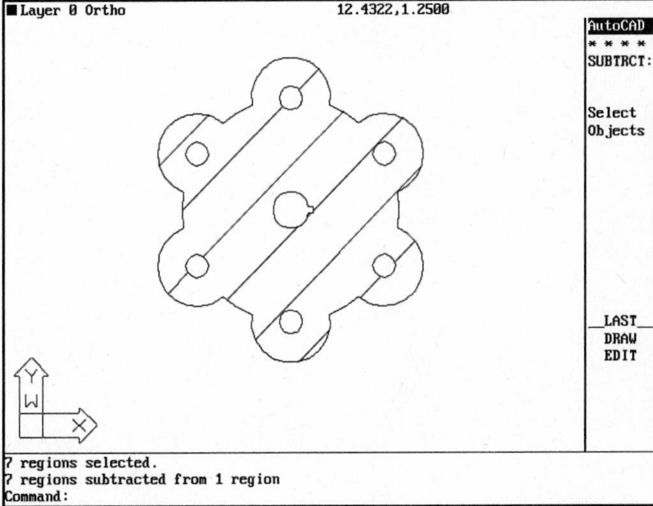

Figure 14.24:

The object modified with the Region Modeler

Once the object has been modified, using Modeler Mass Property from the pull-down menu produces the following information about the geometry:

```
Area:                       22.7144 sq cm
Perimeter:                  33.91323 cm
Bounding box:           X: 3.283945 – 9.006878 cm
                        Y: 1.859719 – 8.205499 cm
Centroid:               X: 6.145179  cm
                        Y: 5.032609  cm
Moments of inertia:     X: 621.9436  sq cm sq cm
                        Y: 904.4192  sq cm sq cm
Product of inertia: XY: 702.4719  sq cm sq cm
Radii of gyration:      X: 5.232689  cm
                        Y: 6.310071  cm
Principal moments(sq cm sq cm) and X-Y directions about cen-
troid:
                        I: 46.65036 about [0 1 ]
                       J: 46.65262 about [1 0 ]
```

This information can be viewed on-screen, or it can be saved as a file on disk.

Summary

AutoCAD provides nearly limitless possibilities for enhancing drawings. In this chapter, you have covered the essentials to get you started. Here are some other reminders about hatching and sketching.

AutoCAD needs fully closed boundaries for hatching; use BHATCH or PLINE to create closed continuous boundaries. Standard AutoCAD patterns are designed to be scaled by your drawing scale factor. Use HATCH U when you just want a quick hatch. You can press Ctrl-C to terminate hatching in progress. Use Erase Last to get rid of hatch patterns as a block. When hatching, take time to find the patterns that work best for your drawings. Do not overlook the possibility of creating your own hatch patterns and linetypes to give your drawings a unique look.

Be careful with SKETCH. Use it with a relatively large increment, set SKPOLY to 1 and curve fit with PEDIT for smooth efficient curves. Use the calibrated digitizer mode when you need to sketch or trace data from existing paper drawings.

Use AutoCAD's inquiry commands to measure, identify, and generally find out the status of entities and what is in a drawing. Consider using the TIME command as a management tool. Use ID to identify coordinates and reset the last point. Use DIST for distances and angles. Use AREA for areas and perimeters. Use LIST to check coordinates and properties of existing entities. Do not forget the system variables that store these data.

15

Dimensioning

To communicate designs, drawings must convey more than just graphic entities and annotations. Many drawings require dimensions, tolerances, and other key information to define the design well enough so that it can be built or manufactured. This information is often just as important as the drawing. An object that is not drawn to scale might not affect the project, as long as the dimensions are correct. If you put down a wrong dimension, however, the chances of an error in production increase dramatically.

This chapter shows you how to dimension your drawings in AutoCAD by defining spatial relationships between objects. You learn about many basic dimensioning techniques and commands. In Chapter 17, "Advanced Dimensioning," you learn more about dimensioning with AutoCAD, including how to use dimension styles and associative dimensions. This chapter, therefore, lays the groundwork for Chapter 17.

Understanding Dimensioning

AutoCAD takes as much work out of dimensioning as possible: distances are calculated automatically; dimension arrows are consistently sized; standards for settings, such as extension line offsets, are maintained and applied to the drawing; and the entities that make up a dimension are created automatically.

After specifying the type of dimensions to draw, identify what to measure (usually endpoints, arcs, or other points of existing entities). For greater accuracy, use object snaps. Then pick a location for the dimension line and text. Finally, accept AutoCAD's measurements as dimension text or enter your own text.

The key to accurate dimensioning relies more on drawing technique than on dimensioning. The accuracy of your drawing controls the accuracy of the drawing's dimensions because AutoCAD calculates dimensions based on the points you specify. When you draw an object out of scale or to an incorrect size, the drawing's dimensions reflect that error unless you override them. Overriding these dimensions defeats the advantage AutoCAD provides by calculating dimensions for you. Accuracy in drawing makes dimensioning much easier.

AutoCAD can create dimensions in many different styles and to nearly any standard. The default style of dimensioning works, but may not suit your standards. To dimension in AutoCAD, you usually create a group of standard settings that control the appearance and placement of your dimensions. Then, you select the type of dimension and the points or entities to dimension, and AutoCAD does the rest. System variables called *dimension variables* (or *dimvars*) provide almost complete control over size, placement, and appearance of dimensions. The easiest way to adjust the dimension variables is by using the Dimension Style option of the Settings pull-down menu. This dialog box contains a list of dimension variable groupings that brings up child dialog boxes that enable those variables to be viewed and adjusted. If you know them quite well, you also can set dimension variables using the SETVAR command, by entering the variable names as commands or by choosing them from the list provided on the screen menu. Table 15.1 lists all of AutoCAD's dimension variables.

You usually have several standard sets of dimension variables that you use. You can save these as *dimension styles* (*dimstyles*). Dimstyles are groups of settings that you can save and recall by name, to easily set up different styles for different applications. Dimension styles are explained in detail in Chapter 17. The following list describes a few of the characteristics you can control by using dimension variables (and dimension styles):

- The appearance and size of your dimension arrows (or what you use instead of arrows)
- The size and style of the dimension text

- What, if any, tolerance ranges are included with the text
- Where the dimension text goes relative to the dimension line
- The layer on which arrows, text, and extension lines are placed (to control plotted line weight by color)

Table 15.1
AutoCAD Dimension Variables

VARIABLE NAME	*DEFAULT SETTING*	*DEFAULT MEANING*	*DESCRIPTION*
DIMALT	0	**DDIM,** DIMALT	Controls the drawing of additional dimension text in an alternative-units system: 1 = On 0 = Off
DIMALTD	2	**DDIM,** DIMALTD	The decimal precision of dimension text in alternative units
DIMALTF	25.4000	**DDIM,** DIMALTF	The scale factor for dimension text alternate units
DIMAPOST	""	**DDIM,** DIMAPOST	The user-defined suffix for alternative dimension text (RO)
DIMASO	1	DIMASO	Controls the creation of associative dimensions: 1 = On 0 = Off
DIMASZ	0.1800	**DDIM,** DIMASZ	Controls the size of dimension arrows and affects the fit of dimension text inside dimension lines when DIMTSZ is set to 0
DIMBLK	""	**DDIM,** DIMBLK	The name of the block to draw, rather than an arrow or tick (RO)
DIMBLK1	""	**DDIM,** DIMBLK1	The name of the block for the first end of dimension lines. *See DIMSAH* (RO)
DIMBLK2	""	**DDIM,** DIMBLK2	The name of the block for the second end of dimension lines. *See DIMSAH* (RO)
DIMCEN	0.0900	**DDIM,** DIMCEN	Controls center marks or center lines drawn by radial DIM commands: Mark size = value Draw center lines = negative (mark size = absolute value)

Table 15.1—continued

VARIABLE NAME	*DEFAULT SETTING*	*DEFAULT MEANING*	*DESCRIPTION*
DIMCLRD	0	**DDIM,** DIMCLRD	The dimension line, arrow, and leader color number: 0 = BYBLOCK 256 = BYLAYER
DIMCLRE	0	**DDIM,** DIMCLRE	The dimension extension line's color
DIMCLRT	0	**DDIM,** DIMCLRT	The dimension text's color
DIMDLE	0.0000	**DDIM,** DIMDLE	The dimension line's extension distance beyond ticks when ticks are drawn (when DIMTSZ is nonzero)
DIMDLI	0.3800	**DDIM,** DIMDLI	The offset distance between successive continuing or baseline dimensions
DIMEXE	0.1800	**DDIM,** DIMEXE	The length of extension lines beyond dimension lines
DIMEXO	0.0625	**DDIM,** DIMEXO	The distance by which extension lines originate from dimensioned entity
DIMGAP	0.0900	**DDIM,** DIMGAP	The space between text and a dimension line; determines when text is placed outside a dimension **(Creates reference dimension outlines if negative)**
DIMLFAC	1.0000	**DDIM,** DIMLFAC	The overall linear dimensioning scale factor; if negative, acts as the absolute value applied to paper space viewports
DIMLIM	0	**DDIM,** DIMLIM	Presents dimension limits as default text: 1 = ON 0 = OFF *See DIMTP and DIMTM*
DIMPOST	""	**DDIM,** DIMPOST	The user-defined suffix for dimension text, such as "mm" (RO)
DIMRND	0.0000	**DDIM,** DIMRND	The rounding interval for linear dimension text
DIMSAH	0	**DDIM,** DIMSAH	Enables the use of DIMBLK1 and DIMBLK2, rather than DIMBLK or a default terminator: 1 = ON 0 = OFF
DIMSCALE	1.0000	**DDIM,** DIMSCALE	The overall scale factor applied to other dimension variables except tolerances, angles, measured lengths, or coordinates 0 = Paper space scale

Table 15.1—continued

VARIABLE NAME	*DEFAULT SETTING*	*DEFAULT MEANING*	*DESCRIPTION*
DIMSE1	0	**DDIM,** DIMSE1	Suppresses the first extension line: 1 = On, 0 = Off
DIMSE2	0	**DDIM,** DIMSE2	Suppresses the second extension line: 1 = On, 0 = Off
DIMSHO	0	DIMSHO	Determines whether associative dimension text is updated during dragging: 1 = On, 0 = Off
DIMSOXD	0	**DDIM,** DIMSOXD	Suppresses the placement of dimension lines outside extension lines: 1 = On, 0 = Off
DIMSTYLE	*UNNAMED	**DDIM,** Dim: SAVE	Holds the name of the current dimension style (RO)
DIMTAD	0	**DDIM,** DIMTAD	Places dimension text above the dimension line, rather than within: 1 = On, 0 = Off
DIMTFAC	1.0000	**DDIM,** DIMTFAC	The scale factor, relative to DIMTXT, for the size of tolerance text
DIMTIH	1	**DDIM,** DIMTIH	Forces dimension text inside the extension lines to be positioned horizontally, rather than aligned: 1 = On, 0 = Off
DIMTIX	0	**DDIM,** DIMTIX	Force dimension text inside extension lines: 1 = O, 0 = Off
DIMTM	0.0000	**DDIM,** DIMTM	The negative tolerance value used when DIMTOL or DIMLIM is on
DIMTOFL	0	**DDIM,** DIMTOFL	Draws dimension lines between extension lines, even if text is placed outside the extension lines: 1 = On, 0 = Off
DIMTOH	1	**DDIM,** DIMTOH	Forces dimension text to be positioned horizontally, rather than aligned when it falls outside the extension lines: 1 = On, 0 = Off

Table 15.1—continued

VARIABLE NAME	*DEFAULT SETTING*	*DEFAULT MEANING*	*DESCRIPTION*
DIMTOL	0	**DDIM,** DIMTOL	Appends tolerance values (DIMTP and DIMTM) to the default dimension text: 1 = On 0 = Off
DIMTP	0.0000	**DDIM,** DIMTP	The positive tolerance value used when DIMTOL or DIMLIM is on.
DIMTSZ	0.0000	**DDIM,** DIMTSZ	When assigned a nonzero value, forces tick marks to be drawn (rather than arrow-heads) at the size specified by the value; affects the placement of the dimension line and text between extension lines
DIMTVP	0.0000	**DDIM,** DIMTVP	Percentage of text height for vertical dimension text offset
DIMTXT	0.1800	**DDIM,** DIMTXT	The dimension text height for non-fixed text styles
DIMZIN	0	**DDIM,** DIMZIN	Suppress the display of zero inches or zero feet in dimension text 0 = Feet & Inches=0 1 = Neither 2 = Inches Only 3 = Feet only

(RO) indicates read only.

Overview of the Exercises

The exercises in this chapter are organized into two major groups:

- The first group explains how to use the dimensioning commands, including center, radius, diameter, angular, and linear dimensions. In this group of exercises, you also learn how to set some dimensioning variables.
- The second group of exercises, beginning with "Dimension Variables Explained," goes deeper into the discussion of AutoCAD's dimension variables by explaining the process of working with and setting these variables.

If you already are familiar with AutoCAD's basic dimensioning features, you might want to begin with the second group of exercises. Before you begin, however, complete the "Setting Up for Dimensioning" and "Setting DIMTXT, DIMASZ, and DIMSCALE" exercises in the first section.

Using Dimensioning Tools

AutoCAD provides many dimensioning commands and settings, and makes them available on various pull-down, screen, icon, and tablet menus that are used throughout this chapter. Because dimensioning has so many options, it has its own command mode and prompt, accessed through the DIM and DIM1 commands.

You can abbreviate any dimensioning command to the fewest characters that are unique to that command, such as HOR for Horizontal. Six commands require three characters: HORizontal, HOMetext, REStore, REDraw, STAtus, and STYle. Six dimensioning commands can be abbreviated to one character: Baseline, Diameter, Newtext, Exit, Leader, and Undo. All others can be abbreviated to their first two characters.

Working with Dim Mode, the Dim Prompt, and Dim Commands

When you enter the dimensioning mode, you see a new prompt, `Dim:`, instead of the usual AutoCAD command prompt. The DIM command places you in dimensioning mode and leaves you there. The DIM1 command automatically exits dimensioning mode after one dimensioning command. All dimensioning is done in dimensioning mode. When you are in dimensioning mode, you cannot execute the regular AutoCAD commands, but function keys, control-key combinations, object snap overrides, and most transparent commands, menus, and dialog boxes still function normally. After you are finished dimensioning, exit the dimensioning mode and return to the regular `Command:` prompt.

Dimensioning has a unique vocabulary, and AutoCAD has its own dialect within that vocabulary. The following lists AutoCAD's dimensioning terms:

- **Alternate Units.** This terms stands for dimensions in which two separate measurement systems are used, such as inch and metric units.
- **Angular.** This term stands for a set of dimension lines, extension lines, arrows, and text that shows the measurement of an angle.
- **Arrow.** Also called *terminator,* this term stands for the block attached to the end of a dimension line. Other entities, such as ticks, dots, and user-defined blocks, also may be used as terminators.
- **Associative Dimension.** This term stands for a dimension created as a single entity instead of individual lines, arrows (solids), arcs, and text. Associative dimensions can be moved, scaled, and stretched along with the entities being dimensioned; and the dimension text adjusts automatically. This option is the default dimensioning mode.
- **Baseline Dimensions.** This term stands for a series of successive linear dimensions, starting at the same extension line.
- **Center Mark/Center Line.** This term stands for a line that identifies the center point of a circle. AutoCAD's dimensioning commands draw these automatically.
- **Continuing Dimensions.** This term stands for a series of successive linear dimensions that follow one another. Also referred to as *chained dimensions.*
- **Datum or Ordinate Dimension.** This term stands for a dimension consisting only of a leader and dimension text indicating the feature's horizontal or vertical distance from a 0,0 base point. Datum dimensions are generally used as a series of dimensions referencing a common base point.
- **Dimension Line.** This term stands for a line that shows which angle or distance is being dimensioned. It usually has arrows at both ends.
- **Dimension Styles.** This term stands for a named group of dimension variable settings that can be stored to disk with the drawing. After you fine-tune your dimension variable settings, you can save that setup by name for future use.
- **Dimension Text.** This term stands for the text string that displays the dimension value. You can use AutoCAD's default value or enter your own value to override the default.

- **Dimension Variables.** This term stands for a set of variables, some user-controlled (also called *dimvars*), which controls size, style, location, and appearance of dimensions.
- **Extension Line.** This term stands for a short line segment that shows each end or extent of the element being dimensioned (also called *witness line*).
- **Leader.** This term stands for a line that extends from the dimension text to the element being dimensioned or annotated.
- **Limits.** This term stands for a type of tolerance dimensioning that shows the minimum and maximum dimensions, rather than a single value.
- **Linear Dimensions.** This term stands for a set of dimension lines, extension lines, arrows, and text that shows the distance between two (or more) points in a straight line.
- **Tolerances.** This term stands for plus and minus amounts that can be attached to a dimension text. To use tolerance dimensions, you must set their values with dimension variables.

Setting Up for Dimensioning

In this chapter, you reuse the MOCKSECT drawing that you created in Chapter 10. You use this drawing to explore a wide variety of dimensioning features. Many of the dimensions you add deviate from what is considered the usual dimensioning for this type of drawing. When you are finished, your completed drawing should resemble figure 15.1. If you use the IA DISK, you can use the IA7MOCKD.DWG file.

Setting Up for Dimensioning

Choose File, then New, and enter drawing name `MOCKDIM=IA7MOCKD`.

Choose File, then New, enter drawing name `MOCKDIM=MOCKSECT`, and check the settings shown in table 15.2.

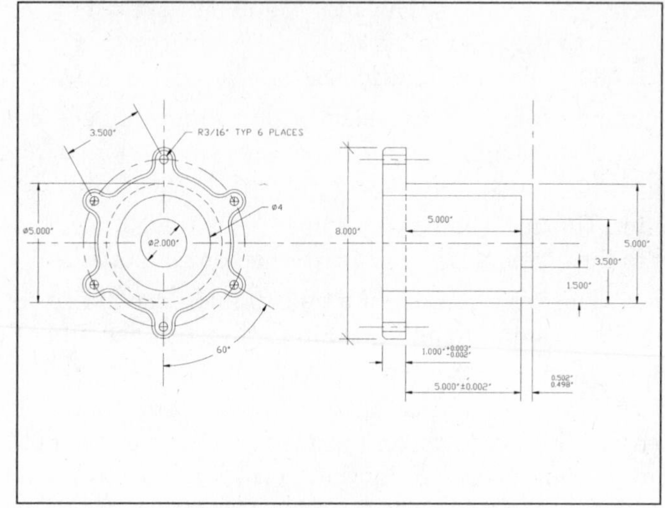

Figure 15.1:

The MOCKDIM drawing with a number of dimensions.

Table 15.2
MOCKDIM Drawing Settings

COORDS	*GRID*	*LTSCALE*	*OSNAP*
On	1	1	NONe

Layer Name	*State*	*Color*	*Linetype*
0	On	7 (White)	CONTINUOUS
DIMS	On/Current	2 (Yellow)	CONTINUOUS

Your MOCKDIM drawing should look like figure 15.2.

Consider the topic of scaling dimensions. Assume that MOCKDIM is scaled 1=2 (a half-scale factor) when plotted or composed in a paper space sheet.

Scaling Dimensions

AutoCAD's defaults make assumptions about dimension setup parameters, including the scale of your dimension text and arrows. The defaults may be acceptable for a drawing that is plotted at full scale, but if your drawing is to be scaled, the default settings may make your dimensions huge or nearly

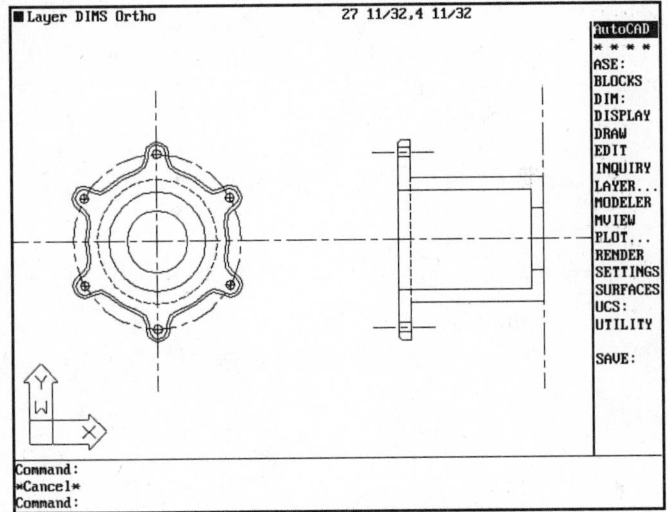

Figure 15.2:
The starting MOCKDIM drawing.

invisible. On a 60′x100' facilities planning drawing, for example, the default arrow of 0.18 inches is invisible at almost any drawing scale and sheet size. Setting a scale factor for sizing dimensions is similar to setting a scale for annotating your basic drawing.

You could reset all the dimension variables to get the right size, but AutoCAD has a better answer: DIMSCALE. Every scalar dimension variable is multiplied by DIMSCALE before it is applied to the drawing. DIMSCALE does not affect the measured value of the dimension, only its physical size relative to the drawing. You can use DIMSCALE to change all the dimensioning variables with a single scale factor. The default for DIMSCALE is 1.0000. Set DIMSCALE to the drawing-scale factor (drawing units divided by plot or paper space sheet units). If you scale the drawing down, you need to scale the dimensions back up to their intended size. If you scale a drawing up when you plot, you need to scale the dimensions down. MOCKDIM will be plotted at half scale (1 plotted inch = 2 drawing units), which means the drawing scale is 2. The DIMSCALE variable can be set at the Feature Scaling setting in the Features dialog box.

Set the scalar dimension variables, such as dimension text and arrow size, to the actual sizes you want in the plotted output. DIMTXT is for text, and DIMASZ is for arrows. These settings are multiplied by DIMSCALE. A .125 DIMTXT setting will be .25" in the drawing (.125×2), but it will plot half that size (.125).

Set these values in the following exercise. Set DIMTXT for the text, set DIMASZ for arrows, and then set DIMSCALE to 2, making your dimension scale offset your drawing scale. Use the screen menus to set various dimension variables. The dialog boxes are used more extensively later in the chapter.

Setting DIMTXT, DIMASZ, and DIMSCALE To Scale Dimensions

`Command:` *From the screen menu, choose* DIM:, *then* Dim Vars	Enters dimensioning mode and displays dimension variable screen menu
`_DIM Dim:` *From the screen menu, choose* dimasz	Issues the DIMASZ variable prompt
`Dim: _DIMASZ Current value <3/16> New value:` **`0.14`**↵	Sets the arrowhead size
`Dim:` *From the screen menu, choose* next	Displays the next page of the Dim Vars screen menu
`Dim:` *From the screen menu, choose* dimscale	
`Dim: _DIMSCALE Current value <1.000000> New value:` **`2`**↵	Sets DIMSCALE to 2
`Dim:` *From the screen menu, choose* next	Displays the next page of the Dim Var screen menu
`Dim:` *From the screen menu, choose* dimtxt	
`Dim: _DIMTXT Current value <3/16> New value:` **`.125`**↵	Makes text 1/4" high in the drawing (.125 DIMTXT×2 DIMSCALE)
`Dim:` *Press Ctrl-C or choose* AutoCAD *from the screen menu*	Exits to `Command:` prompt

Save the drawing.

By choosing the Dimension Style option of the Settings menu, you adjust these variables from dialog boxes. DIMSCALE is found under the Feature Scaling option of Features, and DIMASZ is listed as Arrow Size in that same dialog box. The DIMTEXT can be set from the Text Height setting in the Text Location dialog box.

Be careful when you use UNDO after you exit the dimensioning mode. If you set any variables, a command-prompt level UNDO or U cancels everything from the preceding dimensioning mode session in a single UNDO step. You can easily undo dimension variable settings accidentally. Always exit the dimensioning mode immediately after you set dimension variables, then re-enter dimensioning mode to dimension objects. This step protects settings from an accidental undo.

You can exit dimensioning mode by using the EXIT command, abbreviate it with just an E, or press Ctrl-C.

Using Undo in Dimensioning Mode

The DIM command's Undo option is similar to Undo in the LINE command. DIM's Undo removes the results (extension lines, arrows, text, and so on) of the last dimensioning command. Enter **U** to undo at the `Dim:` prompt. As discussed in the preceding Caution, you also can undo dimensions with the normal UNDO command from the `Command:` prompt, but one Undo then wipes out an entire dimensioning session.

Dimensioning the MOCKDIM Plan View

To start dimensioning, use the plan view (the left side) of the MOCKDIM drawing to test some of the basic dimensioning commands. Figure 15.3 shows the dimension types covered in this first section.

Dimensioning with Center Marks

The plan view has a series of small circles in the lugs on the flange's edge. Begin your dimensioning sequence in the following exercise by using the CENTER command to place center marks in these circles. The CENTER command puts a cross at the center of an arc or circle.

Put the first mark in the circle at the upper right, and then work your way around the flange.

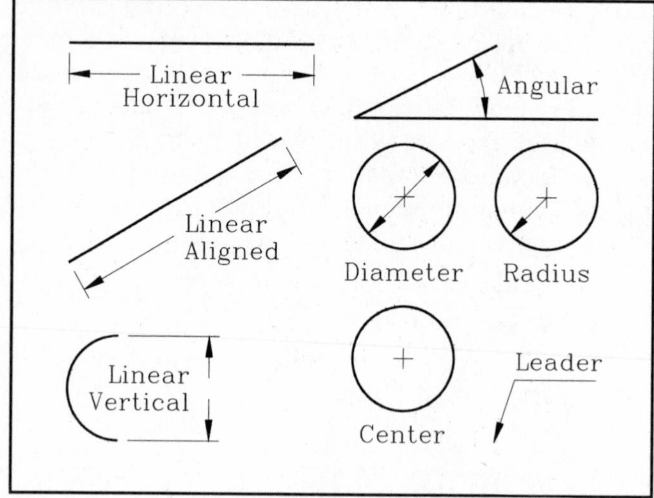

Figure 15.3:
Some dimension examples.

Using CENTER To Place a Center Mark

Use ZOOM with the Window option to zoom in on the flange top view.

`Command:` *Choose* Draw, *then* Dimensions, *then* Radial, *then* Center Mark	Enters dimensioning mode and issues CEN command
`Command: _dim1`	
`Dim: _cen Select arc or circle:` *Pick the hole's circumference at ① (see fig. 15.4)*	Draws a center mark

Next, use the screen menu to access the CENTER command.

`Command:` *From the screen menu, choose* DIM:, *then* next, *then* CENTER	Enters dimensioning mode and issues CEN command
`_CENTER Select arc or circle:` *Pick another hole*	Adds center marks to another hole
`Dim:` *Press Enter*	Repeats CENTER command
`_CENTER Select arc or circle:` *Repeat the process above to add center marks to the remaining holes*	Adds center marks to remaining holes

The center mark should appear as shown in figure 15.4.

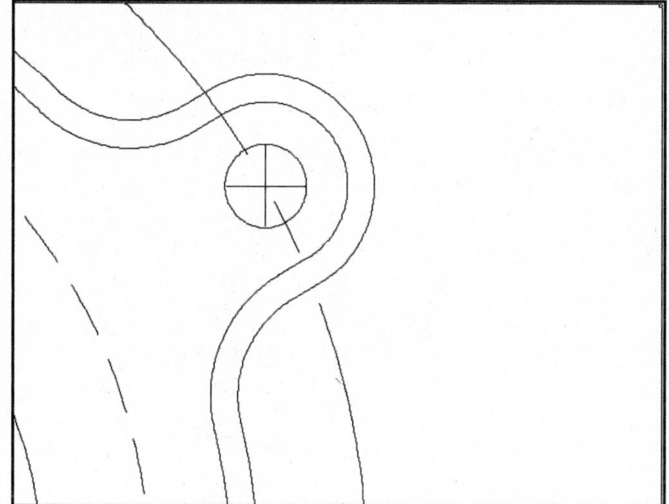

Figure 15.4:

Detail of a center mark.

TIP

The DIMCEN dimension variable sets the size of the center marker. If you give DIMCEN a negative value, center lines extending beyond the circumference are added to the center mark. In either case, the value of DIMCEN is half the width of the cross it creates. To set DIMCEN using the dialog boxes, change the Center Mark Size value in the Features dimensioning dialog box.

Dimensioning a Radius

Place a radius dimension in the inner flange circle. The RADIUS command measures from an arc or circle center point to a circumference point. In the following example, the dimension text does not fit inside the circle. Drag the dimension outside the circle and place it by picking a point. The point determines the leader's length, not its endpoint. The dimensioning screen menu is already displayed; use it instead of the dialog box.

Using RADIUS To Place a Radius Dimension

Continue in the DIM command from the previous exercise.

`Command:` *From the screen menu, choose* previous, *then* RADIUS	Issues RADIUS command
`Dim: _RADIUS Select arc or circle:` *Select the inner circle at point* ① *(see fig. 15.5)*	Specifies dimension line location
`Dimension text <1 1/4>:` *Press Enter*	Accepts default
`Enter leader length for text:` *Pick point outside circle*	Sets leader length and draws dimension

Your drawing should appear as shown in figure 15.5.

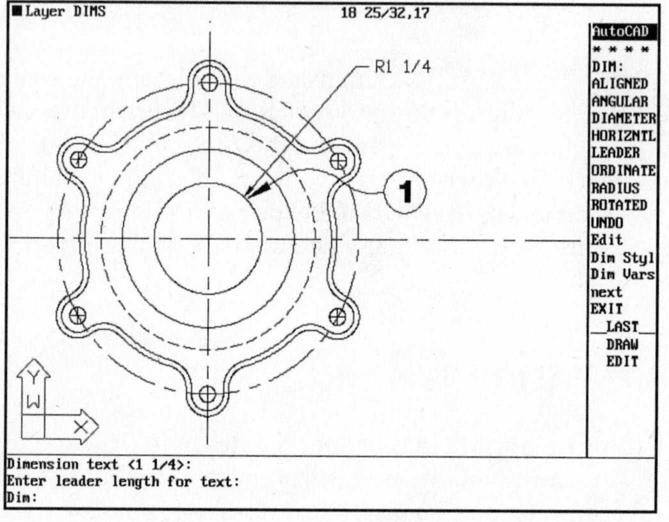

Figure 15.5:
A radius dimension.

AutoCAD measured the radius for you and drew the correct dimension with default text. (You can input your own text instead of using the default dimension text, if necessary.)

Because the dimension lines, arrow, and text would not fit inside the circle, AutoCAD asked you for a leader length. (You are not limited to picking a point; you also can enter a distance for the length.) The angle of the leader

is determined by the center of the circle and the point picked to select the circle.

Forcing the Text inside the Circle or Arc

Text size and pick point determine if the dimension text fits in the circle. What do you do if you want the radius dimension inside the circle in all circumstances? AutoCAD provides a variable for this control. With radial dimensions, the variable DIMTIX On forces the value inside the circle or arc, even if AutoCAD would normally prompt you to place it outside. DIMTIX Off forces it outside.

To see how this variable works, undo this first radius in the following exercise. Then, set DIMTIX On and execute the radius command again. This time, select the circle by picking at about the 85-degree point on the circumference.

Forcing a Radius Dimension inside a Circle

`Dim:` *Choose* Assist, *then* Undo	Undoes the first radius dimension
`Dim:` *Choose* Settings, *then* Dimension Style	Cancels the DIM command, and displays Dimension Styles and Variables dialog box
`*Cancel*` `Command: ddim`	
Choose **T**ext Location	Displays Text Location dialog box
Click on Default *in the* **H**orizontal *edit box, then click on* Force Text Inside, *then choose* OK, *then* OK *again*	Sets DIMTIX on and exits dialog boxes
`Command:` *Choose* Draw, *then* Dimensions, *then* Radial, *then* Radius	Enters dimensioning mode and issues the RADIUS command
`Dim: _rad Select arc or circle:` *Pick circle at point ① (see fig. 15.6)*	
`Dimension text <1 1/4>:` *Press Enter*	Draws dimension with text inside
`Command:` **`QSAVE`** ↵	Saves the file

The dimension should appear as shown in figure 15.6.

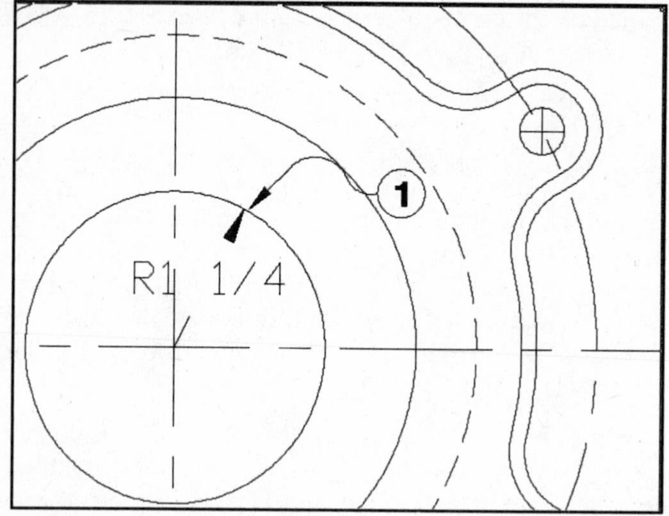

Figure 15.6:
Detail of a radius dimension.

The dimension text was placed in the circle, and you were not prompted for leader length.

Use a text style with a width factor of 0.75 to condense the dimension text.

AutoCAD always writes dimension text horizontally, even for angular dimensions, unless you change the dimension variables.

You get vertical dimension text if your current text style is vertical when you enter dimensioning mode. Reset your text to a horizontal style before executing the dimension commands.

Dimensioning a Diameter

Now that the text fits in the circle, replace the radius with a diameter dimension. *Diameter* measures between two diametrically opposed points on the circumference of a circle or arc. Placing a diameter is similar to placing a radius. When you select the circle that you want to dimension,

Diameter uses the point you pick as a diameter endpoint. AutoCAD automatically determines where the second endpoint goes. (If the text does not fit, a leader also stems from this first picked point.) Diameter dimension text placement is controlled by DIMTIX, just as radius dimensions are.

Undo the radius and put in a diameter dimension in the following exercise. Because DIMTIX is still on, the dimension is automatically placed inside the circle.

Using DIAMETER To Place a Diameter Dimension

Select the previous radius dimension, and then issue the ERASE command.

`Command:` *Choose* Draw, *then* Dimensions, *then* Radial, *then* Diameter	Enters dimensioning mode and issues DIA command
`Dim: _dia Select arc or circle:` *Pick the circle at* ① *(see fig. 15.7)*	
`Dimension text <2 1/2>:` *Press Enter*	Draws the dimension

The diameter dimension should appear as shown in figure 15.7.

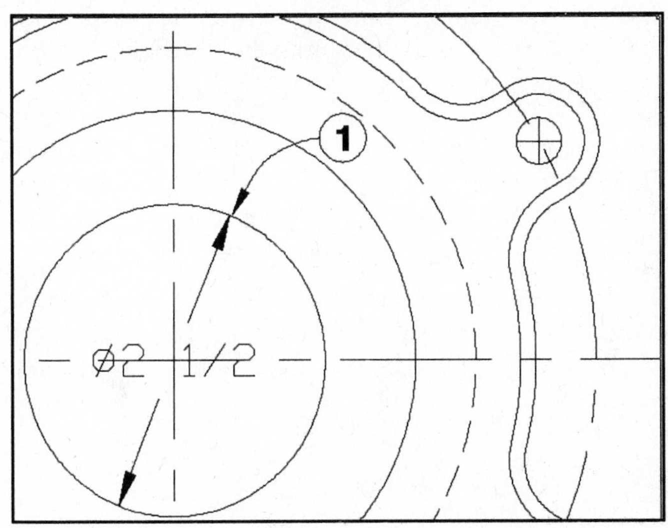

Figure 15.7: Detail of a diameter dimension.

Forcing an Inside Dimension Leader

If DIMTIX is on, it forces the text and leader inside the arc or circle; if DIMTIX is off, it forces them outside. When the leader and text are outside, no leader or arrows are drawn inside. Your dimensioning standards may require a radius or diameter leader drawn from or through the center to the pick point, even if the text is outside. The DIMTOFL dimension variable controls the inside leader. To force AutoCAD to draw outside text with both an outside and inside leader, set DIMTOFL on and DIMTIX off. DIMTOFL off (the default) suppresses the inside leader. If the inside leader is drawn, the arrows are drawn inside.

Adding Text to a Default Dimension

You may have noticed that AutoCAD precedes the radius and diameter text with an R or a diameter symbol, but it does not put a space between the symbol and the measured text. How can you place a space between them? This section discusses working with dimension text, including forcing spaces, adding text, and overriding the measured dimension.

When you create a dimension, AutoCAD measures the value and displays it for you as a default. If you press Enter at the default, AutoCAD uses that value. Sometimes you may want to add text to the dimension, or change it altogether. To do this, enter the desired text at the default dimension text prompt. If you want the text to appear with your added text, represent the dimension in your typed text by a pair of angle brackets. For example, if the default is <2 1/2">, then enter **<> NOT TO SCALE** to create the text as 2 1/2" NOT TO SCALE.

Add text to a measured dimension in the following exercise. Return to the lug circle at the top of the flange and place a radius dimension with some added text. Use the exercise's prompt sequence to get your text input, including the angle brackets, and a leader offset value. Because AutoCAD recognizes the angle brackets as the default text value, the text includes the calculated value, plus any text added after the <>.

Adding Text to a Dimension

`Command:` *Choose* Settings, *then* Dimension Style	Opens dialog box
Choose Text Location	Displays Text Location dialog box
Click on Force Text Inside *in the* Horizontal *edit box, then click on* Default, *then choose* OK, *then* OK *again*	Sets DIMTIX off and exits dialog box
`Command:` *Choose* Draw, *then* Dimensions, *then* Radial, *then* Radius	Enters dimensioning mode and issues RAD command
`Dim: _rad Select arc or circle:` *Pick the top small hole at point ① (see fig. 15.8)*	

Figure 15.8 shows the pick point for the dimension that is to receive text.

`Dimension text <3/16>:` **`<> TYP 6 PLACES`** ↵	Adds to the dimension text
`Enter leader length for text:` *Pick a point at upper right of circle*	Draws dimension (see fig. 15.9)

The inserted text should appear, as shown in figure 15.9.

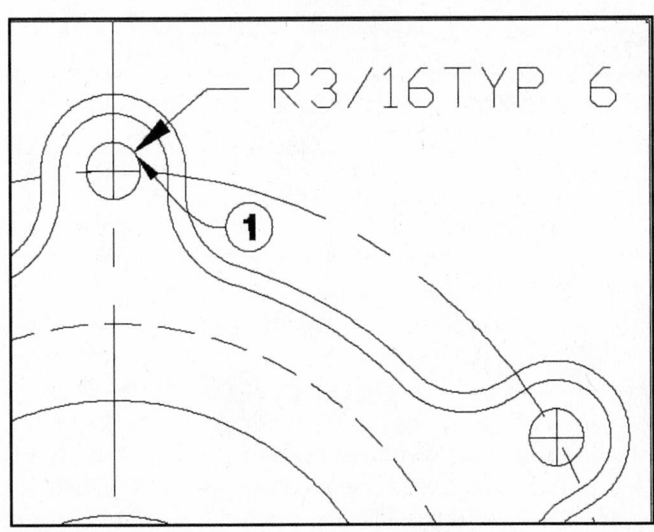

Figure 15.8:
Detail of a radius dimension.

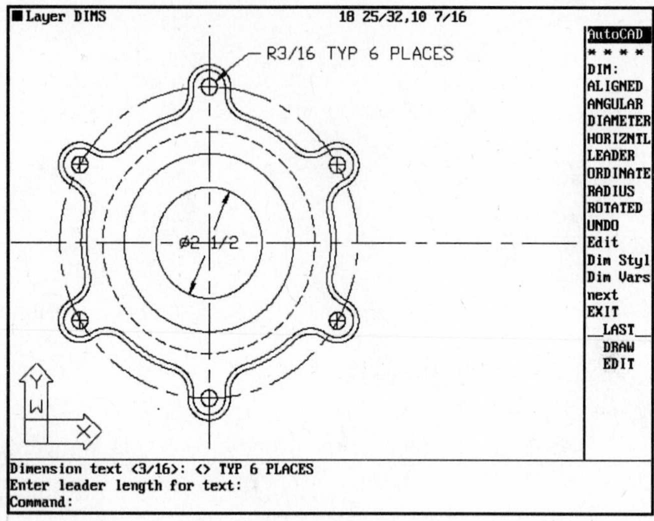

Figure 15.9:

A radius dimension with added text.

Table 15.3 shows some other text examples.

Table 15.3
Alternative Text Examples

When AutoCAD offers:	*Enter this*	*To get this*
`Dimension text <2.5000>:`	*Press spacebar*	
`Dimension text <2.5000>:`	`Not important`	`Not important`
`Dimension text <2.5000>:`	`about <>`	`about 2.5000`
`Dimension text <2.5000>:`	`roughly <>"`	`roughly 2.5000"`

Dimensioning with Leader Dimensions

In both the radius and diameter dimensions, a leader was used to place text outside the circle (or arc). A leader is like a combination of an arrow block insert, the LINE command, and the TEXT command. It enables you to create a *call out* to point text to a specific location. Use the Leader command to create an arrow, with one or more continuous line segments, to place text away from the entities you are dimensioning (see fig. 15.10).

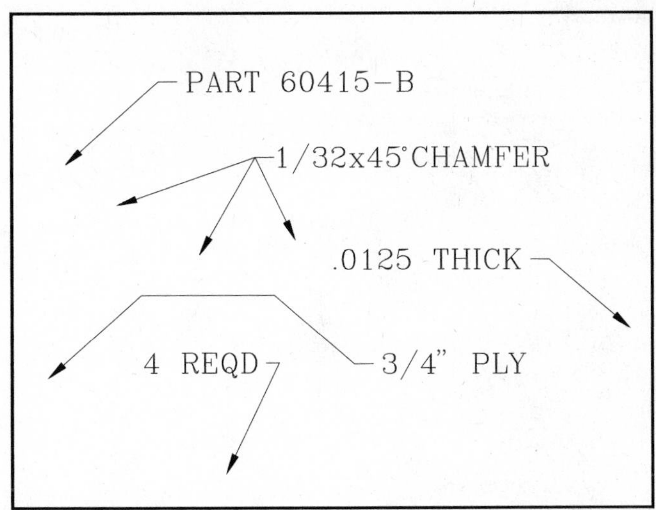

Figure 15.10:

Some leader examples.

Use a leader to dimension the hole in the flange in the following exercise. AutoCAD prompts for a starting point for the leader line. You do not need to pick a point for the leader's short horizontal extension line—AutoCAD automatically places a horizontal extension onto the end of the leader for the text.

Using LEADER To Place a Leader Dimension

`Command:` *Choose* Draw, *then* Dimensions, *then* Leader	Issues the LEADER dimensioning command
`Dim: _lea Leader start:` *From the pop-up menu, choose* Nearest	Issues NEA object snap
`nea to` *Pick right side of the large circle at point ① (see fig. 15.11)*	
`To point:` *Pick point ②*	Defines leader line
`To point:` *Press Enter*	Creates a short line at end of leader
`Dimension text <3/16>:` **`%%C4`** ↵	Adds diameter symbol to text 4

Your drawing should appear as shown in figure 15.11.

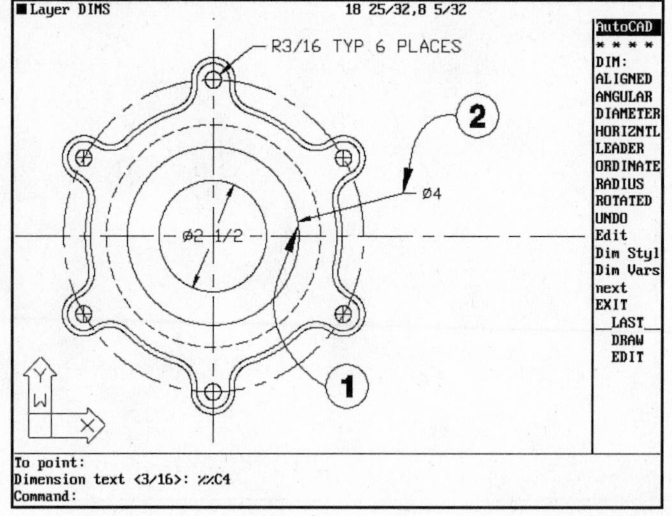

Figure 15.11:

Creating a leader dimension.

If you enter %%C4 as the dimension text, you get the same effect as if you had dimensioned the hole by using the DIAMETER dimensioning command. You can use leaders to annotate any feature with a note—not just circles and arcs—and you can use multisegmented leaders in dense drawings.

New text is usually entered each time a leader is created. After locating the points for the leader and pressing Enter, you are prompted for the text. After you enter the text, the LEADER command places the text at the end of the leader (near the last point indicated). If the last segment of the leader line is pointed toward the right, the text is left-justified. If the last leader segment points left, the text is right-justified. This prevents the text from overwriting its leader.

AutoCAD offers the default text value of the previous radius dimension as the default leader text. This procedure enables you to use the previous dimension value as all or part of the leader text.

To use a previous dimension value, execute any dimension, such as a DIAMETER dimension, then cancel it at the text prompt. Execute the LEADER dimension command and accept the default dimension or use angle brackets with added text.

Dimensioning an Angle

The measure of the angle between two of the outer flange holes is an *angular dimension*. The ANGULAR command measures the inner or outer (acute or obtuse) angle between two specified nonparallel lines, the angle of an arc, or the angle between three points (see fig. 15.12). You can select an arc, circle, line, or polyline entity to dimension; or pick three points for the vertex, start, and endpoints of the angle—virtually any situation you can imagine.

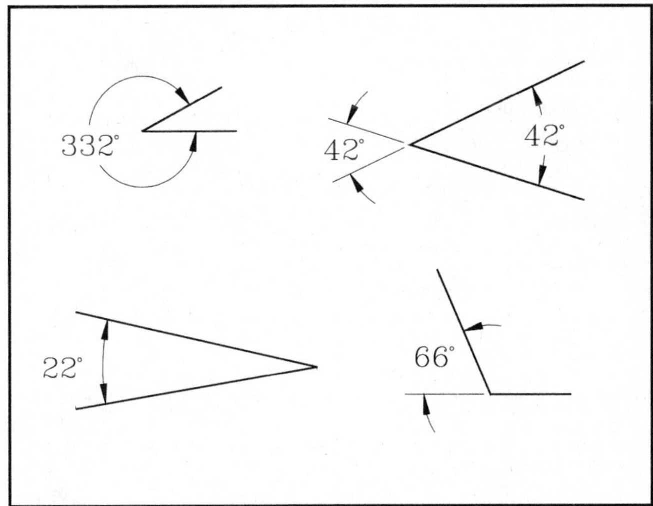

Figure 15.12:
Angular dimension examples.

In the following exercise, dimension the angle between the two outer holes at the lower right of the flange. Use object snaps to pick the points and zoom in if necessary. Notice that using the dimensioning commands from the pull-down menu are like the DIM1 command, which brings you back to the `Command:` prompt instead of the `DIM:` prompt.

Using ANGULAR To Place an Angular Dimension

`Command:` *Choose* Draw, *then* Dimensions, *then* Angular	Enters dimensioning mode and issues the ANGULAR command
`Dim: _ang Select arc, circle, line, or RETURN:` *Press Enter*	Specifies three-point method
`Angle vertex:` *From the pop-up menu, choose* Intersection, *then pick point at ① (see fig. 15.13)*	Sets vertex point
`First angle endpoint:` *From the pop-up menu, choose* Center	
`center of` *Pick hole in tab at ②*	Sets one angle point
`Second angle endpoint:` *From the pop-up menu, choose* End point	
`end of` *Pick bottom center line at ③*	Sets other angle point
`Enter dimension line arc location:` *Pick ④*	
`Dimension text <60>:` *Press Enter*	Accepts text
`Enter text location:` *Press Enter*	Defaults to arc location

Your new dimension should appear as shown in figure 15.13.

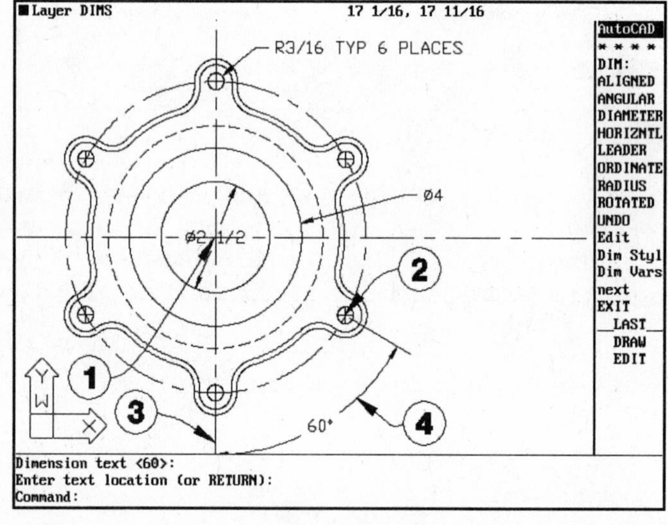

Figure 15.13:

Creating an angular dimension.

Drawing Angular Dimensions

The ANGULAR command gives you a number of options. The following list explains possible Angular selections and the action that occurs:

- **Arc.** This option measures the arc from endpoint to endpoint and prompts you to place the dimension text. The ANGULAR command calculates the angle of the arc automatically, using the arc's center and its two endpoints.
- **Circle.** When this option is used, AutoCAD assumes you want to measure from the pick point to the next point you pick on the circle. The angle is then measured from the center of the circle.
- **Line.** When this option is used, AutoCAD assumes you want to dimension the angle, between two lines and prompts for a second line.
- **Press Enter and pick three points.** This option is used to measure and dimension any angle, instead of selecting an entity. Usually, you use object snap to locate the points on existing entities.

No matter what kind of entity you dimension, the result is an arc angle between two points about a center point. Two angles exist for every set of points: one obtuse angle and one acute angle. The angle that is dimensioned depends on the location you pick for your dimension line arc. If you pick it between the two points, you get an acute angle with a small-dimension arc; if you pick it outside the two points, you get an obtuse angle.

Dimensioning with Linear Dimensions

Linear dimensions refer to a group of dimensioning commands that measure between two points. The points can be endpoints, intersections, arc chord endpoints, or any two points you can identify (usually by selecting an entity or using object snap). Linear dimensions include the following measurements:

- **HORIZONTAL.** This linear dimension creates horizontal dimension lines.
- **VERTICAL.** This linear dimension creates vertical dimension lines.
- **ALIGNED.** This linear dimension creates dimension lines that are aligned (parallel) to an object or two specified points.

- **ROTATED.** This linear dimension creates dimension lines rotated to a specified angle, not necessarily aligned with the points.
- **BASELINE.** This linear dimension creates a series of dimensions, with each dimension using the previous dimension's second extension line as the new dimension's first extension.
- **CONTINUE.** This linear dimension creates a series of dimensions, all from the same first extension line.

Making Horizontal and Vertical Linear Dimensions

The Horizontal and Vertical commands work exactly the same, except that one dimensions horizontally and the other vertically. When using either command, pick two points as the origins of two extension lines, or select an object (like a line, arc, or circle) and automatically dimension the full length or breadth of that object. If space allows (or if you set the variables to force it), the dimension line and text are drawn between the extension lines.

Dimension the dashed (hidden line) circle in the following exercise. Use Vertical and select the circle. The Vertical command selects the circle's top and bottom quadrant points as starting points for your extension lines, then prompts you for the location of the dimension line. Place the dimension line to the left of the circle.

Using Linear VERTICAL To Place a Vertical Dimension

`Command:` *Choose* Draw, *then* Dimensions, *then* Linear, *then* Vertical	Enters dimensioning mode and issues VERTICAL command
`Dim: _vertical`	
`First extension line origin or RETURN to select:` *Press Enter*	Specifies the entity selection method
`Select line, arc, or circle:` *Pick any point on the hidden circle*	
`Dimension line location (Text/Angle):` *Pick point at about 4-1/2,15*	
`Dimension text <5>:` **`%%C<>`**	Adds the diameter symbol to the text and draws dimension

The vertical dimension should appear as shown in figure 15.14.

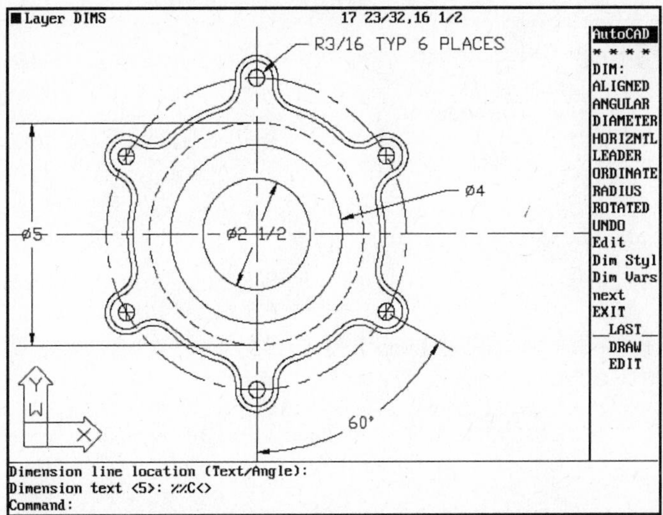

Figure 15.14:

A linear vertical dimension on a circle.

The text conflicts with the center line. The dimension text location is automatically set, but you can control it with dimension variables or change it after placement, as you will see in the associative dimensioning section of Chapter 17.

Aligning Dimensions

The next exercise demonstrates the process of dimensioning a distance that is neither horizontal nor vertical, such as the distance from the center of one outer flange hole to the center of another. A vertical dimension measures only the Y-axis distance from the first hole to the second hole. Aligned, however, measures the actual distance between the two holes. Aligned works the same way as any linear dimensioning command: select an object or pick points to locate your dimension lines. The dimension is drawn parallel to the two points or object. Try this command on the two holes at the upper left of the flange.

Using Linear Aligned To Place an Aligned Dimension

`Command:` *Choose* Draw, *then* Dimensions, *then* Linear, *then* Aligned	Enters dimensioning mode and issues ALIGNED command
`Dim: _ali`	
`First extension line origin or RETURN to select:` *From the pop-up menu, choose* Center	
`center of` *Pick hole at* ①	Sets first alignment point *(see fig. 15.15)*
`Second extension line origin:` *From the pop-up menu, choose* Center	
`center of` *Pick the center of hole at* ②	Sets second alignment point
`Dimension line location (Text/Angle):` *Pick point 8,18*	
`Dimension text <3 1/2>:` *Press Enter*	Accepts AutoCAD's default text

Zoom out a little if necessary to view the dimensions.

The result is an aligned dimension, as shown in figure 15.15. Of course, if the origin points align vertically or horizontally, an aligned dimension produces identical results to vertical or horizontal.

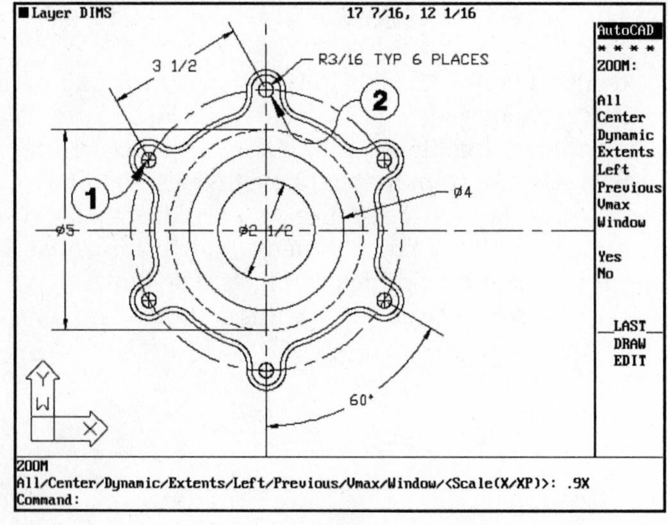

Figure 15.15:

An aligned dimension.

Creating Rotated Dimensions

If you do not want the dimension line to align with the two points you are dimensioning, AutoCAD provides a type of linear dimension called a *rotated dimension*. The rotated linear dimension is similar to the other linear dimensions except that you must specify the angle of the dimension line. Although it is not as practical as the other methods, you can use Rotated for vertical and horizontal dimensioning by specifying an angle of 90 or 0 degrees, respectively.

Use a rotated dimension to mark the distance between the lower right flange hole perpendicular to a line from the center of the 2 1/2" circle through the upper right flange hole. The dimension line should be at 120 degrees.

Using Linear ROTATED To Place a Rotated Dimension

`Command:` *From the screen menu, choose* DIM:, *then* ROTATED	Enters dimensioning mode and issues ROTATED command
`Dim: _ROTATED Dimension line angle <0>:` **`120`** ↵	
`First extension line origin or RETURN to select:` *From the pop-up menu, choose* Center	
`center of` *Pick point on 2 1/2" circle*	
`Second extension line origin:` *From the pop-up menu, choose* Center	
`center of` *Pick point on lower right flange hole*	
`Dimension line location:` **`16.5,15.5`** ↵	
`Dimension text <3 1/32>:` *Press Enter*	Draws the dimension
`Dim:` **`E`** ↵	Exits dimensioning mode

Save the drawing.

The rotated dimension should appear as shown in figure 15.16.

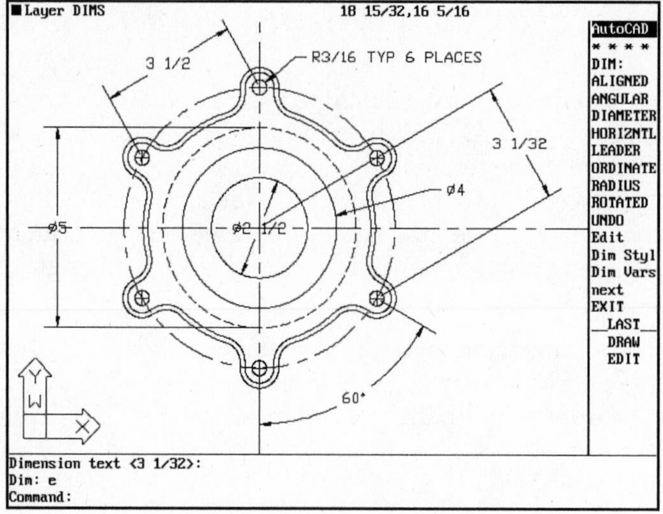

Figure 15.16:

A rotated dimension.

This completes a quick tour through the basics of dimensioning. To dimension, graphically define what you want to dimension, and then define where the dimension entities are to be located. You may have to practice to get the effects you want. Use the MOCKDIM drawing to try some variations, and then undo or discard those practice variations before you proceed.

The next section explores controlling dimension appearance using additional dimension variables and explores more of AutoCAD's dimensioning dialog boxes.

Understanding Dimension Variables

From the dimension variables you already have changed, you can see the effect on the appearance of certain dimensions. AutoCAD has over 40 dimension variables. These can be set in different combinations to create dimensions that match nearly any standard. You will probably use several different combinations in your own work. Chapter 17 explains how to save and restore these sets as customized dimstyles.

The dimension variable names are cryptic acronyms for what the variables do. You should be able to decode them from the list in table 15.1 or the list that the Status dimensioning command provides. The acronyms are easier to remember if you think of them in terms of their functions.

Examining the Default Dimension Variables

The following exercises look at the dimension variables with two different commands and in two different systems of units. Begin a new drawing to ensure that all variables show their default values. Use the SETVAR command with the default decimal units and the Status dimensioning command with fractional units, like the units in the MOCKDIM drawing. The complete lists are not shown in the following exercise—only dimension variables that already have been discussed or that are discussed in this section.

To print a list of dimension variables, turn on your printer, then press Ctrl-Q to turn on printer echo. Issue the SETVAR command, and list variables using the pattern DIM*. Press Ctrl-Q again to turn off printer echo. The next exercise helps you print a list of dimensioning variables—just turn on printer echo before you perform the exercise and turn it off again when you finish.

Looking at Dimension Variables

Choose File, then New, and enter drawing name **DIMVARS**.

Command: **SETVAR** ↵	Issues SETVAR command
Command: Variable name or ?: **?** ↵	Prompts for names
Variable(s) to list <*>: **DIM*** ↵	Lists all dimension variables (they all begin with DIM), including the following:

```
DIMASZ        0.1800
DIMCEN        0.0900
DIMDLI        0.3800
DIMEXE        0.1800
DIMEXO        0.0625
DIMGAP        0.0900
DIMSCALE      1.0000
DIMSTYLE      "*UNNAMED"  (read only)
DIMTIX        0
DIMTOFL       0
DIMTXT        0.1800
```

`Command:` *Press F1 to return to the graphics screen, then choose* Settings, *then* Units Control	Opens the Units Control dialog box

Set Units to Fractional, precision to 1/64, and leave the rest at their defaults.

`Command:` **`DIM`**↵	Enters dimensioning mode
`Dim:` **`STATUS`**↵	Lists the current settings, including the following:

```
DIMASZ      3/16      Arrow size
DIMCEN      3/32      Center mark size
DIMDLI      3/8       Dimension line increment for continuation
DIMEXE      3/16      Extension above dimension line
DIMEXO      1/16      Extension line origin offset
DIMGAP      3/32      Gap from dimension line to text
DIMSCALE    1.000000  Overall scale factor
DIMSTYLE    *UNNAMED  Current dimension style (read-only)
DIMTIX      Off       Place text inside extensions
DIMTOFL     Off       Force line inside extension lines
DIMTXT      3/16      Text height
```

You can discard the drawing at this point.

As you can see, the dimensioning Status list is more than just a list of the variables. Both methods display in current units; the units were changed in the previous exercise to illustrate the following warning:

The current units mislead you when the list rounds off the default settings. For the DIMTXT variable, for example, STATUS with fractional units shows it as 3/16, but .1800 is still its actual value. The values displayed as defaults are rounded to the drawing units settings. This difference becomes important when you mix annotations generated by the dimension commands with ones created with TEXT, DTEXT, and other drawing commands. Text heights will not match, and you will have trouble aligning items. Therefore, you should change all scalar dimension variables to exact fractional values when using any system of units that does not display true values. If, for example, you enter **3/16** as a new value for DIMTXT, it becomes .1875; however, if you press Enter at the default <3/16> prompt, it is unchanged and remains .1800.

In the rest of this chapter, all scalar dimension variables are reset to precise decimal equivalents of these fractions. Several ways to set dimension variables are examined.

Using the Dimensioning Dialog Boxes

Set dimension variables by using the SETVAR command or enter the name of the dimension variable at the Command prompt or the Dim prompt. You also can set the dimension variables by selecting Dim Vars from the dimensioning screen menu. You get a list of dimension variables menu items covering three full-screen menu pages.

Because the dimension variable names are cryptic and sometimes hard to remember, AutoCAD has devoted a group of dialog boxes for setting dimension variables and creating dimension styles. These dialog boxes use check boxes, edit boxes, radio buttons, and list boxes to control dimension features. The DDIM command or Dimension Style item on the Settings pull-down menu displays the main Dimension Styles and Variables dialog box (see fig. 15.17). From this dialog box, you can select an item from the list to access the other dialog boxes.

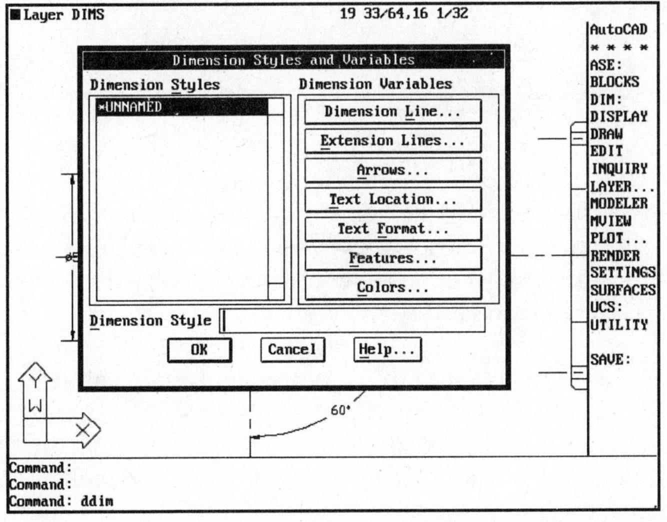

Figure 15.17:
The Dimension Styles and Variables dialog box.

The Features dialog box controls the more popular display characteristics of dimensions (see fig. 15.18). Radio buttons enable selection of the type of arrows to be used and list boxes, such as the one for extension-line visibility, offer several options when the box is chosen. The check boxes can be chosen to turn features off or on. Change the values in the edit boxes by choosing the box and editing the value, or by double-clicking on the box and entering a new value. Another convenience of the dialog boxes is the capability to see the whole group of variables which will affect a certain feature. For this reason, some dimension variables appear in more than one dialog box.

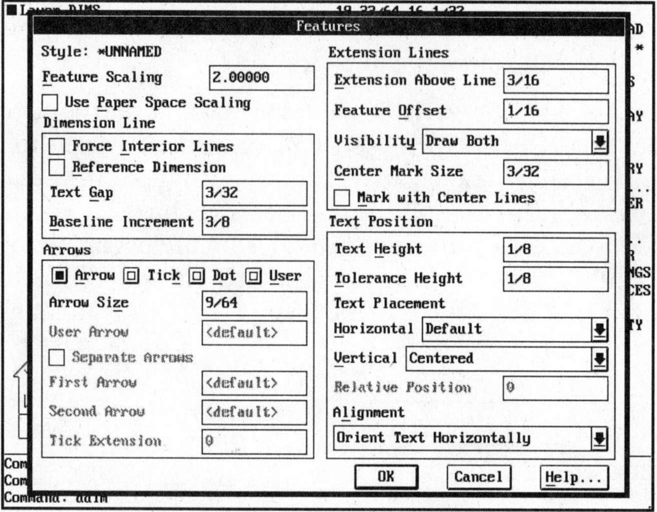

Figure 15.18:

The Features dialog box.

TIP: The dimensioning dialog boxes are most effective when you do not know the name of the dimension variable you need to set or do not know which variables must be set to work together. If you know which ones to set, however, it may be faster to change the dimension variables directly.

The following exercises show both the dimension variable names and values and the dialog box instructions for setting them. As you make dialog box selections, try to keep track of the dimension variables that are affected. With some practice, you will learn the dimension variables well enough to set them manually.

Return to the MOCKDIM drawing in the following exercise and practice controlling the dimension variables from the dialog boxes.

Setting Dimension Variables with Dialog Boxes

Choose File, then New, and enter drawing name `MOCKDIM=IA7MOKD2` replacing your earlier MOCKDIM drawing.

Choose File, then Open, and enter drawing name `MOCKDIM` to edit your existing MOCKDIM drawing.

`Command:` *Choose* Settings, *then* Dimension Style	Opens Dimension Styles and Variables dialog box
Choose Text Location	Opens Text Location dialog box
Click on Default *in the* Horizontal *edit box, then select* Force Text Inside, *and choose* OK	Sets DIMTIX on and returns to previous dialog box
Choose Extension Lines, *then verify that* Feature Offset *is set to 1/16*	Sets DIMEXO variable to 1/16"
Verify that Extension Above Line *is set to 3/16, then choose* OK	Sets DIMEXE variable to 3/16" and returns to previous dialog box
Choose Features, *double-click in the* Baseline Increment *edit box, enter* `5/8`	Sets DIMDLI variable to 5/8"
Verify that Feature Scaling *is set to 2*	Sets DIMSCALE variable to 2" (verifies setting made earlier in chapter)
Verify that Text Gap *is set to 3/32*	Sets DIMGAP variable to 3/32
Choose OK	Returns to main dialog box
Choose Text Location, *and verify that* Text Height *is set to 1/8, then choose* OK	Sets DIMTXT to 1/8" and returns to previous dialog box
Choose OK	Returns to command prompt

Save the drawing to be used in Chapter 17, then quit AutoCAD.

Summary

You now have some experience with most of AutoCAD's basic dimensioning commands; and you can place linear, radius, and diameter dimensions, as well as leaders. Chapter 17 explains the rest of AutoCAD's many dimensioning commands and features.

The most important point to remember about dimensioning with AutoCAD has nothing to do with dimensioning: be as precise as possible when you draw. Always use object snaps or exact coordinates whenever possible. This ensures that AutoCAD calculates the correct values when the drawing is dimensioned.

Control the appearance of your dimensions with dimension variables. As you learned in the last exercise, you can set dimension variables most easily by using AutoCAD's dialog boxes. After you have used the variables for some time, you will remember them by name. Then you can speed up the process of setting dimension variables by entering their variable names at the `Command:` prompt.

The last several chapters have shown that when a drawing has been properly created, it becomes a valuable database. Chapter 16 begins Part Four: "Advanced AutoCAD Features," and provides a rest from dimensioning while you learn about AutoCAD's attributes and data extraction. Chapter 16 shows several examples of how to use attributes—AutoCAD's way of storing non-graphical (ASCII text) information in a drawing. There are limitless possibilities for storing this kind of data with your drawing geometry.

In the next chapter, you will learn how to create attribute definitions, edit them, and combine attribute definitions with graphical entities into blocks. When blocks with attributes are inserted, the data for attributes is requested. Chapter 16 also shows you how to modify attribute data after insertion and how to extract the data for use in other programs for tabulation or reporting. All of these operations can be performed by standard commands or simplified through dialog box alternates. Dimensioning resumes in Chapter 17, called "Advanced Dimensioning."

Part Four

Advanced AutoCAD Features

This book's first three parts taught you how to create an accurate drawing, dimension it, and print it out as hard copy. This is all many users really expect of AutoCAD. If you are a more sophisticated user, however, you probably want to take advantage of AutoCAD's additional built-in capabilities, which can help you enhance your drafting productivity. Part Four of *Inside AutoCAD Release 12* introduces you to AutoCAD's more advanced features, including several new ones.

How Part Four Is Organized

Part Four consists of three chapters, which cover the following topics:

- Storing and retrieving information in drawings, and using attributes to export that information to other programs

- Using dimension styles to control the appearance of dimensions
- Exchanging data and images between AutoCAD and other programs

These topics enable you to add a considerable amount of information to the graphics in your drawing and to use that information and graphics in many other programs.

Using Attributes To Store and Retrieve Information

As a drafter, designer, or artist, you understand that drawings are much more than just collections of graphic entities and annotations. Drawings convey ideas. For example, drawings are often used to keep track of equipment in commercial facilities, to define items to be purchased for a project, and to generate bills of materials for items to be manufactured. Electronic-format drawings, such as those maintained by AutoCAD, have the capability to store many different types of non-graphic information.

In Chapter 16, you learn about AutoCAD's attribute entities. *Attributes* are like informational tags that you can attach to various items in your drawing. These tags maintain information about the items to which they are attached. If you are creating a drawing that shows the equipment in a factory, for example, you can assign attributes to each piece of equipment to keep track of cost, function, manufacturer, purchase date, maintenance data, and other types of information.

Stored information is not useful, however, unless you have a method of retrieving it from the drawing in some meaningful way. Chapter 16 also shows you how to extract data from attributes in a drawing, so that you can export the data to a database program for analysis, create bills of materials, or otherwise collect and analyze the data that is contained in your drawings.

Additional Dimensioning Capability

Chapter 17 increases your dimensioning capability by showing you how to create and use AutoCAD's dimension styles. As you learned in Chapter 15, AutoCAD's dimensions are controlled by a wide range of dimension variables. AutoCAD has so many dimension variables (and their names are so cryptic) that they can be difficult to keep track of—even for experienced AutoCAD users. Dimension styles overcome this problem by enabling you to define a style of dimensioning, save it by name, and then specify the dimension style's name whenever you want to use it again. Chapter 17 also explains several advanced dimensioning features, including commands for ordinate, chain, and datum dimensioning.

Exchanging CAD Data with other Software

The final chapter in this part shows you how to exchange AutoCAD data and images with other software packages. Chapter 18 explains the two file formats that have been used for data conversion with AutoCAD for many years (the IGES and DXF formats). Chapter 18 also discusses a new and exciting feature of Release 12: the capability to import and export graphics file formats, such as GIF, TIFF, PCX and PostScript. The ability to copy a drawing—or part of a drawing—to another document can save considerable time in developing training materials, manuals, reports, and other documents.

16

Attributes and Data Extraction

So far, the drawings in this book have been based on graphic entities or on spatial relationships between graphic entities. AutoCAD also can produce drawings from other types of data. In the Autotown subdivision you created in Chapter 12, for example, you can add "House Model Name," "House Size (Sq. Ft.)," and "House Exterior Finish" data to each house block to provide even more information about the real-world objects that are represented by the graphic blocks. This kind of extra information can be very helpful to the person who is reading your drawing.

In AutoCAD, you can assign attributes to any item in your drawing, to provide extra information about that item. *Attributes* are like paper tags that are attached to merchandise with a string. They can contain all kinds of

information about the item to which they are tied: the item's manufacturer, model number, materials, price, stock number, and so on. The information stored within the attribute is the attribute's *value*.

In this chapter, you learn how to make your drawings more informative by adding text attributes to the drawing's blocks. You also learn how to extract this data in report form. By tagging entities with attributes, you can extract automatic bills of materials, schedules, and other tabular lists of data, or you can view the information in graphic form. You do not need to clutter your drawing with attribute data that you do not want to display. You can store data invisibly in the drawing file until you are ready to turn it into a report.

Understanding Attributes

You store an attribute (such as a name) in a block the same way you store graphic entities in a block. Just as you create and carefully lay out graphic entities before you include them in a block, you define attributes before you create an *attribute-laden* block.

AutoCAD provides an attribute-definition command called ATTDEF and a dialog box (called DDATTDEF) for attribute definition. You use ATTDEF or DDATTDEF to create attribute definitions, which determine how and what kind of attribute values are stored. Then you use the BLOCK command to group graphic entities and attribute definitions to form a block. This places the attribute definitions into the same block definition as the graphic entities.

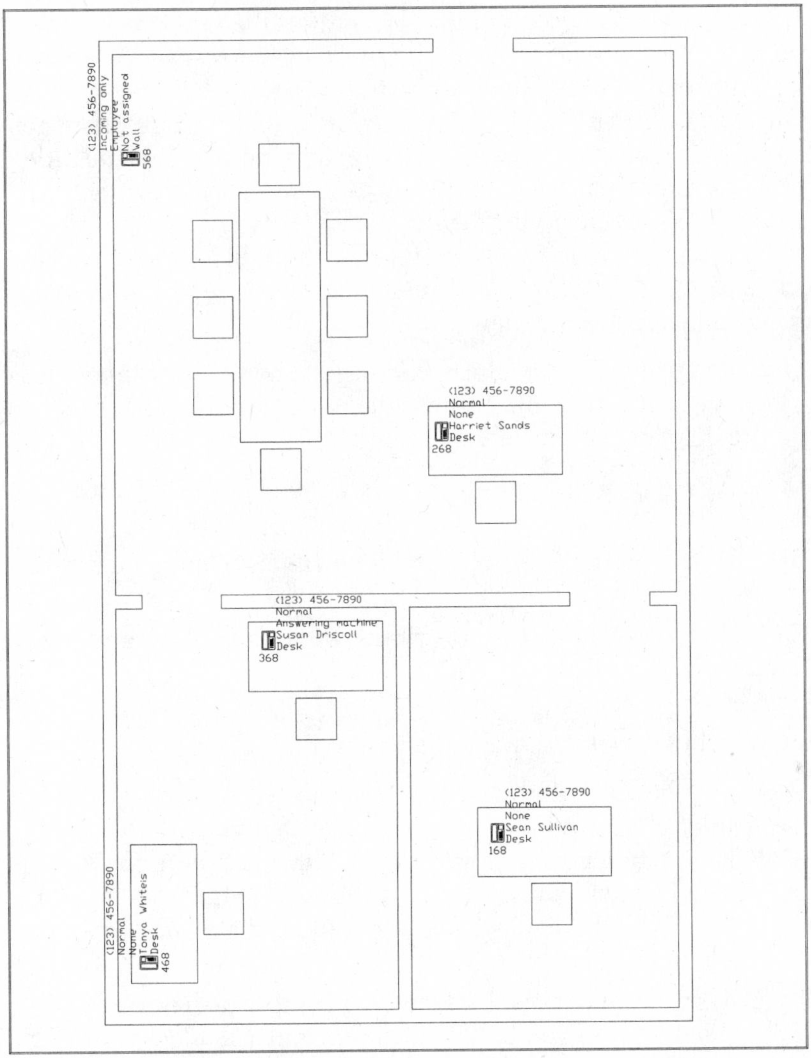

Figure 16.1:

A facility drawing with phone attributes.

You often may want to tag a group of graphic entities that already are in a block. If you design printed circuit boards, for example, you can assign text to an integrated circuit (IC) chip by labeling the chip with the manufacturer's name and pin assignments. If you are the facilities manager of an office building, you can tag each desk with an employee's name, title, department, phone number, and workstation description, as shown in figure 16.1. The desk (or IC chip for the PC board) probably already is stored as a block. In these cases, you can explode and reblock or form a new nested block (a block within a block) by including the attribute definition tags and the original block in the new block definition.

After you form an attribute-laden block, you use the INSERT command to insert the block into your drawing. You use the following commands to control attribute display and attribute editing:

- **ATTDISP.** This command controls the visibility of attributes in the drawing.
- **ATTEDIT.** This command changes attribute values after you insert them in your drawing.
- **ATTEXT.** This command extracts attribute values and block information, which you can place in a report.
- **ATTREDEF.** This command redefines a block and its associated attributes through the Attribute Redefinition dialog box.
- **DDATTEXT.** This command performs attribute extraction through a dialog box.
- **DDEDIT.** This command displays the Edit Attribute Definition dialog box (see fig. 16.2) when you select an attribute definition that has not been blocked. (DDEDIT displays the Text Editing dialog box when you select a text entity.)
- **DDATTE.** This command displays the Edit Attributes dialog box (see fig. 16.3), which enables you to edit attribute values in blocks after they have been inserted into the drawing. When you insert a block and the ATTDIA system variable is set to 1 (the default is 0), this dialog box prompts you for initial attribute data.

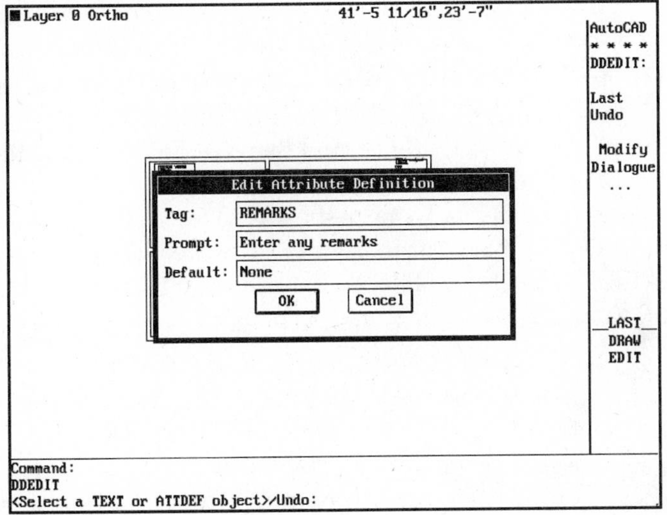

Figure 16.2:
The DDEDIT Edit Attribute Definition dialog box.

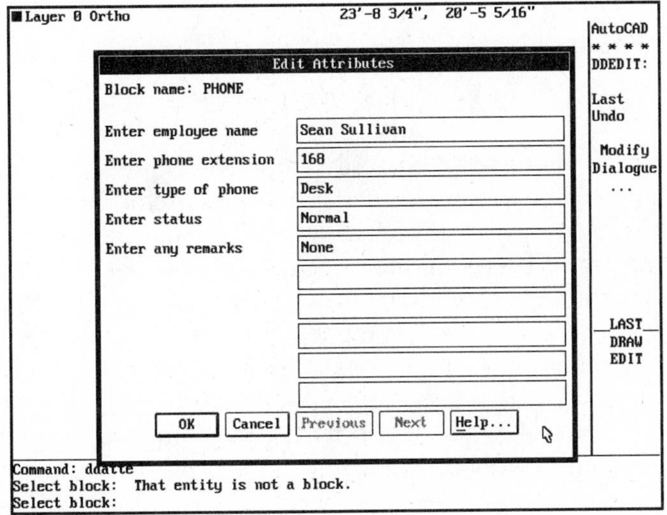

Figure 16.3:
The DDATTE Edit Attributes dialog box.

An *attribute definition* is the attribute entity before it is blocked; an *attribute entity* exists only as a subentity in a block insert.

Menu items for the attribute commands are scattered throughout different screen menus. From the screen menu, choose BLOCKS, then choose ATTDEF to issue the ATTDEF command. You then can choose DISPLAY, and then ATTDISP to issue ATTDISP. Choose EDIT, then DDEDIT, DDATTE, or ATTEDIT to issue those commands. You can choose DDEDIT and then choose Modify Dialogue to issue the DDMODIFY dialog box. Choose UTILITY, then ATTEXT and then choose ATTEXT to issue the ATTEXT command, or choose UTILITY and then Att Ext Dialogue to issue the DDATTEXT command. From the pull-down menu, choose Draw, Text, then Attributes, and then Define to issue the DDATTDEF command, or Edit to issue the DDATTE command, or Extract to issue the DDATTEXT command. To use ATTREDEF, choose File, then Applications, and load ATTREDEF.LSP from the \ACAD\SAMPLE directory; you can then enter AT or ATTREDER to issue the command.

This chapter's attribute exercises are straightforward. First, you set up a facility drawing in which to work. Then you learn how to define attribute definitions, how to insert a block with attributes, and how to display and edit the attributes after they are in the drawing. Finally, you learn how to extract the data in a text report. Once this is done, you redefine the block with different attributes and extract the data to a second text report.

Setting Up for Attributes

Facility management drawings commonly employ attributes. In this chapter, imagine that you are working in the offices of the Acme Tool Co. One of your responsibilities is to maintain drawings and produce reports on the equipment in the office. This equipment includes telephones, copiers, fax machines, and computers. Each piece of equipment in the office has information — such as an identification number and name assignment — which is stored in a drawing in the form of attributes. In the following exercises, you develop a drawing that shows the telephone equipment for a small section of the office complex, and you extract a telephone report. Table 16.1 lists the information that you need to store and extract in your drawing.

Table 16.1
Telephone Report for Acme Tool Co.

Name	*Number*	*Ext*	*Type*	*Status*	*Remarks*
Not Assigned	(123) 456-7890	586	Wall	In only	Employee
Tonya Whiteis	(123) 456-7890	486	Desk	Normal	None
Susan Driscoll	(123) 456-7890	386	Desk	Normal	Ans.Mach.
Harriet Sands	(123) 456-7890	286	Desk	Normal	None
Shawn Sullivan	(123) 456-7890	186	Desk	Normal	None

In this chapter, you are more concerned with manipulating the attributes associated with the graphics than with manipulating the graphic entities. Nevertheless, you still need a drawing. Create a new drawing, named OFFICE, which uses architectural units. The drawing scale factor is 24 for a scale of 1/2" = 1'-0", sized to plot on a 36"×24" sheet.

If you use the IA DISK, the IA7OFFIC.DWG file contains the basic office-layout drawing. Also on the disk is a graphic block drawing called PHN-BLK.DWG and a text file named PHONE.TXT that you use in the data report. If you do not have the disk, you need to create a simple floor plan of the office drawing. You also need to create the phone symbol before you begin your attribute definitions.

Setting Up the Office Drawing

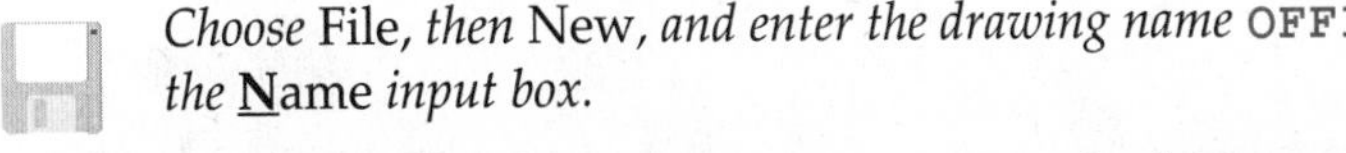

Choose File, *then* New, *and enter the drawing name* `OFFICE=IA7OFFIC` *in the* Name *input box.*

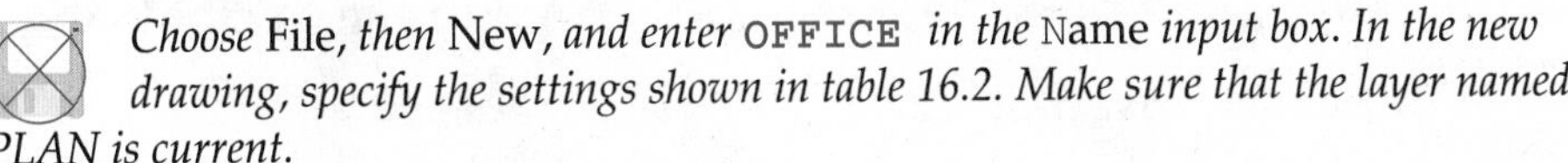

Choose File, *then* New, *and enter* `OFFICE` *in the* Name *input box. In the new drawing, specify the settings shown in table 16.2. Make sure that the layer named PLAN is current.*

Table 16.2
Office Drawing Settings

COORDS	*GRID*	*ORTHO*	*SNAP*	*FILL*	*UCSICON*
ON	24	ON	3	OFF	OR

UNITS	Set UNITS to 4 Architectural, default the rest
LIMITS	Set LIMITS from 0,0 to 72',48'
ZOOM	Zoom All
VIEW	Save view as A

Layer Name	*State*	*Color*	*Linetype*
0	On	7 (White)	CONTINUOUS
DATA	On	7 (White)	CONTINUOUS
PLAN	On/Current	3 (Green)	CONTINUOUS

If you have the IA DISK drawing, your screen shows the drawing in figure 16.4. If you do not have the IA DISK and need to create the drawing, change the layer to PLAN and use the dimensions shown in figure 16.4 to draw the floor plan in the following exercise. When you use the SOLID command, remember to pick the points in an X pattern to avoid drawing bow-tie shapes. See Chapter 12 for more information on the AutoLISP-defined DLINE command.

Creating the Office Floor Plan and Furniture Symbols

You already have the floor plan. Just read this exercise.

Complete the floor plan in this exercise.

`Command:` *Choose* Draw, *then* Line, *then* Double Lines *and draw the walls*

`Command:` *Choose* Draw, *then* Line, *then* Segments, *and draw a table, chair, and desk.*
`Command:` *Choose* Modify, *then* Copy, *and copy the chairs and desks*
`Command:` *Choose* Modify, *then* Rotate, *and rotate the copied desks*

If you do not have the phone symbol, you need to create it (a simplified version is fine). After you draw or insert the telephone symbol, you need to set the UCS at the lower left corner of the phone symbol. This point is your insertion base point. If you are using the disk, you only need to insert the block named *PHN-BLK.

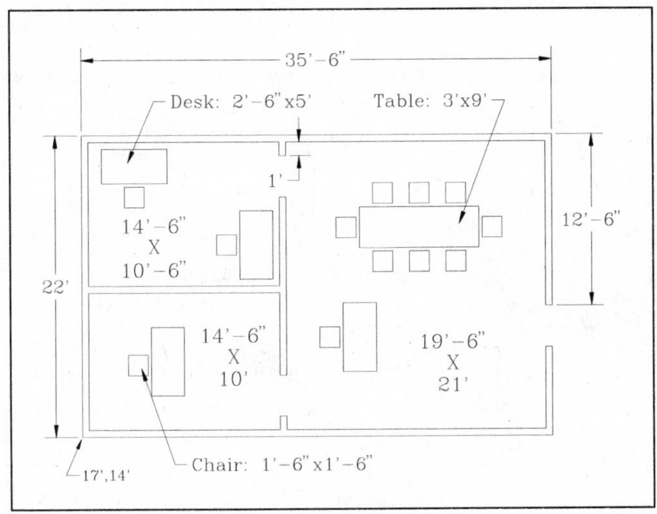

Figure 16.4: The floor plan before attributes are added.

Creating the Telephone Symbol

`Command:` *Use* LAYER *to make layer* 0 *current, then turn off* the PLAN *layer*

`Command:` *Choose* View, *then* Zoom, then Center, *pick a point and zoom to a height of 36"*

`Command:` *Choose* Settings, *then choose* Drawing Aids, *and set snap to .25 and grid to 2"*

`Command:` *Choose* Draw, *then* Insert, *and insert *PHN-BLK at 0,0 as shown in figure 16.5.*

Draw a telephone as shown in figure 16.5.

`Command:` *Choose* UCS:, *then* Next, *then* origin, *and pick the origin point at the lower left corner of the telephone symbol*

`Command:` *Choose* File, *then* Save

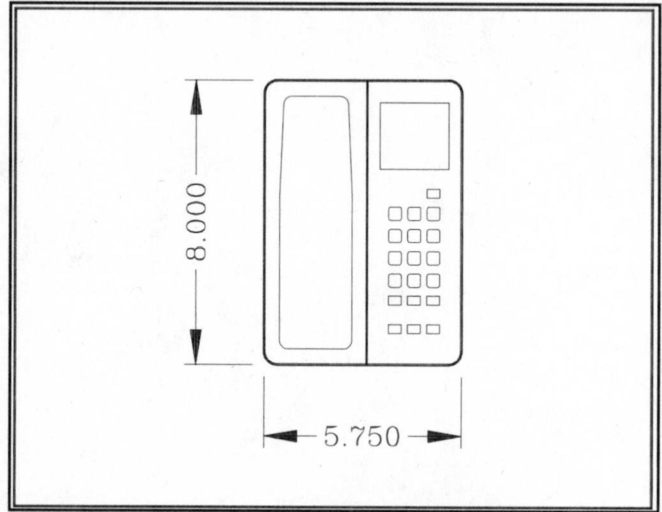

Figure 16.5:
The telephone symbol.

Use figure 16.5 as your guide for drawing the telephone.

You now are ready to add attribute definitions.

Using the ATTDEF Command To Define Attributes

To create an attribute, first use the ATTDEF command. Start by defining the EXTENSION attribute for the phone. Attributes have several definition modes, including normal (the initial default), Invisible, Preset, Constant, and Verify. In this drawing, define the EXTENSION attribute for the phone as normal.

Understanding Variable Attributes

A *variable* attribute is an attribute that is not constant. You usually enter a variable attribute's value when its block is inserted, but you can change it later. You can define a value as a default that appears on the prompt line when you insert the block into the drawing. In addition, you set attribute definition modes and set text parameters to define the way the attribute appears on-screen (and in the drawing).

The process for defining variable attributes sounds more complicated than it really is. The following exercise shows you how to use the ATTDEF command to define a variable attribute.

Using ATTDEF To Define a Variable Attribute

`Command:` *From the screen menu, choose* BLOCKS, *then* ATTDEF:	Issues the ATTDEF command
`Attribute modes - Invisible:N Constant:N Verify:N Preset:N`	Displays the current attribute modes
`Enter (ICVP) to change, RETURN when done: V↵`	Turns on Verify
`Attribute modes - Invisible:N Constant:N Verify:Y Preset:N`	Displays the new attribute modes
`Enter (ICVP) to change, RETURN when done:` *Press Enter*	Accepts the attribute modes' settings
`Attribute tag:` **`EXTENSION ↵`**	Specifies the attribute tag

`Attribute prompt:` **`Enter phone extension`**↵	Specifies the attribute prompt
`Default attribute value:` *Press Enter*	Specifies that no default attribute value will be used
`Justify/Style/<Start point>:` **`C`**↵	Specifies the Center text option
`Center point:` **`2.875,-5`**↵	Centers the attribute under the telephone
`Height <0'-0 3/16">:` **`3`**↵	Specifies 1/8"-high text at 1/2"=1'-0"
`Rotation angle <0>:` *Press Enter*	Creates the attribute definition

Your screen should show the extension attribute tag centered under the telephone, as shown in figure 16.6.

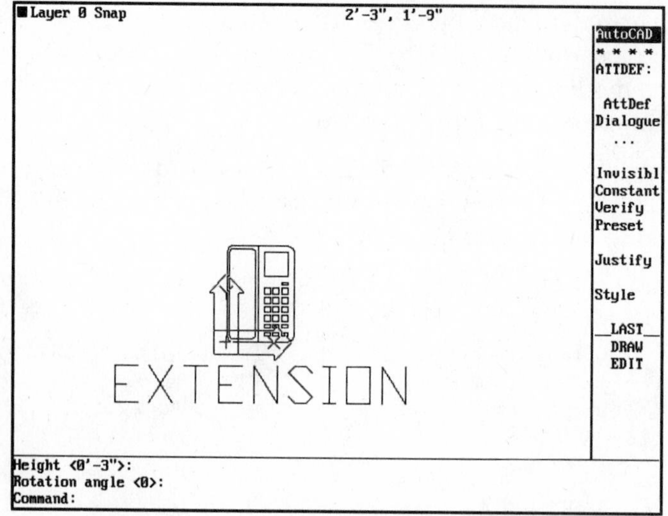

Figure 16.6: The telephone with EXTENSION attribute definition.

Using Attribute Modes

Before AutoCAD prompts you to control the appearance of the attribute text, it prompts you for several attribute modes. These modes control the attribute's visibility and the treatment of block insertions. You can choose from the following modes:

- **Invisible.** The Invisible mode makes the attribute data invisible. Invisible mode is useful when you want to store data in the drawing, but you do not want to display or plot the data, or wait for it to regenerate.
- **Constant.** The Constant mode creates attributes with a fixed text value. Constant mode is helpful when you want to write boilerplate notes with attribute text. You cannot edit a constant attribute after it is inserted as a block without redefining the block. The default is `Constant:N`, which means that the attribute is variable. You can edit variable attributes after you insert them by using the ATTEDIT command or the DDATTE dialog box.
- **Verify.** The Verify mode enables you to check variable attribute values before you insert them into the drawing file. If an attribute has the Verify mode, AutoCAD displays the attribute value on the prompt line after you type it. AutoCAD waits for you to press Enter before inserting the text. You can see what you have typed, check for errors, and correct them before the attribute is inserted.
- **Preset.** The Preset mode enables you to create attributes that automatically accept their default value. When the block is inserted, attribute values are not requested. Preset is the most flexible mode. Preset attributes function the same as Constant attributes, except that you can edit Preset attributes after you insert them by using the ATTEDIT command or the DDATTE dialog box.

Attributes can be Constant, Invisible, Preset, and Verified at the same time, or in any combination. The initial default setting is N (no) for all modes. To turn one of the ATTDEF modes on or off, type I, C, V, or P, then press Enter. AutoCAD redisplays the mode's prompt with a Y (yes) or N (no) next to the item. The last settings are saved as new default modes for the next use of ATTDEF.

Defining Attributes

You define attributes by giving them a tag name, an optional prompt, and an optional default or constant text value. The default value is entered in the drawing, unless you provide a new value when you insert the attribute block. After you define the default value, you set its location, style, alignment, height, and angle, exactly as you do with the TEXT and DTEXT commands.

Using Attribute Tags

Each attribute has a *tag*, such as "Name," "Employee-No.," "Extension," and "Part-Number." You can think of a tag as the name of the attribute value that you insert (such as block names). The only restriction on tag names is that they cannot include blanks. Use a hyphen in place of a blank (as in "Employee-No.") to separate the tag name's elements. AutoCAD translates all tags into uppercase letters, even if you type them in lowercase letters.

Using Attribute Prompts

In addition to naming the attribute, you can assign an instructional prompt to use at insertion time. You can assign, for example, the prompt `Enter the Part Number of this widget here` to the tag name "Part-Numbers." Prompts are most useful when you do not use the Enter Attributes dialog box (you use this dialog box in later exercises).

A prompt longer than 24 characters is truncated in the Enter Attributes dialog box.

You can use any text you want for your prompts. `Gimme the number now, Dummy` is as valid as `Would you please enter the number here...`. If you feel that the attribute tag name says it all, you do not need to add a prompt. The attribute tag name is used as the default prompt if you do not enter a prompt when you define the attribute. Press Enter to use the attribute tag as the attribute prompt.

Using Default Attribute Values

When you define attributes, AutoCAD asks you for the default values. Practical defaults for variable attributes are "Not Yet Entered" or "XXX.NN". These show up in the drawing if you accept the default by pressing Enter instead of entering an attribute value at the time of insertion. Constant and Preset attributes insert automatically, without showing you their default values.

Displaying Attributes

After assigning the attribute value, AutoCAD prompts you for information about how to display attribute-value text. This series of AutoCAD prompts is identical to the standard TEXT prompts. After you set all the text parameters, AutoCAD draws the attribute on-screen just as it draws text. You can edit attribute definitions before they are blocked by using the CHANGE command or the DDEDIT dialog box.

Creating a Block with Many Attributes

Earlier in this chapter, you defined the extension attribute as a variable attribute. Before you build the complete phone block, you need to analyze the other attribute data types that you include in your phone report. Use table 16.1 as a guide to the following attribute definitions.

All the telephones have the same number in table 16.1, which makes the telephone number an obvious candidate for a Constant attribute with the value "(123) 456-7890." The rest of the attribute tags have different values; make them Variable or Preset. Define the status and remarks attributes as Preset to accept their defaults and avoid the prompt on insertion. The status and remarks attributes are not likely to change often.

The extension, telephone type, and employee name are important to this project, so keep them visible. The telephone number, status, and remarks, however, are not pertinent to your report. Define them as Invisible, so that the data is available for other reports.

Creating the Rest of the Attribute Definitions

You create the rest of the attribute definitions in the following exercise. To start, make DATA the current layer. This change gives you the option of displaying or plotting the drawings with only the extension visible (on the layer of insertion), or of including the type and name on the DATA layer.

Look for the different attribute modes, tags, and defaults in the exercise. Notice that you can repeat the ATTDEF command to place the next line of text just below the first, just as you do for the TEXT command. Answer all the attribute-specific prompts first. Then, when the `Justify/Style/`

`<Start point>:` prompt appears, AutoCAD highlights the last attribute-defined line on the screen. If you press Enter, the current attribute definition is placed immediately below the old one.

Using ATTDEF To Define Attributes

`Command:` *Use the LAYER command and make DATA the current layer*

First, you need to make the NUMBER attribute Constant and Invisible, as follows.

`Command:` *From the screen menu, choose* BLOCKS, *then* ATTDEF:	Issues the ATTEXT command
`Attribute modes - Invisible:N Constant:N Verify:Y Preset:N`	Displays the current attribute modes
`Enter (ICVP) to change, RETURN when done:` **V**	Turns off Verify
`Attribute modes - Invisible:N Constant:N Verify:N Preset:N`	Displays the new attribute modes
`Enter (ICVP) to change, RETURN when done:` **I**	Turns on Invisible
`Attribute modes - Invisible:Y Constant:N Verify:N Preset:N`	
`Enter (ICVP) to change, RETURN when done:` **C**	Turns on Constant
`Attribute modes - Invisible:Y Constant:Y Verify:N Preset:N`	
`Enter (ICVP) to change, RETURN when done:` *Press Enter*	Accepts the attribute modes' settings
`Attribute tag:` **NUMBER ↵**	Specifies the attribute tag
`Attribute value:` **(123) 456-7890 ↵**	Specifies the attribute value
`Justify/Style/<Start point>:` **6.75,20 ↵**	Specifies the starting point
`Height <0'-3">:` *Press Enter*	Accepts the height
`Rotation angle <0>:` *Press Enter*	Accepts the rotation angle

Next, make the STATUS attribute Invisible and Preset.

`Command:` *Press Enter*	Repeats the ATTDEF command
`ATTDEF Attribute modes - Invisible:Y Constant:Y Verify:N Preset:N`	
`Enter (ICVP) to change, RETURN when done:`↵	Turns off Constant
`Attribute modes - Invisible:Y Constant:N Verify:N Preset:N`	
`Enter (ICVP) to change, RETURN when done:` **P**↵	Turns on Preset
`Attribute modes - Invisible:Y Constant:N Verify:N Preset:Y`	
`Enter (ICVP) to change, RETURN when done:` *Press Enter*	
`Attribute tag:` **STATUS**↵	
`Attribute prompt:` **Enter status**↵	
`Default attribute value:` **Normal**↵	
`Justify/Style/<Start point>:` *Press Enter*	

Next, make the REMARKS attribute Invisible and Preset.

`Command:` *Press Enter*	Repeats the ATTDEF command
`ATTDEF Attribute modes - Invisible:Y Constant:N Verify:N Preset:Y`	
`Enter (ICVP) to change, RETURN when done:` *Press Enter*	
`Attribute tag:` **REMARKS**↵	
`Attribute prompt:` *Enter any remarks and press Enter*	
`Default attribute value:` **None**↵	
`Justify/Style/<Start point>:` *Press Enter*	

Next, use the DDATTDEF command to make the NAME attribute. The DDATTDEF command displays a dialog box that defines an attribute using the same information as ATTDEF.

`Command:` *From the screen menu, choose* DRAW, *then* ATTDEF:, *and then* AttDef Dialog	Issues the DDATTDEF command and displays the Attribute Definition dialog box
Click in the Invisible and *the* Preset boxes *removing the checkmarks*	Turns off Invisible Preset

Enter `NAME` *in the* **T**ag: *input box*	Specifies the Tag name
Enter `Enter employee name` *in the* **P**rompt: *input box*	Specifies the attribute prompt
Enter `Not assigned` *in the* **V**alue: *input box*	Specifies the default value
Choose the **A**lign below previous attributes *box*	Sets the new attribute location below the last one
Choose OK	Defines the attribute

Finally, make the TYPE attribute by using DDATTDEF.

`Command:` *Press Enter*	Repeats the DDATTDEF command
Enter `TYPE` *in the* **T**ag *input box*	Specifies the Tag name
Enter `Enter type of phone` *in the* Prompt *input box*	Specifies the attribute prompt
Enter `Desk` *in the* **V**alue *input box*	Specifies the default value
Choose the **A**lign below previous attributes *box*	Sets the new attribute below the last one
Choose OK	Defines the attribute

`Command:` *Choose* View, *then* Pan
Pan, if needed, to see everything
`Command:` *Choose* File, *then* Save

Your screen should show all six attribute definitions, even though some of the attributes become invisible when you block the phone (see fig. 16.7).

An attribute definition displays the attribute tag, but when blocked and inserted, the attribute value displays instead.

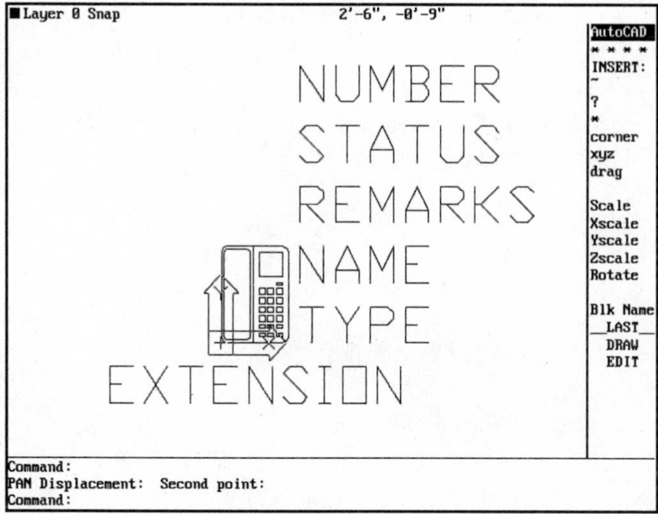

Figure 16.7:

The telephone with all attribute definitions.

Using BLOCK To Group Graphics and Attribute Definitions

The next step is to group all the graphic entities (lines, polylines, and so on) and nongraphic entities (attribute definitions) together by using the BLOCK command. After you block the attribute definitions, you cannot edit the definitions without a block redefinition. Now, you can edit the attribute definitions by using the CHANGE command or the DDEDIT or DDMODIFY dialog boxes, just as you edit strings of text. You also can erase the attribute definitions and replace them by using the ATTDEF command if you need to make major changes.

Block your telephone symbol and use the lower left corner as an insertion base point. The order in which you select attribute definitions is important because the selection order controls the prompting order when you insert the block. Name the block PHONE.

Using BLOCK To Group Graphics and Attribute Definitions into a Block

`Command:` *From the screen menu, choose* BLOCKS, *then* BLOCK:

`Block name (or ?):` **`PHONE`**↵	
`Insertion base point:` **`0,0`**↵	Specifies the UCS point of origin
`Select objects:` *Pick the* NAME *attribute first*	Starts selection with the attribute definition
`Select objects:` *Shift-pick the* EXTENSION *attribute*	Adds to the set
`Select objects:` *Shift-pick the* TYPE *attribute*	Adds the attribute definition to the block
`Select objects:` *Shift-pick the* NUMBER *attribute*	Adds to the set
`Select objects:` *Shift-pick the* STATUS *attribute*	Adds to the set
`Select objects:` *Shift-pick the* REMARKS *attribute*	Adds to the set
`Select objects:` *Shift-pick entities for the PHONE block*	Adds entities to the set
`Select objects:` *Press Enter*	Defines the block from the selection set

All graphic elements and attribute definitions disappear, just as in normal block creation.

You have just formatted your first attribute-laden block. Attribute block creation does not involve anything special, other than remembering to select the attribute definitions in the order that you want them. You can block, insert, redefine an attribute block, and write to disk using WBLOCK the same way you do a normal block.

If you select the attribute definitions by using a Window or Crossing object selection with oct-tree sorting for object selection, the attribute definitions are found starting with the most recently created definition. This order probably is the opposite of the order you want, unless you plan ahead and create them in reverse order. With oct-tree on, the selection order is unpredictable (see Chapter 8 for details).

Using INSERT To Insert Attribute Blocks

When the ATTDIA system variable is on 1 (the default is off or 0), you can use the Enter Attributes dialog box to enter attribute values during block insertions (see fig. 16.8). Fortunately, the dialog box enables you to edit or change the defaults in any order that you want. The dialog box displays all attribute prompts and defaults (including preset attributes), except those defined as Constant. Except for the title, this dialog box is identical to the DDATTE command's Edit Attributes dialog box.

Layer 0 Snap 49'-9",34'-6"

Enter Attributes

Block name: PHONE

Enter employee name	Not assigned
Enter phone extension	586
Enter type of phone	Wall
Enter status	Normal
Enter any remarks	None

OK Cancel Previous Next Help...

AutoCAD
* * * *
INSERT:
?
*
corner
xyz
drag
Scale
Xscale
Yscale
Zscale
Rotate
Blk Name
LAST
DRAW
EDIT

Y scale factor (default=X):
Rotation angle <0>:

Figure 16.8:

The Enter Attributes dialog box.

Locate the telephones in the offices by inserting them at the appropriate places in the floor plan. Turn ATTDIA on, then start by inserting the employee telephone on the wall in the conference room on the right.

Using INSERT To Insert Attribute Blocks

`Command:` *Use LAYER to make 0 the current layer, then turn on the PLAN layer*

`Command:` *Zoom to the view shown in figure 16.9*

`Command:` *From the screen menu, choose* AutoCAD, *then* UCS:, *then* World	Sets the UCS to World
Choose Settings, *then choose* Drawing Aids, *and set snap to 6" and grid to 2'*	
`Command:` **`UCSICON`**↵	
`UCSicon On/Off/OROff`↵	Turns off the UCS icon
`Command:` **`ATTDIA`** ↵	Turns on Enter Attributes dialog box for INSERT
`New value for ATTDIA <0>:1`↵	
`Command:` *From the pull-down menu Choose* Draw, *then* Insert	Issues the INSERT command
Enter **`PHONE`** *in the* **B**lock *input box*	Specifies the block
Choose OK	
`Insertion point:` *Pick a point in the upper right corner of conference room (see fig. 16.9)*	Positions the block
`X scale factor <1> / Corner:` *Press Enter*	Accepts the X scale
`Y scale factor <default=X>:` *Press Enter*	Accepts the Y scale
`Rotation angle <0>:` *Press Enter*	Accepts the rotation angle

The Enter Attributes dialog box automatically displays input boxes for entering the attribute values.

Enter `586` *in the* Enter phone extension *input box*	Specifies the extension
Enter `Wall` *in the* Enter type of phone *input box*	Specifies the phone type
Leave the employee name unchanged and choose OK	Inserts the block and the attributes
`Command:` *Use ZOOM with the window option and zoom in for a look (see fig. 16.10)*	
`Command:` *Use ZOOM with the Previous option to return to the previous view*	

The PHONE block should appear on-screen with all the attributes in their correct positions. The NUMBER, STATUS, and REMARKS attributes are invisible. They are stored in the correct position, but not displayed. If you

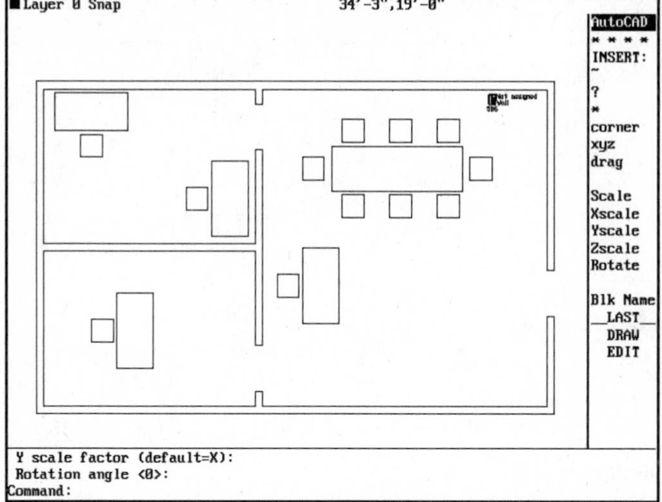

Figure 16.9:

An inserted wall telephone.

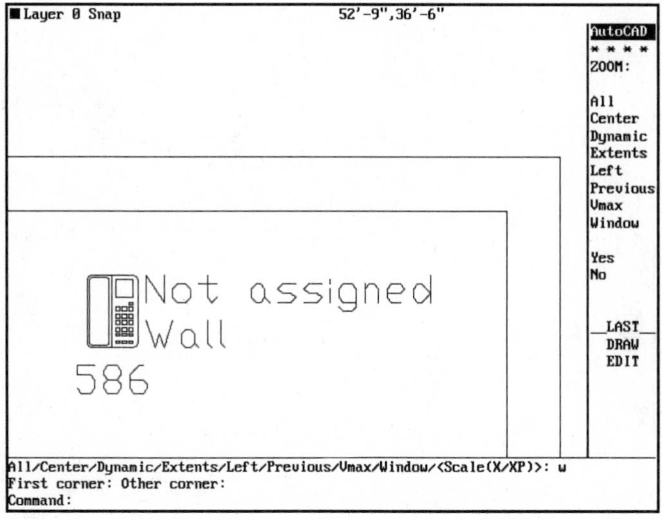

Figure 16.10:

A detail of the telephone.

turn off the DATA layer, only the phone symbol and extension attribute, which were created on layer 0, are visible.

Next, insert three more telephones in the following steps. Use the following list for the attributes:

Rotation	*Name*	*Ext*	*Type*
0	Tonya Whiteis	486	Desk
270	Susan Driscoll	386	Desk
270	Harriet Sands	286	Desk

Inserting Three More Attribute Phones

`Command:` *Choose* Draw, *then* Insert, *and insert the phone for Tonya Whiteis at ① (see fig. 16.11)*

Insert phone for Susan Driscoll at ②

Insert phone for Harriet Sands at ③

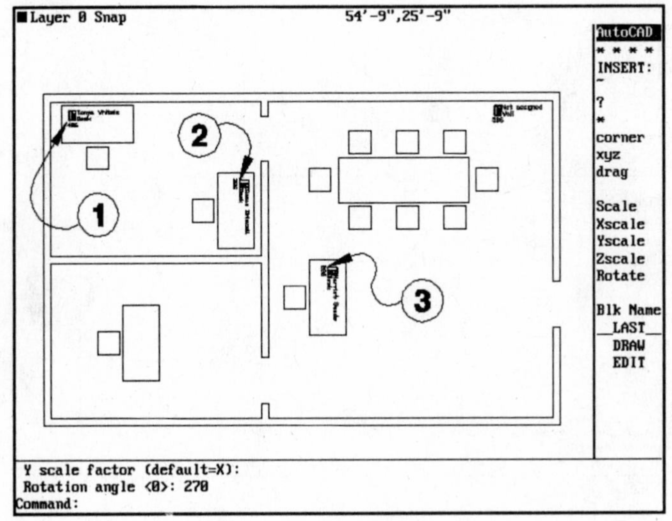

Figure 16.11:

Three more telephones inserted in the office.

Using the Attribute Prompts

In the steps that follow, insert the last telephone by using the attribute prompts you entered when you first made the attribute definitions. The next steps also give you an opportunity to test the verify mode you applied to the EXTENSION attribute. The final telephone goes on the desk in the lower left office. Use the INSERT command, with the ATTDIA system variable set to 0 so that the attribute prompts display to accept attribute values in place of the Enter Attributes dialog box.

Using Attribute Prompts To Insert an Attribute Block

`Command:` **`ATTDIA`**↵

`New value for ATTDIA <1>: 0`↵

`Command:` **`INSERT`**↵

`Block name (or ?):` *Insert the PHONE block at ① at 270 (see fig. 16.12)*

`Enter employee name <Not assigned>:` **`Shawn Sullivan`**↵	Specifies the value for employee name
`Enter phone extension:` **`186`**↵	Specifies the value the for phone extension
`Enter type of phone <Desk>:` *Press Enter*	Accepts the default value
`Verify attribute values`	
`Enter phone extension <186>:` *Press Enter*	Double-checks the value of the EXTENSION attribute

`Command:` *Choose* File, *then* Save

Shawn Sullivan's telephone should be placed on the desk shown in figure 16.12.

The dialog box is easier to use than the standard insertion prompts, and sometimes faster. It enables you to accept defaults and verify entries without any overt action on your part. Later, you learn how to use the same dialog box to change values of an inserted attribute.

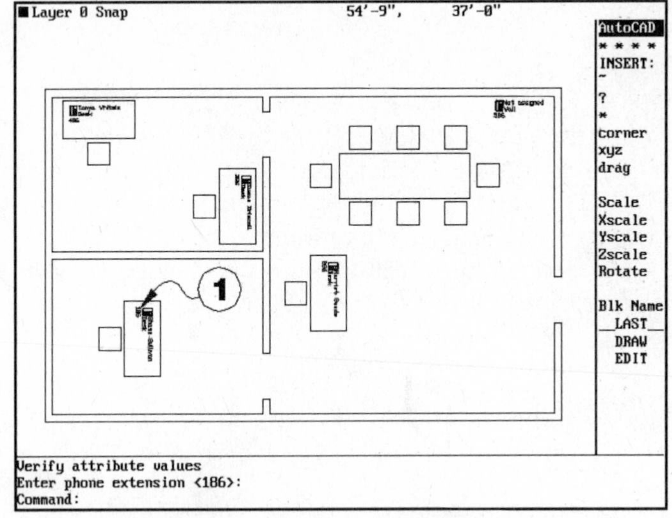

Figure 16.12:

A telephone inserted without a dialog box.

TIP

You can suppress attribute prompting by setting the ATTREQ system variable to 0. This suppression forces block insertion to accept all the attribute defaults, but you still can edit attributes at a later time. If ATTREQ is set to 0, variable attribute block insertions act as if they were preset.

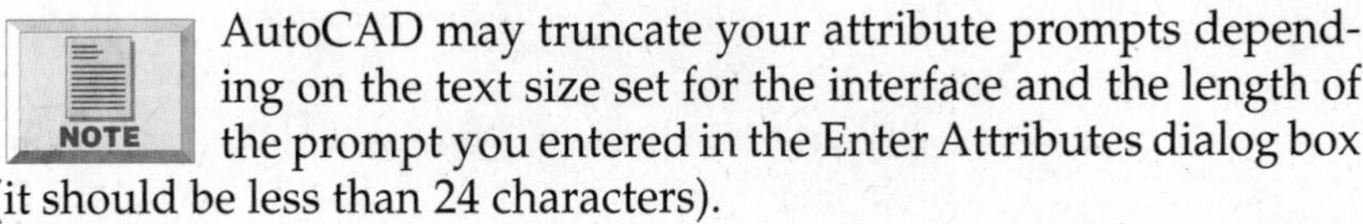

NOTE

AutoCAD may truncate your attribute prompts depending on the text size set for the interface and the length of the prompt you entered in the Enter Attributes dialog box (it should be less than 24 characters).

Your screen should now show the floor plan with all five PHONE blocks (see fig. 16.13).

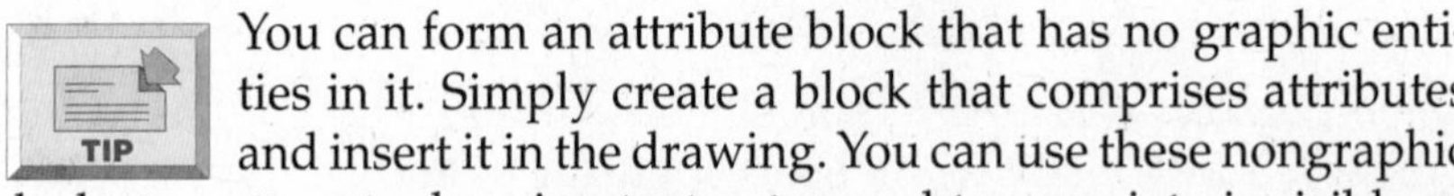

TIP

You can form an attribute block that has no graphic entities in it. Simply create a block that comprises attributes and insert it in the drawing. You can use these nongraphic blocks to automate drawing text entry, and to associate invisible or nongraphic information in a drawing. Be sure at least one attribute has a visible value when inserted, or you insert an invisible block of attributes.

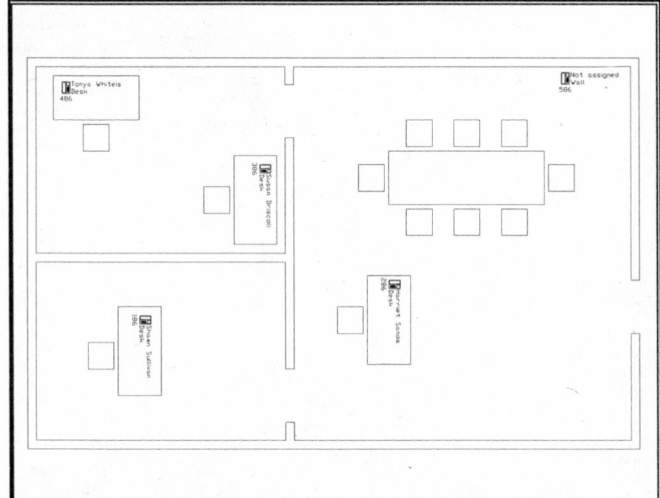

Figure 16.13:

The floor plan, showing five PHONE blocks.

Controlling Attribute Visibility

You can control an attribute's visibility by using the ATTDISP (ATTribute DISPlay) command. ATTDISP temporarily reverses visibility, turning on invisible attributes, or turning off visible attributes. To return to the default condition that is set by the ATTDEF command, set ATTDISP to N (for Normal).

Use ATTDISP first to turn off all the attributes, then change them back to normal, then on. On forces all the attributes to display. When you regenerate the screen, you can see the way you have stored the STATUS, REMARKS, and other DATA layer attributes.

Using ATTDISP To Control Attribute Visibility

`Command:` *Use ZOOM Window to zoom in on the upper left office*	
`Command:` *From the screen menu, choose* DISPLAY, *then choose* ATTDISP:	Issues the ATTDISP command
`Command: ATTDISP Normal/ON/OFF <Normal>:` *From the screen menu, choose* OFF	Turns all attributes off

`Regenerating drawing.`	Regenerates the drawing, turning off all attributes (see fig. 16.14)

Next, you set ATTDISP back to Normal.

`Command:` *Press Enter*	Repeats the ATTDISP command
`ATTDISP Normal/ON/OFF <Off>:` *Choose* Normal *from the screen menu*	Displays attributes as they were defined
`Regenerating drawing.`	Returns the display to normal
`Command:` *Press Enter*	Repeats ATTDISP
`ATTDISP Normal/ON/OFF <Normal>:` *Choose* ON *from the screen menu*	Turns all attributes on
`Regenerating drawing.`	Regenerates the drawing, showing all invisible attributes (see fig. 16.15)

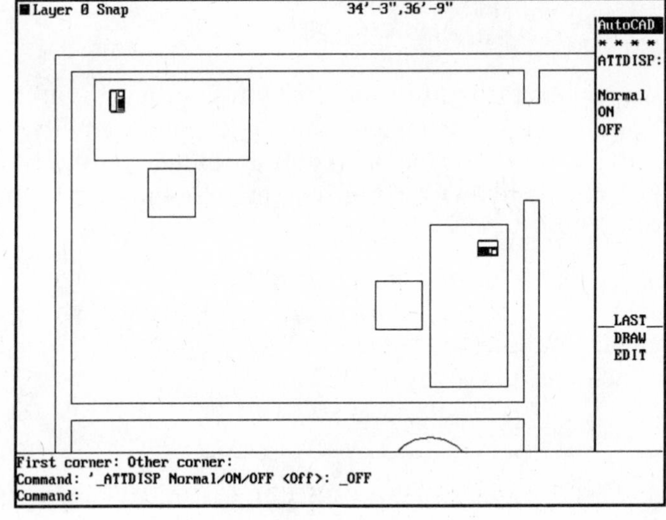

Figure 16.14:

The floor plan, with no attributes showing.

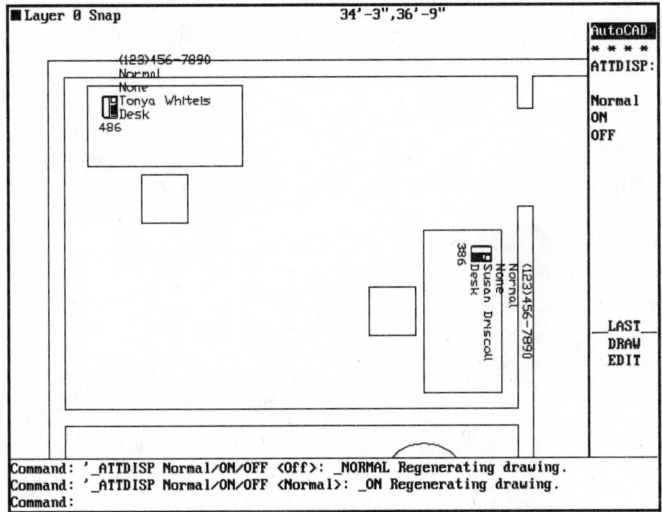

Figure 16.15:

The floor plan, with all attributes showing.

Using Layers To Control Attribute Display

You can extend your control of attribute visibility by putting your attribute data on different layers. Insert or define the attributes on the layer that you normally keep attributes on, then use layer visibility controls to turn data on and off. Do not forget that in paper space, viewports can have independent layer visibility settings.

Using ATTEDIT To Edit Attributes

If attributes could not be edited in AutoCAD, they would not be as useful as they are. If you suddenly realized, for example, that Shawn spells his name Sean, you need some way to change the contents of the attribute. Fortunately, AutoCAD enables you to edit attributes by using the ATTEDIT command.

An attribute must be displayed to be edited. It can be hidden again as soon as all the editing has been completed.

The ATTEDIT (ATTribute EDIT) command enables you to change attributes. When you use ATTEDIT, you first form a selection set for editing the attributes. ATTEDIT provides additional filters to help you select attributes and a graphic X cursor to identify the attribute being edited. You explore these filters and other attribute features in more detail later. For now, try a simple pick selection to change Shawn's name to Sean.

Using ATTEDIT To Edit Individual Attributes

`Command:` *Choose* View, *then* Pan, *and pan down to Shawn's office*	
`Command:` *From the screen menu, choose* EDIT, *then* ATTEDIT:	Starts the ATTEDIT command
`Edit attributes one at a time? <Y>:` *Press Enter*	Specifies editing attributes one at a time
`Block name specification <*>:` *Press Enter*	Specifies all editing attribute tags
`Attribute tag specification <*>:` *Press Enter*	Specifies editing all attributes' values
`Attribute value specification <*>:` *Press Enter*	Specifies all attributes' values are available to edit
`Select Attributes:` *Choose the text string* Shawn Sullivan *and press Enter*	Highlights and displays an X after selection (see fig. 16.16)
`1 attributes selected.`	
`Value/Position/Height/Angle/Style/ Layer/Color/Next <N>:` **`V`** ↵	Specifies an editing value
`Change or Replace? <R>:` **`C`**↵	Tells AutoCAD that you want to change the value
`String to change:` **`Shawn`**↵	Specifies the old value (you cannot use wild cards here)
`New string:` **`Sean`**↵	Specifies new value
`Value/Position/Height/Angle/Style/ Layer/Color/Next <N>:` *Press Enter*	Completes the name change
`Command:` *Choose* File, *then* Save	

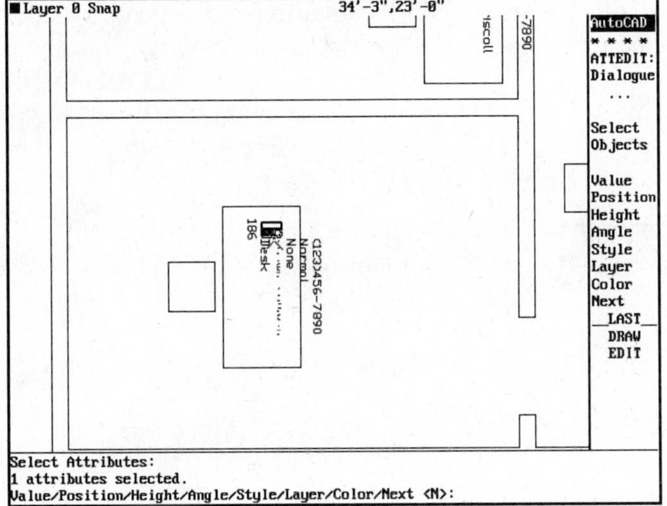

Figure 16.16:

A selected attribute, indicated by an X.

You should notice two nice features on-screen. First, an X appears adjacent to the attribute you want to edit (see fig. 16.16). Second, AutoCAD asks if you want to change part of the attribute value text string or replace it. In this exercise, you changed part of it (see fig. 16.17).

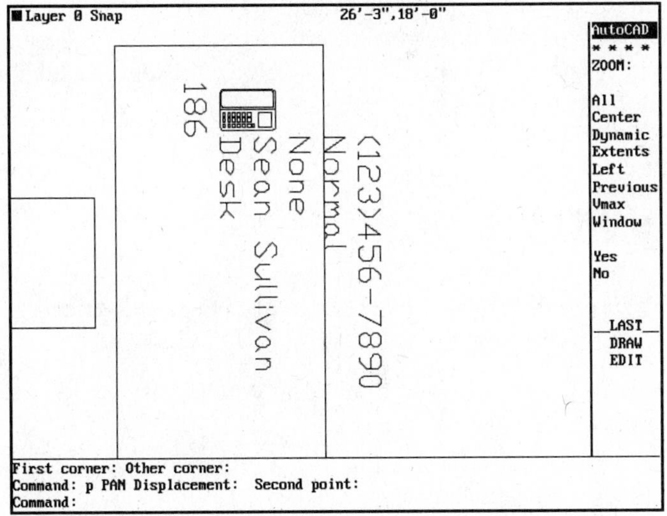

Figure 16.17:

A detail of the corrected attribute.

You can change much more than the text value when you edit attributes individually. Frequently, attributes overlap graphic objects. For the invisible attributes, this may not be a concern. The appearance of visible attributes, however, is an important part of your final drawing. Fortunately, you can use ATTEDIT to fine-tune their appearance by changing the text position and angle, the text style, height, layer, and color.

In the preceding exercise, you changed Sean's name fairly easily. What if you want to make global changes, such as change the 86 in all the extensions to 68, or selectively change 86 to 68 only on employee phones throughout the building?

Making Global Attribute Edits with ATTEDIT

Your facility drawing has only five telephones; individually picking each attribute for editing is not a problem. An entire office complex might have five hundred telephones. A considerable amount of time would be needed to edit five hundred attributes individually. You could gather all the tags named EXTENSION and do the replacement in one window — or could you? You could if you were able to tell AutoCAD exactly which characters in the EXTENSION attribute you want to edit. In other words, you need to set up a selection set filled with just the precise group. Regular selection set techniques do not work for this type of task.

Using Wild Cards To Edit Attributes Selectively

Instead of individually picking attributes from the screen, you can use a combination of wild-card filters and standard selection set options to select your attributes. The following common scenarios can be used:

- Select all attributes in blocks with a name you specify (wild cards are acceptable). Use * to select all blocks.
- Select all attributes that match a tag name you specify (wild cards are acceptable). Use * to select all tag names.
- Select all attributes that match a specified value (wild cards are acceptable). Use * to select all values.
- Narrow the selection process further by picking an individual attribute object, or by using the Window, Last, Crossing, or BOX options.

- Use any combination of the selection options described previously.

You can narrow the field of attributes that you want to edit by using wild cards to filtering the selection. The following wild cards are available:

Wild card	*Meaning*
@	Matches any alphanumeric character.
#	Matches any number.
*	Matches any string, even an empty (null) string. You can use an asterisk at the beginning, middle, or end of a string.
.	Matches any nonalphanumeric character.
?	Matches any single character.
~	Matches any character but the one that follows the tilde. The string ~?86, for example, matches any telephone extension except those ending in 86.
[ ]	Matches any single instance of any of the characters you enclose between the brackets, such as [xyz] to match either an x, y, or z.
[~]	Matches anything except any of the characters enclosed.
-	Matches a range of characters when used in brackets, such as [1-5] to match 1, 2, 3, 4, or 5.
'	Matches the special character that follows, such as '? matches a ? instead of using the ? as a wild card.

You can use individual wild cards or combine them. Do not be overwhelmed by the possibilities; you usually use the question mark and asterisk. The other wild cards are available if you need them.

Using Tag Selection To Edit Attributes

After you select and filter your attributes, AutoCAD prompts you to edit them. If you ask for individual editing (the default), AutoCAD prompts for your changes one at a time. As you saw in the preceding exercise, you can tell which attribute you are editing by looking for the highlighting or X onscreen.

Use AutoCAD's attribute-editing capabilities to change the wall phone status from "Normal" to "Incoming only" by following the next exercise. Narrow your attribute selection by specifying the STATUS attribute to edit, then select all five workstations with a window. Watch the X cursor to know which attribute AutoCAD wants you to edit. Use the <N>, which is the Next default, to skip to the wall phone status. Change the text value of the wall phone status. Then, use the <N> to skip past the rest, or terminate ATTEDIT by pressing Ctrl-C.

Using an Attribute Tag To Specify an Attribute Edit

`Command:` *Choose* View, *then* Zoom, *then* All	Displays the entire office
`Command:` **`ATTEDIT`**`:`↵	
`Edit attributes one at a time? <Y>:` *Press Enter*	
`Block name specification <*>:` *Press Enter*	
`Attribute tag specification <*>:` **`STATUS`**↵	Specifies editing only the attribute tag STATUS
`Attribute value specification <*>:` *Press Enter*	
`Select Attributes:` *Select all of the phones by using a window*	Specifies attributes to edit
`5 attributes selected.`	
`Value/Position/Height/Angle/Style /Layer/Color/Next <N>:` *Press Enter until an X is on the wall phone (see fig. 16.18)*	Moves the X to the next attribute
`Value/Position/Height/Angle/Style /Layer/Color/Next <N>:` **`V`**	Specifies Value
`Change or Replace? <R>` *Press Enter*	Specifies Replace
`New attribute value:` **`Incoming only`**↵	Specifies a new value
`Value/Position/Height/Angle/Style /Layer/Color/Next <N>:` *Press Enter*	Ends the ATTEDIT command

Zoom in to view the wall phone (see fig. 16.19), then use the ZOOM Previous option to resume the previous view.

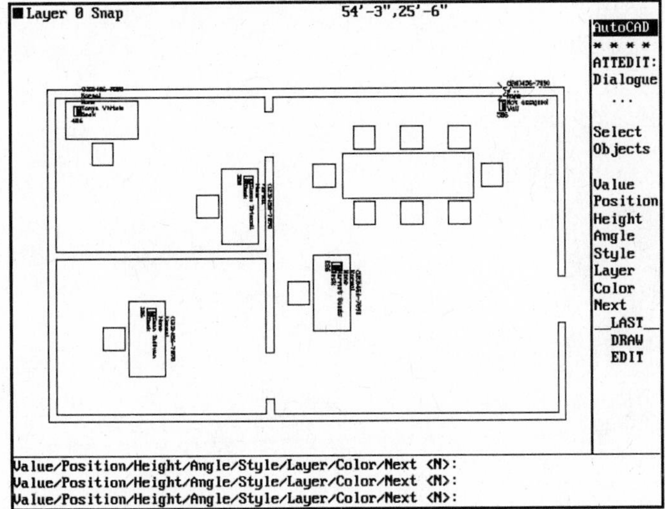

Figure 16.18:

Editing the wall phone by its tag.

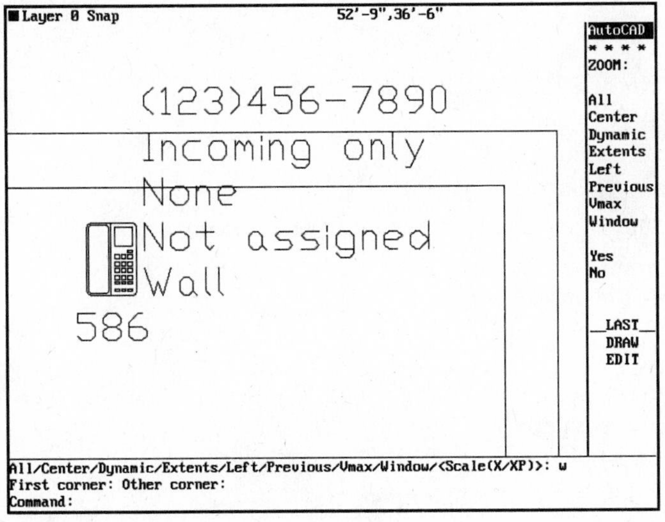

Figure 16.19:

A detail of the wall phone.

The preceding editing sequence is convenient if you are making selective changes to many attributes. If you have a change that applies to all or a filterable subset of a large group of attributes, however, you can use a global selection.

The following exercise shows you how to make a division-wide reorganization by changing the last two digits in all the telephone extensions from

"86" to "68". Use the default * wild card and a window to include all your telephone extensions.

Using ATTEDIT for a Global Edit

Command: **ATTEDIT**↵	
Edit attributes one at a time? <Y>: **N**	Edits all attributes globally
Global edit of Attribute values.	
Edit only Attributes visible on screen? <Y>: *Press Enter*	Specifies editing only attributes on-screen

Even though all the attributes are on-screen, you have the option to include those off-screen.

Block name specification <*>: *Press Enter*	
Attribute tag specification <*>: **EXTENSION**↵	Limits the selection to the specified tag
Attribute value specification <*>: *Press Enter*	
Select Attribute: *Select all the telephones by using a window*	
5 attribute selected.	
String to change: **586**↵	Old text string
New string: **568**↵	New text string

Zoom in to examine the wall phone (see fig. 16.20), then use the ZOOM Previous option to resume the previous view.

All your extensions now should end in 68. If you want to change all but the wall phone (extension 586), enter **~586** at the `Attribute value specification` prompt.

Using the Attribute Dialog Box To Edit Attributes

You can use the DDATTE dialog box to edit attributes. DDATTE presents the Edit Attributes dialog box, which is the same as the Enter Attributes dialog box that you used when you inserted the first PHONE blocks earlier in this chapter. You can edit the text string values of any number of attributes, but you can edit only the text string values of one block at a time. If you use a window selection, AutoCAD edits only the first block it finds.

In the following exercise, use the dialog box to edit two preset REMARKS attributes.

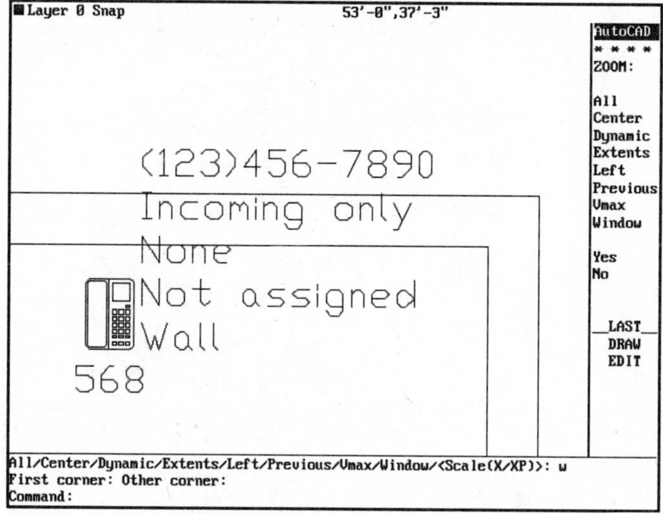

Figure 16.20:

A detail of the wall phone.

Using the DDATTE Dialog Box To Edit Attributes

`Command:` *From the screen menu, choose* EDIT, *then* DDATTE:	Issues the DDATTE command
`DDATTE Select block:` *Select the wall phone*	The Edit Attributes dialog box appears (see fig. 16.21)
Enter `Employee` *in the* Enter any remarks *input box*	Changes the attribute value
Choose OK	Closes the dialog box
`Command:` *Press Enter*	Repeats DDATTE

When the DDATTE `Select block:` prompt appears, select Susan's phone, and enter Answering machine in the Enter any remarks input box. When you are finished, choose OK.

Command: *From the screen menu, choose* DISPLAY, *then* ATTDISP:, *then* Normal	Sets ATTDISP back to normal
Command: **SAVE**↵	

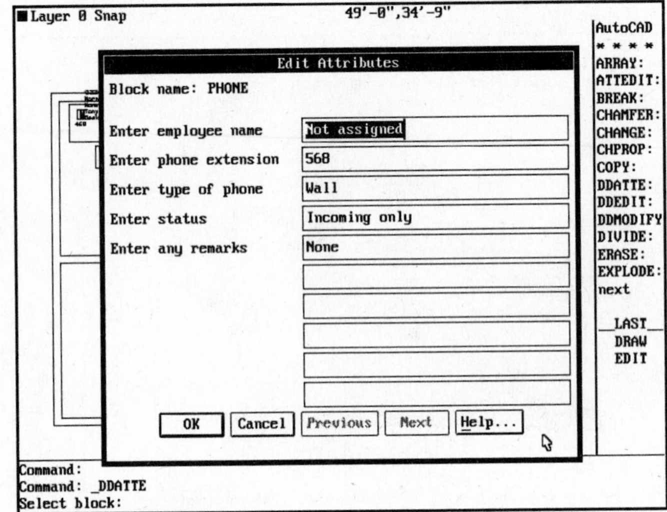

Figure 16.21:

Editing attributes by using the Edit Attributes dialog box.

Plotting the Office Drawing

If you want to see the way AutoCAD plots attributes, make a quick plot of your office plan. AutoCAD offers four ways to plot the drawing attribute data:

- Turn off all the attributes
- Plot the extension number, employee name and phone type (Normal)
- Plot the extension number only (layer 0)
- Turn on all the attributes

The next step is to extract the data to format a telephone report, similar to a simple telephone directory or part of an equipment report. You also use this office drawing in Part Two of the book, when you extrude it into a 3D drawing.

Using the ATTEXT Command To Extract Attributes

Although the ATTEXT command sounds like a text operation, it stands for ATTribute EXTraction. ATTEXT provides a way to extract attribute information from the drawing file and print that information in a text report. In addition to ATTEXT, there is another command, DDATTEXT, that performs the same function with the Attribute Extraction dialog box. DDATTEXT is used later in the chapter.

Setting Up an Attribute Report

When you set up the facility drawing earlier in the chapter, you listed in a simple table the data for the employee names, status, remarks, type, and extension for each of the five telephones. Similar kinds of tables form the basis for bills of materials (BOM), lists, schedules, and specifications that regularly accompany professional drawings. These tables organize the data scattered around drawing files.

Examining ATTEXT Formats

AutoCAD provides three ways to extract attribute values from a drawing file and format them in a disk file. You can print these lists or use the data in other programs, such as dBASE III or IV, Lotus 1-2-3, or a word processor. You also can put the list into a table and bring it back into your drawing. The following attribute extraction formats are templates that define the way the data is formatted in the extracted text file:

- **CDF (Comma Delimited Format).** CDF is easy to use with BASIC programs or with dBASE's "APPEND FROM . . . DELIMITED" operation. (See the following example.)
- **SDF (Standard Data Format).** SDF is for FORTRAN and other programs that read a dBASE "COPY . . . SDF" file, or a dBASE "APPEND FROM . . . SDF" operation. (See the following example.)
- **DXF (Drawing Interchange Format).** DXF is a subset of AutoCAD's full DXF file format that is used by many third-party programs.

You can extract data in any format that is suitable for your application. Many users (and vendors of third-party software) now have applications built around AutoCAD by using one or more of these data extraction interfaces.

Extracting Attribute Data Using CDF or SDF

CDF creates a file that has commas separating the data fields in the attribute extraction. The following is a simple example of a CDF format:

CDF Format

```
'Name1','Type1','Extension1'
'Name2','Type2','Extension2'
 ...
 ...
 ...
'Name9','Type9','Extension9'
'Name10','Type10','Extension10'
```

To format extract files, you need to place alphanumeric characters, commas, and spaces. In the CDF format, each data field is separated by a comma. The spacing of the data field is dependent on the data width in the field. `Name10` in the preceding example takes up more room than `Name9`.

The SDF format creates a file similar to CDF, but without commas and with a standard field length and spacing, as shown in the following list.

SDF Format

```
Name1       Type1  Extension1
Name2       Type2  Extension2
... ...     ...
... ...     ...
Name9       Type9  Extension9
Name10      Type10 Extension10
```

In SDF format, the data field length is standardized and preformatted to a standard value, regardless of the data value length. If the data exceeds the length, the data is truncated.

Creating an Attribute Report Template File

Before you can extract attributes, AutoCAD needs a template file to create the SDF or CDF file. The template file is a format instruction list that tells AutoCAD what to put where in the extract data file. The IA DISK contains a template file called PHONE.TXT. This file provides an SDF template for the telephone data. If you are using the disk, you can use this file to create the report.

If you are not using the disk, create the file as an ASCII text file by using EDLIN, EDIT (in DOS 5), Notepad, Write, or your word processor. Use spaces, not tabs. Make sure you end the last line of your file with a return character (↵). Also, make sure you do not have any extra spaces at the end of lines, or extra returns after the last line of text.

If you do not feel like making the file, just read through the next two exercises to understand the way a report is generated.

The following is the PHONE.TXT file format for your example telephone data. The template assumes that NAME comes first, TYPE second, and EXTENSION third. The NUMBER, STATUS, and REMARKS is not included in the report.

Creating an SDF Template File

Examine the PHONE.TXT file from the disk.

Use EDLIN, EDIT, or your word processor to create a plain ASCII file named PHONE.TXT with the following lines. Make sure you that end the last line by pressing Enter.

```
BL:NAME         C011000
BL:X            N006002
DUMMY1          C002000
BL:Y            N006002
DUMMY2          C002000
NAME            C015000
TYPE            C008000
EXTENSION       N005000
```

Type BL:NAME, not the actual block name

If you look at the right column, you can easily decipher the formatting information. The first C or N says this is a character or a number. The next three digits (011 in the BL:NAME line) tell the number of spaces to leave for the data. The final three digits specify the number of decimal places for floating point (decimal) numeric data. Integer data have 000 in the last three columns.

The BL:X and BL:Y are not blocks or attributes. They extract the X,Y coordinate values for the block.

DUMMY1 and DUMMY2 only appear in the template file. They are not blocks or attributes; they are used to provide space in the report. These dummy lines force a two-space blank between the X,Y coordinates (BL:X,BL:Y) and a two-space blank between the Y coordinate and the NAME, making the output easier to read.

Table 16.3 shows the complete list of the kinds of data that ATTEXT or DDATTEXT can extract.

Table 16.3
ATTEXT Template Fields

FIELD	*DATA TYPE*	*DESCRIPTION*	*FIELD*	*DATA TYPE*
BL:LEVEL	integer	Block nesting level	BL:XSCALE	decimal
BL:NAME	character	Block name	BL:YSCALE	decimal
BL:X	decimal	X insert coord	BL:ZSCALE	decimal
BL:Y	decimal	Y insert coord	BL:XEXTRUDE	decimal
BL:Z	decimal	Z insert coord	BL:YEXTRUDE	decimal
BL:NUMBER	integer	Block counter	BL:ZEXTRUDE	decimal
BL:HANDLE	character	Entity handle	*attribute*	integer
BL:LAYER	character	Insertion layer	*attribute*	character
BL:ORIENT	decimal	Rotation angle		

Integer fields are formatted Nwww000, floating point (decimal) fields are Nwwwddd, and character fields are Cwww000, in which www is overall width (such as 012 for 12 characters wide and 000 is 000) and ddd is the width to the right of the decimal point.

Extracting the Data File

After you have the template file, you can extract data for all or some of the attributes. If you have the PHONE.TXT file, switch to AutoCAD. Extract the attribute data into a file called PHN-DATA.

Using ATTEXT To Create an SDF Data File

`Command:` *From the screen menu, choose* UTILITY, *then* ATTEXT:	
`ATTEXT CDF, SDF, or DXF Attribute extract (or Entities) <C>:` **`S`**↵	Specifies a space-delimited file and displays the Select Template File dialog box
Select the file PHONE.TXT *in your* \IA *directory and choose* OK	Selects thetemplate and displays the Create Extract File dialog box
Enter **`PHN-DATA`** *in the* File Name *input box and choose* OK	Specifies the extract file name and saves the file to disk
`5 records in extract file.`	
`Command:` **`SAVE`**	

In the preceding exercise, if you enter an E for entities, AutoCAD prompts for object selection to extract data from specific blocks, and then prompts for CDF, SDF, or DXF.

Do not use the same name for your template file as that of your extract file, or the extract file overwrites the template.

The extracted SDF report file is shown in the following list. You can examine the file by using a text editor or your word processor. Take a look at your data text file.

SDF Report Example

PHONE	408.33	435.79	Not assigned	Wall	568
PHONE	60.00	441.00	Tonya Whiteis	Desk	468
PHONE	198.00	396.00	Harriet Sands	Desk	268
PHONE	303.00	318.00	Susan Driscoll	Desk	368
PHONE	123.00	294.00	Sean Sullivan	Desk	168

Notice that the extracted data gives useful spatial information about this drawing as well as the attribute data. The X and Y data fields give the X and Y insertion points of each PHONE block. Your X,Y fields can vary from the ones shown here, depending on where you insert the blocks. The PHONE column is set up to print the name of the block that acts as the attribute data source. The PHONE column has character data (see the C in the template) and an 11-character print width.

The next two columns give the X and Y locations of the block insertion point in numeric form (see N in the template). (Your data can vary from the example.) The X and Y data have two decimal places and the decimal point in a six-character print width. The X and Y fields and the employee name would all run together if the two-character dummy fields were not included. The other extracted attribute fields (a character field and a numeric field) are in the last two columns. If an employee's name is unusually long, you can see that the name would be truncated by the print width.

Redefining a Block with Attributes

Redefining a block without attributes is as simple as creating the geometry and using the BLOCK command. To redefine the attributes in a block, you can insert the block exploded, edit its attribute definitions, and then use BLOCK or the AutoLISP-defined ATTREDEF command to redefine it.

In this exercise, use DDEDIT to redefine the attribute REMARKS to BUILDING. Once this is done, use ATTREDEF to redefine the block and update the drawing.

Using DDEDIT To Edit an Attribute

`Command:` *Issue the ZOOM command and zoom to a Center point of 46',18' and a Height of 6'*	
`Command:` **`INSERT`**↵	
`Block name (or ?):` **`*PHONE`**↵	Specifies a * block
`Insertion point:` **`46',18'`**↵	
`Scale factor:` *Press Enter*	
`Rotation angle <0>:` *Press Enter*	Displays the block and attribute definitions

Use DDEDIT to change the values of the attribute definition.

`Command:` *From the screen menu, choose* EDIT, *then* DDEDIT:	Starts the DDEDIT command
`<Select a TEXT or ATTDEF object>/Undo:` *Select the attribute definition* REMARKS	Specifies the attribute definition to modify
Enter **`BUILDING`** *in the* Tag *input box*	Replaces REMARKS
Enter **`Enter building name`** *in the* Prompt *dialog box*	Specifies the new prompt
Enter **`Green Tree`** *in the* Default *dialog box*	Specifies the default value
Choose OK	Closes the dialog box and makes the changes (see fig. 16.22)

The ATTREDEF command is an AutoLISP program that must be loaded before use. You can load it from the File menu's Applications selection. Once loaded, you can modify the attributes associated with a block, redefine the block, and the entire drawing is updated.

Load the ATTREDEF command and redefine the phone block and associated attributes.

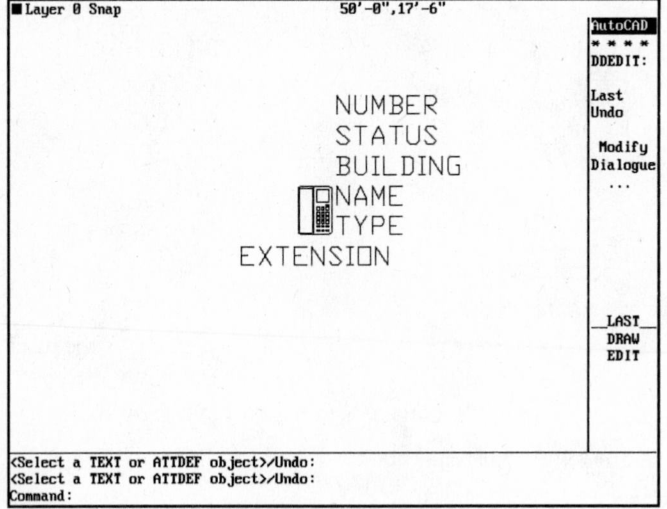

Figure 16.22: The redefined attribute definition.

Using ATTREDEF To Redefine Attributes in a Block

`Command:` *Choose* File, *then* Applications, *then* File	Displays the LISP/ADS dialog box
In the directories list, double-click on the \, *then* ACAD, *then* SAMPLE	Displays the files in the \ACAD\SAMPLE subdirectory
In the Files *list, double-click on* ATTREDEF, *then choose* Load	Loads the ATTREDEF command
`Command:` **`AT`** ↵	Starts the ATTREDEF command
`Name of Block you wish to redefine:` **`PHONE`** ↵	
`Select entities for new Block...`	
`Select objects:` *Select all the attribute definitions and the phone geometry*	Specifies the new block definition
`Select objects:` *Press Enter*	
`Insertion base point of new Block:` *Select the lower left corner of the phone*	
`Command:` *Issue the ZOOM command with the Previous option*	

The finished drawing should now look like figure 16.23. The attributes now display "Green Tree" instead of "None."

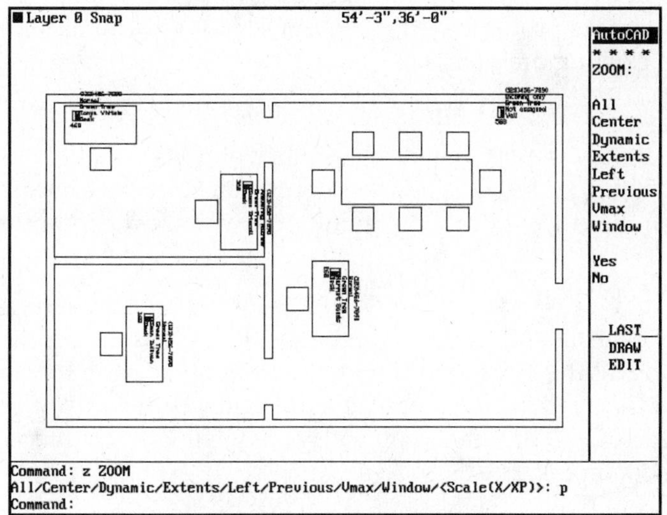

Figure 16.23:

The redefined blocks and attributes.

Attributes versus DXF, DXB, and IGES Drawing Data Exchange

AutoCAD provides additional methods for extracting spatial and graphic data from the drawing file. Block layers and block levels (levels of nesting for nested blocks, block rotation, and scale) are extractable. These spatial attributes are useful for handing off data to engineering programs in which the block orientation or relationship among drawing entities is as critical as the text or numeric data associated with the block.

DXF, AutoCAD's Drawing Interchange Format, is used in many add-on programs and for drawing file exchange. You use the DXFOUT command to extract the DXF file from a drawing. An ATTEXT DXF file includes only block reference and attribute information, but the DXFOUT command exports either the full drawing file or selected entities. A full DXFOUT creates a complete ASCII text description of the drawing. DXFOUT also

utilizes a binary option to create a more compact binary file for faster processing by sophisticated third-party programs.

The DXFIN command imports a DXF file. You can use DXFIN to import an entire drawing, but this requires a new drawing file, created by starting a new drawing with no prototype, such as *NAME* = ↵. You can use DXFIN to import into an existing drawing, but you get the following message:

```
Not a new drawing - only ENTITIES section will be input
```

In such a partial DXF import, data such as block definitions and layer information are not imported. A partial import functions the same as an insert, in which the current drawing definitions override the imported definitions.

The IGES format is another drawing exchange format. You get data in and out by using the Igesin and Igesout commands. IGES is not perfect, and you usually need to edit the resulting drawing. Igesout loses attribute definitions and solid fills, and 3D data may be represented differently. When you register your AutoCAD program, you receive a detailed IGES Interface Specifications document.

DXB, another file format used by AutoCAD, is a binary drawing file format. DXBIN imports binary drawing files. You can output a limited (everything converted to straight line segments) DXB format file by configuring the AutoCAD file output formats ADI driver and selecting AutoCAD DXB file as the output format.

To learn more about attributes, DXF, and other types of file processing with AutoCAD, see Chapter 18 and *Maximizing AutoCAD, Volume II*, from New Riders Publishing.

AutoCAD SQL Extension (ASE)

In addition to attributes, AutoCAD has a Structured Query Language (SQL) extension. Through the use of SQL, AutoCAD can directly pass information back and forth with a traditional relational database. This enables a direct linkage between the graphical information in AutoCAD and the non-graphical information in the relational database. This information need not be associated only with a block.

The advantage of this system is a smaller drawing, because the non-graphical information can be stored in the relational database. Information is shared directly between AutoCAD and the relational database, which increases speed, accuracy, and flexibility. Finally, an expansion in the type of data is enabled because the SQL extension can share any type of graphical data — not just that type stored in a block.

Summary

Attributes provide power and flexibility for annotating your drawings and producing reports. When you use attributes, you make AutoCAD manage both graphic and nongraphic information.

To better use and organize attributes, design your report formats before you define attributes. Develop a rough table to plan ahead for field name, size, and prompting. Good layout and design of attribute fields is critical to creating a useful attribute file. Test your extraction before you fill up your drawing with information in a format you cannot use.

Place your attribute definitions on different layers or create them with different colors to distinguish them from regular text. The names you use for tags are important; try to make them explanatory but also brief. The tag name is the default prompt when no other prompt is given, and it is used in attribute edits and extracts. Break your attribute data into useful fields. Use enough fields to capture all the variable information you need. Avoid fields that are filled with extra long strings of output.

ATTEDIT is an extremely flexible and powerful command. While you work with this command, make sure you check your results often. You can easily introduce an ATTEDIT error that creates global havoc. You can have AutoCAD prompt you for all the changes if you take advantage of grouping attributes by layer, tag name, and value.

Use attributes in place of normal text for standardized boilerplate entries and title blocks. Attributes offer more input control, automation, and sophisticated editing than regular text does.

This chapter has shown you how to do more with AutoCAD than just create and plot drawings. In the next chapter, you learn how to make the most of AutoCAD's dimensioning commands, as well as the important role that associative dimensions play in your design process.

17

Advanced Dimensioning

In Chapter 15, you learned to use AutoCAD's basic dimensioning commands to create linear and radial dimensions. Chapter 15 also introduced you to the use of dimension variables to control the appearance and other characteristics of dimensions.

Working with so many dimension variables, however, can be hard to control. This chapter teaches you how to control dimension variables by introducing you to AutoCAD's dimension styles.

You also learn how to use several advanced dimensioning commands that were not examined in Chapter 15. AutoCAD's commands for creating ordinate, baseline, and chain dimensions, among others, are covered in this chapter's exercises. Perhaps the most important topic in this chapter is the topic of associative dimensions. As you soon learn, *associative dimensions* enable you to update an object or feature while its associated dimensions automatically update to reflect the change as well.

You have several choices for accessing Dimensioning commands and variables. Pull-down menus and dialog boxes with easy-to-follow controls are available, but they require several steps to issue the commands and variables (see fig. 17.1). You also can use screen menus. Or if you know the command and variable names, you can enter them directly from the keyboard, abbreviating the commands if you like. The exercises in this chapter demonstrate all three methods; therefore, you can decide which method you prefer.

Before you begin using these new dimensioning commands, however, you should have a good understanding of dimension styles. The following discussion introduces you to this convenient AutoCAD feature.

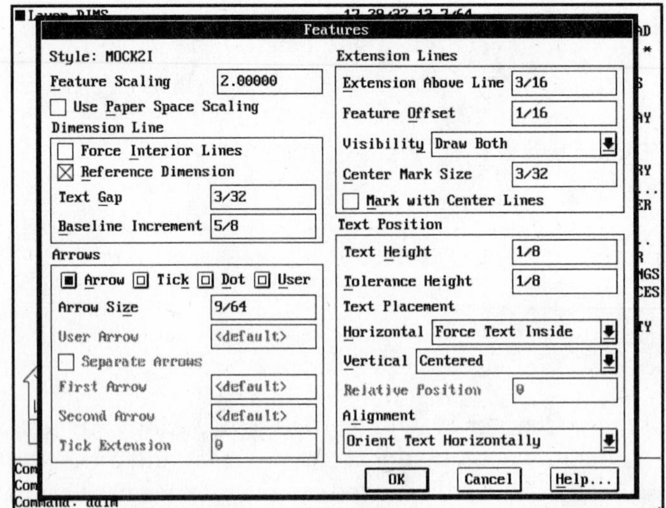

Figure 17.1:

One of AutoCAD's many dimensioning dialog boxes.

Saving Sets of Dimension Variables as Dimension Styles

Even with the help of dialog boxes, dimension variables can be a nuisance to set. Many effects you want to achieve do not depend on a single setting, but rather on many dimension variable settings working together. Remembering all of the combinations necessary for the variety of dimensioning in a typical drawing is difficult at best. Fortunately, the dimension settings in most drawings can be grouped into a few types. AutoCAD's dimension style feature enables you to save named sets of dimension variable settings. (All settings except DIMASO and DIMSHO are saved.) Using dimension styles enables you to easily save as many different groups of settings for as many types of dimensions as you need. You also can restore any style at will.

Furthermore, associative dimensioning saves dimension styles along with the dimension entities. This feature protects the style of the associative dimension from accidental changes while you edit the drawing. It also enables you to update a style simply by selecting a dimension entity that uses it. Associative dimensions are described in detail later in this chapter.

Because the next dimension exercise requires you to change a few dimension variables, save the current settings as a style.

When you save a style, you must assign it a name. The default style name is *UNNAMED, which is not saved in associative dimension entities. Any time you change a dimension variable, it creates a new *UNNAMED style. If you want the dimensions to be protected from change, always have a named style current when you create new dimensions. The easiest way to manage dimension styles is to use the Dimension Styles Variables dialog box. Use the DDIM command or choose Settings, then Dimension Variables to display it.

In the following exercise, load the MOCKDIM drawing you created at the end of Chapter 15, then save the current settings as a style named MOCK2I (2 for half scale, I for Inside text because DIMSCALE and DIMTIX were the only significant deviations from the defaults). If you have not yet created MOCKDIM, but you have the IA DISK, you only need to perform the last exercise in Chapter 15 to create it.

Saving the Current Dimension Variables as Dimension Style MOCK2I

Start AutoCAD by using the IA.BAT batch program.

`Command:` *Enter* `OPEN`, *then enter* `MOCKDIM`	Loads the drawing MOCKDIM
`Command:` *Choose* Settings, *then* Dimension Style	Issues DDIM, which displays the Dimension Styles and Variables dialog box
In the Dimension Style *edit box, enter* `MOCK2I`	Assigns a name to the current settings and creates a style

The message `New style MOCK2I created from *UNNAMED` appears at the bottom of the dialog box when you press Enter, and the new style name appears in the list box in place of *UNNAMED.

Choose OK	Closes the dialog box
`Command: QSAVE ↵`	Saves the drawing with the name MOCKDIM

Dimension styles are that easy to save. When a new style is named, its settings are the same as the current one until some changes are made in the dimension variables. Do not, however, confuse the dimension mode SAVE style command with the drawing SAVE command.

Dimension styles are restored by the Restore dimensioning command or through the Dimension Styles and Variables dialog box. You define and save styles within the drawing, not as separate files on disk such as you do with text fonts or linetypes. Later in this chapter, however, you learn how to save dimension styles within drawing files that you can use as dimension style storage files.

Creating a Dimension Style for Paper Space Dimensioning

Sometimes you may want to dimension objects in a model space viewport while you are preparing to plot in paper space. Most of the preparation is the same as in the plotting chapter in which you composed a paper space plot sheet. You learned to set up the viewport and scale its contents relative to the paper space sheet with Zoom XP.

One disadvantage of dimensioning in paper space versus an mview viewport or tilemode is that associative dimensions are not tied to the model space objects and not automatically updated when the drawing is edited.

Two features make dimensioning model space objects from paper space possible. First, you can snap to model space from paper space by using object snap. Second, a special feature of the DIMLFAC dimension variable also adjusts the dimensions measured in model space to the scale factor of

the viewport. DIMLFAC is a factor by which all measurements are multiplied before dimension text is generated. This global scale factor enables dimensioning at scales other than the current units. Usually this factor is set to 1. If DIMLFAC is set to a negative value, it multiplies all paper space dimensions by the absolute value of that value. (Model space dimensioning ignores a negative setting and uses 1, so you do not have to create a separate dimension style for this purpose.) To simplify setting for paper space, the DIMLFAC dimension variable enables you to select a viewport, and then it calculates the value for you.

The following exercise sets up an mview viewport for dimensioning the section view of MOCKDIM from paper space.

Setting Up for Paper Space Dimensioning

`Command:` *Choose* View, *then* Tilemode, *then* Off (0)	Turns TILEMODE off and enters paper space
`Command:` *From the screen menu, choose* MVIEW, *then* MVIEW:	
`ON/OFF/Hideplot/Fit/2/3/4/Restore/ <First Point>:` *Pick points 3,2 and 10,8*	Defines a viewport and displays the drawing
`Command:` **`MS`** ↵	Enters model space
`Command:` *Select the 3 1/32 rotated dimension, then enter the ERASE command*	Erases the dimension
`Command:` *Use ZOOM and enter a zoom scale factor of* **`.5XP`**	Zooms the image to half-scale relative to paper space
`Command:` *Choose* View, *then* Pan, *and pan from far right to far left to match figure 17.2*	
`Command:` *Choose* Settings, *then* Layer Control, *create a new layer named PSDIMS with color magenta, and make it current*	
Deselect PSDIMS *and select* DIMS *in the* list *box, and click on Cur VP* Frz, *then choose* OK	Freezes DIMS in the current viewport

Command: `DDIM`↵	Displays the Dimension Styles and Variables dialog box
Click on MOCK2I *in the list box*	Selects the MOCK2I style
Choose Text Format, *double-click in the* Length <u>S</u>caling *edit box, and enter* `2`	Displays the Text Format dialog box and sets the inverse of .5 ZOOM XP factor
Choose OK *twice*	Closes the dialog box and saves changes as MOCK2I
Command: `PS`↵	Enters paper space

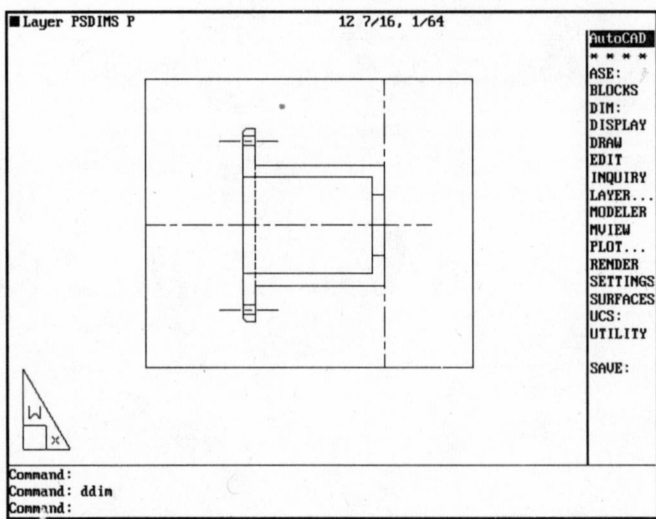

Figure 17.2:

An mview viewport set up for paper space dimensioning.

Affecting Styles with Dimension Variables Changes

If you change any dimension variable at the `Command:` or `Dim:` prompts, a new *UNNAMED style is created. Any change made in the Dimension Styles and Variables dialog box (the DDIM command), however, changes

the settings of the currently selected style. Unfortunately, this makes it difficult to use the dialog box when you want to make only a couple of variable changes to apply to only one or two dimensions. When you create a new style with the dialog box, it inherits the settings of the previously current style, and you can then make changes to that new style. However, you may not want to create a new style each time you encounter such a situation. The solution is to apply the current settings to a new *UNNAMED style.

In the DDIM dialog box, to create a new *UNNAMED style, select the style which you want to base it, make the settings changes you want, and exit the dialog box by choosing OK. The selected style's dimensions are updated, but you then use the U (Undo) command to reverse that update. Fortunately, the settings changes you made in the dialog box are not undone in the resulting *UNNAMED style, which is now current. See the "Overriding a Dimension Style" exercise for an example.

Placing Ordinate Dimensions

Now you are ready to create some ordinate dimensions of the section. *Ordinate dimensions* (sometimes called *datum dimensions*) are a series of dimensions that are offset from a common base point, without dimension lines. They have only one extension line — a leader on which the dimension text is placed. The dimension text is always aligned with the leader, regardless of the values of the dimension variables DIMTIH and DIMTOH. Ordinate dimensions measure the X datum or Y datum of the point you specify from the current 0,0 origin. Use UCS to place the current origin at the desired base point and object snap to ensure accurate datum points. Use ortho to ensure straight leader lines. Otherwise, if you pick a point for the end of the leader that is not in line with the dimension point, AutoCAD draws an offset line or "dogleg" as the leader. Doglegs can be useful, however, for avoiding overlapping dimension text in closely spaced dimensions.

In the following exercise, enter paper space and add a few ordinate dimensions to the section view. Set the UCS, using XYZ point filters to get the bottom left corner at the chamfer. Pick all the dimension leader end points so that they line up. Turn ortho off for the last dimension, however, to keep it clear of the top one.

Placing Ordinate Dimensions

Issue ZOOM with the Extents option to fill paper space with the viewport

`Command:` *Choose* Settings, *then* Drawing Aids, *set snap to 1/8, and turn it on, then turn on* Ortho, *and choose OK*

`Command:` *Choose* Settings, *then* UCS, *then* Icon, *and then* Origin — Sets UCSICON to ORigin

`Command:` *Choose* Settings, *then* UCS, *then* Origin — Issues the UCS Origin prompt

`Origin point <0,0,0>: .X↵` — Specifies an X filter
`of` *Use the INT object snap to pick at* ① *(see fig.17.3)*

`(need YZ):` *Use the INT object snap to pick a point at the bottom* right *of the section* — Moves the UCS to the corner (see fig. 17.3)

`Command:` *Choose* Draw, *then* Dimensions, *then* Ordinate, *then* Y-Datum — Enters dimensioning mode and issues the ORDINATE command with the Y-datum option

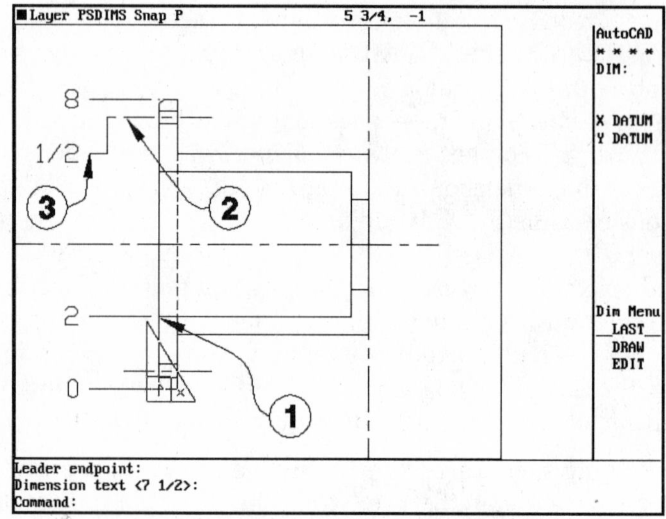

Figure 17.3:
Ordinate dimensions in paper space.

`Dim: _ordinate`	
`Select Feature:` **`0,0`**↵	Dimensions the UCS origin
`Leader endpoint (Xdaturm/Ydatum): -Y`	The menu issues the Y option
`Leader endpoint:` *Pick at @1<180*	Locates the end of the dimension leader
`Dimension text <0>:` *Press Enter*	Places the dimension
`Command:` *Choose* Draw, *then* Dimensions, *then* Ordinate, *then* Y-Datum	
`Select Feature:` *From the pop-up menu, choose* Intersection, *then pick at* ①	
`Leader endpoint:` *Pick at @1<180*	Locates the end of the dimension leader
`Dimension text <2>:` *Press Enter*	
`Command:` **`DIM`**↵	
`Dim:` **`ORD`**↵	
`Select Feature:` *From the pop-up menu, choose* Filters, *and then* .X	
`.X of` *From the pop-up menu, choose* Intersection, *then pick at point* ①	
`(need YZ):` *From the pop-up menu, choose* Endpoint, *and pick a point on the top edge of the flange*	
`Leader endpoint (Xdatum/Ydatum):` **`Y`**↵	Specifies the Y datum option
`Leader endpoint:` *Pick at @1<180*	Locates the leader's end point
`Dimension text <8>:` *Press Enter*	Places the dimension
Turn ORTHO off	
`Dim:` *Press Enter*	Repeats the ORDINATE command
`Select Feature:` *From the pop-up menu, choose* Endpoint, *then pick at* ②	
`Leader endpoint (Xdatum/Ydatum):` **`Y`**↵	
`Leader endpoint` *Pick at point* ③	Specifies the offset point
`Dimension text <7 1/2>:` *Press Enter*	
Turn ORTHO back on	
`Dim:` **`E`**↵	

AutoCAD rounds off the angle between the first and second points in 90-degree increments to determine whether to calculate the X datum or Y datum in the Automatic mode. The Xdatum and Ydatum options of ORDINATE enable you to override AutoCAD and specify whether you want an X coordinate or a Y coordinate.

Although the preceding exercises required you to dimension in paper space, you dimension more often in model space.

Dimensioning the Section View in Model Space

When dimensioning in model space, you must be sure that DIMSCALE is appropriately set for the final plotting scale. The point of composing a drawing in a paper space sheet is to plot the sheet at full scale. Composing the sheet before dimensioning can set DIMSCALE relative to paper space scale. When you set DIMSCALE to 0, it calculates an appropriate scale value relative to the scale of the current viewport in paper space. This value is the inverse of the Zoom XP scale value used for that viewport. When you are in paper space, or using TILEMODE viewports, the 0 setting is ignored and treated as if set to 1.

The following exercise sets up a viewport and uses DIMSCALE to scale the dimensions. Create and zoom the viewport for half scale. Set two other dimension variables to get the dimension appearance you want. Figure 17.4 shows that the 1" and 1/2" dimensions at the bottom of the view have no text or dimension lines between the extension lines. You need to turn off DIMTIX and DIMTOFL to allow the text outside and to suppress the inside dimension line. Save the changes as a new dimension style named MOCK2O (2 for 1/2 scale and the letter O for Outside text and dimension lines). Use the dialog boxes or enter the dimension variables at the dimension mode prompt.

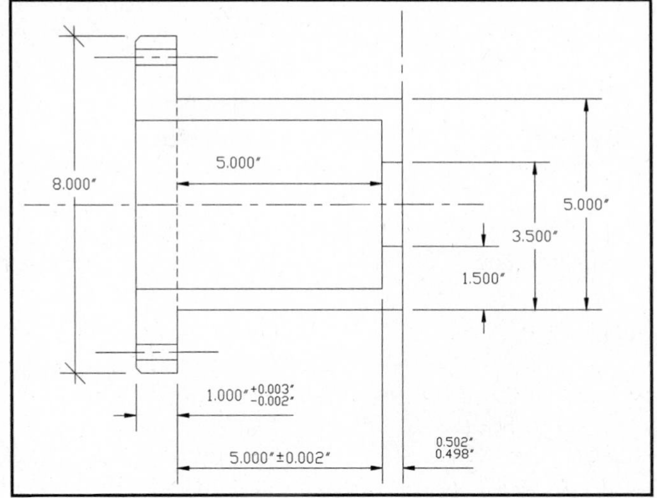

Figure 17.4:

The MOCKDIM section view target drawing.

Setting Up for Dimensioning the Section View in Model Space

`Command:` *Select the viewport border and dimensions, then enter the ERASE command*	Clears the drawing area
`Command:` *Choose* Settings, *then* UCS, *then* Named UCS, *click on* *WORLD*, *then* Current, *and then* OK	Sets the UCS to World
Make DIMS the current layer	
`Command:` *Choose* View, *then* Mview, *and then* Create Viewport	
`ON/OFF/Hideplot/Fit/2/3/4/Restore/ <First Point>:` *Pick or enter* `.5,.5` *and* `12,8`	Creates a new viewport
Issue ZOOM with the Extents option	
`Command:` *Choose* View, *then* Model space	Enters model space
Command: *Enter* Z, *then enter* .5XP	Zooms image half scale relative to paper space
Pan to the view shown in figure 17.5	

`Command:` **`PS`**↵	Switches to paper space
`Command:` *Choose* Settings, *then* Dimension Style	Opens the Dimension Styles and Variables dialog box
In the **D**imension Style *edit* box, *enter* `MOCK2O` *(enter the letter O, not zero)*	Creates a new style MOCK2O from MOCK2I
Choose **T**ext Location, *then open the* **H**orizontal *drop-down list box,* and *select* Default	Turns on DIMTOH
Verify that A**l**ignment *is set to* Orient Text Horizontally	Turns off DIMTIX
Clear the Use **P**aper Space Scaling *check box, double-click in the* **F**eature Scaling *edit box, and enter* 2, *then choose* OK	Sets DIMSCALE to 2
Choose Text **F**ormat, *double-click in the* Length **S**caling *edit box, enter* `1`, *then choose* OK	Sets linear scaling for model space (DIMLFAC=1)
Choose OK	Saves the new style as MOCK2O
`Command:` **`MS`**↵	Enters model space
Save the drawing	

Figure 17.5 shows the completed setup.

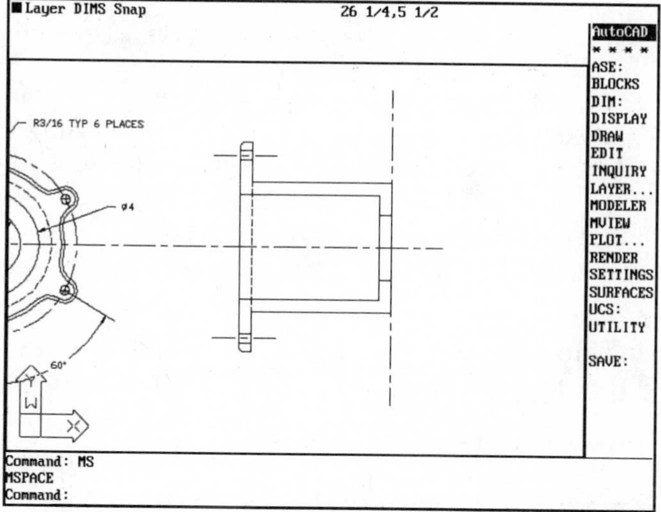

Figure 17.5:

The viewport, ready to dimension.

Even though you only changed three dimension variables, including DIMSCALE, the last exercise is a typical example of modifying a dimension style to create a new one. The DIMSCALE 0 setting for model space dimensioning and the earlier DIMLFAC 2 setting for paper space dimensioning are compatible — this style can now be used for either.

If you need to zoom an image, do not zoom in model space. This action throws off the DIMSCALE sizing of the dimension relative to paper space. Instead, use PAN, or enter paper space and zoom, then re-enter model space.

Take another look at figure 17.4. The linear dimensions along the bottom form a set of continuing dimensions; the dimensions on the right are baseline dimensions.

Dimensioning with Continued Dimensions

Begin with a normal linear dimension. Then use the Continue command to string subsequent dimensions together in a series. Continue begins each new dimension line where the last dimension line left off. Continue uses the previous extension line as the first extension line for the new dimension. If the dimension line needs room to clear the last text, Continue offsets the new dimension line by the DIMDLI value. You previously set DIMDLI to 5/8.

In the following exercise, you draw a horizontal dimension (see fig. 17.6) along the bottom of the section view and continue by adding new extension lines (to the right). Remember to use object snaps to ensure accuracy.

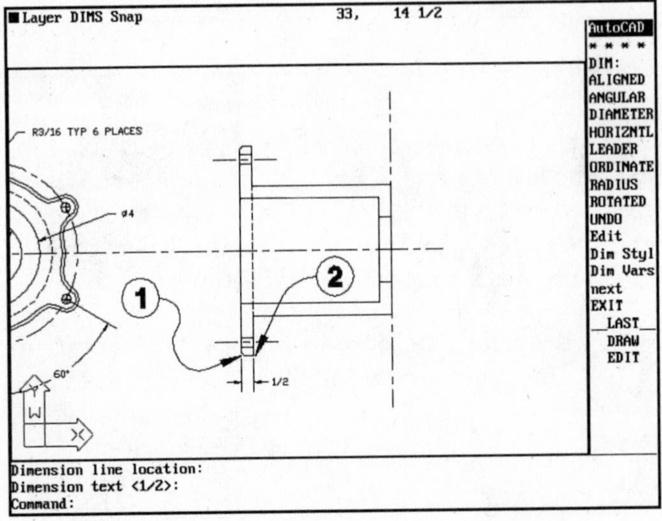

Figure 17.6:

The first horizontal dimension.

Using HORIZONTAL CONTINUE Dimensions

Make sure that you are in model space

`Command:` *Choose* Draw, *then* Dimensions, *then* Linear, *then* Horizontal	Enters dimensioning mode and issues the Horizontal command
`Command: _DIM1`↵	
`Dim: _horizontal`	
`First extension line origin or RETURN to select:` *With snap on, pick at ① (see fig. 17.6)*	
`Second extension line origin:` *Pick at ②*	
`Dimension line location:` *Pick point 21,8*	
`Dimension text <1/2>:` *Press Enter*	Accepts the default dimension text
`Command:` *From the screen menu, choose* DIM:, *then* next, then CONTINUE	Re-enters dimension mode and issues CONTINUE
`Dim: _CONTINUE`	
`Second extension line origin or RETURN to select:` *Pick point at ③ (see fig. 17.7)*	
`Dimension text <5>:` *Press Enter*	Accepts the text
`Dim:` *Press Enter*	Repeats CONTINUE
`_CONTINUE`	
`Second extension line origin or RETURN to select:` *Pick point at ④ and press Enter*	Draws the dimension with default text

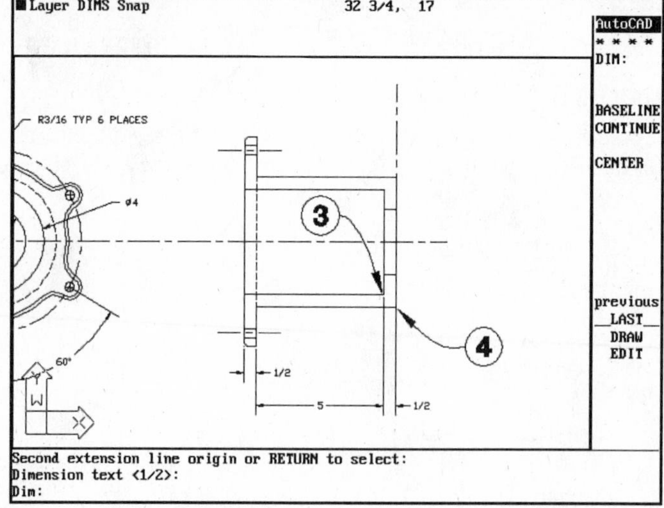

Figure 17.7:

The continued horizontal dimensions.

AutoCAD put the text "1/2" from the first dimension outside the extension line because it could not fit into the dimensioned space. To place the text on the left side, just reverse the pick order of the two points.

AutoCAD automatically placed the continued dimension line below the first one. The distance between the two dimension lines is controlled by DIMDLI. If the first horizontal dimension, 1/2, had been drawn right to left, its text would have been on the left and all three dimension lines would have been drawn aligned with each other.

By default, CONTINUE strings dimensions from the last linear dimension drawn in the current drawing session. The RETURN to select option enables you to select an existing linear dimension from which to continue.

A series of vertical baseline dimensions is next. Like continued dimensions, baseline dimensions begin from an existing linear dimension. You need a normal vertical dimension to begin with, but if you use the current dimension style as it is, it puts the text outside the extension lines (see fig. 17.8). Therefore, restore and redefine the MOCK2I dimension style in the following exercise, change DIMSCALE to 0 for model space, and save it. Use the MOCK2I dimension style because it turns on DIMTIX, forcing AutoCAD to place the dimension text within the dimension lines. Then, turn DIMTOFL off to avoid drawing a dimension line through the text. Update MOCK2I's DIMSCALE to 0 for model space scaling to paper space.

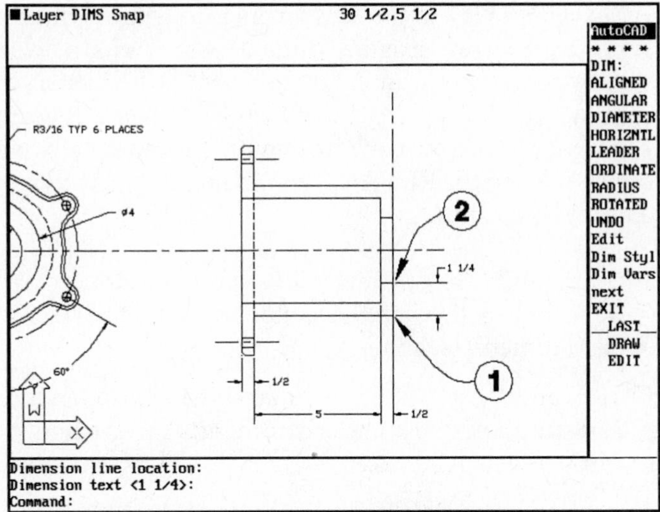

Figure 17.8:

The vertical dimension with DIMTIX off.

Restoring, Redefining, and Examining Existing Dimension Styles

The primary dimension commands for working with existing dimension styles are SAVE, RESTORE, and VARIABLES. (The UPDATE and OVERRIDE commands are examined in the associative dimensioning section of this chapter.) The SAVE command saves changes you make to a style, redefining it.

Use caution when using the DDIM or SAVE commands to redefine an existing dimension style; this process changes every existing dimension entity in the drawing by using that style.

The RESTORE command changes the current dimension style to a previously saved style. Enter a dimension style name to restore or press Enter to adopt the dimension style of an existing dimension entity that you choose.

An excellent way to prevent errors is to restore dimension styles by selecting existing dimensions — what you see is what you get. You can enter the DIMSTYLE system variable as a command to see what the current style name is, but you cannot change it that way. You can, however, rename an existing dimension style by using the RENAME command. (RENAME is not a dimension mode command.)

The VARIABLES command lists the dimension variable settings of any saved dimension style. It lists them in the same format that STATUS lists the settings of the current dimension style.

The SAVE, RESTORE, and VARIABLES commands each have an inquiry option. If you enter a question mark, these commands list existing style names. Use wild cards to list all styles.

In the following exercise, you use RESTORE to reload the MOCK2I dimension style and adjust its DIMSCALE and DIMTIX settings. Remember, a change to any dimension variable changes the current dimension style to *UNNAMED, so use SAVE to redefine MOCK2I and make it the current style before you use it.

Restoring and Redefining a Dimension style

`Dim:` *Choose* Settings, *then* Dimension Style	Opens the Dimension Styles and Variables dialog box
Click on MOCK2I *in the list box*	Selects MOCK2I
Choose **F**eatures, *then put a check mark in the* Use Paper Space Scaling *check box, then clear the* Force **A**nterior Lines *check box, and choose* OK	Effectively sets DIMSCALE to 0 and turns DIMTOFL off
Choose Text F**o**rmat, *then double-click in* Length **S**caling *edit box, enter* `1`, *then choose OK*	
Choose OK	Saves the changes to the style MOCK2I

Now the vertical dimension fits within the extension lines when you create it in the next exercise.

Just as you create a library of blocks, you can create a library of dimension styles. AutoCAD provides two ways to save dimension styles and reload them from separate disk files. One way is to define all of the dimension styles you need in a prototype drawing. Then, when you begin new drawings equal to the prototype (*newname=prototypename*) or set it as the default prototype with the AutoCAD configuration menu, new drawings already contain those dimension styles.

The other method is to create a drawing file containing one or more dimension styles and insert them as blocks into any drawing where you need to use those styles. You can accomplish this in several ways. Use the WBLOCK command to save the dimension entities with those styles to a new file. Then insert it as a block, but cancel the insertion before the entities themselves become part of the drawing. Or, define the styles in an empty drawing and insert it without needing to cancel it. You also can create a style-laden empty drawing by erasing dimension entities from a drawing created with WBLOCK. In any case, the insertion makes any dimension styles in the inserted file a part of the current drawing.

Dimensioning with Baseline Dimensions

Now you can draw the first vertical dimension line (see fig. 17.9), and use the BASELINE command to continue it. BASELINE is a cross between continuous and ordinate dimensioning. It works like CONTINUE, except that it uses the first extension line (base extension line) as the origin for all successive dimension calculations and line placements. Each successive dimension line is offset by the DIMDLI setting.

In previous exercises, you used snap to locate your dimension points. While this works, it is a good habit to use object snaps instead to ensure that you select the exact points for the dimensions. In the rest of the exercises, you turn snap off and use object snaps to locate your points.

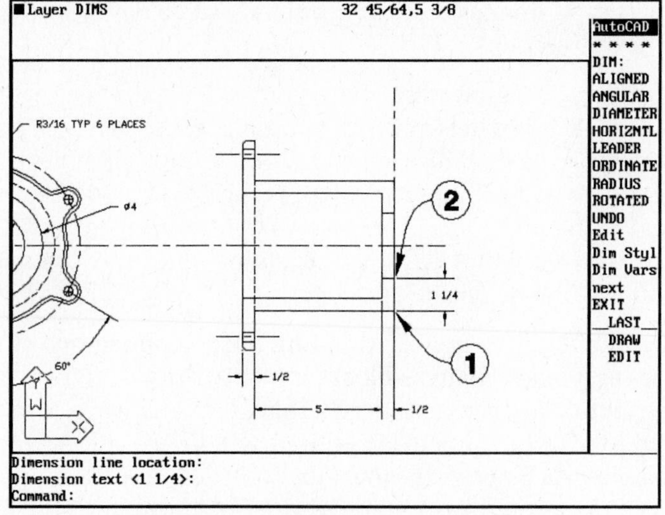

Figure 17.9:

The first vertical dimension for BASELINE.

Using BASELINE for a Series of Vertical Dimensions

`Command:` *Turn off snap and ortho*

`Command:` *Choose* Draw, *then* Dimensions, *then* Linear, *then* Vertical — Enters dimensioning mode and issues the VERTICAL command

`Dim: _vertical`

`First extension line origin or RETURN to select:` *From the pop-up menu, choose* Intersection, *then pick corner at* ① *(see fig. 17.9)*

`Second extension line origin:` *From the pop-up menu, choose* Intersection, *then pick corner at* ②

Dimension line location: 28,11 ↵

`Dimension text <1 1/4>:` *Press Enter* — Places the text inside the dimension line

`Command:` *From the screen menu, choose* DIM:, *then* next, *then* Baseline — Issues the BASELINE command

`Dim: _BASELINE`

`Second extension line origin or RETURN to select:` *With object snap INT, pick corner at ③ (see fig. 17.10)*	Sets the origin point
`Dimension text <3 3/4>:` *Press Enter*	Accepts the text and draws the dimension
`Dim:` *Press Enter*	Repeats BASELINE
`_BASELINE`	
`Second extension line origin or RETURN to select:` *With object snap INT, pick at ④ and press Enter*	Sets point, accepts text, and draws dimension
`Dim:` **E** ↵	Exits dimensioning
Save the drawing	

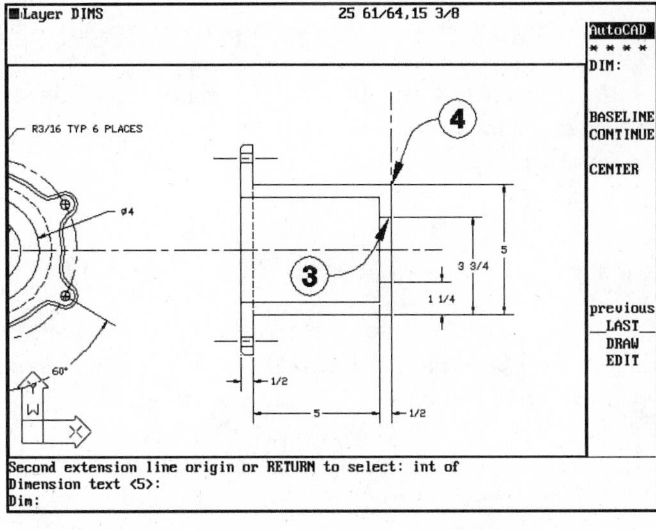

Figure 17.10:

Vertical dimensions after BASELINE.

In the next set of exercises, you stretch, scale, and update the drawing. You also use two more dimension variables to add inch tick marks to the dimension text and to increase the extension line offset.

Appending a Units Suffix to Dimension Text

If you look closely at the current drawing, you see that the dimension text does not show any units. You are using the multipurpose fractional style of units. You can set an automatic dimension suffix with DIMPOST to append any text character or string to dimensions. You set it to a period to clear the suffix. Commonly used suffixes or prefixes include ', ", cm, fathoms, R (radius), or the diameter symbol. The next exercise shows you how to add inch marks to the dimension text.

Add a suffix, prefix, or both by typing custom characters before or after < > at the dimension text prompt. AutoCAD inserts the characters and replaces < > with its calculated text. See Chapter 15 for details on using this feature.

Controlling Extension Line Offset from Objects

When you are setting dimension variables in the next exercise, reset DIMEXO to increase the offset for extension lines. The default 1/16 is too small to clearly separate extension lines from objects.

The Efficiency of Dimension Styles

It might seem that dimension styles add more work to dimensioning. Why not just set the dimension variables and be done with it? That might be easier for a few dimensions. But when you create several types of dimensions over and over, you are constantly resetting dimension variables as you switch between types. With dimension styles, you can just restore the style to switch between types instead of resetting several dimension variables. Overall, dimension styles are faster and easier — well worth the time it takes to set them up.

You have already created associative dimensions whether you knew it or not. In the next section, you use the MOCKDIM drawing to take a closer look. You also learn how to tailor them further by including tolerances, changing the terminator (arrow) type, and editing the characteristics of existing dimensions.

Understanding Associative Dimensions

An associative dimension is a single entity that is linked to the dimensioned entity. As you move, scale, and stretch the dimensioned entity, the associative dimension moves, scales, or stretches as well. The associated dimension's text also adjusts automatically. Associative dimensioning is the default dimensioning mode. If the DIMASO dimension variable is on, AutoCAD creates associative dimensions (except for leader dimensions, which are always individual entities). If DIMASO is off, AutoCAD draws dimensions with individual lines, arrows (solids), arcs, and text entities. DIMASO is on by default.

An associative dimension is a special kind of unnamed block. Exploding an associative dimension creates individual lines, arrows (solids), arcs, and text entities that look the same as the associative dimension block. Individual components of associative dimensions can only be edited with special associative dimensioning commands or by STRETCH. Of course, exploded associative dimensions or dimensions created with DIMASO off can be edited as ordinary entities.

The dimension style name that is current when an associative dimension entity is created is stored with it. If it is a named dimension style, the associative dimension is protected from any subsequent changes to dimension variables (unless the dimension style is redefined). If the current dimension style is *UNNAMED, any associative dimensions change to assume the current dimension style, text style, and units settings, which is usually not wanted. Accidental updates to associative dimensions occur easily with the STRETCH or SCALE commands as well as several dimensioning commands. To protect the integrity of the dimensions, be sure a named dimension style is current whenever you create a new dimension.

AutoCAD has no dimension variables to control associative dimensions. Use the normal AutoCAD UNITS command to set units and the dimension mode STYLE command or the normal AutoCAD STYLE command to set text style. The dimension mode STYLE command is limited to setting styles; it cannot define a style.

A named dimension style does not protect the text style or units from accidental updating. The safest method is to limit the dimensions to a single text style. If you need more than one type of unit, keep one type set with the UNITS command and create the other(s) with the dimension variables DIMALT, DIMALTD, DIMALTF, DIMPOST, and DIMLFAC.

Associative dimensioning creates *definition points*. Associative dimensions use these points to control their rescaling and updating. Definition points are kept on a special layer called DEFPOINTS. They do not plot but are always visible when the dimension is visible. Exploding an associative dimension converts definition points to point entities on layer DEFPOINTS. The point locations vary with the type of dimension. For linear dimensions, there is one at each extension line origin and one at the dimension line intersection with the second extension line. You can snap to definition points with object snap NODe, even though layer DEFPOINTS is frozen. You also can use object snap NODe to snap to the midpoint of the associative dimension text, although it is not a true definition point.

Subentities of associative dimensions respond to the object snap modes just like subentities of ordinary blocks. You can snap, for example, to the end of a dimension arrow by using the ENDPoint object snap.

Using Associative Dimensions

Associative dimensions make it easy to update and rescale a fully dimensioned drawing. In the following exercises, you learn three ways to use associative dimensions: to update dimension variables, including redefining and reassigning dimension styles; to stretch dimensions to relocate dimension text; and to stretch and rescale drawing entities and their associated dimensions to automatically update measurements.

Associative Dimensioning Commands

AutoCAD offers the following seven dimensioning commands for editing existing associative dimensions:

- **HOMETEXT.** This command restores text of selected associative dimensions to its default (home) position.
- **UPDATE.** This command reformats selected associative dimensions to the current dimension style.
- **NEWTEXT.** This command enables editing of associative dimension text or restoration of the default measurement as text.
- **OBLIQUE.** This command changes extension lines of selected associative dimensions to an oblique angle.

- **OVERRIDE.** This command changes one or more dimension variable settings of the current dimension style and applies them to one or more selected associative dimensions as dimension style *UNNAMED.
- **TEDIT.** This command changes the position or rotation of selected dimension text.
- **TROTATE.** This command changes the rotation of selected dimension text.

Updating Associative Dimensions

The UPDATE command changes selected associative dimensions by applying the current dimension style, text style, and units settings to them. Be sure a current named dimension style exists before using UPDATE, or the associative dimension adopts an *UNNAMED dimension style. All non-associative dimension entities are ignored even if they are part of the selection set, so window and crossing selections are easy and convenient.

Update all the associative dimensions in the following exercise with new DIMPOST and DIMEXO settings. For simplicity, return to a single TILEMODE viewport and reset DIMSCALE to 2. Update the current MOCK2I dimension style, and then repeat the process for MOCK2O.

Updating Dimensions with Suffix Text and Increased Extension Line Origin Offsets

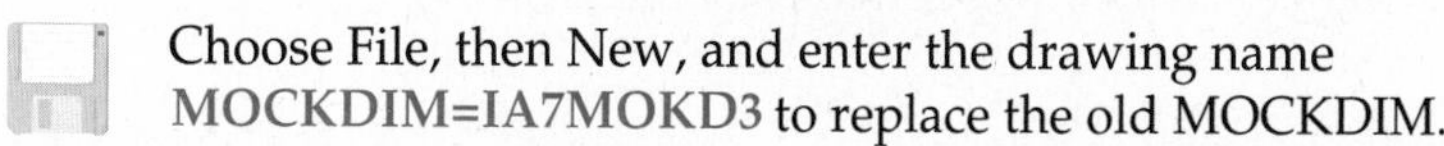
Choose File, then New, and enter the drawing name MOCKDIM=IA7MOKD3 to replace the old MOCKDIM.

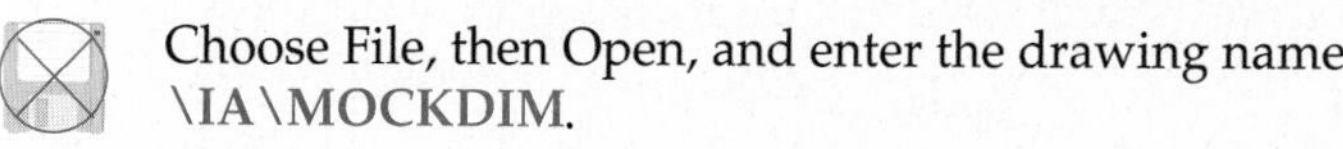
Choose File, then Open, and enter the drawing name \IA\MOCKDIM.

`Command:` **`TILEMODE`**↵	
`New value for TILEMODE <0>:` **`1`**↵	Returns to a single tiled viewport (see fig. 17.11)
Issue ZOOM with the Extents option	
`Command:` *Choose* Settings, *then* Dimension Style	Opens the Dimension Styles and Variables dialog box
Select MOCK2I in the list box	Makes MOCK2I the current style

Choose **E**xtension Lines, *double-click in the* Feature **O**ffset *edit box, enter* `1/8`, *then choose* OK	Sets DIMEXO to 1/8"
Choose Text **F**ormat, *double-click in the* Text **S**uffix *edit box, and enter* `"`, *then choose* OK	Sets DIMPOST to "
Choose **F**eatures, *clear the* Use Paper Space Scaling *check box, double-click in the* **F**eature Scaling *edit box, enter* `2`, *then choose* OK	Sets DIMSCALE to 2
Choose OK	Saves the changes as MOCK2I

The vertical and baseline associative dimensions with the MOCK2I style are immediately redefined with added " and larger offsets.

`Command:` *Choose* Modify, *then* Edit Dims, *then* Update Dimension	Enters dimension mode and issues the UPDATE command
`Dim: _update`	
`Select objects:` *Select all dimensions in the flange top view, but not those in section, then press Enter*	Updates the dimensions in the top view

The dimension entities are redefined to the MOCK2I style, adding " and increasing offsets. Any other entities are ignored. The drawing's continued dimensions still need to be updated; MOCK2I style, however, is unsuitable for the *"R3/16" TYP 6 PLACES"* dimension. The following exercise restores the MOCK2O style from the continued dimensions, makes the same changes to it as to MOCK2I, and updates this dimension. Enter the commands and variables from the keyboard. You can abbreviate them as shown.

Restoring and Updating Dimensions

Command: **DIM**↵	
Dim: **RES**↵	Issues RESTORE
Current dimension style: MOCK2I	
?/Enter dimension style name or RETURN to select dimension: *Press Enter*	
Select dimension: *Pick one of the horizontal continue associative dimensions*	Extracts the style from the dimension
Current dimension style: MOCK2O	Resets the current style
Dim: **DIMEXO**↵	
Current value <1/16> New value: **1/8**↵	Increases the offset
Dim: **DIMPOST**↵	
Current value <> New value: **"**↵	Sets the suffix to "
Dim: **DIMSCALE**↵	
Current value <2.000000> New value: *Press Enter*	
Dim: **SA**↵	Issues SAVE
?/Name for new dimension style: **MOCK2O**↵	
That name is already in use, redefine it? <N> **Y**↵	

The continue dimensions with the MOCK2O style are immediately redefined with added " and larger offsets.

Dim: **UP**↵	Issues UPDATE
Select objects: *Select the* R3/16" TYP 6 PLACES *and the* Ø5 DIA *dimension*	Updates it (see fig. 17.11)
Dim: **E**↵	Ends dimensioning
Save the drawing	

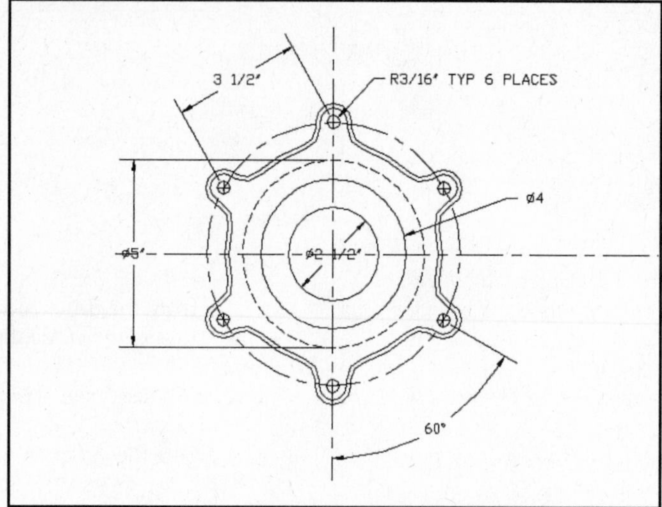

Figure 17.11

Detail of a top view.

Now, as figure 17.11 demonstrates, all the dimension text (except the 60-degree radius dimension) has inch marks. Angular dimensions ignore DIMPOST. With DIMEXO at 1/8, the dimensions are separated more clearly from the objects they dimension. The extension lines on the 5" diameter vertical dimension at the left, however, still look too close because of the circle's large radius. This problem is solved in the next exercise. Before you proceed, however, take a quick look at other controls for dimension line and extension line appearance.

Controlling Dimension and Extension Lines

Do not confuse DIMEXO with the similar-sounding DIMEXE, which controls how far extension lines extend beyond the dimension line. You can also use the following dimension variables for controlling dimension and extension lines:

- **DIMDLE.** This variable extends the dimension line through tick marks by its value when DIMTSZ is on (non-zero).
- **DIMGAP.** This variable controls the gap between text and the break in the dimension line, or optionally draws a box around the text if you set a negative value.

- **DIMTAD.** This variable puts text above the dimension line, with no break, when on. The variable DIMTVP controls how far above the line the text goes.
- **DIMSE1.** When turned on, this variable suppresses the first extension line. Suppression off means draw the line.
- **DIMSE2.** This variable suppresses drawing of the second extension line.

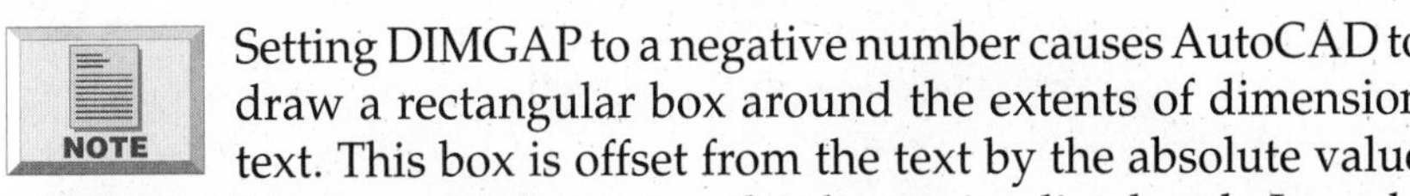

Setting DIMGAP to a negative number causes AutoCAD to draw a rectangular box around the extents of dimension text. This box is offset from the text by the absolute value of DIMGAP, precisely intersecting the dimension line break. In early printings of the *AutoCAD Release 12 Reference Manual*, these are referred to as Reference dimensions, but the negative setting is controlled by the Boxed Text check box of the Dimension Line group of Features dialog box. Note that, according to ANSI Y14.5M standards, this dimension type is known as a Basic dimension.

DIMSE1 and DIMSE2 are commonly used as exceptions to various dimension styles. You might, for example, need a dimension whose extension line would overlap the object itself or another line if an extension line were not suppressed. Suppress DIMSE1 or DIMSE2, especially if the extraneous extension line overlaps a dashed or hidden line. If you do not suppress these extra entities, drawing regenerations are slowed down and drawings may not plot neatly. You also can suppress overlapping lines with plot optimization.

Occasionally, it is more expedient to override one or two dimension variables for a single dimension rather than to create another special dimension style. Try a DIMSE1 and DIMEXO override in the next exercise.

Dimension styles can be overridden in two ways. Change one or more dimension variables before drawing the odd dimension, and then restore the previous style and continue working. Or, use the Override command to change the settings of the current style. Override then prompts you to select one or more associative dimensions to update according to the modified dimension variables. If the associative dimension has a named dimension style, you can update the style (redefining it for all entities assigned to it). The current dimension style is not changed, unless it also is the associative dimension's style.

Alter the 5" diameter vertical dimension at the left of the plan view in the following exercise. Give it an even larger DIMEXO and draw a horizontal dimension inside the flange hole on the section with DIMSE1 on. The setting of DIMSE1 demonstrates the earlier tip on using DDIM to create an *UNNAMED style.

Overriding a Dimension Style for Odd Cases

`Command:` *From the screen menu, choose* DIM:, *then* Dim Styl, *and then* Restore	Issues RESTORE
`Dim: _RESTORE`	
`Current dimension style: MOCK2O`	
`?/Enter dimension style name or RETURN to select dimension:` *Press Enter*	
`Select dimension:` *Select the vertical 5" at the right side.*	
`Current dimension style: MOCK2I`	Restores MOCK2I
`Dim:` *From the screen menu, choose* Override	Issues OVERRIDE
`Dim: Override`	
`Dimension variable to override:` **DIMEXO** ↵	Specifies the DIMEXO variable
`Current value <1/8> New value:` **1/2** ↵	Sets a new override value
`Dimension variable to override:` *Press Enter*	Ends variable specification
`Select objects:` *Select the 5" vertical dimension of the circle* at the left side	Increases the offsets
`Modify dimension style "MOCK2I"? <N>` *Press Enter*	Leaves the style unchanged
`Dim:` *Choose* Settings, *then* Dimension Style	Opens the Dimension Styles and Variables dialog box and cancels DIM mode
With no style name displayed in the Dimension Style *edit box, choose* Extension Lines, *open the* Visibility *drop-down list box, and select* Suppress First	Turns DIMSE1 on to suppress the first extension line

Choose OK, *then* OK again

The MOCK2I dimensions update to suppress the first extension line, but a new style called *UNNAMED has been created and made active, as you see in the next step.

`Command: U ↵`	Undoes the update on the MOCK2I dimensions but leaves *UNNAMED intact
`Command:` Choose Settings, *then* Dimension Style	Opens the Dimension Styles and Variables dialog box
*Notice the current *UNNAMED style, then choose* Cancel	Closes the dialog box without any changes
`Command:` *Choose* Draw, *then* Dimensions, *then* Linear, *then* Horizontal, *and use object snap NEA to draw dimension from ① to ②, picking dimension line location at ② (see fig. 17.12)*	Draws a 5" dimension inside the hole in the section with no extension line at the left side
`Command:` *From the screen menu, choose* DIM:, *then* Dim Styl, *then* Restore	
`Dim: _RESTORE`	
`Current dimension style: *UNNAMED`	
`?/Enter dimension style name or RETURN to select dimension: MOCK2I ↵`	
`Dim: E ↵`	Exits from dimensioning mode
Save the drawing.	

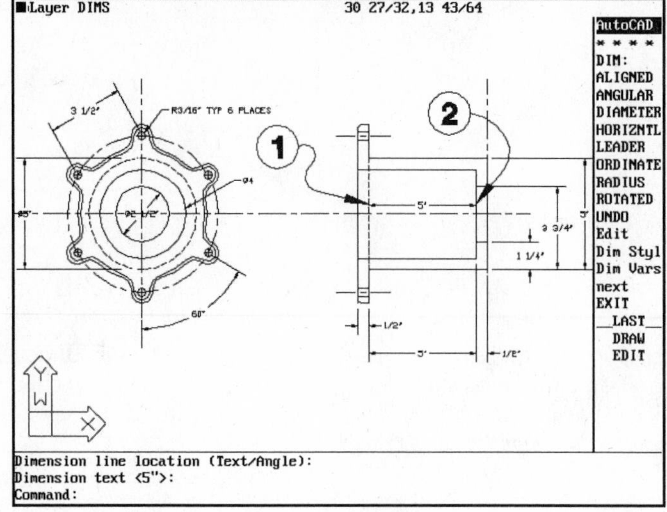

Figure 17.12:

Dimension on a circle after override.

The offset, as illustrated in figure 17.12, should now be quite distinct. You can see no first extension line from the new horizontal dimension over the hidden line. You might be able to see the second extension line in yellow, overlapping the green bottom line of the hole. Notice that changing DIMSE1 changed the current style from MOCK2I to *UNNAMED.

Beware of the difference between OVERRIDE and UPDATE. OVERRIDE assigns dimension style *UNNAMED to the associative dimension(s) unless you ask it to update the dimension style. The dimensions are not protected from accidental updating. UPDATE assigns the current dimension style, named or unnamed.

If the associative dimensions have the current dimension style, answer yes to update the dimension style with OVERRIDE. The result is equivalent to changing dimension variables and redefining the current dimension style.

Until now, you have been using fractional units. Drawings like this one are usually dimensioned in decimal units. Update the current units to decimal.

Controlling Units

Controlling units is simple and automatic — the current drawing units are used in the dimensioning text. Almost as simple is applying a round-off factor with the DIMRND dimension variable. If DIMRND is non-zero, all measurements (except angular dimensions) are rounded to the nearest increment of its value. For example, if set to .5, the dimension text is rounded to the nearest half unit. DIMRND does not truncate trailing zeros; the number of decimal places and display of zeros are controlled by the UNITS command and the DIMZIN dimension variable.

Units are not saved or controlled by dimension styles.

If you use DIMZIN, controlling units can be tricky. Measurements can be formatted in several possible ways. For example, in feet and inches, 1/4", 8", and 3' also can be formatted 0'0 1/4", 0'8", and 3'0". This confusion is controlled by setting DIMZIN to 1, 2,or 3, 4.

- 0 suppresses both zero feet and zero inches (the default).
- 1 includes both zero feet and zero inches.
- 2 includes zero feet but suppresses zero inches.
- 3 suppresses zero feet but includes zero inches.

If a measurement includes fractional inches, zero inches are not suppressed, regardless of the setting. This automatic override helps avoid hard-to-read values like 6'1/2".

DIMZIN also controls decimal zeros, using settings of 4 and 8. These are additive settings; you can use them both for a sum of 12 and you can add them to the 0, 1, 2, or 3 settings for feet and inches control. A value of 4, 5, 6, or 7 suppresses all leading zeros (0.7500 becomes .7500). A value of 8, 9, 10, or 11 suppresses (truncates) trailing zeros (0.7500 becomes 0.75). A value of 12, 13, 14, or 15 suppresses both leading and trailing zeros (0.7500 becomes .75). Update the drawing's dimensions with decimal units and suppress zeros in the horizontal dimensions.

Figure 17.13 shows the section before DIMZIN.

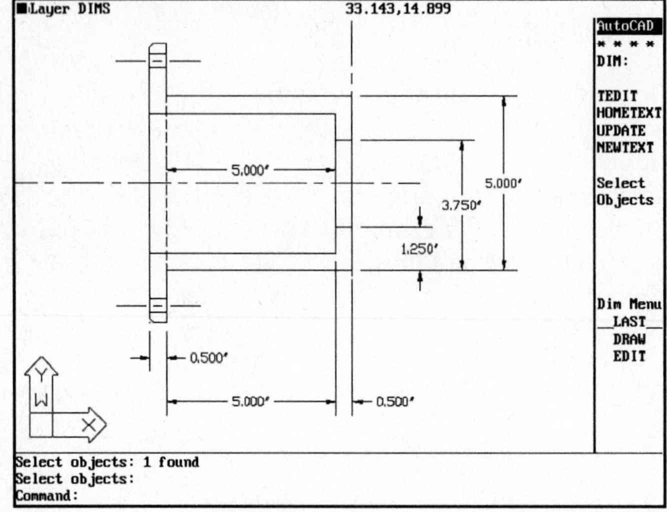

Figure 17.13:
Decimal dimensions before DIMZIN.

Updating to Decimal Units and Controlling Zeros

Use ZOOM with the Window option to zoom to view shown in figure 17.13.

`Command:` *Choose* Settings, *then* Units Control, *and set* Decimal *units, with 0.000 Precision*	
`Command:` *Choose* Modify, *then* Edit Dims, *then* Update Dimension	Issues the UPDATE command
`Dim: _update`	
`Select objects:` *Select all vertical dimensions*	Updates to decimal, but the DIMPOST " suffix remains
`Command:` Choose Settings, *then* Dimension Style, *select MOCK2O in the list box, then choose Features, clear the* Use Paper Space Scaling *check box, and set* Feature Scaling to 2.0	Sets the style MOCK2O and updates three horizontal dimensions
`Command:` *Choose* Modify, *then* Edit Dims, *then* Update Dimension	Issues the UPDATE command
`Dim: _update`	

`Select objects:` *Select the inside 5" horizontal dimension*	Updates to decimal
`Command: DIM ↵`	
`Dim: OV↵`	
`Dimension variable to override: DIMZIN↵`	
`Current value <0> New value: 12↵`	
`Dimension variable to override:` *Press Enter*	
`Select objects:` *Select all the horizontal dimensions and press Enter*	
`Modify dimension style "MOCK20"? <N>` *Press Enter four times*	Answers no for each selected MOCK20 dimension

Examine the dimensions before undoing the DIMZIN override.

`Dim:` *Choose* Assist, *then* Undo	Undoes the override
`Dim:` *Enter* `OV`, *then override the 5" horizontal dimension inside the hole, setting DIMSE1 back on, without modifying the existing style*	Suppresses the first extension line
`Dim: E↵`	Exits from dimensioning mode
Save the drawing	

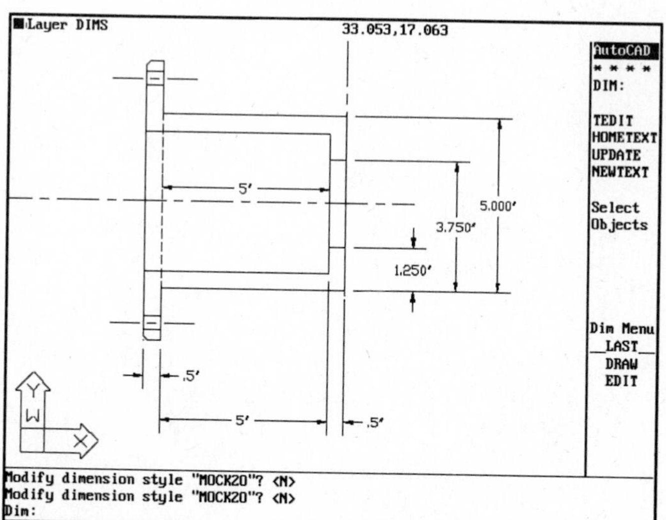

Figure 17.14

Horizontal dimensions after DIMZIN.

Figure 17.14 shows the horizontal dimensions after DIMZIN.

Experiment with different units and DIMZIN settings for other combinations you might use in your work.

You also can alter the linear scale of units and combine two alternate forms of units into one dimension.

Dimensioning with Alternative Units

AutoCAD uses the units settings and actual distances you set up when you draw entities to calculate dimensions. If these units are not the lengths you want to show, apply a standard multiplier to alter the default calculations. You might, for example, use this feature to dimension an inserted scaled-down or metric detail.

To multiply all linear default dimensioning measurements by a standard factor, set the DIMLFAC dimension variable. When DIMLFAC is non-zero, AutoCAD uses the factor as a multiplier to calculate the dimension text. For example, if the measured dimension is 7.05", set DIMLFAC to 2.54 to generate the metric equivalent (17.907). Then to show as 17.907cm, set DIMPOST to cm. DIMLFAC has no effect on angular dimensioning.

Using Two Measurement Systems at the Same Time

To display alternative dimension text strings on a dimension line, set DIMALT on. When you do, AutoCAD formats the dimension to match the *number* [*alternative number*] setting on the dimension line.

The first number is the standard dimension measurement (multiplied by DIMLFAC). The alternative number, shown in brackets, is that number multiplied by DIMALTF (dimension alternative factor). The alternative number of decimal places is set by DIMALTD (dimension alternative decimals). The default for DIMALTF is 25.4, the number of millimeters in an inch. The default for DIMALTD is two decimal places. The optional alternative suffix is set by DIMAPOST. For example, if the measured dimension is 7.05 and you want the text line read 7.05" [17.907cm], set these dimension variables: DIMAPOST to cm: DIMALT on; and DIMALTF to 2.54; and DIMALTD to 3.

Another popular dimensioning task is to include tolerances in dimensions. AutoCAD makes it easy.

Adding Tolerances and Limits to Dimension Text

The dimension variables that control tolerances and limits are DIMTOL, DIMLIM, DIMTM, DIMTP, and DIMTFAC. The DIMRND round-off dimension variable also is useful. DIMTOL On turns tolerances on and DIMLIM On turns limits on. These dimension variables are mutually exclusive; turning one on turns the other off. DIMTP is the plus tolerance/limit value, and DIMTM is the minus value. DIMTFAC controls the size of the plus and minus tolerance and limits text strings (relative to DIMTXT size).

If you have only a few tolerance or limit dimensions in a drawing, use Override. If you use them frequently, create dimension styles for them. A convenient compromise is to create tolerance and limits dimension styles that you can override for specific DIMTP and DIMTM values. This method, however, sacrifices the dimension style protection against accidental changes.

Tolerances and limits work the same whether you update existing dimensions or create new ones with their settings. In the following exercise, update the existing horizontal associative dimensions below the section to try tolerances and limits. Also, turn DIMTAD on to place dimension text above unbroken dimension lines. To create tolerances (see fig. 17.15), set DIMTOL on, DIMTP to .003, DIMTM to .002, and DIMTFAC to .8 (.8 X .125 DIMTXT = .1 text), and save a new dimension style. Then, override those settings to update the lower 5" dimension with equal DIMTP and DIMTM tolerance values. To create limits (see fig. 17.16), update the lower right dimension with DIMLIM on.

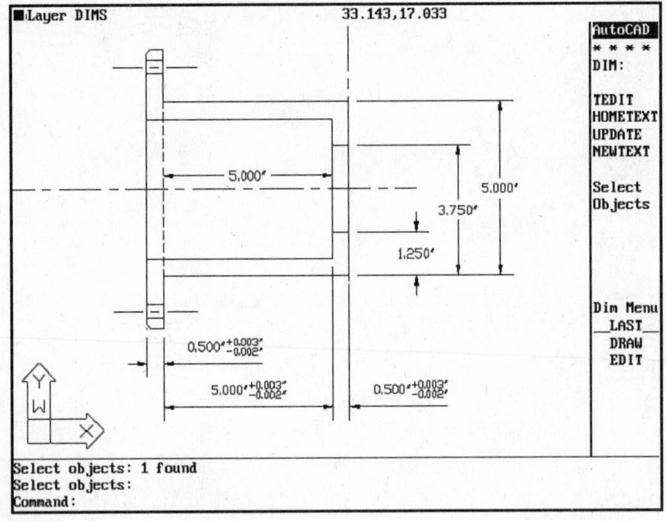

Figure 17.15:

Horizontal dimensions above a line with tolerances.

Creating and Using Tolerance and Limits Dimensions

`Command:` *Choose* Settings, *then* Dimension Style, *click in the* Dimension Style *edit box, and enter* `MOCK2OTP3M2`	Starts a new style

The message `New Style MOCK2OTP3M2 created from MOCK20` appears at the bottom of the dialog box.

Choose Text Location, *open the the* Vertical *drop-down list box, select* Above, *then choose* OK	Turns on DIMTAD
Choose Text Format, *then click on the* Variance *radio button*	Turns on DIMTOL
Double-click in the Upper Value *edit box, then enter* `.003`	Sets DIMTP
Double-click in the Lower Value *edit box, then enter* `.002`	Sets DIMTM

Choose OK	Returns to the main dialog box
Choose Text Location, *then double-click in the* Tolerance Height *edit box and enter* `0.1`	Sets DIMTFAC to .8 (ratio of text height to tolerance text height)
Choose OK, *and then* OK	Saves new settings for MOCK2OTP3M2 and returns to command prompt

The style name was derived from: DIMSCALE *2* *O*utside *T*olerance *P*lus .*003* *M*inus .*002*

`Command:` *Choose* Modify, *then* Edit Dims, *then* Update Dimension, *and select the bottom three horizontal dimensions*	Updates dimensions with tolerances (see fig. 17.15)
`Command:` **`DIM`** ↵	
`Dim:` **`DIMTP`** ↵	
`Current value <0.003> New Value:` **`.002`** ↵	Sets plus tolerance same as minus
`Dim:` *Choose* Modify, *then* Edit Dims, *then* Update Dimension, *and update the toleranced 5.000" dimension*	Overrides its style
`Command:` **`DIM`** ↵	
`Dim:` **`DIMLIM`** ↵	
`Current value <off> New Value:` **`ON`** ↵	Turns limits on and tolerances off
`Dim:` *Choose* Modify, *then* Edit Dims, *then* Update Dimension *and update right-most 0.500" toleranced dimension*	Overrides its style
Save the drawing	

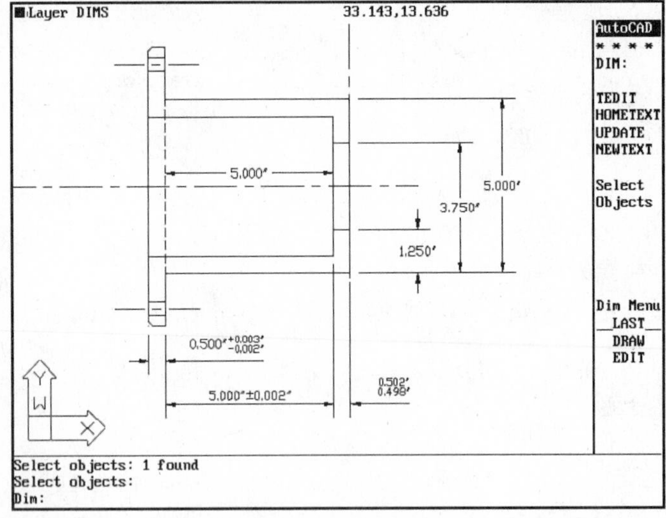

Figure 17.16:

Horizontal dimensions with tolerances and limits.

The left-most horizontal dimension now reads 0.500" +0.003"/-0.002", the middle dimension is 5.000" ±0.002", and the right-most one reads 0.502"/ 0.498".

For more complete coverage of geometric dimensioning and tolerancing to ANSI Y14.5M-1982 (R1988) standards, consult *AutoCAD Drafting and 3D Design* (New Riders Publishing).

Controlling Dimension Text

In addition to the settings you have already used, AutoCAD offers other ways to control dimension text, as described in the following list of dimension commands and dimension variables:

- **HOMETEXT.** This command restores text of selected associative dimensions to their default (home) position.
- **NEWTEXT.** This command enables you to edit the contents of selected associative dimension text, or restore the default measurement as text if you enter <>. Embedded <> measurements and text are accepted.
- **TROTATE.** This command changes the rotation angle of dimension text.

- **TEDIT.** This command changes the location of selected dimension text without affecting its contents. You can justify it left or right, pick a new location, restore it to its home position, or change its angle. Tedit includes the features of Hometext, Newtext, Trotate, and STRETCH, but can only edit one associative dimension at a time.
- **DIMTIH.** This variable keeps text that is inside extension lines horizontal when on (the default). When off, the angle of the text takes on the angle of the dimension line.
- **DIMTOH.** Similar to DIMTIH, this variable places text outside the extension lines.
- **DIMCLRT.** This variable assigns a color to associative dimension text for plotting pen line weight control.

You might want to use the STRETCH command instead of Tedit. The regular STRETCH command is useful for relocating dimension text to locations not allowed by the TEDIT command.

Use STRETCH in the following exercise to relocate the 0.500" +0.003"/-0.002" horizontal section view dimension. Figure 17.17 shows its appearance before editing.

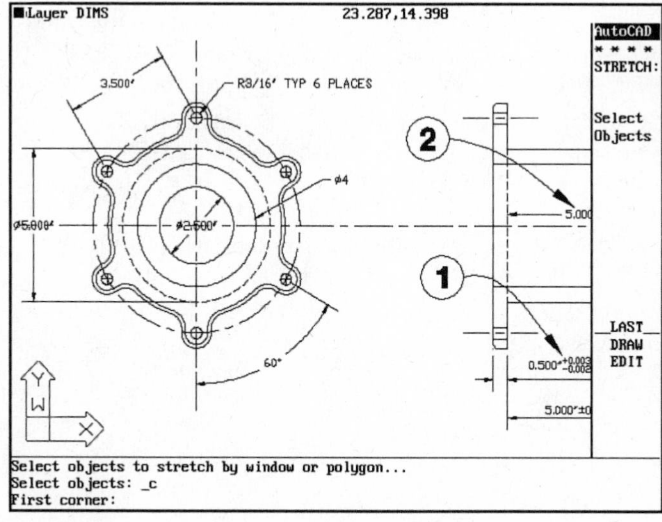

Figure 17.17:

The MOCKDIM drawing before editing.

When you are selecting dimension text with STRETCH, the crossing window only needs to catch the node point in the center of the dimension text. Then use TEDIT to relocate the dimensions shown. The 5" vertical dimension text is located on top of the flange center line, so move it up a little. While you are editing the dimensions, break the center lines going through the inner circle's dimension. Also set DIMCLRT to red, both to try it out and to use it as a visible flag to see which dimension text values are changed by the TEDIT and STRETCH commands.

Relocating Text and Controlling Color with Tedit, STRETCH, and DIMCLRT

Zoom and pan to the view illustrated in figure 17.17.

`Command:` *Choose* Settings, *then* Dimension Style, *and click on* MOCK2I *in the list box, then choose* OK	Restores the MOCK2I style
`Command:` *Choose* Modify, *then* Edit Dims, *then* Update Dimensions *and select all dimensions in top view (except R3/16"...)*	
`Command:` *Choose* Settings, *then* Dimension Style	Opens the Dimension Styles and Variables dialog box
Click on MOCK2I, *choose* Colors, *click in the color box to the right of BYBLOCK in the* Dimension Text Color *drop-down list line, click on red, then choose* OK *three times*	Changes text color of MOCK2I dimensions (changes DIMCLRT variable for MOCK2I)
`Command:` *Choose* Modify, *then* Stretch, *and select the dimension text at ① (see fig. 17.17)* `Base point or displacement:` *With object snap NODe, pick text at ①*	Selects 0.500" toleranced dimension
`Second point of displacement:` *Turn on ortho, drag text to left and pick point to place it where shown in figure 17.18*	Relocates text
`Command:` *Turn off ortho*	

`Command:` *Choose* Modify, *then* Stretch *and stretch the 5.000" dimension at ② to the left and up (see figs. 17.17 and 17.18)*	Makes text red and moves it above the dimension line, which "heals" itself
`Command:` **`DIMSHO`** ↵	
`New value for DIMSHO <1>: 0` ↵	Turns off dynamic updating of dimension during edit
`Command:` *Choose* Modify, *then* Edit Dims, *then* Dimension Text, *then* Move Text	Issues TEDIT
`Dim: _tedit`	
`Select dimension:` *Pick the 5" diameter dimension at the far left of plan view*	
`Enter text location (Left/Right/Home /Angle):` *Pick new location shown in figure 17.18*	Moves it above center line
`Command:` *Choose* Modify, *then* Break, *then* Select Object, Two Points, *and break the center lines to clear the 2.500" diameter dimension*	

Save the drawing.

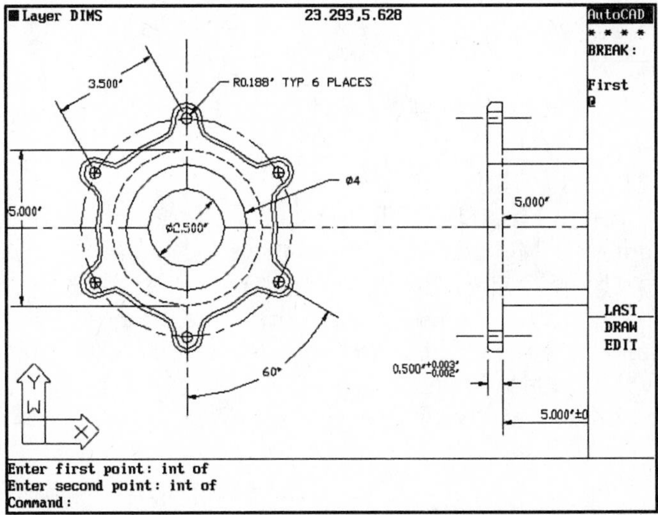

Figure 17.18:

MOCKDIM after STRETCH, TEDIT, and BREAK.

Setting DIMCLRT made the current dimension style *UNNAMED. However, the first STRETCH and the TEDIT did not change their dimension's text values because they had named dimension styles stored with them. Stretching the 5" horizontal dimension updated it to the current dimension variable settings and changed its color because it began as an *UNNAMED associative dimension. When you stretch an associative dimension's text out of the dimension line, the line "heals" itself. The HOMETEXT command makes the associative dimension text snap back to its default home.

Did you notice a difference in dragging with DIMSHO off? If DIMSHO is on, AutoCAD recalculates the dimension value and updates the dimension while dragging; if off, it does not. DIMSHO on might be jerky and slow on some computers; if so, turn it off. DIMSHO is not stored in the dimension style, so changing it does not change the current dimension style to *UNNAMED.

Editing other objects, such as center lines, might be the easiest way to clear up conflicts. When you have a choice in modifying an associative dimension, it is usually better to use dimensioning utility commands rather than normal AutoCAD commands. Instead of using STRETCH to move text, use TEDIT. Instead of exploding a dimension so you can edit its text or change its color, use NEWTEXT or DIMCLRT.

Controlling Dimension Color and Line Weight

In addition to using the DIMCLRT dimension variable to set color for dimension text, you can use DIMCLRD to set color for dimension lines, arrows, and leaders. DIMCLRE similarly controls the color of extension lines. You can set them to any color, or to BYLAYER or BYBLOCK. They are set to BYBLOCK by default, so the entities within the dimension take on current color settings when created or changed with CHPROP. This also is the reason why the leader dimension is white. Leaders and center marks are not associative dimensions; they act like associative dimensions that have been exploded.

Try using EXPLODE on an associative dimension. Because they are really special forms of blocks, EXPLODE changes associative dimensions to individual entities with linetype BYLAYER and the color set by the

DIMCLRx dimension variables. With default DIMCLRx settings, leaders are drawn with color BYBLOCK, which appears white. Change them by setting colors or using CHPROP. Undo is the only way to restore associativity.

The STRETCH and SCALE commands are the links to maintaining associativity of dimensions as you edit drawing objects.

Stretching and Scaling Entities and Associative Dimensions

Remember that associative dimensions contain invisible definition points at their extension line origins. If you select a dimension when using SCALE or catch a definition point in the crossing window when stretching, the dimension text automatically is recalculated.

To examine this effect, use STRETCH in the following exercise to double the flange thickness from .5" to 1" on the left side of the section view. Then use SCALE and STRETCH to resize the inner circle's hole diameter from 2.5" to 2" in both the plan view and the section view. Figure 17.19 shows the selection points for the STRETCH crossing windows.

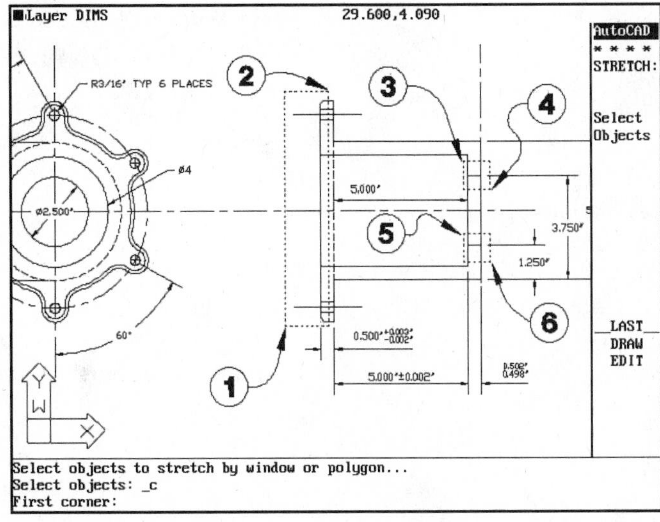

Figure 17.19:

Crossing windows for changing the flange.

Using STRETCH and SCALE To Edit Objects and Associative Dimensions

Zoom to the view shown in figure 17.19.

`Command:` *Choose* Settings, *then* Dimension Style, *click on* MOCK2OTP3M2, *then choose* OK	Restores MOCK2OTP3M2 dimension style
`Command:` *Choose* Modify, *then* Edit Dims, *then* Dimension Text, *then* Home Position	Enters DIM mode and issues HOMETEXT
`Dim: _hometext`	Returns text to default position
`Select objects:` *Select the left-most tolerance 0.500″ dimension*	Returns text to default position

`Command:` *Choose* Modify, *then* Stretch
`Command: Stretch`
`Select objects to stretch by window or polygon...`
`Select objects: _c`	

`First corner:` *Pick point at ① (see fig. 17.19)*	
`Other corner:` *Pick point at ②* `Select objects:` *Press Enter* `Base point:` *Pick any point* `New point:` **`@-.5,0`**↵	Thickens by .5" and increases dimension (see fig. 17.20)
`Command:` *Select the 2.500″ dimension and circle, then pick the center grip*	Creates selection set and enters Stretch mode
`** STRETCH **` `<Stretch to point>/Base point/Copy/Undo/eXit:` **`SC`**↵	Switches to Scale mode
`** SCALE **` `<Scale factor>/Base point/Copy/Undo/Reference/eXit:` **`R`**↵	Specifies the Reference option
`Reference length <1.000>:` **`2.5`**↵	Specifies the reference length

`<New length>/Base point/Copy/Undo/ Reference/eXit: 2↵` — Scales the circle and the dimension

`Command:` *Double-click in an empty space* — Clears the selection set and grips

`Command: R ↵` — Redraws the screen

`Command:` *Choose* Modify, *then* Stretch, *and select crossing ③ and ④ (see fig. 17.19) to stretch edge of hole and vertical 3.750" dimension to 3.500"*

`Command:` *Choose* Modify, Stretch, *and select crossing ⑤ and ⑥ to stretch other edge of hole and vertical 1.250" dimension to 1.500"*

Save the drawing

All of the associated dimensions are selected and updated to match the stretched and scaled entities. As illustrated in figure 17.20, the drawing remains accurate after editing.

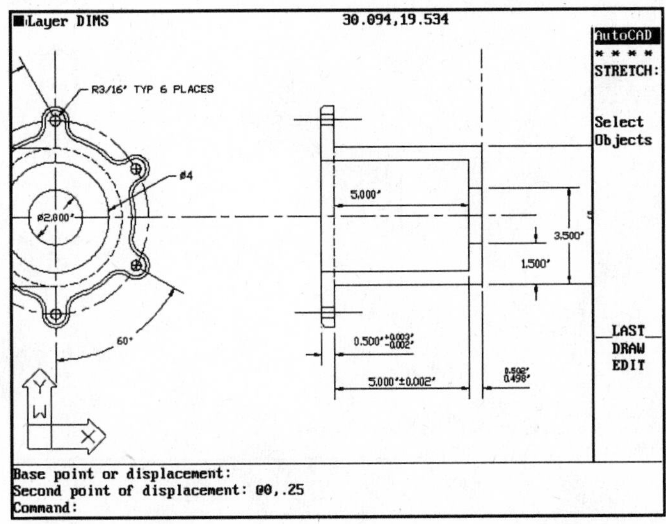

Figure 17.20:

The stretched flange and rescaled holes.

Changing the Dimension Terminator (Arrow)

A terminator is the symbol placed at the intersection of a dimension line and an extension line. The default terminator is an arrow, but ticks or dots can be substituted simply by setting dimension variables. Whenever DIMTSZ (dimension tick size) has a value greater than 0 (the default), ticks of that size are drawn instead of arrows.

In the following exercise, set DIMTSZ to a value of .125 for the tick size. Also set DIMDLE to .125 to extend the dimension line through tick marks. Then place a vertical dimension using tick marks instead of the normal dimension line arrows (see fig. 17.21). Draw the overall vertical dimension of the flange section 1 inch to the left of the face.

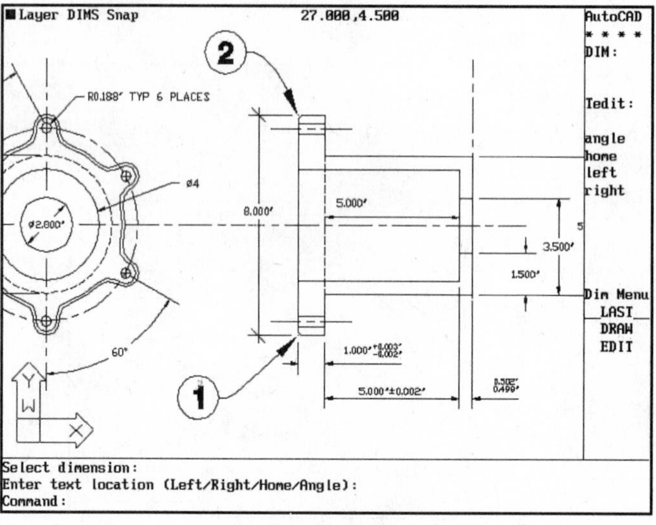

Figure 17.21:
A vertical dimension with tick marks.

Dimensioning with Tick Marks

`Command:` *Choose* Settings, *then* Dimension Style, *and select* MOCK2I	Selects MOCK2I style
Choose **Ar**rows, *click on the* **T**ick *radio button, double-click in the* Tick E**x**tension *edit box, and enter* **`.125`**	Selects ticks instead of arrows and sets DIMDLE to .125
Double-click in the Arrow Si**z**e *edit box, then enter* **`.125`**, *and choose* OK, *then* OK *again*	Sets DIMTSZ, closes dialog boxes, and updates MOCK2I dimensions
`Command:` **`U`**↵	Undoes dimension change, but retains dimension style changes as *UNNAMED
`Command:` *Turn on snap*	
`Command:` *Choose* Draw, *then* Dimensions, *then* linear, *then* Vertical, *and pick extension line origins ① and ② (see fig. 17.21), dimension line location at 18,12 and accept the default text*	Enters dimension mode and draws 8" Vertical dimension
`Command:` *Turn off snap*	
`Command:` *Choose* Modify, *then* Edit Dims, *then* Dimension Text, *then* Move Text, *and move the text up above center line (see fig. 17.21)*	
Save the drawing and quit AutoCAD	

You also can use dots or any drawing or block as a customized dimension terminator.

You easily can set the size of dimension arrows with the DIMASZ dimension variable. You also can substitute dots, custom arrows, or any symbol you want. If the DIMBLK (dimension block) dimension variable contains the name DOT, AutoCAD creates a block named DOT and uses it as a terminator. If DIMBLK contains the name of any other block, AutoCAD uses that block in place of the default arrow (unless overridden by a non-zero DIMTSZ).

If you create a custom symbol oriented for the right end of the dimension line, AutoCAD can flip it 180 degrees for the left side and rotate it for angular dimensions. Dimension blocks can be any shape you want. A few examples are shown in figure 17.22.

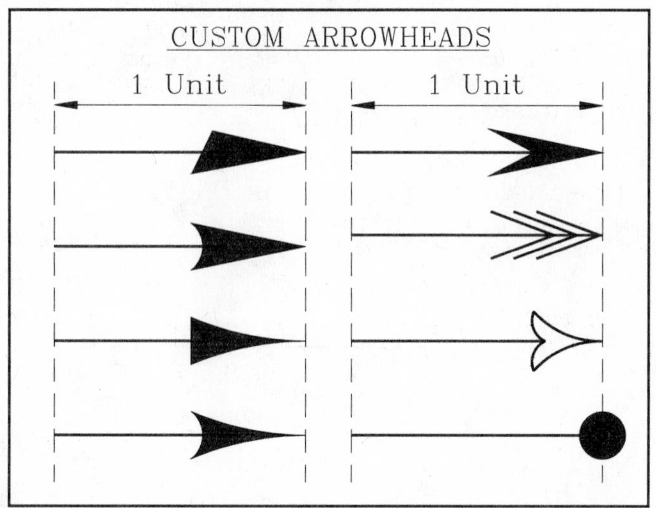

Figure 17.22: Some DIMBLKS examples.

TIP

Make your symbol one drawing unit wide. AutoCAD draws the dimension line or leader up to one unit away from the extension line. If the symbol is not one unit wide, there is a gap between the symbol and the dimension line. Point the symbol or arrow to the right and make the symbol or arrow's tip the block insertion base point. If you do not use a filled symbol, include a one-unit line from the insertion point to where the symbol joins the dimension line.

You can create different dimblocks for the right and left sides. To use them, set the DIMBLK1 dimension variable to the name of the left side dimension block and DIMBLK2 to the name of the right side dimension block. Then, turn the DIMSAH dimension variable on to tell AutoCAD to use the separate blocks.

You can now erase the MOCKSECT and DIMVARS drawing. You do not need them again.

Summary

Associative dimensions are one of the most useful features of any CAD system when used properly. Associative dimensions ensure that the dimension values always reflect the current size of the objects in the drawing. If you change the objects, you do not need to change the dimensions — they are updated automatically. Associative dimensions also make it easier to make global changes to the dimensions. Remember the following points to use associative dimensioning most effectively:

- Draw precisely, so the dimensions are accurate. Do not draw out of scale unless you absolutely have to.
- When modifying the drawing by stretching or scaling, make sure you include the dimensions in the selection set so they are updated as well.
- Let AutoCAD do the work of making changes by using the associative dimension utility commands such as NEWTEXT, TEDIT, and TROTATE.
- Use named dimension styles to protect associative dimensions from accidental updating. Standardize your dimensioning into as few dimension styles as possible. Save those dimension styles in a prototype drawing or in a drawing you can insert as a block. Use the Restore option to set the current dimension style by selecting existing dimensions. You can reduce the chance of error by seeing what you are setting the dimension style to.
- Use overrides to named dimension styles sparingly and check instances of their use before plotting to be sure they have not accidentally changed.

- Put the dimensions on a separate layer with a different color than the one used for the main body of the drawing. Use the DIMCLRX set of dimension variables to assign colors to parts of dimensions so you can plot different line weights. This way, extension lines and dimensions stand out and are not mistaken for actual drawing elements.
- Adjust dimension text to the same height as the annotation text for consistency and to make text changes and additions easier.

18

Data Exchange with Other Applications

In a perfect data processing world, everyone would use the same brand of software for CAD, word processing, desktop publishing, and rendering. If this were the case, file translations would not be an issue to be concerned with. Because this has not happened, many data-exchange formats have been introduced by leading software providers and by third-party developers to handle a wide variety of tasks. Although this chapter cannot cover all the available file formats, it does cover the formats most common to AutoCAD users and several that have been very popular in the broad field of computer graphics.

Most CAD software packages use a proprietary data file that is very efficient for the internal manipulation of data, but which cannot be read into another application. The AutoCAD drawing file (DWG) format is a good example of this. Directly reading from a proprietary drawing file is an ideal method of accurately obtaining entity information. Although this is sometimes done, it is not economical to acquire a different translator for every proprietary format. Also, Autodesk does not publish the format of its DWG file and reserves the right to make changes at any time.

For these reasons, several neutral file formats have been developed to make file exchange between different applications possible. For many years, AutoCAD has used the DXF and IGES formats. IGES (Initial Graphics Exchange Specification) is a public format; DXF (Drawing Interchange File) is an Autodesk proprietary format, but it is well-documented and available for public use. These formats are supported by AutoCAD and many other applications, as shown in figure 18.1. This chapter explains and demonstrates the use of these files.

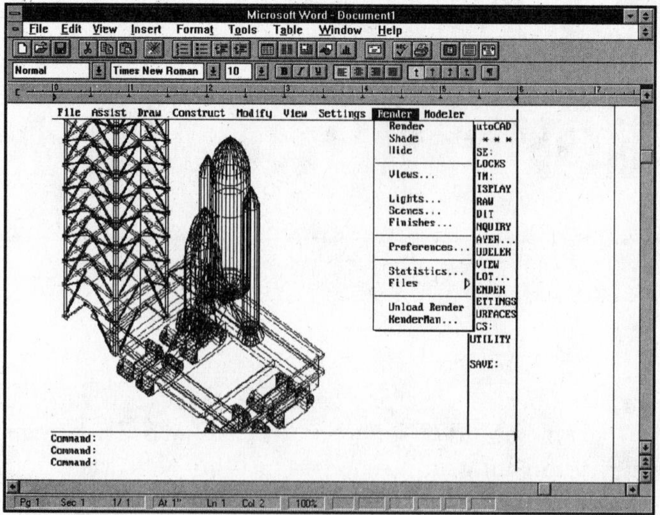

Figure 18.1:

An AutoCAD display copied to a Word for Windows document.

A new and exciting feature of AutoCAD Release 12 is the capability to import and export files in PostScript, TIFF, GIF, and PCX formats. These formats and other graphics formats are popular with presentation, illustration, and desktop publishing applications. These graphics formats also are covered more in depth later in the chapter.

AutoCAD also provides a new interface, called the *AutoCAD SQL Extension* (ASE), which provides powerful links between graphic entities and external database information. This interface will be widely utilized by users and third-party developers to make integrated databases for many computer applications.

Another method of using AutoCAD drawings in other applications is through a variety of screen-capture programs, such as Collage or Hijaak. Often, you can activate these programs by pressing a hot key when you are ready to capture the AutoCAD screen. Of course, this capture is only a

raster image file and is not of much use in another CAD application. The display's resolution greatly affects the file size.

Using DXF for Data Exchange

The Drawing Interchange File (DXF) was developed by Autodesk to accurately describe an AutoCAD drawing file in a text-file format. Although AutoCAD's binary (or compiled) drawing file is efficient for a computer to use, it is difficult to manipulate outside of that software application. An ASCII text file, on the other hand, is a more cumbersome file, but it is one that most software applications can read and write to. Because of AutoCAD's market dominance, the DXF format has become an industry standard.

You can find the DXFIN and DXFOUT commands for DXF files by choosing DXF/DXB from the UTILITY screen menu or the Import/Export option of the Files pull-down menu. The DXFOUT command prompts for a file name, so that you can give the DXF file a different name than the drawing name. The DXF extension is automatically added. You also can specify a number of decimal places of accuracy for the file. Six is the default and works well in most cases. Some high-precision applications may require more decimal places of precision. The DXFOUT command can output to an ASCII file, unless you specify the Binary option. The Binary option outputs to a more efficient binary DXF file. Try creating a DXF file in the next exercise.

Using DXFOUT To Export Data

Start AutoCAD by using the IA.BAT batch program and start a new drawing named DXFTEST, then use the CIRCLE command to draw a 2"-radius circle, and use the LINE command to add lines to create the simple drawing shown in figure 18.2.

`Command:` *Choose* File, *then* Import/Export, *then* DXF Out	Issues the DXFOUT command and displays the Create DXF File dialog box

AutoCAD supplies the drawing name as the default (in this case, DXFTEST) in the File edit box.

Choose OK	Accepts the default DXFTEST.DXF
`Enter decimal places of accuracy (0 to 16)/Entities/Binary <6>:` *Press Enter*	Accepts the default accuracy and creates a DXF file

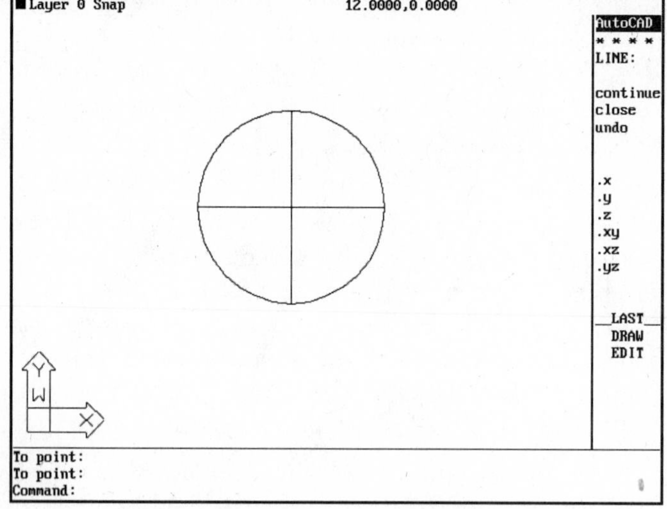

Figure 18.2:

The starting DXFTEST drawing.

Next, use AutoCAD's file utilities to locate the file.

`Command:` *Choose* File, *then* Utilities, *and click on* List Files	Displays File List dialog box
Double-click in the Pattern *edit box and enter* **`*.DXF`**	Lists only DXF files when you press Enter
Choose OK or Cancel, *then* Exit	Closes the File Utilities dialog box

Save the drawing, then exit from AutoCAD.

This simple exercise created a text file that accurately described the drawing database. At first glance, the text file may look a little confusing, but it is not difficult to learn to read this type of file. Because there were so few entities in this drawing, most of the file is filled with the first two sections, called the header and tables, which define all of the drawings variables, settings, and feature definitions. The last part of the file, which lists the entities and their coordinates, is simple. The next exercise shows how to change a coordinate in the DXF file.

Inside a DXF File

You can view an ASCII text file by using the DOS command TYPE, or by opening the file in your favorite word processor. Some word processors require a special save command so that the file is not saved in a special file format other than ASCII. Be sure to retain the DXF extension, or AutoCAD cannot read the file.

To get a feel for how complex a DXF file is, load DXFTEST.DXF into the MS-DOS Editor (see fig. 18.3). If you are not using MS-DOS 5.0, you can use the DOS EDLIN command or any word processor that can read and write ASCII files, or you can enter **MORE < DXFTEST.DXF** at the DOS command prompt in the IA directory to page through, but not edit, the file. If you do not have a text editor that you can use to edit DXFTEST.DXF, follow the exercise, noting the change in the drawing at the end. If you are working on a UNIX-based system, use the `vi` command to edit the file.

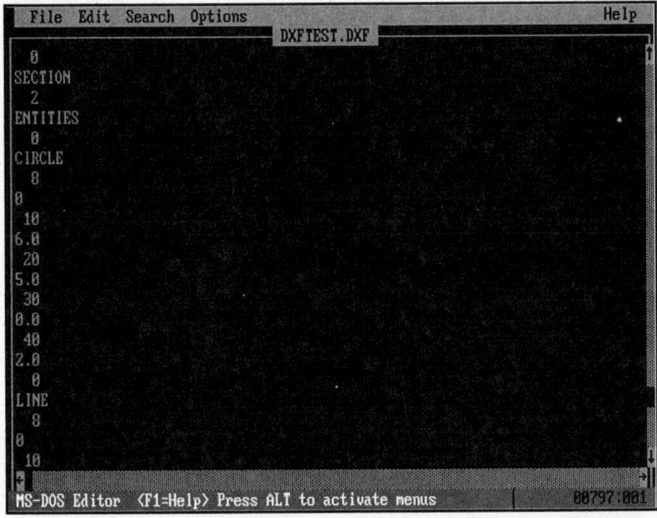

Figure 18.3

DXFTEST.DXF loaded into the MS-DOS Editor.

Viewing and Editing a DXF File

Start from the DOS command line (outside of AutoCAD).

`C:\>`**`CD \IA`**	Changes to the \IA directory
`C:\IA>`**`\DOS\EDIT DXFTEST.DXF`**	Starts the MS-DOS 5 Editor and loads DXFTEST.DXF
Scroll to the bottom of the file and locate the line that reads CIRCLE	
In the CIRCLE section, locate the line that reads 2.0, *and change it to* 4.0	Changes the radius of the circle
Choose File, *then* Save	Saves the changes
Choose File, *then* Exit	Closes the Editor and returns to the system prompt

Next, use the IA.BAT program to start AutoCAD.

`Command:` *Choose* File, *then* Import/Export, *and choose* DXF In	Issues the DXFIN command and displays the Select DXF File dialog box
Double-click on DXFTEST *or enter* **`DXFTEST`**	Issues the DXFIN command and reads the file (see fig. 18.4)

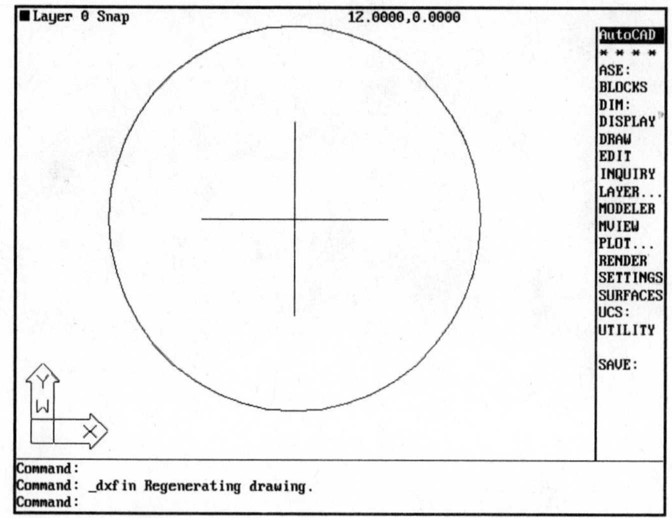

Figure 18.4:

The modified DXF file imported into AutoCAD.

By finding the entity-coordinate information in the DXF file, you were able to modify the circle radius and then see that change after you read the file back into AutoCAD graphics. This technique is the way many third-party applications can manipulate a drawing file. You may have noticed how much other data was in that file. In many cases, the drawing setup information is not required in the DXF file. By using the Entities option of the DXFOUT command, only the entities themselves are exported to the file. This option is used in the following exercise.

Exporting Selected Entities with DXFOUT

`Command:` *Choose* File, *then* Import/Export, *and choose* DXF Out	Opens the Create DXF File dialog box
Enter **`LINES`** in the File box	Specifies the file name LINES.DXF
`Enter decimal places of accuracy (0 to 16)/Entities/Binary <6>:` **`E`**↵	Specifies the Entities option
`Select objects:` *Select the two lines and press Enter*	
`Enter decimal places of accuracy (0 to 16)/Binary <6>:` **`3`**↵	Specifies 3 decimal places of accuracy and creates the DXF file

Next you clear the drawing and use DXFIN at the `Command:` prompt to import the LINES.DXF file.

`Command:` *Enter* **`NEW`**, *click on* Discard Changes, *then choose* OK	Begins a new drawing with no name
`Command:` **`DXFIN`** ↵	Issues the DXFIN command and displays the Select DXF File dialog box
Double-click on LINES	Imports the file LINES.DXF

To import block insertions into a drawing, however, the block definitions must exist in the receiving drawing, or you must import a full (not Entities-only) DXF file into a new drawing. If you look at this DXF file, it appears much shorter than the previous one because only those entities that you chose were included. This method often is preferred to creating a file because the drawing parameter section will not have a potential conflict with the file you to which you want to import. You should use this option if you want to import into an existing drawing file, rather than into a new one.

A full DXF file can only be imported into a new, empty drawing file. To create an empty drawing, you must use the default original ACAD.DWG prototype file, specify no prototype, or specify the new drawing name equal to nothing (blank), such as NAME= in the New Drawing Name: box.

The DXFOUT command also features the Binary option. This option creates a binary DXF file, which is about 25 percent smaller than a text file and can be read much faster by AutoCAD. A binary DXF file can be read and written by sophisticated third-party programs, but you cannot read or edit the file with a text editor.

Using Binary Drawing Interchange (DXB) Files

Another file format that is more compact than a binary DXF file is the DXB format. This file format is not as complete as a the DXF, but it can handle large amounts of entity data very efficiently and it maintains greater accuracy. A special command called DXBIN is used to read in a DXB file. Although AutoCAD has no direct command for creating one of these files, it can be done indirectly by configuring an ADI plotter driver to plot in a DXB format.

Exchanging Data with IGES

The Initial Graphics Exchange Specification (IGES) has been an industry standard file-translation format for many years. It is especially popular for transferring the large three-dimensional product design files used in manufacturing. Because the IGES specification was developed for no specific CAD program, each CAD program conforms differently to the standards. Many different entity types are supported, but not all CAD systems use identical entity definitions. For this reason, you can lose data or have it altered in the exchange process. The success of this translator varies, depending on which CAD software packages are sending and receiving the information. AutoCAD has the IGESIN and IGESOUT commands built into the software, and they are easy to use because they have no options. The following exercise creates an IGES file in model space (because IGES does not support paper space).

Using IGESOUT To Export Data

Open the MOCKDIM drawing, which you created in Chapter 17. Discard changes to the current drawing.

`Command:` *Set TILEMODE to 1, then issue ZOOM with the* Extents *option (see fig. 18.5)*	Switches to a single tiled viewport
`Command:` *Choose* File, *then* Import/Export, *and choose* IGES Out	Issues the IGESOUT command and displays the Create IGES File dialog box
Choose OK	Accepts the default file name (MOCKDIM.IGS) and exports to file

```
Writing Start section
Writing Global section
Writing line type 2 (HIDDEN)
Writing view 1 (A)
Translating AutoCAD entity 70 (DIMENSION)
Copying DE data record 422 of 422
Copying Parameter data record 324 of 324
Writing Terminate section
```

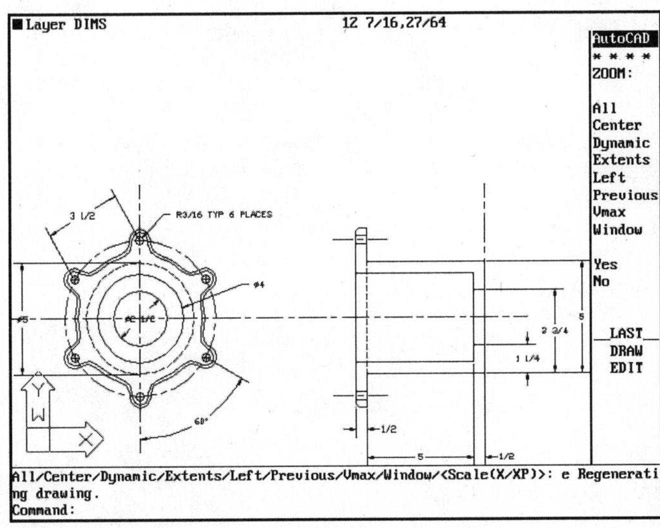

Figure 18.5:
MOCKDIM ready to export.

As you can see from the command prompt activity, the IGES file is a rather substantial file that contains several sections that define its file type, the parameters, and the entity data. Because it is an ASCII text file, you can attempt the same type of coordinate modification as you did with the DXF file. Some of the more advanced features of AutoCAD are not supported in the IGES file; therefore, they may be lost or modified. When you are importing IGES files into AutoCAD, you must start with a new drawing file that contains no defined entities, as previously was noted for a full DXF import. You see an error if you do not follow this procedure.

In the following exercise, you import the IGES file MOCKDIM.IGS that you created in the previous exercise. After you complete the exercise, you see that, although IGES offers a standard by which most CAD applications can exchange data, it loses something in the translation.

Using IGESIN To Import Data

`Command:` *Enter* **NEW**, *choose* Discard Changes, *then choose* OK	Creates a new drawing with no name

Set VIEWRES for fast zooms, and a circle zoom percent of 2000.

`Command:` *Choose* File, *then* Import/Export, *then choose* IGES In	Opens the Select IGES File dialog box
Double-click on MOCKDIM	Imports MOCKDIM.IGS

```
Scanning IGESIN file: C:\IA\MOCKDIM.IGS
Read 422 directory and 324 parameter records.
Found 2 status, 3 global, 422 directory, and 324 parameter records.
Checking T record. Bypassing START section. Reading GLOBAL section.
Product id: C:\IA\MOCKDIM
IGES file created by: AutoCAD-12 Version: IGESOUT-3.04
Processing independent, non-annotation entities.
Read 423 directory and 211 parameter records.
Processing annotation or logically dependent entities.
Read 28 directory and 11 parameter records.
Warning: Inconsistent parameter data for entity in section P, record 226
Read 182 directory and 102 parameter records.
Processing View and Drawing entities.
Read 22 directory and 15 parameter records.
Regenerating drawing.
Drawing extents undefined. Zooming to limits.
Regenerating drawing.
```

`Command:` *Set TILEMODE to 1, then issue ZOOM with the* Extents *option (see fig. 18.6)*

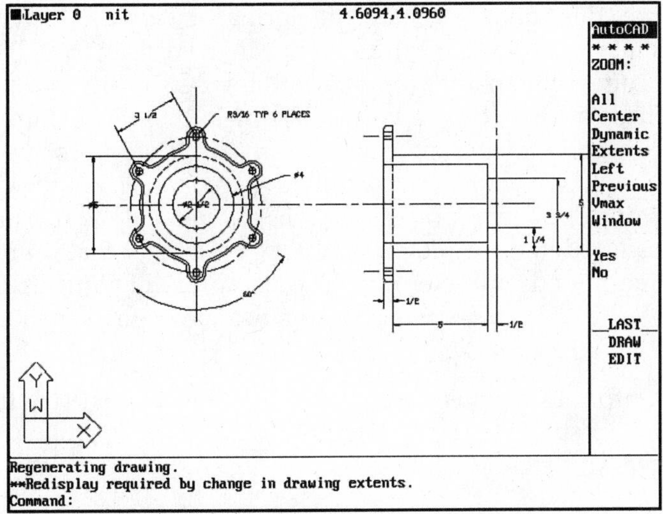

Figure 18.6:

MOCKDIM imported from MOCKDIM.IGS file.

Depending on what type of entities you used in your drawing, you see from the previous exercise that the translation process is not perfect. The *AutoCAD/IGES Interface Specification* document details which AutoCAD entities are supported in IGES, and contains tips on how to obtain the best results in file translations. If you need to exchange IGES files with other sources, it may be beneficial for you to document some drawing-setup procedures to minimize the effects of the IGES translation.

Importing and Exporting to Raster Files

DXF and IGES files can be very large and complex, but they try to maintain the accuracy and flexibility of the entities in a CAD database. If you are interested in the picture itself, a raster image may be much more practical. Similar to the difference between a pen plotter output versus a dot-matrix hard copy, a raster image defines shapes as a series of closely grouped dots on a screen or on paper. AutoCAD Release 12 includes capabilities to create raster files for use in other applications and to import common raster files. Although a raster image does not contain the inherent accuracy of a vector file, this image is much easier to edit and transport between software-application packages.

Some of the more common raster image file formats include FAX, Tagged Image File Format (TIFF), and Graphics Interchange Format (GIF). Bit-map (BMP) files are common to paint programs and the PCX format also is widely used. These types of files have become the industry standard for exchanging raster image files. You can find many applications for using this type of CAD output, in which absolute drawing accuracy is not required. Desktop publishing, rendering and animation, electronic FAX, and logos are commonly transferred in these file formats. One parameter that is important is the resolution of these raster files. The advantage of viewing and printing sharp-looking, high-resolution files must be weighed against the large file sizes that are generated.

AutoCAD can output to various types of raster files by configuring the plotter to the proper specifications, then plotting to a file. The following exercise illustrates this technique.

Configuring a Raster Plot Device

Command: **CONFIG** ↵ — Starts AutoCAD Configuration

Select option 5 to configure a plotter

```
Plotter Configuration Menu
   0. Exit to configuration menu
   1. Add a plotter configuration
   2. Delete a plotter configuration
   3. Change a plotter configuration
   4. Rename a plotter configuration
```

Enter selection, 0 to 4 <0>: **1** ↵

Press RETURN to continue: *Press Enter*

Searching for files. Please wait.

Available plotters:

```
    1. None
    2. ADI plotter or printer (installed - pre v4.1) - by Autodesk
    3. AutoCAD file output formats (pre 4.1) - by Autodesk
    4. CalComp ColorMaster Plotters ADI 4.2 - by Autodesk
    5. CalComp DrawingMaster Plotters ADI 4.2 - by Autodesk
    6. CalComp Electrostatic Plotters ADI 4.2 - by Autodesk
    7. CalComp Pen Plotters ADI 4.2 - by Autodesk
    8. Canon Laser Printer ADI 4.2 - by Autodesk
    9. Epson printers ADI 4.2 - by Autodesk
   10. Hewlett-Packard (HP-GL/2) ADI 4.2 - by Autodesk
```

```
 11. Hewlett-Packard (HPGL) ADI 4.2 - by Autodesk
 12. Hewlett-Packard (PCL) LaserJet ADI 4.2 - by Autodesk
 13. Hewlett-Packard (PCL) PaintJet XL ADI 4.2 - by Autodesk
 14. Houston Instrument ADI 4.2 - by Autodesk
 15. IBM 7300 Series ADI 4.2 - by Autodesk
 16. IBM Graphics Printer ADI 4.2 - by Autodesk
 17. IBM Proprinter ADI 4.2 - by Autodesk
 18. JDL 750 & 750E ADI 4.2 - by Autodesk
 19. NEC Pinwriter P5/P5XL/P9XL ADI 4.2 - by Autodesk
 20. PostScript device ADI 4.2 - by Autodesk
 21. Raster file export ADI 4.2 - by Autodesk
Select device number or ? to repeat list <1>: 21 ↵
Supported models:
  1. 320 x 200 (CGA/MCGA Colour)
  2. 640 x 200 (CGA Monochrome)
  3. 640 x 350 (EGA)
  4. 640 x 400
  5. 640 x 480 (VGA)
  6. 720 x 540
  7. 800 x 600
  8. 1024 x 768
  9. 1152 x 900 (Sun standard)
 10. 1600 x 1280 (Sun hi-res)
 11. User-defined
Enter selection, 1 to 11 <1>: 5 ↵
You can export the drawing in any of the following raster file
formats. Please select the format you prefer.
  1. GIF (CompuServe Graphics Interchange Format)
  2. X Window dump (xwd compatible)
  3. Jef Poskanzer's Portable Bitmap Toolkit Formats
  4. Microsoft Windows Device-independent Bitmap (.BMP)
  5. TrueVision TGA Format
  6. Z-Soft PCX Format
  7. Sun Rasterfile
  8. Flexible Image Transfer System (FITS)
  9. PostScript image
 10. TIFF (Tag Image File Format)
 11. FAX Image (Group 3 Encoding)
 12. Amiga IFF / ILBM Format
In which format would you like to export the file, 1 to 12 <1>: 4
```
Press Enter

```
You can write the file using any of the following colour gamuts.
```

```
The more colours you use, the larger the file will be, usually.
   1. Monochrome
   2. 16 colours
   3. All 256 standard AutoCAD colours
```

`How many colours do you want to use, 1 to 3 <3>:` *Press Enter*

```
You can specify the background colour to be any of AutoCAD's 256
standard
colours. The default of 0 selects a black screen background.
```

`Background colour (0 = black), 0 to 255 <0>:` **7** ↵

```
Plot optimization level = 0
Sizes are in Inches and the style is landscape
Plot origin is at (0.00,0.00)
Plotting area is 640.00 wide by 480.00 high (MAX size)
Plot is NOT rotated
Pen width is 0.010
Area fill will NOT be adjusted for pen width
Hidden lines will NOT be removed
Plot will be scaled to fit available area
```

`Do you want to change anything? (No/Yes/File) <N>:` ↵

`Enter a description for this plotter:` **`Windows DIB (BMP) file`** ↵

```
Your current plotter is: Raster file export ADI 4.2 - by Autodesk
Description: Windows DIB (BMP) file
```

Repeat the process to install any other raster plot drivers you require, then exit from the Configure program and save your changes.

If your system shows only a few plotter options and omits `Raster file export ADI ...`, make sure that you have a SET ACADDRV= line in your startup batch file (IA.BAT) that specifies the AutoCAD driver file path (generally \ACAD\DRV).

Now, try out the raster plot on your MOCKDIM drawing. In the following exercise, you export the drawing to a Windows BMP file. If you have added a different raster plot device to your configuration, simply select it instead.

First, reload MOCKDIM. Then use the PLOT command to create a BMP file.

Plotting to a Raster Plot Device

`Command:` *Choose* File, *then* Open, *click on* Discard Changes, *then enter* `MOCKDIM`	Reloads MOCKDIM
`Command:` *Choose* File, *then* Plot	Displays the Plot Configuration dialog box
Choose Device and Default Selection	Opens the Device and Default Selection dialog box (see fig. 18.7)
Click on Windows DIB (BMP) file *in the Port list box, then choose* OK	
Click on File Name, *then enter* `MOCKDIM.BMP` *(include the BMP file extension)*	Specifies a name for the BMP file
Choose OK	Begins plot

`Command: _plot Effective plotting area: 640.00 wide by 462.91 high`
`Regeneration done nn%`
`Vector sort done nn%`
`Plot complete.`
	Creates the raster file (see fig. 18.8)

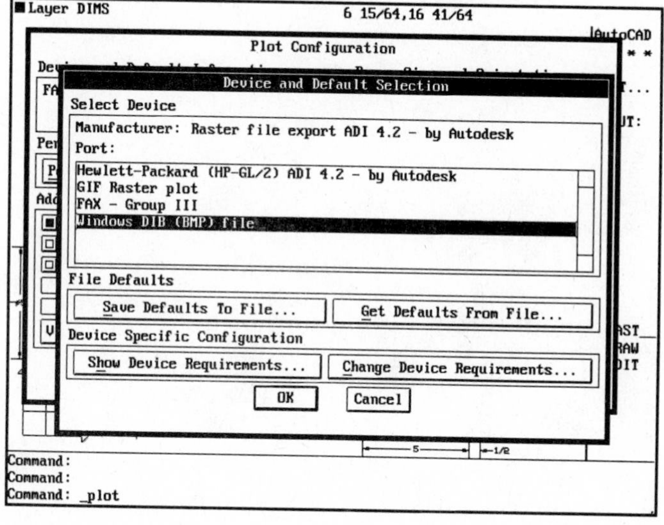

Figure 18.7: The Device and Default Selection dialog box.

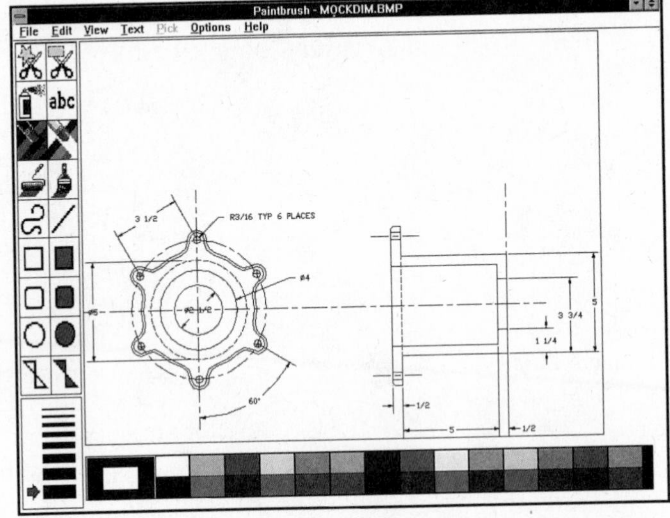

Figure 18.8: MOCKDIM.BMP displayed in Windows Paintbrush.

You may want to try configuring AutoCAD to plot to another type of raster file, especially if you have software that can use that type of file. If AutoCAD does not output to the type of raster file you need, there is a good chance that if you use a standard format, such as PCX, GIF, or BMP, you can later translate the file. Many common programs, such as Graphics Workshop, Paintshop, or WinGIF are readily available, often as shareware. They can read or write to several of the popular formats (see fig. 18.9).

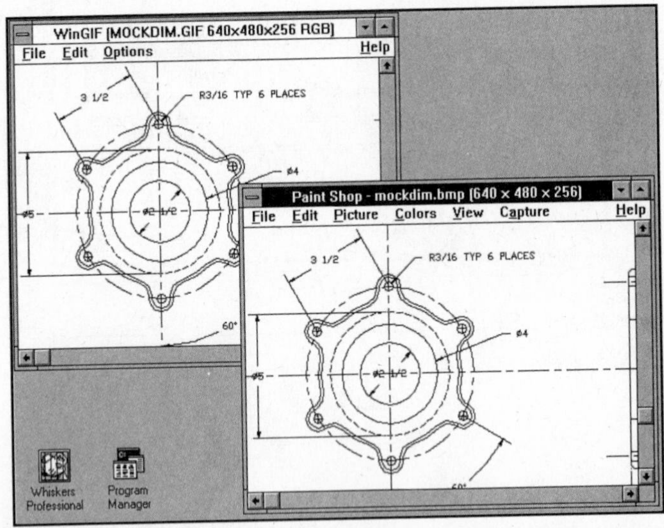

Figure 18.9: MOCKDIM converted to PCX and GIF using Paintshop and WinGIF.

Importing Raster Images

One of the new ADS applications available in AutoCAD is the capability to read raster files into the drawing editor. Raster files can be useful for graphics, such as logos or images, which are often available in popular formats such as GIF, PCX, or TIF. Some images are easier to create using other graphics software and can be imported into AutoCAD to enhance a drawing created in a CAD environment. Unless a scanned image has been converted into a vector file, it is often a raster image and must be brought into CAD accordingly.

Three separate commands, depending on the type of file to be read, can be issued: GIFIN, PCXIN, and TIFFIN. These commands, named for the type of file to be read, are very similar in the way they operate. Entering the command will produce prompts very similar to the BLOCK command. The file name must be entered, along with the appropriate path. The extension is not needed if it is the standard GIF, TIF, or PCX extension. An insertion point and scale factor must also be given. While dragging in the image, it will appear as a rectangle with the file name shown inside. This helps visualize the location and scale factor for fast and efficient dragging.

A raster file is brought in as a block containing many solid entities that define the shape of the image. The colors may be a little unpredictable due to the process of assigning AutoCAD color numbers to all the dithered entities. As you might have guessed, best results occur with small files of well-defined images. Once you import the image you can leave it as is, explode and modify it, or simply trace over and discard it.

Six ADS functions, which operate just like system variables, can be altered to change the way the raster image is imported. Each of them begins with the RI (Raster In) designation.

- **RIASPECT.** The image ASPECT ratio controls the roundness of circles or the X to Y ratio, to compensate for different graphics resolutions.
- **RIBACKG.** The BACKGround color is adjustable, depending on the predominant background color of the image and what your screen background is set to. This variable controls which predominant color will not be converted to solid images. The most common settings are 0 for a black screen background and 7 for a white screen background.
- **RIEDGE.** This integer controls the EDGE detection capabilities for importing an image where you want highly defined edges. The higher

the number (up to 255), the more contrast is required on an image to show the edges.

- **RIGAMUT.** The number of colors used (GAMUT) is defined by this variable. Popular settings are 256, 16, or 8.
- **RIGREY.** A GREYscale image can be obtained by setting this variable to 1, which turns on the greyscale option. This can reduce the file size by effectively reducing the number of colors available.
- **RITHRESH.** This TRESHhold feature enables filtering out some of the background "noise" by enabling only the brighter entities to be captured. The higher the number, the more filtering will take place.

As you can see, this business of importing raster images is hard to define with hard and fast rules. You will have to experiment on your hardware.

Exchanging Data through PostScript

PostScript is a type of graphics file that is popular if you create illustrations and do desktop publishing. The advantage that PostScript has over regular raster images is that it contains special shapes and fonts that are stored more efficiently and generated with better resolution than most raster images. You can use PostScript fonts in AutoCAD drawings, rather than the AutoCAD fonts. PostScript makes the file much more compatible with other devices or applications that recognize PostScript entities. The standard file extension for PostScript is EPS (Encapsulated PostScript). This file is a text file and can be read by many different graphics software packages, as well as by hard copy output devices (see fig. 18.10).

The PostScript commands, PSOUT and PSIN, can be accessed from the Import/Export option of the Files pull-down menu. Creating an EPS file is very similar to plotting. If you have used a PostScript text font (by using a style defined with a font file that has a PFB extension) or a PostScript fill pattern (by using the PSFILL command), these fonts and fills will be exported along with the rest of the image. If FILEDIA is set to 1, a file dialog box appears to name the file. The next prompt offers the same five choices as plotting for the area to output: Display, Extents, Limits, View, or Window. A screen preview may be added to the EPS file in either an EPSI or TIFF format, and several choices are offered for the resolution of that image. Then the scale and output size is specified. The next exercise shows how to plot to a PostScript file.

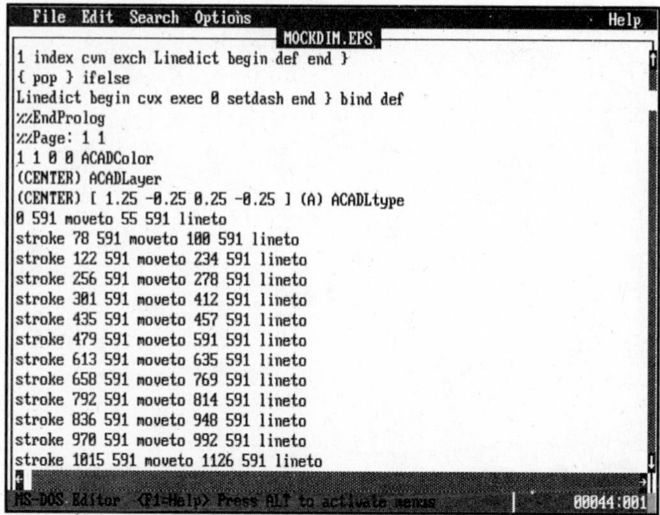

File Edit Search Options Help
MOCKDIM.EPS
1 index cvn exch Linedict begin def end }
{ pop } ifelse
Linedict begin cvx exec 0 setdash end } bind def
%%EndProlog
%%Page: 1 1
1 1 0 0 ACADColor
(CENTER) ACADLayer
(CENTER) [1.25 -0.25 0.25 -0.25] (A) ACADLtype
0 591 moveto 55 591 lineto
stroke 78 591 moveto 100 591 lineto
stroke 122 591 moveto 234 591 lineto
stroke 256 591 moveto 278 591 lineto
stroke 301 591 moveto 412 591 lineto
stroke 435 591 moveto 457 591 lineto
stroke 479 591 moveto 591 591 lineto
stroke 613 591 moveto 635 591 lineto
stroke 658 591 moveto 769 591 lineto
stroke 792 591 moveto 814 591 lineto
stroke 836 591 moveto 948 591 lineto
stroke 970 591 moveto 992 591 lineto
stroke 1015 591 moveto 1126 591 lineto
MS-DOS Editor <F1=Help> Press ALT to activate menus 00044:001

Figure 18.10:

A portion of MOCKDIM.EPS viewed in the MS-DOS Editor.

Plotting to a PostScript File

Continue with the MOCKDIM drawing from the previous exercise.

`Command:` *Choose* File, *then* Import/Export, *then* Postscript Out	Starts the PSOUT command and displays the Create PostScript File dialog box
`Command: psout`	
Choose OK *to accept the default file name MOCKDIM.EPS*	
`What to plot — Display, Extents, Limits, View or Window <D>` E↵	Specifies the Extents option
`Include a screen preview image in the file? (None/EPSI/TIFF) <None>:` T↵	Includes the TIFF screen preview image in the file
`Screen preview image size (128 x 128 is standard)? (128/256/512) <128>:` *Press Enter*	Accepts the default resolution for the preview
`Size units (Inches or Millimeters) <Inches>:` *Press Enter*	
`Specify scale by entering: Output Inches=Drawing Units or Fit or ? <Fit>:` *Press Enter*	

```
Standard values for output size
Size      Width      Height
A             8      10 1/2
B            10          16
C            16          21
D            21          33
E            33          43
F            28          40
G            11          90
H            28         143
J            34         176
K            40         143
A4      7 51/64    11 13/64
A3     10 45/64    15 19/32
A2     15 19/32    22 13/32
A1     22 13/32    32 13/64
A0     32 13/64    45 29/32
USER      7 1/2      10 1/2
Enter the Size or Width,Height
(in Inches) <USER>: A↵
Effective plotting area: 8.00 wide
by 3.76 high
```

Exports to the file

Using PostScript To Import Data

The PSIN command inserts an EPS file similarly to inserting a block. If FILEDIA is set to 1, a file dialog box assists in selecting the EPS file. The PSQUALITY system variable is used to define the resolution of the image. A higher number provides higher resolution. A negative number outlines the polygons instead of filling them.

Because you have the MOCKDIM.EPS file, use it in the following exercises to experiment with the PSIN command. First, import the file with the default PSQUALITY setting of 75. Then decrease the setting to see what effect it has on the imported drawing quality.

Using PSIN To Import an EPS File

`Command:` *Enter* `NEW`, *choose* Discard Changes, *then choose* OK	Clears the drawing
`Command:` *Choose* File, *then* Import/Export, *then* Postscript In	Starts PSIN command and displays Select PostScript File dialog box
Double-click on MOCKDIM	Starts the import process, then displays drawing
`Command: psin ....................`	The command line displays dots as the file imports
`Insertion point<0,0,0>:` *Press Enter*	Accepts the default insertion point
`Scale factor: 1`	Specifies scale factor of 1
Zoom to the extents of the imported image to view the results (see fig. 18.11)	

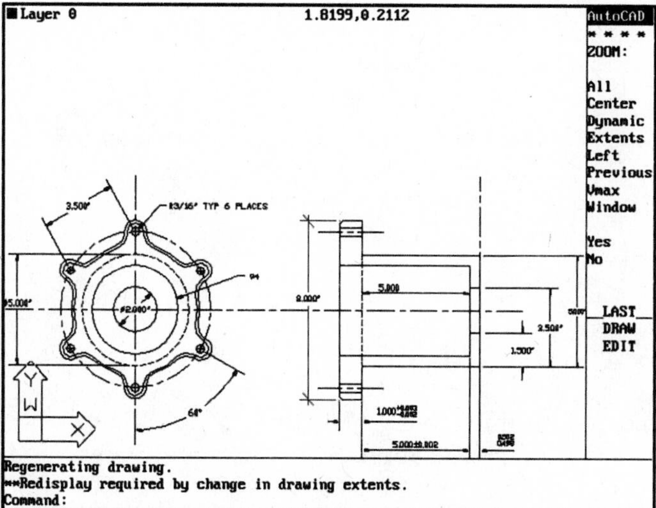

Figure 18.11:
The MOCKDIM.EPS file imported into AutoCAD with PSQUALITY=75.

You may need to experiment with the PSQUALITY variable to see what resolutions work the best for graphics display and hard copy output. A balance between a good image and a reasonable file size must be maintained. Figure 18.12 shows the MOCKDIM drawing with a PSQUALITY setting of 10.

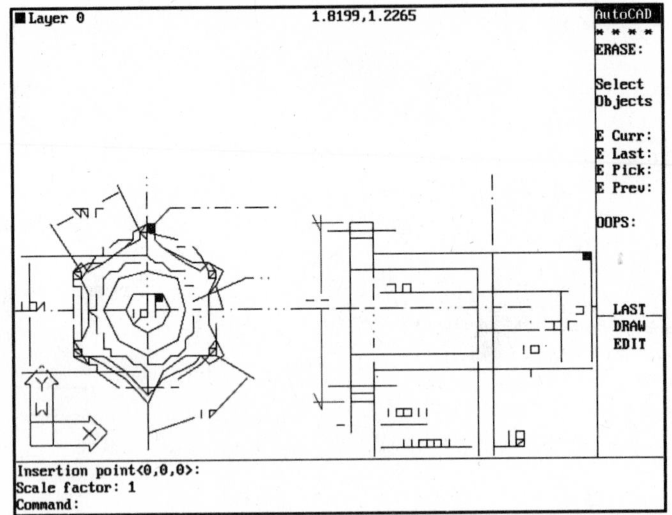

Figure 18.12:
MOCKDIM.EPS imported with PSQUALITY=10.

PostScript capability enables you to use AutoCAD to exchange information with other software packages without converting the image to a raster image. PostScript also gives AutoCAD a better interface with output devices that directly support this type of file.

Using ASCTEXT To Import Text

Standard text files, conforming to the ASCII format, are commonly used in software programs because most application packages can read and write to that format. On a DOS computer, the CONFIG.SYS and AUTOEXEC.BAT files are ASCII files. UNIX configuration files, such as .profile, also are ASCII files. Some of the AutoCAD files, such as the ACAD.PGP file, are ASCII. AutoCAD has an AutoLISP-defined command called ASCTEXT, which can read an ASCII text file into the drawing editor. This command, which is actually a Lisp routine that uses the TEXT command, works much like a block insertion.

Because AutoCAD is really a poor text editor, you may find it more practical to create your notes and product descriptions in a text editor, then insert them into your drawings as needed. The DOS commands EDLIN or EDIT (for DOS 5.0) create an ASCII text file. Keeping your text in ASCII files is preferable to having blocks that contain nothing but text, because you can use them in documents other than AutoCAD drawings. Much like a block library, you can create a library of common text strings that you can use in your drawings. Of course, you can edit the text after it is imported by using the regular AutoCAD text-editing options.

If the ASCTEXT command is executed, you must specify the path and file name, including the extension. The rest of the prompts look similar to the prompts you see when you use the TEXT command. You must specify the placement and justification, along with the text height and rotation angle. If you choose the change text options, you can specify several other parameters that affect the appearance and placement of the text. You see these options in the next exercise, in which you import a text file by using the ASCTEXT command.

In the next exercise, you begin a new drawing, then import your CONFIG.SYS and AUTOEXEC.BAT files. If you want to use different ASCII files (or are working on a different operating system), substitute the appropriate file names.

Using ASCTEXT To Import Text

Begin a new drawing named TEXTIN.

Command: **ASCTEXT** ↵	Starts the ASCTEXT command
File to read (including extension): **\CONFIG.SYS** ↵	
Start point or Center/Middle/Right/?: *Pick a point near .5,8.5 (the upper-left corner of drawing area)*	Specifies the text's starting location, left-justified
Height <0.2000>: *Press Enter*	Accepts the default text height
Rotation angle <0>: *Press Enter*	Accepts the default text rotation
Change text options? <N>: *Press Enter*	Places text
Command: *Press Enter*	Repeats the ASCTEXT command
File to read (including extension): <\CONFIG.SYS>: *Press Enter*	Specifies same file

`Start point or Center/Middle/Right /?: C` ↵	Specifies the Center option
`Center point:` *Pick a point near 6,3*	Sets the text's location, center-justified
`Height <0.2000>:` *Press Enter*	Accepts the default text height
`Rotation angle <0>:` *Press Enter*	Accepts the default text rotation
`Change text options? <N>: Y` ↵	
`Distance between lines/<Auto>: .5` ↵	Sets line spacing
`First line to read/<1>: 2` ↵	Starts at line 2
`Number of lines to read/<All>: 3` ↵	Tells AutoCAD to read from line 2 to line 4
`Underscore each line? <N>:` *Press Enter*	
`Overscore each line? <N>: Y` ↵	
`Change text case? Upper/Lower/<N>: U` ↵	
`Set up columns? <N>:` *Press Enter*	ASCTEXT imports the text in uppercase (see fig. 18.13)

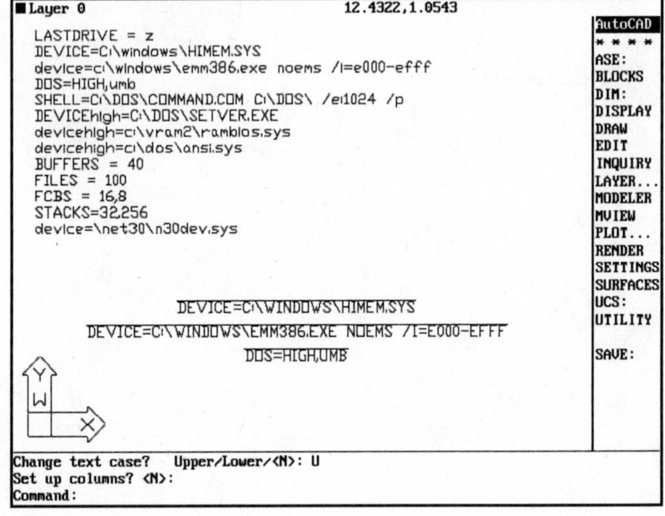

Figure 18.13:
Text imported with ASCTEXT.

The first time you used the ASCTEXT command in this exercise was similar to the way you used the TEXT command, except that you did not type the text. Using it the second time with the case options showed the additional capabilities of the command.

Understanding the AutoCAD SQL Extension

Another feature that is new to AutoCAD in Release 12 is the module called the AutoCAD SQL Extension (ASE). This interface uses Structured Query Language (SQL) to manipulate information in a standard relational database-management system (DBMS). The capability to form strong links between graphic entities and non-graphic data helps develop a small drawing file with a great deal of external data connected to it. This feature provides many advantages over the attribute definition and extraction that is presently being done.

To use the ASE, you must have a database program that uses SQL and is supported by database drivers supplied with AutoCAD or your database vendor. Using the ASE is not difficult, but a strong knowledge of database operation is recommended. See the *AutoCAD SQL Extension Reference Manual* for more information.

Summary

Because many of your suppliers or customers may use other CAD packages, you probably will be faced with data translation. IGES and DXF files are commonly used for this. IGES is more of an industry standard, but DXF usually provides better results when AutoCAD files are used. Try to develop drawing standards to obtain the best results as you translate files. Although you don't often have to read an IGES or DXF file in its ASCII format, it is nice to know that it can be done.

Most people would not purchase and implement a CAD package as extensive as AutoCAD just to create and export graphic files. Because you already learned to use the software and created many graphic files for engineering and design purposes, there are many things you can do with that file in other software packages.

As computers and software applications continue to mature, it is becoming easier to transport data successfully between application packages. AutoCAD Release 12 has provided many new features for doing this. Try to use some of the examples shown in this chapter for your own applications.

Part Five

AutoCAD and 3D Drawing

At this point, you should realize how easily you can increase your design and drafting productivity by using AutoCAD, rather than a drafting machine or drawing board. When you know AutoCAD's commands, you can create, edit, and plot drawings in much less time than is required to draw them manually. You can store more information in an AutoCAD drawing file than you can on a typical paper drawing, and AutoCAD's drawing information is portable.

The techniques you have learned so far, however, are similar to those used in manual drafting, in that you have concentrated on flat 2D drawings. In this final part of *Inside AutoCAD Release 12*, you learn how to take advantage of AutoCAD's third dimension. Instead of showing you how to create more 2D drawings, the following chapters show you how to build 3D models. You also learn how to define a 2D drawing as one or more views of a 3D model.

You can use AutoCAD's 3D-modeling capabilities to increase your drafting productivity, but this is not the only consideration. When you develop a design, you generally must describe one or more three-dimensional objects. You must convey the design to others, including those who must create the real objects from your information. You may think that your 2D drawings accurately convey your 3D design, but others may miss points that you think are obvious. Indeed, your 2D drawings may actually convey something other than the message you originally intended because of conflicts between views, missing elements, or other errors. When you create a 3D model to document your design, however, you can rest assured that all views are consistent. In many—but not all—applications, 3D modeling is essential.

Understanding the Benefits of 3D Modeling

So far, you have worked with two-dimensional images on your screen, much as you do on paper. But paper drawings are hopelessly inadequate when you need to manipulate a 3D object. In AutoCAD, you can draw, edit, rotate, scale, and stretch 3D objects in much the same manner as you work with 2D objects. You can move your viewpoint around the 3D model, using different views of it as you visualize, create, and present the design. If you need a side view, you just move your viewpoint around to that side. If you need to see the model's underside, you simply move your viewpoint again. This flexible visualization capability can solve many difficult design problems.

You can use three-dimensional models to create complex shapes or to find intersections and other design relationships that are difficult or impossible to draw manually.

Learning the Building Blocks of 3D

The task of building a 3D model is not difficult if you take it one step at a time. You can build complex objects from simple shapes, such as cubes, spheres, surfaces, and cones. You can use 2D entities, such as lines, polylines, and circles to build part of your model, and then switch to 3D entities and objects, such as faces, surfaces, spheres, cubes, and cylinders.

But no matter how you put your model together, you are simply making smaller parts and assembling them into larger parts.

How Part Five Is Organized

Part Five leads you step-by-step through the entire process of building 3D models. The explanations and exercises in Part Five take you from building simple 3D shapes with planar and extruded 2D entities, to full 3D surface modeling, and finally to creating presentations and renderings. The five chapters comprising Part Five cover the following topics:

- The basics of 3D drawing
- Creating 3D surface entities
- Viewing your 3D drawings
- Shading and rendering for presentation
- Solid modeling

By the time you complete Part Five, you may find yourself envisioning uses for 3D that you had never before considered.

3D Basics

Chapter 19 teaches you how to manipulate the user coordinate system (UCS) for positioning construction planes anywhere in 3D space. In Chapter 19, you draw on these construction planes by using standard 2D drawing commands. You learn how to use UCSs to move, rotate, and tilt your X,Y,Z axes so that you can create a 3D model from extruded 2D entities.

Viewports take on additional importance when you need to visualize a model in three dimensions. The exercises show you how to see a more realistic view of your model with hidden lines removed. Chapter 19 shows you how to create a 3D model of a drafting board—ironically, a furnishing you may no longer need.

3D Entities

Chapter 20 introduces you to new entities, such as 3D polylines, 3D faces, and 3D surface meshes. You model an office chair by creating 3D parts and inserting them as blocks for assembling the chair. In addition to the basic surface commands, Chapter 20 shows you how to use AutoLISP-defined commands that create 3D objects, such as boxes, wedges, cones, and spheres. Surface shading is used for hidden-line removal and for viewing your model quickly and clearly.

Viewing in 3D

Chapter 21 shows you how to adjust your 3D viewpoint dynamically and create perspective views by using the DVIEW command as a single 3D substitute for the VPOINT and ZOOM commands. You learn advanced 3D-viewing techniques that make 3D drawing easier and help you plan and preview 3D presentations. The chapter shows you how to put together dynamic views, slides, and scripts to create a walk-through of successive views in a simple 3D office model.

Shading and Rendering

AutoCAD Release 12 features powerful rendering capabilities, which can achieve a more realistic picture of a surfaced 3D model. Chapter 22 covers AutoCAD's new rendering commands and shows you how to create a shaded image, beginning with an explanation of the fundamentals of rendering. These new commands provide the shading capabilities that formerly required the separate AutoShade program. A simple exercise using most of the default settings is included, followed by explanations of many of the options that utilize more fully the features of rendering.

Solid Modeling

Chapter 23 covers AutoCAD's capability to perform solid modeling. You can purchase the solid-modeling package, called the *Advanced Modeling Extension* (AME), at an additional cost. Although solid modeling does not

entirely replace the traditional 3D-drawing techniques, it certainly introduces some exciting new capabilities to AutoCAD.

Learning When To Use 3D

One of your goals in this 3D section is to learn how to determine when 3D modeling is useful and when it is not. Many projects do not require 3D modeling. Good examples are simple plans, diagrams, and flowcharts.

On the other hand, much of what you design and build is three-dimensional, and 3D modeling can be the most natural way to create and document your design. Three-dimensional modeling may add time and complexity to the design process, so you need to know how to determine when the added complexity is worthwhile. Only you can make this determination, but you first must be proficient in 3D.

In any case, once you see how easy 3D can be, you can probably find some indispensable use for it in your everyday work.

19

Getting Started with 3D

In a 3D view, what you see is one of many possible views of the 3D model that you are creating in AutoCAD. You need to remember this distinction between the model itself and the view of the model. AutoCAD provides one set of tools that you use to build 3D models, and provides another set of tools that you use to view your models.

This chapter teaches you the basics of working in 3D. First, you learn how to create a 2D drawing—called an *isometric drawing*—that emulates 3D. After that, you create a *wireframe drawing*, consisting of familiar AutoCAD entities, but built in 3D dimensional space. This chapter shows you how to use the VPOINT command to control the angle from which you view your 3D model, and then shows you how to use viewports in 3D. You learn about moving and rotating your UCS and about drawing and editing in 3D with extruded 2D entities.

This chapter also shows you how to use the HIDE command to remove hidden lines for more realistic 3D images, how to create and insert 3D blocks into your drawings, and how to compose multiple 3D views.

In the following lessons, you focus on using the UCS and 2D entities to build 3D models. AutoCAD provides two methods for using 2D entities to represent 3D objects. First, you can draw isometrically, just as you do in manual drafting. Second, you can create a true 3D drawing with 2D entities by controlling the entities' positions in 3D space and by extruding them along their Z axes.

Before you begin working with a true 3D drawing, consider the ways in which you can create 3D views by working entirely in 2D with an isometric drawing.

Understanding Isometric Drawing

Isometric drawings are 2D representations of a 3D object. Why should this chapter include a section on 2D drawing? Mechanical and piping designers frequently use isometric drawings to help the fabricator visualize the product, as shown in figure 19.1.

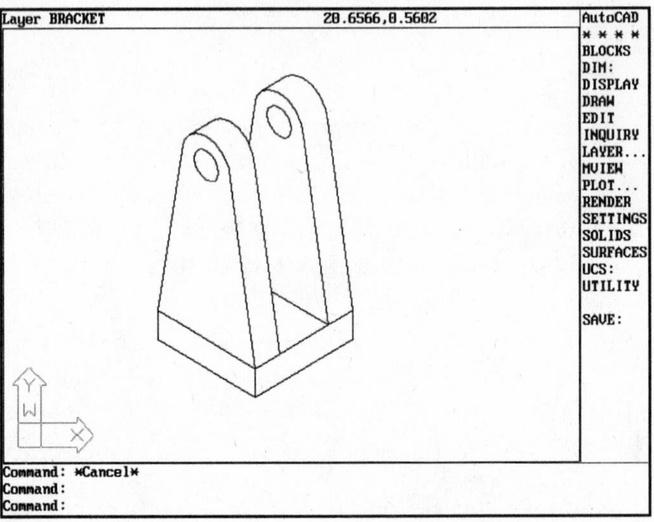

Figure 19.1:

An isometric drawing of a pulley bracket.

Isometric drawing offers several advantages, which make it a viable alternative to true 3D drawing. Here are several of the advantages of isometric drawing:

- In AutoCAD, isometric drawing uses familiar 2D commands. You do not need to master new commands or concepts.

- In some cases, you can create an isometric drawing more quickly than you can generate a 3D model.
- You can draw isometrics alongside other standard 2D drawings without using multiple viewports or paper space.

Isometric drawing also has a few disadvantages, including the following:

- You cannot view isometrics from different angles, as you can a 3D model.
- You cannot view isometrics in perspective mode.
- You cannot automatically remove hidden lines from an isometric drawing.
- When you make changes to one isometric view, all views do not automatically update, as 3D models do.

In this section, you learn how to create an isometric drawing by using some of AutoCAD's basic 2D tools. As you develop your isometric drawing and as you continue to learn about 3D construction, you begin to understand how each technique can be applied for specific needs.

Setting Up for an Isometric Drawing

AutoCAD provides several tools to assist in the creation of isometric drawings. Of these tools, the two most frequently used are AutoCAD's isometric grid option and the ISOPLANE command. The isometric grid option enables you to rotate your drawing's snap and grid settings to create an isometric drawing. The ISOPLANE command enables you to set the current drawing plane to the top, right side, or left side.

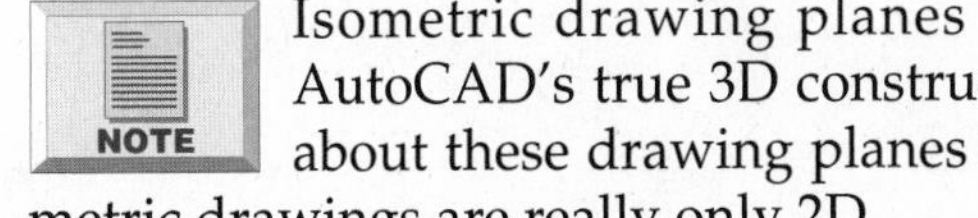

Isometric drawing planes are entirely different from AutoCAD's true 3D construction planes. You learn more about these drawing planes later, but remember that isometric drawings are really only 2D.

In the following exercise, you learn how to create a 2D isometric drawing of a pulley bracket. You begin by setting up a new drawing, called ISO, using the settings shown in table 19.1. You then define a single working viewport.

Table 19.1
Isometric Drawing Settings

COORDS	*TILEMODE*	*GRID*	*ORTHO*	*SNAP*	*UCSICON*
ON	OFF (0)	ON	OFF	.5	OR

UNITS	Use defaults for all UNITS settings.
LIMITS	Set LIMITS from 0,0 to 17,15.
ZOOM	Zoom All.

Layer Name	*State*	*Color*	*Linetype*
0	On	White	CONTINUOUS
BRACKET	On/Current	White	CONTINUOUS

Starting an Isometric Drawing

Choose File, then Open, and enter `ISO=IA7150` and skip to the end of the exercise.

Choose File, then New, enter `\IA\ISO`, and make the settings shown in table 19.1.

`Command:` *Choose* View, *then* Mview, *then* Fit	Defines a single, working viewport
`Command: mview`	
`ON/OFF/Hideplot/Fit/2/3/4/Restore/` `<First Point>: fit Regenerating drawing`	
`Command:` **`MS`**	Returns to model space

Working with ISOMODE

At this point your drawing is not unlike most 2D drawings. You can draw an isometric by using lines and ellipses, but you can get the angles correct much more simply by using AutoCAD's built-in isometric drawing tools.

To begin working in isometric mode, you must first change the snap style. AutoCAD provides two preset snap styles: standard and isometric. *Standard* is the default style, in which the crosshair cursor's X and Y axes are

perpendicular. *Isometric* skews the crosshairs and the snap angle to an isometric angle.

Figure 19.2 illustrates the three isometric planes you can work in: Right, Left, and Top. The ISOPLANE command enables you to set the isometric plane you want to use.

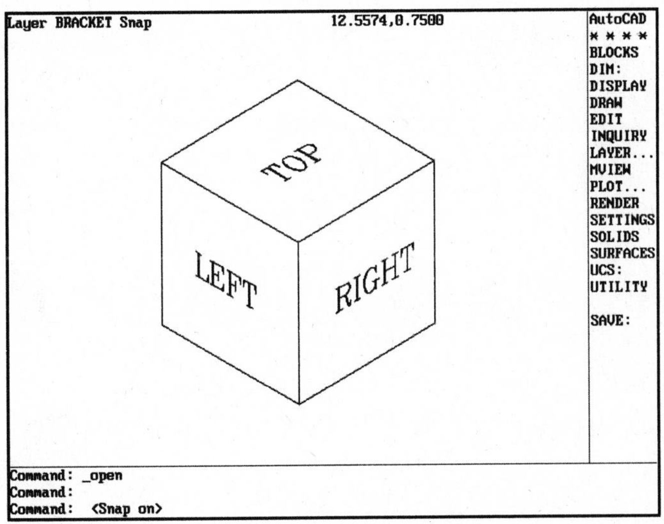

Figure 19.2:

The Right, Left, and Top ISOPLANE options.

The following exercise enables you to practice using the SNAP command's Style option and the ISOPLANE command as you prepare to draw the baseplate for the pulley bracket. Continue working in the drawing you began in the previous exercise.

Using the ISOPLANE Command

`Command:` **`SNAP`** ↵	
`Snap spacing or ON/OFF/Aspect/Rotate/Style <0.5000>:` **`S`** ↵	Specifies the snap Style option
`Standard/Isometric <S>:` **`I`** ↵	Specifies the Isometric style
`Vertical spacing <0.5000>:`↵	Sets the snap spacing
`Command:` **`ISOPLANE`** ↵	Prompts for a new isometric plane
`Left/Top/Right/<Toggle>:` **`R`** ↵	Specifies the Right isometric plane

Notice how the grid dots and the crosshairs change orientation, as shown in figure 19.3.

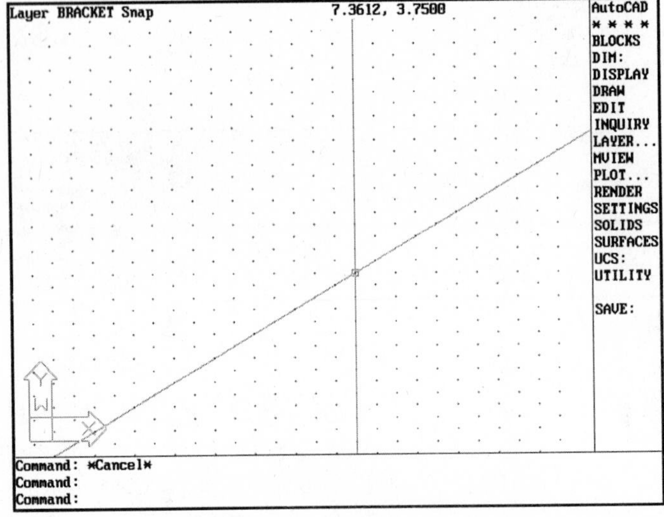

Figure 19.3:
The effect of an isometric snap style on a drawing.

Now you are ready to begin drawing your isometric pulley bracket. Begin by using the LINE command to create isometric rectangles to outline the baseplate. When the snap and grid settings are properly defined, you should be able to use the coordinate display to pick the coordinates directly from the screen, without typing them in.

Creating an Isometric Baseplate

Continue drawing in the ISO drawing.

`Command:` **LINE** ↵	Issues LINE command
`From point:` *Pick the first corner at 9.0933,2.25*	
`To point:` *Pick the second corner at 1.0<90*	
`To point:` *Pick the third corner at 4.0<30*	
`To point:` *Pick the final corner at 1.0<270*	
`To point:` **C** ↵	Closes the rectangle
`Command:` *Choose* Construct, *then* Mirror	Begins the MIRROR command
`Command: _mirror`	

`Select objects:` *Use a crossing window to select lines, as shown in figure 19.4*	Selects three lines for mirroring
`Select objects:` *Press Enter*	Ends object selection
`First point of mirror line:` *Use ENDP object snap to pick at ①*	
`Second point:` *Use ENDP object snap to pick at ②*	
`Delete old objects? <N>` *Press Enter*	Copies the lines in a mirror image

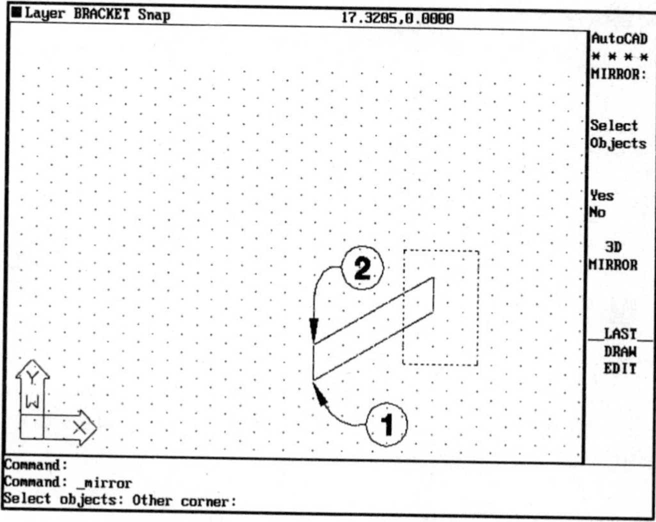

Figure 19.4:
The first half of the baseplate.

You have now created your first isometric drawing. Next, you learn a fast way to switch between isometric planes and a way to easily create isometric circles.

Drawing the Support Arms

Now you create the bracket's support arms. You can create one arm, using the LINE and ELLIPSE command, then copy and modify the other arm.

Creating the Bracket Arms

`Command:` **`ISOPLANE`** ↵	
`Left/Top/Right/<Toggle>:` **`L`** ↵	Specifies the left isometric drawing plane
`Current Isometric plane is: Left`	
`Command:` **`LINE`** ↵	
`From point:` *Pick at 9.0933,3.25*	
`To point:` *Pick at 8.2272,9.75*	
`To point:` *Pick at 6.4952,10.75*	
`To point:` *Pick at 5.6292,5.25*	
`To point:` *Press Enter*	Ends the LINE command
`Command:` **`ELLIPSE`** ↵	
`<Axis endpoint>/Center/Isocircle:` **`I`** ↵	Chooses the Isocircle option
`Center of circle:` *Use MID object snap to pick the short line at* ① (see fig. 19.5)	
`<Circle radius>/Diameter:` *Use ENDP object snap to pick the short line at* ②	Draws an isometric circle

You have now drawn the support arm's basic outline, as shown in figure 19.5. The short line at the top of the arm is a temporary construction line. Next, you clean up and complete the arm.

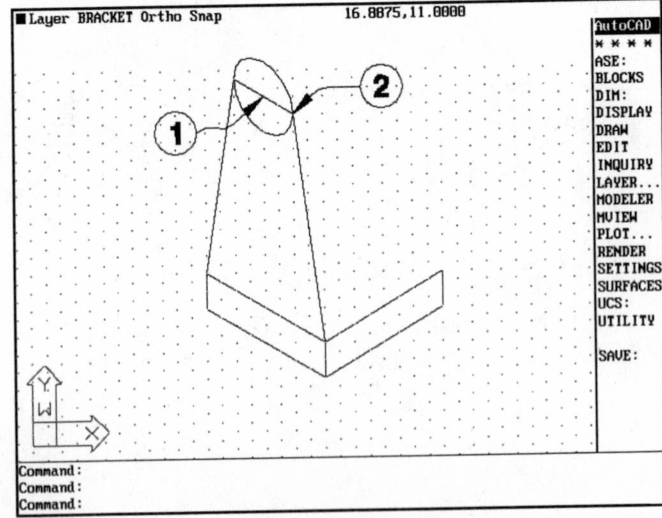

Figure 19.5:

The support arm begins to take form.

You have learned how to use the ISOPLANE command to change the current isometric plane, but there is an easier way. You can press Ctrl-E you to switch modes, even during another command, in Left-Top-Right order.

You also can change the current isometric plane by using the Drawing Modes dialog box. To reach the dialog box, choose Settings, then Drawing Modes. In this dialog box, you can change the current isometric plane and turn the isometric snap style on or off.

In the next exercise, you complete the support arm. First use the ELLIPSE command to create a "hole," then copy the first support arm to create the second arm.

Completing the Support Arm

`Command:` **`ELLIPSE`**↵	
`<Axis endpoint>/Center/Isocircle:` **`I`**↵	Specifies the Isocircle option
`Center of circle:` *Use MID object snap to pick the short line at the top of the arm*	Uses the same center as the last circle
`<Circle radius>/Diameter:` **`0.5`**↵	Specifies the radius
`Command:` **`COPY`**↵	
`Select objects:` *Select the outer ellipse and the three support arm lines*	
`<Base point of displacement>/Multiple:` *Pick any point on the screen*	
`Second point of displacement:` *Pick at 1<30 with snap on*	
`Command:` **`L`**↵	Issues the LINE command
`line From point:` *Use TAN object snap to pick at* ① (see fig. 19.6)	
`To point:` *Use TAN object snap to pick at* ②	
`To point:` *Press Enter*	Ends the LINE command

In the following steps, you trim the large ellipse.

`Command:` **`TRIM`**↵	
`Select cutting edge(s)`	
`Select objects:` *Select the short line at* ③ (see fig. 19.6)	Selects the cutting edge

`<Select object to trim>/Undo:` *Pick the lower half of the large ellipse*	Removes the lower half of the ellipse

Repeat the TRIM command on the second large ellipse, then erase the hidden lines and the construction guide lines so that your drawing matches figure 19.7.

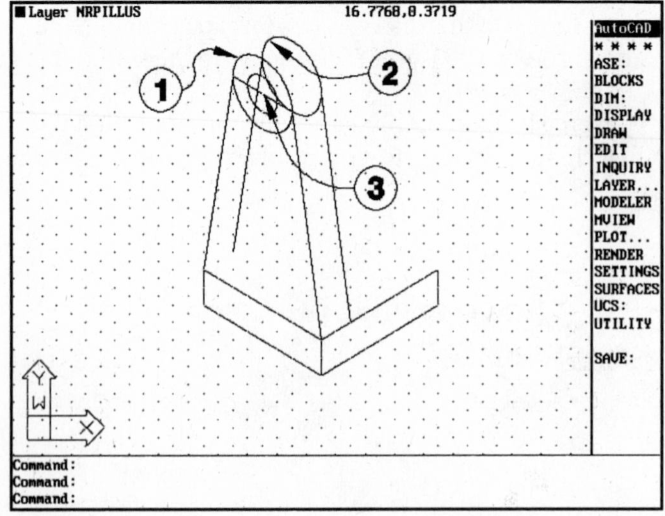

Figure 19.6:

Finishing the support arm.

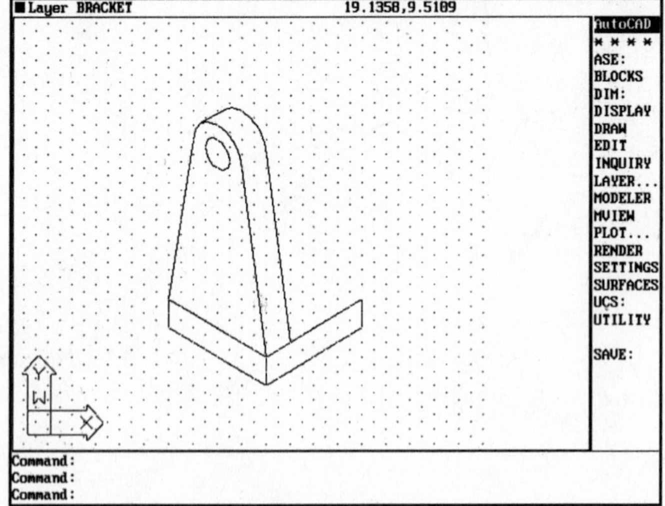

Figure 19.7:

A completed support arm.

To complete the bracket, you must copy the first support arm, trim the hidden lines, and add a line where the second support arm meets the baseplate. To simplify the process of picking points from the screen, work in the TOP isometric plane.

Completing the Pulley Bracket

`Command: COPY↵`

`Select objects:` *Pick the entities that make the first bracket*

`<Base point or displacement>/Multiple:` *Pick a point near the baseplate corner*

`Second point of displacement:` *Drag the selected entities 3 units at 30 degrees* — Copies the support arm

Finally, draw a line where the arm meets the base and use the TRIM command to clean up the second arm, which is obscured by the first arm. Your finished bracket should look like the one shown in figure 19.8.

This is a good time to save your drawing and take a break.

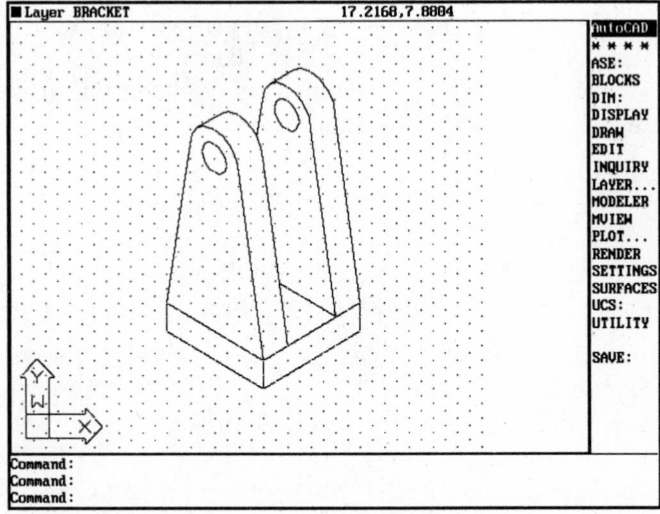

Figure 19.8:

The completed isometric pulley bracket drawing.

You can reset the Snap Style to Standard and annotate your isometric drawing, or you can combine isometric and orthographic drawings in the same drawing without using paper space. You also save the processing time normally required for AutoCAD to perform the HIDE command on a true 3D model. If you need to see another view of the pulley, however, you have to draw it. Your isometric drawing is not truly 3D and cannot be properly viewed from different angles.

As you see, AutoCAD's isometric tools are quick and easy, but not well-suited for multiple views. If your drawing requires a single, simple 3D view for illustrative purposes, isometric drawing works well.

But what if you need to generate multiple views of a model? You can do this by using AutoCAD's powerful 3D tools. AutoCAD has many 3D commands; many of the 2D commands work in 3D space, too. One of the key concepts behind 3D in AutoCAD is the *User Coordinate System*, or *UCS*. Before you begin working with 3D tools, you must learn how to use the UCS to your advantage.

Using the User Coordinate System (UCS)

Up to this point, you have been working in AutoCAD's basic coordinate system—the *World Coordinate System*, or *WCS*. In fact, you have been working in the X,Y plane of the WCS. The WCS is the coordinate system of AutoCAD's model space. All drawing entities are defined in terms of their coordinate values in this coordinate system.

The principal difficulty of 3D modeling lies in the 2D nature of your workstation. Your workstation's input and output devices are two-dimensional devices. You can use the mouse or digitizer to interactively specify X and Y coordinates, but not Z coordinates. To construct 3D models, however, you must specify X, Y, and Z coordinate values for points and displacements.

To solve this problem, AutoCAD enables you to define your own coordinate systems, or UCSs. You have only one WCS, but you can create as many UCSs as you want. You can define your UCSs at any angle and location in the 3D space that is defined by the WCS. The X,Y plane of a UCS is its default construction plane, as is the X,Y plane of the WCS. A *construction plane* is like a transparent sheet of plastic on which you can draw by using standard 2D or 3D AutoCAD commands. You can rotate and align that transparent sheet to any orientation in 3D space by using the UCS command.

The Z elevation of points defaults to the construction plane, unless you explicitly specify a different elevation above or below the construction plane. You can give the construction plane a non-zero Z elevation, or you can relocate the UCS to control the Z coordinate. In both cases, the end result is the same, because entities are defined in terms of WCS coordinate values, regardless of how they are specified.

Look at the table drawings in figure 19.9. The four views are of a single table drawn in 3D. Each view has an associated UCS that enables you to work on a different plane, as if it were a 2D X,Y plane. In the following exercises, you learn how to create and edit this table by using 2D drawing entities and editing commands. The key to using 3D efficiently is learning how to locate your UCS in your drawing.

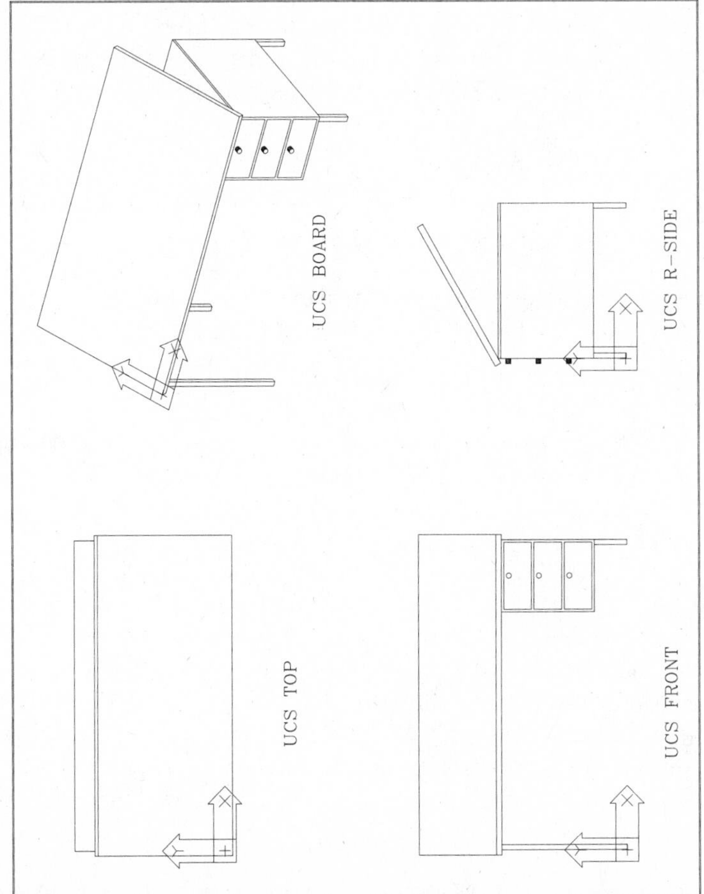

Figure 19.9:

The table drawings, with UCS icons.

You can draw 2D entities in any UCS construction plane and then extrude them in the Z direction. The drawing board, for example, is drawn at a 30-degree angle to the table top. It was drawn by first placing the UCS on the table top, then rotating the UCS' X-axis angle 30 degrees to the top of the table. To give the board thickness, the artist extruded it in the Z direction. All 2D drawing and editing commands work for drawing and editing in any construction plane, set by the UCS anywhere in 3D space. If you know how to locate and use your UCS, you have an immediate advantage because you can use everything you already know about 2D drawing and editing to create work in 3D.

Setting Up for a 3D Drawing

Later you will draw a drafting table in 3D, but first, draw a few simple 3D entities and then view them from several different angles to become familiar with viewpoints in 3D space. To begin, set up a new drawing called UCS.

Setting Up the 3D UCS Drawing

Choose File, then New, and enter the drawing name `\IA\UCS`. Turn on the coordinate display and grid, and set snap to .5.

If you encounter problems in any exercise, check your current UCS, thickness, and object snap settings.

Getting Around in Simple 3D Drawings

Every entity you have drawn so far has been in the same plane as the WCS construction plane. All the entities' X and Y values have been in a flat plane, and the Z value for all these entities has been 0. Just as you have control over X and Y locations for entities, AutoCAD gives you Z-axis control for creating 3D objects.

You can draw some entities directly in 3D. A point or line does not have to lie flat on the X,Y construction plane. The simplest way to give 3D life to your drawing is to add a Z coordinate when you pick point coordinates. The LINE command, the full 3D-entity commands (3DPOLY, 3DFACE, and 3DMESH), and several surfacing commands accept Z input for any point. Other 2D-entity commands accept a Z coordinate for their first point only, and that coordinate is applied to the rest of their points so that they are created parallel to the current construction plane.

Although many 3D objects look complex, they are easy to draw. The following simple exercise shows you how to use all three coordinates (X,Y,Z) to create lines in 3D space.

Using LINE To Make 3D Lines

Zoom Center with a center point of 0,0 and a height of 3

`Command:` **`UCSICON`**↵

`ON/OFF/ALL/Noorigin/ORigin<ON>:` **`OR`**↵	Displays the UCS icon at the drawing's origin
`Command:` *Choose* Draw, *then* Line, *then* 1 Segment *and draw a line along the X axis from 0,0,0 to 1,0,0*	Draws a white horizontal line
`Command:` *Choose* Settings, *then* Entity Modes, *and set the color to red*	Changes the default entity color from BYLAYER to red
`Command:` *Choose* Draw, *then* Line, *then* 1 Segment, *and draw a line along the Y axis from 0,0,0 to 0,1,0*	Draws a red vertical line
`Command:` *Choose* Settings, *then* Entity Modes, *and set the color to green*	
`Command:` *Choose* Draw, *then* Line, *then* 1 Segment *and draw a line along the Z axis, picking point 0,0,0 and entering point* `0,0,1`↵	Draws a green line toward you, which appears as a dot

Notice that you used three values for each coordinate. The third value is for the Z axis. Although the first two lines did not actually require a Z value, the Z coordinates are included to clarify the exercise. Your drawing should resemble the one shown in figure 19.10, with the lines in different colors.

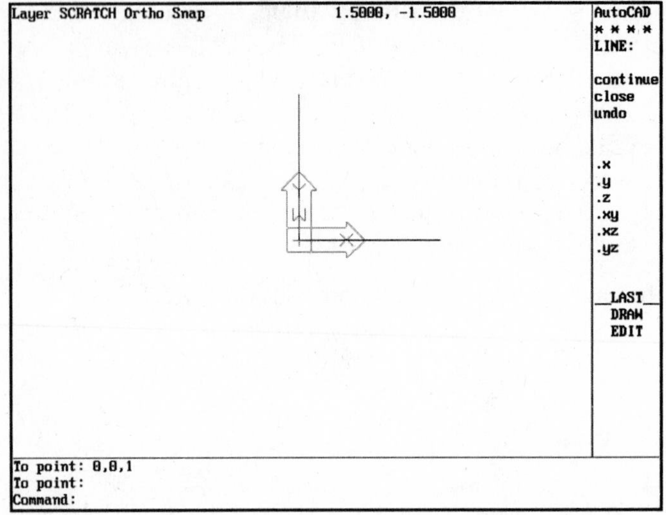
Layer SCRATCH Ortho Snap 1.5000, -1.5000
AutoCAD
* * * *
LINE:
continue
close
undo
.x
.y
.z
.xy
.xz
.yz
LAST
DRAW
EDIT
To point: 0,0,1
To point:
Command:

Figure 19.10:

Three lines in 3D space (the Z-axis line appears as a green dot).

Take a look at your drawing. You see two lines and the UCS icon. Although you drew three lines, only the two lines in the X,Y plane are clearly visible (see fig. 19.10). From your current viewing direction, you cannot see the third line because you are looking directly down at its endpoint. It looks as if the line is coming directly out of the screen at you, so you see it as a single point. You need a way to view the drawing from a better angle. Fortunately, you can use AutoCAD's VPOINT command to change your viewing angle.

Using VPOINT To Get Around

Until now, your graphics window has represented the X,Y plane only. Your vantage point, in front of the screen, is actually some distance above the X,Y plane, looking down along the Z axis. If the plane of the screen represents flat ground, you look at that flat ground from a perch on top a flagpole. Figure 19.11 shows you how the real-world X, Y, and Z axes are oriented on your screen in a normal plan view.

In AutoCAD, the direction from which you view your drawing or model is called the *viewpoint*. AutoCAD's VPOINT command controls this direction in relation to the drawing. The default viewpoint is 0,0,1, which indicates that your viewpoint is directly over the X,Y origin. Your line of sight is

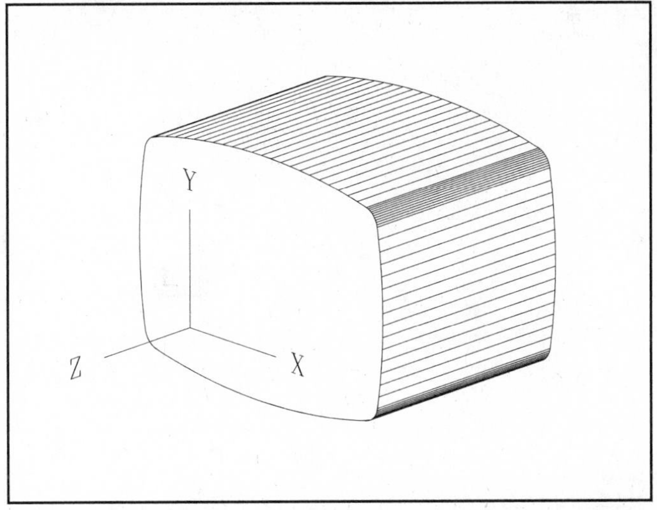

Figure 19.11:

The orientation of the X, Y, and Z axes, relative to the screen.

along a line from 0,0,1 to 0,0,0 (the origin). This view of a drawing is called the *plan view.* As long as you are directly above your drawing and looking down the Z axis, everything you create with 2D entities looks flat.

To see 3D, you have to move to a point that is not looking straight down at your model. Your viewpoint must have a non-zero X or Y, or both. For example, a 1,1,1 setting gives you a 45-degree angle in the X,Y plane and a 45-degree angle above the X,Y plane. This perspective enables you to look back at 0,0,0, where your lines are located. You can use VPOINT to set the viewpoint to any X, Y,Z location.

Although you can enter values to locate your viewpoint, the easiest way to use VPOINT is by using its predefined icon selections or by using the VPOINT command's globe and axes. Figure 19.12 shows the Viewpoint child pull-down menu, including Axes, which issues the VPOINT command with the globe and axes option. The child menu also offers the Presets option for the Viewpoint Presents dialog box (the DDVPOINT command), which enables you to preset views and coordinate-defined viewpoints. The menu also offers the Set Vpoint option, which issues the VPOINT command.

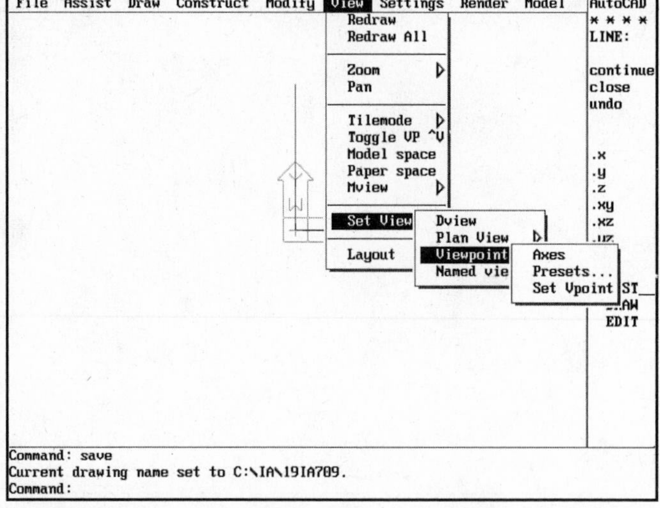

Figure 19.12:

The Viewpoint child pull-down menu.

Using the VPOINT Globe and Axes

The viewpoint globe (see fig. 19.13) looks like a bull's-eye with crosshairs. You can display the viewpoint globe by entering **VPOINT** at the VPOINT command's `Rotate/<0.0000,0.0000,1.0000>:` prompt. You also can choose Set View, Viewpoint, Axes from the View pull-down menu.

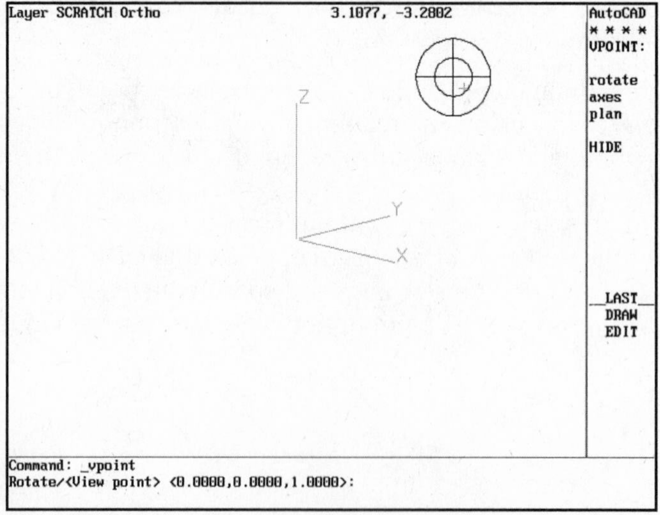

Figure 19.13:

The VPOINT globe and axes.

To understand VPOINT, think of your drawing as being located at the center of a transparent globe, so that the X,Y plane is in the same plane as the globe's equator. The default viewpoint is sitting at the North Pole, looking down to the center of the globe, at your drawing. The globe's concentric circles represent the world's globe; the center point represents the North Pole, the inner circle represents the equator, and the outer circle represents the South Pole.

When you move the cursor around the viewpoint globe, you move around the outside of the world globe's sphere. If the cursor is in the inner circle, as shown in figure 19.13, you are above the equator, looking down on your model (that is, you are in the northern hemisphere, looking down toward the equator). If the cursor is in the outer circle, you are looking up at the drawing from *underneath* it (that is, you are in the southern hemisphere, looking up toward the equator).

If you move the cursor to a point directly on the inner circle, you are looking directly at the drawing's edge. From this view, a 2D drawing appears as a single line. The horizontal and vertical lines represent the X and Y axes, dividing the globe into four quadrants, just as the AutoCAD X and Y axes divide your drawing.

The dynamically moving X,Y,Z axes shown in your graphics window (see fig. 19.13) reflect the position of your viewpoint as you move the cursor. For some users, this process is an intuitive way to select a viewpoint, although it does take some getting used to.

In the following exercise, you display the VPOINT globe, use the illustrations to position your cursor in the concentric circles, and then pick your viewpoint. Your drawing regenerates to reflect your VPOINT position.

Using the VPOINT Globe and Axes

Continue working in the drawing \IA\UCS.

`Command:` *Choose* View, *then* Set View, Viewpoint, Axes	Displays the globe and axes and prompts for a viewpoint
`Rotate/<0.0000,0.0000,1.0000>:` *Move your pointing device until it matches figure 19.13, then press the pick button*	Displays the lines in 3D, in the lower left of the drawing area
`Command:` *Choose* View, *then* Pan, *and pan your three drawn lines to the screen's center (see fig. 19.14)*	

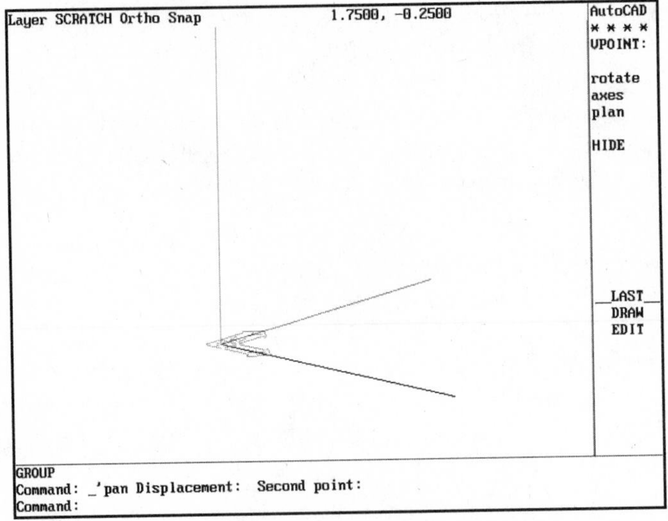

Figure 19.14:

The view of the lines, after VPOINT and PAN.

The VPOINT command always causes a regeneration and displays the image zoomed to the drawing extents. You can cancel the regeneration as soon as you see how the drawing will be displayed, and then you can zoom in to the desired view. For frequently used viewpoints, you can save and restore named views by using the VIEW command, described in Chapter 5.

Selecting Predefined Viewpoints

You also can select any of nine predefined viewpoint directions from the Viewpoint Presents dialog box (the DDVPOINT command), shown in figure 19.15. You can select the viewpoint by choosing one of the eight preset angles (0 degrees through 315 degrees), then selecting the angle from the X,Y plane. If none of the preset angles suits you, you can enter a specific angle X Axis and the XY Plane boxes. To return to a plan view, select Set to Plan View. This sets you viewpoint to 0,0,0. You also can control which coordinate system the viewpoint is set to by selecting either the Absolute to WCS or Relative to UCS button. Normally, you set the viewpoint absolute to the WCS, as is the case in the following exercises. After you specify both angles, AutoCAD calculates the viewpoint and regenerates the drawing.

The Viewpoint Presets dialog box is quick and foolproof. To get a precise view angle, use the angle entry boxes to type in the angle.

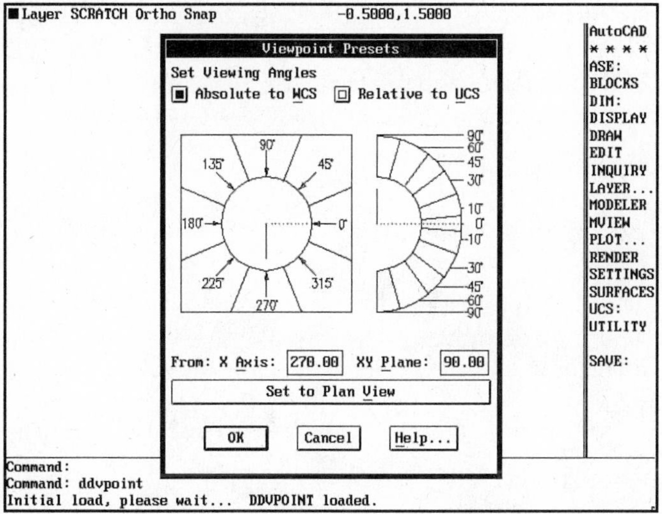

Figure 19.15:

The Viewpoint Presets dialog box.

Using Polar Angles To Select a Viewpoint

If you look at the VPOINT prompt on the command line, you see the Rotate option. The VPOINT icon menu uses Rotate to set its two angles. You also can set the viewpoint by entering two angles at the command prompt. The first angle determines the rotation in the X,Y plane from the X axis (X axis equals 0 angle) and the second angle determines the Z angle (inclination) from the X,Y plane. The Rotate option seems more natural to many users than specifying an X,Y,Z coordinate point in space. Use the following exercise to experiment with the VPOINT options to see which you like. First, use the dialog box again.

Using VPOINT Options

`Command:` *Choose* View, *then* Set View, Viewpoint, *then* Presets, *and click in the area labeled 225 degrees (arrow pointing to upper right), then enter* `30` *in the* X,Y Plane *edit box, then* OK.	Displays the Viewport presets dialog box

Menu supplies angle and regenerates view in figure 19.16.

Next, you use the VPOINT command and coordinate values.

`Command:` *Select* View, *then* Set View, *then* Viewpoint, *then* Set Vpoint

`_vpoint Rotate/<View point> <-6.5358,-6.5358,5.3364>: 1,1,.5 ↵`	Regenerates the view shown in figure 19.17

Now use the VPOINT command and rotate option.

`Command: VPOINT↵`	
`Rotate/<View point> <1.0000,1.0000,0.5000>: R↵`	
`Enter angle in X-Y plane from X axis <45>: 200 ↵`	
`Enter angle from X-Y plane <19>: 50↵`	Regenerates the view shown in figure 19.18

Finally, use the Rotate option to view lines from below the X,Y plane:

`Command:` *Press Enter*	Repeats command
`vpoint Rotate/<View point> <-0.9060,-0.3298,1.1491>: R↵`	
`Enter angle in X-Y plane from X axis <200>:` *Press Enter*	
`Enter angle from X-Y plane <50>: -50↵`	Regenerates the view shown in figure 19.19

Notice that the box is now gone from the UCS icon (see 19.19). It appears only when your viewpoint is above the X,Y plane, as shown in figure 19.18.

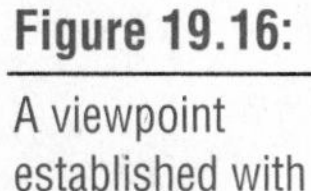
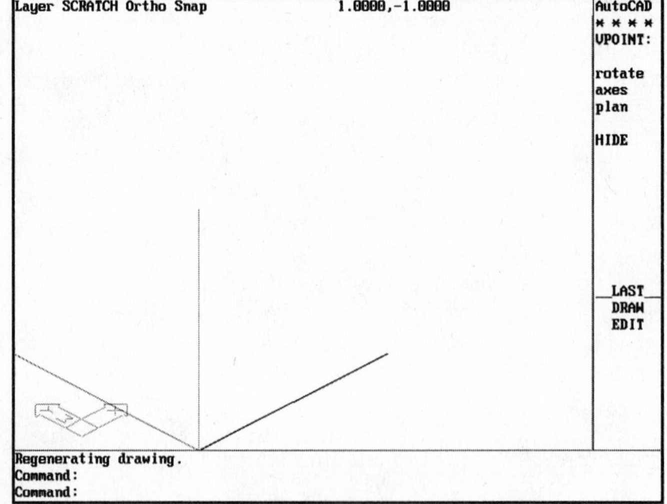

Figure 19.16:

A viewpoint established with a dialog box.

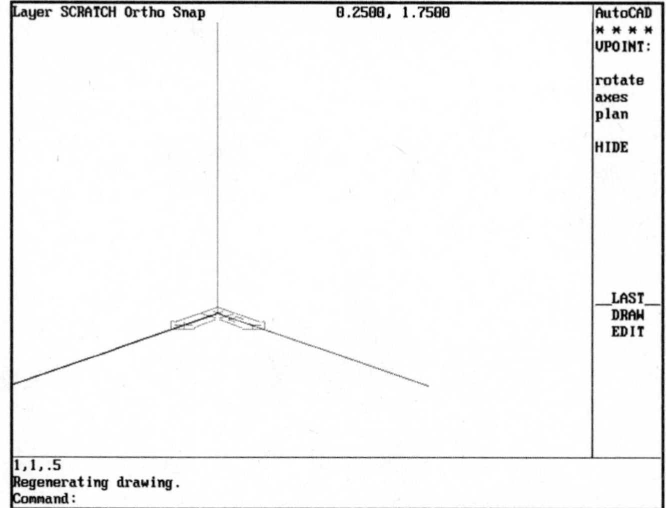

Figure 19.17:

A viewpoint established with coordinate values.

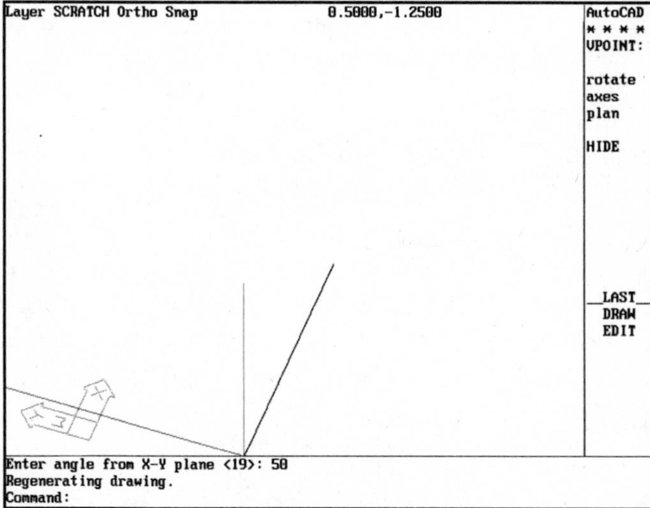

Figure 19.18:

A viewpoint established with the Rotate option.

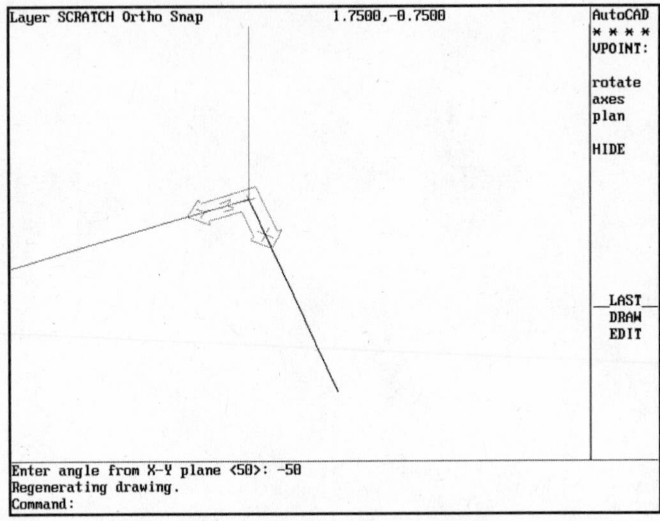

Figure 19.19:

A bottom view, using the Rotate option.

Practice with VPOINT for a few minutes to get a feel for the way it works. VPOINT makes sense if you remember that you are always looking through the specified viewpoint toward 0,0,0 (and beyond). Remember, too, that you are moving around the drawing; it does not move around. The entire drawing is always displayed. As you try different options, you find that the X,Y,Z axes icon matches your three lines. The lines' three colors and their intersection at 0,0,0 help you identify your vantage point.

If you select a viewpoint that is parallel to the current X,Y construction plane, the UCS icon turns into a *broken pencil* icon. Because AutoCAD projects distances from the screen to the X,Y plane, a small distance on the screen projects to a large one on the X,Y plane, resulting in a loss of precision. If the broken pencil appears, AutoCAD cannot project the points with acceptable precision.

If you have trouble picking a viewpoint, try to set the angle in the X,Y plane first, and then adjust the inclination.

The WORLDVIEW System Variable

By default, VPOINT always bases your views on the World Coordinate System, not on the current UCS. The WORLDVIEW system variable's

setting determines whether VPOINT bases the view on the WCS or UCS. The default WORLDVIEW of 1 enables you to specify your viewpoint relative to the WCS. If you set WORLDVIEW to 0, your coordinates and viewpoint-rotation angles are interpreted by VPOINT in the current UCS rather than the WCS. If you want to specify a viewpoint relative to the WCS while a UCS is current and WORLDVIEW is set to 0, prefix the coordinates with an asterisk and the UCS is ignored.

Generally, you should set WORLDVIEW to 1 (the default). It then provides a constant viewpoint reference to the World Coordinate System and makes it easier not to get "lost in space." As you become more comfortable in AutoCAD's 3D world, you can use the WORLDVIEW system variable for greater flexibility in positioning your models in the graphics window. Regardless of the WORLDVIEW setting or current UCS, the VPOINT command always regenerates the drawing looking through your viewpoint at the WCS origin.

Using the PLAN Command

What do you do if you lose your bearings? The PLAN command quickly returns your view to the default orientation. It automatically resets the viewpoint to 0,0,1 in the current UCS (default), the WCS, or a named UCS you have saved.

Try using a quick PLAN command in the following exercise.

Using PLAN To Return to a Plan View

`Command:` *Choose* View, *then* Set View, Plan View, World	Displays the lines at the lower left corner in plan view in the World UCS
Zoom Center at 0,0,0 with a height of 2	Centers the lines

Save the drawing and continue, or end the drawing session and take a break.

You could have chosen Plan View, Current UCS because the WCS is the current UCS in this exercise.

The preceding drawing exercise showed that you can use AutoCAD's basic LINE command in 3D space. The next section shows you how to use other 2D commands in the 3D drawing world.

Drawing 2D Entities in 3D Space

You can draw most of AutoCAD's basic 2D entities with a Z-coordinate value. 2D entities, such as polylines, circles, arcs, and solids, are constrained to the X,Y plane of the UCS. For these entities, the Z value is accepted only for the first coordinate to set the elevation of the 2D entity above or below the current plane.

When you pick entity coordinates, AutoCAD assumes a Z value of 0 (unless you use object snap). Until you began the 3D section of this book, you allowed AutoCAD to operate this way. Picking coordinates above or below the X,Y plane (when a Z value is allowed) is as easy as adding a Z value when AutoCAD asks for a point. When you pick a point by using an object snap mode, AutoCAD uses the X,Y, and Z values of the matching point.

The following tips can assist you in creating 3D objects from familiar 2D entities:

- Circles are best for making closed cylinders. Donuts make good open-ended cylinders with thick walls.
- Solids quickly make rectilinear closed objects. Keep Fill turned off to speed up regenerations.
- Lines and polylines make good open rectilinear objects. Polylines show their width.
- Lines can approximate any object in wireframe but cannot hide anything unless extruded.
- Solids, wide polylines, and traces fill only in plan view and do not plot filled in other views.

Three-Dimensional Thickness

You can create a 3D model by positioning flat 2D entities at various angles in 3D space. You can create 3D models more efficiently, however, by extruding 2D entities (lines, polylines, arcs, circles, and solids) to give them a

thickness in their Z direction. When you assign a thickness to a 2D entity, you give the entity *height* in its Z direction. If you draw a line on the X,Y plane, for example, its thickness appears as a wall, stretching from the line itself to the height of the thickness given it. Figure 19.20 shows how a 3D object "grows" from flat 2D entities.

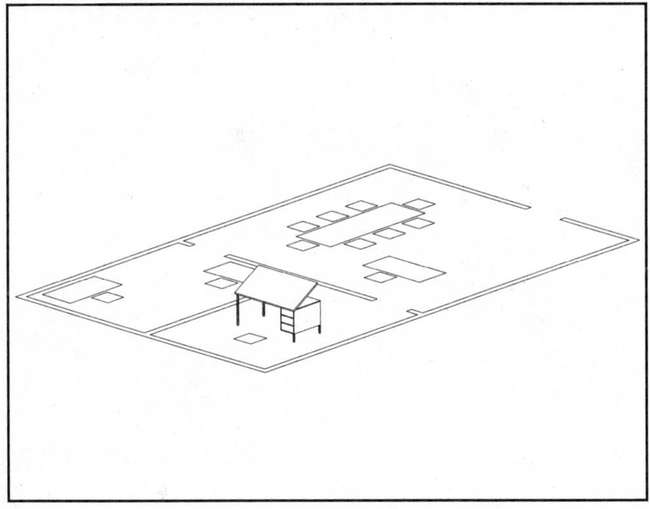

Figure 19.20:

Growing a 3D drawing from 2D entities.

You can create new entities with thickness by first setting a value for the THICKNESS system variable. All entities are created with a thickness equal to the value of the THICKNESS variable. The default value is 0, which produces planar entities—that is, entities with no thickness. You also can use the CHPROP command to edit the thickness of an existing entity.

NOTE

Thickness can be positive (up in the Z direction) or negative (down in the Z direction). Thickness is relative to the Z axis of 2D entities, even if applied by CHPROP with the current UCS in a different orientation. For 3D entities that can accept thickness, such as points and lines, thickness is always relative to the current UCS. These entities appear oblique if they do not lie in or parallel to the current UCS. If thickness is added to a line drawn directly in the Z direction, it appears that the line extends beyond its endpoint in the positive or negative thickness direction.

Using THICKNESS To Draw Table Legs

Your table drawing begins with its legs. Make TABLE the current layer and then set a thickness for the extruded height of the legs. Draw one table leg with lines and a second with a polygon, and then copy both to create the table's other two legs. You may find this process easier if you first turn on ORTHO. Create the table by using the settings shown in table 19.2.

Table 19.2
Table Drawing Settings

COORDS	*FILL*	*GRID*	*ORTHO*	*SNAP*	*UCSICON*
ON	OFF	2	ON	.25	OR
UNITS	Use defaults for all UNITS settings.				
LIMITS	Set LIMITS from 0,0 to 68,44.				
ZOOM	Zoom All.				

Layer Name	*State*	*Color*	*Linetype*
0	On	White	CONTINUOUS
SCRATCH	Off	White	CONTINUOUS
TABLE	On/Current	White	CONTINUOUS

Using the THICKNESS Variable To Extrude a 2D Entity

Choose File, then New, enter drawing name `\IA\TABLE`, and then make the settings shown in table 19.2. Be sure that TABLE is the current layer and that the SCRATCH layer is off.

`Command:` *Choose* View, *then* Zoom, *then* All — Zooms to show grid

`Command:` *Choose* Settings, *then* Entity Modes, *enter* `25` *in the* Thickness *box, and then choose* OK

`Command:` *Choose* Draw, *then* Line, *then* Segments, *and draw a 1" square with its lower left corner at 4,7.5*

`Command:` *Choose* Draw, *then* Polygon, *then* Circumscribed, *and draw a polygon with four sides at center point 51.5,8 circumscribed around a .5 radius circle*

`Command:` *Choose* Construct, *then* Copy, *and copy the two legs 29 inches up in the Y direction*

As figure 19.21 shows, you now have four squares for table legs, but you need to view the legs from a different viewpoint to see the thickness. A common problem of drawing in 3D is that you cannot see what you have done unless you first change your viewpoint. Multiple views of your drawing help you work most effectively in 3D.

```
Layer TABLE Ortho Snap          61.0000,1.5000        AutoCAD
                                                      * * * *
                                                      COPY:

                                                      Select
                                                      Objects

                                                      Multiple

                                                      LAST
                                                      DRAW
                                                      EDIT
Select objects:
<Base point or displacement>/Multiple: Second point of displacement:
Command:
```

Figure 19.21:

Table legs drawn with THICKNESS, as seen from plan view.

Using Multiple Viewports To Control Drawing Display and 3D Viewing

You can view your 3D model in several viewports, which can have different snap, grid, zoom, and viewpoint settings. MVIEW and VPORTS are the commands that create multiple viewports.

Chapters 5 and 13 taught you how MVIEW and VPORTS set up and control 2D drawing viewports. As you may recall, the VPORTS command divides the AutoCAD graphics window into as many as 16 tiled viewports, and the MVIEW command creates up to 15 MVIEW viewports. (One viewport number is reserved by the system for the main paper space viewport in paper space.)

You can work in only one viewport at a time—that is, the *current* viewport. Make the viewport current by clicking on it with your pointer. When you work in a viewport, you can use all your normal display controls, as if you were working with a single viewport. As you draw or edit in one viewport, however, the drawing is updated in all viewports.

When you work in 3D, you should set up three viewports as a starting configuration. Set up one viewport for your UCS plan view, use a second viewport as a 3D viewport for visualizing and building your 3D model, and use the third viewport to hold a WCS view or a second 3D view of your drawing.

Using Viewports To View the 3D Table's Construction

In the next exercise, you set up three viewports so that you can see the 3D table construction as you draw it (see fig. 19.22). Split the graphics window into a large top view for construction and two smaller views below. The lower left viewport gives you a left-front 3D view of the table from above. The lower right viewport gives you a right-front 3D view of the table from below. The top view is your plan view. The table you are building appears in each viewport. When your views are set up, save the viewport configuration with the name TABLE.

Using MVIEW To Set Three Viewports

`Command:` *Choose* View, *then* Tilemode, *then* Off	Enters paper space
`Command:` *Choose* View, *then* Mview, *then* 3 Viewports	Issues Mview with the 3 option

```
Command: _mview
ON/OFF/Hideplot/Fit/2/3/4/Restore/
<First Point>: 3
```

`Horizontal/Vertical/Above/Below /Left/<Right>: A`	Specifies Above
`Fit/<First Point>: F`	Fits three viewports to the screen
`Command: MS`	Returns to model space
`Command:` *Click in the bottom left viewport*	Makes the viewport current
Use VPOINT to set the viewpoint to -.6,-1,.8	
`Command:` *Select the lower right viewport*	
Set the viewpoint to -1,-1,-.4	
`Command:` *Select the lower left viewport*	
Use VIEW *with the* Save *option to save the view as* TABLE	Saves the model-space view
`Command: PS`	Enters paper space
Use VIEW *with the* Save *option to save the view as* TABLEP	Saves the three-viewport paper-space view

The table legs should be visible in all three viewports (see fig. 19.22). Their thickness makes them 25 inches high.

When you use multiple viewports and you want to redraw or regenerate all viewports, use the REDRAWALL or REGENALL command.

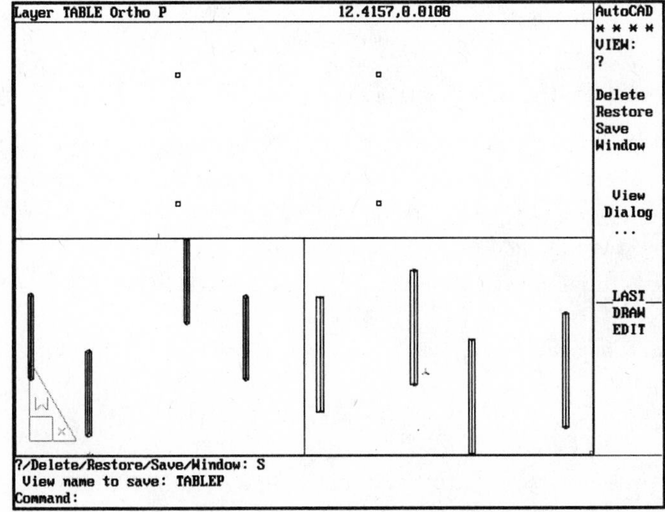

Figure 19.22:

The table legs shown in three viewports.

Using the SOLID Command To Make a 3D Object

Now you are ready to put a top on the table. You want the table top to show as a solid surface, so you make it a solid entity. The top is 1/2" thick; you can extrude the top by assigning a thickness to it. The only constraint on using solids in 3D is that all the extruded Z points must lie in a plane parallel to the X,Y plane.

Using XYZ Filters in 3D

How do you get the table top up on top of the legs? You have two choices. You can assign a thickness of 0.5 inches for your table top, and then begin your solid at the Z height of 25 inches above the current UCS construction plane. The second option is to set a new UCS that is 25 inches above the current one—so that the X,Y plane is at the top of the legs—and to begin drawing the solid from that spot.

You use the first method in the following exercise, which shows how to start the solid at the correct Z height by using XYZ filters. First, set THICKNESS to 0.5 inches. Then use the SOLID command to create the table top by picking the X,Y coordinates and entering the Z value at the keyboard.

Using SOLID and XYZ Filters To Make a 3D Table Top

`Command:` **`MS`**	Enters model space
`Command:` *Click in the top viewport*	Makes the viewport current
`Command:` *Choose* Settings, *then* Entity Modes, *enter* **`.5`** *in the* Thickness *box, and choose* OK	
`Command:` *Choose* Settings, *then* Object Snap	Opens the Running Object Snap dialog box
Select the ENDpoint snap mode, then choose OK	Selects the running object snap mode
`Command:` *From the screen menu, choose* DRAW, *then* next, *then* SOLID:	
`Command: SOLID First point:` **`.XY`** ↵	Specifies the XY filter
`of` *Pick near corner of leg at ① (see fig. 19.23)*	Sets the XY values
`(need Z):` **`25`** ↵	Specifies the elevation

`Second point:` *Pick the second, third, and fourth corners in the sequence shown by the bubbles in fig. 19.23, then press Enter*	Draws solid top (see fig. 19.24) and ends the command
`Command:` *Choose* Settings, *then* Object Snap	Opens the Running Object Snap dialog box
Click to clear the ENDpoint snap mode, then choose OK	Turns off the running object snap mode

Save the drawing.

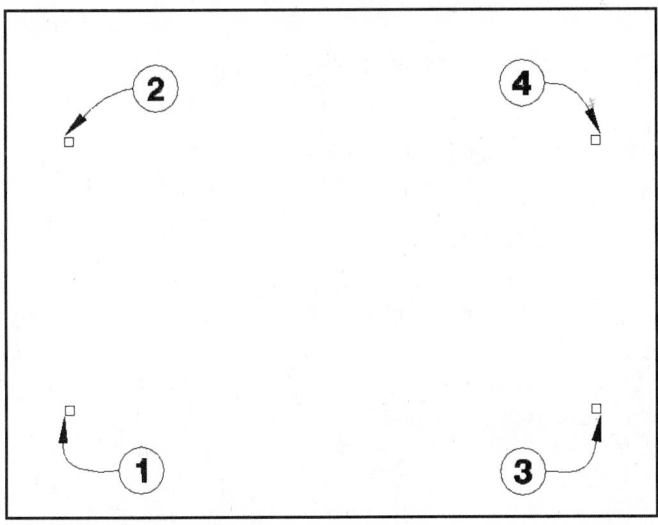

Figure 19.23:

Detail of the pick points.

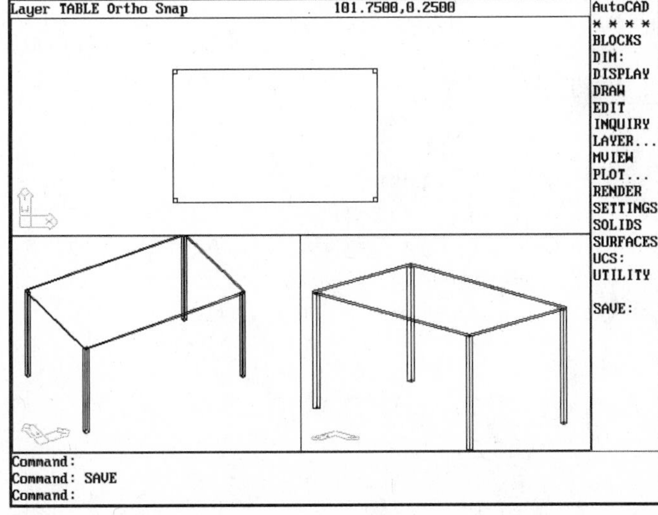

Figure 19.24:

The table top, added with SOLID.

Note that you had to enter only the Z value for the first coordinate point; AutoCAD assumed the same Z value for the three remaining points. This technique works for all extrudable 2D entities, but it does not work for 3D entities, such as the lines, that accept different Z coordinates for their different points.

XYZ point filters are efficient for creating entities at various Z elevations without changing your UCS. You can use object snap to snap the X,Y point to an existing object, and then enter a Z value. You also can use object snap to pick the Z elevation from an entity in a different viewport.

You can quickly access the XYZ filter by using the cursor pop-up menu. Click the pop-up button on your pointing device, then select Filters from the pop-up menu.

Z Values and Thickness

You made a simple 3D table by extruding the legs and top, assigning thickness values, and drawing the entities at the Z height you wanted. When you draw in 3D, remember that the draw commands do not prompt for thickness. You can check the current thickness setting by using the THICKNESS system variable or by displaying the Entity Creation dialog box. You can find the Z value and thickness of an existing entity by using the LIST command. If you want to change the thickness of an existing entity, use the CHPROP or DDLIST command. You select the entity, respond with thickness as the property you want to edit, and then input a new value. You can check the X,Y,Z coordinates of existing entities with the ID command by snapping to them with object snap in a suitable view.

The ELEV command can assign a thickness value, but it is better to control thickness by using the THICKNESS system variable. ELEV also can set an ELEVATION variable, but it is better to enter elevations directly by using object snaps when appropriate. The ELEV command may eventually be eliminated from AutoCAD, and it can be confusing to use with varying UCSs.

AutoCAD ignores the thickness setting when you create text. If you want text with a 3D thickness, use CHPROP or DDLIST to set a thickness after you create the text.

You now have a good 3D drawing of a simple table. Before moving on to more 3D drawing and editing, take a minute to see how the table drawing looks with its hidden lines removed.

Using HIDE To Remove Hidden Lines

In the bottom viewports, the different views of the table are *wireframe* representations. These wire edges help you visualize the table's appearance in 3D space. When AutoCAD generates a wireframe image, it does not consider whether a line would be visible from your viewpoint if the objects on the screen were solid. Instead, AutoCAD shows it as if it were transparent or constructed of wires. This is the quickest way the program can display the view.

Once you get a view you like, you can make it look more realistic by using the HIDE command to remove lines that should be hidden. The HIDE command is simple to use and takes only a little longer than a screen regeneration. While HIDE works, AutoCAD keeps you informed by displaying the percentage of hiding that has been completed.

Try hiding the table in the following exercise; it uses a simple drawing, so the process is rapid.

Using HIDE To Remove Hidden Lines in the Table

`Command:` *Click in the bottom left viewport*	Makes the viewport current
`Command:` *Choose* Render, *then* Hide	
`Command: _HIDE Regenerating drawing.` `Hiding lines: done 100%`	Regenerates and displays the HIDE operation's progress

The results are shown in figure 19.25.

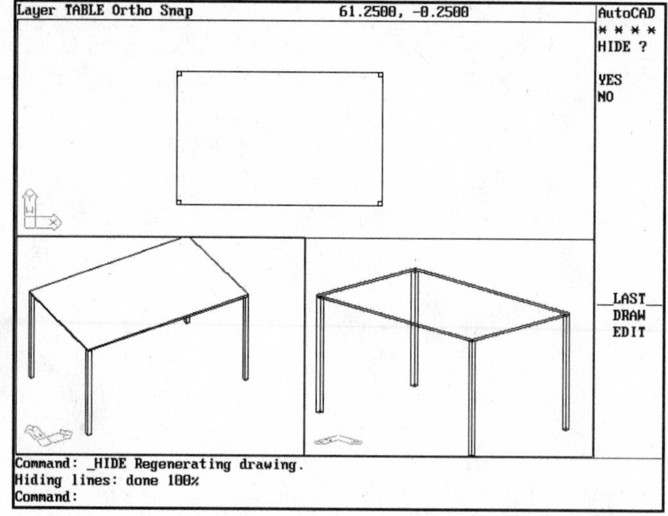

Figure 19.25:

The table after HIDE.

AutoCAD clears the viewport, regenerates the drawing, processes the drawing, and finally displays the drawing with the hidden lines removed. Now, the table top obscures the back leg.

The HIDE command performs hidden-line removal only on the current viewport. Be sure you are in model space and that the correct viewport is active before issuing the HIDE command.

What Gets Hidden with HIDE?

Here is a way to think about hidden lines. Imagine that your 3D wireframe model is constructed of clear, non-reflective plastic; you can see all the edges in the model, regardless of their positions. If you then paint the model so that the surfaces are opaque, you can see only the edges that are not hidden by surfaces. AutoCAD simulates the painting process in software and displays the result.

It helps to know the ways that AutoCAD treats various entity surfaces when it calculates hidden-line removal. AutoCAD puts an opaque cap on the bottom and top of most graphic entities that surround an area. Circles and solids, for example, have top and bottom surfaces that hide lines enclosed within or behind them. (You saw the effect of the solid table top in

your table view.) A polyline (or trace) hides only what is behind its thickness extrusion or what is concealed by its width. Areas enclosed by closed polylines are not hidden because they have no top or bottom. Remember that polygons, ellipses, and donuts are really polylines. Other 2D extruded entities hide only what is behind their extrusions.

When the HIDE command determines what to display, it includes entities on layers that are turned off. This can result in invisible objects hiding visible ones. Use frozen layers if you want to suppress unwanted objects when hiding.

All normal editing commands work on 3D-generated displays, but a regeneration or any zoom unhides the drawing. When you edit a hidden-line display, turn REGENAUTO off to avoid accidentally regenerating the drawing.

You should freeze layers that contain extraneous information before you use the HIDE command. AutoCAD should not spend time removing hidden lines unnecessarily.

If you have created top and bottom objects from entities that do not hide lines behind them, fill in the surface boundaries with circles, solids, or wide polylines.

The HIDE command hides one entity when it is behind another. If two entities intersect or coincide in the same plane, small rounding errors make it impossible to predict which one will hide the other. When two entities intersect, cut a tiny slice out of one at the intersection. If they coincide, move one a short distance in front of the other.

Remember that all the editing tools you have learned so far also can be applied to 3D.

Using Familiar Editing Commands as 3D Tools

The editing commands that reposition entities are valuable in 3D drawing. You often can more easily draw an entity in the current UCS and then move, copy, or rotate it than you can by using more advanced 3D techniques. The COPY and MOVE commands accept 3D points or displacements. COPY Multiple is useful for positioning several identical entities at different points in 3D space. The ROTATE command rotates only objects that are parallel to the current UCS, but, by setting different UCSs, you can rotate objects to any orientation in space.

Using MOVE as a 3D Construction Tool

In the following exercise, you construct a cabinet on the table's right side. The new cabinet overlaps the legs. Later, you shorten the legs and add drawers. You draw the cabinet at the UCS origin and then move it into place, instead of picking the corner points in space. You can set a new color to distinguish the cabinet from the table. Use SOLID to draw the cabinet and extrude it in the Z direction with a thickness of 18 1/2 inches.

Drawing and Moving the Cabinet in 3D

`Command:` *Press F8 to turn on Ortho Mode*

`Command:` *Choose* Settings, *then* Entity Modes, *enter* `18.5` *in the* Thickness *box, and choose* OK

`Command:` *From the screen menu, choose* Draw, *then* next, *then* SOLID:

`Command: _SOLID First point: 0,0,0↵` — Specifies the UCS origin

`Second point:` *Enter* `14,0`, `0,30`, *and* `14,30` *for the second, third, and fourth corners and press Enter* — Draws a solid cabinet (see fig. 19.26) and ends the command

ZOOM in close on the table top's right corner (see fig. 19.28)

Next, you move the cabinet to below the top at the right front corner.

`Command:` *Choose* Modify, *then* Move

`Command: _move`

`Select objects:` *Click in the lower right viewport and select the cabinet*

`Base point or displacement:` **`ENDP`**`↵`

`ENDP of` *Pick corner at ① (see fig. 19.27)*

`Second point of displacement:` **`ENDP`**`↵`

`ENDP of` *Click in the lower left viewport and pick the outside corner of the right leg at ② (see fig 19.28)*

`Command:` *Choose* View, *then* Zoom, *then* Previous

Use SAVE and continue, or END and take a break.

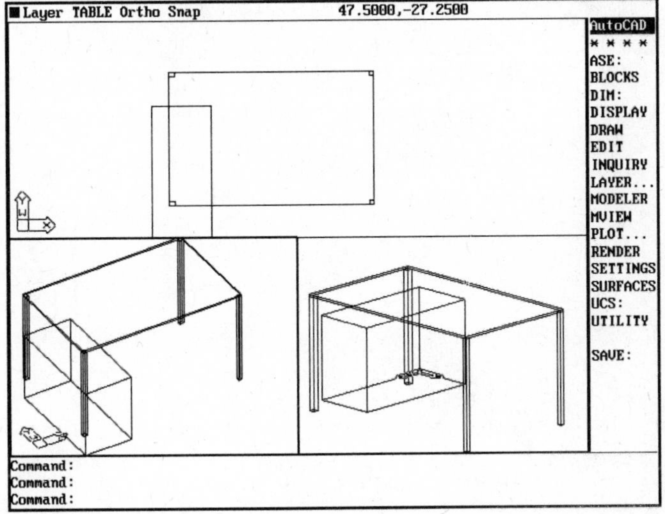

Figure 19.26:

The table with the cabinet at UCS origin.

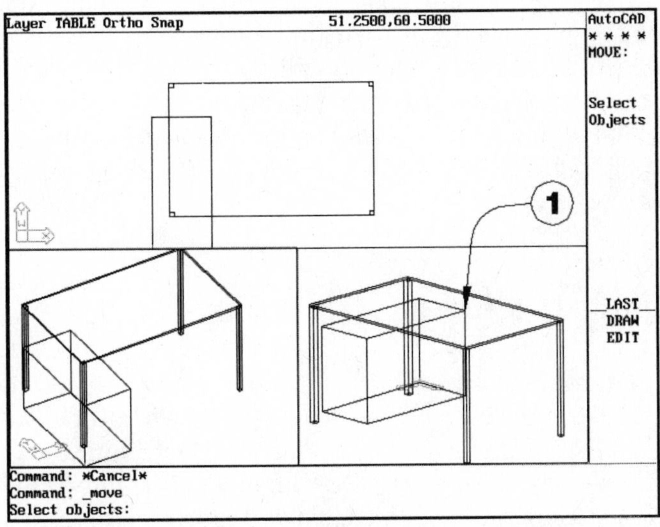

Figure 19.27:

Detail of the MOVE command's base point.

If all went well, you should have a good solid cabinet mounted under the right side of the table, as shown in figure 19.28. The cabinet overlaps the legs, but that will be fixed later.

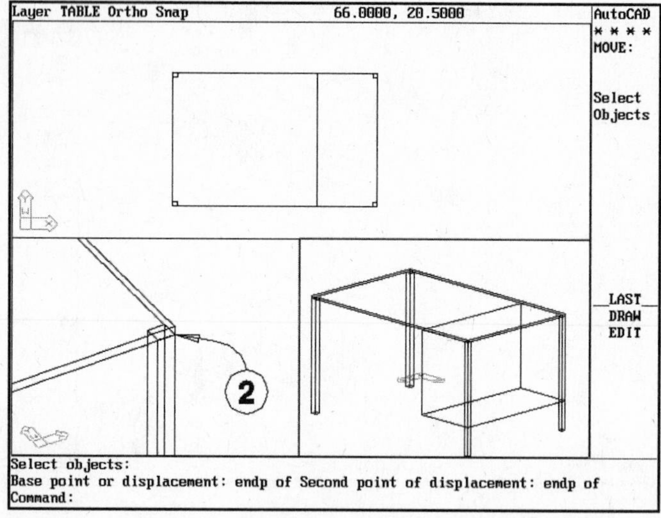

Figure 19.28:

The table with the cabinet moved below top.

Although THICKNESS settings, Z coordinate values, object snap, and the editing commands are useful for constructing 3D drawings, they cannot handle all 3D construction tasks that you will encounter. In the next set of exercises, you add drawers and a drawing board at a 30-degree slant on top of the table. Think about ways to draw these entities by using the tools you have used so far. The drawers are pretty simple, but the slanted drawing board is easier to do with a reoriented UCS.

Establishing a UCS in 3D

Start this section by taking a closer look at the UCS command and the UCS icon. So far, you have been using AutoCAD's WCS, the default coordinate system, and UCSs that share its X,Y plane. You can create your own coordinate system, however, by using the UCS and UCSICON commands. These commands were developed for 3D to enable you to work with 2D entities and editing commands by locating your coordinate system anywhere in 3D space.

You can establish or modify a UCS by using the UCS command, the UCS screen menu, the UCS item on the SETTINGS screen menu, or the UCS item in the Settings pull-down menu, which displays a child menu of five UCS menu items. The Named UCS Control pull-down item uses the DDUCS command to display the UCS Control dialog box (see fig. 19.29). The UCS

Presets selection displays the UCS Orientation dialog box with a group of predefined UCSs (see fig. 19.30). The UCS Icon selection enables you to change the origin and visibility of the UCS icon. The Axis option enables you to rotate the current UCS about the X, Y, or Z axis. Finally, the Origin option enables you to change the origin of the current UCS.

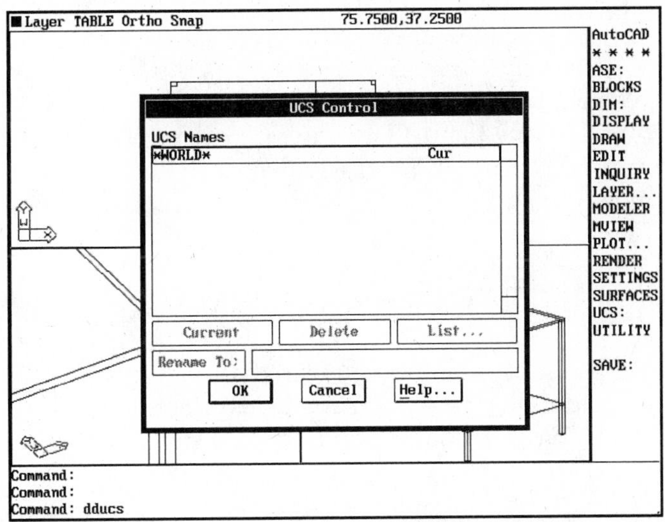

Figure 19.29: The UCS Control dialog box.

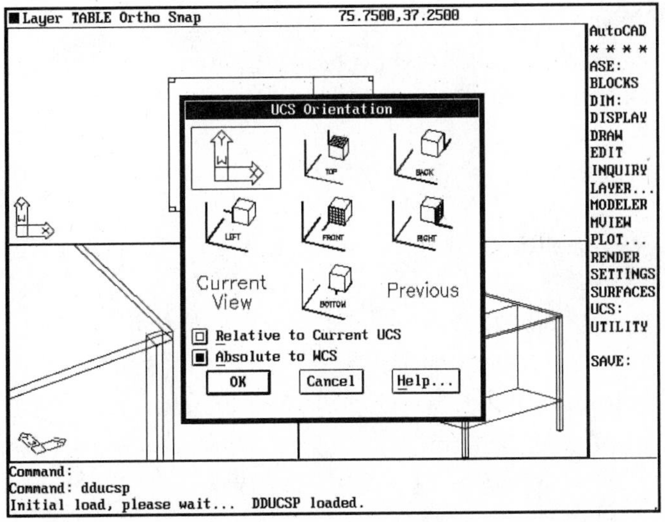

Figure 19.30: The UCS Orientation dialog box.

You can establish a new UCS in 3D in the following ways:

- Specify a new origin; a new X,Y plane; or a new Z axis
- Copy the orientation of an existing entity
- Align the new UCS to your current view
- Rotate the current UCS around any one or all X, Y, or Z axes

You can set a UCS by using these methods, or you can combine them by executing the UCS command several times in succession. A complex UCS move is easier to visualize in several steps. You can define any number of UCSs by naming and saving them. Only one UCS can be current at any one time, however, and the current UCS defines all coordinate input. If you are using multiple viewports, they all share the current UCS.

Understanding the UCS Command's Options

As you construct the rest of the table, you learn how to use most of the command options to define, name, and save UCSs. The following list describes all of the UCS command's options (more details appear in the exercises):

- **Origin.** This option specifies a new UCS origin point, without changing the orientation.
- **Z Axis.** This option specifies a new UCS origin point and defines a new UCS by specifying a positive point on the Z axis.
- **3-point.** Use this option to define a new UCS by specifying three points: an origin, a positive point on the X axis, and a positive point on the Y axis.
- **Entity.** This option aligns the current UCS with the coordinate system of the selected entity.
- **View.** You can use the view option to align the UCS to your current viewpoint.
- **X.** Use this option to rotate the UCS about the X axis.
- **Y.** Use this option to rotate the UCS about the Y axis.
- **Z.** Use this option to rotate the UCS about the Z axis.
- **Prev.** This option restores the previous UCS. You can repeat this option to step back up to ten previous coordinate systems in paper space or ten in model space.

- **Restore.** This option restores a previously named and saved UCS. Enter a question mark for a list of named UCSs.
- **Save.** This option saves the current UCS. You specify a name (up to 31 characters). Enter a question mark for a list of named UCSs.
- **Del.** This option deletes a saved UCS by name. Enter a question mark for a list of named UCSs.
- **?.** This option lists named UCSs. You can use wild cards to create a specific list. A current unnamed UCS is listed as `*NO NAME*`, unless it is the WCS, which is listed as `*WORLD*`.
- **World.** This default option restores the WCS.

The X,Y plane of the current UCS also is the current construction plane, unless you have used the ELEV command to set a non-zero elevation. A *non-zero elevation* creates a current construction plane above or below the UCS X,Y plane and can make drawing in 3D confusing. Thus, you should not use ELEV to set elevations. For brevity and simplicity, the term *UCS* is often used rather than the term *construction plane.*

In the following section, you return to the table drawing, in which you define and save two UCSs.

Defining and Saving a 3Point UCS

In the following exercises, you establish two more UCSs: at the front of the table and on the right side. You use the 3point option for the front UCS. (You can use 3point to establish any UCS.) If you do not pick up all the options immediately, pick this option to learn first.

You define the UCS by entering three coordinate points: the first point defines the origin, the second point defines the positive X axis from the new origin point, and the third point defines the X,Y plane (and, consequently, the Z axis). The third point need not be on the Y axis (because the Y axis must be perpendicular to the X axis), but it defines the direction of the positive Y axis. The only constraint for the 3point option is that all three points cannot lie in a straight line. The prompts for each of the points present defaults that set that point or axis equal to the current UCS.

In the following exercise, you define the UCS so that it lies at the base of the table's left front leg. You pick the first origin point on the front lower left corner of the leg, the second on the right leg, and the third on the front edge of the top. After picking the points, you save the UCS with the name **FRONT**. The exercise also shows you how to return to a single viewport and set a larger grid, so that you can more easily see the object snap points and UCS icon as you work.

Using 3Point To Create a UCS

Continue from the preceding exercise in the TABLE drawing and select the bottom left viewport.

`Command:` **PS**↵	Enters paper space
`Command:` *Choose* View, *then* Zoom, *then* Window, *and fill the graphics window with the lower left viewport*	
`Command:` **MS**↵	Returns to model space
`Command:` *Choose* View, *then* Zoom, *then* All	
`Command:` *Choose* Settings, *then* Drawing Aids, *and set the grid to 6*	
`Command:` *From the screen menu, choose* UCS, *then* Next, *then* 3point	Issues UCS 3point option
`Origin point <0,0,0>:` **INT**↵	
`INT of` *Pick at* ① *(see fig. 19.31)*	
`Point on positive portion of the X-axis <5.0000,7.5000,0.0000>:` **INT**↵	
`INT of` *Pick at* ②	
`Point on positive-Y portion of the UCS X-Y plane <4.0000,8.5000,0.0000>:` **MID**↵	
`MID of` *Pick at* ③	Creates the UCS
`Command:` *Press Enter, and from the screen menu choose* SAVE	
`?/Desired UCS name:` **FRONT**↵	

Your UCS icon's origin should be on the base of the front left leg, with the X axis pointing toward the right leg and the Y axis pointing up the left leg. Notice that you did not change your view of the drawing by setting the UCS. By saving the UCS, the FRONT UCS will be listed as an option the next time you display the UCS Control dialog box.

Now you can define a second UCS on the right side.

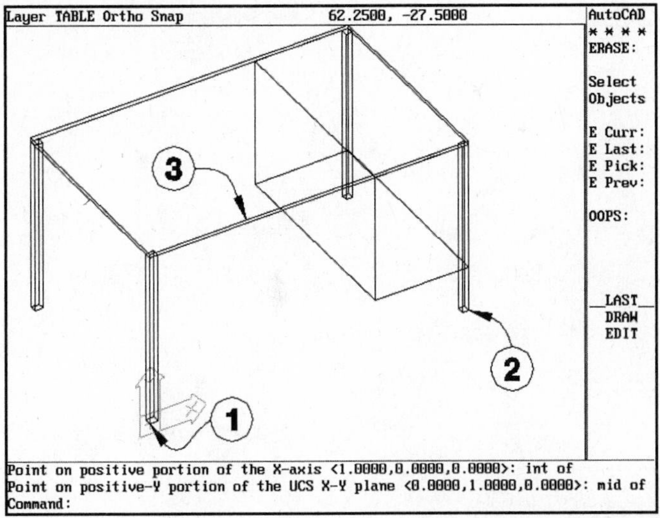

Figure 19.31:

The table with a 3point UCS at the front.

Using the ZAxis Option To Define a UCS

In the following exercise, you use the ZAxis option to define a UCS at the right leg, with the X,Y plane on the table's right side. The ZAxis option enables you to specify a new positive Z axis by picking an origin and a point on the Z axis. This option rotates the X,Y plane, based on your new Z axis. Again, this is an easy option to use.

In this case, the new Z direction must face out from the table's right side, as shown in figure 19.32. After you pick your origin point at the corner of the right front leg, you specify the second point with relative polar coordinates at 0 degrees. The new UCS is saved with the name R-SIDE.

Using ZAxis To Create R-Side UCS

Command: **UCS** ↵

Origin/ZAxis/3point/Entity/View/XYZ/Prev/Restore/Save/Del/?/<World>: **ZA**↵

Origin point <0,0,0>: **INT**↵

INT of *Pick at ② from previous exercise (see fig. 19.31)*

Point on positive portion of Z-axis <48.0000,0.0000,1.0000>: **@1<0**↵ — Positions UCS, as in figure 19.32

From the screen menu choose UCS, *then* SAVE

?/Desired UCS name: **R-SIDE**↵

Save the drawing

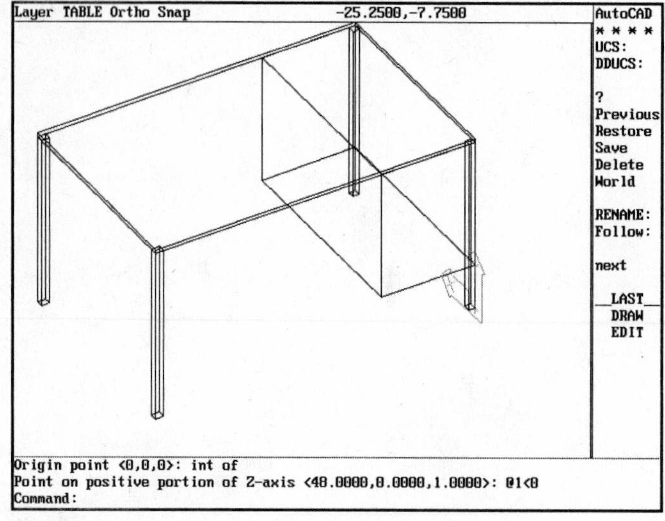

Figure 19.32:

The table with the new UCS at the right side.

Your new UCS icon origin should be at the base of the right front leg with the X axis pointing toward the back of the table, the Y axis pointing toward the table top, and the Z axis pointing to the right.

Using the UCS Icon To Keep Track of UCS Orientation

You will come to rely heavily on the UCS icon as a reminder of your construction plane's orientation and to confirm that you have defined your UCS the way you want it.

Looking closely at your drawing, you see that the icon's X and Y axes point along the axes of the table. The + on the icon means that it is located at the origin of the current UCS. The W on the Y axis is missing, which indicates that your current coordinate system is not the WCS. The box at the icon's base means that you are viewing the UCS from above (a positive Z direction). No box means that you are looking at the icon from below (a negative Z direction). Figure 19.33 shows a collection of icon views that you will encounter. When you see a *broken pencil* icon, your view is within one degree of parallel (edge-on) to the current UCS, making point picking unreliable. When you see the paper-space icon, you know to switch to model space in order to draw.

To control the visibility and location of the UCS icon, use the UCSICON command. You can find this command by choosing Settings, then UCS, then Icon. The UCSICON settings can be controlled separately in each viewport allowing the user to selective turn the icon on or off.

The UCSICON settings do not have any effect on the UCS. It is recommended that you keep the UCS icon on. This serves as a reminder of the current UCS.

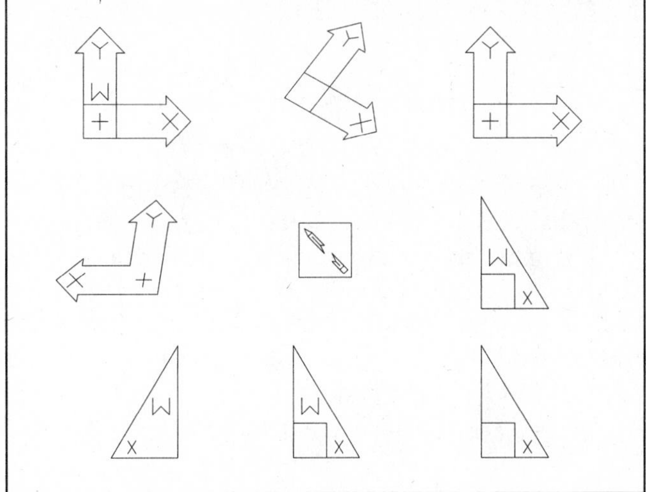

Figure 19.33: Different views of the UCS icon.

UCSICON Options

The following list reviews the UCSICON options for controlling the UCS icon's display.

- **ON.** This option turns on the UCS icon, so that it appears on the screen.
- **OFF.** This option turns off the UCS icon.
- **All.** This option displays the UCS icon in each viewport when you use multiple viewports.
- **Noorigin.** This option always displays the UCS icon at the lower left corner of each viewport.

- **ORigin.** This option displays the UCS icon at the 0,0 origin of the current UCS, unless the origin is off-screen or too close to the edge for the icon to fit. The icon then displays at the lower left corner of the viewport.

When you are working with three viewports, AutoCAD displays the UCS icon in each viewport. You can set different display settings for the icon in each viewport.

Setting the UCS Origin and a Plan View

Depending on what you are doing, it may be clearer to draw in a 3D viewpoint or in a plan view of the current UCS. Use the PLAN command to set a plan view if it is easier to find your pick points that way.

In the following exercise, you restore the FRONT UCS and use the UCS origin options to set the UCS at the lower left corner of the cabinet. Then you use the PLAN command to set a plan view for constructing the drawers. When the view is set, you can draw the first (lower) drawer on the cabinet face with a 2D polyline, and then use the COPY command's Multiple option to add the next two drawers. When you are done, you restore your 3D view named TABLE.

Using UCS in Plan View To Add Drawers to the Table

`Command:` *Choose* Settings, *then* UCS, then Named UCS, *highlight* FRONT, *click on the* Current *button, then* OK	Makes FRONT the current UCS
Choose Settings, *then* UCS, *then* Origin	Prompts for a new UCS origin
`Origin point <0,0,0>:` **INT**↵	
`INT of` *Pick the cabinet's lower left corner*	
Save the current UCS as CABINET	

Set a thickness of .01 because, when entities are in the same plane, you cannot always predict when one entity will hide another. The .01 thickness makes the drawer polylines protrude slightly beyond the face of the cabinet, ensuring that they will not be hidden accidentally.

`Command:` *Choose* Settings, *then* Entity Modes, *then enter* **.01** *in the* *Thickness box, then OK*	
`Command:` *Choose* View, *then* Set View, *then* Plan View, *then* Current UCS	Displays PLAN viewpoint
ZOOM in on the cabinet, as shown in figure 19.34	
`Command:` *Choose* Draw, *then* Polyline, *then* 2D, *then draw from .5,.5 to @13<0 to @5.5<90 to @13<180 and enter* `Close`	Creates the first drawer
`Command:` *Choose* Construct, *then* Copy, *and select the drawer, and then choose* Multiple *from the screen menu and add two drawers above the original at a 6" spacing*	Creates a total of three drawers, as shown in figure 19.35
Use VIEW to restore the view named TABLE (see fig. 19.35)	
Save the drawing.	

Aside from the Origin, 3point, and ZAxis options that you have used so far, there are several other ways to set a UCS.

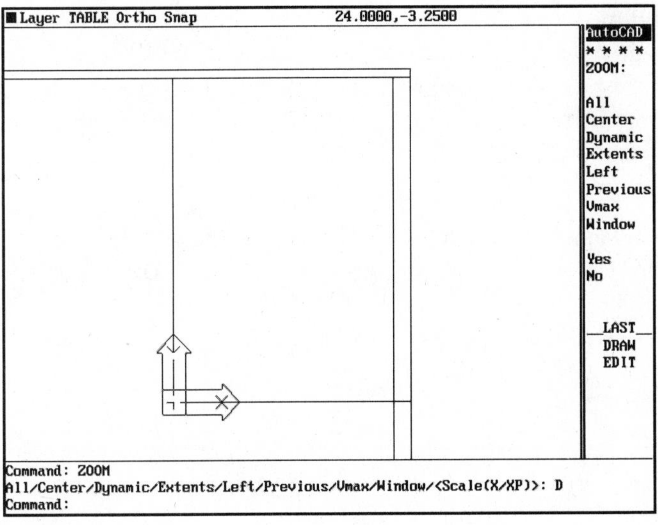

Figure 19.34:

The cabinet in a plan with the UCSICON at the CABINET UCS origin.

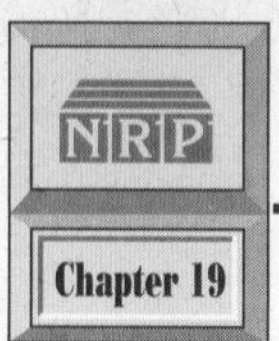

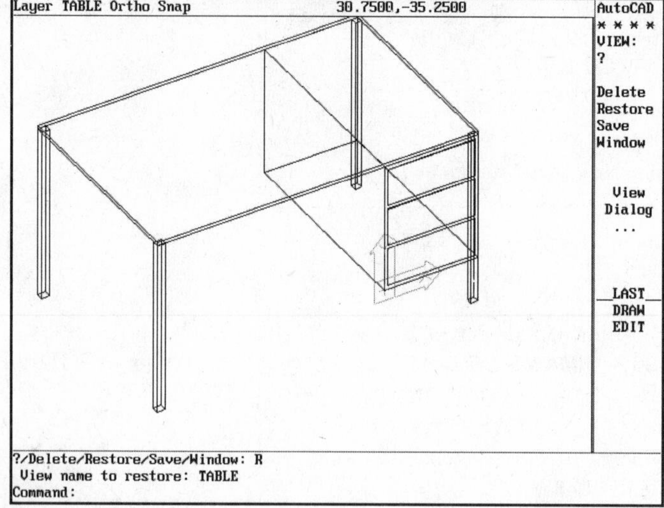

Figure 19.35:

The table with drawers added.

Setting a UCS with the X/Y/Z, View, and Entity Options

The X/Y/Z options enable you to rotate the current UCS around either the X, Y, or Z axis. The angle of rotation is relative to the specified axis of the current UCS through the right-hand rule of rotation. The *right-hand rule of rotation* means that if you close your right fist and extend your thumb to point in the positive direction of the specified axis, your curled fingers point in the direction of positive rotation. Figure 19.36 shows the direction of the rotations. If you want to rotate more than one axis, re-execute the UCS command to rotate the second (or third) axis. (You use the X/Y/Z options in some of the remaining exercises.)

The View option is simple; it sets the UCS' X,Y plane so that it is parallel to the screen's orientation. The origin does not change. The Entity option is a bit more complex.

Using Entity Selection To Establish a UCS

You can define a new UCS by selecting an existing entity. This action aligns the UCS with the entity. You use entity selection in the next set of exercises when you create and insert a block to form the drawing board. If you select an entity, the entity type and your pick point determine the new UCS. You cannot, however, base a UCS on either 3D polyline entities or 3D meshes. (You learn about these two entities in the next chapter.) The following list describes the ways in which entities can determine a new UCS:

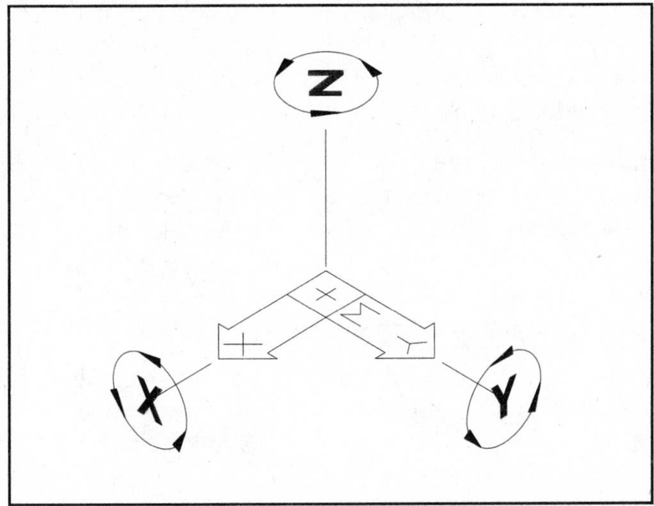

Figure 19.36:

Rotation angles from viewpoint 1,1,1.

- **Arc.** The arc's center becomes the new origin point, and the X axis goes through the end point nearest your pick point.
- **Circle.** The circle's center becomes the new origin point, and the X axis passes through your pick point.
- **Line.** The endpoint nearest your pick point becomes the new origin, and the second endpoint is on the positive X axis. (The second point's Y coordinate is 0.)
- **Point.** The point becomes the new origin point.
- **2D Polyline.** The polyline's start point becomes the new origin point; the X axis lies along the line to the first vertex point. (The first vertex Y coordinate is 0.)
- **Solid.** The first point becomes the new origin point, and the X axis lies along the line between the first two points.
- **Trace.** The first point of the trace becomes the new origin point, and the X axis lies along the trace's center line.
- **3DFace.** The first point determines the new origin point, the X axis lies along the first and second points, and the positive Y axis is determined by the first and fourth points.
- **Dimension.** The new origin is the middle of the dimension text, and the X axis is parallel to the X axis that was in effect when the dimension text was drawn.

- **Text, Attribute, Attdef, Shape, Insert.** The new origin is the entity's insertion point. The X axis is defined by the entity's rotation about the extrusion direction (Z axis). In effect, the entity you select will have a zero rotation angle in the new UCS.

For all these entities, the positive Z axis of the resulting UCS is parallel to the Z extrusion direction of the selected entity. Because each entity type behaves differently, you should play with each to see how it behaves when you establish a new UCS. Set an undo mark and use your SCRATCH layer to draw and test any entity type, then use it to define a new UCS. When you are done, undo back, and resume with the next exercise on blocks.

You now have a table with a decent set of drawers. The last item to add to the drafting table is the drawing board.

Using BLOCK and INSERT To Insert Blocks in 3D

The drawing board is 1 1/4 inches thick and overlaps the table top on all sides by 1 inch. The next two exercises show you how to create the drawing board and insert it as a block, slanted at a 30-degree angle.

You can insert 3D blocks into a drawing the same way you insert 2D blocks. The standard INSERT command accepts a 3D-insertion point and gives you the options of X-scaling, Y-scaling, and Z-scaling the block's entities. The current UCS defines the X,Y plane for the block when it is created.

Using BLOCK To Create a Unit 3D Block

As in 2D, unit-scaled blocks are versatile in 3D. To make the drawing board, you use SOLID to build a 1×1×1 block, name it CUBE, and extrude the solid in the Z direction by setting its thickness to 1. The resulting block can be inserted with various scales to represent any rectilinear 3D box.

In the following exercises, you use the UCS Entity and Z options to set the construction plane on the table top to build the block. Save the UCS with the name TOP, and then make the block.

Using the SOLID Command To Make a Building Block

Continue in the table drawing.

`Command:` **`UCS`** ↵	
`Origin/ZAxis/3point/Entity/View/XYZ/ Prev/Restore/Save/Del/?/<World>:` **`E`** ↵	
`Select object to align UCS:` *Pick the table top*	Sets the UCS on top
`Command:` *Press Enter*	Repeats the UCS Command
`Origin/ZAxis/3point/Entity/View/XYZ/ Prev/Restore/Save/Del/?/<World>:` **`Z`** ↵	
`Rotation angle about Z axis <0>:` **`-90`** ↵	Aligns X and Y axes with edges of top
`Command:` *Press Enter*	Repeats the UCS command
`Origin/ZAxis/3point/Entity/View/XYZ/ Prev/Restore/Save/Del/?/<World>:` **`S`** ↵	
`?/Desired UCS name:` **`TOP`** ↵	
`Command:` *Choose* Settings, *then* Entity Modes, *then set THICKNESS to 1*	Enables CUBE block to assume properties of layer inserted on
Make layer 0 current	
ZOOM Center to a height of 3 in a clear area of the drawing	
`Command:` *Choose* Settings, *then* Drawing Aids *and set Grid to 1*	
`Command:` *From the screen menu, Choose* DRAW, *then* next, *then* SOLID: *and draw a 1″ square*	Creates a 1×1×1 cube
`Command:` *From the screen menu, Choose* BLOCKS, *then* BLOCK:	Issues the BLOCK command
`Command: BLOCK Block name (or ?):` **`CUBE`** ↵	
`Insertion base point:` *Pick ① at lower left corner of solid (see fig. 19.37)*	
`Select objects:` *Select the solid*	Defines the CUBE block and erases the solid
Set THICKNESS to 0, set grid back to 6, and ZOOM Previous	

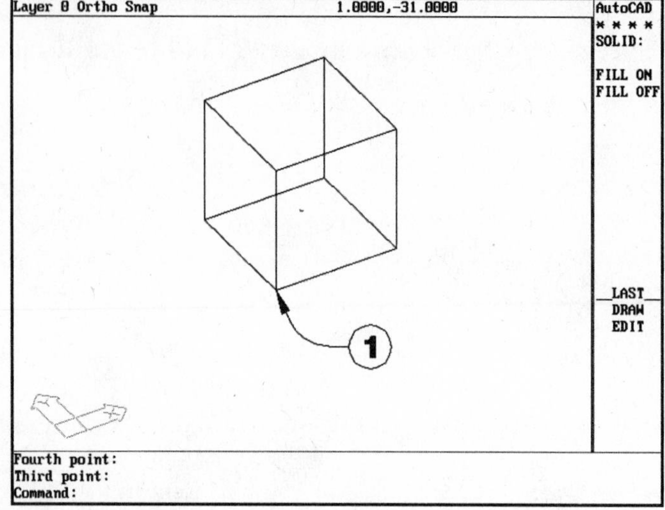

Figure 19.37:

A 1×1×1 building block with an insertion point.

The cube is now defined and stored in your drawing.

Using INSERT To Insert a 3D Block

You can use the INSERT command to insert the cube into the drawing, stretching its scale into a drawing board. When you insert a 3D block, the block's X,Y plane is aligned so that it is parallel to the current UCS.

The TOP UCS is the current UCS. To slant the drafting board 30 degrees, use the UCS X option and rotate the UCS 30 degrees about the X axis. Offset the insertion by one inch to provide an overlap at the front of the table. The INSERT command's Corner option tells INSERT to prompt first for the opposite X,Y corner, then the Z scale. The following exercise uses an X that extends the board 12 inches beyond the right side of the table. You can later edit the drawing to make it fit.

Inserting a 3D Block as a Drawing Board

`Command:` *Make TABLE the current layer*

`Command:` **`UCS`** ↵

`Origin/ZAxis/3point/Entity/View/XYZ/`
`Prev/Restore/Save/Del/?/<World>:` **`X`** ↵

`Rotation angle about X axis <0>: 30↵`	Tilts UCS 30 degrees
`Command:` *Press Enter*	Repeats the UCS command
`Origin/ZAxis/3point/Entity/View/XYZ/ Prev/Restore/Save/Del/?/<World>: S↵`	
`?/Desired UCS name: BOARD↵`	
`Command:` *Choose* Draw, *then* Insert	Opens the Insert dialog
Enter `CUBE` *in the* Block NAME *edit box, then clear the specific parameters on screen check box, and set insertion point to -1,-1,0, and scale to 62, 31, 1.25*	Predefines insertion parameters

ZOOM Extents and save the drawing.

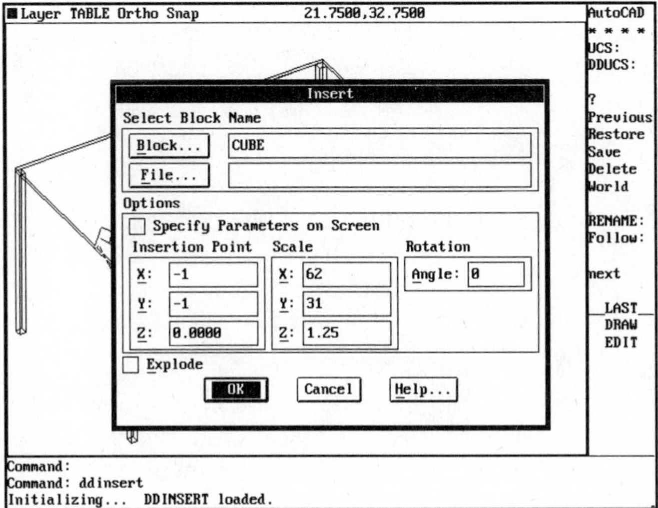

Figure 19.38:
The Insert dialog box (DDINSERT).

When you finish, the drawing board lies in the same X,Y plane as your X-rotated UCS. The UCS icon should appear to lie just under the drawing board at the table's left corner (see fig. 19.39). The Z-scale value of 1.25 scaled the board's thickness in the positive Z direction from the rotated UCS icon. You also could have rotated the block. When you provide a rotation angle, it rotates the block in the current X,Y plane around the insertion point.

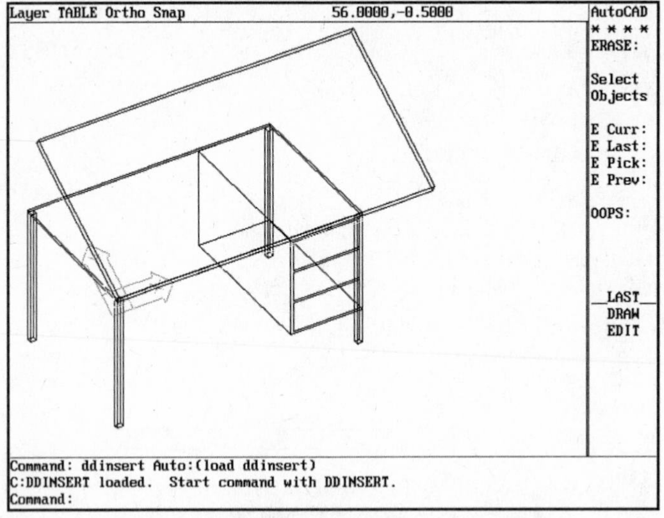

Figure 19.39:

The table, with the drawing board added.

Building a Library of 3D Blocks

As you work in 3D, you can build a library of blocks like the CUBE—a wedge, a pyramid, a cone, various roof shapes, and a pipe elbow are examples of useful shapes that you can easily insert and scale in different drawings. By using the same blocks repeatedly, you can create drawings quickly and reduce the size of your drawing files.

AutoCAD also provides AutoLISP routines that create primitive shapes made of 3D meshes. These routines are accessed from the 3D Surfaces pull-down menu (see fig. 19.40) and the 3D Objects icon menu under the Draw pull-down menu (see fig. 19.41).

These mesh commands are documented in the *AutoLISP Programmer's Reference*, but you do not have to be a programmer to use them. The routines form custom shapes from 3D meshes. Although they are not blocks, 3D mesh objects behave somewhat like blocks. You can select an entire object with a single pick, just like a block. You also can explode these objects into individual 3DFace entities. Unlike multiple occurrences of scaled blocks that all reference the same block definition, each occurrence of these mesh objects is composed of separate data. If you use the same primitives frequently, you can block and insert them for greater efficiency. You will make and use 3D meshes in the next chapter.

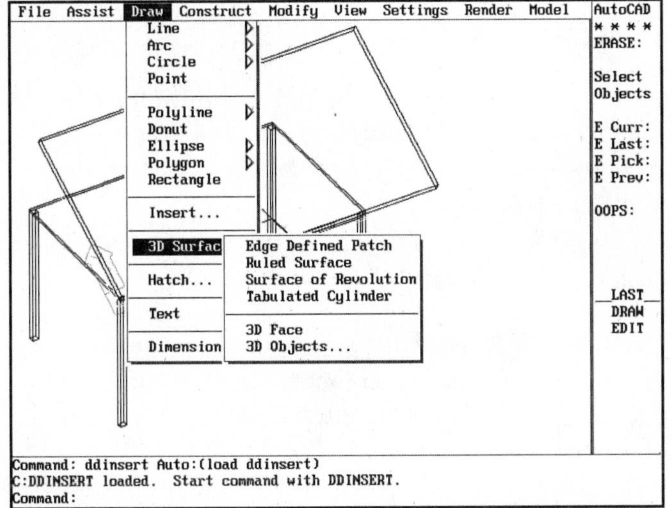

Figure 19.40:

The 3D mesh surfaces pull-down menu.

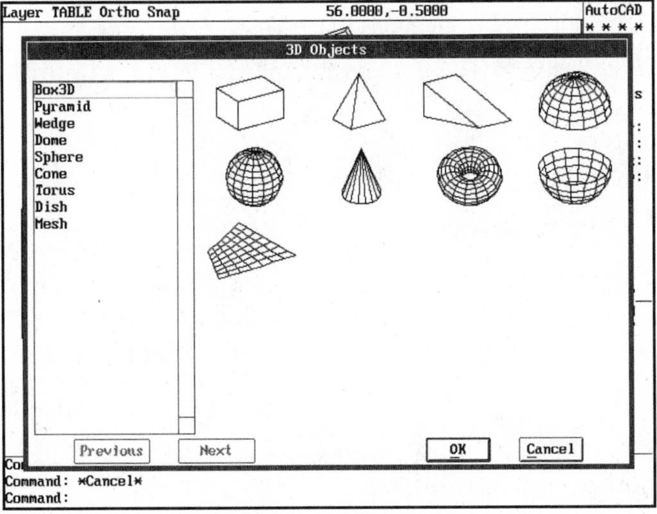

Figure 19.41:

The 3D mesh objects icon menu.

Editing in 3D

Meanwhile, back at the table, the drawing looks a bit funny. The board overhangs on the right, and the two right legs extend up through the cabinet. Now it is time for you to start editing your 3D drawing.

Wireframes can quickly become confusing. As you edit, you can do several things to avoid picking the wrong entities or getting lost in 3D space. First, use color extensively to help identify entities. Second, keep track of the UCS you used when you created an entity. Many users encounter problems during wireframe editing because they pick objects that are at an oblique angle to the UCS. Several 2D editing commands work only with entities that are parallel to the current construction plane. In these cases, you must adjust your UCS to match the entity's UCS. The easiest way to do this is to use the UCS Entity option. If you have any doubts about the outcome of your edits, work in multiple viewports.

You have already used MOVE and COPY in 3D. In the following section, you use CHPROP, STRETCH, TRIM, EXTEND, BREAK, FILLET, CHAMFER, and OFFSET. You also try HATCH, another drawing command.

Using CHPROP and DDMODIFY To Edit an Entity's Thickness

The CHPROP, DDCHPROP (CHange PROPerties dialog box), and DDMODIFY commands work on any entity with any current UCS setting. It can often be easier to create or copy entities with the current settings and then use CHPROP, DDCHPROP, or DDMODIFY to alter them, than it is to change settings, create an entity, and change the settings back. CHPROP and DDMODIFY are the only commands that can assign a thickness to text, shape, and attribute-definition entities.

In the following exercise, you fix the right two legs of the table by using DDCHPROP to change their thickness.

Using DDCHPROP To Edit Entity Thickness

`Command:` *Choose* Modify, *then* Change, *then* Properties	Displays the Change Properties dialog box
`Command:` **`ddchprop`**	
`Select objects:` *Select the two right legs*	
Change the Thickness *to 6.5, then click on* OK	
`Command:` *Choose* View, *then* Redraw	

Figures 19.42 and 19.43 show the table before and after the change to the right legs.

The CHANGE command is "pickier" than CHPROP and DDLIST. Several of its options require that selected entities be parallel to the current UCS, so it will not select nonparallel entities. Use CHPROP or DDLIST instead, whenever possible.

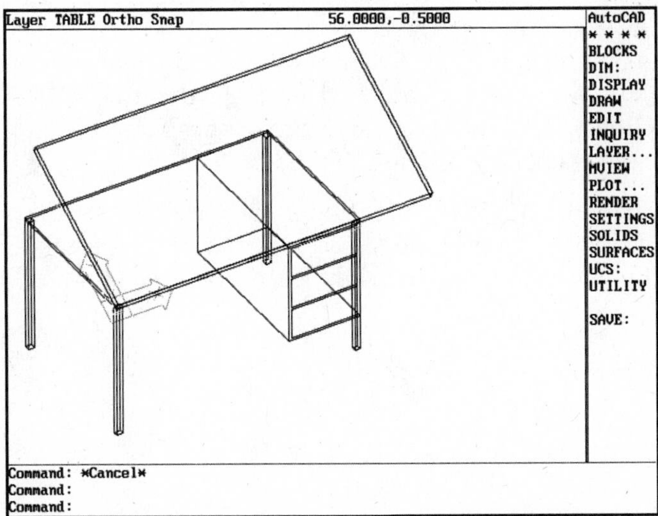

Figure 19.42:

The original table legs.

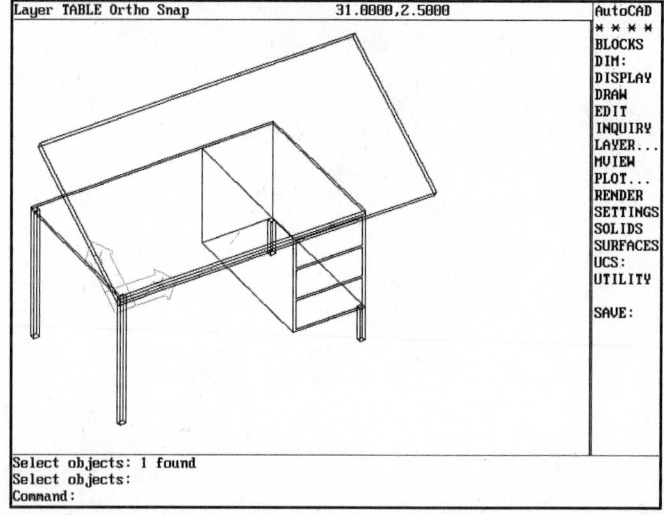

Figure 19.43:
The table legs after being edited.

Using STRETCH To Edit in 3D

The results of STRETCH depend on the entity and current UCS. 3D entities, such as lines (and 3D meshes), can be stretched from and to any point in 3D space, regardless of the current UCS. For 2D and extruded 2D entities, it is safest when all the entities being stretched are aligned with the STRETCH displacement. Otherwise, entities' construction planes may be changed by STRETCH, and the results are difficult to predict.

In the next exercise, you stretch the table to fit the length of the drawing board. All the entities align with the X axis of the current BOARD UCS. You stretch the cabinet, drawers, top, and right legs 12 inches along this X axis.

Stretching the Table

`Command:` *Choose* Modify, *then* Stretch

`stretch`
`Select objects to stretch by window...`
`Select objects: crossing`

`First corner:` *Pick at* ① *(see fig. 19.44)*

`Other corner:` *Pick at* ②

`Select objects:` *Press Enter*

`Base point or displacement:` *Pick any point*	
`Second point of displacement: @12<0` ↵	Stretches the table 12 inches along the X axis from the basepoint (see fig. 19.45)
`Command:` *Choose* View, *then* Redraw	

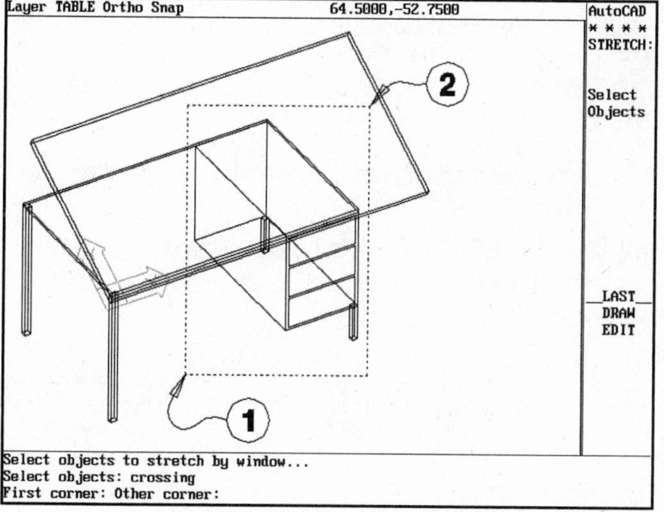

Figure 19.44:

The crossing window for STRETCH.

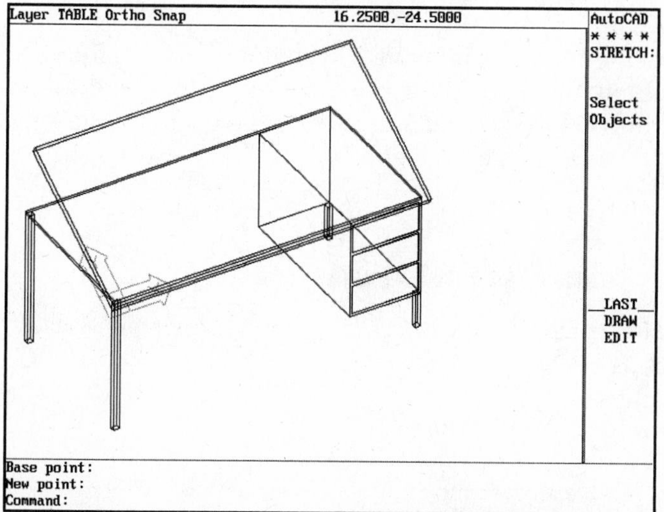

Figure 19.45:

The stretched table.

Like CHANGE and STRETCH, several other editing commands require more care and attention in 3D.

The following editing commands work correctly only for entities in which the current UCS is in or parallel to the construction plane of their entity coordinate system(s). The easiest way to use these commands is to use the UCS Entity option to make your UCS parallel to the entities you want to edit. Use special care when you use the following editing commands in 3D:

- **BREAK.** This command projects the entity and break points to the current UCS.
- **TRIM.** This command projects the trim edge and entities to the current UCS.
- **EXTEND.** This command projects the extend edge and entities to the current UCS.
- **FILLET and CHAMFER.** All objects being filleted or chamfered must lie in a plane parallel to the current UCS (the extrusion thickness is parallel to the current Z axis).
- **OFFSET.** This command performs relative to the current UCS.

You may find it easiest to work with these commands in plan view while observing the results in multiple 3D viewports.

Using FILLET To Edit in 3D

To demonstrate the FILLET command's behavior in 3D, the following exercise shows you how to fillet the polylines of the cabinet drawers by using a 0.5 radius in the next exercise. First, you try it in the current UCS to see the type of error messages that appear.

Using FILLET To Fillet Drawers in 3D

ZOOM in to the front of the cabinet, so that all the drawer fronts are visible.

Choose Construct, *then* Fillet

`Command: _fillet`

`View is not plan to UCS. Command results may not be obvious.`

`Polyline/Radius/<Select first object>:` *From the screen menu, choose* radius

`Enter fillet radius <0.000>: .5↵`	Specifies the radius and repeats the command
`Command: _FILLET` `View is not plan to UCS. Command resultsmay not be obvious.`	Warns you that results may not be visible
`Polyline/Radius/<Select first object>:` *From the screen menu, choose* polyline	Specifies the polyline option
`Select 2D polyline:` *Pick any drawer*	
`The entity is not parallel to the UCS.`	Rejects selection
`Select 2D polyline:` *Press Enter*	Ends the FILLET command
`Command:` *Choose* Settings, *then* UCS, *then* Named UCS, *then highlight* CABINET, *choose* Current, *and click on* OK	Restores the CABINET UCS, which is used to create the drawers
`Command:` *Choose* Construct, *then* Fillet	
`Command: _fillet` `View is not plan to UCS. Command results may not be obvious.`	Warns you that results may not be clear, but try it anyway
`Polyline/Radius/<Select first object>:` *From the screen menu, choose* polyline	
`Select 2D polyline:` *Pick any drawer*	Fillets the drawer
`4 lines were filleted`	
Repeat to fillet the second and third drawers	Fillets all the drawers, as shown in figure 19.46
`Command:` *Choose* View, *then* Zoom, *then* Previous	

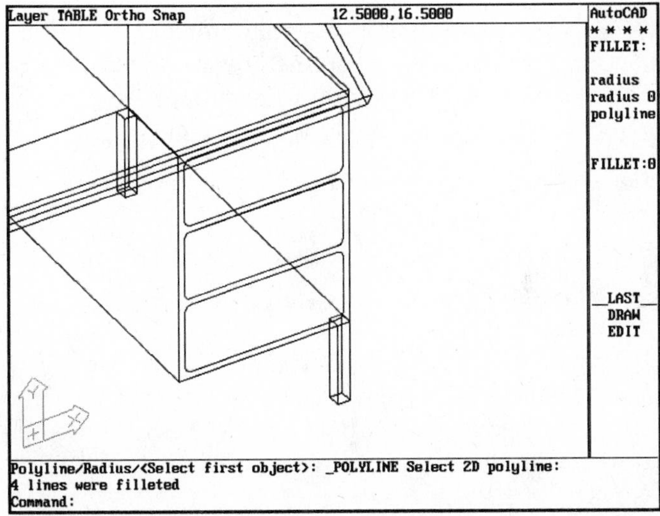

Figure 19.46:

The filleted drawers.

If you are wondering why your CABINET UCS icon seems to be floating in space, remember that you stretched the table 12 inches to the right, away from the UCS origin. The FRONT UCS also works for these fillets.

When you edit in 3D, you find that it pays to name and save your UCSs so that you can later restore them. If you forget their names, you can get a list by using the UCS command or the UCS Control dialog box.

Supplemental 3D Editing Commands

If you have installed AutoCAD's supplemental programs, you have access to additional editing commands that are designed specifically for editing 3D models. You can load these commands through the applications dialog box; just load /ACAD/SUPPORT/GEOM3D.ADS (substituting your path name). This ADS application defines the following new commands:

- **3DARRAY.** This command enables you to create rectangular and polar arrays that, unlike the standard ARRAY command, can be non-parallel to the current UCS. 3DARRAY does not, however, enable you to create an array in three directions at once.
- **ALIGN.** This command works like an efficient combination of the MOVE and ROTATE commands. Uses three pairs of points; source and destination points.
- **MIRROR3D.** This command enables you to mirror a selection set about a 3D plan. The plane can be defined by an existing entity, the last-used plane, a viewpoint, or by user-definition.
- **PROJECT.** This command creates a 2D copy of a 3D view.
- **ROTATE3D.** This command enables rotation in the X, Y, or Z direction.

Hatching in 3D

You can spruce up your 3D images by filling their surfaces with hatch patterns. You usually have to set the UCS on the surface to be hatched and then draw new boundary edges to hatch in. The HATCH command projects the hatch boundaries onto the X,Y plane of the current UCS. In the

following exercise, you create a boundary with lines on layer 0 and try to hatch the board.

Trying To Hatch the Drawing Board

Make layer 0 current, set INT as the running object snap mode, then draw four lines around the top of the drawing board. You may have to turn snap off and transparently zoom in on the front left corner to pick it.

`Command:` *Choose* Draw, *then* Hatch

`bhatch`

Choose the Hatch Options *button, then the* Pattern *button, select the* LINE *pattern, set the scale to* 6, *click on* OK, *then click on* Select objects	Defines the hatch parameters
`Select objects:` *Select the four boundary lines, and press Enter*	
Choose Preview hatch	Displays the hatch pattern (see fig. 19.47)
Press Enter to return to the Boundary Hatch dialog, then Choose Cancel	Cancels the HATCH command

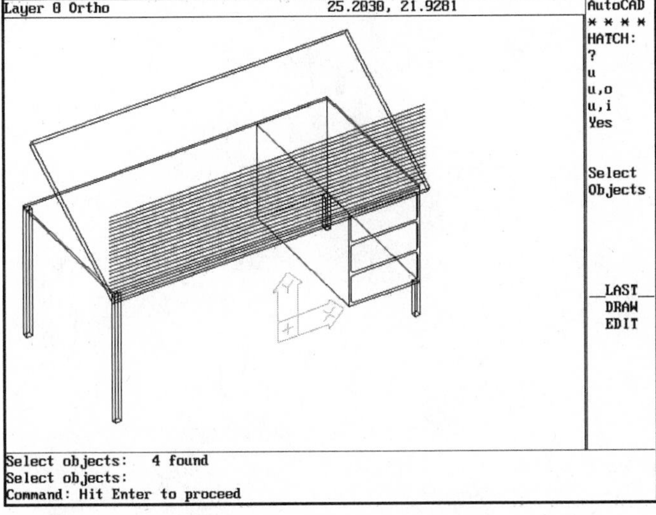

Figure 19.47:

The table with an incorrect hatch.

The hatch was projected to the current UCS, which is not the effect you want. To get the hatch right, locate the UCS on the plane of the drawing board's surface.

Erase the first hatch, restore your BOARD UCS and try again to get the hatch right. The BOARD UCS is on the underside of the board, so use the UCS Origin option to move the origin 1.25 inches up to the board top.

Hatching the Drawing Board

`Command:` *Choose* Settings, *then* Object Snap, *then* Select, *clear all check boxes, and click on* OK	Turns off running object snaps
`Command:` **`UCS`**↵	
`Origin/ZAxis/3point/Entity/View/XYZ/Prev/Restore/Save/Del/?/<World>:` **`O`**↵	
`Origin point <0,0,0>:` **`0,0,1.25`**↵	Moves the UCS to the top of the board

Repeat the BHATCH command from the previous exercise, this time finishing by clicking on Apply rather than Cancel. Save the drawing.

Your table should now have a hatch on the plane of the drawing board (see fig. 19.48).

Figure 19.48:

The correctly hatched table.

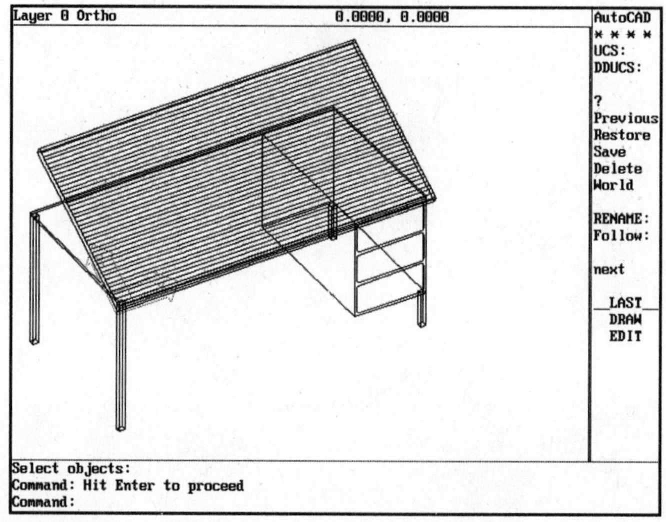

Both the TRIM and EXTEND commands behave like HATCH, projecting their boundary edges and entities onto the construction plane of the current UCS to calculate the trim or extension. The trimmed or extended entities, however, remain in their own planes after modification.

Viewing the Table

Before you put the table drawing to rest, clean up the drawing by erasing the hatch and boundary lines, and then review its construction by looking at the plan views of the TOP, FRONT, and R-SIDE UCSs you saved.

Using UCSFOLLOW To Automate Plan Views

Viewing the TOP, FRONT, and R-SIDE UCSs in their plan views shows the top, front, and right sides of the model. When the UCSFOLLOW system variable is set to 1, AutoCAD automatically generates a plan view whenever you change UCSs. Set UCSFOLLOW to 1 in the next exercise, and look at your drawing's UCSs in plan view. Try this with both the UCS command and the dialog box.

Using UCSFOLLOW To View Saved UCS Planes in Plan

Erase the hatch and boundary lines on layer 0

Command: **UCSFOLLOW**↵

New value for UCSFOLLOW <0>: **1**

Command: **UCS**↵

Origin/ZAxis/3point/Entity/View/X/Y/Z/Prev
/Restore/Save/Del/?/<World>: **R**↵

?/Name of UCS to restore: **TOP**	Restores the TOP UCS, as shown in figure 19.49
Regenerating drawing.	Displays plan view
Command: *Choose* Settings, *then* Named UCS, *highlight* FRONT, *choose* Current, *then* OK	Restores FRONT UCS and displays the plan view (see fig. 19.50)
Use either method to restore the R-SIDE UCS	Restores R-SIDE UCS (see fig. 19.51)

Set UCSFOLLOW back to 0 (off)

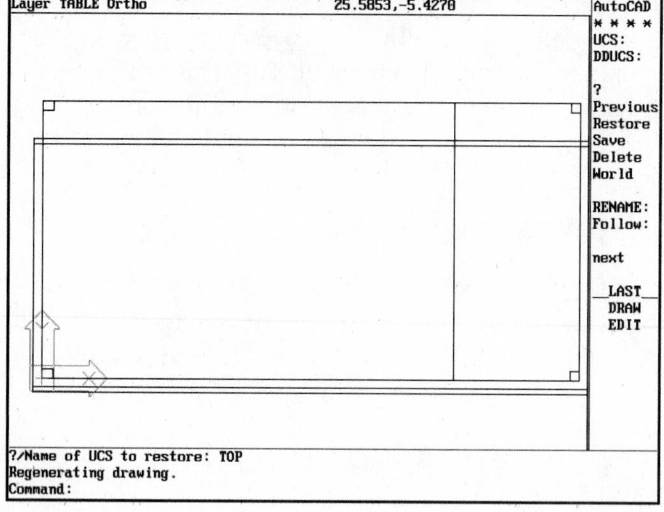

Figure 19.49:

Plan view of the top.

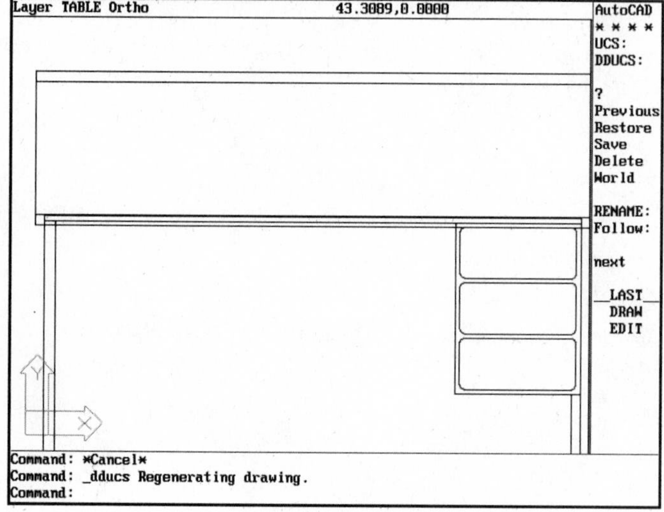

Figure 19.50:

Plan view of the front.

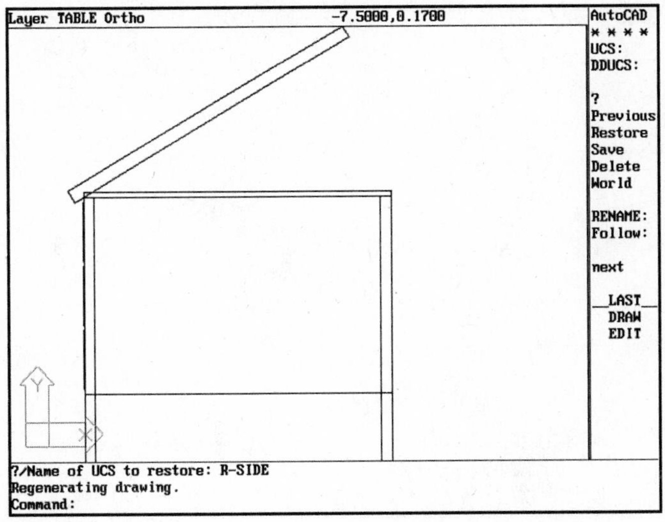

Figure 19.51:

Plan view of the right side.

Now that you have reviewed your drawing, you can restore your 3D view and hide the table's hidden lines in the next exercise. The following exercise also shows you how to change some settings for later use. Finally, you end the drawing session.

Hiding the Table's Hidden Lines

`Command:` **`PSPACE`**↵	Enters paper space
`Command:` *Choose* View, *then* Zoom, *then* All	
Erase all three viewports	
`Command:` *Choose* View, *then* Tilemode, *then* On (1)	Returns to a single tiled viewport
Use VIEW to restore the 3D view TABLE, then ZOOM Extents	
`Command:` *Choose* Settings, *then* UCS, *then* Presets, *and double-click on the UCS icon*	Sets the UCS to the WCS
Choose Render, *then* Hide	
`Regenerating drawing.` `Hiding lines: 100% done`	The drawing regenerates as in figure 19.52

End the drawing; the table model is complete.

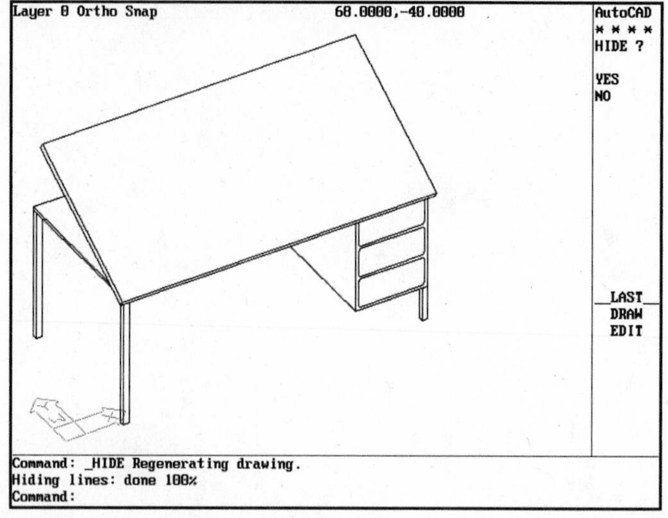

Figure 19.52:

The hidden table.

When you edit 3D views that have had hidden lines removed, the hidden lines may reappear. If so, execute HIDE again when you finish editing.

Congratulations! You have created (and edited) a 3D table from start to finish. You should have gained a feel for the power and ease built into 3D drafting. Once you get the hang of it, using a UCS is like 2D drafting. The only difference is that, like a fly, you can climb all over your drawing.

To document the results of your 3D designs, you can create assembly drawings. The next section shows you how to assemble a multiple-view drawing.

Creating 3D Multiple-View Drawings

Once you have a basic 3D drawing, you can easily create a multiple-view drawing. The next exercise shows you how to have a plan, top, right side, and 3D view in the same drawing. You will use MVIEW viewports in paper space to view the same 3D model from several viewpoints.

Setting up a multiple-view drawing is easy. All you have to do is enter paper space, insert your title block (if you have one), and open up as many viewports as you need to contain the different views of your model (see fig. 19.53). Then you orient the views by simply setting the desired UCS in each viewport and using the PLAN command. The ZOOM command, when used with the XP options, scales the viewport contents relative to the paper-space sheet for plotting.

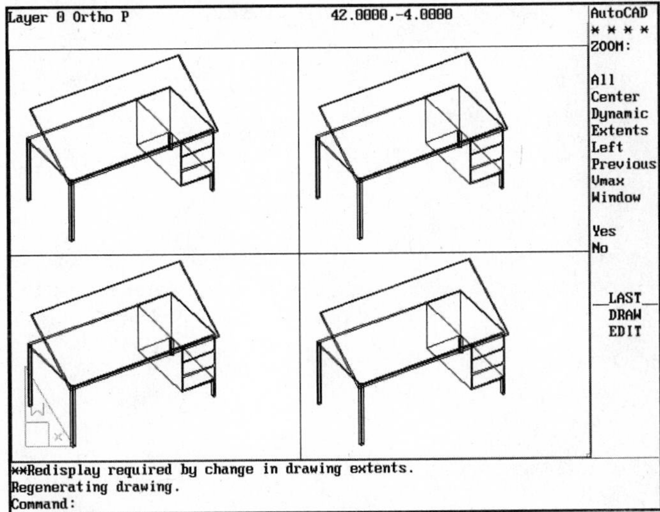

Figure 19.53:
MVIEW viewports before reorienting views.

Assembling a Multiple-View Drawing in Paper Space

Choose File, then New, and enter the drawing name as `\IA\MV-TABLE=\IA\TABLE`

`Command:` *Press Ctrl-G to turn off the grid*	
`Command:` *Choose* View, *then* Tilemode, *then* Off	Turns off TILEMODE
`Command:` *Choose* View, *then* Mview, *then* 4 Viewports	Enters paper space and issues MVIEW with the 4 option
`Command: _mview`	
`ON/OFF/Hideplot/Fit/2/3/4/Restore/<First Point>: 4`	
`Fit/<First Point>:` **`1,2↵`**	Sets the lower left corner
`Second point:` **`20,15↵`**	Opens four viewports
`Command:` *Choose* Settings, *then* Drawing Limits	
`Command: _limits`	
`Reset Paper space limits:`	

`ON/OFF/<Lower left corner>` `<0.0000,0.0000>:` *Press Enter*	
`Upper right corner` `<12.0000,9.0000>:` **`22,17`**↵	Sets the limits for a 22"×17" sheet
Use ZOOM Extents	Displays the views shown in figure 19.53
`Command:` **`MSPACE`**↵	Enters model space
`Command:` *Select the upper left viewport*	
`Command:` *Choose* View, *then* Set View, *then* Plan View, *then* World	Reorients viewpoint for top view
`Command:` **`ZOOM`**↵	
`All/Center/Dynamic/Extents/Left/` `Previous/Vmax/Window/<Scale(X/XP)>:` **`.125XP`**↵	Scales the viewport relative to paper space sheet for 1=8 scale

The following steps reorient the viewpoint for the front view.

`Command:` *Select the lower left viewport, then restore* UCS FRONT

`Command:` *Choose* View, *then* Set View, *then* Plan View, *then* Current UCS

ZOOM .125XP (1=8 scale)

The following steps reorient the viewpoint for the side view.

`Command:` *Select the lower right viewport, then restore* UCS R-SIDE

`Command:` *Choose* View, *then* Set View, *then* Plan View, *then* Current UCS

ZOOM .125XP (1=8 scale)

Select the upper right viewport and ZOOM .6 (not .6XP)

`Command:` **`PS`**↵	Enters paper space
Make TABLE the current layer and freeze layer 0	Makes the viewport borders disappear (see fig. 19.54)

End or close and save the drawing.

You now have four different views of your table, and you did not have to copy or insert anything to do it. To align the viewports and get the drawing ready for plotting, see Chapter 13.

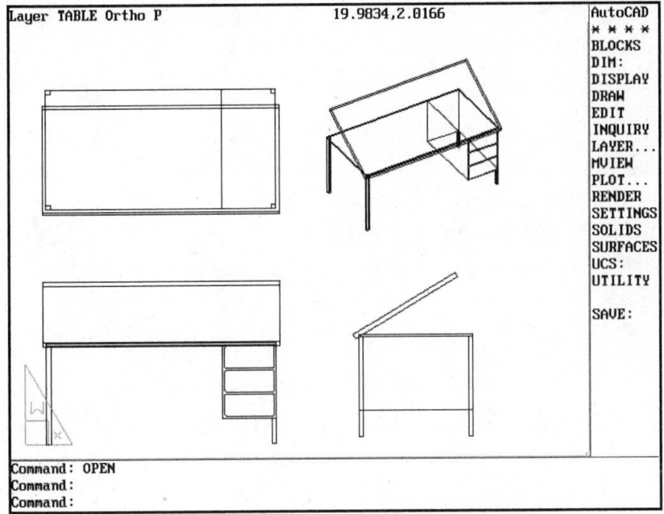

Figure 19.54:

The completed multiple-view table drawing in paper space.

You also can create 2D copies of your 3D model from any viewpoint, projected onto any UCS. The PROJECT command is a supplemental program which "projects" a view of your model onto the desired 2D plane. This command is particularly useful when you need to include a two-dimensional 3D view within a 3D model. If you like, experiment with this concept by creating a block of a projected 3D view, and then inserting that block on your drafting table. The result is a 2D "drawing" (of a 3D view) lying on the desktop of your 3D model. Load PROJECT.LSP using the applications dialog box, and run the program by typing **PROJECT** and then pressing Enter.

Summary

2D isometric drawings provide a quick and simple method of emulating 3D views. They work well for simple drawings in which multiple views are not required.

Good layer and color management can greatly ease and speed 3D work. Colors help clarify a mass of overlaid wireframe images. Layers enable you to turn objects off to help with picking points in complex drawings and to freeze unneeded layers in order to speed up regenerations and hidden-line

removal. Paper space gives you individual layer visibility control in each viewport.

Use multiple viewports when drawing in 3D. Sometimes it can be hard to select objects and pick points in a single viewport, particularly when using object snap to select an existing object. Remember that you can use XYZ point filters, and even switch viewports in the middle. You can, for example, select your objects in one or more viewports, pick your X,Y point in another viewport, and then switch to a third viewport to pick the Z value by using object snap.

A standard set of named UCSs, views (viewpoints), and viewports makes moving around in 3D a breeze. Remember that each viewport can have its own set of snap and grid settings. Save your settings in a 3D prototype drawing. Use the UCS Entity option for quick edits to existing entities or to add new entities parallel to existing ones. The X,Y orientation may look unusual, but it seldom matters.

For 2D entities that are constrained to be parallel to the current UCS, you need not change the UCS just to place them above or below the current UCS. A Z value entered for their first coordinate point establishes their position in 3D space. Do not confuse things by setting elevation or by using the ELEV command.

Remember that you can use editing commands in 3D. COPY and MOVE, for example, can place any entity up and down in the current Z axis.

The next chapter shows you how to work with 3D entities. Now that you have created a drafting table, you need a chair—a 3D chair.

20

Using 3D Entities

In the last chapter, you used 2D entities and extrusions to build a table in 3D space. In this chapter, you learn how to draw and edit objects by using true 3D entities, including 3D polygon meshes. You can use these 3D entities to construct complex shapes bounded by flat and curved surfaces. You can also combine these 3D objects into complex assemblies by making and inserting blocks of 3D entities to build a drawing.

Because you have a table, you need a comfortable chair to sit in while AutoCAD does all of its 3D work. As you draw the chair, shown in figure 20.1, you use all of AutoCAD's 3D entities.

Selecting 3D Entities and Meshes

AutoCAD has only four true 3D entities: points, lines, 3Dfaces, and a family of special polylines. The simplest of the polylines is the 3D polyline, which is a polyline without width or curvature, and whose vertices can be at any X, Y, or Z coordinate in space. The 3Dface entity is much like a 2D solid entity except that each of its three or four corners can be at any X, Y, and Z coordinate in space, whereas a solid is planar. The sides of the chair's legs are constructed of 3Dfaces. Although you can create multiple 3Dfaces in a single 3DFACE command, these 3Dfaces exist as individual entities. More efficient and versatile are the polyline mesh entities.

Figure 20.1: The completed 3D chair.

Most 3D commands you work with in this chapter construct faceted surface meshes. The chair's seat, back, and pedestal have multiple faces. Although you can build these surfaces by using individual 3Dfaces, AutoCAD's 3D mesh commands automatically generate 3D polygon meshes that can approximate any possible surface in 3D space. They can be either planar, like the square center of the seat; or curved, like the pedestal, back, edges, corners, and casters.

AutoCAD has various types of polyline meshes. Polyface meshes are the most general and versatile because they can be arbitrarily irregular. You can create polyface meshes with the PFACE command, and they can contain any number of edges and vertices and any number of visible or invisible interior divisions. Other polygon meshes are less general. The 3DMESH command, for example, is used to create topologically rectangular meshes; although they can be warped and distorted, they must be bounded by four

lines or curves. Opposite sides must have the same number of subdivisions, although a side can converge to a single point (that is, it can have a zero length).

Applying 3D Drawing Tools

AutoCAD provides numerous commands, menu items, and AutoLISP and ADS routines for constructing regular polyline meshes. On the Draw pull-down menu is the 3D Surfaces option, which provides access to the 3D surface commands, as well as to the 3D Objects icon menu. The 3D Objects icon menu, which includes selections that use AutoLISP to create 3D geometric objects like spheres, cones, and tori from the surface meshes, is shown in figure 20.2. The 3D Surfaces pull-down menu of surfacing-command selections is shown in figure 20.3.

The 3D commands also are found on the screen menu. Choose SURFACES or DRAW, and then choose 3D Surfs to find items for the following 3D drawing commands: 3DFACE, 3DPOLY, PFACE, 3DMESH, EDGESURF, REVSURF, RULESURF, and TABSURF. The 3D and objects selections at the bottom of the menu open a menu of the same AutoLISP routines as the 3D Objects icon menu.

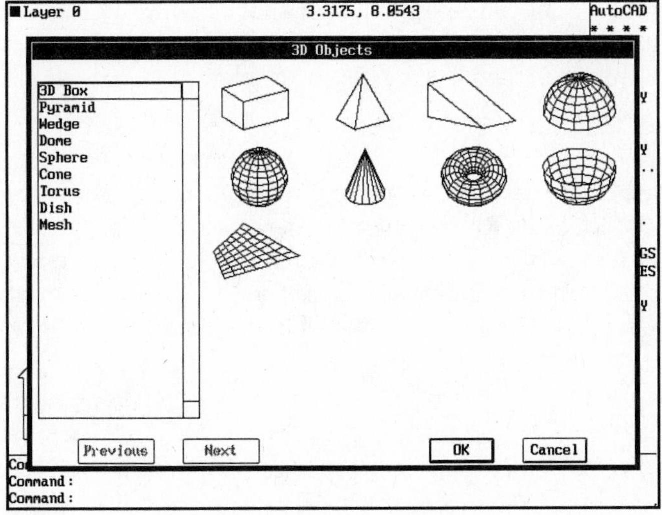

Figure 20.2:
The 3D Objects icon menu.

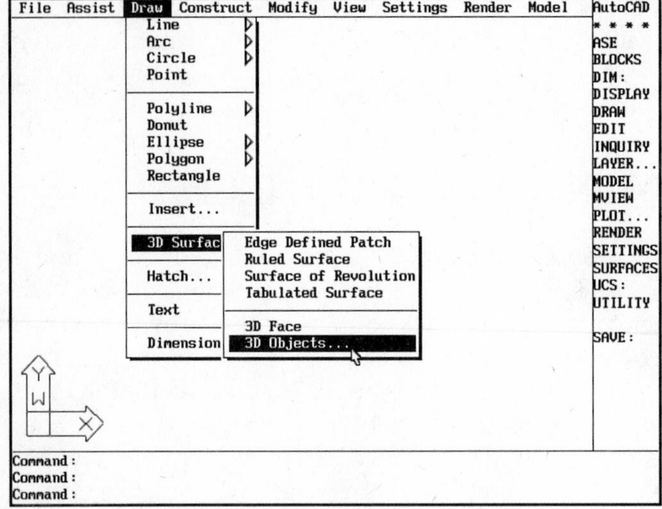

Figure 20.3:

The 3D Surfaces child pull-down menu.

Understanding Mesh Generation

Think of a mesh as a piece of net or chicken wire that you can mold or stretch into various shapes. The wires or cords that make up the net enable you to visualize the shape of a surface, even though your model is essentially transparent. You can model simple shapes with a coarse net, but you need a finer net to model complex shapes or shapes with small features. AutoCAD creates meshes with a preset number of four-sided areas, which you can control through the use of system variables.

You can use the PFACE and 3DMESH commands to create irregularly shaped surfaces, but, in most cases, you want to use commands that take advantage of symmetry or regularity about which or in which a mesh can be generated. The RULESURF command generates a surface defined by ruling lines between two existing edges, which may be lines or curves—two of the ruling lines form the other two edges. The EDGESURF command generates a mesh that fills the area bounded by four existing lines or curves.

The process of generating a mesh often involves specifying the profile of the mesh and line it is to be rotated about or translated (moved) along. The REVSURF command makes a circular mesh when you specify a path profile and an axis of rotation (the *path profile* is a cross section of the surface that you want). If you rotate the profile 360 degrees, you get a cylindrical or globular surface, similar to the chair's pedestal or casters.

You also can generate a mesh by using the TABSURF command, translating a direction vector along a path curve (profile). The results of using TABSURF look like the results of extruding a 2D entity into 3D, except that the TABSURF command can create oblique or skewed surfaces. Figure 20.4 shows how these commands are used to create your chair.

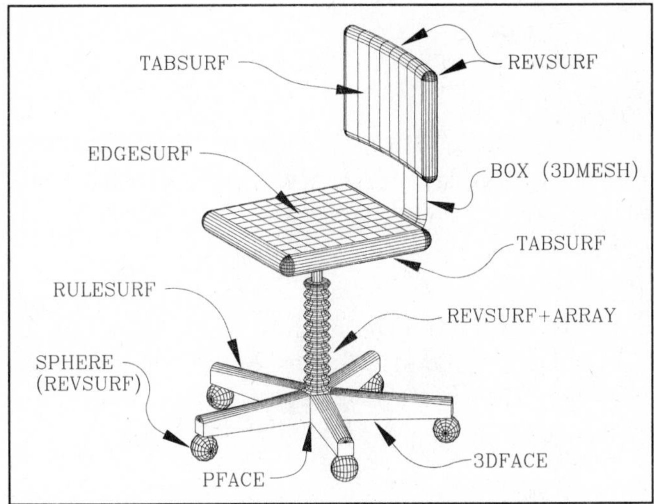

Figure 20.4:
The 3D commands for the chair.

That is all there is to meshes: defining edges, path profiles, direction vectors, or rotation axes, and a few system variable settings.

Following the Chair Exercises

As you use each 3D drawing command to build the parts of the chair, you get some practice and tips on using UCSs to draw and edit entities in 3D space. You also edit some of the chair's meshes by using the PEDIT command. As you create the parts, you make them into 3D blocks. Then you assemble the chair by inserting the casters on the legs, the legs on the pedestal, the pedestal on the seat, and so on, just as you might assemble a real chair. You use 3D blocks by applying the standard BLOCK and INSERT commands.

Because the chair is built in parts, you can do it all or pick and choose the commands that you want to learn by working on particular components.

The IA DISK contains the component blocks, which you can use to assemble the chair, even if you do not want to draw all the parts.

Set up the drawing by using the upper-right viewport as a scratch viewport. Use the SCRATCH layer for practicing the 3D commands. When you are through practicing, restore the previously current layer and freeze the SCRATCH layer.

Setting Up for Using 3D Entities

The CHAIR drawing uses two layers, CHAIR and BUILD, with default drawing units and limits large enough to contain the chair at full scale. The chair is 35 inches high and about 25 inches wide at the base, with varied entity colors to help your viewing in 3D.

If you are using the IA DISK, you have the drawing setup in the IA7CHAIR.DWG file. Load it and skip the rest of the following setup. Otherwise, create a new CHAIR drawing, make the settings as shown in table 20.1, and set up your viewports. The initial setup uses three viewports: a full-height viewport on the left (in which you spend most of your time building the chair); a lower-right viewport with a plan view of the chair; and an upper-right viewport to use as a scratch viewport.

Table 20.1
3D Chair Drawing Settings

COORDS	*FILL*	*GRID*	*SNAP*	*UCSICON*
ON	OFF	Off	.25	OR

UNITS	Use defaults for all settings.
MODEL SPACE LIMITS	0,0 to 68,44

Layer Name	*State*	*Color*	*Linetype*
0	On	7 White	CONTINUOUS
BUILD	On	1 Red	CONTINUOUS
CHAIR	On/Current	7 White	CONTINUOUS
SCRATCH	On	4 Cyan	CONTINUOUS

Setting Up for 3D Entities

Choose File, then New, and enter `\IA\CHAIR=\IA\IA7CHAIR`.

Choose File, then New, and enter `\IA\CHAIR` and make the settings shown in table 20.1.

Choose View, *then* Set View, Viewpoint, Axes	
`Rotate/<View Point><0.0000,0.0000, 1.0000>:` **`-1,-1,0.5`** ↵	
Choose View, *then* Tilemode, *then* Off	Sets TILEMODE to 0 and enters paper space
Choose View, *then* Mview, *then* 3 Viewports	Issues MVIEW command
`Command:` **`MVIEW`**	
`ON/OFF/Hideplot/Fit/2/3/4/Restore /<First Point>: 3` ↵	
`Horizontal/Vertical/Above/Below/Left /<Right>:` **`L`** ↵	
`Fit/<First Point>:` **`F`**↵	Fits three viewports to the screen
`Command:` **`MS`**	Enters model space
Click in the upper right viewport to make it current	
Use ZOOM with the Center option at 0,0 with a height of 10	
Turn the UCS icon off	
Use VIEW *to save the current view as CHAIR*	
Make the left viewport current	
Choose Settings, *then* UCS, *then* Origin	
`Origin point <0,0,0>:` **`0,88,0`** ↵	Creates new UCS named HUB
Save the chrrent UCS as HUB	
Zoom Center at 0,0 and a height of 20	
Save view as BUILD	
Select lower right viewport	
Choose View, *then* Set View, *then* Plan View, *then* Current UCS	
Zoom Center at 0,0 and a height of 5	
Save your drawing.	

When you finish this first exercise, your screen should look like figure 20.5, with layer CHAIR current and the UCS icon located in the center of the left viewport and in the center of the lower-right viewport. The lower-right viewport should be current.

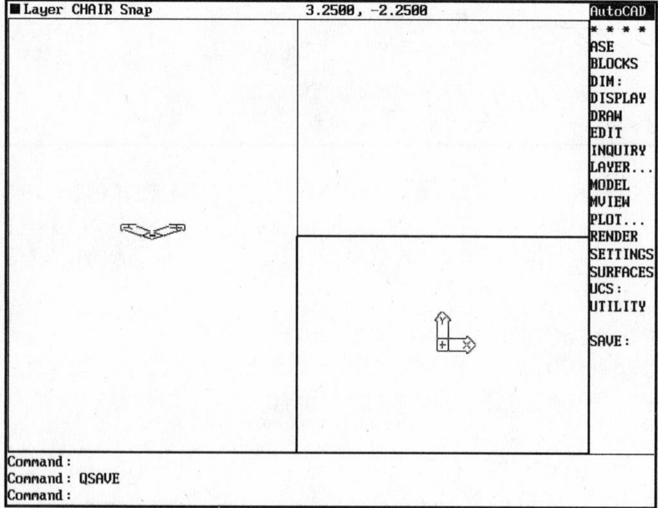

Figure 20.5:
Viewports for the chair.

The job of creating 3D entities requires preparation. Drawings can become complex and difficult to visualize. Your ability to visualize and select entities depends on your display resolution—a high-resolution, large-screen display makes matters easier, especially for tired eyes. The following exercises specify the required ZOOM, SNAP, ORTHO, and object snap settings, but you may want to zoom in further, and more often. If this is the case, follow each additional "zoom in" with a ZOOM Previous, so that you can track the exercises and illustrations.

Using the 3D Objects Mesh Commands

You can extrude a 2D polyline to create the chair's hub, but you should create it as a true 3D surface. The *hub* is a pentagon-shaped cylinder. AutoCAD does not have a specific command to draw five-sided cylinders,

but it does include some AutoLISP routines that you can use to draw many different types of 3D objects. These routines are included in the AutoLISP file, 3D.LSP, and can be used just like built-in commands—by selecting them from the 3D Objects icon menu. The routines are Cone, Wedge, Torus, Sphere, Pyramid, Mesh, Dome, Dish, and Box.

This 3D AutoLISP file also defines the general command, 3D, which you can use to access any of these commands. The 3D command issues the following prompt so that you can select the surface shape you want:

```
Box/Cone/DIsh/DOme/Mesh/Pyramid/Sphere/Torus/Wedge:
```

These options are documented in the AutoCAD *Extras* manual, but they are so easy to use that you probably do not need to look them up.

Although the 3D object commands are AutoLISP programs, they are easily accessed through the 3D Objects icon menu. Choose Draw, then 3D Surfaces, then 3D Objects to display the icon menu. Selecting an icon or a command name from this menu automatically loads and executes the requested command in much the same way as AutoCAD's built-in commands are loaded and executed.

The 3D objects mesh commands do not include a pentagon, but you can use the CONE command to create one because of the way that AutoCAD draws surface entities.

Using CONE To Construct the Chair's Five-Sided Hub

The AutoLISP CONE command is versatile. It enables you to specify a top as well as a bottom diameter for drawing a truncated cone. If the diameters are equal, the result is a cylinder. You also can specify the resolution (number of segments) that it uses to represent the cone or cylinder. The AutoLISP routine normally uses 16 segments to approximate a circular cone; five segments generates a pentagon.

Use CONE in the following exercise to create the hub of the chair.

Drawing a Five-Sided CONE

Choose Draw, *then* 3D Surfaces, *then* 3D Objects, *and double-click on* Cone *or the cone icon*	Loads 3D.LSP and issues the CONE command
`cone Auto: (load 3d)`	
`Base center point:` **`0,0,-2.5`** ↵	
`Diameter/<radius> of base:` **`1.55`** ↵	
`Diameter/<radius> of top <0>:` **`1.55`** ↵	
`Height:` **`2.5`** ↵	
`Number of segments <16>:` **`5`**↵	Specifies 5 "sides"

The hub created in this exercise look like figure 20.6. You should have a plan view of the hub polygon in the right viewport and a 3D view of it in your left viewport.

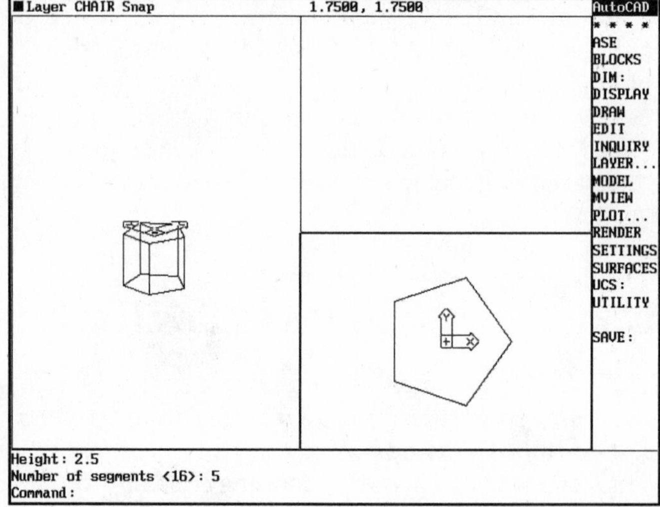

Figure 20.6:

The hub of the chair.

Using 3DFACES To Create the Chair Leg

Next, create the chair's leg with 3Dface entities. 3Dfaces are defined by three or four edges (they always have four corner points, but the third and fourth may coincide). The 3DFACE command prompts are similar to those for a 2D solid entity (not an AME solid), but the pick-point order is more natural.

You can pick clockwise or counterclockwise, rather than in a crisscross bow tie (if you pick the points in the same sequence as for the SOLID command, the result is a bow-tie shape). A 3D solid is confined to a single plane (in any UCS); edges and points of a 3Dface can be anywhere in space. A non-extruded 2D solid and a 3Dface may look the same if they both lie in the same plane, but they have different edge and transparency properties. If all points and edges of a 3Dface lie in a single plane, the HIDE command treats the 3Dface as opaque. If the 3Dface is not planar, it is transparent and does not hide. Unlike a 2D solid, you cannot extrude a 3Dface; it always has zero thickness.

Use 3Dfaces when you want to draw simple three-point or four-point planar faces. For the chair leg, you want an end cap, an underside, and two simple planar sides.

Create a four-sided 3Dface as the leg's end cap in the following steps, working in the left viewport. The easiest method is to create the 3Dface at the origin, then move it where you want it. After you create and move the end cap, use 3DFACE again to create the bottom and the two sides, snapping to end points on the cap and hub. You can leave the top open for now.

Using 3DFACE To Make the First Leg

Make the left viewport current.

Choose Draw, *then* 3D Surfaces, *then* 3D Face

`Command:` **`3DFACE`**	
`First point:` **`0,0`** ↵	Specifies first corner
`Second point:` **`0,0,1.25`** ↵	
`Third point:` **`0,1.5,1.25`** ↵	
`Fourth point:` **`0,1.5,0`** ↵	
`Third point:` *Press Enter*	Ends the 3DFACE command and creates end cap of leg at the UCS origin (see fig. 20.7)

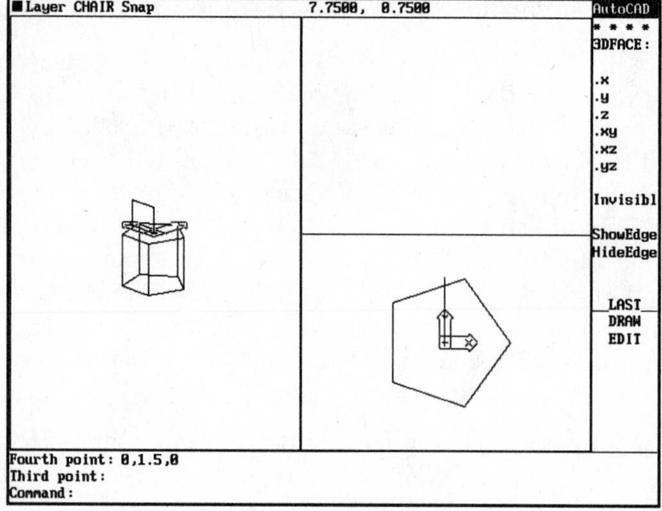

Figure 20.7:

The end cap of the leg at UCS origin.

Choose Modify, *then* Move, *and move the 3Dface with a displacement of –12.5,–.75,–2 (see fig. 20. 8)*	
Pan to view shown in figure 20.8 to see end cap	
Choose Settings, *then* Object Snap	Displays OSNAP dialog
Click on the Endpoint *box, then* OK	Sets running ENDP object snap to draw the leg faces
Choose Draw, *then* 3D Surfaces, *then* 3D Face, *and draw leg's left face first, then remaining faces, selecting points ① (see fig. 20.9) through ⑧ in sequence in clockwise order, then press Enter to exit*	
Set the running object snap mode back to NONE	
Choose Render, *then* Hide	Hides drawing to confirm drawing (see fig. 20.10)
Save the drawing.	

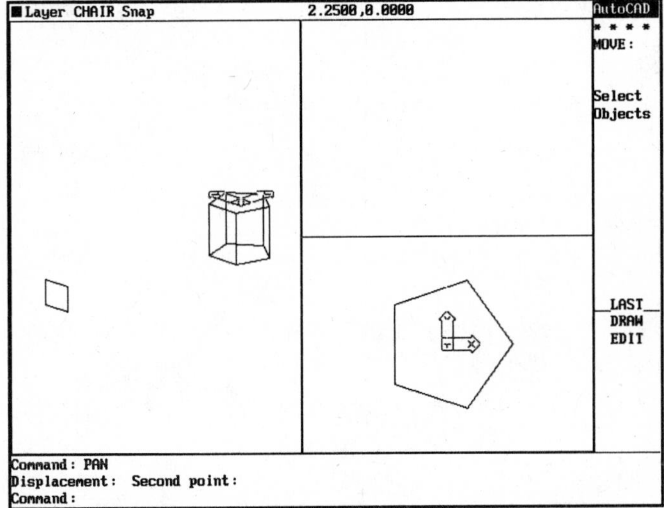

Figure 20.8: The end cap of the leg moved into place.

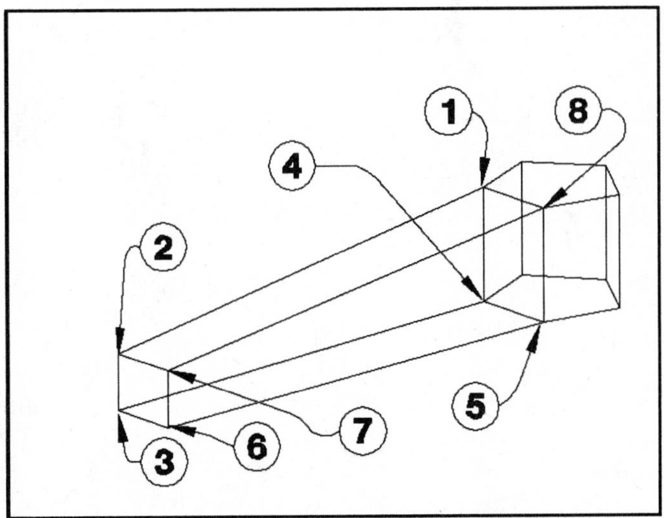

Figure 20.9: Detail of pick points.

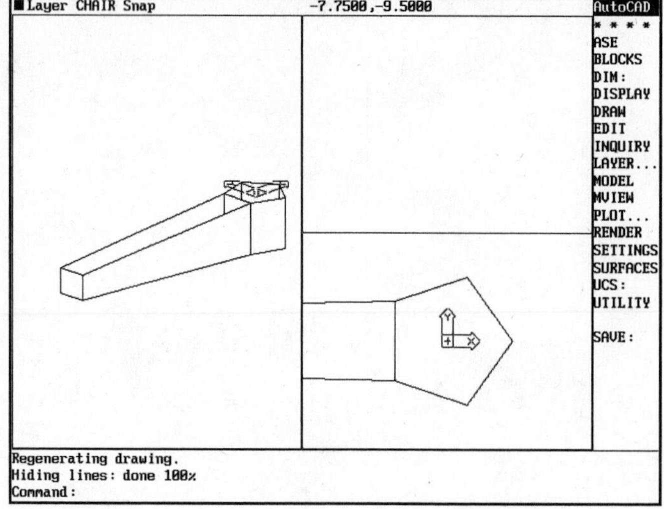

Figure 20.10:
The chair leg constructed with 3Dfaces.

Utilizing 3Dfaces with Invisible Edges

By using multiple adjoining 3Dfaces with invisible edges, you can create what appears to be a single surface. The SPLFRAME system variable controls whether the invisible edges display. SPLFRAME is the same variable that you use to control the frame points for a curve fit polyline in 2D.

When SPLFRAME is 0, invisible edges are invisible; when SPLFRAME is 1, all edges are visible. To draw an invisible edge during a 3DFACE command, enter an **I** before the first pick for that edge.

You can use invisible edges to make the top of the chair hub look like one piece, even though you create it with five separate 3Dfaces. Use 3DFACE to create a triangular surface that you can later array with the leg to complete the chair base. Use SPLFRAME to make invisible edges visible to confirm the results.

Using 3DFACE with Invisible Edges To Cap the Chair Hub

Make the lower right viewport current.

Choose Draw, *then* 3D Surfaces, *then* 3D Face

`Command:` **`3DFACE`**	
`First point:` *Enter* `I` *and use the ENDP object snap to pick polygon's first corner at ① (see fig. 20.11)*	Begins invisible edge
`Second point:` *Enter* `I` *and use the ENDP object snap to pick the polygon's second corner at ②*	Completes first invisible edge
`Third point:` *Enter* `I`*, then enter* `0,0`	Specifies center of cap at ③
`Fourth point:` *Press Enter*	Makes it three-sided, but invisible
`Third point:` *Press Enter*	Exits 3DFACE
Set SPLFRAME system variable to 1	Turns on edge visibility
Regenerate the drawing	Displays the 3Dface

Save the drawing.

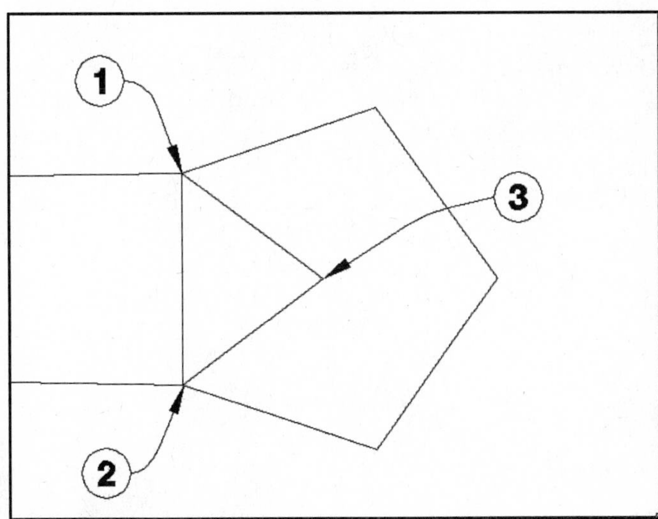

Figure 20.11: Detail of edges and pick points.

Leave SPLFRAME on until you hide or end. If you create a 3Dface with all edges invisible and SPLFRAME off, AutoCAD does not select it, even with Window or Last. You may even forget the 3dface is there.

Invisible edges can be hard to set up correctly when drawing 3D faces. The AutoCAD Sample disk includes the EDGE.LSP AutoLISP program, which is probably installed in your ACAD\SAMPLE directory. It edits the visibility of existing 3Dface edges after they are drawn, making 3D face constructions much easier. Enter **(load "\\ACAD\\SAMPLE\\EDGE")** to load it and **EDGE** to use it as a command. You can also load EDGE.LSP through the Applications dialog box, found on the File pull-down menu.

So far, you have used simple, flat 3D entities. The rest of the chair construction involves curves and contours. The following section discusses the mesh tools for such 3D surface constructions. You then come back to the chair leg and put a ruled surface on top of it.

Introducing 3D Polyline Meshes

AutoCAD has only two 3D mesh entities, both of which are polyline variants: polyface meshes, created by the PFACE command, and polygon meshes, for which there are five drawing commands. All mesh commands, except PFACE, create meshes of *n* rows by *m* columns. The basic polygon mesh command is 3DMESH. Although the 3DMESH command generates a mesh directly, point-by-point, the other four commands rely on existing entities to establish the edges, directions, paths, and profiles of the resulting surface.

Working with Polyface and Polygon Meshes

The following is a list of the commands that create polyface and polygon meshes:

- **3DMESH.** This command creates a wireframe rectilinear blanket, composed of *m* column lines by *n* row lines, passing through a matrix of *mxn* 3D points in space. You have complete control over *m*, *n*, and the coordinate location of each of the 3D points.

- **RULESURF.** This command creates a ruled surface. RULESURF is like stretching and bending a ladder in 3D space. You select any two lines, polylines, or curves that make up the rails, and AutoCAD fills in the ladder with straight rungs. If you select a point, the rungs converge to that point.
- **TABSURF.** This command creates a tabulated surface. AutoCAD sweeps or translates a line you select (called a direction vector or *generatrix*) along any curve you select (called the *directrix*) to define the surface. If, for example, you translate a straight line along a circle, you create a cylinder.
- **REVSURF.** This command creates a surface of revolution. AutoCAD sweeps any curve you select about an axis of revolution. If, for example, you sweep a 90-degree arc about a line through one of its end points, you create a bowl shape.
- **EDGESURF.** This command creates a four-sided surface defined by four boundary lines or curves you select. AutoCAD fills in *mxn* column and row lines to define the surface, as in a 3D meshed flying carpet.
- **PFACE.** This command constructs a mesh of any topology you want. You specify arbitrary locations of vertices and then specify which vertices are part of which face. You can have any number of edges and any number of faces, each with any number of sides or vertices. Any side can be any color, be located on any layer, or be invisible.

Figure 20.12 shows examples of these entities.

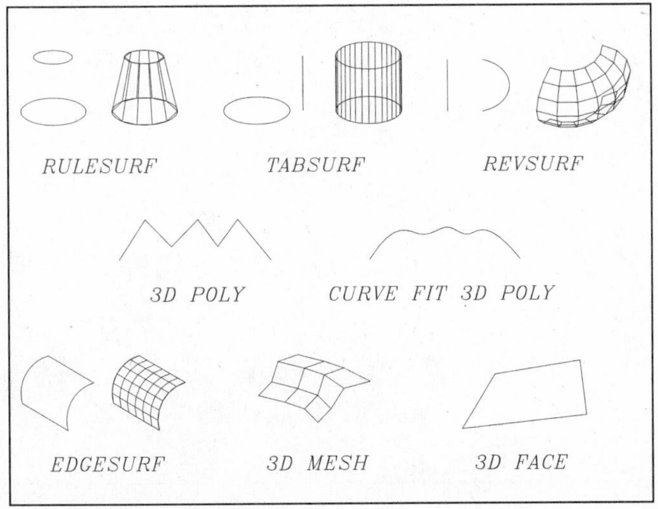

Figure 20.12:
Mesh entity primitives.

The 3DMESH command is provided primarily to enable AutoCAD application developers a tool for building 3D meshes without using other entities as paths. The following section shows how the 3DMESH command works—keep in mind, however, that usually the other mesh commands provide simpler solutions.

Using the 3DMESH Command

You rarely use the 3DMESH command unless you are using AutoLISP to generate mesh points automatically. A 3D mesh is made up of rows and columns. The directions *m* and *n* are indices that specify the number of rows and columns that make up the mesh, up to 256×256. These indices determine the number of vertices required in the mesh. After you set *m* and *n*, you input each vertex as X,Y,Z coordinates. Meshes can be open or closed, depending on whether the mesh joins in either the *m* or *n* direction, or both.

Figure 20.13 shows an example of a 3D mesh, showing the *m* and *n* directions. This is an open mesh. A donut mesh is an example of a mesh closed in both directions. An example of a mesh closed in *m* and open in *n* is a tube; an auto tire (without a rim) is open in *m* and closed in *n*. Later, when you edit a mesh, you identify the vertices to see how the mesh vertex information is displayed.

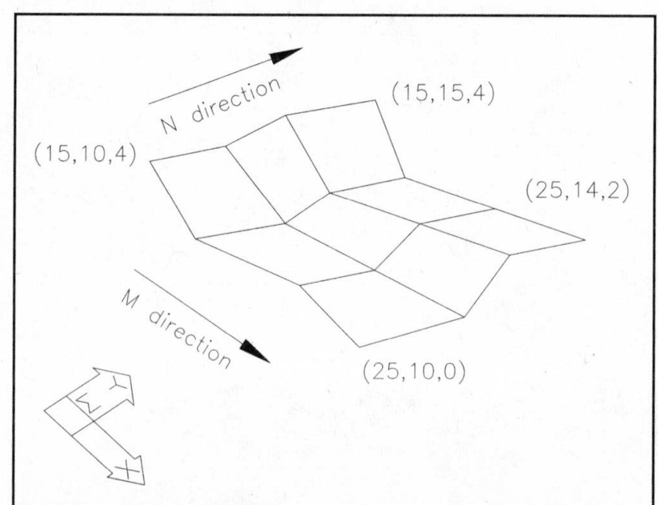

Figure 20.13:

A 3D mesh example.

The 3DMESH command is difficult to use because the points must be entered in rigid row-by-row, column-by-column order. The PFACE command is more flexible.

Using the PFACE Command

Like the 3DFACE command, PFACE can create surfaces with invisible interior divisions. Unlike the other meshes, you can specify any number of vertices and create any number of faces by using PFACE. First, pick all of the vertex points, remembering their numerical order, and then you create faces by entering the vertex numbers that define their edges. To make an edge invisible, you respond to the first vertex prompt of that edge with a negative, instead of a positive vertex number. Like 3Dfaces, invisible polyfaces are visible when SPLFRAME is set to 1 and invisible when it is set to 0.

You also can assign a color or layer by responding to any `Face n, vertex n:` prompt using C for color or L for layer. It then re-prompts for the vertex number. If you do so, the current face and all subsequent faces get that color or layer until you specify otherwise.

Although the PFACE command is capable of making more complex surfaces, you can use it in place of 3DFACE to cap the hub. You use it to put a bottom on the hub, for comparison. Use the ENDP running snap mode to pick all except the center vertex point. SPLFRAME is set to 1 so that all edges are visible until you set it to 0 and regenerate.

Putting a Bottom Surface on the Hub with PFACE

Make the left viewport current, zoom in on the hub, and set a running object snap to ENDP.

`Command:` *From the screen menu, choose* SURFACES, *then* PFACE:

`Command:` **`PFACE`**
`Vertex 1:` **`0,0,-2.5`** ↵ — Specifies the center vertex ① (see fig. 20.14)

`Vertex 2:` *Pick* ②

`Vertex 3:` *Pick* ③

`Vertex 4:` *Pick* ④

`Vertex 5:` *Pick* ⑤

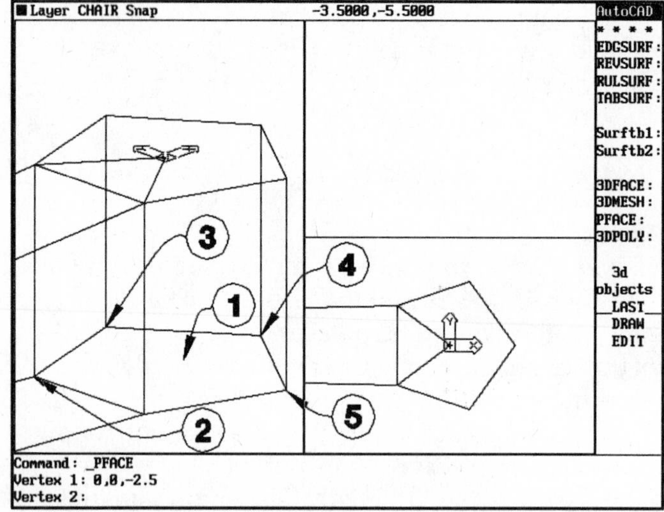

Figure 20.14:
PFACE vertex numbers and pick points.

`Vertex 6:` *Pick* ⑥	
`Vertex 7:` *Press Enter*	Ends vertex specification

Next, you specify which vertex numbers define each face.

`Face 1, vertex 1: -1 ↵`	Negative makes following edge invisible
`Face 1, vertex 2: 2 ↵`	Positive makes outside edge visible
`Face 1, vertex 3: -3 ↵`	
`Face 1, vertex 4:` *Press Enter*	Completes face 1
`Face 2, vertex 1: -1 ↵`	
`Face 2, vertex 2: 3 ↵`	
`Face 2, vertex 3: -4 ↵`	
`Face 2, vertex 4:` *Press Enter*	
`Face 3, vertex 1: -1 ↵`	
`Face 3, vertex 2: 4 ↵`	
`Face 3, vertex 3: -5 ↵`	
`Face 3, vertex 4:` *Press Enter*	
`Face 4, vertex 1: -1 ↵`	
`Face 4, vertex 2: 5 ↵`	
`Face 4, vertex 3: -6 ↵`	
`Face 4, vertex 4:` *Press Enter*	
`Face 5, vertex 1: -1 ↵`	

`Face 5, vertex 2:` 6 ↵	
`Face 5, vertex 3:` -2 ↵	
`Face 5, vertex 4:` *Press Enter*	
`Face 6, vertex 1:` *Press Enter*	Completes all faces (see fig. 20.15)
Set SPLFRAME to 0, and regenerate	Makes edges invisible
Set object snap back to NONE, *set SPLFRAME back to 1, and Zoom Previous*	

Save your drawing.

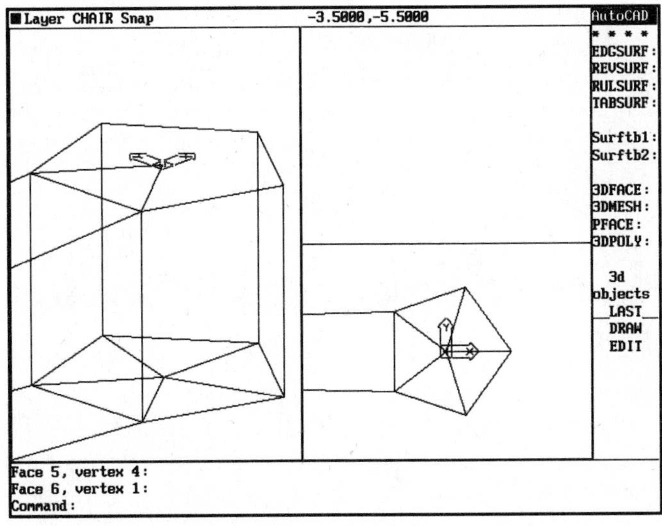

Figure 20.15:

A completed PFACE bottom of a hub.

You generally do not know all the surface points required to create a surface entity; calculating these points may be too difficult. You can use the four "surf" commands, however, to generate 3D surfaces based on boundaries, curves, and direction vectors that are relatively easy to specify or determine. AutoCAD then handles the tedious calculations.

The IA DISK includes an AutoLISP command named PFACE2. You load it by entering (load "pface2") and use it in place of the PFACE command. PFACE2 displays numbered markers at the vertices during the command to make it easier to keep track of the vertices. The AutoCAD Sample disk includes the MFACE.LSP AutoLISP program, which is probably installed in your ACAD\SAMPLE directory. It enables you to generate a polyface with

invisible interior edges by entering only the perimeter vertices. Enter **(load "\\ACAD\\SAMPLE\\MFACE")** to load it and **MFACE** to use it as a command. You also can use the APPLOAD command (choose File, then Applications) to load PFACE2.LSP or MFACE.LSP from the IA directory.

Although you may not use the 3DMESH command often, you still need to set the system variables that control the *m* and *n* indices to control mesh density in the other commands. The SURFTAB1 system variable sets the *m* index, and SURFTAB2 sets the *n* index. Although you can use values up to 256 for either, you should use the lowest values that generate acceptably smooth surfaces. Values of 8 to 16 are suitable for most purposes. Dense meshes significantly increase your drawing processing time. If you do not like the mesh that appears, you cannot re-specify these variables for an existing mesh. You have to erase the mesh, reset the SURFTAB values, and then create a new mesh.

Using RULESURF To Create the Leg Top

The RULESURF command creates a ruled surface between two boundaries of nearly any type. RULESURF creates a 2x*m* polygon mesh between the two boundaries; that is, it defines a one-way mesh of straight ruled lines between the boundaries. The entities that define the boundaries can be points, lines, arcs, circles, 2D polylines, or 3D polylines. (If you use a point, only one edge can be a point.) You only need to set the SURFTAB1 system variable, which controls the spacing of the rules.

You use RULESURF to finish the leg's top surface and to add a little arched cap to the end. The top surface runs as a ruled surface from an arc drawn above the end cap to the top edge of the hub top. To create the arc, use the UCS Entity option to set the UCS in the plane of the end cap.

Preparing for RULESURFs

Make the left viewport the current layer, and set the current layer to BUILD.

```
Command: UCS ↵
Origin/ZAxis/3point/Entity/View/X/Y/Z
Prev/Restore/Save/Del/?/<World: E↵
```

`Select object to align UCS:` *Pick the end cap at ① (avoid selecting the 3Dface sides (see fig. 20.16)*	Aligns the UCS with the leg's end cap
Set PDMODE system variable to 66	Makes points visible
Use the POINT command and MID object snap to put a point at ①	
Use the ENDP object snap to draw a line from ② to ③	
Use the ARC command's Start, End, Angle *options with the ENDP object snap to pick start and end points at ④ and ⑤, then enter angle* `135`.	
Use UCS to restore the HUB UCS.	

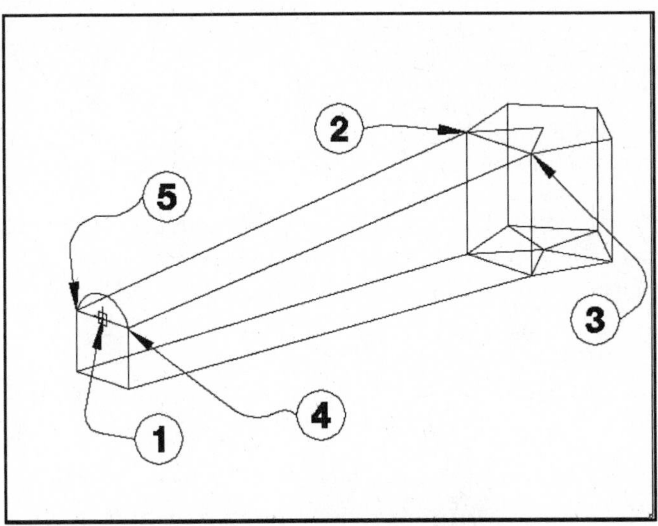

Figure 20.16:

Detail of curves.

After you have defined the curves for RULESURF, you can begin the surfacing. The arc defines a curve for the top of the leg and the space at the end cap. After you draw the top mesh surface, it is impossible to pick the arc for the arched end cap surface because the top surface gets in the way. To use the arc for both surfaces, you temporarily erase the top mesh. After making the arched mesh, you can use OOPS to bring the top mesh back.

Using RULESURF To Complete the Leg

Make CHAIR the current layer, and set SURFTAB1 to 8.

Choose Draw, *then* 3D Surfaces, *then* Ruled Surface	Begins RULESURF command
`Command:` **`RULESURF`**	
`Select first defining curve:` *Pick* ① *(see fig. 20.17)*	

If AutoCAD can't find the line at ①, turn off the CHAIR layer, complete both RULESURF commands and turn the CHAIR layer back on.

`Select second defining curve:` *Pick* ②	Draws the surface
Erase the top surface	
Redraw the viewport	Redraws construction entities
`Command:` **`RULESURF`** ↵	
`Select first defining curve:` *Use NODe object snap and pick* ③	
`Select second defining curve:` *Pick arc at* ②	
`Command:` **`OOPS`** ↵	Restores the erased top surface
Save the drawing.	Figure 20.18 shows the les surfaces

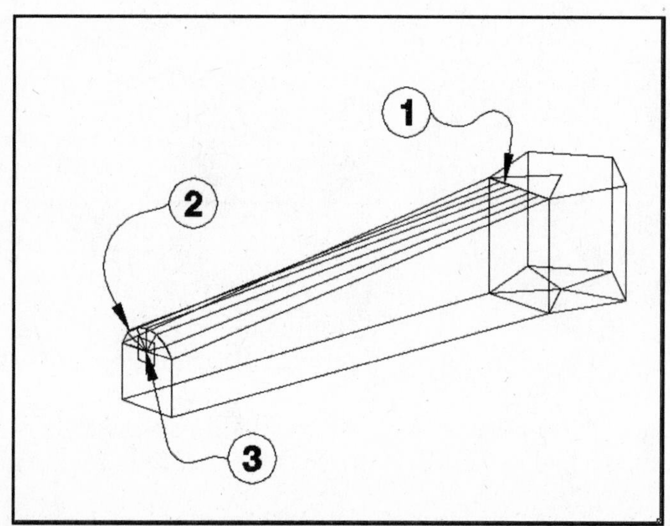

Figure 20.17:

Detail of RULESURF.

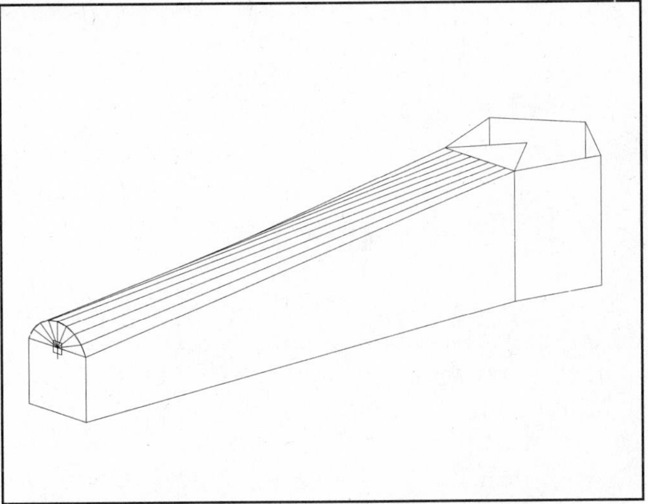

Figure 20.18:

The completed leg surfaces.

When you work with RULESURF, your pick points can be critical. If your edge curves are open, the rule is built from the end point nearest your pick point on each entity. The ruled surface can twist if you do not pick the nearest end points on the edge entities. You also can get a twist with closed entities. The generated mesh starts from the 0-degree point of circles and from the starting vector of closed polylines. If you are generating a mesh between two circles or a circle and closed polyline, make sure that your zero points and first points are aligned in order to avoid a twist in the mesh.

You may want to use RULESURF between a circle and a polyline ellipse. Aligning the zero point on the circle with the starting vector of the ellipse is almost impossible. It is easier to achieve the correct alignment if both entities are created by using the ELLIPSE command.

The mesh commands require that you pick the entities to be used to create the ruled surface. When creating meshes with a common boundary entity, get the first mesh out of the way to pick the boundary entity for the second mesh. Otherwise, it is almost impossible to pick it. You can put your profiles on a different layer, which also helps control the selection of profile entities.

Besides temporary erasures, other methods for temporarily removing an entity include blocking it to a temporary name and performing an *insert later, or moving it to another location and back again later.

Completing the Base Assembly

To complete the base, draw a caster, and then duplicate the leg and caster to make the other four legs. You can use the caster to take advantage of one of the AutoLISP 3D mesh drawing commands from the 3D Objects icon menu. Select the Sphere icon from the 3D Objects menu—this command is an AutoLISP routine that uses the REVSURF command to revolve an arc about an axis line.

Using a 3D SPHERE To Construct the Chair's Casters

You select the Sphere icon from the 3D Objects icon menu. You are prompted for the sphere's center point and radius. The routine draws the arc and axis line, generates the sphere, and then automatically cleans up by erasing the arc and axis line.

Using the AutoLISP SPHERE Command To Make a Caster

Choose Draw, *then* 3D Surfaces, *then the 3D Objects icon, then double-click on the Sphere icon*

`sphere`

`Center of sphere:` **0,0** ↵

`Diameter/<radius>:` **1.25** ↵

`Number of longitudinal segments <16>:` **12** ↵

`Number of latitudinal segments <16>:` **12** ↵ — Draws the sphere (see fig. 20.19)

Zoom in for a closer look

Move the caster with displacement –12,0,–3.25 (see fig. 20.20) — Completes one leg

`Command:` **REDRAWALL** ↵ — Redraws all viewports

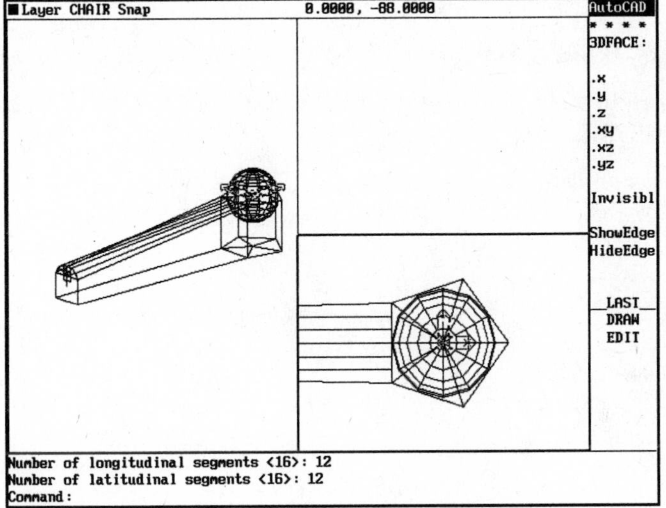

Figure 20.19:

The chair caster before MOVE and UCS previous.

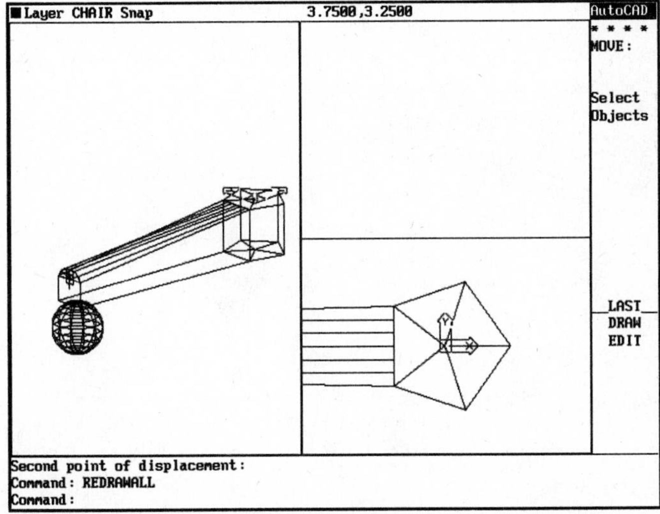

Figure 20.20:

The chair caster after MOVE.

Using ARRAY to Complete the Chair Base

Now you can array the first leg and caster to complete the chair's base, and then block the base as a finished component. Use the standard ARRAY command to array the leg and BLOCK to create the BASE block.

Using ARRAY To Complete the Base

Make the lower right viewport current, and ZOOM Center at 0,0, with a height of 28. Turn off the BUILD layer.

Use ARRAY to polar array all entities except the hub and bottom cap, about center point 0,0—5 items to fill 360 degrees and rotate as copied (see fig. 20.21)

`Command: HIDE ↵`

Use BLOCK to block everything to name BASE with insert base point 0,0

Save and continue, or end and take a break.

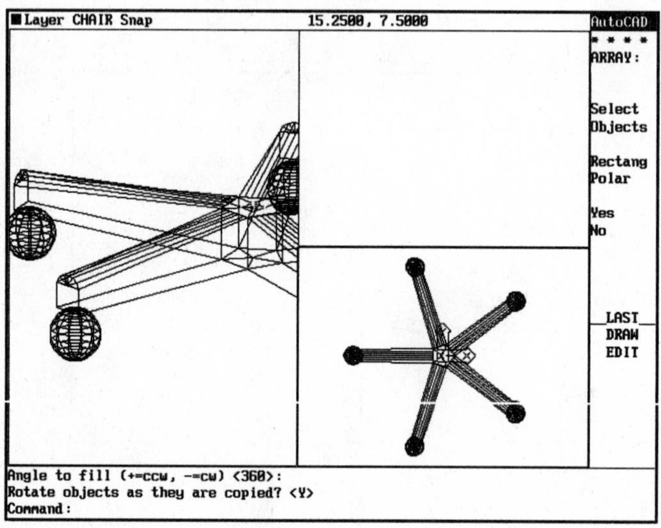

Figure 20.21:
The completed base after array.

The BASE block is stored in your current CHAIR drawing. If you are using the IA DISK, you also have the base stored on disk as BASE.DWG.

Using the REVSURF Command

You saw REVSURF in action, generating the sphere, although you did not actually enter the command by name. REVSURF creates a surface by re-

volving a path curve around an axis of revolution. In the case of the sphere, the SPHERE routine created the path curve, an arc, and the axis of revolution for you. You can select a line, arc, circle, or 2D or 3D polyline as the path curve. You can select a line or open polyline to specify the axis of rotation. If you select a polyline as the axis of revolution, AutoCAD uses an imaginary line between the first and last vertices as the axis, ignoring the intermediate vertices.

You then enter the angle at which the rotation starts, and the included angle of rotation: 360 degrees for a full cylinder or sphere. You can offset the start angle if you do not want to start from a 0-degree angle.

Creating a Shaft Profile of the Pedestal

You use REVSURF to create a complex surface (the chair's accordion-shaped pedestal cover), which covers the shaft. The pedestal mesh is made up of two different revolved shapes. Create a single pleat at the bottom and the top closure as two polyline profiles, and then revolve them into 3D surfaces by using REVSURF. You array the bottom piece vertically to complete the pedestal.

In the following exercise, you set up a UCS, create a vertical line for the axis of revolution, and create a polyline path profile for the bottom pleat. You use PEDIT to add tangent information to the first and last vertices, and then curve fit the polyline so that it smoothly meets adjoining sections.

Preparing Axis and Bottom Path Curve for REVSURF

Make the left viewport current and set BUILD as the current layer.

Erase the arc, line, and point left from the base construction	
Use UCS with the X option and rotate the UCS 90 degrees about the X axis	
Draw a line from 0,0 to 0,13	Designates axis of revolution
Choose View, *then* Set View, *then* Plan View, *then* Current UCS	Displays plan view
Zoom in on bottom half of the line	
Draw a polyline from 1.25,0 to .75,.5 to 1.25,1	

Next, you set tangents and curve fit the profile.

Choose Modify, *then* PolyEdit

```
Command: ai_peditm
Select objects: L ↵
Select objects: Press Enter
PEDIT Select polyline:
Close/Join/Width/Edit vertex/Fit/Spline/
Decurve/Ltype gen/Undo/eXit <X>: E ↵
Next/Previous/Break/Insert/Move/Regen
/Straighten/Tangent/Width/eXit <N>: T ↵
Direction of tangent: 90 ↵
Next/Previous/Break/Insert/Move/Regen
/Straighten/Tangent/Width/eXit <N>:
Press Enter twice
Next/Previous/Break/Insert/Move/Regen
/Straighten/Tangent/Width/eXit <N>: T ↵
Direction of tangent: 90 ↵
Next/Previous/Break/Insert/Move/Regen
/Straighten/Tangent/Width/eXit <N>: X ↵
Close/Join/Width/Edit vertex/Fit curve
/Spline curve/Decurve/Undo/eXit <X>: F ↵
Close/Join/Width/Edit vertex/Fit/Spline/
Decurve/Ltype gen/Undo/eXit <X>:
Press Enter
```

The results appear in figure 20.22.

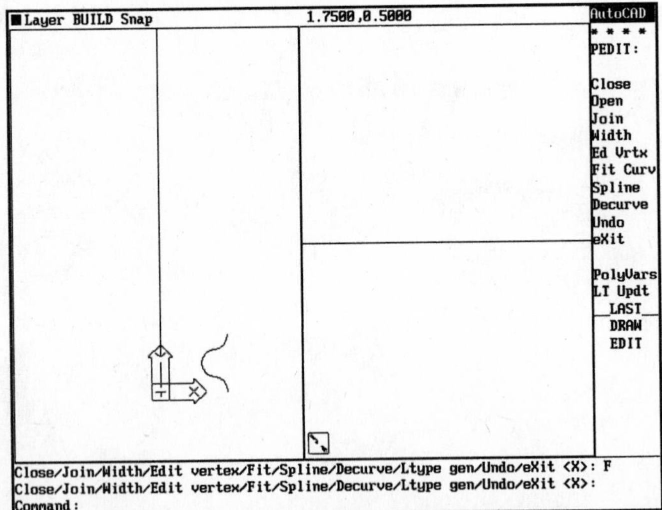

Figure 20.22:

The bottom path curve and axis for REVSURF.

The top of the pedestal terminates with a shaft. Draw the second path curve to establish the top shaft profile and a closure where it meets the arrayed bottom piece. This shaft profile combines polyline arc and line segments.

Creating Top Path Curve for the Shaft Top

ZOOM to the top half of the line,

Choose Draw, *then* Polyline, 2D

```
Command: _PLINE
From point: .5,13 ↵
Current line-width is 0.0000
Arc/Close/Halfwidth/Length/Undo/Width/
<Endpoint of line>: @0,-2.75 ↵
Arc/Close/Halfwidth/Length/Undo/Width/
<Endpoint of line>: @.5,0 ↵
Arc/Close/Halfwidth/Length/Undo/Width/
<Endpoint of line>: A ↵
Angle/CEnter/CLose/Direction/Halfwidth/
Line/Radius/Second pt/Undo/Width/
<Endpoint of arc>: @.25,-.25↵
Angle/CEnter/CLose/Direction/Halfwidth
/Line/Radius/Second pt/Undo/Width/
<Endpoint of arc>: Press Enter
```

The results appear in figure 20.23.

Using REVSURF To Complete the Shaft

You now can complete the shaft by using REVSURF. Adjust the SURFTAB1 and SURFTAB2 settings to achieve acceptably smooth surfaces. When you execute REVSURF, pick your profile entity first, then pick the axis line. Accept the default start angle of 0 degrees and the default included angle of 360 degrees for a full circle. After you have revolved the bottom, repeat REVSURF for the top. Finish the pedestal by using a rectangular array to create nine copies (ten rows, one column) of the bottom piece. When done, reset your UCS and define the block, PEDESTAL, which includes the top shaft and all the pleats in the cover.

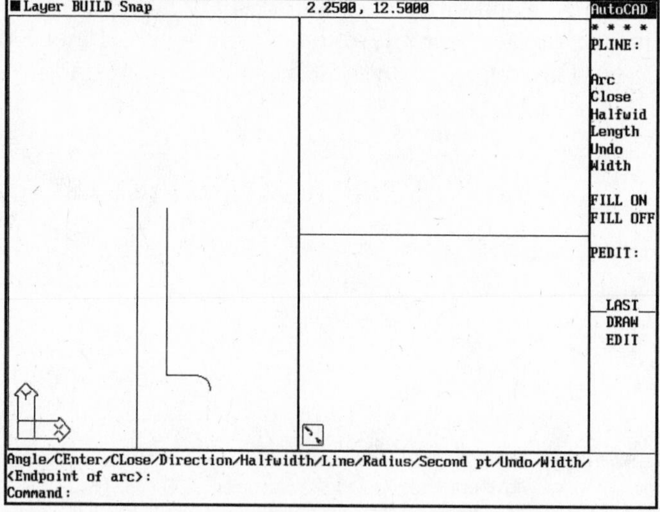

Figure 20.23:

The top path curve for the pedestal shaft top.

Using REVSURF To Make the Pedestal Surface

Restore BUILD view and Zoom to see both path profiles, then make CHAIR the current layer

Set SURFTAB1 to 12 and SURFTAB2 to 4

Choose Draw, *then* 3D Surfaces, *then* Surface of Revolution — Issues REVSURF command

`Command:` **`REVSURF`**

`Select path curve:` *Pick top profile at ① (see fig. 20.24)*

`Select axis of revolution:` *Pick the axis at ②*

`Start angle <0>:` *Press Enter*

`Included angle (+=ccw, -=cw) <Full circle>:` *Press Enter* — Creates top of pedestal

Set SURFTAB2 to 6

Repeat REVSURF on the bottom profile, picking path curve at ③ and axis of revolution on line at ② with included angle a full circle — Creates bottom of pedestal

Use ARRAY to create a rectangular array of the bottom piece, 10 rows and one column at one unit spacing (see fig. 20.25) — Completes pedestal

Restore HUB UCS and turn layer BUILD off

Zoom in on lower right viewport for a better look

Create a block named PEDESTAL selecting everything and using insert base point 0,0

Save your drawing.

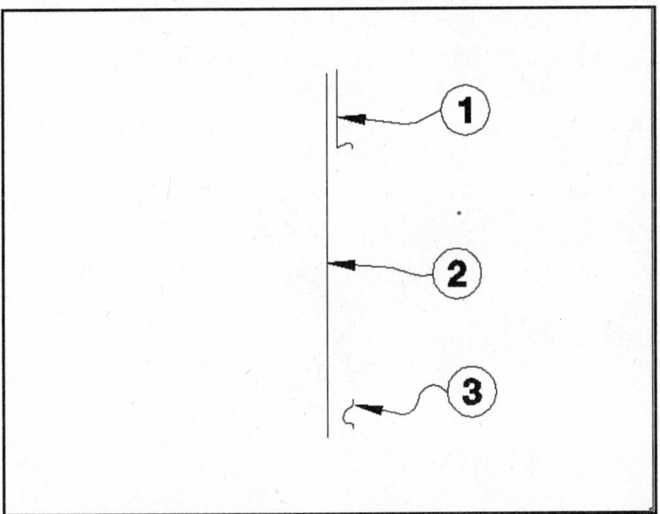

Figure 20.24:
Detail of REVSURF pick points.

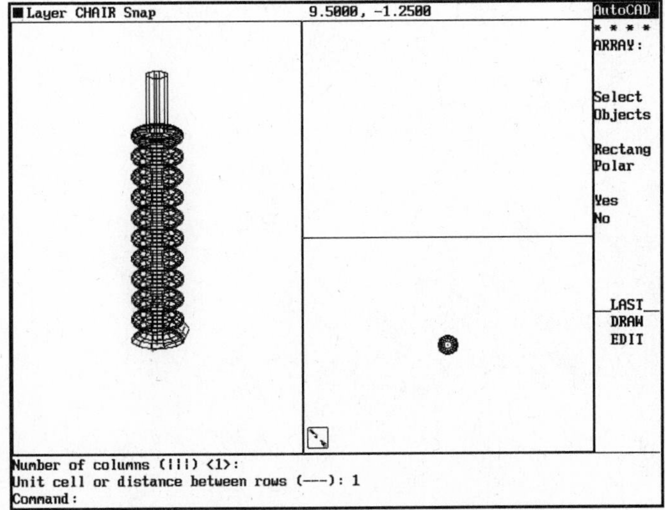

Figure 20.25:
The completed pedestal.

The pedestal used the default (full-circle) rotation. The next exercise uses a partial, 90-degree REVSURF to connect rectangular frames made with BOX, one of the AutoLISP 3D mesh drawing commands. You make the frames first, and then connect them with a partial REVSURF.

Using the BOX AutoLISP Command

BOX is one of the AutoLISP 3D mesh drawing commands on the 3D Objects icon menu. This command prompts for the starting corner, length, width, height, and rotation angle. You can enter the values or pick points. The cube option requires only one dimension. Remember that length is measured along the X axis of the current UCS, width along the Y axis, and height along the Z axis.

Use BOX to draw the three frame pieces. After the menu has loaded the BOX command, you also can enter it at the command prompt to create the seat support base (see fig. 20.26).

Using BOX To Create Seat and Back Support Frames

Make sure that the left viewport and CHAIR layer are still current.

Choose Draw, *then* 3D Surfaces, *then* 3D Objects, *and then double-click on the Box icon*

`ai_box`

`Corner of box:_`**`-1.5,-1.25`** ↵

`Length:` **`10.5`** ↵

`Cube/<Width>:` **`2.5`**_↵

`Height:` **`1`** ↵

`Rotation angle about Z axis:` **`0`**↵ — Draws seat support base (see fig.20.26)

Zoom all viewports to views shown in fig 20.26

`Command:` **`AI_BOX`**↵

`Corner of box:` **`10,-1.25,2`** ↵

`Length:` **`1`** ↵

`Cube/<Width>:` **`2.5`** ↵

`Height:` **`13`** ↵

`Rotation angle about Z axis:` **`0`** — Creates back support (see fig. 20.27)

`Command:` *Press Enter*	Repeats IA_BOX command
`Corner of box: 9.25,-1.25,11.5↵`	
`Length: .75↵`	
`Cube/<Width>: 2.5 ↵`	
`Height: 1.5↵`	
`Rotation angle about Z axis: 0 ↵`	Creates back support spacer (see fig. 20.27)

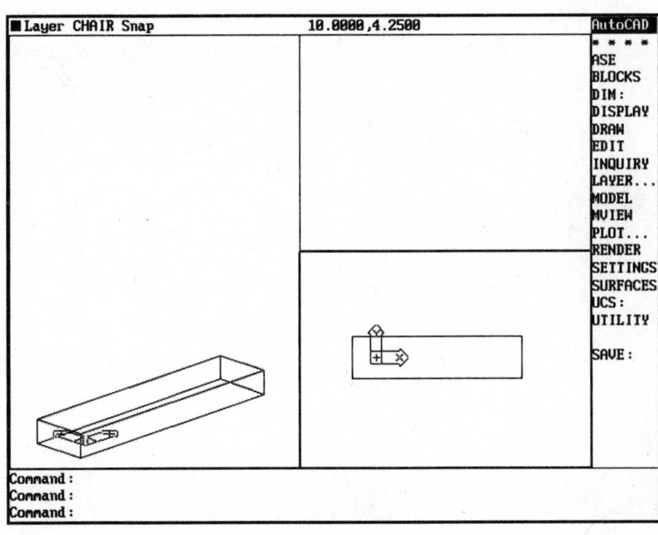

Figure 20.26:

The seat support made with BOX.

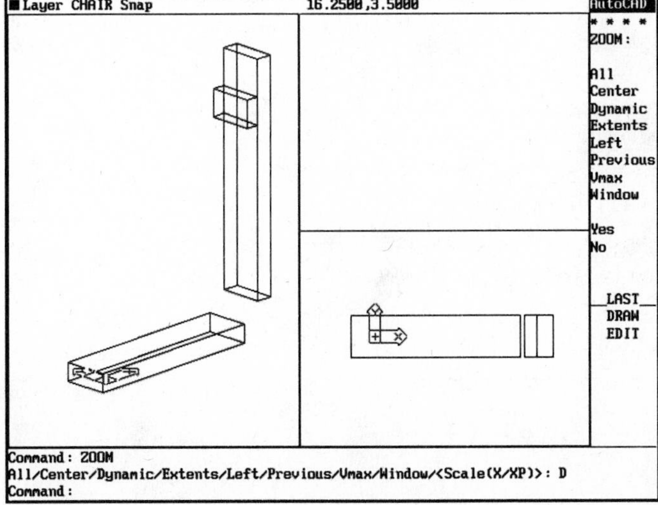

Figure 20.27:

The back support, made with BOX.

Using 3D Polylines

Now, connect the frames by using REVSURF to revolve a 3D polyline. Use 3D polylines when you need to draw a polyline with vertices that do not lie in a single plane. 3DPOLY draws polylines with independent X,Y, and Z axis coordinates for each vertex. 2D polylines can exist in any 3D construction plane, but all of its vertices must lie in a single plane. A 3D polyline is not subject to this limitation. A 3D polyline, however, consists of straight-line segments only, with no thickness. You can spline fit 3D polylines by using PEDIT; the resulting "curve" consists of short, straight segments (this also is true of spline fit 2D polylines).

The process of editing a 3D polyline with PEDIT is similar to editing a 2D polyline, but with fewer options. You cannot join 3D polylines, curve fit them with arc segments, or give them a width or tangent. The PEDIT prompt for 3D polylines looks like this:

```
Close/Edit vertex/Spline/Decurve/Ltype gen/Undo/eXit <X>
```

You use the LINE command to draw the axis of rotation for REVSURF, and you use a 3D polyline to create a rectangular path curve. You do not need to adjust the UCS to draw with 3DPOLY.

Creating the Axis and Path Curve for REVSURF

Make BUILD the current layer and erase the leftover pedestal construction entities.

Draw a line from 9,1.25,2 to @0,–2.5	Designates the axis *(see fig. 20.28)* of revolution
Choose Draw, *then* Polyline,*then* 3D *(use the ENDP object snap to pick the points shown)*	
`Command:` **`3DPOLY`**	
`From point:` *Pick at* ① *(see fig. 20.29)*	
`Close/Undo/<Endpoint of line>:` *Pick at* ②	
`Close/Undo/<Endpoint of line>:` *Pick at* ③	
`Close/Undo/<Endpoint of line>:` *Pick at* ④	
`Close/Undo/<Endpoint of line>:` **`C`** ↵	Completes the rectangle

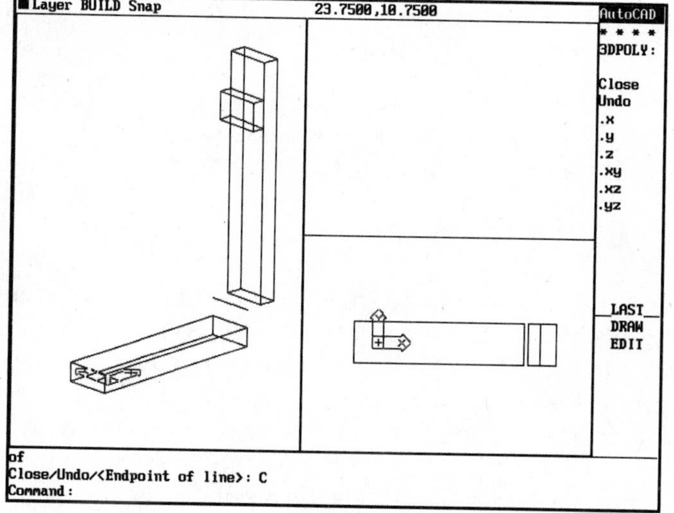

Figure 20.28: The axis and 3D polyline path curve.

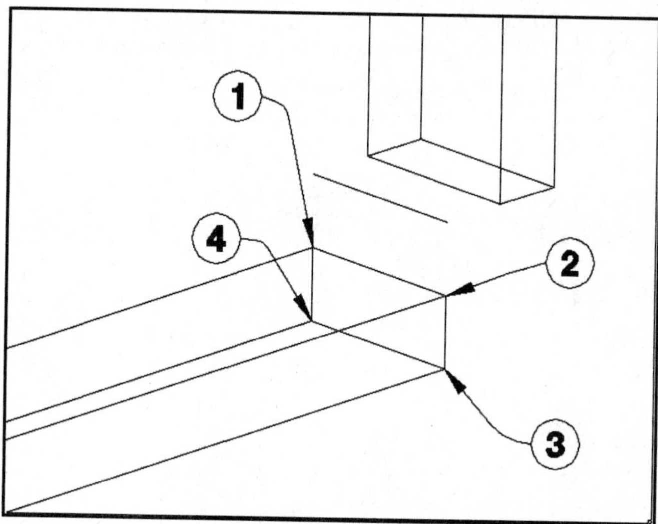

Figure 20.29: Detail of 3DPOLY pick points.

Now that you have the axis and polyline path profile, you can connect the two frames by using a partial REVSURF.

Understanding Partial REVSURFS and the Direction of Rotation

The direction of surface rotation for REVSURF is determined by your pick point on the axis of rotation and the right-hand rule. When you pick an axis of rotation, the end nearest your pick point is considered the origin of that axis. Recall the *right-hand rule of rotation* from Chapter 19: if you curl your fingers around that axis and point with your thumb pointing away from the origin, your fingers naturally curl in the direction of positive rotation. The assigning of a non-zero start angle offsets the mesh in this direction, and a partial rotation sweeps in this direction from the starting angle.

Revolve the 3Dpoly profile through a 90-degree arc to create a mesh section that connects the two frames. After you get the supports connected, define a block named SUPPORT, consisting of the frames and the mesh. As you do the REVSURF, visualize the right-hand rule.

Using a 90-Degree Revsurf To Connect Back and Seat Frames

Make CHAIR the current layer, and set SURFTAB1 to 6.

Choose Draw, *then* 3D Surfaces, *then* Surface of Revolution

`Command:` **`REVSURF`** ↵

`Select path curve:` *Select rectangle on near side edge at ① (see fig. 20.30)*

`Select axis of revolution:` *Select line at ② (see fig. 20.30)*

`Start angle <0>:` *Press Enter*

`Included angle (+=ccw, -=cw) <Full circle>: -90` ↵

Turn off BUILD layer

Create a block named SUPPORT, selecting everything and using base point 0,0

Save your drawing.

Figure 20.31 shows the connected supports.

The seat and back support construction involves simple surfaces. In the next section, you encounter curved surfaces and corners that require more complex meshes.

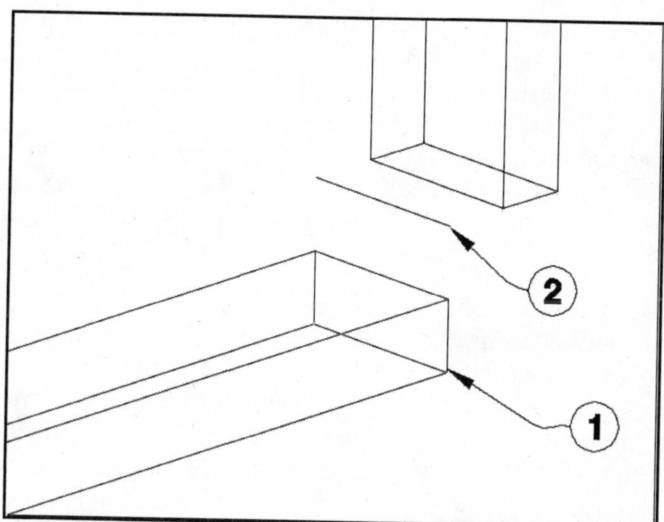

Figure 20.30:

Detail of REVSURF pick points.

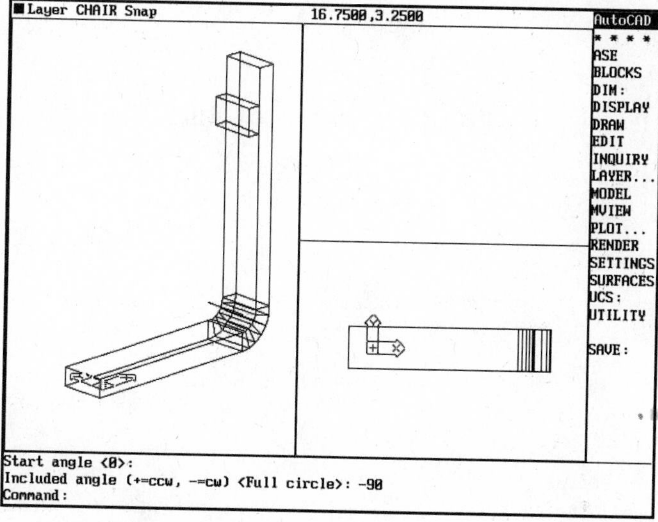

Figure 20.31:

The supports after REVSURF.

Combining 3D Surfaces for Complex Mesh Construction

Many 3D objects are made by combining different 3D meshes. You need to make a curved back cushion with curved corners and edges. You can create the backrest with seven mesh entities. When you work with multiple mesh entities, you frequently encounter edges that coincide. When the arched ruled surface mesh was added to the end cap of the chair leg, you temporarily erased the preceding mesh from the top of the leg to get it out of the way. As you work with several meshes at once in the following exercises, you use the alternate technique mentioned earlier— temporarily moving meshes out of your way.

In plan view, the main body of the chair back is slightly curved and is 1.5 inches thick with semicircular ends. You create its profile as a polyline by drawing a large arc, offsetting it 1.5 inches, and closing the ends with two small arcs. You create a major axis line at the center of the large arc to use with surfacing commands (discussed later). The top, bottom, and corners of the back also are curved. You create another small arc and minor axis at one corner to use with the surfacing commands as you define the curved parts of the back. You build these profiles and axes in plan view in the lower right viewport.

Creating a Polyline Path Curve of Back Cushion

Make the lower right viewport current, and ZOOM Center at 0,0 with height 20. Make BUILD the current layer and erase leftover entities.

Next, you draw an arc for the inside profile of the back.

Choose Draw, *then* Arc, *then* Start, End, Angle

`Arc Center/<Start point>:` **0,-7** ↵

`Center/End/<Second point>:` E
`End point:` **0,7** ↵

`Angle/Direction/Radius/<Center point>:` A `Included angle:` **20** ↵

Draw a line from center of arc to @0,0,–9 in the Z direction — Designates direction vector and rotation axis line

Make the left viewport current and ZOOM Extents to see the line, and then make the lower right viewport current again.

Use OFFSET with distance 1.5 to offset the arc to the right	Creates outside profile of back
Draw another Start, End, Angle *arc, using ENDP object snaps to pick start point at ② and end point at ①, and enter* `180` *degree included angle (see fig. 20.32)*	Connects end of large arcs with a short arc
Use PEDIT to join all three arcs into single polyline and close it	Creates fourth arc segment at other end of large arcs (see fig. 20.33)

Make the left viewport current (to draw small arc and axis for path curve of both rounded corner and top surfaces), and zoom to the left end of the polyline.

Draw a line between ① and ② (see fig. 20.34)	Connects the ends of the small arc segment
Use UCS Entity *option to align the UCS with the line just drawn, and then rotate the UCS 90 degrees about the X axis*	
Draw another Start, End, Angle *arc, using object snaps to pick start point at ②, end point at ①, and then enter* `180` *as angle*	
Zoom out to see major axis line and profile paths (see fig. 20.35)	

Save the drawing.

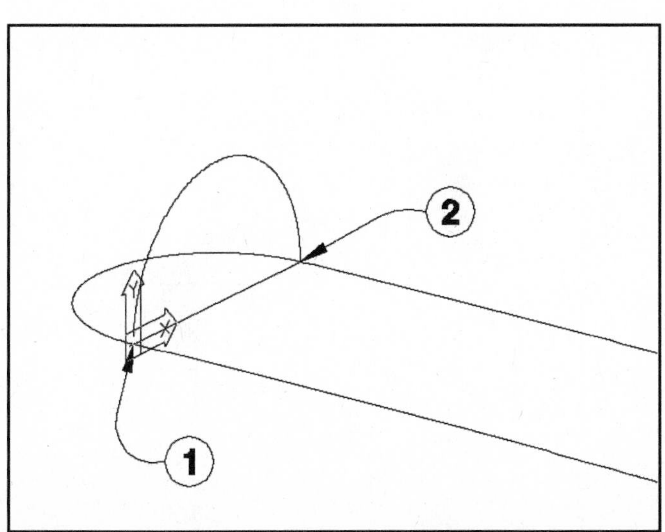

Figure 20.32:

Detail of arc pick points.

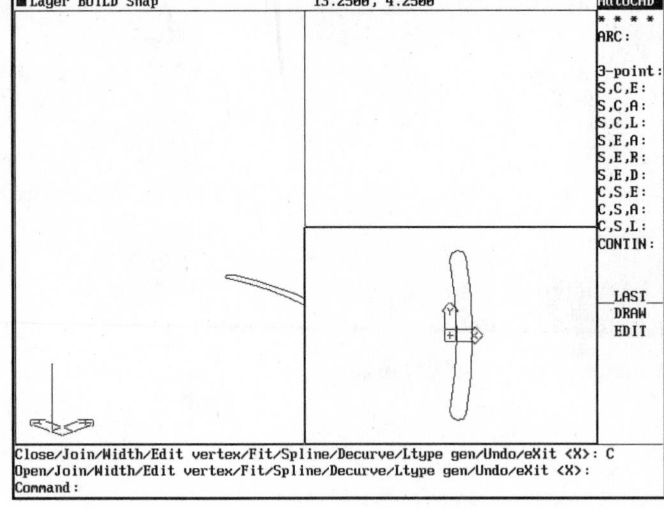

Figure 20.33:

The backrest profile and axis line.

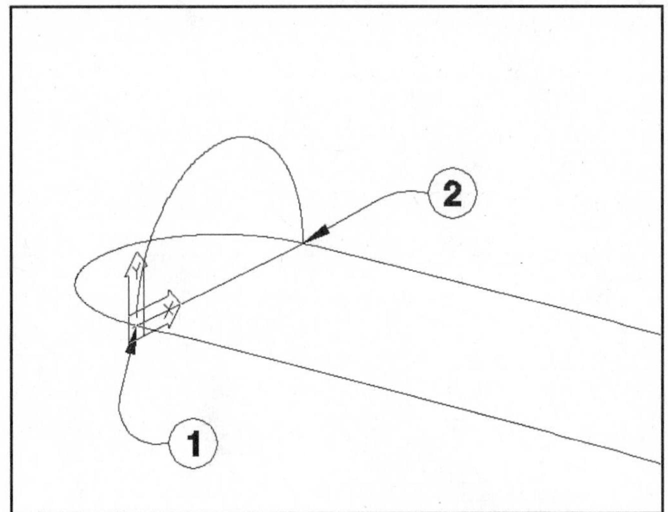

Figure 20.34:

Detail of arc pick points.

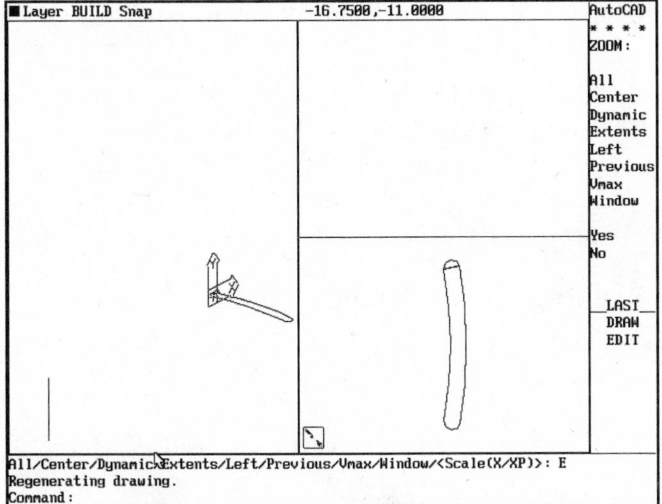

Figure 20.35:

An axis and path curve for rounded edges and corners.

Now you are ready to create the mesh entities, starting with TABSURF for the main body of the backrest.

Using the TABSURF Command

TABSURF creates a *tabular* surface by using a path curve (directrix) and a direction vector (generatrix). Like RULESURF, you only need to set SURFTAB1. TABSURF uses the usual set of entities for the path curve: line, arc, circle, or 2D or 3D polyline. After you select the entity to use for the path curve, select the direction vector. The surface lines it creates are parallel to the direction vector. The direction vector does not need to be on the path curve; it defines the direction and distance in which TABSURF extrudes your path profile. The direction of extrusion is away from the direction vector pick point.

As noted earlier, you need to move surfaces out of the way as you create them. Move them to the WCS origin, using a special form of coordinate input, so that they appear in the upper-right viewport.

Prefixing any coordinate value with an asterisk makes AutoCAD interpret the coordinate value in the WCS. Using the MOVE command with a first point of 0,0 (in the current UCS) and a second point of *0,0 moves the mesh

surfaces to the WCS coordinate point that corresponds to their current UCS locations.

Now use TABSURF to create the main part of the chair's back, and then move it to *0,0 so that you can create the top and corner meshes.

Using TABSURF and *0,0 To Create and Move the Back

Make CHAIR the current layer, and set SURFTAB1 to 8.

Choose Draw, *then* 3D Surfaces, *then* Tabulated Surface	Issues TABSURF command
`Command: _tabsurf`	
`Select path curve:` *Pick the joined polyline profile*	
`Select direction vector:` *Pick top of major axis line at ① (see fig. 20.36)*	Specifies direction and draws back
*MOVE the mesh from 0,0 to *0,0 (see fig. 20.37)*	Moves mesh to 0,0 of WCS
`Command:` **`REDRAWALL`** ↵	Redraws all viewports

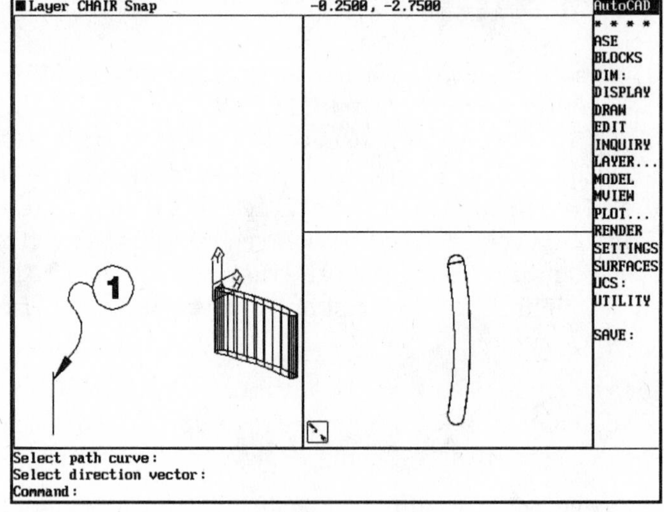

Figure 20.36:

The body of the back before moving.

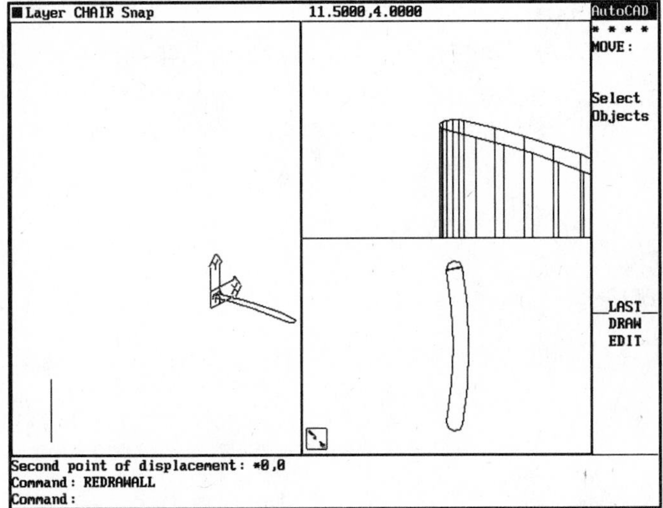

Figure 20.37:

The body of the back moved to WCS.

Using REVSURF To Create Revolved Surfaces

Use REVSURF to surface the top edge and a corner of the backrest. First, create a 20-degree partial Revsurf by revolving the small arc at the corner about the major axis. This surface becomes the top edge of the back. Move the Revsurf to 0,0 in the WCS. Finally, use a 90-degree Revsurf to create the first rounded corner with the same arc, but revolve it 20 degrees (matching profile angle) about the short axis between its end points.

Using REVSURF To Surface Top Edge and Corner of Backrest

Set SURFTAB2 to 8

Choose Draw, *then* 3D Surfaces, *and then* Surface of Revolution

Command: **REVSURF**

Select path curve: *Pick arc at ① (see fig. 20.38)*

Select axis of revolution: *Pick line at ③ (see fig. 20.39)*

`Start angle <0>:` *Press Enter*	
`Included angle (+=ccw, -=cw) <Full circle>:` **`20`** ↵	Creates top edge of chair back
*Move the mesh from 0,0 to *0,0*	
Zoom in on left end of polyline, as shown in fig. 20.40	

Next, you use REVSURF to make the first corner of the backrest.

Choose Draw, *then* 3D Surfaces, *and then* Surface of Revolution	
`Command:` **`REVSURF`**	
`Select path curve:` *Pick the arc at* ①	
`Select axis of revolution:` *Pick the short line at* ②	
`Start angle <0>:` *Press enter*	
`Included angle (+=ccw, -=cw) <Full circle>:` **`90`** ↵	Draws first corner
*Move the meshes in upper right viewport from *0,0 back to 0,0*	
Zoom to fill left viewport with back surfaces (see fig. 20.41)	

Save your drawing.

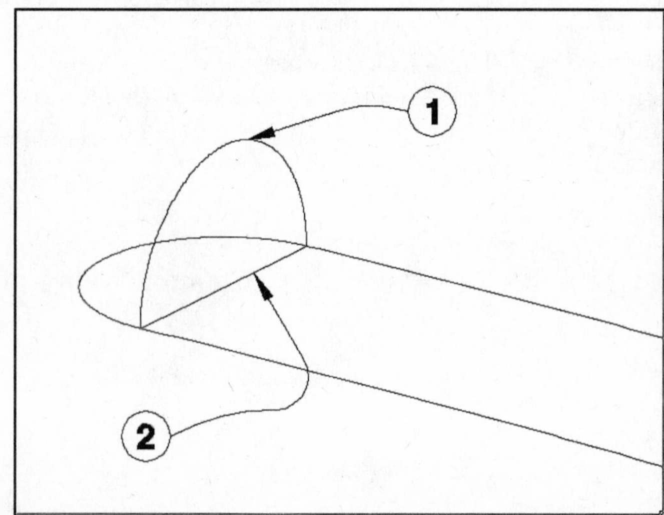

Figure 20.38:

Detail of path curve pick point.

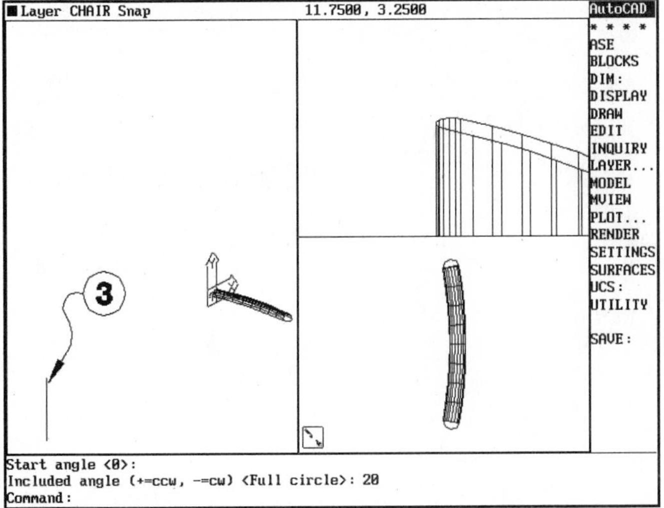

Figure 20.39:

Surface on the top edge of the backrest.

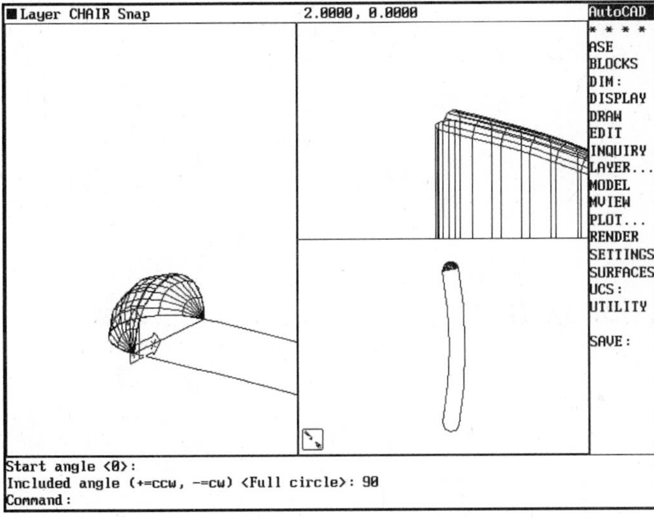

Figure 20.40:

Create the corners.

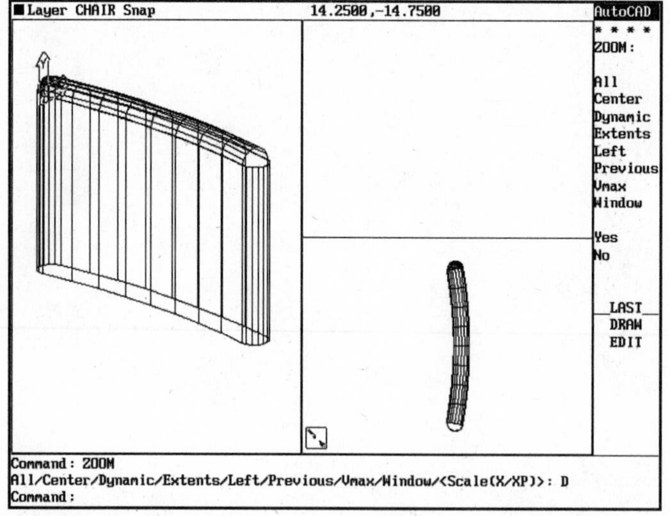

Figure 20.41:
A backrest with three mesh entities.

You now have all the entities you need to complete the backrest. You can create the remaining edges and corners of the backrest in the same way, but it is much easier to mirror the existing entities. Before you mirror the entities, make the mirroring easier by changing the UCS and moving the back to center its back surface on the UCS origin. After completing the backrest with two MIRROR commands, select everything to create a block named BACK.

Using MIRROR To Complete the Backrest

Make the lower right viewport current.

Restore UCS HUB	Returns UCS to top front center of backrest
Choose Modify, *then* Move	
`Command:` **`MOVE`**	
`Select objects:` *Select everything*	
`Base point or displacement:` *Use object snap ENDP to pick middle of back side at ① in lower right viewport (see fig. 20.42)*	
`Second point of displacement:` **`0,0,4.5`** ↵	Moves the back
Use UCS with the Y option to rotate the UCS –90 degrees around the Y axis (see fig. 20.43)	

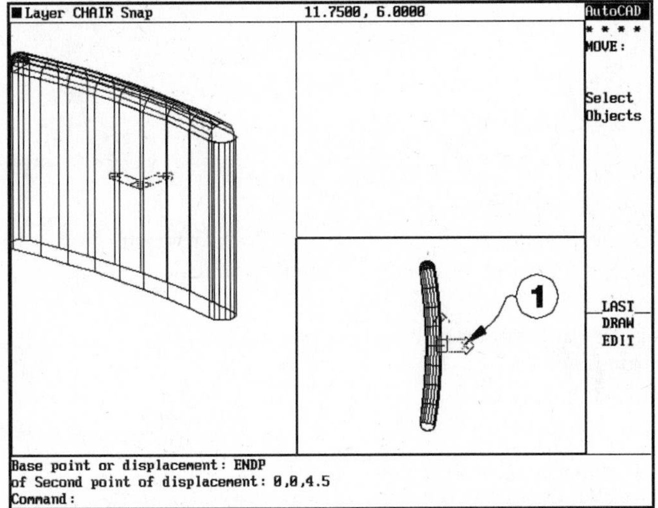

Figure 20.42:

The back midpoint to move 4.5" above HUB UCS origin.

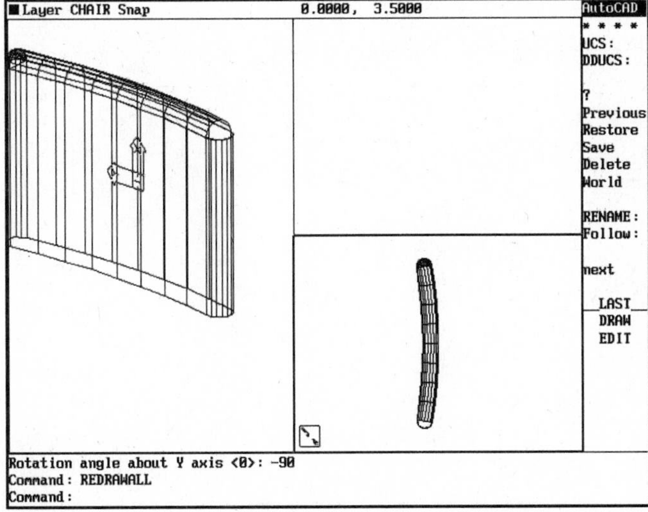

Figure 20.43:

UCS oriented for mirroring.

Next, you mirror the corner mesh to the other side.

Choose Construct, *and then* Mirror

```
Command: MIRROR
Select objects: Select corner mesh
First point of mirror line: 0,0 ↵
Second point: 1,0 ↵
Delete old objects? <N> Press Enter
```

Draws opposite corner (see fig. 20.44)

Repeat the MIRROR command and mirror top edge and both corner meshes to bottom of back, specifying mirror line from 0,0 to 0,1 and not deleting old objects (see fig. 20.45)

Restore UCS HUB and turn layer BUILD off

Create a block named BACK, selecting everything and using base point 0,0

Save and continue or end and take a break.

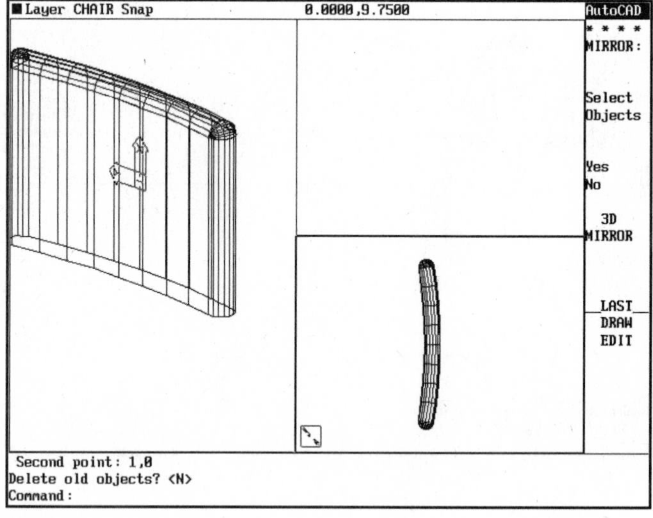

Figure 20.44:

The mirrored backrest corner.

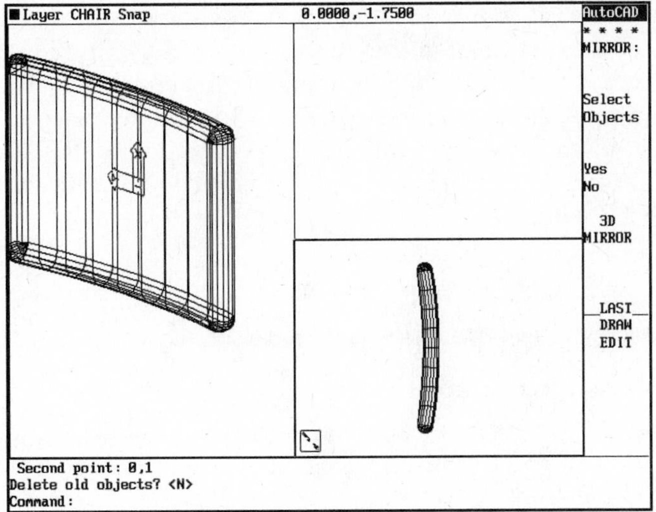

Figure 20.45:

The completed backrest.

You now have all the chair components except the seat itself. In the next section, you create the chair's seat and explore the use of PEDIT to change the surface contours of the seat. You can use PEDIT to move mesh vertices and to smooth meshes by spline fitting. First, use EDGESURF to create the seat body. Later, finish the seat construction by using a 3Dface for the seat bottom and by using REVSURF and TABSURF to create rounded edges and corners. Finally, assemble the chair by inserting the blocks that store its component parts.

Creating a Surface Using the EDGESURF Command

EDGESURF creates a polygon mesh from four adjoining edges. The edges can be lines, arcs, or open 2D or 3D polylines, but the four edges must touch at their end points. A polyline is a single edge, no matter how many vertices it has. You need to set SURFTAB1 and SURFTAB2 to specify your *m* and *n* mesh density. The EDGESURF command is simple; simply select the four edge entities. The first pick sets the SURFTAB1 *m* mesh direction along the edge picked.

In the following exercise, you create four lines to define the planar edges of the top surface of the seat cushion, and then use EDGESURF to fill it in with a 10×10 mesh. Pick the edges so that the *m* and *n* directions match the illustrations in figure 20.46. Temporarily go back to a single viewport, so that you can better see the results when you experiment with PEDIT mesh smoothing. Because the cushion is two inches thick, begin by drawing the line edges with a Z value of 2.

Using EDGESURF To Create the Top Surface of the Seat Cushion

Make sure the left viewport is current.

Set TILEMODE to 1 — Exits from the mview viewports and returns to single viewport

Zoom Center at 0,0,3 with height 15

Set layer BUILD current, and erase leftover entities

Set SURFTAB1 to 10 and SURFTAB2 to 10

Draw a line from 7,7,2 to 7,–7,2 to –7,–7,2 to –7,7,2, and Close it

Make CHAIR the current layer

Next, use EDGESURF to create a 10x10 mesh 2" above seat bottom.

Choose Draw, *then* 3D Surfaces, *and then* Edge Defined Patch — Issues EDGESURF command

`Command:` **`EDGESURF`**
`Select edge 1:` *Pick line at ① (see fig. 20.46)*
`Select edge 2:` *Pick line at ②*
`Select edge 3:` *Pick line at ③*
`Select edge 4:` *Pick line at ④* — Draws seat bottom (see fig. 20.47)

Save your drawing.

You can change the surface contours of a 3D polyline polygon mesh by editing the 3D vertex points with PEDIT.

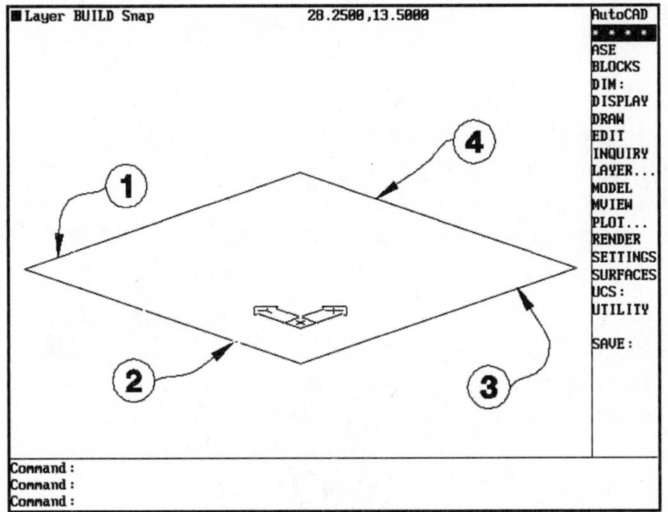

Figure 20.46:

Creating the seat edges.

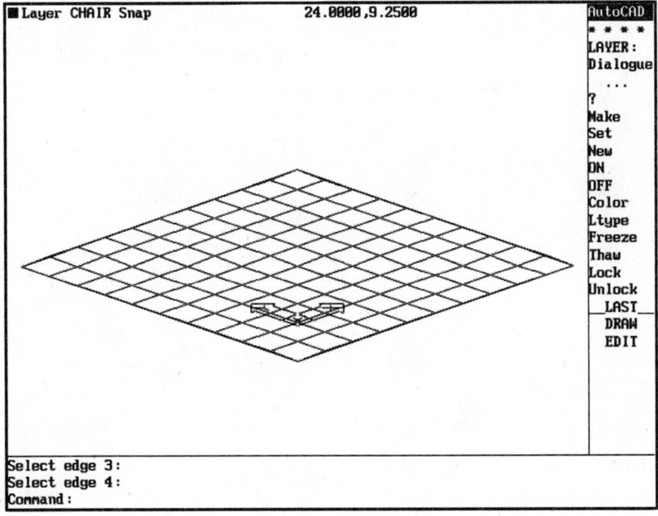

Figure 20.47:

The EDGESURF mesh.

Using PEDIT To Edit 3D Meshes

PEDIT is an intelligent command. When you select a mesh, PEDIT prompts with the only options available for editing meshes. (The options also change with 2D or 3D polylines, but polyface meshes cannot be edited.) You can use PEDIT to move a mesh vertex point by identifying the vertex point and entering a new 3D coordinate. You also can smooth and unsmooth the mesh by spline fitting the vertex mesh points.

When editing meshes, PEDIT has several options for moving the vertex editing X marker from vertex to vertex, in addition to the familiar Next and Previous options. Look at the prompt line in the following exercise. The X starts at the corner nearest the first pick point used in EDGESURF. The Vertex (*m,n*) prompt indicates your current vertex (the location of the X). You move the X up (away from the starting corner) and down the *m* direction or right (away from the starting corner) and left in the *n* direction. The Next option initially moves in the right direction.

To get a feel for editing vertices and spline fitting meshes, try the following exercise. It exaggerates the movement of the vertex points so that you can see the effects of different curve fits. Watch the (*m,n*) prompt and X mark as you work. Set an undo mark so you can easily undo the experiment. First, move vertex (3,3).

Using PEDIT To Edit Mesh Vertex Points

`Command:` **`_UNDO`** ↵
`Auto/Back/Control/End/Group/`
`Mark/<number>:` **`M`** ↵ — Sets a mark

Choose Modify, *then* PolyEdit

`Select objects:` *Pick mesh and press Enter*

`PEDIT Select polyline:`
`Edit vertex/Smooth surface/Desmooth/`
`Mclose/Nclose/Undo/eXit <X>:` **`E`** ↵

`Vertex (0,0). Next/Previous/Left/Right/`
`Up/Down/Move/REgen/eXit <N>:` *Press Enter*

`Vertex (0,1). Next/Previous/Left/Right/`
`Up/Down/Move/REgen/eXit <N>:` **`R`** ↵

`Vertex (0,2). Next/Previous/Left/Right`
`/Up/Down/Move/REgen/eXit <R>:` **`U`** ↵

`Vertex (1,2). Next/Previous/Left/Right /Up/Down/Move/REgen/eXit <U>:` *Press Enter twice*	
`Vertex (3,2). Next/Previous/Left/Right /Up/Down/Move/REgen/eXit <U>:` **R** ↵	
`Vertex (3,3). Next/Previous/Left/Right /Up/Down/Move/REgen/eXit <R>:` **M** ↵	
`Enter new location:` **@0,0,3** ↵	Moves vertex (3,3) 3" in Z direction
`Vertex (3,3). Next/Previous/Left/Right /Up/Down/Move/REgen/eXit <R>:` *Press Enter*	
`Vertex (3,4). Next/Previous/Left/Right /Up/Down/Move/REgen/eXit <R>:` **M** ↵	
`Enter new location:` **@0,0,2** ↵	Moves vertex (3,4) 2" in Z direction
Go to vertex (4,4) with Up option and move the vertex 2" in Z by entering **@0,0,2**	
Go to vertex (4,3) with Left option and move the vertex 2" in Z by entering **@0,0,2**	
Go to vertex (7,4) with Up Up Up Right and move the vertex 1" in Y and 9" in Z by entering **@0,1,9**	
Go to vertex (8,5) with Up Right and move the vertex -5" in Z by entering **@0,0,-5** *(see fig. 20.48)*	
`Vertex (8,5). Next/Previous/Left/Right /Up/Down/Move/REgen/eXit <R>:` **X**	Exits vertex editing
`Edit vertex/Smooth surface/Desmooth /Mclose/Nclose/Undo/eXit <X>:` *Press Enter*	

The smooth surface option enables you to perform three types of spline fitting. Each type produces a different smooth surface, based on formulas that produce a surface passing near the vertex points. You control the type of spline fit by setting the SURFTYPE system variable. Two other system variables, SURFU and SURFV, control the fineness of the fit in the *m* and *n* mesh directions. You use the SPLFRAME system variable to control whether the spline fit or original mesh displays. A value of 0 (off—the default) displays the spline fitting, if any, and a value of 1 (on) displays the original mesh and vertices regardless of spline fitting.

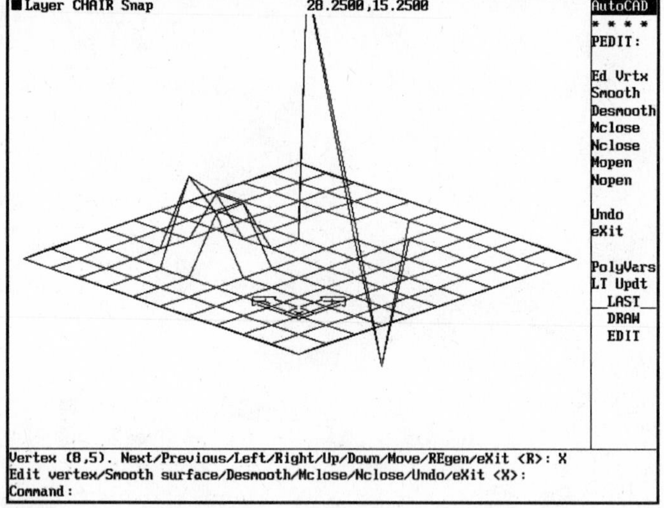

Figure 20.48:

The seat mesh after editing.

Choosing Smooth Surface Options

The three smooth surface options and their variables are as follows:

- **Cubic B-spline curve.** SURFTYPE 6 (AutoCAD's default).
- **Quadratic B-spline curve.** SURFTYPE 5.
- **Bezier curve.** SURFTYPE 8.

Try all the smoothing options on the mesh to see the effect each has. Use the exercise that follows to configure the SURFU, SURFV, and SURFTYPE settings. Use PEDIT to smooth the mesh to a cubic B-spline surface, with default SURFTYPE 6.

Using PEDIT To Smooth Mesh Surface Fitting

Set SURFU system variable to 24 and SURFV to 24.

Choose Modify, *then* PolyEdit

`Select objects:` *Pick mesh and press Enter*

`PEDIT Select polyline:`
`Edit vertex/Smooth surface/Desmooth`
`/Mclose/Nclose/Undo/eXit <X>:` **S** ↵

`Edit vertex/Smooth surface/Desmooth`
`/Mclose/Nclose/Undo/eXit <X>:` *Press Enter*

Nothing happened because SPLFRAME was set to 1 for polyface and 3Dmesh visibility in an earlier exercise.

Set SPLFRAME to 0 and regenerate drawing	Makes spline fitting visible (see fig. 20.49)
Set SURFTYPE to 5	Specifies quadratic B-spline surface
Use PEDIT Smooth again (see fig. 20.50)	
Set SURFTYPE to 8	Specifies Bezier surface
Use PEDIT Smooth again (see fig. 20.51)	
`Command:` **`UNDO`** ↵	
`Auto/Back/Control/End/Group/ Mark/<number>:` **`B`** ↵	Restores flat mesh

You have to look closely to see the difference between SURFTYPEs 5 and 6, but 8 is dramatically smoother. You can regenerate to see the effects of a SPLFRAME change, but you have to use PEDIT to resmooth the mesh to see the effects of changing SURFTYPE, SURFU, or SURFV. When you finish, you should have the flat starting mesh restored. If you like, try to edit the mesh into a comfortable seat contour.

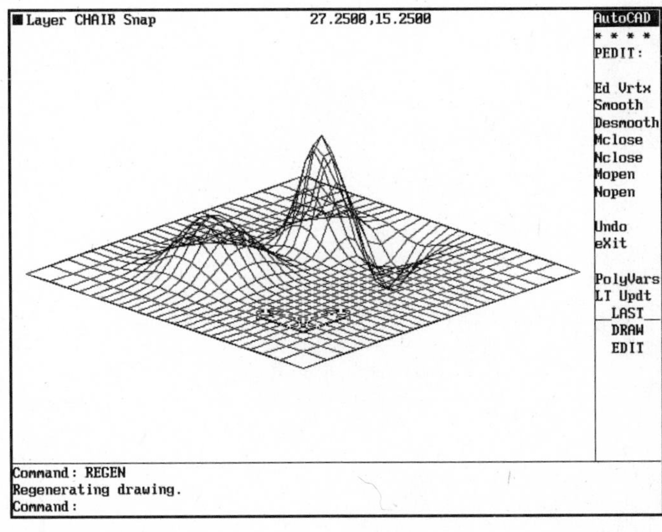

Figure 20.49: SURFTYPE 6 smoothing.

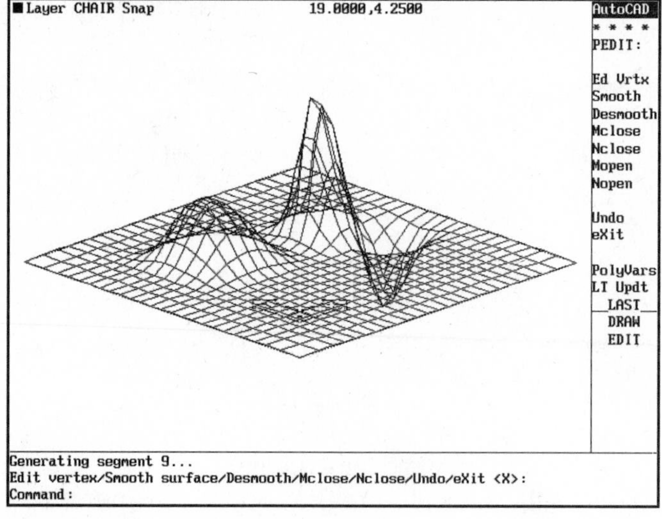

Figure 20.50:
SURFTYPE 5 smoothing.

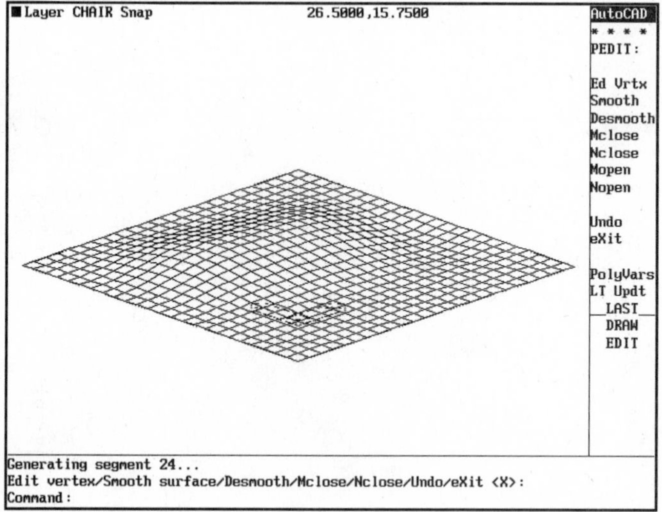

Figure 20.51:
SURFTYPE 8 smoothing.

Other PEDIT Mesh Options

The Mclose and Nclose options control whether a mesh connects the first vertex to the last vertex of the mesh. A mesh in the shape of a dish (half of a sphere) is closed in the M direction and open in the N direction. If you open

the dish in the M direction by selecting Mclose, the dish is redrawn with a wedge segment missing. Likewise, if you close the dish in the N direction, the dish is redrawn with a mesh going from the edge to the center of the dish, creating a cone inside the dish. The M and N options display either close or open prompts, depending on the current status of the mesh being edited.

Finishing the Seat by Using 3DFACE, TABSURF, and REVSURF

Now you can finish the seat. Make a simple seat bottom with the 3DFACE command, and then use REVSURF to make curved corners and TABSURF to close the curved edges.

After drawing the seat bottom by using 3DFACE, you create the arc and axis for REVSURF. You also move the existing mesh out of the way so that you can select one of its edge lines when you use TABSURF to create the arc. You utilize the same techniques here that you used to build the backrest.

Using 3DFACE and Creating Arc Path and Axis for REVSURF and TABSURF

Set TILEMODE to 0 viewports	Returns to mview
Make left viewport current, and ZOOM Center 0,0 to height 36	
Choose Draw, *then* 3D Surfaces, *then* 3D Face, *and draw seat bottom from 7,7 to 7,–7 to –7,–7 to –7,7, then press Enter*	Draws seat bottom (see fig. 20.52)
Make BUILD the current layer	
Draw a line from –7,7 to @0,0,2	Designates axis for corner Revsurf
*Move seat top mesh from 0,0 to *0,0*	Makes mesh appear in upper right viewport
*Zoom top right viewport with center point *0,0 and height 16*	
Use UCS Entity option and pick bottom of axis line in left viewport	Aligns UCS with line

Rotate UCS –90 degrees about Y axis (see fig. 20.53)	
Use ARC *with* Start, End, Angle *option, entering start point* `2,0`*, end point* `0,0`*, and angle* `180` *degrees*	Creates path curve for seat corner REVSURF and edge TABSURF (see fig. 20.53)

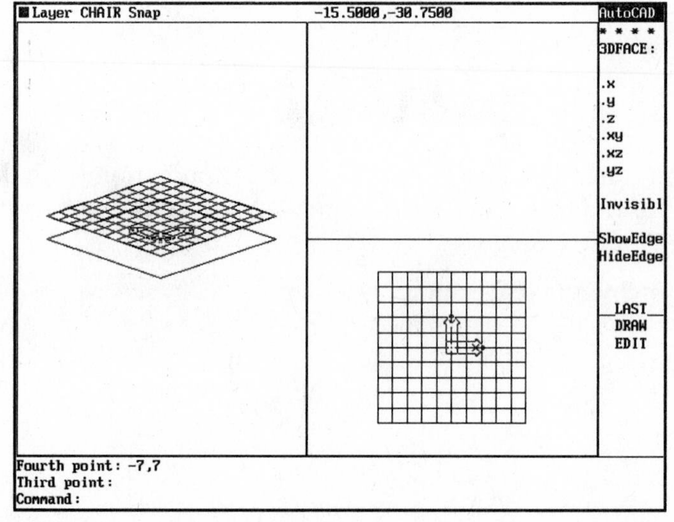

Figure 20.52:
The seat with a 3DFACE bottom.

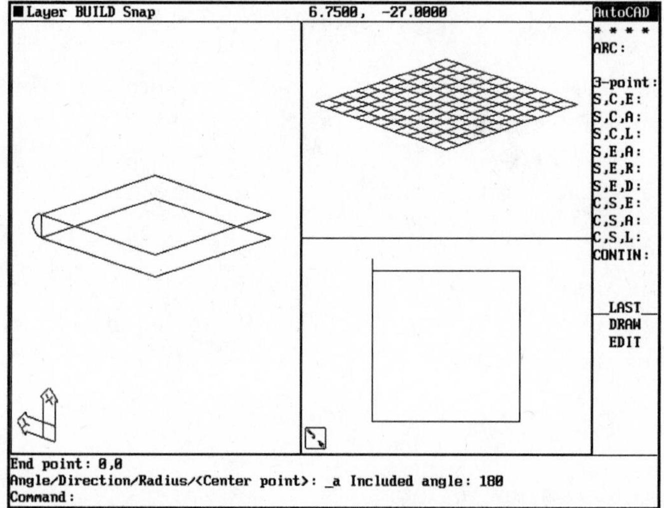

Figure 20.53:
Arc and construction lines ready for surfacing.

Now you can use REVSURF and TABSURF to create the first corner and edge. Afterward, use a polar array to complete the seat cushion. The use of ARRAY takes advantage of the fact that the seat is symmetrical and saves mirroring (or individually creating) the edges and corners.

Using REVSURF, TABSURF, and ARRAY To Complete the Seat

Make CHAIR the current layer

Choose Draw, *then* 3D Surfaces, *then* Surface of Revolution

`Command:` **`REVSURF`**

`Select path curve:` *Pick arc at* ① *(see fig. 20.54)*

`Select axis of revolution:` *Pick line at* ②

`Start angle <0>:` *Press Enter*

`Included angle (+=ccw, -=cw) <Full circle>:` **`90`** ↵ — Forms the corner

When picking points with the REFSURF command, use care to pick the point shown in figure 20.54.

Restore UCS HUB — Centers UCS on seat

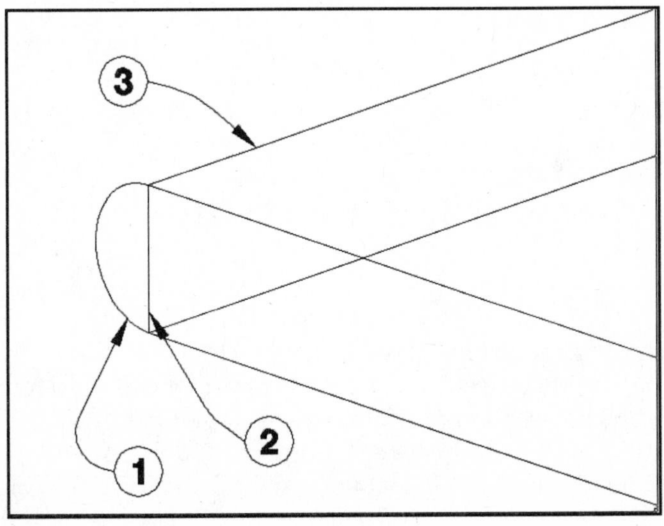

Figure 20.54:

Detail of pick points.

*Move seat corner from 0,0 to *0,0 and redraw*

Choose Draw, *then* 3D Surfaces, *then* Tabulated Surface

`Command:` **`_tabsurf`**
`Select path curve:` *Pick arc at* ①

`Select direction vector:` *Pick line at* ③ — Creates seat edge

*Move meshes from upper right viewport, back from *0,0 to 0,0*

Turn BUILD layer off

Next, create a polar array of the edge and corner mesh to create the three remaining sides.

Choose Construct, *then* Array

`Command:` **`ARRAY`**
`Select objects:` *Select TABSURF edge mesh and REVSURF corner mesh*

`Rectangular or Polar array (R/P):` **`P`** ↵

`Center point of array:` **`0,0`** ↵

`Number of items:` **`4`** ↵

`Angle to fill (+=ccw, -=cw) <360>:` *Press Enter*

`Rotate objects as they are copied? <Y>` *Press Enter* — Creates rest of corners and edges (see fig. 20.55)

Create a block named SEAT selecting everything and using base point 0,0

Save your drawing.

Congratulations. You now have all your chair components stored in your drawing as blocks.

Inserting 3D Blocks

In 3D, building complex parts as a series of smaller blocked parts offers several productivity benefits. First, you only have to work with a limited number of entities on the screen for a particular part, which makes construction and editing less confusing (other parts do not get in your way). This technique also makes redraws, regenerations, and interim hidden-line removals faster. Another benefit is that you can easily change the compo-

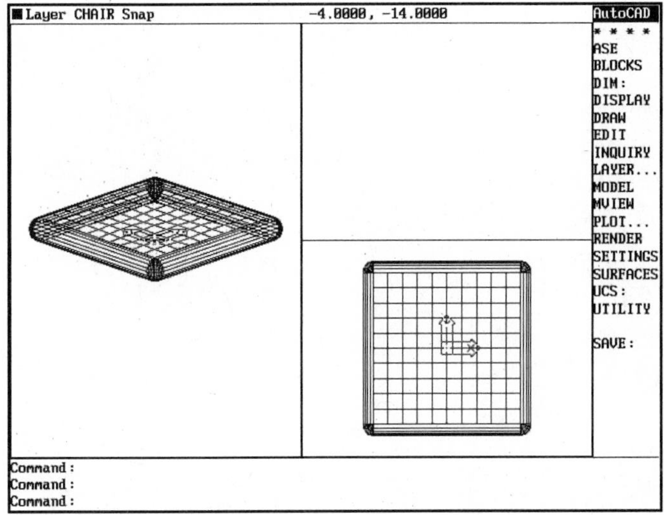

Figure 20.55:

The completed seat cushion.

nents. For example, with a variety of seat, back, pedestal, and base blocks, you can use block redefinition to build a different chair from other parts.

Use the INSERT command to construct the chair from the components you have blocked. Even if you did not create all the blocks, they are on the IA DISK (they still can be inserted). When all parts are inserted, use the BASE command to set an insertion base point at floor level so that you can easily insert this drawing into other drawings.

Using INSERT To Assemble the 3D Chair

Choose File, then New, and enter `\IA\CHAIR=\IA\IA7CHAIR`, replacing your preceding CHAIR drawing.

Choose File, then Open, and enter `\IA\CHAIR`.

Set TILEMODE to 1 — Returns to single viewport

Set UCS Origin to 30,22,0

Turn on all layers, zoom extents, and erase any leftover entities

Zoom center at 0,0,18 with a height of 42

Insert BASE block at 0,0,4.5 with default scale and rotation

Insert PEDESTAL at 0,0,4.5 with default scale and rotation

Insert SUPPORT at 0,0,17.5 with default scale and rotation

Insert SEAT at 0,0,18.5 with default scale and rotation

Insert BACK at 9.25,0,30 with default scale and rotation

Command: **BASE**

Base point <-30.0000,-110.0000,88.0000>:
0,0,0↵

Choose Render, *then* Hide

Save your drawing.

Now the chair is complete (see fig. 20.56).

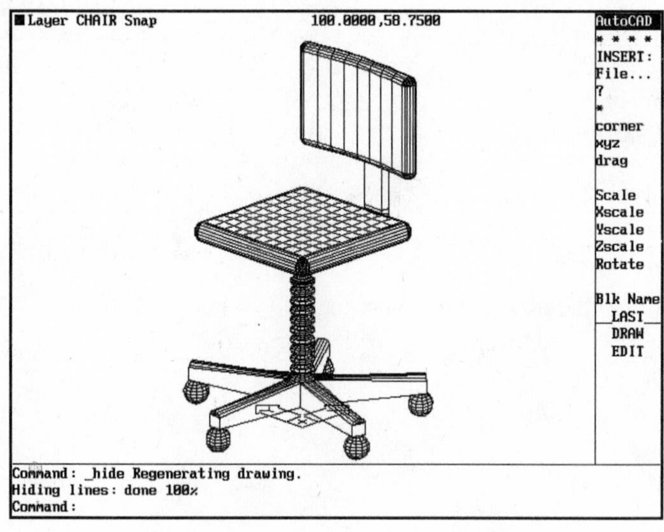

Figure 20.56:

The assembled chair, with hidden lines removed.

Summary

When you construct a 3D drawing, use the entities and commands necessary for your needs. Meshes may not always be the most efficient drawing entities. Extruded 2D entities require less memory and hard disk space, so use them if they adequately represent what you need to show.

You usually should use a mix of 2D extruded entities and 3D mesh entities. If you are building a complex drawing, consider using the approach taken in this chapter: build your drawing in components and assemble it by using the BLOCK and INSERT commands.

When you use meshes, set reasonable surface mesh density by using SURFTAB1 and SURFTAB2. Keep track of these settings; if you forget to set the desired values, you have to erase the mesh and create a new one. Keep mesh profile entities on a separate layer to avoid conflicts with 3D model entities. If you have meshes with common edges, use temporary blocks, moves, or erasures to remove one mesh so that you can pick the edge entity for the second mesh. If you really want to control your meshes, create some AutoLISP routines. For details, consult *Maximizing AutoCAD, Volume II: Inside AutoLISP* (available from New Riders Publishing).

In Chapter 21, you are shown how to walk through a 3D drawing. You generate perspectives and partial hides and view an office drawing dynamically.

With these techniques, you will be able to present your 3D drawings to others with the greatest possible impact. Even simple schematic drawings and mass models are impressive when displayed using tools like perspective projection, shading, hidden-line removal, and clipping planes.

21

Dynamic 3D Displays

In the preceding two chapters, you used extruded 2D entities and 3D surface entities to draw 3D models. This chapter presents advanced 3D viewing techniques that make drawing in 3D easier and helps you plan and preview your 3D presentations. When you create a presentation, you use a variety of views in 3D space. This chapter teaches you how to use the DVIEW command to dynamically adjust your viewpoint and other parameters that control the appearance of the display so you can create the individual views that comprise a 3D presentation.

Often, the correct 3D view can save you time and money. Systematically revolving a drawing in 3D space might reveal an unanticipated design condition, such as interference between machinery and a wall. Learning to use tools such as DVIEW in your presentations can help you win projects.

This chapter shows you how to use DVIEW as an interactive 3D substitute for the VPOINT and ZOOM commands, as well as how to display perspectives in AutoCAD. You also learn how to create slides of these views and construct a slide show using a script file.

Viewing Drawings Dynamically

By combining DVIEW with paper space viewports, you can draw and annotate a single drawing with any combination of views, including perspectives. By combining DVIEW, the RENDER and SHADE commands, slides, and scripts, you can quickly create preliminary or simple presentations. Then you can go on to create impressive full-motion video presentations by using Autodesk RenderMan, 3D Studio, AutoFlix, and Autodesk Animator (all Autodesk products).

The IA DISK drawing for this chapter includes saved views that correspond to this chapter's three series of exercises. The first series starts at the beginning of the chapter. The series continues at the "Rotating the View with the Target Option" and at the "Making a 3D Slide Presentation" sections. You can use the disk to begin in any of these sections.

DVIEW includes all the facilities of the VPOINT and ZOOM command, plus a few additional features. Rather than using the VPOINT globe and axes, DVIEW enables you to display all or part of your drawing as you adjust your viewpoint directly. Using DVIEW, you can zoom, pan, and adjust your viewpoint in a single command. Unlike VPOINT, DVIEW provides parallel (orthographic) or perspective views. Figure 21.1 shows both parallel and perspective views of an office. In the perspective view, parallel lines recede from your view toward a vanishing point. In the parallel view, parallel lines always remain parallel. Note that VPOINT is limited to defining parallel views. Parallel views often seem unnatural because your eyes are accustomed to viewing the real world. Parallel lines appear to converge as they recede from your viewpoint.

The VPOINT command zooms the new view to the drawing extents, but DVIEW gives you full control over the display of your view. VPOINT forces you to look through the entire drawing toward 0,0,0. DVIEW enables you to look from any point to any other point, control the zoom factor, and you can clip the foreground or background to temporarily remove objects that obscure the object you want to see.

DVIEW uses an interactive camera and target metaphor to control your drawing view. To select a view, you point an imaginary camera at a target in your drawing. The line from the camera to the target is your line of sight. You can move the camera and target to get different views. The camera metaphor is carried further in perspective views to enable you to change your field of view by changing the lens length. You also can cut away

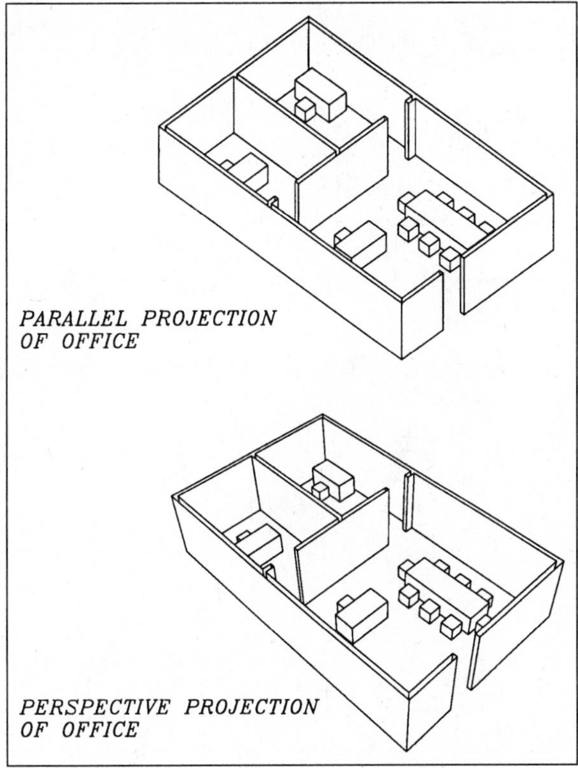

Figure 21.1:
Parallel and perspective projections of an office.

sections of your drawing by clipping the front or back plane of your view. This useful feature enables you to look at an office interior in a building plan or create a section view of a part.

Although each of these features gives you more control over your drawing views, DVIEW's most powerful advantage is its *interactive interface*. The VPOINT command displays the globe and axes to preview the line-of-sight orientation, which requires trial and error to find the correct view. DVIEW, however, displays a selection set of drawing objects or a 3D icon if no objects are selected so that you can visualize the orientation of the line of sight in complex drawings. You can easily adjust the viewpoint using only a few selected entities and then regenerate the view of the entire drawing from this new perspective.

Using Dynamic Display with the Slide and Script Commands

You can access DVIEW from the Set View option of the View pull-down menu. You also can select DVIEW on the Display screen menu.

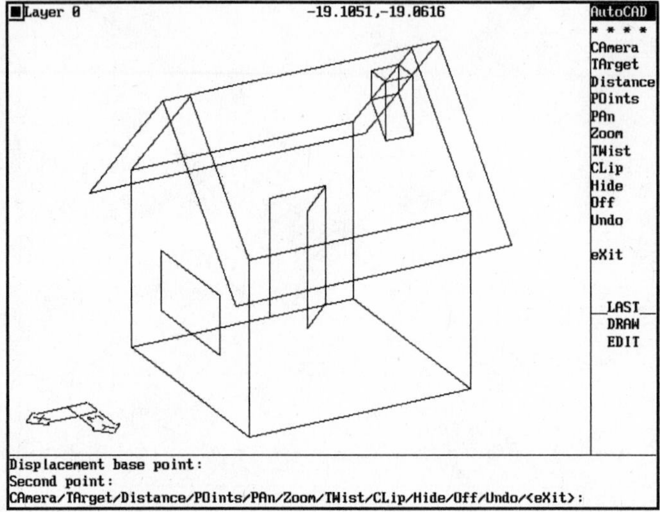

Figure 21.2:
The Dview Options screen menu.

In addition to DVIEW, you use the SCRIPT, MSLIDE, and VSLIDE commands in this chapter. You use the MSLIDE and VSLIDE commands to make and view slides. These commands appear on the Utility screen menu.

Setting Up for DVIEW

For the exercises in this chapter, use the office plan from Chapter 16 that you saved as OFFICE.DWG (see fig. 21.3). This drawing provides a variety of perspective views from the different rooms, and it regenerates quickly.

Although the OFFICE.DWG drawing is simple, it illustrates a time-saving technique. You can work with simple shapes that regenerate quickly, such as those in this draw-

ing to develop a presentation, then replace them with complex blocks before plotting or presenting your work.

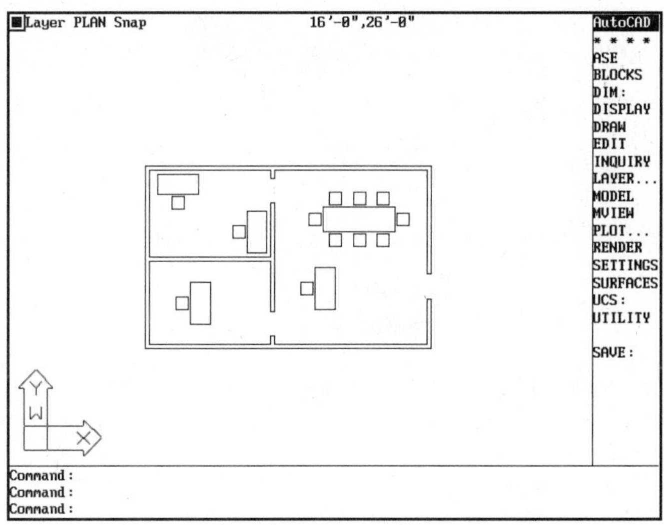

Figure 21.3:

The office with primitive table, desks, and chairs.

If you are using the IA7 DISK, you have IA7OFF3D.DWG extruded and ready for the first DVIEW exercise. If you do not have a copy of the OFFICE drawing, you can create it quickly by doing the first two exercises from Chapter 16.

After you load the drawing, freeze the attributes layer. You need only the floor plan for this chapter's exercises. Then extrude the plan into a 3D drawing by giving height to the walls, desks, table, and chairs.

Setting Up the Dynamic View Office Drawing

Select File, then New, enter `\IA\OFFICE3D=\IA\IA7OFF3D`, and skip the rest of this exercise.

Select File, then New, enter `\IA\OFFICE3D=\IA\OFFICE`, and make sure that the current settings match table 21.1.

Set layer PLAN current and freeze layers 0 and DATA (see fig. 21.3)

Use CHPROP *to change the thickness of desks and table to 30"*
Use CHPROP *to change the thickness of all chairs to 18"*
Set VPOINT to -2, -3, 4
Set a running object snap of ENDP
Add a 3DFACE *(picking points clockwise) to each desk, chair, and the table*
Zoom previous
Set OSNAP *to* NONE
Use CHPROP *to change the thickness of all walls to 8'*
Zoom window 16',13' to 34',26' (see fig. 21.4)

Table 21.1:
Dynamic View Office Drawing Settings

COORDS	*GRID*	*ORTHO*	*FILL*	*SNAP*	*UCSICON*
ON	2'	OFF	OFF	3"	ON and OR

UNITS	Set to 4 Architectural, default the rest.
LIMITS	Set LIMITS from 0,0 to 72",48'.
VIEW	Saved view named A.

Layer Name	*State*	*Color*	*Linetype*
0	Frozen	7 White	CONTINUOUS
DATA	Frozen	7 White	CONTINUOUS
PLAN	On/Current	3 Green	CONTINUOUS

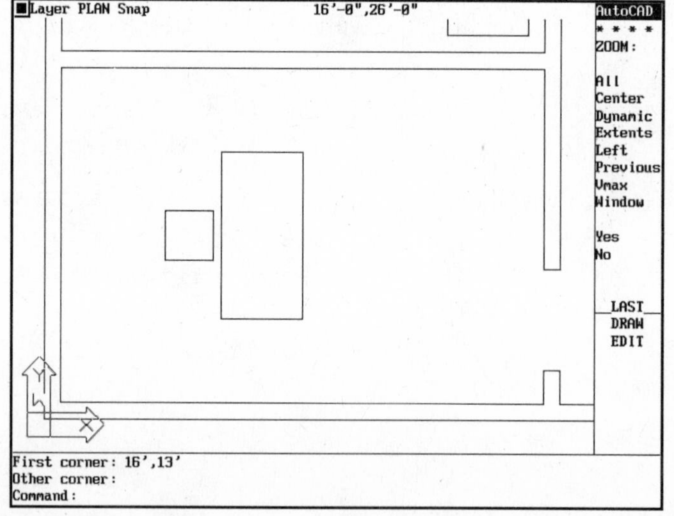

Figure 21.4:
A magnified view of the room.

You now see the lower left room of the floor plan, which contains a simple chair and desk in the center of the room. You should be in the WCS with the UCS icon showing in the lower left corner of the drawing area. The thickness of the extrusions does not appear until the first dynamic view because your viewpoint is at 0,0,1—directly above the WCS origin.

Understanding the DVIEW Command

DVIEW is complex because it has twelve options; however, the command is easy to use after you learn these options and their effects. First, DVIEW asks for a selection set to use as the dynamic display. After you select objects or accept AutoCAD's default house icon, set your *viewpoint* (camera location) and the *focus* (target) by picking or setting points. These two points establish a line of sight or viewing direction. Then refine the view by zooming, panning, clipping, or hiding. After you have the view you want, exit DVIEW. AutoCAD regenerates the drawing according to the parameters you set. DVIEW's default view is parallel projection, but you can specify a perspective view.

Understanding DVIEW Options

Use the following options to control DVIEW:

- **CAmera.** This option rotates the viewpoint. CAmera is similar to the VPOINT Rotate option, but rotates the viewpoint around the target point rather than around 0,0.

The target point default is 0,0,0 until you change it by using the TArget option.

- **TArget.** This option rotates the target point around the camera viewpoint. The TArget option is the opposite of the CAmera option. CAmera rotates the viewpoint around the target point.
- **Distance.** This option changes the distance from the camera to the target along the current line of sight. It switches the view from parallel to perspective.

- **POints.** This option sets the camera position (viewpoint) and target point. These points define the viewing direction.
- **PAn.** This option moves the camera and target points parallel to the current view plane. Because both points move by the same displacement, the angles between the viewing direction vector and the axes do not change.
- **Zoom.** This option enlarges or shrinks the image on the screen without changing the camera and target locations in the WCS-perspective angles are not affected.
- **TWist.** This option rotates the image around the line of sight.
- **CLip.** This option removes foreground or background objects from the image by setting clipping planes perpendicular to the line of sight.
- **Hide.** This option performs a temporary hidden-line removal in the Dview command. The image regenerates after you exit Dview.
- **Off.** This option turns off perspective mode and returns the image to parallel projection.
- **Undo.** This option undoes the other options.
- **eXit.** This option ends the DVIEW command. AutoCAD displays the `Command:` prompt and regenerates all drawing entities except portions that are clipped or outside of the current view as specified with the DVIEW command. If perspective mode is set, the drawing regenerates in perspective.

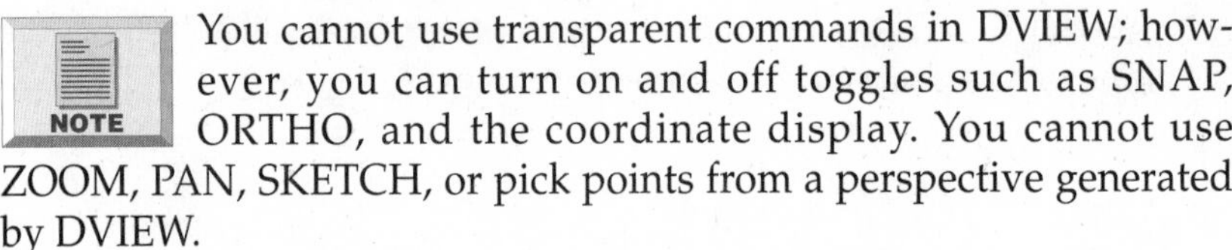

You cannot use transparent commands in DVIEW; however, you can turn on and off toggles such as SNAP, ORTHO, and the coordinate display. You cannot use ZOOM, PAN, SKETCH, or pick points from a perspective generated by DVIEW.

Setting a Line-of-Sight View with POints

In the following exercise, you use the POints option and select the entire room to dynamically view your drawing. Then you set the camera position in the upper left corner of the room at approximately eye level and set a target point on the center of the desk top. Locate the target point, then the camera point with XYZ point filters. After you pick the target point, a

rubber-band line appears from the target point to the camera point to help you visualize the line of sight.

Using POints To Set the DVIEW Camera Line of Sight

Select View, *then* Set View, *and then* Dview

Command: **DVIEW**	
Select objects: *Use a window to select room and contents*	Specifies objects to view dynamically
CAmera/TArget/Distance/POints/PAn/Zoom/TWist/CLip/Hide/Off/Undo/<eXit>: Type **PO** *and press Enter, or select* Options, *and then* POints *from the screen menu*	
Enter target point <25'-0 7/16", 19'-6", 4'-0">: **.XY** ↵	
Pick point in middle of desk top with point filter	Specifies XY coordinates of the "look at" point
(need Z): **3'6** ↵	
Enter camera point <26'-5 1/8", 19'-6", 4'-1">: **.XY** ↵	Specifies XY coordinates of the "look from" point
of *Pick upper left corner of room*	
(need Z): **5'6** ↵	Sets camera point at eye level
CAmera/TArget/Distance/POints/PAn/Zoom/TWist/CLip/Hide/Off/Undo/<eXit>: *Press Enter*	Regenerates the entire view using DVIEW parameters

Figure 21.5 shows your drawing after you input the points.

Figure 21.6 shows what you see after you exit DVIEW.

Your drawing regenerates after you exit DVIEW. The drawing should show a view of the desk with the office doorway in the left background. If you study the location of the camera and target points in relation to the plan view and the new view, you discover that the display includes objects in back of the camera location as well as in front of it. These objects appear because you did not set clipping planes to remove objects from the display that a real camera cannot see.

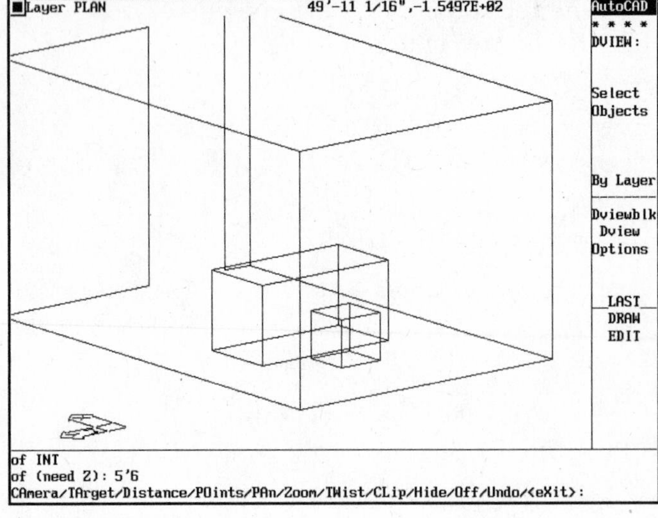

Figure 21.5:

The DVIEW display after point selection.

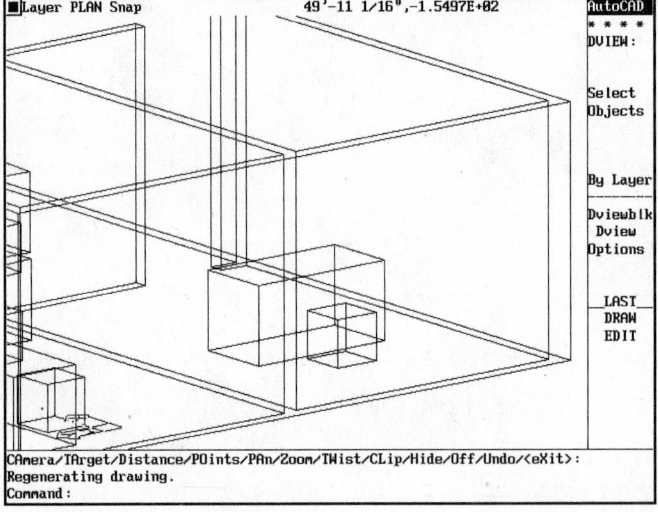

Figure 21.6:

Offices viewed from the corner of the room.

DVIEW automatically turns off snap, but you can turn it back on for snapping to points by pressing F9 or Ctrl-B. You also can use object snap overrides to pick points.

The DVIEW default target and camera point prompts, as well as other default values and pick points, vary from those shown in this book. The exact defaults and points depend on your display and on the locations of your desks and chairs.

Using DVIEW's Undo Option

Like other complex commands, DVIEW has an Undo option to step back through the settings, angles, and point changes made during the use of the current DVIEW command. If you have exited DVIEW, you can use the UNDO command to undo an entire DVIEW operation.

Understanding the DVIEW House Icon

If you press Enter in response to the DVIEW object selection prompt instead of selecting objects, AutoCAD displays a 3D house icon to orient you in space during a DVIEW operation. As you adjust your DVIEW settings, the house icon moves dynamically. After you exit DVIEW, your drawing regenerates in the view you established by manipulating the house icon.

You can replace the house icon with your own icon by defining a block named DVIEWBLOCK. You might prefer an icon that relates better to the subject of your drawings-a car, airplane, tool, video camera, or just a set of arrows. DVIEW scales the icon to fit your drawing and aligns it to the axes of your current UCS; therefore, create your block as a 1x1x1 unit block. Align the X,Y,Z axes with an origin point at the front lower left corner. Use a custom icon block instead of selecting complex objects to make DVIEW use quick and efficient. The house icon can be seen in figure 21.2.

Create an easily recognizable DVIEW block with a unique top, bottom, left, right, front, and back side so that its orientation is easy to determine at a glance. Keep the block simple so that it drags smoothly in DVIEW.

Changing the Camera Location

The CAmera option rotates the point of view around the target point. The CAmera option is like the VPOINT Rotate option except that the order of the angle prompts is reversed. The first CAmera prompt asks for the angle from the X,Y plane. You can adjust this angle to move the camera up and down. The second prompt asks for the angle from the X axis (in the X,Y plane). This angle moves the camera from side to side. You can input the angles from the keyboard, or you can dynamically rotate your view by moving your crosshairs up, down, left, and right. Moving your crosshairs up increases the camera angle from the X,Y plane, while moving them to the right increases the angle from the X axis (in the X,Y plane). This dynamic rotation enables you to effectively select both angles with a single pick.

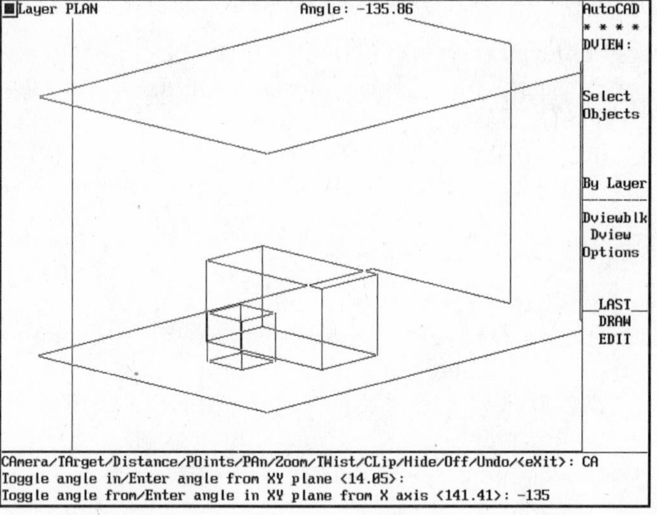

Figure 21.7:
The DVIEW display during camera selection.

Using Dynamic Rotation

If you know the angles that produce the desired line of sight in advance, you can produce the view best by keying in the angles. If not, you can use the cursor to find the right image interactively. As you move the cursor, AutoCAD dynamically redraws the selected objects to represent the new view. AutoCAD updates the angle display and the image as you move the

cursor. AutoCAD provides similar dynamic editing features, such as slider bars to change distance settings.

The angles in DVIEW always are in the WCS unless you set the WORLDVIEW system variable to 0. If you have a UCS current, and WORLDVIEW is 1 (the default), AutoCAD switches to the WCS during DVIEW, and then switches back to the UCS. A camera angle of 0 from the X,Y plane looks edge-on to the UCS or WCS construction plane.

Next, you try the CAmera option by changing the angle in the X,Y plane to a view from the lower left corner of the room (with respect to the original plan view), looking back at the desk. The office doorway appears on the right (see fig. 21.7). Leave the angle above the X,Y plane unchanged.

Using CAmera Option To Locate DVIEW Camera

Continue from the preceding exercise.

Choose View, *then* Set View, *then* Dview

`Select objects:` **`P`** ↵	Selects walls of room, desk, and chair
From the screen menu, choose Dview Options, *then* CAmera	
`Toggle angle in/Enter angle from XY plane <14.36>:` *Press Enter*	Retains the current angle
`Toggle angle from/Enter angle in X-Y plane from X axis <141.95>:` **`-135`** ↵	
`CAmera/TArget/Distance/POints/Zoom/ TWist/CLip/Hide/Off/Undo/<eXit>:` *Press Enter*	Exits DVIEW command and regenerates screen
`Regenerating drawing.`	

The resulting view appears in figure 21.8.

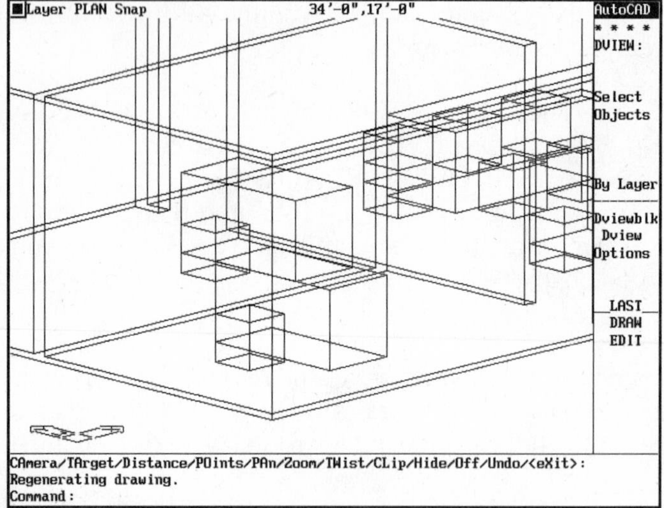

Figure 21.8:

The camera moved to the lower left corner.

NOTE

If you select an option that uses slider bars, the initial image depends on your cursor location and usually is different than the view that was displayed when you selected the option. To restore the view you just lost, move the diamond on the slider back to the end of the slider control. The illustrations with slider bars show the cursor and slider at their current default positions.

The disadvantage of dynamically picking the camera's viewpoint is that precise values are hard to pick. Use the CAmera option's dynamic rotation ability to pick approximate views, but for precise views, enter the specific angles required.

If you want to experiment with the dynamic rotation, move the "camera" around. After you are done, use the Undo option to return the camera to -135 degrees.

Setting a Distance for Perspective Views

You switch from parallel to perspective view by using the Distance option. AutoCAD prompts you for a new distance from the camera to the target, with your current distance as the default. The line of sight remains unchanged. You can enter a distance or use the top slider bar. The slider values range from 0X (on the left) to 16X (on the right). Your current distance factor

is 1X. Move to the right, and you are farther away from the target; 2X is twice the distance. A continuous update of your distance displays on the status line.

Remember that the default prompt and status lines show the distance, but the slider is a multiplication factor, not a distance.

If you select the Distance option, you also see your UCS icon replaced with a perspective icon (a small cube) in the lower left corner of the graphics window. This icon reminds you that you are in perspective mode. To turn off perspective, use the Dview Off option.

In the next exercise, you set a new camera/target distance to get a perspective view. The current distance is about seven or eight feet. Press Enter to accept the default distance so that you can see the desk in perspective at the current distance (see fig. 21.9). Then increase the distance to about 19 feet (about 2.7X). Use the VIEW command to save this view as a named view so that you can return to it later.

Using Distance Option To Create a Perspective View

Continue from the preceding exercise.

Select View, *then* Set View, *then* Dview

`Command:` **`DVIEW`** ↵

`Select objects:` *Select the previous* entities — Selects walls of room, desk, and chair

`CAmera/TArget/Distance/POints/PAn/Zoom/`
`TWist/CLip/Hide/Off/Undo/<eXit>:` **`D`** ↵

`New camera/target distance <8'-2 7/8">:`
`8'` ↵ — See fig. 21.9

`CAmera/TArget/Distance/POints/PAn/Zoom/`
`TWist/CLip/Hide/Off/Undo/<eXit>:` **`D`** ↵

`New camera/target distance <8'-0 13/16">:`
Enter `19'` *or select approximate distance*

`CAmera/TArget/Distance/POints/PAn/Zoom/`
`TWist/CLip/Hide/Off/Undo/<eXit>:`
Press Enter

Your drawing should resemble the one shown in figure 21.10. Save the view with the name OFFICE1.

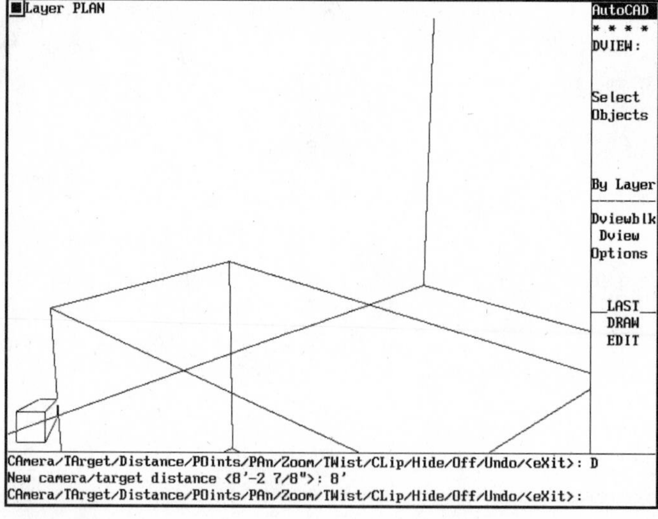

Figure 21.9:

The desk at a distance of 8'-0".

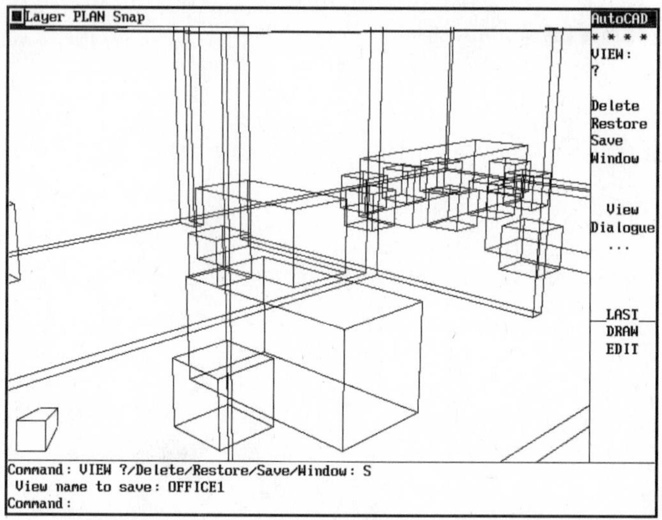

Figure 21.10:

The desk at a distance of 19'-0".

When you change the distance, you change the perspective. You can magnify an image by using the Zoom option without changing distance. Zoom acts like switching or zooming on a camera lens. After you set the perspective, you can use the POints, CAmera, and TArget options to change the perspective by changing points.

In the next section, you leave perspective on and change the target point.

Rotating the View Using the TArget Option

One frustration of the VPOINT command is that it always looks at the WCS origin point. DVIEW's POints and TArget options, however, enable you to move the target point as well as the viewpoint. The TArget option prompts are similar to the CAmera prompts. The first prompt is for a new angle from the X,Y plane, and the second prompt is for a new angle in the X,Y plane from the X axis. The effect is the opposite of the CAmera option's effect; you are changing the target's angles relative to your vantage point (camera point). If you adjust only the angle in the X,Y plane, the effect at the camera is like turning your head to look around the room (or rotating the room around your head).

In the following exercise, you use the TArget option to aim the point of view at the office door on the right (see fig. 21.11). Change the target angle in the X,Y plane to get a view with the doorway near the center, leaving the angle from the X,Y plane unchanged.

Using the TArget Option To Get a Viewpoint of Door

Continue from the preceding exercise.

Select View, *then* Set View, *then* Dview

`Command:` **`DVIEW`**

`Select objects:` **`P`** ↵ — Selects walls of room, desk, and chair

`CAmera/TArget/Distance/POints/PAn/`
`Zoom/TWist/CLip/Hide/Off/Undo/<eXit>:`
Select Options, *and then* TArget *from the screen menu*

`Enter angle from XY plane <-14.36>:`
`-14` ↵

Your display should resemble figure 21.11.

`Enter angle in X-Y plane from X axis`
`<45.00>:` *Enter* **22** *or pick approximate point*

`CAmera/TArget/Distance/POints/PAn/`
`Zoom/TWist/CLip/Hide/Off/Undo/<eXit>:`
Press Enter

You should see the corner of the building in the upper right of the drawing area (see fig. 21.12).

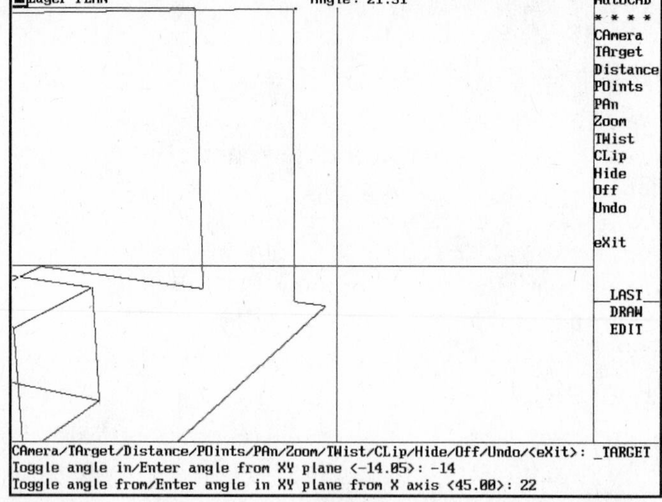

Figure 21.11: The DVIEW target option.

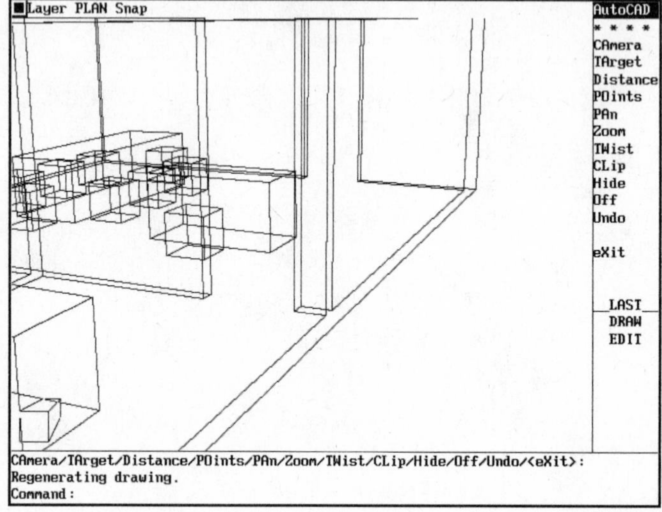

Figure 21.12: The room with a new target.

Selection Sets and Dragging in DVIEW

As you adjust these perspective images, you get a feel for your system's performance in updating DVIEW's preview image. Complex images slow the responsiveness. If your entities are extremely complex (with 3D

meshes), you might not get a fully formed preview. The solution is to select only enough entities to orient you in the drawing while you are in DVIEW. Remember that the whole drawing regenerates with the view after you exit DVIEW.

Using the PAn Option To Center the Room View

The PAn option enables you to change your view by moving the camera and target point side to side and up and down relative to the plane of your current view. The target and camera points move by the same displacement, so that the angle of the viewing direction and distance between the target and camera points remains unchanged. You pan by picking a base point and second point to show the displacement. AutoCAD dynamically drags the image as you drag the second point. In parallel projection, this effect is just like the effect of the PAN command. The entire image shifts, but the relative visual positions of objects remain unchanged. In perspective projection, the relative visual positions shift in the perspective as the image pans.

Try centering the desk in your current view of the room with the next exercise until it looks like figure 21.13.

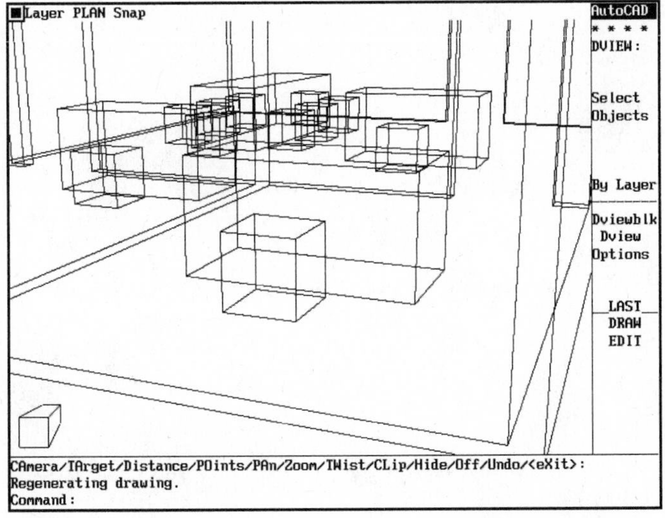

Figure 21.13:
Panned to the center of the room.

Centering the Room with PAn

Command: **DVIEW** ↵

`Select objects:` **P** ↵ — Selects walls of room, desk, and chair

`CAmera/TArget/Distance/POints/PAn/Zoom/ TWist/CLip/Hide/Off/Undo/<eXit>:` **PA** ↵

`Displacement base point:` *Pick any point near the desk*

`Second point:` *Drag desk to center of viewport and pick*

You should have a perspective view with the desk centered in the room (see fig. 21.13).

Sometimes it can be difficult to make the perspective view pan to fill the drawing area. But you should be able to achieve the effect you want by using a combination of PAn and Distance. Use, for example, PAn to center your view, and then use the Distance slider bar or try entering different distances to get the view you want.

Organizing Your Views

After you set up perfect perspectives, you can save and later restore them by using the VIEW command or its dialog-equivalent: DDVIEW. In the Distance option exercise, you saved the original perspective view as a view named OFFICE1. You use the DDVIEW command to restore it in the next exercise. DDVIEW, like VIEW, can name and save perspective views just like normal views. Saving a view stores all of the current DVIEW settings so that you can go about your work and later use DDVIEW to return your saved perspective view to the current viewport.

You also can save a collection of views including perspectives in multiple viewports. See Chapter 5 for details.

Previewing Hidden-Line Removal Using the Hide Option

DVIEW's Hide option has two purposes. The first is to check your clipping settings while you are in DVIEW. (You do clipping in the next section.) The second is to preview a selection of objects and get the view you want before doing a more time-consuming hidden-line removal with HIDE. DVIEW Hide works like the HIDE command, except you see the hide in perspective. DVIEW Hide, however, is temporary and affects only the entities selected. When you exit DVIEW, AutoCAD regenerates the drawing without the hide. To hide the full drawing, use the HIDE command.

You already have a perspective view that you saved as the OFFICE1 view, so use DDVIEW to restore it (see fig. 21.14). Then try the Hide option.

Using DVIEW's Hide Option

Choose View, *then* Set View, *then* Named view *and click on view OFFICE1 (see fig. 21.14), and then click on* Restore, *then* OK

Choose View, *then* Set View, *then* Dview

`Command:` **`DVIEW`**

`Select objects:` **`P`** ↵ — Selects walls of room, desk, and chair

`CAmera/TArget/Distance/POints/PAn/Zoom/TWist/CLip/Hide/Off/Undo/<eXit>:` **`H`** ↵

`CAmera/TArget/Distance/POints/PAn/Zoom/TWist/CLip/Hide/Off/Undo/<eXit>:` *Press Enter*

Figure 21.15 shows that everyhting is hidden. You cannot see anything but the nearest corner of the wall. You need to clip it away to see what is inside.

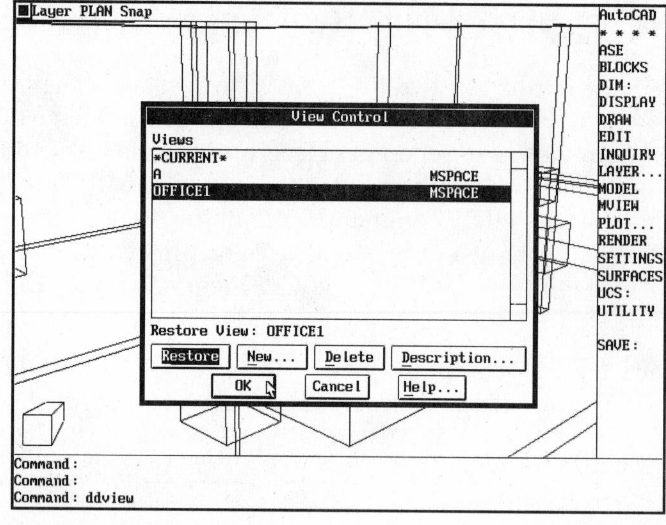

Figure 21.14:

Using DDVIEW to restore view OFFICE1.

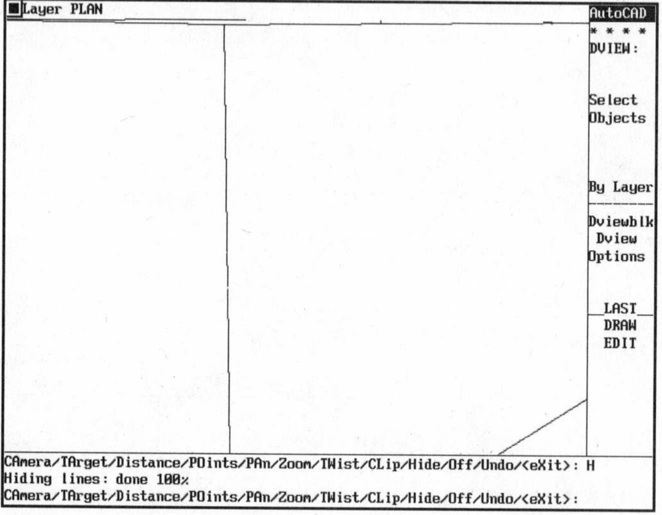

Figure 21.15:

The completely hidden DVIEW perspective.

Using DVIEW To Clip Away Obstructions

When you hid the office, the two walls forming the nearest corner obstructed your view. To present your drawing, you often must clip away objects in the foreground to reveal the objects of interest. As you work in

complex 3D wireframes, you often need to suppress the display of objects in the foreground or background that cannot be turned off with the LAYER command. The DVIEW CLip option enables you to place a front and a back clipping plane (or both) to get these effects. A *back clipping plane* obscures all objects behind it; a *front clipping plane* removes all objects in front of it. Clipping works in both parallel and perspective projection.

Clipping planes are perpendicular to the line of sight between the camera and the target. You place clipping planes by specifying their distances from the target. A positive distance puts the plane between the target and the camera (or behind the camera) whereas a negative distance puts it beyond the target. You also can set the front clipping plane to be at the camera with the CLip Front Eye option sequence. The CLip option gives you a `Back/Front/<Off>` prompt, which you use to set the back or front clipping distances or turn clipping off. Off turns both planes off, but the Back option also has an independent on/off option to control it.

When working with the first perspective drawing, before setting the camera-to-target distance to 19 feet, you might have noticed the front plane clipping effect. After you switch perspective mode on, it turns the front clip on and defaults its location to the current camera position (like the Eye option).

Next you try clipping the nearest corner and background (see fig. 21.16). Put your front clipping plane about two-and-a-half feet from the target. Then issue the HIDE command again for an unobstructed view of the desk and chair (see fig. 21.17). Before you exit Dview to see the full drawing, set the back clipping plane to about minus 10 feet (just beyond the room) to clip out the background clutter. Then issue a SHADE or HIDE command.

Using CLip To See into the Room and Remove Background Clutter

Select View, *then* Set View, *and then* Dview

`Command:` **`DVIEW`**

`Select objects:` **`P`** ↵ — Selects walls of room, desk, and chair

`CAmera/TArget/Distance/POints/PAn/Zoom/TWist/CLip/Hide/Off/Undo/<eXit>:`
Select Options, *and then* CLip *from the screen menu*

`Back/Front/<Off>:` **`F`** ↵

`Eye/<Distance from target> <19'-0">:` **`2'8`** ↵

Next, use the Hide option to see into the room.

`CAmera/TArget/Distance/POints/PAn/Zoom/ TWist/CLip/Hide/Off/Undo/<eXit>:` **H** ↵	
`CAmera/TArget/Distance/POints/PAn/Zoom/ TWist/CLip/Hide/Off/Undo/<eXit>:` **CL** ↵	Clips the back by turning the back plane on
`Back/Front/<Off>:` **B** ↵	
`ON/OFF/<Distance from target> <4'-0">:` *Move slider bar back and forth, and then position it just beyond the back corner at about -10' and pick (see fig. 21.18)*	Moves clipping plane forward and back, and then sets it
`CAmera/TArget/Distance/POints/PAn/Zoom/ TWist/CLip/Hide/Off/Undo/<eXit>:` *Press Enter*	

Now you can see the objects you want to present. It becomes easier to work in the drawing because most of the background clutter is gone. A little clutter remains in front of the back clipping plane.

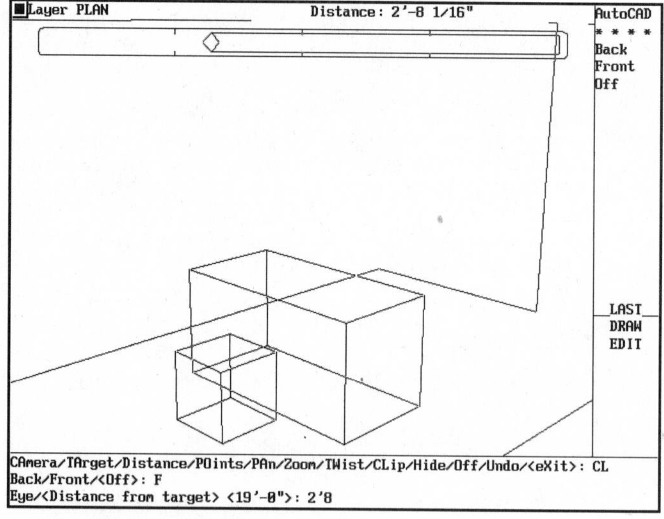

Figure 21.16:
During DVIEW with front clipping set to see into a room.

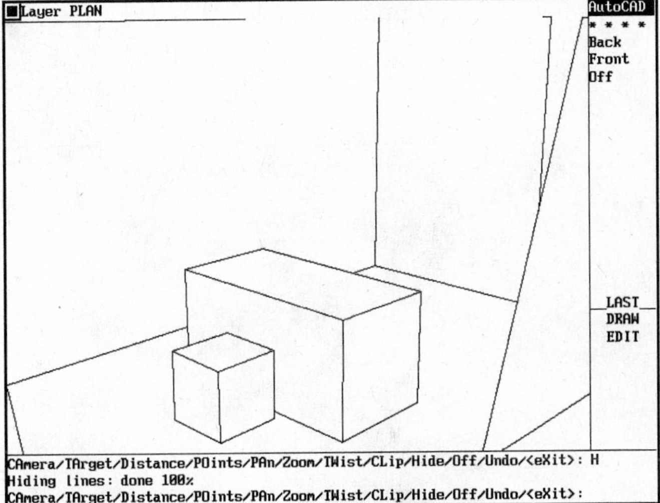

Figure 21.17:

HIDE with the nearest corner clipped.

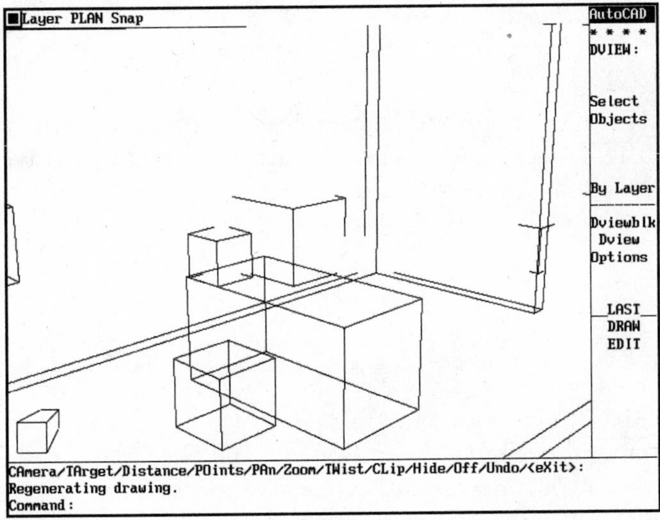

Figure 21.18:

View of drawing with the front and background clipped.

Using the HIDE command is faster than using the SHADE command in simple drawings, but in complex drawings using the SHADE option is much quicker (see fig. 21.19).

Figure 21.19:

The clipped room with SHADE.

Watch your clipping values. These values remain in effect after you exit the DVIEW command. If you think you have suddenly lost portions of your drawing, you probably left clipping on. If so, turn DVIEW CLip off.

Zooming To Change Camera Lenses

You cannot use the ZOOM command in a perspective view, but you can use the DVIEW command to change your field of view. The Dview Zoom option enables you to "change lenses" to include more (or less) of the image in your view, without changing the location of camera and target points. The default lens length is 50mm, which provides a field of view that looks natural—just as a normal lens (50mm to 55mm lens for a 35mm camera) does for a real camera. An increased lens length (105mm in the next exercise) has a telephoto effect (see fig. 21.20). A decreased lens length (35mm) gives a wide-angle effect (see fig. 21.21). The Zoom command used on parallel projection acts just like AutoCAD's standard ZOOM Center. The

Zoom slider and the coordinate readout show the zoom ratio, instead of a lens length.

Use your current view in the following exercise to try switching lenses.

Using ZOOM To View Room with Different Lenses

`Command:` *Select* View, *then* Set View, *and then* Dview	
`Select objects:` **P** ↵	Selects walls of room, desk, and chair
`CAmera/TArget/Distance/POints/PAn/Zoom/ TWist/CLip/Hide/Off/Undo/<eXit>:` **Z** ↵	
Drag the slider back and forth	Changes only the image scale, not the perspective
`Adjust lens length <50.000mm>:` **105** ↵	Creates a telephoto effect
`CAmera/TArget/Distance/POints/PAn/Zoom/ TWist/CLip/Hide/Off/Undo/<eXit>:` **Z** ↵	
`Adjust lens length <105.000mm>:` **35** ↵	Creates a wide-angle effect
`CAmera/TArget/Distance/POints/PAn/Zoom/ TWist/CLip/Hide/Off/Undo/<eXit>:` **X** ↵	
Save the drawing and continue.	

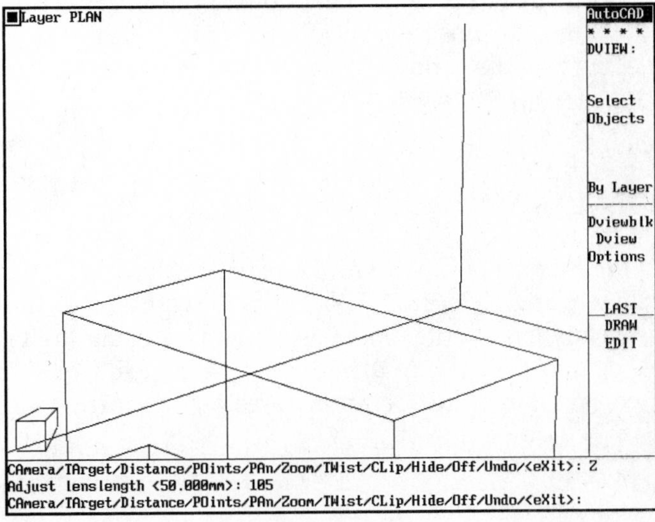

Figure 21.20:

View with a 105mm lens.

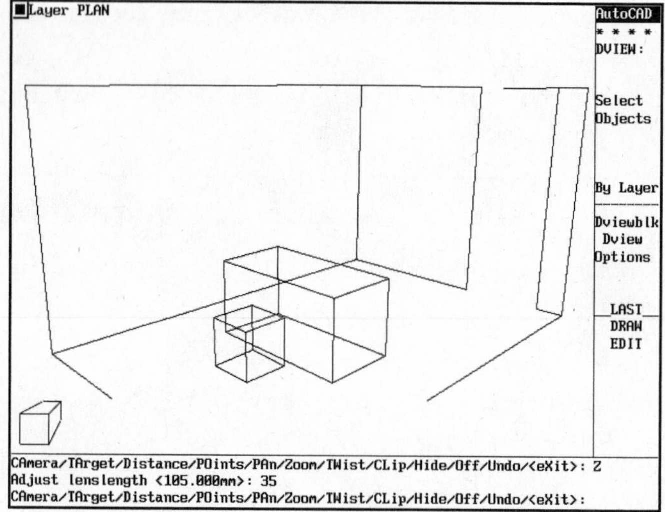

Figure 21.21:
View with a 35mm lens.

The 35mm lens is a good choice for interior room views because its wider angle encompasses more of the room.

Contrary to popular belief, the lens length does not affect perspective. Only the distance and angle from camera to target determine perspective. The lens length only determines the width of the view. Many people think lens length affects perspective because wide-angle (short) lenses coincidentally tend to be used for close distances and telephoto (long) lenses are used for distant subjects. Unlike real lenses (especially short fish-eyes), AutoCAD's lenses are perfect with no distortion. They always yield a geometrically true perspective.

Using the TWist Option

DVIEW's TWist option enables you to rotate your view around your line of sight by specifying an angle. Because TWist uses the right-hand rule of rotation, a positive angle is counterclockwise. If you try using the TWist option, you can see how easy it is to turn the room upside down. After you try this option, you can undo the operation to restore the current view.

As you develop a set of views, you might want to capture them as slides for later reference or presentation.

Making a 3D Slide Presentation

Slides are the mainstay for AutoCAD presentations because of their early use in computer shows. When you make a slide, you save a screen image that AutoCAD can quickly recreate on-screen.

Using the MSLIDE Command To Make a Slide

The MSLIDE (Make slide) command creates a disk file with the extension SLD. AutoCAD does not store all the drawing file information in the SLD file. It only stores the display vector list and colors needed to paint the screen quickly. AutoCAD cannot edit slides. If you want to change a slide, you must edit the drawing file that was used to create the slide and then create a new file.

You make a slide of your current office view in the next exercise (see fig. 21.22). You must exit the DVIEW command and use the HIDE or SHADE commands to get a hidden or shaded view. Then you can use MSLIDE to make a slide named VIEW-1.

Using MSLIDE To Create a Slide of the Office

Continue in the OFFICE3D drawing from the previous exercise.

`Command:` **`HIDE`** ↵	Removes hidden lines
`Command:` **`MSLIDE`** ↵	
Enter `VIEW-1` *in the* File *box* ↵	Stores image on disk as VIEW-1.SLD

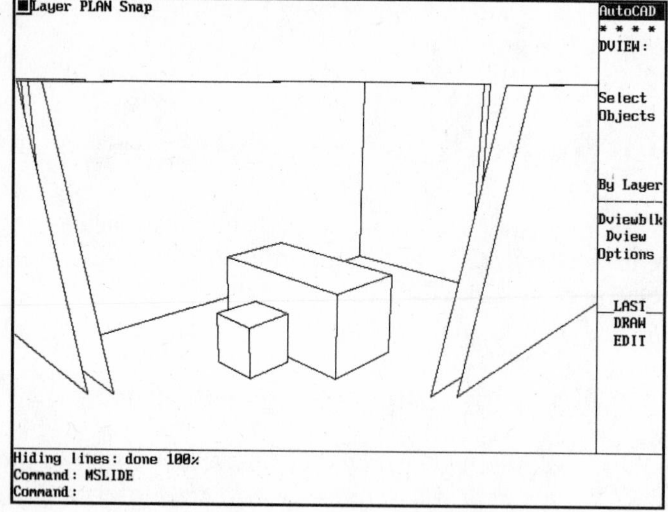

Figure 21.22: View of the office for slide.

Using VSLIDE To Display a Slide

The VSLIDE (View slide) command recalls the SLD file from the disk and displays the slide image. When you display a slide, it temporarily paints over the graphics window and leaves whatever you were working on intact and active, but invisible.

To see how this feature works, follow the next instructions to put back a plan view (WCS) of the office, then display the VIEW-1 slide.

Using VSLIDE To View the Slide

Select View, *then* Set View, *then* Plan View, *then* World	
`Command: VSLIDE`	
Enter `VIEW-1` *in the* File *box, and press Enter, or double-click on* VIEW-1 *in the file list*	Displays the slide, (see fig. 21.22)
Select View, *then* Redraw	Removes the slide

After you redraw the window, you should be back in plan view.

Slides appear over your actual drawing. Any attempt at drawing on or editing the slide actually appears on the drawing, which is obscured by the slide.

Use a viewport to display a slide for reference while you work in another viewport.

Making Slides for a Slide Show

Next you produce a brief slide show, but first you need to create at least three more slides. You create three more perspective views and make a slide of each. These next three views take you around the office plan. VIEW-2 and VIEW-3 provide two views of the large room on the right (see figs. 21.23 and 21.24). VIEW-4 gives a view of the office with two desks in the upper left (see fig. 21.25). Remember these view names because you need them to prepare corresponding AutoCAD Render images in the next chapter. After you create the slides, end the drawing and exit AutoCAD to create a script file.

Using MSLIDE To Create Three More Slides

`Command:` **`DVIEW`** ↵

Select a representative sampling of walls, desks, and chairs

Use POints *to set target to 33',33', 2' and camera to 51'6,21'6,5'6*	Sets viewpoint for VIEW-2 slide
Use Distance *and accept default*	Turns on perspective
Use Zoom *to set lens to 35mm, then exit*	
Use HIDE *or* SHADE *on the drawing*	
Use MSLIDE *to make a slide with name VIEW-2 (see fig. 21.23)*	

`Command:` **`DVIEW`** ↵

Select Previous objects *and use* POints *to set target to 52',35'6,0' and camera* perspective *to 33',14'6,6', and then exit*	Adjusts viewpoint, but not lens
Use SHADE *or* HIDE *and make a slide with name VIEW-3 (see fig. 21.24)*	

`Command:` **`DVIEW`** ↵

Select Previous objects *and use* POints *to set target to 38',33'6,0' and camera to 17'6,25',6', and then exit*

Use SHADE *or* HIDE *and make a slide with name VIEW-4 (see fig. 21.25)*

Return to WCS plan view of office

Zoom all

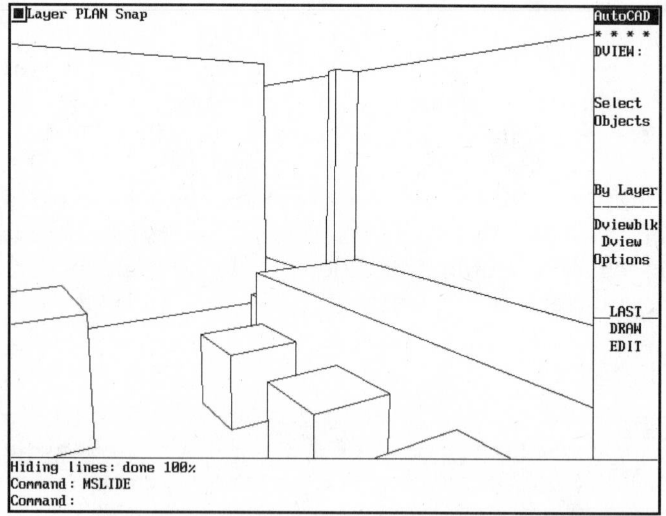

Figure 21.23:

Slide VIEW-2.

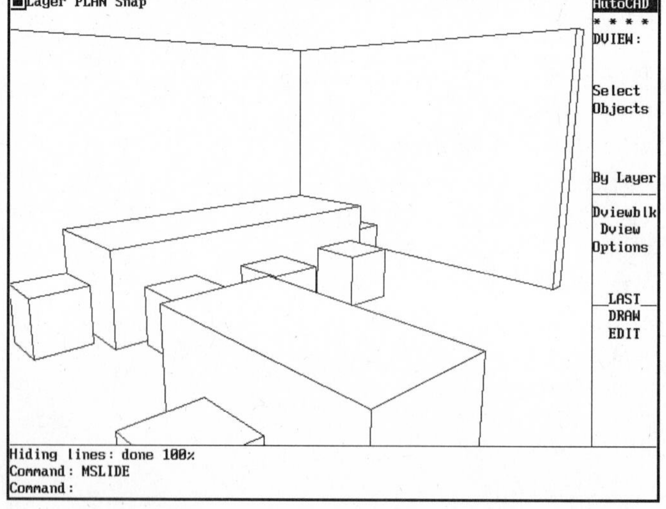

Figure 21.24:

Slide VIEW-3.

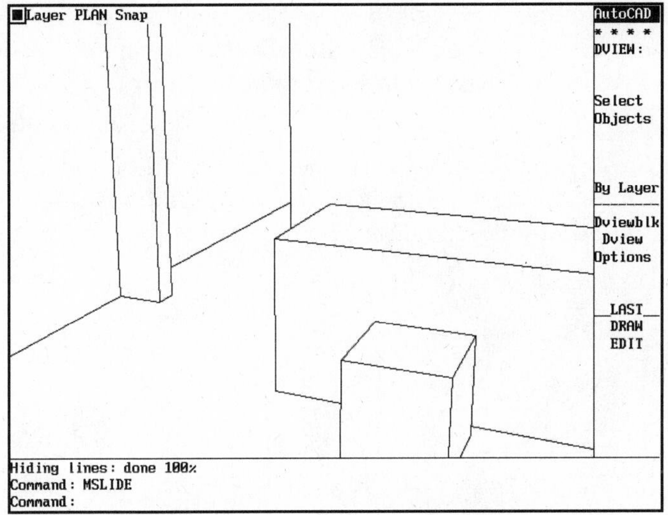

Figure 21.25:

Slide VIEW-4.

Automating Slide Shows Using Script Files

You have the slides. Now how do you make a script? SCRIPT is a utility command for hands-free operation. A *script file* is a list of commands, input, and responses stored in a text file and played character for character exactly as if it were typed directly at the keyboard. Like slides, scripts are designed for self-running demonstrations of AutoCAD at presentations and shows.

Making a Script File for Slide Presentations

Scripts are ideally suited for controlling AutoCAD shows. Script files are ASCII text files and have an SCR extension. In order to create or modify a script, you need a text editor or word processor that creates ASCII text files. Edlin, DOS 5.0's Edit, or any word processor that can create unformatted text files works fine.

If you are using the IA7 DISK, you have the SLIDSHO.SCR script file to run the four-slide show. If you do not have the IA7 DISK, you can create the script with Edit. Enter it exactly as shown in the next exercise.

The SCRIPT command loads and starts a script. Scripts use a DELAY command to control each slide's display time. Delays are in milliseconds (2000 is 2 seconds). The RSCRIPT command repeats a script.

The SLIDSHO.SCR script (shown following) controls the display of the slides, VIEW-1 through VIEW-4, by stringing together a series of VSLIDE and DELAY commands. The final RSCRIPT command loops the script to start over. After you create the file, move on to the next exercise to run the script.

Creating a Script for a Slide Show

You have the SLIDSHO.SCR script. Look at it if you like, and then test it in the next exercise.

Create the SLIDSHO.SCR text file, and then test it in the next exercise.

Use Edlin, Edit, or your word processor to create or look at SLIDSHO.SCR. Do not use tabs or any trailing spaces. Press Enter to end the last line.

Enter the following:

```
vslide view-1
delay 2000
vslide view-2
delay 2000
vslide view-3
delay 2000
vslide *view-4
delay 2000
rscript
```

Save SLIDSHO.SCR and exit your editor.

Using Scripts for Other Purposes

Scripts can do other things besides run slide shows. Scripts offer three unique advantages. First, you can start them outside the drawing editor from the operating system prompt. Second, they can end a drawing, run through the main menu, the configuration menu, the plot dialogues, and go

back into a drawing. The third advantage is that scripts can loop indefinitely. Scripts are sometimes used to modify or plot a batch of drawing files. For details, see Chapter 11 on plotting.

Using Script To Run a Slide Show

You now have a script for AutoCAD's SCRIPT command to run. Run the script, sit back, and enjoy the slide show. The slides show in the drawing area, cycling through in sequence and repeating until you cancel the script by pressing Backspace or Ctrl-C.

Using SCRIPT To Run the Slide Show

Command: **SCRIPT** ↵

Enter **SLIDSHO** *in the* File *text box, and select* OK

The script commands scroll by on the command line, and the slides display.

```
Command: vslide
Slide file <OFFICE3D>: view-1
```

Other script commands and slides appear.

`Command: delay Delay time in milliseconds: 2000`	
`Command: rscript`	Repeats the script sequence
`Command: vslide`	
`Slide file <OFFICE3D>: view-1`	
`Command: vslide`	
`Slide file <OFFICE3D>: *view-2`	
`Command: delay Delay time in milliseconds: 2000`	
`Command: vslide`	
`Command:` *Press Backspace*	Halts the script

If a script has an error, it stops and returns to the command prompt. You can correct it with your text editor. Look for the error following the last command that executed correctly.

After you run the slide show, you can adjust the delay or slide name sequence to alter the show. If you want to show slides of your own, substitute your own names and extend the script by repeating the VSLIDE *name*, DELAY pattern.

Stopping and Resuming Scripts

You can stop a script by pressing Backspace or Ctrl-C. The script finishes its current command and returns to the `Command:` prompt. You can do some work, and then pick up where you stopped the script by using the RESUME command.

Slide Library Files

Although slides were invented for presentations, they now have an important use as images for icon menus. To avoid cluttering your disk with dozens of slide files, you can group and store slides in slide library (SLB) files.

To display a slide from a library, use the format *libraryname(slidename)* as the slide name in your script or with VSLIDE at the `Command:` prompt. When you display an icon menu, you are displaying slides from the standard ACAD.SLB slide library file.

Making a Slide Library File

You can create your own slide library files by using AutoCAD's SLIDELIB.EXE program. The process of creating a slide library requires the following three steps:

- Make all the needed slides.
- Create an ASCII text file (as an example call it SLDLIST.TXT), listing each slide name (without the SLD extension) on a separate line. Do not include any extra carriage returns or spaces. Make sure that you press Enter after the last name.

- Run the SLIDELIB.EXE program from the DOS prompt to create a SLB library file from your *slidelist*.TXT file and the listed slide files.

Assuming that the slides and a slide list file named SLDLIST.TXT are in your current IA directory and that the SLIDELIB.EXE program is in the ACAD directory, the command line format to create a slide library named IA-LIB.SLB is as follows:

```
C:\IA> \ACAD\SLIDELIB IA-LIB <SLDLIST.TXT
```

Using AutoFlix, the Low-Cost Animator

If you like slide shows, you should look into AutoFlix, another Autodesk program. AutoFlix can combine AutoCAD and AutoShade slides with text files and even simple musical notes to create a movie. AutoFlix includes AutoLISP programs to automate the production of slides and shaded images. It can even follow animation sequences. You can make the movies self-running or interactive. Interactive movies prompt the user for a choice and then branch to various movie subsections or even run external programs. AutoFlix requires an EGA (or VGA) standard video card. The AutoFlix program is *shareware*, meaning that you can copy and distribute it freely. But if you find AutoFlix useful, you are required to pay Autodesk $35 for it.

If you are a member of CompuServe, you can download AutoFlix from the ACAD Forum. AutoFlix is available in a file called AFEGA.ZIP for EGA card owners, or AFVGA.ZIP for VGA card owners. Before you download either file, though, you might want to read the file AFLIX.TXT, which describes what AutoFlix can do in more detail. Many ready-made AutoFlix movies also are available in the ACAD forum. All of the files mentioned here are located in the Shade/Flix/Rman files library. AutoFlix also is included with the AutoShade program.

Using Autodesk Animator, Animator Pro, and 3D Studio for Creating Presentations

Sometimes putting together a group of slide files using AutoFlix or a script file is not an impressive enough presentation. Maybe you need to add a splash of color, add text and titling, use special effects such as dissolves and wipes, or even add real character animation. For those times, Autodesk has other answers—Autodesk Animator (320 x 200 pixels), Animator Professional (resolution-independent), and 3D Studio.

Animator offers all the features just mentioned and more. Animator can add color, special effects, and titles to your animation to achieve professional-quality animated sequences.

In addition to AutoCAD slides, AutoCAD Render and AutoShade RenderMan rendering files, Animator can import GIF images. GIF is the popular graphic format standardized by CompuServe. With additional hardware, you can even incorporate videotaped sequences and photographs in your presentation and export presentations to videotape. For an in-depth look at Animator, see *Inside Autodesk Animator* (New Riders Publishing).

Autodesk 3D Studio is a combined modeling, rendering, and animation package designed for presentation graphics. It features a low price and an easy-to-use interface. You can load AutoCAD models into 3D Studio by using DXF or filmroll files, and then manipulate the models in 3D Studio. Or you can create 3D models in 3D Studio with its integrated modeling tools. The modeler in 3D Studio is not as precise as AutoCAD, however, and cannot take advantage of the AutoCAD third-party products available. Nor can you plot out your 3D designs from 3D Studio; you can only print them or output to video tape. You can, however, render and animate your models in 3D Studio in many ways. The quality of renderings made in 3D Studio approaches those of real photographs because you can assign life-like materials and textures to surfaces. You also can simulate realistic shadows and atmospheric effects. When animated to produce motion effects, your 3D models come alive with presentation power. *AutoCAD 3D Design and Presentation* (New Riders Publishing) details the integrated use of Animator Pro, 3D Studio, and AutoShade RenderMan with your 3D AutoCAD models to create professional presentations.

Drawing and editing commands normally work in parallel projection views created by VPOINT or DVIEW, with or without clipping. But drawing and editing are restricted in perspectives.

Editing, Annotating, and Plotting Perspectives

How do you edit perspective drawings? The big limitation in perspective is not being able to pick points. Several commands do not enable entity selection in perspective because they require picking by point. These commands include BREAK, FILLET, CHAMFER, TRIM, EXTEND, the UCS Entity option, and dimensioning by entity picking, but you can still use these commands by typing coordinates or picking in other viewports. Normal object selection, including entity picking, still works with some exceptions.

The PAN, ZOOM, and SKETCH commands are not enabled in perspective. These commands cancel themselves, and AutoCAD prompts: `This command may not be invoked in a perspective view.` Rather than use PAN and ZOOM, use DVIEW's PAn and Zoom options. These limitations are not severe, largely because you can easily use DVIEW in multiple viewports.

Using Viewports To Work with Perspective Views

Rather than trying to work directly in a perspective view, you can use multiple viewports. Enter points in one viewport while you observe your perspective in another. Any command that you execute in a normal viewport is reflected in the perspective viewport. As you modify your drawing, the perspective view updates to match the changes.

In this last exercise, set up three viewports and use one for a perspective view, another for editing in parallel projection, and a third for plan view editing (see fig. 21.26). Use the HIDE option in the perspective viewport because you cannot select objects after invoking the SHADE command.

Editing a Perspective in Viewports

Use View *to restore the OFFICE1 view*

Select View, *then* Tilemode, *then* Off

Select View, *then* Mview, *then* 3 Viewports, *and create three viewports with the* Right *and* Fit *options*

`Command:` **`MS`**↵ — Return to model space

Use DVIEW *with the* Clip *options and re-create a 2'8" front clipping plane*

Use HIDE *on the right viewport*

Use DVIEW *with the* Off *option and select any object(s) to return top left viewport to parallel view*

Use plan *to set bottom left viewport to WCS plan view*

Zoom center 25',20' with height 12' in bottom left viewport (see figure 21.26)

Make right viewport current.

Select Modify, *then* Move

`Command: _move`

`Select objects:` *Select desk and chair* — Object selection works fine

`Base point or displacement:` *Try to pick a point in perspective*

`Pointing in perspective view not allowed here`

Make upper left viewport current

`Base point or displacement:` *Use object snap INT in top left viewport to pick rightmost bottom corner of desk*

Make lower left viewport current

`Second point of displacement:` *Drag and pick in lower left viewport to place desk in upper right corner (see fig. 21.27)*

As you dragged the desk and chair in the lower left viewport, the images dragged with you in all viewports (see fig. 21.27). A REDRAW cleans up the upper left viewport, but the right viewport requires re-hiding. If the right viewport was not hidden, a REDRAW also cleans it up.

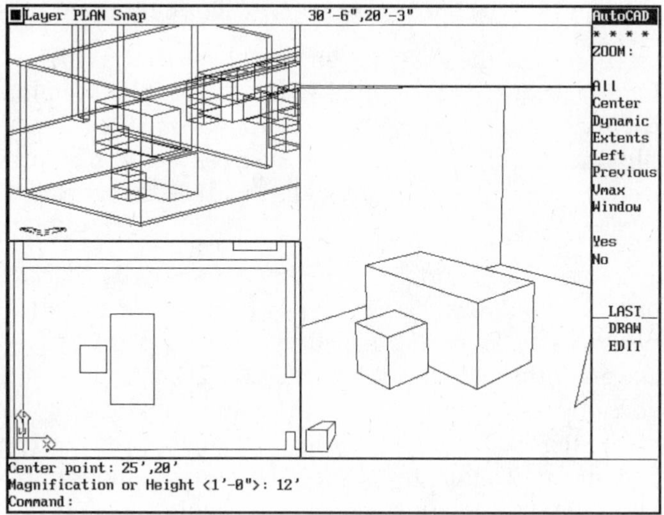

Figure 21.26:

The three viewports before editing.

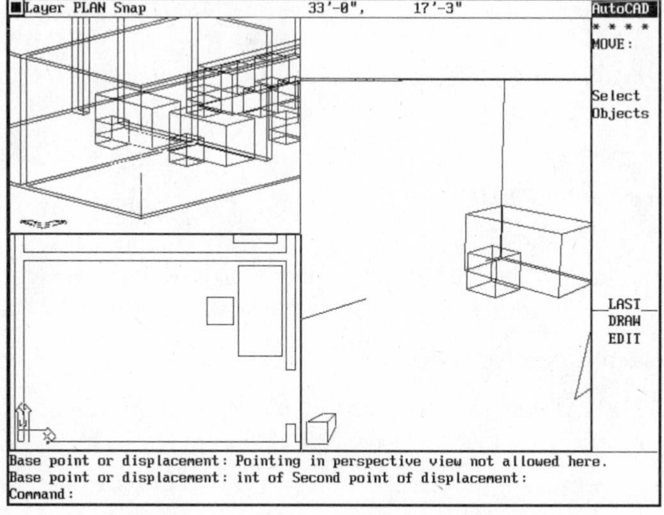

Figure 21.27:

The three viewports after editing.

Annotating and Plotting Perspective Drawings

Sooner or later, you will want to enhance or annotate a 3D perspective image. You can plot a single perspective image by plotting the current viewport. What you see is what you get, except for any hides or shades. You can use the PLOT command's hidden-line removal option if you like.

But you might want to plot the perspective on a sheet with a title or other images, or with annotations, or do a bit of rendering to it before plotting. Adding title text, annotations, or drawing a border around a perspective view is practically impossible in 3D. Placing 3D trees and shrubs around a building perspective is impractical and makes the drawing slow to regenerate.

The best way to compose and annotate a perspective is to use paper space. Then you can use all of AutoCAD's commands to annotate and add rendering details to the drawing. Treat a perspective view in a paper space viewport just like any other viewport. You can add 2D annotation and other details to the view in paper space and plot the results. If you plot in paper space, the view(s) that are current at plot time, parallel or perspective, clipped or not, are the views that get plotted. To have the plot remove hidden lines in a particular viewport, select it by using the MVIEW Hideplot option. See Chapter 13 for details on composing and plotting in paper space.

You can delete OFFICE.DWG, which you no longer need, but keep OFFICE3D.DWG for the next chapter.

Summary

Do not get carried away with 3D and perspectives. Use them for what you need, but 2D is simpler and quicker if 3D is not really required.

Here are some techniques for speed and efficiency when you use DVIEW:

- Use the DVIEW house icon (or your own custom icon) instead of selecting complex entities.
- Select a representative subset of entities to use in DVIEW.

- Use block redefinition, substituting simple blocks for complex ones until you get it right, and then swap them back for the final presentation images.
- Use object snaps and point filters to set points in DVIEW instead of using trial and error (unless in perspective). If you know where you want to look from (camera point) and what you want to look at (target point), then you can use object snaps and XYZ point filters to align them with known geometry. If setting perspectives, get the points ahead of time using the ID command.
- Use sliders for dynamic image adjustment, and then enter exact values if you need precision in your views.
- Use named views to save and restore your perspectives and other DVIEW settings after you get them right.

In the next chapter you learn how to create realistic renderings within AutoCAD using the AutoCAD Render commands. You place lights, define multiple "cameras", and assign material properties such as color and reflectivity. Using AutoCAD Render, you learn how to create more realistic images for more effective presentations.

22

Inside Shading and Rendering

Shading or rendering can turn your 3D drawing into an eye-catching image. The AutoCAD SHADE command and AutoCAD Render (also called the *AutoCAD Visualization Extension*, or AVE) let you illuminate and shade your 3D drawings to achieve more realistic 3D images. These tools can help you better visualize and present the drawing.

On a 256-color (or better) display, rendered 3D drawings are absolutely impressive. For example, figure 22.1 shows the rendering of the chair you created in Chapter 20. Think of SHADE and AutoCAD Render as an art studio for your drawings. Whether you use SHADE, AutoCAD Render, or AutoShade 2.0 with RenderMan to add photorealistic textures and reflections, you will impress your clients with improved presentations.

The emphasis in this chapter is on AutoCAD's built-in shading and rendering capabilities. How you prepare your drawings in AutoCAD has a big impact on the appearance and efficiency of your renderings. Seemingly slight differences between 2D or 3D commands, extruded 2D entities or 3D surfaces, and the order of entity creation in AutoCAD can make a big difference in the results you get with SHADE or AutoCAD Render. In this chapter you learn how the use of the 3D tools provided in AutoCAD. You also learn how to work out good lighting schemes, which are keys to creating render-efficient 3D drawings in AutoCAD.

Figure 22.1:

The 3D shaded chair.

Deciding To Hide, Shade, or Render

You already have used the HIDE command to remove hidden lines from 3D wireframe drawings. HIDE works well when you need to quickly visualize your 3D drawing. AutoCAD also features the SHADE and RENDER commands to help you visualize your 3D drawings. The SHADE command produces several types of surface renderings, and takes only about as much time to work as two screen regenerations. SHADE is quick and can produce shaded images without light sources or materials.

The RENDER command provides still greater control over lighting and materials, enabling you to create more realistic images. RENDER also enables you to save your images in a number of popular image formats. You can use these images to create impressive presentations in AutoFlix or Animator Pro.

If the Release 12 HIDE command does not properly remove hidden lines in your drawings, you can configure AutoCAD to use the old Release 11 HIDE command. You can change this setting by using the CONFIG command's operating parameters submenu. Be aware that the old HIDE command can be 10 to 100 times *slower* than the standard Release 12 HIDE command, but it handles intersecting entities better.

Using SHADE

The SHADE command can produce up to four types of renderings, depending on the number of colors your screen can display. You can use the SHADEDGE system variable to control the type of rendering produced by the SHADE command.

You can set SHADEDGE to one of the following four values:

- **SHADEDGE 0.** A value of 0 results in shading without highlighted edges. This type of shading requires a 256-color display.
- **SHADEDGE 1.** A value of 1 creates shading with edges highlighted in the background color. This type of shading requires a 256-color display.
- **SHADEDGE 2.** A value of 2 simulates hidden-line removal. This type of shading works with all displays.
- **SHADEDGE 3.** A value of 3 draws faces filled with their original colors and highlights the edges in the background color. This type of shading works with all displays.

Figure 22.2 illustrates the results of the various shading options when they are applied to the chair you created in Chapter 20. Notice that highlighted edges (SHADEDGE 1) break the images into many small faces. Highlighted edges work best with simple drawings.

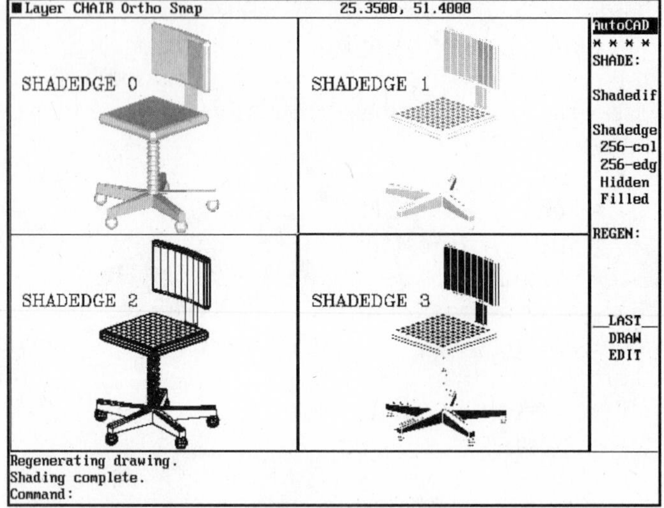

Figure 22.2:

The four SHADEDGE options, applied with the SHADE command.

If you have a 256-color display that uses AutoCAD's standard color scheme, you can create shaded images by setting SHADEDGE to 0 or 1. The SHADE command uses over-the-shoulder lighting, automatically providing a light source from directly behind your viewpoint, regardless of your view. The default lighting uses 70 percent direct light reflecting from this source and 30 percent ambient background light. You can set the SHADEDIF system variables to adjust these percentages. The SHADEDIF setting can range from 0 to 100; the default value is 70. Higher values increase reflectivity and contrast. The intensity of the shading on a particular face is greatest if it is perpendicular to the light source. The shading's intensity decreases as the angle of the face increases.

Notice how a rendering created with SHADEDGE 2 produces similar results to the HIDE command. SHADE may be faster in some cases, but HIDE still has two advantages over SHADE. You can select entities after a HIDE, but you must regenerate the screen after a SHADE before you can select entities. HIDE also can put the hidden lines on a special layer for viewing or plotting.

In the following exercise, you use the SHADE command on the 3D chair from Chapter 20. You begin by using VPOINT to get a view you like; then you can SHADE the chair.

Shading the Chair

Begin a new drawing named **\IA\CHAIR=\IA\IA7CHAIR**, replacing your previous CHAIR drawing.

Open the drawing CHAIR, which you created in Chapter 20.

Turn off the grid and set SPLFRAME to 0 to hide invisible edges.

`Command:` **VPOINT**↵	
`Rotate/<0.0000,0.0000,1.0000>:` **R**↵	Specifies the Rotate method
`Enter angle in X:Y plane from X axis <0>:` **240**↵	
`Enter angle from X:Y plane:` **19**↵	Regenerates the display with the 3D view
Zoom Center at 0,0,18 with a height of 42	Centers the image
`Command:` *Choose* Render, *then* Shade	Issues the SHADE command
`Regenerating drawing` `Shading complete`	Displays percentage of completion while calculating, and shades the chair
`Command:` **SAVE**↵	

Experiment with different SHADEDGE and SHADEDIF values, noting the effect they have on the rendered image.

After the SHADE command shades the drawing, you must regenerate the display before you can select entities. Both shaded and hidden-line images disappear with a regeneration, but you can make slides to save them for later viewing. You cannot plot a shaded image, so AutoCAD still must remove hidden lines for plotting.

When you are finished using the SHADE command to test various viewpoints, go to the next section and use the RENDER command to create a more realistic image. The rendered image can be output to an image file, for use in desktop publishing, presentations or hard copy.

Using AutoCAD Render

The AutoCAD Render incorporates most of the functionality of AutoShade 2.0 into AutoCAD. The key element of an AutoCAD Render rendering is the *scene*. When you make an image, you *shoot* a scene in your drawing. A scene consists of a 3D drawing, a view, and one or more light sources. Making a scene is like setting up a real-world scene for a still or motion picture. When you create your scene in AutoCAD, you set your viewpoint and lighting, then you execute the SCENE command. Think of a scene as an individual frame of film. You can create as many scenes as you like.

The realism of your shaded images depends on the number of colors that AutoCAD Render can use. You can obtain the best results by using a 256-color (or better) display driver.

Setting Up for AutoCAD Render

The exercises in this chapter assume that AutoCAD Render and its supporting files are installed, and that AutoCAD Render is properly configured. You may also want to go through the *AutoCAD Render Reference Manual* tutorial to explore the AutoCAD Render commands and menus.

Using the AutoCAD Render Tools

You can find the AutoCAD Render tools on the Render pull-down menu (see fig. 22.3). The principal AutoCAD Render command is RENDER. You can use other AutoCAD Render commands to adjust the type and quality of the rendering, setup lights and scenes, or save and replay images. You can use the RENDER command without any other AutoCAD Render setup. By default, RENDER uses the same over-the-shoulder lighting as SHADE, and creates a rendered image of the current view. In the following exercise, you test the RENDER command on the CHAIR drawing, which already is loaded.

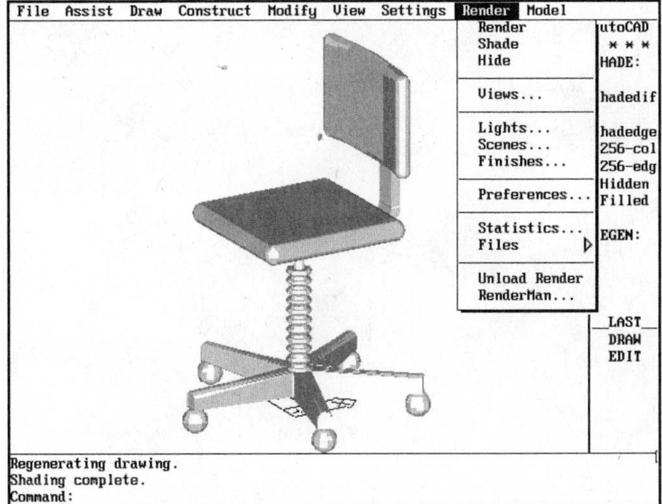

Figure 22.3:

The Render pull-down menu.

Quick Rendering

```
Command: RENDER↵
Initial load, please wait...
Initializing AutoCAD Render Render
Using current view.
Default scene selected.
Projecting objects into view plane.
Processing face 2624.
Applying parallel projection.
Calculate extents for faces.
Calculate shading and assign colors.
Z-buffering polygons in 1 band.
Outputting scanlines of current band.
```

Renders the drawing, providing progress messages during the process

After a few moments, the rendering appears as shown in figure 22.4.

The first time you run AutoCAD Render, you may receive configuration prompts. These prompts must be properly answered for AutoCAD Render to function. Refer to the *AutoCAD Interface, Installation and Performance Guide* and the documentation for your video display hardware for further information.

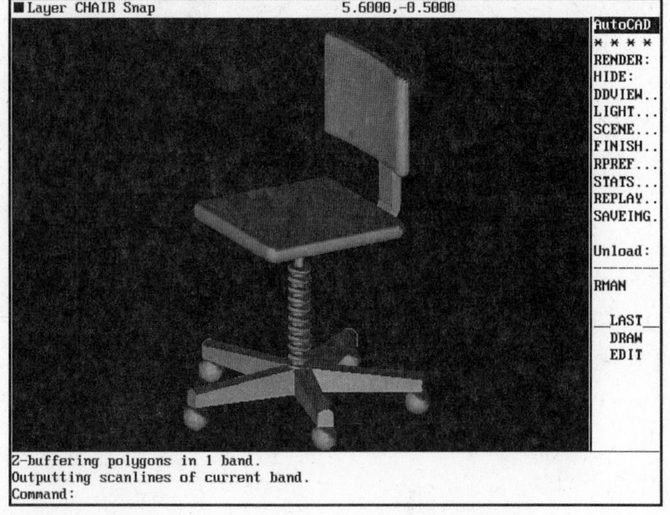

Figure 22.4:

The first chair rendering.

RENDER gives a quick preview of the chair, showing the effects of the default lighting and finishes (see fig. 22.4). You may notice some faces apparently missing. These faces are *back* faces. By default, AutoCAD Render does not render back faces, as rendering back faces can double the processing time.

The chair may appear quite dark. This darkness is due to default lighting conditions assumed by the RENDER command and the colors the chair was drawn in. By default, RENDER uses a Quick Render mode, giving you a quick method for previewing a rendering. A Quick Render, as its name implies, can be much faster than a Full Render (which is explored later). A Full Render provide more control over the rendering, but those controls can lengthen the image processing time.

Be careful when you construct 3Dfaces. In AutoCAD Render, *front* faces obscure *back* faces. Faces whose vertexes are in a clockwise order from the current viewpoint are considered front faces, while counterclockwise faces are considered back faces. You can set UCS to Entity to check an existing face. If the Z axis points toward the camera, it is a front face. The MIRROR command flips a face. The wrong order can create a rendering where the back faces obscure the front faces. The Back Face Normal is Negative check box on the More Options dialog of the Rendering Preferences dialog reverses the order of the rendering if you get the wrong order.

Preparing 3D Drawings for AutoCAD Render

Any of AutoCAD's entities can be used in a 3D wireframe image drawing. The RENDER command, however, ignores all entities without surfaces or thickness. It recognizes only the following entities:

- 3Dfaces and 3D polyline meshes
- Extruded entities (entities with a thickness)
- AME solids

If your shaded images have missing areas, they may have been created as wireframe lines, which RENDER does not recognize. You need to go back and reconstruct your 3D drawing with extrusions or surfaces.

When it becomes necessary to overlap or nest entities, small changes in Z values or thickness can control the final order and appearance of your image.

Sprucing Up the Drawn Image

The RENDER command renders each face with a single shade of color, which may cause a large surface to look wrong when it is rendered. For example, a long wall receding away from your point of view should normally become darker as it recedes. Because RENDER applies a single shade of color, however, you can get this shading effect only by making the wall's surface out of many smaller faces. Try to anticipate the need for mesh surfaces where you want complex or graduated surface effects. You can control the number of faces on curved surfaces by adjusting VIEWRES and the surface system variables SURFTAB1, SURFTAB2, SURFU, and SURFV.

Hatch patterns can add texture to 3D drawings. The hatch pattern must first be exploded and the resulting entities given a small thickness. You can apply a small thickness to other entities (such as lines and points) so that RENDER can recognize them.

Defining objects with surfaces to create RENDER-ready drawings usually requires more work and more entities than the typical 3D line drawing. The more faces you use in constructing your drawing, the better your rendering will look. However, there is a trade-off. The more faces you have, the larger the drawing file becomes, and AutoCAD's processing time increases. For example, a Full Render rendering of the chair drawing takes anywhere from moments to minutes (or longer), depending on your hardware and the rendering options.

Using Perspective in AutoCAD Render

AutoCAD Render renders orthographic and perspective views. In perspective views, smaller objects may not display the perspective well. You can enhance perspective views and show relative scale by adding foreground and background objects. In architectural scenes, these objects can be walls, trees, and vehicles. You can enhance mechanical drawings by adding contrasting surfaces in the background of the view. Patterns—such as a checker-board or parallel lines—also make good perspective-enhancing backgrounds.

The rendered chair looks good, although it is floating in space. Now you can move on to work with the office drawing. The remainder of the exercises use the office drawing to show you how to control views, lighting, and material finishes in making shaded scenes. These perspective renderings match the perspective-view slides that you created in Chapter 21.

Calling for Lights, Camera, Action!

Before you can get anything onto a roll of film, you need a camera and lights. You shoot a scene with the RENDER command in much the same way you do with a camera. AutoCAD Render provides two types of light blocks (three with RenderMan) and commands to establish *scenes* and material *finishes* in your drawing. Once you create the views, assign finishes and place the lights, you can create one or more scenes.

Making Scenes for Drawings

You have two options for working with the office drawing. You can either work with the simple, rather primitive, office drawing from Chapter 21, or create a more realistic office by inserting the CHAIR drawing from Chapter

20 and the TABLE drawing from Chapter 19 into the corner office of the office drawing. The table and the chair contain many faces and require more processing time. If you do not want to tie up your workstation by processing complex images, use the simple office drawing to do the following exercises. Then, to create the more complex and realistically shaded images, you can come back later, substitute the complex table and chair, and redo the rendering.

This is a good technique to remember: use a simple drawing to get your cameras, lights, and perspectives right, then substitute complex 3D objects for the final renderings. The exercise illustrations show both the simple and complex drawings.

Using DVIEW To Create Perspective Views

You create two scenes of the floor plan by defining two saved views in the drawing. Point the first view at the office chair and set it at about eye level. Point the second view at the right corner of the room, also at eye level. The coordinates are given in the exercise sequence.

You need the OFFICE3D drawing from Chapter 21. If you do not have the OFFICE3D drawing, you can quickly create it from the Chapter 16 OFFICE drawing by doing the *Setting Up the Dynamic View Office Drawing* exercise near the beginning of Chapter 21. If you have the IA DISK, you can use the IA7OFF3D drawing instead.

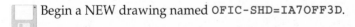

Using DVIEW To Locate a Views for RENDER

Begin a NEW drawing named `OFIC-SHD=IA7OFF3D`.

Begin a NEW drawing named `OFIC-SHD=OFFICE3D`, using OFFICE3D from Chapter 21.

Turn TILMODE on, then zoom in on the lower left office with chair and table to fill the screen (see fig. 22.5).

`Command:` **`DVIEW`** ↵

`Select objects:` *Use a window to select room and contents*	Specifies objects dynamically to view

`CAmera/TArget/Distance/POints/PAn/Zoom/ TWist/CLip/Hide/Off/Undo/<eXit>:` *Enter* **PO** ↵ *or from the screen menu choose* Options, *and then* POints	Specifies the POints option
`Enter target point:` **24',19'6,1'6** ↵	
`Enter camera point:` **18',15',5'6** ↵	
`CAmera/TArget/Distance/POints/PAn/Zoom/ TWist/CLip/Hide/Off/Undo/<eXit>:` **D**↵	Selects Distance
`New camera/target distance <8'-6">:` *Press Enter*	Enables perspective
`CAmera/TArget/Distance/POints/PAn/Zoom/ TWist/CLip/Hide/Off/Undo/<eXit>:` **Z**↵	Selects Zoom
`Adjust lenslength <50.000mm>:` **35**↵	Modifies the lens length
`CAmera/TArget/Distance/POints/PAn/Zoom/ TWist/CLip/Hide/Off/Undo/<eXit>:` *Press Enter*	Ends the DVIEW command
Use the VIEW command and save the current view as VIEW-1	Saves the first view
Repeat DVIEW command with POints option and specify a target point of 32'6,15',0 and a camera point of 18',24',5'6	
Use the VIEW command and save the new view as VIEW-2	Saves the second view

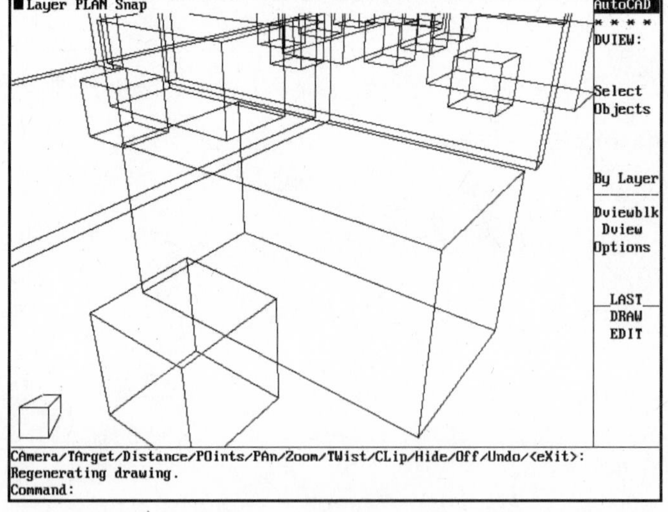

Figure 22.5:

The office room for shading.

Now that you have defined a couple of views, the next step is to create some lights.

Using LIGHT To Set Lights

To design your lighting, AutoCAD Render provides two types of light sources: point sources and distant lights. A *point source* is a light that radiates in all directions. A bare light bulb or an overhead light is a good example of a point source. A *distant light* provides parallel rays in a given direction. Think of a distant light as sunlight through a window. The sun is a point source in the scale of the solar system, but to objects on earth, it is a distant source, with relatively parallel rays.

There is a third light type available if you are using AutoShade with RenderMan: the spot light. The RENDER command does not recognize spot-type lights.

You place lights in much the same way you define views with the DVIEW command's POints option. A light requires a location and a name. A distant source also needs an aim point. In the next exercise, you place four lights in the drawing to represent an ceiling light (point); a light from a window (DISTANT); and a flash (DISTANT) aimed from each camera towards the camera's target. Again, use the location values given in the exercise sequence.

Using LIGHT To Locate Lighting Types

Choose Render, *then* Lights	Issues the LIGHT command and opens the Lights dialog box
Choose New, *then* Point Light, *then* OK, *enter* `CEILING` *in the* Light Name *box, then choose* Modify *in the* Position *settings*	Defines the light and prompts for its location
`Enter light location <current>:` `26',20',10'` *Press Enter*	
Choose OK	Creates a new point light and returns to the Lights dialog box
Choose New, *then* Distant Light, *then* OK, *enter* `WINDOW` *in the* Light Name *box, then choose* Modify	Defines the light prompts for its location

```
Enter light target <current>:
21',20',2' ↵
Enter light location <current>:
26',15',6' ↵
```

Choose **O**K — Creates a new point light and returns to the Lights dialog box

Create two more DISTANT lights in the same manner. Name the first `DISTANT1` using a target of `22',20',2'` and a location of `18',16',6'`. Name the second `DISTANT2`, using a target of `32',15',6'` and a location of `18',23',6'`.

The **L**ights list box now includes four lights (see fig. 22.6).

Choose **O**K *to exit from the Lights dialog box.*

As you place the lights, light icons appear with their names (see fig. 22.7). Each DISTANT light source is pointing at its aim point. Lights DISTANT1 and DISTANT2 simulate a camera flash.

Use XYZ point filters for light placement. They enable you to pick the light's XY location from the screen, the enter the elevation separately.

You can construct complex lights, like linear and fluorescent lights, by using many small lights. In Lights/Modify dialog box, you can adjust the intensity of each light, its color, and other parameters.

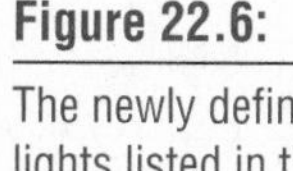

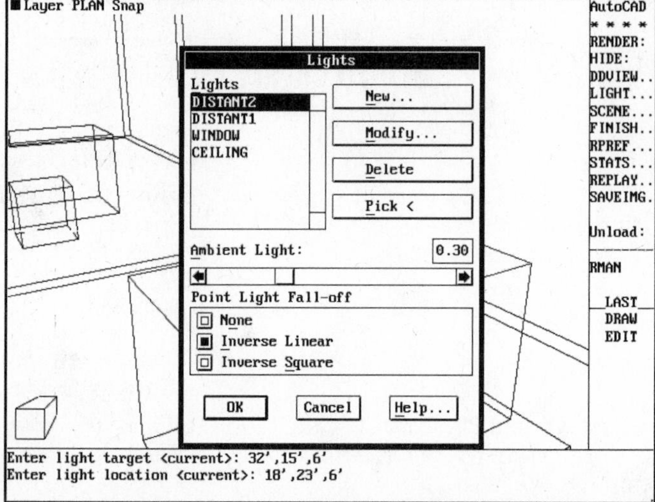

Figure 22.6:

The newly defined lights listed in the Lights dialog box.

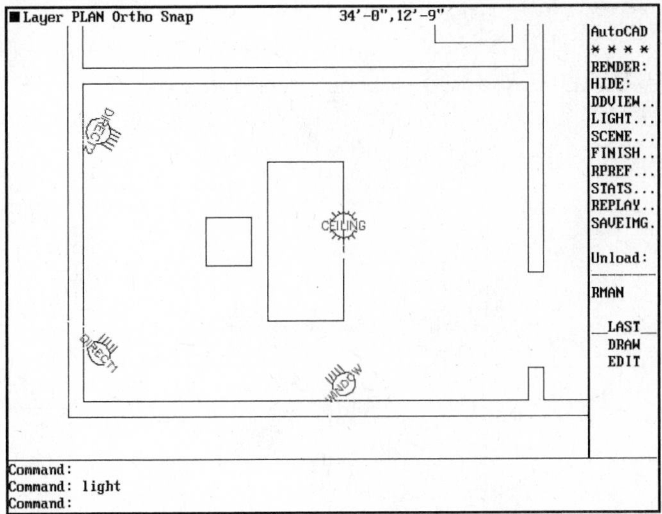

Figure 22.7:

An office with lights.

Creating Action!

All that remains is to group your views and lights into a scene. A scene consists of one view and as many lights as you want. Try creating two scenes using the window and ceiling lights in both, and each camera's flash in its scene.

Defining a Scene

Choose Render, *then* Scenes, *then* **N**ew	Issues the SCENE command and opens the SCENES, then the New Scene dialog box (see fig. 22.8)
Enter **SCENE1** *in the* Scene **N**ame *box*	
Select VIEW-1 *from the* **V**iews *list, and select lights* CEILING, WINDOW, *and* DISTANT1 *from the* **L**ights *list, then choose* OK	Defines the view and lights for SCENE1 and returns to the Scenes dialog
Choose **N**ew, *then enter* **SCENE2** *in the* Scene **N**ame *box*	
Select VIEW-2 *from the* **V**iews *list, and select lights* CEILING, WINDOW, *and* DISTANT2 *from the* **L**ights *list, then choose* OK	Defines SCENE2 and returns to the Scenes dialog (see fig. 22.9)
Highlight SCENE1, *then choose* OK	Sets SCENE1 as the current scene and exits from the Scenes dialog box

The newly defined scenes appear in the Scenes dialog box. The active scene is highlighted. If *CURRENT* is highlighted, RENDER shades the current view, otherwise RENDER shade the current scene. Render the *CURRENT* scene for a quick check of the view angle, lights and settings, but be sure to create a named scene for any scenes you want to save.

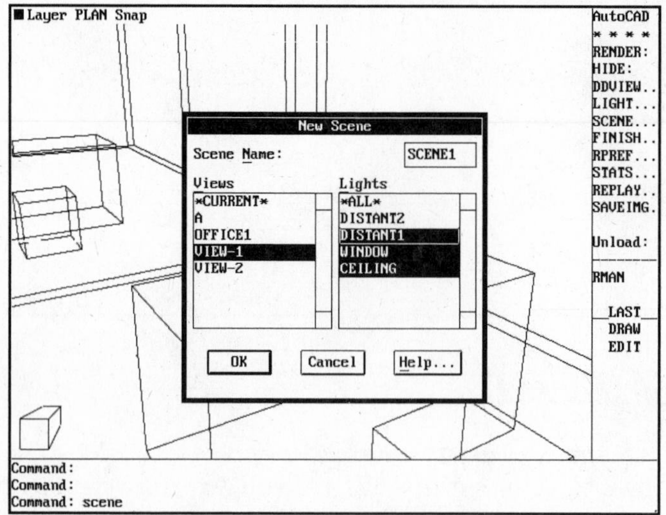

Figure 22.8: The New Scene dialog box.

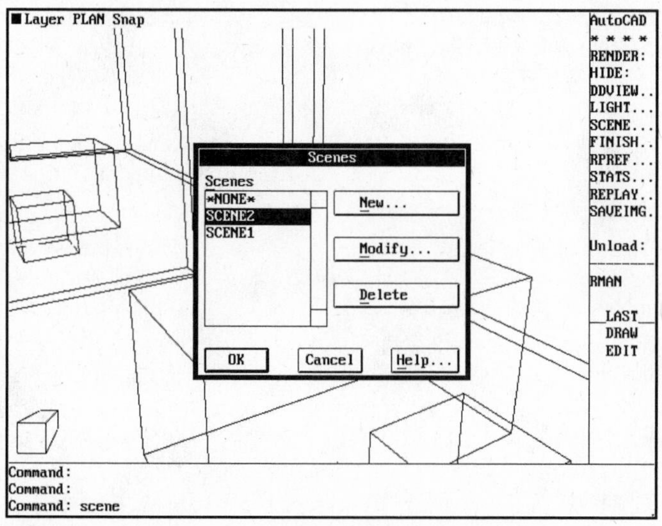

Figure 22.9: The Scenes dialog box with SCENE1 and SCENE2 defined.

Using the Full Render Option

In the next exercise, you use the Full Render option to render SCENE1 and SCENE2. You adjust the render options through the Rendering Preferences dialog box, and then render each scene in order.

Using Full RENDER To Render a Scene

Choose Render, *then* Preferences, *then make the* Rendering Type *and* Rendering Options *settings shown in figure 22.10*	Issues the RPREF command and opens the Rendering Preferences dialog and sets preferences
From the Rendering Preferences *dialog, choose* More Options	Opens the Render Options dialog box
Turn Discard Back Faces *off, then choose* OK	Forces back face rendering (only necessary if rendering the complex chair)
Choose OK *to exit dialog*	
Choose Render, *then* Render	Renders SCENE1

`Scene SCENE1 selected.`
`Projecting objects into view plane.`
`Processing face: 1552`
`Sorting 5435 triangles by depth.`
`Checking 5435 triangles for obscuration.`
`Calculate shading and assign colors.`
`Outputting triangles.`
	RENDER keeps you informed about the rendering's progress

Examine the rendering, and then render SCENE2 in the following steps.

`Command:` **`SCENE`** ↵	Opens the Scenes dialog box
Choose SCENE2, *then choose* OK	Selects SCENE2
`Command:` **`RENDER`** ↵	Renders SCENE2

Your completed renderings should look like figures 22.11 through 22.14. Each scene is rendered with the lighting and viewpoints you defined.

The renderings are fine, but see if you can improve on SCENE1, where there is relatively little contrast between the table top and the walls behind it. AutoCAD Render provides tools for adjusting the light and material finish settings.

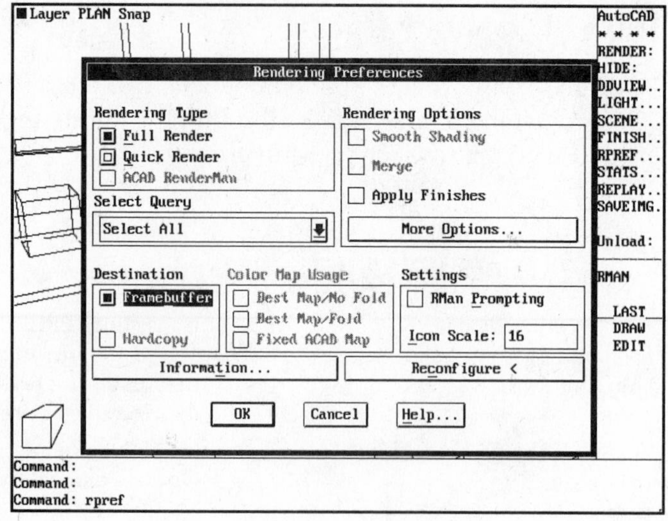

Figure 22.10:

The Render Preferences dialog box with settings defined.

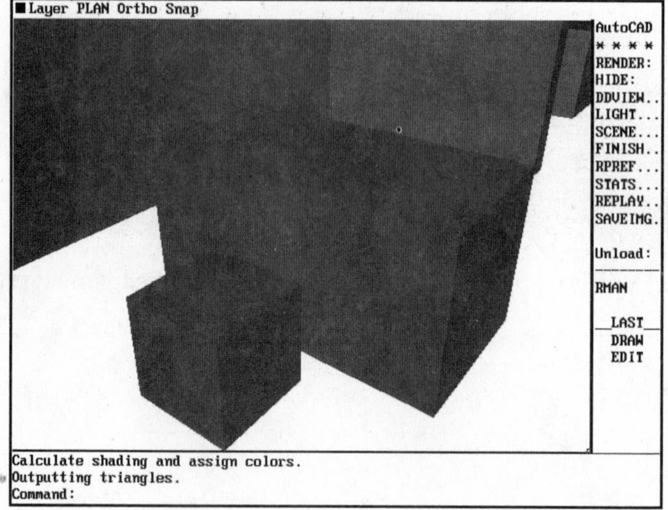

Figure 22.11:

A simple rendering of SCENE1.

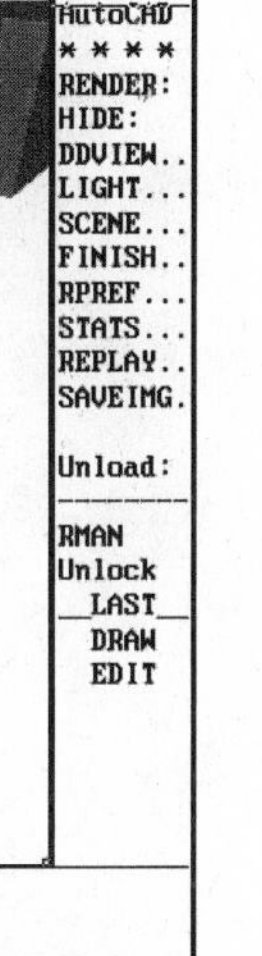

Figure 22.12:

A complex rendering of SCENE1.

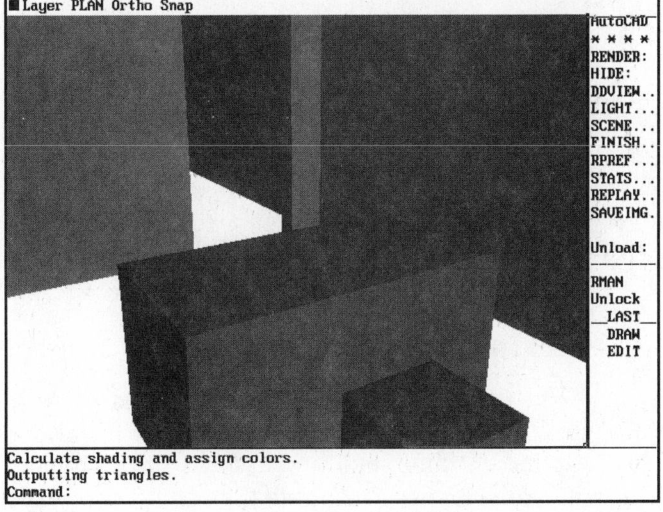

Figure 22.13:

A simple rendering of SCENE2.

Figure 22.14: A complex rendering of SCENE2.

Using Lighting and Finishes To Enhance Images

You can adjust your lighting and material finishes in AutoCAD Render. The Lights dialog box, which is accessed through the Render menu, lists all the lights that are defined in the current drawing. Double-click on a light name to open the Modify Light dialog box. You can make a light brighter or dimmer by increasing or decreasing its intensity value. A zero value is the same as turning the light off. In fact, a negative value can actually subtract light (like a black hole).

The Finishes dialog box, which also is accessed through the Render menu, enables you to load, define, modify, save, and assign finishes to entities or colors in your drawing. You can use finishes to give objects and colors a shiny or matte appearance (and everything in-between).

You can give faces the effect of different colors and finishes on each side of the face by duplicating the entity with an extremely small distance separating the face and the duplicated face, and then changing the color or finish of the duplicated face.

Use COPY or MIRROR, and then the LAYER, FINISH, or COLOR command.

In real life, objects appear to get darker as their distance from you increases. The RENDER command does not depict shading differences relative to distance from a light source unless it has been told to do so. The Point Light Fall-off section of the Lights dialog box offers three ways to adjust your lighting. These settings adjust how the light reflects from the objects in your drawing. The settings affect the look and texture of the rendering. Changing the settings controls visual depth by having RENDER make objects with the same color brighter in the foreground than in the background.

The factors you adjust in the next exercise include the ambient lighting factor (controlling overall light level), and the diffuse and specular finish factors (controlling reflectivity). The ambient factor setting uniformly controls the brightness of stray light (such as is bounced off walls, ceilings, and all objects in the real world) as opposed to light from specific sources. An ambient setting of 0 contributes no stray light (unrealistic) and a maximum setting of 1.0 floods all surfaces equally, so light sources have no effect. While the ambient factor controls how much light hits the surfaces, other factors control how it is reflected.

The finish settings (see figs. 22.15 and 22.16) control how light is reflected off surfaces. The ambient light setting controls how ambient light is reflected off the surface. This value can range from 0 (no ambient light reflected) to 1.00 (all ambient light reflected).

Diffuse reflection is light reflected equally in all directions, relative to the amount of light striking the surface (from 0 to 1.00), regardless of the direction of the source. Higher diffuse settings create a "dull" material, with no shiny highlights.

The specular setting (from 0 to 1.00) controls the amount of shiny surface reflection versus diffuse reflection. As a rule, the sum of the ambient, diffuse, and specular factors should equal 1.0. The roughness setting (from 0 to 1.00) controls how widespread the specular highlight is. A higher roughness value makes the specular highlight larger.

Try enhancing SCENE1 with some lighting and finish adjustments in the following exercise. These adjustments are most dramatic when using the complex table and chair.

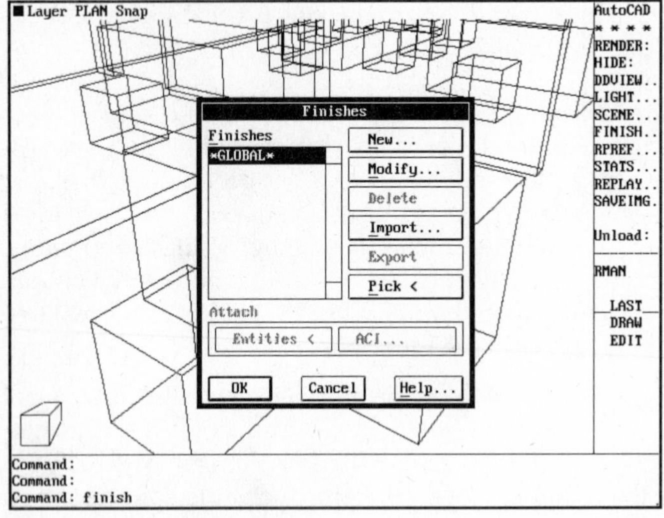

Figure 22.15:

The Finishes dialog box.

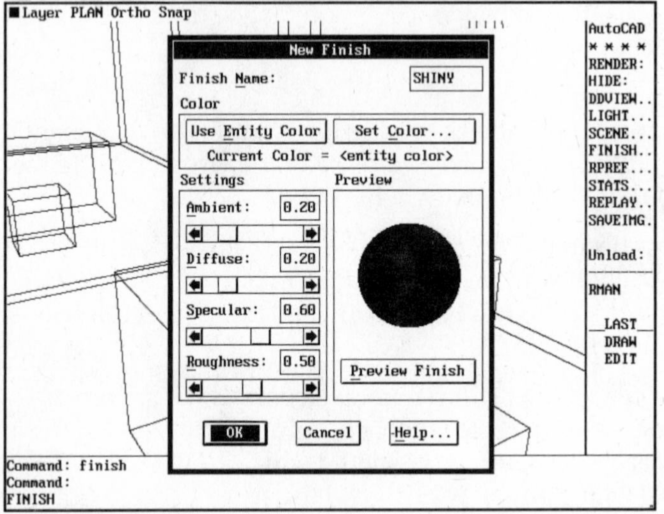

Figure 22.16:

The New Finish dialog box.

Using Lights and Finishes To Enhance Contrast

`Command:` **`LIGHT`** ↵	Opens the Lights dialog
Double-click on light DISTANT1, *change* Intensity *to* `.8`, *then choose* OK *twice*	
Choose Render, *then* Finishes, *then* New	Issues the FINISH command and opens Finishes, then New Finish dialog box
Enter **`SHINY`** *in the* Finish Name *box, then set* Ambient *to* `0.2`, Diffuse *to* `0.2`, Specular *to* `0.6`, *and* Roughness *to* `0.5`	Defines a new material
Choose Preview Finish	Renders a sphere using the new finish settings
Look at the finish, then choose OK	Prompts for location
`Enter New Finish location <current>:` *Press Enter*	
Select Attach Entities, *select the table and the chair and press Enter, then* OK	Attaches the SHINY finish to the table and chair
`Command:` **`RENDER`** ↵	Renders the scene

When you are done, your screen should show an image with differing contrasts (see figs. 22.17 and 22.18).

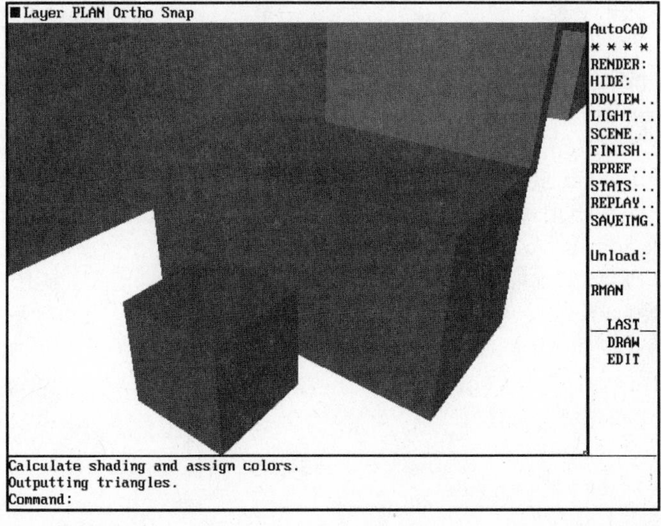

Figure 22.17:

A simple SCENE1 rendered with new settings.

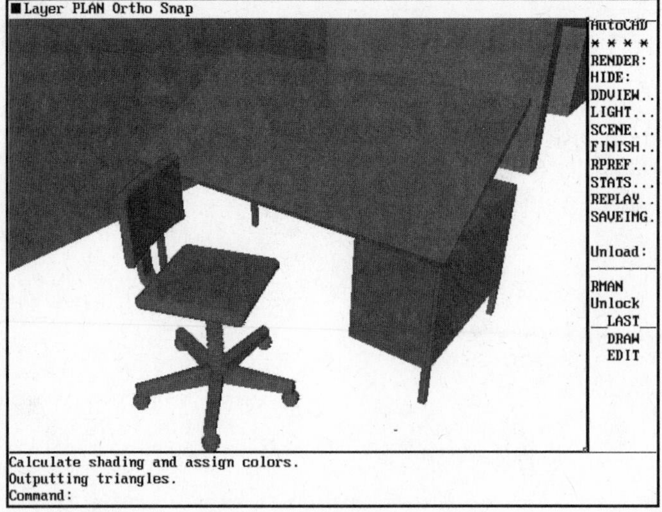

Figure 22.18:

A complex SCENE1 rendered with new settings.

The new light and shading model settings show AutoCAD Render's flexibility. With practice, you can make settings to simulate actual lighting situations. Take a look at SCENE2 to see the effect of the light changes. Experiment with different settings. Try your own hand at using a wide variety of values to see new effects. The best way to understand lighting is to experiment.

Shading Model Distance Factors

Several factors adjust the shading of surfaces relative to their distance from light sources or from the camera. *Inverse square* causes light intensity to decrease as the square of the distance from the light source to the object face. *Linear lighting* causes light intensity to decrease linearly from the light source to the object face. Linear lighting does not produce distance shades of color as dark as inverse square. *Inverse contrast* is used in conjunction with linear lighting to produce an effect similar to fluorescent lighting. *Z shading* produces a rendering with the foreground brighter than the background. Light placements, intensities, and shading factors (except stretch contrast) are ignored. This is adequate for most quick studies, and easier than setting linear and inverse factors.

Compare figures 22.19 through 22.21 to see the effects of the various fall-off options.

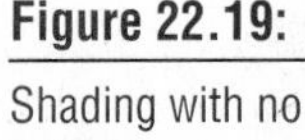

Figure 22.19:

Shading with no fall-off.

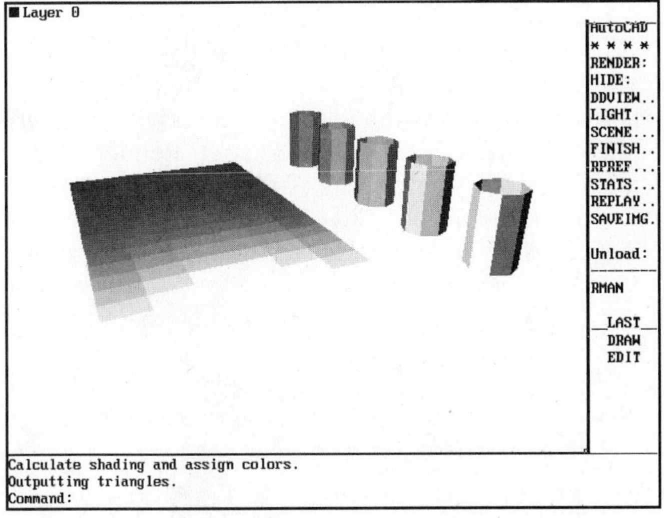

Figure 22.20:

Shading with inverse linear fall-off.

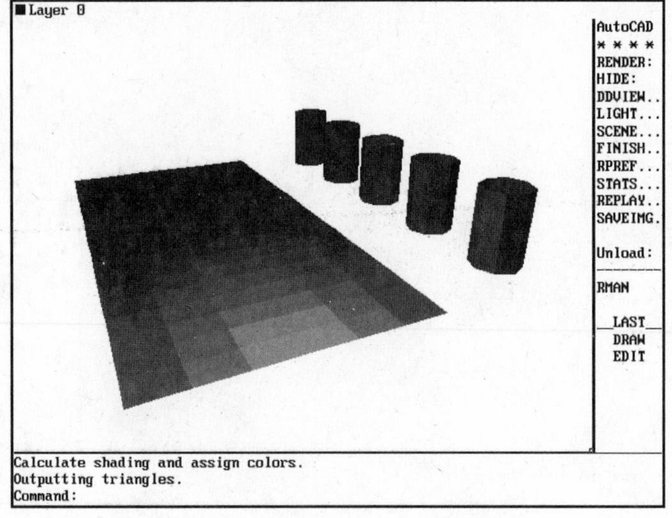

Figure 22.21:

Shading with inverse square fall-off.

Saving and Printing Renderings

Unlike AutoCAD's SHADE command, images created with RENDER cannot be stored in an AutoCAD slide file. AutoCAD Render renderings can be saved in a number of other formats. Saving renderings to an external file allows you to replay the images inside AutoCAD in much less time than it takes to re-render them. Saved images can also be sent to a printer, image editor, or desktop publishing program. The next exercise takes you through the necessary steps to save a rendered image to an external file.

Render files (RND) are display-device-specific. Files created with one type of video configuration cannot be displayed on any other type of video.

In the next section, you set up four final scenes to create renderings of the office plan. These renderings correspond to the perspective views that you developed with DVIEW.

Developing Scenes for a Replay

So far, you have explored AutoCAD Render's finish and lighting settings to get a desired rendering. The office with the chair and table are small objects and you can control their renderings easily. Larger and more complex drawings require more control in AutoCAD Render, and more forethought when you create your views, finishes, lights, and scenes.

Return to the simple office drawing and create four new camera positions using the DVIEW command. You create a set of renderings that can be replayed similarly to the slide show in Chapter 21. The difference this time is that each image is fully shaded. First, make a new drawing named RENDER from the simple office plan and prepare it for rendering. Use figure 22.22 and table 22.1 to create the four scenes for rendering.

Creating Four Scenes Rendering Replay

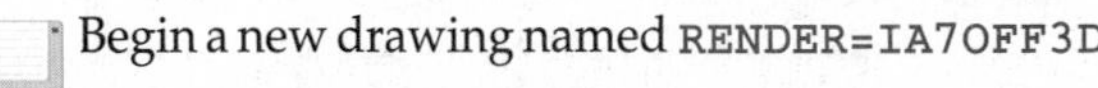
Begin a new drawing named `RENDER=IA7OFF3D`.

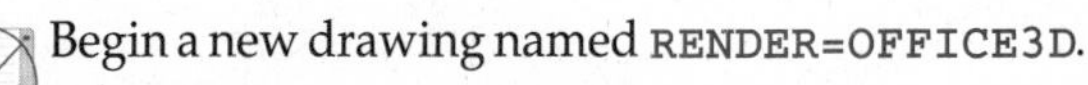
Begin a new drawing named `RENDER=OFFICE3D`.

ZOOM All, then use table 22.1 to define the views and lights, and to create scenes to match figure 22.22. Save your drawing.

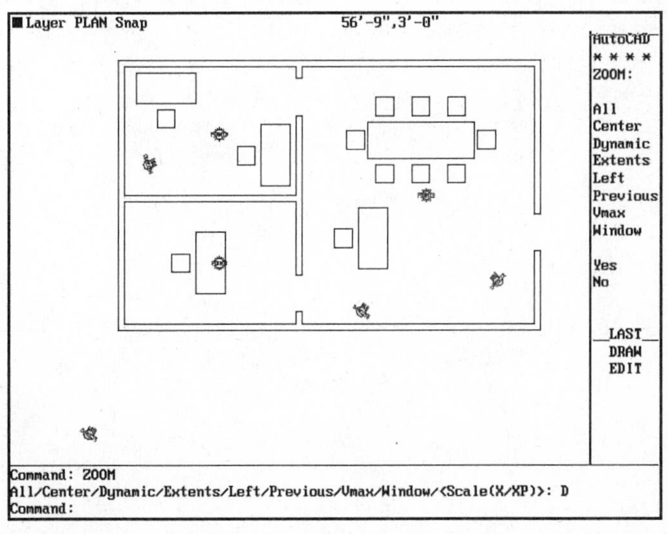

Figure 22.22: The RENDER drawing ready for rendering.

Table 22.1
Settings for the Office Scenes

SCENE1	*Target Location*	*Viewpoint/Light Location*
VIEW1	24',19'6,2'	18',15',5'6
POINT1(point)	25'6,19'6,10'0	
DISTANT1 (distant)	23'9,19'6,3'6	14'6,5'6,8'6
SCENE2	*Target Location*	*Icon Location*
VIEW2	33'0,33'0,2'0	51',21',5'6
POINT2 (point)	43'0,25'0,10'0	
DISTANT2 (distant)	33'0,33'0,2'0	49'0,18'0,5'6
SCENE3	*Target Location*	*Icon Location*
VIEW3	52'0,35'6,0'0	33'0,15',6'0
POINT2	43'0,25'0,10'0	
DISTANT3 (distant)	52'0,35'6,0'0	37'6,15'6,6'0
SCENE4	*Target Location*	*Icon Location*
VIEW4	38'0,33'6,0'0	18',25'6,6'0
POINT3 (point)	25'6,30'0,1'0	
DISTANT4 (distant)	38'0,33'6,0'0	19'6,27'6,6'0

Now that you have the four scenes safely stored in the drawing file, use the RENDER command to render each image.

Rendering the Four Scenes

Choose Render, *then* Scenes, *select* SCENE1, *then choose* OK	Makes SCENE1 current
Choose Render, *then* Render Render	Renders SCENE1
Choose Render, *then* Files, *then* Save Image	Issues the SAVEIMG command and displays the Save Image dialog box

Enter `\IA\RENDER-1` *in the* Image Name *box, then choose* OK	Saves the first image as RENDER-1

Repeat this sequence for each of the four scenes. Name the next three image files \IA\RENDER-2, RENDER-3, and RENDER-4, respectively. Your images should match figures 22.23 through 22.26

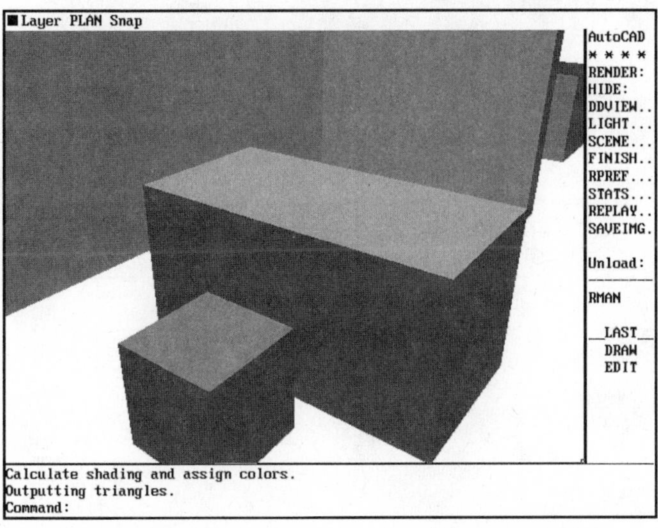

Figure 22.23:

Rendering of SCENE1.

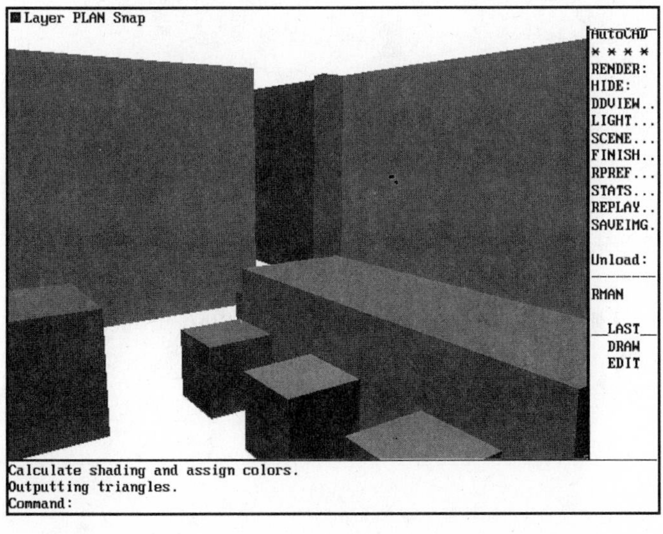

Figure 22.24:

Rendering of SCENE2.

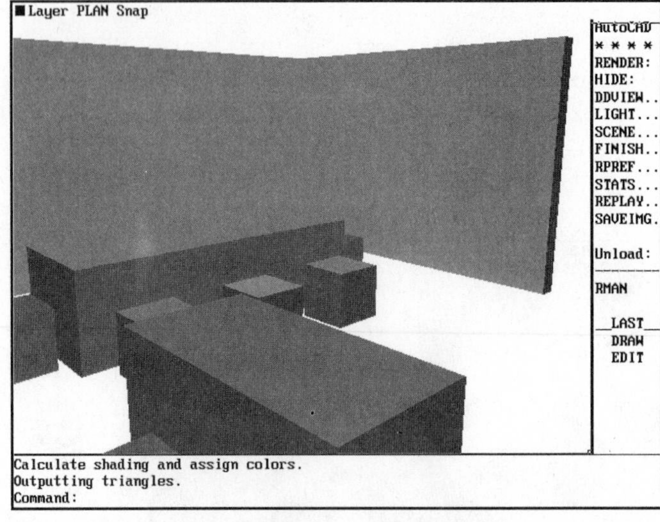

Figure 22.25:

Rendering of SCENE3.

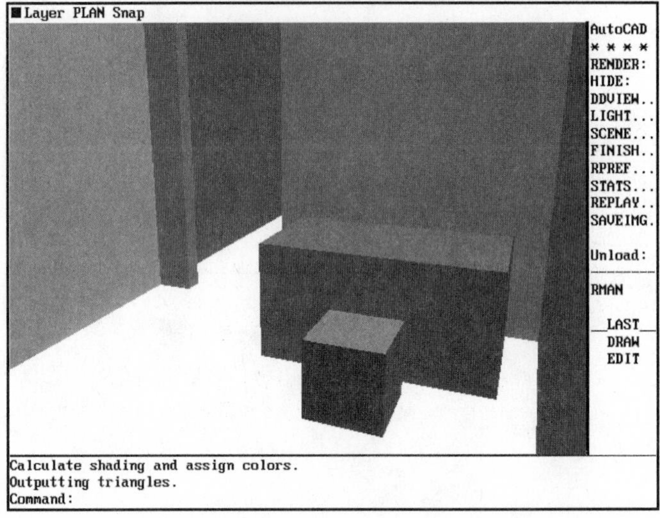

Figure 22.26:

Rendering of SCENE4.

Once you have all the rendering files created, you can replay them individually, using the REPLAY command. From the Render menu, choose Files, then Replay Image. This opens the Replay Image dialog box. You can browse directories for files matching the extension provided. You can also change the filename extension to search for. Valid extensions include TGA, TIF, GIF, and RND.

You can use the Save Image dialog to save just the current viewport, the entire drawing area, or the entire screen (including menus). The latter is useful for exporting to word-processing or desktop publishing programs for use in documents such as training manuals.

Creating Photorealism with AutoShade and RenderMan

AutoCAD Render duplicates the rendering capabilities that required AutoShade 2.0 with earlier versions of AutoCAD. However, when used with the Autodesk RenderMan option, AutoShade can produce more lifelike renderings than AutoCAD Render. RenderMan can create rendered images that rival photographs. Autodesk RenderMan produces high-resolution, anti-aliased images of models. You have full control over shading and shadow casting, and you can assign textures, materials, and surface properties in AutoCAD.

To output to AutoShade, you must create a *filmroll*, which is a file that has an FLM extension and is used by AutoShade to define the 3D model for lights and scenes. If you are using Autodesk RenderMan, you can assign additional properties to entities, including material and texture maps. For more information on the AutoCAD-to-AutoShade (and RenderMan) process, refer to your *AutoShade Reference Manual.*

You can delete OFFICE.DWG, RENDER.DWG, *.FLM, and *.RND from your IA directory.

Summary

From planning and creating your 3D model in AutoCAD, to using the AutoCAD Render commands to prepare lights, finishes, and scenes for rendering to the screen or printer, the following tips make the process quicker and the results better.

Use simple entities to get your scenes right and test the shading, then substitute complex meshed objects for final renderings.

Plan and create your 3D model with extrusions, surfaces, and surfaced solids, or objects won't show up when rendered. Create 3Dfaces in a counterclockwise order (the 3D Objects commands ensure the right order).

When setting colors, consider how they appear after shading darkens and lightens them.

Use object snaps, XYZ point filters, and DVIEW to plan your scenes before putting in lights and saving views.

Balance the efficiency of entities versus smoothness of shading. Simple extrusions and low mesh densities regenerate and process faster, but fine surface meshes create smoother shading. Use the smooth shading option with coarse meshes wherever possible.

Use AutoCAD and AutoShade scripts to automate rendering production. *INSIDE Autodesk Animator,* from New Riders Publishing, includes a chapter on using the Autodesk Animation Tool Kit (ATK) to create an animated movie of AutoCAD Render or AutoShade renderings. The ATK is available from your AutoCAD or Animator dealer, in AutoShade 2.0, or from the Autodesk forum on CompuServe (GO ACAD).

What you see on screen is not necessarily what you get in hard copy, particularly with black and white printers. It may be necessary to adjust your colors in AutoCAD to get the effects you want. In general, rendering destined for hard-copy output require higher light intensities than rendering to the screen.

The RENDER command can produce quality shaded images but requires some patience and a good understanding of how lighting, reflection, and shading is calculated. Trial and error focuses you on the settings you use most of the time, but experimenting with the more obscure settings and studying the *AutoCAD Render Reference Manual* helps you get an even better understanding and produce better renderings.

Wireframes, surface meshes, and shaded surfaces all are useful approximations of 3D objects. But sometimes you need more precision and mass in your 3D objects. In the next chapter, you move on to AutoCAD's AME and create a *solid* model with real-world properties like density, yield strength, coefficient of linear expansion, centroid, and moment of inertia.

23

Inside Solid and Region Modeling

In the 3D work you did in previous chapters, you used two modeling techniques — wireframe and surface modeling. AutoCAD Release 12 also includes two additional types — region and solid modeling. To understand exactly what region and solid modeling is and how to use them, take a quick look at how they differ from wireframe and surface modeling.

The Three Types of 3D Modeling

Wireframe models not only are often the hardest to create but also convey the least amount of information. All a wireframe can describe is that two 3D coordinates are connected by a line or by some other 2D entity. With enough coordinates and lines, you can create a respectable looking 3D image. The wireframe, however, is ambiguous in representing where surfaces exist between lines and intersections. You can make some visual assumptions, but the model lacks associative information that is useful in design. And, without surface data, wireframes cannot be shaded and used for visualization.

Surface models add another layer of complexity to the model by associating entities with surfaces and by maintaining relationships between surfaces (like edge-to-edge intersection). Surface models enable you to model much more complex designs and shade them. But even with that added associativity, surface models can only visually imitate real-world objects. In reality, objects contain more complexity than either wireframe or surface models can convey. Real objects can be measured by area, mass, weight, and other properties which wireframe and surface models cannot provide. These properties can be valuable, or even essential, to the design process.

To answer the need for objects with "real-world" properties, AutoCAD provides two additional types of modeling: region and solid modeling. The Region Modeler is included with AutoCAD and enables you to create closed, two-dimensional areas or regions. The Advanced Modeling Extension (AME) is AutoCAD's optional solid modeler, enabling you to create 3D solid models. Both add real-world properties to the model, enabling you to analyze the model according to its physical properties.

The Region and solid modelers share many of the same commands. Using a region or solid model, you can calculate mass properties such as area, weight, center of gravity and moments of inertia. One of the best aspects of region and solid modeling is that this type of modeling usually is easier to use than the other two types of modeling. This is because you build a region or solid model in much the same way you would actually manufacture the item being modeled. You can, for example, start with a block, punch holes in it (subtract a cylinder), and perform other modeling operations that mimic the actual manufacturing operation.

Who Needs Region and Solid Modeling?

Although solid modeling generally has been the province of mechanical designers, AutoCAD's region and solid modeling features also are useful to spatially oriented designers such as architects and to drafters of many disciplines. Using regions, you can easily define closed areas that contain voids. You can easily calculate a region's area or other properties. Using solids, you can resolve complex intersections and penetrations that might take arduous calculations in 2D drafting. Solids can quickly demonstrate conflicts and interferences between components. Architects can use solids to create mass studies of models, then transfer the results to 3D surfaces for presentation drawings or to 2D for production drawing development. Just pretend that the mechanical parts in this chapter's exercises are mass models for a strange-looking building.

Getting Started in Region Modeling

Region modeling is the 2D-cousin of solid modeling. AutoCAD's region modeler uses many of the same commands used in the solid modeler. The region modeler creates 2D objects, but like other AutoCAD entities, these objects can be located in any orientation and location in 3D space. You can convert 2D region models into 3D solid models. The following exercise demonstrates some region modeling basics, as you learn to create, edit, and analyze a region. You can complete the next exercise even if you do not have the AME option.

Creating a Region Model

Defining regions is a simple process. You can combine lines, arcs, circles, polylines, or any AutoCAD entities that enclose an area, and join them to define a region. The command to join them is SOLIDIFY. When you solidify entities, they become a new entity; a region. You can use the SOLDELENT variable to choose to retain the defining entities or discard them. In this exercise, you define several simple 2D entities that form a closed area. You set SOLDELENT to ask you if you want to discard the defining entities as the region is created. Finally, you solidify the entities, to create a region.

Creating a Region

Begin a new drawing named \IA\IA7-REG. Set snap to 0.25, grid to 1, and turn on coordinate display. Set the limits from 0,0 to 17,11, and then zoom all.

```
Command: PLINE ↵
From point: 4,1 ↵
Current line-width is 0.0000
```

```
Arc/Close/Halfwidth/Length/Undo
/Width/<Endpoint of line>: 14,1 ↵
Arc/Close/Halfwidth/Length/Undo
/Width/<Endpoint of line>: 14,11 ↵
Arc/Close/Halfwidth/Length/Undo
/Width/<Endpoint of line>: 4,11 ↵
Arc/Close/Halfwidth/Length/Undo            Closes polyline
/Width/<Endpoint of line>: C ↵
```

Next, give the polyline rounded corners using the FILLET command.

```
Command: FILLET ↵
Polyline/Radius/<Select first
object>: R ↵
Enter fillet radius <0.0000>: 1 ↵          Defines fillet radius
Command: FILLET ↵
Polyline/Radius/<Select first
object>: P ↵
Select 2D polyline: L ↵                    Selects the last visible object
                                           created (the polyline)
```

Your polyline should resemble figure 23.1. Next, set the SOLDELENT variable to prompt before deleting entities, then use the SOLIDIFY command to create the initial region. The Region Modeler may need to be loaded.

```
Command: SOLDELENT ↵
Delete the entity after extrusion,
revolution or solidification?
(1=never, 2=ask, 3=always)<3>: 2 ↵
```

Choose Model, *then* Solidify

```
Command: _solidify
Command: solidify Delete the entities
that are solidified? <N> Y ↵
Select objects: Select the polyline
and press Enter
```

Boundary evaluation and tessallation occur (see fig. 23.2).

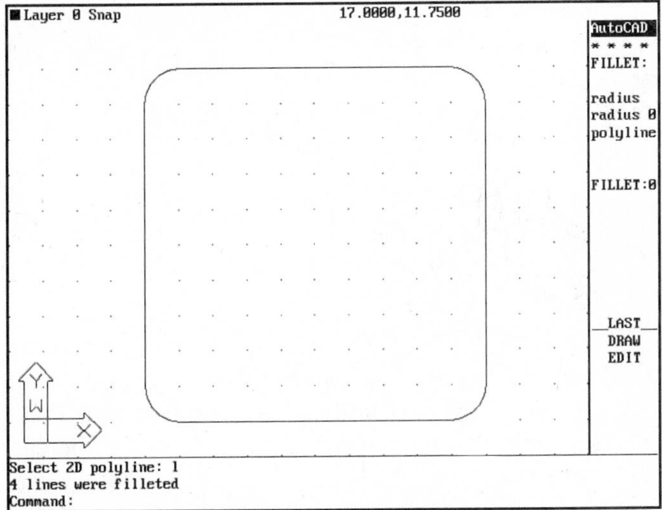

Figure 23.1:

The 2D polyline with rounded corners.

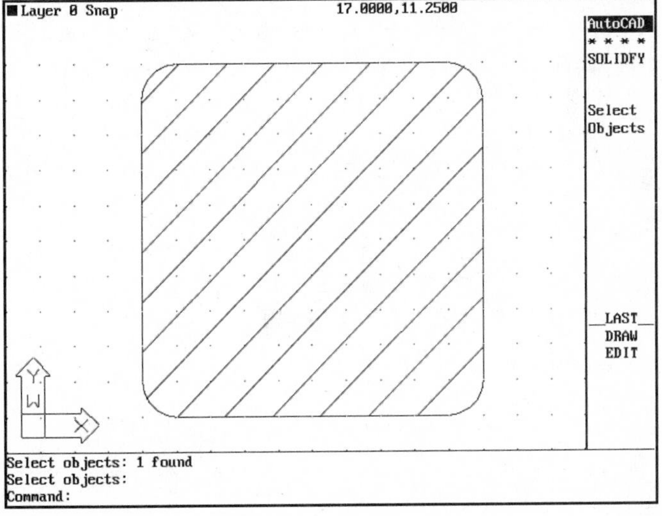

Figure 23.2:

The newly defined region, evident by its hatch pattern.

The SOLIDIFY command uses the closed polyline to define a new entity: a region. The region is, by default, automatically cross-hatched. This helps you to visually discern a region from any other collection of 2D entities. You can further control the region's display with the SOLHANGLE, SOLHPAT, and SOLHSIZE variables.

The SOLHANGLE variable sets the angle of region hatching. For this exercise, you use the default 45 degree angle, but SOLHANGLE accepts any real number, just like the Angle option of AutoCAD's HATCH command. Changing this value does not effect existing regions unless that region is modified.

SOLHPAT enables you to instruct AutoCAD to use a particular hatch pattern on regions. SOLHPAT uses that same pattern file used by the AutoCAD HATCH command. Like SOLHANGLE, SOLHPAT does not effect existing regions until they are modified.

The SOLHSIZE variable defines the current region hatch scale, similar to the HATCH command's Scale option. The advantage to using variables for these values, rather than simply duplicating the HATCH command's prompts, becomes apparent when creating multiple regions. You can simply set the values once, and then go about the process of creating your regions, without unnecessary prompts.

In the first exercise, you used the default region hatching values. In the next exercise, you adjust those settings and review the results after editing the region. To modify the region, you define a new region, subtracting it from the first region with the SOLSUB command to create a "hole." Then you use a basic AutoCAD command, COPY, to create an overlapped copy of the new region. Finally, you use the SOLUNION command to define the final region.

Subtracting and Joining Regions

Draw a circle with center point at 7,4 and a radius of 2 units

`Command:` **`SOLHANGLE`** ↵

`Hatch angle <45.0>:` **`135`** ↵

`Command:` **`SOLIDIFY`** ↵

`Delete the entities that are solidified <N>`**`Y`**↵

`Select objects:` *Select the circle and press Enter*

Boundary evaluation and hatching occurs. Note how the hatch angle has changed (see fig. 23.3). Next, copy the circular region and unify it with the first region.

`Command:` **`SOLSUB`** ↵

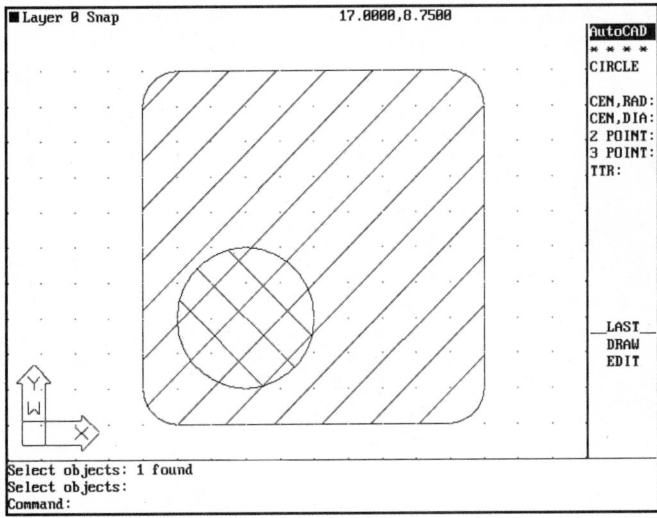

Figure 23.3:

A second region is defined.

```
Source objects...
Select objects: Select the original rectangular region and press Enter
```

```
Objects to subtract from them...
Select objects: Select the lower left circular region and press Enter
```

Boundary evaluation and hatching occur. You now have a single region with a void or a hole in the lower left-hand side (see fig. 23.4). Finally, use the basic AutoCAD COPY command to duplicate the region, and then unify the two regions with SOLUNION.

```
Command: COPY ↵
Select objects: Select the region
Select objects: Press Enter
<Base point or displacement>/
Multiple: 4,4 ↵
Second point of displacement: Press Enter        Copies the region
Command: SOLUNION ↵
Select objects: Select the two regions, then press Enter
```

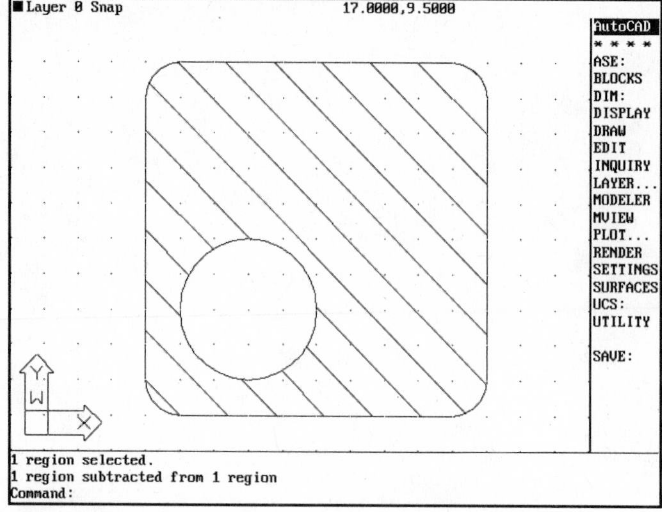

Figure 23.4:

A region with a "hole."

Boundary evaluation and hatching occurs (see fig. 23.5). Notice how the hatching of the original region took on the new angle specified by the SOLHANGLE variable. You have seen a few of the basic region modeling commands. Now take a look at one way you can evaluate regions.

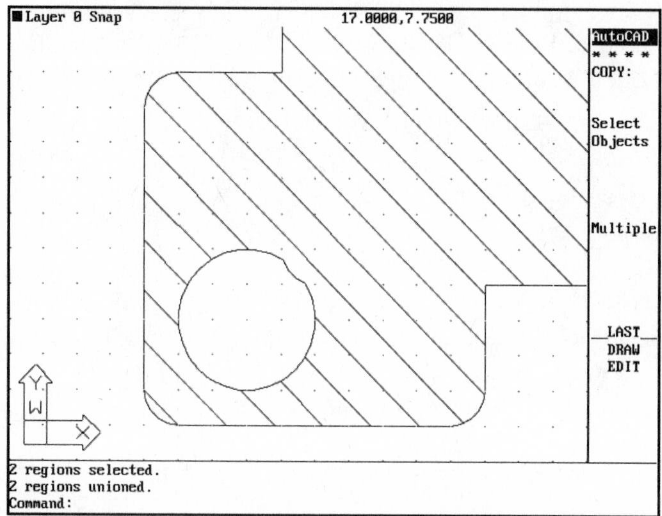

Figure 23.5:

The new, composite region.

Region models can be analyzed much like solid models. You can, for instance, calculate the region's area, or its material properties. In the following exercise, you calculate the area of the region you generated in the first two exercises.

Calculating the Area of a Region

Continue working in drawing \IA\IA7-REG

`Command:` **`SOLAREA`** ↵

`Select objects:` *Select the region and press Enter*

`Surface area of regions is 150.254 sq cm` — SOLAREA calculates area of region

You can discard drawing \IA\IA7-REG; it is no longer needed.

SOLAREA returns the area of the selected regions. You can create, edit, and analyze region models with many AME commands. The following list describes AME commands that work with region models:

Most of these commands can be used with regions or solids but not with both simultaneously. For example, the SOLUNION command enables you to unify regions or solids, but not regions and solids.

- **SOLAREA.** The SOLAREA command, as exemplified by the preceding exercise, calculates the combined area of all selected regions.
- **SOLCHP.** This command enables you to change the properties of a solid or region primitive. With this one command, you can change the color, copy, move, replace, delete, or resize any primitive. This command is described in further detail later in this chapter.
- **SOLFEAT.** Using the SOLFEAT command, you can create standard AutoCAD entities from any region or solid model.
- **SOLINT.** The Boolean intersection operator, SOLINT creates a new region by calculating the common area of two intersecting regions.
- **SOLLIST.** This command displays the information that defines a region.

- **SOLMASSP.** This command calculates and displays the mass properties of the selected regions and solids. Mass properties calculated for regions include moments of inertia, product of inertia, radii of gyration, principal moments, and principal directions.
- **SOLMAT.** This command enables you to assign the current material, edit an existing material, or create a new material. AutoCAD uses the material assignments to perform the mass property calculations.
- **SOLMESH.** This command displays regions as a 3D mesh. Use SOLMESH where the model must be processed with the SHADE or HIDE commands.
- **SOLMOVE.** This command enables you to move and rotate regions in one command.
- **SOLPURGE.** This command erases the entities from which a composite region is built, reducing file size and improving performance.
- **SOLSEP.** This command separates composite regions created using the SOLUNION, SOLINT, and SOLSUB commands. SOLSEP enables you to separate the specific primitives you select.
- **SOLSUB.** This Boolean function subtracts one region from another.
- **SOLUCS.** This command aligns the current UCS with the face or edge of an existing region.
- **SOLUNION.** This is the Boolean union function, which creates composite regions by combining the area of two or more existing regions.
- **SOLWIRE.** This command displays selected regions as wireframes.

These commands are a subset of the AME command, but they work in much the same way. Even if you do not have AME, you can use the region modeler to familiarize yourself with most of the same commands and techniques used in AME. Of course, you also can use most of the standard AutoCAD drawing and editing commands as well.

The remainder of this chapter focuses on the fourth type of modeling: solid modeling. Many of the technique demonstrated in the AME section also apply to AutoCAD's region modeler.

Getting Started in Solid Modeling

Everything you have learned about 3D modeling in previous chapters applies to solid modeling. You use the same types of coordinate systems (UCSs) and many of the same basic techniques. AutoCAD helps by providing special functions to create solid primitives (simple geometric solids), as well as functions to add solids together, subtract them from each other, and analyze mass properties.

The exercises in this chapter are grouped into three sections. In the first, you create simple primitives and combine them to form more complex models. You also create revolved and extruded solids and use many of the solid-editing functions. In the second section, you learn how to list, manipulate, and change many of the properties of your completed model. In the final section, you translate a solid model's information into a 2D drawing.

Setting Up a 3D Solid Modeling Environment

Because the best way to learn is by doing, begin by using AutoCAD's AME functions to create a simple mechanical part in a new drawing called 3D. The first thing to do is to create the viewports and User Coordinate Systems needed for working in 3D (see fig. 23.6). Then, save the drawing as a prototype to use in the rest of the exercises. If you have the IA DISK, this prototype is called IA7-3D.

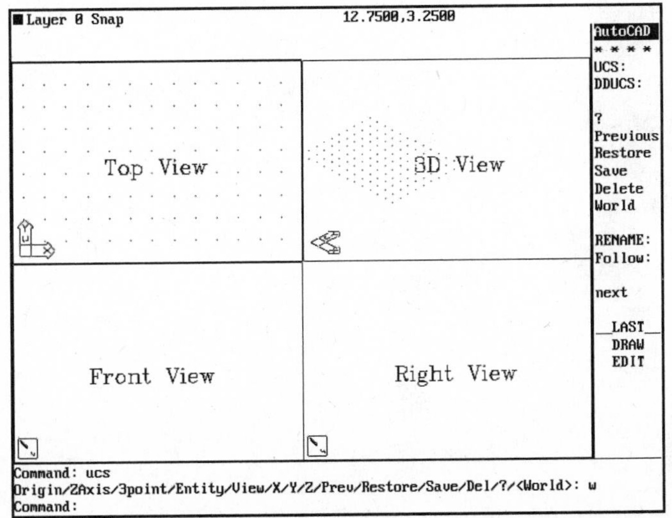

Figure 23.6:
The 3D prototype drawing setup.

Setting Up the Modeling Environment

Copy \IA\IA7-3D.DWG to \IA\3D.DWG and skip this setup.

Begin a newdrawing named 3D and continue.

Set snap to 0.25, grid to 1, and turn on coordinate display, load linetype HIDDEN, set TILEMODE to 0 (off) to enter paper space, set LIMITS from 0,0 to 36,24, use MVIEW to create four viewports from 0,0 to 36,24, ZOOM All, use MSPACE to enter model space, and select lower left viewport to make it current.

`Command:` **`LINETYPE`** ↵

`?/Create/Load/Set:` **`L`** ↵ — Loads a linetype stored in a *.LIN file

`Linetype to load:` **`HIDDEN`** ↵

Press Enter to accept default linetype file

`Command:` **`TILEMODE`** ↵

`New value for TILEMODE <1>:` **`0`** ↵ — Enters paper space

`Entering Paper space. Use MVIEW to insert Model space viewports.`

`Regenerating drawing.`

`Command:` **`MVIEW`** ↵

`ON/OFF/Hideplot/Fit/2/3/4/ Restore/<First Point>:` **`4`** ↵ — Divides a window into 4 equal sized viewports

`Fit/<first point>:` **`0,0`** ↵

`Second point:` **`36,24`** ↵ — Creates the four viewports

`Regenerating drawing.`

Zoom All

`Command:` **`MS`** ↵ — Enters model space

Next, use VPOINT to set up each of the four views and UCS to define and save three new user coordinate systems.

`Command:` **`VPOINT`** ↵ — Alters the perspective of a viewport

`Rotate/<View point> <0.0000,0.0000,1.0000>:` **`R`** ↵ — Selects the Rotate option

Enter angle in XY plane from X axis <270>: **270** ↵

Rotates the X,Y plane 270 degrees from the X axis

Enter angle from XY plane <90>: **0** ↵

Sets the Z angle from the X,Y plane to 0, creating a front elevation view

Select the lower right viewport

Command: **VPOINT** ↵

Rotate/<View point>

<0.0000,0.0000,1.0000>: **R** ↵

Enter angle in X-Y plane from X axis <270>: **0** ↵

Rotates the X,Y plane 0 degrees from the X axis

Enter angle from X-Y plane <90>: **0** ↵

Sets the Z angle from the X,Y plane to 0, creating a right elevation view

Select the upper right viewport

Command: **VPOINT** ↵

Rotate/<View point>

<0.0000,0.0000,1.0000>: **R** ↵

Enter angle in X-Y plane from X axis <270>: **315** ↵

Rotates the X,Y plane 315 degrees from the X axis

Enter angle from X-Y plane <90>: **30** ↵

Sets the Z angle from the X,Y plane to 30, creating an isometric view

Select the lower right viewport (right side view)

Command: **UCS** ↵

Origin/ZAxis/3point/Entity/View/X/Y/Z/Prev/Restore/Save/Del/?/<World>: **V** ↵

Sets current UCS to the current view

Command: **UCS** ↵

Command: **SOLWDENS**↵

Sets wire density of wireframe for representations of curved surfaces

Wireframe mesh density (1 to 12):**4**↵

`Origin/ZAxis/3point/Entity/View/ X/Y/Z/Prev/Restore/Save/Del/?/ <World>:` **S** ↵	
`?/Desired UCS name:` **RIGHT** ↵	Saves the new UCS
Select the lower left viewport (front view)	
`Command:` **UCS** ↵	
`Origin/ZAxis/3point/Entity/View/ X/Y/Z/Prev/Restore/Save/Del/?/ <World>:` **V** ↵	Sets the current UCS to the current view
`Command:` **UCS** ↵	
`Origin/ZAxis/3point/Entity/View/ X/Y/Z/Prev/Restore/Save/Del/?/ <World>:` **S** ↵	
`?/Desired UCS name:` **FRONT** ↵	Saves new UCS
Select the upper left viewport (top view)	
`Command:` **UCS** ↵	
`Origin/ZAxis/3point/Entity/View/ X/Y/Z/Prev/Restore/Save/Del/?/ <World>:` *Press Enter*	Restores the WCS
`Command:` **QSAVE** ↵	Saves the drawing

The drawing you just created will be the prototype for the following solid modeling exercises.

Making Something from Nothing—Almost

Like any complex operation, solid modeling is made up of many smaller, simpler operations. When you bring all of those simple operations together, you have a complex model. AutoCAD's solid modeling commands give you tools to create simple solids (primitives) and to merge them together to quickly create complex models. These functions are similar to the AutoCAD functions for creating surface primitives covered in previous chapters.

You can, for example, use commands to create solid boxes, cylinders, cones, spheres, toruses, and wedges. You can use these primitives to construct complex designs from simple geometric shapes. You might start with a box or extrusion, and add other primitives to it. Or you might start with a complex extrusion and use utility commands to remove material from it.

Take a look at AutoCAD's solid modeling commands and use them to create a few simple primitives. Then, merge those primitives into a more complex part.

AutoCAD's Solid Modeling Tools

AutoCAD groups all of the solid modeling functions into a module called the Advanced Modeling Extension. Although the AME commands act like an integral part of AutoCAD, they are actually a separate program which is loaded into AutoCAD and run through ADS and AutoLISP. AME functions are located in the Modeler pull-down and screen menus. You can use either. The pull-down menu uses plain-English command syntax whereas the screen menu uses the actual AME command names. To use, for example, the AME command SOLFILL, you can select Fillet Solids from the Modify submenu of the Modeler pull-down menu or SOLFILL: from the MODIFY submenu of the MODELER screen menu. The first selection of any of the AME commands from either menu in a drawing session automatically loads AME.

To use AME, you must purchase the AME option. When you purchase the AME option, all you get is an authorization code; the program is on your original AutoCAD disks but does not run without the code. If you did not install AME when you installed AutoCAD, rerun the AutoCAD install program from a backup copy of your original AutoCAD disks and select only AME as the option to install. The Region Modeler is a subset of AME that is included with the AutoCAD program and needs no authorization code.

You can load AME or the Region Modeler after you start a new drawing by selecting any of the modeling commands from the pull-down or screen menu. AutoCAD automatically loads the solid modeling functions and initializes the 3D environment for modeling. If you want to load AME without using a menu, you can enter **(xload "AME")** at the command line or load AME.EXP through the Applications dialog box.

Creating a Simple Model Using Primitives

Many solid models can be created from little more than boxes, cylinders, and other simple shapes. AutoCAD provides the following six commands for creating 3D solid primitives:

- **SOLBOX.** This command creates a box shape defined by diagonally opposite corners and a height you specify. You also can specify a box by length, width, and height or use the Cube option to create a cube of a specified size.
- **SOLCONE.** This command creates a circular or elliptical conic solid. If circular, you provide a center point, radius or diameter, and height. For elliptical cones, you specify two axes, as you do for the ELLIPSE command, along with the height.
- **SOLCYL.** This command creates a solid cylinder given a center point, radius or diameter, and a height. It may be elliptical; the prompts are identical to SOLCONE.
- **SOLSPHERE.** This command creates a solid sphere, given a center point and radius or diameter.
- **SOLTORUS.** This command creates a torus, like its surface counterpart in AutoCAD's 3D objects icon menu. You specify the center point, radius or diameter of the torus, and radius or diameter of the tube.
- **SOLWEDGE.** Creates a wedge defined by opposite corners and the height of the wedge; or by the width, length, and height you specify. The first point specifies the thick end of the wedge.

These commands can be entered at the `Command:` prompt or selected from the tablet, screen, or pull-down menu. Many AME commands have three-character abbreviations defined in the ACAD.PGP file. The DDSOLPRM command opens the AME Primitives dialog box shown in figure 23.7. To access DDSOLPRM, select Primitives from the Modeler pull-down menu. If the Primitives selection us unavailable, reload the menu with the MENU command. To select a primitive, first click on the desired primitive's icon, and then on OK. As with most dialog box selections, you also can just double-click on the primitive's icon to both select and accept the command.

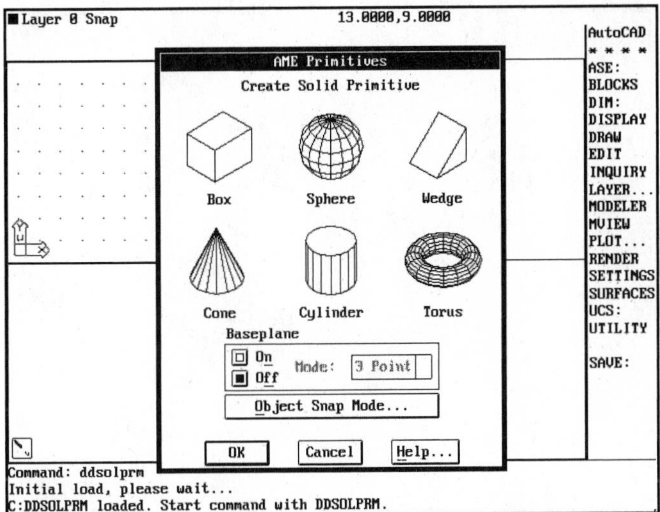

Figure 23.7:

The AME Primitives dialog box (DDSOLPRM command).

The height of these solids is parallel to the Z axis. The bases of wedges and boxes always are parallel to the X and Y axes of the current UCS, so to create rotated wedges or boxes, you first must either adjust your UCS or use the Baseplane option. The Baseplane option enables you to define a temporary UCS for the current primitive. Baseplane uses the same options as the UCS command but operates within the solid primitive commands. The current UCS is restored following command completion.

Although you can control the Z elevation of these primitives by presetting an elevation with the ELEV command or ELEVATION system variable, setting ELEVATION and adjusting UCSs can lead to confusing combinations. Instead, control elevation with UCSs, the Baseplane option, or by specifying a Z value as part of the first coordinate. Specifying a Z value (relative to the current UCS) as part of the first coordinate is the easiest method; the solid is created relative to that point.

In the next exercise, use the SOLBOX and SOLCYL commands to rough out your first solid model — a guide block (see fig. 23.8).

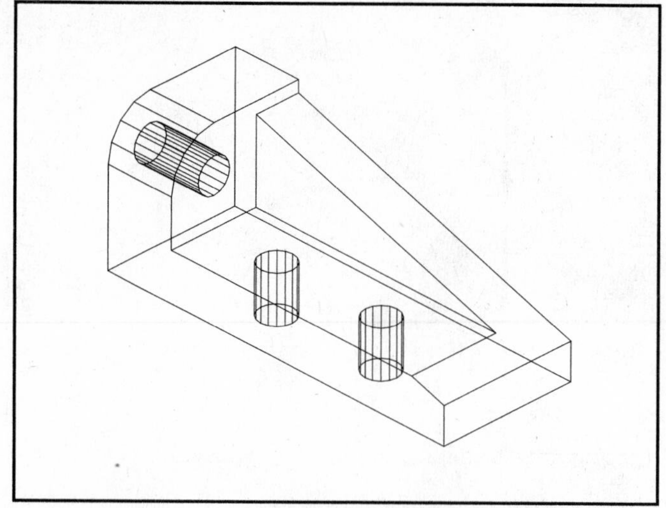

Figure 23.8:
The finished guide block 3D solid model.

Creating Your First Solid Model

Begin a new drawing named `GUIDBLOK=3D` and select the 3D isometric (upper right) viewport to make it current.

`Command:` **`ZOOM`** ↵	
`All/Center/Dynamic/Extents/Left/ Previous/Vmax/Window/<Scale(X/XP)>:` **`C`** ↵	Selects Center option
`Center point:` **`3,3`** ↵	Specifies center
`Magnification or Height <17.8164>:` **`8`** ↵	Specifies height
`Command:` *Restore the* Right *UCS*	
Choose Modeler, *then* Primitives, *and double-click on the* Box *icon*	Issues DDSOLPRM, displays AME primitives dialog box, then issues SOLBOX command

`Command: solbox`
`Initial load, please wait...`
`Initializing Advanced Modeling Extension.`	

`Baseplane/Center/<Corner of box> <0,0,0>:` *Press Enter*	Accepts default corner of 0,0,0

`Cube/Length/<Other corner>: 3,3 ↵`	Specifies other corner
`Height: 1.5 ↵`	Specifies height
`Phase I - Boundary evaluation begins. Phase II - Tessellation computation begins. Updating the Advanced Modeling Extension database.`	and draws box
Restore the FRONT UCS	
Choose Modeler, *then* Primitives, *and double-click on the* Box *icon*	Issues SOLBOX
`Command: solbox`	
`Baseplane/Center/<Corner of box> <0,0,0>: 1.5,0,-3 ↵`	Specifies first corner
`Cube/Length/<Other corner>: L ↵`	Specifies Length option
`Length: 6.5 ↵`	
`Width: 2.75 ↵`	
`Height: 1 ↵`	

Boundary evaluation and tessellation occurs, and the box is drawn.

Set the UCS to WORLD	
Choose Model, Primitives, *then* **O**bject Snap Mode	Displays AME Primitives object, then Running Object Snap dialog boxes
Turn on **E**ndpoint *object snap mode, then* OK	Sets running ENDPoint object snap and returns to the AME Primitives dialog box
Double-click on the Box *icon*	Executes SOLBOX
`Baseplane/Center/<Corner of box> <0,0,0>:` *Pick point near* ① *(see fig. 23.9)*	Specifies first corner
`Cube/Length/<Other corner>:` *Pick point near* ②	Specifies opposite corner

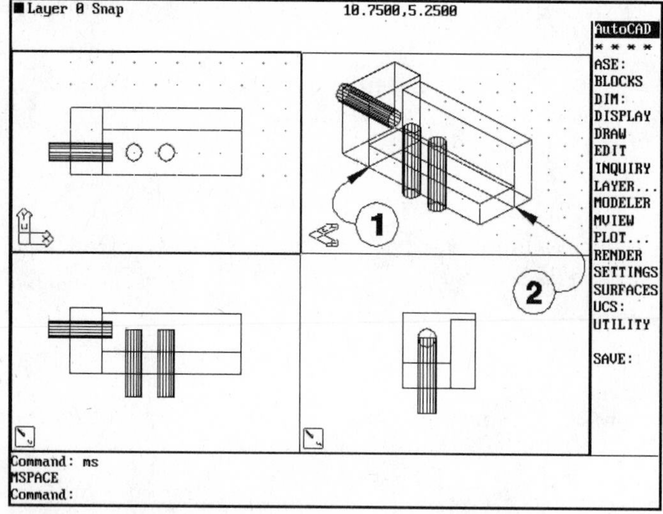

Figure 23.9:

The roughed-out guide block model.

`Height:` **`1`** ↵	Specifies height

Boundary evaluation and tessellation occur, and the box is drawn.

Restore the RIGHT UCS

Choose Modeler, *then* Primitives, *then* <u>O</u>bject Snap Mode, and turn off <u>E</u>ndpoint *object snap mode, then choose* OK	Turns off running object snap and returns to the Solid Primitives dialog box
Double-click on the Cylinder *option*	Issues SOLCYL
`Baseplane/Elliptical/` `<Center point>:` **`1,2,-1`** ↵	Specifies center
`Diameter/<Radius>:` **`.375`** ↵	Specifies radius
`Center of other end/<Height>:` **`3`** ↵	Specifies height

Boundary evaluation and tessellation occur, and the cylinder is drawn.

Set the UCS to WORLD

`Command:` **`CYL`** ↵	Issues SOLCYL command
`Elliptical/<Center point>:` **`3,1,-1`** ↵	
`Diameter/<Radius>:` **`.375`** ↵	
`Center of other end/<Height>:` **`3`** ↵	

Boundary evaluation and tessellation occur, and the cylinder is drawn.

```
Command: CYL ↵
Elliptical/<Center point>: 4.5,1,-1 ↵
Diameter/<Radius>: .375 ↵
Center of other end/<Height>: 3 ↵
```

Boundary evaluation and tessellation occur, and the cylinder is drawn.

Zoom in each of the viewports to match the views illustrated in figure 23.9

Your model should look like figure 23.9. But, the model still has one mistake. The last cylinder created was located at the wrong coordinate. It should be one inch farther away from cylinder number 2. To show that solids can be edited like any other type of entity, use the stretch grip editing mode to move it over one inch along the X axis.

Moving Solids Using the MOVE Command

Select the 3D isometric viewport.

Command: *Select the right-most cylinder*	Highlights it and displays grip at base
Pick the grip	Enters Stretch mode
<Stretch to point>/Base point/Copy Undo/eXit: **@1,0** ↵	Specifies displacement and moves cylinder
Command: **REDRAWALL** ↵	
Command: **QSAVE** ↵	Saves drawing

You also can use other editing commands to change solids. You can, for example, use ROTATE to rotate solids in 3D space. Or you could have simply copied the second cylinder to create the third.

Boolean Operations — AutoCAD's Solids Modifiers

Operations that combine solids, subtract one solid from another, and find the intersection of solids are called *Boolean operations*. AutoCAD includes three Boolean functions for performing those three tasks: SOLUNION, SOLSUB (SOLid SUBtraction), and SOLINT (SOLid INTersection).

Adding two solids together to form a single homogeneous solid is called a union. AutoCAD provides the SOLUNION command to do just that. The SOLSUB command is used to subtract one solid from another, such as subtracting a cylinder from a box to form a hole. Finally, the SOLINT command enables you to find the intersection of two solids (the common space shared by the two solids).

When you use the SOLUNION command, you build a selection set of solids. Then you press Enter to finish the set, and AutoCAD combines all of the individual solids in the set to form a composite solid.

The SOLSUB command acts a little differently. SOLSUB prompts you to select entities in two sets. The first set of entities comprises the main group of solids. The second set of entities includes the entities to be subtracted from the main group. So, if you want to subtract a cylinder from a box to form a hole, select the box first (as the main group), and then select the cylinder as the second set.

SOLINT finds the intersection between two solids. (You use it a little later in the chapter.) For now, use the SOLUNION and SOLSUB commands on the guide block to join the boxes and create the holes. These solid utility commands are located in the Modeler screen and pull-down menus. In the Modeler pull-down menu, they are Union, Subtract, and Intersect.

In this next exercise, you use these commands to further refine your guide block model.

Using SOLUNION and SOLSUB To Modify Solids

Choose Modeler, *then* Subtract — Issues SOLSUB command

`Command: solsub`
`Source objects...`
`Select objects:` *Select the bottom horizontal box at ① and left vertical box at ② (see fig. 23.10)* — Selects the primitives to subtract from

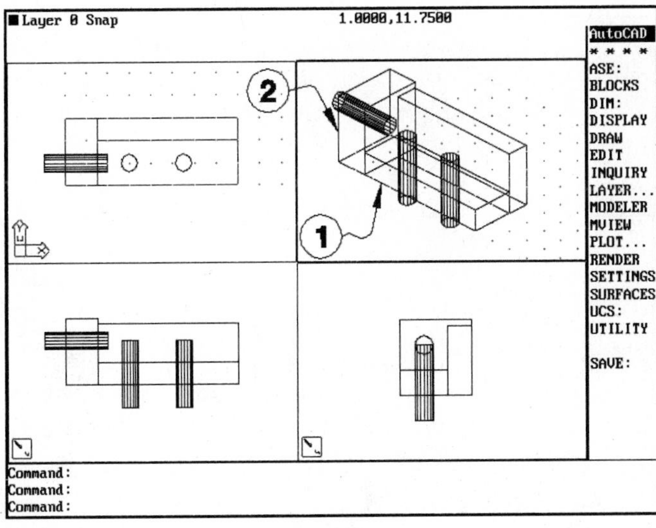

Figure 23.10: The guide block before subtraction and union.

`Select objects:` *Press Enter* — Ends selection

`2 solids selected.`
`Objects to subtract from them...`

`Select objects:` *Select the three cylinders* — Selects the primitives to subtract

`Select objects:` *Press Enter* — Ends selection

`3 solids selected.`

Boundary evaluation and tessellation occur, and the two boxes are redrawn as a single solid with 3 holes through it. In this case, SOLSUB performed a union (of the two boxes) as well as a subtraction. You also can use SOLUNION to join solids.

Choose Modeler, *then* Union	Issues SOLUNION command
`Command: solunion`	
`Select objects:` *Select the newly created single solid, and the right vertical box*	
`Select objects:` *Press Enter*	Ends selection
`2 solids selected.`	

Boundary evaluation and tessellation occur (see fig. 23.11).

`Command: QSAVE ↵`	Saves drawing

As figure 23.11 shows, the lines on the right side and front dividing the horizontal box from the vertical box are gone. The drawing is all one solid entity now.

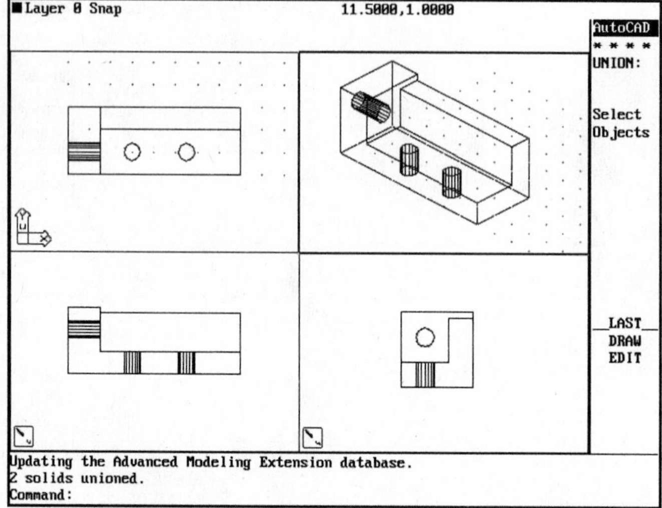

Figure 23.11:
The guide block after subtraction and union.

Creating Solid Tools for Removing Material

In manufacturing, you use different tools to remove material from stock to create a finished part. Drill bits (cylinders) are used to form holes, milling cutters can be used to cut rectangular shapes from stock, and broaches (extruded shapes) can be used to form keyways, keyseats, and other broached shapes.

The same concept applies in solid modeling, and that is why using a solid model is one of the easiest ways to model in 3D. Many of the operations you perform to create your design are just like the operations you would perform in the shop to manufacture the part. You do not have to learn a new way of doing things.

If you need to punch a slot in your model, you can create the outline of the slot, extrude it to a solid, then subtract it from the main body, forming a void. If you need to mill a circular pocket out of your model, draw the profile of the pocket and rotate it to form a solid, then subtract it from the main body. In both cases, you are making tools out of 2D geometry that can be used to modify your model.

In the real world, two bodies cannot coexist in the same space at the same time. Inside the computer, it is different. You can create two solids and put one inside the other. The main, or outside, solid is still completely solid — at least as far as the computer is concerned. But when you subtract the inside solid from the main body, you form a void where the interior solid used to be.

Now use that technique on the guide block. Create a wedge using the SOLWEDGE command. Then, position the wedge in the same space as the guide block, using it as a subtraction tool to form a sloped surface.

Using a Wedge as a Machining Tool

Choose Model, *then* Primitives	Opens Solid Primitives dialog box
Double-click on the Wedge *icon*	Issues SOLWEDGE

```
Baseplane/<Corner of wedge>:0,-3.5↵
Length/<Other corner>: L ↵
Length: 9 ↵
Width: 3 ↵
Height: 2.75 ↵
```

Boundary evaluation and tessellation occur, and the wedge is drawn.

Restore UCS FRONT

`Command:` **`ROTATE`** ↵

`Select objects:` **`L`** ↵ — Selects the wedge

`Base point:` *Pick a point near front middle of base of wedge*

`<Rotation angle>/Reference:` **`180`** ↵ — Rotates wedge

Zoom extents as required to see the wedge and the guide block

`Command:` **`MOVE`** ↵

`Select objects:` **`L`**↵ — Selects the wedge

`Base point or displacement:` *Use* ENDP *object snap to pick left rear endpoint of wedge at ① (see fig. 23.12)*

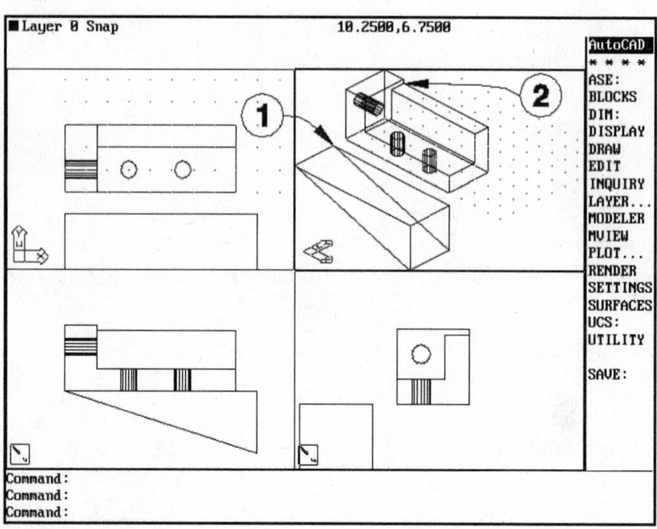

Figure 23.12:

The wedge, ready to move and subtract.

`Second point of displacement:` *Use* ENDP *object snap to pick rear vertical box at ②*

`Command:` **`Sub`** ↵ — Issues SOLSUB command

`Source objects...`
`Select objects:` *Select the rear vertical box*

`1 found`

`Select objects:` *Press Enter* — Ends selection

`1 solid selected.`

`Objects to subtract from them...`

`Select objects:` *Select the wedge*

Select objects: *Press Enter* Ends selection

`1 solids selected.`

Boundary evaluation and tessellation occur, and the block is redrawn beveled (see fig. 23.13).

Zoom extents

`Command:` **`QSAVE`** ↵

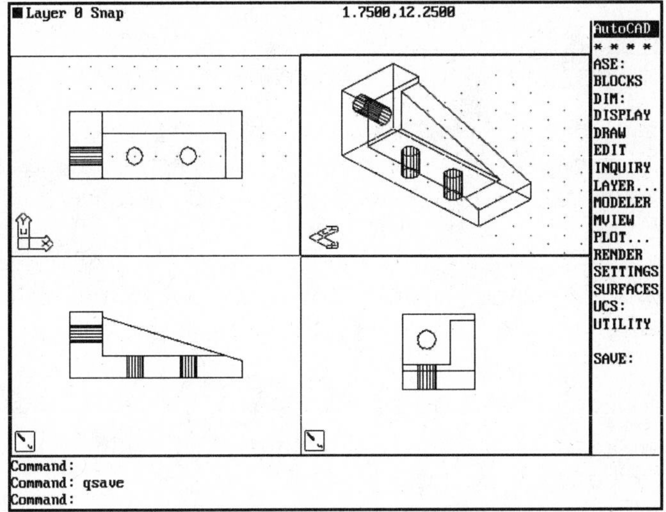

Figure 23.13:

The wedge removed from guide block.

If your finished profile required a more complex shape, you could draw the shape in 2D, extrude it to form a solid, then subtract it from the main body. Extrusions are covered a little later in this chapter.

Creating Fillets and Chamfers on Existing Solids

When you draw fillets and chamfers in 2D, drawing rectangular shapes and then filleting the corners is often the easiest method. You also can do the same thing with 3D solids using the SOLFILL and SOLCHAM utility commands. These are located in the Modeler Modify menus.

SOLCHAM can add to the solid to chamfer an inside edge or subtract from it to bevel an outside edge. SOLFILL also can fillet an inside edge or round off an outside edge. Both SOLFILL and SOLCHAM work on straight, convex, or concave edges of a solid. Where two or more edges come together at a corner, SOLFILL and SOLCHAM correctly resolve the corner.

When you use SOLCHAM, AutoCAD first prompts for a base surface, then for the edge(s) to chamfer. Then, you specify the distance to chamfer back along the base surface (which is why you specify a base surface). Finally, you specify the distance to chamfer along the second surface. If you pick an edge that is not adjacent to the base surface, it is not chamfered. When you press Enter, AutoCAD creates a primitive called a chamfer and automatically subtracts or unions (adds) it to the solid.

Because a fillet is symmetrical along an edge, SOLFILL prompts only for the edge(s) you want to fillet. You can select one or more edges. Then, you specify the radius of the fillet. AutoCAD calculates the resulting fillet primitive, then subtracts or unions it to the solid.

Use SOLFILL to finish up the guide block model by filleting the corner of the left vertical box.

Filleting a Corner Using SOLFILL

Choose Model, *then* Modify, *then* Fillet Solids — Issues SOLFILL command

`Command: solfill`

`Pick edges of solids to be filleted (Press ENTER when done):` *Pick left vertical plate at ① (see fig. 23.14), then Press Enter*

```
1 edges selected.
Diameter/<Radius> of fillet< 0.00>: 1 ↵
```

Boundary evaluation and tessellation occur, and the fillet appears (see fig. 23.15).

```
Command: QSAVE ↵
```

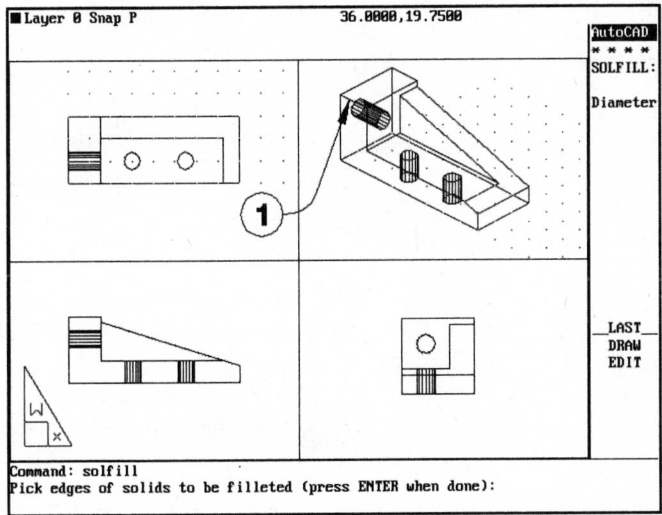

Figure 23.14:
The guide block before the fillet.

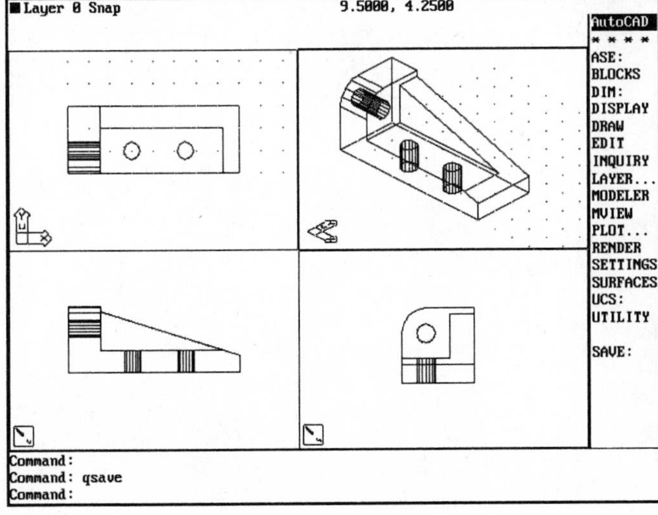

Figure 23.15:
The finished guide block after the fillet.

There is one thing to keep in mind when you are creating multiple fillets on a model. If you select a single edge to fillet, then come back and fillet an edge that intersects the fillet, you will get the effect shown in figure 23.16. If you want the two edges to fillet together smoothly, as shown in figure 23.17, pick both edges within the same SOLFILL command. If, for example, you wanted to fillet all twelve edges of a cube to model a die (as in a pair of dice), you would have to select all twelve edges in the same operation.

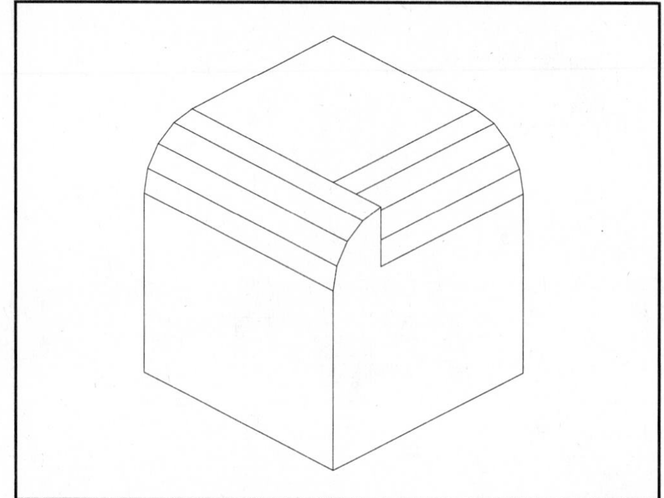

Figure 23.16: Non-simultaneous fillets.

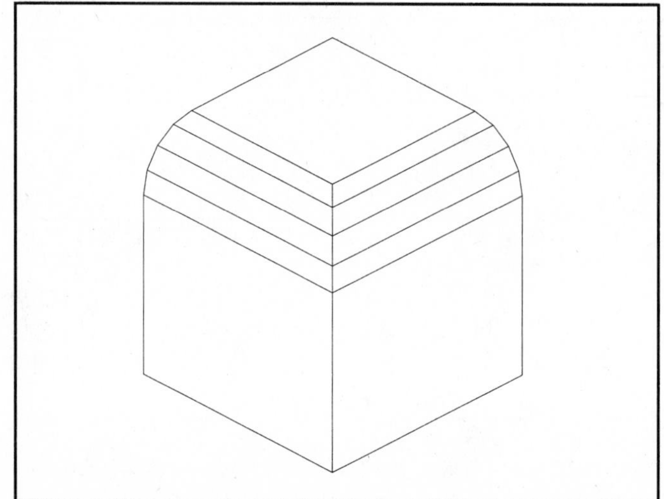

Figure 23.17: Simultaneous fillets.

By now, you may wish you could remove hidden lines and view your solid clearly. You can, but you need to prepare your model before you can use the HIDE command on it.

Controlling How Solid Models Display

You can choose to display your solids in wireframe (the default) or with surface meshes. The two methods do not produce much difference in how the model looks. But when you perform a hidden line removal with the HIDE command or shade your model with SHADE, it does not display properly unless you first put a surface mesh on it.

AutoCAD provides commands to convert solids between wireframe and mesh representations and to control the resolution of your wireframe or surface mesh. The resolution can be set by command or by setting a variable. The following are some of the commands that control solid model display:

- **SOLWIRE.** This command enables you to select and display a solid as a wireframe.
- **SOLMESH.** This command enables you to select and display solids using a surface mesh. Solids must have a surface mesh for the HIDE and SHADE commands to work properly.
- **SOLWDENS.** (SOLid Wire DENSity) This command sets the *wire density* (number of tessellation lines) for curved surfaces of wireframes and the mesh density of meshes. It can be a number from 1 to 8. Higher numbers give higher resolutions and take longer to calculate images.
- **SOLVAR.** Like the SETVAR command, SOLVAR enables you to assign values to variables. SOLVAR controls only variables that relate to solid modeling. You can set wire density with the SOLWDENS command, or you can use SOLVAR to set the variable SOLWDENS.

The RENDER command automatically performs surface meshing on AME solids; however, be certain to set the SOLWDENS variable beforehand.

These commands are located in the Modeler pull-down menu under Display, or you can access them from the Display option in the Modeler screen menu.

These settings affect only how solids display — internally, they still are calculated as solids with complete precision, unlike AutoCAD 3D surface entities, which are only approximations.

The choice of wireframe or mesh has other effects beyond how it displays. Meshes and wireframes are both specially controlled blocks, and only one can display at a time. A mesh explodes into pface entities while a wireframe explodes into lines and polylines. You can use object snaps such as TAN, CEN, and QUA on arcs and circles in a wireframe, but you will be restricted to osnaps such as ENDP, INT, and MID in mesh representations.

Try the solid display functions to place a mesh on the guide block model, and then use HIDE to perform a hidden line removal on the isometric view.

Checking the Model With HIDE

Choose Modeler, *then* Display, *then* Mesh	Issues SOLMESH

`Command: solmesh`
`Select solids to be meshed ...`
`Select objects:` *Select the solid*	

`1 solid selected.`
`Surface meshing of current solid is completed.`
`Creating block for mesh representation...`	

`Done.`	
Select the isometric viewport to make it current.	
Choose Render, *then* Hide	Issues the HIDE command

`Command: _hide`
`Regenerating drawing.`
`Hiding lines: done 100%`
	Performs hidden-line removal on the guide block (see fig. 23.18)

`Command:` **`QSAVE`** ↵	Saves drawing for later in this chapter

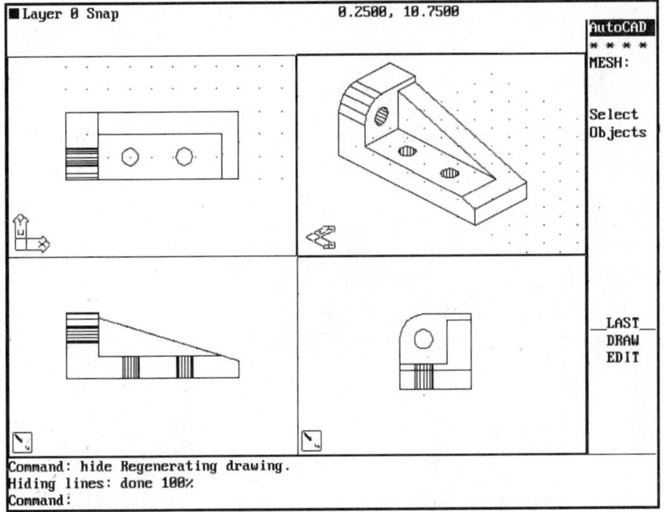

Figure 23.18:

The finished guide block, after using the SOLMESH and HIDE commands.

To round out our tour of solid primitives, you will next work with spheres and toruses.

Creating Toroidal and Spherical Primitives

AutoCAD's AME and AMElite modules include functions to create toruses and spheres. Both functions work much like the functions for creating toroidal and spherical surfaces that you can access from the 3D menu, but they create solid primitives rather than a surface mesh.

The SOLSPHERE command prompts you for a center point, which can be picked or entered at the `Command:` prompt. Then, you supply either a radius value or diameter value.

The SOLTORUS command prompts you to specify the center of the torus, the radius or diameter of the torus, and the radius or diameter of the tube (see fig. 23.19). As with the TORUS surface mesh command, you can pick points for the distance values or type them in.

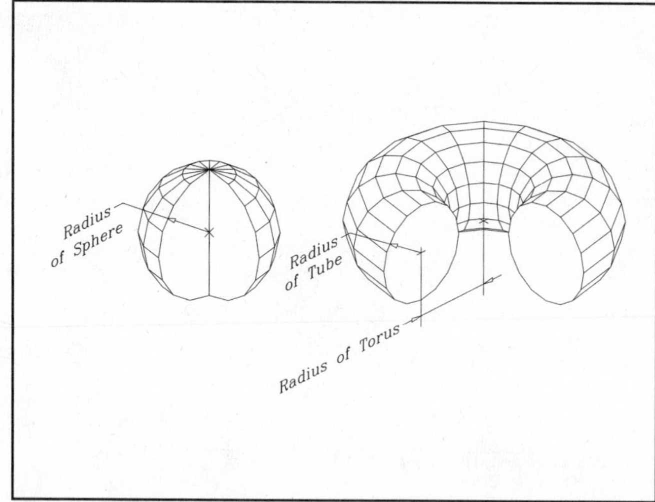

Figure 23.19:
SOLSPHERE and SOLTORUS examples.

If you specify a radius for the tube that is greater than the radius of the torus, you create a self-intersecting torus. A *self-intersecting torus* has no center hole and looks like an apple. If you specify a negative torus radius, the resulting solid has a football shape.

Creating Extrusions and Revolved Solids

Often, three-dimensional solids are patterned from a two-dimensional model. This might be the 2D profile of a part that you extrude or a cross section that you revolve to form a solid. AutoCAD AME and AMElite provide SOLEXT for extrusions and SOLREV for revolved solids. Both use 2D geometry as a basis for the solids.

The SOLEXT command extrudes polylines, polygons, circles, ellipses, and 3D polylines. If the polyline you select has a width associated with it, SOLEXT ignores the width and extrudes the shape from the center line of the polyline. There are other limits to what SOLEXT can do. The geometry must consist of at least two line segments. If the polyline is not closed, SOLEXT assumes it to be closed by a line from the first segment to the last. If the polyline has segments that intersect (whether real or assumed by SOLEXT), SOLEXT does not extrude the shape.

Extrusions can be straight or tapered. The extrusion taper angle must be zero or greater, and must be less than 90 degrees, so the 2D base is always larger than the tapered end of the extrusion. In other words, you cannot taper out from the base — only in.

In this exercise, use the SOLEXT command to create the basic solid that will be used to model the hinge block. Begin a new drawing, setting it equal to your 3D prototype drawing, draw the profile, and extrude it.

Using an Extruded Solid to Create HINGBLOK

Begin a NEW drawing named `HINGBLOK=3D`, select the lower left viewport (front view) to make it current, and restore the FRONT UCS.

`Command:` **`ZOOM`** ↵

`All/Center/Dynamic/Extents/Left/Previous/ Vmax/Window/<Scale(X/XP)>:` **`L`** ↵	Specifies left corner option

`Lower left corner point:` **`-1,-1`** ↵

`Magnification or Height:` **`5`** ↵

Use the PLINE command to draw the front profile with lower left corner at 0,0 as shown in figure 23.20. Use the Line and Arc options, and close it. Then draw the hinge pin hole with a .375 radius circle at 1.25,1.5.

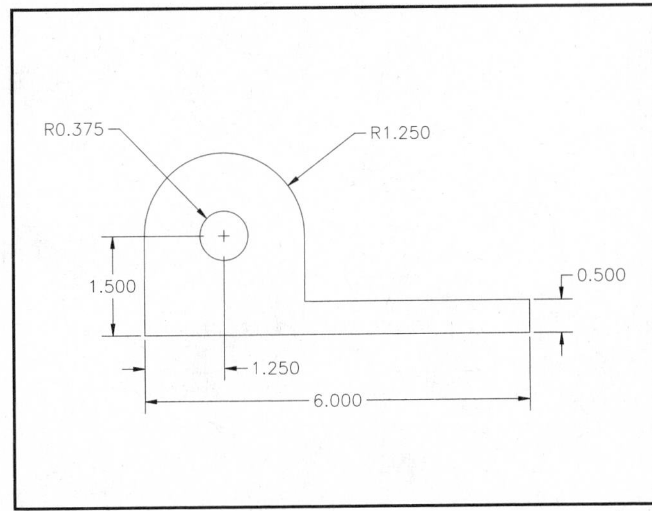

Figure: 23.20.

The front profile of a hinge block.

Choose Modeler, *then* Extrude	Issues SOLEXT
`Command: solext` `Select regions polylines and circles for extrusion...`	
`Select objects:` *Select the polyline and circle*	
`2 found`	
`Select objects:` *Press Enter*	Ends selection
`Height of extrusion:` **3** ↵	
`Extrusion taper angle <0>:` *Press Enter*	Accepts default taper angle (none) and extrudes the profile and hole (cylinder)
Set the UCS to WORLD	
Move the hinge and hole with a displacement of 0,3	

Zoom each of the viewports to match figure 23.21.

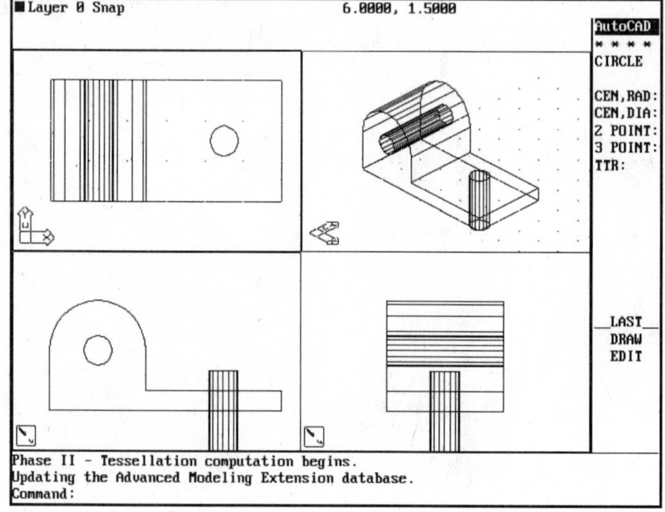

Figure 23.21:

The hinge block before using the SOLSUB command.

Select the top view

Draw the bolt hole with a circle at `4.5,1.5,-1` *with a radius of* `.375`

Command: **SOLEXT** ↵

Select polylines and circles for extrusion...

Select objects: *Select the circle*

Height of extrusion: **2** ↵

Extrusion taper angle <0>: *Press Enter* — Extrudes the cylinder

Your drawing should resemble figure 23.21.

Using the SOLSUB *command, select the main body and subtract the two holes (see fig. 23.22)*

Command: **QSAVE** ↵

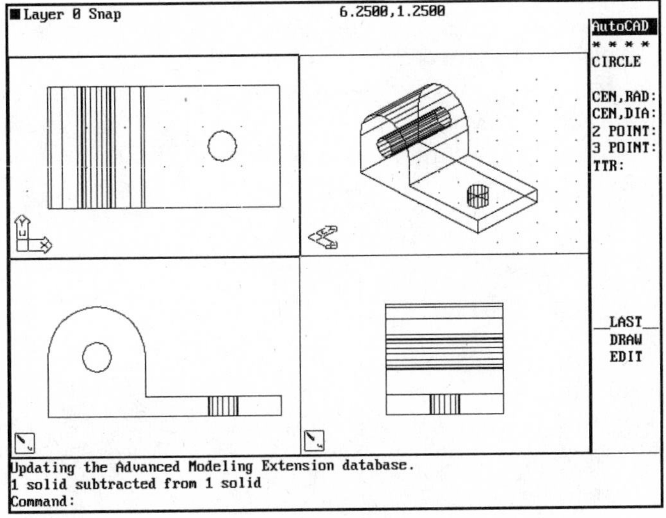

Figure 23.22:
The hinge block after the SOLSUB command.

Before you finish modeling the hinge block, practice separating joined solids from another using the utility command called SOLSEP.

Separating Joined Solids Using SOLSEP

When you perform a union on two solids, you are joining them together. When you subtract one solid from another, you are still joining them together in the sense that both original primitives still exist, although one exists as a void.

AME provides the SOLSEP command to enable you to separate solids that have been joined together with a union or subtraction. If, for example, you had subtracted a cylinder from a solid to form a hole only to find that the hole should have been countersunk, you would need to separate the original cylinder from the rest of the model.

Go back to the hinge block drawing and separate the hole in the horizontal plate from the main body of the model. Then, erase the cylindrical solid and put in the countersunk hole.

Creating a Countersink Using SOLREV

The next exercise also gives you a chance to use the SOLREV command to create a revolved solid. Separate the original hole, erase it, and draw the profile of the countersink as you would see it in section. Then revolve the countersink to create a solid countersink tool to be used to remove material from the main body.

Separating and Revolving Solids

Choose Modeler, *then* Modify, *then* Separate	Issues SOLSEP
`Command: solsep`	
`Select objects:` *Select the solid*	
`1 found.`	
`Select objects:` *Press Enter*	
`1 solid selected.`	Separates cylinder from hinge block
Erase the cylinder.	
`Select objects:` *Press Enter* *Select the lower left viewport (front view)*	

Restore UCS FRONT

Using the PLINE command, draw a profile of countersink from `4.5,0,-1.5` to `@.375,0` to `@0,.25` to `@.25,.25` to `@-.625,0` and close (see fig. 23.23).

Set the UCS to WORLD

Choose Modeler, *then* Revolve — Issues SOLREV

`Command: solrev`

`Select region, polyline or circle for revolution...` *Select polyline profile of countersink*

`Axis of revolution - Entity/X/Y/<Start point of axis>:` *Use* ENDP *object snap to pick the bottom point of countersink at center line*

`End point of axis:` *Use* ENDP *object snap to pick top of center line*

`Angle of revolution <full circle>:` *Press Enter* — Revolves profile and draws countersink

Select the isometric view

Using the SOLSUB command, select the main body and subtract the hinge pin hole and countersink. Your drawing now should resemble figure 23.24.

`Command:` **`QSAVE`** ↵

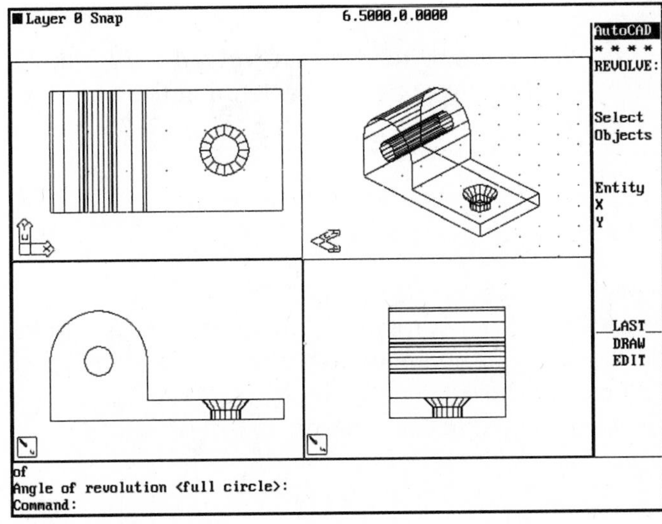

Figure 23.23:

The hinge block after revolving the countersink.

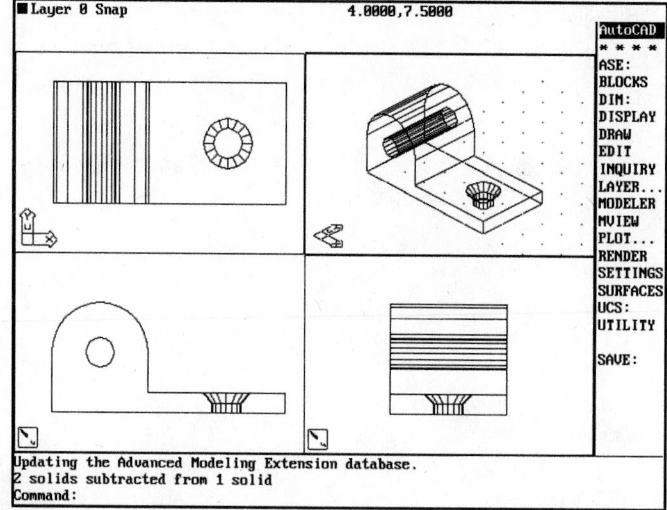

Figure 23.24:

Hinge block after subtracting the pin hole and countersink.

You may have realized that you could have just used a SOLCHAM on the original cylinder. But then you would not have an excuse to use SOLSEP and SOLREV.

More about Revolved Solids

The last exercise showed you how to create a revolved solid from 2D geometry. SOLREV provides four options for defining the axis of revolution.

SOLREV Options

- **Entity.** This option enables you to select a line or single-segment polyline to use as the axis of rotation. You cannot use one of the segments of your profile geometry as the axis of rotation. If necessary, osnap a 2D line over the segment you want as the axis, then pick the 2D line when prompted for the axis entity.

- **X.** This option defines the X axis of the current coordinate system as the axis of revolution. The axis passes through the origin.
- **Y.** This option defines the Y axis of the current coordinate system as the axis of revolution. The axis passes through the origin.
- **<Start Point>.** This option enables you to pick two points to define the axis of revolution. Using this option, you can pick endpoints of segments in your profile or pick any other two points.

You have the basic blank stock for the hinge block, along with the countersunk hole. Next, switch to the right side view and create a rectangular tool to cut the material out between each of the vertical hinge plates. After you create the extruded cutting block, subtract it from the main body.

Using an Extruded Solid as a Cutting Tool

Select the lower right viewport (right side view).

Restore UCS RIGHT.

Using the PLINE command, draw a profile of the cutout between the two vertical plates from point `.75,.5,-2` to `@1.5<0` to `@3<90` to `@1.5<180` and close (see lower right viewport in fig. 23.25).

`Command:` **`EXT`** ↵	Issues SOLEXT
`Select regions, polylines and circles for extrusion...` `Select objects:` **`L`**↵	Selects the polyline
`Height of extrusion:` **`6`** ↵	
`Extrusion taper angle <0>:` *Press Enter*	Extrudes cutting tool (see fig. 23.25)

Using the SOLSUB command, select the main body of the model and subtract the block (see fig. 23.26).

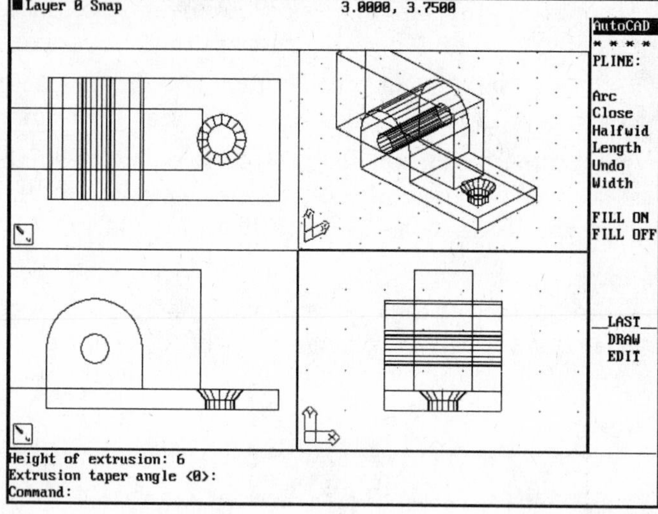

Figure 23.25:

An extruded block as a cutting tool.

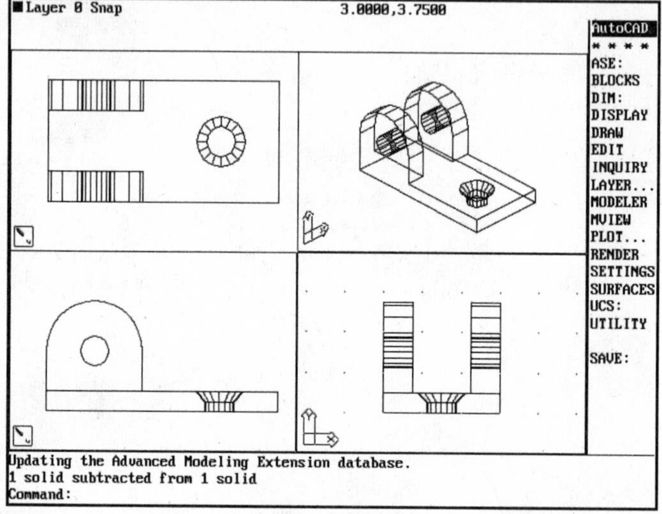

Figure 23.26:

The hinge block after the block is removed.

Finishing the Hinge Block with Fillets and Holes

To finish the hinge block round off the end of the horizontal plate with two fillets.

Pick both corners of the horizontal plate and fillet them at the same time. Finally, place a mesh on the finished model and perform a hidden line removal on the isometric view to visually check it.

Finishing the Hinge Block with Fillets and Holes

Select the isometric view and zoom in to right front end of horizontal plate

`Command:` **`SOLFILL`** ↵

`Pick edges of solids to be filleted (Press ENTER when done):` *Select vertical edges of plate at ① and ② (see fig 23.27), then press Enter*

`2 edges selected.`

`Diameter/<Radius> of fillet< 0.00>: 1.5` ↵

Boundary evaluation and tessellation occur. Figure 23.28 shows the filleted plate.

Set the UCS to WORLD

Zoom previous

Finally, visually check the model by putting a mesh on it and doing a hide or shade.

Choose Modeler, *then* Display, *then* Mesh

`Command: solmesh`

`Select objects:` *Select the solid*

`Command:` **`HIDE`** ↵ *(or SHADE)*	Removes hidden lines
`Command:` **`END`** ↵	Saves drawing and exits AutoCAD

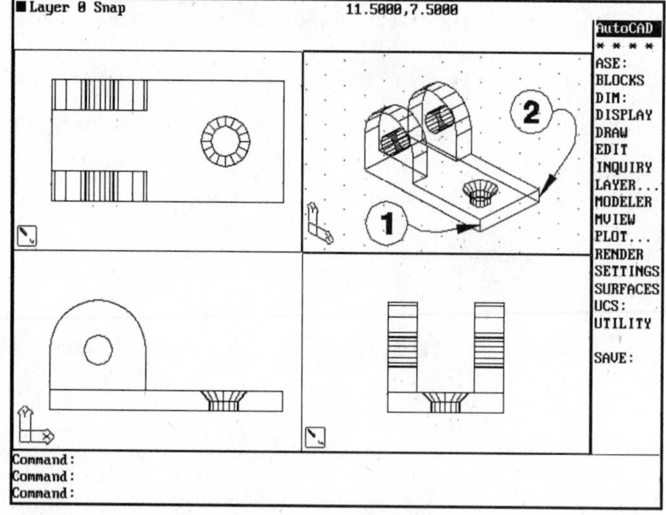

Figure 23.27:

The fillet pick points.

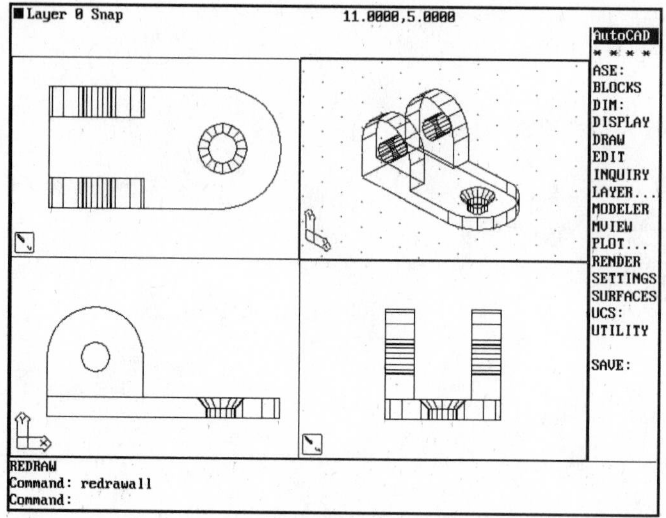

Figure 23.28:

The hinge filleted plate.

That takes you through all of the modeling primitives except cones. Next, you use the SOLCONE and SOLINT commands to find the intersection of two solids.

Intersections, Interferences, and SOLINT

AME includes a Boolean function called SOLINT that enables you to model the intersection of two or more solids. The *intersection* is the common mass shared by the solids you select. You can use SOLINT to do such things as take a slice out of a cone. In fact, that is just what you are about to do!

Start a new drawing and set it equal to 3D. Create a cone with a diameter of 4" and a height of 6". Then, create a box 6" high to use as a tool to create a slice of the cone.

Finding the Intersection of a Cone and Box

Begin a new drawing named `CONE=3D`.

Command: **SOLCONE** ↵

Baseplane/Elliptical/<Center point>: *Pick a point in the middle for center of cone*

Diameter/<Radius>: **2** ↵

Apex/<Height>: **6** ↵

Command: **SOLBOX** ↵

Baseplane/Center/<Corner of box>: *Draw the box to intersect the cone as shown in figure 23.29*

Cube/Length/<Other corner>:

Height: **6** ↵

Command: **SOLINT** ↵

Select objects: *Pick the cone and the box*

Select objects: *Press Enter*

2 solids selected.

Command: **REDRAW** ↵

Command: **QUIT** ↵

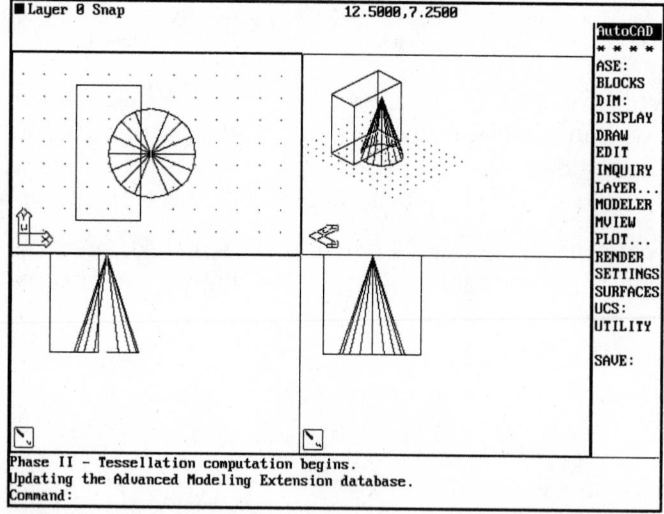

Figure 23.29:

The cone and box before using the SOLINT command.

As figure 23.30 shows, SOLINT finds the material that is common to both solids and subtracts the rest.

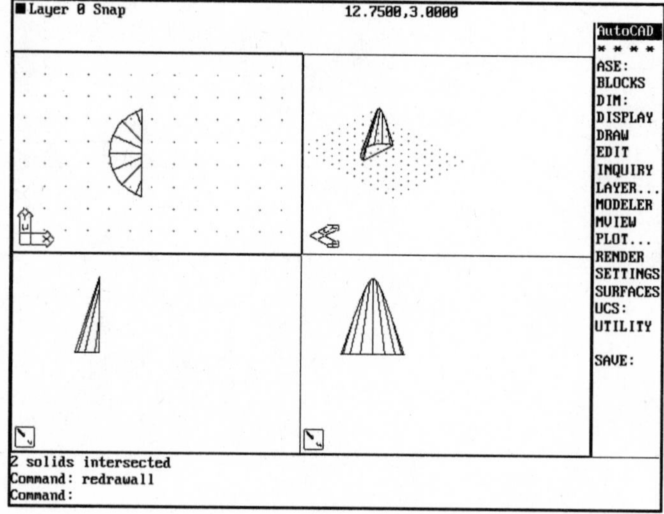

Figure 23.30:

Common material shared by the cone and box.

This is a good place for a break. You have covered all of the solid primitives and most of the utility commands. Most of what you have covered so far is not very different from basic 3D surface modeling.

In the next section, you learn how to specify material types for your model, how to change the material specification, and how to determine some of the mass properties of your model. You also learn to use a few more of the solids utility commands.

Adding Properties to Your Solid Model

Although creating a 2D drawing from a 3D solid model is one of the easiest ways to draw a complex part, the emphasis in solid modeling has traditionally been on designing rather than drafting. A large part of design involves not only defining the geometry of a part but also defining and determining other characteristics such as weight, center of gravity, surface area, and moments of inertia.

AutoCAD's AME enables you to determine those properties and others by first specifying certain parameters, like the type of material from which the solid would be made. Then, after setting a few variables to control the accuracy of your calculations, you can evaluate the design with a single command.

Adding a Material Specification Using SOLMAT

AME includes the SOLMAT and DDSOLMAT commands for controlling a solid's material properties. SOLMAT enables you to choose from a list of common materials to set a solid's default material. If the material you need is not already defined, you can easily create, save, and load your own material specifications.

All of the defined material properties are used when evaluating a solid. For example, the density is used when calculating the weight of a solid. The variables and the units you can assign in a material specification are as follows:

- Density, kg/cu_m
- Young's modulus, GN/sq_m
- Poisson's ratio
- Yield strength, MN/sq_m not,
- Ultimate strength, MN/sq_m
- Thermal conductivity
- Linear expansion coefficient, alpha/1e6
- Specific heat, kJ/(kg deg_C)
- Convection coefficient

SOLMAT Options

The SOLMAT command enables you to manipulate most properties of a solid's material definition. The SOLMAT options are as follows:

- **Change.** This option enables you to change the material assigned to a solid.
- **Edit.** This option enables you to edit specific properties of a material.
- **eXit.** This option exits the SOLMAT command.
- **LIst.** This option displays the current property settings of a material.
- **LOad.** This option enables you to load a material definition from an external ASCII file.
- **New.** This option creates a new material definition.
- **Remove.** This option removes a material definition from the current model.
- **Save.** This option saves a material definition in an external file.
- **Set.** This option sets the default material definition of newly created solids.
- **?.** This option displays a list of all materials currently defined in your model.

Before you calculate the properties of a solid, remember to first assign the correct material to the solid. The default material is MILD_STEEL.

Using the Materials Browser Dialog Box

The DDSOLMAT command provides SOLMAT's functionality with a dialog box interface (see figure 23.31). Enter DDSOLMAT or choose Utility, then Material from the Modeler pull-down to use the Materials Browser to edit existing materials, define new materials, and change the material assignments of existing solids. The options provided in the DDSOLMAT dialog box parallel the SOLMAT options, but the dialog box interface makes editing materials a breeze.

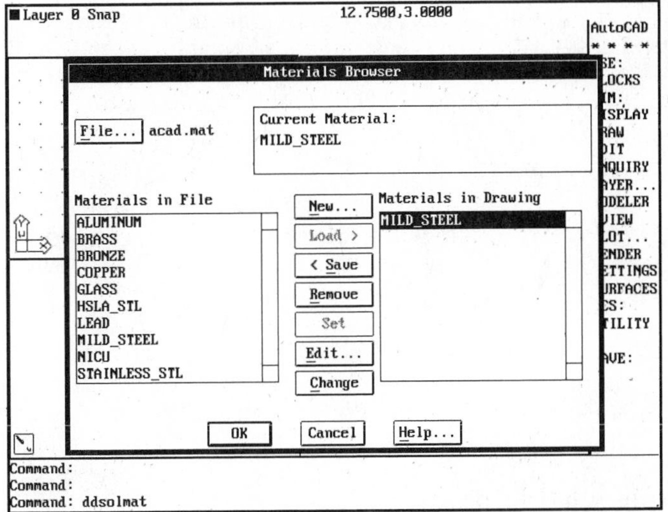

Figure 23.31: The Materials Browser dialog box (DDSOLMAT command).

Calculating the Properties of a Solid

SOLMASSP, and its dialog box version, DDSOLMASSP, are the AME commands for calculating the mass properties of solids in your models. After you have assigned a material definition to the solid, you use SOLMASSP or DDSOLMASSP to calculate and display all of the available properties. You can use these commands to calculate mass, volume, bounding box (3D extents), centroid, moments of inertia, products of inertia, radii of gyration, and principal moments of a solid. When AME is finished calculating those values, you have the option of writing the values to a file. You can type in the command, or Choose Modeler, then Inquiry, then Mass Property.

Changing the Characteristics of a Solid

Standard AutoCAD editing commands, such as STRETCH, do not work on solids and cannot change the size and shape of individual features in a solid. A composite solid is much like a block — you cannot get at the individual entities that make it up, which prevents you from accessing the individual primitive features. You need a way to change solids and their features. One of the most important utility commands for editing solids is the SOLCHP command, which requires the full AME. SOLCHP enables you to change many characteristics of solid primitives. What makes it so important is that you can use the command to change primitives that are part of a larger, composite solid. Here is why.

When you perform a union on two solids, AutoCAD calculates the resulting union and displays the result. But, the original primitives that were unioned still exist in memory, and AutoCAD maintains these along with the composite solid. You cannot see the original primitives, but they still are there and can be accessed by the SOLCHP command (choose Modify, then Change Prim from the Modeler menu.)

SOLCHP enables you to perform such edits as changing the color of a hole, moving a hole in a solid (by relocating the cylinder that created it), deleting a hole, or changing its size. You even can use SOLCHP to change the overall size of the main body. Before using the SOLCHP command, take a look at its options for editing your solids.

The following are SOLCHP options:

- **Color.** This option changes the color assigned to a primitive.
- **Delete.** This option deletes a primitive from the model. If it is a stand-alone primitive (not part of a composite solid), the primitive is deleted altogether. If it is part of a composite, it is deleted from the CSG tree, but you have the option of retaining it as a stand-alone primitive. (The CSG tree is defined following this list.)
- **Evaluate.** This option causes a re-evaluation of the CSG tree, updating the solid and is similar in concept to a drawing regeneration.

- **Instance.** This option creates a copy of the primitive you select, in the same location as the original. This is most useful when you want to copy or replace a feature.
- **Move.** This option enables you to move a primitive around in the solid. You can, for example, relocate a hole (subtracted cylinder) using the Move option.
- **Next.** This option cycles through the solid to the next primitive in the composite solid.
- **Pick.** Although similar to Next, this option enables you to pick the primitive to be edited.
- **Replace.** This option replaces the selected primitive with another solid. You can, for example, create a rectangular solid and replace a hole in a solid with a square cutout simply by replacing the hole's defining cylinder with the new rectangular primitive.
- **Size.** This option gives you control over the size of a selected primitive. You can resize individual components of a composite solid, such as changing the diameter of an existing hole. Size can change the size of a box; the x radius, y radius, and height of a cone; the radius of a sphere; the major and minor radii of a torus; the shape, height, and taper of an extrusion; and the included angle of a revolved solid.
- **eXit.** This option exits the SOLCHP command and returns you to the `Command:` prompt.

The *Constructive Solid Geometry* (CSG) tree is a hierarchical structure of the Boolean operations, like union and subtraction, that were used to create a composite solid. At the top of the tree structure is the composite solid. In descending levels under that are the Boolean operations that make up the composite and the primitives that help define the composite. Think of the CSG tree as the parts list and instructions for building a composite solid.

In this exercise, you use the SOLCHP command to make a few changes to the guide block model you created earlier in this chapter. If you have the IA DISK, you have the GUIDBLOK drawing as IA7GUID.DWG. Load the drawing, change the size of the outermost hole in the horizontal plate, and move the hole half an inch toward the matching hole.

Changing the Size and Shape of a Composite Solid Model

 Begin a NEW drawing named `GUIDBLK=IA7GUIDB`.

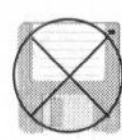 Begin a NEW drawing named `GUIDBLK=GUIDBLOK`.

Set the UCS to World.

Select upper right viewport.

Choose Model, Modify, *then* Change Prim	Issues SOLCHP
`Command: solchp`	
`Select a solid or region:` *Select the solid*	

Each primitive flashes as it updates.

`Select primitive:` *Select any of the primitive features*	
`Color/Delete/Evaluate/Instance/Move/ Next/Pick/Replace/Size/eXit <N>:` *Press Enter*	Cycles through primitives with Next option

Pressing Enter cycles through primitives until the right-most vertical cylinder is highlighted.

`Color/Delete/Evaluate/Instance/Move/ Next/Pick/Replace/Size/eXit <N>:` **`S`** ↵	Specifies Size option
`Radius along X axis <0.375>:` **`.25`** ↵	
`Radius along Y axis <0.25>:` *Press Enter*	
`Length along Z axis <3>:` *Press Enter*	

Boundary evaluation and tessellation occur and the cylinder shrinks.

`Color/Delete/Evaluate/Instance/Move/ Next/Pick/Replace/Size/eXit <N>:` **`M`** ↵	Specifies Move option
`Base point of displacement:` **`-.5,0`** ↵	Specifies displacement if you press Enter at second point prompt
`Second point of displacement:` *Press Enter*	Moves it (see fig. 23.32)
`Color/Delete/Evaluate/Instance/Move/ Next/Pick/Replace/Size/eXit <N>:` **`X`** ↵	

Boundary evaluation, tessellation, and meshing occur.

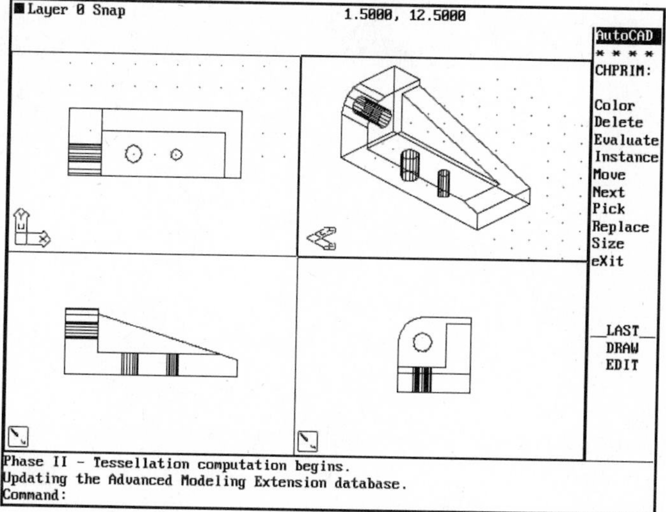

Figure 23.32:

The guide block after resizing and moving the hole.

If you want to change both of the holes in the horizontal plate, you could change both within the same SOLCHP command. The same results could be achieved with three commands instead of one by: (1) using SOLSEP, (2) editing (or re-creating) the target primitives, and (3) rebuilding the composite solid. SOLCHP, however, is a more efficient means of editing, as you saw in the previous exercise.

In a composite solid SOLCHP enables you to select not only the primitives that create positive mass but also those that create voids from a previous SOLSUB operation.

Take a look at another change. Suppose, for example, that you have a hole that you want to highlight, to identify a special tolerance consideration. One way to do that would be to change the color of the hole to make it plot differently from the rest of the composite. Because the hole is really a primitive that is buried inside a composite solid, you cannot use the standard AutoCAD CHANGE and CHPROP commands. Instead, use the Color option of SOLCHP to change the color of the last hole to red.

Changing the Color of Primitives in a Composite Solid

Command: **SOLCHP** ↵

Select a solid or region: *Select the composite solid*

Select primitive: *Select the smaller vertical hole, remember you can use the next option to cycle through the entities*

Color/Delete/Evaluate/Instance/Move/
Next/Pick/Replace/Size/eXit <N>: **C** ↵

New color <7 (white)>: **RED** ↵

Color/Delete/Evaluate/Instance/Move/
Next/Pick/Replace/Size/eXit <N>: **X** ↵

Not just the primitive but also the inside face of the hole changes color. If you perform a HIDE on the view, the hole still retains its new color.

Deleting Features from a Composite Solid

As with many other changes to a composite solid, erasing a feature cannot be accomplished with the standard AutoCAD ERASE command. But, the SOLCHP Delete option enables you to delete primitives from the composite. Use the SOLCHP command to delete the last hole (the red one) from the model.

Deleting Primitives from a Composite Solid

Command: **SOLCHP** ↵

Select a solid or region: *Select the composite*

Select primitive: *Select the red hole*

Color/Delete/Evaluate/Instance/Move/
Next/Pick/Replace/Size/eXit <N>: **D** ↵

`Retain detached primitive? <N>:` *Press Enter* Erases hole

`Color/Delete/Evaluate/Instance/Move/`
`Next/Pick/Replace/Size/eXit <N>:` **`X`** ↵

Boundary evaluation, tessellation, and meshing occur.

The primitive is removed and the change is reflected when the model is updated. If you had answered yes to the question about retaining the detached primitive, AME would have separated the cylinder from the composite but would not have deleted it from the drawing (like a selective version of the SOLSEP command).

Replacing Features in a Composite Solid

Another operation you often need to perform on a solid involves updating the geometry of some of the features. You may need to change a slope, change the shape of a cutout, or change a hole to a square slot. The SOLCHP Replace option enables you to do that. To see how it works, replace the remaining hole in the horizontal plate with a square slot.

Replacing Primitives in a Composite Solid

Use the SOLBOX *command to draw a 1×1×4" high box*

`Command:` **`SOLCHP`** ↵

`Select a solid or region:` *Select the composite*

`Select primitive:` *Select the remaining vertical hole (see fig. 23.33)*

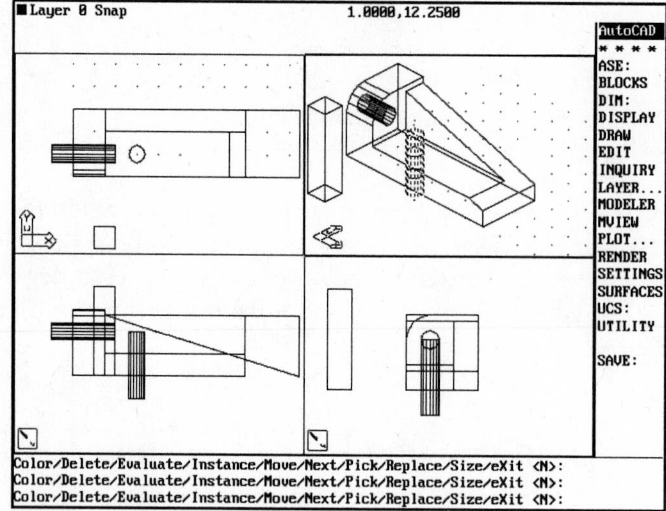

Figure 23.33:

Selecting a cylinder to replace with a box.

`Color/Delete/Evaluate/Instance/Move/`
`Next/Pick/Replace/Size/eXit <N>:` **R** ↵

`Select solid to replace primitive:` *Select the box*

`Retain detached primitive? <N>:` *Press Enter*

`Color/Delete/Evaluate/Instance/Move/Next/`
`Pick/Replace/Size/eXit <N>:` **X** ↵

Boundary evaluation, tessellation, and meshing occur.

`Creating block for mesh representation...`
`Done.`

What happened to the box? It disappeared. It became a part of the composite solid, but because it does not touch the rest of the solid, you cannot tell that it has been subtracted.

The Replace option does not automatically place the new primitive in the same location as the original. If you do not position the new primitive before you execute the Replace, you can use the Move option to move the new primitive into position. Try this technique with the box.

Moving a Primitive into Position

Command: **SOLCHP** ↵	
Select a solid or region: *Select the composite*	The box becomes visible
Select Primitive: *Select any primitive*	
Color/Delete/Evaluate/Instance/Move/ Next/Pick/Replace/Size/eXit <N>: *Press Enter several times to cycle through primitives until the box is selected*	
Color/Delete/Evaluate/Instance/Move/ Next/Pick/Replace/Size/eXit <N>: **M** ↵ Base point of displacement: *Use INT object snap to pick a corner point on the box*	
Second point of displacement: *Pick a point inside base of composite*	Relocates box
Color/Delete/Evaluate/Instance/Move/ Next/Pick/Replace/Size/eXit <N>: **X** ↵	

Boundary evaluation, tessellation, and meshing occur, and the slot appears (see fig. 23.34).

Command: **END** ↵	Saves the model and exits

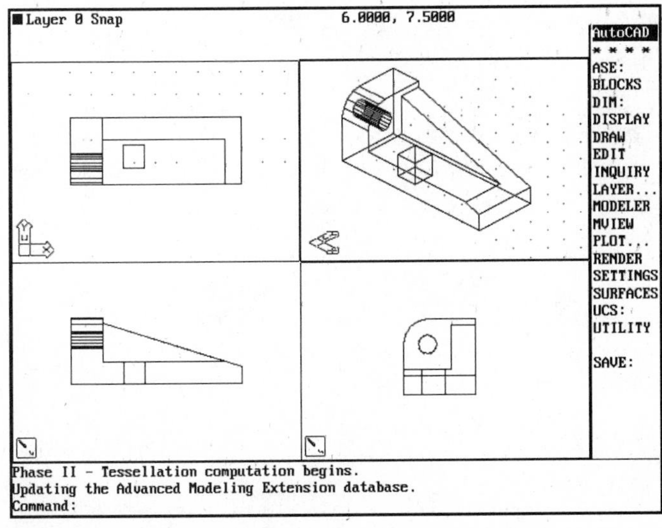

Figure 23.34:

The box moved to create a slot.

That is it. Now the solid is complete, and you had an opportunity to use most of the options for SOLCHP. SOLCHP gives you a way to modify existing 3D solids. But what about modifying other types of 3D data, like polylines that have a thickness assigned to them? The following section shows how to do just that; turn non-solid 3D data into a true, 3D solid model.

Turning Non-Solid 3D Geometry into Solids

Sometimes it is easier to create models by adding thickness to 2D entities such as polylines. Or, you may need to take existing 3D models you have created with previous versions of AutoCAD and turn them into solid models.

AutoCAD's AME includes the SOLIDIFY command, which converts several types of AutoCAD objects into solids. The entities can be polylines, polygons, circles, ellipses, traces, donuts, or solids (standard AutoCAD *solid* entities, not AME solid models). Any polyline width is ignored. The objects without a thickness are converted into regions. Objects with a non-zero thickness become solid primitives. A positive thickness extrudes up; negative extrudes down.

The results of SOLIDIFY on objects with thickness are almost exactly like those of SOLEXT. But SOLIDIFY requires a predefined thickness while SOLEXT prompts for thickness, ignoring any preset thickness. SOLEXT also allows taper, whereas SOLIDIFY does not. Like the SOLEXT command, if the object is not closed, SOLIDIFY assumes a closing line from the end of the last segment to the beginning of the first segment. And, the object cannot have intersecting segments, whether real or assumed.

Try out the SOLIDIFY command in a new drawing. To test SOLIDIFY, set thickness to 4. Then, draw a closed polyline of any shape. Draw another polyline inside the first. Solidify both polylines, then subtract the second from the first one to prove that they are now solids.

Turning 3D Wireframes into Solids with SOLIDIFY

Begin a new drawing named SOLIDIFY, and then turn on grid.

```
Command: VPOINT ↵
Rotate/<View point> <0.0000,0.0000,
0.0000>: R ↵
```

```
Enter angle in XY plane from X axis
<270>: 315 ↵
Enter angle from XY plane <90>: 30 ↵
Command: THICKNESS ↵
New value for THICKNESS <0.0000>: 4 ↵
```

Draw the first closed polyline, then a second inside the first (see fig. 23.35).

`Command: SOLIDIFY ↵`

`Select objects:` *Select the first polyline* — Creates an extended solid

Repeat the SOLIDIFY for the other polyline

`Command: REDRAW↵` — Redraws the new solids

Using the SOLSUB *command, select the outside solid and subtract the inside solid*

Check the results by meshing the model with SOLMESH and using the HIDE command(see fig. 23.36).

`Command: QUIT ↵`

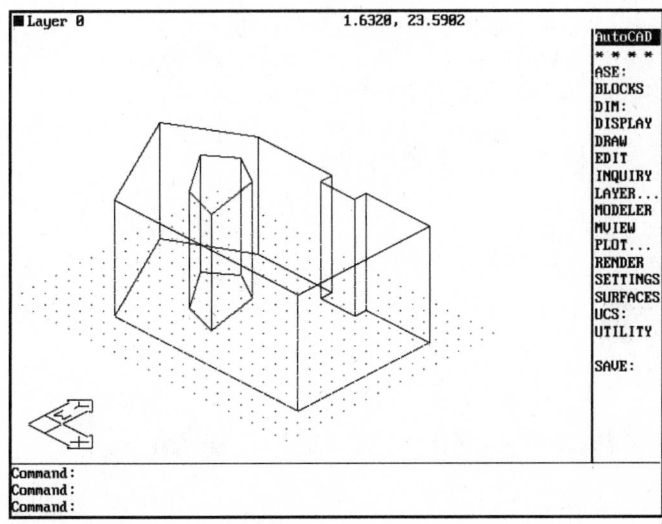

Figure 23.35:

Sample polylines before solidifying.

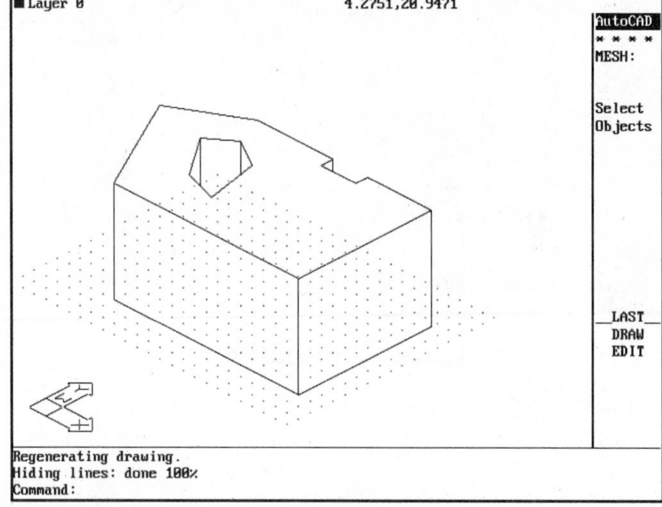

Figure 23.36:

Meshed solid with Hide.

Use SOLIDIFY when you need to update 3D models that were created without the benefit of the AME module. This allows designing on multiple stations that do not have access to AME, then bringing all of the models onto one station that does have AME to convert 3D shapes to solids.

Listing Solids Information and Controlling Variables

Finish up this section of the chapter by taking a look at the variables that the solid modeling module adds to AutoCAD. You also find a command that enables you to list information about a solid and one that finds the surface area of a solid.

Setting and Listing Solid Modeling Variables

The AME module uses its own set of system variables to control and list parameters such as the wire density of solids, the units of measurement for the volume of a solid, and the display mode. When you are working with the standard AutoCAD drawing environment, you can use the SETVAR command to list and set system variables like PDMODE and TILEMODE. SETVAR cannot be used to set solid modeling system variables, however, AME includes similar commands like SOLVAR which work very much like SETVAR. You also can use the AME system variable dialog box (the DDSOLVAR command — choose Setup, then Variables from the Modeler pull-down menu) to make settings. Use these commands to tailor your solid modeling environment.

Like standard system variables, AME variables come in two types — read only, and ones that you can change. To use SOLVAR, you issue the command, then the name of the variable you wish to change. AutoCAD then prompts you to supply a new value for the variable. DDSOLVAR works in much the same way as SOLVAR but uses the now-familiar dialog box interface. Here is a list of some of the most common variables you will set with SOLVAR:

- **SOLAReau.** The SOLid AREA Unit variable sets the unit of measure used in area calculations. AutoCAD maintains a list of valid unit types in the file ACAD.UNT.
- **SOLDELent.** The SOLid DELete ENTity variable controls whether a 2D entity used as the basis for extrusion is automatically deleted after the extrusion takes place.
- **SOLDIsplay.** The SOLid DISPLAY variable controls the display mode of a solid, whether wireframe or mesh. You also can control this using the display options in the Solids menu.
- **SOLHAngle.** The SOLid Hatch ANGLE variable sets the hatch pattern angle used to crosshatch sections created with the SOLSECT command. SOLSECT is covered in the third section of this chapter.
- **SOLHPAT.** The SOLid Hatch PATtern variable sets the hatch pattern used on sections created with SOLSECT.
- **SOLHSize.** The SOLid Hatch SIZE variable sets the hatch size of crosshatch patterns used on sections created with SOLSECT.
- **SOLLength.** This variable sets the unit of measure used for length calculations of solids. When you change SOLLength, AME asks if you also want to update SOLVolume and SOLAReau to the new length unit.
- **SOLMASs.** This variable sets the unit of measure for the mass of the solid.
- **SOLVolume.** This variable sets the unit of measure for volume calculations of solids.
- **?.** Not a variable, but like a help request in other AutoCAD commands, entering a question mark lists the SOLVARs along with their current settings.

The SOLAREA command uses the SOLLength variable to calculate surface area, and then converts the results into SOLAReau units.

Listing Information Attached to a Solid

Like other entities in AutoCAD, solids have data attached to them that you do not normally see. The SOLLIST command enables you to extract and display that information. You can list information associated with an edge or face of a solid, or you can list the CSG tree for a solid.

You can use the Edge option of SOLLIST to display such information as the type of edge (line, circular, and so on), its endpoints, center point, and radius. The Face option lists the type of surface, such as planar, cylindrical, conical, spherical, or toroidal. Depending on the type of surface, you will get other information such as radius, direction of the outward normal vector (direction away from the solid), and center point if it is a spherical or toroidal surface.

Finding the Surface Area of a Solid

Whether you are calculating the amount of surface finish required for a part or some other surface-related value, you sometimes need to find the surface area of a solid you have created. AME includes the SOLAREA command to do that.

The area is computed as the sum of the areas of the mesh faces used to represent the solid. Because the surface mesh is an approximation of the solid, a higher SOLWDENS setting increases accuracy.

Run through a quick exercise and calculate the surface area of the guide block. Set SOLLENGTH and calculate the surface area in square inches first (the default), then change the SOLAREA variable and recalculate in square centimeters.

Calculating the Surface Area of a Solid

Begin a new drawing named GUIDBLOK=IA7GUIDB, replacing your old GUIDBLOK drawing.

Edit an existing drawing named GUIDBLOK.

Set the UCS to World

Select upper right viewport

Command: **SOLLENGTH** ↵	Calculates surface area
Length units <cm> **IN** ↵	Sets the surface area measurement units to inches
Change area and volume units also <N>? **Y** ↵	Changed area and volume units
Command: **SOLAREA** ↵	Calculates the total surface area of a solid
Select objects: *Select the solid*	
1 solid selected Updating object. Surface area of solids is 100.2 sq in	
Command: **SOLVAR** ↵	Sets a solid modeling system variable
Variable name or ?: **SOLAREA** ↵	
Area units <sq in>: **sq cm** ↵	Sets area measurement units to sq cm
Command: **SOLAREA** ↵	
Select objects: *Select the solid again*	
1 solid selected Surface area of solids is 646.7 SQ cm	
Command: **QUIT** ↵	

That wraps up the utility and inquiry commands. In the last section of this chapter, you will turn a 3D solid model into a 2D drawing using a few more of the AME commands. You will cut a section through a solid, transfer the profile of a solid to a 2D representation, and transfer a face or edge of a solid into 2D.

Turning Your Solid Model into a Finished Drawing

Solid modeling really has two sides — the design side and the documentation side. Some users need solid modeling to facilitate design, while others use it to help generate 2D drawings of complex 3D parts. Whichever your case, you probably will want to turn your solid model into a finished 2D drawing, complete with notes, dimensions, and other annotation. AutoCAD AME and paper space make this easy.

Starting Your 2D Drawing with Profile Views

When you begin laying out a 2D drawing, you normally start by drawing the outline of your design in three orthographic views. AME provides SOLPROF to automatically extract the profile of a solid.

SOLPROF is most useful in conjunction with paper space; in fact, it does not work in tiled viewports. You model your design in model space, use SOLPROF to create a profile for each view, then create a named block out of each profile. Enter paper space, insert your title block, insert each view in its correct orientation, and add annotations and dimensions.

SOLPROF does a hide on the current viewport and creates new 2D entities on new layers to represent the hidden view. You then can erase entities that you do not need in the final view. SOLPROF has an option to automatically place hidden lines on a layer separate from visible lines. If the HIDDEN linetype is loaded, it automatically is set for the layer containing the hidden lines so hidden lines will display properly on your finished drawing.

Two important points to remember when creating profiles are that first, the profile is created relative to your current viewport and second, the profile is created relative to the current UCS.

SOLPROF takes the viewpoint of that viewport into account when it determines which lines should be visible and which lines should be hidden. The number of that viewport determines how it names the layers it creates. These new layers do not show up in other viewports unless you thaw them there.

Also, because the profile is created relative to the current UCS, you should set the UCS normal to the view before you create the profile. This makes it easy to insert the views into your final drawing in their correct orientations.

Use the hinge block model to create profiles of each of the top, front, and right side views of HINGBLOK. The next three exercises take you through creation of each of these profiles and have you write them to disk so you can insert them into your final drawing.

Creating a Front Profile of Hinge Block

Begin a new drawing named `HINGBLOK=IA7HINGB`, replacing your old HINGBLOK drawing.

Edit an existing drawing named `HINGBLOK`.

Select the front view

Restore the UCS FRONT

`Command:` **`SOLPROF`** ↵

`Select objects:` *Select the solid*

`1 found`

`Select objects:` *Press Enter*

`Display hidden profile lines on separate layer ? <Y>` **`Y`**↵

`Project profile lines onto a plane? <Y>:` **`N`**↵

`Delete tangential edges? <Y>` **`Y`**↵

`Hidden line removal computation of current solid is completed.`

`Command:` **`DDLMODES`** ↵

Turn off layer 0, which contains your solid object; change layer PV-4 to yellow, and AME_FRZ to cyan (see fig. 23.37); turn off AME_FRZ, and set current layer to PV-4

Zoom in and examine the profile (see fig. 23.38)

Command: **DDLMODES** ↵

Turn off PV-4, and set PH-4 current to see hidden lines

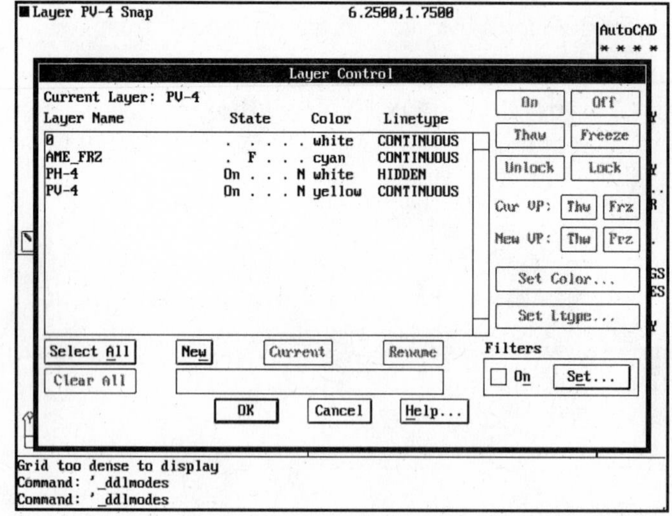

Figure 23.37:

DDLMODES shows new layers.

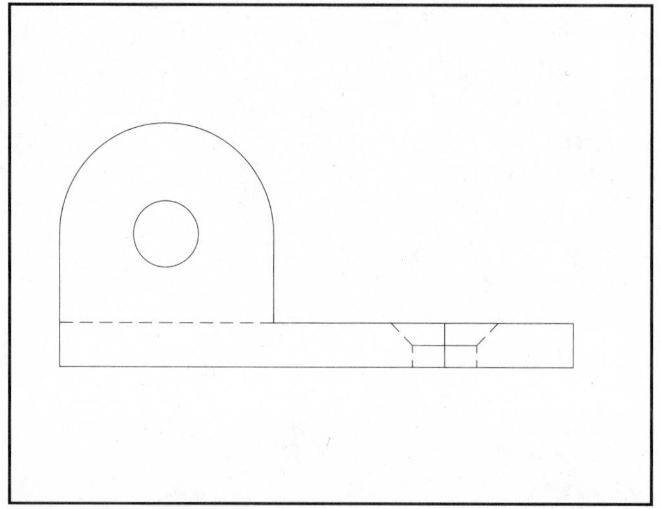

Figure 23.38:

The hinge block profile.

Notice that AME and SOLPROF have created several new layers. AME_FRZ is the layer AME uses to store the primitives that make up the solid. You normally keep it off and should never need to use it directly. The SOLPROF command creates two layers, one for hidden lines (in this case, PH-4) and one for visible lines (PV-4). It names the layers by combining PV (for ProfileVisible) or PH (ProfileHidden), a hyphen, and the viewport number (in this case, 4). If the HIDDEN linetype is loaded in the drawing, it automatically sets it for the PH layer. The check N in the State column of the layer control dialogue box show that these new layers are automatically frozen in new viewports so the profiles do not interfere with other entities.

The visible and hidden profiles are created as blocks on their respective layers. You probably noticed that the hidden profile contained lines that you would not normally draw as hidden because they would be behind the visible profile lines. In your normal work, you may want to explode the hidden line block and erase the extra lines. When you explode it, the lines take on color BYBLOCK, so you want to reblock the remaining lines or use CHPROP to change them to BYLAYER.

Now write the profile to disk as the drawing file \IA\HING-F for later insertion into our final drawing.

Saving the Profile as a Drawing File

`Command:` **`DDLMODES`** ↵

Turn on layer PV-4

Use the WBLOCK command, selecting both the hidden and visible profiles, then writing them to file \IA\HING-F with an insertion base point at the lower left corner of the profile

`Command:` **`DDLMODES`** ↵

Turn on layer 0

The WBLOCK command saved the front profile in its own file. Next, create the profile of the right side view (see fig. 23.39), the top view (see fig. 23.40), and the 3D view.

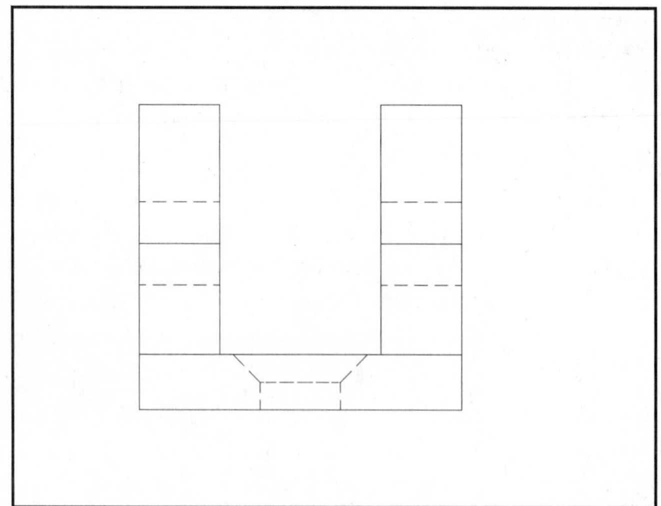

Figure 23.39:
The hinge block's right profile.

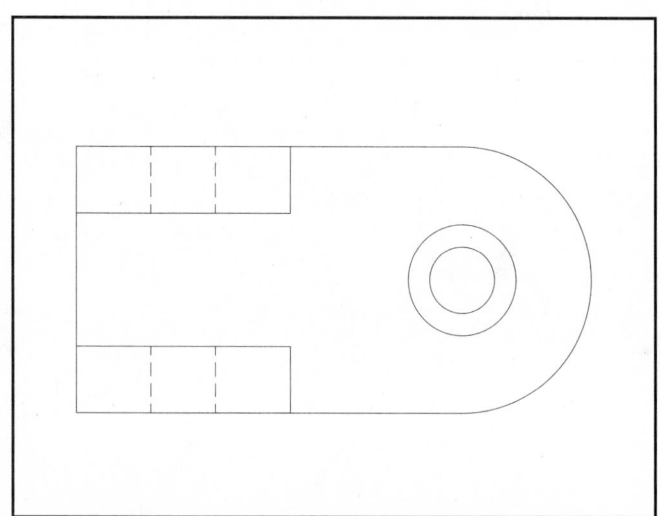

Figure 23.40:
The hinge block's top profile.

Creating the Right Side and Top Profiles of Hinge Block

Select the right-side viewport

Restore the UCS RIGHT

`Command: SOLPROF ↵`

Select the solid and the create profile with a separate hidden layer

`Command: DDLMODES ↵`

Turn off layer 0, set new PV layer to yellow, PH layer to blue

`Command: WBLOCK ↵`

Select both hidden and visible profiles and write to file \IA\HING-R with insertion base point at lower left corner of profile

`Command: DDLMODES ↵`

Turn on layer 0

Select the top (plan) viewport

Set the UCS to World

`Command: SOLPROF ↵`

Select the solid and create the profile with a separate hidden layer

`Command: DDLMODES ↵`

Turn off layer 0, set new PV layer to yellow, PH layer to blue

`Command: WBLOCK ↵`

Select both hidden and visible profiles and write to file \IA\HING-T with insertion base point at lower left corner of the plan view

`Command: DDLMODES ↵`

Turn on layer 0

Select the isometric (plan) viewport

```
Command: SOLPROF ↵
```

Select the solid and create the profile with a separate hidden layer

```
Command: DDLMODES ↵
```

Turn off layer 0, set new PV layer to yellow, PH layer to blue

```
Command: WBLOCK ↵
```

Select both hidden and visible profiles and write to file \IA\HING-3D with insertion base point at lower left corner of front plane

```
Command: DDLMODES ↵
```

Turn on layer 0

```
Command: QSAVE ↵
```

At this point, you could load each of the drawings you just created and clean them up before inserting them into your final drawing. For now, however, exercise the two other commands that AME provides for converting your solid model into a drawing. Start by cutting a section.

Cutting a Section through a Solid

Documenting a design requires more than just drawing and dimensioning three views. Many times, you need section views of your design. With a 2D drawing, or with a 3D wireframe, you would have to draw the section from scratch, laying it out like any other part of your drawing. But one of the main benefits of creating your design using solid modeling is the fact that once the geometry is created, you can cut sections through it and automatically convert that data to a 2D representation.

The full AME command SOLSECT enables you to cut a section through a solid, transferring it to 2D. It does not create the section on a special layer, but it automatically crosshatches the section if you set a pattern. SOLSECT uses the X,Y plane of the current UCS as the cutting plane. So, the secret to using SOLSECT is to set up the UCS so it passes through the solid where you want the section taken.

To see how the SOLSECT command works, take a vertical section through the centers of the two vertical hinge plates.

Cutting a Section through a Solid Using SOLSECT

Select the front view

Restore the UCS FRONT

`Command:` **SOLVAR** ↵

`Variable name or ?:` **SOLHPAT** ↵

`Hatch pattern <U>:` **STEEL** ↵

`Command:` **SOLSECT** ↵

`Select objects:` *Select the solid*

`1 solid selected.`

`Sectioning plane by Entity/Last/Zaxis/`
`View/XY/YZ/ZX/<3points>:` *Press Enter*

`1st point on plane:` **1.25,0,0**↵

`2nd point on plane:` **1.23,0,-3**↵

`3rd point on plane:` *Pick the center of the circle, (you cannot use object snaps)*

Evaluation takes place.

Select the right view

Restore UCS RIGHT

`Command:` **WBLOCK** ↵

`File name:` **HING-S** ↵

`Block name:` *Press Enter*

`Insertion base point:` *Pick the lower left corner*

`Select objects:` **C** ↵

Select everthing

`3 found`

`Select objects:` **R** ↵

`Remove objects:` *Remove the solid model, by selecting at ① (see fig. 23.41)*

`1 selected, 1 found, 1 removed`

`Remove objects:` *Press Enter* — Writes the file

`Command:` **REDRAWALL** ↵

`Command:` **QSAVE** ↵

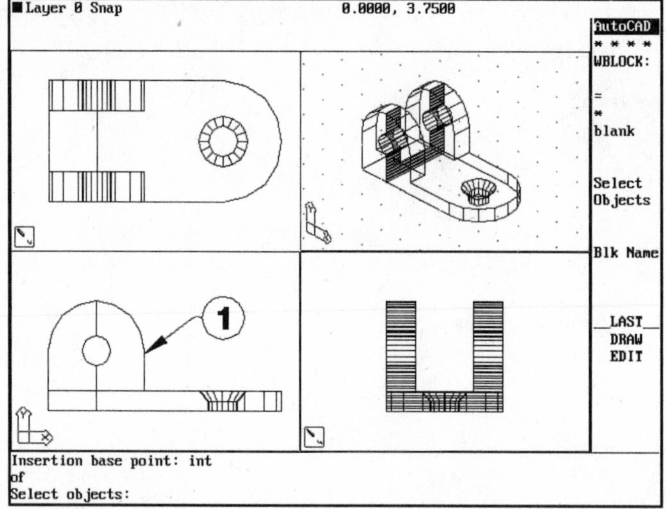

Figure 23.41:
A hatched section through the solid.

The section is made up of two blocks: the section outline and the hatch. The two are not tied together in any way. You can change them to different layers if you want to alter their colors for plotting. Using the SOLVAR command, you can specify the scale of the hatch pattern with the SOLHSIZE variable and the angle with the SOLHANGLE variable.

Copying an Edge or Face of a Solid to 2D

The last full AME command for translating your 3D solid into a 2D drawing is called SOLFEAT (SOLid FEATure). SOLFEAT is similar to the SOLPROF command, except that instead of generating an entire profile, it creates a 2D representation of a single edge or face. As with the other translation tools, SOLFEAT creates an unnamed block containing the resulting geometry and places it at the same location as the original edge or face.

When you are using the Edge option, SOLFEAT enables you to select only one edge at a time, so you cannot use a window selection set. The same holds true with the Face option. You can convert only one face at a time. To select a face, you must pick one of its edges. Every edge, however, is an edge between two faces; AME cannot tell which one you want. So the Face option enables you either to accept the face that it initially highlights or to use its Next option to cycle to the adjacent face.

In either case, the 2D entity that is created by SOLFEAT becomes the last entity created and can be accessed by the Last selection option. This makes it easy to select the 2D geometry to move it away from the solid or to put it in a block.

Use the SOLFEAT command to pull a single edge, then a single face off the hinge block model.

Copying Edges and Faces from a 3D Solid to a 2D Drawing

Select the isometric view

Set the UCS to World

Command: **SOLFEAT** ↵

Edge/<Face>: **E** ↵

All<Select>: *Press Enter*

Pick an edge: *Select any edge*

PMESH solid. Change it to WIREFRAME for feature selection? <Y>: *Press Enter*

Repeat selection: *Pick the same edge again and press Enter*

Command: **MOVE** ↵

Use Last to select a new 2D entity and then move it off the solid

Command: **REDRAW** ↵

Command: **SOLFEAT** ↵

Edge/<Face>: **F** ↵

All/<Select>: *Press Enter*

Select the arc between the front vertical face and the curved top of the nearest hinge plate

Pick a face:

<OK>/Next: **N** ↵	Highlights the P-shaped front face
<OK>/Next: *Press Enter*	Accepts the face

Pick a face: *Press Enter*

Command: **MOVE** ↵

Use Last to move the face away from the solid

Command: **REDRAWALL** ↵

Erase the P-shaped 2D face and 2D edge line

Command: **END** ↵

After you select the circular edge of the front face, AutoCAD selects the tops of the two vertical hinge plates, which it considers as a single face. Selecting the Next option cycles through to the next adjacent face, which is the front face.

That wraps up the translation utilities for converting 3D solids to 2D geometry. Now, go through one final exercise that brings those views together in paper space to make a final drawing.

Composing a Drawing from Profiles, Sections, and a 3D View

In the final 3D exercise, you clean up the HINGBLOK drawing, saving only its 3D viewport. Then you insert the ANSI-C title block created in Chapter 13 using MVSETUP, change to paper space, and compose the finished drawing within it. You use MVIEW to tell the 3D viewport to do a hide when plotted and to change its border to a new layer which is turned off to make it invisible. Then inserting the other views and any optional annotations that you want to make completes the project.

Composing Your Drawing from Viewports, Profiles, and Sections

Begin a new drawing named HINGE=IA7HINGB.

Begin a new drawing named HINGE=HINGBLOK.

Select the 3D viewport

Turn off grid

Command: **ZOOM** ↵

All/Center/Dynamic/Extents/Left/Previous/

`Vmax/Window/<Scale(X/XP)>:` **`1XP`** ↵	
`Command:` **`PSPACE`** ↵	Returns to paper space
Erase the viewport frames of TOP, FRONT, *and* RIGHT *views*	
Reset LIMITS *to* `0,0` *and* `22,17`	
Set GRID *to* `1`	
Insert ANSI-C *at 0,0 with default scale and rotation*	
`Command:` **`MVIEW`** ↵	
`ON/OFF/Hideplot/Fit/2/3/4/ Restore/<First Point>:` **`H`** ↵	
`ON/OFF:` **`ON`** ↵	Turns on Hideplot
`Select objects:` *Pick the top edge of the 3D viewport border*	
`1 selected, 1 found`	
`Select objects:` *Press Enter*	
`Command:` **`MOVE`** ↵	
Move the 3D viewport to position the 3D image to the upper right of the title block	
`Command:` **`DDLMODES`** ↵	
Make a new 3D-VP layer, turn it off, and thaw layers 0-PH-? and 0-PV-?	
`Command:` **`CHPROP`** ↵	
Change frame of 3D viewport to 3D-VP layer	It disappears, but 3D image remains
Zoom All	
Insert HING-T *at 3,11 with default scale and rotation*	Inserts the TOP profile
Insert HING-F *at 3,4 with default scale and rotation*	Inserts the FRONT profile
Insert HING-R *at 12,4 with default scale and rotation*	Inserts the RIGHT profile
Insert HING-S *at 17,4 with default scale and rotation*	Inserts the SECTION profile

Your drawing should resemble figure 23.42.

`Command:` **`QSAVE`** ↵

You can dimension and annotate the drawing or plot it as-is. When you are finished, end the drawing.

Now you can dimension your views and place notes and other annotations on the drawing to finish it. For a cleaner plot, you want to explode the top, front, and right images and erase the extraneous hidden lines that are overlapped by visible lines. The 3D image will plot with hidden lines removed.

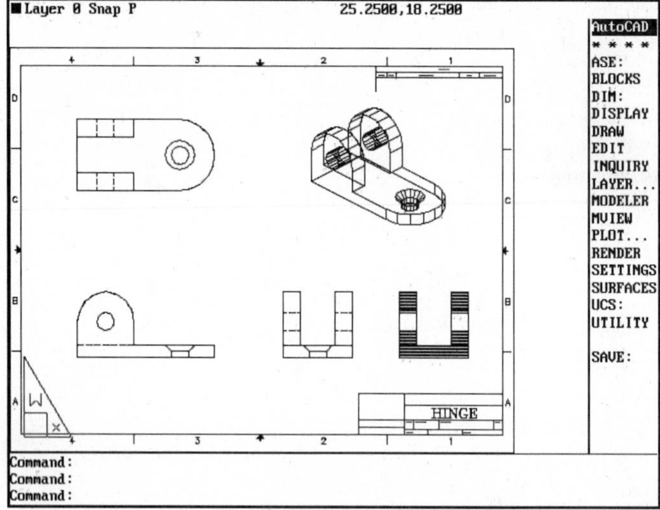

Figure 23.42:

The finished hinge block drawing.

NOTE

You can safely erase the drawings 3D, GUIDBLOCK, HINGBLOCK, CONE, GUIDBLK, and HINGE if you want to. You do not need them any longer.

Summary

Solid modeling probably will be most useful to you if you are doing mechanical design or a type of design related to mechanical engineering. In any case, solid modeling gives you two major benefits. The first benefit is that it makes it much easier to create a design and check it against other parts for fit and function. You can, for example, model two parts, place them in their proper 3D orientation to each other, then perform a Boolean intersection on them to see if there is any interference between the two. If you end up with solids left over, you have interference between the solids.

The other benefit to solid modeling is that it makes creating a drawing for a complex part much simpler. Instead of laying out 2D geometry to make up your drawing, you can model the part as a solid, then let AutoCAD pull off profiles and sections for your drawing.

Most of the functions for creating solid primitives work virtually the same as their surface modeling counterparts do. And, working with coordinate systems and axes is no different whether you are creating wireframes, surface models, or solid models. Only your model is different.

One of the keys to using solid modeling effectively is to model your design in much the same way you would actually manufacture the part. Start with a solid that represents your blank stock, then create tools and perform union and subtraction operations to "machine" your design from that blank stock.

When you are comfortable with solid modeling, you may find it is really so much easier to create your 2D drawings from it that you may do all of your design work in 3D! When working in 2D, use Regions when you need to calculate material or mass properties of an object or you need to treat a complex object as a single entity that, unlike a block, can be modified.

Installing, Configuring, and Troubleshooting AutoCAD

This appendix offers solutions to some of the most common problems that you may encounter when installing and configuring AutoCAD. The information in the following pages also should give you a better understanding of the AutoCAD manuals.

Because AutoCAD becomes more complex with each release, however, this appendix cannot cover all the different operating environments, hardware configurations, and other variables that may affect your particular setup. For complete information on the settings that you can make to fine-tune your particular system, see the *AutoCAD Interface, Installation, and Performance Guide* or the *AutoCAD Reference Manual*. If you are running AutoCAD on a DOS-based system and you run into problems, you may find the solution in a DOS guide, such as the *Microsoft MS-DOS User's Guide and Reference*, or in New Riders Publishing's *Maximizing MS-DOS 5*.

For AutoCAD to run properly, you must set up your system environment properly. On UNIX-based systems, the system administrator is typically responsible for setting up and maintaining the operating environment, as well as for setting up applications such as AutoCAD. On DOS systems, however, that responsibility often falls on the user. The first section of this appendix, therefore, examines the DOS bootup environment.

Setting Up To Use AutoCAD in the DOS Environment

When a DOS system starts up, the computer system performs a self-test and checks the system's memory. It then looks for two system files. On MS-DOS systems, these files are called IO.SYS and MSDOS.SYS. These files are *hidden* and do not show up in a directory listing. IO.SYS controls interaction between the upper levels of the operating system and the hardware. MSDOS.SYS is the MS-DOS *kernel*; that is, it controls file input and output, memory allocation, and general operating-system services.

When the self-test is complete, the computer loads the command shell, COMMAND.COM. The shell provides the internal portion of DOS; that is, those commands and functions that are loaded into (and remain in) the system's memory, instead of existing as executable files on disk. The shell is the interface to the kernel.

The operating system then looks for two additional files—CONFIG.SYS and AUTOEXEC.BAT. You can modify the contents of these two files to customize your system's setup. These files generally are created by the person who sets up the system, and they often are created or modified by applications software during the application's installation. Because AutoCAD depends on the operating-system environment, you should understand these two DOS files.

CONFIG.SYS primarily contains statements that define the system's hardware configuration. It often includes commands that load *device drivers* (programs that control a device such as a mouse), sets the number of files that can be open concurrently, and allocates the number of *disk buffers* (temporary storage areas). Your system may or may not have a CONFIG.SYS file. Some systems require device drivers to configure their memory, hard disks, or other storage devices. Some kinds of settings, such

as buffers and files, may not be necessary for DOS to boot successfully, but AutoCAD relies on them just the same. DOS 5 creates a CONFIG.SYS file when it is installed.

Once the CONFIG.SYS file has been executed, DOS searches for a file called AUTOEXEC.BAT. While CONFIG.SYS primarily controls the system's hardware configuration, AUTOEXEC.BAT controls the software environment. Statements commonly found in AUTOEXEC.BAT load device drivers with COM and EXE file-name extensions, set environment variables, and execute start-up commands. AUTOEXEC.BAT does not need to exist for the system to boot, but, as with CONFIG.SYS, most systems have an AUTOEXEC.BAT file.

Understanding CONFIG.SYS

CONFIG.SYS is a file that DOS executes automatically each time the operating system is booted. CONFIG.SYS must reside in the root directory of the boot drive, which in most DOS systems is drive C. The following lines represent a typical minimum CONFIG.SYS file, which your system must have if you run AutoCAD:

```
FILES=40
SHELL=C:\DOS\COMMAND.COM /P /E:256
```

The FILES line defines the maximum number of files that the system can keep open at one time. If the FILES setting is too low, AutoCAD may generate a `Too many open files` error message when it attempts to open additional files. An increased value of FILES requires a relatively small amount of memory, so you should set FILES to a minimum of 40.

The SHELL line in the CONFIG.SYS file enables you to change the way COMMAND.COM functions. DOS requires a certain amount of RAM to store environment-variable settings and other global information. AutoCAD itself also uses environment variables (a typical AutoCAD installation requires at least 256 bytes of environment space). The SHELL line in CONFIG.SYS changes the amount of memory allocated to the DOS environment. The previous example specifies an environment space of 256 bytes for DOS 3.3 or later. A setting of 256 is a good starting size. This number specifies the actual size setting. For 512 bytes, use 512. The maximum is 32768 bytes.

Modify or add a SHELL line to your CONFIG.SYS file if you get a DOS `out of environment space` message. This error message may be difficult to see because often it scrolls off the screen quickly when the AUTOEXEC.BAT or the AutoCAD startup batch file (described later in this appendix) executes. Remember to substitute your boot drive for `C:` if your boot drive is not C. You must include the `/P` switch on the SHELL line to make COMMAND.COM reside in memory permanently, or the system will be unresponsive after booting.

Your CONFIG.SYS file probably must include other lines, particularly device drivers. For example, to configure memory and initialize a mouse, CONFIG.SYS might include the following lines:

```
DEVICE=C:\BOOT\EMM.SYS
DEVICE=C:\MOUSE\MOUSE.SYS
```

Understanding AUTOEXEC.BAT

AUTOEXEC.BAT is a standard batch file that resides in the root directory of the boot drive (typically drive C). During start-up, DOS automatically looks for a file called AUTOEXEC.BAT. If DOS finds this file, it executes the statements contained in the file.

AUTOEXEC.BAT usually installs any terminate-and-stay-resident (TSR) device drivers required by your system, such as mouse and digitizer drivers, ADI drivers with COM and EXE extensions, and utility programs such as DOSKEY. AUTOEXEC.BAT also sets the system prompt, sets global environment variables, and performs other standard start-up functions.

At a bare minimum, a typical AUTOEXEC.BAT file should include the following lines:

```
PROMPT=$P$G
PATH C:\;C:\DOS
```

The preceding PROMPT statement causes DOS to display the current directory in the system prompt.

The PATH line should contain, at a minimum, your root directory (`C:\`) and DOS directory (`C:\DOS`). Your system's path probably includes other directories, as well. Your path does not need to include the directory that contains AutoCAD if you execute AutoCAD explicitly from its program directory.

In addition to PATH and PROMPT statements, your AUTOEXEC.BAT file may include commands to load ADI drivers and other device drivers, and to set environment variables.

Using Multiple DOS Configuration Files

Some programs cannot run properly on a system that is set up for AutoCAD. Similarly, AutoCAD cannot always run on a system that is set up for other programs. One solution is to use multiple DOS configuration files, and switch between them whenever necessary. You can create one set of configuration files (with alias names for CONFIG.SYS and AUTOEXEC.BAT) for AutoCAD and a second set with different aliases for the alternative configuration. For example, create files called ACADCFG.SYS and ACADAUTO.BAT for use as your system configuration files when running AutoCAD. Then create a set of files called ALTCFG.SYS and ALTAUTO.BAT for use with the alternative configuration. Each file should include the appropriate commands and settings for each configuration.

Next, create two batch files that copy the correct configuration files to the names CONFIG.SYS and AUTOEXEC.BAT, depending on your configuration. Then reboot the system to make the new configuration take effect. You use one batch file to copy your AutoCAD-specific files for use, and the other to copy the alternate configuration files. The following two batch files, called GOALT.BAT and GOACAD.BAT, offer examples of this process.

The GOALT.BAT file, for example, should contain the following lines:

```
COPY C:\ALTCFG.SYS C:\CONFIG.SYS
COPY C:\ALTAUTO.BAT C:\AUTOEXEC.BAT
@ECHO REBOOT system to run the ALT configuration.
```

The GOACAD.BAT file should contain the following lines:

```
COPY C:\ACADCFG.SYS C:\CONFIG.SYS
COPY C:\ACADAUTO.BAT C:\AUTOEXEC.BAT
@ECHO REBOOT system to run AutoCAD.
```

To run AutoCAD, type **GOACAD** and press Enter. The correct configuration files are copied into place. Then reboot the system by pressing Ctrl-Alt-Del. After the system has rebooted, start AutoCAD as you normally do. Use the same process with **GOALT** to switch configuration files for the alternative configuration.

Creating and Editing Environment Files

You can create and edit CONFIG.SYS and AUTOEXEC.BAT by using any text editor that can read and write ASCII files. Before you change your CONFIG.SYS or AUTOEXEC.BAT files, make sure that you have a backup of your current CONFIG.SYS file, as well as a bootable DOS diskette. If you make an error, you may need to reboot from a diskette and copy the backup files onto your hard disk. See your DOS manual if you need assistance.

Writing ASCII Text Files

Many of the files used by the operating system and applications are stored in a simple text format called *ASCII* (which stands for American Standard Code for Information Interchange). ASCII files can be read by almost all word processors and text editors. Several DOS commands are designed specifically to work with ASCII files. Many applications (including AutoCAD) use ASCII files to store data that can be modified by the user, but these programs also have their own special formats for their other data files.

You can use the DOS TYPE command to examine the contents of ASCII text files, such as your AUTOEXEC.BAT file. You can use TYPE to display the contents of other types of data files, but their contents may not be recognizable. Because other data files usually contain special characters that may cause your system to make strange noises, flash the screen, or even crash (forcing you to reboot), you should use TYPE only on files that you know are in ASCII format. The TYPE command takes the following general format:

```
TYPE filename.ext
```

In this generic form, *filename.ext* is the name of the file (including the extension) that you want to display. The file name can include the path information. The TYPE command does not accept wild cards.

Suppose that your AUTOEXEC.BAT file resides in the root directory of the current drive. To display the file's contents, issue the following command:

```
TYPE \AUTOEXEC.BAT
```

If the file contains more information than fits on a single screen, you can use the command **MORE** < *filename.ext* to make the display pause after each full screen of information.

If you do not have a text editor or word processor, you can create ASCII files by using the DOS COPY command. To start the command and name the new file, use the following format of the COPY command:

```
COPY CON: filename.ext
```

In this generic format, `filename.ext` is the name of the file to be created. The CON: portion of the command stands for *console* and instructs the COPY command to take the information that you type with the keyboard (the console) and copy it into the specified file. When you type this command and press Enter, the new file is created, and any further text you type is stored in that file. Enter a Ctrl-Z character (hold down the Control key and press Z, then release) and then press Enter to stop entering text and mark the end of the file.

If you want to create the AUTOEXEC.BAT file shown earlier, for example, you can enter the following lines at your DOS prompt:

```
COPY CON: AUTOEXEC.BAT
PROMPT=$P$G
PATH C:\;C:\DOS
<^Z>
```

When you are finished, DOS displays a message and the system prompt reappears, as follows:

```
        1 File(s) copied
C:\>
```

This file-creation method works for extremely simple files that do not need modification after their creation. Unfortunately, however, it also has a number of limitations. Once you press Enter at the end of a line, you cannot change the line. Further, you cannot edit an existing file. This makes it difficult to create long files. This method does offer some advantages, however, in that it is always available to you in DOS, and it is quick.

For editing files (rather than simply creating them), DOS includes the EDLIN (EDitor LINe) command. EDLIN has all the commands necessary for modifying an existing file, but it is primitive and tedious to use compared to most text editors and word processors. See your DOS manual or a book about DOS for information on its use.

Using the DOS 5.0 EDIT Command

If you use DOS 5.0, you have access to a full-screen, menu-based editor, called EDIT, which you can use for working with ASCII files.

The DOS Editor has a complete help system, works with either a mouse or the keyboard, and offers a variety of keyboard shortcuts and useful features. You issue the EDIT command to activate the program. When you issue the EDIT command at the DOS prompt, you can include the name of the file you want to create or edit, as follows:

```
EDIT CONFIG.SYS
```

If you do not specify a file name with the EDIT command, you can use the program's File menu to open any file once the program has started. EDIT is more powerful and easier to use than EDLIN, and it offers many of the advantages of a word processor for editing text files.

If you are using an earlier version of DOS, you probably will find EDLIN to be cumbersome and confusing. If so, you can use a commercial text editor or word processor to display, print, and edit ASCII files. Many people prefer using a familiar word processor rather than using DOS commands to edit files.

Selecting a Text Editor

To create or modify your CONFIG.SYS and AUTOEXEC.BAT files, you need a text editor that can edit and save ASCII files. You can create ASCII files with Norton's Editor, Sidekick, PC Write, WordStar in non-document mode, the WordPerfect Library Program Editor, WordPerfect's DOS text-file option, Microsoft Word in text-only format, and most other word processors.

The default format of most word processors is not ASCII, so be sure to create and save files in an ASCII format. Also be sure to specify the correct file-name extension for your ASCII file, such as SYS and BAT, because most word processors automatically assign their own document-file extension. If you are not sure whether your word processor can produce ASCII files, use the following exercise as a test:

Testing Your Text Editor

Load your text editor or word processor. Get into its edit mode, and create a new file named TEXT.TXT. Write a paragraph of text, and copy it to get a few screens full. Save the file, and exit to DOS. Then test the file. Start by using the DOS CD command to change to the directory that contains the TEXT.TXT file. (In this example, the file resides in the IA-ACAD directory.) Conduct the test by issuing the following commands:

`C:\IA-ACAD>TYPE TEXT.TXT↵`	Displays all the text you entered, if your editor produced a standard ASCII file
`C:\IA-ACAD>DEL TEXT.TXT↵`	Deletes the file

Your text editor is working fine if your text is identical to what you typed in your editor, and no extra characters or control codes (which might look like åÇäæ^L) appear. If any "garbage" appears on your screen during the test, particularly at the top or bottom of the file, then your text editor either is not suitable for saving ASCII files, or it is not configured correctly for use as an ASCII editor.

After you determine that your text editor can create and edit ASCII files, you are ready to customize your system's configuration files.

Recommended Hardware Configurations

The purpose for which you use AutoCAD determines which type of hardware is best suited to your application. Whether you work in an educational or production environment, an 80386- or an 80486-based system is required to run the DOS version of AutoCAD Release 12. If you are not using AutoCAD in a production environment, consider a 386SX system. If your drawings are not very large or complex, a 386SX provides performance comparable to a full 80386DX system.

The following minimum configuration is recommended for the DOS version of AutoCAD:

- An 80386-based system (or better) for production use, or an 80386SX-based system for educational use.
- 640K conventional memory plus at least 8M or more extended memory. AutoCAD 386 makes the best use of extended memory. AutoCAD also can use expanded memory in addition to the extended memory required, but extended memory is faster.
- A hard disk with at least 23M of free disk space before AutoCAD is installed. This includes space for all of AutoCAD's program files; it does not include your drawing files.
- One or more floppy disk drives with 1.2M or 1.44M capacity.
- PC or MS-DOS version 3.3 or later (5.0 is recommended), with program files loaded in a hard disk directory named C:\DOS.
- AutoCAD program files loaded in a hard disk directory named C:\ACAD.

If you have not yet done so, you should update your DOS operating system to at least version 5. Although it is easy to remember to keep AutoCAD software up to date, it also is easy to forget to update PC DOS or MS-DOS. DOS versions 3.3 and later offer valuable features for a customized environment, including a better capability to deal with space limitations. See the section on DOS 5 later in this appendix.

Installing AutoCAD

AutoCAD Release 12 for DOS comes with a menu-driven installation program that automatically creates the necessary directories, copies files, and personalizes AutoCAD for you. It also enables you to install only those groups of files that you want, which saves disk space if you do not want to install the AME, ASE, ADS, IGES, AutoCAD Render, source, bonus, or sample files.

IMPORTANT! Before you begin any software installation, always make a backup copy of your software program disks (often called the *distribution disks*). Install the software from the backup set of disks, not the originals. You also should keep a backup copy of your DOS distribution disks.

Backing Up Your Original Diskettes

Before you make backup copies of your distribution disks, cover the notch (if any) in the upper right corner of 5 1/4-inch disks with a write-protect tab or a piece of tape. For 3 1/2-inch disks, slide open the write-protect button on the back of the upper right corner. These measures prevent accidental erasure or damage. You need the same number and type of backup disks as your distribution set.

Using DISKCOPY To Back Up Your Disks

If you have only one floppy disk drive of the correct type, insert the first original (source) disk in it.

C:>**CD \DOS**↵	Changes to the \DOS directory
C:\DOS>**DISKCOPY A: A:**↵	

If you are using drive B, use the letter B rather than A. Change disks when prompted.

If you have two disk drives that are the same size and density (both 5 1/4-inch or both 3 1/2-inch), place the first distribution disk in drive A and a backup (target) disk in drive B, and type the following command:

C:>**CD \DOS**↵	
C:\DOS>**DISKCOPY A: B:**↵	Copies everything on the disk in drive A to the disk in drive B

Repeat the process for each source disk.

Remember that the *source* disk is the disk you are copying (your original distribution disk), and the *target* disk is your duplicate (backup) disk. Your target disk does not have to be formatted. The DISKCOPY command formats it for you.

Preparing Your Hard Drive

A minimal configuration for AutoCAD Release 12 requires at least 11M of free space on your disk for executable and support files and 4M for working space. If you install the sample drawings, you will need an additional 2.6M. A complete installation, including ADS (which only developers need) and the Advanced Modeling Extension (AME), an extra-cost option, AutoCAD SQL Extension (ASE), AutoCAD Render, and the AutoCAD tutorial requires a minimum of 23M. If you do not have enough space to install the files you have selected, the INSTALL program warns you.

The installation program creates the necessary directories, so you do not need to create them beforehand. The INSTALL program prompts you to enter information about your installation, including your name, company name, dealer name, and dealer's telephone number. You must enter each item, or INSTALL cannot continue to personalize your software. This information is written to your first distribution diskette and becomes a permanent part of your AutoCAD executable file that INSTALL creates on your hard disk.

The INSTALL program is fully menu-driven, so you should have no difficulty installing AutoCAD. During the installation process, INSTALL asks if you want it to create a start-up batch file named ACAD386.BAT. If this file is on your path (it is created in your root directory, so it should be), you can enter **ACAD386** at the DOS prompt to start AutoCAD from any current directory.

Installing AutoCAD Release 12

Insert Disk #1 in drive A.

```
C:\>A:↵
A:\>INSTALL↵
```

Follow the instructions and prompts.

If your source disk drive is not drive A, substitute its drive letter for A. If your hard disk is not drive C, substitute its drive letter for C.

To finish the installation, run AutoCAD and configure your system. If any of your hardware requires an ADI driver, install it according to the manufacturer's instructions before you configure AutoCAD.

AutoCAD Configuration

If you have just installed AutoCAD, or if you need to reconfigure AutoCAD for a different hardware device, the AutoCAD configuration menu prompts you to identify selected parameters for the appropriate video display, digitizer, plotter, and printer/plotter that make up your workstation configuration.

You must run AutoCAD to configure it. If you have not configured AutoCAD, it skips to the configuration menu automatically when you start the program. During a first-time configuration sequence, AutoCAD automatically takes you through the steps required to select your display, input device, plotter, and printer.

Using the Configuration Menu

If AutoCAD has already been configured once, you can examine your configuration setup by entering the **CONFIG** command at the AutoCAD `Command:` prompt. AutoCAD displays the current configuration and prompts you with the configuration menu.

Examining Your AutoCAD Configuration

Start AutoCAD. If you are using a start-up batch file, such as ACAD386.BAT or ACAD.BAT, type **`ACAD386`** or **`ACAD`** at the DOS prompt and press Enter. If your AutoCAD directory is part of your path and AutoCAD's environment variables have been set, you can start the program from any working directory by typing **`ACAD`** and pressing Enter. Otherwise, change to your AutoCAD directory, type **`ACAD`** and press Enter.

If AutoCAD has not been configured, it prompts you through the configuration choices and then displays the current configuration.

To reconfigure AutoCAD, enter **`CONFIG`** at the `Command:` prompt.

```
Current AutoCAD configuration
  Video display:      Your current display
    Version: Your current display driver version
  Digitizer:          Your current input device
    Version: Your current input device driver version
  Plotter:            Your current output device
    Port: Your current output device connection
    Version: Your current output device driver version
Press RETURN to continue: ↵
Configuration menu
  0.  Exit to drawing editor
  1.  Show current configuration
  2.  Allow detailed configuration
  3.  Configure video display
  4.  Configure digitizer
  5.  Configure plotter
  6.  Configure system console
  7.  Configure operating parameters
Enter selection <0>:
```

Enter the number corresponding to the part of AutoCAD you want to reconfigure. Depending on which option you select, additional menus and prompts appear. Enter your choices when requested to do so.

During configuration, AutoCAD creates a configuration file called ACAD.CFG in the current directory. This configuration file contains the settings of the CONFIG command and certain AutoCAD system variables.

Reconfiguring Your System

Reconfiguring AutoCAD is simple and straightforward. AutoCAD asks you several questions about your hardware setup, and you respond with answers or a number selection from a list of choices that AutoCAD provides. Configuration is dependent on your hardware.

To configure or change a device driver, select the item you want to change from the configuration menu. AutoCAD then prompts you for values to supply for each device.

Using ADI Drivers

Autodesk Device Interface (ADI) drivers are device-driver programs for plotters, printers, digitizers, and video cards. Two types of ADI drivers are available: real-mode ADI drivers and protected-mode ADI drivers. *Real-mode* ADI drivers are memory-resident (TSR) programs that operate in conventional memory. If you are using a real-mode ADI driver, you must install it in memory before you start AutoCAD. Install this type of driver by entering its name at the DOS prompt, just like any other program. You can install an ADI driver in your CONFIG.SYS file, AUTOEXEC.BAT file, or your AutoCAD start-up batch file. Examples of both files are shown in this appendix. You can configure AutoCAD to use real-mode ADI drivers by choosing the proper ADI version from the configuration menu.

If you are using a *protected-mode* ADI driver, AutoCAD loads the driver automatically into extended memory; you do not have to load the driver before you start AutoCAD. AutoCAD automatically loads the names of protected-mode drivers into the configuration menu. To configure AutoCAD for a protected-mode driver, choose the correct driver from the configuration menu.

For AutoCAD to load the names of protected-mode ADI drivers into the configuration menu automatically, the driver must be named with a *magic prefix*. The magic prefix identifies the type of protected-mode driver. AutoCAD searches for, and then loads the driver names into an appropriate configuration menu, based on the magic prefix. See the *AutoCAD Interface, Installation, and Performance Guide* for more information on protected-mode drivers and magic prefixes.

Using AutoCAD's Standard Tablet Menu

AutoCAD comes with a standard tablet menu (see fig. A.1) and includes a plastic template for an 11-by-11-inch digitizer tablet. To use the standard AutoCAD tablet menu, affix the AutoCAD standard plastic template to your digitizer and use AutoCAD's TABLET command to let the program know where the tablet's "boxes" are located.

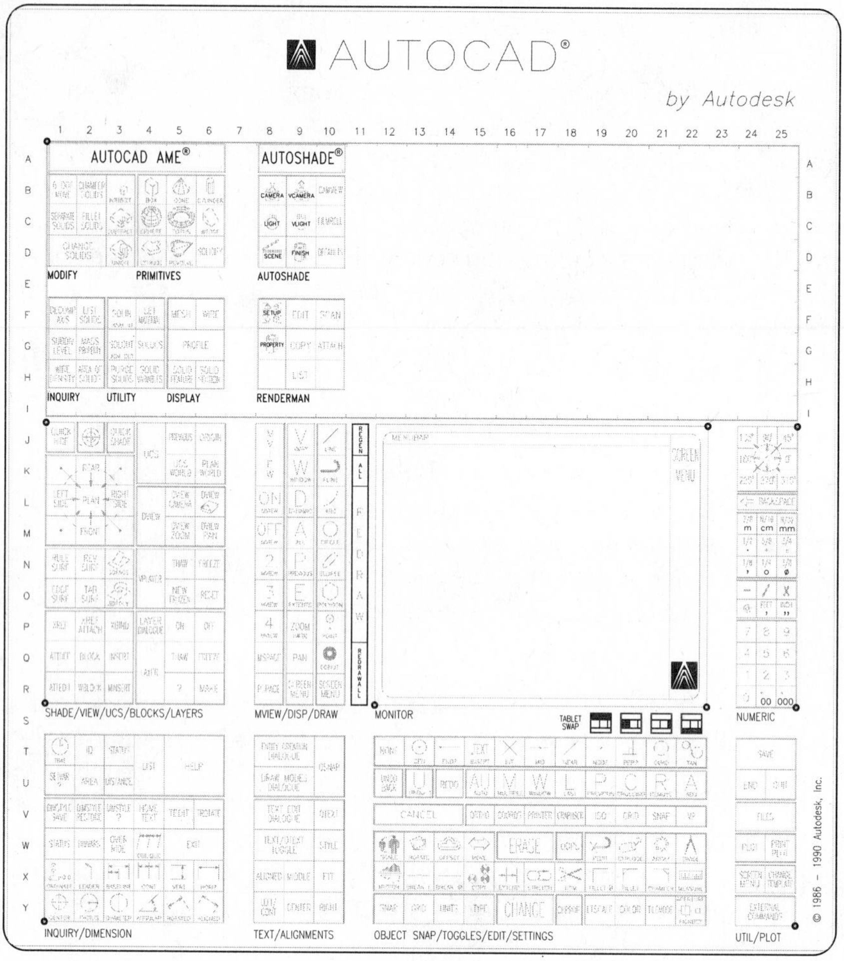

Figure A.1:

The standard AutoCAD tablet menu.

Understanding the TABLET.DWG Drawing

AutoCAD also comes with a drawing file, TABLET.DWG in the SUPPORT directory, which reproduces the plastic template menu. You can use this drawing to create a custom template drawing for your digitizer.

If you know how to edit drawings and customize the tablet menu, you can make your own tablet drawing, supporting the menu with your own tablet menu programs, print it out, and affix it to the tablet. If you customize

your tablet menu, make a backup copy of TABLET.DWG, call it MYTABLET.DWG, and make your changes to the copy, not to the original.

Configuring the Tablet Menu

This section assumes that you are using an 11-by-11-inch or larger digitizer that has been configured according to the *AutoCAD Interface, Installation, and Performance Guide.*

If you are using the AutoCAD template, place it on your digitizer. If you are using the plotted TABLET drawing, trim the drawing, leaving about a 1/2-inch border, and tape it to your digitizer. Because every tablet is different, and because every user trims and tapes differently, you must configure the tablet to let AutoCAD know exactly where the tablet commands are located on the tablet's surface.

Use the TABLET command from inside the drawing editor to configure the tablet. You see a series of donuts—tablet pick points on the drawing (or template)—that you can use as a guide when picking each of the four menu areas prompted for by the TABLET command.

The standard menu is divided into four menu areas by columns and rows. In figure A.1, for example, the columns are numbered 1 to 25 across the top and the rows are lettered A to Y on the left. Menu area 1 is the top rectangular area. The first donut pick point is near A and 1 in the top left corner. Menu area 1 has 25 columns and 9 rows of menu "boxes."

The following exercise steps you through configuration of the AutoCAD tablet menu. To configure the tablet, pick the three points specified for each menu area and enter the number of columns and rows. Use figure A.2 as a guide for picking points.

Configuring the AutoCAD Tablet Menu

Begin a NEW drawing named **TEST**. The drawing screen appears with the screen menu.

```
Command: TABLET ↵
Option (ON/OFF/CAL/CFG): CFG↵
Enter the number of tablet menus
desired (0-4) <0>: 4 ↵
```

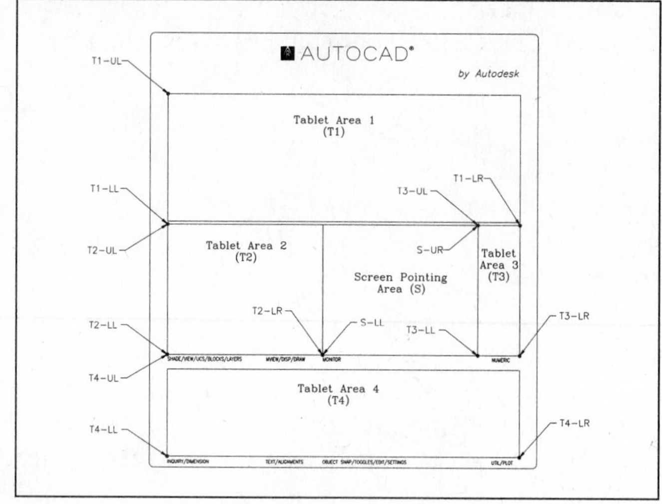

Figure A.2:

Pick points for configuring the AutoCAD standard tablet menu.

Digitize the upper left corner of
menu area 1: *Pick point T1-UL*

Digitize the lower left corner of
menu area 1: *Pick point T1-LL*

Digitize the lower right corner of
menu area 1: *Pick point T1-LR*

Enter the number of columns for
menu area 1: **25** ↵

Enter the number of rows for
menu area 1: **9** ↵

Digitize the upper left corner of
menu area 2: *Pick point T2-UL*

Digitize the lower left corner of
menu area 2: *Pick point T2-LL*

Digitize the lower right corner of
menu area 2: *Pick point T2-LR*

Enter the number of columns for
menu area 2: **11** ↵

Enter the number of rows for
menu area 2: **9** ↵

Digitize the upper left corner of
menu area 3: *Pick point T3-UL*

Digitize the lower left corner of
menu area 3: *Pick point T3-LL*

`Digitize the lower right corner of`
`menu area 3:` *Pick point T3-LR*

`Enter the number of columns for`
`menu area 3:` **9**↵

`Enter the number of rows for`
`menu area 3:` **13**↵

`Digitize the upper left corner of`
`menu area 4:` *Pick point T4-UL*

`Digitize the lower left corner of`
`menu area 4:` *Pick point T4-LL*

`Digitize the lower right corner of`
`menu area 4:` *Pick point T4-LR*

`Enter the number of columns for`
`menu area 4:` **25**↵

`Enter the number of rows for`
`menu area 4:` **7**↵

`Do you want to respecify the screen`
`pointing area (Y)` *Press Enter*

`Digitize lower left corner of screen`
`pointing area:` *Pick point S-LL*

`Digitize upper right corner of screen`
`pointing area:` *Pick point S-UR*

Try picking a few commands from the tablet and drawing in the screen-pointing area to test the configuration.

`Command:` **QUIT**↵ Quits the TEST drawing

The standard AutoCAD tablet menu is configured for your digitizer, and the configuration parameters are stored on your disk in a file.

Swapping the Tablet Menu Areas

The process of swapping a menu area changes its function from the default to a different, predefined menu. To swap a particular menu area, select one of the four corresponding tablet-swap icons located on the digitizer overlay below the monitor area. The following list describes the default and alternative menus for each swap icon:

- **Menu Area 1**. This is the top menu area. By default, this menu area contains the AME and AutoShade menus. Alternatively, you can

replace the AME and AutoShade menus with a blank menu area that can be used for personal applications and menu items.

- **Menu Area 2**. This is the left menu area. By default, this area's display commands are transparent, and VPOINT and DVIEW refer to the WCS. Alternatively, you can configure display commands to cancel a command in progress, and VPOINT and DVIEW to refer to the current UCS.
- **Menu Area 3**. This is the right menu area. By default, this area is set for American units. Alternatively, you can configure this area for metric units.
- **Menu Area 4**. This is the lower menu area. By default, object-snap picks are temporary in this area. Alternatively, you can change object-snap picks so that they act as running object-snap picks.

When you swap a menu area, the corresponding asterisk in the screen menu below [AutoCAD] changes to a number to indicate which menu has been switched. Select [AutoCAD] to reset all menu areas to their defaults.

For more information on tablet swapping and customization, see *Maximizing AutoCAD, Volume I* from New Riders Publishing.

Using Start-Up Batch Files

You can preset several of AutoCAD's start-up settings that control its memory usage and support file search order. The installation program gives you the option of creating a start-up batch file called ACAD386.BAT. A typical ACAD386.BAT file for Release 12 looks like this:

```
SET ACAD=C:\ACAD\SUPPORT;C:\ACAD\FONTS;C:\ACAD\ADS
SET ACADCFG=C:\ACAD
SET ACADDRV=C:\ACAD\DRV
C:\ACAD\ACAD %1 %2
SET ACAD=
SET ACADCFG=
SET ACADDRV=
```

This start-up batch file sets the AutoCAD file search paths, executes AutoCAD, then clears the environment variables when you exit from AutoCAD.

A more sophisticated start-up batch file also can optimize AutoCAD's use of memory, specify other AutoCAD operating parameters, and change the current drawing directory.

Optimizing Memory and Controlling Directories

The following example shows a more sophisticated start-up batch file, named STARTUP.BAT. You can create a file like this for each of your jobs or applications, and give each batch file a unique name.

The STARTUP.BAT file assumes that your AutoCAD program directory path is C:\ACAD. If it is not, substitute your own path.

Creating the STARTUP.BAT File

In the following sample start-up batch file, the lines in the `special typeface` represent actual statements that your STARTUP.BAT file should include. The lines in *italic* represent lines that should consist of settings or statements that are appropriate for your particular system. Do not put any blank lines in your batch file, or it will not work.

```
SET ACAD=C:\ACAD\SUPPORT;C:\ACAD\FONTS;C:\ACAD\ADS
SET ACADCFG=C:\ACAD
SET ACADDRV=C:\ACAD\DRV
Your version and hardware-dependent memory settings and other operating parameters
go here.
C:
CD \PROJECT
\ACAD\ACAD %1 %2
CD\
SET ACAD=
SET ACADCFG=
SET ACADCFG=
Memory release statements go here.
```

The following list describes each of the statements in the sample STARTUP.BAT file:

- **SET ACAD=.** In this statement, you define the directory that AutoCAD should search if it does not find a needed support file in the current directory. The support files include shape files, slide files, and other support files.

- **SET ACADCFG=.** This statement defines the directory that AutoCAD searches for configuration files. You can create several configuration directories and corresponding start-up batch files if you must support more than one environment or more than one device, such as different graphics adapters.
- **SET ACADDRV=.** This statement specifies the directory or directories that AutoCAD must search for protected-mode ADI driver files. If you want to use protected-mode drivers, you must set this variable to a directory that contains them. If your third-party drivers are installed in separate directories, you can add the directory name to this variable. This statement makes updating AutoCAD or your drivers easier and helps to keep files organized.
- **Version and Hardware-Dependent Memory Settings.** The start-up file can also control the amount of memory AutoCAD uses. (This is controlled by the SET ACADMAXMEM= statement). Memory that is in use before you load AutoCAD is *not* available for AutoCAD's use.

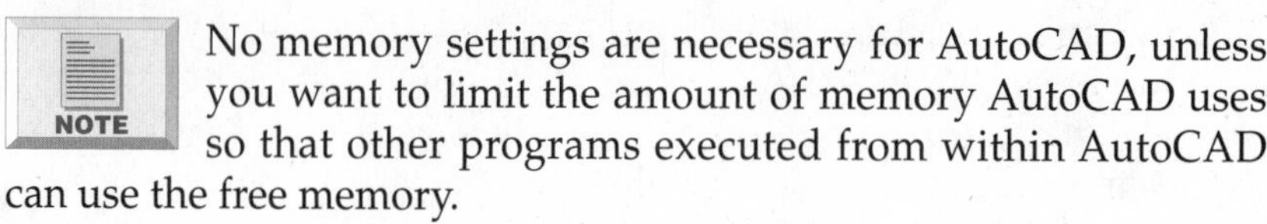

No memory settings are necessary for AutoCAD, unless you want to limit the amount of memory AutoCAD uses so that other programs executed from within AutoCAD can use the free memory.

- **C:**. This statement ensures that the correct disk drive is current when you start AutoCAD. Substitute another letter if AutoCAD is not on drive C.
- **CD \PROJECT.** This statement changes to the working directory (in this example, PROJECT); your STARTUP.BAT file can change to any working directory you specify in this statement. You can create multiple start-up batch files, each with its own CD command, for each project directory you use.
- **\ACAD\ACAD %1 %2.** This statement executes the ACAD.EXE program file. If ACAD.EXE is on your system's path, you can use ACAD alone here, but you can prevent DOS from searching the path if you specify the directory. The %1 and %2 are replaceable parameters for which you can enter a drawing name (%1) and script name (%2) when you run the STARTUP.BAT batch file. For example, to run a script with the name MYSCRIPT on a drawing MYDWG, enter STARTUP MYDWG MYSCRIPT, and the batch file executes this line as \ACAD\ACAD MYDWG MYSCRIPT. AutoCAD then executes MYSCRIPT at the main menu with MYDWG as the default drawing.

- **CD\.** This statement returns you to the root directory.
- **SET ACADDRV=, SET ACADCFG=, and SET ACAD=.** Clear these settings to avoid conflict with any other AutoCAD configurations that you might use, and to free up environment space.
- **Memory Release Statements.** If you made any other memory or environment settings, insert lines here to clear them as well.

Use the SET variable= statement to clear any settings that you make in a start-up batch file, such as STARTUP.BAT. If you do not clear your settings, your other AutoCAD-related applications will find the settings and be directed to the wrong configuration and support files.

Consult the *AutoCAD Interface, Installation, and Performance Guide* for more information on memory settings for running AutoCAD. If you are unfamiliar with the various types of memory, the following descriptions should help.

Understanding Types of Memory

RAM is commonly expressed in bytes and bits. A *bit* is the smallest unit of storage, representing either a 0 or a 1. A *byte* is eight bits, and it represents a single alphanumeric character. You do not need to concern yourself with this or with data storage, but you do need to know how much memory you have because AutoCAD needs a great deal. A given memory location is accessed by its *address*, commonly expressed in bytes (usually in K, or 1024-byte increments). For example, the lowest memory address is at 0K, and on a system with 1M of RAM, the maximum address is 1024K (which equals 1M). Figure A.3 shows how DOS typically uses memory in a PC.

Your system can include any of the following five types of memory:

- **Conventional memory.** This is the range of memory addresses from 0K to 1024K. Because the upper 384K of conventional memory is reserved, the first 640K of memory addresses is often considered (incorrectly) to be where conventional memory ends. Conventional memory is most crucial for standard DOS applications, and one of the benefits of DOS 5 is that it can make more memory between 0K and 640K available to applications.

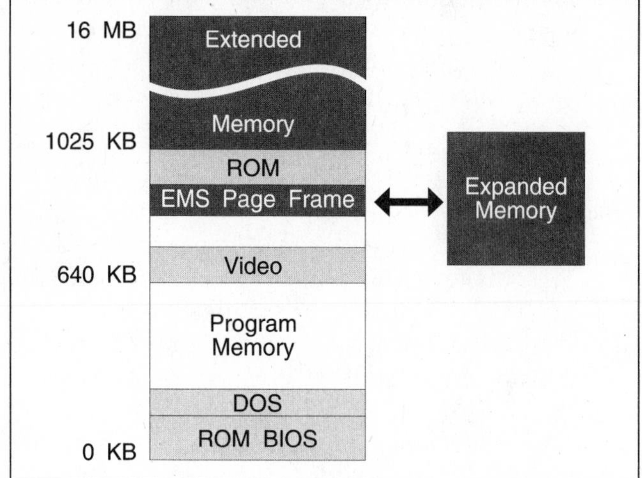

Figure A.3:

A DOS memory map.

- **Reserved I/O Address Space, or Upper Memory Area (UMA).** This area is the 384K of memory between 640K and 1024K. It is primarily reserved for video adapters and other peripheral device-address mapping (the device is assigned an address within that range). In addition, a range of memory is sometimes allocated from the UMA as an expanded-memory page frame, which is a range of memory that an expanded-memory manager uses to make expanded memory available to the system. Standard applications do not normally access this reserved memory area.
- **High Memory Area (HMA).** The HMA is either the 64K address range between 1024K and 1088K or the 64K of memory addresses between the end of conventional memory at 1024K and the beginning of extended memory at 1088K. Only one program at a time may use the HMA. In DOS 5, a portion of the operating system may be loaded into this region.
- **Extended memory.** Sometimes referred to as XMS, this is the memory above the 1088K mark, which can be as much as 15M on 80286 systems and as much as 4G on 80386 and 80486 systems. (A gigabyte is equal to 1024 megabytes.) This memory is addressed directly by applications that are specifically written to address it. A program called an *extended-memory manager* is used to manage extended memory access by applications.

- **Expanded memory.** Also referred to as EMS, expanded memory is memory configured for the Lotus/Intel/Microsoft (LIM) expanded-memory specification (EMS). Physical expanded memory comes in the form of a card installed in the computer. All types of processors can access expanded memory. A special driver must be used to permit applications to address this memory. On 80386 and 80486 systems, a device driver can be used to emulate expanded memory by using extended memory.

Using AutoCAD with Microsoft Windows

AutoCAD can run as a full-screen DOS application under Microsoft Windows 3.1. This arrangement enables you to switch between AutoCAD and Microsoft Windows applications. You need to take two steps to set up Windows to work with AutoCAD. The first step is to add a line to the `[386Enh]` section of your Windows SYSTEM.INI file with a text editor. The second step is to create a Windows Program Information File (PIF) for AutoCAD. The following exercise details these steps.

Setting Up Windows for AutoCAD

Start your word processor and open your Windows SYSTEM.INI file. The file is usually located in C:\WINDOWS. Then find the `[386Enh]` section and add the following line below the `[386Enh]` label:

```
device=c:\acad\pharlap.386
```

Start Windows and run the PIF Editor. The PIF Editor is usually located in the Main program group.

In the Program Filename: *text box, enter* `COMMAND.COM`

In the Window Title: *text box, enter* `AutoCAD 12`

In the Optional Parameters: *text box, enter* `/E:256 /C STARTUP.BAT`

In the Start-up Directory: *text box, enter* `C:\PROJECT`

Click on High Graphics — Highlights the radio button

In the EMS Memory: KB Limit *text box, enter* `0`

In the XMS Memory: KB Limit
text box, enter at least `2048`

Leave all other settings at their default values.

Choose File, *then* Save

In the File Name: *text box, enter* `ACAD12.PIF`

Choose File, *then* Exit

Select a program group to add the AutoCAD program item.

Choose File, *then* New *and click on* OK

In the Command Line: *text box,*
enter `ACAD12.PIF`

Now Windows is set up to run AutoCAD. To start AutoCAD, double-click on the AutoCAD 12 icon.

Using Windows-Compatible Third-Party Memory Managers

Microsoft Windows uses a memory manager that is compatible with AutoCAD. HIMEM.SYS is the memory manager commonly used with Windows and DOS 5.

Quarterdeck Office Systems' QEMM memory manager, version 5.1 or greater, is compatible with AutoCAD and Windows. It also may give you more available conventional memory than HIMEM.SYS does.

In addition to QEMM, other third-party memory managers are compatible with both Windows and AutoCAD. Check the documentation for the memory manager, or consult the manufacturer to make sure that the memory manager you are considering is compatible.

Finding Solutions to Your Problems with AutoCAD Release 12

This section offers some suggestions for dealing with common problems encountered in setting up and running AutoCAD. Some problems originate

in AutoCAD itself, others in DOS, others from device drivers, and others from interactions. The following sections discuss system components and their errors.

Solving Problems with AutoCAD

If you have a problem with any exercise, you probably overlooked something. The following list includes tips for solving AutoCAD-related problems.

- When errors occur, use AutoCAD's UNDO command to clean up the drawing and restore system variables. Then try the command again.
- Go back to the previous exercises to see if you made an error that did not show up immediately.
- Check defaults, such as snap, object snaps, aperture, current layer, and layer visibility.
- Check the *AutoCAD Reference Manual.*
- Call your AutoCAD dealer. If you have no current dealer, Autodesk can recommend one.
- Try the ACAD forum on CompuServe, the world's largest AutoCAD user group and most knowledgeable source of support.
- If you find a specific problem in this book, particularly a problem with an exercise, you can call New Riders Publishing at (503) 661-5745. Be ready to give us the page number where you are having the problem. Remember, however, that New Riders Publishing cannot give general AutoCAD support; your AutoCAD dealer can answer general AutoCAD questions.

Solving Problems with CONFIG.SYS

If your CONFIG.SYS settings do not run smoothly, your only indication may be that some programs do not work. You may, for example, see the following DOS error message:

```
Bad or missing FILENAME
```

When this message appears, DOS cannot find the file as it is specified. Open your CONFIG.SYS file and look for the statement that specifies that the file be opened. Check the command for proper spelling, syntax, and a full path.

The following message also may appear if a problem exists in CONFIG.SYS:

```
Unrecognized command in CONFIG.SYS
```

This message means that you made a syntax error, or that your version of DOS does not support the configuration command. Open the CONFIG.SYS file and check the command's spelling.

Watch closely when you boot the system. These error messages flash by very quickly. If you suspect an error, temporarily rename your AUTOEXEC.BAT file so that the system stops after loading CONFIG.SYS. You can also try to send the screen messages to the printer by pressing Ctrl-PrintScrn as soon as DOS starts reading the CONFIG.SYS file. Press Ctrl-PrintScrn again to turn off the printer echo.

Solving Problems with ADI Drivers

If you have a problem with a device that uses an ADI driver, suspect the driver first. Verify that the driver is properly installed, see that AutoCAD is configured properly, then consult the driver's documentation. If all else fails, contact your dealer or the manufacturer for help.

Solving Problems with AUTOEXEC.BAT

Errors in AUTOEXEC.BAT are harder to troubleshoot, for many reasons. Often, the system just does not behave as you think it should. Here are some troubleshooting tips:

- Isolate errors by temporarily editing your AUTOEXEC.BAT file. You can disable a line by placing a leading colon before the line, as follows:

  ```
  : NOW DOS WILL IGNORE THIS LINE!
  ```

- Many AUTOEXEC.BAT files use the command ECHO OFF or @ECHO OFF to turn off echo to the screen. Disable ECHO OFF to see what these files are doing. To disable ECHO OFF, put a leading colon on the line.
- Direct the contents of AUTOEXEC.BAT to the printer. Press Ctrl-PrintScrn while the system is booting to see what is happening.
- Make sure that the prompt, path, and other environment settings precede any TSR (memory-resident) programs in the file.

- Check your path for completeness and syntax. Directories do not need to be in the path unless you want to execute files in them from other directories, or the program requires it. (An example of a PATH statement is in the section on AUTOEXEC.BAT.)
- APPEND (DOS 3.3 or later) works like PATH to enable programs to find their support and overlay files in other directories. It uses about 5K of RAM. All files in an appended directory are recognized by programs as if they were in the current directory. If you use APPEND, use it cautiously. If you modify a file in an appended directory, the modified file will be written to the current directory, not to the appended directory. Loading an AutoCAD MNU file from an appended directory creates an MNX file in the current directory. AutoCAD searches an appended directory before completing its normal directory search pattern, so appended support files get loaded instead of those in the current directory.
- SET environment errors are often obscure. Type **SET** and press Enter to see your current environment settings. If a setting is truncated or missing, you are probably out of environment space. Fix it in your CONFIG.SYS file, using what you learn in the next section. Do not use extraneous spaces in a SET statement.
- If you are fighting for memory, insert temporary commands in the AUTOEXEC.BAT to check your available memory. Once you determine what uses how much, you can decide what to sacrifice. Use the following commands:

  ```
  CHKDSK
  PAUSE
  ```

  Insert these commands at appropriate points in the AUTOEXEC.BAT file to display the remaining memory. Reboot to see the effect. Remove the commands when you are done.

  Run **CHKDSK /F** at the DOS prompt on a regular basis. It will verify your hard disk file structure and free up any "lost clusters" that it finds. *Lost clusters* are sometimes created when programs crash. Answer **N** when CHKDSK asks if you want to convert the clusters to files. Do not run CHKDSK /F from the SHELL command while in AutoCAD.

  If you have unusual occurrences or lockups, and you use TSRs, suspect the TSRs as your problem source. Cause and effect may be hard to pin down. Disable TSRs one at a time in your AUTOEXEC file. Reboot and test.

Solving Problems with DOS Environment Space

If you run out of space to store DOS environment settings, the following error message appears at the DOS prompt:

```
Out of environment space
```

You may see this message when executing a batch file. An environment space problem also may show up in unusual ways, such as a program failing to execute, AutoLISP not having room to load, or a block insertion not finding its file on disk. This occurs because the path; AutoCAD settings limiting extended or expanded memory; and AutoCAD configuration, memory, and support file settings are all environment settings.

To find out how much environment space you need:

- Type SET>TEMP.$ at the DOS prompt.
- List the TEMP.$ file with the DIR command. The file size is the number of characters. Delete the file.
- Add the number of characters for new SET statements. Include revisions to your AUTOEXEC.BAT and start-up files, such as IL.BAT.
- Add a safety margin of ten percent.

DOS defaults the environment size to 160 bytes. The space expands if you type in settings, but it cannot expand during execution of a BAT file, including your AUTOEXEC.BAT file. Loading a memory-resident (TSR) program or utility (such as SIDEKICK, PROKEY, some RAM disks and print buffers, or the DOS PRINT and GRAPHICS commands) freezes the environment space to the current size. Fortunately, DOS 3.0 or later versions can easily expand the space. See the earlier section on CONFIG.SYS in this appendix for details.

Solving Problems with Memory Settings

So many possible variations of operating system environment settings and version-specific switches that deal with AutoCAD's memory usage exist that they cannot all be covered here. The wrong settings can cause random crashes and conflicts with other software. These settings and switches are explained in the *AutoCAD Interface, Installation, and Performance Guide.*

Losing the Display or Digitizer Configuration

Sometimes your digitizer configuration or screen gets disturbed when you are drawing. This can happen when you use memory-resident programs or AutoCAD's SHELL command to access other programs from AutoCAD. Instead of ending your drawing and starting again, use the REINIT command. The REINIT command displays a dialog box that enables you to re-initialize the digitizer and plotter port, digitizer, display, and ACAD.PGP file. If your display becomes garbled and you cannot see the dialog box clearly, press Ctrl-C three times and then enter the following command in AutoCAD:

```
RE-INIT 8
```

This automatically re-initializes the display. You can reverse any errors that may have occurred while the screen was garbled by issuing the UNDO command.

Finding Support Files

When you ask AutoCAD to find a support file (such as a menu file), it searches your disk in a particular order. A typical search order is:

```
"STUFF.mnu": Can't open file
```

`in C:\PROJECT\ (current directory)`	First the current directory.
`or C:\DWGS\`	Then the current drawing's directory.
`or C:\ACAD\SUPPORT\`	Then the directory(ies) designated by SET ACAD=.
`or C:\ACAD\`	Last, the program directory, home of ACAD.EXE.

```
Enter another menu file name (or RETURN for none):
```

If you keep AutoCAD's search order in mind, it helps you avoid errors caused by AutoCAD's finding the wrong support files. Sometimes AutoCAD finds the wrong support files because the ACAD environment variable's setting is in a start-up batch file. Be sure to clear your settings with SET ACAD= at the end of your start-up batch files. Remember that appended directories are always searched first.

Deciphering Current Directory Errors

If you use AutoCAD's SHELL command to change directories from within AutoCAD, you may get strange results. Although new drawings will not default to the new current directory, the SAVE command defaults to save files in the changed current directory. After you change directories in this manner, subsequent attempts to load support files (such as MNX files) can cause AutoCAD to crash.

If you must change directories on SHELL excursions to run other programs, automate the directory change with a batch file so that it also changes back to the original directory.

Solving other AutoCAD SHELL Errors

This section discusses some other common error messages that you may encounter when you use AutoCAD's SHELL command. Most problems with SHELL stem from insufficient memory. The memory environment created by the SHELL command is inhibiting.

The following message may be caused by an ill-behaved program executed during a previous SHELL or before entering AutoCAD:

```
SHELL error: insufficient memory for command
```

Some programs do not clean up after themselves; they leave behind unreclaimed memory, which causes AutoCAD to believe (erroneously) that insufficient memory exists. Even with well-behaved programs, you may not have enough free memory, and you see the following message:

```
Unable to load XYZABC: insufficient memory
Program too big to fit in memory
```

If SHELL got this far, the preceding messages are correct. You need to modify your system configuration to allow more conventional memory space. Try removing TSRs from memory as a first step. The second step is to use the SHROOM.COM utility that is in the AutoCAD SAMPLE subdirectory. SHROOM swaps additional AutoCAD program code to disk, leaving more memory available to SHELL.

This error can be caused by not having enough free conventional memory to load DOS. The solutions are the same as those for the preceding error.

```
SHELL error in EXEC function (insufficient memory)
```

Handling File Errors

You may encounter file-error messages when AutoCAD cannot open a file. This may happen because by too few files are requested in the `FILES=` statement of the CONFIG.SYS file, or because too many files were left open by AutoLISP's OPEN function. This error can show up as the following message:

```
Can't find overlay file C:\ACAD\ACAD.OVL
```

Tracing Errors

You are your best source for error diagnosis. When problems occur, record them so you can recognize patterns. Here are some troubleshooting tips:

- Use a screen-capture program to document the text screen.
- Echo the screen's contents to the printer.
- Write down what you did in as much detail as possible, as far back as you can remember.
- Echo a copy of AutoCAD's STATUS screen to the printer.
- Check the DOS SET command's settings and current directory by using SHELL.

Solving File Problems after a System Crash

When your system goes down unexpectedly in the middle of an AutoCAD session, you may end up with extraneous files on the disk or with files that are locked and inaccessible.

First, run CHKDSK /F at the DOS prompt to restore any disk space that is occupied by abandoned files. Do not run CHKDSK /F from AutoCAD's SHELL program.

Removing Extraneous Swap Files

When AutoCAD 386 terminates abnormally, you may find files on your hard drive with names that are hexadecimal numbers, such as 092A314F.SWR or 103B272D (no extension). Typically, these files have file

sizes of 0K, 100K, or nearly 400K. Normally, AutoCAD erases these files when you end a drawing session correctly. If the system locks up for some reason, however, the files remain on your disk until you erase them.

Use the DOS DEL or ERASE commands to erase these files. You can erase all files with an extension of SWR by entering the following command at the DOS prompt:

```
DEL *.SWR
```

If you have a number of these files without extensions, they probably begin with the same one or two digits. For example, if they all begin with 0, you can delete them all by entering the following command:

```
DEL 0*.
```

Be aware, however, that this command deletes every file in the current directory that begins with 0 and has no extension. If you have data or other files in the current directory that do not have extensions, and you wish to keep them, you have to erase the swap files individually or use a wild-card combination that is common to them all.

Unlocking Locked Files

If file locking is enabled and your AutoCAD session terminates abnormally, the drawing file you were editing remains locked. If you try to edit it again, AutoCAD refuses to let you access the file.

To unlock a locked file, first verify that the file is not actually in use by someone else, such as on a network. If it is not, choose File, then Utilities to access the File Utilities dialog box. Click on Unlock file. A standard AutoCAD file dialog box appears. Select all the files you want to unlock and click on OK. AutoCAD then unlocks the files. The File Utilities dialog box reappears and tells you how many files were unlocked.

Solving Login Errors

After a system crash, you may see an AutoCAD Alert dialog box that contains the following error message:

```
Login Failed: The maximum number of users has been reached.
Try again later.
```

You must restart AutoCAD with the same ACAD.CFG configuration file that was in use at the time of the crash. AutoCAD then can automatically repair the situation.

Dealing with Corrupted Drawings

If you receive an error message that begins with words such as EREAD or SCANDR when you try to load a drawing, the file may be corrupted. If the drawing was made with Release 11 or 12, AutoCAD itself may be able to salvage some or all of it. If the drawing was created with a prior release, you must either redraw the file or use a third-party drawing-recovery utility.

The RECOVER command attempts to recover as much of your drawing as possible. It performs an automatic audit of the file and presents you with the results in the drawing editor. Any warning messages AutoCAD displays are also written to a log file with the same name as the recovered drawing, but with an ADT extension if the AUDITCTL system variable has been set to 1 (the default is 0).

DOS Basics and Performance

To use AutoCAD, you should first know something about your computer and how it works. Most computer programs—applications such as AutoCAD or most word processors—require the user to understand basic computer functions. Some programs "insulate" the user from the computer system by performing these basic functions automatically, but such programs still are the exception rather than the norm.

Fortunately, getting started in AutoCAD requires only a modest knowledge of your system. If you are new to computers or to the DOS operating system, this appendix can help get you up to speed. If you are already familiar with DOS, skim this appendix to learn what applies to AutoCAD.

You need to understand seven basic elements about your computer system. On the hardware side (the physical equipment that makes up the system), you need to know something about:

- The individually identifiable components, such as a mouse or digitizer, video monitor, and printer or plotter.
- The computer's internal processor.

- The system's internal working memory.
- The disk drives, in which the software programs and data (such as AutoCAD drawings) are stored.

On the software side (the instructions that tell the system what to do), you need to know something about:

- The operating system's commands and utilities.
- Data files (such as AutoCAD drawings) and how to manage them.
- Applications software (such as the AutoCAD program) and how its commands and functions interact with the operating system.

To begin, consider the difference between two fundamental components of your computer system—the hardware and software.

Understanding Hardware and Software

Hardware is your computer's physical equipment, including the keyboard, video monitor, disk drives, and any other tangible components it may have. *Software* is a set of instructions that controls these physical components. Software is stored electronically on disk or in the system's internal memory. The computer reads the software from the disk into memory, where it exists only as electrical charges that tell the computer system how to function.

Hardware is divided into *system hardware* and *peripherals*. The system hardware includes the keyboard, monitor, central processing unit (CPU), internal working memory (RAM), and internal storage memory (usually disks). Peripherals include external storage memory (diskette or tape drives), digitizers, printers, plotters, modems, mice, and so on. The type of CPU, the amount and type of memory, and the storage capacity and speed of the disks are all related to the system's *performance*—overall speed. Your monitor's resolution, image quality, and availability of color also affect your productivity when you do computer-aided design or drafting (CAD).

Other peripherals, which vary widely from system to system, also affect your productivity. For example, a digitizer generally offers quicker command entry and greater precision and flexibility than a mouse or keyboard does. A printer often produces a drawing faster than a plotter, but the plotter produces a better quality drawing.

Software can be categorized into two main groups: *operating system software* and *application software*. Operating system software provides various levels of interaction (called the *interface*) between the computer hardware and the user, as well as between the computer hardware and application software. *Application software* (often called programs, such as AutoCAD and AutoSHADE) is what you interact with most often. The operating system is general-purpose software; a program is special-purpose software.

Picture a computer system as a stack of blocks. The top block represents your applications, below that is the operating system, and at the bottom is the system's hardware. Figure B.1 illustrates this concept.

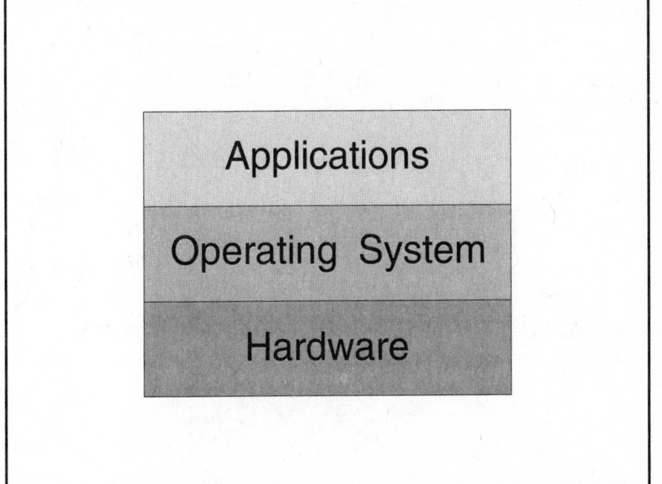

Figure B.1:

The various levels of a typical computer system.

You deal most actively with the top block (your applications) while the operating system makes it all happen behind the scenes, or *transparently* for the user. On IBM-compatible systems, the operating system software is generally DOS (disk operating system). The standard DOS commands are the same, whether you are using MS-DOS (Microsoft DOS), PC DOS (IBM's version), or an OEM (original equipment manufacturer) version, which is slightly customized by the hardware supplier.

The Many Levels of DOS

The operating system provides commands for managing your system and data. One of the most important functions of the operating system is to display a screen *prompt*, such as `A:\>` or `C:\>`. A prompt is a cue that the system is ready to receive and execute a command. When you type a command after a prompt and press Enter, DOS interprets what you typed and acts accordingly. If what you typed is neither a valid DOS command nor a program name that DOS recognizes, the system displays an error message and repeats the prompt.

You generally have two *entry points* into your computer system. You can control it from within an application, such as AutoCAD, or you can control it from the operating-system level. But before you learn to control the system, you should have an understanding of its hardware components.

The CPU and Memory

What many users perceive as the main body of the system, the CPU and memory, are physically two of the smallest components in the system. Nevertheless, they are the most important. The next section examines the first of these pieces—the brain of the system.

The Central Processing Unit

The central processing unit (CPU) is responsible for the work done in your computer. Most of the "computing" takes place in the CPU. The type of CPU in your computer system determines both its speed and its capabilities. Four classes of processors are used in IBM compatibles: the 8088 or 8086, the 80286, the 80386, and the 80486. The 80486 is the newest and most powerful.

The outdated 8088 and 8086 processors (used in the original IBM PC) and the 80286 (used in the IBM AT) are limited in their memory-management and processing capabilities, compared to today's 80386 and 80486 CPUs. AutoCAD is a complex program that needs all the power you can afford. To run AutoCAD Release 12, you must have at least an 80386- or 80486-based system.

The 80386 requires a *math coprocessor* to run AutoCAD. A math coprocessor, also called an *FPU* (floating-point unit), processes floating-point math operations many times faster than the CPU does. Math coprocessors manufactured by Intel have numbers the same as the CPU they were designed to work with, except that the last digit is a 7. For example, the 80386 requires an 80387 FPU. The 80486 has a built-in math coprocessor and does not require an external one.

NOTE

References to the 80386 or 80486 mean the 80386DX and 80486DX parts. The 80386SX has half the external data-transfer capacity of the 80386DX. For production AutoCAD use, the slight cost savings of an 80386SX are not worth the performance loss. Beware of the 80486SX—it is an 80486 with the FPU disabled! The money you save on an 80486SX purchase can easily be used up by the 80487 FPU you have to buy.

Computer systems are classified by the type of CPU because the CPU imposes absolute limits on performance and software compatibility. Memory is a more flexible resource, and you can easily improve a computer system's performance by adding more working memory.

Primary Storage Memory

Your computer system's primary storage area, or working *system memory*, is the CPU's workspace. When you copy a file from one disk to another, the file is momentarily stored in that system memory workspace before being copied to the destination disk. Programs use the same workspace for calculations or data manipulations. The applications software and operating-system software must also be loaded into this workspace when they are executing. Because of the way in which the CPU retrieves data from it, this memory is called *random-access memory* (RAM).

Although RAM chips vary in type and storage capacity, what is important to system performance is the location of the memory and the way the processor addresses it. (For more details about memory and for definitions of terms used in the following list, see Appendix A or your *AutoCAD Interface, Installation and Performance Guide*.)

The primary types of system memory are:

- **Conventional memory.** The range for conventional memory is 0K to 1024K. (With personal computers, memory is usually measured in *kilobytes*, abbreviated as K. A kilobyte contains 1,024 bytes of data.) All AutoCAD systems need at least 640K, but only part of that memory is actually available to AutoCAD because DOS uses part of it. DOS version 5.x can make more of this 640K available to applications than in previous DOS versions.
- **Extended memory.** Sometimes referred to as *XMS*, extended memory is the memory over 1088K. A program called an *extended memory manager* (EMM) can manage your application software's access to extended memory.
- **Expanded memory.** Also referred to as *EMS*, expanded memory may be on a physical expanded memory card installed in the computer and controlled by expanded memory manager software, or provided by an extended memory manager.

Extended and expanded memory are addressed directly only by applications, such as AutoCAD, that are specifically written for them. AutoCAD 386 needs extended memory. At least 8M (8 *megabytes* equals 8192K) total system memory is recommended for AutoCAD 386, of which 7M probably should be configured as extended memory.

Secondary Storage Memory

The system memory (RAM) provides a place for the CPU to manipulate data. But the system must also have a place to store that data, as well as application programs, operating system files, and so on. The system's secondary storage—its hard drives, disk drives, tape drives, and CD-ROM drives—serves that function. Because the disk drive slot is visible on your computer but the hard disk is not, some users confuse hard-disk storage with system RAM. Data is stored in the system's RAM storage as transient electrical charges; data is stored as relatively permanent magnetic codes on a tangible, though hidden, disk. Hard disks work like floppy disks, except they are much faster and have a much larger storage capacity, due to being manufactured more precisely and being sealed airtight to eliminate dust. The more secondary storage available to the system, the more information you can store.

Although secondary storage can consist of tape and various devices other than disks, this discussion refers only to disks. Your main disk is probably a hard disk, designated C. If your hard disk is not drive C, substitute its actual drive letter wherever C is shown throughout this book.

Hard disks are useful for storing large amounts of data. Floppy disks are used to distribute software, transfer files between computers that are not connected by a network, and create backup copies of important files. Floppy disks (also called diskettes) come in two sizes. The older size is 5 1/4 inches, with a flexible jacket. At 3 1/2 inches, the newer size is smaller, with a hard plastic case. Each size comes in several densities. *Density* refers to the relative amount of information that can be stored on the disk. The standard DSDD (double-sided double-density) 5 1/4-inch floppy disk holds 360K; the standard DSDD (or just DD) 3 1/2-inch floppy disk holds 720K of memory. High-density (HD) 5 1/4-inch floppies hold about 1.2M of information, and high-density 3 1/2-inch floppies hold approximately 1.44M. Drives that are designed for high-density disks can usually read and write to lower-density disks, but low-density drives cannot read high-density disks.

The combination of physical size and density determines the *format* of the disk. Any application you want to install and any data you want to copy on your system must be in the appropriate format. Most software manufacturers make their products available on both 5 1/4-inch and 3 1/2-inch floppies in standard densities.

The floppy disk is made of a flexible magnetic material similar to that used for audio tapes. Disk care is important. Avoid temperature extremes, do not touch the actual recording material, and store diskettes in sleeves or containers to avoid contamination by dirt. Handle 5 1/4-inch floppies carefully to avoid creasing the jacket, and do not write on the disk (or its label) with a ballpoint pen.

Hard disks are classified by their data-access speed, such as 15 milliseconds, or ms (lower is better); their data-transfer rate, such as 15M/sec (higher is better); and their total capacity, such as 40M (a suitable minimum for AutoCAD). Hard disks are protected from your touch, but be careful not to expose them to physical shock. Once you have purchased a hard disk, all that is really important to you is the amount of currently available storage space on the disk.

Referencing a Drive

A single computer system may have several storage devices connected to it at once. In fact, most systems have at least two disk drives. In DOS, disk drives are addressed by an identifying *drive letter.* If a system has only one floppy drive, that drive is referred to as drive A. If a second floppy drive is available, it is drive B. The first hard disk drive is referred to as drive C.

The drive letters are *logical* references, not physical references. A single physical drive may be assigned more than one logical drive letter. A hard disk may be divided into several logical disks, each with its own drive letter.

An important concept with DOS is the *current drive*—the drive the system uses for its current operations unless you instruct it otherwise. Many programs and DOS commands work with information that is stored on the computer. If you do not specify a drive letter, DOS attempts to execute the command using information from the current drive.

Most systems use the DOS command prompt `$P$G` to make the current drive letter appear as part of the DOS prompt (for example, `C:\>`). See "Checking the Current Directory" later in this appendix.

You reference a drive by its drive letter followed by a colon (:), for example, `C:` for drive C. To change to a different current drive, enter the new drive letter, followed by a colon, and then press Enter. For example, to change from drive C to drive A, type A: and press Enter. If you are changing to a floppy disk drive, the floppy disk should be in the drive ready for the system to use. See "Checking Disks with CHKDSK" for an example.

The DOS Operating System

Information management on your computer system occurs at two levels: in the processor and where files are organized and stored on disk. The control in the processor is automatic, though its efficiency is affected by which version of operating system you have and by the way the system is configured. File management, on the other hand, is an ongoing process that you are responsible for.

To obtain the best performance from your computer system, you should have an up-to-date operating system that is configured properly. To check

your DOS version, type **VER** and press Enter at the DOS prompt. Your version is important because many programs benefit from or require features available only in DOS version 3.0 or later, and DOS 5.x (the current version) has features that maximize the amount of memory available to applications.

Booting the System

Generally, a computer system must have a *system disk*. A system disk is one that contains all of the operating system files necessary to start the computer. Most systems are set up to start (boot) from a hard disk. Otherwise, you start the computer from a floppy disk containing these files. As the system starts, the operating system is copied from the disk to RAM, where the processor can use it.

Once the basic portion of the operating system has been installed, the system checks for any special configuration instructions in a file called CONFIG.SYS, which must be located on the system disk. The settings in CONFIG.SYS establish memory management and install device drivers. For more information about CONFIG.SYS and configuring your system for use with AutoCAD, see Appendix A.

After the system is configured, it searches for a file called AUTOEXEC.BAT (AUTOmatically EXECuting BATch file), containing instructions about standard DOS commands that are to be automatically executed. Many of these commands control how the operating system manages file access; others set *system variables*. Programs use system variables to obtain information about your computer system's configuration. Appendix A tells you how to customize your AUTOEXEC.BAT file.

When the operating system is booted, it is ready for you to use its utility commands, organize your files and directories, or start your application programs. One of the first things you may want to do is check memory and disk space.

Checking Disks with CHKDSK

The DOS CHKDSK (ChecK DiSK) command checks the total amount of storage space on a disk and the amount that is currently available. It also reports the total and available amounts of conventional RAM. To use the CHKDSK command, type **CHKDSK** at the DOS prompt and press Enter. To check a disk in a drive other than the current one, include the drive letter in the command, for example **CHKDSK B:**. The operating system responds to your CHKDSK command with a report (in this case, for a hard disk) that looks something like this:

```
Volume AUTOCAD1 created 04-18-1991 3:41p
Volume Serial Number is 169A-5C83
   65468416 bytes total disk space
    4270080 bytes in 3 hidden files
     118784 bytes in 53 directories
   32727040 bytes in 967 user files
     655360 bytes in bad sectors
   27697152 bytes available on disk
       2048 bytes in each allocation unit
      31967 total allocation units on disk
      13524 available allocation units on disk
     655360 total bytes memory
     181088 bytes free
```

Generally, the most useful information is the `bytes available on disk` line, which indicates how much room is available for new programs and data files. Although the figure is reported in bytes, it is much more convenient to think of available storage in terms of megabytes. To convert from bytes to megabytes, divide by 1,024,000 (or 1,000,000 for a rough estimate). In the sample listing, approximately 27.5M of free space is available on the hard disk.

CHKDSK provides other information about the hard disk. The first two lines identify the disk. The next section presents a summary of disk usage by reporting the total disk space and the number and total size of hidden files, directories, and user files. The `bytes total disk space` line indicates the size of the hard disk (again, divide by 1,024,000 to convert to megabytes). Many disks have portions that are no longer usable, reported as `bytes in bad sectors.`

The final two lines indicate the amount of working RAM installed in the system and the amount currently available. The DOS 5.x MEM command also reports this information.

CHKDSK also reports any disk problems, for example, lost clusters, which are usually harmless leftovers created when programs crash (terminate due to error or power failure). Enter **CHKDSK /F** at the DOS prompt and answer **N** when DOS asks whether you want to convert the clusters to files in order to delete them. See your DOS manual for details.

Using Directories and Files

Information on your computer is stored in *files*. They include documents, drawings, and other data files you create, as well as the support files for the operating system and various applications. *Support files*, such as AutoCAD's text font definition files, contain data used by the program.

You refer to files by their *file names*. To avoid sorting through several hundred files to find the one you need, organize the files into groups, just as you organize your paper files in file folders and file cabinets. You do this by creating *directories* and *subdirectories*. Directories also have names by which you refer to them, and one directory can contain any number of other directories and files.

Most people use the terms *subdirectory* and *parent directory* when talking about the relationship between two directories. For example, if you have a directory named DRAWING within your ACAD directory, you can say that the DRAWING directory is a subdirectory of the ACAD directory, or that the ACAD directory is the parent of the DRAWING directory.

Your hard disk is probably already organized into a collection of directories, with each program contained in its own subdirectory and with data files organized under their own directories and subdirectories. This organization is called the *directory structure* or the *directory tree*. Each subdirectory is a branch of the directory tree. The main directory that contains all the other directories, subdirectories, and files on your disk is called the *root directory*.

Displaying the Directory Tree

The DOS 3.3 or DOS 5.x TREE command lists directories and subdirectories. Figure B.2 shows a sample directory tree. In DOS 3.3, the listing starts with the root directory; in DOS 5.x, it starts with the current directory.

To specify a subdirectory or a file in a subdirectory, you need to specify the *path* of directory names that you follow from the root directory or current directory to the desired subdirectory. The full path name of a directory starts with the drive letter and the root directory. The root directory has no name but is indicated with a backslash (\). For example, the root directory of the first hard disk on your system is `C:\`. If the ACAD directory is a subdirectory of the root, it is specified as `C:\ACAD`. Subdirectories of ACAD are prefaced with additional backslashes. If the DRAWING

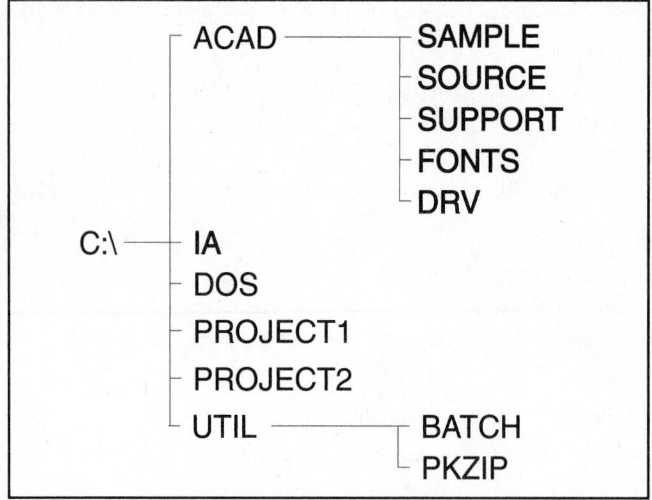

Figure B.2:

A directory tree.

directory is a subdirectory of C:\ACAD, you use the path name C:\ACAD\DRAWING. If drive C is the current drive, you can omit the drive designation, and the path name is \ACAD\DRAWING.

You can abbreviate the current directory with a single period (.) and the parent directory with a double period (..). For example, if the current directory is \ACAD\ DRAWING, and if DRAWING2 is also a subdirectory of ACAD, you specify the path of DRAWING2 as ..\DRAWING2 instead of \ACAD\DRAWING2.

Checking the Current Directory

In working with directories, you always need to be aware of what your current directory is. Unless your AUTOEXEC.BAT file is set up to change the current directory, you always start up in the root. You change the current directory with the CD (change directory) command or with an appropriate command from your application program. To change your directory, type CD *path* at the DOS prompt and press Enter, where *path* is the path of the desired directory.

Be careful not to lose track of the current directory. If you do lose track, you can enter CD without designating a path, and DOS displays the name of the current directory.

If your DOS prompt is the default (such as C>), and you want it to display the current directory (such as C:\>), follow the steps in the following exercise to reset it.

Setting the Prompt To Show the Current Directory

Type CD\ and press Enter at the DOS prompt to make sure the root directory is current.

```
C> PROMPT $P$G↵
C:\>
```

Your prompt should now display a backslash, for the root directory.

You can put the PROMPT PG command in your AUTOEXEC.BAT file so that your prompt automatically displays the current path. See Appendix A for details.

Listing Directories and Files

The DOS DIR (DIRectory) command lists the subdirectories and files in the current directory. It also lists the volume label of the current disk, the disk serial number (for DOS 4.x and 5.x hard disks only), and the name of the current directory. To display the listing, type **DIR** and press Enter. A listing might look like this:

```
 Volume in drive C has no label
 Volume Serial Number is 2A35-17EB
 Directory of  C:\AB1DOC
.            <DIR>     06-17-92   4:14p
..           <DIR>     06-17-92   4:14p
CMDREF       <DIR>     06-17-92  10:36p
PM           <DIR>     06-17-92   4:16p
AB1CHP02 DOC     16896 06-21-92   3:51p
AB1CHP03 DOC     24576 06-25-92  12:14p
AB1CHP04 DOC     26112 06-25-92   1:35p
AB1CHP05 DOC     27648 06-20-92  11:34a
AB1CHP06 DOC     25088 06-20-92  11:34a
AB1CHP01 DOC     66560 06-25-92   9:05p
      10 File(s)   67223552 bytes free
```

The directories, including the abbreviations for current directory (.) and parent directory (..) , are indicated with <DIR>. The other items in the listing are files. File and directory names in DOS can contain up to eight characters, with an optional *extension* of up to three characters. In the preceding sample listing, the file names have DOC extensions. When you enter a file name at the DOS prompt, you must separate the name from its extension with a period, for example AB1CHP01.DOC. The directory listing on the screen does not show the periods.

The DIR /AD command in DOS 5.x lists only subdirectories within the current directory. In other DOS versions, the command DIR *. lists all files or directories that do not have extensions. Because files are often named with extensions and directories are not, DIR *. usually lists only subdirectories.

Try listing your directories, and look for your AutoCAD directory.

Listing Directories

Type `CD\` and press Enter at the DOS prompt to make sure the root directory is current.

For DOS 5.x:

`C:\>`**`DIR /AD`**↵	Displays a listing of directories

For DOS 5.x or DOS 3.x:

`C:\>`**`DIR *.`**↵	Displays a listing of directories

Your listing might be similar to the following:

```
 Volume in drive C has no label
 Volume Serial Number is 2A35-17EB
 Directory of  C:\
ACAD         <DIR>     04-01-91   9:32p
BAT          <DIR>     11-30-90   9:04a
BOOT         <DIR>     11-30-90   8:14a
DOS          <DIR>     11-27-90   4:37p
DWG          <DIR>     12-18-90  10:45p
AB1DOC       <DIR>     06-17-91   4:14p
UTIL         <DIR>     12-15-90   9:16a
WORD         <DIR>     01-03-91   9:19a
       8 File(s)   66408448 bytes free
```

Try to identify your AutoCAD program directory. The one shown in the sample listing is ACAD.

If your AutoCAD program directory is not named ACAD, substitute its name wherever ACAD is shown throughout the book.

Many directory listings are too long to display on a single screen. The DIR /P command causes the listing to stop after each screen full of information. The DIR /W command lists names and extensions only, in a five-column-wide listing.

The /AD, /P and /W are *parameters* that modify the action of the directory command. Any number of parameters can be used with a single directory command. DOS 5.x includes several additional parameters.

Using the DIR Command in DOS 5.x

The /O parameter organizes the DOS output into a sorted list. In addition to the parameter, you must specify how you want the files organized. You can use the following parameters:

N Name

E Extension

S Size

D Date and Time

For example, DIR /ON displays all of the files and directories sorted by name. DIR /OD displays the files sorted by date starting with the oldest file. You can use the minus sign to reverse the direction of any sort. DIR /OD reverses the date order and displays the newest file first. DIR /OG groups the directories at the start of the listing.

DIR /S specifies that the contents of each subdirectory are displayed as an individual listing. The DIR /S command first displays the contents of the current directory (including all files and subdirectories), then the contents of the first directory in the list are displayed. If that subdirectory contains a subdirectory, its contents are then displayed, and so on.

Creating and Removing Directories

Many programs and applications automatically create directories, during installation, that store their program files. You can also create directories for your data files by using the MD or MKDIR command (MaKe DIRectory). To remove a directory, use the RD or RMDIR command (remove directory).

To use the MD (or MKDIR) command, enter the command followed by the name (or path) of the subdirectory to be created. For example, MD \ACAD\DRAWING creates the \ACAD\DRAWING directory. If you specify just the new directory name (with no path), a new subdirectory in the current directory is created. Unless a problem occurs, the MD command works quietly without giving you any feedback or messages.

The RD (or RMDIR) command works exactly like MD, except that it removes, rather than creates, the specified directory. You can only remove a directory that contains no files or subdirectories. Use the DEL command to remove any files before you remove the directory. If you enter **DEL \ACAD\DRAWING*name.ext***, where *name* is a particular file name and *ext* is its extension, that particular file is deleted. If you enter **DEL \ACAD\DRAWING*.***, all files in the DRAWING directory are removed.

Changing Directories

The CD or CHDIR (CHange DIRectory) command changes the current directory. To move to a new directory, type **CD** (or **CHDIR**) followed by the path of the destination directory. For example, to move to the ACAD subdirectory, enter **CD \ACAD** (or **CHDIR \ACAD**). If you specify a drive letter, like **CD B:\PROJECTS**, it does not change to drive B, but changes the current directory of drive B. If you later change the current drive to drive B, you find that PROJECTS is the current directory on drive B.

Several shortcuts for changing directories are available. Consider the parent directory \ACAD and its two subdirectories \ACAD\DRAWING and \ACAD\ DRAWING2 as examples. If the destination directory is a subdirectory of the current directory, you can enter **CD**, followed by the subdirectory name. When \ACAD is current, CD DRAWING changes to \ACAD\DRAWING. To move back up one level to the current

directory's parent, enter CD and two periods. For example, enter CD.. to change to \ACAD when \ACAD\DRAWING is current. If the current directory is \ACAD\DRAWING, you can move to DRAWING2 by entering CD ..\DRAWING2 instead of CD \ACAD\DRAWING2.

Most applications have their own methods and commands for moving between directories to locate a data file. Generally, you only need to use the CD command to locate and manage files in DOS, or to change to an application's subdirectory before starting the application program.

Managing Files

All the information in your computer system is stored in the form of files. Program files with EXE, COM, and BAT extensions contain instructions that execute when you start up an application. The application program itself usually manages these files and any special support data files it needs. As you work, you create your own data files, such as word processing documents, spreadsheets, or AutoCAD drawings.

Every file takes up storage space. In time, your disks begin to fill up. To maintain your system performance and avoid confusion, you should manage your files wisely. Proper file management includes naming your files properly, using subdirectories to organize your files, maintaining backup copies of your data files, and deleting unnecessary files.

Naming Files

File and directory names in DOS can be up to eight characters long, with an optional extension of up to three characters. Permissible characters include all of the letters and numbers on your keyboard as well as the punctuation characters: ' ~ ! @ # $ ^ & ( ) _ - { }. A period separates the file name from the extension. Each combination of file name and extension must be unique within each directory.

Like most application programs, AutoCAD assigns certain specific extensions to its data files. The following are common file extensions that you see when working with AutoCAD:

- **DWG.** The DWG extension denotes an AutoCAD drawing file. AutoCAD assigns the DWG extension automatically—you do not need to assign it when you save a drawing. You just enter a file name; AutoCAD adds the extension.

- **SCR.** An SCR file is an AutoCAD script file, containing a list of AutoCAD commands. *Script files* are similar in concept to DOS batch files, except that they work within AutoCAD, not within DOS. You can automate many processes in AutoCAD with script files.
- **LSP.** LSP identifies an AutoLISP file. AutoLISP is AutoCAD's programming language. By using LISP programs, you can automate complex tasks that cannot be performed with a script.
- **CFG.** The CFG extension denotes a configuration file, containing information about your system hardware setup.
- **MNU.** MNU files are *menu-source files*. You can customize your AutoCAD menu or create custom menus by creating and editing menu source files.
- **MNX.** *Compiled-menu files* have the extension MNX. Before AutoCAD can use a menu, it compiles (translates) the menu source file (MNU file) into a more efficient form. AutoCAD then uses the MNX file as the menu file.
- **SHP.** *Shape-definition source files* have the extension SHP. *Shapes* include text fonts and simple symbols. You can create your own text styles by creating shape-definition files.
- **SHX.** SHX identifies a *compiled shape file*. As with menus, AutoCAD compiles shape definitions into a more efficient form.

Using Wild Cards To Locate Files

DOS enables you to use wild cards when specifying file names. A *wild card* is a special character that represents one or many unknown characters. The asterisk matches any number of letters in either the file name or the extension. The question mark matches a single unknown character. For example, *.DWG matches any file with the DWG extension (AutoCAD drawings). R*.* matches any file that has a file name starting with the letter R, regardless of how many total letters are in the file name. R??.* matches any file with a three-letter file name that starts with R, regardless of extension. Using *.* matches any file name. Wild cards are useful when listing files or when copying a group of files.

The asterisk makes DOS fill in the file name (or extension) from its position to the end of the file name (up to the period) or extension. Any characters to the right of the asterisk are ignored. You cannot place an asterisk between two letters to match characters at the beginning and end of a file name. For example, R*Z matches all files that start with the letter R, not just those that start with R and end with Z.

You can use wild cards with the DIR command to list certain types of files. The command DIR R* is the same as the DIR R*.* command and lists all file names starting with the letter R (regardless of their extension). The commands DIR, DIR *, DIR., DIR .*, and DIR *.* all produce a listing of all files in the directory. The command DIR *. lists only those files with a blank extension, which includes most directories.

Copying Files

An important aspect of file management is maintaining current *backups*. A backup is a duplicate set of files to use if you lose one. You should create a backup whenever the nuisance of re-creating your work would exceed the minor inconvenience of backing up your file(s)—in other words, almost always. The simplest way to create backups is to use the COPY command to duplicate the file(s) onto another disk (or, in AutoCAD, use the SAVE command to save a copy of a drawing to a different disk).

The COPY command can be used to replicate a file with a new name or to duplicate a file in a new location as a backup. To copy a series of files, use wild cards. The general form of the COPY command is:

```
COPY source target
```

where *source* is the file(s) to be copied and *target* is either the new name or the new location (or a combination of both). The command **COPY TEMPLATE.DWG WORKING.DWG** creates a duplicate of the file TEMPLATE.DWG with the name WORKING.DWG in the current directory. The command **COPY TEMPLATE.DWG B:** creates a backup of the TEMPLATE.DWG file, also named TEMPLATE.DWG, on the disk in the B drive.

Wild cards and paths are permitted within the COPY command. For example, the command **COPY *.* B:** copies all the files in the current directory to the disk in the B drive. The command COPY \ACAD\DRAWINGS*.* B: copies all the files in the \ACAD\DRAWINGS directory on the current drive to drive B. COPY *.DWG B: copies those files with a DWG extension (AutoCAD drawing files) from the current directory to the disk in the B drive.

NOTE

Restoring the directory organization, programs, and data of your entire system can be a huge task in the event of a major system failure or error. Backing up your entire system regularly with a tape drive or commercial backup program can make this task much easier if disaster strikes. Tape drives and backup programs are also good for backing up large sets of files.

Deleting Unwanted Files

File management includes getting rid of files that you no longer need on your system. Periodically, you should back up and delete the files that you are no longer using regularly. The DEL command (or its synonym ERASE) deletes files. It accepts both wild cards and path information. The command DEL OLD.DWG (or ERASE OLD.DWG) deletes the file OLD.DWG from the current directory. The command DEL \ACAD\DRAWINGS\OLD.DWG deletes the file OLD.DWG from the \ACAD\DRAWINGS directory. The command DEL \ACAD\DRAWINGS*.DWG removes all of the files with the extension DWG (AutoCAD drawing files) from the directory \ACAD\DRAWINGS. Obviously, you should be extremely careful when using wild cards with the DEL command. If you try to delete all of the files in a directory with the command DEL *.*, you see this prompt:

```
All files in directory will be deleted!
Are you sure (Y/N)?
```

You must enter a Y (upper- or lowercase does not matter in DOS) to confirm the deletion of all the files. You can also delete all files in a subdirectory by specifying the name of the directory rather than a file name. For example, the command DEL \ACAD\DRAWINGS is the same as DEL \ACAD\DRAWINGS*.*.

NOTE

You may unexpectedly get an `All files in directory will be deleted! Are you sure (Y/N)?` message when you did not intend to delete an entire directory. For example, accidentally entering **DEL *A.*** instead of **DEL A*.*** deletes the entire current directory instead of all files beginning with the letter A. If you make such a mistake and get the warning prompt, answer **N** to its message.

File Recovery

Sooner or later, when you are manipulating files, you lose one. In DOS 5.x, you can sometimes restore a mistakenly deleted file with the UNDELETE command. However, any changes made to other files on the disk after the unintended deletion reduce your chances of successfully restoring the deleted file. The DOS 5.x UNFORMAT command can retrieve information from a disk that has been formatted by mistake.

If you have an earlier version of DOS, you can use utility programs such as the Norton Utilities QU (Quick Unerase) or the PCTOOLS program to undelete files.

You may think you have lost or deleted a file when it was merely created in the wrong directory, or you may simply forget where you stored a file. In DOS 5, you can search multiple directories for files. Just add a **/S** to the DIR command, and it searches all subdirectories of the current directory (or path, if you specify a path). For example, the command **DIR \ACAD*.DWG /S** searches for and lists all drawing files in the \ACAD directory and all of its subdirectories.

With earlier versions of DOS, you can use utility programs, such as the Norton Utilities FF (Find File) or the PCTOOLS program, to search for files.

Program Execution

Many common commands, such as DIR and CD, are built into the DOS COMMAND.COM file. Because COMMAND.COM is loaded when DOS is booted, these commands are always available at the DOS prompt. Other commands, application programs, and utility functions are contained in

executable files (those with EXE extensions), command files (with COM extensions), and batch files (with BAT extensions). To execute EXE, COM, and BAT program files, enter their file names (with or without extensions) at the DOS prompt. Of course, DOS has to find the files to execute them.

If you have EXE, COM, and/or BAT files with the same file names, DOS first executes the EXE file. If no EXE file is found, DOS looks for a COM file, and, if neither is found, it looks for a BAT file to execute.

You can enable DOS to find a program that is not located in the current directory in three ways. The first way is to use CD to change to another directory and then enter the program's file name. The second way is to enter the program's file name with the full path to its directory. For example, if ACAD.EXE is in C:\ACAD, you could enter \ACAD\ACAD to start AutoCAD from another current directory or enter C:\ACAD\ACAD to start AutoCAD from another drive. If the current directory is \ACAD\AB, you could start ACAD.EXE by entering ..\ACAD rather than \ACAD\ACAD.

The third way to enable DOS to find a program that is not located in the current directory is to include the location of the program file in the PATH environment variable in your AUTOEXEC.BAT file. See Appendix A for more information.

Files in AutoCAD

Most of AutoCAD's file functions are accessed by using the FILES command. The File Utilities dialog box provides an alternative to DOS (or your operating system) for managing your files. To display the File Utilities dialog box, enter the FILES command. You can also access the File Utilities by choosing File, then Utilities. Start AutoCAD and try the File Utilities dialog box.

Accessing Files from AutoCAD

`C:\>CD \ACAD↵`	Changes to the AutoCAD directory
`C:\ACAD>ACAD↵`	Starts AutoCAD and displays the opening screen

Choose File, *then* Utilities	Accesses the File Utilities dialog box
Click on List files	Displays an AutoCAD file dialog box with all the DWG files in the current directory in the Files: scroll box
Click on Cancel, *then* Exit	Exits the file and File Utilities dialog box

File Utilities

The following is a list of the File Utilities dialog box options.

- **List files.** Lists AutoCAD drawing files by default, but lists other files by changing the file display pattern.
- **Copy file.** Enables you to copy a file from a drive and directory (source) into another drive and directory (destination). You can also specify a different name for the copied file. You can copy a file from one drive and directory to another and rename the file at the same time. This action does not delete the original file.
- **Rename files.** Enables you to rename a file and (optionally) place the file in a different directory at the same time. RENAME copies a file from one directory to another (you can keep the same file name) and deletes the original file.
- **Delete files.** Enables you to specify one or more files to delete. You are prompted to answer no or yes before each file is actually deleted.
- **Unlock file.** Enables you to unlock one or more files after a system crash, using wild-card options if you choose.
- **Exit.** Closes the File Utilities dialog box.

When you refer to a file name, do not forget to include the extension (such as DWG for drawing files).

When you use the file utilities, do not delete the current drawing file (DWG), temporary files (AC, AC, or $A), or lock files (??K).

New computer users generally find AutoCAD's FILES command helpful for manipulating files. Experienced users, however, may feel more comfortable with the operating system's file-manipulation commands. When you are in an AutoCAD drawing, you can *shell out* to the operating system and execute operating system commands without exiting AutoCAD to execute those commands. You shell out with AutoCAD's SHELL or SH commands.

SHELL (or SH) functions as a gateway between AutoCAD, the operating system (such as DOS), and other external programs. If you press Enter once after typing **SHELL** or **SH**, AutoCAD presents an `OS Command:` prompt, at which you can issue a single operating-system command and immediately return to AutoCAD. If you press Enter at the OS command prompt, you stay in the operating system until you type **EXIT** to return to AutoCAD. Once in the operating-system, you can execute most operating-system commands and software programs, depending on their memory requirements.

You can easily forget that you have shelled out of AutoCAD and into the operating system or another program. If you are shelled to the operating system, you see a double "greater than" symbol (>>) at the command prompt, instead of the normal single symbol.

AutoCAD 386 owners can use the SHROOM utility, included with AutoCAD, to increase the amount of memory SHELL provides for external programs. See the AutoCAD README.DOC and SHROOM.DOC files for more information.

The following are most common things to be aware of when working with the SHELL command:

- **Changing directories.** Make sure the current directory when you exit the SHELL command is the same directory as when you entered it.
- **CHKDSK.** Do not issue a CHKDSK /F when using SHELL.
- **Temporary files**. Do not delete temporary AutoCAD files with a $ symbol in the file name or extension, or lock files with the extension ??K.
- **TSRs.** Do not load any RAM-resident or TSR programs from the shell. Load them before you start AutoCAD.
- **Resetting Ports.** Do not run programs (such as BASIC) that reset the I/O (input/output) ports.

Increasing AutoCAD Performance

Because AutoCAD accesses and manages your system resources efficiently, you do not need to tweak AutoCAD or your system to increase performance. Any general system-performance enhancers speed up AutoCAD. Four main bottlenecks commonly occur in computer systems: disk access, application workspace in RAM, graphics processing, and computing speed.

Speeding Up Disk Access

Because AutoCAD can be very *disk-intensive* (it accesses the disk frequently), your system's hard drive access speed affects AutoCAD's performance.

You can increase the disk access speed in several ways. The most inexpensive and dramatic way to increase disk performance is to use a disk-cache. A disk cache is a TSR program that stores recent and frequently accessed disk information in RAM. Norton's N-CACHE, PCTOOLS' PC-CACHE, and Microsoft Windows 3.1's SMARTDRV.EXE are popular disk-cache programs.

The amount of RAM allocated to the disk cache does not have to be large to significantly increase performance. A good starting size is 512K. Increasing the size of the cache improves disk access; however, the amount of improvement diminishes quickly. AutoCAD can use the RAM more efficiently after a certain point.

When DOS stores files on your hard disk, it must sometimes break the files up and scatter them around the disk, rather than store the file in contiguous (side-by-side) sectors (units of disk storage). The more files are added to or deleted from the disk, the more likely your files are to be fragmented. To maintain good disk performance, you should reorganize (*pack, defragment,* or *optimize*) the disk at least once a month. This process reorders the files, moving the data for each file into contiguous sectors so DOS can access their contents more efficiently. You find that periodically reorganizing your hard disk improves performance in your other applications as well as in AutoCAD.

Several commercial disk-management programs not only pack the disk but also check and adjust other performance parameters of your hard drive, such as the disk's *interleave factor* (the ordering of the sectors on the disk).

See any software dealer for recommendations. Before you pack your hard disk, make sure you have a complete backup of all files on the disk and that you know how to restore them in case of any problems.

Keep each of your software programs, like AutoCAD, in its own subdirectory. File access is faster, data files do not get mixed up, and future program upgrades are easier to install. Backing up your file system is also easier when programs are separated into individual directories. If you have more than one hard disk, consider installing software programs on one and using another for data. Because your software is relatively static (the files do not change often), you need not defragment software disks as often as your data disk.

Another way to improve disk performance is to buy a faster disk drive.

Increasing Application Workspace

You can also enhance AutoCAD's performance cost-effectively by installing more RAM. When your drawings grow in size so that they no longer can fit in RAM while you work on them in AutoCAD, AutoCAD begins paging drawing data to disk. You begin to lose time as AutoCAD reads to and from your disk. The more RAM you can install in your computer, the longer you can put off paging. To determine how much RAM you might need, use this rule of thumb:

3× drawing size + 2M AutoCAD

A 1M drawing requires 5M RAM to forestall paging. If you typically create 1M drawings, you should have 5M RAM (or more) to accommodate AutoCAD and maximize performance.

Free as much RAM as you possibly can before running AutoCAD, so that AutoCAD has as much RAM as possible. Load only those memory-resident TSR programs that you absolutely need.

Use a memory manager, such as MS-DOS 5.x's HIMEM.SYS or QEMM386.SYS from QuarterDeck Office Systems, along with DOS=HIGH and/or DOS's LOADHIGH or QEMM's LOADHI to maximize your available DOS memory. See an MS-DOS 5 or QEMM 386 manual, or *Maximizing DOS 5*, from New Riders Publishing, for details.

Using Faster Video

A number of manufacturers offer video-adapter boards that are optimized for AutoCAD, and that improve screen regeneration and redraw speed in AutoCAD. A number of these manufacturers, as well as other third-party ADI driver developers, offer software video drivers that optimize AutoCAD video performance. See your AutoCAD dealer for details.

Increasing Computing Speed

The only thing that can be done to increase computing speed is to use a faster CPU. Usually this means purchasing a new computer (or at least a new mother board). Some computers have upgradeable CPU modules or accept the INTEL DX2 line of CPUs.

Keeping Current

Although it is easy to remember to keep your AutoCAD software up-to-date, it is also easy to forget to update your DOS or ADI drivers. Keep in contact with your hardware manufacturer and AutoCAD dealer for updates. Install MS-DOS 5.x if you are not using it already.

Utilizing Other Tips

For other performance tips, see the *AutoCAD Interface, Installation and Performance Guide* and README.DOC file in your AutoCAD directory.

C

Customizing AutoCAD

In previous chapters, you learned to use AutoCAD's functions and commands to create and annotate drawings. This appendix examines a completely new topic—customization.

Experienced AutoCAD users have discovered that the best way to get more power out of AutoCAD is to customize the program. You can use the following tools to customize AutoCAD:

- **Command Scripts.** You can automate repetitive operations by creating scripts of AutoCAD commands and parameters, which are processed by the SCRIPT command.
- **Custom linetype, shape, font, and hatch patterns.** These patterns give you control over the visual appearance of many entity types. You can use these patterns with the LINETYPE, COMPILE, LOAD, SHAPE, STYLE, BHATCH, and HATCH commands.
- **Custom Menus.** You can organize AutoCAD's menus any way you like and create macros that make AutoCAD work the way you want it to.
- **Custom status line.** By using the DIESEL programming language, you can make AutoCAD's status line display almost any information you need. You also can make the status line update automatically.
- **Command aliases.** You can define short keystroke combinations to execute any AutoCAD command.

- **External commands.** You can launch other programs or work at the system's command prompt directly from within AutoCAD.
- **Custom help information.** By customizing AutoCAD's Help system, you can add any information you want to the HELP command.
- **Prototype drawings.** You can modify default parameters and initial drawing geometry for your new drawings.
- **Special configurations.** You can modify and switch among different AutoCAD configurations for your hardware or to suit the way you work.
- **The AutoLISP Programming Language.** AutoLISP is a user programming language that is easy to learn and use, yet powerful enough to create almost any custom command.
- **The AutoCAD Development System (ADS).** The ADS is an advanced programming interface that enables developers to create AutoCAD applications by using powerful programming languages, such as C.
- **Programmable dialog boxes.** AutoCAD Release 12 features a special programming language that enables anyone to define custom dialog boxes for use by AutoLISP and ADS commands.
- **The AutoCAD SQL Extension.** AutoCAD Release 12 also contains a library of AutoLISP and ADS functions, which enables you to link AutoCAD entities to external databases at the workstation or across a network.
- **Redefined commands.** You can replace native AutoCAD commands with ones you create yourself.

You can do so much to customize AutoCAD that New Riders Publishing offers two other books on the subject, *Maximizing AutoCAD, Vol. I: Customizing AutoCAD with Menus and Macros*, and *Maximizing AutoCAD Vol. II: Inside AutoLISP.* These two books cover almost every aspect of AutoCAD customization in detail. To give you a head start on customizing AutoCAD and to show you a few easy techniques, this appendix examines a few of the previously mentioned customization methods.

You start by learning how to use prototype drawings to quickly customize your AutoCAD drawings. You then learn about the ACAD.PGP file and command aliases. Finally, you get an overview of menu macro creation and a quick lesson on how to modify the AutoCAD menus.

Some of the changes you can make to AutoCAD, such as creating custom menus, affect your productivity directly by providing quick access to often-

used commands and features. Other changes, such as changing your prototype drawing, also can increase your productivity with AutoCAD, but in a more subtle way.

Using Custom Prototype Drawings

Many users overlook the fact that they can customize their drawing setup by starting a drawing session with a prototype drawing that they can modify. This simple task can save time-wasting setups.

Chapter 1 shows you how to establish a default working environment for the units, grid, and snap settings by loading a prototype drawing called ACAD.DWG. The ACAD.DWG file comes with the AutoCAD program. (All the ACAD.DWG variables and their default values are listed in the table of system variables, which appears at the end of this appendix.)

Instead of always using the ACAD.DWG prototype drawing, however, you can create your own prototype drawing and use it to initialize your drawings. After you create this drawing with the defaults (and any standard graphics, such as a title block) that you want, you can save it on disk with a name that you prefer. Then you can load the drawing as an option, or set up AutoCAD to load it automatically.

Use the following exercise as a guide to creating a prototype drawing file with your own default settings and standard graphics. In this example, the new prototype drawing is named IA-PROTO.

This exercise is just an example. Do not set up for this book's exercises by using the following exercises. If you perform the following exercises, set your default prototype drawing back to ACAD when you are finished.

For simplicity, IA-PROTO uses an 8 1/2 by 11-inch setup at full scale with engineering units. If you use a different scale factor and sheet size, adjust your text and dimension scales accordingly. Start your drawing with the standard defaults from the Create Drawing File dialog box by setting IA-PROTO= or by checking the No Prototype box.

If you are using the IA DISK, you already have the IA-PROTO drawing. You might want to read the exercise, however, to see how the drawing is set up.

Table C.1
IA-PROTO Drawing Settings

APERTURE	*COORDS*	*GRID*	*LTSCALE*	*SNAP*	*ORTHO*
6	ON	.5	.375	.0625	ON

UNITS	Engineering units, default all other settings
LIMITS	0,0 to 11,8.5
ZOOM	Scale of .75X
VIEW	Save view ALL

Layer Name	*State*	*Color*	*Linetype*
0	On	White	CONTINUOUS
CENTER	On	Green	CENTER
DASHED	On	Yellow	DASHED
DIM	On	Yellow	CONTINUOUS
HATCH	On	Red	CONTINUOUS
HIDDEN	On	Blue	HIDDEN
NO-PLOT	On	Magenta	CONTINUOUS
OBJECTS	Current	Green	CONTINUOUS
TEXT	On	Cyan	CONTINUOUS
TITLE	On	Yellow	CONTINUOUS

Customizing a Prototype Drawing

Choose File, then Open, enter the drawing name `\IA\IA-PROTO`. Examine the layers and settings shown in table C.1 and in the rest of this exercise.

Choose File, then New, enter the drawing name `\IA\IA-PROTO=`, then make the layers and settings shown in table C.1 and in the rest of this exercise. Use Style to create the STD text style with the ROMANS font. Default all other options.

Set the TEXTSIZE system variable to .125

Set the following dimension variables:

DIMDLI to 0.375 *DIMTXT to 0.125* *DIMASZ to 0.1875* *DIMEXE to 0.1875* *DIMCEN to 0.0625* *DIMEXO to 0.9375*	
Choose File, *then* Save	Saves IA-PROTO for future use

Optionally Loading a Prototype Drawing

Now that you have preserved IA-PROTO, you can load it as an option by setting any new drawing so that the new drawing is equal to IA-PROTO. This technique is used throughout the book. You can use it now to check IA-PROTO in the following exercise.

Testing a Prototype Drawing

Choose File, *then* New, *and enter drawing name* `TEST=IA-PROTO`	Starts new drawing; if it is identical to IA-PROTO, it is okay

Loading a Prototype Drawing Automatically

You can set up AutoCAD to automatically use IA-PROTO for your new drawing in two ways. One is to copy IA-PROTO.DWG to the name ACAD.DWG in the AutoCAD program directory, replacing the original default ACAD.DWG. If you do this and later you want to restore the standard ACAD.DWG prototype drawing, just begin a new drawing in your AutoCAD program directory named ACAD= and then save it.

The other way to automate IA-PROTO is to set it as the default prototype drawing in AutoCAD's configuration menu. The following exercise shows you the steps for automating a prototype drawing by reconfiguring AutoCAD.

Configuring a Prototype Drawing

Choose File, *then* New	Displays the Create New Drawing dialog box
In the text box beside Prototype, *enter* `IA-PROTO`	
Click on Retain as Default, *then* OK	

Now, when you create a new drawing with the current configuration, the drawing starts up with IA-PROTO's defaults.

Using the PGP File

You can run other programs, utilities, or operating-system commands without ending your AutoCAD drawing session. With most applications, you must leave the application if you want to run another program or use operating-system commands. With AutoCAD, you can enter these names directly at the command prompt. To enable AutoCAD to do this, a few *external commands*, such as SHELL, are defined in a file named ACAD.PGP. An *external command* is any program that is external to AutoCAD. You can use the external commands to run a text editor, for example, or to design third-party AutoCAD applications.

The PGP extension stands for ProGram Parameters. AUTOCAD.PGP contains all the information that AutoCAD needs to partially unload itself from memory, execute the external program, and reload when the external program finishes. Initially, AutoCAD uses the ACAD.PGP file, which is supplied with AutoCAD and resides in the AutoCAD program directory. This file can be easily modified to add external programs of your own choosing.

You can use the SHELL command to run the programs or commands you want. The SHELL and SH commands are generic external commands that unload portions of AutoCAD from memory and allow you temporarily access to the operating-system prompt. Enter EXIT to return to AutoCAD.

Using AutoCAD Command Aliases

In addition to providing access to external DOS commands and other applications, ACAD.PGP contains abbreviated aliases for AutoCAD commands. For example, instead of entering REDRAW, you can simply enter R, because R has been defined as an alias for REDRAW.

You can use your preferred ASCII editor to display the contents of the standard ACAD.PGP file, which should be in the SUPPORT directory. The following exercise shows a partial list of the aliases that are stored in the standard ACAD.PGP file.

Viewing the PGP File

```
; acad.pgp - External Command and Command Alias definitions
; External Command format:
;  <Command name>,[<DOS request>],<Memory
;   reserve>,[*]<Prompt>,<Return code>
; Examples of External Commands for DOS
CATALOG,DIR /W,33000,File specification: ,0
DEL,DEL,      33000,File to delete: ,0
DIR,DIR,      33000,File specification: ,0
EDIT,EDLIN,    42000,File to edit: ,0
SH,,          33000,*OS Command: ,0
SHELL,,      127000,*OS Command: ,0
TYPE,TYPE,    33000,File to list: ,0
; Command alias format:
;  <Alias>,*<Full command name>
; Sample aliases for AutoCAD Commands
; These examples reflect the most frequently used commands.
; Each alias uses a small amount of memory, so don't go
; overboard on systems with tight memory.
A,      *ARC
C,      *CIRCLE
CP,     *COPY
DV,     *DVIEW
E,      *ERASE
L,      *LINE
LA,     *LAYER
M,      *MOVE
MS,     *MSPACE
```

```
P,      *PAN
PS,     *PSPACE
PL,     *PLINE
R,      *REDRAW
Z,      *ZOOM

3DLINE, *LINE

; easy access to _PKSER (serial number) system variable
SERIAL, *_PKSER
; These are the local aliases for AutoCAD AME commands.
; Comment out any you don't want or add your own.
; Note that aliases must be typed completely.
```

The ACAD.PGP file contains aliases for a number of AutoCAD commands, but not for all of them. You can add alias names for any AutoCAD command. Typically, the alias is a one- or two-letter mnemonic that you can type in place of the command's full name. Unless your system has lots of available memory (over 4M), you should define aliases only for those commands you use frequently, because each alias uses a small amount of memory.

To add command aliases, make a backup of ACAD.PGP in the AutoCAD program directory. Then use your text editor to edit the file. Enter the alias, followed by a comma and the command to be referenced by that alias. The AutoCAD command must be prefixed with an asterisk, as shown in the preceding listing. The IA DISK includes an IA-ACAD.PGP file with aliases for every command; you can append it to your existing ACAD.PGP file. You can edit it to remove any aliases you do not need.

After editing the ACAD.PGP file, you can either exit and reload the drawing to load the new definitions, or you can use the REINIT command.

Using AutoCAD Command Macros

The term "macro" is shorthand for *macro-command*, which means a large or long command. In AutoCAD, a *macro* is a series of one or more AutoCAD

commands and parameters that are strung together to perform a task. You can make macros that pause for user input and execute any of AutoCAD's commands, or even automatically repeat commands. Here is a simple macro that executes three Ctrl-Cs to cancel any pending command, even if you are deep into dimensioning mode or the PEDIT command.

```
[^C]^C^C^C
```

If you place this macro in a screen menu and select the [^C] item, AutoCAD executes three Ctrl-Cs just as if you had typed them from the keyboard. You build macros by writing keyboard command sequences in a text file. You group macros into menu files.

A *menu* is a text file that lists each menu item or macro for every box on the screen, tablet, button, pull-down menus, and icon menus. You can make items in a menu extremely short, even a single character, or extremely complex, involving many commands. You also can use AutoLISP in menu items. When you create your own commands using menu macros, you automate your drawing command sequences.

Menu Macros

Any custom menu performs a common set of tasks. As you think about the procedures that you can automate, use the following list as a starting point. A custom menu system can help you do the following:

- Standardize your drawings
- Set up, format, and fill in data for title sheets
- Place text in the drawing
- Locate, draw, and insert components, assemblies, and materials
- Dimension and annotate components

If you must routinely perform any of these tasks, then you have good candidates for custom menu macros.

Take some macros apart to show how they are made. They have just two basic types of ingredients: AutoCAD commands and parameters, and a group of special character codes used by the AutoCAD menu (and command) interpreter.

Labeling Macro Commands

As you look at menu items, the first special character you encounter is a pair of square brackets [ ]. You control what is displayed on the screen by putting a macro label in square brackets.

The square brackets signify labels to the menu interpreter. The characters that follow the right-hand bracket (]) make up the macro itself. Only eight characters display on the screen menu label, but you can make labels longer for documentation. Labels can include letters, numbers, and any displayable character. Control and extended ASCII characters are simply ignored. You can use an empty pair of brackets to make a blank menu item.

Using Ctrl-C To Cancel Macros

Most command macros start with two or three ^Cs. In a menu, Ctrl-C keystroke combination is a special code that cancels a command. The Ctrl-C works in the macro to cancel a command, just as it does when you issue it from the keyboard.

Because you want most macros to execute from AutoCAD's `Command:` prompt, starting a macro with three Ctrl-Cs ensures that any pending commands are canceled. Why three? Some commands in AutoCAD require three Ctrl-Cs to get you back to the `Command:` prompt. If you look at the way macros are constructed, you see that the actual command in the macro comes after the ^C entries. In effect, you cancel everything, then start your macro.

To put a Ctrl-C in a macro, type a caret (^) followed by a C. The caret enables menus to include codes for any control character without interfering with the meaning that a real control character might have to your text editor.

Using Command Options and Parameters

To put options or parameters in a macro, use the same characters that you would normally type at the keyboard. For example, you use P for the Previous option in the ZOOM command in a [ZOOM:P] macro:

```
[ZOOM:P]^C^CZoom P
```

Using Semicolons versus Spaces in Macros

If you look again at the macros in ACAD.MNU, you see that they have some spaces and semicolons in them.

The semicolon (;) is the special character that represents a press of the Enter key. In macros, spaces are like pressing the spacebar and semicolons are like pressing Enter from the keyboard. You usually can use semicolons and spaces interchangeably in macros; AutoCAD generally treats either as entering a preceding command or option. AutoCAD also treats each line in the menu file is if it ended with a space, unless it ends in a special character such as a semicolon. If you need an Enter rather than, or in addition to, a space at the end of a macro, use semicolons. Do not use trailing spaces because you cannot easily see them in a text editor.

Repeating Commands and Macros

Use an asterisk (*) as the first character of the macro if you want the macro to repeat indefinitely. Put the asterisk immediately after the closing right bracket.

The asterisk tells the menu interpreter to repeat the macro in its entirety. The asterisk must be followed by at least one "^C" (or "^X"). Otherwise, the asterisk is interpreted as part of the following command or input. In the following example, AutoCAD would see *MOVE, not recognize it, and an error would result:

```
[Move]*MOVE
```

The correct menu macro follows:

```
[Move]*^C^CMOVE
```

You can repeat single commands without an asterisk by using the Multiple command. In the following [ARC:] macro, for example, the Multiple command modifier causes AutoCAD to repeat the command until you press Ctrl-C to cancel it. Multiple only repeats the command, ignoring any options or parameters used in the first execution.

```
[ARC:]^C^C^CMULTIPLE ARC
```

Multiple works for simple menu items, or you can use it to repeat the last command in a macro. If you try to make Text automatically repeat a mode (such as M for Middle), however, it uses the mode the first time, then ignores the mode thereafter. Multiple is intended primarily for on-the-fly keyboard use or for single commands. The asterisk method works better for most macros.

Pausing for Input

Many macros pause for input from the user. The backslash (\) is the special character that makes a macro pause for input and then resume execution with more commands or options. The pause lets you string together multiple commands and input.

A single backslash (\) tells AutoCAD to wait for a single piece of input. In the following [INSERT:S] macro, the macro pauses for the insertion point. Without a backslash, AutoCAD would continue taking its input from the macro and would pass the next item along to the command processor. It would read the SCALE entry and cause an error. You must supply one backslash for each point that you want for input.

```
[INSERT:S]*^C^C^CINSERT \SCALE
```

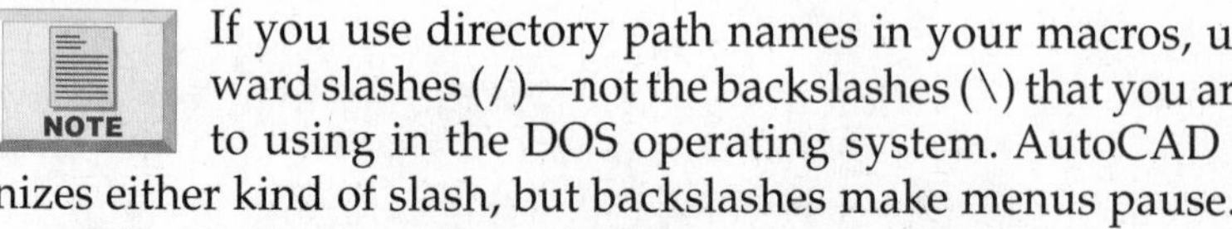

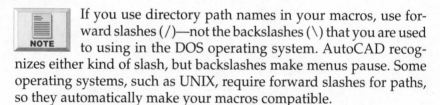

If you use directory path names in your macros, use forward slashes (/)—not the backslashes (\) that you are used to using in the DOS operating system. AutoCAD recognizes either kind of slash, but backslashes make menus pause. Some operating systems, such as UNIX, require forward slashes for paths, so they automatically make your macros compatible.

Using Transparent Commands

Transparent operations (such as 'ZOOM) do not use up backslashes present in the macro. In other words, you do not have to add backslashes to compensate for one or more transparent commands entered by the user. When you use a backslash to make a macro pause for point input, you can use a transparent command, and the macro continues to pause while the transparent command executes.

Object snaps and XYZ point filters also are transparent. Other common transparent commands are 'GRAPHSCR, 'HELP, 'RESUME, 'SETVAR, 'TEXTSCR, 'PAN, and the 'DDXXXX dialog box commands.

Using Special Characters in Menus

You can use about a dozen special characters in macros. You have already seen the backslash for pause, a semicolon for Enter, square brackets for labels, asterisk to repeat, and ^C to clear previous commands. AutoCAD automatically reads the end of a menu line as if it ended in a space, unless the line ends with a special character.

Table C.2 provides a complete list of the special characters used by AutoCAD's menu interpreter. The @ (lastpoint) is not a special character because it does not receive special treatment from the AutoCAD menu interpreter.

When you use control characters in your macros, type them into the menu file as two characters. Use a caret followed by the uppercase letter, such as `^B`.

Using Selection Sets with Macros

AutoCAD macros can work on an existing selection set when Noun/Verb Selection is active, or you can make object selection a part of your macro for more control. Noun/Verb object selection makes editing more intuitive, but makes macro design more complicated — your macros must accommodate virtually every possible combination of objects. Incorporating object selection in your macro enables you to control how your macro selects objects. This limits your macro writing by allowing only a fixed number of picks. Whether you use Window, Last, or another selection mode, you still need to predefine one backslash per pick. AutoCAD's SELECT command is indispensable in macros because it has the unique feature of pausing the macro indefinitely until the entire selection process is complete. It pauses even when other commands follow. The following macro is an example:

```
[CH:LAYER]^C^C^CSELECT AU \CHPROP P ;LAYER (getvar "CLAYER") LAYER \;
```

As you saw in the [CH:LAYER] macro, SELECT does not do anything except create a selection set of entities, allowing an indefinite number of picks. This is invaluable because you can use a subsequent command, such as MOVE, to select that selection set with the P (Previous) selection option.

Table C.2
Special Menu Characters

Character	*Function*
\	Pauses for input
+	Continues macro to next line
*	Automatically repeats, or marks page
	The space character
^D	Turns coordinate display on or off
^G	Turns the grid on or off
^C	*Cancel*
^Q	Turns printer echoing on or off
^X	*Delete* input buffer
^Z	Does nothing; put at end of line to suppress automatic space
;	Issues Enter
[]	Encloses Label
^B	Turns snap on or off
^M	Issues Enter
^E	Turns Isoplane on or off
^H	Issues Backspace
^O	Turns orthographic mode on or off
^P	Turns Menuecho on or off
^T	Turns Tablet on or off
~	Grays out a pull-down menu label
->	Displays a cascading submenu
—	Displays a separator line
<-	Indicates the last item in submenu
<-<-	The last item in submenu; terminates the parent menu
!*c*	Displays the symbolic character *c* (. equals check mark)
$(	Beginning of a DIESEL expression
/*c*	Menu accelerator key *c*
<*c*	Character format code: B = Bold O = Outline S = Shadow I = Italic U = Underline
^*name*^	Icon *name* displayed in place of the label on supported platforms

AutoCAD features the following three selection modes, which you may find especially useful in macros:

- **SIngle.** When this option is used, AutoCAD remains in selection mode until one object or one set is successfully picked.
- **BOX.** This option acts like either Crossing or Window, depending on the relative position of the two points picked.
- **AUto.** If the first point finds an object, AUto picks it. Otherwise, AUto acts like BOX.

You can combine SIngle with other modes, such as BOX, Crossing, or AUto. You also can use it with SELECT if you want to force the creation of a previous set with only a single selection. Although SIngle ends object selection when an object or set is picked, it does not suspend the rest of a macro.

Use SELECT and BOX or AUto for most macros. BOX is clean and simple. Pick left to right for a window and right to left for a crossing. AUto gives the most flexibility, combining picking by point with the BOX mode. If your first point misses, you go into BOX mode; otherwise, AUto selects the entity at the first pick point.

Creating Text Input in Macros

When you enter text in a macro command, all special characters, except spaces, act exactly the same, whether they are in the middle of a text string or not. Since you must be able to type space characters between words in text strings, AutoCAD's menu interpreter treats them as true spaces in your text, not as the Enter key as in the AutoCAD program itself. If you want a macro to continue after text input, you need some way to tell AutoCAD that the string of text is complete. You cannot use the automatic space at the end of the menu line for text, so use a semicolon.

Writing Long Macros

Menu items can get extremely long, especially macros that set many parameters or set up layers. You can continue a macro for many lines by ending each line with a plus sign (+). When AutoCAD sees a plus sign at the end of a line, it treats the next line as part of the same macro.

You can add blank lines to a menu macro, each line containing only a solitary plus sign. This makes macros easier to read by providing a visual break. AutoCAD ignores the solitary plus sign, and it has no effect on the macro.

Menu Macro Tips

The following [BOLT:] macro, shown in table C.3, is a working example of how much power you can put into a macro. To develop good macros, you need to carefully work out the drawing sequences that you want to automate. When you write menu macros, your command syntax must be exact. Use your drawing editor interactively as a testbed so that you know what options and input parameters are expected in your macros. Write your sequences down. Make your mistakes in the drawing editor; it is a lot easier to work out the sequences in the drawing editor, then type them into your text editor when you think you have them down pat. Here are some notes on menu macros.

Make sure that you are creating simple ASCII files for your menus and macros. These files are sometimes called DOS text files, programmer's mode files, or nondocument files. Use existing menu items as templates. It can often be easier to overtype or copy complex text containing commas, control characters, and brackets than to type the information again.

Look for tricks that you have picked up by using AutoCAD, like the sequence LINE;;^C that resets the last point (@) to the end of the last line drawn. This is great for inserting blocks at the end of a line.

Start new macros with three Ctrl-Cs to cancel the previous command. Use an asterisk (*^C^C^C) at the beginning of macros for automatic repeating. (You also can use *^X.) Use the Multiple command modifier for simple single or last command repetitions. Give all your menu items [LABELS], including blank labels for blank lines [ ].

If you enter the following macro into a menu file, omit the comments that are shown on the right.

Be careful not to leave any extra spaces at the end of lines; AutoCAD reads spaces in macros as the Enter character. Watch out for extra blank lines. Never use two spaces in a row; they are too hard to count. Use one space and then semicolons for subsequent returns.

Table C.3
The Annotated [BOLT:] Macro

Macro Line Contents	*Description*
`[BOLT:  Pick 2 end points and enter scale to create a bolt.]`	A long label containing comments
`^C^C^C^P+`	^P suppresses commands
`LINE;\\;`	Prompts for the two end-points
`INSERT SCALE S;\@ 0`	Prompts for the scale and inserts the SCALE block
`SETVAR MENUECHO 3;+`	Suppresses everything possible
`INSERT NUT S @ CEN,QUI @`	Presets the NUT scale by snapping to the SCALE block with object snaps
`@ MID,QUI @;+`	Insert point for NUT; rotates it to the line's midpoint
`ERASE L ;`	Gets the NUT out of the way
`MOVE L ;@ MID,QUI @`	Moves SCALE to the line's midpoint
`OOPS;+`	Restores the NUT
`ERASE QUA,QUI @ ;`	Gets the SCALE out of the way
`PEDIT MID,QUI @ Y E I ;^C+`	Turns the line into a polyline; resets the last point to its start point
`OOPS`	Restores SCALE
`PEDIT END,QUI @ W MID,QUI @ CEN,QUI @;;+`	Changes polyline's width, and snaps to SCALE with object snaps.
`INSERT HEAD S MID,QUI @ CEN, QUI @ @ MID,QUI @`	Inserts HEAD like NUT
`ERASE P ;`	Erases SCALE
`SETVAR MENUECHO 0`	

Make your macro set your defaults. You never know what was used last before your macro. A good practice is to explicitly set defaults, modes, and settings, like text styles, if they are important for your macro to function.

Use the SELECT command to automatically pause for a selection set. Use SELECT to make the set and then pass the set to other editing commands by using the Previous option. Look for ways to use object snaps as tools in macros, like using rotated block insertions to get correct angles. When you use *intelligent* blocks (blocks including attributes) in macros, give your blocks and macros unique yet explanatory names. DESK1 and [DESK2] do not say much. DeskEXEC and [DeskREG] are more descriptive.

AutoCAD System Variables

This section contains a table of AutoCAD system variables. You can use the following table to look up AutoCAD's environment settings and their values. Table C.4 presents all the variables available through AutoCAD, AutoLISP, or the AutoCAD Development System (ADS). Each system variable's name and the default AutoCAD prototype drawing (ACAD.DWG) settings for the variable are shown. A brief description is given for each variable, and the meaning is given for each code. Some variable names appear in italic; you use the SETVAR command to set their values. You can set all other variables directly by entering their name at the `Command:` prompt or indirectly through AutoLISP, ADS, or by using the command shown in the *Command Name* column.

Variable names and features shown in bold are new to Release 12. All values are saved with the drawing unless noted with (CFG) for ConFiGuration file, or (NS) for Not Saved. Variables marked (RO) are read only; you cannot change them.

Table C.4
AutoCAD System Variables

Variable Name	*Default Setting*	*Command Name*	*Variable Description*
ACADPREFIX	C:\ACAD;C:ACAD\SAMPLE;...		Directory search path set by DOS environment variable ACAD (NS),(RO)
ACADVER	12		The release number of your copy of AutoCAD
AFLAGS	0	**DDATTDEF**, ATTDEF	Current state of ATTDEF modes. The value is the sum of the following: 1 = Invisible 2 = Constant 4 = Verify 8 = Preset
ANGBASE	0	**DDUNITS**, UNITS	The direction of angle 0 in the current UCS
ANGDIR	0	**DDUNITS**, UNITS	The direction of angle measure: 1 = Clockwise 0 = Counter-clockwise
APERTURE	10	**DDOSNAP**, APERTURE	Half the OSNAP target size in pixels (CFG)
AREA	0.0000	AREA, LIST	The last computed area in square drawing units
ATTDIA	0		Controls the attribute-entry method: 1 = DDATTE dialogue box 0 = Attribute prompts
ATTMODE	1	ATTDISP	Attribute display: 1 = Normal=1 2 = ON 3 = OFF
ATTREQ	1		Attribute values used by Insert: 1 = Prompts for values 0 = Uses defaults
AUDITCTL	**0**		**Controls the creation of an ADT log file containing AUDIT results:** **0 = No file** **1 = ADT file** **(CFG)**

Table C.4—continued

Variable Name	*Default Setting*	*Command Name*	*Variable Description*
AUNITS	0	**DDUNITS**, UNITS	The angular unit display code: 0 = Decimal deg. 1 =Degrees/min/sec 2 = Grads 3 = Radians 4 = Surveyors
AUPREC	0	**DDUNITS**, UNITS	The number of angular units decimal places
BACKZ	0.0000	DVIEW	The DVIEW back clipping plane offset in drawing units. *See VIEWMODE* (RO)
BLIPMODE	1	BLIPMODE	Controls blip display: 1 = Blips 0 = No Blips
CDATE	19881202.144648898	TIME	Current date and time in YYYYMMDD.HHMMSSmsec format (NS),(RO)
CECOLOR	BYLAYER	DDEMODES, COLOR	The current entity color (RO)
CELTYPE	BYLAYER	DDEMODES, LINETYPE	The current entity linetype (RO)
CHAMFERA	0.0000	CHAMFER	The first chamfer distance
CHAMFERB	0.0000	CHAMFER	The second chamfer distance
CIRCLERAD	**0.0000**		**The default radius value for new circle entities:** **0 = None (NS)**
CLAYER	0	DDLMODES, LAYER	The current layer (RO)
CMDACTIVE	**1**	**CMDACTIVE**	**Indicates that an AutoCAD command is active (used primarily by ADS):** **1 = None** **2 = Transparent** **4 = Script** **8 = Dialog box** **(NS),(RO)**
CMDECHO	1		Controls AutoCAD `Command:` prompt echoing by AutoLISP: 1 = Echo 0 = No Echo (NS)

Table C.4—continued

Variable Name	*Default Setting*	*Command Name*	*Variable Description*
CMDDIA	**1**		**Controls whether the PLOT command issues dialog boxes or prompts; a nonzero setting issues dialog boxes, and 0 issues prompts (CFG)**
CMDNAMES	**""**		**Names of any active commands**
COORDS	0	[^D] [F6]	Controls the updating of the coordinate display: 0 = Absolute upon picks 1 = Absolute continuously 2 = Relative only during prompts
CVPORT	1	VPORTS	The current viewport's number
DATE	2447498.61620926	TIME	The current date and time in Julian format (NS),(RO)
DBMOD	**4**	**Most**	**Describes modifications to the current drawing database:** **0 = None** **1 = Entities** **2 = Symbol table** **4 = Database variable** **8 = Window** **15 = View** **(RO)**
DIASTAT	0	DD?????	The last dialog box exit code: 0 = Canceled 1 = OK button (RO)
DIMALT	0	**DDIM,** DIMALT	Controls the drawing of additional dimension text in an alternative-units system: 1 = On 0 = Off
DIMALTD	2	**DDIM,** DIMALTD	The decimal precision of dimension text when alternative units are used
DIMALTF	25.4000	**DDIM,** DIMALTF	The scale factor for dimension text when alternate units are used

Table C.4—continued

Variable Name	*Default Setting*	*Command Name*	*Variable Description*
DIMAPOST	""	**DDIM,** DIMAPOST	The user-defined suffix for alternative dimension text (RO)
DIMASO	1	DIMASO	Controls the creation of associative dimensions: 1 = On 0 = Off
DIMASZ	0.1800	**DDIM,** DIMASZ	Controls the size of dimension arrows and affects the fit of dimension text inside dimension lines when DIMTSZ is set to 0
DIMBLK	""	**DDIM,** DIMBLK	The name of the block to draw rather than an arrow or tick (RO)
DIMBLK1	""	**DDIM,** DIMBLK1	The name of the block for the first end of dimension lines. *See DIMSAH* (RO)
DIMBLK2	""	**DDIM,** DIMBLK2	The name of the block for the second end of dimension lines. *See DIMSAH* (RO)
DIMCEN	0.0900	**DDIM,** DIMCEN	Controls center marks or center lines drawn by radial DIM commands: Mark size = value Draw center lines = negative (mark size = absolute value)
DIMCLRD	0	**DDIM,** DIMCLRD	The dimension line, arrow, and leader color number: 0 = BYBLOCK 256 = BYLAYER
DIMCLRE	0	**DDIM,** DIMCLRE	The dimension extension line's color
DIMCLRT	0	**DDIM,** DIMCLRT	The dimension text's color
DIMDLE	0.0000	**DDIM,** DIMDLE	The dimension line's extension distance beyond ticks when ticks are drawn (when DIMTSZ is nonzero)
DIMDLI	0.3800	**DDIM,** DIMDLI	The offset distance between successive continuing or baseline dimensions

Table C.4—continued

Variable Name	*Default Setting*	*Command Name*	*Variable Description*
DIMEXE	0.1800	**DDIM,** DIMEXE	The length of extension lines beyond dimension lines
DIMEXO	0.0625	**DDIM,** DIMEXO	The distance by which extension lines originate from dimensioned entity
DIMGAP	0.0900	**DDIM,** DIMGAP	The space between text and a dimension line; determines when text is placed outside a dimension **(Creates reference dimension outlines if negative)**
DIMLFAC	1.0000	**DDIM,** DIMLFAC	The overall linear dimensioning scale factor; if negative, acts as the absolute value applied to paper space viewports
DIMLIM	0	**DDIM,** DIMLIM	Presents dimension limits as default text: 1 = ON 0 = OFF *See DIMTP and DIMTM*
DIMPOST	""	**DDIM,** DIMPOST	The user-defined suffix for dimension text, such as "mm" (RO)
DIMRND	0.0000	**DDIM,** DIMRND	The rounding interval for linear dimension text
DIMSAH	0	**DDIM,** DIMSAH	Enables the use of DIMBLK1 and DIMBLK2, rather than DIMBLK or a default terminator: 1 = ON 0 = OFF
DIMSCALE	1.0000	**DDIM,** DIMSCALE	The overall scale factor applied to other dimension variables except tolerances, angles, measured lengths, or coordinates 0 = Paper space scale
DIMSE1	0	**DDIM,** DIMSE1	Suppresses the first extension line: 1 = On 0 = Off

Table C.4—continued

Variable Name	*Default Setting*	*Command Name*	*Variable Description*
DIMSE2	0	**DDIM,** DIMSE2	Suppresses the second extension line: 1 = On 0 = Off
DIMSHO	0	DIMSHO	Determines whether associative dimension text is updated during dragging: 1 = On 0 = Off
DIMSOXD	0	**DDIM,** DIMSOXD	Suppresses the placement of dimension lines outside extension lines: 1 = On 0 = Off
DIMSTYLE	*UNNAMED	**DDIM,** `Dim:` SAVE	Holds the name of the current dimension style (RO)
DIMTAD	0	**DDIM,** DIMTAD	Places dimension text above the dimension line, rather than within: 1 = On 0 = Off
DIMTIH	1	**DDIM,** DIMTIH	Forces dimension text inside the extension lines to be positioned horizontally, rather than aligned: 1 = On 0 = Off
DIMTIX	0	**DDIM,** DIMTIX	Force dimension text inside extension lines: 1 = O 0 = Off
DIMTM	0.0000	**DDIM,** DIMTM	The negative tolerance value used when DIMTOL or DIMLIM is on
DIMTOFL	0	**DDIM,** DIMTOFL	Draws dimension lines between extension lines, even if text is placed outside the extension lines: 1 = On 0 = Off

Table C.4—continued

Variable Name	*Default Setting*	*Command Name*	*Variable Description*
DIMTOH	1	**DDIM,** DIMTOH	Forces dimension text to be positioned horizontally, rather than aligned when it falls outside the extension lines: 1 = On 0 = Off
DIMTOL	0	**DDIM,** DIMTOL	Appends tolerance values (DIMTP and DIMTM) to the default dimension text: 1 = On 0 = Off
DIMTP	0.0000	**DDIM,** DIMTP	The positive tolerance value used when DIMTOL or DIMLIM is on
DIMTSZ	0.0000	**DDIM,** DIMTSZ	When assigned a nonzero value, forces tick marks to be drawn (rather than arrowheads) at the size specified by the value; affects the placement of the dimension line and text between extension lines
DIMTVP	0.0000	**DDIM,** DIMTVP	Percentage of text height to offset dimension vertically
DIMTXT	0.1800	**DDIM,** DIMTXT	The dimension text height for non-fixed text styles
DIMZIN	0	**DDIM,** DIMZIN	Suppress the display of zero inches or zero feet in dimension text 0 = Feet & Inches=0 1 = Neither 2 = Inches Only 3 = Feet only
DISTANCE	0.0000	DIST	The last distance computed by the DISTANCE command (NS)(RO)
DONUTID	**0.5000**		**The default inner diameter for new DONUT entities; may be 0 (NS)**

Table C.4—continued

Variable Name	*Default Setting*	*Command Name*	*Variable Description*
DONUTOD	**1.0000**		**The default outer diameter for new DONUT entities; must be nonzero (NS)**
DRAGMODE	2	DRAGMODE	Controls object dragging on screen: 0 = Off 1 = If requested 2 = Auto
DRAGP1	10		The regen-drag sampling rate (CFG)
DRAGP2	25		The fast-drag sampling rate (CFG)
DWGCODEPAGE	**ascii**		**The code page used for the drawing**
DWGNAME	UNNAMED		The current drawing name supplied by the user when the drawing was begun (RO)
DWGTITLED	**0**	**NEW**	**Indicates whether the current drawing has been named or not.** **1 = Yes** **0 = No** **(RO)**
DWGPREFIX	C:\ACAD\		The current drawing's drive and directory path (NS)(RO)
DWGWRITE	**1**	**OPEN**	**Indicates that the current drawing is opened as read-only:** **0 = No** **1 = Yes**
ELEVATION	0.0000	ELEV	The current elevation in the current UCS for the current space
ERRNO	0		An error number generated by AutoLISP and ADS applications. (See the *AutoLISP Reference Manual* or the *ADS Programmer's Reference Manual*)

Table C.4—continued

Variable Name	*Default Setting*	*Command Name*	*Variable Description*
EXPERT	0		Suppresses successive levels of `Are you sure?` warnings: 0 = None 1 = REGEN/LAYER 2 = BLOCK/WBLOCK/SAVE 3 = LINETYPE 4 = UCS/VPORT 5 = DIM
EXTMAX	-1.0000E+20,-1.0000E+20		The X,Y coordinates of the drawing's upper right extents in the WCS (RO)
EXTMIN	1.0000E+20,1.0000E+20		The X,Y coordinates of the drawing's lower left extents in the WCS (RO)
FILEDIA	1		Controls the display of the dialog box for file name requests: 0 = Only when a tilde (~) is entered 1 = On (CFG)
FILLETRAD	0.0000	FILLET	The current fillet radius
FILLMODE	1	FILL	Turns on the display of fill traces, solids, and wide polylines: 1 = On 0 = Off
FRONTZ	0.0000	DVIEW	The DVIEW front clipping plane's offset, in drawing units; *see VIEWMODE* (RO)
GRIDMODE	0	DDRMODES, GRID	Controls grid display in the current viewport: 1 = On 0 = Off
GRIDUNIT	0.0000,0.0000	DDRMODES, GRID	The X,Y grid increment for the current viewport
GRIPBLOCK	**1**	**DDGRIPS**	**Controls the display of grips for entities in blocks:** **1 = On** **2 = Off** **(CFG)**

Table C.4—continued

Variable Name	*Default Setting*	*Command Name*	*Variable Description*
GRIPCOLOR	**5**	**DDGRIPS**	**The current color code of unselected grips; can be a value of 0 to 255 (CFG)**
GRIPHOT	**1**	**DDGRIPS**	**The current color code of selected grips; can be a value of 0 to 255 (CFG)**
GRIPS	**1**	**DDSELECT**	**Controls the display of entity grips and grip editing 1 = ON 0 = OFF (CFG)**
GRIPSIZE	**5**	**DDGRIPS**	**The size of grip box in pixels; equals PICKBOX = 0 (CFG)**
HANDLES	0	HANDLES	Controls the creation of entity handles for the current drawing: 1 = On 0 = Off (RO)
HELPFILE	**""**	**HELP**	**The default help file's name; also set by the ACADHELP environment variable (NS)**
HIGHLIGHT	1		Determines whether the current object selection set is high-lighted: 1 = On 2 = On (NS)
HPANG	**0**	**BHATCH, HATCH**	**The default angle for new hatch patterns (NS)**
HPDOUBLE	**0**	**BHATCH, HATCH**	**Controls user-defined hatch-pattern doubling: 1 = On 0 = Off (NS)**
HPNAME	**""**	**BHATCH, HATCH**	**The default name for new hatch patterns (NS)**
HPSCALE	**1.0000**	**BHATCH, HATCH**	**The default scale factor for new hatch patterns; must be nonzero (NS)**

Table C.4—continued

Variable Name	*Default Setting*	*Command Name*	*Variable Description*
HPSPACE	**1.0000**	**BHATCH, HATCH**	**The default spacing for user-defined hatch patterns; must be nonzero (NS)**
INSBASE	0.0000,0.0000	BASE	Insertion base point X,Y coordinate of current drawing in current space and current UCS
INSNAME	""	**DDINSERT, INSERT**	**The default block name for new insertions (NS)**
LASTANGLE	0	ARC	The end angle of the last arc in the current-space UCS (NS)(RO)
LASTPOINT	0.0000,0.0000,0.0000		The current space and UCS coordinate of the last point entered (recall with "@") (NS)
LENSLENGTH	50.0000	DVIEW	The current viewport perspective view lens length, in millimeters (RO)
LIMCHECK	0	LIMITS	Controls limits checking for current space: 1 = On 0 = Off
LIMMAX	12.0000,9.0000	LIMITS	The upper right X,Y limit of current space, relative to the WCS
LIMMIN	0.0000,0.0000	LIMITS	The lower left X,Y limit of current space, relative to WCS
LOGINNAME	""	**CONFIG**	**The name entered by the user or configuration file during login to AutoCAD (CFG)(RO)**
LTSCALE	1.0000	LTSCALE	The global scale factor applied to linetypes
LUNITS	2	**DDUNITS,** UNITS	The linear units format: 1 = Scientific 2 = Decimal 3 = Engineering 4 = Architectural 5 = Fractional
LUPREC	4	**DDUNITS,** UNITS	Units precision decimal places or fraction denominator

Table C.4—continued

Variable Name	*Default Setting*	*Command Name*	*Variable Description*
MACROTRACE	**0**		**Controls the DIESEL macro-debugging display** **1 = On** **0 = Off**
MAXACTVP	16		The maximum number of viewports to regenerate (NS)(RO)
MAXSORT	200		The maximum number of symbols and file names sorted in lists, up to 200 (CFG)
MENUCTL	**1**		**Command-line input-sensitive screen menu-page switching:** **1 = On** **0 = Off** **(CFG)**
MENUECHO	0		Suppresses the display of menu actions on the command line; the value is the sum of the following: 1 = Menu input 2 = Command prompts 4 = Disable ^P toggling (NS)
MENUNAME	ACAD	MENU	The current menu name, plus the drive/path, if entered (RO)
MIRRTEXT	1		Controls reflection of text by the MIRROR command: 0 = Retain text direction 1 = Reflect text
MODEMACRO	**""**		**A DIESEL language expression to control status-line display**
OFFSETDIST	**-1.0000**	**OFFSET**	**The default distance for the OFFSET command; negative values enable the Through option (NS)**
ORTHOMODE	0	[^O] [F8]	Sets the current Ortho mode state: 1 = On 0 = Off

Table C.4—continued

Variable Name	*Default Setting*	*Command Name*	*Variable Description*
OSMODE	0	**DDOSNAP,** OSNAP	The current object snap mode; the value is the sum of the following: 1 = Endp 2 = Mid 4 = Cen 8 = Node 16 = Quad 32 = Int 64 = Ins 128 = Perp 256 = Tan 512 = Near 1024 = Quick
PDMODE	0		Controls the graphic display of point entities
PDSIZE	0.0000		Controls the size of point graphic display
PERIMETER	0.0000	AREA, DBLIST, LIST	The last computed perimeter (NS)(RO)
PFACEVMAX	4		The maximum number of vertices per face in a PFACE mesh (NS)(RO)
PICKADD	**1**	**DDSELECT**	**Controls whether selected entities are added to, or replace (added with Shift+select) the current selection set:** **0 = Added** **1 = Replace** **(CFG)**
PICKAUTO	**0**	**DDSELECT**	**Controls the implied (AUTO) windowing for object selection:** **1 = On** **0 = Off** **(CFG)**

Table C.4—continued

Variable Name	*Default Setting*	*Command Name*	*Variable Description*
PICKDRAG	**0**	**DDSELECT**	**Determines whether the pick button must be depressed during window-corner picking in set selection (MS Windows style): 1 = On 0 = OFF (CFG)**
PICKFIRST	**0**	**DDSELECT**	**Enables entity selection before command selection (noun/verb paradigm): 1 = On 0 = Off (CFG)**
PICKBOX	3		Half the object-selection pick box size, in pixels (CFG)
PLATFORM	*Varies*		Indicates the version of AutoCAD in use: a string such as "386 DOS Extender," "Sun 4/SPARCstation," "Apple Macintosh," etc.
PLOTID	**""**	**PLOT**	**The current plotter configuration description (CFG)**
PLOTTER	**0**	**PLOT**	**The current plotter configuration number (CFG)**
PLINEGEN	**0**		**The control points for polyline generation of noncontinuous linetypes: 0 = Vertices 1 = End points**
PLINEWID	**0.0000**	**PLINE**	**The default width for new polyline entities**
POLYSIDES	**4**	**POLYGON**	**The default number of sides (3 to 1024) for new polygon entities (NS)**

Table C.4—continued

Variable Name	*Default Setting*	*Command Name*	*Variable Description*
POPUPS	1		Determines whether the Advanced User Interface (dialog boxes, menu bar, pull-down menus, icon menus) is supported: 1 = Yes 0 = No (NS)(RO)
PSPROLOG	**""**		**The name of the PostScript post-processing section of ACAD.PSF to be appended to the PSOUT command's output**
PSQUALITY	**75**	**PSQUALITY**	**The default quality setting for rendering of images by the PSIN command**
PSLTSCALE	**1**		**Paper-space scaling of model space linetypes: 1 = On 0 = Off (DWG)**
QTEXTMODE	0	QTEXT	Sets the current state of Quick text mode: 1 = On 0 = Off
REGENMODE	1	REGENAUTO	Indicates the current state of REGENAUTO: 1 = On 0 = Off
SAVEFILE	**AUTO.SV$**	**CONFIG**	**The default directory and file name for automatic file saves (CFG)(RO)**
SAVETIME	**120**	**CONFIG**	**The default interval between automatic file saves, in minutes: 0 = None (CFG)**

Table C.4—continued

Variable Name	*Default Setting*	*Command Name*	*Variable Description*
SAVENAME	**""**	**SAVEAS**	**The drawing name specified by the user to the last invocation of the SAVEAS command in the current session (NS) (RO)**
SCREENBOXES	**25**	**CONFIG**	**The number of available screen menu boxes in the current graphics screen area (RO)**
SCREENMODE	**0**	**[F1]**	**Indicates the active AutoCAD screen mode or window:** **0 = Text** **1 = Graphics** **2 = Dual screen** **(RO)**
SCREENSIZE	572.0000,414.0000		The size of current viewport, in pixels, X and Y (RO)
SHADEDGE	3		Controls the display of edges and faces by the SHADE command: 0 = Faces shaded, edges unhighlighted 1 = Faces shaded, edges in background color 2 = Faces unfilled, edges in entity color 3 = Faces in entity color, edges in background
SHADEDIF	70		Specifies the ratio of diffuse-to-ambient light used by the SHADE command; expressed as a percentage of diffuse reflective light
SHPNAME	**""**	**SHAPE**	**The default shape name (NS)**
SKETCHINC	0.1000	SKETCH	The recording increment for SKETCH sements
SKPOLY	0		Controls the type of entities generated by SKETCH: 1 = Polylines 0 = Lines

Table C.4—continued

Variable Name	*Default Setting*	*Command Name*	*Variable Description*
SNAPANG	0	**DDRMODES,** SNAP	The angle of SNAP/GRID rotation in the current viewport, for the current UCS
SNAPBASE	0.0000,0.0000	**DDRMODES,** SNAP	The X,Y base point of SNAP/ GRID rotation in the current viewport, for the current UCS
SNAPISOPAIR	0	**DDRMODES,** SNAP [^E]	The current isoplane for the current viewport: 0 = Left 1 = Top 2 = Right
SNAPMODE	0	**DDRMODES,** SNAP	Indicates the state of [^B] [F9] Snap for the current viewport: 1 = On 0 = Off
SNAPSTYL	0	**DDRMODES,** SNAP	The snap style for the current viewport: 1 = Isometric 0 = Standard
SNAPUNIT	1.0000,1.0000	**DDRMODES,** SNAP	The snap X,Y increment for the current viewport
SOLAMEVER	**2.1**		**The Region Modeler software's version number**
SOLAREAU	**sq cm**		**The unit system for area calculations**
SOLAXCOL	**3**		**The color number of the SOLMOVE MCS icon**
SOLDELENT	**3**	**SOLIDIFY**	**Controls prompting for original entity deletion by the SOLIDIFY command.** **1 = Don't delete** **2 = Ask** **3 = Delete**
SOLDISPLAY	**WIRE**	**SOLMESH, SOLWIRE**	**Controls the default display mode for new solids**
SOLHANGLE	**45.000000**	**SOLIDIFY**	**The default angle of new solid entity hatch patterns**

Table C.4—continued

Variable Name	*Default Setting*	*Command Name*	*Variable Description*
SOLHPAT	U	SOLIDIFY	The default pattern name for new solid entity hatching
SOLHSIZE	1.000000	SOLIDIFY	The default scale for new solid entity hatch patterns
SOLLENGTH	cm	SOLLIST, SOLMASSP	The unit system for perimeter calculations
SOLMATCURR	MILD_STEEL	SOLMAT	The default material assigned to new solid entities
SOLPAGELEN	25	SOLLIST, SOLMASSP SOLMAT	The length of message pages, in lines
SOLRENDER	CSG	SHADE, SOLMESH SOLWIRE	The display type for solids CSG = By primitive UNIFORM = As composite
SOLSERVMSG	3	MANY	The level of details displayed by Region Modeler messages 0 = None 1 = Errors 2 = Errors+progress 3 = All
SOLSOLIDIFY	3	MANY	Controls prompting for entity conversion to solid regions 1 = Don't convert 2 = Ask 3 = Convert
SOLWDENS	4	MANY	Controls the number of edges used to represent curved solid surfaces displayed as wire-frames (SOLWDENS*4)
SORTENTS	0	DDSELECT	The optimization codes for oct-tree spatial database organiza-tion; the value is the sum of the following: 0 = OFF 1 = Object selection 2 = OSNAP 4 = REDRAW 8 = MSLIDE 16 = REGEN 32 = PLOT 64 = PSOUT (CFG)

Table C.4—continued

Variable Name	*Default Setting*	*Command Name*	*Variable Description*
SPLFRAME	0		Controls the display of control polygons for spline-fit polylines, defining meshes of surface-fit polygon meshes, invisible 3D face edges: 1 = On 0 = Off
SPLINESEGS	8		The number of line segments in each spline curve
SPLINETYPE	6		Controls the spline type generated by the PEDIT command's Spline option: 5 = Quadratic B-Spline 6 = Cubic B-Spline
SURFTAB1	6		The number of RULESURF and Tabsurf tabulations, also the REVSURF and EDGESURF M-direction density
SURFTAB2	6		The REVSURF and EDGESURF N-direction density
SURFTYPE	6		Controls type of surface generated by Pedit smooth option: Quadratic B-Spline=5 Cubic B-Spline=6 Bezier=8
SURFU	6		The M-direction surface density of 3D polygon meshes
SURFV	6		The N-direction surface density 3D polygon meshes
SYSCODEPAGE	**ascii**		**The code page used by the system**
TABMODE	**0**	**TABLET, [F10]**	**Controls tablet mode:** **1 = On** **0 = Off**
TARGET	0.0000,0.0000,0.0000	DVIEW	The UCS coordinates of the current viewport's target point (RO)
TDCREATE	2447498.61620031	TIME	The date and time of the current drawing's creation, in Julian format (RO)

Table C.4—continued

Variable Name	*Default Setting*	*Command Name*	*Variable Description*
TDINDWG	0.00436285	TIME	The total amount of editing time elapsed in the current drawing, in Julian days (RO)
TDUPDATE	2447498.61620031	TIME	The date and time when the file was last saved, in Julian format (RO)
TDUSRTIMER	0.00436667	TIME	User-controlled elapsed time in Julian days (RO)
TEMPPREFIX	""		The directory configured for placement of AutoCAD's temporary files; defaults to the drawing directory (NS)(RO)
TEXTEVAL	0		Controls the checking of text input (except by DTEXT) for AutoLISP expressions: 0 = Yes 1 = NO (NS)
TEXTSIZE	0.2000	TEXT	The height applied to new text entities created with nonfixed-height text styles
TEXTSTYLE	STANDARD	TEXT, STYLE	The current text style's name (RO)
THICKNESS	0.0000		The current 3D extrusion thickness
TILEMODE	1	TILEMODE	Release 10 VPORT compatibility setting; enables/disables paper space and viewport entities: 1 = On 0 = Off
TRACEWID	0.0500	TRACE	The current width of traces
TREEDEPTH	**3020**	**DDSELECT**	**The maximum number of node subdivisions for oct-tree spatial database organization in model space and paper space for the current drawing**

Table C.4—continued

Variable Name	*Default Setting*	*Command Name*	*Variable Description*
TREEMAX	**?**	**TREEMAX**	**The maximum number of nodes for oct-tree spatial database organization for the current AutoCAD configuration (CFG)**
UCSFOLLOW	0		Controls automatic display of the plan view in the current viewport when switching to a new UCS: 1 = On 0 = Off
UCSICON	1	UCSICON	Controls the UCS icon's display; the value is the sum of the following: 0 = Off 1 = On 2 = At origin
UCSNAME	""	**DDUCS**, UCS	The name of the current UCS for the current space: "" = Unnamed (RO)
UCSORG	0.0000,0.0000,0.0000	**DDUCS**, UCS	The WCS origin of the current UCS for the current space (RO)
UCSXDIR	1.0000,0.0000,0.0000	**DDUCS**, UCS	The X direction of the current UCS (RO)
UCSYDIR	0.0000,1.0000,0.0000	**DDUCS**, UCS	The Y direction of the current UCS (RO)
UNDOCTL	**5**	**UNDO**	**The current state of UNDO; the value is the sum of the following: 1 = Enabled 2 = Single command 4 = Auto mode 8 = Group active (RO)(NS)**
UNDOMARKS	**0**	**UNDO**	**The current number of marks in the UNDO command's history (RO) (NS)**

Table C.4—continued

Variable Name	*Default Setting*	*Command Name*	*Variable Description*
UNITMODE	0		Controls the display of user input of fractions, feet and inches, and surveyor's angles: 0 = Per LUNITS 1 = As input
USERI1 - 5	0		User integer variables USERI1 to USERI5
USERR1 - 5	0.0000		User real-number variables USERR1 to USERR5
VIEWCTR	6.2518,4.5000	ZOOM, PAN, VIEW	The X,Y center point coordinate of the current view in the current viewport (RO)
VIEWDIR	0.0000,0.0000,1.0000	DVIEW	The camera point offset from target in the WCS (RO)
VIEWMODE	0	DVIEW, UCS	The current viewport's viewing mode; the value is the sum of the following: 1 = Perspective 2 = Front clipping on 4 = Back clipping on 8 = UCSFOLLOW On 16 = FRONTZ offset in use (RO)
VIEWSIZE	9.0000	ZOOM, VIEW	The current view's height, in drawing units (RO)
VIEWTWIST	0	DVIEW	The current viewport's view-twist angle (RO)
VISRETAIN			Controls retention of XREF file-layer settings in the current drawing 0 = Off 1 = On
VSMAX	12.5036,9.0000,0.0000	ZOOM,PAN,VIEW	The upper right X,Y coordinate of the current viewport's virtual screen for the current UCS (NS)(RO)

Table C.4—continued

Variable Name	*Default Setting*	*Command Name*	*Variable Description*
VSMIN	0.0000,0.0000,0.0000	ZOOM,PAN,VIEW	The lower left X,Y coordinate of the current viewport's virtual screen for the current UCS (NS)(RO)
WORLDUCS	1	UCS	The current UCS, equivalent to WCS: 1 = True 0 = False (RO)
WORLDVIEW	1	DVIEW,UCS	Controls the automatic changing of a UCS to the WCS during the DVIEW and VPOINT commands: 1 = On 0 = Off
XREFCTL	**0**		**Controls the creation of an XLG log file that contains XREF results:** **0 = No file** **1 = XLG file** **(CFG)**

Index

Symbols

A

B

NRP

NRP
Index

D

NRP
Index

E

F

M

N

NRP
Index

T

U

V

W

X

Z

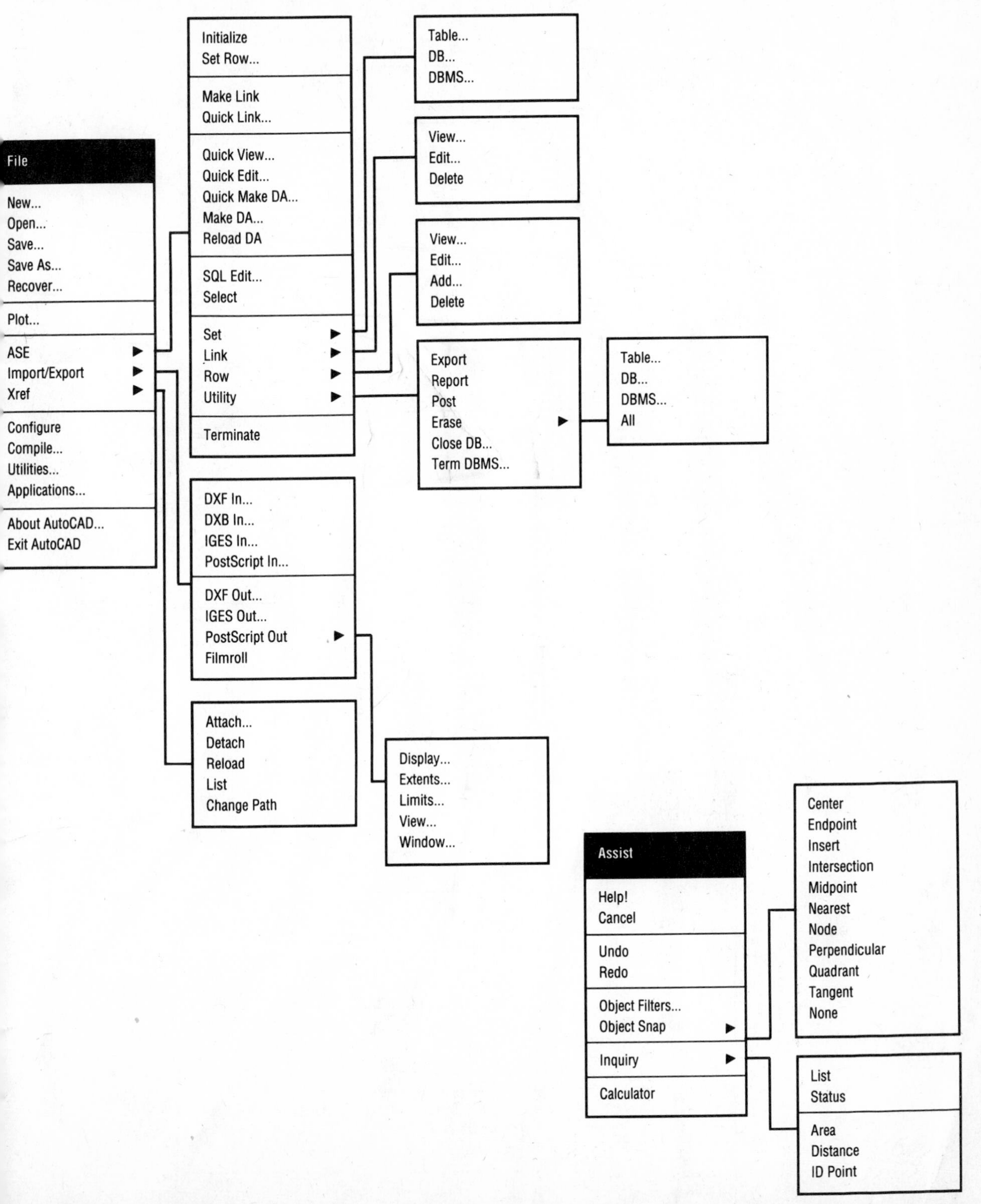
File
New...
Open...
Save...
Save As...
Recover...
Plot...
ASE
Import/Export
Xref
Configure
Compile...
Utilities...
Applications...
About AutoCAD...
Exit AutoCAD
Initialize
Set Row...
Make Link
Quick Link...
Quick View...
Quick Edit...
Quick Make DA...
Make DA...
Reload DA
SQL Edit...
Select
Set
Link
Row
Utility
Terminate
Table...
DB...
DBMS...
View...
Edit...
Delete
View...
Edit...
Add...
Delete
Export
Report
Post
Erase
Close DB...
Term DBMS...
Table...
DB...
DBMS...
All
DXF In...
DXB In...
IGES In...
PostScript In...
DXF Out...
IGES Out...
PostScript Out
Filmroll
Display...
Extents...
Limits...
View...
Window...
Attach...
Detach
Reload
List
Change Path
Assist
Help!
Cancel
Undo
Redo
Object Filters...
Object Snap
Inquiry
Calculator
Center
Endpoint
Insert
Intersection
Midpoint
Nearest
Node
Perpendicular
Quadrant
Tangent
None
List
Status
Area
Distance
ID Point

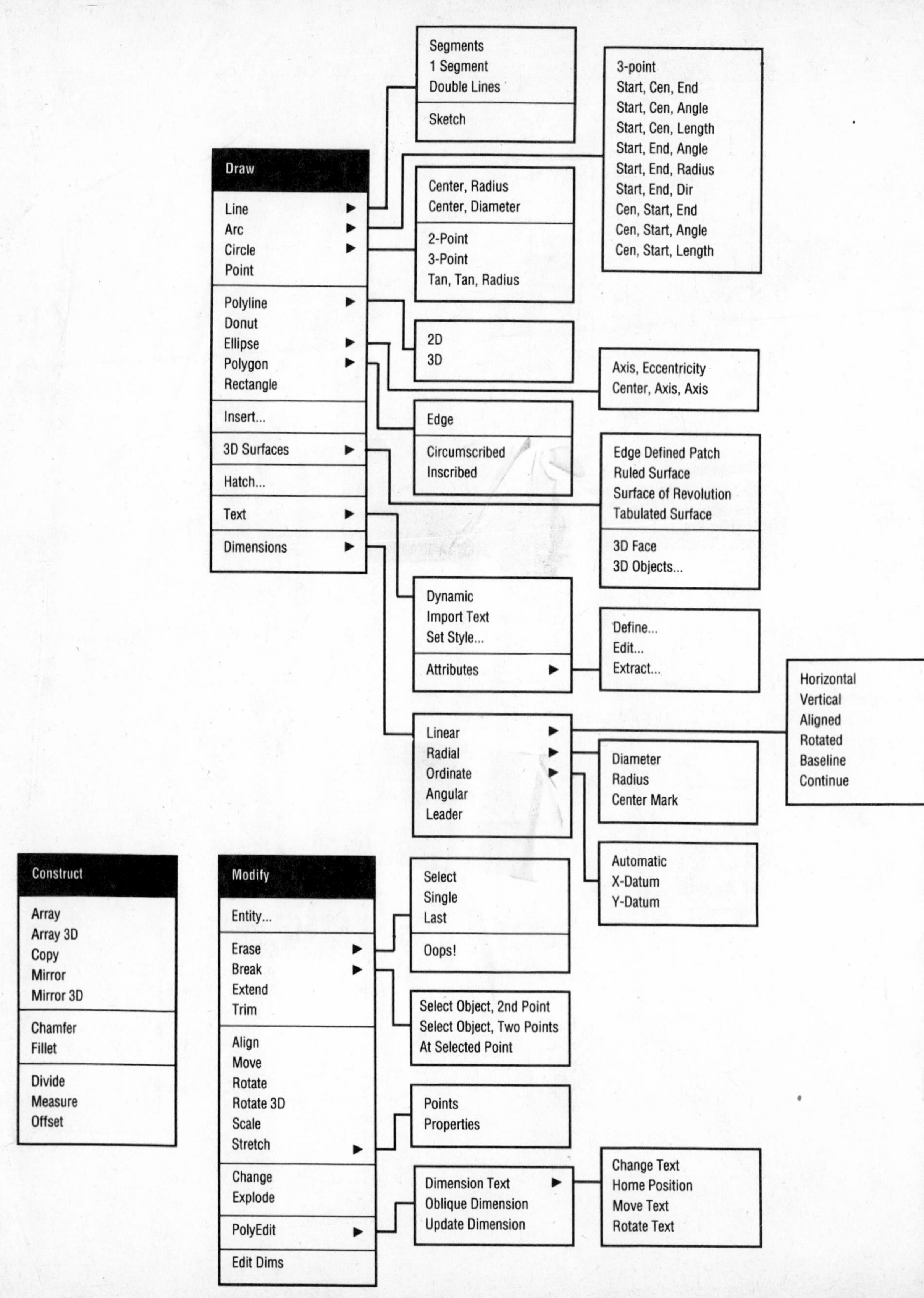

Segments
1 Segment
Double Lines
Sketch
3-point
Start, Cen, End
Start, Cen, Angle
Start, Cen, Length
Start, End, Angle
Start, End, Radius
Start, End, Dir
Cen, Start, End
Cen, Start, Angle
Cen, Start, Length
Draw
Line
Arc
Circle
Point
Polyline
Donut
Ellipse
Polygon
Rectangle
Insert...
3D Surfaces
Hatch...
Text
Dimensions
Center, Radius
Center, Diameter
2-Point
3-Point
Tan, Tan, Radius
2D
3D
Axis, Eccentricity
Center, Axis, Axis
Edge
Circumscribed
Inscribed
Edge Defined Patch
Ruled Surface
Surface of Revolution
Tabulated Surface
3D Face
3D Objects...
Dynamic
Import Text
Set Style...
Attributes
Define...
Edit...
Extract...
Horizontal
Vertical
Aligned
Rotated
Baseline
Continue
Linear
Radial
Ordinate
Angular
Leader
Diameter
Radius
Center Mark
Automatic
X-Datum
Y-Datum
Construct
Array
Array 3D
Copy
Mirror
Mirror 3D
Chamfer
Fillet
Divide
Measure
Offset
Modify
Entity...
Erase
Break
Extend
Trim
Align
Move
Rotate
Rotate 3D
Scale
Stretch
Change
Explode
PolyEdit
Edit Dims
Select
Single
Last
Oops!
Select Object, 2nd Point
Select Object, Two Points
At Selected Point
Points
Properties
Dimension Text
Oblique Dimension
Update Dimension
Change Text
Home Position
Move Text
Rotate Text

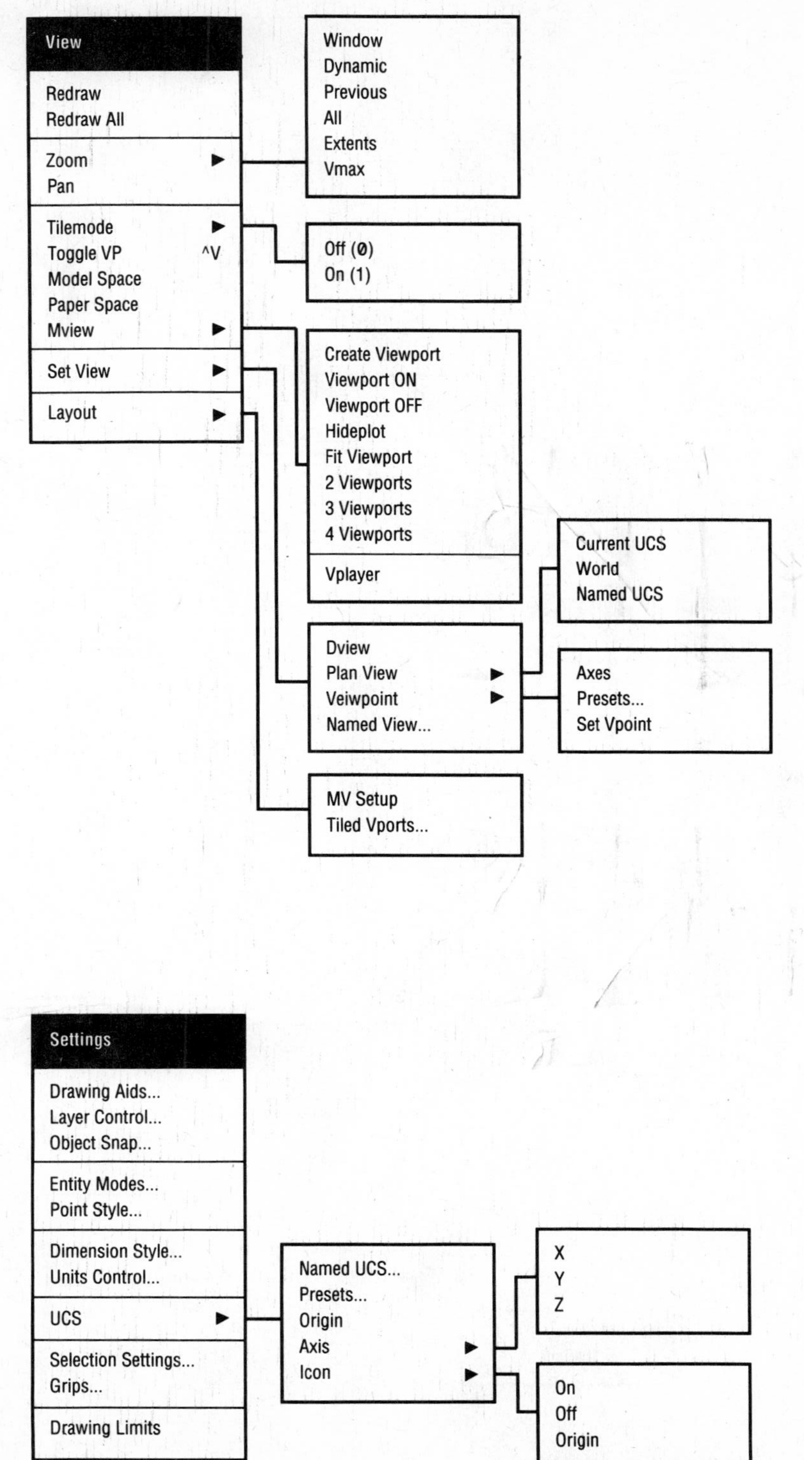
View
Redraw
Redraw All
Zoom
Pan
Tilemode
Toggle VP ^V
Model Space
Paper Space
Mview
Set View
Layout
Window
Dynamic
Previous
All
Extents
Vmax
Off (Ø)
On (1)
Create Viewport
Viewport ON
Viewport OFF
Hideplot
Fit Viewport
2 Viewports
3 Viewports
4 Viewports
Vplayer
Dview
Plan View
Veiwpoint
Named View...
Current UCS
World
Named UCS
Axes
Presets...
Set Vpoint
MV Setup
Tiled Vports...
Settings
Drawing Aids...
Layer Control...
Object Snap...
Entity Modes...
Point Style...
Dimension Style...
Units Control...
UCS
Selection Settings...
Grips...
Drawing Limits
Named UCS...
Presets...
Origin
Axis
Icon
X
Y
Z
On
Off
Origin

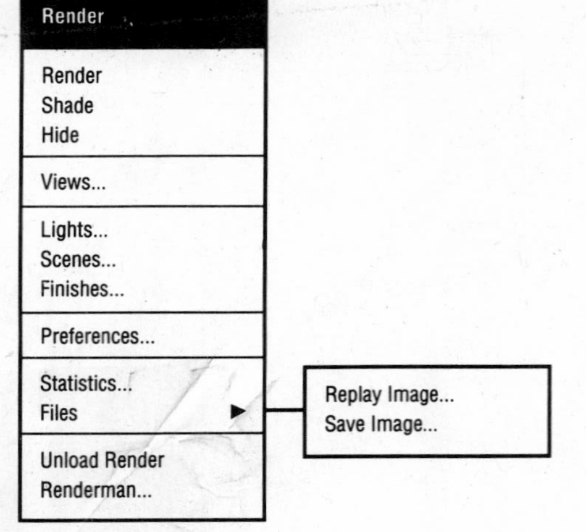
Render
Render
Shade
Hide
Views...
Lights...
Scenes...
Finishes...
Preferences...
Statistics...
Files
Unload Render
Renderman...
Replay Image...
Save Image...

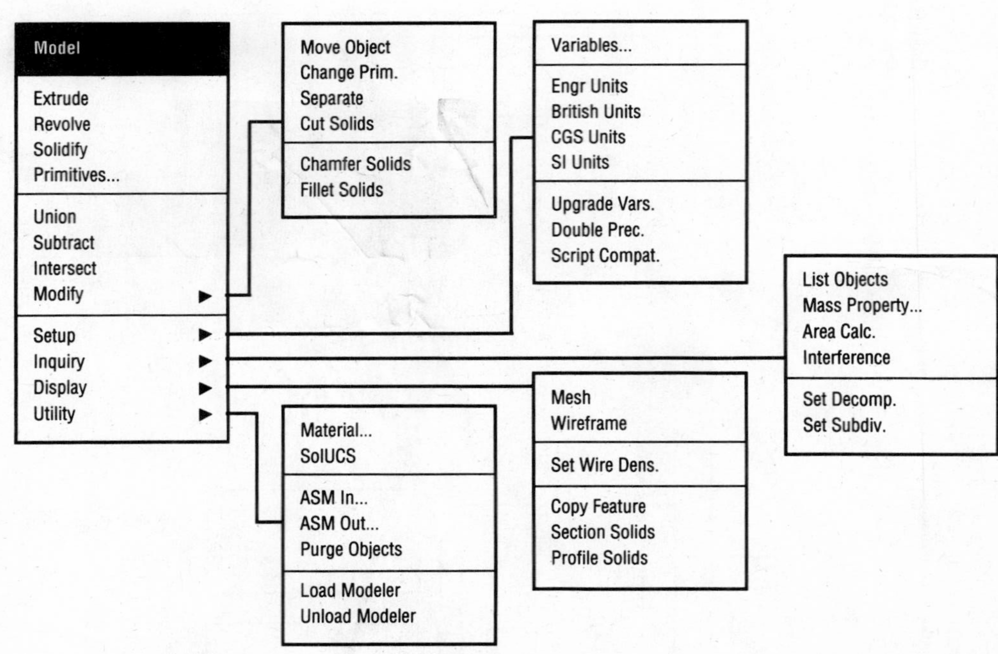
Model
Extrude
Revolve
Solidify
Primitives...
Union
Subtract
Intersect
Modify
Setup
Inquiry
Display
Utility
Move Object
Change Prim.
Separate
Cut Solids
Chamfer Solids
Fillet Solids
Variables...
Engr Units
British Units
CGS Units
SI Units
Upgrade Vars.
Double Prec.
Script Compat.
List Objects
Mass Property...
Area Calc.
Interference
Set Decomp.
Set Subdiv.
Mesh
Wireframe
Set Wire Dens.
Copy Feature
Section Solids
Profile Solids
Material...
SolUCS
ASM In...
ASM Out...
Purge Objects
Load Modeler
Unload Modeler

Add to Your New Riders Library Today with the Best Books for the Best Software

Yes, please send me the productivity-boosting material I have checked below. Make check payable to New Riders Publishing.

❑ **Check enclosed.**

Charge to my credit card:

❑ **VISA** ❑ **MasterCard**

Card # ______________________

Expiration date: ______________________

Signature: ______________________

Name: ______________________

Company: ______________________

Address: ______________________

City: ______________________

State: ______________ ZIP: __________

Phone: ______________________

The easiest way to order is to pick up the phone and call 1-800-541-6789 between 9:00 a.m. and 5:00 p.m., EST. Please have your credit card available, and your order can be placed in a snap!

Quantity	Description of Item	Unit Cost	Total Cost
	Inside CorelDRAW!, 2nd Edition	$29.95	
	AutoCAD 3D Design & Presentation*	$29.95	
	Maximizing Windows 3 (Book-and-Disk set)	$39.95	
	Inside AutoCAD, Special Edition (for Releases 10 and 11)*	$34.95	
	Maximizing AutoCAD: Volume I (Book-and-Disk set) Customizing AutoCAD with Macros and Menus	$34.95	
	AutoCAD for Beginners	$19.95	
	Inside Autodesk Animator*	$29.95	
	Maximizing AutoCAD: Volume II (Book-and-Disk set) Inside AutoLISP	$34.95	
	Inside AutoSketch, 2nd Edition*	$24.95	
	AutoCAD Reference Guide, 2nd Edition	$14.95	
	AutoCAD Reference Guide on Disk, 2nd Edition	$14.95	
	Inside CompuServe (Book-and-Disk set)	$29.95	
	Managing and Networking AutoCAD*	$29.95	
	Inside AutoCAD, Release 11, Metric Ed. (Book-and-Disk set)	$34.95	
	Maximizing MS-DOS 5 (Book-and-Disk set)	$34.95	
	Inside Generic CADD*	$29.95	
	Inside Windows	$29.95	
	AutoCAD Bible	$39.95	
	*Companion Disk available for these books	$14.95 ea.	

❑ **3½″ disk**

❑ **5¼″ disk**

Shipping and Handling: See information below.	
TOTAL	

Shipping and Handling: $4.00 for the first book and $1.75 for each additional book. Floppy disk: add $1.75 for shipping and handling. If you need to have it NOW, we can ship product to you in 24 to 48 hours for an additional charge, and you will receive your item overnight or in two days. Add $20.00 per book and $8.00 for up to three disks overseas. Prices subject to change. Call for availability and pricing information on latest editions.

New Riders Publishing • 11711 N. College Avenue • P.O. Box 90 • Carmel, Indiana 46032

1-800-541-6789
Orders/Customer Service

1-800-448-3804
FAX

To order: Fill in the reverse side, fold, and mail

NO POSTAGE NECESSARY IF MAILED IN THE UNITED STATES

BUSINESS REPLY MAIL

FIRST CLASS PERMIT NO. 6008 INDIANAPOLIS, IN

POSTAGE WILL BE PAID BY ADDRESSEE

NEW RIDERS PUBLISHING

P.O. Box 90

Carmel, Indiana 46032